Social Inequality

Social Inequality

Kathryn M. Neckerman
Editor

Russell Sage Foundation
New York

The Russell Sage Foundation

The Russell Sage Foundation, one of the oldest of America's general purpose foundations, was established in 1907 by Mrs. Margaret Olivia Sage for "the improvement of social and living conditions in the United States." The Foundation seeks to fulfill this mandate by fostering the development and dissemination of knowledge about the country's political, social, and economic problems. While the Foundation endeavors to assure the accuracy and objectivity of each book it publishes, the conclusions and interpretations in Russell Sage Foundation publications are those of the authors and not of the Foundation, its Trustees, or its staff. Publication by Russell Sage, therefore, does not imply Foundation endorsement.

Library of Congress Cataloging-in-Publication Data

Social inequality / Kathryn M. Neckerman, editor.
    p.   cm.
    Includes bibliographical references and index.
    ISBN 0-87154-620-5 — ISBN 0-87154-621-3 (pbk.)
    1. Equality—United States.   I. Neckerman, Kathryn M.

HN90.S6S55 2004
305—dc22   2003069340

Text design by Genna Patacsil

RUSSELL SAGE FOUNDATION
112 East 64th Street, New York, New York 10021
10 9 8 7 6 5 4 3 2 1

Contents

Contributors

KATHRYN M. NECKERMAN is associate director of the Institute for Social and Economic Research and Policy (ISERP) at Columbia University.

SUZANNE BIANCHI is professor of sociology and director of the Maryland Population Research Center at the University of Maryland, College Park.

HENRY E. BRADY is Class of 1941 Monroe Deutsch Professor of Political Science and Public Policy at the University of California, Berkeley.

CORAL CELESTE is a doctoral candidate in the Department of Sociology at Princeton University.

TIFFANI CHIN is a postdoctoral scholar at the UCLA School of Public Policy and Social Research.

PHILIP N. COHEN is assistant professor of sociology at the University of California, Irvine.

SEAN CORCORAN is assistant professor of economics at California State University, Sacramento.

JANET CURRIE is professor of economics at the University of California, Los Angeles, and research associate at the National Bureau of Economic Research.

PAUL DIMAGGIO is professor of sociology at Princeton University.

CHRISTINE E. EIBNER is associate economist at RAND Corporation in Santa Monica, California.

DAVID T. ELLWOOD is Lucius N. Littauer Professor of Political Economy at the John F. Kennedy School of Government, Harvard University.

WILLIAM N. EVANS is professor of economics at the University of Maryland, College Park.

NEIL FLIGSTEIN is Class of 1939 Chancellor's Professor in the Department of Sociology at the University of California, Berkeley.

RICHARD B. FREEMAN is Herbert Ascherman Professor of Economics at Harvard University, codirector of the Labor and Work Life Forum at the Harvard Law School, director of the Labor Studies Program at the National Bureau of Economic Research, codirector of the Centre for Economic Performance at the London School of Economics, and visiting professor at the London School of Economics.

JENNIFER GODWIN is senior statistician at the Center for Child and Family Policy at Duke University.

ESZTER HARGITTAI is assistant professor of communication studies and sociology and faculty associate of the Institute for Policy Research at Northwestern University.

ROBERT M. HAUSER is Vilas Research Professor and director of the Center for Demography of Health and Aging in the Department of Sociology at the University of Wisconsin-Madison.

ROBERT HAVEMAN is John Bascom Emeritus Professor of Economics and Public Affairs at the University of Wisconsin-Madison

V. JOSEPH HOTZ is professor of economics at the University of California, Los Angeles, and research associate at the National Bureau of Economic Research.

MICHAEL HOUT is professor of sociology and demography at the University of California, Berkeley.

CHRISTOPHER JENCKS is Malcolm Weiner Professor of Social Policy at the John F. Kennedy School of Government, Harvard University.

THOMAS J. KANE is professor of policy studies and economics at the University of California, Los Angeles.

MEREDITH KLEYKAMP is a doctoral candidate in the Department of Sociology at Princeton University.

GABRIEL S. LENZ is a doctoral candidate in the Department of Politics at Princeton University.

KARA LEVINE is a doctoral candidate in economics at the University of Wisconsin-Madison.

STEVEN P. MARTIN is assistant professor of sociology at the University of Maryland, College Park, and a member of the Maryland Population Research Center.

SUSAN E. MAYER is dean and associate professor of sociology at the Irving B. Harris Graduate School of Public Policy Studies, University of Chicago.

MARCIA K. MEYERS is associate professor of social work and public affairs at the University of Washington.

JOHN MULLAHY is professor of population health sciences and economics at the University of Wisconsin-Madison.

SHEILA E. MURRAY is an economist at RAND.

KEI NOMAGUCHI is a postdoctoral fellow in the Department of Sociology at the University of Calgary, Canada.

LARS OSBERG is McCulloch Professor of Economics at Dalhousie University in Nova Scotia, Canada.

ANNE R. PEBLEY is Bixby Professor of Public Health and Sociology at the University of California, Los Angeles, and senior research associate at RAND.

MEREDITH PHILLIPS is assistant professor of policy studies and sociology at the University of California, Los Angeles.

SARA RALEY is a doctoral candidate in the Department of Sociology at the University of Maryland.

STEPHANIE ROBERT is assistant professor of social work at Population Health Sciences at the University of Wisconsin-Madison.

DAN ROSENBAUM is a doctoral candidate in the Department of Sociology at Princeton University.

JAKE ROSENFELD is a doctoral candidate in the Department of Sociology at Princeton University.

HOWARD ROSENTHAL is Roger Williams Straus Professor of Social Science at Princeton University and Distinguished Visiting Professor of Economics and Political Science at Brown University.

CHRISTOPHER RUHM is Jefferson-Pilot Excellence Professor of Economics at the University of North Carolina, Greensboro.

GARY SANDEFUR is professor of sociology at the University of Wisconsin-Madison.

NARAYAN SASTRY is senior social scientist in the Labor and Population Program at RAND.

KAY LEHMAN SCHLOZMAN is John Joseph Moakley Professor of Political Science at Boston College.

JOHN KARL SCHOLZ is professor of economics and director of the Institute for Research on Poverty at the University of Wisconsin-Madison.

ROBERT M. SCHWAB is professor of economics at the University of Maryland, College Park.

JONATHAN SCHWABISH is senior director in the Project and Policy Department of the Partnership for New York City.

STEVEN SHAFER is a doctoral candidate in the Department of Sociology at Princeton University.

TAEK-JIN SHIN is a doctorial candidate in the Department of Sociology at the University of California, Berkeley.

THEDA SKOCPOL is Victor S. Thomas Professor of Government and Sociology and director of the Center for American Political Studies at Harvard University.

TIMOTHY M. SMEEDING is the Maxwell Professor of Public Policy at the Maxwell School of Syracuse University and overall director of the Luxembourg Income Study.

SIDNEY VERBA is Carl H. Pforzheimer University Professor in the Department of Government at Harvard University.

ANDREA VOYER is a doctoral candidate in sociology at the University of Wisconsin-Madison.

JANE WALDFOGEL is professor in the School of Social Work at Columbia University.

BRUCE WESTERN is professor of sociology at Princeton University.

BARBARA WOLFE is professor of economics, public affairs, and population health sciences at the University of Wisconsin-Madison.

Foreword

Too much talk about social inequality generally makes Americans uncomfortable. We are, after all, a nation founded on the premise that "all men are created equal," and most Americans see themselves as part of a vast middle class that encompasses the greater part of society. The evident economic differences between rich and poor do not dislodge the popular conviction that America still provides equal opportunities for all. In a free market economy, open to individual enterprise and ability, some people will inevitably work harder, or get a better education, or invest more fortunately, and as a result, accumulate more resources than others. In principle, these inequalities of outcomes need not threaten equality of opportunity, so long as the children of rich and poor can still start life's race on equal footing. In fact, of course, an individual's chances in life have always been shaped to some degree by family resources of all kinds—income, education, social connections, political influence. America's promise of equal opportunity has, at best, been approximated by social reality—much more closely at some periods in our history than others.

The three decades after World War II were a particularly promising time in this regard. Pent-up demand fueled an industrial boom after the war that produced strong economic growth and put Americans back to work, erasing memories of the Great Depression. High rates of unionization reduced wage competition between firms in many industries. American business, with little challenge from abroad, could afford generous labor settlements. Wages for manufacturing and other workers made steady gains, and economic disparities between rich and poor declined. The GI Bill made college available to returning veterans, and the subsequent expansion of state-supported higher education brought college within reach of more families than ever before. The civil rights movement ended legal discrimination and began to pry open educational and economic opportunities for previously excluded groups. Economic mobility rose significantly, and an individual's chances to prosper were less tightly determined by family resources. The great American social project of growing the middle class and broadly sharing prosperity appeared to be an inexorable and irreversible trend. We know now that it was not.

Beginning late in the 1970s, the United States experienced a series of economic shocks and demographic changes that caused economic inequality to rise sharply. Although there are still arguments about exactly how and why this happened, the broad outlines of the story are, by now, familiar. Stagflation in the 1970s, the two oil price crises, and loss of market share to reviving foreign competition led to a period of restructuring in many U.S. industries. The dismantling of regulations and the de facto weakening of labor protections, undertaken to shore up U.S. competitiveness, put strong downward pressure on wages, particularly for male workers with limited education in previously unionized industries. At the same time, the increasing penetration of information technology into all sectors of the economy began to automate many production jobs and substitute computer power for many repetitive, low-skill clerical jobs. The result was declining demand for workers with no more than a high school education, a trend that has persisted ever since. Finally, and most notoriously, globalization—in the form of increased trade with low-wage countries, increased outsourcing of production and service jobs to offshore locales, and increased immigration to the United States of workers willing to accept very low wages—has put American workers, and particularly those with modest skills and training, into competition with a much larger labor pool on a worldwide scale. Not surprisingly, the result has been a long downtrend in wages at the bottom of the labor market.

To be sure, many Americans have benefited from the new economy. Globalization has put downward pressure on prices and made many consumer goods dramatically cheaper. Investments in information technology eventually led to a welcome burst of productivity growth in the 1990s, which ushered in an unprecedented period of low unemployment and low inflation toward the end of the decade. All workers gained ground in the strong economy of the late 1990s, but college-educated workers benefited most. The wage premium paid to college graduates rose to about 85 percent above the wages of high school graduates. While the 1980s saw a dramatic widening of the wage structure across the board, in the 1990s workers in the bottom 10 percent made up some lost ground against the median, but workers in the top 10 percent continued to pull away from everyone else. Family incomes, which reflect changes in family composition and employment as well as wages, showed even more pronounced trends. Overall, mean family income grew about 30 percent in real terms from the end of the 1970s to the beginning of the new century. But the distribution of aggregate national income became dramatically more unequal. From 1979 to 2002, families in the top fifth of the income distribution increased their share of the national income from 44 percent to just under 50 percent, with almost all of this gain going to families in the top 5 percent. Every other quintile lost income share, and losses became progressively steeper (in percentage terms) going down the income scale. The bottom fifth of all American families saw their meager share of national income decline from 4.3 percent to 3.5 percent.

Although these facts are well known, we still understand very little of their larger social significance. Is the recent burst of economic inequality nothing but a temporary consequence of the transition to a new and more productive economy? Can Americans respond to the increasing economic importance of education by going to college in greater numbers and insulating themselves from computerization and global competition? Or will inequality, once under way, prove difficult to reverse? This might happen if the families who have fallen behind economically also fall behind in other ways that will make it more difficult for them, and for their children, to compete with the more advantaged. If, for example, as economic inequality rose over the past twenty-five years, the children of families at the bottom of the income distribution were increasingly likely to live in single-parent families, grow up in distressed neighborhoods, receive substandard child care and health care, attend poor-quality schools, and have less of an opportunity to go to college, then economic inequality might become a self-reinforcing trend. Inequality might also tend to reinforce itself at the other end of the economic spectrum if high-income families became wealthy enough to purchase private substitutes for public goods and withdraw political support for public investments in schools and social insurance systems that benefit the poor.

In 2000 the Russell Sage Foundation and the Carnegie Corporation of New York joined forces in support of a program of research designed to examine whether the recent rise in economic inequality has in fact exacerbated social inequalities of the kind that might make economic inequality more difficult to reverse. We commissioned forty-eight social scientists organized into six working groups to examine many different dimensions of social life in an effort to determine, from the available social data, the *level* of social inequality observed between rich and poor in each social domain and the *changes* in levels of inequality that appear to be correlated with the recent rise in inequality. For each social domain, we asked how the lives of rich and poor changed over the last three decades as economic inequality rose. Did inequality in family structure and investments in children, in educational quality and opportunity, in health care and outcomes, in job quality and satisfaction with work, in political participation and influence, and in many other aspects of social life become more or less pronounced?

This large and diverse volume provides a first installment on the answers to these questions derived from reviewing the research literature and analyzing available data. The pattern of answers is complicated but by no means unintelligible. In domains where social participation depends, even partially, on the private ability to pay, social inequality tended to rise in step with economic inequality. The gaps between rich and poor in enrollment in four-year colleges, use of quality day care, and access to the Internet all became more pronounced as economic inequality increased. But when public funding of a social resource expanded, this pattern was reversed. For example, expenditures per pupil in primary and secondary schools became more equal as state governments responded to court-ordered equalization, and states with underfunded public schools began to invest more in education. Clearly, public investment can be effective in reducing social inequality where there is political support. Other observed trends in social inequality were more subtle, and if there are economic influences, they are less direct and obvious than just the ability to pay. For example, voting rates among the poor have declined more than among higher-income, higher-education groups. Is this because the poor believe that the political system is unresponsive to their needs, or are they simply too hard-pressed to take time off from low-wage jobs to vote? To take another example, single-parenthood has recently risen most rapidly among women with the least education. Is this because less-educated women have little to gain economically from marrying men whose economic prospects are increasingly limited? Or is it because they have so much less to lose economically by having a child out of wedlock than more-educated women?

The chapters that follow wrestle with these and many other questions about the recent trends in social inequality. Subsequent publications in the social inequality project will attempt to delve more deeply into the causes and consequences of these social changes and attack the big and difficult questions about whether the ways in which social inequality has increased appear likely to reduce economic mobility in the future and weaken America's promise of equal opportunity. In the meantime, this landmark volume offers an unprecedented statistical portrait of the many differences in the lives of rich and poor Americans. It is, like America itself, a complex picture.

Eric Wanner
President
Russell Sage Foundation

Introduction

About twenty-five years ago, economic inequality began to rise in the United States. Poverty increased and incomes fell among the poor, while the affluent enjoyed a substantial increase in their standard of living. This inequality has grown through both recession and recovery, and shows few signs of abating. Debate continues about the causes of rising inequality, but most experts agree that any explanation should include global trade, immigration, a decline in union strength, the computerization of work, and the decline in the real value of the minimum wage. This dramatic change in the distribution of incomes jeopardizes the progress made after World War II in reducing poverty and improving standards of living across the board, and also in reducing racial and ethnic inequality.

By itself, this economic inequality would be ample cause for concern, but its impact could well be compounded by its social consequences. Rising social inequality—in many different domains, such as family life, education, or civic engagement—could magnify the burden of rising poverty for the most vulnerable and sustain the effects of inequality far into the future. To take one not entirely hypothetical example, economic inequality could lead to a widening gap in education outcomes because rising incomes among affluent families bring new resources to suburban school districts, or because more affluent families opt out of the public schools into higher-quality private education, while falling incomes among the poor make it more difficult for them to improve or escape their underfunded public schools. Rising economic inequality might also widen the gap in access to high-quality preschool, to private college education, and to other privately financed educational services, such as tutoring or prep courses for college entrance tests. With so much riding on education—particularly access to secure, well-paying jobs—it is clear that rising educational inequality could have very significant long-term effects.

Despite the possibility of these far-reaching implications, the rise in economic inequality has received little public attention. Perhaps this is because inequality has risen so gradually over the last twenty-five years, or because changes in inequality are distributed over the entire population and are therefore difficult to perceive in any immediate way. In addition, although inequality is an intuitively meaningful idea, measures of inequality are less familiar to the public than are the indicators used to track other economic phenomena. We regularly see the ups and downs of the unemployment rate reported in the news, for instance. By contrast, the Gini coefficient, the most commonly used measure of inequality, is very far from being a household word.

Four years ago, the Russell Sage Foundation and the Carnegie Corporation of New York began a special project to promote research on social inequality. Working groups of social scientists were established at six leading universities to examine the social implications of rising economic inequality in a wide range of areas including family functioning, neighborhood quality, education, health, working conditions, political participation, and involvement with crime and the criminal justice system. With support from the two foundations, the scholars in these working groups have begun to generate a stream of new research intended to help the nation understand the deeper significance of the recent rise in inequality.

Social Inequality is the first major product of this Russell Sage–Carnegie project. It reflects the initial charge given to the six working groups, which was to conduct a thorough review of what we know about recent changes in inequality in specific social domains. The individual chapters in this volume are quite varied. Some draw from a large and well-established base of research, providing incisive reviews and sometimes a re-analysis of current work. In other chapters, for instance one on Internet access, the topic was novel enough that the authors had to map out a new field of study. A number of authors went beyond the existing evidence to present their own new research findings, providing a preview of the original empirical research that will be forthcoming from the social inequality project in the future.

Publishing these diverse papers together, in this rather hefty volume, seemed important for several reasons. At the simplest level, it reminds us that we cannot reckon the full cost of economic inequality unless we consider its impact across a wide range of social domains: family life, education, health, the body politic, and much else. More subtly, inequality in one domain may well have implications for another. Changes in family life could spill over into the schools. A decline in job quality for low-skilled workers could affect their health or their ability to form and maintain stable families. Although each of these chapters focuses on a single topic, juxtaposing them in this volume allows us to explore connections among these multiple domains. Finally, scholars who study inequality face some common problems of research design and method. By including work from a variety of disciplines, the volume can promote exchange of insights and research strategies across the fields.

This book examines a number of dimensions of social inequality, including inequality in family and neighborhood, education and work, health, and political participation and the formation of public policy. It pays special attention to recent trends that may threaten to sustain inequality into the future.

The remainder of this introduction offers a tour through the subsequent chapters, highlighting findings about these trends. We begin with a preview of conceptual and methodological issues underlying the analysis of inequality presented here. The final section of this volume provides a more technical and complete treatment of these issues. William Evans, Michael Hout, and Susan Mayer review the different types of inequality effects and the problems of estimating them independently. Michael Hout discusses strategies for modeling the relationship between inequality and intergenerational mobility. Readers interested in precise coverage of these issues would do well to consult these chapters at the outset. For others, the conceptual guidelines in the following section should be sufficient.

METHODS AND CONCEPTS

Our project is concerned primarily with dimensions of participation in social life that are correlated with economic resources. So, in the first instance, we are concerned to know whether there is a positive gradient relating the *levels* on some economic scale with *levels* on the social dimension under study. Although income is usually the economic scale of choice, education is sometimes substituted for income, since annual income can vary a great deal from year to year, and educational attainment is an excellent predictor of lifetime earnings.

In tracking *trends* over time, we are interested in whether increasing economic inequality is matched by increasing inequality in the social dimension under study. This could happen because the correlation between the economic and social variables remains constant over time and increased dispersion on the economic scale is simply reflected by increased dispersion on the social scale. Or, it could happen because the correlation between the two variables increased over time. So, for example, there may be increasing differences between the college enrollment rates of students from rich and poor families if increasing inequality of family incomes makes it more likely that rich families can pay the bill and less likely that poor families can. Or, it might be that families' economic resources become a more important determinant of college enrollment because scholarship aid and student loans fail to keep up with rising tuition, and a family's ability to pay becomes an even more important factor in a student's decision to go to college. Finally, of course, it is possible that both these changes (rising economic inequality and an increasing correlation of economic and social trends) could happen at once.

Although the effects of changing trends in economic inequality are often referred to as a unitary phenomenon, it is important to keep in mind that inequality may rise in quantitatively distinct ways. The poor may fall behind the rest of the population, for example, or the rich can leap ahead of everyone else. These are obviously very different kinds of economic changes, and they are likely to have different social consequences. While studies of inequality are increasingly recognizing these differences, traditional measures of inequality, such as the Gini coefficient, are insensitive to them. Ratios of the income available at various points in the distribution are more informative, such as the 90/50 ratio, which compares the well-off to the median, or the 50/10 ratio, which compares the median to the poor.

In addition to affecting the economic resources available to an individual at a given position in the distribution, economic inequality also changes the distribution of resources available to others. Does the shape of the distribution of economic resources available to others influence an individual's outcomes, even while his own resources remain the same? For example, is it healthier for an individual, let's say with the median income, to live in a society where most people have incomes fairly similar to his own, or to live in a society with the same median income but a large difference between rich and poor? Only one of the chapters in this volume (by Christine Eibner and William Evans) examines a variant of this stronger claim about the social effects of inequality of the resources available to others, but it is well to keep the difference in mind.

Finally, economic inequality may exert effects on the political system in ways that reflect the overall shape of the distribution. So, for example, if the well-to-do pull away from the rest of the population, then the upper tail of the distribution will become fatter, and the income of the median citizen will fall below the mean. If the distribution is still sufficiently bell-shaped that most votes are to be found in the vicinity of the median voter, then there should be increasing political pressure for redistributive policies, such as progressive taxation and social insurance programs. Most of the chapters in the section on inequality and public policy are at pains to explain why something of the sort has *not* happened, at least in the United States.

FAMILY AND NEIGHBORHOOD

Family life and neighborhood are highly salient for the immediate well-being of children, and for the eventual economic and social status of the next generation. We know, for example, that growing up in a single-parent family can marginally but significantly impair school performance, raise the odds of teen pregnancy and criminal involvement, and depress future employment and earnings. It is therefore particularly worrisome that in this volume, both David Ellwood and Christopher Jencks, and Steven Martin report growing class differences in the incidence of single-parent families. Well-educated women are increasingly postponing both childbirth and marriage, but they marry when they have children. Less-educated women are also postponing or eschewing marriage, but not childbirth. As a result, nonmarital births have risen much more quickly among less-educated women during the past thirty years. Although the causes of these trends are complex, Ellwood and Jencks argue that decisions to marry and bear children have become more a matter of individual choice in the past thirty years due to changing social norms, which have made unwed motherhood more acceptable, and more effective methods of birth control, which enable women to postpone childbirth. As women consider their options, implicitly or explicitly, rising economic inequality may well influence their decisions. Less-educated women may have little economic incentive to marry, given the increasingly limited economic prospects of their likely partners. Nor do they have as much to lose from early childbearing as more educated women with increasingly brighter career prospects, so they have less reason to put off having a child.

While family structure was becoming more unequal over the period, many other family and community resources show more favorable trends. Robert Haveman and his colleagues find that parental education, time spent on child care, and preschool care have all increased since the mid-1970s, while family size declined. But the distribution of most family resources—including both financial assets and expenditures on children—remained highly unequal, as did more intangible aspects of family life. For example, Suzanne Bianchi and her colleagues present new research on parents' investments in children, showing among other things that college-educated parents report spending about 20 percent more time with their children than noncollege-educated parents. These large differences did not increase over the last thirty years of rising inequality, leading Bianchi et al. to speculate that increasingly hard-pressed parents in poor families are able to protect the time they spend with their children from other encroachments, even if they cannot match the level of parental time put in by more advantaged parents.

Neighborhoods with high concentrations of poverty and scarce social resources have long been linked to developmental problems for the children living in them. Neighborhoods with high crime rates, high residential turnover, poor institutional supports, and weak communal ties make it difficult for poor families to provide the kind of environment in which children can thrive. In the 1970s and 1980s, concentrated poverty became more prevalent in American cities, as economic inequality increased at the bottom of the income distribution. The growth of concentrated poverty leveled off in the 1990s, perhaps because much of the increased inequality in the 1990s occurred at the top of the income distribution. Anne Pebley and Naran Sastry review these trends in their chapter and discuss the difficulties of disentangling the causal impact of poor neighborhoods from the problems of the poor families that live there. While research on economic segregation largely focuses on the isolation of the poor, the increasing geographic detachment of the wealthy from the rest of society (for example, in gated communities) may eventually pose problems for a democracy that depends upon a broadly shared sense of social solidarity to sustain political support for public facilities. Investigation of these more subtle "neighborhood effects" at the top of the income distribution is an important item for future research.

EDUCATION AND WORK

Education is another dimension of inequality with transparent importance for the next generation. Over the last three decades, the economic value of education has risen dramatically. High school dropouts are marginalized in a very competitive job market, and strong cognitive skills and college credentials are increasingly important to economic attainment. Americans have responded to this rising demand for skill by getting more and better education wherever they can. Our question is whether families at the bottom of the income distribution have the opportunity to improve their educational preparation as effectively as more advantaged groups. By and large, the answer appears to be no.

This is most clearly the case at the beginning and end of the educational process, where access to educational facilities depends in part on private financing and the ability of individual families to foot the bill. In their chapter, Marcia Meyers and her colleagues show that the wealthiest fifth of American families spend almost five times as much for preschool child care as the bottom fifth. The type of daycare used also reveals inequalities; well-off families are more likely to use regulated day care centers and poorer families are more likely to rely on informal arrangements. This difference between rich and poor is echoed at the other end of the educational spectrum, where Thomas Kane finds that students from well-off families have been able to increase their enrollment in four-year colleges more rapidly than students from poor families. This is true, even after differences in educational preparation between these groups are taken into account. Again, the problem appears to be financial. As tuition increases for four-year colleges have outstripped available financial aid, students from poor families have been increasingly unable to keep up with the rich.

The picture is more mixed in K–12 education, where fully funded public schools are available to all. The question here is whether the quality of public schools available to the poor matches the quality of schools in richer neighborhoods. Because public schools have been funded largely by local property taxes in the past, there have long been large differences between rich and poor school districts in expenditures per pupil. As Sean Corcoran and his colleagues show, however, these differences have actually declined over the past thirty years, due largely to successful legal challenges to the inequities of local financing. In state after state, courts have ordered state governments to step in and make school budgets more equal. The result is a significant decline in the inequality of expenditures per pupil across the nation's school districts. But large financial differences remain: expenditures per pupil in the richest 5 percent of all public schools are still more than twice the expenditures in the poorest 5 percent of all schools. Moreover, many non-economic measures of school quality still show large differences, as Meredith Phillips and Tiffani Chin show in their chapter. Schools with high concentrations of poor students have a higher incidence of school violence, less-well-maintained physical plants, fewer advanced placement courses, less-well-stocked school libraries and less-well-prepared teachers than schools in richer districts. Evidently, overcoming inequalities of these kinds will take more than the degree of financial equalization between schools achieved to date.

Patterns of achievement and attainment in the K–12 years are also mixed. As Robert Hauser shows, income and race differentials in grade retention and school dropout rates have diminished over the last three decades. The gaps in achievement between rich and poor students, and between white and minority students, remain large, however. Given these gaps in academic achievement, Hauser suggests that class and race differences in grade retention and school dropout rates are likely to widen again as school reform increasingly mandates high-stakes testing for grade promotion.

Two chapters in this section concern topics loosely related to education—Internet access and working conditions. Use of the Internet has become so widespread in both school and work that we must take seriously its implications for inequality. Despite extensive federal investments to provide Internet connections for the nation's public schools, higher-income families continue to have better access to advanced Internet technology. Moreover, individuals with higher cognitive and technical skills are likely to use the Internet more for education and research, and less for entertainment. It is too soon to know whether the Internet will reinforce existing class inequality or ameliorate it. It is not too soon to map out a research agenda, however, and Paul DiMaggio and his colleagues take a major step in that direction.

Educational inequality has its most immediate consequences in the labor market, as new workers are sorted into good and bad jobs. With the deregulation of business, the decline of unions, and the rise of contingent labor, some analysts fear that protections for workers have weakened and job quality has deteriorated, particularly for low-skilled workers. Neil Fligstein and Taek-Jin Shin present evidence showing that inequality in benefits, workplace safety, and nonstandard shift work have all widened roughly at the same time that earnings inequality has increased—with low-paid workers losing ground on all fronts. Not surprisingly, the gaps between high- and low-earning workers in self-reported satisfaction with one's work and financial situation also grew over the same period. Interestingly, managers and professionals worked increasingly longer hours, and felt more pressure at work, but also enjoyed their jobs more.

HEALTH

Given the very strong relationship between economic status and health, we might expect growing economic inequality to be mirrored in the health status of the population. There are many channels through which income might improve health, including better material living conditions, access to better medical care, and protection from environmental hazards. If inequality in health widens, there may be long-term reciprocal consequences for economic inequality; for just as income can affect health, so health can impact income. Illness and disability make it more difficult to hold a job, of course, and as recent research shows, poor health in childhood leads to lower education and earnings in adulthood. Through its effect on health, then, the long-term implications of economic inequality could be substantial. Rising inequality in health is difficult to measure in the short term, however, because some medical problems may take years to appear. As John Mullahy and his colleagues show, there have been large and stable differences in self-reported health between the poor and nonpoor since the mid-1970s. But there is no indication in the data that these differences increased as inequality rose over the past years. However, as Janet Currie and Joseph Hotz note in their chapter about child mortality, improvements in product safety, environmental protection, intensive-care technology, and other changes have improved health across the board in the past two decades, and may offset the effects of the rise in economic inequality.

Epidemiologists have speculated that living in a more unequal society has an impact on health that goes beyond the material deprivations of poverty. Inequality may be stressful for those who are not doing as well as the rest of their peer group, and people may respond to the stress of relative deprivation with unhealthy behavior such as smoking, over-eating, and binge drinking, which is likely to raise their mortality. Intriguing evidence for this idea comes from field studies of primates, which show higher levels of stress hormones among those who are lower in the status hierarchy. Christine Eibner and William Evans present new evidence that when relative deprivation is higher—as it is under conditions of greater inequality—people are more likely to smoke and to be overweight, and more likely to die from coronary disease or lung cancer. These patterns give credence to epidemiologists' ideas about the psychosocial effects of inequality, and have implications beyond the field of health.

POLITICAL PARTICIPATION

The book devotes two sections to politics and public policy. The reason is not hard to see. There is virtually no dimension of social inequality that is unaffected by law and public policy. Consider, for instance, the divorce laws that affect the formation and well-being of single-parent families, or the legal action driving school finance reform, or public investments in health and environmental protection. If economic inequality reduces the political influence of the poor while it empowers the wealthy, public policy is likely to shift toward the interests of upper-income constituencies, deepening economic inequality. This concern is heightened by the cross-national differences that we already see: the United States has higher economic inequality than any other country in the industrialized world, and this country's social safety net is weak compared to those of other developed countries.

Political participation is central to this concern about the policy effects of economic inequality. Many types of participation in electoral politics are already quite stratified by income and education. Rising economic inequality gives the affluent even more resources and the poor less, which could widen inequality in political participation and influence, particularly as financial contributions become the key to electoral success in modern, mass market campaigns. Inequality might also have more subtle effects. The poor might become demoralized by the growing disparity between their own condition and that of the majority. The affluent, who can afford private schools, gated communities, and the like, might withdraw their support for public services. More broadly, we might see an erosion of the public sphere, and of a sense of solidarity and shared interests that crosses class lines.

Chapters by Sidney Verba, Henry Brady, and Richard Freeman take different approaches to the inequality of political participation, analyzing different data sets with different measures, and arriving at somewhat different pictures of recent change in political participation and its relation to rising inequality. Verba reviews the evidence indicating that high-income, high-education citizens participate more than poor, less-educated citizens on every dimension of political activity—from voting to working for candidates, making financial contributions to campaigns, joining political organizations, and contacting political representatives. Combining all forms of activity into a single scale, and tracking this scale over time, Verba finds no increase in inequality with regard to the sheer number of different political activities engaged in by rich and poor since the mid-1970s. But there may be differences in the intensity, or the impact of various activities. Not surprisingly, Verba finds the gap between rich and poor is largest where campaign contributions are concerned and much smaller where political activities involve contributing time, not money. To the extent that money has become more important to electoral success, the influence of the rich may have grown.

Richard Freeman looks exclusively changes in inequality in voting behavior between rich and poor. Although well-educated, well-off citizens have traditionally voted at higher rates than the poor, inequality on this key dimension of political activity has not been as extreme as in other types of political participation. Freeman finds, however, that inequality in voting behavior has increased significantly over the past forty years. While all income and education groups are voting less in presidential elections than they did in 1964, the poor show by far the largest decline. Over this period, the voting rate among the poorest fifth of the population dropped by 14 percent—more than twice the decline in voting among the rest of the population. Freeman estimates that this differential decline in electoral participation among the poor had the effect of raising the income of the median voter from the 53rd percentile (of the whole population) to the 59th. To the extent that politicians try to cater to the needs of the median voter, this change moves the center of gravity of the political system significantly toward the more well-to-do.

In her chapter, Theda Skocpol points out that we should also consider the institutional context in which political participation takes place. The contours of civic involvement have changed over the years, with less emphasis on face-to-face participation in grassroots organizations, and more on lobbying groups and other national organizations that rely on direct mail, financial contributions, and the mass media. As Skocpol shows, these institutional changes have led to a striking decline in the kinds of civic organizations that bring people of different class backgrounds together and give people from modest backgrounds an opportunity to gain political experience and leadership skills. Poor and working-class people now face a political environment that offers them fewer opportunities for meaningful participation. To take one telling example, the number of members of professional societies with at least some college education has ballooned to more than four times the number of non-college-educated workers in unions—an advantage that has grown by 50 percent since 1975.

PUBLIC POLICY

There are long-standing differences of opinion about the implications of economic inequality for public policy. As inequality rises and the affluent become increasingly capable of purchasing private substitutes for public social provisions (such as education, heath care, and retirement pensions), they might use their increasing economic and political resources to lobby for reductions in progressive taxation and cuts in social programs. On the contrary, growing economic inequality might spur more redistributive public policies, if the ranks of the have-nots begin to outnumber the ranks of the haves, and politicians respond to the growing constituency of economically-frustrated voters by taxing the rich and distributing benefits to the poor. Three chapters examine these alternative scenarios, looking at evidence across countries, across states, and over the course of U.S. history.

Lars Osberg and his colleagues review the cross-national evidence showing that among a set of comparably developed countries, the United States has the highest level of economic inequality and the lowest level of cash assistance to the poor. When noncash benefits, such as education, health insurance, and food stamps are taken into account, however, the United States moves toward the middle of the pack. So, at this general level, international comparisons do not support the simple idea that more inequality inevitably leads to less social spending, but inequality may influence the form in which social transfers are made. As Osberg and his colleagues point out, cash benefits require trust that the recipient will choose to use the support provided in a responsible way. Noncash benefits, such as food stamps, pre-empt that choice. If, as many studies suggest, high levels of inequality lead to low levels of community involvement and trust in others, then the high levels of inequality in the United States might account for our preference for noncash benefits.

Gabriel Lenz reviews evidence for the relationship between inequality and redistributive policy within the United States. He points out that the recent rise in inequality in the United States corresponds exactly with a decline in the generosity of welfare programs, such as Aid to Families with Dependent Children (AFDC). Analyzing cross-sectional variation across the fifty states, Lenz finds that the relationship between inequality of a state's income distribution and the generosity of its AFDC benefits is negative. But the relationship is weak, and Lenz suggests that we will need to develop more sophisticated models of political factors at the state level in order to get a true test of the relationship between inequality and welfare generosity.

Howard Rosenthal looks at the long sweep of U.S. political history in the twentieth century and shows a remarkable coincidence between inequality and political polarization between the two parties on a single liberal-conservative dimension: the more inequality, the greater the polarization. Polarization tends to make the political process "sticky" because it is more difficult to achieve a legislative consensus. Therefore, as inequality rises, it may become more difficult to respond legislatively with effective countermeasures. For example, the real value of the minimum wage, which is not indexed and must be raised legislatively to keep up with inflation, has fallen by about one-third since inequality started rising in the late 1970s. Rosenthal also points out that the rise of inequality has been accompanied by reasonably strong economic growth, so that real income of the median household has not suffered, even as incomes have grown fastest at the top. This is not, as Rosenthal suggests, a scenario likely to lead to strong political demands for redistribution. In fact, top marginal tax rates have generally declined since the 1970s, and the exemption from estate tax liability has risen.

Bruce Western and colleagues turn from distributional issues to examine the effects of rising inequality on criminal justice policy. Since 1980, there has been an unprecedented increase in the U.S. incarceration rate, just as inequality was rising. Tellingly, these increases were much steeper among high school dropouts than among graduates of high school or college. Was this because those with limited educational preparation faced increasingly bleaker prospects as inequality rose and therefore turned to crime, or was it because rising inequality leads to a perceived need to control increasingly marginalized groups who come to be considered a threat to social order? Certainly, the criminal justice system became a great deal more punitive over the past twenty-five years with the adoption of mandatory minimum sentencing laws, habitual offender laws, and truth in sentencing laws. It is difficult to account for these systemic changes by any aggregate increase in crime, which generally declined over the period. But a conclusive test of the social control hypothesis will need to compare the relative risks of incarceration among those who lost ground economically with the risk of those who advanced, holding criminal propensities constant. Western's group is at work on just such a test.

WEALTH

Economic inequality can be reproduced over the generations as families accumulate wealth and bequeath it on to their children. Questions remain about trends in wealth inequality over the last twenty-five years, but it is clear that racial inequality in wealth is very large. Much of the research on this question has investigated the role of racial differences in labor market position, family characteristics, returns on investment, and other factors. As John Karl Scholz and Kara Levine write, the research on racial inequality in wealth provides resources for thinking about wealth inequality more generally, and particularly for finding the connections between economic inequality and inequality in other domains, such as families.

DIRECTIONS FOR RESEARCH

It is clear that social inequality has risen in a number of domains. On family life, the results of Ellwood and Jencks's research have already been noted. Similarly, Steven Martin notes growing class differences in the timing of family formation. Marcia Meyers and colleagues report that the cost burden of day care and early childhood education has become more unequal, and that the gap in access to quality care may also have widened. At the other end of the educational spectrum, Thomas Kane reports similar trends for college access. As Fligstein and Shin write, working conditions have improved for high-skilled workers and deteriorated for low-skilled workers (although work for everyone became less secure). Richard Freeman finds evidence that class inequality in voting has increased.

There are exceptions to this pattern. By and large, Suzanne Bianchi and her colleagues did not find rising inequality in parents' investments in children, although class differences in these resources remain quite large. Sean Corcoran and his colleagues found that spending by local school districts has become more equal over the last three decades. As noted earlier, we might expect the effect of economic inequality to vary reflecting the relative role of market and public institutions, as the example of education suggests. When most students attend public school, their access to educational resources reflects school finance policies that, whatever their flaws, have some redistributive elements. In early childhood education, however, and at college, parents face a complex mix of public and private schools, and the quality of education depends much more on the ability to pay. In these more market-driven sectors, it is not surprising to find evidence that access to quality schooling has widened as economic inequality has grown.

The research reported here should stimulate further work about the contextual effects of economic inequality. Rising economic inequality could, some fear, have social implications beyond those stemming from changes in individual and family incomes. The context of inequality itself, with wide disparities between rich and poor, could have subtle consequences for morale, civic engagement, and commitment to public institutions. It is important to know what economic inequality may mean for our political lives, and for the public policies that result. In addition, a new stream of research on inequality and health, represented here by the work of Eibner and Evans, suggests that the context of economic inequality might have a variety of social and psychological effects on individuals, for instance on marital stability, educational aspirations, and mental health, that we should not ignore.

Clearly, economic inequality may have far-reaching and long-term social consequences that bear further investigation. This volume provides a foundation for research on these consequences. It is just a beginning, however. As we would expect from this foray into a new field, the chapters that follow raise more questions than they answer. To resolve these empirical questions, and to extend our understanding of social inequality into new areas, will require a large and interdisciplinary research effort. We hope this volume will stimulate such an effort.

Kathryn M. Neckerman
Associate Director
Institute for Social and Economic Research and Policy

Part I

Family and Neighborhood

Chapter 1

The Uneven Spread of Single-Parent Families: What Do We Know? Where Do We Look for Answers?

David T. Ellwood and Christopher Jencks

Amerchant families changed dramatically during the last third of the twentieth century. From 1900 until the late 1960s, roughly three-quarters of all American sixteen-year-olds had lived with both of their biological parents. By 2000 only about half of all sixteen-year-olds were living with both biological parents. During the first half of the twentieth century, moreover, most parents who were not living with their children had no choice about the matter: they were dead. By the end of the twentieth century, most of the parents who were not living with their children were alive but living elsewhere (see figure 1.1).

The focus of this chapter, however, is not simply the fact that family structures changed, but the fact that they changed very differently depending on parents' education and race. All groups are postponing marriage, but not all are postponing parenthood. As a result, the rise in single-parent families is concentrated among blacks and among the less educated. It hardly occurred at all among women with college degrees.

Children's families have changed in broadly similar ways throughout the developed world, but no other nation has changed as much as the United States. The best evidence on this comes from the Fertility and Family Surveys (FFS), which provide data on the stability of both marriages and cohabiting unions in Europe during the late 1980s and early 1990s. Gunnar Andersson (2002) used these data to estimate the fraction of fifteen-year-olds who would live with both of their biological parents if parents continued to split up at the same rate as that found at the time of the FFS.[1] Figure 1.2 shows his projections for the United States and six countries in western Europe. If nothing changed, roughly seven-eighths of southern European fifteen-year-olds and two-thirds of northern European fifteen-year-olds would live with both of their biological parents at age fifteen, compared to only half of all American fifteen-year-olds.

The transformation of the American family since 1960 has been both an intellectual challenge and a recurrent source of frustration for social scientists. Some of the nation's best-known social theorists, including Gary Becker and William Julius Wilson, have sought to explain the change. Yet no consensus has emerged about why American families changed or why the amount of change varied by race and education. The most widely cited empirical papers seem to be those that disprove a popular explanation, not those that support one. Indeed, it is only a slight exaggeration to say that the main contribution of empirical social science to our understanding of family change has been to show that *nothing* caused it. Yet despite the absence of an identifiable culprit or a smoking gun, families did change.

FIGURE 1.1   *U.S. Children Not Living with Their Own Parents at Age Sixteen Because a Parent Died or for Other Reasons, 1910s to 1990s*

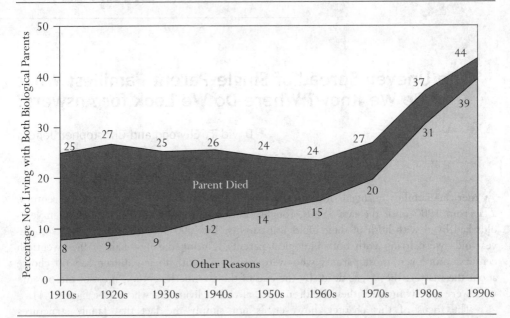

Source: Retrospective reports from 40,090 surviving adults interviewed by the General Social Survey between 1972 and 2000 (tabulations by Zoua Vang). The number of respondents turning sixteen in a decade ranges from a maximum of 8,530 in the 1960s to as low as 876 in the 1990s and 1,074 in the 1910s. The question was "Were you living with both your own mother and father around the time you were sixteen?" If "No" "With whom were you living around that time?" If the respondent had married or left home by age sixteen, the interviewer was supposed to ask whom the respondent lived with before that. If respondents were not living with both their own mother and father at sixteen, a follow-up question asked, "What happened?" Aside from a parent dying, the most common answer was that the respondent's parents divorced or separated. There is no separate category for parents who never lived together. Some respondents born out of wedlock may have described their parents as having "separated." Others may have given answers that the GSS records as "other."

This report is divided into five sections. The first section discusses which changes in family structure should worry us. We argue that:

- Those whose primary goal is to reduce child poverty should mainly worry about the increased proportion of children living with only one adult, especially adults with relatively low potential earnings.

- Those whose primary goal is to improve children's overall well-being should also worry about the fact that even children in two-adult households are less likely to be living with both of their biological parents and more likely to be living with a stepparent or their mother's live-in boyfriend.

- Those whose primary goal is to bring American behavior into line with traditional moral rules should worry about the rising age of marriage (which has led to a large increase in premarital sex), the decline of shotgun weddings (which has led to a large increase in nonmarital births), and the high rate of divorce.

FIGURE 1.2   *Projected Percentage of Children Not Living with Both Biological Parents at Age Fifteen in the United States and Six Western European Nations, Based on Split-Up Rates Around 1990*

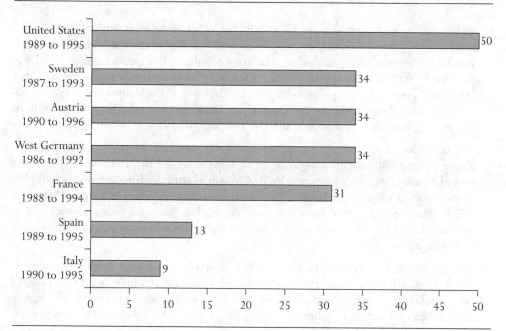

Source: Andersson (2002). Cumulative dissolution rates for marriages and cohabiting unions are estimated from life tables for these six-year intervals by assuming that the current dissolution rates for children of different ages persist.

The next section describes the most important changes affecting children's living arrangements over the past generation.

• Single-parent families have become more common in all demographic groups, but the increases have been greatest among less-educated women and African Americans.

• Women in all demographic groups are marrying later than they did a generation ago. But while highly educated women have postponed both marriage and parenthood, less-educated women have postponed marriage more than parenthood. As a result, nonmarital births have risen dramatically among less-educated women but more modestly among the highly educated.

• Compared to white women, African American women have also postponed marriage more than childbearing, so nonmarital births have risen faster among African Americans than among whites.

• White women with a college degree seldom have children out of wedlock. Most of those who become single mothers marry before their child is born but then divorce. Divorce rates among the highly educated have not risen since the early 1980s, so the fraction of highly educated mothers raising children on their own has not changed much since 1980.

- The increase in nonmarital births, which continued into the 1990s, was confined to the bottom two-thirds of the educational distribution. As a result, the association between a woman's educational attainment and her chances of being a single mother rose after 1980.

- Cohabiting couples now account for nearly half of all nonmarital births in the United States. Among whites, cohabiting couples account for almost all of the increase in non-marital births since 1980. But unlike cohabiting couples in Europe, cohabiting couples in the United States usually split up within a few years of their baby's birth. The fact that "high-risk" couples have been switching from marriage to cohabitation since 1980 prob-ably played a role in stabilizing the divorce rate. It is not clear whether the switch from marriage to cohabitation increased the risk that any given couple would split up.

- Attitudes toward premarital sex, gender roles, the value of marriage, and the accept-ability of nonmarital childbearing changed rapidly during the late 1960s and 1970s. Such attitudes have changed far less since 1980. Changes in attitudes have not always moved in tandem with changes in behavior. Premarital sex increased sharply in the 1960s and 1970s, when attitudes were becoming more permissive. But premarital sex continued to increase during the 1980s and early 1990s, when attitudes towards premarital sex were not changing much.

- The age at which individuals first have sexual intercourse (whether marital or premari-tal) fell only a little between 1960 and 1990, while the age at which individuals married rose substantially. Taken together, these two facts suggest that premarital sex mainly replaced marital sex, not abstinence. This pattern does not vary much by education.

- In the early 1960s, most marriages were closely followed by a first birth. That linkage has now been broken. More women are having their first child well before they marry, and more women are marrying well before they have their first child.

The third section discusses the social science literature on the role of wages, welfare benefits, and the sex ratio in explaining family change. The following section discusses the role of non-economic influences, such as changes in women's sense of control and efficacy, changes in attitudes toward nonmarital sex, cohabitation, nonmarital births, and divorce, and improvements in contraception, the legalization of abortion, and no-fault divorce. In the next section, we present some new evidence regarding some of these theories. We then present our conclusions in the final section.

We come to several conclusions regarding the existing literature on changes in family composition:

- Traditional economic models emphasize the economic advantages that flow from the fact that one partner can specialize in child-rearing while the other specializes in market labor. These models predict that improvements in men's earning power will make mar-riage more common, while improvements in women's earning power will make mar-riage less common. These models also predict that lower welfare benefits will make marriage more common, while a lower ratio of men to women will make marriage less common.

- The wages available to men, the wages available to women, welfare benefits, and the sex ratio can explain a large fraction of the change in single-parenthood for different racial and educational groups. But the estimated impact of these variables is extremely sensi-tive to how we specify the statistical model. A cross-group time series gives properly signed and significant results for all four variables. In a model that includes a linear time trend and race dummies, however, many signs reverse and the estimates become unstable.

- The literature provides consistent evidence that declines in men's economic opportunities reduce marriage rates. But men's real wages have not changed enough over the past generation to explain much of the change in family structure, even among the least educated.

- The literature also provides consistent evidence that the ratio of men to women in a given geographic area or demographic group has a significant impact on marriage rates. But the ratio of men to women has not fallen enough to explain a substantial fraction of the decline in marriage.

- The literature is divided on how women's economic opportunities affect marriage. Comparisons across geographic areas and time periods usually suggest that increases in women's economic opportunities reduce the fraction who are married at any given age, but this may indicate only that higher wages allow women to marry later. Longitudinal data on individuals usually suggest that women with higher wages and hours are more likely to marry eventually.

- Recent literature suggests that higher welfare benefits reduce marriage but that the effect is small. Real welfare benefits have fallen since 1980, so changes in the welfare system cannot explain the spread of single-motherhood since that time.

- Traditional economic models focus on whether individuals gain from marriage, not on whether they gain more from marrying early or marrying late, so they are not helpful in explaining delays in marriage.

- The traditional economic model also treats marriage and childbearing as nearly synchronous, so it cannot explain why a rising fraction of highly educated women marry well before they have children or why a rising fraction of less-educated women have children well before they marry.

- Psychological theories sometimes make different predictions from economic theories. Psychological theories that focus on an individual's sense of control and confidence, for example, predict that better job opportunities will induce women to eschew early childbearing but could also make women more likely to marry later.

- The timing of technical advances in birth control, the legalization of abortion, and no-fault divorce is broadly consistent with the timing of changes in sexual activity and marriage, including the decline in "shotgun" marriages. But the case for a causal link between these changes is mostly circumstantial.

- Some sociological theories stress the possibility that the cultural and attitudinal determinants of behavior can change for non-economic reasons, but we did not find many testable hypotheses regarding these sources of change in family composition. The slow pace of most normative changes makes it hard to estimate the impact of such changes on behavior, because the most common way of showing that a change in A leads to a change in B is to identify the precise times at which A has changed and then see whether changes in A are followed by changes in B.

We also conclude that both theoretical and empirical work on family change needs to address three gaps in the existing literature:

1. Instead of treating marriage and childbearing as essentially simultaneous events, social scientists need to treat them as separate (though potentially related) outcomes.

2. Social scientists also need to draw a clearer distinction between factors that delay marriage or childbearing and factors that lead people to eschew marriage or parenthood entirely.

3. Social scientists need to integrate economic, social, and technological changes into unified models of changes in marriage and fertility patterns.

We conclude by offering a working hypothesis about the sources of family change that seems to us consistent with the data, but we do not try to test this hypothesis in a rigorous way.

WHICH CHANGES IN AMERICAN FAMILIES SHOULD WE WORRY ABOUT?

When legislators, policy analysts, and opinion leaders discuss "the decline of the family," they usually focus on two issues: out-of-wedlock births and fatherless families. They often discuss these two issues as if they were identical. In reality, however, nearly half of all fatherless families are created by death, imprisonment, or divorce, and cohabiting couples now account for nearly half of all out-of-wedlock births. As a result, it is important to figure out precisely what forms of family change worry us before we try to explain the changes. Americans seem to worry about family change for at least three kinds of reasons, which we label economic, developmental, and moral. Each of these concerns implies a different definition of "the problem."

The Economic Problem

From an economic perspective, the most troubling feature of family change has been the spread of single-motherhood. Few fathers want to devote a large share of their income to supporting children they do not live with, especially when the money actually goes to their former wife or girlfriend. Furthermore, even the most generous fathers cannot do as much to support their children when they also have to maintain another household as when they live in the child's household. This problem is compounded by the fact that single mothers tend to be less educated and seldom command high wages. Nor can many single mothers make up for low wages by working long hours, since they must also care for their children. And while poor single mothers are eligible for public assistance, legislators have kept such benefits very low, lest generosity encourage even more women to raise children on their own.

Most mothers avoid poverty by living with someone else who has a regular job, and even unmarried mothers usually find that this is the easiest way to raise their standard of living. Mothers who have divorced often remarry, and they tend to be about as well off economically in their second marriage as in their first (McLanahan and Sandefur 1994). Unmarried mothers often cohabit with the father of their children or a more recent boyfriend. Young unmarried mothers often live with their parents or with another relative. But not all mothers can find a steady worker who wants to help support them and their children, and even mothers who can find such a person often feel that the non-economic costs of such a living arrangement outweigh the economic benefits. As a result, only 26 percent of all unmarried mothers with children under eighteen lived with another adult who worked full-time all year in 1999, and only 15 percent did so in 1969.

The spread of single-mother families has played a major role in the persistence of poverty. In 1964, when President Lyndon Johnson declared war on poverty, only 30 percent of poor families with children were headed by single mothers. Since the late 1970s the figure has been about 60 percent (calculated from U.S. Department of Commerce 2000b, table B-3). Adam Thomas and Isabel Sawhill (2002) argue that if single-motherhood had not increased between 1970 and 1998, the child poverty rate for 1998 would have been reduced by about one-fifth.

The Child Development Problem

Most Americans probably believe that growing up poor is bad for children, but they also seem to believe that growing up in a single-parent family is bad for children even when the family is not poor. Indeed, the idea that two parents can raise a child better than one usually seems self-evident to couples who get along reasonably well. But when parents do *not* get along, the assumption that their children will always fare better if the parents stay together becomes problematic. Much is likely to depend on what form the parents' incompatibility takes. Getting a violent or abusive parent out of a child's household is often a good idea. Getting a father out of the house when he is having an affair may make the mother feel better while making her children feel worse.

Sara McLanahan and Gary Sandefur (1994) have assembled data from a number of American surveys showing that children who grow up with both of their biological parents perform better on school achievement tests, have fewer children as teenagers, finish high school more often, attend and complete college more often, and are more likely to be employed in early adulthood than those living with a single parent in adolescence. Those whose parents have divorced are only marginally better off than those whose parents have never married. Those with a parent who died are, in contrast, significantly better off than those whose parents divorced or never married. These differences persist with controls for parental education, race, number of siblings, and place of residence.

About half of the disadvantage associated with living in a single-parent family is explained by the fact that these families have less income than two-parent families.[2] Income is not the whole story, however, because children living with a stepparent in adolescence have about the same family income as children living with both of their biological parents. Yet despite enjoying roughly the same family income as adolescents living with both biological parents, adolescents living with a stepparent are far more likely to drop out of high school or to have a child while still a teenager. Indeed, children living with a stepparent are at least as disadvantaged as children living with a single parent. A key finding is thus that children raised by both of their biological parents do better than children raised by mothers who never married, mothers who married and then divorced, or mothers who married, divorced, and remarried.

The claim that family disruption is bad for children must, however, be assessed against some explicit counterfactual alternative. Consider nonmarital births. One possible question is, what would happen if unmarried women never became pregnant or always got abortions? To answer this question, we need to know how marriage and fertility patterns would change. If marriage and fertility patterns remained unchanged, the birth rate would fall by about one-third, and the couples having children would be identical to the married couples who currently have children. If these children's test scores, behavior, and other outcomes remained unchanged, almost all measures of children's well-being would show a marked improvement. Reducing the birth rate by one-third would, however, create strong pressures to admit more immigrants, whose children also tend to have more problems than the children of married natives.

Many critics of nonmarital childbearing envision a different counterfactual world in which couples who conceive children out of wedlock always get married before the child is born. If these couples also stay married, we would see a rise in the number of children whose parents have a "bad" marriage. Some children would presumably be better off with two somewhat incompatible parents than with only one, while other children would be worse off. No one has yet proposed a convincing way to estimate the net effect of such a change on either parents or children.

Nonetheless, the trend that should worry those who believe that children's social and psychological outcomes would improve if more biological parents stayed together is not the percentage of children living with a lone mother but the percentage who do not live with their biological parents—a group we refer to as coming from "non-intact" families. Because unmarried mothers often marry (or remarry), the percentage of children living in a non-intact family is considerably larger than the percentage living in a single-parent family.

If we were exclusively concerned with parents' welfare, we might not worry much about the fact that fewer biological parents are choosing to stay together. After all, if parents choose to split up, at least one of them must think he or she will be better off living elsewhere. In many cases, moreover, both parents think they will be better off apart. They may be wrong, of course, but they have usually given the matter more thought and know more about their own situation than either social scientists or legislators.

But even if the current system maximizes parents' welfare, we cannot assume that it maximizes children's welfare. Parents embroiled in a conflictual relationship cannot know how splitting up will affect their children. Even well-meaning parents may exaggerate the degree to which their children's interests coincide with their own. A system in which the stability of parental unions depends entirely on the parents' choices is therefore likely to put less weight on children's welfare than society as a whole would like. Children's long-term welfare might, for example, be optimized when 80 percent of parents stay together until their children are grown, while parents' welfare might be optimized when only 40 percent do so. If a laissez-faire system in which each parent is free to do what he or she thinks best resulted in 50 percent of biological parents staying together, laissez-faire would not serve children's interests very well.

The Moral Problem

When American politicians and citizens talk about changes in the family, they often use traditional moral language, asserting that the spread of premarital sex, out-of-wedlock births, and divorce violates moral rules that allow no exceptions. Such moralists often claim that immoral behavior has negative social consequences, but their assessment of the behavior seldom depends on the validity of such empirical claims. Those who believe that premarital sex is morally wrong mostly think it is wrong even for individuals who practice birth control effectively, do not spread AIDS, and marry before having children. Likewise, those who believe that divorce violates immutable religious principles seldom exempt divorces that make both partners happier, divorces that make particular children better off, or divorces involving childless couples.

Because traditional moral rules about sex, marriage, divorce, and childbearing are not sensitive to the particular circumstances in which individuals find themselves, many Americans reject the idea that violating these rules is always wrong. As violations of traditional norms have become more common, reluctance to condemn the violations seems to have increased, even among those who follow the rules themselves. For those who favor traditional moral rules, the public's growing willingness to make exceptions in particular cases is part of the problem.

WHEN AND HOW DID FAMILIES CHANGE?

Children Living with Unmarried Mothers

Broadly speaking, there are two ways of measuring the spread of single-motherhood. If your primary concern is measuring changes in the welfare of children, the most natural approach is to treat children as the unit of observation and ask how many of them lived with unmarried mothers in a given year. But if your primary concern is understanding why some mothers are married and others are not, it makes more sense to treat mothers as the unit of observation and ask how many mothers raising children are currently unmarried.

This chapter focuses on mothers, partly because we want to understand why mothers have made different choices in different periods and partly because treating mothers as the unit of observation makes it easier to track changes in the association between mothers' marital status and their education, race, employment status, and other characteristics. Here and throughout we define "children" as individuals under the age of eighteen and "mothers" as either biological mothers or stepmothers living with such children. We define women as "married" only if they live with their husband, and we use the term "unmarried" and "single" interchangeably to subsume all women are not living with a husband, regardless of whether they are separated, divorced, widowed, never married, or cohabitating.

Figure 1.3 shows changes between 1940 and 2000 in the proportion of mothers with children under eighteen who were not married and living with a husband. Note that the numbers are all much lower than the numbers in figure 1.1. Figure 1.3 counts only mothers who were unmarried in a given year. Mothers are thus counted as "married" even if they were married to someone other than their children's father. Figure 1.3 also covers mothers with children of all ages, whereas figure 1.1 describes the probability of a family disruption before a child is sixteen. Nonetheless, the trend lines in the two figures are roughly parallel. Both are essentially flat between 1940 and 1960. Both rise sharply between 1960 and 1990. The only difference is that the trend line in figure 1.1 continues to rise in the 1990s, whereas the trend line in figure 1.3 levels off.

This chapter focuses primarily on the question of how and why American families changed differentially by education and race between 1960 and 2000. In her excellent survey of trends in the well-being of American women, Francine Blau (1998) breaks down family structure changes by level of education—a type of analysis that is surprisingly uncommon in the literature—and demonstrates sharp differences in the trends by education between 1970 and 1995. We extend our look to the period between 1940 and 2000. Figure 1.4 shows the fraction of mothers who were unmarried broken down by the number of years of school the mother had completed, using the decennial censuses. The trend lines for mothers with some high school, a high school diploma, some college, and a college diploma

FIGURE 1.3   *U.S. Mothers Not Living with a Husband, 1940 to 2000*

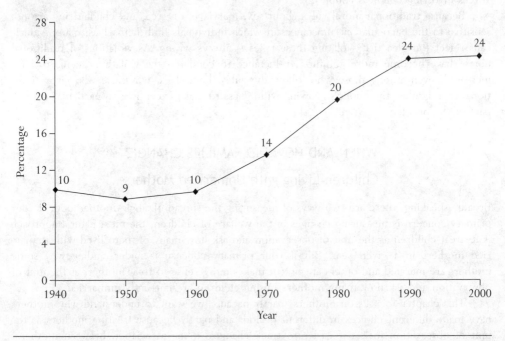

Source: Tabulations by Andrew Clarkwest using Integrated Public Use Micro Samples from the decennial census.

diverge dramatically. The line for women with some college is almost indistinguishable from that for women with only a high school diploma. To minimize clutter, we have also suppressed the post-1970 trend line for mothers with no high school, which is almost flat. (After 1970, mothers with less than nine years of schooling were increasingly likely to be immigrants, whose chances of becoming single mothers are relatively low.)

Here and throughout we focus on percentage point changes in the fractions of different groups who are married, divorced, or single mothers, not on the proportional changes. If we ask what proportion of mothers were unmarried in 2000 compared to the proportion in 1960, for example, the proportion rose from 11.3 to 39.5 percent among mothers with nine to eleven years of school and from 7.2 to 25.5 percent among mothers with thirteen to fifteen years of school. In absolute terms the increase is much larger for the less-educated mothers (28.2 versus 18.3 percentage points). In proportional terms, the rate grew by a factor of about 3.5 for both groups. We focus on percentage point differences because doubling a big number matters more than doubling a small number. If we were to emphasize proportional changes or changes in the logged odds of different outcomes, differences by race and education would often look quite different.

In theory, the widening gaps between high school dropouts, high school graduates, and college graduates could also reflect compositional change. Mothers' educational attainment rose substantially between 1960 and 2000. As a result, high school dropouts were far more disadvantaged, at least in relative terms, in 2000 than in 1960. Similarly, college graduates were less advantaged in 2000 than in 1960. Thus, if a mother's marital status depended on her relative rather than her absolute level of education, the percentage of single mothers

FIGURE 1.4   *U.S. Mothers Not Living with a Husband, by Years of School Completed, 1940 to 2000*

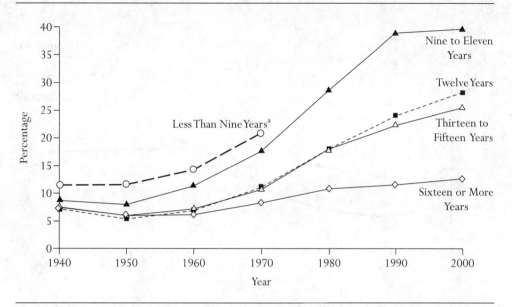

Source: Tabulations by Andrew Clarkwest using Integrated Public Use Micro Samples from the decennial census.
[a]Post-1970 data for mothers with less than nine years of school were omitted because the category is increasingly composed of mothers raised in countries other than the United States.

would rise at every educational level simply because every level ranked lower in relative terms.

To avoid this problem, we usually define educational attainment in relative terms, comparing mothers in the top, middle, and bottom thirds of the educational distribution for any given year.[3] Figure 1.5 presents the data in this way. The percentage of mothers who were unmarried rose sharply throughout the educational distribution between 1960 and 1980. After 1980 the increase continued among mothers in the bottom and middle thirds of the distribution, but not among mothers in the top third.

Divorce

The trend line for highly educated women flattens out after 1980 because these women were mostly becoming single mothers by marrying and divorcing rather than by having a child out of wedlock, and divorce rates leveled off after about 1980. Figure 1.6 shows the annual divorce rate per 1,000 married women from 1920 through 1996, when the federal government stopped reporting such data. If we set aside the spike right after World War II, the rate shows a very modest upward trend between 1920 and 1960 (from 8.0 to 9.2 per 1,000). From 1960 to 1980, the rate rose sharply, peaking at 22.6 per 1,000 in 1980 and edging down after that.

Our concern here, of course, is not with the overall divorce rate but with the rate among couples with children. About half of all divorces involve children under eighteen. The small squares in figure 1.6 estimate the cumulative probability that a child would experience a divorce before the age of eighteen if the divorce rate among couples with

FIGURE 1.5   *U.S. Mothers Not Living with a Husband, by Rank in the Educational Distribution for a Given Year, 1940 to 2000*

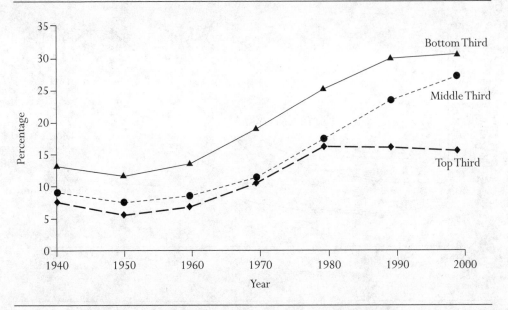

Source: Tabulations by Andrew Clarkwest using Public Use Micro Samples from the decennial census.

children in the year shown had persisted for eighteen years. The estimates do not precisely parallel the divorce rate for all married women, but both trends begin to climb in the 1960s and both peak around 1980. Unfortunately, this series ends in 1984.

To assess post-1984 trends among couples with children, we draw on calculations by Steven Martin using the June Current Population Survey (CPS). Martin's estimates cover the firstborn children of women in their first marriage and show the percentage of these children who experienced a divorce before the age of ten. These results are arranged with the year in which the children were five years old on the horizontal axis, since age five is roughly the midpoint of the interval during which each cohort was at risk. Martin's data also suggest that children's chances of living through a divorce climbed in the 1970s, flattened out in the early 1980s, and declined slightly in the 1990s.[4]

Figure 1.7 provides crude estimates of how divorce rates affected mothers at different educational levels. It shows the percentage of mothers in each third of the educational distribution who were either separated from their husband or divorced and not remarried. In the 1980s, these percentages fell for women in the top third of the education distribution. In the 1990s, they level off or fall for everyone.

Nonmarital Births

Among mothers in the bottom two-thirds of the education distribution, single-motherhood continued to rise during the 1980s, largely owing to a sharp rise in the share of children born out of wedlock.

Figure 1.8 shows the fraction of all mothers with children who were never married broken down by rank in the education distribution. This measure shows a dramatic fanning

FIGURE 1.6   *U.S. Children's Experience of Divorce, 1920 to 1996*

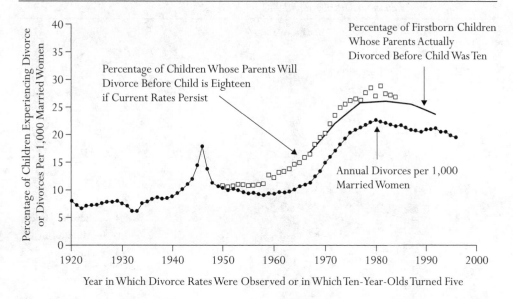

Sources: Divorces per 1,000 married women are annual estimates from U.S. Census Bureau, *Historical Statistics of the United States*, series B-217, and *Statistical Abstract of the United States*, various years. Percentages of children whose parents will divorce before the child is eighteen are based on the percentage of children whose parents divorced in the year shown and come from London (1989, table 1). We converted these annual estimates (P_{D1}) to eighteen-year risks (P_{D18}) by assuming $P_{D18} = 1 - (1 - P_{D1})^{18}$. The percentage of firstborn children experiencing a divorce within ten years of birth is for children from first marriages and is based on hazard models for five-year birth cohorts estimated by Steven Martin using the June Current Population Survey. We used linear interpolation to estimate probabilities for one-year birth cohorts. Each cohort's probability of experiencing a divorce before age ten is shown for the midpoint of the interval during which the cohort was at risk, which is the year in which the cohort was five years old.

out since 1970, with the greatest growth among less-educated women and far more modest changes among the well-educated. But this figure does not capture patterns of out-of-wedlock childbearing very accurately, since many women who are not married at the time of their child's birth either marry later or have been married earlier. Thus, as an alternative, figure 1.9 shows the proportion of mothers with children under the age of one who report they are not currently living with a husband.[5] Here we see even less growth in the proportion of highly educated mothers with who are not married. More interestingly, we see real evidence that the incidence of out-of-marriage childbearing has declined in the most recent period.

Racial Differences

Figures 1.10 and 1.11 show the percentage of all women with children (married and unmarried) who are widowed, separated or divorced, and never married. These estimates come from the March Current Population Survey and cover the years from 1965 through 2002. The fraction of black mothers who were unmarried was already higher in 1965 than the fraction of white mothers who were unmarried in 2002. Black mothers are much more

FIGURE 1.7   *U.S. Mothers Either Divorced and Not Remarried or Separated, by Rank in the Education Distribution, 1940 to 2000*

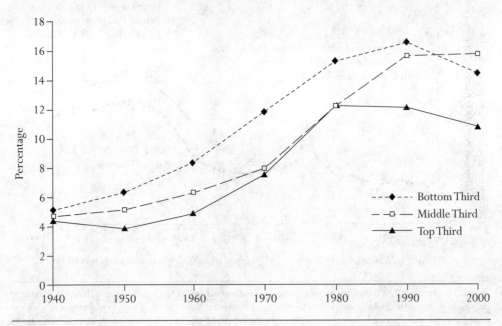

Source: Tabulations by Andrew Clarkwest using the Integrated Public Use Micro Samples from the decennial census.

FIGURE 1.8   *All U.S. Mothers with Children Under Eighteen Who Have Never Been Married, by Rank in Education Distribution, 1940 to 2000*

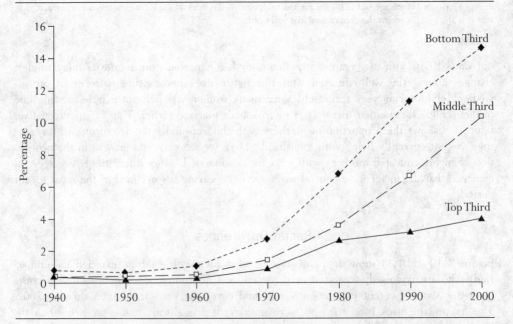

Source: Tabulations by Andrew Clarkwest using the Integrated Public Use Micro Samples from the decennial census.

FIGURE 1.9   *U.S. Mothers with Children Less Than One Year Old Not Living with a Husband, by Rank in the Educational Distribution, 1940 to 2000*

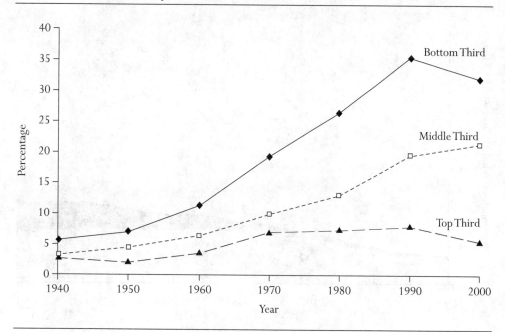

Source: Tabulations by Andrew Clarkwest using Integrated Public Use Micro Samples from the decennial census.

likely than whites to be single parents owing to parental death, divorce, or having never been married. Still, having never been married is the most common reason for being a single parent among blacks, while separation and divorce is the most common reason among whites.

The high fraction of black mothers who have never married has several sources. First, teenage mothers accounted for 20 percent of black births but only 11 percent of white births in 2000, and very few teenage mothers of either race now marry. But older blacks are also less likely than whites to marry before their children are born. Indeed, blacks are less likely than whites ever to marry. Among women age forty to forty-four in 2000, for example, 91 percent of whites but only 71 percent of blacks had been married.[6] Whites of almost any age are more likely to have married than to have had a child. Blacks of almost any age are more likely to have had a child than to have married.

Cohabitation

The post-1980 increase in nonmarital births is closely related to the fact that more couples live together without marrying. According to Larry Bumpass and Hsien-Hen Lu (2000), 29 percent of unmarried American mothers were cohabiting with their baby's father in the early 1980s. By the early 1990s the figure had reached 39 percent. In the Fragile Families Study, which covers children born between 1998 and 2000 in American cities of more than 200,000, almost half of all unmarried mothers were living with the father when the baby was born.[7]

Furthermore, Bumpass and Lu (2000) report that among whites the increase in non-

FIGURE 1.10   *Marital Status of White Mothers 1965 to 2002*

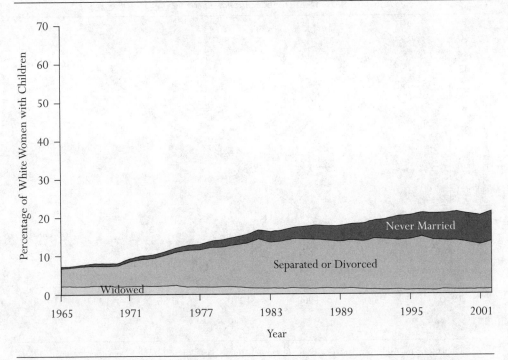

Source: Authors' tabulations of March CPS data.

marital childbearing between the early 1980s and the early 1990s was almost entirely trace-able to the increase in cohabitation. The fraction of white babies born to mothers who were not living with their child's father was essentially flat, although this fraction did rise among blacks. We follow the British practice of using the term "lone mothers" to identify those who are neither married nor cohabiting. This designation should not be taken literally, however, since some of these mothers have boyfriends and others live with relatives.

The uneven spread of cohabitation makes cross-national comparisons of nonmarital childbearing almost uninterpretable. Figure 1.12, for example, shows the fraction of chil-dren born to unmarried couples around 1990 in the United States and eight western Euro-pean nations covered by the FFS study described earlier. If we simply look at the overall percentage of children born to unmarried couples, the United States falls in the middle of the distribution: above Italy, Spain, Finland, and West Germany, but below Austria, Norway, and France, and far below Sweden. However, American children were far less likely than children in other rich countries to be born into a household that included both of their biological parents. Unpartnered mothers of newborns were three times as common in the United States as in Sweden, even though unmarried parents were almost twice as common in Sweden as in the United States.

One reason American scholars have neglected the spread of cohabitation is that the American variant of cohabitation is unusually unstable. Using the FFS data from around 1990, Andersson (2001) estimates that in the United States only 22 percent of children born to cohabiting couples will be living with both of their parents at age fifteen, compared to 65 percent of children born to married couples, as shown in figure 1.13. Andersson's

FIGURE 1.11   *Marital Status of Black Mothers 1965 to 2002*

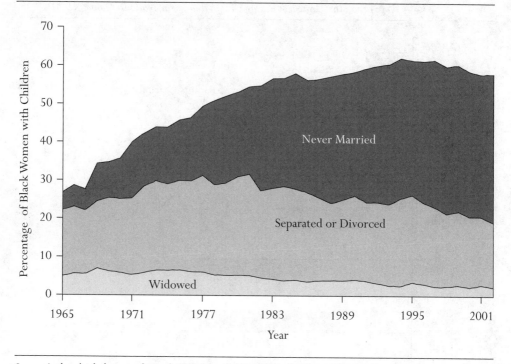

Source: Authors' tabulations of March CPS data.

estimates for the United States are based on data from 1989 to 1995, but the Fragile Families Study, which covers children born between 1998 and 2000, found that such relationships were very unstable. Cohabiting parents are more likely to stay together in western Europe. As figure 1.13 shows, in all nations married couples are more likely than cohabiting couples to stay together. But cohabiting European couples are about as likely to stay together as married American couples. (France is the exception.)

Premarital Sex

Many Americans attribute the spread of premarital sex to advertising, television, and parental permissiveness, which are said to have encouraged young people to experiment with sex at ever earlier ages. Yet adults' retrospective reports suggest that women's age at first intercourse has declined little. Figure 1.14, from the National Survey of Family Growth, shows the age at which adult women said they first engaged in sexual intercourse, arranged by the year in which respondents turned twenty-one. We show the ages at which 25, 50, and 75 percent of each cohort said that it had first had intercourse. There is some decline in age at first intercourse, but it is very small.

Figure 1.15 shows the percentage of each birth cohort that was unmarried at the time of first intercourse. The fraction of the population engaging in premarital sex rose from around half among those who turned twenty-one in the late 1950s to almost 90 percent among those who turned twenty-one in the early 1990s. The increase in premarital sex is

FIGURE 1.12   *Couples Who Were Either Not Living Together or Cohabiting When Their Child Was Born, the United States and Eight European Nations Around 1990*

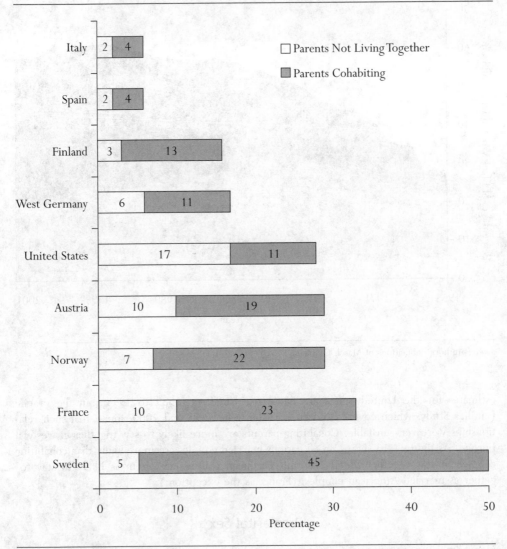

Source: Andersson (2002).

almost entirely due to the fact that young women were marrying much later but were not postponing sexual intercourse.

The increase in premarital sex does, however, help explain the increase in nonmarital childbearing. American couples who have sexual relations are not very careful about contraception, and a significant fraction of the women who conceive a child are unwilling or unable to get abortions. These problems are especially common among American teenagers. Births to teenagers are more frequent in the United States than in other rich countries. Births to teenagers account for a significant fraction of all nonmarital births, especially those to mothers who are not cohabiting.

FIGURE 1.13   *Newborns Expected to Live with Both Biological Parents at Age Fifteen, by Type of Union at Birth, Around 1990*

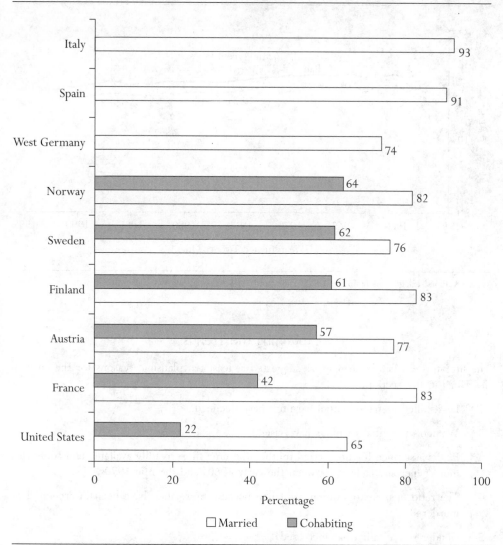

Source: Projections by Andersson (2002) using FFS data on union stability in the late 1980s and early 1990s. The German, Italian, and Spanish surveys did not include enough cohabiting couples with children over nine to estimate fifteen-year dissolution rates. The German and French dissolution rates were very similar up to age nine. The Italian dissolution rates prior to age nine were by far the lowest in Europe.

All of our cross-national comparisons suggest that parents are less committed to one another (or perhaps less committed to their children) in the United States than in western Europe. American parents are less likely to be living together when their baby is born, and those who are living together are more likely to split up before the child is grown, regardless of whether they started out married or cohabiting.[8] We are not aware of any empirical research that seeks to explain this form of American exceptionalism.

FIGURE 1.14   *U.S. Women's Age at First Intercourse, Regardless of Marital Status, by Year Turned Twenty-One, 1958 to 1991*

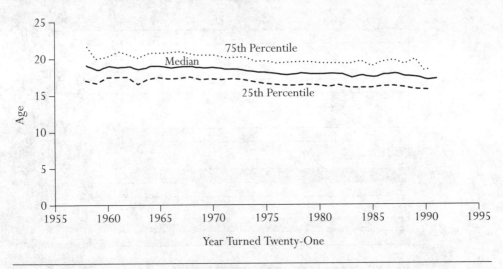

Source: Authors' calculations from the 1982, 1988, and 1995 National Surveys of Family Growth.

Explaining the Trends

The literature on family change has suggested at least ten plausible reasons for the changes described in this section:

1. Less-skilled men's potential earnings have declined.

2. Women's potential earnings have risen.

3. Public assistance for unmarried mothers became more readily available and somewhat more generous, at least between the early 1960s and the mid-1970s.

4. The ratio of men to women has fallen because more men have been incarcerated or murdered.

5. Gender role conflict has increased.

6. Women's sense of control and efficacy has changed.

7. Attitudes toward premarital sex, cohabitation, out-of-wedlock childbearing, and divorce have become more permissive.

8. Better methods of contraception have become available.

9. Abortion was legalized.

10. Divorce laws have been liberalized.

The next section discusses the first four explanations; the following section takes up the remaining six.

FIGURE 1.15   *Fraction of All U.S. Women Who Had Had Premarital Sex as of Age*
Twenty-Five, by Year Turned Twenty-One, 1958 to 1991

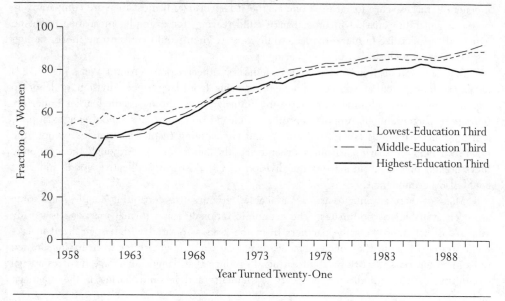

Source: Authors' calculations from the 1982, 1988, and 1995 National Surveys of Family Growth.
Note: Numbers are five-year moving averages.

ECONOMIC DETERMINANTS OF FAMILY CHANGE

The literature that invokes changes in wages, public assistance, or the sex ratio to explain changes in family structure has been heavily influenced by the pathbreaking work of Gary Becker (1991). Becker mainly sought to explain why people marry, not why they have children, and most of the literature that builds on his work does the same. The theory holds that people become unmarried parents when no available marriage looks attractive but raising children remains attractive nonetheless. Work in this tradition relies on a cluster of ideas that we label the traditional economic model (TEM). Some of this work uses economic terminology, like the division of labor, gains from trade, economies of scale, and insuring against risk. But many non-economists have also invoked changes in people's economic alternatives to explain changes in marriage and fertility.

The Traditional Economic Model

The traditional economic model treats marriage as a contract from which both husbands and wives expect to reap economic benefits.[9] These benefits arise because a long-term contract allows both partners to share the potential gains associated with specialization and the household division of labor. Individuals derive utility from market goods, household goods (such as children), and leisure. Market goods are purchased with earnings generated by family members. Household goods (such as supper or children) are produced by some combination of market goods (groceries, books, clothes) and home production (cooking, childrearing) supplied by one or both partners. In such a model, if one partner has a comparative advantage in either market work (because of higher wages) or home production (because they are more efficient nurturers or find such work more rewarding, for example), it generally makes sense for at least one partner to specialize. If most men are comparatively better at generating market income than at child-rearing, for example, most men might be expected to specialize in market work, while most women would concentrate more, though not necessarily exclusively, on childrearing.

Marriage can also yield economic benefits for other reasons. Yoram Weiss (1997, 82) highlights four potential sources of economic gains from marriage: "division of labor to exploit comparative advantage or increasing returns"; overcoming credit market imperfections (one partner might support the other while he or she attends school, for example); sharing collective goods (such as a home); and risk-pooling (if one partner loses a job, the other can help by sharing earnings or entering the labor force). Although the economic literature on marriage emphasizes the division of labor, sharing collective goods and risks could also be important.

Many of these advantages are also available, of course, to cohabiting couples, and some are even available to roommates. The economic rationale for a formal marriage is usually said to be that it protects the partners from the risks associated with a specialized investment strategy. Should the partnership dissolve, one party might suffer from having limited skills in either market work or childrearing. To reduce that danger, marriage involves a legal commitment, with adjudicated property settlements and income-sharing if the marriage ends.

The traditional economic model yields fairly straightforward predictions. If male and female wages converge, or if the value that men and women assign to the non-economic benefits of employment becomes more similar, the advantages of specialization and thus the gains from marriage decline. Conversely, if the gender gap in either wages or the subjective value of market work widens, the advantages of both specialization and marriage grow.

Some of the other economic advantages of marriage should be more sensitive to absolute income levels than to the relative incomes of men and women. High-income individuals can afford to live alone rather than sharing their household with someone they do not find especially congenial. Thus, when incomes rise, we expect to see fewer adults doubling up. That is precisely what we observe among unmarried adults. But while low-income adults are more likely to have roommates or to live with relatives, they are less likely to live with a spouse. Similarly, low-income adults tend to save a smaller fraction of their income than high-income adults, so those with low incomes should be more eager to pool risks with a spouse.

All economic models also predict that improvements in external economic support for single adults, particularly single parents, will make marriage less common. If a single parent can specialize in household production and still get money or noncash benefits from public assistance or relatives, the advantages of marriage diminish. Raising welfare benefits should therefore reduce marriage, while lowering benefits should make marriage more common. Note, however, that what matters is not the absolute benefit level but the difference between a mother's standard of living when she is unmarried rather than married. Thus, if real welfare benefits fall but unskilled men's wages fall even more, marriage rates should also fall.

The sex ratio is obviously not an economic variable in any ordinary sense of the word, but because economic models often include it, we have included it under this heading. At a minimum, the sex ratio is important because in the absence of polygamy any deviation from fifty-fifty means that some members of the more numerous sex are unable to find partners of the less numerous sex. In addition, if both sexes find marriage equally attractive, the scarcer sex should be able to bargain for a larger share of the gains from marriage. If men are in short supply because many men are in prison or dead, for example, women who want to marry have to compete for husbands by offering better "deals"—for example, more earnings, more housework, more child care, or fewer complaints about infidelity. Household resources may also go disproportionately to the men. If a shortage of men allows them to gain many of the advantages of marriage without actually marrying, marriage rates may decline even further.

The traditional economic model suggests that divergent trends in single-parenthood by race and education should be traceable to changes in the ratio of male to female wages for different groups, in welfare benefits or parental support for unmarried mothers, and changes in the ratio of marriageable men to marriageable women. These factors also figure prominently in the work of sociologists, though with some twists. Perhaps the best-known theoretical work is by William Julius Wilson and Kathryn Neckerman (1986). Unlike Becker and other economists, these authors focus on disadvantaged groups, particularly blacks living in inner cities. But like many economists, Wilson and Neckerman emphasize the importance of male earning power and the ratio of young black men to young black women. They argue that high levels of unemployment, weak connections to mainstream employers, rising levels of imprisonment, and a low ratio of men to women have created a shortage of marriageable black men. They argue that the decline in the male marriageable pool (MMP) is a more plausible explanation for changes in black families than are the changes in welfare benefits. They spend relatively little time on the question of whether improved economic opportunities for black women contributed to marriage declines.

All these models share a number of important limitations. First, they are not framed in a life-cycle context. As Valerie Oppenheimer (1997b) points out, the models are meant to explain *whether* people will marry, not *when* they will marry. If the economic gains to marriage decline, more unmarried individuals should permanently eschew marriage, and more married individuals should divorce and not remarry.

A second significant limitation is the lack of attention to fertility decisions (Hotz, Klerman, and Willis 1997).[10] Implicitly, the TEM assumes that decisions about marriage and childbearing are combined into one. The gains from marriage come chiefly from specialization in the care and nurturing of children. Credit market constraints, risk-sharing, and sharing collective goods remain potentially important even when couples do not have children, but gains from specialization sharply diminish when home production does not involve the care and nurture of the children. Failure to model marriage and childbearing separately can blur the distinction between explanations for the prevalence of marriage, nonmarital childbearing, and children living in families headed by a single mother. This is particularly evident when rising welfare benefits are invoked to explain declining marriage rates, since welfare benefit levels alter the economic consequences of marriage only if couples have children. Without the assumption that childbearing and marriage are closely linked, some key predictions of the traditional economic model also change. When married couples have no children, the gains to specialization are far smaller.

A third limitation of the TEM, at least to date, is that it does not seem to explain the spread of cohabitation. The main difference been cohabitation and marriage is that marriage involves a stronger long-term commitment, both legally and normatively. This could be an economic advantage under three circumstances. First, marriage somewhat reduces the economic risks to women who want to specialize in home production. Julie Brines and Kara Joyner (1999) find that married couples are in fact slightly more likely to stay together if they specialize, whereas cohabiting couples are more likely to stay together if their earnings are approximately equal. A second advantage of marriage over cohabitation is that marriage makes it safer for one partner to put the other through school, since marriage provides more of a guarantee that the partner who invests in the other's human capital will realize some of the subsequent benefits. A third advantage of marriage is that if partners want to insure one another against the risk of unemployment or illness, marriage makes such commitments easier to enforce.

One possible reason for the spread of cohabitation may be that the combination of high divorce rates and low alimony payments has reduced the expected value of all these potential benefits. Marriage has less economic advantage over cohabitation for couples who merely want to enjoy the economies of scale associated with sharing living space and consumer goods, although institutions such as banks sometimes treat married and unmarried couples differently. Indeed, marriage has no economic advantage over living with a roommate if the goal is merely to share living space and consumer goods.

A fourth limitation of the TEM derives not from the theory itself but from the way in which it is often applied. The TEM is supposed to describe a long-run equilibrium, but those who use it to predict marriage rates often fail to distinguish between the effects of long-run and short-run economic changes. Initially, of course, long-term and short-term changes in a spouse's earnings may be indistinguishable. But if couples use marriage to insure themselves against short-term risks or against the ups and downs of the business cycle, changes of this kind should not have an immediate impact on family structure. The length of the lag between an economic change and a change in living arrangements remains an open question.

A fifth limitation of the TEM is that it does not predict *how* adjustments will occur when long-run economic conditions change. A reduction in the prevalence of marriage can be achieved either by a rise in divorce or a fall in marriage. The model predicts changes in the percentage of the population who are married, not how these changes come about.

Basic Trends Among Twenty-Five- to Thirty-Four-Year-Olds

Since the traditional economic model focuses on the equilibrium probabilities of marriage rather than flows in and out of marriage, we begin by looking at changes in the fraction of American adults who are married. Then we explore how male economic performance, female market participation and performance, sex ratios, and welfare benefits have changed over time and whether these patterns are roughly consistent with the changes in family structure. Unlike the figures presented earlier, most of which cover only mothers living with children of their own under eighteen, the data presented in this section also cover childless men and women, since one of our goals is to explain changes in childbearing patterns. Furthermore, while earlier sections covered mothers of all ages, this section looks at men and women between the ages of twenty-five and thirty-four. We then compare trends for the top, middle, and bottom thirds of the education distribution for men or women of this age in the relevant year. We separate blacks from whites, but when we assign individuals to the top, middle, or bottom third of the educational distribution, we use the same thresholds for both races. Our data come from the March Current Population Survey and cover the years from 1964 to 2000. Because the black samples are relatively small in any given year, we show three-year moving averages for blacks.

Figures 1.16 and 1.17 show the fractions of black and white women in each third of the education distribution who were unmarried mothers in a given year. Among women in

FIGURE 1.16   *U.S. White Women Age Twenty-Five to Thirty-Four Who Were Single Mothers, by Education Thirds, 1964 to 2000*

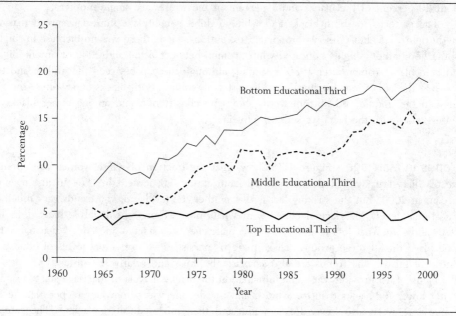

Source: Authors' calculations.

FIGURE 1.17   *U.S. Black Women Age Twenty-Five to Thirty-Four Who Were Single Mothers, by Education Thirds, 1964 to 2000*

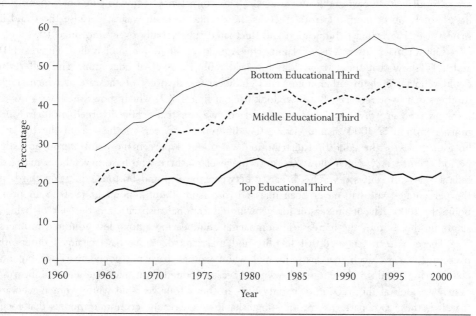

Source: Authors' calculations.
Note: Numbers are three-year moving averages.

the bottom third of the overall education distribution, roughly half the blacks and one-fifth of the whites are now single mothers. Among women in the top third of the distribution, about 20 percent of the blacks and 5 percent of the whites are single mothers.

The patterns for both blacks and whites exhibit roughly the same fan spread that we saw in figure 1.5, but with two important exceptions. First, there was no increase in single-motherhood among highly educated white women between 1964 and 2000 or among highly educated black women after 1980.[11] Second, although the gap between the middle and top thirds of the education distribution widens steadily among both blacks and whites, the gap between the middle and bottom thirds shows no consistent trend among either blacks or whites. These are the facts we seek to explain.

Trends in Marriage   Figure 1.18 shows that the fraction of white women age twenty-five to thirty-four who were married fell from almost 90 percent in 1964 to just over 60 percent in 2000. But the striking fact is that neither the levels nor the trends vary much by educational level. Marriage declined somewhat more among the highly educated in the 1970s and somewhat less in the 1990s, but marriage rates started and ended at roughly the same place for all three groups. These patterns persist if we use actual levels of education instead of thirds. The trends are also surprisingly linear and relatively constant.

Figure 1.19 provides the same information for blacks. Levels of marriage started significantly lower for blacks than for whites, and the decline was somewhat steeper. The levels of marriage were also lower for less-educated than more-educated blacks.[12] The rate of decline was somewhat steeper between 1965 and 1980 than in more recent years, and there is some evidence of an increase after 1995 among blacks in the bottom third of the distribution. But with this exception, the trends are remarkably similar across educational levels.

Any explanation of marriage trends must therefore account for the fact that the trends are so similar at different educational levels. This consistency seems to rule out explanations based solely on economic factors, such as the decline in male wages, because the trend in male wages has varied by education and fluctuated substantially over time since 1964.

Our primary interest is explaining the spread of single-parent families. Figures 1.16 and 1.17 show that these trends differ considerably by level of education. This difference could reflect trends in either nonmarital childbearing, divorce, or the rate at which single mothers marry or remarry. But if we look back at figure 1.7, which shows the fraction of all mothers who are divorced and not remarried, we see that while divorced mothers were more common is 2000 than in 1960, the difference between mothers from the top and bottom thirds of the education distribution was about 4 percentage points throughout this period. Figure 1.8, which shows the percentage of mothers who have never been married, tells a very different story. The disparity between the top and bottom education thirds in the percentage who had never been married rose from about 1 point in 1960 to about 13 points in 2000. The main reason for growing educational disparities in the risk of being a single mother is thus the increase in nonmarital childbearing among less educated mothers.

These patterns suggest that fertility and marriage decisions have changed differently over time. As we shall see, less-educated white women have postponed marriage but not childbearing, while more-educated women have postponed both marriage and childbearing. When we look at the fraction of twenty-five- to thirty-four-year-old white women who are married, these two patterns are indistinguishable. As a result, economic models that focus exclusively on marriage are likely to have trouble explaining the spread of single-parent-hood. We return to this issue in a later section. For now, we continue to examine the

FIGURE 1.18   *U.S. White Women Age Twenty-Five to Thirty-Four Who Were Currently Married, by Education Thirds, 1964 to 2000*

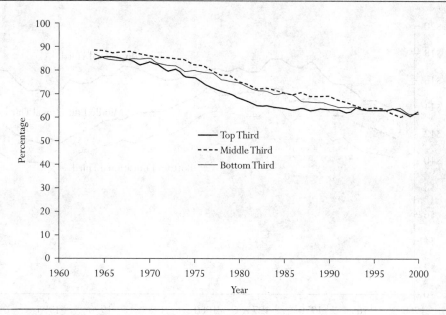

Source: Authors' calculations.
Note: Numbers are three-year moving averages.

FIGURE 1.19   *U.S. Black Women Age Twenty-Five to Thirty-Four Who Were Currently Married, by Education Thirds, 1964 to 2000*

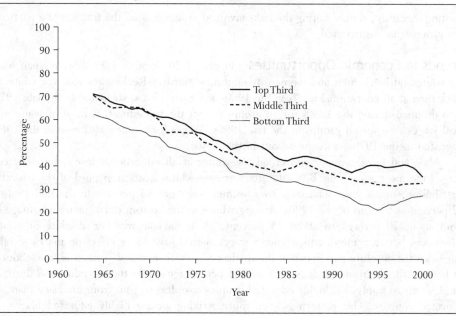

Source: Authors' calculations.
Note: Numbers are three-year moving averages.

FIGURE 1.20   *Median Wage of U.S. White Men Age Twenty-Five to Thirty-Four, by Education Thirds, 1962 to 2000*

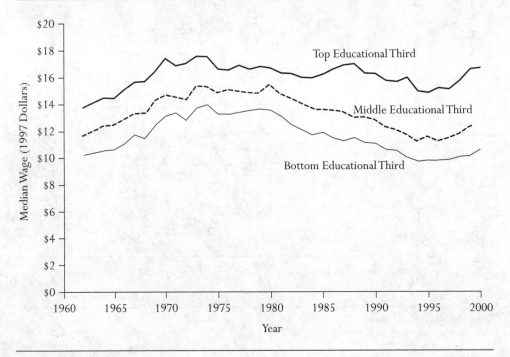

Source: Authors' calculations.

existing literature, simply noting the risks involved in focusing on the fraction of a particular age group who are married.

Trends in Economic Opportunities

Figures 1.20 through 1.23 show median wages for white and black men and women by education thirds.[13] Real wages rose for white and black men at all educational levels in the 1960s and early 1970s, stagnated in the late 1970s, then dropped during the 1980s for all groups except the top education third of white men. Real wages rose for all groups in the late 1990s. Wages for women also rose in the 1960s, stagnated in the 1970s, and spread out in the 1980s.

Male and female wages converged for whites at all educational levels, but they converged the most among the best educated. Among whites in the top third of the education distribution, men's wage advantage over women fell from 55 percent in the mid-1960s to 12 percent at the end of the 1990s. Among whites in the bottom third, men's advantage fell from about 70 percent to about 25 percent.[14] It is unclear whether absolute or relative differences between men's and women's wages should have more effect on marriage rates. But since the absolute gap between the median wages of men and women is now about $2 an hour in all education thirds, with a smaller percentage gap in the top education third, the TEM seems to imply that highly educated couples have less to gain from marriage than less-educated couples. This pattern is even more striking among highly educated blacks, for whom male and female wages were almost identical by 2000. Among the least-educated third of blacks, men still earned roughly one-third more than women in 2000.

FIGURE 1.21   *Median Wage of U.S. White Women Age Twenty-Five to Thirty-Four, by Education Thirds, 1962 to 2000*

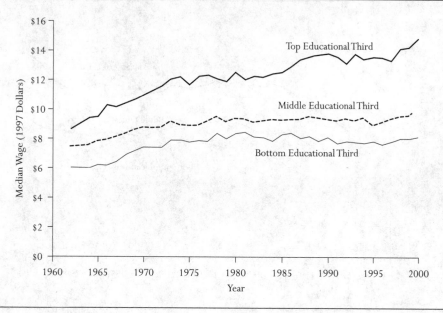

Source: Authors' calculations.

FIGURE 1.22   *Median Wage of U.S. Black Men Age Twenty-Five to Thirty-Four, by Education Thirds, 1964 to 2000*

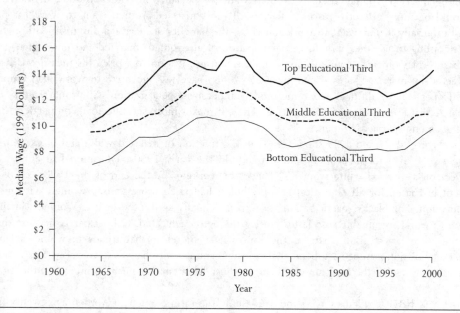

Source: Authors' calculations.
Note: Numbers are three-year moving averages.

FIGURE 1.23   *Median Wage of U.S. Black Women Age Twenty-Five to Thirty-Four, by Education Thirds, 1964 to 2000*

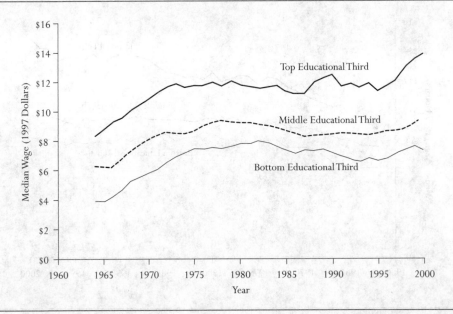

Source: Authors' calculations.
Note: Numbers are three-year moving averages.

Another measure of the potential gains from marriage involves the extent of paid work among married women. If many women want to specialize in home production, marriage should be more attractive to both parties. If most married women want to work for pay, and especially if they want to work full-time, the benefits of marriage diminish. Although it is tempting to use the labor force participation of all women, married and unmarried, as a measure of women's economic opportunities and motivation to work, this measure is itself affected by marriage rates, since married women have less incentive to work than unmarried ones. The traditional economic model emphasizes specialization within marriage as the vehicle that creates returns to marriage. Thus, it makes more sense to focus on participation rates among married women.

Figures 1.24 and 1.25 show trends in the fraction of married white and black women age twenty-five to thirty-four who worked. In the early 1960s, education had almost no effect on a married white woman's chances of working. By the end of the 1990s, employment had risen for all education groups, but it had risen more among women with more education. For blacks, participation rose pretty equally across the board. Women's inclination to work presumably rose faster among the better educated, at least partly because their wages rose fastest. But whatever the cause, it seems clear that trends in women's labor market position cannot have been the main determinant of changes in marriage rates, since marriage rates fell the least among women whose labor market position improved the most.

The Sex Ratio   Figures 1.26 and 1.27 show the ratio of men to women age twenty-five to thirty-four in the civilian, non-institutional population. (Using this population obviously involves some oversimplification, since members of the armed forces and even prison in-

FIGURE 1.24   *U.S. White Married Women Age Twenty-Five to Thirty-Four Who Work, by Education Thirds, 1964 to 2000*

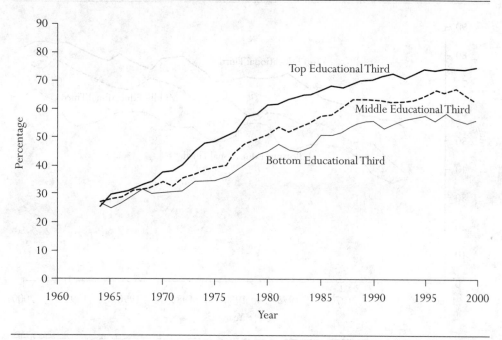

Source: Authors' calculations.
Note: Numbers are three-year moving averages.

mates are often married.) For whites, the sex ratio is close to even and shows a very weak trend. For blacks, the number of "missing" men is substantial.

It is not clear whether we should think about marriage markets in relative or absolute terms. When men get more education than women, they often marry women with less education than themselves. When women get more education than men, however, they may be less inclined to "marry down." This issue is even more important to blacks than whites, because more black women than men have been attending college. Unlike earlier figures, figures 1.26 and 1.27 use the same education categories for men and women, so we do not end up with exactly one-third of each sex in each category. This makes no difference for whites, but for blacks it means that the ratio of men to women in the top education third is remarkably low before 1980. The low ratio of black men to women could play a role in low marriage rates, particularly among highly educated blacks in the 1960s and 1970s.

Welfare Benefits   Welfare generosity is difficult to characterize. Benefit levels can be computed, but administrative practices affect how difficult it is to get these benefits and what recipients must do in return. Most scholars report that welfare benefits rose sharply in real terms up to the early 1970s and then failed to keep pace with inflation, but this conclusion is somewhat sensitive to the way in which we think recipients value Medicaid. One simple way to see how welfare might have influenced family change is to track the ratio of welfare cases to female-headed households.

Figure 1.28 shows that the welfare rolls rose faster than the number of female-headed

FIGURE 1.25   *U.S. Black Married Women Age Twenty-Five to Thirty-Four Who Work, by Education Thirds, 1964 to 2000*

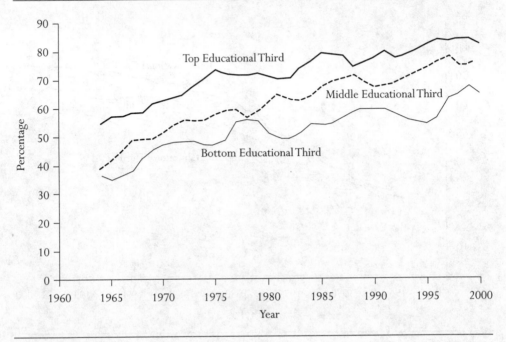

Source: Authors' calculations.
Note: Numbers are three-year moving averages.

households with children from 1965 to 1971. From 1971 to 1989, the ratio fell steadily. It rose again from 1989 to 1993 and then fell sharply after that. This decline began before Temporary Assistance to Needy Families (TANF) replaced Aid to Families with Dependent Children (AFDC) in 1996, but it became more precipitous after that. If welfare alone were driving trends in marriage, we should see a sharp increase in single-motherhood among the least-educated women during the late 1960s and early 1970s, followed by a gradual decline between 1972 and 1992, and then a sharp decline after 1992. Yet in figure 1.16 the increase in single-motherhood among the least-educated white women was essentially linear, and the increase was about as steep among women in the middle third of the distribution as among women in the bottom third. Until 1990 these patterns also held for black women. Figure 1.17 does suggest, however, that single-parenthood declined among the least-educated black women after 1990. This decline could be linked to welfare reform, which began to make it harder for single mothers both to qualify for welfare and to stay on the rolls.

How Much Can the TEM Explain?

Taken one at a time, men's wages, women's wages, married women's employment rate, the sex ratio, or welfare cannot explain the educational variation in the spread of single-parent families. But these five factors together could still account for a significant fraction of the variation. Rising work rates by women could have disproportionately depressed marriage among the best educated, while falling male wages could have depressed marriage among

FIGURE 1.26   *Male-Female Sex Ratio for Whites Age Twenty-Five to Thirty-Four, by Education Thirds, 1964 to 2000*

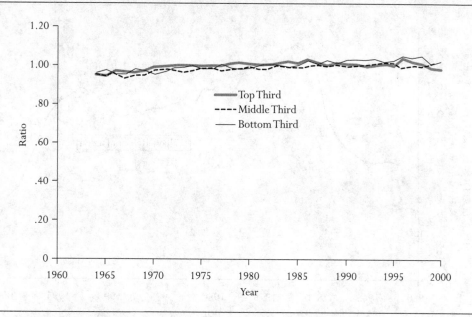

Source: Authors' calculations.
Note: Numbers are three-year moving averages.

FIGURE 1.27   *Male-Female Sex Ratio for Blacks Age Twenty-Five to Thirty-Four, by Education Thirds, 1964 to 2000*

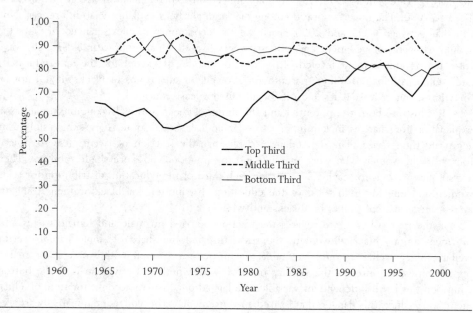

Source: Authors' calculations.
Note: Numbers are three-year moving averages.

FIGURE 1.28   *Ratio of Cases on AFDC/TANF to Female-Headed Family with Children, 1960 to 2000*

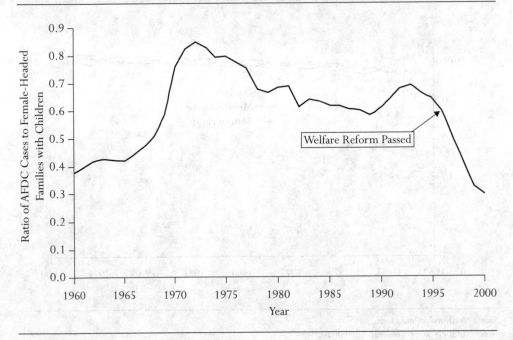

Source: Authors' calculations.

the less educated after 1973; the combination could explain declines for all groups from 1973 to 2000. The lower sex ratio among blacks might help explain racial differences. Note too that between 1995 and 2000 nearly all the economic variables changed in ways that should have encouraged marriage among twenty-five- to thirty-four-year-olds: male wages rose, female employment leveled off, sex ratios stabilized (except for the least educated), and welfare receipt fell. Single-parenthood also fell for all groups of blacks. It did not fall for whites, but at least it leveled off for all but the least educated.

To illustrate both the potential and the limits of the traditional economic model as an explanation for changes in family structure, table 1.1 shows some regression results using aggregate time series. The dependent variables are the fraction of twenty-five- to thirty-four-year-old women who were married and the fraction who were single mothers. There are six observations for each year: one for each third of the education distribution for white women and one for each third of the education distribution for black women (using the same educational cut points for blacks and whites).

In the first column, we regress the fraction married on male and female wages, employment among married women, the sex ratio, and the share of single parents getting welfare. Since welfare should have a larger impact for women with worse labor market opportunities, we interact the welfare measure with whether the woman is in the bottom education third. All independent variables are lagged one year to account for time of adjustment and reduce the danger that shared measurement error will contaminate the regressions. The model is not sophisticated, but it does provide a sense of the potential connections between variables.

TABLE 1.1   *Cross-Group OLS Time-Series Regressions of Marriage or Female Head Fraction Among Women Age Twenty-Five to Thirty-Four*

	Fraction Married			Fraction Single Parents		
	(1)	(2)	(3)	(4)	(5)	(6)
Median male wage	0.021		0.002	−0.013		0.004
	(.004)	—	(.003)	(.004)	—	(.002)
Median female wage	−0.010		−0.007	−0.019		−0.018
	(.005)	—	(.003)	(.004)	—	(.003)
Fraction of married women who are working	−0.605		−0.120	0.306		−0.215
	(.041)	—	(.045)	(.04)	—	(.04)
Fraction of single parents receiving welfare (AFDC/TANF)	−0.068		0.003	0.131		0.069
	(.031)	—	(.018)	(.03)	—	(.017)
Fraction of single parents receiving welfare (AFDC/TANF) × lowest education third	−0.057		−0.052	0.032		0.025
	(.015)	—	(.009)	(.014)	—	(.008)
Male-female sex ratio	0.604		−0.127	−0.640		0.098
	(0.042)	—	(.043)	(.041)	—	(.038)
Year		−0.008	−0.006		0.002	0.006
	—	(.0002)	(.001)	—	(.0003)	(.0005)
Black		−0.300	−0.319		0.297	0.320
	—	(.006)	(.013)	—	(.01)	(.012)
Other race		−0.015	−0.023		−0.019	−0.015
	—	(.011)	(.012)	—	(.018)	(.01)
_cons	0.306	16.793	13.161	0.832	−4.417	−12.152
	(.042)	(.374)	(1.056)	(.041)	(.611)	(.952)
Adjusted R-squared	0.83	0.93	0.94	0.78	0.750	0.930

Source: March CPS. Groups based on education thirds and race.

- Economic variables alone can explain 83 percent of the variance in marriage rates by education, race, and year (column 1 of table 1.1). Every variable is significant and has the sign predicted by the traditional economic model.

The fact that the variables are all correctly signed is quite remarkable, given how uniform the patterns of marriage were. It is worth emphasizing that the two variables with by far the highest significance are the employment rates of married women and the sex ratio. That should come as no surprise: the employment rate for married women is the only variable that rose continuously over the period when marriage rates fell, and the sex ratio is the variable that best differentiates blacks from whites. These results suggest that economic models could have great potential.

Column 2 shows an even simpler model for predicting marriage that includes only a linear time trend (year) and race dummies. The combination of a linear trend and race dummies explains even more of the variation in marriage rates than the traditional economic model does. R-squared rises from 0.83 to 0.93. Column 3 investigates how much of the time trend the TEM can explain by adding the economic variables to the equation in column 2. When we use standard economic variables to explain the linear trend in marriage, they perform poorly: the coefficient of the time trend falls only from −0.008 to −0.006. In addition, male wages become insignificant and the sex ratio is wrongly signed.

The same basic pattern recurs when we use the standard economic model to explain variation in the proportion of twenty-five- to thirty-four-year-old women who are both unmarried and raising a child under eighteen, except that increases in female wages seem to reduce the fraction of unmarried mothers. This result is at odds with the notion that higher wages make it easier for a woman to have children without marrying. Perhaps higher female wages also serve as a proxy for the availability of more interesting and rewarding work for women, which makes childrearing less attractive by comparison.

Economic variables are even worse at explaining the long-term increase in single-motherhood than the long-term decline of marriage among twenty-five- to thirty-four-year-olds. In column 5, which controls only race dummies, the average annual increase in the proportion of single mothers is 0.002. In column 6, which also controls male and female wages, the fraction of married women working, welfare recipiency rates, and the sex ratio, the unexplained linear trend is larger (0.006) instead of smaller. Both coefficients are highly significant. Including the economic variables thus deepens the mystery of why single-motherhood became more common rather than throwing light on it.

Of course, this model is not particularly well specified, and a simple time series would not be the preferred method of estimation. A rigorous test of the traditional economic model would require far more sophisticated empirical work. Furthermore, these results do show that economic forces can sometimes explain a lot. The trouble is that even minor changes in functional form can lead to results that contradict the theory.

The Empirical Literature on Marriage

Turning now to a review of the literature, we consider marriage, divorce and separation, and the formation of single-parent families separately, because that is what most of the literature does. We begin with the literature on marriage, which uses three methodological strategies:

1. Comparisons of geographic areas at one or more points in time

2. Comparisons of individuals, each of whom is surveyed once, who may be drawn either from a single survey or from a series of surveys in different years

3. Comparisons of *changes* in marital status for specific individuals followed over time

Each of these strategies has different strengths and limitations.

Area Comparisons   Area comparisons use the decennial census or the Current Population Survey to generate data for different geographic areas (typically metropolitan areas) that can plausibly be seen as separate marriage markets. The dependent variable is usually the fraction of an age group (often subdivided by race and sex) who are married. The independent variables are the area's economic and social characteristics. The biggest challenges to such models come from uncertainty about the direction of causality, omitted variable bias, and measurement error.

The causality problem can be illustrated by an otherwise strong article by Sara McLanahan and Lynne Casper (1995). The authors regress the fraction married among women age twenty-five to twenty-nine on indicators of male economic opportunity and employment rates for women of this age in different geographic areas. They find a strong negative association between work by women and marriage. But as Oppenheimer (1997b) points out, married women tend to work less than unmarried women, so the direction of causality might run from marriage to work instead of from work to marriage. The work of Mark

Fossett and Jill Kiekolt (1993) and Cynthia Cready, Fossett, and Kiekolt (1997) on African Americans has similar limitations.

Omitted variable bias is another obvious problem. Suppose attitudes toward both marriage and work are more "traditional" in an area such as the South. This fact would create a negative correlation between marriage rates and married women's employment rates. But such a correlation would not imply that increased work by married women had caused the decline in marriage rates. Both could have a common cause.

Measurement error is also a major problem. Some authors use data broken down by metropolitan area, education, and age, for example. Setting aside the question of whether the metropolitan area is the appropriate level of aggregation, this approach usually yields estimates based on relatively small samples for some subgroups in smaller metropolitan areas. As a result, there is a lot of random measurement error in the independent variables, which not only inflates the standard errors but biases coefficients toward zero. Work by Michael Brien (1997) suggests this could be a larger issue than is commonly realized, particularly for blacks.

Robert Wood (1995) and Francine Blau, Lawrence Kahn, and Jane Waldfogel (2000) do the best job of solving these problems. Both analyses use changes over time to eliminate unmeasured fixed effects of particular geographic areas. Both also use a measure of the area's industrial mix to estimate the effect of exogenous changes in demand for male and female workers. Blau and her colleagues (2000) calculate the national mix of workers by sex and education for each industry. They then multiply the share of employment in each industry in the local area by the national composition of the industry to determine which local areas have an industrial mix that favors persons of a particular gender and education. We would expect opportunities for, say, low-skill women to be better in locales where the industrial mix increases demand for their services. Lynn White (1981) does the same thing, though she predicts the mix only by race and sex, not by education. Wood (1995) uses a similar method except that he predicts pay rates, multiplying local industrial mix by the average national wages for black and white women in that industry. Of course, the industrial mix is at least partially endogenous—industries needing low-skill women are drawn to areas with larger numbers of such women seeking work. Still, a great many factors besides availability of workers of a particular type are likely to drive the industrial mix in an area.

Daniel Lichter, Felicia LeClere, and Diane McLaughlin (1991) use the labor force participation rate of unmarried women (which presumably is not heavily influenced by the proportion women who are married) and the average earnings of full-year, full-time female workers as measures of opportunity. They use a single year of census data and thus cannot implement fixed-effects models.

Table 1.2 summarizes the results of these papers. We would like to compare the magnitudes of effects across papers, but the plethora of dependent variables and the large variation in samples make such comparisons almost impossible.

- Most area models find positive effects on marriage for job opportunities for men, negative effects for job opportunities for women, and positive effects of the sex ratio—all as predicted.[15] Welfare performs inconsistently, often being wrongly signed as well as insignificant.

Oppenheimer (1997b) has questioned the credibility of such analyses, particularly as a test for the "female independence" hypothesis. She argues that the causality question is extremely hard to resolve. Where marriage is less common, more women are working or the industrial mix has adjusted to the presence of more women. Questions about omitted

TABLE 1.2   Summary of Empirical Results for Marriage Using Economic Variables—Grouped by Method

Method/Data	Dependent Variable (Sample)	Male Work Opportunities	Female Work Opportunities/Participation	Public Aid	Sex Ratio (Male/Female)
Predicted effect in TEM		+	−	−	+
Blau, Kahn, and Waldfogel (2000)	Area; 1980 and 1990 census	Proportion married (women 16 to 24, 25 to 34) + whites i blacks	− whites i blacks	− whites i blacks	+ whites + blacks
Cready, Fossett, and Kiekolt (1997); Fossett and Kiekolt (1993)	Area; 1960, 1970, 1980, and 1990 vital statistics	Proportion married (black men and women) +		−	+
Lichter, LeClere, and McLaughlin (1991)	Area; 1980 census	Proportion married, ever married, newly married (women 20 to 29) +	−	−	
McLanahan and Casper (1995)	Area; 1970, 1980, and 1990 census	Proportion married (women 25 to 29) +	−	+	i
White (1981)	Area; 1960 and 1970 census	Proportion married (women 22 to 24) i	i white − blacks	o	i
Wood (1995)	Area; 1970 and 1980 census	Proportion ever married (women 20 to 34) i whites + blacks	− whites i blacks	i	i
Hoffman, Duncan, and Mincy (1991)	Micro, cross-section time series; PSID	Marital status/AFDC receipt (women at age 25) +	−	−	o
Lichter, McLaughlin, and Ribar (2002)	Micro, cross-section time series; CPS 1986 to 1996	Currently married (women 19 to 54) Negative impact of predicted gain in total income if marry (opposite sign expected)		i	+

Study	Dependent variable	Data and method				
Mare and Winship (1991)	First marriage probability (race, sex, and age subgroups)	Micro, cross-section; census for 1940, 1950, 1960, 1970, and 1980; CPS for 1985 to 1987	ø	ø		+ (male models) ø (female models)
Schultz (1994)	Probability of being married (women 15 to 64 and subgroups)	Micro, cross-section; 1980 census	ø	– whites i blacks	– whites i blacks	+ whites i blacks
Brien (1997)	Transition to marriage (women)	Hazard; NLHS Class of 1972	+ (entered in place of male opportunity)	ø	i	+
Ellwood and Rodda (1990)	Transition to first marriage (men)	Hazard; NLSY 1967 to 1971, 1980 to 1986		ø	ø	+
Koball (1998)	Transition to marriage (men)	Hazard; NSFH 1987 to 1988			ø	+
Lichter et al. (1992)	Transition to first marriage (women age 18 to 28, 1979 to 1986)	Hazard; NLSY	+ (entered in place of male opportunity)	ø	+ (employed prior to marriage)	+
Oppenheimer (1997a)	Transition to marriage (men)	Hazard; NLSY 1979 to 1990		ø		+
Raley (1996)	Transition to first union (women age 19 to 34)	Hazard; NSFH 1987 to 1988		ø	+	ø
Smock and Manning (1997)	Transition from cohabitation to marriage (cohabiting couples)	Hazard; NSFH, 1987 to 1988, 1992, 1993, and 1994		ø	i	+
Testa and Krogh (1995)	Transition to first marriage (men)	Hazard; Urban Poverty Survey 1987	ø	ø	ø	+

Source: Authors' compilation.
+ = positive and significant effect
– = negative and significant effect
i = insignificant effect
ø = not included

variable bias also remain unresolved. The fixed-effects and industrial mix models of Blau, and her colleagues (2000) and Wood (1995) address these difficulties to some degree. Nonetheless, as Oppenheimer points out, Zhenchao Qian and Samuel Preston (1993) show that the marriage propensity of college-educated women rose somewhat relative to other women, even though their work patterns inside of marriage also rose more than those of other women. David Ellwood and Jonathan Crane (1990) also emphasize this point. But of course, opportunities for male college graduates rose disproportionately as well, so it is plausible that gains by men and women offset one another and that marriage declined less among college graduates for other reasons.

- The most serious criticism of all this work is that it cannot distinguish women who will never marry from women who will marry when they are older. Samples of twenty-five- to thirty-four-year-old women, for example, include a lot of unmarried women who will marry relatively soon. Women who are successful in the labor market may postpone marriage and childbearing until they have established themselves in a career. In models that concentrate on younger women, such delays would show up as a negative effect of "female independence," even if what we were really observing was a change in the timing of marriage and fertility.

Individual Comparisons   Individual comparisons estimate the odds that individuals with different characteristics are married at the time they are surveyed. There are two challenges to overcome with this methodology. First, most surveys observe individuals' marital status, employment status, and wages at the same time. People's employment status and wages may depend on their marital status, as well as the other way around. Second, while one usually has detailed social and economic characteristics of the observed individual, one has no individual-level information on the individuals they could marry. The characteristics of potential spouses must either be inferred in some way or ignored. In the models we reviewed, the sex ratio was simply ignored. Mare and Winship (1991) also omit the labor market opportunities of potential spouses (and welfare generosity), though they do estimate separate models for men and women in which the man's or woman's own potential earnings enter.

Saul Hoffman and his colleagues (1991) estimate actual spousal income for the subset of women who are married. This equation is then used to estimate potential spousal income for those who are not married. In addition, they use predicted rather than actual wages to avoid reverse causality (since current marital status may influence current wage). Their independent variables include both individual-level variables such as the woman's education or her sister's wage rate and local labor market characteristics such as industrial mix and unemployment rate. Paul Schultz (1994) uses a similar method with a less rich set of explanatory variables. By contrast, Daniel Lichter and his colleagues (2002) simultaneously estimate marriage, combined family income if married, and income if unmarried in a switching model that allows for correlated residuals. They then use predicted financial gain from marriage as their measure of economic opportunities. Table 1.2 summarizes the results of these studies as well.

- When marital status and other characteristics are observed simultaneously, the results tend to be broadly consistent with the TEM. Men with better jobs are more likely to be married, and women with better jobs are less likely to be married. The one exception is the study by Lichter, McLaughlin, and Ribar (2002), which has a specification that seems inconsistent with the underlying theory.[16]

It is hard to see what advantages these individual-level models have over the area models, since characteristics of the marriage market information must still be estimated from area data. When characteristics of the respondent are used to estimate the income of potential spouses, one is arguably identifying the model by assuming differences in functional form. In practice, moreover, these models usually focus on women under thirty-five, making it hard to distinguish the timing of marriage from the probability of ever marrying.

Longitudinal Data on Individuals   In principle, following the same individuals over time can overcome some problems of cross-sectional data by explicitly modeling the timing of marriage. In most cases, however, such surveys still provide no information on the individual's potential marriage partners, whose characteristics must be either inferred or omitted. Longitudinal models estimate the effect of economic variables by looking at the association between year-to-year changes in survey respondents' economic positions and their chances of being married. Using year-to-year changes in an individual's economic situation to infer how their potential marriage partners have changed is problematic.

Most investigators, including Ellwood and Rodda (1990), Koball (1998), Oppenheimer (1997a), and Testa and Krogh (1995) for men and Raley (1996) for women, summarize marriage market conditions using measures of general economic conditions. Lichter and his colleagues (1992) and Brien (1997), in contrast, use 1980 census data to create measures of men's economic opportunities that vary by race, age, and geographic area. Lichter and his colleagues merge these measures with data on women tracked from 1979 to 1986. Brien merges the same measures with data on the high school class of 1972 tracked through 1986. The only year-to-year variation in the data comes from the fact that women age and sometimes move to new locations.

A more promising approach may be that adopted by Pamela Smock and Wendy Manning (1997), who use data collected from cohabiting partners to predict their chances of marrying. Using cohabiting couples provides data on both partners instead of just one. But the influence of economic variables on the transition from cohabitation to marriage may be quite different from their influence on whether couples decide to cohabit, decide to date, or ever meet at all.

A second problem with studies that rely on longitudinal data is that these surveys never track a cohort of individuals over their entire life. Lichter and his colleagues (1992) look at eighteen- to twenty-eight-year-olds, so they miss the marriage behavior of persons over twenty-eight, who account for a large and growing fraction of all marriages. In longitudinal surveys where initial age varies widely, we can attempt to stitch together a model that covers individuals of all ages, but then we cannot test for cohort effects. Without data for long periods, it is very difficult to distinguish between delay and permanent avoidance of marriage. Indeed, a number of authors explicitly say that they are modeling the *timing* of marriage.

A third problem, which is closely related to the second, involves the functional form of the equation that is estimated. Most models use some form of proportional hazard, which assumes that an independent variable such as employment or earnings has the same percentage effect on the odds of marriage regardless of the respondent's age. If women with high earnings and skills are less likely to marry early in their career but more likely to marry later, a proportional hazard model could yield an earnings coefficient of zero. Such hypotheses are testable, but the limited duration and modest samples of most longitudinal surveys would make such tests imprecise. In any case, none of the papers we reviewed allowed for such a flexible form.

With these caveats in mind, there is nonetheless striking consistency in the hazard model findings.

- All the hazard models show a strong effect of male economic success on marriage. Whether this is simply a timing effect is less clear.

- In sharp contrast to the area results and the cross-sectional individual results, hazard models for women and cohabiting couples typically show a positive or insignificant impact of women's work on marriage.

- Welfare and sex ratios are rarely modeled in this work.[17]

The fact that women's work appears to have a different effect on marriage in models that track women over time than in models that measure marital status and economic status simultaneously requires some explanation. Oppenheimer (1997b) argues that the longitudinal models are likely to be the more accurate, since the dangers of endogeneity are less than in cross-section models.

One hypothesis about these seemingly contradictory findings is that economically successful women marry later, but ultimately marry more than other women. Goldstein and Kenney (2001) present data consistent with this hypothesis. According to this hypothesis, the hazard models capture the higher eventual level of marriage, while the area models, by focusing on younger women, capture the impact of high earnings on a woman's propensity to delay mariage. This view seems to be supported by the fact that models of marriage that include only education (not work variables), such as Qian and Preston (1993), typically find that education is positively related to marriage despite the fact that the labor force participation of educated married women has increased disproportionately. But the hazard models could also be capturing a timing phenomenon within a cohort. Within a cohort, women with high earnings might be more likely to marry because they are also more appealing spouses. But cohorts in which more women work might still be less likely to marry, because the returns to marriage have fallen.

Conclusions About Marriage   Taken together, the literature on marriage seems to us to support the following conclusions:

- All methods suggest a strong positive influence of male economic performance on marriage rates. It is unclear how much of this effect is simply one of timing versus permanence.

- Women's work lowers marriage in area comparisons and cross-sections of individuals but rarely shows up in longitudinal data on individuals. These divergent findings cast doubt on the "women's independence" hypothesis, except perhaps as a factor in *delaying* marriage.

- Sex ratios show a clear impact on marriage in all settings.

- Welfare performs ambiguously. In some specifications, it has a significant negative impact on marriage, but it is often insignificant or wrongly signed.

Several authors have also tried to use these variables to explain changes over time in national marriage patterns. Changing patterns of male work and earnings cannot explain much of the trend in marriage. Ellwood and Rodda (1990) employ a hazard model with little control for female work. This combines both timing and avoidance effects, thus providing an upper bound for the impact of male earnings. Yet even they conclude, along with

Jencks (1992) and Wood (1995), that male labor market performance can explain only a tiny share of the decline in marriage. The empirical literature on marriage does not really allow us to determine whether the models predict stability or change in educational differentials. Since these models have not performed very well in explaining the overall decline in marriage, it seems unlikely that they would do well in explaining the relatively uniform declines within educational groups.

The Empirical Literature on Divorce

The literature on the economic factors that influence divorce is far smaller than that on marriage, but the findings are similar. Recent models of divorce tend to be hazard models. Since both parties can be observed before (and sometimes after) the divorce, there is less guesswork about partners' economic situation than in marriage models.

Endogeneity is the biggest challenge in this literature. Married women who are uncertain about their marriages may be more inclined to work in order to ensure they can support themselves should the marriage dissolve. Indeed, William Johnson and Jonathan Skinner (1986) have shown that women raise their labor supply significantly in the three years prior to divorce. This problem may be present in both area and hazard models.

Endogeneity remains an issue in several of these papers. Steven Ruggles (1997) uses census data from as far back as 1880 and as recently as 1990 to estimate the connection between the probability of a sample member being divorced and area measures of labor force participation rates for both married women and men, as well as measures of male and female opportunity. He reports strong and economically meaningful impacts in nearly all years, but he does not consider the possibility that the same cultural influences that make divorce more common in a given area or period could also make married women more inclined to work.

Several of the hazard models also use contemporaneous information on the labor supply or wages of married women. Theodore Greenstein (1990) includes information on both marital and premarital work experience. He finds that married women's hours are strongly and positively related to the odds of divorce. Although that could be because women in precarious marriages decide to work more, women who worked more *prior* to marriage are also more likely to divorce. After conditioning on hours, however, women with higher earnings are less likely to divorce, perhaps because they are more attractive partners.

Meei-Sheen Tzeng (1992) and Jessie Tzeng and Robert Mare (1995) address the theoretically interesting question of whether levels of work by husbands and wives, changes in work after marriage, or differences between husbands and wives are destabilizing. But work is often observed only in the year prior to divorce, so they cannot rule out the possibility that wives go to work when they sense that their marriage is failing. Moreover, all of the ways in which male and female earnings might influence outcomes are constructed from some combination of the same work status variables for the husband and wife, and all are entered simultaneously, making it difficult to disentangle the effects of male and female work and pay. The model suggests that rising female work and earnings actually stabilize marriages, but their impact depends heavily on the earnings of the husband and other factors.

Other authors do address the endogeneity problem, but with mixed success. Rand Ressler and Melissa Waters (2000) use area data and simultaneous equations to attack the problem. They use the median earnings of all (married and unmarried) full-time, full-year female workers as their measure of opportunity. By looking at the pay rather than the employment of married women, they reduce the simultaneity problem. Full identification is achieved by assuming that religion, region, and age affect divorce but not female earnings, while occupational structure affects earnings but not divorce. Most of these assumptions strike us as problematic. The authors find positive but significant effects of female earnings on divorce for 1960, but not for later years.[18]

Johnson and Skinner (1986) and Hoffman and Duncan (1995) probably do the best job of dealing with endogeneity. Both estimate two-stage models. Johnson and Skinner assume that the duration of the marriage and various psychological and religious variables affect divorce but not wives' labor force participation. Hoffman and Duncan use predicted wage rates as their measure of female opportunity. They include education and city size variables only in their first-stage wage equations. None of these identification strategies is entirely satisfactory. Neither paper explains why factors such as religion and education do not belong in the models of pay and labor force participation as well as the model of divorce. Ultimately, Johnson and Skinner find a positive but insignificant impact of female earnings on divorce, while Hoffman and Duncan unexpectedly find a significant negative effect.

The results of these studies are summarized in table 1.3.

• Stronger male earnings seem to reduce divorce. But in several studies, the impact is small and insignificant, while in others the impact is much larger.

• Female earnings have inconsistent effects. In the area studies and cross-sectional comparisons of individuals, female participation or opportunity has the right sign and at least in one case is highly significant. But in the hazard models, its impact varies enormously from study to study.

These findings are broadly consistent with the results of the marriage papers. Male employment performs roughly as expected, but female employment behaves one way in area and micro models and another in the hazard context.

The Empirical Literature on Female Headship and Single-Motherhood

In many respects, the most problematic literature in this area is that focused on explaining variations in the prevalence of single-motherhood. Because relatively few parents now die before their children leave home, almost all single-parent families are created either by a divorce (or separation) or by an out-of-wedlock birth. But the prevalence of families headed by single mothers also depends on how many single mothers marry or remarry. These three factors have been changing at different rates, and their distribution also varies by race and education. Furthermore, there are good reasons to believe that economic factors might influence them differently.

The TEM portrays improvements in economic opportunities for women as a deterrent to marriage, which might in turn lead to an increase in the fraction of unmarried mothers. If children were a normal good, both married couples and unmarried couples would tend to have more children as their income rose. But children do not appear to be a normal good in this sense. Thus, it is unclear whether improvements in women's economic status should increase or decrease their chances of becoming unmarried mothers. Many sociologists interpret nonmarital childbearing among the less advantaged as a consequence of poor labor market opportunities and as an opportunity for women with few marketable skills to have

TABLE 1.3   *Empirical Results for Divorce and/or Separation Using Economic Variables, Grouped by Method*

	Method/Data	Dependent Variable (Sample)	Male Work Opportunities	Female Work Opportunities/ Participation	Public Aid	Sex Ratio (Male/ Female)
Predicted Effect			−	+	+	−
Greenstein (1990)	Hazard; NLSYW 1968 to 1982	Hazard of divorce (married women)	i	− earnings + hours + premarital weeks worked	ø	ø
Hoffman and Duncan (1995)	Hazard; PSID 1968 to 1987	Hazard of divorce (married women)	−	−	+	ø
Johnson and Skinner (1986)	Hazard; PSID 1972 to 1978	Hazard of divorce (married women)	i	i	ø	ø
Ressler and Waters (2000)	Area; census 1960, 1970, 1980, 1990	Divorce rates in area	i	i	−	ø
Ruggles (1997)	Micro; census 1880, 1910, 1940, 1970, 1980, and 1990	Probability of being divorced or separated (men and women 20 to 39)	−	+	ø	ø
Tzeng and Mare (1995); Tzeng (1992)	Hazard; NLSY 1979 to 1987, NLSYM 1966 to 1981, NLSYW 1968 to 1985	Hazard of divorce (married men and women)	−	+ − work at time of marriage	ø	ø

Source: Authors' compilation.
+ = positive and significant effect
− = negative and significant effect
i = insignificant effect
ø = not included

control over a portion of their lives. Both economic and sociological theories suggest that we should probably model marriage and childbearing jointly, but this is rarely if ever done.

Welfare and Single-Motherhood   Most of this literature is preoccupied with whether welfare plays a major role in encouraging the formation of female-headed families. A much smaller literature investigates whether there is a sizable intergenerational element in female headship. The literature on welfare seeks to exploit changes in welfare policy and either ignores or "differences out" other features of the marriage market. For example, David Ellwood and Mary Jo Bane (1985) use state fixed effects or natural control groups (a variation on difference in differences methods) to remove state differences in attitudes or tastes, while Jeff Grogger and Stephen Bronars (1997) use twins to control for unmeasured differences in family background and genetics. Often the marriage market issues are not mentioned at all. Hilary Hoynes (1997b, 961) notes that we can think of a potential spouse's wage or women's opportunities as being a function of observable variables already included in the model (such as education or age). She concludes that, "while the results of this reduced form model cannot be used to determine the importance of changes in employment and earnings of men and women, they are appropriate to explore the role of welfare benefits." We could argue about whether such methods effectively control for marriage market effects, but studies of welfare and family structure almost always make this assumption.

The primary goal of this review is not to understand the effects of welfare but to understand why family structure has changed in different ways for different groups. If the literature has succeeded in measuring the short-term impact of changes in welfare policy on family structure, however, we should be able to use these estimates to determine how large a contribution long-run changes in welfare policy could have made to long-run changes in family structure. Welfare seems to be a particularly promising hypothesis for explaining increases in the effect of maternal education on family structure, since welfare is a particularly attractive alternative for less-educated women.

Several careful reviews have summarized the literature on welfare and family structure, most notably that of Robert Moffitt (1998, 75), who writes:

> Based on this review, it is clear that a simple majority of the studies that have been conducted to date show a significant correlation between welfare benefits and marriage and fertility, suggesting the presence of such behavioral effects. However, in addition to this finding not being able to explain the time-series increase in non-marital fertility and decline in marriage, the majority finding itself is weakened by the sensitivity of the result to the methodology used and to numerous other differences in specification. A neutral reading of the evidence still leads to the conclusion that welfare has incentive effects on marriage and fertility, but the uncertainty introduced by the disparities in research findings weakens the strength of that conclusion.

Reviews by Gregory Acs (1995) and Hoynes (1997a) are even less supportive of welfare playing a major role in the spread of single-parent families. Hoynes (1997a, 129) comments:

> Taken together, this evidence suggests that marriage decisions are not sensitive to financial incentives. The literature on the effect of welfare on out-of-wedlock births is also quite conclusive. . . . Overall these effects are often insignificant and when they are not, they are small.

It has proven strikingly difficult to find large welfare effects, and the high sensitivity to functional form is worrisome. But even if welfare impacts were large and precisely estimated, welfare would not be a promising explanation for the spread of single-parent families since the early 1970s. As discussed earlier, the real value of cash welfare benefits has eroded fairly steadily since the early 1970s. Since 1979 the combined value of cash benefits and food stamps has also eroded steadily. Only the value of Medicaid has risen since 1979. The rising value of Medicaid probably made welfare more attractive to families with serious medical problems, but for most mothers the overall value of the benefit package fell between 1979 and 1996. These declines should have reduced the proportion of single mothers, especially among mothers in the lowest third of the education distribution. That is precisely the opposite of what we observe.

Charles Murray (1993) argues that we should think of welfare as an enabler rather than a cause of single-motherhood: once a certain threshold is reached, welfare enables persons to get by as single parents. Fluctuations in benefits above the threshold level may matter little. This argument strikes us as unconvincing. Surely different people have different thresholds. If so, changes in benefits should change the percentage of women who think the benefit level is enough to support a family.

Combining Welfare and Marriage Market Effects   The findings of the few authors who have examined the determinants of female headship using changes in both welfare and the marriage market are summarized in table 1.4. Among the papers cited earlier, Cready, Fossett, and Kiekolt (1997) and Fossett and Kiekolt (1993) also examine the fraction of families with children that are married and the fraction of births to married women. Once again, their results are consistent with theory. But they include the labor force participation of women as an independent variable, even though it could be endogenous, making their results highly suspect. In an otherwise similar paper, Scott South and Kim Lloyd (1992) use measures of the female and male wage rates rather than participation rates. This method reduces but does not eliminate the endogeneity problem. Strangely, their results for whites are consistent with theory, while their results for blacks are the opposite.[19]

William Darity and Samuel Myers have written a series of papers (notably Darity and Myers 1995) that examine the impact of the available pool of men on the number of female-headed families. To infer marriage market characteristics, they first use the demographic characteristics of each household head, such as whether the head is an unmarried mother, to estimate the number of employed males per female. This appears to be an effort to determine whether female heads are part of a population group facing poor marriage prospects. The ratio of employed men to women becomes their male marriageable pool index (MMPI), which they use to predict the odds of a female being a single-parent. We find their methodology confusing and nearly tautological: they seem to condition on family status to determine the MMPI, which they then use to estimate family status. This is essentially identification through functional form. Variables like education, region, and central-city residence are included in the MMPI models but excluded from the main equation. Even more surprising is their apparent decision to exclude information on female labor market opportunities in a marriage market model. Darity and Myers report that male availability alone can account for virtually all of the change in the rate of female headship among blacks. But their finding depends entirely on their peculiar measure of male availability. Few other measures of black employment declined noticeably over this time frame. If we use the more plausible Wilson-Neckerman measure of the MMPI, namely, the ratio of employed males to all females, there is virtually no change in the measure between the two years that Darity and Myers studied.

Two other papers try to estimate the effect that being married might have on a mother's income and then examine how the difference affects the proportion of mothers who are unmarried. Sheldon Danziger and his colleagues (1982) estimate first-stage equations for family earnings, welfare income, other income, and labor force participation for both married and unmarried women. They then estimate the income and work status that a woman might have if married and if unmarried and use these estimates of "potential gains from marriage" as independent variables in a second equation predicting family headship. They find that higher income and lower labor force participation of unmarried women raises female headship. Higher labor force participation inside marriage depresses marriage for whites but not for blacks. Unfortunately, their estimates use identical variables (though differing functional forms) to estimate each component of the potential gains from marriage, so their procedure amounts to identification through functional form.

Motivated by the paradox of cross-sectional results showing some impact of welfare and

TABLE 1.4   Empirical Results for Single-Parent-Family and/or Out-of-Wedlock Childbearing Using Economic Variables, Grouped by Method

	Method/Data	Dependent Variable (Sample)	Male Work Opportunities	Female Work Opportunities/ Participation	Public Aid	Sex Ratio (Male/Female)
Predicted effect			−	+	+	−
Cready, Fossett, and Kiekolt (1997); Fossett and Kiekolt (1993)	Area; census 1960, 1970, 1980, and 1990; vital statistics	Proportion of families with children unmarried, proportion of births married (black men and women)	−	+	+	−
Danziger et al. (1982)	Micro; CPS 1975	Probability of being a female head (women 25 to 54)	i	ø	+ (not directly measured)	ø
Darity and Myers (1995)	Micro; CPS 1976 and 1985	Probability a family head is female (family heads age 14 or older)	− (combined with sex ratio)	ø	+	(incorporated into male work)
Moffitt (2001)	Aggregate national time series; CPS 1968 to 1996	Fraction female heads (women age 18 to 65)	−	+	+	−
South and Lloyd (1992)	Area; census 1980; vital statistics	Nonmarital fertility rate (women age 15 to 34)	− whites + blacks	+ whites i blacks	i	i

Source: Authors' compilation.
+ = positive and significant effect
− = negative and significant effect
i = insignificant effect
ø = not included

time-series patterns showing that single-parenthood rose as benefits fell, Moffitt (2001) has recently estimated a time-series model that includes both welfare benefits and marriage market characteristics. His dependent variable is the prevalence of female headship by birth cohort. The independent variables are the ratio of male to female wages (to capture a sense of specialization-related gains marriage), the sum of husbands' and wives' wages (to give a sense of what a couple's joint income might be in marriage), and a measure of welfare benefits. Like the models shown in table 1.1, Moffitt's model simply asks whether a small set of economic variables, taken together, can explain changes in the prevalence of single-motherhood over the past generation.

The key economic variables in Moffitt's model have the right signs, just as they do in table 1.1. This model indicates that if all else had been equal, the decline in welfare benefits since the mid-1970s would have reduced single-motherhood. The reason this did not happen was that the effects of declining welfare benefits were more than offset by the effects of changes in male and female wages. Moffitt emphasizes that his simple time series is not a rigorous test of the economic model, but his findings certainly support his conclusion that models exploring the effects of welfare need to be more attentive to changes in the marriage market, since changes in the marriage market dominate changes in welfare benefits over most of this period.

In many respects, Moffitt's article leaves our discussion of economic influences on family structure where it began. A simple time-series model with only the main economic variables can explain most of the variation across groups and over time. But these findings become unstable as soon as we add even a few obvious control variables, such as a linear time trend and education. As a result, we cannot be sure of a great deal.

NON-ECONOMIC DETERMINANTS OF FAMILY STRUCTURE

Marriage and childbearing practices depend partly on the economic incentives facing individuals, partly on the degree to which sexually active couples can control their fertility, and partly on social conventions and moral judgments that differ across societies and over time. Changing norms regarding premarital sexual activity, out-of-wedlock childbearing, male responsibility, acceptable roles for men and women, and appropriate ways of caring for children could therefore play a central role in changing family structure. Normative changes can influence both legal and technical changes. No-fault divorce laws, legal abortion, and widespread use of the pill all reflect changing norms, but they may also influence behavior directly. Moreover, divorce laws, abortion laws, and contraceptive technologies can also influence social norms, because ideas about how people ought to behave depend in part on the likely consequences of the behavior. Clearly this kind of back-and-forth causation poses a challenge for those seeking to understand changing family patterns, because the underlying causal structure may be indeterminate.

This section considers six interrelated causal factors:

1. Gender role conflict

2. Changes in women's sense of control and efficacy

3. More permissive attitudes toward premarital sex, cohabitation, nonmarital childbearing, and divorce

4. New contraceptive technologies

5. Legalization of abortion

6. No-fault divorce

Gender Role Conflict

One popular explanation for the rise of single-motherhood is that women are less willing to "put up with" the way men often treat them. Explanations of this kind are often attributed to the breakdown of consensus about "gender roles" (Furstenberg 1996, 2001). Both the women's movement and the increase in women's employment have probably changed the way husbands and wives think about their obligations to one another. If male and female expectations change in different ways or at different rates, there might be an extended period when old marriages dissolve and new marriages are slow to form because the parties cannot agree on appropriate roles.

Orlando Patterson (1998, 160) makes a related argument about blacks, arguing that African American men and women are moving on "very different socioeconomic trajectories," with men "falling behind in both absolute and relative terms." He sees high levels of gender conflict as endemic in African American culture and traces this to the legacy of slavery, not poverty. Patterson's work remains highly controversial, since it is not obvious why these cultural legacies should suddenly have become more important in the last half of the twentieth century. Patterson argues that there has always been a big difference between black and white families, but that the underlying conflict between black men and women has a bigger impact on living arrangements today than in the past because black men's economic position has deteriorated while black women's position has improved.

Stories about gender role conflict also imply changes in interpersonal dynamics as women seek to redistribute the costs and benefits of marriage and childbearing. Beliefs about women's roles changed sharply in the late 1960s and 1970s. If women's expectations changed more than men's, this could have contributed to the spread of single-motherhood. If these changes were unevenly distributed by education or race, they could also help explain why single-motherhood increased more among black women and those without a college degree.

Arland Thornton and Linda Young-DeMarco (2001) review changes in the role expectations of men and women. Using data on the attitudes of high school seniors from 1976 to 1998, they report that disagreement with the statement that "the husband should make all the important decisions in the family" rose from 72 to 85 percent among women and from 44 to 49 percent among men. Disagreement with the statement that "it is usually better for everyone involved if the man is the achiever outside the home and the woman takes care of the home and family" rose from 42 to 71 percent among women and from 17 to 37 percent among men. If this pattern also holds at the behavioral level, it could help explain why men and women have become more reluctant to marry and have more trouble staying married. But these data do not tell us how such attitudes change as people age or whether the gender gap narrows among those who attend college.

The General Social Survey (GSS) also asks two questions about gender roles that can be construed as measuring beliefs about equality between the sexes. One question asks whether respondents agree or disagree with the statement that "women should take care of running their homes and leave running the country to men." The second asks whether the respondent approves of "a married woman earning money in business or industry if she has a husband capable of supporting her." Each succeeding birth cohort was more likely than its predecessors to endorse gender equality. Among those who had completed college, the trend was the same for men and women. Among those who had not completed college, egalitarian responses to the question about women's place being in the home increased significantly more among women than among men. This area deserves more systematic study.

Efficacy and Control

Following Ellwood (1994), we distinguish between expectancy models, which focus on confidence and expectations, and cultural models, which look to larger social norms. In practice, these are often mixed together, but important distinctions remain.

Expectancy models are normally the domain of social psychologists. They typically posit an interactive relationship between confidence and perceptions of control, on the one hand, and the results of actual behavior, on the other. Behavior that is validated by success (however perceived) is reinforced, and confidence is built. Behavior that leads to perceived failure can lead to loss of self-esteem, reduced sense of control, and even dysfunctional behavioral responses. Poor information on subjects such as contraception can also lead to a limited sense of control.

These models are often invoked to explain early pregnancy. The National Academy of Science Panel on Adolescent Pregnancy and Childbearing (1987, 120), for example, notes that "several studies of social and psychological factors associated with adolescents' sexual behavior conclude that self-perception (not self-esteem)—that is who one is, can be, and wants to be—is at the heart of teenagers' sexual decision making." Robert Plotnick (1992) finds that measures of self-esteem, attitudes toward school, educational expectations, and employment of an adult female in the household all influence teen pregnancy and its resolution. Lack of knowledge about contraception and an inability to resist peer influences and pressures from males are frequent themes here as well.

Power and control can also play a big role in explaining decisions not to marry. Kathryn Edin's (1999, 22, 24) powerful ethnographic study of the factors leading inner-city mothers to eschew marriage emphasizes control:

> In a non-marital relationship, women often felt they had more control than they would have had if they were married. Even if the couple cohabited, they nearly always lived with her mother or in an apartment with her name on the lease. Thus, mothers had the power to evict fathers if they interfered with child-rearing or they tried to take control of the financial decision making. . . .
>
> When we asked single mothers what they liked best about being a single parent, their most frequent response was "I am in charge," or "I am in control." . . .
>
> Finally, mothers often expressed the view that if they married, their men would expect them to do all of the household chores, plus "cook and clean" and otherwise "take care of" them.

Edin emphasizes that the women want to marry, but that they feel men must bring something valuable to the table—namely, economic resources. Much of Edin's work focuses on men's inability to provide income. But control is also central. She reports that women want to continue to exercise control and that the "primary way that mothers thought they could maintain power in a marriage relationship was by working and contributing to the family budget" (Edin 1999, 25).

The expectancy models often yield the same predictions as economic models. Women who have fewer opportunities in the labor market—where they experience failure, lack of control, and no positive sense of identity—turn to child-rearing as an arena where they can gain a greater sense of self-worth and importance. Nurturing children can provide such women with avenues for success that the market does not provide. This description is reminiscent of Becker's model for individuals whose comparative advantage is in "home production," although the language is obviously very different. The potential importance of the male marriageable pool problem is also strongly echoed in the work of Edin and others.

But efficacy and control models do point to a different role for work and opportunity among women. Unlike economic models, in which better work opportunities for women reduce the gains from marriage and may thus increase single-parent families, efficacy models suggest that better job opportunities could make women *more* inclined to marry, since they would expect to have more power in the marriage. (Of course, men would have less power, so if the effects are symmetric, marriage rates might not change.)

Expectancy models have traditionally been applied to highly disadvantaged women and teenagers. But the notion that better employment opportunity for women might lead to the postponement of childbearing and make marriage more (not less) attractive in the long run is consistent with the data. As we noted earlier, labor market success is positively correlated with marriage in longitudinal studies. Still, expectancy and control models by themselves cannot go very far in explaining altered family patterns. Women's job opportunities have improved in tandem with rising numbers of single-parent families. And declining male opportunities alone seem unable to explain a large share of marital changes.

Norms, Attitudes, and Culture

Most sociologists and anthropologists see culture as people's collective interpretation of their situation. In some cases, this interpretation offers individuals a guide to behavior. Socioeconomic classes are said to have distinctive norms and subcultures that affect behavior by defining what is rational and reasonable as well as what is desirable and good. These norms are generally seen as at least partially adaptive. When norms of behavior begin to have undesirable consequences, the norms often change. If norms of behavior are widely felt to have failed, they may be replaced by new ones. New definitions of success and failure (new "values") may also emerge. Unfortunately, the adaptive nature of norms and values makes it unusually hard to investigate their independent causal role unless they can be measured directly and exogenous sources of change can be identified.

Both popular writers and empirical social scientists sometimes treat words like "norms," "attitudes," "values," and "beliefs" as if they were interchangeable. In principle, this is a mistake. In practice, however, distinguishing these constructs is often difficult. Norms are informal social rules that can affect the behavior of individuals who do not endorse them as well as the behavior of those who do. The norm that unmarried couples should not have sex can affect the behavior of couples who do not themselves believe nonmarital sex is wrong— for example, because they want to avoid the disapproval of others. Norms are thus an attribute of people's social environment. Of course, people can choose the places in which they live, work, and play with a eye to the norms that prevail there. In addition, individuals have a choice about how they will respond when other people violate a given norm of behavior. If individuals are unwilling to enforce a norm by imposing costs on violators, the norm loses its force. Indeed, we could argue that the spread of "tolerance" is not so much evidence of cultural pluralism or open-mindedness as evidence of growing reluctance on the part of individuals to pay the personal costs associated with enforcing norms of behavior that serve the common good. If parents who think premarital sex is bad for the young are unwilling to risk alienating their children by enforcing this norm, for example, it will collapse.

Unlike norms, attitudes and beliefs are attributes of individuals and are usually colored by personal experiences. In practice, however, social scientists usually measure changes in norms by measuring changes in individuals' attitudes, not by measuring changes in the way individuals' respond to behavior that is at odds with the attitudes they express. Scholars measure changes in norms regarding premarital sex, for example, as the percentage of adults who say that premarital sex is "always" or "almost always" wrong, not by asking unmarried couples who take vacations together whether they get disapproving glances from hotel clerks or lectures from their relatives.

Values are judgments that individuals make about the relative desirability of different things. The term is sometimes reserved for judgments about the relative importance of ultimate ends, like a high standard of living versus a large family, or patriotism versus salvation. But there is no clear dividing line between values of this kind and what economists usually label "tastes," which are preferences about more mundane matters, like the choice between material possessions and leisure time, or between one car and another.

Anthropologists originally used the term "culture" to describe values, attitudes, beliefs, and social norms that were widely shared throughout a society. In very small groups there may be something close to a consensus about values, attitudes, beliefs, and norms. In large groups, however, such matters are likely to be contested. When this is the case, "cultural differences" are little more than group differences in the percentage of individuals expressing a particular attitude or belief, endorsing a particular value, or enforcing a particular norm of behavior.

The role of culture in shaping family structure comes up most prominently in discussions of the "culture of poverty" and the "underclass." Murray (1984) argues, for example, that social policies adopted during the 1960s rewarded behavior that was dysfunctional within the larger society and ultimately undermined the norm that couples were morally obligated to marry before having children. Wilson (1987) argues that lack of economic opportunities for less-educated blacks, coupled with rising economic segregation among blacks, created poor black neighborhoods where few black men were employed in the regular economy. In the absence of either role models or social networks that could help residents find regular jobs, an "underclass" emerged.

Altered attitudes and values could change family patterns in several ways. First, some set of relatively exogenous forces might alter attitudes. Consider the "sexual revolution," which destigmatized premarital sexual activity. The origins of the sexual revolution might be traced to technological changes, such as the development of the contraceptive pill or antibiotics that cure many sexually transmitted diseases. Lowering the risks associated with nonmarital sex need not change people's judgments about whether nonmarital sex is morally wrong. But if lowering these risks leads couples to delay marriage, making nonmarital sex more common, those who try to enforce the traditional norm may feel that their efforts are more difficult and have less effect. If this change makes the norm enforcers less aggressive, the social cost of violating the norm will fall and nonmarital sex will become even more common. Nonetheless, technology is still the prime mover in this story, and changes in social norms are an endogenous response to technical innovation. Normative change simply explains why the effect of the innovation is gradual, not immediate.

Norms can play a similar role when economic incentives change. Suppose new economic conditions make marriage less desirable. This change is likely to reduce marriage and increase divorce. But since norms change slowly, we would not expect these changes to be instantaneous. Instead, changes in economic incentives are likely to generate normative feedbacks that make the long-term effects larger than the short-term effects. Consider Murray's (1993) argument regarding welfare. Welfare encouraged the formation of female-headed families, which in turn changed norms regarding the appropriateness of forming such families. Even if the incentives were slowly reversed later on, the altered norms would change only slowly, so behavior would be slow to change. Murray even implies that it may be impossible to return to the earlier set of norms. Once there is such a large stock of single-parent families, it becomes impossible to condemn them.

The uncertain pace of normative change poses a problem for empirical social science. Normative accounts imply that the determinants of family change exert their influence gradually and cumulatively. This claim, while plausible, makes it hard to assess the impact of legal and economic changes because we have no way of knowing how long these changes take to exert their full effect. If normative changes are gradual, it is also very hard to distinguish between endogenous and exogenous shifts. Those who emphasize attitudes, values, and norms therefore tend to focus on explaining persistent differences between groups rather than changes within groups.

Parental religion is one relatively exogenous cultural influence on children's behavior, and there is substantial evidence that religion has a significant influence on teenage sexual activity, age of marriage, and childbearing behavior. For example, even after controlling for parental SES, education, family structure, and the like, Evelyn Lehrer (2000) finds that children raised in fundamentalist Protestant households marry younger than mainstream Protestants, who in turn marry younger than Jews. Mormons marry the youngest of all. Similarly, Shelly Lundberg and Robert Plotnick (1995) find that Catholics are less likely than others to have an out-of-wedlock birth. Melvin Zelnik, John Kantner, and Kathleen Ford (1981) report that religion affects the odds of premarital intercourse, but not the likelihood of becoming pregnant before marriage. Presumably, religions with a more tolerant attitude toward sexual activity are also more likely to encourage birth control.

The evidence that parental religion (or its non-economic correlates) influences patterns of family formation in the next generation seems quite strong. The evidence does not tell us whether this influence operates through differential willingness to enforce norms regarding appropriate behavior, through differences in parental attitudes and beliefs that influence children's attitudes and beliefs, or through other non-economic features of the environments in which different religions are embedded. Nor have we been able to find evidence on whether changes over time in the distribution of religious beliefs can explain changes in family structure.

There is also abundant evidence of major attitudinal shifts over time, particularly during the 1960s and early 1970s. Shifts since then have been far smaller. Thornton (1989) reports that in a 1965 National Opinion Research Center (NORC) survey, 69 percent of women under the age of thirty responded that it was always or almost always wrong if a woman "has intimate relations with a man . . . she is engaged to and intends to marry." By 1972 the General Social Survey found that only 34 percent of women under thirty thought it was always or almost always wrong "if a man and a woman have sex relations before marriage." Since the GSS question is not explicit about the couple's intention to marry, the true change was probably even larger than these numbers suggest. By 1974 the GSS found that only 24 percent of women thought premarital sex was always or almost always wrong. The figure has hardly changed since 1974. In the course of a decade reported attitudes about sex were dramatically transformed.

More permissive attitudes toward nonmarital sex have been accompanied by greater acceptance of women who choose not to marry. A 1957 national survey found that 80 percent of respondents considered a woman who remained unmarried to be "sick, neurotic, or immoral." By 1978, only 25 percent endorsed this view (Veroff, Douvan, and Kulka 1981). Axinn and Thornton (2000) find virtually no further changes in attitudes toward marriage after the mid-1970s. But while remaining single has become more acceptable, both ethnographic and survey data still show widespread support for and interest in marriage, even among inner-city blacks whose actual marriage rate is low (Edin 1999). Unfortunately, none of the trend data are reported separately by race or education.

Thornton (1989) also shows that attitudes toward divorce changed dramatically between the early 1960s and the mid-1970s. In 1962 only half of all respondents disagreed with a statement suggesting that parents who do not get along should stay together for the children. By 1977 over 80 percent disagreed with the same statement. Here too attitudes have changed little since the 1970s. Thornton also shows that mothers' attitudes regarding the roles of men and women grew far more egalitarian between 1962 and 1977, with only modest change in the 1980s.

Attitudes toward cohabitation have, in contrast, continued to grow more liberal since the 1970s. For example, Axinn and Thornton (2000) report that the percentage of female high school seniors who agreed that "living together before marriage is a good idea" rose from 33 percent in the mid-1970s to 39 percent in the mid-1980s, and 51 percent by the mid-1990s. Attitudes toward out-of-wedlock childbearing may also have grown more permissive since the 1970s. Whereas 23 percent of female high school seniors in the mid-1970s thought that childbearing outside of marriage was destructive to society, only 15 percent felt that way in the 1990s.

- All surveys seem to show a rather radical change between the mid-1960s and the early 1970s on attitudes toward premarital sex, remaining single, divorce, and gender roles. With the exception of attitudes toward cohabitation, there is far less evidence of change in attitudes regarding these issues since the 1970s.

- Published time series seldom distinguish attitudes by level of education, making it difficult to determine whether the pattern of attitudinal change matches the pattern of behavioral change across groups.

Overall, attitudinal changes may explain behavioral changes in the 1960s and 1970s, but they are not promising explanations for more recent changes in behavior. In a richer story that distinguishes individual attitudes from societal norms, we might find that norms have changed more gradually, but that is pure speculation.

Even when survey questions ask whether behavior is "wrong," many respondents' answers seem to reflect their perception of whether the behavior is socially acceptable rather than deeply felt personal beliefs about what is right and wrong. As a result, attitudinal surveys may be more useful for assessing the prevalence or strength of various social norms than for predicting how individuals will behave. For example, while Thornton (1989) reports that 69 percent of women between the ages of eighteen and thirty said in 1965 that premarital sex was always or almost always wrong, our analysis of the 1982, 1988, and 1995 National Surveys of Family Growth (NSFG) show that 55 percent of women who were in this age range in 1965 later said that they had had premarital sex. This discrepancy suggests that many respondents in Thornton's survey were condemning actions that they either had already engaged in or would soon engage in.[20]

Assuming the 1965 reports are accurate, it would seem either that a lot of women believed that the behavior they engaged in was wrong (or "almost always wrong," which leaves a lot of wiggle room) or that they were giving the socially acceptable answer in 1965.[21] Either way, we interpret the data as showing that societal norms about what was acceptable changed between 1965 and the early 1970s, but that many women ignored these norms even in 1965. That said, the change in norms could still have had *some* effect on behavior. We conclude that:

- Changes in attitudes toward premarital sex were concentrated between 1965 and 1975. Those who were already adults became more liberal during this period, and those who came of age after this period were more liberal than those who came of age earlier (Harding and Jencks 2003). After the mid-1970s, new cohorts did not become more liberal, and existing cohorts, if anything, became slightly more conservative as they aged.

- Reported behavior changed far less rapidly than attitudes (see figures 1.14 and 1.15).

- Roughly half of those who turned twenty-one in the early 1960s report that they engaged in premarital sex. After that the proportions begin to rise significantly for all education groups.

- Among the least-educated third, premarital sex rose by about one percentage point per year between the late 1950s and 1990 (from about 55 to 90 percent). Among the most educated third, who were less likely to have had premarital sex in the late 1950s, the increase was somewhat steeper between the late 1950s and the early 1970s (from 40 to 65 percent). Since the early 1970s, premarital sex has been about equally common for all educational groups (see figure 1.15).[22]

- The fact that premarital sex rose fairly uniformly in all education groups while premarital births rose fastest among the least educated (see figure 1.9) suggests that the effect of education on premarital births rose because less-educated unmarried women were less likely to use contraception.

Assuming we are right in seeing delayed marriage as the most important proximate cause for increases in premarital sex, we still need to ask whether changes in sexual attitudes led to delays in marriage or whether delays in marriage led to changes in sexual attitudes. To settle this question, we need to identify exogenous shocks that could have influenced sexual attitudes only by influencing age at marriage or vice versa.

The Pill, Abortion, and No-Fault Divorce

George Akerlof, Janet Yellen, and Michael Katz (1996) argue that new contraceptive technologies and the legalization of abortion altered the character of sexual relations. Until abortion became legal, women could usually assume that if they engaged in premarital relations and became pregnant, the man would marry them. This norm was supported by older adults of both sexes, and "shotgun" marriages were the result. Akerlof and his colleagues argue that the invention of the pill and the legalization of abortion made unmarried women more willing to participate in "uncommitted" premarital sex by lowering the risk that any given sexual act would lead to motherhood. At the same time, they argue, women who sought to hold men to the old rules (no sex without a commitment to marry) found it harder and harder to compete for boyfriends.

The authors claim that this change made the traditional implicit contract between unmarried couples unenforceable and led to the decline of shotgun marriages. By their calculations, about three-fourths of the increase in the white out-of-wedlock first-birth ratio and about three-fifths of the black increase between 1965 to 1969 and 1985 to 1989 can be traced to a decrease in the fraction of premarital pregnancies that led to marriage. The authors note that the changes in contraception, abortion, and shotgun weddings occur at about the same time, although the shifts in shotgun weddings were not instantaneous. They trace the loose temporal connections partly to the fact that norms and attitudes shift more slowly than technology.

This argument rests primarily on a clever theoretical construction and a loose connection between the timing of different changes. Several other authors have sought to tighten the case by investigating whether easier access to abortion leads to changes in teen birth rates. There is an obvious direct effect. If pregnancy rates are unchanged, birth rates should fall when abortion is legalized. But there might be an offsetting indirect effect, since the availability of abortion might lead to more risky behavior and thus to more pregnancies.

Phillip Levine and his colleagues (1996) and June Sklar and Beth Berkov (1974) have shown that birth rates among both married and unmarried women fell earlier in states where abortion became legal earlier. But the number of abortions was far greater than the estimated reduction in births. This could mean that the number of pregnancies increased, but it could also mean either that there were a lot of unreported illegal abortions prior to legalization or that a lot of pregnancies that would have ended in a miscarriage prior to legalization ended in an abortion after legalization.

Thomas Kane and Douglas Staiger (1996) have also found evidence that modest new abortion restrictions reduced teen motherhood. In addition, they find fairly strong evidence that in counties where access became more restrictive, birth rates fell. They argue that small increases in the "costs" of obtaining an abortion may have made some people more careful about avoiding pregnancy without reducing abortions among those women who were likely to abort before the costs rose.

Claudia Goldin and Lawrence Katz (2000) relate women's marriage decisions to the diffusion of the pill among college-educated women. They argue that by facilitating sexual activity prior to marriage, the easy availability of the pill reduces the cost of delaying marriage and staying in school. This change in sexual opportunity encourages "impatient" women to postpone marriage and invest more in their human capital. As the timing of marriage shifts, even women who are not "impatient" will stay in school and delay marriage, since they will not have to worry that fewer partners will be available when they finish school. Like Akerlof and his colleagues (1996), Goldin and Katz rest their case heavily on timing, but with a tighter connection. Cohorts with greater access to the pill delayed marriage and increased their professional education. The authors also exploit the variation in the timing of both state laws that gave minors access to birth control services without parental consent and laws that legalized abortion. They conclude that there were "modest but detectable increases in the delay of marriage of college-educated women in states where young unmarried women had greater legal access to the pill" (Goldin and Katz 2000, 26). One difficulty with the Goldin-Katz story is that better contraceptive technology should allow delayed childbearing and greater investments in schooling among women of all skill levels. But as we shall see, less-educated women did not postpone childbearing to any significant extent. Nor did premarital sexual activity rise much faster among college-bound women than among the less educated.

Other legal changes, such as the liberalization of divorce laws, have also been investigated as possible determinants of divorce rates, marriage rates, property settlements, and even suicide and domestic homicide (see, for example, Friedberg 1998; Stevenson and Wolfers 2000). In virtually every case there is evidence that the legal and institutional changes had an impact.

- The newly emerging literature on new contraceptive technologies and legal changes is far from definitive, but it does make a fairly plausible case that sexual behavior, fertility, and marriage have been influenced by changes in both technology and the law.

- The literature on contraception, abortion, and the legal environment either does not consider how the impact of these factors differed by education and income or focuses only on college students.

Taken together, legal, technical, and normative changes probably help explain why family-related behavior began to change in the late 1960s and early 1970s, even though the economy was strong and wages were growing. None of these factors seem capable of explaining changes in family structure since 1980 unless we assume quite long lags between legal and technical changes and changes in individual behavior.

SEARCHING FOR BETTER ANSWERS

Quantitative models have not provided a compelling explanation for most of the changes in family structure since 1960. Estimates often seem sensitive to functional forms. Differences among geographic areas, individuals surveyed at a point in time, and individuals tracked over time often suggest different conclusions. Still, some fairly strong findings emerge.

What Do We Know?

- In virtually all models and samples, weaker male economic performance is associated with reduced or delayed marriage. But the economic position of men has not changed enough to explain most of the changes in marriage patterns. Put differently, marriage patterns have changed nearly as much for advantaged and employed males as for others.

- The influence of increases in women's economic opportunities is ambiguous. In cross-section and time-series models, better economic opportunities for women usually have a negative influence on marriage. In longitudinal data, improvements in a woman's economic situation either have no effect or increase the chance that she will marry. Theories about the likely effect of improving women's economic opportunities are also ambiguous. Economic models generally suggest that better job opportunities for women deter marriage, while some expectancy models and ethnographic reports suggest the opposite.

- Sex ratios typically influence marriage in predictable ways, but changes in the sex ratio have not been large enough to account for a large share of family change.

- Welfare benefits seem to have some effect on family structure, but the effects are not robust. Moreover, welfare benefits have fallen since the 1970s, so they cannot explain much of the change since then.

- Attitudes toward sex and marriage changed sharply in the 1960s and early 1970s. Premarital sexual activity and divorce patterns shifted sharply at the same time. There have been relatively minor changes in attitudes since the mid-1970s. Divorce leveled off after 1980, but premarital sexual activity continued to rise.

- New contraceptive technology and the legalization of abortion played some role in the changing patterns of marriage and divorce prior to 1980, but have probably had little impact since then.

Taken together, we might argue that these changes can perhaps explain the decline of marriage, as long as we recognize that their importance changed over time. As in the Agatha Christie book *Murder on the Orient Express,* "they all did it," but not all at once. In the 1960s and early 1970s, more women began working outside the home, attitudes about sex and women's roles changed, the pill and abortion became available, and welfare benefits rose. All these changes made early marriage less attractive. After 1974 attitudinal change slowed and welfare benefits stopped rising, but men's real earnings began to fall, both absolutely and relative to women's potential earnings. These changes also made marriage less attractive.

Perhaps this approach can even explain why marriage declined at roughly the same rate for individuals with different amounts of education. In the 1960s and early 1970s, rising labor force participation by women led to less marriage for all groups, even though men's earnings remained strong. Work increased more among more-educated women during this period, but rising welfare benefits discouraged both marriage and work among the less educated, so marriage declined across the board. From the mid-1970s to the early 1990s, marriage declined among the less educated because less-educated men's wages were falling while less-educated women's wages were merely stagnating. Highly educated men held their own during this period, but highly educated women's wages and labor force participation were growing. The net result was that the economic benefits of marriage fell for all groups. In the late 1990s, when men's wages began to rise and welfare benefits were harder to get, the decline in marriage slowed, and even reversed itself among blacks in the bottom third of the educational distribution.

Unfortunately, this scenario cannot really explain the growing impact of education on the proportion of women who are single mothers, which is our primary concern in this chapter. For that we need a theory that can explain why some women delay fertility but not marriage, while others delay both.

One reason it is hard to pinpoint a single cause for family change is that the effect of changing economic and social conditions is filtered through changing norms and culture, which evolve rather slowly, with fewer sharp breaks or turning points. Attitudes acquired by age twenty-one are slow to change. Social science does best with sharp turning points and tight links between dependent and independent variables. Thus, one interpretation is that quantitative models have done about as well as could be expected given the limits of our methods for investigating a complex system. This is an unsatisfying conclusion. Thus, we conclude by looking at the limitations of the theories and methods used in past work in order to suggest ways in which we might get a clearer and more convincing picture of what happened.

Modeling Both Marriage and Childbearing

Becker's model of family formation treats marriage and childbearing as inextricably linked, and with a handful of exceptions, subsequent economic treatments of the family have done the same thing. Surprisingly little work has been done on how the links between marriage and parenthood have changed over time, and how the absence of children affects marital stability.

Table 1.5 uses retrospective data from the June CPS to examine changes in the interval between first marriage and first birth among all women who married in different years, regardless of their age. We examine when their first child was born relative to this date. The changes between 1960 and 1990 are quite dramatic. Among women who married for

TABLE 1.5   *Timing of First Births Relative to First Marriage, 1960 to 1990*

Year of First Marriage	Child Born More Than Thirty-Six Months Prior to Marriage	Child Born One to Thirty-Six Months Prior to Marriage	Child Born Zero to Thirty-Six Months After Marriage	Child Born More Than Thirty-Six Months After Marriage, if at All
All women				
1960	3%	5%	71%	22%
1970	3	5	56	36
1980	7	7	48	49
1990	13	10	37	40
White women				
1960	2	3	73	22
1970	2	4	57	38
1980	4	6	49	41
1990	10	10	39	42
Black women				
1960	10	17	53	19
1970	14	18	47	21
1980	27	16	36	22
1990	42	9	21	28

Source: Authors' calculation.

the first time in 1960, 71 percent had a first birth within the first thirty-six months after marriage. Among women who first married in 1990, only 37 percent had their first child in the first thirty-six months after marriage.

Some decoupling of marriage and childbearing is an inevitable consequence of the rising number of out-of-wedlock births. But even among women who had their first child within marriage, delay became much more common. Among women who were childless at the time of marriage, the fraction who had a baby within three years fell from 77 percent among those married in 1960 to 48 percent among those married in 1990.

The bottom panel of table 1.5 shows that marriage and childbearing were never as closely linked among blacks as among whites. Because nonmarital childbearing has become so common among blacks, the connection between the two is now even weaker. But when childless black women marry, a majority now postpone childbearing more than three years.

Table 1.6 shows similar information for women divided by educational thirds. The disconnection between marriage and immediate childbearing has occurred for all education groups, but the reasons differ significantly.

- For the less educated, childbearing is increasingly occurring before marriage, though childbearing within marriage is being postponed somewhat as well.

- For the most educated, there still is little childbearing before marriage, but childbearing within marriage is occurring much later.

In light of this radical decoupling of marriage and childbearing, both theories and empirical strategies that implicitly treat marriage and parenthood as synonymous are hard to justify. There is still some connection between childbearing and marriage, but it seems clear that they need to be modeled separately, although probably simultaneously.

A few economic models do seek to separate the two. The best so far is by Robert

TABLE 1.6   *Timing of First Births Relative to First Marriage*

Year of First Marriage	Child Born More Than Thirty-Six Months Prior to Marriage	Child Born One to Thirty-Six Months Prior to Marriage	Child Born Zero to Thirty-Six Months After Marriage	Child Born More Than Thirty-Six Months After Marriage, if at All
Women in the bottom education third				
1960	3%	7%	70%	20%
1970	5	8	62	26
1980	10	11	51	28
1990	18	15	38	29
Women in the middle education third				
1960	3	4	73	21
1970	3	5	58	34
1980	7	7	51	36
1990	17	9	36	39
Women in the top education third				
1960	2	3	70	25
1970	2	3	46	49
1980	3	2	41	54
1990	5	4	37	54

Source: Authors' calculation.

Willis (1999), who shows that under certain marriage market conditions an equilibrium may be created in which it makes sense for some women to eschew marriage while having children. His model says nothing about fertility within marriage (fertility is still presumed to accompany marriage). Nor does it explain marriage after childbearing.

A modest but growing literature also examines marriage patterns after a child is born out of wedlock. Neil Bennett, David Bloom, and Cynthia Miller (1995), Daniel Lichter and Deborah Graefe (2001) and Dawn Upchurch, Lee Lillard, and Constantijn Panis (2001) all report that women who have a child out of wedlock are significantly less likely to marry. According to Lichter and Graefe, only 72 percent of such women will marry by the time they reach forty, compared to 88 percent of women who do not have a child while they are unmarried. Still, the vast majority of unmarried mothers will eventually marry (at least in the United States). This raises the question of whether it is marriage or childbearing that is being postponed or permanently rejected.

Delays Versus Permanent Declines

Many economic models assume that when marriage market conditions change the equilibrium level of marriage will change as a result. Barring any further change in conditions, the change should be permanent. But there is abundant evidence that many people are postponing marriage or childbearing without avoiding them altogether.

A number of authors have commented on the question of whether marriage is being eschewed or delayed. Andrew Cherlin (1992) suggests that much of what is being observed is marriage delay. Empirical treatments, including those using hazard models, and the birth control work of Goldin and Katz (2000), treat postponement as the dependent variable. But confusion remains about whether childbearing, marriage, or both are being postponed or eschewed permanently, and by whom.

We used CPS data to explore the ways in which marriage and childbearing are changing. We examined the fraction of women in various birth cohorts who have been married or have had a first child by various ages. We also looked at these fractions separately by race and education thirds.[23] Table 1.7 summarizes the results by contrasting women born in the early 1940s with women born in the mid-1960s. The first two columns of the table show declines in the percentages of women who had a baby by age twenty-five and age thirty, while the third column shows the projected decline in the percentage who will have had a baby by age forty. The fourth and fifth columns show declines in the percentages of women who had married by age twenty-five or age thirty, while the last column shows declines in the percentage who were expected to have married by age forty. Changes at age twenty-five or even age thirty may simply be delays. Changes at age forty are likely to be permanent, particularly in childbearing. Several patterns stand out:

- For both childbearing and marriage, there is far more delay than permanent avoidance. The overall decline in the fraction with a child at age twenty-five is twenty-one percentage points. By age forty, the decline is only six points. The declines are comparable for marriage.

- The patterns for blacks and whites differ dramatically. White women are postponing both childbearing and marriage. Black women are postponing childbearing far less and postponing marriage far more than whites. Indeed, many black women are no longer marrying at all.

- There are also large differences by education. The proportion of women who have married by the age of thirty or forty declined by about the same amount regardless of where women fell in the distribution of schooling. The proportion who had not had a child by the age of thirty or forty declined far more among highly educated women.[24] The fraction of highly educated women who are not having children at all rose substantially.[25]

These tables raise serious questions about the correct interpretation of work that investigates marriage rates among women age eighteen to twenty-four or age twenty-five to thirty-four. Most of the changes found in these studies involve delay rather than permanent avoidance of marriage. Table 1.7 also illustrates the necessity of understanding the forces driving both childbearing *and* marriage if we are to understand changes in family structure. Why are more-educated women postponing childbearing far more than less-educated ones? Why are less-educated women postponing marriage nearly as much as more-educated women? And why are racial patterns of marriage and childbearing so different?

A small but growing literature examines the "optimal" timing of motherhood. This work is ably summarized in Hotz, Klerman, and Willis (1997) and in Gustafsson (2001). Most of the work treats the mother's opportunity cost as an important element in her decisions about when to have children. The literature itself is theoretically and empirically complex, in part because closed models with endogenous fertility and labor supply typically require dynamic programming techniques and estimates based on truncated longitudinal data.[26] The complexity arises even when very strong assumptions are made about wage profiles (which are often assumed to be either flat or affected only by experience) and about

TABLE 1.7   *Actual or Projected Change in the Proportion of Women Having a Baby or Marrying by Ages Twenty-Five, Thirty, and Forty: Women Born in the Early 1940s Versus Women Born in the Mid-1960s*

	Projected Decline in Proportion Who Will Have Had a Baby			Projected Decline in Proportion Who Will Have Married		
	By Age Twenty-Five	By Age Thirty	By Age Forty	By Age Twenty-Five	By Age Thirty	By Age Forty
Overall	.21	.14	.06	.25	.16	.07
By race						
White women	.22	.15	.07	.23	.12	.05
Black women	.09	.07	.03	.44	.28	.17
By education						
Lowest third	.10	.06	.03	.20	.16	.06
Middle third	.17	.13	.05	.24	.16	.08
Highest third	.32	.20	.09	.29	.16	.07

Source: Authors' tabulation of June and March CPS data. Based on tables available from the authors. Projections for the cohort born in the mid-1960s are based on proportions observed at age thirty to thirty-five and changes between ages thirty and thirty-five and age forty in previous cohorts.

the opportunity costs of parenting (all mothers withdraw from the labor market for a fixed period). Furthermore, this literature either looks only at childbearing conditional on marriage or ignores marriage entirely. Hotz and his colleagues (1997, 310, n. 49) report: "To date no dynamic models have been developed which incorporate marriage decisions within a life cycle context." Thus, illogically, the marriage decision is completely independent of and usually prior to the childbearing decision (an interesting reversal of the TEM, which treats child-rearing as one of the primary reasons for marrying).

Theoretical models differ somewhat in their predictions regarding the effect of women's economic opportunities on fertility timing. James Walker (1995) theorizes that a flatter life-cycle profile leads to later births, while Alessandro Cigno and John Ermisch (1989) predict the opposite (for a discussion, see Gustafsson 2001). Like the early work of Moffitt (1984), recent work usually predicts that women with more opportunities to invest in human capital will have children later.

Interestingly, most of the empirical literature that examines the timing of first births focuses on countries other than the United States. Heckman and Walker (1990) and Walker (1995) examine Swedish behavior. Joan Kahn and Leslie Whittington (1994) study Puerto Rico. Adriaan Kalwij (2000) examines the Netherlands. Philip Merrigan and Yvan St.-Pierre (1998) examine Canada. This literature almost uniformly finds that increases in women's work and wages diminish their fertility. Most of the literature also reports that increases in husbands' wages raise fertility. Thus, there appears to be some theoretical and empirical basis for seeing the differential postponement of childbearing as having an economic basis.

Cohabitation

Starting with Bumpass, Sweet, and Cherlin (1991), a growing literature has sought to describe and explain changes in cohabitation. Cohabitation has increased in recent years, both in the United States and in other affluent countries, especially Scandinavia. Using a fairly liberal definition of cohabitation (persons of the opposite sex and roughly the same age in shared living quarters) and correcting for various coding inconsistencies over time, our tabulations of CPS data indicate that:

- The fraction of all women age twenty-five to thirty-four who cohabited rose from less than 1 percent in the 1960s to roughly 10 percent in 2000. Over the same period the fraction of women in this age range who were married and living with a spouse fell from roughly 85 to 55 percent. Thus, up to one-third of the decline in marriage has been replaced by cohabitation. But cohabitation is still relatively rare among American women with children, accounting for only about 4 percent of households with children. (The percentages are higher in many other countries.)

- It is not clear how work on family structure should treat cohabitation. The traditional solution is to treat cohabiters as single, but this is clearly unsatisfactory for assessing a household's current resources or poverty status. The simplest alternative is to treat cohabiting couples as married. Unfortunately, a sizable body of research indicates that cohabiting couples are rather different from both married couples and individuals who live alone.

Smock and Manning (1997) report that roughly one-third of partners who are cohabiting at a point in time will marry within two years, while another one-fifth will split up within two years. Michael Brien, Lee Lillard, and Linda Waite (1999) report that 33 to 40 percent of the high school class of 1972 cohabited before their first marriage. They argue that cohabitation is often a step to marriage and sometimes motherhood, since marriage rates jump sharply when the woman becomes pregnant. They speak of cohabitation as a kind of trial marriage. As we might expect, cohabiting relationships are far more likely than marriages to end in separation.

Bumpass, Sweet, and Cherlin (1991) show that only 51 percent of cohabiting males report that an important reason why they wanted "to live with someone of the opposite sex without being married" is that "couples can be sure they are compatible before marriage." Other important reasons include the desire to "share living expenses" (28 percent), greater independence than marriage (17 percent), and more "sexually satisfying than dating" (17 percent). Thus, cohabitation can be a number of different things: a modest step up from dating, a trial marriage, or an alternative to marriage. In the United States, however, most cohabiting couples with children either marry fairly soon or split up.

Another recent line of work sees cohabitation as part of the marital search process. Brien, Lillard, and Stern (2000) posit a model in which partners reduce uncertainty about match quality by first cohabiting. A search model could predict a longer transition to marriage and an increase in cohabitation either when uncertainty about partners' characteristics or prospects increases or when the benefits to a longer search rise. David Loughran (2000) argues that the increasing variance in male wages increases the time required for searching. He suggests that between 1970 to 1990 from 20 to 35 percent of the reduction in marriage between the ages of twenty-two and twenty-eight derived from the growing inequality of male earnings. His empirical findings have some limitations (he finds that a variance-preserving rise in male wages would reduce marriage), but he does find that a rising wage gap between the bottom and the middle of the male distribution affects marriage rates among less-educated women, while a rising gap between the middle and top affects marriage rates among the more-educated—a finding consistent with the theory.

What Needs to Be Explained and a Working Hypothesis

A few facts seem to hold the key to a better understanding of family change:

- Marriage and childbearing are less and less connected. Childbearing often precedes marriage, but it also often follows marriage by a longer interval than in the past.

- More-educated women are postponing childbearing and marriage. Less-educated women are postponing marriage but not childbearing, at least not nearly as much.

- African American women have only delayed childbearing a little, but they have postponed marriage a lot, often permanently.

- Cohabitation is more common than ever before, particularly among couples who do not have children.

Our review of existing research presents a somewhat discouraging picture. We do find evidence that improving job opportunities for men somewhat increases marriage and reduces single-parenthood. Both the theoretical and empirical literature is far more ambiguous about the effects of female labor market opportunities. Contraceptive technology, access to abortion, and attitudes regarding premarital sex and the family all changed in the 1960s and early 1970s, but family change continued well into the 1990s, possibly because technical, legal, and attitudinal changes take a long time to exert their full influence. Other factors, however, may also have been at work.

Yet if we take a broad view of the trends and findings, we believe a fairly plausible hypothesis emerges. Like Sweeney (2002), we think that the relationship between economic opportunity and marriage has changed over the years. Three factors are likely to have altered the preferred timing of marriage and parenthood.

First, *the pill and legalized abortion* gave couples, and particularly women, far more control over the timing of births and thus allowed other factors (including economic incentives) to play more of a role. Previous forms of contraception, such as condoms, withdrawal, rhythm, and diaphragms, were often less reliable, required the interruption of sexual activity, or gave males control. The pill and abortion weakened the link between marriage and childbearing.

Second, *changing sexual mores* made it far more acceptable for unmarried couples to engage in sexual activity and live together. The non-economic incentives to marry therefore fell. All else being equal, this change could have made economic considerations more important and could have also allowed them to influence the timing of marriage and childbearing differently.

Finally, *gender roles and expectations changed dramatically, particularly with respect to maternal employment.* As late as March 1968, fewer than one-quarter of married mothers whose youngest child was under five were working. This varied little by education. Even among mothers with elementary school children, only about 40 percent worked, and even fewer worked full-time. By March 2000, roughly two-thirds of married mothers with children under five were working, and the numbers were even higher for mothers with older children. Despite welfare reform, moreover, maternal employment in 2000 rose sharply with education. Because potential mothers expect to work far more over their lifetime, they know that their decisions about the timing of fertility have greater financial implications.

These changes can influence fertility and marriage directly, but they are also likely to increase the impact of traditional economic variables. If women gain greater control over the timing of parenthood, and if they have more opportunities in the labor market, some of them will find it advantageous to delay childbearing. If women delay childbearing, many will delay marriage as well.

Why should these changes lead college-educated women to delay childbearing more than women with less schooling? First, college-educated women have more attractive labor market options, so they may choose to postpone motherhood simply because it would interfere with another satisfying activity. Second, the career costs associated with early childbearing may be greater for more skilled women. College-educated women may need to invest more heavily during the early part of their career in order to maximize their lifetime earnings (by becoming a partner in a law firm, for example). In preliminary work, we have found strong evidence that early childbearing reduces the earnings of highly skilled women more than the earnings of less-skilled women. Finally, college-educated women may be more likely to anticipate using paid child care and may therefore want to wait until they can afford such help.

If women's economic opportunities have come to play a more important role in the timing of motherhood, we would expect educated women to delay childbearing longer than less-educated women even if their relative economic opportunities had not changed.[27] But in fact economic opportunities *did* improve more for college-educated women, so there is even more reason for them to delay having a child.

Less-educated women who still want to have children at a relatively early age face the problem that their male counterparts have fared badly in the labor market. As a result, many of these women cannot find economically attractive mates. This might lead them to delay marriage but not childbearing. More-educated women, who are in no rush to have children, would also be in no rush to get married. Hence, they would delay both marriage and childbearing, even though their prospective husbands are doing relatively well economically.

This hypothesis can also help to explain the sudden change in many trends during the late 1990s. For the first time in almost thirty years, both marriage and delayed childbearing became more common. The wages of less-skilled men and women rose. Jobs became plentiful. The Earned Income Tax Credit and other supports made work even more lucrative for unskilled parents. Welfare reform pushed more women into paid employment. Welfare reform may also have convinced some women that single-parenthood was becoming less acceptable to others.

This explanation is far from perfect. It probably still fails to fully explain the racial differences that have grown so large. It says nothing about divorce or remarriage. We offer this loose hybrid hypothesis only as a starting point. But it does suggest that social science may yet be able to explain far more of what has happened to families.

In this simple form, our story suggests that changing technology, attitudes, and norms made economic forces far more important in influencing fertility and marriage decisions. Women gained more control over fertility and saw more potential payoff from doing so (owing to better job opportunities). At the same time, our hypothesis represents a significant shift in focus from the usual economic model. Instead of assuming that marriage is synonymous with having children, our hypothesis assumes that the timing of fertility is more important than the timing of marriage. The timing of childbearing is driven primarily by female job opportunities or the lack thereof. Marriage decisions are made within this context. Of course, a full model would require that decisions about the timing of fertility and marriage be made jointly, since the economic opportunities available to men surely affect the childbearing calculations of women.

A critical element in our hypothesis is that improved opportunities led women to postpone childbearing. Our story requires that highly educated women see the costs and benefits of early childbearing differently from less-educated women. The most obvious economic source of such a difference is that accumulating more labor market experience has a bigger payoff for better educated women. There is some evidence that women with greater market opportunities tend to postpone childbearing more. But we found no evidence on whether early childbearing leads to a larger percentage reduction in lifetime earnings among women with better economic prospects.

Indeed, we found very little evidence on how the timing of childbearing (after one's teens) influenced women's labor market outcomes, regardless of education. Charles Calhoun and Thomas Espenshade (1988) have examined the impact of childbearing on forgone earnings of women (because of reduced work hours) in the United States. They find that lost earnings are five times greater for whites than blacks, and higher for those with more education. Similar work has been done by Heather Joshi (1990) for Britain and by Oystein Kravdal (1992) for Norway. But none of these authors examine whether the *timing* of childbearing influences its lifetime costs, and they look only at the short-term impact of reduced hours of work, not at the possible long-term impact on earnings after a woman returns to the labor force.

Teenage childbearing is the one major exception to our claim that little is known about how the timing of childbearing affects future earnings. Until recently, most social scientists assumed that adolescent childbearing reduces the mother's future earnings. But some recent literature, nicely summarized in Cherlin (2001), suggests that disadvantaged women who postpone childbearing until their twenties often fare no better than those who do not postpone. Arline Geronimus and Sanders Korenman (1992) find that when sisters are compared, the differences between teen parents and older parents drop by as much as two-thirds. Hotz, McElroy, and Sanders (1997) compare women who miscarry with women who do not and find virtually no impact of teen childbearing (although their estimates are not very precise). Saul Hoffman (1998) raises legitimate questions about this literature. None of it asks whether the consequences of early childbearing are larger for women from more advantaged backgrounds or with greater academic promise. If the costs of early childbearing vary systematically, this could help explain the puzzle of family structure change.

CONCLUDING THOUGHTS

We reviewed the literature on family structure in the hope of finding explanations for the dramatic increase in single-parenthood and nonmarital childbearing among all but the best-educated American women. We have found some consistent findings and some tantalizing hints. Male earnings and sex ratios clearly influence marriage, but not enough to explain the bulk of recent changes. Female market opportunities have a more ambiguous effect. New methods of birth control have become available, and delays in marriage have led to an increase in premarital sex. Social norms have also changed, although we do not know whether this is a cause or a consequence of changed behavior.

The challenge now is to understand why fertility patterns have changed so differently among more- and less-educated women while marriage patterns changed so similarly. Ultimately, that will require weaving together our stories. We are more optimistic now than we were when we began this project about social scientists' ability to offer a credible account of what has caused families to change, but a great deal remains to be done.

APPENDIX

FIGURE 1A.1   *Children in Single-Mother Homes, by Education of the Mother, 1960 to 2002*

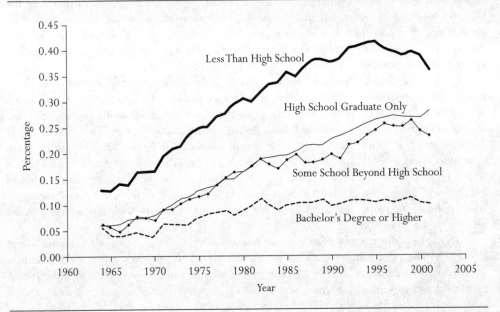

Sources: Authors' calculations.

FIGURE 1A.2   *Forty- to Forty-Four-Year-Old American Women Who Have Never Had a Child, by Birth Cohort, 1916–1920 to 1956–1960*

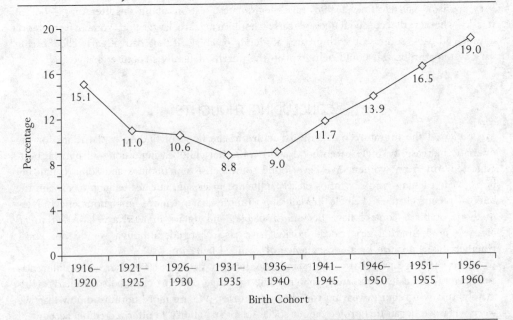

Sources: U.S. Department of Commerce (2000a) and U.S. Department of Health and Human Services (1998).

The authors gratefully acknowledge generous support from the Russell Sage Foundation's New Inequality Project. Jencks was also supported by a Hewlett Foundation Fellowship at the Center for Advanced Study in the Behavioral Sciences while working on these issues. We also thank Andrew Clarkwest, David Harding, Elisabeth Riviello, Joseph Swingle, Zoua Vang, Beth Welty, and Chris Wimer for excellent research work and thoughtful suggestions; Seth Kirshenbaum for careful editing of an earlier draft; and Steve Martin for sharing his unpublished data on divorce. Francine Blau, Andrew Cherlin, Paula England, Frank Furstenberg, Irv Garfinkel, Patrick Heuveline, and Eric Wanner provided very helpful comments, as did other participants in the New Inequality Project, the MacArthur Network on the Family and the Economy, and seminars at Cornell University, Harvard University, Syracuse University, and the University of Wisconsin.

NOTES

1. The percentage of fifteen-year-olds living with both biological parents at the end of 2000 depends on the 1985 dissolution rate for unions involving children under the age of one, the 1986 rates for unions involving children between one and two, and so on. Andersson's life-table estimates are based on average dissolution rates during the seven-year interval shown for each country. In countries where dissolution rates rose in the 1990s, the life-table method underestimates the actual rate.

2. One potential limitation of McLanahan and Sandefur's (1994) findings is that they generally control income in a single year, which is a very imperfect proxy for long-term income or for most forms of consumption. To the extent that family structure is a proxy for unmeasured income differences, their estimates underestimate the importance of family structure's economic effects and exaggerate the importance of its non-economic effects. Studies that use multiyear measures of parental income often show very small effects of family structure.

3. Because individuals are concentrated at certain levels of schooling (such as high school graduate), we must split groups with the same schooling to generate thirds. To do this, we simply draw randomly from the schooling group that spans the thirty-third or sixty-seventh percentile to fill out our thirds. The mean schooling of each third is quite different, even though there is some overlap at the margin.

4. There is some evidence that the divorce rate for firstborn children under five turned up again in the early 1990s, but this could be due to chance.

5. *Vital Statistics* publishes a different series that is often cited in determining the share of children born out of wedlock. That series is derived from data on birth certificates that every state collects from hospitals and doctors. Birth certificate data vary from state to state, and their accuracy has often been questioned. Even today five states (including California) do not actually ask mothers whether they are married, preferring to make educated guesses that probably exaggerate the percentage of unmarried parents. From 1940 through 1970, the proportion of infants not living with a married parent was quite similar to the proportion whose birth certificates indicated that the mother was unmarried. By 1990, however, the trend lines had diverged substantially, and by 2000 the census estimate was less than three-fifths of the *Vital Statistics* estimate (19.3 versus 33.2 percent). We cannot fully explain this discrepancy. In some cases, couples who were unmarried at the time of a birth may have married before the child turned one. The Fragile Families Study of births in cities of more than 200,000 finds that roughly 9 percent of couples who were unmarried when the baby was born had married within a year, while 6 percent of those who were married had separated (Cynthia Osborne, unpublished tabulations, July 28, 2002). Because so many births in these cities were to unmarried parents, the parents of one-year-olds were slightly more likely than the parents of newborns to be married. Still, this can explain only a modest part of the divergence, and we are troubled by the methodology used in the *Vital Statistics* series. Moreover, *Vital Statistics* data are not available by level of education; for this we rely exclusively on the census and on CPS data.

6. Joshua Goldstein and Catherine Kenney (2001) estimate that 93 percent of white women but only 64 percent of black women born in the early 1960s will eventually marry.

7. We do not know whether the higher rate of cohabiting in the Fragile Families Study is due to a continuing secular trend, the fact that the sample excludes rural areas, suburbs, and cities of less than 200,000, or the

fact that the initial interview occurs within a few days of the baby's birth, when couples whose relationship is somewhat ambiguous may be especially likely to say that they are living together.

8. The estimates in figures 1.12 and 1.13 also include split-ups due to death, but mortality rates are relatively similar in all these countries.

9. For excellent recent reviews of the theoretical literature see Weiss (1997) and Hotz, Klerman, and Willis (1997).

10. As discussed later, there have recently been a few attempts to integrate models of fertility and childbearing; see, for example, Willis (1999).

11. The difference between figure 1.5 and figure 1.16 in the trends for highly educated mothers is not explained by race but may be a function of age selection.

12. Recall that educational thirds are defined the same way for all women. Black women in the top third of the overall education distribution are actually in the top 20 percent of blacks.

13. Median wages are calculated from March CPS data by dividing total earnings by weeks worked and usual hours worked per week. Persons with no earnings or with an estimated wage of less than $1 per hour are excluded. All earnings were price-adjusted using the CPI-U-X1.

14. These ratios are based on observed medians and are adjusted for neither the fact that men typically have more labor market experience than women nor the fact that the experience gap has narrowed over time. Neither are they adjusted for anything else.

15. The coefficients of these variables are sometimes insignificant, but they usually have the correct signs. The large standard errors may just reflect measurement error for small subgroups in smaller metropolitan areas.

16. Theory suggests that increased work or pay for married women reduces marriage while increased work and pay for men tends to increase it. Yet Lichter and his colleagues (2000) use a specification suggesting that only the gain in total income from marriage matters, regardless of whether the gain is caused by male or female married work.

17. Lichter and his colleagues (1992) and Brien (1997) do include a sex ratio measure that yields a significant positive effect as predicted by theory, though it is used as an alternative to the male market measure, not simultaneously.

18. Strangely, Ressler and Waters (2000) emphasize that they find negative and significant effects of female earnings. But when we add the base impact of earnings times the added effects for 1970, 1980, or 1990, the sign reverses and the overall impact becomes negligible.

19. Their coefficients on women's pay are wrong signed and nearly significant.

20. Nor is it likely that their attitudes and behavior changed later. Roughly half of those who were over twenty-five in 1965 said they had engaged in premarital sex before age twenty-five.

21. Unfortunately, we have been unable to locate the original data from the 1965 survey, and prior to the advent of the GSS in 1972 there were not many other surveys that asked the same questions about sexual attitudes in more than one year. But there are other surveys. One shows that 63 percent of men and women age twenty to thirty said that "two people who are in love and engaged to be married should wait until marriage to have sexual relations" (Erskine 1967b, 122). Our favorite is a question from a 1939 survey asked about members of the opposite sex: "Do you consider it all right, unfortunate, or wicked when young women (men) have sexual relations before marriage?" Counterintuitively, men were more forgiving of women (28 percent wicked) than women of men (47 percent wicked) (Erskine 1967a).

22. Similar trends in premarital sexual behavior among women at all educational levels may seem surprising given the apparent beginnings of the sexual revolution on college campuses. And there does appear to be a modest jump in premarital sex among the most educated in the early 1960s, bringing their behavior closer to that of their less-educated counterparts.

23. The detailed tables are available from the authors on request.

24. Education, of course, may be partly endogenous. Women who have children early are presumably less likely to get as much education and thus are more likely to show up in the bottom education third. Ideally, we might like to do such tables based on parental education or some other exogenous variable.

25. The June 2000 CPS, which was not available when we constructed the appendix tables or table 1.7, is roughly consistent with these projections.

26. Hotz, Klerman, and Willis (1997, 309) report that their "solutions do not lead to straightforward and robust implications about what life cycle patterns of fertility should be observed and how they vary as prices and income vary." In a footnote they add that "the solutions to these programs do not lend themselves to simple econometric specifications, either."

27. Heckman and Walker (1990) examine the timing of fertility using Swedish data and find some evidence of changing economic impacts over time. They report that their finding of "declining male income coefficients for the first Cigno and Ermisch (1989) transition is consistent with the view that more recent cohorts of women are less dependent on male income in initiating the fertility process." But international evidence points in a somewhat different direction. McDonald (2002) argues that fertility is lower in affluent countries when there is more economic uncertainty and fewer supports for raising children.

REFERENCES

Acs, Gregory. 1995. "Do Welfare Benefits Promote Out-of-Wedlock Childbearing?" In *Welfare Reform: An Analysis of the Issues,* edited by Isabel V. Sawhill. Washington, D.C.: Urban Institute.

Akerlof, George A., Janet L. Yellen, and Michael L. Katz. 1996. "An Analysis of Out-of-Wedlock Childbearing in the United States." *Quarterly Journal of Economics* 111(2, May): 277–317.

Andersson, Gunnar. 2002. "Children's Experience of Family Disruption and Family Formation: Evidence from 16 FFS Countries." *Demographic Research* 7(August): 344–63.

Axinn, William G., and Arland Thornton. 2000. "The Transformation in the Meaning of Marriage." In *The Ties That Bind: Perspectives on Marriage and Cohabitation,* edited by Linda J. Waite. New York: Aldine de Gruyter.

Becker, Gary. 1991. *A Treatise on the Family.* Enlarged edition. Cambridge, Mass.: Harvard University Press.

Bennett, Neil G., David E. Bloom, and Cynthia K. Miller. 1995. "The Influence of Nonmarital Childbearing on the Formation of First Marriages." *Demography* 32(1, February): 47–62.

Blau, Francine D. 1998. "Trends in the Well-being of American Women, 1970–1995." *Journal of Economic Literature* 36(March): 112–65.

Blau, Francine D., Lawrence M. Kahn, and Jane Waldfogel. 2000. "Understanding Young Women's Marriage Decisions: The Role of Labor and Marriage Market Conditions." *Industrial and Labor Relations Review* 53(4, July): 624–47.

Brien, Michael J. 1997. "Racial Differences in Marriage and the Role of Marriage Markets." *Journal of Human Resources* 32(4): 741–78.

Brien, Michael J., Lee A. Lillard, and Steven Stern. 2000. "Cohabitation, Marriage, and Divorce in a Model of Match Quality." Unpublished paper. University of Virginia, Charlottesville.

Brien, Michael J., Lee A. Lillard, and Linda J. Waite. 1999. "Interrelated Family-Building Behaviors: Cohabitation, Marriage, and Nonmarital Conception." *Demography* 36(4, November): 535–51.

Brines, Julie, and Kara Joyner. 1999. "The Ties That Bind: Principles of Cohesion in Cohabitation and Marriage." *American Sociological Review* 64(June): 333–55.

Bumpass, Larry, and Hsien-Hen Lu. 2000. "Trends in Cohabitation and Implications for Children's Family Contexts in the United States." *Population Studies* 54(March): 29–41.

Bumpass, Larry L., James A. Sweet, and Andrew Cherlin. 1991. "The Role of Cohabitation in Declining Rates of Marriage." *Journal of Marriage and the Family* 53(November): 913–27.

Calhoun, Charles A., and Thomas J. Espenshade. 1988. "Childbearing and Wives' Forgone Earnings." *Population Studies* 42(1, March): 5–37.

Cherlin, Andrew J. 1992. *Marriage, Divorce, Remarriage.* Cambridge, Mass.: Harvard University Press.

———. 2001. "New Developments in the Study of Nonmarital Childbearing." In *Out of Wedlock: Causes and Consequences of Nonmarital Fertility,* edited by Lawrence L. Wu and Barbara Wolfe. New York: Russell Sage Foundation.

Cigno, Alessandro, and John Ermisch. 1989. "A Microeconomic Analysis of the Timing of Births." *European Economic Review* 33(4, April): 737–60.

Cready, Cynthia M., Mark A. Fossett, and K. Jill Kiekolt. 1997. "Mate Availability and African American Family Structure in the U.S. Nonmetropolitan Areas." *Journal of Marriage and the Family* 59(February): 192–203.

Danziger, Sheldon H., George Jakubson, Saul Schwartz, and Eugene Smolensky. 1982. "Work and Welfare as Determinants of Female and Household Leadership." *Quarterly Journal of Economics* 97(3, August): 519–34.

Darity, William A., Jr., and Samuel L. Myers Jr. 1995. "Family Structure and the Marginalization of Black Men: Policy Implications." In *The Decline in Marriage Among African Americans,* edited by M. Belinda Tucker and Claudia Mitchell-Kernan. New York: Russell Sage Foundation.

Edin, Kathryn. 1999. "Why Don't Low-Income Mothers Get Married (or Remarried)?" Unpublished paper. University of Pennsylvania, Philadelphia.

Ellwood, David T. 1994. "Understanding Dependency." In *Welfare Realities: From Rhetoric to Reform,* edited by Mary Jo Bane and David T. Ellwood. Cambridge, Mass.: Harvard University Press.

Ellwood, David T., and Mary Jo Bane. 1985. "The Impact of AFDC on Family Structure and Living Arrangements." In *Research in Labor Economics,* edited by Ronald Ehrenberg. Greenwich, Conn.: JAI Press.

Ellwood, David T., and Jonathan Crane. 1990. "Family Change Among Black Americans: What Do We Know?" *Journal of Economic Perspectives* 4(4, Autumn): 65–84.

Ellwood, David T., and David Rodda. 1990. "The Hazards of Work and Marriage: The Influence of Employment on Marriage." Unpublished paper. Harvard University, Cambridge, Mass.

Erskine, Hazel Gaudet. 1967a. "The Polls: Morality." *Public Opinion Quarterly* 30(4, Winter): 669–80.

———. 1967b. "The Polls: More on Morality and Sex." *Public Opinion Quarterly* 31(1, Spring): 116–28.

Fossett, Mark A., and K. Jill Kiekolt. 1993. "Mate Availability and Family Structure Among African Americans in U.S. Metropolitan Areas." *Journal of Marriage and the Family* 55(May): 288–302.

Friedberg, Leora. 1998. "Did Unilateral Divorce Raise Divorce Rates? Evidence from Panel Data." *American Economic Review* 88(8, June): 608–27.

Furstenberg, Frank. 1996. "The Future of Marriage." *American Demographics* (June): 34–40.

———. 2001. "The Fading Dream: Prospects for Marriage in the Inner City." In *Problem of the Century: Racial Stratification in the United States,* edited by Elijah Anderson and Douglas Massey. New York: Russell Sage Foundation.

Geronimus, Arline T., and Sanders Korenman. 1992. "The Socioeconomic Consequences of Teen Childbearing Reconsidered." *Quarterly Journal of Economics* 107(4, November): 1187–1214.

Goldin, Claudia, and Lawrence F. Katz. 2000. "The Power of the Pill: Oral Contraceptives and Women's Career and Marriage Decisions." Working paper 7527. Cambridge, Mass.: National Bureau of Economic Research (February).

Goldstein, Joshua, and Catherine Kenney. 2001. "Marriage Delayed or Marriage Forgone? New Cohort Forecasts of First Marriage for U.S. Women." *American Sociological Review* 66(August): 506–19.

Greenstein, Theodore N. 1990. "Marital Disruption and the Employment of Married Women." *Journal of Marriage and the Family* 52(August): 657–76.

Grogger, Jeff, and Stephen G. Bronars. 1997. "The Effect of Welfare Payments on the Marriage and Fertility Behavior of Unwed Mothers: Results from a Twins Experiment." Working paper 6047. Cambridge, Mass.: National Bureau of Economic Research (May).

Gustafsson, Siv. 2001. "Optimal Age at Motherhood: Theoretical and Empirical Considerations on Postponement of Maternity in Europe." *Journal of Population Economics* 14(2): 225–47.

Harding, David, and Christopher Jencks. 2003. "Changing Attitudes Toward Premarital Sex: Cohort, Period, and Aging Effects." *Public Opinion Quarterly* 67(2, Summer): 211–26.

Heckman, James J., and James R. Walker. 1990. "The Relationship Between Wages and Income and the Timing and Spacing of Births: Evidence from Swedish Longitudinal Data." *Econometrica* 58(6, November): 1411–41.

Hoffman, Saul D. 1998. "Teenage Childbearing Is Not So Bad After All . . . Or Is It? A Review of the New Literature." *Family Planning Perspectives* 30(5, September–October): 236–39.

Hoffman, Saul D., and Greg J. Duncan. 1995. "The Effect of Income, Wages, and AFDC Benefits on Marital Disruption." *Journal of Human Resources* 30(1, Winter): 19–41.

Hoffman, Saul D., Greg J. Duncan, and Ronald Mincy. 1991. "Marriage and Welfare Use Among Young Women." Paper presented to the meeting of the Population Association of America, Washington, D.C. (March).

Hotz, V. Joseph, Jacob Alex Klerman, and Robert J. Willis. 1997. "The Economics of Fertility in Developed

Countries." In *Handbook of Population and Family Economics,* edited by Mark R. Rosenzweig and Oded Stark. Amsterdam: Elsevier Science.

Hotz, V. Joseph, Susan Williams McElroy, and Seth G. Sanders. 1997. "The Impacts of Teenage Childbearing on the Mothers and the Consequences of Those Impacts for Government." In *Kids Having Kids: Economic Costs and Social Consequences,* edited by Rebecca A. Maynard. Washington, D.C.: Urban Institute Press.

Hoynes, Hilary Williamson. 1997a. "Work, Welfare, and Family Structure: What Have We Learned?" In *Fiscal Policy: Lessons from Economic Research,* edited by Alan Auerbach. Cambridge: Cambridge University Press.

———. 1997b. "Does Welfare Play Any Role in Female Headship Decisions?" *Journal of Public Economics* 65(2, August): 89–117.

Jencks, Christopher. 1992. *Rethinking Social Policy: Race, Poverty, and the Underclass.* New York: HarperCollins.

Johnson, William R., and Jonathan Skinner. 1986. "Labor Supply and Marital Separation." *American Economic Review* 76(3, June): 455–69.

Joshi, Heather. 1990. "The Cash Opportunity Costs to Childbearing: An Approach to Estimation Using British Data." *Population Studies* 44(1, March): 41–60.

Kahn, Joan R., and Leslie A. Whittington. 1994. "The Transition to Parenthood in Puerto Rico: Occupational Status and the Timing of First Births." *Population Research and Social Policy* 13: 121–40.

Kalwij, Adriaan S. 2000. "The Effects of Female Employment Status on the Presence and Number of Children." *Journal of Population Economics* 13(2): 221–39.

Kane, Thomas J., and Douglas Staiger. 1996. "Teen Motherhood and Abortion Access." *Quarterly Journal of Economics* 111(2, May): 467–506.

Koball, Heather. 1998. "Have African American Men Become Less Committed to Marriage? Explaining the Twentieth-Century Racial Cross-over in Men's Marriage Timing." *Demography* 35(2, May): 251–58.

Kravdal, Oystein. 1992. "Forgone Labor Force Participation and Earning Due to Childbearing Among Norwegian Women." *Demography* 29(4, November): 545–63.

Lehrer, Evelyn. 2000. "Religion as a Determinant of Entry into Cohabitation and Marriage." In *The Ties That Bind: Perspectives on Marriage and Cohabitation,* edited by Linda J. Waite. Hawthorne, N.Y.: Aldine de Gruyter.

Levine, Phillip B., Douglas Staiger, Thomas J. Kane, and David J. Zimmerman. 1996. "*Roe v. Wade* and American Fertility." Working paper 5615. Cambridge, Mass.: National Bureau of Economic Research (June).

Lichter, Daniel T., and Deborah Roempke Graefe. 2001. "Finding a Mate? The Marital and Cohabitation Histories of Unwed Mothers." In *Out of Wedlock: Causes and Consequences of Nonmarital Fertility,* edited by Lawrence L. Wu and Barbara Wolfe. New York: Russell Sage Foundation.

Lichter, Daniel T., Felicia B. LeClere, and Diane K. McLaughlin. 1991. "Local Marriage Markets and the Marital Behavior of Black and White Women." *American Journal of Sociology* 96(4, January): 843–67.

Lichter, Daniel T., Diane K. McLaughlin, George Kephart, and David J. Landry. 1992. "Race and the Retreat from Marriage: A Shortage of Marriageable Men?" *American Sociological Review* 57(6, December): 781–99.

Lichter, Daniel T., Diane K. McLaughlin, and David C. Ribar. 2002. "Economic Restructuring and the Retreat from Marriage." *Social Science Research* 31(June): 230–56.

London, Kathryn. 1989. "Children of Divorce." *Vital and Health Statistics,* series 21(46). DHHS (PHS)89-1924. Washington: U.S. Government Printing Office.

Loughran, David S. 2000. "Does Variance Matter? The Effect of Rising Male Wage Inequality on Female Age at First Marriage." Labor and Population Program working paper 00-12. Santa Monica, Calif.: Rand Corporation (July).

Lundberg, Shelly, and Robert D. Plotnick. 1995. "Adolescent Premarital Childbearing: Do Economic Incentives Matter?" *Journal of Labor Economics* 13(April): 177–200.

Mare, Robert D., and Christopher Winship. 1991. "Socioeconomic Change and the Decline of Marriage for Blacks and Whites." In *The Urban Underclass,* edited by Christopher Jencks and Paul E. Peterson. Washington, D.C.: Brookings Institution.

McDonald, Peter. 2002. "Low Fertility: Unifying the Theory and the Demography." Available at: http://eprints. anu.edu.au/archive/00001113/01/PAA_Paper_2002.pdf.

McLanahan, Sara, and Lynne Casper. 1995. "Growing Diversity and Inequality in the American Family." In *State of the Union, America in the 1990s: Social Trends,* edited by Reynolds Farley. New York: Russell Sage Foundation.

McLanahan, Sara, and Gary Sandefur. 1994. *Growing Up with a Single Parent.* Cambridge, Mass.: Harvard University Press.

Merrigan, Philip, and Yvan St.-Piere. 1998. "An Econometric and Neoclassical Analysis of the Timing and Spacing of Births in Canada from 1950 to 1990." *Journal of Population Economics* 11(1): 29–51.

Moffitt, Robert. 1984. "Optimal Life-Cycle Profiles of Fertility and Labor Supply." *Research in Population Economics* 5: 29–50.

———. 1998. "The Effect of Welfare on Marriage and Fertility." In *Welfare, the Family, and Reproductive Behavior,* edited by Robert Moffitt. Washington, D.C.: National Academy Press.

———. 2001. "Welfare Benefits and Female Headship in U.S. Time Series." In *Out of Wedlock: Causes and Consequences of Nonmarital Fertility,* edited by Lawrence L. Wu and Barbara Wolfe. New York: Russell Sage Foundation.

Murray, Charles. 1984. *Losing Ground.* New York: Basic Books.

———. 1993. "Welfare and the Family: The U.S. Experience." *Journal of Labor Economics* 11(1–2, January): S224–62.

National Academy of Science. Panel on Adolescent Pregnancy and Childbearing. 1987. *Risking the Future: Adolescent Sexuality, Pregnancy, and Childbearing.* Washington, D.C.: National Academy Press.

Oppenheimer, Valerie Kincade. 1997a. "Men's Career Development and Marriage Timing During a Period of Rising Inequality." *Demography* 34(3, August): 311–30.

———. 1997b. "Women's Employment and the Gain to Marriage: The Specialization and Trading Model." *Annual Review of Sociology* 23: 431–53.

Patterson, Orlando. 1998. *Rituals of Blood.* Washington, D.C.: Civitas/Counterpoint.

Plotnick, Robert D. 1992. "The Effects of Attitudes on Teenage Premarital Pregnancy and Its Resolution." *American Sociological Review* 57(6, December): 800–11.

Qian, Zhenchao, and Samuel H. Preston. 1993. "Changes in American Marriage, 1972 to 1987: Availability and Forces of Attraction by Age and Education." *American Sociological Review* 58(4, August): 482–95.

Raley, R. Kelly. 1996. "A Shortage of Marriageable Men? A Note on the Role of Cohabitation in Black-White Differences in Marriage Rates." *American Sociological Review* 61(6, December): 973–83.

Ressler, Rand A., and Melissa S. Waters. 2000. "Female Earnings and the Divorce Rate: A Simultaneous Equations Model." *Applied Economics* 32(14, November): 1889–98.

Ruggles, Steven. 1997. "The Rise of Divorce and Separation in the United States, 1880–1990." *Demography* 34(4, November): 455–66.

Schultz, T. Paul. 1994. "Marital Status and Fertility in the United States: Welfare and Labor Market Effects." *Journal of Human Resources* 29(Spring): 637–69.

Sklar, June, and Beth Berkov. 1974. "Abortion, Illegitimacy, and the American Birth Rate." *Science* 185(4155, September 13): 909–15.

Smock, Pamela J., and Wendy D. Manning. 1997. "Cohabiting Partners' Economic Circumstances and Marriage." *Demography* 34(3, August): 331–41.

South, Scott J., and Kim M. Lloyd. 1992. "Marriage Markets and Nonmarital Fertility in the United States." *Demography* 29(2, May): 247–64.

Stevenson, Betsy, and Justin Wolfers. 2000. "'Til Death Do Us Part': Effects of Divorce Laws on Suicide, Domestic Violence, and Spousal Murder." Unpublished paper. Harvard University, Department of Economics, Cambridge, Mass.

Sweeney, Megan. 2002. "Two Decades of Family Change: The Shifting Economic Foundations of Marriage." *American Sociological Review* 67(1, February): 132–47.

Testa, Mark, and Marilyn Krogh. 1995. "The Effect of Employment on Marriage Among Black Males in Inner-City Chicago." In *The Decline in Marriage Among African Americans,* edited by M. Belinda Tucker and Claudia Mitchell-Kernan. New York: Russell Sage Foundation.

Thomas, Adam, and Isabel Sawhill. 2002. "For Richer or for Poorer: Marriage as an Antipoverty Strategy." *Journal of Policy Analysis and Management* 21(4): 587–99.

Thornton, Arland. 1989. "Changing Attitudes Toward Family Issues in the United States." *Journal of Marriage and the Family* 51(November): 873–93.

Thornton, Arland, and Linda Young-DeMarco. 2001. "Four Decades of Trends in Attitudes Toward Family Issues in the United States: The 1960s Through the 1990s." *Journal of Marriage and the Family* 63(November): 1009–37.

Tzeng, Jessie M., and Robert D. Mare. 1995. "Labor Market and Socioeconomic Effects on Marital Stability." *Social Science Research* 24: 329–51.

Tzeng, Meei-Sheen. 1992. "The Effects of Socioeconomic Heterogamy and Changes on Marital Dissolution for First Marriages." *Journal of Marriage and the Family* 54(August): 609–19.

Upchurch, Dawn M., Lee A. Lillard, and Constantijn W. A. Panis. 2001. "The Impact of Nonmarital Childbearing on Subsequent Marital Formation and Dissolution." In *Out of Wedlock: Causes and Consequences of Nonmarital Fertility,* edited by Lawrence L. Wu and Barbara Wolfe. New York: Russell Sage Foundation.

U.S. Department of Commerce, Bureau of the Census. 2000a. "Fertility of American Women: Current Population Survey: Detailed Tables" (June). Available at: www.census.gov/population/www/socdemo/fertility/p20-543.html.

———. 2000b. "Poverty in the United States, 1999." *Current Population Reports.* P-60-210. Washington: U.S. Government Printing Office

U.S. Department of Health and Human Services, National Center for Health Statistics. 1998. Table 4. In *Health, United States, 1998.* Available at: ftp://ftp.cdc.gov/pub/Health_Statistics/NCHS/Publications/Health_US/hus98/table004/wk1.

———. 2002. *National Vital Statistics Report* 50(6, March 21).

Veroff, Joseph, Elizabeth Douvan, and Richard A. Kulka. 1981. *The Inner American.* New York: Basic Books.

Walker, James R. 1995. "The Effect of Public Policies on Recent Swedish Fertility Behavior." *Journal of Population Economics* 8(3): 223–51.

Weiss, Yoram. 1997. "The Formation and Dissolution of Families: Why Marry? Who Marries Whom? and What Happens Upon Divorce?" In *Handbook of Population and Family Economics,* edited by Mark R. Rosenzweig and Oded Stark. Amsterdam: Elsevier Science.

White, Lynn. 1981. "A Note on Racial Difference in the Effect of Female Economic Opportunity on Marriage Rates." *Demography* 18(3, August): 349–54.

Willis, Robert J. 1999. "A Theory of Out-of-Wedlock Childbearing." *Journal of Political Economy* 107(6, pt. 2): S33–64.

Wilson, William Julius. 1987. *The Truly Disadvantaged: The Inner City, the Underclass, and Public Policy.* Chicago: University of Chicago Press.

Wilson, William Julius, and Kathryn M. Neckerman. 1986. "Poverty and Family Structure: The Widening Gap between Evidence and Public Policy Issues." In *Fighting Poverty: What Works and What Doesn't,* edited by Sheldon H. Danziger and Daniel H. Weinberg. Cambridge, Mass.: Harvard University Press.

Wood, Robert G. 1995. "Marriage Rates and Marriageable Men: A Test of the Wilson Hypothesis." *Journal of Human Resources* 30(1): 163–93.

Zelnik, Melvin, John F. Kantner, and Kathleen Ford. 1981. *Sex and Pregnancy in Adolescence.* Beverly Hills, Calif.: Sage Publications.

Chapter 2

Women's Education and Family Timing: Outcomes and Trends Associated with Age at Marriage and First Birth

Steven P. Martin

In the United States the decades from the 1970s to the 1990s were a time of increasing social and economic inequality, as well as a time when family patterns diverged across social and economic strata. A well-known changing family pattern was a shift in family *structure*—the dramatic increase in single-parent families that David Ellwood and Christopher Jencks discuss in chapter 1 of this volume; this particular shift in family structure has been identified as a factor that exacerbates income inequality (Karoly and Burtless 1995). The other dramatic divergence in family patterns, and the focus of this chapter, is a shift in family *timing*—an increase in the proportion of men and women who postpone marriage and childbearing.

In simplistic terms, the case for a link between single-parent families and social inequality rests on two observations: single-parenthood is most common among socially disadvantaged groups, and single-parenthood appears to compound social disadvantage in numerous ways. This chapter examines the case for a comparable but opposite link between delayed family formation and social inequality: delayed family formation may be most common among socially *advantaged* groups, and it may confer compounded *advantage* in numerous ways. In a review across several disciplines, I find growing evidence for such a link, although neither the distributional patterns nor the consequences of delayed family formation are as clearly aligned with social inequality as is the case for nonmarital family formation.

In the first part of this chapter, I review the implications of marriage and birth timing for women, couples, and children, based on published findings in the sociological, psychological, economic, and medical literatures. In the second part, I review descriptive studies on the recent divergence in marriage and first-birth timing and supplement them with my own descriptive analyses.

ADVANTAGES AND DISADVANTAGES OF DELAYED MARRIAGE AND CHILDBEARING

Is marrying and having children at a later age a "good" thing for the families who do it, or is it a potentially harmful side effect of other sweeping changes in the life course, such as young women's increasing career orientation and young men's declining earning power? This is a difficult question to answer because delayed marriage and childbearing tend to occur in families with high educational attainment and other clear social advantages. Thus, it is often not sufficient to identify the family advantages associated with delayed marriage and child-bearing; we must also make a plausible case that such family advantages exist or are larger *because* of marriage and birth timing. Furthermore, delayed family formation has economic, social, psychological, and biological effects that are fundamentally incommensurate, so it is difficult to make a summary assessment of delayed family formation on which all interested readers would agree. However, as I shall argue, the balance of research across several fields shows that the advantages of later family formation are increasing relative to the disadvantages, for both parents and children.

I begin this portion of the chapter with a review of research on marriage timing, with an emphasis on the association between marriage timing and divorce, and of research on the processes that might mediate such an association. Next, I review the broad literature on birth timing, which includes research on the economic, social, psychological, and biological outcomes associated with delayed childbearing. After that, I review research on the relationship between delayed childbearing and childlessness.

Delayed Marriage

Delayed marriage is an unmistakable trend in the United States. By the early 1990s, the median marriage age had risen to its highest level in the twentieth century, for both women and men (U.S. Department of Commerce 1992). Hence, whatever consequences follow from delayed marriage are affecting increasing numbers of American couples.

Before I undertake a discussion of delayed marriage, I must acknowledge the potential importance and confounding effects of *cohabitation*. Part of the recent delay in marriage reflects not a delay in union formation but an increase in the proportion of unions that do not begin with a marriage ceremony (Bumpass, Sweet, and Cherlin 1991; Wu 1999). In many respects, cohabitation is more like being single than being married (Rindfuss and VandenHeuvel 1990), but sharing a household and a life with one partner is an important respect in which marriage and cohabitation are quite similar. Furthermore, several proposed mechanisms by which delayed marriage supposedly affects life outcomes (such as maturity and length of partner search) may make more sense in relation to *union* timing than in relation to *marriage* timing. Nevertheless, I proceed here with some confidence that the literature on marriage timing and marriage outcomes is providing useful information on unions in general, for two reasons. First, cohabitation is not concentrated in any racial or educational group but is increasing among couples of all classes in the United States (Bumpass and Lu 2000; see also Gaughan 2002). Second, the small amount of research on trends in the timing of *union* formation has produced results comparable to those of other studies on the timing of *marriage* formation (for example, Raley and Bumpass 2002 and Castro Martin and Bumpass 1989).

Of the various dimensions and outcomes of marriage associated with delayed marriage, the most widely studied is the rate of marital dissolution. Age at marriage is generally the strongest social predictor of marital stability in a half-century of research on the subject (Monahan 1953; Moore and Waite 1981; Teachman 1983; Larson and Holman 1994). However, this relationship is not linear; in the United States most of the age differences in marital stability reflect differences between teen marriage and marriage up to the midtwenties; delaying marriage past age twenty-four appears to have little relationship to the probability of a marital dissolution (Heaton 2002). In fact, some authors have found that people who marry well past the normative age for their cohort have relatively *higher* rates of marital dissolution (Bitter 1986; Booth and Edwards 1985). Thus, from descriptive statistics alone, one might conclude that recent trends in delayed marriage (which increasingly are pushing marriages into the late twenties and later) might not be associated with any additional advantages in marital stability.

There are at least three mechanisms that can help explain the empirical relationship between marriage timing and marital stability. One is an increase in "maturity" (including qualities of patience, experience, calmness under stress, and willingness to cooperate) that couples may experience when they live more years of their adult lives before marrying (see Booth and Edwards 1985). In support of this perspective, Gary Lee (1977) found a positive relation between age at marriage, spouse's marital role performance, and marital satisfaction. Stephen Bahr, Bradford Chappell, and Geoffrey Leigh (1983) were not able to replicate this result, but their study had a fairly low response rate (approximately 59 percent) and further excluded a large number of couples (about 27 percent) with a previously married spouse, as well as an unknown number of divorced or separated couples.

More recent research indicates that men who marry later tend to do a more significant share of housework (Pittman and Blanchard 1996). However, the notion of increasing maturity at marriage does not explain the observed pattern of no gains in marital stability after age twenty-four or so.

A second possible explanation for links between delayed marriage and marital stability is that they are simply correlated with the same social variables. The most obvious of these is education; highly educated individuals marry late and tend to have low rates of marital dissolution (Castro Martin and Bumpass 1989). However, empirical patterns suggest that education *does not* explain the effect of age at marriage on marital dissolution rates (Bumpass and Sweet 1972; Martin 2002a).

A third possible explanation is that couples who delay marriage have more time to locate a highly compatible marriage partner. The notion of extended search time for a marriage partner has commonsense appeal, and it has been theorized in various ways (Becker 1974; Becker, Landes, and Michael 1977; Oppenheimer 1988). In general, extended search time can be seen as reducing uncertainty about a partner, especially in a time when men's and women's earning potential does not become evident until they have established their career trajectories. Valerie Oppenheimer (1988) also suggests that as women's earnings increase, their desirability as marriage partners may extend across more years of their lives. This extended search time may allow women to be more selective of their marriage partners, resulting in increasingly compatible and stable marriages. Furthermore, women with extended time available for searching could afford to be most selective early in adulthood, when they can anticipate a large number of potential future partners.

Selectivity due to different search times would suggest that *within* a group of women with a given available search time, those marrying late may be at less leisure to hold out for an optimally compatible partner, while *between* groups of women with different available search times, the groups with the longer search times should have both later and more stable marriages, on average. These counterbalancing influences on marital stability could explain the apparent flattening of the relationship between marital stability and marriage timing after age twenty-four. Such patterns could also explain recent findings that suggest that as *educational groupings* of women have increasingly disparate ages at marriage, there have been strongly diverging patterns of marital stability *between these groups* regardless of relative age at marriage within the group (Martin 2002a).

Here is a final comment on the potential benefits of delayed marriage. Timothy Chandler, Yoshimori Kamo, and James Werbel (1994) have reported that delaying marriage significantly increases married women's wages. However, as in most research on income and family formation, it is very difficult to identify the direction of the causal links, and it is very likely that favorable wage trajectories for women lead to lower marriage rates and later marriage (Teachman and Schollaert 1989).

Up to now I have discussed only the potential *advantages* associated with delayed marriage. The literature on the *disadvantages* associated with delayed marriage has also identified several important patterns. First of all, physical appearance and other factors related directly to age might reduce a woman's ability to enter a marriage if she has postponed marriage past young adulthood. Oppenheimer (1988) has argued, however, that as women increase their labor force involvement, income and other characteristics that increase with age are increasingly important for their marriage market status. Megan Sweeney (2002) has found evidence supporting this argument.

Other negative consequences of delayed marriage arise when a person postpones marriage later than most of the rest of his or her cohort and encounters a severely depleted marriage market. Individuals who delay marriage in this way might face a choice between remaining unmarried or marrying a relatively poor-quality partner (see Schoen 1983).

However, this negative consequence of delayed marriage also appears to be diminishing in importance. One reason for this trend is that the shift toward increasing age at marriage has moved the depletion of the marriage market to a much later point in women's life courses. Another reason is an increasing adaptation to the age distribution of partners—in effect, more people are ignoring traditional standards for men's and women's appropriate relative marriage ages (NiBhrolchain 2000).

We can compare the current environment of delayed marriage to the postwar baby boom, when universal early marriage arguably created a marriage "trap" that left women with severely depleted marriage opportunities if they postponed marriage past their very early twenties (Goldman, Westoff, and Hammerslough 1984). The option of marrying young or not at all arguably diminished both the quality of marriages and women's opportunities for personal development outside of marriage.[1]

Delayed marriage is also linked to at least one negative social outcome that is *increasing* in importance; all else being equal, delayed marriage increases nonmarital childbearing by increasing exposure to the possibility of a nonmarital birth. The proportion of U.S. births occurring out of wedlock has increased to about one in three (Ventura and Bachrach 2000), and much of this increase has been due to the declining proportion of women married at a given age, especially among black women, but also increasingly among white women (Smith, Morgan, and Koropeckyj-Cox 1996).

Of course, nonmarital childbearing is not a necessary consequence of delayed marriage. White college graduate women have very low rates of nonmarital childbearing despite marrying at relatively old ages. Clearly, women who have access to highly effective hormonal contraceptives (and who wish to avoid nonmarital births) can delay marriage without having nonmarital births. By comparison, cheaper and widely available barrier contraceptives (such as condoms) are not ideal for preventing pregnancies across sexually active spans of five to ten years or more.

In summary, delayed marriage appears to be associated with marital stability and better marital quality. It is not clear how strongly any advantages of delay continue to accrue to women who marry at ages well beyond their midtwenties, but there are clear advantages to having the *flexibility* to marry at a later age, even if a marital search happens to produce a compatible match at an earlier age. Of the potential disadvantages of delayed marriage, the relative depletion of the marriage market has turned out to be only a minor problem for recent cohorts of women. However, for women who may not have the means to reliably control their fertility for an extended period of unmarried adulthood, the risk of a nonmarital birth is a growing problem.

Delayed Childbearing

In comparison with postponing a marriage, postponing a first birth is more clearly associated with negative outcomes, including not being able to have a child at all. However, these negative outcomes are becoming less common and less important over time, and delayed childbearing is also associated with positive economic and psychological outcomes. In this section, I review the economic, social and psychological, and biomedical effects associated with childbearing.

Birth Timing and Income

When women take time from their careers to have children, they clearly suffer deficits in income relative to what they would have earned had they not had children. Part of the literature on this "wage gap" for mothers examines whether the deficits in income vary by the age at which women have children, and the limited evidence available suggests that early childbearing is worse for women's careers than later childbearing. Hiromi Taniguchi (1999) reports that early child-bearers are likely to experience a higher wage penalty, possibly because their careers are interrupted during a critical period of career-building, while Ellen Van Velsor and Angela O'Rand (1984) report that interrupting a career for childbearing brings a smaller wage penalty than starting a career after childbearing, and that the wage penalty for a woman's career interruption has declined over time. In addition, women who delay childbearing have been more likely to remain in the labor force throughout their working lives (Pienta 1999).

While studies of the wage penalty for motherhood compare the wages of mothers with the wages of comparable nonmothers, another line of research compares wage trajectories of women who have children at different ages. Late childbearers clearly have higher and steeper income trajectories than early childbearers (Hofferth 1984), but they also have other demographic characteristics that would predict steep income growth across ages. Attempts to disentangle childbearing age from women's other, unmeasured characteristics have produced ambiguous results (Blackburn, Bloom, and Neumark 1993; Meyer 1999).

One likely explanation for the association between a woman's income and age at first birth is that birth timing and income are mutually reinforcing—delaying a first birth increases women's wage rates, and higher wage rates increase age at first birth (Mertens et al. 1998). The availability of quality child care could be a crucial element of this reinforcing pattern. Births bring breaks in employment that lead to lost work time, both full- and part-time, and lost human capital (along with many other factors), and this lost time explains much of the wage penalty of motherhood (Joshi, Paci, and Waldfogel 1999; Phipps, Burton, and Lethbridge 2001). Women who make enough money to pay for high-quality organized child care out of their wages can greatly reduce their lost career time; thus, economically successful women can have smaller wage penalties even though they have much higher wages at risk of a wage penalty. Deborah J. Anderson, Melissa Binder, and Kate Krause (2002) report findings from fixed-effects models that support this interpretation: among four-year college graduate women (who earn more and have children later in life than other women), most or all of the wage difference between mothers and nonmothers appears to be explained by heterogeneous selection into motherhood. For women with less educational attainment, comparable wage differences between mothers and nonmothers are explained instead by variables consistent with a wage "penalty": length of job disruption and part-time employment.

The research I have cited so far suggests that working women may benefit economically from delayed childbearing, but other studies indicate a more complex and uncertain story. The wage penalty is substantial even for women who delay childbearing (Grindstaff 1996). In addition, the relationship between birth timing and income appears to vary with women's other demographic characteristics. For example, high school dropouts and other women with poor employment prospects (who often have children quite young) experience little or no wage penalty (Anderson, Binder, and Krause 2002; Dex et al. 1996); their incomes would probably be depressed even if they had not had children early.

The studies cited here add up to an interesting and important discussion about whether delayed childbearing *causes* women to have more favorable income trajectories; this discussion could help to explain some women's motivation to postpone childbearing. However, when we look at how family resources affect children's outcomes, it is more important to simply note that increasing age is *correlated* with higher income. Hence, parents with young children generally have more resources available for their children if they delayed childbearing than if they had their children early in their careers.

The general relationship of higher earnings and income with age has two noteworthy patterns with implications for birth timing. First, workers of all education levels have earnings that increase with age from the midtwenties past the midthirties, but the increase with age is much more pronounced for college graduates than for high school graduates (Spain and Bianchi 1996). Second, there is growing evidence of "stickiness" in the low-wage sectors: compared with previous cohorts, recent cohorts of persons with low education and/or low-wage jobs are more likely to stay at low hourly wages through their midthirties (Bernhardt et al. 2001). These patterns imply that the resource advantages of delaying childbearing are most pronounced among the educational groups that are most likely to delay childbearing.

As a final note, the standard use of constant-dollar accounting based on the consumer price index may not properly capture trends in the relationship between a worker's age and his or her ability to support children, because the economic costs of raising children have been rising (Casper 1995; England and Folbre 1999). Thus, delaying a family may be less of a way for parents to gain additional *advantages* for their children than a strategy for providing resources comparable to those they had themselves as children of younger parents.

In addition to earnings, various other indicators of economic resources show strong age patterns. Median net worth increases between age twenty-five to thirty-four and thirty-five to forty-four for household heads of all education levels (Keister 2000). More specifically, Robert Mare and Meei-Shenn Tzeng (1989) report that when other aspects of sons' socioeconomic background are controlled, sons born to older fathers enjoy significantly higher levels of educational and occupational achievement than do sons born to younger fathers. The authors attribute this pattern to the fact that parents' education, employment, and economic wealth improve with age. In the context of families experiencing divorce, Ann Nichols-Casebolt and Sandra Danziger (1989) find that children born to older parents suffer fewer economic consequences of divorce, because both fathers and mothers have higher income and employment rates.

In summary, parents who delay childbearing may be starting families at an age when they have more resources to pass on to their children. The relationship between age and economic resources is most pronounced (and increasingly so) among highly educated adults, who are the most likely to postpone childbearing. However, much of the evidence for these assertions is indirect, and the causal relationships between age, income, and childbearing are complicated.

Birth Timing and Social and Psychological Effects of Age   Outside of income effects, there are other direct effects of delayed childbearing on the well-being of parents and children. Older parents may be more emotionally prepared for the particular stresses of parenthood, have stronger social support networks (Reece 1993), and have educational and other characteristics that put them at an advantage relative to other parents. On the other hand, older parents may experience disadvantages such as less energy and greater psychological distance from their children (Morris 1988). In addition, much of the research on this topic uses in-depth ethnographic analysis that captures the richness of the concept of "well-being" but also uses small nonrandom samples that sacrifice generalizability. As a result, different studies of the social and psychological effects of delayed childbearing have often produced conflicting results.

Studies of the social and psychological effects of delayed childbearing tend to focus on specific dyads, such as mother-child, father-child, and husband-wife (Parke 1988). The quality of mother-child interactions generally increases with maternal age, with different studies showing correlations between delayed parenthood and positive maternal affect (Ragozin et al. 1982), more positive maternal behavior (and less negative maternal behavior) (Conger et al. 1984), and less anger and frustration during the transition to parenthood (Walter 1986). Most of these studies do not measure nonlinear effects of delayed childbearing because they compare only two or three age categories, but John Mirowsky and Catherine Ross (2002) have found that the relation between maternal depression and age is curvilinear, with the lowest predicted depression for women with a first birth around age thirty. These studies tend to focus on the critical time just after a child is born, when the emotionally stabilizing effects of age presumably are most important (see Wilkie 1981).

The father-child dyad also appears to benefit from delayed parenthood. Teresa Cooney and her colleagues (1993) find that late fathers are more likely to be highly involved with their children, with positive paternal affect and low depression. Late fathers spend more time in leisure activities with their children, have higher expectations of their children's behavior, and are more nurturant toward their children (Heath 1994). Also, while older fathers may engage in less physical play with their children in comparison with younger fathers, older fathers establish stronger connections to extrafamilial contexts and rely more on verbal mechanisms to engage children during play (Neville and Parke 1997).

Research on delayed childbearing and the husband-wife dyad shows more mixed outcomes. Jeffrey Wright, Scott Henggeler, and Lisa Craig (1986) report that the wife's age is a strong predictor of the husband's marital adjustment following a first birth. Heather Helms-Erikson (2001) reports that overall, having a first birth later in a marriage leads to a better evaluation of the marriage ten years after the transition to parenthood, especially if the couple has a nontraditional division of labor. This pattern of marital adjustment may be mediated by housework; late birth timing strongly predicts the father's contribution to household labor (Coltrane and Ishii-Kuntz 1992; Coltrane 1990). However, other studies have found no consistent relation between marital adjustment and childbearing age (Roosa 1988; Garrison et al. 1997), and some have found a *decline* in marital satisfaction for older parents (Cowan and Cowan 1992).[2]

The increased maturity associated with delayed childbearing may be offset by several age-related factors, including: emotional distance from children, lack of energy, and the non-normative age at which the transition to parenthood occurred. Both Monica Morris (1988) and Alice Rossi (1980) report that older mothers describe feelings of distance from their much younger children, and that children also report a sense of separation from and lack of intimacy with their mothers when they reach adulthood (see also Daniels and Weingarten 1982; Yarrow 1991; Frankel and Wise 1982). However, this pattern of emotional distance from children may be an artifact of nonrandom samples; other studies have found opposite effects of delayed childbearing on emotional distance. For example, Audrey VandenHeuvel (1988) reports a *positive* effect of delayed childbearing on the closeness of adult children with their same-sex parent, operating through the parents' marital happiness. More convincingly, Gordon Finley (1998) uses a relatively unbiased sample to test the hypothesis that children born to older parents see greater disadvantages to late childbearing; he finds that, in contrast to Morris's (1988) study of twenty-two nonrandom children of older parents, adolescent children perceive older fathers *more favorably* in the parenting role than younger fathers, and older mothers about the same as younger mothers.

As adults age, their energy level drops. Benjamin and Rachel Schlesinger (1989) found that parents who delay childbearing encounter an unexpected energy cost, accompanied by role conflicts and other problems. However, this study did not involve a comparison group, so it is not clear how delayed parents differ from other parents in the stressful transition to parenthood.

A final potentially negative effect of delayed childbearing is its "non-normativeness," both with respect to other parents' birth timing and the usual ordering of life-course events. Children of delayed parents often report childhood embarrassment about their parents' non-normative ages and declining health and physical appearance (Yarrow 1991). However, these responses seem to be diminishing across cohorts as delayed parenthood becomes less unusual (Daniels and Weingarten 1982). For the parents, the problems of being "off-schedule" do not appear to be serious. For example, N. Maxine Soloway and Rebecca M. Smith (1987) do *not* find evidence of transitional crises when older, career-oriented parents shift to a family orientation.

In conclusion, the literature on well-being and birth timing indicates mostly positive effects of delayed childbearing on parent-child relationships, particularly in early childhood, when parents need the maturity to cope with new stresses. Potentially negative effects of delayed childbearing, such as emotional distance and non-normativeness, are not consistently evident across studies and are probably decreasing over time.

Birth Timing and Biomedical Outcomes: The "Less Favored Years for Human Procreation"

Although the economic and psychological correlates of delayed childbearing are generally positive, the biological effects are clearly not. In fact, medical care providers have historically recognized delayed childbearing as an important risk factor in maternal and infant health outcomes (Feldman 1927; Bleyer 1958). This part of the literature review surveys the types of poor health outcomes associated with delayed childbearing, along with important trends in those outcomes.

In contrast to studies of psychological well-being, studies of birth timing and biomedical outcomes involve very large numbers of cases, often from vital statistics registries for entire states or nations. These research methods make it much easier to detect statistically significant differences between groups, but statistical significance may belie the relative importance of group differences in a potential outcome that is extremely unlikely for all parents, such as maternal mortality.

Another difference between the biomedical and social research on delayed parenthood is the definition of "delay." In the social scientific literature, a "delayed" first birth generally means about age thirty or later, but it could mean the midtwenties or later. In biomedical research, the commonest standard for "delay" is age thirty-five or older, because women who have first births between the ages of thirty and thirty-four generally have medical outcomes indistinguishable from those of most younger mothers. Hence, the negative biomedical consequences of delayed childbearing apply to a relatively small proportion of the childbearing population.

The medical outcomes of a delayed first birth can be divided into two broad classes. One class includes dangerous but potentially remediable circumstances defined broadly as maternal and fetal/infant morbidity, as well as medical complications arising during pregnancy and delivery. Such outcomes occur fairly often, particularly for older mothers. The other class of outcomes includes permanent or long-term deficits in maternal or child outcomes, with the most extreme being maternal mortality and fetal and neonatal mortality. These outcomes occur very infrequently but are more likely to occur with older mothers than with younger mothers.

I discuss the first class of outcomes at some length. Medical research has linked delayed childbearing to the following dangerous but usually temporary outcomes:

1. Problems during pregnancy, such as hypertension, hyperthyroidism, gestational diabetes, macrosomia, premature contractions, and uteroplacental bleeding, all of which may lead to a preterm delivery (van Katwijk and Peeters 1998; Ananth et al. 1996; Astolfi and Zonta 1999; Jolly et al. 2000; Dildy et al. 1996).

2. Problems during delivery, such as postpartum hemorrhage, multiple births, and fetal and maternal distress, reflected in rates of operative deliveries such as cesarean sections (Peipert and Bracken 1993; Kullmer et al. 2000; Jolly et al. 2000; Gilbert, Nesbitt, and Danielsen 1999).

3. Low birthweight (Berkowitz et al. 1990; Aldous and Edmondson 1993; Reichman and Pagnini 1997; Ananth et al. 2001; Tough et al. 2002).

This list of negative outcomes, while imposing, does not necessarily make a compelling case against delayed childbearing, because most of the outcomes are not directly caused by delayed pregnancy. Instead, the problems are generally due to preexisting conditions such as hypertension and adult diabetes that are more common in mid-adults than in young adults (Newcomb, Rodriguez, and Johnson 1991; Yuan et al. 2000). Healthy mid-adult women have healthy deliveries, as do healthy young adult women.

Medical researchers differ in their assessments of the individual costs of delayed childbearing and their suggested advice to potential older parents. In the 1970s and earlier, medical care providers tended to be greatly concerned about the health consequences of delayed childbearing, and they readily volunteered that information to their childless patients. In the more recent papers mentioned in this section, some authors, in recognition of the persistent risks, recommend that medical care providers advise women about the potential hazards of postponing childbearing (Gilbert, Nesbitt, and Danielsen 1999) or at least that they note maternal age as a potentially complicating factor (Yuan et al. 2000). Other authors emphasize that delayed childbirth has few if any long-term consequences for women who receive proper health care and is probably *less* dangerous than most women believe (Windridge and Berryman 1999). However, some researchers have noted that even though these complicated pregnancies almost always have positive outcomes, they are considerably more expensive than routine pregnancies and deliveries. Because most women who have children at older ages are covered by medical insurance, this added expense of late child-bearing becomes an overall social burden (see Tough et al. 2002).

Given that most women who postpone childbearing come from higher educational and social strata, it is important to note that the medical studies cited so far do not consider whether social variables might influence the relationship between delayed childbearing and birth outcomes. The few studies on this topic have reached mixed conclusions. Research by Arline Geronimus and her colleagues (Geronimus 1996; Geronimus, Bound, and Waidman 1999) has indicated that low-income black women in Michigan suffer an increasing incidence of low-birthweight first births if they postpone childbearing past their teen years. This finding supports the "weathering hypothesis" that the stressful lives of poor women lead to deteriorating health starting in early adulthood, thus making teen childbearing a rational response to social hardship (Geronimus 1994; Chisholm 1993). However, Cande Ananth and her colleagues (2001) are not able to replicate this finding in a study using nationwide vital registration data for black women. These researchers do not select on poor women (which may weaken their findings) or on first births (which should have no effect on their findings).

The medical outcomes discussed so far are dangerous but generally remediable. Of greater concern are the long-term (or permanent) negative birth outcomes associated with delayed fertility. These outcomes include maternal mortality, fetal mortality, neonatal mortality, long-term negative health consequences for mothers, and long-term negative health consequences for children.

Studies of delayed childbearing and maternal, fetal, and neonatal mortality generally use sample sizes in the hundreds of thousands. Most of these studies find the odds of fetal or neonatal mortality for first-time mothers who are age thirty-five or older to be about twice the odds for other first-time mothers (Cnattingius et al. 1992; Fretts et al. 1995), but some find smaller or unclear effects (Bianco et al. 1996; Prysak, Lorenz, and Kisly 1995). Rates of adverse outcomes for women giving birth for the first time between the ages of thirty and thirty-four may be slightly higher than for younger mothers but are clearly lower than the rates for first-time mothers at age thirty-five or older.

Event if overall rates of fetal and infant deaths are quite low, a doubling in the odds of such deaths may seem to be a serious cost of delayed childbearing. However, this difference in odds in cross-section does not necessarily mean that a woman is increasing her own odds of an infant death by postponing childbearing. A study by Ruth C. Fretts and colleagues (1995), which encompasses all births at a major Montreal hospital across thirty-three years, shows that fetal and neonatal death rates have been plummeting over time (more than death rates at any other age) and have indeed fallen more quickly than the increases a woman might experience with advancing age. Thus, in retrospect, it was *less* safe for a woman born in the mid-1950s to have a birth in young adulthood in the 1970s than to have a birth in mid-adulthood in the early 1990s.[3] Of course, medical improvements may or may not continue to reduce fetal mortality in the future.

Aside from the relatively remote possibility of maternal mortality, there are some persistent negative effects of delayed childbearing for mothers. These include hormonally mediated effects, such as an increase in breast cancer rates for women who have later or fewer children, compared with women who have more children early in adulthood (White 1987). In examining a range of possible long-term health outcomes, Adrian Alonzo (2002) does indeed find several outcomes at age fifty associated with having children at age thirty-five or older. These include systolic blood pressure, blood glucose, physician assessment of patient health, and limited mobility. However, of the women in the sample with a birth at age thirty-five or older, fewer than 10 percent had a *first* birth at age thirty-five or older; thus, this is essentially a study of health problems associated with late age at *last* birth, a variable strongly correlated with large family size for the 1938 to 1940 birth cohort of mothers in the study. Furthermore, this bivariate analysis does not attempt to control for any social variables that might be associated with having a last birth at age thirty-five or older. Thus, the most comprehensive study available provides no compelling evidence of overall long-term maternal health consequences of delayed childbearing.

Delayed first birth could have long-term negative effects on *children's* health by several mechanisms, including obstetric complications, fetal and perinatal problems, and a higher likelihood of genetic problems like trisomy, mitochondrial DNA disorders, or inheritable mutation disorders (Tarin, Brines, and Cano 1998). Mutation disorders are perhaps the most widely recognized outcome associated with delayed childbearing, but such disorders are now routinely detected during pregnancy screening. Women generally have the option to terminate these pregnancies, but an abortion is not an acceptable or available choice for some women, so the association between age at childbearing and mutation disorders should not be discounted completely.

Other long-term health effects are more difficult to measure. One study that attempts to identify possible long-term effects of delayed childbearing on children uses data from a large sample of ten-year-olds in Great Britain (Pollock 1996). As in similar studies, a lack of statistical controls limits the strength of the conclusions, but there were no clear adverse outcomes and modest educational and behavioral advantages among ten-year-olds with older (age thirty or older) first-time mothers. The educational and behavioral advantages were probably due to the association of delayed childbearing with relative social advantage.

In summary, delayed childbearing has clearly negative biomedical consequences. However, these consequences have become much *less* negative over time, particularly for women with full access to the best and most modern health care.

Delayed Childbearing and Childlessness   A final concern about delayed childbearing is that many women or couples who postpone a birth might remain involuntarily childless or with fewer children than desired. Coital inability, conceptive inability, and pregnancy loss all increase with age, along with some social barriers to childbearing (McFalls 1990), so there is clearly some relationship between fertility delay and unintended childlessness. However, the extent of this effect is less clearly established, and men and women who remain involuntarily childless often do not suffer as devastating an impact as we might suppose.

Jane Menken and Ulla Larsen (1986) provide a useful estimate of the proportion of women who postpone a birth who will remain involuntarily childless due to biological subfecundity. In an analysis of seven historical populations with late marriage ages and little or no deliberate fertility control, the authors counted the proportion of women at each marriage age who either remained childless or had only one child by age fifty; they attribute the patterns in childlessness to the decline of fecundity due to age. The authors report that childlessness increases monotonically with age at marriage and is increasingly pronounced for women marrying in their early thirties (15 percent childless), late thirties (30 percent), and early forties (64 percent). Women who wait until they are in their thirties to try to have a child clearly experience an increased probability of remaining childless, but they still have a high probability of having at least one child.

The social effects of delayed fertility on childlessness are much stronger than the biological effects. In the United States many women who delay childbearing remain childless because of social constraints such as age-specific fertility and marriage norms, lack of either a suitable marriage partner or the economic resources for childbearing, and a gradual shift in life goals (Rindfuss and Bumpass 1978). Across most of the twentieth century, only 35 to 40 percent of women who remained childless to age thirty had a first birth after age thirty (Rindfuss, Morgan, and Swicegood 1988).

In recent decades the difference between delayed and forgone childbearing has increasingly depended on a woman's educational attainment. The proportion of women who are childless at age thirty who have births after that age has increased to about 50 percent, but only among women with a four-year college degree (Martin 2000). The proportion of delayed child-bearers having *two or more* children has also increased—again, only among women with a four-year college degree. Thus, it appears that diverging patterns in delayed childbearing are in part explained by diverging fertility outcomes among women who delay childbearing. I discuss age-specific first birth and marriage rates in detail in the second half of this chapter.

A new factor in the association between postponed childbearing and childlessness is the recent increase in the availability and effectiveness of medical reproductive technology. In 1995, 10 percent of U.S. women age fifteen to forty-four reported some form of reproductive impairment, and 44 percent of these had sought medical help or advice (Chandra and Stephen 1998). However, most of the medical help or advice offered to women with such impairments is fairly basic. Only a small fraction of U.S. women opt for involved procedures such as oocyte donation or in vitro fertilization, and fewer than 1 percent of all U.S. births result from such procedures, though this proportion is increasing rapidly (Stephen 2000). It should be noted that because these procedures are very expensive (about $10,000 per cycle), are generally not covered by health insurance, and have low success rates per cycle (Szamatowics and Grochowski 1998), only women and couples with substantial resources can afford them. To a small but growing extent, then, the likelihood of involuntary childlessness as a negative outcome of delayed childbearing depends on a couple's ability to afford medical reproductive assistance.

Various social and medical researchers disagree, often vehemently, about how concerned women should be about the link between delayed childbearing and childlessness. Many authors emphasize the risks of remaining childless (with vivid references to "gambling" and "reproductive roulette") and argue that women are not sufficiently aware of these risks (Toulemon 1996; Gosden and Rutherford 1996; McFalls 1992; Hewlett 2001). Others argue that these risks are generally overstated and that women might become more willing to postpone childbearing if they had a realistic estimate of those risks (Menken 1985).

To estimate the probabilistic cost of childlessness associated with delayed childbearing, we need to know not only the likelihood that delay will lead to childlessness but also the relative cost for women who become involuntarily childless. The costs of childlessness can include the stress of failed attempts to have a child, the loss of life experiences for which there is no substitute, smaller or weaker social support networks, and the considerable social stigma attached to childlessness by the often strongly pronatalist American culture (May 1995). On the other hand, childless persons avoid the substantial economic and career costs of raising children, can direct their social energies to building support networks not based on lineal descent, and often establish relationships with children through extended family ties, adoption, or other means.

The numerous studies that have attempted to measure the net costs of childlessness directly have produced mixed findings of very mixed quality. The "psychological distress" literature on the consequences of childlessness (often based on samples of infertile persons undergoing medical treatment for infertility) shows consistent negative associations between childlessness and health, life satisfaction, and marital satisfaction. These studies have been criticized, however, for nonrandom sampling, inappropriate statistical procedures, over-reliance on self-reports, and failure to account for the processual and socially conditioned nature of the infertility experience (Greil 1997). The few studies of the long-term conse-quences of childlessness indicate that the health and emotional well-being (including loneli-ness and depression) of older persons is generally not related to childlessness per se, but that gender and marriage play important roles. Childless older women tend to have a comparable quality of life to older women who are mothers, while childless, unmarried older men tend to have a diminished quality of life relative to other men (see Bengel et al. 2000).

To summarize the literature on delayed childbearing and childlessness, the conse-quences of delayed childbearing related to involuntary childlessness are certainly negative because delaying a birth necessarily increases the possibility of remaining involuntarily child-less, and because involuntary childlessness is by definition not a preferred outcome for those who experience it. However, it appears that increasing proportions of college graduate women are postponing births without remaining childless. Also, advances in medical repro-ductive technology have reduced involuntary childlessness somewhat, although this effect is not yet demographically significant. Lastly, childlessness may have few long-term negative consequences for many individuals, particularly for women, but more research on the life-course effects of involuntary childlessness is clearly needed.

The Cumulative Advantages or Disadvantages of Delayed Marriage and Child-bearing

So far, this chapter has compared delayed family formation with "on-time" family formation and discussed how delayed marriage and childbearing have advantages and disad-vantages across economic, social, psychological, and biological dimensions. Although these dimensions are to some extent incommensurable, a review of the literature suggests two patterns in delayed family formation that have implications for social inequality. First, over time the relative advantages of delayed family formation have increased while the relative disadvantages have diminished. Compared with a few decades ago, women and couples who delay family formation today are more likely to avoid negative consequences of a depleted marriage market, to have medical care that mitigates any pregnancy or birth complications, and to have access to medical assistance for fertility problems.

Second, for women and couples with higher income and higher educational attainment, the advantages of delay are consistently larger, and the disadvantages consistently smaller, than for other women. College-educated men, and perhaps women as well, are more likely than the less educated to see their incomes increase substantially with age; if they delay family formation, their children benefit from higher family income, while children of less-educated parents see less economic benefit. Moreover, college-educated women may face smaller wage penalties for a birth than women with lower education. In addition, among women who delay family formation, four-year college graduates may be more likely to avoid both nonmarital births prior to delayed marriage and involuntary childlessness.

These patterns satisfy some of the conditions for a link between social inequality and marriage and fertility timing. Delaying marriage until one has matured and found a highly compatible partner and delaying childbearing until the late twenties or early thirties (but perhaps not much later) often provide net advantages for adults and their children. To the extent that families who are already well off time their marriages and childbearing later than other families, social differences in birth timing could compound the inequalities that al-ready exist in children's and parents' circumstances.

It would be premature to conclude from this review that less-educated or minority women and couples could improve their family outcomes by postponing marriage and childbearing. As I shall show in the second part of this chapter, women and couples of all groups are postponing marriage and childbearing to some extent, but the outcomes that *follow* delay are diverging across educational and racial categories. Delayed family formation leads primarily to later marriage and marital childbearing for some groups, but it may increasingly lead to nonmarriage, childlessness, and/or nonmarital childbearing for other groups.

OBSERVED TRENDS IN DELAYED MARRIAGE AND CHILDBEARING

To this point I have discussed the quality of outcomes associated with delayed marriage and childbearing. For the rest of the chapter, I discuss whether demographic trends in marriage and fertility timing in recent decades are increasingly unequal across education and racial groups. It turns out that age at marriage and age at first birth are increasing for all groups of women to some degree; in this respect, the timing of family formation has not become much more unequal in recent decades. However, the demographic implications of delay for outcomes such as nonmarriage, childlessness, and nonmarital childbearing may be quite different for women of different educational levels. To show how similar trends in delay can produce dissimilar outcomes, I present an analysis of the *age-specific rates* for the transition to marriage for never-married women, and for the transition to parenthood for childless women.

Birth and Marriage Delayed

In the United States (and most everywhere else), husbands and wives who delay family formation are better educated than other couples. This pattern persists to a lesser or greater extent across time and across racial and ethnic groups, for both differences in childbearing (Baldwin and Nord 1984; Rindfuss, Morgan, and Swicegood 1988) and differences in marriage timing (Dobson and Houseknecht 1998). This pattern has persisted for most of the twentieth century and through periods of rising and falling social inequality.

Although recent delays in marriage and childbearing are well documented (see, for example, Espenshade 1985) there is relatively little work on whether educational or racial differences in family timing have been increasing in recent decades. Ronald Rindfuss, S. Philip Morgan, and Kate Offutt (1996) report that educational differences in the timing of fertility increased from 1960 to the late 1980s. Much of this divergence occurred in the 1960s, however, and these researchers' data show increases in delayed fertility among *all* educational groups of women starting in the 1970s.

To evaluate changes in the timing of marriage and childbearing across more recent time periods, I used data from the combined June 1985, June 1990, and June 1995 Current Population Surveys (CPS), which I discuss in more detail later. Table 2.1 shows the mean age at marriage for women of different race and educational categories, for 1970 to 1974 and for 1990 to 1994. The first time period corresponds roughly to the start of the recent increase in income inequality. Across this two-decade span, mean age at marriage increased by 4.1 years. The increase was smaller for women with no four-year college degree (3.5 years) than for women with a four-year college degree (4.8 years), but it was substantial for both groups.

The increase in mean age at marriage was larger for black women than for whites;

TABLE 2.1   *Trends in the Mean Ages of First Marriages for U.S. Women, by Race and Education, for 1970 to 1974 and 1990 to 1994*

	1970 to 1974		1990 to 1994		
	Mean Age	Standard Deviation	Mean Age	Standard Deviation	Difference
All races	21.3	(4.0)	25.4	(5.9)	4.1
No four-year college degree	20.9	(4.1)	24.4	(6.0)	3.5
Four-year college degree	22.8	(3.6)	27.6	(5.3)	4.8
White non-Hispanic					
No four-year college degree	20.6	(3.8)	24.1	(5.6)	3.5
Four-year college degree	22.8	(3.6)	27.5	(5.1)	4.6
Black non-Hispanic					
No four-year college degree	22.3	(5.4)	27.1	(7.0)	4.8
Four-year college degree	22.4	(4.0)	29.7	(5.7)	6.5
All races, detail by education					
No high school diploma	20.8	(5.4)	22.2	(5.6)	1.4
High school graduate	20.7	(4.0)	24.6	(6.3)	3.8
Some college	21.2	(3.4)	24.9	(5.6)	3.8
B.A. degree only	22.6	(3.5)	27.0	(5.0)	4.5
Master's or professional degree	23.5	(3.8)	29.7	(5.8)	6.2

Source: June 1985, 1990, and 1995 CPS.
Note: Standard errors are in parentheses.

much of this increase for blacks was no doubt a consequence of declining marriage rates, as I discuss later. Detailed breakdowns by education present some concerns because of endogeneities between marriage, childbearing, and the timing of educational attainment. For women with no high school diploma *and* for women with a master's or professional degree, the difference in mean age at marriage across the two time periods is biased by numerous cases censored before they completed their education. The distinction between women with a four-year college degree and women without a four-year college degree is less subject to this sort of bias, so I restrict most of the remaining analyses to this two-category breakdown of education at interview.

The data on delayed childbearing tell much the same story as the data on delayed marriage. As shown in table 2.2, mean age at first birth is increasing for all women, but more dramatically for women with a four-year college degree than for women with no four-year college degree. A comparison of table 2.2 with table 2.1 shows that the timing of a first birth is diverging more than the timing of a first marriage. This difference between trends in birth and marriage timing is partially explained by increases in nonmarital first births.

Tables 2.1 and 2.2 do not show a complete picture of trends in marriage and fertility timing, because they contain no information about women who never marry and/or never have children. Indeed, it will be some time before researchers can observe the proportions who remain childless or never-married among women who reached their early adult years in the late 1980s and 1990s. Hence, forecasts of family formation for these cohorts must be based on partial data and some conjecture.

We might expect that as women postpone marriage and childbearing, more are forgo-

TABLE 2.2   *Trends in the Mean Ages of First Births for U.S. Women, by Race and Education, for 1970 to 1974 and 1990 to 1994*

	1970 to 1974		1990 to 1994		
	Mean Age	Standard Deviation	Mean Age	Standard Deviation	Difference
All races	22.6	(4.3)	25.1	(5.8)	2.5
No four-year college degree	22.0	(4.2)	23.5	(5.3)	1.5
Four-year college degree	24.9	(4.1)	29.7	(4.3)	4.8
White non-Hispanic					
No four-year college degree	22.2	(4.0)	24.2	(5.3)	2.0
Four-year college degree	25.2	(4.0)	29.8	(4.3)	4.6
Black non-Hispanic					
No four-year college degree	20.8	(4.7)	21.6	(5.3)	0.8
Four-year college degree	22.9	(4.0)	28.6	(5.7)	5.7
All races, detail by education					
No high school diploma	21.3	(5.1)	19.5	(4.1)	−1.8
High school graduate	22.0	(4.1)	23.7	(5.2)	1.7
Some college	22.5	(3.8)	25.1	(5.0)	2.6
B.A. degree only	24.7	(4.0)	29.0	(4.2)	4.3
Master's or professional degree	25.6	(4.3)	31.9	(4.0)	6.3

Source: June 1985, 1990, and 1995 and CPS.
Note: Standard errors are in parentheses.

ing such transitions entirely. Indeed, numerous theoretical perspectives on the family make little distinction between delayed family formation and forgone family formation, because both patterns would presumably result from the same social processes. These theoretical perspectives are based variously on the rising value of women's time (Schultz 1974); the lower utility of marriage for women who are not economically dependent on men (Becker 1981; Parsons 1949); cultural shifts toward an individualist orientation, including dilation of the early adult part of the life course as more adults and particularly women take time for themselves (Dion 1995; Presser 2001); and even a general shift away from collective values in a society (Popenoe 1993).

The common element to these perspectives is that there are no effects associated with *declining* age-specific marriage and birth rates in young adulthood that explicitly *increase* the age-specific rates in later adult years. Hence, age-specific marriage and birth rates at later ages should *not* rise across cohorts, although the average age at marriage and first birth of those who do form families increases because more women are exposed to the possibility of births and marriages at later ages. As a result, the net proportion of those who eventually marry or have children necessarily declines across cohorts.

On the other hand, there are perspectives that could be consistent with delayed family formation and *high* cumulative proportions of women who have ever formed a family. For example, women who are committed to having children but also need or want to have a career may postpone childbearing if they perceive that they can better afford child care by waiting a few years until their earning power increases (see Rindfuss, Morgan, and Offutt 1996). In this case, women would become more likely to postpone childbearing because *delayed* childbearing is becoming *more* attractive across cohorts, not because *young adult* childbearing is becoming *less* attractive across cohorts. Finally, there are perspectives somewhere in the middle that focus on the social shifts affecting young adults that may or may not have effects into middle adulthood. An example is the observation that declining incomes among young adult men decrease marriage rates for young adult women (Oppenheimer, Kalmijn, and Lim 1997).

To summarize this argument so far, if we observe only the average age at first marriage and average age at first birth, we may be missing important social trends that affect the timing of family formation, and thus we may be missing important points of divergence in family timing in an increasingly unequal society. Women with different social characteristics could have divergent experiences at different parts of the life course, so we must examine marriage and childbearing patterns at specific ages.

Age-Specific Rates of Marriage and Childbearing

Although we cannot observe all the marriage and childbearing years of the most recent cohorts of women, we can get detailed information from the years we can observe by looking at *age-specific* rates of entry into marriage and childbearing for unmarried or childless women of different educational groups and races. Figures 2.1 through 2.8 present age-specific marriage rates for never-married women. Figures 2.9 through 2.14 present age-specific first birth rates for childless women. These analyses use the combined June 1985, June 1990, and June 1995 Current Population Surveys. Full details of the analyses are provided in the appendix to this chapter.

Figures 2.1 and 2.2 show trends across cohorts for first marriage rates of U.S. women of all races, first for women with no four-year college degree and next for women with a four-year college degree. There is clear evidence of declining first marriage rates for women with no four-year college degree who are in their teens and twenties. These rates are apparently not declining for women in their thirties and may be slightly increasing at age thirty or older for the 1960 to 1969 birth cohort. Women with a four-year college degree have also had declining marriage rates to about age twenty-five. Hence, declining marriage in early adulthood is common to women of all educational levels; this decline is producing the universal increases in marriage ages shown in table 2.1. However, starting in the late twenties, the trends for women with a four-year college degree are quite different from trends for less-educated women. The college graduates have shown pronounced increases in marriage rates in their late twenties and thirties for both the 1950 to 1959 and 1960 to 1969 birth cohorts.

Figures 2.3 and 2.4 show trends across cohorts for first marriage rates of non-Hispanic white U.S. women. Marriage rates at older adult ages are strongly increasing among four-year college graduates, but they are also increasing somewhat for white women with less educational attainment.

Given that there are some increases in delayed marriage rates for non-Hispanic white women of all educational levels, we might wonder whether women are really changing their behavior at older ages, or whether we are simply seeing a different population of women unmarried at age thirty and older. The growing cohorts of "new delayers" could be socially distinct from the small cohorts of women who delayed marriage in the past, and the new delayers are likely to be more family-oriented. Hence, it would not be surprising to see rising overall marriage rates for unmarried thirty-year-old women simply because a wider range of women are remaining unmarried to age thirty. In other words, the increase in

FIGURE 2.1   *First Marriage Rates for U.S. Women with No Four-Year College Degree*

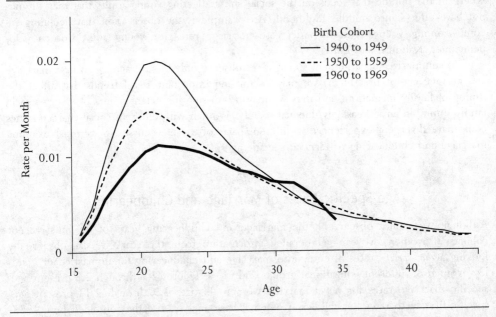

Source: June 1985, 1990, and 1995 CPS.

FIGURE 2.2   *First Marriage Rates for U.S. Women with a Four-Year College Degree*

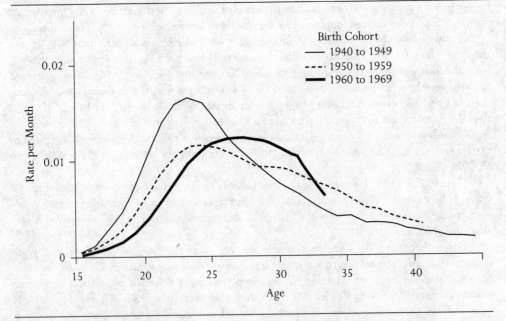

Source: June 1985, 1990, and 1995 CPS.

FIGURE 2.3   *First Marriage Rates for U.S. Non-Hispanic White Women with No Four-Year College Degree*

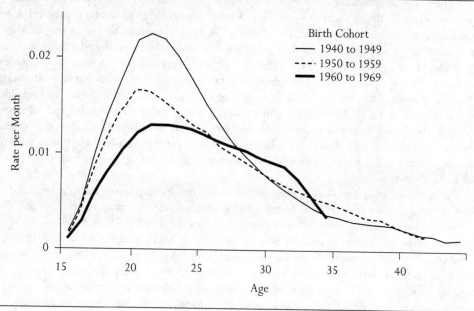

Source: June 1985, 1990, and 1995 CPS.

FIGURE 2.4   *First Marriage Rates for U.S. Non-Hispanic White Women with a Four-Year College Degree*

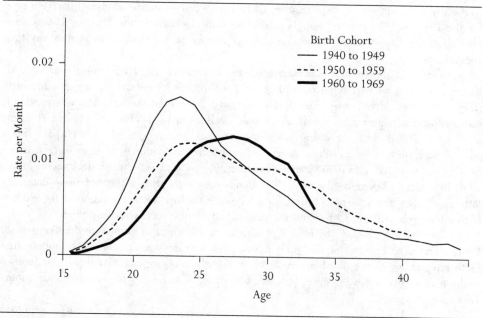

Source: June 1985, 1990, and 1995 CPS.

marriage rates at age thirty may be due to *unmeasured heterogeneity* in the population of women who delay marriage.

There are various ways to estimate the effects of unmeasured heterogeneity in a statistical model, and all of them involve considerable uncertainty. In another paper, I have applied various assumptions about the distribution of unmeasured heterogeneity in these analyses of age-specific marriage rates, and they have consistently produced results such as those shown in figures 2.5 and 2.6 (Martin 2002b). According to a model that assumes normally distributed unmeasured heterogeneity in each age cohort of women, white non-Hispanic women with no four-year college degree show consistently lower age-specific marriage rates in the 1960 to 1969 cohort than in the 1940 to 1949 cohort at all ages, although the decline is not as pronounced at older ages. In comparison, white non-Hispanic college graduates at age thirty and older still have a pattern consistent with increasing marriage rates at older ages, even when we account for the heterogeneous composition of the birth cohorts.

Why, then, are controls for unmeasured heterogeneity important only in models for women with no four-year college degree? There appear to be two reasons. First of all, the trends toward increasing marriage rates at older ages are much weaker for less-educated women and so are easier to explain away. Second, only a tiny proportion of the 1940 to 1949 cohort of white women with no four-year college degree remained unmarried at age thirty or even at age twenty-five, so an increase in delayed marriage could produce a dramatic change in the composition of the population of women unmarried at age twenty-five and older. Meanwhile, college graduates in all birth cohorts have been more likely to remain unmarried past their young adult years, so the compositional shifts in the population unmarried after age twenty-five or thirty have been much more modest over time.

Figures 2.7 and 2.8 show the trends in age-specific first marriage rates for non-Hispanic black women. For non-Hispanic black women with no four-year college degree, marriage rates are clearly low and declining across most or all ages. For non-Hispanic black women with a four-year college degree, there is no clear evidence of rising marriage rates for the 1950 to 1959 cohort, but there may be some increase in the 1960 to 1969 cohort starting in the late twenties. However, the sample sizes are too small to permit any firm conclusions.[4]

Having analyzed the data on marriage rates in some detail, I will move more quickly through the data on first birth rates. Figures 2.9 through 2.14 show the age-specific birth rates for women of different races and educational attainment, and the story is much the same as for marriage rates. Across all groups, declines in birth rates are evident at young adult ages. The declines at young adult ages are not pronounced for non-Hispanic black women with no four-year college degree. However, recent national declines in teen childbearing suggest that this demographic group may have had substantial declines in young adult first birth rates since the mid-1990s (and outside the time frame of these data). At later adult ages, the age-specific first birth rates clearly increase across cohorts for women with a four-year college degree and increase slightly for women with less education.

It is possible to model the effects of various distributions of unmeasured heterogeneity for birth rates, as I have done in figures 2.7 and 2.8 for marriage rates. In such models, first birth rates at age thirty or older are level or slightly declining across cohorts for women with no four-year college degree, but they are strongly increasing for women with a four-year college degree.

(*Text continues on p. 104.*)

FIGURE 2.5   *First Marriage Rates for U.S. Non-Hispanic White Women with No Four-Year College Degree, Assuming Normally Distributed Heterogeneity*

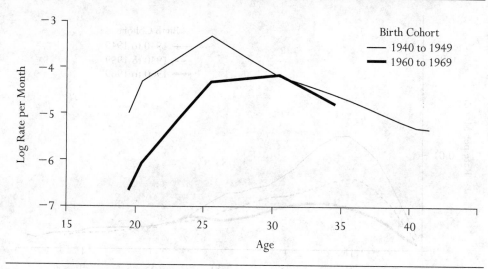

Source: Martin (2002b).
Note: exp(σ) = 2.

FIGURE 2.6   *First Marriage Rates for U.S. Non-Hispanic White Women with a Four-Year College Degree, Assuming Normally Distributed Heterogeneity*

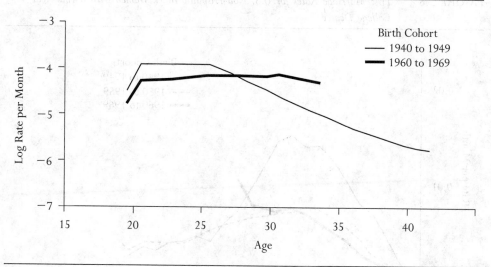

Source: Martin (2002b).
Note: exp(σ) = 2.

FIGURE 2.7   *First Marriage Rates for U.S. Non-Hispanic Black Women with No Four-Year College Degree*

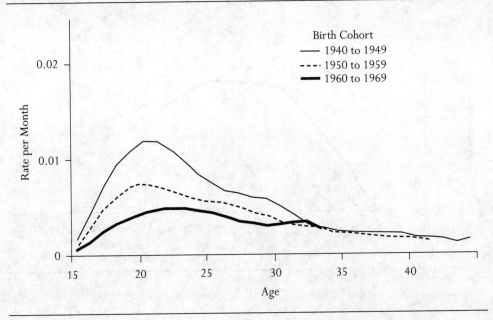

Source: June 1985, 1990, and 1995 CPS.

FIGURE 2.8   *First Marriage Rates for U.S. Non-Hispanic Black Women with a Four-Year College Degree*

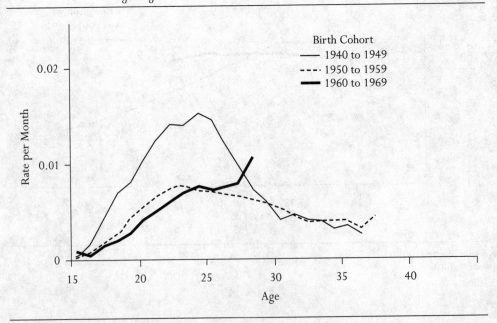

Source: June 1985, 1990, and 1995 CPS.

FIGURE 2.9   *First Birth Rates for U.S. Women with No Four-Year College Degree*

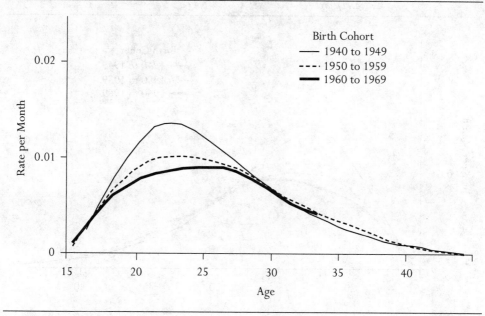

Source: June 1985, 1990, and 1995 CPS.

FIGURE 2.10   *First Birth Rates for U.S. Women with a Four-Year College Degree*

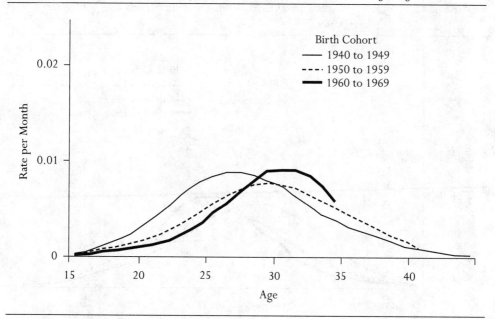

Source: June 1985, 1990, and 1995 CPS.

FIGURE 2.11   *First Birth Rates for U.S. Non-Hispanic White Women with No Four-Year
College Degree*

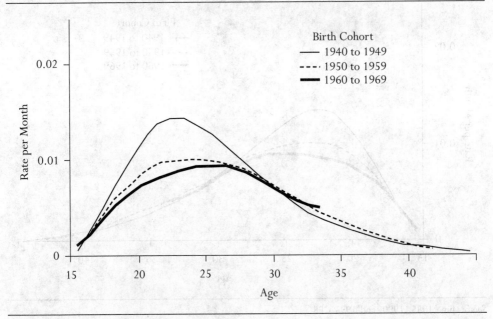

Source: June 1985, 1990, and 1995 CPS.

FIGURE 2.12   *First Birth Rates for U.S. Non-Hispanic White Women with a Four-Year
College Degree*

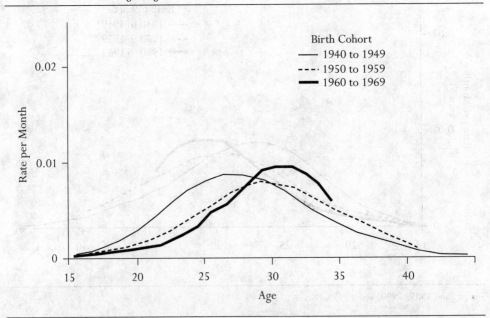

Source: June 1985, 1990, and 1995 CPS.

FIGURE 2.13   *First Birth Rates for U.S. Non-Hispanic Black Women with No Four-Year College Degree*

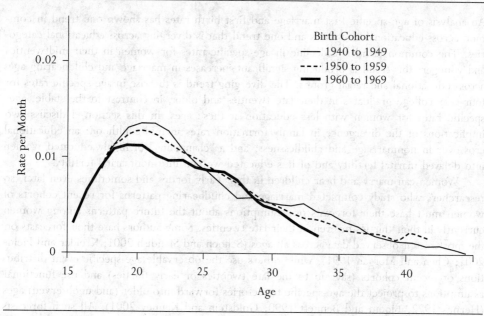

FIGURE 2.14   *First Birth Rates for U.S. Non-Hispanic Black Women with a Four-Year College Degree*

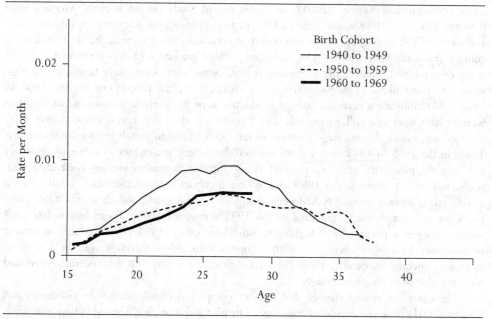

Implications of Trends in Age-Specific Marriage and Birth Rates

An analysis of age-specific first marriage and first birth rates has shown one trend in common across educational categories and one trend that is diverging across educational categories. The common trend is a decline in age-specific rates for women in their midtwenties and younger; this trend is producing significant increases in marriage and childbearing ages across educational and racial groups. The diverging trend is the rise in age-specific rates for four-year college graduates in their late twenties and older, in contrast to the stable, age-specific rates for women with less education at these ages. In this section, I discuss two implications of the divergence in family formation rates in mid-adulthood: an educational crossover in nonmarriage and childlessness, and a "channeling" of highly educated women into delayed marital fertility and of less-educated women into nonmarital fertility.

Women can marry and bear children in their early forties and sometimes even later, so researchers who study completed marriage and childbearing patterns for recent cohorts of women must base their forecasts on assumptions about the future patterns among women currently in their thirties or even in their late twenties. Some authors base their forecasts on the most recent observed data across all ages (Schoen and Standish 2001; Kreider and Fields 2001; Chen and Morgan 1991), while others use the observable age-specific event distributions of recent cohorts (say, up to the late twenties or early thirties) and use functional assumptions to project the age-specific trajectories forward into older (and unobserved) ages (Hernes 1972; Bloom and Bennett 1990; Goldstein and Kenney 2001). All such forecasts necessarily involve some uncertainty.

Allowing for the uncertainty of these forecasts, there is growing evidence for an educational crossover in marriage: the most educated women have historically been the most likely to remain unmarried, but in the future they may be more likely to marry than their less-educated counterparts. Table 2.3 shows estimated proportions of women ever marrying from Goldstein and Kenney (2001), the most recent study on the subject. Women born between 1945 and 1949 would have had the highest proportions marrying in the late 1960s and early 1970s; among the never-married in this cohort, there were higher proportions of college graduates than women who were not college graduates (8.9 percent and 5.5 percent, respectively). Hence, the groups of women who were most likely to delay marriage were also most likely to forgo marriage. By comparison, the projections for the 1960 to 1964 cohort indicate a reversal: college graduates were *less* likely to remain unmarried than women who were not college graduates (5.4 percent and 13.6 percent, respectively).

We can match the marriage patterns in table 2.3 to recent trends in income inequality. Those in the 1945 to 1949 birth cohort reached their early adult years at a time of relatively low income inequality and experienced rising income inequality during their mid-adult years. In contrast, those in the 1960 to 1964 birth cohort reached their early adult years at a time when income inequality had been rising for several years, and their mid-adult years were not yet completed by the time of the 1995 survey interview. These incomplete projections suggest a potentially disturbing trend: historically, high levels of education among women may have been correlated with willingness to *eschew* marriage, but in a time of increasing income inequality, these high education levels may instead become correlated with the ability to *obtain* marriage.

There are no recent studies that project completed childbearing—as Goldstein and Kinney (2001) project completed marriage—in part because childbearing behavior in mid-adulthood often does not follow predictions from mathematical models (cf. Bloom 1982;

TABLE 2.3   *Projected Percentage of U.S. Women Never Marrying, by Education, Race, and Birth Cohort*

	1945 to 1949	1950 to 1954	1955 to 1959	1960 to 1964
All races				
Not college graduate	5.5%	8.5%	12.0%	13.6%
College graduate	8.9	10.2	8.2	5.4
Whites				
Not college graduate	4.0	6.8	8.6	7.9
College graduate	8.6	9.9	6.5	3.7
Blacks				
Not college graduate	15.4	21.6	34.4	40.5
College graduate	—	—	—	—

Source: Goldstein and Kenney (2001).

Bloom and Trussell 1984; for another discussion on the subject, see Rindfuss, Morgan, and Swicegood 1988). A conservative way to evaluate trends in completed childbearing is to look only at cohorts in their forties or older. Table 2.4 shows the proportions of women remaining childless at age forty to forty-four, from recent CPS data. In 1980 women with a college degree were about twice as likely to remain childless (17.6 percent) as women of lower educational attainment (8.0 to 9.5 percent). By 2000, childlessness had increased among women of all educational levels, but the gap has closed since 1990 because the odds of remaining childless rose most rapidly for less-educated women. Allowing for a twenty-year lag between early adult childbearing years and age forty to forty-four, this period of rising childlessness among less-educated women corresponds to the onset of increasing income inequality in the United States.

If recent trends continue, there may be an educational crossover in childlessness similar to the one that may be occurring for marriage, and women with less education may become more likely to remain childless than more-educated women. There would be a historical precedent for this sort of crossover. In a study of racial differences across a longer time span, Robert L. Boyd (1989) reported that childlessness among blacks was less common

TABLE 2.4   *Observed Percentage of U.S. Women Childless at Age Forty to Forty-Four, by Education and Year*

	Year			Odds Ratio	
	1980	1990	2000	1990/1980	2000/1990
Less than high school	8.0%	10.9%	15.9%	1.41%	1.55%
High school, four years	9.2	12.5	16.8	1.41	1.41
Less than college degree	9.5	15.2	18.4	1.71	1.26
College degree and above	17.6	25.7	27.3	1.62	1.09

Source: June 1980, 1990, 2000 CPS.
Note: Excludes women known to be born outside the United States.

than among whites for cohorts that reached adulthood during the baby boom, but that childlessness had been higher for blacks than for whites during and after the Great Depression.

An educational crossover in nonmarriage and childlessness has not yet occurred, but another pattern associated with diverging family formation can already be seen: the correlation between the timing of a first birth and a woman's marital status at first birth. Figures 2.15 through 2.18 display this correlation graphically using CPS data.[5]

In figures 2.15 through 2.18, the proportion of women with a marital first birth at age fifteen to twenty-four has declined for women of all educational and racial categories. For white non-Hispanic women with no college degree, this decline has been offset in part by increases in marital first births at older ages and in part by increases in nonmarital first births before age twenty-five. For white non-Hispanic women with a four-year college degree, virtually all of the change in the circumstances of first births has been a shift to marital first births after age twenty-five, while for black non-Hispanic women with no four-year college degree, virtually all the change in first births has been a shift to nonmarital births before age twenty-five. We cannot draw conclusions about black non-Hispanic college graduates because the sample was too small.

Note that none of the groups of women has seen a large increase in nonmarital first births *after* age twenty-five. Hence, in a time of decreasing marital fertility in early adulthood, some women postpone childbearing, while other women have nonmarital births, but very few women do both. Furthermore, white college graduates are the most likely to have a delayed first birth and the least likely to have a nonmarital first birth, while black noncollege graduates are the least likely to have a delayed first birth and the most likely to have a nonmarital first birth. In other words, delayed childbearing is inversely correlated with nonmarital childbearing at both the individual and the group level. This pattern suggests that nonmarital childbearing and delayed childbearing are not complementary trends but rather mutually exclusive alternatives to marital childbearing in early adulthood.

We could offer a speculative interpretation for this exclusive relationship between delayed and nonmarital fertility if we start with two assumptions: most women of all races and educational levels would like to have children, preferably within marriage; and women of all races and educational levels are finding marriage in early adulthood less feasible or less desirable. If postponing a marriage and a first birth led to a high probability of a later marriage and marital first birth, women would be strongly motivated to postpone both marriage and childbearing past early adulthood. This would be the case for women with high educational attainment. However, if postponing a marriage and a first birth led to a relatively low probability of a later marriage and marital first birth, women might be more willing to bear children outside of marriage in early adulthood rather than risk remaining childless. This may increasingly be the case for women with moderate or low educational attainment.[6]

The relationship between education, age-specific marriage and fertility rates, and marital status at birth may be interpreted in terms of *flexibility*. Women with four-year college degrees do not all desire to marry and have children after age thirty, but they often have the social and economic resources to keep that timing pattern as an option. They can anticipate having a good chance of marrying if they wait until age thirty or older, being able to pay for child care without spending most of their earnings, or even being able to pay for any medical fertility assistance not covered by standard health insurance. Having the option to form families later in life can give college graduates the flexibility to initiate family formation at younger adult ages only under favorable conditions. Women with fewer resources

FIGURE 2.15   *Age and Marital Status at First Birth for U.S. Non-Hispanic White Women with No Four-Year College Degree*

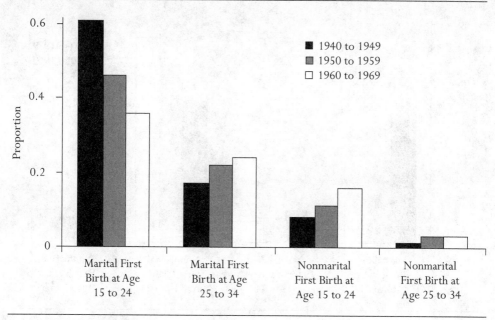

Source: June 1985, 1990, and 1995 CPS.

FIGURE 2.16   *Age and Marital Status at First Birth for U.S. Non-Hispanic White Women with a Four-Year College Degree*

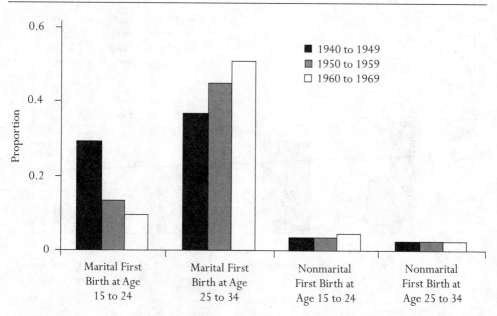

Source: June 1985, 1990, and 1995 CPS.

FIGURE 2.17   *Age and Marital Status at First Birth for U.S. Non-Hispanic Black Women with No Four-Year College Degree*

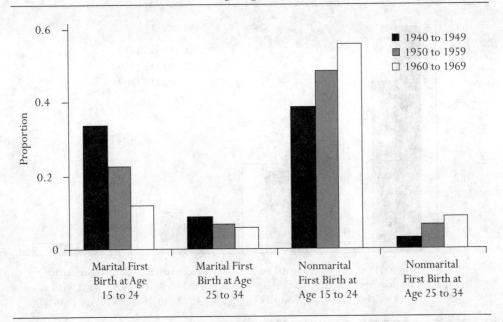

Source: June 1985, 1990, and 1995 CPS.

FIGURE 2.18   *Age and Marital Status at First Birth for U.S. Non-Hispanic Black Women with a Four-Year College Degree*

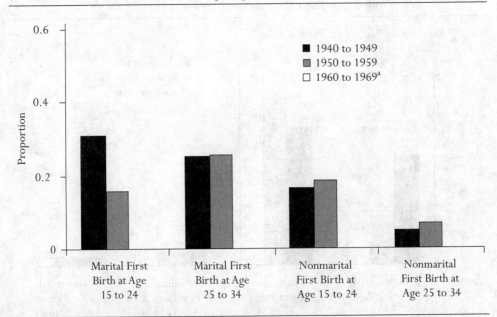

Source: June 1985, 1990, and 1995 CPS.
[a]The sample for the 1960 to 1969 birth cohort of black college graduates has fewer than fifty respondents.

have less flexibility to position their family formation later in the life course, so they could be more constrained to initiate childbearing by their midtwenties, even if their relationships and careers are not ideal at that age.

DISCUSSION

The outcomes associated with delayed family formation satisfy some but not all of the conditions for a link between social inequality and marriage and fertility timing. The literature review at the beginning of this chapter indicated that delayed marriage and childbearing are associated with some positive and some negative outcomes when compared with "on-time" childbearing in early adulthood. However, there has been a diminution over time in the negative sequelae of postponing marriage and childbearing, such as difficulty entering a marriage or having a child later in life or medical complications of pregnancy and birth at older ages. As a result, delayed family formation can be seen as an increasingly appealing alternative to early adult family formation for many women and couples. To the extent that highly educated women marry and have children later than other women, timing differences could increasingly exacerbate other inequalities that already exist between families.

Demographic trends in delayed marriage and childbearing also satisfy some but not all of the conditions for a link between social inequality and marriage and fertility timing. The empirical analysis in the second part of this chapter has shown that marriage and childbearing ages have been increasing among women of all races and educational levels. However, within this general shift, there is some evidence of divergence. Women with a four-year college degree (non-Hispanic white and possibly non-Hispanic black as well) are increasingly likely not only to postpone marriage and childbearing but to marry and have children at later ages when they postpone family formation, rather than remaining unmarried and/or childless. By comparison, the increasing proportions of women with no four-year college degree (both non-Hispanic white and non-Hispanic black) who postpone marriage and childbearing past early adulthood continue to have relatively low rates of marriage and first births at older ages; though many will go on to have a delayed marriage and/or birth, many more will probably remain unmarried and/or childless.

Why might we be seeing this divergence in age-specific marriage and first birth rates across cohorts? One possible reason is that women with a four-year college degree recognize that they can expect significant gains from postponing a marriage or birth and know that they have a substantial possibility of marrying and having children even if they do postpone family formation. From this reasoning it would follow that college graduates are more frequently postponing family formation as a deliberate strategy of repositioning family formation within the life course, while women of lower educational attainment are postponing marriage and childbearing largely as a reaction to difficulties in family formation in early adulthood. Another possible reason could be group differences in the discounting of time preference. It is a common economic observation that the wealthy tend to show more patience than the poor (Fisher 1930). Recently, Gary Becker and C. B. Mulligan (1997) have expanded on this observation to postulate a mechanism for it: the greater the future utility and certainty associated with postponing a present act to the future, the more likely a person is to anticipate and visualize the future event, and this visualization can reduce the extent to which future pleasures are discounted. Conversely, poor or uncertain prospects can induce rational actors to heavily discount the future. In the current context, this means that even if women from disadvantaged backgrounds could expect some net benefit from postponing marriage or childbearing, they would be unlikely to do so because the small expected gains and large uncertainty would reduce their anticipation and planning for that future outcome.

What are the social implications of these findings? For one, there is the possibility that nonmarital fertility and the timing of family formation are linked phenomena. Part of the reason for the increase in nonmarital fertility of women of lower socioeconomic status may be that they anticipate neither a high likelihood of delayed marital fertility nor strong benefits of delayed marital fertility should they postpone family formation past their mid-twenties. Other possibilities are that the educational crossover in nonmarriage will come about and become more pronounced in the future and that an educational crossover in childlessness will also occur. A society in which the more-educated women are also the most likely to have children and to marry could have advantages from certain policy perspectives, but it would also clearly be unequal across several dimensions of social life.

However, it is also possible that recent demographic trends will not persist in the future. For one thing, college graduates may not continue to maintain the same total proportions who are marrying at later ages. It is possible that the full recovery of marriage for recent cohorts is a transitory phenomenon, since the normative and social constraints against *delayed* marriage and childbearing are falling more rapidly in the short term than the normative and social barriers to nonmarriage and childlessness.

Similarly, recent trends predict declining family formation among women with no four-year college degree, but as a result of more women experiencing marriage at later ages, some of the social and normative variables that have previously limited women's entry into marriage at later ages could quite easily weaken. For example, norms favoring younger marriage ages for women than for men appear to be weakening (NiBhrolchain 2000). By this argument, college graduates may have different patterns of family timing than other women simply because they are at a more advanced stage in the transition of marriage—a transition where all couples will eventually adapt their marriage and parenthood patterns to the new challenges and opportunities presented by modern society. However, many social obstacles must be overcome before this can happen. Recent trends in marriage among black women show that continued and accelerated decline in marriage is certainly possible, and recent increases in economic inequality may make obstacles to flexible marriage and birth timing all the more formidable.

Perhaps the most important message of this chapter is that the social circumstances of marriage and childbearing are changing for all women and men. Recent decades have brought important changes in the social and cultural foundations of family life. New opportunities and constraints have made the traditional life-course pattern of early marriage and marital fertility unworkable for an increasing number of women and men of all educational levels and races.

Across the same time span, income inequality has been increasing. Increases in income inequality have certainly not been a sole or even a primary cause of the decline of early adult marriage and marital childbearing, but inequality appears to be playing an important part in how families adapt to the new opportunities and constraints. Individuals with more resources appear to have more flexibility to time marriages and births across a wider part of the adult life course. Individuals with fewer resources may have less flexibility to adapt their family formation to increasingly complex social conditions, and their family outcomes may be poorer as a result.

APPENDIX

The June 1985, 1990, and 1995 Current Population Surveys contain nearly complete marriage and fertility histories, and their large samples allow tests for interactions between period trends and educational attainment of respondents. The CPS fertility and marriage histories record the dates of births, marriages, separations, divorces, and remarriages for women age fifteen to sixty-five at interview. The U.S. Department of Labor (2001) has published a full description of the procedures used in collecting the CPS data. I show separate results for non-Hispanic white women, non-Hispanic black women, and all U.S. women, including Hispanic women and women of other racial and ethnic backgrounds. I restrict the sample to women born from January 1940 to December 1969, and I further restrict the sample to women age twenty-five or older at interview, to reduce artificial correlations between age at interview and education at interview. With these cohort and age restrictions, the final sample contains 75,680 women, including 64,206 non-Hispanic white women and 7,185 non-Hispanic black women.

From the CPS combined birth and marriage histories, I identify women who experienced a first marriage and/or a first birth and record the woman's age at the birth or marriage, to the nearest month. Women's retrospective accounting of the timing of marriage or first birth may be less accurate for events that happened a long time before the interview and among those women with multiple marriages; this may create problems for an analysis of trends over time. To test the accuracy of women's retrospective accounts over time, I estimated models separately for the 1985, 1990, and 1995 Current Population Surveys and found that patterns of marriage and childbearing were substantively the same whether women recalled events across a short (CPS 1985) or long (CPS 1995) time span.

In addition to distinctions by race, I use the educational attainment of the mother at interview as the key explanatory variable. Education at interview is not a perfect measure to use in an analysis of family trends and social inequality, for several reasons. First of all, education at interview is increasingly correlated with age at interview, because many women pursue additional years of education across the life course. An endogenous relationship between education, fertility, and marriage may be a particular problem for high school completion or equivalency, or for enrollment in some college courses after high school, so I limit most of my analyses to differences between four-year college graduates and other women, and to women age twenty-five or older at interview.

Second, women's educational attainment has increased across recent decades, so the population of women with a four-year college degree is somewhat different in the 1990s than it was in the 1970s. The sample proportion of all U.S. women over age twenty-five reporting a four-year college degree at interview changed from 22.5 percent of the sample of women born between 1940 and 1949 to 25.5 percent of the sample of women born between 1960 and 1969; this difference is artificially reduced by the fact that the 1940 to 1949 cohort was older at interview than the 1960 to 1969 cohort. The argument could be made that the latent tendency to marriage has an inverted-U distribution across educational categories, with the lowest marriage levels at the highest and lowest educational levels. In that case, moving a small proportion of women into the category of college graduates might increase the proportions ever marrying among college graduates and reduce it among other women. It is unclear how this sort of argument would explain observed patterns in the *timing* of marriage or the incidence or timing of first births.

A final concern with the use of education as an indicator of relative socioeconomic level is that income inequality within educational groups increased more quickly than between-group inequality during the 1970s and 1980s (Katz and Murphy 1992; Levy and Murnane 1992). This increased variance might dilute any association between education and family outcomes that was mediated by income inequality. However, the increase in within-group inequality was concentrated among workers of lower educational attainment and was largely explained by declines in organized labor and the stagnation of the minimum wage (DiNardo, Fortin, and Lemieux 1996). Thus, any negative effects of increasing within-group income inequality on family formation were probably most pronounced at lower educational levels, and comparisons by educational attainment almost certainly capture much of the recent increase in income inequality.

The Current Population Surveys contain large samples but have a limited number of variables suitable for statistical controls. In analyses of age-specific marriage and birth rates, I include no statistical controls. However, in sensitivity analyses (not shown), I estimate models that exclude the few cases with imputation flags for race, education, and the timing of marriages and births. The results are substantively the same as those shown.

I gratefully acknowledge research funding from a Russell Sage Foundation grant on the consequences of social inequality for families, schools, and communities. I would also like to thank Amy Erdman and Sangeeta Parashar, who have provided invaluable research work and helpful assistance.

NOTES

1. Among poor minority and urban women, there has recently been a marriage squeeze associated with a lack of available men with steady jobs, but delayed marriage has not been an important factor in creating this depleted marriage market.
2. Cowan and Cowan (1992) do find that older parents are *less* likely to experience diminishing self-esteem and feelings of incompetence, relative to younger parents.
3. Fretts and colleagues (1995) found essentially identical time trends for neonatal mortality.
4. In separate parametric models for non-Hispanic black women, the cohort increases for women with a four-year college degree at age thirty were marginally statistically significant at $p < .1$.
5. Some respondents were censored by interview before they finished the listed age and cohort categories; for these categories, I assumed that respondents with incomplete age-cohort records would have the same fertility patterns as respondents with complete age-cohort records.
6. Another interpretation for the exclusive relationship between delayed and nonmarital fertility would be that most nonmarital fertility is an unintended result of contraceptive non-use or contraceptive failure, and most women who have an unintended first birth would be likely to do so before age twenty-five. However, the intention status of a birth is often more of a relative than an absolute measure, reflecting the woman's, or the couple's, motivation to contracept. Hence, this alternative interpretation is not fully distinct from the main interpretation discussed here.

REFERENCES

Aldous, Michael B., and M. Bruce Edmondson. 1993. "Maternal Age at First Childbirth and the Risk of Low Birthweight and Preterm Delivery in Washington State." *Journal of the American Medical Association* 270(21): 2574–77.

Alonzo, Adrian A. 2002. "Long-term Health Consequences of Delayed Childbirth: NHANES III." *Women's Health Issues* 12(1): 37–45.

Ananth, Cande V., Dawn P. Misra, Kitaw Demissie, and John C. Smulian. 2001. "Rates of Preterm Delivery Among Black Women and White Women in the United States over Two Decades: An Age-Period-Cohort Analysis." *American Journal of Epidemiology* 154(7): 657–65.

Ananth, Cande V., Allen J. Wilcox, David A. Savitz, Watson A. Bowes Jr., and Edwin R. Luther. 1996. "Effects of Maternal Age and Parity on the Risk of Uteroplacental Bleeding Disorders in Pregnancy." *Obstetrics and Gynecology* 88(4): 511–16.

Anderson, Deborah J., Melissa Binder, and Kate Krause. 2002. "The Motherhood Wage Penalty: Which Mothers Pay It, and Why?" *American Economic Review* 92(2): 354–58.

Astolfi, Paula, and Laura A. Zonta. 1999. "Risks of Preterm Delivery and Association with Maternal Age, Birth Order, and Fetal Gender." *Human Reproduction* 14(11): 2891–94.

Bahr, Stephen J., Bradford C. Chappell, and Geoffrey K. Leigh. 1983. "Age at Marriage, Role Enactment, Role Consensus, and Marital Satisfaction." *Journal of Marriage and the Family* 45(4): 795–803.

Baldwin, Wendy H., and C. W. Nord. 1984. "Delayed Childbearing in the United States: Facts and Fictions." *Population Bulletin* 39(4): 3–42.

Becker, Gary S. 1974. "Theory of Marriage: Part 2." *Journal of Political Economy* 82(2): S11–26.

———. 1981. *A Treatise on the Family*. Cambridge, Mass.: Harvard University Press.

Becker, Gary S., Elizabeth M. Landes, and Robert T. Michael. 1977. "An Economic Analysis of Marital Instability." *Journal of Political Economy* 85(6): 1141–88.

Becker, Gary S., and C. B. Mulligan. 1997. "The Endogenous Determination of Time Preference." *Quarterly Journal of Economics* 112(3): 729–58.

Bengel, Jurgen, C. Carl, U. Mild, and B. Strauss. 2000. "Long-term Psychological Consequences of Childlessness: A Review." *Zeitschrift fur Klinische Psychologie—Forschung und Praxis* 29(1): 3–15.

Berkowitz, Gertrud S., Mary L. Skovron, Robert H. Lapinski, and Richard L. Berkowitz. 1990. "Delayed Childbearing and the Outcome of Pregnancy." *New England Journal of Medicine* 322(10): 659–64.

Bernhardt, Annette, Martina Morris, Mark S. Handcock, and Marc A. Scott. 2001. *Divergent Paths: Economic Mobility and the New American Labor Market*. New York: Russell Sage Foundation.

Bianco, Angela, Joanne Stone, Lauren Lynch, Robert Lapinski, Gertrud Berkowitz, and Richard L. Berkowitz. 1996. "Pregnancy Outcome at Age Forty and Older." *Obstetrics and Gynecology* 87(6): 917–22.

Bitter, Robert G. 1986. "Late Marriage and Marital Instability: The Effects of Heterogeneity and Inflexibility." *Journal of Marriage and the Family* 48(3): 631–40.

Blackburn, Mark L., David E. Bloom, and David Neumark. 1993. "Fertility Timing, Wages, and Human Capital." *Journal of Population Economics* 6(1): 1–30.

Bleyer, Adrien. 1958. *Childbearing Before and After Thirty-five: Biologic and Social Implications*. New York: Vantage Press.

Bloom, David E. 1982. "What's Happening to the Age at First Birth in the United States? A Study of Recent Cohorts." *Demography* 19(3): 351–70.

Bloom, David E., and Neil G. Bennett. 1990. "Modeling American Marriage Patterns." *Journal of the American Statistical Association* 85(412): 1009–17.

Bloom, David E., and James Trussell. 1984. "What Are the Determinants of Delayed Childbearing and Permanent Childlessness in the United States?" *Demography* 21(4): 591–611.

Booth, Alan, and John Edwards. 1985. "Age at Marriage and Marital Instability." *Journal of Marriage and the Family* 47(1): 67–75.

Boyd, Robert. L. 1989. "Racial Differences in Childlessness: A Centennial Review." *Sociological Perspectives* 32(2): 183–99.

Bumpass, Larry L., and Hsien-Hen Lu. 2000. "Trends in Cohabitation and Implications for Children's Family Contexts in the United States." *Population Studies* 54(1): 29–41.

Bumpass, Larry L., and James A. Sweet. 1972. "Differentials in Marital Stability." *American Sociological Review* 37(4): 754–66.

Bumpass, Larry L., James A. Sweet, and Andrew Cherlin. 1991. "The Role of Cohabitation in Declining Rates of Marriage." *Journal of Marriage and the Family* 53(4): 913–27.

Casper, Lynne M. 1995. "What Does It Cost to Mind Our Preschoolers?" *Current Population Report,* series P70, no. 52. Washington: U.S. Government Printing Office for U.S. Census Bureau.

Castro Martin, Teresa, and Larry Bumpass. 1989. "Recent Trends in Marital Disruption." *Demography* 26(1): 37–51.

Chandler, Timothy D., Yoshimori Kamo, and James D. Werbel. 1994. "Do Delays in Marriage and Childbirth Affect Earnings?" *Social Science Quarterly* 75(4): 838–53.

Chandra, Anjani, and Elizabeth H. Stephen. 1998. "Impaired Fecundity in the United States: 1982 to 1995." *Family Planning Perspectives* 30(1): 34–42.

Chen, Renbao, and S. Philip Morgan. 1991. "Recent Trends in the Timing of First Births in the United States." *Demography* 28(4): 513–33.

Chisholm, James S. 1993. "Death, Hope, and Sex: Life History Theory and the Development of Reproductive Strategies." *Current Anthropology* 34: 1–24.

Cnattingius, Sven, Michele R. Forman, H. W. Berendes, and L. Isotalo. 1992. "Delayed Childbearing and the Risk of Adverse Perinatal Outcome." *Journal of the American Medical Association* 268(7): 886–90.

Coltrane, Scott. 1990. "Birth Timing and the Division of Labor in Dual-Earner Families: Exploratory Findings and Implications for Future Research." *Journal of Family Issues* 9: 132–48.

Coltrane, Scott, and Masako Ishii-Kuntz. 1992. "Men's Housework: A Life-Course Perspective." *Journal of Marriage and the Family* 54(1): 43–57.

Conger, Rand D., John A. McCarthy, Raymond K. Yang, Benjamin B. Lahey, and Robert L. Burgess. 1984. "Mother's Age as a Predictor of Observed Maternal Behavior in Three Independent Samples of Families." *Journal of Marriage and the Family* 46(2): 411–24.

Cooney, Teresa M., Frank A. Pedersen, Samuel Indelicato, and Rob Palkovitz. 1993. "Timing of Fatherhood: Is 'On-Time' Optimal?" *Journal of Marriage and the Family* 55(1): 205–15.

Cowan, Carolyn Pape, and Philip A. Cowan. 1992. *When Partners Become Parents.* New York: Basic Books.

Daniels, Pamela, and Kathy Weingarten. 1982. *Sooner or Later: The Timing of Parenthood in Adult Lives.* New York: W. W. Norton.

Dex, Shirley, Heather Joshi, Andrew McCulloch, and Susan Macran. 1996. "Women's Employment Transitions Around Childbearing." Working paper 1408. London: Center for Economic Policy Research.

Dildy, Gary A., G. Marc Jackson, Gary K. Fowers, Bryan T. Oshiro, Michael W. Varner, and Steven I. Clark. 1996. "Very Advanced Maternal Age: Pregnancy After Age Forty-five." *American Journal of Obstetrics & Gynecology* 175(3, Part 1): 668–74.

DiNardo, John, Nicole M. Fortin, and Thomas Lemieux. 1996. "Labor Market Institutions and the Distribution of Wages, 1973 to 1992: A Semiparametric Approach." *Econometrica* 64: 1001–44.

Dion, Karen K. 1995. "Delayed Parenthood and Women's Expectations About the Transition to Parenthood." *International Journal of Behavioral Development* 18: 315–33.

Dobson, Coretta D., and Sharon K. Houseknecht. 1998. "Black and White Differences in the Effect of Women's Educational Attainment on Age at First Marriage." *Journal of Family Issues* 19(2): 204–23.

England, Paula, and Nancy Folbre. 1999. "Who Should Pay for the Kids?" *Annals of the American Academy of Political and Social Science* 563: 194–207.

Espenshade, Thomas N. 1985. "Marriage Trends in America: Estimates, Implications, and Underlying Causes." *Population and Development Review* 11(2): 193–245.

Feldman, W. M. 1927. *The Principles of Ante-Natal and Postnatal Hygiene.* London: John Bale, Sons, and Danielsson.

Finley, Gordon E. 1998. "Parental Age and Parenting Quality as Perceived by Late Adolescents." *Journal of Genetic Psychology* 159(4): 505–6.

Fisher, Irving. 1930. *The Theory of Interest.* New York: Macmillan.

Frankel, Steven A., and Myra J. Wise. 1982. "A View of Delayed Parenting: Some Implications of a New Trend." *Psychiatry: Interpersonal and Biological Processes* 45(2): 220–25.

Fretts, Ruth C., Julie Schmittdiel, Frances H. McLean, Robert H. Usher, and Marlene B. Goldman. 1995. "Increased Maternal Age and the Risk of Fetal Death." *New England Journal of Medicine* 333(15): 953–57.

Garrison, M. E. Betsy, Lydia B. Blalock, John J. Zarski, and P. B. Merritt. 1997. "Delayed Parenthood: An Exploratory Study of Family Functioning." *Family Relations* 46(3): 281–90.

Gaughan, Monica. 2002. "The Substitution Hypothesis: The Impact of Premarital Liaisons and Human Capital on Marriage Timing." *Journal of Marriage and the Family* 64(2): 407–19.

Geronimus, Arline T. 1994. "The Weathering Hypothesis and the Health of African-American Women and Infants: Implications for Reproductive Strategies and Policy Analysis." In *Power and Decision: The Social Control of Reproduction,* edited by Gita Sen and Rachel C. Snow. Cambridge, Mass.: Harvard University Press.

———. 1996. "Black-White Differences in the Relation of Maternal Age to Birthweight: A Population-Based Test of the Weathering Hypothesis." *Social Science and Medicine* 42: 589–97.

Geronimus, Arline T., John Bound, and Tim A. Waidman. 1999. "Health Inequality and Population Variation in Birth Timing." *Social Science and Medicine* 49(12): 1623–36.

Gilbert, William M., Thomas S. Nesbitt, and Beate Danielsen. 1999. "Childbearing Beyond the Age of Forty: Pregnancy Outcomes in 24,032 Cases." *Obstetrics and Gynecology* 93(1): 9–14.

Goldman, Noreen, Charles F. Westoff, and Charles Hammerslough. 1984. "Demography of the Marriage Market of the United States." *Population Index* 50: 5–26.

Goldstein, Joshua R., and Catherine T. Kenney. 2001. "Marriage Delayed or Marriage Forgone? New Cohort Forecasts of First Marriage for U.S. Women." *American Sociological Review* 66(4): 506–19.

Gosden, Roger, and Anthony Rutherford. 1996. "Delayed Childbearing." *Student British Medical Journal* 4(37): 5–9.

Greil, Arthur L. 1997. "Infertility and Psychological Distress: A Critical Review of the Literature." *Social Science and Medicine* 45(11): 1679–1704.

Grindstaff, Carl F. 1996. "The Costs of Having a First Child for Women Aged Thirty-three to Thirty-eight, Canada 1991." *Sex Roles* 35(3–4): 137–51.

Heath, D. Terri. 1994. "The Impact of Delayed Fatherhood on the Parent-Child Relationship." *Journal of Genetic Psychology* 155(4): 511–30.

Heaton, Tim B. 2002. "Factors Contributing to Increasing Marital Stability in the United States." *Journal of Family Issues* 23(3): 392–409.

Helms-Erikson, Heather. 2001. "Marital Quality Ten Years After the Transition to Parenthood: Implications of the Timing of Parenthood and the Division of Housework." *Journal of Marriage and Family* 63(4): 1099–1110.

Hernes, Gudmund. 1972. "The Process of Entry into First Marriage." *American Sociological Review* 37(2): 173–82.

Hewlett, Sylvia A. 2001. *Creating a Life: Professional Women and the Quest for Children.* New York: Talk Miramax Books.

Hofferth, Sandra L. 1984. "Long-term Economic Consequences for Women of Delayed Childbearing and Reduced Family Size." *Demography* 21(2): 141–55.

Jolly, M., N. Sebire, J. Harris, S. Robinson, and L. Regan. 2000. "The Risks Associated with Pregnancy in Women Age Thirty-five Years and Older." *Human Reproduction* 15(11): 2433–37.

Joshi, Heather, Pierella Paci, and Jane Waldfogel. 1999. "The Wages of Motherhood: Better or Worse?" *Cambridge Journal of Economics* 23(5): 543–64.

Karoly, Lynn A., and Gary Burtless. 1995. "Demographic Change, Rising Earnings Inequality, and the Distribution of Personal Well-being, 1959 to 1989." *Demography* 32(3): 379–406.

Katz, Lawrence F., and Kevin M. Murphy. 1992. "Changes in Relative Wages, 1963 to 1987: Supply and Demand Factors." *Quarterly Journal of Economics* 107(1): 35–78.

Keister, Lisa A. 2000. *Wealth in America: Trends in Wealth Inequality.* New York: Cambridge University Press.

Kreider, Rose M., and Jason M. Fields. 2001. "Number, Timing, and Duration of Marriages and Divorces: Fall 1996." *Current Population Reports,* series P70, no. 80. Washington: U.S. Government Printing Office for U.S. Census Bureau.

Kullmer, Uwe, Marek Zygmunt, Karsten Munstedt, and Uwe Lang. 2000. "Pregnancies in Primiparous Women Thirty-five and Older: Still Risk Pregnancies?" *Geburtshilfe Und Frauenheilkunde* 60(11): 569–75.

Larson, Jeffry H., and Thomas B. Holman. 1994. "Premarital Predictors of Marital Quality and Stability." *Family Relations* 43: 228–37.

Lee, Gary R. 1977. "Age at Marriage and Marital Satisfaction: A Multivariate Analysis with Implications for Marital Stability." *Journal of Marriage and the Family* 39: 493–504.

Levy, Frank, and Richard J. Murnane. 1992. "U.S. Earnings Levels and Earnings Inequality: A Review of Recent Trends and Proposed Explanations." *Journal of Economic Literature* 30: 1333–81.

Mare, Robert D., and Meei-Shenn Tzeng. 1989. "Fathers' Ages and the Social Stratification of Sons." *American Journal of Sociology* 95(1): 108–31.

Martin, Steven P. 2000. "Diverging Fertility Among U.S. Women Who Delay Childbearing Past Age Thirty." *Demography* 37(4): 523–33.

———. 2002a. "Unequal Trends in Marital Stability: Women's Educational Attainment and Marital Dissolutions Involving Young Children from 1975 to 1995." Unpublished paper. University of Maryland, College Park.

———. 2002b. "Predicting the Near Future: An Examination of Models for Forecasting Proportions Ever Marrying." Paper presented to the Fortieth Anniversary Conference for the Center for Demography and Ecology. University of Wisconsin, Madison (October 2002).

May, Elaine Tyler. 1995. *Barren in the Promised Land: Childless Americans and the Pursuit of Happiness.* Cambridge, Mass.: Harvard University Press.

McFalls, Joseph A., Jr. 1990. "The Risks of Reproductive Impairment in the Later Years of Childbearing." *Annual Review of Sociology* 16(1): 491–519.

———. 1992. "Reproductive Roulette: Women Who Delay Childbearing." *USA Today Magazine* 121 (2570, November).

Menken, Jane. 1985. "Age and Fertility: How Late Can You Wait?" *Demography* 22(4): 469–83.

Menken, Jane, and Ulla Larsen. 1986. "Fertility Rates and Aging." In *Aging, Reproduction, and the Climacteric,* edited by Luigi Mastroianni and Charles Alvin Paulsen. New York: Plenum.

Mertens, N., A. Van-Doorne-Huiskies, J. Schippers, and J. Siegers. 1998. "Women's Wage Rates and the Timing of Children: A Simultaneous Analysis." *Netherlands Journal of Social Sciences* 34(1): 61ff.

Meyer, Christine Segwarth. 1999. "Family Focus or Career Focus: Controlling for Infertility." *Social Science and Medicine* 49(12): 1615–22.

Mirowsky, John, and Catherine E. Ross. 2002. "Depression, Parenthood, and Age at First Birth." *Social Science and Medicine* 54(8): 1281–98.

Monahan, Thomas P. 1953. "Does Age at Marriage Matter in Divorce?" *Social Forces* 32(1): 81–87.

Moore, Kristin, and Linda J. Waite. 1981. "Marital Dissolution, Early Motherhood, and Early Marriage." *Social Forces* 60(3): 20–40.

Morris, Monica B. 1988. *Last-Chance Children: Growing up with Older Parents.* New York: Columbia University Press.

Neville, Brian, and Ross D. Parke. 1997. "Waiting for Paternity: Interpersonal and Contextual Implications of the Timing of Fatherhood." *Sex Roles* 37(1–2): 45–59.

Newcomb, W. W., M. Rodriguez, and J. W. C. Johnson. 1991. "Reproduction in the Older Gravida: A Literature Review." *Journal of Reproductive Medicine* 36(12): 839–45.

NiBhrolchain, Mare. 2000. "Flexibility in the Marriage Market." *Population* 55(6): 899–939.

Nichols-Casebolt, Ann, and Sandra K. Danziger. 1989. "The Effect of Childbearing Age on Child Support Awards and Economic Well-being Among Divorced Mothers." *Journal of Divorce* 12(4): 35–48.

Oppenheimer, Valerie Kincade. 1988. "A Theory of Marriage Timing." *American Journal of Sociology* 94(3): 563–91.

Oppenheimer, Valerie Kincade, Matthijs Kalmijn, and Nelson Lim. 1997. "Men's Career Development and Marriage Timing During a Period of Rising Inequality." *Demography* 34(3): 311–30.

Parke, Ross D. 1988. "Families in Life-Span Perspective: A Multidimensional Developmental Approach." In *Child Development in Life-Span Perspective,* edited by E. Mavis Hetherington, Richard M. Lerner, and Marion Perlmutter. Hillsdale, N.J.: Lawrence Erlbaum Associates.

Parsons, Talcott. 1949. "The Social Structure of the Family." In *The Family: Its Function and Destiny,* edited by Ruth Anshen. New York: Harper & Row.

Peipert, Jeffrey F., and Michael B. Bracken. 1993. "Maternal Age: An Independent Risk Factor for Cesarean Delivery." *Obstetrics and Gynecology* 83: 388–90.

Phipps, Shelley, Peter Burton, and Lynn Lethbridge. 2001. "In and Out of the Labor Market: Long-term Income Consequences of Child-Related Interruptions in Women's Paid Work." *Canadian Journal of Economics* 34(2): 411–29.

Pienta, Amy. 1999. "Early Childbearing Patterns and Women's Labor Force Behavior in Later Life." *Journal of Women and Aging* 11(1): 69–84.

Pittman, Joe F., and David Blanchard. 1996. "The Effects of Work History and Timing of Marriage on the Division of Household Labor: A Life-Course Perspective." *Journal of Marriage and the Family* 58(1): 78–90.

Pollock, J. I. 1996. "Mature Maternity: Long-term Associations in First Children Born to Older Mothers in 1970 in the United Kingdom." *Journal of Epidemiology and Community Health* 50(4): 429–35.

Popenoe, David. 1993. "American Family Decline 1960 to 1990: A Review and Appraisal." *Journal of Marriage and the Family* 55(3): 527–55.

Presser, Harriet. 2001. "Comment: A Gender Perspective for Understanding Low Fertility in Post-transitional Societies." *Population and Development Review* 27(S): 177–83.

Prysak, Michael, Robert P. Lorenz, and Anne Kisly. 1995. "Pregnancy Outcome in Nulliparous Women Thirty-five Years and Older." *Obstetrics and Gynecology* 85(1): 65–70.

Ragozin, Arlene S., Robert B. Basham, Keith A. Crnic, Mark T. Greenberg, and Nancy M. Robinson. 1982. "Effects of Maternal Age on Parenting Role." *Developmental Psychology* 18(4): 627–34.

Raley, R. Kelly, and Larry Bumpass. 2002. "The Topography of the Divorce Plateau: Levels and Trends in Union Stability After 1980." Working paper 92–27 (revised version). Madison: University of Wisconsin, Center for Demography and Ecology.

Reece, S. M. 1993. "Social Support and the Early Maternal Experience of Primiparas over Thirty-five." *Maternal–Child Nursing Journal* 21(3): 91–98.

Reichman, Nancy E., and Deanna L. Pagnini. 1997. "Maternal Age and Birth Outcomes: Data from New Jersey." *Family Planning Perspectives* 29(6): 268–272, 295.

Rindfuss, Ronald R., and Larry Bumpass. 1978. "Age and the Sociology of Fertility: How Old Is Too Old?" In *Social Demography,* edited by Karl E. Taeuber, Larry L. Bumpass, and James A. Sweet. New York: Academic Press.

Rindfuss, Ronald R., S. Philip Morgan, and Kate Offutt. 1996. "Education and the Changing Age Pattern of American Fertility: 1963 to 1989." *Demography* 33(3): 277–90.

Rindfuss, Ronald R., S. Philip Morgan, and Gray Swicegood. 1988. *First Births in America.* Berkeley: University of California Press.

Rindfuss, Ronald R., and Audrey VandenHeuvel. 1990. "Cohabitation: A Precursor to Marriage or an Alternative to Being Single?" *Population and Development Review* 16(4): 703–26.

Roosa, Mark W. 1988. "The Effect of Age in the Transition to Parenthood: Are Delayed Child-bearers a Unique Group?" *Family Relations* 37(3): 322–27.

Rossi, Alice S. 1980. "Aging and Parenthood in the Middle Years." In *Life-Span Development and Behavior,* edited by Paul G. Baltes and O. G. Brim Jr. New York: Academic Press.

Schlesinger, Benjamin, and Rachel Schlesinger. 1989. "Postponed Parenthood: Trends and Issues". *Journal of Comparative Family Studies* 20: 355–63.

Schoen, Robert. 1983. "Measuring the Tightness of a Marriage Squeeze." *Demography* 20(1): 61–78.

Schoen, Robert, and Nicola Standish. 2001. "The Retrenchment of Marriage: Results from Marital Status Life Tables from the United States, 1995." *Population and Development Review* 27(3): 553–64.

Schultz, Theodore W. 1974. "The High Value of Human Time: Population Equilibrium." *Journal of Political Economy* 82(2): S2–10.

Smith, Herbert L., S. Philip Morgan, and Tanya Koropeckyj-Cox. 1996. "A Decomposition of Trends in the Nonmarital Fertility Ratios of Blacks and Whites in the United States, 1960 to 1992." *Demography* 33(2): 141–51.

Soloway, Maxine N., and Rebecca M. Smith. 1987. "Antecedents of Late Birth Timing Decisions of Men and Women in Dual-Career Marriages." *Family Relations* 36(3): 258–62.

Spain, Daphne, and Suzanne M. Bianchi. 1996. *Balancing Act: Motherhood, Marriage, and Employment Among American Women.* New York: Russell Sage Foundation.

Stephen, Elizabeth H. 2000. "Demographic Implications of Reproductive Technologies." *Population Research and Policy Review* 19(4): 301–15.

Sweeney, Megan M. 2002. "Two Decades of Family Change: The Shifting Economic Foundations of Marriage." *American Sociological Review* 67(1): 132–47.

Szamatowics, Marian, and Dariusz Grochowski. 1998. "Fertility and Infertility in Aging Women." *Gynecological Endocrinology* 12(6): 407–13.

Taniguchi, Hiromi. 1999. "The Timing of Childbearing and Women's Wages." *Journal of Marriage and the Family* 61(4): 1008–19.

Tarin, Juan J., Juan Brines, and Antonio Cano. 1998. "Long-term Effects of Delayed Parenthood." *Human Reproduction* 13(9): 2371–76.

Teachman, Jay D. 1983. "Early Marriage, Premarital Fertility, and Marital Dissolution: Results for Blacks and Whites." *Journal of Family Issues* 4(1): 105–26.

Teachman, Jay D., and Peter T. Schollaert. 1989. "Economic Conditions, Marital Status, and the Timing of First Births: Results for Whites and Blacks." *Sociological Forum* 4(1): 27–46.

Tough, Suzanne C., Christine Newburn-Cook, David W. Johnston, Lawrence W. Svenson, S. Rose, and Jaques Belik. 2002. "Delayed Childbearing and Its Impact on Population Rate Changes in Lower Birthweight, Multiple Birth, and Preterm Delivery." *Pediatrics* 109(3): 399–403.

Toulemon, Laurent. 1996. "Very Few Couples Remain Voluntarily Childless." *Population* 8: 1–25.

U.S. Department of Commerce. U.S. Census Bureau. 1992. *Current Population Reports,* series P-20-468, "Marital Status and Living Arrangements, March 1992." Washington: U.S. Government Printing Office.

U.S. Department of Labor. U.S. Bureau of Labor Statistics. 2001. *Current Population Survey,* technical paper 63RV, "Design and Methodology." Washington: U.S. Department of Commerce.

Van Katwijk, Cornelis, and Louis L. H. Peeters. 1998. "Clinical Aspects of Pregnancy After the Age of Thirty-five Years: A Review of the Literature." *Human Reproduction Update* 4: 185–94.

Van Velsor, Ellen, and Angela M. O'Rand. 1984. "Family Life Cycle, Work Career Patterns, and Women's Wages at Midlife." *Journal of Marriage and the Family* 46(2): 365–73.

VandenHeuvel, Audrey V. 1988. "The Timing of Parenthood and Intergenerational Relations." *Journal of Marriage and the Family* 50(2): 483–91.

Ventura, Stephanie J., and Christine A. Bachrach. 2000. *Nonmarital Childbearing in the United States, 1940 to 1999.* National Vital Statistics Reports 48(16). Hyattsville, Md.: National Center for Health Statistics.

Walter, Carolyn A. 1986. *The Timing of Motherhood.* Lexington, Mass.: D. C. Heath.

White, Emily. 1987. "Projected Changes in Breast Cancer Incidence Due to the Trend Toward Delayed Childbearing." *American Journal of Public Health* 77(4): 495–97.

Wilkie, Jane Riblett. 1981. "The Trend Toward Delayed Parenthood." *Journal of Marriage and the Family* 43(3): 583–91.

Windridge, K. C., and J. C. Berryman. 1999. "Women's Experiences of Giving Birth After Age Thirty-five." *Birth: Issues in Prenatal Care* 26(1): 16–23.

Wright, P. Jeffrey, Scott W. Henggeler, and Lisa Craig. 1986. "Problems in Paradise? A Longitudinal Examination of the Transition to Adulthood." *Journal of Applied Developmental Psychology* 7(3): 277–91.

Wu, Zheng. 1999. "Premarital Cohabitation and the Timing of First Marriage." *Canadian Review of Sociology and Anthropology* 36(1): 109–27.

Yarrow, Andrew L. 1991. *Latecomers: Children of Parents over Thirty-five.* New York: Free Press.

Yuan, W., F. H. Steffensen, G. L. Nielsen, M. Moller, J. Olsen, and H. T. Sorensen. 2000. "A Population-Based Cohort Study of Birth and Neonatal Outcome in Older Primipara." *International Journal of Gynecology and Obstetrics* 68(2): 113–18.

Chapter 3

Neighborhoods, Poverty, and Children's Well-Being

Anne R. Pebley and Narayan Sastry

Income inequality in the United States increased between 1970 and 2000 (Danziger and Gottschalk 1995; DeNavas-Walt, Cleveland, and Roemer 2001). For example, the percentage share of all household income earned by the top 25 percent of the population increased from 43 percent in 1970 to almost 50 percent in 2000 (DeNavas-Walt, Cleveland, and Raemer 2001, table C). This volume examines the consequences of rising income inequality for social and political inequalities in American society. One mechanism through which rising income inequality may have affected social inequality is by increasing residential segregation by income—and also by ethnicity as a consequence, since ethnic minorities make up a disproportionately large share of the poor. In other words, poor and affluent Americans and Americans of different ethnic backgrounds may have become increasingly likely to live in different neighborhoods.

Susan Mayer (2001) shows that rising income inequality did indeed contribute to the increase in residential segregation by income and ethnicity between 1970 and 1990. During this period the poor were increasingly concentrated into urban neighborhoods that were largely populated by other poor people and ethnic minorities (Wilson 1987, 1996; Massey and Eggers 1990; Massey and Denton 1993; Jargowsky 1997). Although the increases in residential segregation by ethnicity and income appear to have leveled off between 1990 and 2000, residential segregation remained at high levels in 2000 (Logan et al. 2001; Mare and Cort 2003).

Residential segregation increases the exposure of poor and ethnic minority individuals to the social problems that characterize high-poverty neighborhoods. Numerous studies have shown that problems such as poor health status, lagging school performance, behavior problems, substance abuse, early sex and parenthood, delinquency, and violence are geographically clustered in concentrated-poverty neighborhoods.[1]

Residential segregation can also play an important role in the intergenerational transmission of poverty if growing up in a poor neighborhood negatively affects children's social and behavioral development and opportunities for success. There is a solid basis in social theory for the idea that social environments, including home, school, peers, and neighborhoods, strongly influence children's development (see, for example, Bronfenbrenner 1986; Coleman 1988; Wilson 1987, 1996). However, prior to Christopher Jencks and Susan Mayer's influential review in 1990, there was little persuasive evidence that neighborhood conditions are causally related to child outcomes, and, if so, exactly how and why.

In the last decade a tidal wave of new "neighborhood effects" studies has appeared (see figure 1 in Sampson, Morenoff, and Gannon-Rowley 2002), some of which employ novel methodological approaches and make theoretical advances. The best of these new studies provide stronger evidence of neighborhood effects on children that are not due to selectivity or family characteristics (see, for example, Del Conte and Kling 2001; Aaronson, 1997, 1998; Solon, Page, and Duncan 2000). Nonetheless, Greg Duncan and Stephen Raudenbush (2001, 107) recently concluded that "the task of securing precise, robust and unbiased estimates of neighborhood effects has proved remarkably difficult."

In this chapter, we examine recent research in the area of neighborhood effects on children's development. We begin by reviewing the literature on the mechanisms through which neighborhoods may influence child development. Then we consider four issues that are fundamental to neighborhood effects research: the definition of "neighborhood"; the aspects of neighborhood environments that are important and how they should be measured; neighborhood selection; and children's residential mobility. Next, we assess recent empirical work on neighborhood effects. Recent reviews by Robert Sampson et al. (2002), Donna Ginther et al. (2000), Greg Duncan and Stephen Raudenbush (1999, 2001), and Tama Leventhal and Jeanne Brooks-Gunn (2000) catalog studies since 1990 and provide thorough reviews of their results. Rather than duplicate their efforts, we briefly summarize and compare their conclusions and then focus on the results of selected studies that provide novel approaches or insights. The final section of the chapter summarizes the current state of knowledge about poor neighborhoods and their role in the intergenerational transmission of poverty.

WHY WOULD NEIGHBORHOODS AFFECT CHILDREN'S WELL-BEING?

Research on neighborhood effects suggests that neighborhood characteristics such as poverty, crime, and residential turnover influence several interrelated aspects of the neighborhood environment that, in turn, affect families and children. These mechanisms can be summarized in four categories: child and family-related institutions; social organization and interaction; normative environment; and labor and marriage markets. We will briefly describe each of these.

Child and family-related institutions include schools, child care providers, public libraries, recreational programs and activities (such as music lessons, youth organizations, sports activities, arts and theater activities, and mentoring programs), parks, religious institutions, and social service providers. These institutions play a vital role in the general process of socialization, but many also impart important skills and provide specific services. While the availability and quality of these institutions may be affected directly by public policy (for example, by school improvement programs in poorer neighborhoods), they are also likely to be determined by neighborhood socioeconomic characteristics (Jencks and Mayer 1990; Aber et al. 1997). For example, child care centers and after-school programs may be more readily available, hire better staff, and provide better service in more affluent or well-educated neighborhoods, because residents demand it and can afford to pay for it. As described later, more socially organized neighborhoods may also be able to demand better institutions through collective action and the political process, even if income and educational levels are low. Poorer neighborhoods may be worse off than others not only because they have weaker institutions but also because the greater needs of families are likely to overtax the existing institutions (Aber et al. 1997).

Neighborhood *social organization and interaction* has recently received considerable attention in research on neighborhood effects. Social disorganization theory suggests that some neighborhood characteristics (such as poverty, ethnic heterogeneity, high residential turnover rates, low homeownership rates, and concentration of recent immigrants) make it harder for residents to establish social ties and agree on the values needed to exercise social control and work together on common goals. As a result, socially disorganized neighborhoods are more difficult, dangerous, and stressful places to live. Parents and children in these neighborhoods are both more likely to participate in deviant behavior (delinquency, crime, violence, substance abuse) and to suffer the consequences of this behavior in others (Shaw and McKay 1969; Sampson, Morenoff, and Gannon-Rowley 2002). Sampson and his colleagues (Sampson, Morenoff, and Earls 1999; Sampson, Morenoff, and Gannon-Rowley 2002) argue that neighborhood collective efficacy—that is, shared expectations and the involvement of neighborhood residents in active support and social control of children—is key to a positive neighborhood environment for children. In neighborhoods with higher collective efficacy, residents are more likely to monitor and, when necessary, correct children's behavior. They are also more likely to work together on neighborhood problems and to build and maintain strong local institutions.

Two other theoretical perspectives—William Julius Wilson's (1987, 1996) collective socialization model and James Coleman's (1988) social capital theory—suggest related ways in which neighborhood social interaction may be important for children. Collective socialization models posit that neighborhood adults play an important role by monitoring children's behavior (as Sampson and his colleagues emphasize) and by providing role models. For example, Wilson argues that the selective out-migration of middle-class professionals from African American inner-city neighborhoods has resulted in fewer positive role models for the children in those neighborhoods. Social capital models suggest that the key elements are the dense and overlapping social ties among adults and children. In neighborhoods with more social capital, children know that they will be held accountable for their actions and that they can rely on neighborhood adults for support. However, as Wilson (1996) and Sampson, Morenoff, and Earls (1999) note, high levels of social capital can facilitate the enforcement of *both* negative and positive norms and behavior. Wilson (1996, 62) points out, for example, that in neighborhoods "characterized by high levels of individual and family involvement in aberrant behavior," a high degree of social integration among adults can in fact help to create and reinforce problem behavior among children.

Connections with the world outside the neighborhood may also be important. Especially in disadvantaged neighborhoods, extralocal social ties can provide access to information about, or assistance with, opportunities, services, or normative feedback from those who move in other social circles (Coleman 1988; Stack 1974; Edin 1991; Tigges, Browne, and Green 1998). Melvin Oliver's (1988) study of social networks in urban African American communities in Los Angeles shows that extralocal social ties vary considerably among neighborhoods. He concludes that in poor neighborhoods the lack of outside social ties may be a significant disadvantage. In recent decades urban sociologists have argued that despatialized social networks have displaced the role of neighborhoods in urban life; neighborhoods are increasingly *un*important, they argue, in individuals' lives (South 2001; Fischer 1984; Wellman 1999). However, Barry Wellman (1999, 27), a proponent of this view, admits that "communities have not totally lost their domestic roots. . . . Local relationships are necessary for domestic safety, controlling actual land use, and quickly getting goods and services." He shows, for example, that much of Toronto residents' telephone contact is with neighbors rather than with extralocal ties (Wellman 1996). As Sampson and his colleagues

(2002) point out, social ties among neighbors do not need to be strong or close in order to be effective. In fact, social disorganization theory suggests that neighborhood environments depend on weak and limited ties among neighbors who share a minimum level of trust, agreement on basic standards, and willingness to live by and enforce those standards. Nonetheless, the relative importance for children's development of urban neighborhood environments versus social networks is an empirical question for which we do not yet have complete answers.

The economic models suggest that *labor and marriage markets* are key elements in neighborhood effects on families and children (Duncan and Hoffman 1990; Haveman and Wolfe 1994). Local labor markets, marriage markets, and, in some neighborhoods, the illicit economy provide constraints and opportunities for neighborhood residents. Market conditions affect adults and adolescents most directly. However, by affecting their *parents'* probabilities of employment and marriage, local markets may have indirect effects on younger children. For example, in neighborhoods with poor labor markets, higher rates of parental unemployment may affect children by increasing stress on parents, depressing household income, and creating a more stressful home environment.

Neighborhood characteristics, such as high levels of marriage, are thought to affect children's well-being both directly, by providing a positive normative environment, strong institutions, effective monitoring and social control, and a supportive climate for children, and indirectly, through effects on parents and the home environment. As noted earlier, neighborhood labor market and marriage market conditions can affect parents' income, family structure, and the home environment. Neighborhoods may also directly affect parenting behavior and family dynamics (Aneshensel and Sucoff 1996; Klebanov et al. 1997; Coulton 1996; Korbin and Coulton 1997). For example, parents in extremely disadvantaged neighborhoods are more likely to exhibit more punitive, authoritarian, and coercive parenting styles and to use corporal punishment (McLoyd 1990; Sampson and Laub 1994) as well as to withdraw emotionally from their children (Klebanov, Brooks-Gunn, and Duncan 1994). These responses are likely to have detrimental consequences for children's emotional, cognitive, and social development, and those consequences may later be reinforced by other negative aspects of neighborhood life.

Several theorists emphasize the key role of the *normative environment* itself in linking neighborhood compositional characteristics (such as poverty or high turnover rates) and child outcomes. Neighborhood norms may be a consequence of the characteristics of the people who live in the neighborhood—their income level, ethnic background, education, or immigrant experience. Those norms may also be affected by the social organization and interaction and by marriage and labor markets, as described earlier. The central idea in this literature is that the greater the concentration of like-minded people, the stronger the normative climate and the greater the exposure of neighborhood residents to these norms. For example, black children in poor inner-city neighborhoods may be more likely to be exposed to social problems, because the extreme concentration of poverty in inner-city African American neighborhoods since 1970 has created negative normative environments in which behavior considered negative by the middle class is reinforced and valued (Massey, Gross, and Eggers 1991; Massey and Denton 1993; Wilson, 1987, 1996; Fordham and Ogbu 1986). However, this process is not necessarily limited to concentrated-poverty neighborhoods or to negative outcomes—for example, some observers have argued that concentrated immigrant communities in Los Angeles can provide supportive climates for social mobility (Waldinger 1996). The "epidemic" hypothesis (Crane 1991; Case and Katz 1991) is a specific version of theories about normative environments. Jonathan Crane (1991) argues that concentrated-poverty neighborhoods dramatically increase adolescents' exposure to problem behavior and negative norms through contacts with peers. Epidemics of social problems can occur once neighborhoods reach a critically high level of negative social behaviors.

ALTERNATIVE APPROACHES TO DEFINING NEIGHBORHOODS

"Neighborhood" is a relatively flexible and amorphous concept that is generally defined spatially. Our review of neighborhood-effects mechanisms suggests that neighborhoods can be viewed in at least two ways. The first view is that neighborhoods are spaces in which residents are exposed on a regular basis to specific types of people, individual and collective behaviors, and social and physical environments, purely because of where they live. For example, many hypotheses suggest that children in poor neighborhoods are disadvantaged because of the greater risk of *exposure* to negative environments and social problems. A second view is that neighborhoods are places in which individuals can develop neighborly relationships and collectively influence the social and physical environment. In other words, neighborhoods can be defined as geographic areas for which individuals have a sense of attachment, ownership, or belonging. These two views of "neighborhood" can yield substantially different definitions of neighborhood boundaries.

Social scientists have defined neighborhoods in several ways. Early social ecologists saw urban neighborhoods as organic or "natural" entities created as a result of the isolation of small geographic areas by physical barriers, such as railroads, rivers, and boulevards (Burgess 1930) and/or through competition over land for residential and commercial use (Sampson, Morenoff, and Gannon-Rowley 2002; Park, Burgess, and McKenzie 1967). Over time these neighborhoods develop distinct identities, including names, which in turn influence the characteristics of in- and out-migrants to and from the neighborhood. Most cities and towns have at least rough definitions of the boundaries of neighborhoods and some consensus about their names: for example, the Lower East Side in Manhattan, Hyde Park in Chicago, and Pico-Union in Los Angeles. Empirical studies by Albert Hunter (1974, 1975) and Avery Guest, Barrett Lee, and Lynn Staeheli (1982) in Chicago, Rochester, and Seattle have shown that these neighborhood names (and presumably identities) can be quite persistent over time. However, traditional neighborhoods are rarely used in neighborhood-effects studies because their boundaries are often ambiguous and change over time. Moreover, traditional neighborhoods may be considerably larger and more diverse than the "neighborhoods" whose conditions are hypothesized to affect children's outcomes.

Almost all neighborhood-effects studies are based on census tracts, zip codes, other administrative units, or aggregates of these units. The primary reason is that most studies are based on census, vital statistics, and administrative data on neighborhood characteristics that are generally available only for census geographies (blocks, block groups, tracts, metropolitan statistical areas) and for zip codes, cities, and towns. Census tracts and block groups were developed by the U.S. Census Bureau and local collaborators to approximate, at least when initially drawn, ecologically meaningful areas. However, researchers often argue that census and other administrative geographies may be less salient to families and children than geographies defined in other ways (Burton, Price-Spratlen, and Spencer 1997; Coulton et al. 2001; Duncan and Raudenbush 2001; Elliott and Huizinga 1990).

Several alternatives to administrative units have been proposed for neighborhood studies. The first approach is to use residents' own definitions of their neighborhood boundaries based on mapping exercises or questions on neighborhood boundaries or size (Coulton et al. 2001; Lee and Campbell 1997; Guest and Lee 1984).[2] For example, Claudia Coulton and her colleagues (2001) asked a sample of 140 respondents living in seven census block groups in Cleveland to draw the boundaries of their neighborhood on a map of the eight-mile radius surrounding their home. The maps were subsequently digitized using mapping software, and the maps of respondents within each block group were compared. The results showed that the average area in respondents' neighborhood maps was about equal to the average size of census tracts. However, the boundaries of resident-defined neighborhoods were quite different from those of the census tracts in which they lived. Using residents' consensus neighborhood boundaries often yielded considerably different average neighborhood characteristics than using census tract boundaries.[3] Coulton and her colleagues also found substantial within-block group variation in all dimensions of neighborhood definition that they examined, and that made it even more difficult to arrive at a single resident-determined definition.

Although the authors conclude that their mapping approach is feasible, they also caution that implementation is difficult. The level of intra-neighborhood agreement on boundaries varies considerably among neighborhoods and is likely to depend on the spatial dispersion of the sample interviewed. For example, a sample of respondents in a census block group is likely to yield more tightly overlapping responses than a sample dispersed across a tract. Furthermore, while this approach is feasible for a limited number of spatially separate neighborhoods, it would be less feasible for defining boundaries for all neighborhoods in a large metropolitan area, because of the expense and the extensive overlap of resident-defined boundaries in adjacent areas.[4] Resident-defined boundaries combine the dual views of neighborhoods described earlier: while residents' responses are likely to delineate areas over which they feel some control and attachment, they are also likely to be affected by the frequency of their exposure to areas around their home. For example, whether a particular block is included in an individual's "neighborhood" may be determined by how frequently he or she travels in that direction.

A second approach comes from the geographic literature on the space and time dimensions of human activities (Newsome, Walcott, and Smith 1998; Rindfuss et al. 2002; Crawford 2002). Torsten Hägerstrand (1970) originally proposed the idea that an individual's activities could be seen as a series of movements through space and time. Subsequent research has modeled these "activity spaces" for individuals, social groups, and local areas. Simpler strategies use information about average travel time in a particular location to draw areas such as radial buffers around a centroid. The radial buffers represent the average distance that can be traveled in a reasonable amount of time to carry out regular activities. For example, Ronald Rindfuss and his colleagues (2002) use radial buffers around rural Thai villages to represent the average distance a farmer is likely to walk to his fields each day. In complex urban areas another approach is to use information about average travel time on specific segments of specific streets and highways to draw time-specific areas around individual residences. For example, in another paper (Pebley, Sastry, and Zonta 2002) we have examined areas that are within fifteen minutes' walking distance in each direction of respondents' homes in Los Angeles based on average travel times. Unlike circular radial buffers, these spaces are irregular in shape because travel times along each radius can vary.

Other geographic approaches describe the regular travel patterns of individuals using other shapes, including prisms and ellipses (Newsome, Walcott, and Smith 1998). For a sample of individuals living in the same geographic area (for example, a block group or tract) the shapes describing each individual's travel path can be superimposed to provide a measure of the spread of the sample members' regular activities. For example, we can examine the spatial patterns of children living in a particular block group as they travel to day care, to school, or to a place of worship, go shopping, or engage in leisure activities. Geographic approaches focused on activity spaces reflect not only the area immediately around families' dwellings but also other neighborhoods to which residents are regularly exposed, such as the area between a child's street and a local school or park. Thus, these approaches are more consonant with the concept of neighborhoods as the places to which children are regularly exposed.

Rick Grannis (1998) proposes a third and very different strategy. Following in the tradition of urban social ecologists (for example, Jacobs 1961; Burgess 1930; Park, Burgess, and MeKenzie 1976), he suggests that social interaction, at least in urban areas, is affected by the physical design of city streets rather than by spatial proximity alone. In particular, he argues that small residential (or tertiary) streets are key to social interaction among neighbors. Grannis divides the urban landscape into tertiary street communities (t-communities) in which "every household . . . is reachable from every other household by only using tertiary streets" (1533). In t-communities, Grannis argues, residents can have neighborly relationships because they encounter each other regularly. In census tract or other units, by contrast, residents often do not even encounter each other because they have to cross busy streets or other obstacles. Grannis's analysis shows that residential segregation patterns by race in central Los Angeles and San Francisco are more closely approximated by t-communities than by census tracts. His definition of t-communities fits squarely with the concept of neighborhoods as spaces in which residents can interact and exercise some control over their local environment.

All of these approaches to neighborhood measurement seek to establish a single set of neighborhood boundaries, either for specific neighborhoods or for an entire landscape (for example, all neighborhoods in San Francisco). Yet common sense suggests that a single, "crisp" set of neighborhood boundaries often does not adequately describe individuals' experience of neighborhood life. Not only do definitions of neighborhood boundaries vary among individuals living on the same block (Lee, Campbell, and Miller 1991; Guest and Lee 1984; Logan and Collver 1983; Coulton et al. 2001), but they also may vary for a single household or individual over time (for example, as children age) and may depend on context. For instance, a person may define only individuals living on his block as neighbors, but define his neighborhood as a larger space when determining whether he works or shops in his neighborhood. From residents' perspective, the "neighborhood" is probably best described as an area relatively close to their home with fuzzy boundaries that may expand or shrink depending on context and personal experience. Moreover, suggest Sampson and his colleagues (1999), there are important spatial externalities to positive neighborhood social interaction. Specifically, they show that, regardless of their own population composition, neighborhoods benefit from being close to other neighborhoods with high levels of collective efficacy. Both the fuzziness of neighborhood definitions and the potential importance of spatial externalities suggest that research based on a fixed set of neighborhood boundaries may be missing much of the action.

Several promising strategies for future neighborhood-effects research do not require the assumption that neighborhood boundaries are fixed. One straightforward, albeit data-intensive, approach is to model neighborhood effects using a decay function in which each child's outcomes are a function of the characteristics of all points in the area surrounding his or her home. (These points may extend out for several miles in each direction.) The effects of the characteristics at a given point are assumed be weaker the further away in distance or travel time the point is from the child's home or block. Thomas Crawford (2002) proposes using fuzzy set theory and grade of member of membership models to define the fuzzy neighborhoods surrounding a central area of residences.[5] In these models, the grade of membership score reflects the probability that a point or area is within the "neighborhood" for a given group of residents (for example, the residents of a particular block). A simpler alternative is to examine the effects of spatially lagged characteristics of neighborhoods that form concentric rings around the study neighborhood, beginning with all adjacent neighborhoods.

In summary, the theoretical literature suggests that neighborhoods can be viewed both as: (a) spaces that define residents' exposure to specific types of people, individual and collective behaviors, and social and physical environments and (b) places to which individuals can have a sense of attachment, ownership, belonging, and control. Neighborhood-effects research has relied almost exclusively on predefined administrative boundaries that may have limited its scope for uncovering and understanding neighborhood effects. Several novel approaches described in this section accord more closely with theoretical conceptualizations of neighborhoods and may yield clearer findings in future research. It is important to note that administrative units will remain a key element of neighborhood-effects research because census and other data are primarily available for these units. However, they should be viewed as a starting point, not an ending point. The novel approaches described here and standard geographic information systems methods allow researchers to estimate neighborhood characteristics for spaces that more closely approximate the roles they play in daily life.

MEASURING NEIGHBORHOOD CHARACTERISTICS

A significant limitation of almost all neighborhood-effects studies is that they use compositional characteristics (such as income, ethnicity, unemployment rate, and household structure) as proxies for the social mechanisms through which neighborhood effects are thought to operate. For example, while many studies show a strong correlation between neighborhood poverty rates and poor child outcomes, they provide little evidence on *how* this effect occurs because they do not measure the intervening mechanism. To study collective socialization models, for example, one must have information on aspects of neighborhood social organization such as: the density of social ties and levels of interaction among neighbors; neighborhood norms about monitoring others' children and about acceptable behavior; the availability of successful role models and neighborhood leaders; and the extent of residents' social ties outside the neighborhood. Institutional models suggest that the availability and quality of social services directed to children and families (schools, day care, after-school and recreational programs; housing, food, and cash assistance) are also likely to account for part of observed neighborhood effects.

Because most of these characteristics are not readily available from census, vital statistics, or other administrative sources, they must generally be collected by researchers themselves through interviews or observation. There is a growing literature on assessing the social and physical dimensions of neighborhood context (see, for example, Burton, Price-Stratlen, and Spencer 1997; Kingston et al. 1999; Caughy, O'Campo, and Patterson 2001; Cook, Shagle, and Degirmencioglu 1997; Diez Roux et al. 2001). Among the most influential and theoretically grounded is a set of approaches developed by Robert Sampson and Stephen Raudenbush and their colleagues in the Project on Human Development in Chicago Neighborhoods (Raudenbush and Sampson 1999; Sampson and Raudenbush 1999).

The PHDCN uses two methods of assessing neighborhood environments: a survey of neighborhood residents exclusively designed to measure neighborhood-level characteristics and systematic social observation (SSO)—that is, direct observation of neighborhoods by trained observers. The neighborhood residents survey was undertaken in all 343 PHDCN-defined neighborhood clusters in Chicago. In each cluster, approximately 25 adult respondents were interviewed. They were asked about their neighborhoods, including items for scales designed to capture key theoretical concepts such as informal social control, social cohesion, and trust.[6] The research group then constructed neighborhood-level measures by aggregating responses by neighborhood. This strategy increases the precision of estimates because the large sample size in each neighborhood minimizes sampling variability.[7] The PHDCN neighborhood survey sample was also selected independently of the sample for the household survey. This independence eliminates potential contamination between individuals' reports of their own and their neighborhood's characteristics, but it requires that two separate, large-scale surveys be conducted—an expensive proposition.[8]

The PHDCN scales appear to be closely related to neighborhood compositional characteristics in Chicago, although not always in the ways that the literature would predict. Sampson, Raudenbush, and Earls (1997) show that the measure of collective efficacy (a scale based on the social cohesion, informal social control, and trust measures) is strongly associated with concentrated disadvantage, immigrant concentration, and residential stability, as social disorganization theory predicts. Collective efficacy also accounts for a substantial portion of the relationship between residential stability and disadvantage, on the one hand, and neighborhood violence, on the other. As the authors recognize, causal direction in these relationships is unclear because their analysis is cross-sectional. Sampson, Morenoff, and Earls (1999) examine the aspects of their collective efficacy measures that theory suggests would be most important for children. Specifically, they reorganize their measures into scales representing child-centered social control, reciprocated exchange, and intergenerational closure. Their results indicate that intergenerational closure and neighborly exchange are in fact *not* related to concentrated disadvantage, as the literature on neighborhood poverty would suggest. Instead, they find that these aspects of collective efficacy are related to concentrated affluence, residential stability, and low population density, consistent with the research described later in this chapter.

A second strategy employed in the PHDCN was direct observation by trained observers (SSO). The advantage of direct observation is elimination of the subjective nature of residents' reports and of an unknown amount of variation in the quality of these reports among neighborhoods.[9] PHDCN staff videotaped both sides of the streets in all sampled Chicago neighborhoods using a specially equipped vehicle traveling at five miles per hour. These staff members also recorded physical and social observations on each block using a standard form. The videotapes were subsequently coded using standard forms by independent raters. The objective was to code specific signs of physical and social disorganization, including trash on the sidewalks and street, graffiti, broken windows, poorly maintained buildings, gangs hanging out, and drug deals. Raudenbush and Sampson's (1999) results show that measures derived from these observations are generally strongly related to measures of social disorder from the neighborhood survey described earlier and from census and administrative data.

Although videotaping and subsequent independent rater coding can be extremely expensive, surveys that involve in-person visits by listing teams or interviewers can incorporate direct observation methods by these field staff (with appropriate training and standardization methods) at a more reasonable cost. The Los Angeles Family and Neighborhood Survey (L.A.FANS) conducted systematic social observations using a modified version of the PHDCN observation forms. Three trained observers independently walked each block face included in the survey and completed check sheets, reflecting the social and physical charac-

TABLE 3.1   *Selected Characteristics of L.A.FANS Neighborhoods, by Neighborhood Poverty*

Neighborhood Characteristic	Very Poor Stratum	Poor Stratum	Low-Income Nonpoor Stratum	High-Income Nonpoor Stratum	All Tracts in Los Angeles County
Census					
Mean household income (1990)	$18,250	$26,060	$38,330	$62,510	$38,263
Homeownership (percentage of					
dwellings owner-occupied)	24%	36%	52%	78%	50%
Ethnicity					
Latino	69	67	31	14	38
White	4	11	40	60	34
African American	16	6	8	4	11
Asian and Pacific Islander	4	9	16	17	12
Population density (units)	22,501	17,790	10,463	5,470	11,969
Single female-headed households, with					
children as percentage of all house-					
holds with children	16%	11%	8%	4%	8%
Systematic social observations					
Trash index (high = more trash)	1.4	0.6	−0.9	−1.4	—
Housing quality index (high = better)	−1.2	−0.4	0.6	1.2	—
Social environment					
Social cohesion	15.8	16.4	17.7	18.9	
Collective efficacy	25.6	26.8	28.8	30.9	—
Child-centered social control	9.8	10.4	11.0	11.9	—
Trust	3.2	3.3	3.7	4.0	—
Number of voluntary associations	0.2	0.3	0.5	0.9	—

Source: Authors' tabulations of the Los Angeles Family and Neighborhood Survey, 2000 to 2001.
Note: Entries are means across all tracts in each neighborhood poverty stratum. All census figures are for 2000 unless otherwise indicated. SSO indices are the tract means of first principal components of an analysis based on all observations for each block in L.A.FANS.

teristics of the block. Table 3.1 shows the variation in these SSO observations by neighborhood income status.[10] The first panel of the table ("Census") presents socioeconomic compositional data from the census. In the second panel ("Systematic social observations"), we show two direct observation indicators, trash and housing quality; these are the tract means of first principal components of an analysis based on all observations for each block in L.A.FANS, averaged across all blocks in each income category. The third panel ("Social environment") presents several PHDCN-based indicators of the neighborhood social environment drawn from interviews with a random sample of adults in each neighborhood.

The L.A.FANS SSO results show that lower-income neighborhoods in Los Angeles have consistently poorer housing quality and a more disordered environment (more trash, drug paraphernalia, broken bottles) compared with the others. However, these indicators and others also show considerable variations *among* neighborhoods in each income group (not shown). For example, some poor neighborhoods in the sample have considerably better housing quality and are much better cared for than others. The third panel includes four scales drawn from the PHDCN (Sampson, Morenoff, and Earls 1999) that were described earlier and a variable indicating the mean number of voluntary organizations to which respondents belong in the neighborhoods in each group. Because these scales are sums of Likert-type items, the values are not meaningful except in relative terms. In a simple analysis of variance, the differences between the four income groups for all variables are statistically significant.

In summary, there have been several recent developments in measuring neighborhood social and physical environments. For example, results from PHDCN and L.A.FANS suggest that both respondent perceptions of social interaction and direct observation of the social and physical environment are significantly related to neighborhood socioeconomic composition in cities as different as Chicago and Los Angeles.

Nonetheless, considerable work remains to be done in determining which aspects of neighborhood environments are most salient to family life and how these aspects can be measured most reliably. In particular, basic methodological studies using techniques such as cognitive interviewing, focus groups, and other qualitative techniques are required to determine how neighborhood residents interpret and respond to questions such as those in the PHDCN and other surveys. Another promising approach is to combine survey-based neighborhood studies with in-depth ethnographic studies of a subsample of the neighborhoods included in the larger study. Qualitative research conducted in the same neighborhoods included in major neighborhood surveys holds the promise of refining and extending our tools for neighborhood measurement.

NEIGHBORHOOD SELECTION

A serious problem in studying neighborhood effects on children's well-being is the potential endogeneity of neighborhood (and school) characteristics.[11] Endogenous characteristics are independent variables that may be correlated with unobserved factors not included in the model. In the case of neighborhood selection, the problem is that parents can choose the neighborhood in which they live but they can also affect children's development in many other ways. Thus, parents' attitudes about child development may affect both the type of neighborhood their children grow up in and other factors that affect their children's development, such as parenting and the home environment. Parents who move to help their children escape the influences of gang activity, drug use, teenage pregnancy, or crime, or who choose a neighborhood for the quality of its schools, may also be better parents in other ways. Other neighborhood attributes that may influence both parents' choice of where to live and children's behavior and development include the strength of neighborhood ties and characteristics of other families and children in the neighborhood. To the extent that neighborhood of residence is a choice, all neighborhood characteristics should be treated as endogenous. It is important, however, to understand the source of the endogeneity in order to identify appropriate analytic strategies.

Neighborhood attributes may be endogenous because place of residence is a choice variable and is determined in part by factors that also influence children's behavior and development. Thus, a common set of parent and family characteristics determines both children's behavior and development *and* neighborhood choice. Some of these characteristics, such as household income and parents' education, are measurable and can be controlled in models of children's behavior and development. However, some are unobserved and hence are picked up in the random component of statistical models, where correlation with included regressors—neighborhood characteristics—leads to biased and inconsistent estimates of all model parameters. As Greg Duncan and his colleagues explain (see, for example, Duncan, Connell, and Klebanov 1997), the problem of neighborhood selection is thus really one of omitted variables. Specific unobserved (omitted) parent and family factors are the parents' cognitive ability and family motivation and aspirations, which may influence the degree to which a family values its children's behavior and development (as well as its choice of place of residence).

If panel data are available, there are several statistical approaches to control for omitted/ unobserved child- or family-specific effects and hence to account for the potential endogeneity of neighborhood characteristics when studying their effects on children's behavior and development. For example, fixed-effects models have been used in the previous literature on neighborhoods effects, as described later. If the omitted variables (and their correlation with observed variables) are time-invariant, then each family or child can be used as its own control, by regressing changes in outcomes on changes in neighborhood characteristics. A second strategy is to use correlated random-effects models (for example, Chamberlain 1980, 1984). This is a more general approach than the fixed-effects models; it has all the strengths of these models but in addition allows researchers to examine the nature and strength of the association between unobserved heterogeneity and the regressors; permits the estimation of time-invariant covariates; and allows for possibly time-varying, unobserved heterogeneity—including changes over time in the correlation between the unobservables and the regressors.

A third approach for which panel data are helpful but not necessary is to use instrumental variables or, more generally, to undertake the joint estimation of child outcomes and neighborhood choice. The challenge is to find convincing instruments that are correlated with the neighborhood measures but uncorrelated with child- or family-level unobserved heterogeneity. For example, an analyst could assume that employment location is exogenous and that residential choice depends on neighborhood characteristics and on the commute to work. In that case, information on the availability of public transportation could provide instruments. However, previous neighborhood-effects studies have had a very difficult time identifying credible instruments, and this approach has only rarely been attempted.

Apart from statistical models that account for endogeneity, another strategy is to collect more extensive and reliable data on children, parents, and families. Improvements in measuring key variables can reduce the problem of neighborhood endogeneity considerably. As Duncan and Raudenbush (1999, 117) note, "The best non-experimental approach to the endogenous [neighborhood] membership problem is to locate data that measure crucial family and individual-level omitted variables." For example, important family characteristics to measure might include parental cognitive skills, attitudes toward child development, priorities and preferences for time use, and family dynamics. Although these variables are often omitted from surveys and their measurement is still rudimentary, neighborhood-effects studies could reduce the chance that their results are due to endogeneity and unobserved variables by making more intensive efforts to measure salient attributes of families and neighborhoods.

A final approach to overcome problems related to the endogeneity of neighborhood choice is social experiments. In theory, experiments have significant advantages over non-experimental research because they allow investigators to control unobserved heterogeneity through random assignment. As described later, the results of several recent experiments do suggest that moving from a poor to a better neighborhood leads to some improvement in adult and child outcomes. However, experiments also have some limitations. First, as the Moving To Opportunity (MTO) example shows, social experiments often suffer from unanticipated sources of heterogeneity that reduce the reliability of the results, such as the failure of some participants to accept the treatment offered and less than adequately implemented treatments. Second, experiments provide evidence on the existence and potential size of neighborhood evidence, but little information on how parents who are not involved in mobility programs choose neighborhoods and why neighborhoods may affect children's outcomes.[12]

CHILDREN'S RESIDENTIAL MOBILITY

Another important aspect of residential mobility for analyses of neighborhood effects is that many American children live in several different neighborhoods during childhood and some children move very frequently. For example, the March 2000 Current Population Survey results show that approximately 18 percent of children age zero to nineteen moved during the *single-year* period 1999 to 2000 (Schachter 2001, calculated from table B). Furthermore, this high annual rate is not primarily due to post–high school moves for older children: the mobility rates are highest for younger children (an average of 23 percent for one- to five-year-olds) and decline to 15 percent for ten- to nineteen-year-olds. These rates imply that many children move at least once, if not more often, during childhood. Yet most neighborhood-effects analyses examine only the association between characteristics of the neighborhood that children currently live in with developmental outcomes.[13]

As a consequence, analyses that relate the characteristics of the neighborhood that a child currently lives in (or a single neighborhood in the past) with current developmental outcomes may seriously misstate the size and direction of neighborhood effects for children who have lived in multiple neighborhoods. If children who move frequently live in the same type of neighborhood each time, it would be more tenable to use current neighborhood characteristics as a proxy for attributes of all their childhood neighborhoods.[14] However, there is substantial evidence that families often move in an effort to find better neighborhoods, schools, and housing for their children (Ludwig, Duncan, and Pinkston 2000; Ludwig, Ladd, and Duncan 2001; Furstenberg et al. 1999; Rossi 1955). This motivation for moving combined with increases in parents' income across the life cycle suggest that the quality of children's neighborhoods is likely to improve on average during childhood. Furthermore, siblings often differ in their exposure to neighborhoods depending on their birth order, as upwardly (or downwardly) mobile families move to better (or worse) neighborhoods over the parents' life cycle. The literature on residential mobility also suggests that some groups find upward residential mobility easier than other groups (Massey, Gross, and Shibuya 1994; Gramlich, Laren, and Sealand 1992; South and Crowder 1998; Crowder 2001). For example, Scott South and Kyle Crowder (1997a, 1997b, 1998) show that African American families are less likely to move to better neighborhoods than whites even holding constant socioeconomic status.

To provide credible estimates of neighborhood effects, analyses must consider not only the process of family selection into and out of neighborhoods but also the effects of residential mobility on the variety of neighborhoods in which many children live during childhood.

NEIGHBORHOOD-EFFECTS ANALYSES

The extensive neighborhood-effects literature published since 1990 has generally sought to answer one or more of the following three questions:

1. Are children who grow up in poor neighborhoods worse off than other children?

2. Are disparities in children's welfare by neighborhood poverty level due to differences in their families' characteristics, or do neighborhood conditions themselves play a role?

3. What mechanisms link concentrated-poverty neighborhoods to poorer outcomes for children?

Studies addressing these questions have generally been of two types. The largest group is non-experimental or observational studies, generally based on sample survey data. More recently, several experimental studies have assessed the consequences for poor families of moving into nonpoor neighborhoods. Both types of studies have usually sought to investigate the first two questions—whether children's outcomes differ by neighborhood characteristics and whether this variation persists if family attributes are held constant. A smaller number of studies have attempted to answer the third question by exploring the mechanisms that may link the characteristics of concentrated-poverty neighborhoods to poorer outcomes for children.

Recent reviews by psychologists, economists, and sociologists have thoroughly cataloged and critiqued this literature (Leventhal and Brooks-Gunn 2000; Ginter, Haveman, and Wolfe 2000; Duncan and Raudenbush 1999, 2001; Sampson, Morenoff, and Gannon-Rowley 2002). In this section, we draw on these critiques and our own reading of the literature to summarize the results of non-experimental research on neighborhood effects. We then consider more recent experimental studies.

Observational Studies

Observational studies are typically based on individual and household data from sample surveys linked with census data on the local areas (usually census tracts) in which children and families live. These studies have employed a wide range of study designs, survey datasets, theoretical approaches, neighborhood, family, and outcome measures, and statistical methods. Here we summarize the results of this very diverse group of studies.

First, basic descriptive analyses have shown that many dimensions of children's well-being (including teen sexual behavior, substance abuse, mental health, cognitive and achievement scores, high school completion, youth violence, delinquency, and child abuse) vary significantly by neighborhood income levels and, less often, by other neighborhood characteristics such as residential stability, high school completion rate, female headship, social disorder, and social cohesion. Children and teens living in poorer neighborhoods generally have worse outcomes.

Second, a substantial part of the variation in children's outcomes by neighborhood income level is accounted for by differences in family income and other family characteristics. In other words, when family characteristics such as income, family structure, and parents' educational attainment are held constant, the relationship between children's outcomes and neighborhood income levels is substantially reduced. Moreover, Ginter and her colleagues (2000) show that the more complete the set of family characteristics that is held constant, the greater the decline in the size and significance of coefficients on neighborhood variables. They conclude that the results of many neighborhood-effects studies are likely due, at least in part, to omitted variables at the family level. Nonetheless, these researchers and others find that some neighborhood characteristics retain significant effects even after extensive controls for family and individual characteristics are introduced.[15]

Third, the size of neighborhood effects on children's outcomes is generally modest and considerably smaller than the effects of family and individual characteristics. For example, in studies reviewed by Leventhal and Brooks-Gunn (2000), neighborhood characteristics accounted for 5 to 10 percent of the variance in children's outcomes. Duncan and Raudenbush

(2001, 132) argue, however, that "the degree of neighborhood-based 'action' may still be large enough to be consistent with cost-effective, neighborhood based interventions."

Fourth, results from these studies, not surprisingly, suggest that the effects of neighborhood conditions (net of family SES) vary by type of child outcome investigated (behavior problems, school readiness, teen sex, delinquency) and by the child's age, ethnicity, and gender. For example, Brooks-Gunn, Duncan, and their colleagues examined an extensive set of child development indicators across a broader age range (Brooks-Gunn, Duncan, and Aber 1997). Duncan and Raudenbush (1999) summarize the results as follows: (1) neighborhood effects appear in the preschool years but are most consistent for school-age children; (2) neighborhood effects appear to be stronger for cognitive and achievement outcomes than for behavior and mental health measures; and (3) white children appear to be more affected by neighborhood conditions than African American children. Sampson and his colleagues (2002) argue that the evidence of neighborhood effects on crime rates is stronger than the evidence for other types of outcomes.

Fifth, several studies suggest that the presence of affluent neighbors has a greater impact on children's outcomes than neighborhood poverty (Brooks-Gunn, Duncan, and Aber 1997; Duncan and Raudenbush 1999; Sampson, Morenoff, and Earls 1999). However, Ginter and her colleagues (2000) dispute this conclusion. Their reanalysis of the PSID data includes variables indicating the percentage of households with high and low income as well as the income of the child's family relative to that of other families in the neighborhood. Their results suggest that "the income of the family relative to that of its neighbors—rather than the extent to which the neighborhood is populated by high (low) income families— may be the more relevant consideration" (628). This is an important topic for future neighborhood-effects research.

Sixth, reliable methods for assessing neighborhood social and physical environments are not well developed and tested. Those studies that have examined intervening processes have investigated a broad range of potential mechanisms. For example, Sampson and his colleagues (Sampson et al. 1997; Sampson and Raudenbush 1999; Morenoff, Sampson, and Raudenbush 2001) show that informal social control, collective efficacy, and social ties are significantly related to outcomes such as delinquency, crime, and homicide. Scott South and Eric Baumer's (2000; Baumer and South 2001) results suggest that peer attitudes and behaviors account for a substantial proportion of neighborhood effects on adolescents, particularly teen parenthood and sexual activity. Dawn Upchurch and her colleagues (1999) and Carol Aneshensel and Clea Sucoff (1996) show that perceived "ambient hazards" (for example, neighborhood disorder, disorganization, and threats) are an important mediating factor between neighborhood disadvantage and teen sexual behavior and mental health.

Finally, a few studies have tackled endogenous residential choice using non-experimental data and statistical models. William Evans, Wallace Oates, and Robert Schwab (1992), Anne Case and Lawrence Katz (1991), and Eric Foster and Sara McLanahan (1996) used instrumental variables to eliminate the correlation between unobserved parent attributes and neighborhood variables. However, finding credible and viable instruments is a very difficult task. Instead, Daniel Aaronson (1997, 1998) and Robert Plotnick and Saul Hoffman (1996) have used sibling fixed effects in analyses of educational attainment, adult economic status, and teen pregnancy in the PSID. While Aaronson found significant neighborhood effects once unobserved family characteristics were controlled, Plotnick and Hoffman did not. Aaronson (1998) suggests that the difference in results lies in the types of sibling pairs included and the measurement of neighborhood variables. Gary Solon, Marianne Page, and

Greg Duncan (2000) take another approach: they compare correlations for sibling pairs with correlations among neighbors within sampling clusters in the PSID. Their results suggest that the size of neighborhood effects is small and considerably smaller than family effects.

Experimental Studies

More recently, several experimental or quasi-experimental studies have attempted to tackle the issue of endogenous neighborhood selection. The initial effort was the Gautreaux Program, in which low-income African American families from Chicago housing projects were given Section 8 housing vouchers that could be used only in predominantly white or multi-ethnic neighborhoods (typically in suburban areas). The control group was Section 8 voucher recipients who used their vouchers in the city of Chicago. James Rosenbaum (1991, 1995) shows that children who move to the suburbs rather than cities are less likely to drop out of school and more likely to attend college, have a job, and receive higher pay. However, the study has several methodological limitations, including self-selection into the study and substantial sample attrition.

The Moving To Opportunity (MTO) experiment was a more carefully designed outgrowth of the Gautreaux Program developed by the U.S. Department of Housing and Urban Development (HUD) and implemented by local public housing authorities and nonprofits between 1994 and 1999 in Baltimore, Boston, Chicago, Los Angeles, and New York (Brennan 2002). Participants were volunteers from very low-income families with children in public housing or Section 8 project-based housing in inner-city, high-poverty neighborhoods. Each participant family was assigned randomly to one of three groups: the *experimental group,* which received vouchers that could be used only in low-poverty areas plus counseling and assistance locating housing; the *comparison group,* which received geographically unrestricted vouchers and standard housing authority briefings and assistance; and the *control group,* which continued to receive project-based assistance. The study sought to answer two questions: What impact does mobility counseling have on families' residential choices and housing and neighborhood conditions? And what are the effects of neighborhood conditions on the well-being of MTO families?

The follow-up design and analyses of MTO in each city have been conducted by separate groups of researchers using different data collection and analytic strategies.[16] This approach has the disadvantage that it is harder to make comparisons across cities (and hence generalizations beyond each city). But it also has the advantage that the multiple research strategies used provide a richer picture of the experimental process and outcomes. The one commonality among all five sites is that HUD conducted a self-administered baseline survey of all families who volunteered to participate. Researchers in most study sites conducted follow-up telephone surveys two to three years after families were assigned to treatment groups. The Boston and Los Angeles projects also conducted qualitative studies with a sample of participants. In contrast, analyses of Boston participants have relied on baseline passive and active tracking of respondents and administrative data on arrests and school performance. Furthermore, the project in each city focused on a somewhat different set of children's outcomes.

As in almost all social experiments, the MTO project encountered significant problems in implementation of the experimental treatment (Matulef 1999). Large proportions of families who were offered vouchers did not move during the period when the vouchers were valid, and analyses comparing movers to nonmovers in the experimental and comparison groups show that movers are significantly different from nonmovers. As a result, most (but not all) MTO analyses adopt analytic strategies that account for this selection. For example, Jens Ludwig and his colleagues (Ludwig, Duncan, and Pinkston 2000; Ludwig, Ladd, and Duncan 2001) in Baltimore and Lawrence Katz and his colleagues (Katz, Kling, and Liebman 2001) in Boston produce both intent-to-treat (ITT) and treatment-on-treated (TOT) estimates. ITT analyses compare outcomes for families assigned to the two treatment groups whether or not they actually moved with outcomes for the control group. Thus, ITT results are "lower bounds" on the effects of the treatment because the two treatment groups include substantial proportions of families who never moved. These researchers also estimate an "effects of TOT" parameter, which is a measure of the effect of moving on those who actually moved during the program. The TOT analysis uses instrumental variables methods to estimate the difference between families in the treatment groups who moved with those in the control group who would have moved if offered the opportunity. In the New York study, Leventhal and Brooks-Gunn (2003) use a conceptually similar approach by comparing treatment group movers with both treatment group nonmovers and those who were assigned to the control group.

Because the MTO experiment was conducted in the mid to late 1990s, the results now available apply only to the first few years after families moved. The results to date for children's outcomes are summarized in table 3.2. In general, most studies show some improvements in children's outcomes in the treatment groups compared with the controls. In particular, the Boston and Baltimore studies show significant differences in behavior problems, including juvenile arrests and respondent-reported behavior problems. This result is particularly striking since both studies report that children in the experimental group were more likely than those in the other groups to be arrested prior to their move. Experimental group children in New York, especially boys, experienced fewer depressive and anxiety-related behaviors.

Baltimore children in the treatment groups also had better test scores. Compared with the control group, children in the experimental group had better test scores overall, while those in the comparison group had better reading scores. There is some evidence in the Baltimore results that experimental-group children were more likely to be suspended from and drop out of school. Ludwig, Ladd, and Duncan (2001) suggest that middle-income schools are less likely to tolerate behavior that is acceptable in schools in poor neighborhoods. Health outcomes were better for children in the experimental group in Boston. The Boston and Chicago studies also report significant declines in fears about safety and increases in feelings of safety, a point of view echoed in the Los Angeles and New York studies.

An important concern of the New York and Los Angeles studies was the impact of moving into middle-class neighborhoods on poor children's social adjustment, social capital, and friendship patterns. If children move to better neighborhoods but feel left out or are socially isolated, they may not be better off in the long run. In general, the results to date are reassuring. Children in all three groups were as likely to have a friend in the neighborhood. In some cases, children were less likely to participate in extracurricular activities in the experimental group. Maria Hanratty, Sara McLanahan, and Becky Pettit (1998) speculate that experimental group families may face more stringent financial situations because of higher rents and large security deposits compared with other groups.

In summary, the early results of the MTO experiments provide important new evidence that neighborhood social and physical conditions affect family life and at least some aspects of children's well-being. The results of these experimental studies are limited by implementation problems and unexpected events as well as by difficulties in generalizing to the rest of the population. Nonetheless, the results of experiments combined with those

TABLE 3.2 *Summary of the Results for Child Outcomes of the Moving to Opportunity Studies*

	Baltimore: Ludwig et al. (2000); Ludwig et al. (2001)	Boston: Katz et al. (2001); Kling et al. (2001)	Chicago: Rosenbaum and Harris (2000, 2001)	Los Angeles: Hanratty et al. (1998); Pettit and McLanahan (2003)	New York: Leventhal and Brooks-Gunn (2003)
Study design	Passive and active tracking results; match to administrative data; ITT and TOT results	Follow-up survey of participants; qualitative study; ITT and TOT results	Follow-up survey of movers	Follow-up survey of participants; qualitative study	Follow-up survey of participants; compare movers, non-movers, and controls
Juvenile arrests; delinquency	EG: Violent crime arrest reduced by 30 to 50 percent; property crime arrests go up initially, but not significant when pre-program-controlled. S8: Does almost as well as EG				No significant treatment effects.
School performance	EG: Five- to twelve-year-olds have much better test scores. S8: Five- to twelve-year-olds have much better scores for reading only. EG and S8: Teens may have more expulsions and dropouts, but slightly higher retention rates?				
Behavior problems		EG and S8: Significant reductions for boys; declines for girls not significant			EG: Had lower depressive symptoms and anxiety, especially boys. No significant group differences.
Health		EG: Significant reduction in injury and asthma attack. S8: No significant differences from controls.		EG and S8: Less likely to use emergency rooms for regular care.	

Safety	EG: Large and significant increase in safety. S8: Same effects, but smaller.	EG and S8: Significant declines in fears for personal safety compared to pre-move.	EG and S8: Report significantly better safety than CG	
Children's activities			EG: Young children less likely to participate in activities than S8 or CG; older kids more likely to be tutored.	Very little difference among groups, but EG and S8 fourteen- to eighteen-year-olds more likely to be involved in student government.
Social interaction			Children in all three groups equally likely to have at least one friend in neighborhood.	
Teen employment			EG and S8: Teens *less* likely to earn money.	
Teen substance abuse				EG: Girls more likely to use alcohol.

Source: Authors' configuration.

Notes: EG is the experimental group that received housing vouchers that could be used only in low-poverty neighborhoods plus counseling and assistance in locating housing. S8 is the comparison group that received a standard Section 8 housing voucher with no geographic restrictions. This group did not receive supplemental counseling or assistance. CG is the control group that continued to receive project-based assistance. "Significant" means statistically significant as defined by the authors of the cited papers. MTO articles, papers, and reports are available at Kling et al. (2001).

from observational studies will play an important role over the next several years in helping us understand the role of residential patterns in children's well-being.

DISCUSSION

In this chapter, we have surveyed the literature on the effects of neighborhood conditions on children's well-being. We reviewed social theory about why and how poor neighborhoods may detrimentally affect children's development and chances in life. We also considered several issues that have limited the results of previous empirical research on neighborhood effects, and we outlined new directions in research in these areas. The final sections assessed observational and experimental neighborhood-effects research.

Despite the serious methodological problems that are only beginning to be addressed adequately, a review of previous experimental and observational studies suggests that growing up in a poor neighborhood negatively affects children's outcomes over and above the effects of family socioeconomic status. However, the effects may be complex and difficult to observe. For example, the MTO results suggest that a major effect of moving to a better neighborhood is feeling safer and less anxious and depressed. Although we might expect a greater sense of safety and lower anxiety and depression to have very important long-run effects on children's emotional development and outlook on life, the effects may be less immediately apparent on school performance, skills acquisition, and behaviors, outcomes that are more typically measured in surveys and administrative data.

Research to date also suggests that family effects on children's outcomes are significantly larger than neighborhood effects. However, it is important to keep in mind that the measurement of neighborhood characteristics is at a much more rudimentary stage of development than measurement of family processes in large-scale surveys. Because of their pervasive role in most children's lives, it makes sense that families would have a greater influence on children's well-being than neighborhoods or other social environments. However, public policy generally has considerably less ability to influence parents' behavior and attributes directly than to affect neighborhood quality. Hence, even modest neighborhood effects may be of considerable interest to policymakers.

Moreover, it is important to consider residential segregation and neighborhood and family effects on children's well-being in a larger context. The finding that neighborhood effects are more modest in size than family effects can be misleading to the extent that neighborhood conditions, and residential segregation more generally, have an important influence on families' socioeconomic status and family dynamics. Residential segregation has been implicated by many scholars as a key mechanism for the intergenerational transmission of inequality (Massey and Denton 1993; Wilson 1987, 1996; Jargowsky 1997). The argument is that restriction to concentrated-poverty neighborhoods compounds the difficulty that poor, minority families face in escaping poverty because in poor neighborhoods housing values remain low, the chances of criminal victimization remain higher, high-paying jobs are less available, exposure to disease and substance abuse is greater, and individuals are more socially isolated. Thus, residential segregation and residence in concentrated-poverty neighborhoods may be an important determinant of the family socioeconomic status and a major indirect influence on children's outcomes.

If residence in a poor and dangerous neighborhood affects parents' attitudes, mental health, and parenting practices (Furstenberg et al. 1999; Kling, Liebman, and Katz 2001; Brooks-Gunn, Duncan, and Aber 1997), it is even more difficult to disentangle "family" effects from "neighborhood" effects. Nonetheless, several recent experimental and observational studies promise to provide clearer answers than past research on the direct and indirect pathways through which residential segregation affects children growing up in poor neighborhoods.

The authors are grateful to the Russell Sage Foundation for support of this research. Additional funding for this research was provided by the National Institute of Child Health and Human Development and the Office of Behavioral and Social Science Research at the National Institutes of Health. We thank our colleagues at UCLA and RAND for comments and suggestions. We would also like to thank Kathryn Neckerman for her thoughtful comments and suggestions.

NOTES

1. See reviews by Jencks and Mayer (1990), Gephart (1997), Aneshensel and Sucoff (1996), Robert (1999), Sampson, Morenoff, and Gannon-Rowley (2002), Leventhal and Brooks-Gunn (2000), and Ginther, Haveman, and Wolfe (2000). The geographic clustering of disadvantage and negative outcomes in American cities and its importance for public policy is, of course, not a new observation; see, for example, Burgess (1930).

2. Survey questions not involving mapping include the Panel Study of Income Dynamics (PSID) Child Development Supplement question, which asks respondents whether they think of their neighborhood as: the block or street they live on, several blocks or streets in each direction, the area within a fifteen-minute walk from their house, or an area larger than a fifteen-minute walk from their house.

3. Consensus boundaries are those on which 70 percent or more of the sample living in the block group agreed (Coulton et al. 2001).

4. The Project on Human Development in Chicago Neighborhoods (PHDCN) did collect neighborhood boundary information using maps from respondents in their neighborhood survey for all neighborhoods in Chicago. To our knowledge, however, PHDCN has not yet published analyses of these data.

5. Fuzzy set theory lets analysts take into account the fact that neighborhood boundaries may not be clearly defined. For example, using a conventional or "crisp" neighborhood boundary, every point in space would be either inside or outside the boundary. In a fuzzy set approach, on the other hand, each point has a *probability* of being inside the neighborhood depending on its location in space. For example, a point closer to an individual's house might have a higher probability of being in the individual's neighborhood whereas a point further away would have a lower probability. Grade of membership models are a statistical application of fuzzy set theory.

6. Most items were five-point Likert scales. For example, they included questions about whether the respondent thinks it is very likely, likely, neither likely nor unlikely, unlikely, or very unlikely that neighbors would intervene if neighborhood children were skipping school, showing disrespect to an adult, or spray-painting graffiti. Other questions asked about social interaction in the neighborhood—for example, whether the neighborhood is close-knit and whether residents do favors for each other. Sampson and his colleagues have proposed several strategies for scale construction using these items (see Sampson, Raudenbush, and Earls 1997; Sampson, Morenoff, and Earls 1999).

7. By contrast, most other studies that ask respondents about their neighborhood rely on one or two respondents' reports of local conditions in each neighborhood.

8. An example of an alternative approach is the Los Angeles Family and Neighborhood Survey (L.A.FANS), which interviewed respondents in an average of forty-one households per neighborhood and replicated the PHDCN measures with the adult sample in the household survey (Sastry et al. 2000).

9. However, as Catherine Ross, John Mirowsky, and Shana Pribesh (2001, 571) caution, "independent assessments made by researchers are no more 'objective' than those made by residents. A description of place as

assessed by a researcher simply substitutes the researcher's subjectivity for the resident's." Nonetheless, assessment of all neighborhoods in a sample by a single group of observers does provide comparable measures across neighborhoods.

10. Neighborhood income status is based on the three sampling strata used in L.A.FANS: very poor (tracts in the top 10 percent of the poverty distribution in 1997), poor (tracts in the sixtieth to eighty-ninth percentiles), and nonpoor (tracts in the bottom 60 percent of the distribution). For this table, nonpoor tracts were further divided into those with median household incomes higher or lower than $50,000.

11. A characteristic or variable is "endogenous" if its value is determined by an individual's choice and hence may be influenced by other variables. In contrast, an "exogenous" variable is one that is fixed and outside the realm of an individual's choosing. Thus, an individual's age, race, and sex are exogenous while his or her neighborhood of residence, employment, and marital status are potentially endogenous. In studying the effects of endogenous variables on child outcomes, it is important to control for the factors that influence people's choices of the endogenous variable as well as the outcome being examined and to recognize that the outcome variable and the endogenous variable may cause each other.

12. An important exception is the Boston Moving To Opportunity study, which conducted extensive qualitative research focused on the mechanisms through which residential mobility affects outcomes (see Kling, Liebman, and Katz 2001).

13. The study of Ginther, Haveman, and Wolfe (2000) is an exception. They use PSID data over a twenty-one-year period matched with tract-level data on all the locations in which the sampled children lived during the period. Other PSID-based analyses, such as that undertaken by Brooks-Gunn and her colleagues (1993), have included characteristics from a single neighborhood in which each child lived prior to the behavior under study.

14. Even in this case, children who move frequently may have different long-run outcomes than stationary children simply because of the experience of moving (Myers 1999).

15. Ginther and her colleagues (2000) suggest that the neighborhood characteristics most closely associated with the outcome being investigated (for example, local school dropout rates for an analysis of individuals' level of educational attainment) are most likely to remain significant.

16. See Kling (2002) for published and unpublished papers from all five sites.

REFERENCES

Aaronson, Daniel. 1997. "Sibling Estimates of Neighborhood Effects." In *Neighborhood Poverty: Policy Implications in Studying Neighborhoods,* vol. 2, edited by Jeanne Brooks-Gunn, Greg J. Duncan, and J. Lawrence Aber. New York: Russell Sage Foundation.

————. 1998. "Using Sibling Data to Estimate the Impact of Neighborhoods on Children's Educational Outcomes." *Journal of Human Resources* 33(4): 915–46.

Aber, J. Lawrence, Martha A. Gephart, Jeanne Brooks-Gunn, and James P. Connell. 1997. "Development in Context: Implications for Studying Neighborhood Effects." In *Neighborhood Poverty: Context and Consequences for Children,* vol. 1, edited by Jeanne Brooks-Gunn, Greg J. Duncan, and J. Lawrence Aber. New York: Russell Sage Foundation.

Aneshensel, Carol S., and Clea A. Sucoff. 1996. "The Neighborhood Context of Adolescent Mental Health." *Journal of Health and Social Behavior* 37: 293–310.

Baumer, Eric P., and Scott J. South. 2001. "Community Effects on Youth Sexual Activity." *Journal of Marriage and the Family* 63: 540–54.

Brennan, Brian. 2002. "Background on MTO." *Moving To Opportunity Research.* Created August 30, 2000; last modified August 22, 2002. Available at: www.princeton.edu/~kling/mto/background.htm.

Bronfenbrenner, Urie. 1986. "Ecology of the Family as Context for Human Development." *Developmental Psychology* 22(6): 723–42.

Brooks-Gunn, Jeanne, Greg J. Duncan, and J. Lawrence Aber, eds. 1997. *Neighborhood Poverty.* New York: Russell Sage Foundation.

Brooks-Gunn, Jeanne, Greg J. Duncan, Pamela K. Klebanov, and Naomi Sealand. 1993. "Do Neighborhoods Influence Child and Adolescent Development?" *American Journal of Sociology* 99(2): 353–95.

Burgess, Ernest. 1930. "The Value of Sociological Community Studies for the Work of Social Agencies." *Social Forces* 8(4): 481–491.

Burton, Linda M., Townsand Price-Spratlen, and Margaret Beale Spencer. 1997. "On Ways of Thinking About Measuring Neighborhoods: Implications for the Study of Context and Developmental Outcomes for Children." In *Neighborhood Poverty: Policy Implications for Studying Neighborhoods,* vol. 2, edited by Jeanne Brooks-Gunn, Greg J. Duncan, and J. Lawrence Aber. New York: Russell Sage Foundation.

Case, Anne C., and Lawrence F. Katz. 1991. "The Company You Keep: The Effects of Family and Neighborhood on Disadvantaged Youth." Working paper. Cambridge, Mass.: National Bureau of Economic Research.

Caughy, Margaret O., Patricia J. O'Campo, and Jacqueline Patterson. 2001. "A Brief Observational Measure for Urban Neighborhoods." *Health and Place* 7: 225–36.

Chamberlain, Gary. 1980. "Analysis of Covariance with Qualitative Data." *Review of Economic Studies* 47: 225–38.

———. 1984. "Panel Data." In *The Handbook of Econometrics* 2(22), edited by Zvi Griliches and Michael D. Intrilligator. Amsterdam: Elsevier.

Coleman, James S. 1988. "Social Capital in the Creation of Human Capital." *American Sociological Review* 94 (supp.): S95–120.

Cook, Thomas D., Shobha C. Shagle, and Serdar M. Degirmencioglu. 1997. "Capturing Social Process for Testing Mediation Models of Neighborhood Effects." In *Neighborhood Poverty: Policy Implications for Studying Neighborhoods,* vol. 2, edited by Jeanne Brooks-Gunn, Greg J. Duncan, and J. Lawrence Aber. New York: Russell Sage Foundation.

Coulton, Claudia J. 1996. "Effects of Neighborhoods on Families and Children: Implications for Services." In *Children and Their Families in Big Cities: Strategies for Service Reform,* edited by A. J. Kahn and S. B. Kamerman. New York: Columbia University.

Coulton, Claudia J., Jill Korbin, Tsui Chan, and Marilyn Su. 2001. "Mapping Residents' Perceptions of Neighborhood Boundaries: A Methodological Note." *American Journal of Community Psychology* 29(2): 371–83.

Crane, Jonathan. 1991. "The Epidemic Theory of Ghettos and Neighborhood Effects on Dropping Out and Teenage Childbearing." *American Sociological Review* 96(5): 1226–59.

Crawford, Thomas W. 2002. "Spatial Modeling of Village Functional Territories to Support Population-Environmental Linkages." In *Linking People, Place, and Policy: A GIScience Approach,* edited by Stephen J. Walsh and Kelley A. Crews-Meyer. Norwell, Mass.: Kluwer Academic Publishers.

Crowder, Kyle D. 2001. "Racial Stratification in the Actuation of Mobility Expectations: Microlevel Impacts of Racially Restrictive Housing Markets." *Social Forces* 79: 1377–96.

Danziger, Sheldon, and Peter Gottschalk. 1995. *America Unequal.* Cambridge, Mass.: Harvard University Press.

Del Conte, Alessandra, and Jeffrey Kling. 2001. "A Synthesis of MTO Research on Self-sufficiency, Safety and Health, and Behavior and Delinquency." *Poverty Research News* 5(1): 3–6.

DeNavas-Walt, Carmen, Robert W. Cleveland, and Marc I. Roemer. 2001. "Money Income in the United States: 2000." *Current Population Reports,* series P60, no. 213. Washington: U.S. Government Printing Office for U.S. Census Bureau.

Diez Roux, Ana V., C. I. Kiefe, D. R. Jacobs, M. Haan, S. A. Jackson, F. J. Nieto, C. C. Paton, and R. Schulz. 2001. "Area Characteristics and Individual-Level Socioeconomic Position Indicators in Three Population-Based Epidemiologic Studies." *Annals of Epidemiology* 11(6): 395–405.

Duncan, Greg J., James P. Connell, and Pamela K. Klebanov. 1997. "Conceptual and Methodological Issues in Estimating Causal Effects of Neighborhoods and Family Conditions on Individual Development." In *Neighborhood Poverty: Context and Consequences for Children,* vol. 1, edited by Jeanne Brooks-Gunn, Greg J. Duncan, and J. Lawrence Aber. New York: Russell Sage Foundation.

Duncan, Greg J., and Saul D. Hoffman. 1990. "Welfare Benefits, Economic Opportunities, and Out-of-Wedlock Births Among Black Teenage Girls." *Demography* 27(4): 519–35.

Duncan, Greg J., and Stephen W. Raudenbush. 1999. "Assessing the Effects of Context in Studies of Child and Youth Development." *Educational Psychologist* 34(1): 29–41.

————. 2001. "Neighborhoods and Adolescent Development: How Can We Determine the Links?" In *Does It Take a Village? Community Effects on Children, Adolescents, and Families,* edited by Alan Booth and Ann C. Crouter. Mahwah, N.J.: Lawrence Erlbaum Associates.

Edin, Kathryn. 1991. "Surviving the Welfare System: How AFDC Recipients Make Ends Meet in Chicago." *Social Problems* 38(4): 462–74.

Elliott, Delbert, and David Huizinga. 1990. *Mediating Effects of Social Structure in High-Risk Neighborhoods.* Boulder: University of Colorado.

Evans, William N., Wallace E. Oates, and Robert M. Schwab. 1992. "Measuring Peer Group Effects: A Study of Teenage Behavior." *Journal of Political Economy* 100(3): 966–91.

Fischer, Claude S. 1984. *The Urban Experience.* New York: Harcourt, Brace, Jovanovich.

Fordham, Signithia, and John U. Ogbu. 1986. "Black Students' School Success: Coping with the Burden of 'Acting White.'" *The Urban Review* 18: 176–206.

Foster, Eric M., and Sara McLanahan. 1996. "An Illustration of the Use of Instrumental Variables: Do Neighborhood Conditions Affect a Young Person's Chance of Finishing High School?" Unpublished paper. Princeton University.

Furstenberg, Frank F., Jr., Thomas D. Cook, Jacquelynne Eccles, Glen H. Elder Jr., and Arnold J. Sameroff. 1999. *Managing to Make It: Urban Families and Adolescent Success.* Chicago: University of Chicago Press.

Gephart, Martha A. 1997. "Neighborhoods and Communities as Contexts for Development." In *Neighborhood Poverty,* vol. 1, edited by Jeanne Brooks-Gunn, Greg J. Duncan, and J. Lawrence Aber. New York: Russell Sage Foundation.

Ginther, Donna, Robert Haveman, and Barbara Wolfe. 2000. "Neighborhood Attributes as Determinants of Children's Outcomes: How Robust Are the Relationships?" *Journal of Human Resources* 35(4): 603–42.

Gramlich, Edward, Deborah Laren, and Naomi Sealand. 1992. "Moving into and out of Poor Urban Areas." *Journal of Policy Analysis and Management* 11: 273–87.

Grannis, Rick. 1998. "The Importance of Trivial Streets: Residential Streets and Residential Segregation." *American Journal of Sociology* 103(6): 1530–64.

Guest, Avery M., and Barrett A. Lee. 1984. "How Urbanites Define Their Neighborhoods." *Population and Environment* 71(1): 32–56.

Guest, Avery M., Barrett A. Lee, and Lynn Staeheli. 1982. "Changing Locality Identification in the Metropolis: Seattle, 1920 to 1978." *American Sociological Review* 47(4): 543–49.

Hägerstrand, Torsten. 1970. "What about People in Regional Science?" *Papers of the Regional Science Association* 24: 7–21.

Hanratty, Maria, Sara McLanahan, and Becky Pettit. 1998. "The Impact of the Los Angeles Moving To Opportunity Program on Residential Mobility, Neighborhood Characteristics, and Early Child and Parent Outcomes." Working paper 98-18. Princeton, N.J.: Princeton University, Center for Research on Child Well-being.

Haveman, Robert, and Barbara Wolfe. 1994. *Succeeding Generations: On the Effects of Investments in Children.* New York: Russell Sage Foundation.

Hunter, Albert. 1974. *Symbolic Communities: The Persistence and Change of Chicago's Local Communities.* Chicago: University of Chicago Press.

————. 1975. "The Loss of Community: An Empirical Test Through Replication." *American Sociological Review* 40(5): 537–52.

Jacobs, Jane. 1961. *The Death and Life of Great American Cities.* New York: Random House.

Jargwosky, Paul A. 1997. *Poverty and Place: Ghettos, Barrios, and the American City.* New York: Russell Sage Foundation.

Jencks, Christopher, and Susan E. Mayer. 1990. "The Social Consequences of Growing up in a Poor Neighborhood." In *Inner-City Poverty in the United States,* edited by Laurence E. Lynn Jr. and Michael G. H. McGeary. Washington, D.C.: National Academy Press.

Katz, Lawrence F., Jeffrey R. Kling, and Jeffrey B. Liebman. 2001. "Moving To Opportunity in Boston: Early Results of a Randomized Mobility Experiment." *Quarterly Journal of Economics* (May): 607–54.

Kingston, Sharon, Roger Mitchell, Paul Florin, and John Stevenson. 1999. "Sense of Community in Neighborhoods as a Multilevel Construct." *Journal of Community Psychology, Special Issue: Sense of Community II.* 27(6): 681–94.

Klebanov, Pamela K., Jeanne Brooks-Gunn, P. Lindsay Chase-Lansdale, and R. A. Gordon.1997. "Are Neighborhood Effects on Young Children Mediated by Features of the Home Environment?" In *Neighborhood Poverty*, vol. 1, edited by Jeanne Brooks-Gunn, Greg J. Duncan, and J. Lawrence Aber. New York: Russell Sage Foundation.

Klebanov, Pamela K., Jeanne Brooks-Gunn, and Greg J. Duncan. 1994. "Does Neighborhood and Family Poverty Affect Mother's Parenting, Mental Health and Social Support?" *Journal of Marriage and the Family* 56: 441–55.

Kling, Jeffrey. 2002. "MTO Research—Quick Document Access." *Moving To Opportunity Research*. Created October 8, 2000; last modified August 6, 2002. Available at: www.wws.princeton.edu/~kling/mto/quick.htm.

Kling, Jeffrey R., Jeffrey B. Liebman, and Lawrence F. Katz. 2001. "Bullets Don't Got No Name: Consequences of Fear in the Ghetto." Working paper 225. Chicago: Northwestern University and the University of Chicago, Joint Center for Poverty Research.

Korbin, Jill E., and Claudia J. Coulton. 1997. "Understanding the Neighborhood Context for Children and Families: Combining Epidemiological and Ethnographic Approaches." In *Neighborhood Poverty*, vol. 2, edited by Jeanne Brooks-Gunn, Greg J. Duncan, and J. Lawrence Aber. New York: Russell Sage Foundation.

Lee, Barrett A., and Karen E. Campbell. 1997. "Common Ground? Urban Neighborhoods as Survey Respondents See Them." *Social Science Quarterly* 78(4): 922–36.

Lee, Barrett A., Karen E. Campbell, and Oscar Miller. 1991. "Racial Differences in Urban Neighboring." *Sociological Forum* 6(3): 525–50.

Leventhal, Tama, and Jeanne Brooks-Gunn. 2000. "The Neighborhoods They Live In: The Effects of Neighborhood Residence on Child and Adolescent Outcomes." *Psychological Bulletin* 126(2): 309–37.

———. 2003. "The Early Impacts of Moving To Opportunity on Children and Youth in New York City." In *Choosing a Better Life: Evaluating the Moving To Opportunity Social Experiment*, edited by John Goering and Judith Feins. Washington, D.C.: Urban Institute Press.

Logan, John, et al. 2001. "Metropolitan Racial and Ethnic Change—Census 2000." State University of New York at Albany, Lewis Mumford Center for Comparative Urban and Regional Research. Available at: http://mumford1.dyndns.org/cen2000/data.html

Logan, John R., and O. Andrew Collver. 1983. "Residents' Perceptions of Suburban Community Differences." *American Sociological Review* 48(3): 428–33.

Ludwig, Jens, Greg J. Duncan, and Joshua C. Pinkston. 2000. "Evidence from a Randomized Housing-Mobility Experiment." Unpublished paper. Georgetown University, Washington, D.C.

Ludwig, Jens, Helen F. Ladd, and Greg J. Duncan. 2001. "Urban Poverty and Educational Outcomes." *Brookings-Wharton Papers on Urban Affairs* 2001: 147–201.

Mare, Robert D., and David Cort. 2003. "Residential Segregation by Income, 1990 to 2000." Unpublished paper, UCLA, California Center for Population Research.

Massey, Douglas S., and Nancy A. Denton. 1993. *American Apartheid: Segregation and the Making of the Underclass.* Cambridge, Mass.: Harvard University Press.

Massey, Douglas S., and Mitchell L. Eggers. 1990. "The Ecology of Inequality: Minorities and the Concentration of Poverty, 1970 to 1980." *American Journal of Sociology* 95(5): 1153–88.

Massey, Douglas S., Andrew B. Gross, and M. L. Eggers. 1991. "Segregation, the Concentration of Poverty, and the Life Chances of Individuals." *Social Science Research* 20(4): 397–420.

Massey, Douglas S., Andrew B. Gross, and K. Shibuya. 1994. "Migration, Segregation, and the Concentration of Poverty." *American Sociological Review* 59: 425–45.

Matulef, Mark. 1999. "Moving To Opportunity (MTO) Demonstration for Fair Housing Program, Los Angeles Demonstration Site Interim Outcomes of Housing Search and Counseling Strategies: Early Lessons for Experimental Design and Implementation." Available at: www.wws.princeton.edu/~kling/mto/quick.htm.

Mayer, Susan E. 2001. "How the Growth in Income Inequality Increased Economic Segregation." Working paper 230. Chicago: Northwestern University and the University of Chicago, Joint Center for Poverty Research. Available at: www.jcpr.org//wp/WPprofile.cfm?ID=256.

McLoyd, Vonnie C. 1990. "The Impact of Economic Hardship on Black Families and Children: Psychological Distress, Parenting, and Socioemotional Development." *Child Development* 61: 311–46.

Morenoff, Jeffrey D., Robert J. Sampson, and Stephen W. Raudenbush. 2001. "Neighborhood Inequality, Collective Efficacy, and the Spatial Dynamics of Urban Violence." *Criminology* 39(3): 517–59.

Myers, Scott M. 1999. "Childhood Migration and Social Integration in Adulthood." *Journal of Marriage and the Family* 61(3): 774–89.

Newsome, Tracy H., Wayne A. Walcott, and Paul D. Smith. 1998. "Urban Activity Spaces: Illustrations and Application of a Conceptual Model for Integrating the Time and Space Dimensions." *Transportation* 25: 357–77.

Oliver, Melvin L. 1988. "The Urban Black Community as Network: Toward a Social Network Perspective." *Sociological Quarterly* 29(4): 623–45.

Park, Robert E., Ernest W. Burgess, and Roderick D. McKenzie. 1967. *The City*. Chicago: University of Chicago Press.

Pebley, Anne R., Narayan Sastry, and Michela Zonta. 2002. "Neighborhood Definitions and the Spatial Dimensions of Daily Life in Los Angeles." Paper presented to the annual meeting of the Population Association of America, Washington, D.C., March 29–31.

Pettit, Becky, and Sara McLanahan. 2003. "Residential Capital and Children's Social Capital: Evidence from an Experiment." Working paper 98-11. Princeton, N.J.: Princeton University, Center for Research on Child Well-being.

Plotnick, Robert D., and Saul D. Hoffman. 1996. "The Effect of Neighborhood Characteristics on Young Adult Outcomes: Alternative Estimates." Working paper 1106-96. Madison: University of Wisconsin, Institute for Research on Poverty.

Raudenbush, Stephen W., and Robert J. Sampson. 1999. "Ecometics: Toward a Science of Assessing Ecological Settings, with Application to the Systematic Social Observation of Neighborhoods." *Sociological Methodology* 29: 1–41.

Rindfuss, Ronald R., B. Entwisle, Stephen J. Walsh, Pramote Prasartkul, Yothin Sawangdee, Thomas W. Crawford, and Julia Reade. 2002. "Continuous and Discrete: Where They Have Met in Nang Rong, Thailand." In *Linking People, Place, and Policy: A GIScience Approach*, edited by Stephen J. Walsh and Kelley A. Crews-Meyer. Norwell, Mass.: Kluwer Academic Publishers.

Robert, Stephanie A. 1999. "Socioeconomic Position and Health: The Independent Contribution of Community Socioeconomic Context." *Annual Review of Sociology* 25: 489–516.

Rosenbaum, Emily, and Laura Harris. 2000. "Low-Income Families in Their New Neighborhoods: The Short-term Effects of Moving from Chicago's Public Housing." *Journal of Family Issues* (March): 183–210.

———. 2001. "Residential Mobility and Opportunities: Early Impacts of the Moving To Opportunity Demonstration Program in Chicago." *Housing Policy Debate*: 321–46.

Rosenbaum, James E. 1991. "Black Pioneers: Do Their Moves to the Suburbs Increase Economic Opportunity for Mothers and Children?" *Housing Policy Debate* 2(4): 1179–1213.

———. 1995. "Changing the Geography of Opportunity by Expanding Residential Choice: Lessons from the Gautreaux Program." *Housing Policy Debate* 6(1): 231–70.

Ross, Catherine E., John Mirowsky, and Shana Pribesh. 2001. "Powerlessness and the Amplification of Threat: Neighborhood Disadvantage, Disorder, and Mistrust." *American Sociological Review* 66(4): 568–91.

Rossi, Peter H. 1955. *Why Families Move: A Study in the Social Psychology of Urban Residential Mobility*. New York: Free Press.

Sampson, Robert J., and John H. Laub. 1994. "Urban Poverty and the Family Context of Delinquency: A New Look at Structure and Process in a Classic Study." *Child Development* 65: 523–40.

Sampson, Robert J., Jeffrey D. Morenoff, and Felton Earls. 1999. "Beyond Social Capital: Spatial Dynamics of Collective Efficacy for Children." *American Sociological Review* 64(5): 633–60.

Sampson, Robert J., Jeffrey D. Morenoff, and Thomas Gannon-Rowley. 2002. "Assessing 'Neighborhood Effects': Social Processes and New Directions in Research." *Annual Review of Sociology* 28: 443–78.

Sampson, Robert J., and Stephen W. Raudenbush. 1999. "Systematic Social Observation of Public Spaces: A New Look at Disorder in Urban Neighborhoods." *American Journal of Sociology* 105(3): 603–51.

Sampson, Robert J., Stephen W. Raudenbush, and Felton Earls. 1997. "Neighborhoods and Violent Crime: A Multilevel Study of Collective Efficacy." *Science* 277(August 15): 918–24.

Sastry, Narayan, Bonnie Ghosh-Dastidar, John Adams, and Anne R. Pebley. 2000. "The Design of a Multilevel Longitudinal Survey of Children, Families, and Communities: The Los Angeles Family and Neighborhood Study." Labor and Population working paper DRU-2400/1-LAFANS. Santa Monica, Calif.: Rand Corporation.

Schachter, Jason. 2001. "Geographic Mobility." *Current Population Reports,* series P20, no. 538. Washington: U.S. Government Printing Office for U.S. Census Bureau.

Shaw, Clifford R., and McKay, Henry D. 1969. *Juvenile Delinquency and Urban Areas.* Chicago: The University of Chicago Press.

Solon, Gary, Marianne E. Page, and Greg J. Duncan. 2000. "Correlations Between Neighboring Children in Their Subsequent Educational Attainment." *Review of Economics and Statistics* 82(3): 383–92.

South, Scott J. 2001. "Issues in the Analysis of Neighborhoods, Families and Children." In *Does It Take A Village? Community Effects on Children, Adolescents, and Families,* edited by Alan Booth and Ann C. Crouter. Mahwah, N.J.: Lawrence Erlbaum Associates, Inc.

South, Scott J., and Eric P. Baumer. 2000. "Deciphering Community and Race Effects on Adolescent Premarital Childbearing." *Social Forces* 78: 1379–1407.

South, Scott J., and Kyle D. Crowder. 1997a. "Residential Mobility Between Cities and Suburbs: Race, Suburbanization, and Back-to-the-city Moves." *Demography* 34: 525–38.

———. 1997b. "Escaping Distressed Neighborhoods: Individual, Community, and Metropolitan Influences." *American Journal of Sociology* 102: 1040–84.

———. 1998. "Leaving the 'Hood: Residential Mobility Between Black, White, and Integrated Neighborhoods." *American Sociological Review* 63: 17–26.

Stack, Carol. 1974. *All Our Kin: Survival Strategies.* New York: Harper Torchback.

Tigges, Leann M., Irene Browne, and Gary P. Green. 1998. "Social Isolation of the Urban Poor: Race, Class and Neighborhood Effects on Social Resources." *Sociological Quarterly* 39(1): 53–77.

Upchurch, Dawn M., Carol S. Aneshensel, Clea A. Sucoff, and Lene Levy-Storms. 1999. "Neighborhood and Family Contexts of Adolescent Sexual Activity." *Journal of Marriage and the Family* 61: 920–33.

Waldinger, Roger. 1996. "Ethnicity and Opportunity in the Plural City." In *Ethnic Los Angeles,* edited by Roger Waldinger and Mehdi Bozorgmehr. New York: Russell Sage Foundation.

Wellman, Barry. 1996. "Are Personal Communities Local? A Dumptarian Reconsideration." *Social Networks* 17(2): 423–36.

———. 1999. "Preface." In *Networks in the Global Village,* edited by Barry Wellman. Boulder, Colo.: Westview Press.

Wilson, William Julius. 1987. *The Truly Disadvantaged.* Chicago: University of Chicago Press.

———. 1996. *When Work Disappears: The World of the New Urban Poor.* New York: Alfred A. Knopf.

Part II

Investments in Children

Chapter 4

Trends in Children's Attainments and Their Determinants as Family Income Inequality Has Increased

Robert Haveman, Gary Sandefur, Barbara Wolfe, and Andrea Voyer

The increase in family income inequality since the early 1970s is one of the most cited economic changes during this three-decade period. As family income inequality increases, those families below the median are further from the social norm than before; similarly, those at the top of the distribution see a larger gap between themselves and the rest of the population. Such growing disparities are not inconsistent with increases over time in the absolute level of income and well-being for both high- and low-income families. Indeed, since the early 1970s, the real (inflation-adjusted) incomes of both rich and poor have increased. At the bottom of the distribution, income growth has been slow, while at the top very large increases in income have been recorded.

Clearly, the increases in real income across the entire distribution suggest improved levels of family economic well-being over time, and hence an improved environment for the nurturing and development of children. This "income effect" suggests that we should find improved levels of attainments for America's children in a number of social indicators over time. However, many fear that the growth in income disparities among families has had a variety of adverse consequences for both families and communities.

The processes by which changes in overall income inequality may affect both the *level* of children's attainments and the *inequality* in children's attainments are complex and ill understood. Let us consider a few of them.

Because family well-being directly affects children, increasing income gaps among families are likely to directly increase disparities among children in their progress and attainments. However, growth in income disparities may also affect the overall level of children's attainments. Growing income gaps are likely to affect the perceptions and aspirations of children and their families at both the top and bottom of the distribution. Children living in families at the bottom of the distribution are likely to have parents who are discouraged and disheartened. Moreover, these same families are likely to experience increased tensions that may erode self-confidence, marital stability, and mental health as their attainments appear to fall increasingly short of the American mainstream. The communities in which such families live are also likely to erode relative to mainstream communities, and this will have its own negative effect on the level of children's attainments.

The growth in disparities in income may also create greater motivation among those in the top deciles of the income distribution to find ways to improve their children's opportunities to succeed and reap higher incomes. Thus, to the extent that parents respond by spending more time with their children and/or conveying the importance of success in school and success in extracurricular activities, the growth in inequality may lead to an overall increase in the level of children's attainments.

It is clear that growing economic distance between people can reduce common interests and increase social separation. As the status of families at the bottom of the distribution drifts further from the mainstream, they are likely to experience an increased sense of alienation as those with many resources see them as more distant and as undeserving. Such growing economic distance between families may also influence citizens' views about the potential role and functions of government (for example, the size and structure of the education system), and this may also influence children's well-being and progress.

The growth in income inequality may also have indirect effects on a variety of other social changes that affect the overall *level* of children's attainments and *inequality* among them. For example, increased family income inequality may contribute to changed *levels* of a variety of other social variables, such as community health status, life expectancy, crime rates, and participation in civic activities. Although the linkage between growing inequality and health has been examined in several research studies, the findings are controversial; there is little knowledge regarding the other potential linkages.

The increase in family income inequality may also contribute to changes in *inequality* among families in a variety of other dimensions, such as inequality in housing quality, child care quality, neighborhood services, school expenditures, teacher quality, and leisure time. These linkages between increases in family income inequality and increases in disparities in other important social dimensions have not been systematically explored and are poorly understood.

Clearly, then, the economic developments over the past few decades leave us with a difficult puzzle. The increase in economic well-being for both rich and poor American families leads us to expect that children's overall attainments have also increased. Simultaneously, the growth in family income inequality may impede the performance of children overall, through some of the linkages identified here, while other linkages suggest reasons for more optimism regarding children's attainments. The critical question, then, is: As real income has increased and income inequality has also increased, what has happened to the overall levels of children's attainments? A second critical question concerns disparities among children in attainments: Do the children of families at the top of the income distribution show more progress in attainments than children at the bottom? Has the rich-poor gap in children's attainment increased?

In our review, we adopt an "investment in children" framework in which the family and the community are seen as production units that employ real inputs in order to encourage the attainments of children. In the first section, we briefly discuss this framework, posing the following questions:

- What is likely to be the independent effect of the increase in inequality of family income and family investments in children on the *level* of children's attainments? Can this effect be identified if, at the same time, the level of family income has increased?

- What is likely to be the independent effect of the increase in inequality of family income and family investments in children on *inequality* among children in terms of their attainments? Can this effect be identified when simultaneous changes in other important factors influence children's well-being?

Hypothesizing about the first set of questions is the more difficult task, and we discuss three possible linkages between changes in the inequality of investments and changes in the average level of children's attainments. With respect to the second set of questions, our hypothesis is that as inequality of inputs into children's attainments increases, the disparities among them in terms of attainments will also increase.

The next section presents a historical perspective on the changes in the *level* and *inequality* of family income. We find that family income grew slowly during the 1970s and 1980s but displayed robust growth during the 1990s. The level of income inequality among families increased persistently over these three decades, with the greatest increases occurring during the decade of the 1980s. The third section discusses trends in both the *level* and *inequality* of inputs to children's attainments and the *level* and *inequality* in the attainments themselves. The inputs into children's attainments on which we focus are those that a sizable research literature has identified as most closely related to children's attainments. The following section presents our review of the voluminous recent research that has attempted to establish the existence and strength of the linkages between family and community inputs and children's attainments.[1]

LINKAGES IN THE LEVEL AND INEQUALITY OF INVESTMENTS IN CHILDREN AND CHILDREN'S ATTAINMENTS

In our discussion of the linkages between the level and inequality of investments in children and children's attainments, we adopt a standard economic investment framework: we view the family and the community as production units that employ real inputs in order to generate well-being for their members. One of the uses of these inputs is to influence the attainments of the children in the family, reflecting the view that children's success yields well-being to the parents.

As Gary Becker and Nigel Tomes (1986, 55) have observed, parents can influence the attainments of their children by making "expenditures on their skills, health, learning motivation, 'credentials,' and many other characteristics." Arleen Leibowitz (1974) presented an economic model of this view (see figure 4.1). In this model, the genetic endowments of parents are to some extent passed along to children through heredity. These abilities and the education choices of the parents jointly determine the level of family income and the quantity and quality of both the time and goods inputs that parents allocate to their children. Parents make decisions about allocating time and goods to their children in conjunction with decisions on the allocation of time and goods to other family priorities. Examples of such inputs to children are nutrition, health care, child care quality, extracurricular activities (such as art or music classes), reading material in the home, tutors if performance lags, and sanitation. Children's ability and the levels of parental income and home investments in time and goods determine in part the attainments of their children in terms of schooling, earnings, and the avoidance of teen nonmarital childbearing.

This general family-based framework can be made more comprehensive by including both the choices made by communities (or government) that influence the opportunities available to children and to their parents (the "social investment in children") and the choices that children themselves make, given the investments in and opportunities available to them. In this framework, communities can employ a wide variety of policy instruments (for example, investments in school and neighborhood quality, changes in taxation policies that affect family net income, moral suasion) in setting the basic environment and opportunities within which families and children make their constrained choices. Some authors

FIGURE 4.1   *Model of the Relationship Between Parental Investments and Children's Attainments*

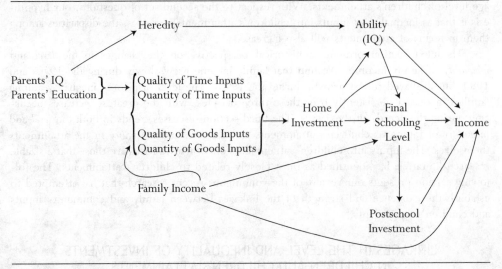

Source: Leibowitz (1974, S111–31).

have suggested that by their teen years children are also decisionmakers seeking to make themselves as well off as possible.[2] However, the age at which children begin to weigh the costs and benefits associated with the options available to them and the care with which they make these calculations vary widely. The information that children have about the options available to them varies widely as well. Consequently, a poor decision may be the result of either poor decisionmaking or bad information.

Consider a society of families with children, each of which invests in a variety of inputs to their children. Many of these inputs are financed by the family's income. Parents use their income to buy a variety of things that give them satisfaction, and increasing the probability that their children will succeed as young adults is one element in this package. Hence, the greater the average level of income of the families in this society, the more successful we would expect their children to be; there is likely to be a positive relationship between average family income and children's attainments.[3]

The families in this society will vary, however, both in terms of the income that they have available and in their propensity to allocate this income to "inputs to children." As a result, families will vary widely in the levels of investment in their children. If there was an increase in the inequality among families in either the income that they have available or their propensity to allocate it to their children, both the average level of children's attainments and the variation around this level are likely to change.

Researchers and other observers have offered reasons to expect that an increase in the inequality of inputs allocated to children will result in an increase in the inequality in children's attainments, and the basis for this conjecture seems firm. If parental income and the level of investments in children are positively related to children's attainments, then inequality in the distribution of children's attainments is likely to increase if the distribution of income or investments becomes more unequal.

Scholars and other observers have also speculated about the relationship between changes in the inequality in income or parental investments and changes in the average level of children's attainments. What is likely to be the effect on the level of children's attainments if inequality among children in the allocation of parental investments is increased? This is a most difficult question, and speculations about the relationship are only that.

The following three examples illustrate how difficult it is to posit a firm linkage between changes in inequality of investments in children and changes in the average level of children's attainments. First, consider a world in which children who are below some absolute threshold in terms of investments demonstrate substantial positive responses to increases in investments in them, whereas children with investment levels above this threshold do not gain from increases in investments in them.[4] Additional income, for example, allows a poor family to purchase a neighborhood environment (or school quality, peers of their children, access to medical care, or birth control information) that exceeds a minimum threshold. In this case, an increase in the inequality of investments in children (for example, increased income inequality) without an increase in average income implies an increase in the number of children with investments below the minimum cutoff, and hence a reduction in the average level of children's attainments.

A second possible link between increases in income inequality and the average level of children's attainments would exist if the relationship between children's attainments and investments in them (for example, income) diminishes as the level of investments (income) increases. If this is the case, an average level of children's attainments can be increased by simply redistributing the constant average level of income (or other investments) from the rich to the poor—that is, by decreasing income inequality. Children with access to little income will gain a great deal in terms of attainments, while children with access to substantial income will lose little. Again, an increase in inequality in investments in children leads to a decrease in the average level of children's attainments. However, if this relationship is linear and not decreasing in income, there is "no free lunch," and redistribution toward the poor does not increase children's attainments.

A third linkage may come through indirect effects related to levels of investment or income. Consider a situation in which increasing income inequality leads to diminished overall public support for children's schooling. Increasing inequality in the distribution of family income lowers the quality of some schools, while other schools gain quality teachers and funding. The use by high-income parents of private schools is another such dynamic interaction. However, the relationship may work in the other direction. For example, increasing income inequality sometimes leads to an increase in society's investment in services to poor families and children. Past history suggests that American society is responsive primarily to severe crises involving the low end of the income distribution. The New Deal and the War on Poverty, for example, developed in response to public awareness of extreme poverty and its consequences and led to the investment of public funds in efforts to assist poor families with children as well as other disadvantaged sectors of society. The growing inequality during the past two decades was not of a sort to spread this kind of alarm and provoke this societal response.[5]

The point then is clear: the links between increases in inequality and the overall *level* of children's attainments is complex and ill understood by researchers concerned with the determinants of children's attainments.

OVERALL TRENDS AND RACIAL DIFFERENCES IN
INCOME AND POVERTY

Since the 1970s, there has been a striking divergence in the economic fates of individual workers. For both men and women, but especially for men, earnings inequality has increased substantially as labor market rewards for people with skills and training have eclipsed the growing supply of such workers. The earnings of college-educated men and women have risen substantially, while those with less education have done well to hold their own. Indeed, those with the fewest skills have experienced real decreases in wage rates and earnings (see Gottschalk 1997; Johnson 1997; Topel 1997; Haveman and Buron 1998).

It is not clear that these labor market developments pertaining to individual workers translate directly into changes in family income inequality. In addition to changing labor market returns, the economic status of families reflects a number of other factors—changes in family structure, changes in labor market participation (for example, the increase in two-worker families), and changes in governmental income support policy, to mention only some of the more important. For this reason, we here examine trends in family income and poverty to see whether the widening inequality in wages is mirrored in the economic status of families at the bottom of the income distribution. We pay particular attention to changes in income poverty, as that is perhaps the most trenchant potential effect of increased family income inequality.[6]

A substantial body of research has examined trends in income and income inequality in family resources (see, for example, Conley 1999; Danziger and Gottschalk 1995; Karoly 1992; Levy and Murnane 1992). We first summarize these trends in income levels, income inequality, and poverty and then seek to understand these developments by tracing some important changes in the underlying determinants of inequality and poverty. We have used a variety of income concepts and indicators of inequality, and we report measures for various population groupings. Because we are interested in the effects of growing income inequality on children, we concentrate on measures for families with children.

Family Income Trends

Table 4.1 contains the mean and median incomes for families with at least one child under age eighteen for the period 1975 to 2000. Between 1975 and 2000, median income (in 2001 dollars) for these families increased from $41,297 to $52,113; most of the increase occurred in the late 1990s. During much of the 1980s and the early 1990s, the median income of these families with children was actually lower than in 1974. Mean family income increased by a larger amount—from $45,894 to $67,559—over the same period. This difference between the median and the mean is a reflection of the growth in income inequality: the very large increases in income experienced by the families at the top of the distribution pulled up the mean without affecting the median.

In 2000 the median income of white families with children was about 175 percent of that of black and Hispanic families ($55,964, as compared to $31,306 for black families and $33,565 for Hispanic families). Between 1987 and 2000 (the period for which the data enable a comparison), the ratio of black to white income varied between .52 and .56, while the ratio of Hispanic to white income declined in the early 1990s, from .60 in 1990 to .55 in 1995, probably reflecting the impact of high levels of immigration over this period. By the year 2000 the ratio of Hispanic to white income had returned to .60.

TABLE 4.1   *Mean and Median Income and the Ratio of Mean to Median for Families with at Least One Child Under Age Eighteen, by Race, 1975 to 2000*

Type of Family and Year	Number (Thousands)	Median Income	Mean Income	Ratio
All families				
2000	38,190	$52,113	$67,559	1.30
1995	36,719	46,157	57,859	1.25
1990	34,503	44,954	53,144	1.18
1985	31,670	43,471	50,065	1.15
1980	31,227	43,472	48,363	1.11
1975	30,177	41,297	45,894	1.11
White families				
2000	30,422	55,964	71,793	1.28
1995	29,713	49,704	61,352	1.23
1990	28,117	47,937	56,347	1.18
1987	27,930	48,931	56,546	1.16
Black families				
2000	5,568	31,306	41,514	1.33
1995	5,340	26,150	37,220	1.42
1990	5,089	25,424	33,724	1.33
1987	4,880	25,281	33,611	1.33
Hispanic families				
2000	5,669	33,565	44,703	1.33
1995	4,422	26,607	35,802	1.35
1990	3,497	28,896	36,124	1.25
1987	3,201	28,683	36,418	1.27

Source: U.S. Department of Commerce (2002a).
Note: Families with at least one child under age eighteen as of March of the following year. "Related" children was used beginning in 1987; "own" children was used in earlier years. Data by type of family are not available by race before 1987. Income in 2001 CPI-U-RS adjusted dollars.

Trends in Family Income Inequality

Our discussion of trends in mean and median income has suggested an increase in income inequality. Column 4 of table 4.1 presents the ratio of mean to median income—a rough indicator of inequality in the distribution—over the period from 1974 to the end of the decade.[7] Among all families, this ratio increased from 1.11 to 1.30, reflecting the growth in inequality.

A second indicator of income inequality among families is the ratio of income to the poverty line at different quintiles. For families with children under age eighteen, this ratio increased from 2.40 to 3.28 between 1967 and 1994. Notably, the ratio for the highest quintile increased from 4.77 to 7.14, while the ratio for the lowest quintile actually decreased from .74 to .66 (U.S. Department of Health and Human Services 2000), indicating that the highest-income families were pulling away from the middle of the income distribution far more rapidly than those at the bottom of the distribution. Because of these changes at the top and the bottom of the distribution, the gap between the highest and lowest quintiles widened considerably during this period.

In table 4.2, we present the trend in family income inequality in the United States by

TABLE 4.2   *Poverty Rates, Poverty Rate Reduction, Mean Income, and Gini Coefficients, by Race, 1975 to 2000*

	All Families				White Families			
Year	Poverty Rate	Poverty Rate Reduction	Mean Income[a]	Gini Coefficient	Poverty Rate	Poverty Rate Reduction	Mean Income[a]	Gini Coefficient
2000	8.7%	1.3%	$67,609	0.433	7.1%	0.9%	$70,386	0.425
1995	10.8	0.8	59,234	0.421	8.5	0.6	61,821	0.409
1990	10.7	−0.4	56,015	0.396	8.1	−0.3	58,484	0.384
1985	11.4	0.2	51,692	0.389	9.1	0.0	53,937	0.378
1980	10.3	−1.2	48,781	0.365	8.0	−1.1	50,744	0.353
1975	9.7	−0.9	45,082	0.357	7.7	−0.9	46,720	0.349
Mean of all years in interval	10.60	−0.03	52,922.69	0.39	8.22	−0.03	55,237.15	0.38

Source: U.S. Department of Commerce (2002b, 2002c, 2002d).
[a]In 2001 constant dollars.

racial group from 1975 to 2000, using the Gini coefficient as our indicator of inequality. Over this twenty-five-year period, income inequality trended upward within each racial group. The bulk of the increase was concentrated in the period after 1975 and before 1990. Two interesting features are apparent in these series. First, economic inequality among families was higher for blacks than for either whites or Hispanics in the 1970s. By the end of the 1990s, however, the level of inequality among the groups had decreased. At the same time, as overall and race-specific income inequality was increasing, income gaps between the races were receding. Second, the timing of the increases in inequality among these racial groups differs substantially. Among whites, the big increase in income inequality came about a decade after the increase recorded for Hispanics, from about 1985 to 1995, compared to the late 1970s and early 1980s. Perhaps immigration during that earlier period accounts for the early increase in Hispanic inequality. Interestingly, income inequality among black families shows no particular period of intense increase; it actually declined during the latter part of the 1990s, perhaps reflecting either the growth of a black middle class, which has been noted by several observers, or the increased incarceration of lower-skilled black men, who are not included in the statistics (see Chandra 2003; Landry 1987).

Trends in U.S. Poverty

From the start of the War on Poverty in the mid-1960s until 1971, the nation's overall poverty rate (among individuals; not in table 4.2) fell. The overall poverty rate reached 11.1 percent in 1971, and the children's poverty rate stood at 15.3 percent. Since 1973, the official poverty rate for all persons has always exceeded 11 percent. In the early 1980s the most severe recession since the 1930s raised the overall poverty rate to about 15 percent. Although the recovery of the 1980s was a long one, the real wages of low- and medium-skilled males continued the erosion that had begun in the mid-1970s, and inequality rose primarily because incomes at the top of the distribution increased. The overall poverty rate fell slowly, but it remained above 13 percent for the rest of the 1980s.

Black Families				Hispanic Families			
Poverty Rate	Poverty Rate Reduction	Mean Income[a]	Gini Coefficient	Poverty Rate	Poverty Rate Reduction	Mean Income[a]	Gini Coefficient
19.3%	4.1%	$45,078	0.442	19.2%	3.5%	$47,092	0.444
26.4	0.9	39,231	0.457	27.0	0.8	37,665	0.439
29.3	−1.5	36,187	0.445	25.0	−1.6	38,494	0.416
28.7	2.2	33,514	0.430	25.5	−0.3	36,327	0.406
28.9	−1.1	32,161	0.410	23.2	−2.9	35,842	0.386
27.1	−0.2	30,162	0.386	25.1	−3.9	32,177	0.371
28.48	0.22	34,348.31	0.43	24.37	−0.08	37,044.00	0.41

During the recession of the early 1990s the overall poverty rate rose to nearly 15 percent. However, the prolonged expansion of the 1990s brought the rate down to 11.7 percent in 2001 the rate increased to 12.1 percent in 2002. These declines were the first noticeable successes against poverty since the gains of the early 1970s.

Table 4.3 shows the trend in the children's poverty rate from 1980 through 2000. As with the overall poverty rate, the children's poverty rate fell from the mid-1960s to 1971. By 1971 the children's poverty rate stood at 15.3 percent. After 1971 the children's poverty rate drifted up, and by 1980 it had risen to 18.3 percent. Over the entire 1980 to 2000 period the percentage of children residing in families with incomes below the poverty line remained relatively constant, around 20 percent. Even though mean incomes were increasing during the 1980s, children's poverty appeared resistant to this growth. Offsetting changes such as the continued growth of one-parent families, teen nonmarital childbearing, and immigration of Hispanic families contributed to the stickiness of the children's poverty rate.

When the recession of the early 1990s struck, the children's poverty rate also increased. Not until the prolonged period of economic growth during the 1990s did the children's poverty rate begin to fall. The prosperity of that period had a powerful effect on the rate—it dropped from 20 percent in 1996 to 18 percent in 1998, and fell again to 15.8 percent in 2001 (not shown in the table), its lowest rate since 1979. The percentage of children living in extreme poverty (incomes below half the poverty line) ranged between 7 and 9 percent during the same period and declined to 6.6 percent in 2001.[8]

In 2001, 12.8 percent of white children, 30 percent of black children, and 27.4 percent of Hispanic children were in families with incomes below the poverty line. Indeed, by 2001 the percentage of black children in poverty was at its historic low point. Children in married-couple families experience substantially lower poverty rates than those for all children, though the racial gaps are still very large: 5 percent of white, 8 percent of black, and 21 percent of Hispanic children in such families lived in poverty in 2000.

TABLE 4.3   *Related Children Under Age Eighteen Living Below Selected Poverty Levels, by Age, Family Structure, Race, and Hispanic Origin, 1980 to 2000*

Poverty Level	1980	1985	1990	1995	2000
Under 100 percent of poverty					
Children in all families					
Related children	18%	20%	20%	20%	19%
White, non-Hispanic	n.a.	n.a.	12	11	9
Black	42	43	44	42	30
Hispanic[a]	33	40	38	39	27
Related children under age six	20	23	23	24	17
Related children age six to seventeen	17	19	18	18	15
Children in married-couple families					
Related children	n.a.	n.a.	10	10	8
White, non-Hispanic	n.a.	n.a.	7	6	5
Black	n.a.	n.a.	18	13	8
Hispanic[a]	n.a.	n.a.	27	28	21
Related children under age six	n.a.	n.a.	12	11	9
Related children age six to seventeen	n.a.	n.a.	10	9	8
Children in female-householder families, no husband present					
Related children	51	54	53	50	40
White, non-Hispanic	n.a.	n.a.	40	34	28
Black	65	67	65	62	49
Hispanic[a]	65	72	68	66	48
Related children under age six	65	66	66	62	47
Related children age six to seventeen	46	48	47	45	36
All children[b]	18	21	21	21	16
Under 50 percent of poverty					
Children in all families					
Related children	7	8	8	8	6
White, non-Hispanic	n.a.	n.a.	4	3	3
Black	17	22	22	20	14
Hispanic[a]	n.a.	n.a.	14	16	9
Under 150 percent of poverty					
Children in all families					
Related children	29	32	31	32	26
White, non-Hispanic	n.a.	n.a.	21	19	16
Black	57	59	57	56	45
Hispanic[a]	n.a.	n.a.	55	59	47

Source: Federal Interagency Forum on Child and Family Statistics (2002a).
Note: Estimates refer to children who are related to the householder and who are under age eighteen. The poverty level is based on money income and does not include noncash benefits, such as food stamps. Poverty thresholds reflect family size and composition.
n.a. = not available
[a]Persons of Hispanic origin may be of any race.
[b]Includes children not related to the householder.

TRENDS IN CHILDREN'S ATTAINMENTS AND THE INPUTS TO ATTAINMENTS

Increased inequality in the distribution of family income and the persistence of poverty motivate our current study. In the previous section, we described these trends, briefly discussed some of the primary causes, and set these developments in a historical context. The primary goal of this part of our review is to examine trends in the level of, and inequality in, a variety of other family and community inputs into the process that yields children's attainments. We also examine trends in those aspects of children's attainments identified earlier. As we have noted, an increase in family economic inequality may not necessarily lead to an increase in inequality in outcomes for children. A review of trends in children's attainments over time may show, for example, that although family income inequality has increased, inequality in educational attainment has remained about the same or even declined.

When studying the potential effects of growing family income inequality, it is particularly important to consider trends in the level and inequality of inputs to children's attainments, as well as trends in those attainments. Changes in the level and distribution of both inputs to children and their eventual attainments are the direct manifestation of economic inequality; they are the elements that reflect the intergenerational transmission of economic status and the means through which the strong links between children's success and family background are weakened. In short, this section of our review considers the various factors that, as a result of income inequality, are distributed unevenly among children. This review also highlights some inputs that appear to be unrelated to increasing inequality.

Examining inequality in inputs and attainments is a difficult task. Unlike income, an interval measure, family status and access to child care, for example, do not lend themselves easily to the conventional measures of inequality such as Gini coefficients. A more appropriate way to think about inequality in these measures is to see the presence of some characteristics as positive factors that support desirable child attainments and the presence of other characteristics as negative factors that impede desirable child attainments. In this context we can define a worsening situation as one in which the proportion of individuals who have a negative characteristic increases or the proportion who have a positive characteristic decreases. So, for example, an increase in the proportion of children living with only one of their parents would be defined as a deteriorating situation, while an increase in the proportion of children living with two parents would be defined as an improving situation. A measure of inequality would be the absolute percentage differences in the proportion of poor or minority children who have a negative (positive) characteristic minus those nonpoor or nonminority children with the same characteristic or a ratio of these proportions. Thus, we ask whether the black-white gap in educational attainment has narrowed or widened over time, and we ask whether the black-white difference in the proportion of children living with two parents has narrowed or widened over time.

Trends in Inputs to Children's Attainments

Although there is a great deal of information on trends in the levels of family and community inputs, we have found very little research on trends in the inequality of these inputs. For example, information on the educational level of parents over time is readily available, but few researchers have examined inequality in parental education and changes in this inequality over time. The major exceptions are variables describing the economic position of the families in which children grow up, namely, the wages, earnings, and income of their parents or families. We discussed trends in the economic position of families earlier, relying on the substantial body of research that has documented growing inequality in each of these dimensions. In addition, we compare the levels of important parental and family characteristics for racial and ethnic groups.

Here we examine the trends in the levels of factors that a sizable research literature has identified as related to children's outcomes.[9] In addition to family income, three other sets of factors have attracted the most attention from researchers: parental education, family structure (see in particular McLanahan and Sandefur 1994), and family size. Clearly these three sets of factors are closely related to family income. Parental education is a fairly robust indicator of permanent income. Moreover, family incomes vary across types of family structure, the most obvious differences being between single-parent and couple-headed families. Family size is important in assessing the "equivalent" resources available to children in families with different numbers of members, since the number of children affects the time and goods a family can invest in each child; it is considered in establishing the national poverty thresholds. We first discuss what is known about trends in the levels of these three sets of factors. We discuss racial and ethnic inequality in most of the factors as well. Then we discuss additional factors thought to contribute to child outcomes, although the links may be somewhat less clear: overall distributional inequality in family assets, parental time spent with children, and the inequality in school expenditures and use of child care during the preschool years.

Trends in Parental Characteristics and Choices   Table 4.4 contains information on the educational attainment of white, black, and Hispanic parents of children age six to eighteen from 1974 through 1999. In 1974 over 27 percent of white mothers had not completed high school. This had declined to around 7 percent by 1999. Among black mothers the decline was from 58 percent to 20 percent, and among Hispanic mothers the decline was from 62 percent to 49 percent. In the case of Hispanics, immigration has played a significant role in retarding the decrease in the prevalence of high school dropouts. Were we to look at figures for only native-born families, we would find a substantially larger improvement in the educational level of Hispanic parents.

Looking at the upper tail of the educational distribution, we find that the percentage of white mothers with a bachelor's degree or higher grew from 9 percent in 1974 to 26 percent in 1999. Among blacks the percentage grew from 4 percent to 14 percent, and among Hispanics the percentage grew from 4 percent to 7 percent. Again, immigration is largely responsible for the smaller increase among Hispanics.

From this evidence, parents in these three racial-ethnic groups have experienced significant improvement in educational levels over time. This bodes well for the well-being of children, since more highly educated parents generally have higher incomes; moreover, as discussed later, parental education is a direct contributor to children's success. In addition to the growth in educational levels, the gap between whites and blacks in high school completion and college graduation also narrowed somewhat. For example, the percentage of white mothers who had completed a college degree in 1974 was 2.25 times the percentage for black mothers in 1974, while in 1999 it was 1.86 times the percentage for black mothers. Nevertheless, by the end of the twentieth century a good deal of racial and ethnic inequality in parental education still existed.

Table 4.5 contains information on the percentage of children under age eighteen who live in one of four family types (two-parent, single-mother, single-father, no-parent), by race

TABLE 4.4   *Distribution of Six- to Eighteen-Year-Olds According to Parents' Highest Education Level, by Child's Race-Ethnicity, 1974 to 1999*

Parents' Highest Education Level and Child's Race-Ethnicity	1974	1979	1984	1989	1994	1999
White families						
Mother's highest education level						
Less than high school diploma	27.1%	22.1%	16.8%	12.0%	9.5%	6.9%
High school diploma or GED	51.4	50.4	50.3	48.8	37.9	35.2
Some college	12.2	16.1	18.3	21.3	31.0	31.4
Bachelor's degree or higher	9.3	11.4	14.6	17.9	21.6	26.4
Father's highest education level						
Less than high school diploma	28.6	22.4	16.2	12.2	9.1	8.1
High school diploma or GED	38.3	38.7	39.0	38.4	32.2	31.5
Some college	13.2	15.5	18.3	20.1	27.4	26.8
Bachelor's degree or higher	19.9	23.4	26.5	29.3	31.3	33.6
Black families						
Mother's highest education level						
Less than high school diploma	57.6	46.4	34.8	26.3	20.0	19.6
High school diploma or GED	32.1	36.1	42.6	44.4	40.0	37.1
Some college	6.8	12.5	15.6	19.8	30.0	29.5
Bachelor's degree or higher	3.6	4.9	7.0	9.4	10.1	13.9
Father's highest education level						
Less than high school diploma	61.3	44.3	33.1	25.4	18.2	14.6
High school diploma or GED	27.1	35.7	38.4	40.4	42.2	39.3
Some college	7.6	12.7	16.3	20.6	23.5	29.7
Bachelor's degree or higher	4.0	7.3	12.2	13.7	16.1	16.5
Hispanic families						
Mother's highest education level						
Less than high school diploma	61.8	60.4	60.5	55.8	51.8	49.2
High school diploma or GED	28.9	28.3	28.2	28.7	26.9	25.2
Some college	5.7	7.2	7.7	10.2	15.6	18.2
Bachelor's degree or higher	3.5	4.1	3.7	5.2	5.7	7.4
Father's highest education level						
Less than high school diploma	58.3	57.2	56.3	51.6	51.1	48.9
High school diploma or GED	24.9	25.0	25.0	27.2	23.2	26.2
Some college	8.4	9.5	10.5	13.4	17.5	14.7
Bachelor's degree or higher	8.4	8.3	8.2	7.7	8.3	10.1

Source: U.S. Department of Education (2001).

Note: Information on parents' highest education level is available only for those parents who live in the same household with their child.

and ethnicity, from 1980 through 2000. For all children, the percentage who lived with two parents decreased from 77 percent in 1980 to 69 percent in 2000. In other words, a smaller percentage of children lived in the most economically well-off type of family at the end of this period than at the beginning. These figures differ significantly by race. By 2000, 77 percent of non-Hispanic white children were living with two parents relative to 65 percent of Hispanic children and 38 percent of non-Hispanic black children. The figure for black children, however, was at a low of 33 percent in 1995 and has increased slightly since then.

Although changes in the proportion of children who live with two parents has pro-

TABLE 4.5   *Children Under Age Eighteen, by Presence of Parents in Household, Race, and Hispanic Origin, 1980 to 2000*

Race	1980	1985	1990	1995	2000
Total					
Two parents[a]	77%	74%	73%	69%	69%
Mother only[b]	18	21	22	23	22
Father only[b]	2	2	3	4	4
No parent	4	3	3	4	4
White, non-Hispanic					
Two parents[a]	n.a.	n.a.	81	78	77
Mother only[b]	n.a.	n.a.	15	16	16
Father only[b]	n.a.	n.a.	3	3	4
No parent	n.a.	n.a.	2	3	3
Black					
Two parents[a]	42	39	38	33	38
Mother only[b]	44	51	51	52	49
Father only[b]	2	3	4	4	4
No parent	12	7	8	11	9
Hispanic[c]					
Two parents[a]	75	68	67	63	65
Mother only[b]	20	27	27	28	25
Father only[b]	2	2	3	4	4
No parent	3	3	3	4	5

Source: Federal Interagency Forum on Child and Family Statistics (2002b, 73).
Note: Family structure refers to the presence of biological, adoptive, and stepparents in the child's household. Thus, a child with a biological mother and stepfather living in the household is said to have two parents.
n.a. = not available
[a]Excludes families where parents are not living as a married couple.
[b]Includes some families where both parents are present in the household but living as unmarried partners.
[c]Persons of Hispanic origin may be of any race.

duced a less favorable situation for children on average, declines in family size over the past few decades have benefited children. With smaller family sizes, parents have more resources to invest in fewer children on average. The change is most obvious in the percentage of families with three children, which declined from 11 percent of all families in 1970 to 7 percent in 2000, and in the percentage of families with four or more children, which declined from 10 percent in 1970 to 3 percent in 2000. The number of families with no children also increased over this period, from 43 percent in 1960 to 52 percent in 1999. In 2000, 10 percent of white families had three or more children compared to 12 percent of black families and 19 percent of Hispanic families.

In sum, if we look at three key indicators of family inputs—parental education, family structure, and family size—we see that the situation for children has improved substantially on two of these, parental education and family size, but worsened in terms of family structure.

Other parental and family characteristics may also reflect the inputs available to children. Asset holdings (including homeownership) and parental time available for child nurturing are two of them. Edward Wolff (2001) suggests that family asset holdings increased modestly between 1989 and 1998. He finds that median family net worth increased from

$58,400 to $60,700 (in 1998 dollars) and that mean family net worth increased from $243,600 to $270,300. Unfortunately, these estimates are for all families, not just families with children, our primary interest.

Wealth is very highly concentrated in the United States. In 1998, for example, the top 0.5 percent of families held 26 percent of net worth (Kennickell, Starr-McCluer, and Surette 2000). This is an increase from the concentration of wealth in 1989, when about 23 percent of net worth was held by the top 0.5 percent of families. Arthur Kennickell and his colleagues (2000) find no statistically significant changes in the Gini coefficient of family wealth holdings across the 1989 to 1998 period, but this conclusion is controversial. For example, Wolff (2001) finds that wealth disparities continued to widen from 1989 to 1998. Over a longer period of time, Wolff (1998) also finds that wealth inequality in the United States has increased, especially relative to other developed countries. Increases in wealth inequality between 1984 and 1994 are also shown by James Smith and his colleagues (1999), using the Panel Study of Income Dynamics (PSID). The conclusion that wealth inequality has increased across families is consistent with both the large increase in the value of financial assets during the strong stock market performance of the 1990s and the increases in income inequality over time.[10]

One aspect of asset holding that may be more relevant to children is homeownership. Not only is homeownership an important element of economic and personal well-being, but families who own their own homes tend to live in better neighborhoods than renters. Furthermore, in general, owning a home tends to be less expensive than renting, enabling homeowning families to invest resources elsewhere—for example, in quality child care (Conley 1999). According to the U.S. Census Bureau, about 68 percent of all householders in the United States in 2001 owned a home. The percentage of householders who owned their own home increased very little from 1965 to 1990, from around 63 percent in 1965 to 64 percent in 1990. Much of the increase, then, in homeownership took place during the 1990s, from 64 percent to 68 percent. Over 70 percent of non-Hispanic whites owned a home in 2002, as compared to 46 percent of blacks and 46 percent of Hispanics. What little evidence we have suggests that homeownership among blacks and native-born Hispanics increased during the 1990s as well. For this component of wealth, racial disparities appear to have eroded over time.

The time that parents allocate to their children is yet another potentially important factor influencing children's attainments. Patterns in the level of parental time allocations to children and in inequalities in such allocations have been studied by Suzanne Bianchi and her colleagues (2003), using time diary information; we simply summarize their findings here.[11] Their most basic finding is shown in the time series in table 4.6, which shows the mean and standard deviation of child care time (in minutes per day) for all parents. Both the level (mean) and the inequality (standard deviation) of child care time increased between 1975 and 2000. Clearly these patterns reflect both the increase in the prevalence of single-parent families over this period and the rapid rise in the time that mothers spend in market work.

Holding other things equal, college-educated mothers appear to invest more time in child-rearing than do mothers with no higher education, but the authors found that this differential did not increase during the period. The distribution of child care time among fathers was highly bifurcated, with a sizable minority spending considerable time in child care and the majority doing little or none.[12]

Overall, the authors conclude that the trends in time spent with children were increasing for both parents with a college education and those without a college education during the period of growing income inequality. However, they found little evidence that parental

TABLE 4.6   *Time (Minutes per Day) Spent by All Parents in Child Care, 1965 to 2000*

	1965	1975	1985	1995	1998	2000
Total parents						
Mean	57	51	48	63	85	87
(Standard deviation)	(78)	(76)	(85)	(96)	(106)	(115)

Source: Biachi et al. (2003, table 1.3).

time investments were becoming more differentiated by educational attainment, suggesting that any inequality in parental investment of time in children by education level has not grown larger during the period of increased income inequality.

Trends in Inputs Outside the Family   Child care and school quality are also relevant to understanding the support provided to children. Marcia Meyers and her colleagues (this volume) discuss trends in child care and child care quality in depth. Sean Corcoran and his colleagues (this volume) examine the level and trend in inequality of per pupil expenditures across school districts in the United States.[13] The information in these two chapters suggests that we have seen steady improvements in the level of preschool and school resources available to children during the period when family economic inequality has been increasing. Both the level of racial inequality in access to quality preschool care and overall inequality in per pupil expenditures among school districts appear to have narrowed while family income inequality has increased. However, the data do not tell us whether individuals at the bottom of the income distribution have become more or less successful in utilizing these resources. A number of scenarios are possible. It could be that those at the bottom of the income distribution have not benefited as much as those at the top from improvements in preschool care and school resources. On the other hand, it is also possible that improvements in child care and public education have countered some of the increases in family economic inequality.

The trend in neighborhood quality seems to vary by indicator of quality of neighborhood. Using crime, the proportion of parents who believe crime is a problem in their neighborhood increased from the 1973 to 1975 period to the 1991 to 1993 period, and the ratio of responses comparing the response of middle-quintile-income parents to those in the bottom quintile increased over this period from 1.17 to 1.53.[14] This evidence suggests a worsening of the environment in which children are being raised, along with increasing inequality in that environment. Alternatively, the concentration of poverty declined in the 1990s after substantial increases in the 1980s; the proportion of urban poor living in census tracts with poverty levels of over 40 percent went from 13 percent (1980) to 17 percent (1990) to 12 percent (2000). The education level in these poverty tracts also increased, as captured by the declining proportion of the population without a high school degree. The racial composition of these concentrated-poverty neighborhoods also changed: in 1980 nearly half of the concentrated-poverty areas were dominated by non-Hispanic blacks, but this was reduced to 39 percent as of 2000; instead, concentrated-poverty rates were more heavily dominated in 2000 by Hispanics, whose dominance in these areas increased from 13 to 20 percent (see Kingsley and Pettit 2003). By these indicators, neighborhood quality would seem to be improving, especially for those living in the worst areas—a suggestion that inequality in this dimension decreased.

Trends in Inputs: Summary Our review of trends in some of the family-based inputs to children over the period of increasing income inequality reveals that in most respects the overall level of these inputs has increased. Parents are more educated than in the past, and families are smaller. The quality of education during the preschool years has also improved, as measured by the percentage of children who have been placed in center-based preschool care, by teacher-student ratios, and by per pupil expenditures. The per family level of net worth has also increased, and in recent years parents appear to be spending more time in activities related to the care of their children than in prior years. The primary factor with an adverse trend is family composition: there has been a decrease in the proportion of children living with two parents. However, this trend appears to have leveled off or slowed down in recent years.

Although research on trends in inequality of these inputs is limited and some inputs, such as family structure, do not lend themselves easily to the measurement of inequality, we have discovered some patterns of interest. The level of inequality in asset holdings among families appears to have increased, though there is some controversy about this. Similarly, inequality among children in the amount of parental time that they are allocated has increased. On the other hand, racial and income differences in access to quality preschool care seem to have declined, and inequality among school districts in per pupil expenditures as well as the concentration of poverty in neighborhoods is smaller at the end of the 1990s than it was in the 1970s. It is possible that the impact on children of increasing income and wealth inequality and increasing inequality of parental time has been compensated for by a general improvement in the level and inequality of other inputs into their well-being. This is an empirical question that needs to be addressed.

Trends in Children's Attainments

In this section, we review trends in attainments or outcomes that have been widely studied in research on the effects of family income on child and adolescent well-being. These outcomes include teen fertility, educational attainment, labor force participation, and earnings.

Teen Fertility Table 4.7 shows the trends in rates of births to adolescents during the 1980 through 2000 period. Although the birth rate was fairly stable in the 1980s, with 50 to 53 births per 1,000 teenage women between the ages of fifteen and nineteen, it rose significantly and stayed above the 1980s levels in the first half of the 1990s. At its peak in 1991 the birth rate was 62.1 births per 1,000 females age fifteen to nineteen. The rate of births to adolescent mothers has decreased since that time. In 2001, 43.6 of 1,000 women between the ages of fifteen and nineteen had a child, fewer than recorded in 1980.

These rates vary widely across racial and ethnic groups, although the recent decline in teen childbearing is apparent in all racial and ethnic groups. Among non-Hispanic whites age fifteen to nineteen, the birth rate peaked at 43.4 in 1991 and declined to 32.5 in 2000. The rate also peaked among non-Hispanic blacks in 1991, at 118.9; the rate had declined substantially by 2000, to 81.9, but was still well above the white rate for the entire 1980 to 1998 period. The pattern is the same for American Indians, whose rate peaked at 85.0 in 1991 and declined to a low of 67.8 in 2000. The teen birth rate for Asians and Hispanics peaked in 1994 at 27.1 and 107.7, respectively, and declined to 21.6 for Asians and 94.4 for Hispanics by 2000. The somewhat different patterns for Asians and Hispanics relative to the other groups are undoubtedly due in part to the impact of immigration on these two

TABLE 4.7   *Adolescent Birth Rate, by Age, Race, and Hispanic Origin, 1980 to 2000 (Live Births per 1,000 Females in Specified Age Group)*

Characteristic	1980	1985	1990	1995	2000
All races					
Age fifteen to nineteen	53.0	51.0	59.9	56.8	48.5
White, total					
Age fifteen to nineteen	45.4	43.3	50.8	50.1	43.6
White, non-Hispanic					
Age fifteen to nineteen	41.2	n.a.	42.5	39.3	32.5
Black, total					
Age fifteen to nineteen	97.8	95.4	112.8	96.1	79.4
Black, non-Hispanic					
Age fifteen to nineteen	105.1	n.a.	116.2	99.3	81.9
Hispanic[a]					
Age fifteen to nineteen	82.2	n.a.	100.3	106.7	94.4
American Indian/Alaska native					
Age fifteen to nineteen	82.2	79.2	81.1	78	67.8
Asian/Pacific Islander					
Age fifteen to nineteen	26.2	23.8	26.4	26.1	21.6

Source: Federal Interagency Forum on Child and Family Statistics (2002c).
n.a. = not available
[a]Persons of Hispanic origin may be of any race. Trend data for Hispanics are affected by expansion of the reporting area in which an item on Hispanic origin is included on the birth.

groups. Although non-Hispanic blacks had higher teen fertility rates than Hispanics in 1991, by 1998 the Hispanic teen birth rate was the highest among the major racial and ethnic groups in the United States.

In sum, teenagers are less likely to have children now than they were in the early 1990s, so on this dimension the level of attainment has improved. There are substantial differences in the rates of teen childbearing among racial groups, and these racial patterns have changed over recent years: by the end of the 1990s, Hispanic rates exceeded those for non-Hispanic blacks (which continued to exceed those for non-Hispanic whites).

Table 4.8 shows the trend in high school graduation rates for individuals age eighteen to twenty-four.[15] The top row shows that the percentage of all individuals in this age group who completed high school has remained relatively constant at near 85 percent over the period 1980 to 2000. However, the information available for the 1990 to 1995 period shows that the percentage who received an equivalent degree increased from 4 percent to 8 percent, and correspondingly, that the percentage who received a diploma declined from 81 percent to 78 percent. Obviously, equivalency programs are becoming increasingly impor- tant in producing high school graduates. We must take into account the changes in Census Bureau procedures noted in the table in interpreting these trends.

The trends for non-Hispanic whites since 1980 follow this same general pattern, which is what we would expect, since they constitute the large majority of those age eighteen to twenty-four. The trend for non-Hispanic blacks is somewhat different, however: high school completion among them rose from 75 percent in 1980 to 85 percent in 1995, declined to 81 percent in 1998, and rose to 84 percent in 2000.[16] The numbers for Hispanics show much more year-to-year variation, owing in part to the smaller numbers of Hispanics in the

TABLE 4.8   *Adults Age Eighteen to Twenty-Four Who Have Completed High School, by Race, Hispanic Origin, and Method of Completion, 1980 to 2000*

	1980	1985	1990	1995[a]	2000
Total[b]					
Total completing high school[c]	84%	85%	86%	85%	87%
Method of completion					
Diploma	n.a.	n.a.	81	78	n.a.
Equivalent[d]	n.a.	n.a.	4	8	n.a.
White, non-Hispanic					
Total completing high school[c]	88	88	90	90	92
Method of completion					
Diploma	n.a.	n.a.	85	83	n.a.
Equivalent[d]	n.a.	n.a.	5	7	n.a.
Black, non-Hispanic					
Total completing high school[c]	75	81	83	85	84
Method of completion					
Diploma	n.a.	n.a.	78	75	n.a.
Equivalent[d]	n.a.	n.a.	5	9	n.a.
Hispanic[e]					
Total completing high school[c]	57	67	59	63	64
Method of completion					
Diploma	n.a.	n.a.	55	54	n.a.
Equivalent[d]	n.a.	n.a.	4	9	n.a.

Source: Federal Interagency Forum on Child and Family Statistics (2002d, 110).
Note: Data are for those not currently enrolled in high school or below.
n.a. = not available
[a]Data for 1995 and subsequent years are not strictly comparable with data for 1980 to 1993, because of major revisions in the CPS questionnaire and data collection methodology and because of the inclusion of 1990 census-based population controls in the estimation process.
[b]Percentages are not shown separately for non-Hispanic Asians/Pacific Islanders and American Indians/Alaska natives, but they are included in the total.
[c]From 1980 to 1991, high school completion was measured as completing four years of high school rather than the actual attainment of a high school diploma.
[d]Diploma equivalents include alternative credentials obtained by passing exams such as the GED test.
[e]Persons of Hispanic origin may be of any race.

samples collected in the October Current Population Surveys. The trend is one of a gradual increase from 57 percent in 1980 to percentages in the mid-60s range in the late 1990s, to 64 percent in 2000. The percentage of degrees earned through equivalency programs has increased for Hispanics as well. Hence, in terms of high school completion, there is a strong upward trend over time. Moreover, since 1980 the racial disparities in high school completion have decreased substantially.

Table 4.9 shows the trends in the percentage of those age twenty-five to twenty-nine who attained a bachelor's degree from 1980 through 2000, and the percentage of the same age range who attained an associate's degree from 1992 through 2000. The percentage who attained a bachelor's degree increased from 26 percent in 1980 to 33 percent in 2000. The percentage who attained an associate's degree increased from 8 percent in 1992 to 10

TABLE 4.9   *High School Graduates Age Twenty-Five to Twenty-Nine Attaining Higher Degrees, by Race and Hispanic Origin, 1980 to 2000*

Characteristic	1980	1985	1990	1995[a]	2000[a]
Bachelor's degree or higher[b]					
Total	26%	26%	27%	28%	33%
Race and Hispanic origin					
White, non-Hispanic	28	27	29	31	35
Black, non-Hispanic	15	14	16	18	20
Hispanic[c]	13	18	14	16	18
Associate's degree					
Total	n.a.	n.a.	n.a.	10	10
Race and Hispanic origin					
White, non-Hispanic	n.a.	n.a.	n.a.	10	10
Black, non-Hispanic	n.a.	n.a.	n.a.	8	10
Hispanic[c]	n.a.	n.a.	n.a.	7	9

Source: Federal Interagency Forum on Child and Family Statistics (2002e, 113).
Note: Analyses of the 1993 Baccalaureate and Beyond Longitudinal Study indicate that about 10 percent of all persons attaining a bachelor's degree in that year had previously earned an associate's degree. *Source:* National Center for Education Statistics.
n.a. = not available
[a]Data for 1994 and subsequent years are not strictly comparable with data for prior years because of major revisions in the CPS questionnaire and data collection methodology and because of the inclusion of 1990 census-based population controls in the estimation process.
[b]Prior to 1992, this indicator was measured as completing four or more years of college rather than the actual attainment of a bachelor's degree.
[c]Persons of Hispanic origin may be of any race.

percent in 2000. Although the overall trend shows increasing attainment of post–high school degrees, there is a persistent and substantial gap between non-Hispanic whites and Hispanic and non-Hispanic black young people when it comes to educational attainment. The attainment levels of all three racial groups—blacks, whites, and Hispanics—increased over this period. By 2000 over one-third of non-Hispanic whites had attained a bachelor's degree, as compared to 20 percent of non-Hispanic blacks and 18 percent of Hispanics. Roughly equal percentages of the three groups had attained associate's degrees. Overall, the trends in educational attainment suggest general improvement over the past two decades accompanied by persistent racial and ethnic gaps.

Human Capital and Its Utilization

The standard assessment of labor market performance uses employment and earnings over time. However, these indicators combine both the opportunities in the labor market that are open to people and their own choices regarding labor supply and work. Moreover, demographic and macroeconomic changes have had a significant influence on trends in young adult employment and earnings, and these also need to be taken into account. Therefore, we turn to an alternative approach to studying human capital utilization by employing a recently developed concept, earnings capacity (EC) (see Haveman, Bershadker, and Schwabish 2003). Because earnings capacity measures the level of potential earnings—the amount that could be earned if people worked full-time, full-year (FTFY)—of people with varying human capital characteristics, it is independent of labor supply choices. EC is estimated statistically and reflects several human capital considerations, including education, age, gender, and health status. It is an annual value—the amount that a person with a given level of EC could earn if he or she worked FTFY. A person with that level of EC who earns less may do so for several reasons—because of taking a job that pays less than he or she could earn, for instance, or working less than FTFY (for which there may be several reasons). This concept can be used to describe both patterns of human capital attainment for various groups of people and the extent to which this human capital is utilized. As such, EC can be viewed as a superior measure of both labor market potential and attainments to education or employment.

Here we present patterns of EC and its utilization over the twenty-six-year period from 1975 to 2000 along racial and education dimensions for young persons age eighteen to twenty-four. These are shown by race and sex in figures 4.2 and 4.3, for male youths by education in figures 4.4 and 4.5, and for female youths by education in figures 4.6 and 4.7. As the figures indicate, over the entire period the largest decreases in earnings capacity are recorded by high school dropouts. This group experienced a decrease of more than 11 percent in their ability to earn. For example, the EC of young male high school dropouts fell from an already low level of $23,500 in 1975 to $16,900 by 1994. We also examined educational groups separately by race, but these are not shown in the figures. Except for nonwhite men, high school graduates experienced much smaller losses. Women with a high school degree experienced smaller losses than their male counterparts. For all of the vulnerable groups—those with little education and minorities—the period from 1975 to the early 1990s saw reductions in their capacity to earn, with all groups except white females experiencing reductions in excess of 18 percent. The sustained period of economic growth after the recession in the early 1990s benefited all of these groups. With the exception of white women, all have EC increases over that period of at least 7 percent.

In terms of capacity utilization rates (CURs), it is useful to distinguish the period from 1975 through the early 1990s from the subsequent recovery after the recession at the start of the 1990s. The experiences of youths between the two subperiods were quite different. The earlier period witnessed increases in CUR for females but decreases for low-education males, except for nonwhite high school dropouts. Female high school dropouts and the subgroup of nonwhite female high school dropouts enjoyed increases in CUR of over 19 percent. In the later period, the early 1990s to 2000, every subgroup enjoyed an increase in CUR. In fact, all groups of young women, except white high school graduates, recorded increases in CUR of over 20 percent, with higher percentage increases observed for high school dropouts than for graduates. The rapidly growing economy combined with welfare reform efforts appears to have brought substantial numbers of young women with low education into employment. The robust economy also helped young nonwhite men with low schooling levels enjoy at least small increases in utilization over this period.

Although these gains in utilization are impressive, the rather low level of the CURs of these groups at the end of the later period should not be overlooked. None of the dropout groups except nonwhite men had utilization rates as high as 50 percent, with the rates for women remaining at or below about 40 percent. Only young men with a high school degree recorded a 2000 CUR that approached the nation's overall rate of utilization of 72 percent.

Among both young men and women with low levels of schooling, then, EC at the beginning of the period was very low—about $23,500 for young men without a high school degree and less than $17,500 for young women who had dropped out. By the end of the period human capital for both groups had fallen—to below $21,000 for young men and to

(Text continues on p. 176.)

FIGURE 4.2 Per Capita Earnings Capacity of Youths Age Eighteen to Twenty-Four, by Race and Sex, 1975 to 2000

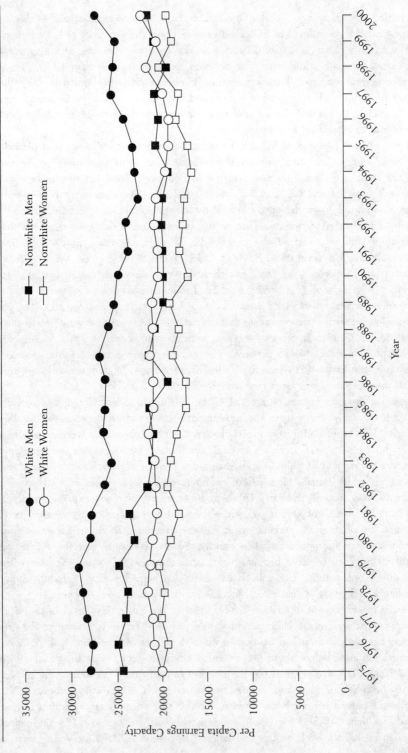

Source: Authors' compilation.

FIGURE 4.3   Capacity Utilization Rates of Youths Age Eighteen to Twenty-Four, by Race and Sex, 1975 to 2000

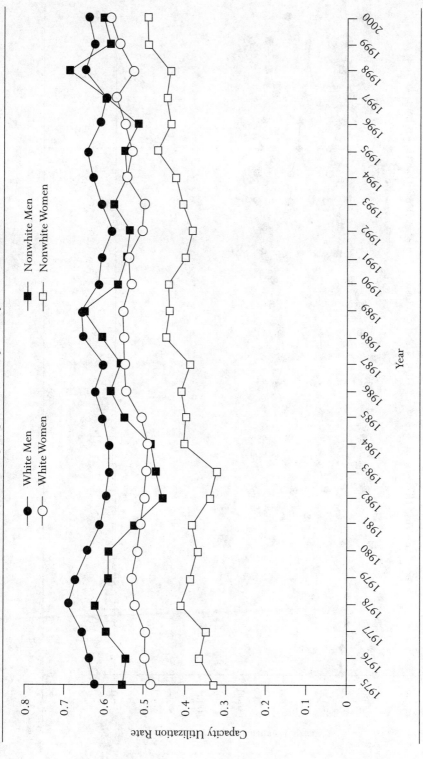

● White Men   ■ Nonwhite Men
○ White Women   □ Nonwhite Women

Source: Authors' compilation.

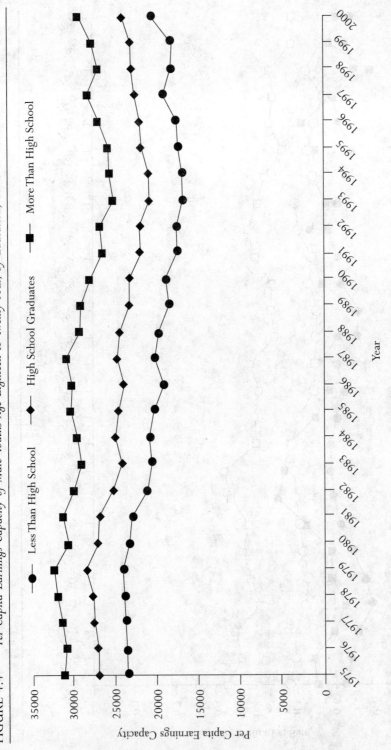

FIGURE 4.4   *Per Capita Earnings Capacity of Male Youths Age Eighteen to Twenty-Four, by Education, 1975 to 2000*

Per Capita Earnings Capacity

35000
30000
25000
20000
15000
10000
5000
0

Year

1975 1976 1977 1978 1979 1980 1981 1982 1983 1984 1985 1986 1987 1988 1989 1990 1991 1992 1993 1994 1995 1996 1997 1998 1999 2000

●— Less Than High School   ◆— High School Graduates   ■— More Than High School

Source: Authors' compilation.

FIGURE 4.5   *Capacity Utilization Rates of Male Youths Age Eighteen to Twenty-Four, by Education, 1975 to 2000*

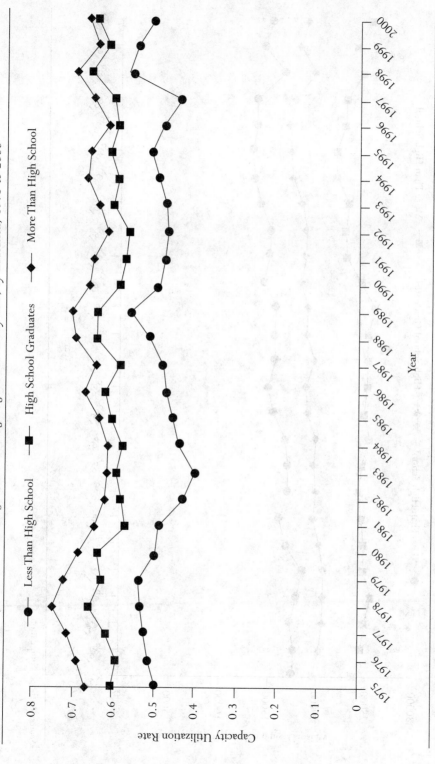

Source: Authors' compilation.

FIGURE 4.6   Per Capita Earnings Capacity of Female Youths Age Eighteen to Twenty-Four, by Education, 1975 to 2000

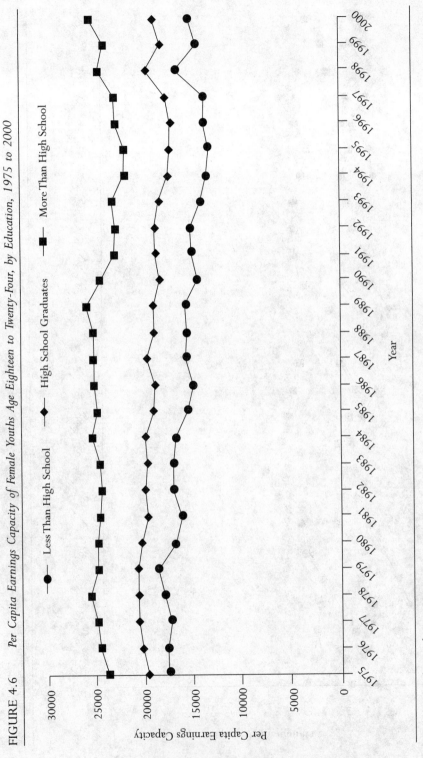

Source: Authors' compilation.

FIGURE 4.7   *Capacity Utilization Rates of Female Youths Age Eighteen to Twenty-Four, by Education, 1975 to 2000*

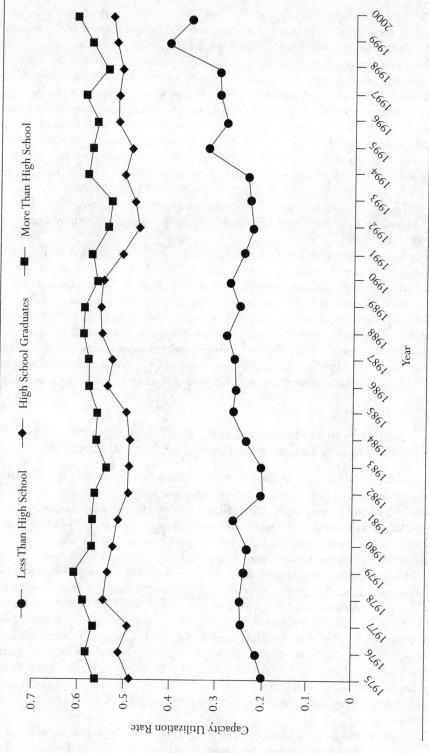

Source: Authors' compilation.

about $15,000 for young women who had failed to complete high school. The earnings potential of these youths who were nonwhite males or single women with children had fallen by 2000 to even lower levels. Clearly inequality in terms of EC had increased. Most of this decrease in the value of human capital occurred between 1975 and the early 1990s, with reductions in EC of between 10 and 30 percent among the high school dropout groups that we have distinguished. However, after the recession of the early 1990s, all of these groups of young males with a high school degree or less experienced substantial increases in EC, ranging from 7 to 34 percent. Smaller gains were recorded for low-education women during this robust growth period, and those were concentrated among nonwhite women.

Among low-education youths, capacity utilization levels were very low. From 1975 through the early 1990s, there was a small decrease in utilization levels for young men without a high school degree, while utilization for young female dropouts increased about 17 to 28 percent. This pattern turned to substantial growth in capacity utilization levels for young low-education women, especially nonwhite young women, from the recession of the early 1990s until 2000.

In terms of earnings capacity by sex by education group, we find a decrease among all three education groups for males over the period 1975 and 2000. At the end of the period all three educational groups had lower EC than in 1975, but the reductions were far larger for those with less schooling. In comparison, CUR in 2000 was nearly identical to that in 1975 for each education group; the trend shows an increase from 1975 to 1978 and then a general decline until very recent years. In contrast for young women, EC increased for the highest education group—those with more than a high school education. Women with less schooling saw a very slight decline in EC over these years. CUR increased for all women, but the biggest increase was for those with the least schooling. In this dimension, inequality decreased.

Summary of Evidence on Levels and Trends in Family and Community Characteristics and Children's Attainments

Making sense out of all these trends in *levels* of inputs and outcomes, trends in *overall inequality* in inputs and outcomes, and trends in *racial and ethnic inequality* in inputs and outcomes is a daunting undertaking. The evidence suggests that in most domains the *levels* of family resources and young adult outcomes have improved over time. This is especially the case for education. Today's parents are more educated than yesterday's parents, and today's adolescents and young adults are more educated than yesterday's adolescents and young adults. These two trends are, of course, really one trend that characterizes successive cohorts over time—that of increasing educational attainment. Other trends in the direction of improvement are declines in family size, improvements in class size and expenditures per pupil in the public schools, increases in the average amount of time spent by parents in child-rearing activities, and modest increases in the level of wealth holdings of families. (Interestingly, the overall level of real spending on children by parents failed to increase.) Also, the teen fertility rate has begun to decrease after increasing in the late 1980s and early 1990s. On the other hand, children are less likely to live with two parents than they were in the past. However, they are more likely to be in quality child care as infants, toddlers, and preschoolers.

There are relatively few statistics or research studies that address trends in *inequality* in family resources. To the extent that this research has been done, it has focused on school-based resources, family economic resources, and parental time allocations. The results show clearly that the 1980s and the early through mid-1990s was a period of increasing inequality in family economic resources. However, there were some promising signs in the late 1990s, when the child poverty rate reached its lowest level since 1979. The poverty rate for black children reached its lowest recorded rate ever in the 1990s. The level of wealth inequality among all families has increased over time, but the evidence on changes in the inequality of wealth holdings of families with children is unclear. The inequality among children in the availability of their parents' child-rearing time appears to be increasing. Across public school districts, there has been a reduction in the inequality of expenditures per student and in pupil-teacher ratios, and across neighborhoods poverty is less concentrated and education levels are increasing.

Tracking *racial and ethnic inequality* over time is complicated by the need to take into account significant Hispanic and Asian immigration during the past few decades. The nature of these populations is changing dramatically owing to immigration, and the well-being of the native-born and foreign-born within these populations differs greatly. In addition, significant differences also occur across groups from different countries of origin. The Asian Indian population is doing much better economically, for example, than the Southeast Asian population. Nonetheless, one can broadly characterize the changes of the past few decades as representing a relative improvement in the well-being of minority children and a narrowing of the gap between the resources of white families and those of Asian and black families in the United States. The situation of children in Hispanic families relative to those in white non-Hispanic families does not seem to have narrowed as much, possibly because of increases in immigration. While racial differences in the level of human capital seem to have increased over the past three decades, racial differences in the utilization of human capital have eroded. Significant gaps remain, however, in both family resources and children's outcomes.

FAMILY AND COMMUNITY CORRELATES OF CHILDREN'S ATTAINMENTS: A REVIEW OF THE LITERATURE

In this section, we review recent research that has attempted to establish the existence and strength of relationships between family and community inputs and children's attainments. A review of the research at this time is important for two reasons. First, while the literature on this subject was reviewed and critiqued several years ago (Haveman and Wolfe 1994, 1995), substantial additional evidence has been forthcoming in recent years. Our review seeks to bring the earlier review up to date. Second, we narrow our review by identifying those aspects of children's environments that appear to be most closely related to their ultimate attainments. Hence, we seek to understand which among the various factors that have been studied appear to have the most persistent and robust (statistically significant) relationship to the attainments of children when they become young adults.

A Review of the Existing Literature

The first step in our review is to identify those factors that appear to be related to success in young adulthood and whose distribution over time we wish to analyze. On the basis of both the pre-1990 studies reviewed by Haveman and Wolfe (1994, 1995) and the more recent literature on which we concentrate here, we have identified the following family and community inputs to children related to their success as young adults:

- Parental education
- Family economic resources during childhood
- Parental assets
- Female-headed family
- Number of siblings
- Immigrant status
- Neighborhood quality during childhood
- Schooling quality during childhood
- Child care quality
- Changes in family location or composition during childhood
- Family composition during childhood

In addition to variables that describe family or community characteristics, nearly all of the studies that we review include in the estimated models a wide range of other background variables, such as race, gender, child's IQ, year of child's birth, and parental age at child's birth.

Although a large number of indicators of children's attainments have been studied in the research literature, the vast bulk of them have focused on a limited set. These include: fertility choices (in particular, the decision of young women to have a nonmarital birth while a teenager), education (schooling) outcomes (high school graduation, years of schooling), and labor market success (employment, earnings, and income and needs). Our review accepts these as the primary outcomes on which we will concentrate.

Summary of Important Relationships Between Children's Attainments and Their Correlates

Comprehending this extensive documentation of research studies and their results is a daunting task. Table 4.10 summarizes our findings on the linkages between those investments in children on which we have chosen to focus and the set of attainment variables we have identified.[17] The first column of table 4.10 lists the number of studies on which our overall assessment of the sign of the relationship is based; this assessment is shown in the second column. The remaining columns of the table provide a breakdown of the estimated relationships between positive and negative coefficients and for each category indicates the number of estimated relationships that are statistically significant. A much more detailed compilation of the studies, their sources, and the findings in the studies is available from the authors.

Parental Education   The level of schooling of the mothers and fathers of the children being studied are among the most commonly explored relationships between family characteristics and children's attainments. Virtually all models indicate that parental education is positively tied to child outcomes, because parents with more education are likely to have aspects of human capital that contribute in several ways to children's attainments—improved ability to nurture children, increase family income through both increased earnings in the market place and more efficient consumption, and create a positive role model in terms of the child's own expected level of schooling.

TABLE 4.10   *Research on the Relationship of Family and Community Investments in Children and Children's Attainments as Young Adults*

	Number of Studies	Overall Relationship	Positively Related to Attainment		Negatively Related to Attainment	
			Significant	Nonsignificant	Significant	Nonsignificant
Parental education	50	Positive	38	10	0	2
Family economic resources	47	Positive	27	18	0	2
Parental assets	15	Positive	6	8	0	1
Female-headed family	39	Negative	0	7	18	14
Number of siblings	28	Negative	1	2	19	6
Immigrant status	6	Positive	0	3	1	2
Neighborhood quality	16	Positive	10	5	0	1
School quality	13	Positive	5	6	1	1
Child care quality	6	Positive	5	1	0	0
Changes in family location	8	Negative	0	0	7	1
Changes in family composition	7	Negative	0	0	3	4

Source: Authors' compilation.

With only a few exceptions, parental schooling is positively associated with children's attainments (interpreting the absence of a teen marital or nonmarital birth as a positive achievement). Of the fifty estimated relationships reported in the first row of table 4.10, forty-eight indicate this positive relationship, and of the two estimates indicating a negative relationship, neither is statistically significant. Of the forty-eight estimates suggesting a positive relationship between parental education and children's attainments, thirty-eight indicate that this relationship is statistically significant.

Family Economic Resources During Childhood   Building on a standard human capital framework, it has often been hypothesized that the level of family economic resources is positively related to the level of children's attainments when they become young adults. It is presumed that, controlling for other factors, the level of income of a family enables the family to purchase those inputs to children's environments that foster well-being and achievement. Consistent with this view, lack of income, or poverty, is expected to reduce children's achievement, since it reduces the level of purchased inputs such as books, outings, and medical care. Poverty may also be associated with parental stress, which may have its own negative association with child outcomes.

As table 4.10 indicates, there are numerous studies of the relationship between indicators of this variable and the three children's attainments identified. In nearly all cases the estimated relationship is positive; only two of the forty-seven studies found a negative relationship, and neither of these is statistically significant. Of the forty-five estimates of a positive relationship, twenty-seven indicate that the relationship is statistically significant.

Parental Assets   Assets, reflecting a stock of resources that can be turned into economic support, are often distinguished from the flow of annual income as an indicator of economic position. Consistent with the expected positive relationship of income to child outcomes, a higher level of parental assets is expected to be associated directly with higher outcomes; assets may also be associated with less uncertainty and a greater feeling of security, which again may be tied to better child outcomes.

In addition to the numerous estimates of the relationship between family economic resources and children's attainments, we have identified fifteen estimates of the relationship between family assets and children's success. The majority of these estimates concern the holding of equity in an owned home, while the others focus on the level of wealth and assets or the existence of wealth and asset holdings. As table 4.10 indicates, only one of the fifteen estimates suggests a negative relationship between family assets and children's attainments, and that estimate is not statistically significant. Of the fourteen estimates indicating a positive relationship, six are statistically significant and eight are not.

Female-Headed Family During Childhood   Growing up in a single-parent family is often interpreted as reflecting a lower level of potential parental time investment in children, detracting from children's ultimate attainments. Less time may mean fewer opportunities to read to young children, help with homework, go on outings, or participate in the PTA. It may also mean difficulties in securing medical care or being involved in the child's after-school activities. Single parents may also face higher levels of stress and anxiety along with greater demands on their time. This single-parent variable is typically included along with family income in the estimated models in order to measure the independent effect of this aspect of family structure apart from its relationship to family income.

Although single-parent status may include father-only status, nearly all of the reported studies measure single-parent status as growing up in a mother-only family. Most of the studies of children's attainment contain a variable indicating this status. As reported in table 4.10, there are a total of thirty-nine estimates of the effect of this variable in the literature that we have surveyed. Of these thirty-nine, thirty-two indicate a negative relationship between being exposed to a female-headed family living arrangement while growing up and children's attainments. Of these thirty-two negative relationships, eighteen are statistically significant. The relationship between this family variable and labor market outcomes is the most uncertain, since an equal number of studies show positive and negative signs. However, two of the five studies indicating a negative relationship are statistically significant, while none of the estimates suggesting a positive relationship are significant.

Number of Siblings   The number of siblings in a family may also reflect the level of parental time available to a child, and hence the level of potential parental investment in that child. Time demands include not only time in the home spent with the children (some of which can be shared across children) but also time in arranging children's activities, time in learning about school and homework, and time spent monitoring children's activities.

The number of siblings is also a standard control variable in many studies of the determinants of children's attainments. Our survey has revealed twenty-eight estimates of the effect of this variable on the three categories of attainment that we study. Of the twenty-eight estimates summarized in table 4.10, twenty-five indicate a negative relationship between number of siblings and attainment, and nineteen of the twenty-five indicate that this negative relationship is statistically significant.

Immigrant Status   Several studies include immigrant status. In thinking about this factor, it is not clear what association we might expect it to have with child outcomes. On the one hand, immigrant status might be tied to English as a second language, which may create difficulties for the child in school and in the community, and it may also be associated with fewer social ties, which might limit opportunities for the child. On the other hand, many immigrant families bring strong traditions and close family ties with them, and these may be associated with positive child outcomes.

We have been able to identify six studies that seek to identify the independent relationship between immigrant status and children's attainments. Two variables have been used to identify immigrant status: living in a household that is non-English-speaking and having a father who is foreign-born. The results of this characteristic are mixed. Only three of the six estimates listed in table 4.10 suggest a positive effect of immigrant status on children's success, and none of them are statistically significant. Three of the six estimates indicate a negative relationship, and only one of these estimates is statistically significant.

Neighborhood Quality During Childhood   Indicators of the quality of the neighborhood in which a child grows up are interpreted as proxies for the level of community support or investment in the child or as reflections on the quality of the peers and role models whom a child encounters while growing up. The growing literature on the impact of neighborhoods includes a new set of studies based on the Moving To Opportunity projects. Within the broad, somewhat controversial literature, there are models that indicate a positive relationship between community (neighborhood) resources and child outcomes. Other models argue that it is individual family resources that matter and that neighborhood resources reflect only parental selection of the neighborhood in which the family resides (for a review of studies of neighborhood effects on children's attainments, see Pebley and Sastry 2002).

Our review identified sixteen coefficients relating some indicator of neighborhood quality to children's attainments. The greatest concentration of these variables are in the teen childbearing outcome, for which seven estimates are available. Fifteen of the sixteen estimates suggest a positive relationship between neighborhood quality and children's success, and of these, ten are statistically significant.

School Quality During Childhood   Only a limited number of studies have looked at the quality of the schools in either the child's neighborhood while he or she was growing up or the quality of the schools that the child attended. The expectation is that better school quality will be associated with better child outcomes, especially educational outcomes. As with the neighborhood literature, there is considerable controversy on whether school resources matter.[18]

Three sorts of variables have been used in these studies: one providing a variety of indicators of school quality (such as the education or experience of teachers and the level of financial support), another indicating whether the high school is "academic," and the third measuring the grading standards applied in the school. Only thirteen estimates for the two school quality variables are included in table 4.10, and of them, eleven suggest a positive relationship with children's success. Of the three estimates that relate grading standards to children's success, only one suggests a positive relationship, and it is not statistically significant.

Child Care Quality   Although the quality of out-of-home child care has recently become an important research and policy issue, only a few studies have been able to relate the quality of child care to the attainments of children when they become young adults. Most of the existing studies attempt to tie child care quality to early indicators of child outcomes, such as school readiness, behavior, and cognitive development (for a recent review of this literature, see Vandell and Wolfe 2000). Whether or not any short-term gains from child care continue into later childhood and young adulthood is largely unexplored. We have been able to identify only six estimates in the literature, and most of these are the results of evaluations of participation in various child care arrangements. All six of the available estimates shown in table 4.10 suggest a positive relationship, and five of the six are statistically significant.

Changes in Family Location During Childhood   The disruption involved in changing geographic location (and schools) is viewed by many as having a potentially negative effect on children's progress and ultimate success. Moving is viewed as a disturbing experience for children almost regardless of age: moving to a new area or school is stressful and anxiety-provoking. Moving to a new school may be challenging in terms of a new curriculum, new expectations, and new friends. Our review identified eight estimates of this relationship, and all of them indicated that the extent of such moves is negatively related to children's attainments. Seven of the eight estimates are statistically significant.

Changes in Family Composition During Childhood   Parental divorce or remarriage during childhood is also widely viewed as disruptive and stressful, with potentially negative effects on children's attainments. The event itself may be anxiety-provoking, and it often leads to less parental time and less quality parental time with a child. Sometimes it may also be associated with a geographic and school move. Seven empirical estimates of the relationship between these events and children's success are summarized in table 4.10, and all of them suggest a negative relationship. However, only three of the seven estimates are statistically significant.

SUMMARY AND CONCLUSIONS

We find evidence that both the *level of family resources* (defined in various ways) and the *level of attainments* of young people have improved over time. This is especially the case for parental education, an important input that reflects the increase in educational attainment that has characterized successive cohorts. Other family and community trends that have improved include homeownership, family size (which has decreased), school class size, expenditures per pupil in the public schools, and overall federal expenditures on children. On the other hand, children are less likely to live with two parents than they were in the past, and they are likely to spend more time in child care as infants and toddlers. Children's schooling in a variety of dimensions has increased over the last three decades, paralleling the changes in parental education. While the teen fertility rate increased during the late 1980s and early 1990s, it has fallen over the last decade. However, as children in recent cohorts have left school and entered the labor market, they have done less well than young adults in earlier cohorts.

We have also provided evidence that a number of the important factors associated with children's attainments became more unequal over the last two decades. These factors include income, assets, and the allocation of parental time to children. Offsetting this growth in the inequality of various aspects of family resources is the reduction in the inequality of expenditures per student and in pupil-teacher ratios across public school districts, the reduction in the concentration of neighborhood poverty, and the convergence among income and racial groups in the quality of child care provided for their children.

Finally, we have learned that in general parental education is a significant and positive determinant of a child's attainments and that one's family's economic resources are a positive and significant determinant of the years of education, postsecondary schooling (college attendance), and employment, earnings, and income of the child as a young adult. We also found that growing up in a single-parent household or experiencing a parental separation or divorce is significantly associated with the probability of giving birth as a teen and reducing the probability of graduating from high school. We also noted some evidence that changes in family location tend to be associated with poorer outcomes as an adult, although this has not been extensively studied.

We found limited evidence that better quality of what might be thought of as social capital—neighborhood quality and school quality—is associated with better outcomes. For neighborhood quality, the association seems to run across all three outcomes, while school quality seems to be associated significantly only with more years of schooling and high school graduation. For quality of child care, the limited evidence consistently suggests a positive association between child care quality and all three outcomes reviewed, but the studies are small and limited. Regarding other aspects of a child's experience, we found evidence of negative associations between having more siblings and outcomes as a young adult, but no consistent evidence of any tie between outcomes and immigrant status, though again, there is only limited evidence on this family characteristic. When it comes to parental assets or wealth, the few existing studies suggest that more assets are associated with better outcomes—again, across all outcomes that we reviewed. Since greater assets are associated with a greater ability to purchase more inputs for one's child, this association is consistent with both an economic model and the possibility that greater inequality in inputs (wealth) leads to greater inequality in outcomes.

Our review leaves us with a puzzle: income inequality among American families has risen over the past few decades, as has wage inequality among American workers. Many observers believe that this growth in inequality has had adverse effects on a variety of social and economic indicators. The bases for these concerns are several—the discouragement faced by children at the bottom of the distribution, the erosion of family stability among lower-income households as a response to economic attainments that appear further from the American mainstream, and an erosion of community and "solidarity" as those with many resources see those with few as more alien and undeserving. Yet in the face of this growth in income inequality, the attainments of American children and adolescents have generally improved. This is especially true with respect to schooling—dropout rates have fallen, and mean years of school completion have increased, as have the prevalence of postsecondary schooling and the rate of college completion. And as we indicated, since the early 1990s, rates of teen nonmarital childbearing have been decreasing. Only in the labor market have youth wages and employment eroded relative to older cohorts, and this development appears to be due more to the evolution of labor market demands than to the capabilities of young labor market participants. Perhaps competition for opportunities is a primary factor that lies behind the observed patterns.

Given the trends that we have studied here, we can speculate on the expected changes.

By necessity, this means we are reinterpreting "association" to suggest a causal connection. We do this only for the purpose of this speculation; establishing causal relationships in this area remains high on the research agenda.

To the extent that the absolute level of some resources improved, we expect that outcomes may have improved. The overall increase in parental education is one of the most important of these changes in levels, and we speculate that it is associated with an increase in the education of children and an improvement in their earnings. However, the trends we have studied suggest that while education levels have increased, earnings have not on average, and family incomes and assets have increased slowly. The absolute decrease in family size (number of siblings) is also expected to be associated with an improvement in outcomes, as are the increase in expenditures on schooling and the decrease in the ratio of students to teachers in the public system, the increase in parental time devoted to childrearing, and the increase in the number of children who are in higher-quality child care programs. In contrast, the increase in the number of children who live with only a single parent leads us to expect a decline in child attainments.

Relative to a benchmark of no change in levels and inequality of inputs to children, the trends in the factors we have reviewed suggest improvement in the level of each of the outcomes we have studied—that is, fewer teen births, more high school graduates, increased years of schooling including college, and higher employment and earnings. However, we also project an increase in the inequality of these outcomes among the more recent cohort of children. We expect that the increases in inequality will be found primarily across income groups and will be reflected among racial and ethnic groups largely to the extent that the income differences overlap with racial and ethnic groups. The racial-ethnic group that seems to be faring the least well in terms of improvement is Hispanics, but this may largely reflect recent immigration. Overall, our working hypothesis is that, because of these trends in inputs, more recent cohorts of children have experienced greater inequality in a variety of (primarily) family inputs while growing up than have earlier cohorts, and that this inequality of inputs will be revealed to be associated with higher levels of inequality in outcomes when they grow up. We suggest that the increase in inequality will stem from the pulling away (greater success) of those with more resources rather than from an absolute decline in the outcomes among those at the lower end of the income distribution.

NOTES

1. Our review includes a series of detailed appendix tables summarizing more than one hundred studies of the relationship between family and community investments in children and children's attainments as young adults; these are available from the authors on request and available on the Russell Sage Foundation website.

2. Barbel Inhelder and Jean Piaget (1958) argued that children's capacity for understanding the relationship between behavior and outcomes—the ability to reason in an "if/then" framework—is developed between the ages of thirteen and fifteen.

3. The level of income may be negatively related to children's attainments, however, in some of its aspects. For example, if earning more income requires that parents spend less time with their children, a side effect of increasing income may be a reduction in this other input. Overall, however, increasing income is expected to increase children's attainments.

4. The absolute poverty line concept may be helpful in thinking about this case. For example, being below the poverty threshold may have serious negative consequences for a family and its children, whereas increases in income above the poverty threshold (or two to three times the poverty threshold) may have no payoff.

5. Another such linkage might occur when family stress is reduced by increased family income or when stress is created by parental perceptions of the gap in resources between them and other families related to substantial income inequality. Susan Mayer (1997) makes a distinction between an investment model and a good-parent model. In the investment model, parents invest time and money in their children. Income is important for "what it buys." In the good-parent model, parental stress related to family income plays the key role in influencing children. Through such linkages, an increase in income inequality might lead to decreases in the average level of investments of other forms in children, and hence a decrease in overall children's attainments.

6. Note that increased family income inequality may have no effect on the level of poverty if all of the increased spread comes from income increases for high-income families without losses for families at the low end of the distribution—those below some absolute income cutoff level.

7. For distributions that are skewed to the right, mean income, being strongly affected by very high values, will exceed median income, which is not at all affected by outlying values. The ratio of the mean to the median indicates the extent of such high values relative to values toward the middle of the distribution and is hence an indicator of income gaps or inequality.

8. However, there is some evidence that the rate of extreme poverty among mother-only families actually increased during the expansion of the 1990s (see Primus et al. 1999).

9. The next section of this chapter identifies the literature that measures these relationships and documents their strength and importance.

10. The discussion in this paragraph draws heavily from Scholz and Levine (2002).

11. Bianchi and her colleagues (2003) also study trends in the level and inequality of child-rearing expenditures among families and in the health status and health-related behaviors of parents. Over the period studied the overall level of parental real spending on children has remained relatively constant, while the overall level of inequality has increased. Both increases and decreases in the health status of mothers and fathers are reported, depending on the health indicator. For example, while the prevalence of smoking decreased, obesity worsened. There is evidence that self-reports of fair or poor health declined over the period. In terms of the gaps in health and health behaviors, the differences in smoking behavior between college-educated and less-than-college-educated parents increased over the period studied, while the gaps in other health indicators between college-educated and less-than-college-educated parents have changed little.

12. Multivariate analysis of paternal time in child care indicates that, although college-educated fathers do more child care, the educational differential did not increase significantly during the period.

13. Corcoran and his colleagues also studied changes in the distribution of nonpecuniary resources in schools, such as safety, quality of physical capital, teacher quality, curriculum, and computer use. Some of their indicators of nonmonetary inputs into schooling are not distributed as equally as expenditures per pupil, including reports of violent incidents, the quality of physical structures, and experienced teachers. However, for their measures of curriculum and Internet access, differences by the poverty and minority status of schools have also declined.

14. Tabulations by David Harris, using the National Crime Victimization Survey as reported in Mayer (1997).

15. Meredith Phillips and Tiffani Chin (2003) have analyzed trends in the level and inequality (both racial and socioeconomic) of schooling attainments in a number of dimensions, including attendance at highly racially segregated schools and academic achievement as reflected in test scores and grades. In both reading and math, average test scores have risen since the mid-1970s. The authors find that test score gaps among ethnic and socioeconomic groups narrowed during the 1970s and 1980s, but not in the 1990s. In the 1990s some of the gaps widened. Robert Hauser (2002) has reviewed trends in the level and racial gaps in grade retention and dropout since the early 1970s.

16. Both blacks and whites show an increase in the percentage of degrees that are earned through equivalency programs.

17. The construction of table 4.10 required the application of numerous conventions and assumptions:

    • In several instances, the correlates of interest are studied as a series of dummy variables, making it difficult to arrive at an overall assessment of their relationship to the outcome and their statistical significance. Where most of the dummy variables have the same sign, we report that sign; similarly, we indicate statistical significance when most of the coefficients of interest are statistically significant at conventional levels.

- The studies that include variables reflecting arrangements over the childhood period are inconsistent in the definition of this variable. Some use the number of years during childhood with a particular exposure, but even these use different periods for measuring status. Others use a dummy variable indicating whether a particular status ever occurred during childhood. In our assessment, we interpret the sign and significance level of the variables that are reported and do not distinguish among these various specifications.

- For the teen childbearing outcome, we did not distinguish between teen nonmarital and teen marital childbearing.

- The effect of particular variables of interest may be camouflaged by the inclusion of variables closely related to the variable of interest in the estimated models. For example, the effect of homeownership may be hidden in a model in which the amount of net worth is also included. We simply record the sign and statistical significance as indicated in the study.

- Neighborhood quality is often reported in several dimensions, including indicators of income level, education level, family composition, and unemployment rate. We take high-income, high-education, two-parent family prevalence, and low unemployment as reflecting higher-quality neighborhoods.

- When effects were same signed for subgroups (for example, whites, nonwhites) but statistically significant for one of the groups, the finding for the largest group was recorded in the table.

- Finally, we accepted a 0.1 level of significance as indicating a statistically significant relationship.

18. This controversy is of long standing. See Coleman and others (1966), Jencks (1972), Summers and Wolfe (1977), and especially Hanushek (1986). The question of the impact of school expenditures on children's attainments is of substantial importance, as most educational expenditures are public and hence are regularly scrutinized and modified.

REFERENCES

Becker, Gary S., and Nigel Tomes. 1986. "Human Capital and the Rise and Fall of Families." *Journal of Labor Economics* 4(3, part 2): S1–S39.

Bianchi, Suzanne, Philip Cohen, Sara Raley, and Kei Nomaguchi. 2003. "Inequality in Parental Investment in Child-rearing: Time, Expenditures, and Health." Working paper. New York: Russell Sage Foundation (February). Available at: www.russellsage.org/programs/proj—reviews/si/revbianchi01.pdf (last accessed August 20, 2003).

Chandra, Amitabh. 2003. "Is the Convergence of the Racial Wage Gap Illusory?" Working paper w9476. Cambridge, Mass.: National Bureau of Economic Research.

Coleman, James S., et al. 1966. *Equality of Educational Opportunity*. Washington: U.S. Department of Health, Education, and Welfare.

Conley, Dalton. 1999. *Being Black, Living in the Red: Race, Wealth, and Social Policy in America*. Berkeley: University of California Press.

Danziger, Sheldon, and Peter Gottschalk. 1995. *America Unequal*. New York: Russell Sage Foundation.

Federal Interagency Forum on Child and Family Statistics. 2002a. "Table ECON1.A: Child Poverty: Percentage of Related Children Under Age Eighteen Living Below Selected Poverty Levels, by Age, Family Structure, Race, and Hispanic Origin, 1980–2000." In *America's Children: Key National Indicators of Well-being*. Washington: U.S. Government Printing Office.

———. 2002b. "Table POP5: Family Structure and Children's Living Arrangements: Percentage of Children Under Age Eighteen, by the Presence of Parents in Household, Race, and Hispanic Origin, Selected Years 1980–2001." In *America's Children: Key National Indicators of Well-being*. Washington: U.S. Government Printing Office.

————. 2002c. "Table HEALTH8: Adolescent Births: Birth Rates by Mother's Age, Race, and Hispanic Origin, Selected Years 1980–2000." In *America's Children: Key National Indicators of Well-being.* Washington: U.S. Government Printing Office.

————. 2002d. "Table ED5: High School Completion: Percentage of Adults Ages Eighteen to Twenty-four Who Have Completed High School, by Race, Hispanic Origin, and Method of Completion, Selected Years 1980–2000." In *America's Children: Key National Indicators of Well-being.* Washington: U.S. Government Printing Office.

————. 2002e. "Table ED7: Higher Education: Percentage of High School Graduates Ages Twenty-five to Twenty-nine Attaining Higher Degrees, by Highest Degree Attained, Race, and Hispanic Origin, Selected Years 1980–2001." In *America's Children: Key National Indicators of Well-being.* Washington: U.S. Government Printing Office.

Gottschalk, Peter. 1997. "Inequality, Income Growth, and Mobility: The Basic Facts." *Journal of Economic Perspectives* 11(1): 21–40.

Hanushek, Eric A. 1986. "The Economics of Schooling: Production and Efficiency in Public Schools." *Journal of Economic Literature* 24: 1141–77.

Hauser, Robert M. 2002. "Progress in Schooling: A Review." Working paper. New York: Russell Sage Foundation (June). Available at: www.russellsage.org/programs/proj_reviews/si/revhauser01.pdf (last accessed August 20, 2003).

Haveman, Robert, Andrew Bershadker, and Jonathan Schwabish. 2003. *Human Capital in the United States from 1975 to 2000: Patterns of Growth and Utilization.* Kalamazoo, Mich.: W. E. Upjohn Institute for Employment Research.

Haveman, Robert, and Larry Buron. 1998. "The Growth in U.S. Male Earnings Inequality: Changing Wage Rates or Working Time." *Journal of Income Distribution* 8: 255–76.

Haveman, Robert, and Barbara Wolfe. 1994. *Succeeding Generations: On the Effects of Investments in Children.* New York: Russell Sage Foundation.

————. 1995. "The Determinants of Children's Attainments: A Review of Methods and Findings." *Journal of Economic Literature* 33: 1829–78.

Inhelder, Barbel, and Jean Piaget. 1958. *The Growth of Logical Thinking from Childhood to Adolescence.* London: Routledge & Kegan Paul.

Jencks, Christopher, et al. 1972. *Inequality: A Reassessment of the Effect of Family and Schooling in America.* New York: Basic Books.

Johnson, George E. 1997. "Changes in Earnings Inequality: The Role of Demand Shifts." *Journal of Economic Perspectives* 11(1): 41–54.

Karoly, Lynn A. 1992. "The Trend in Inequality Among Families, Individuals, and Workers in the United States: A Twenty-five-year Perspective." Working paper R-4206-rc. Santa Monica, Calif.: Rand Corporation.

Kennickell, Arthur B., Martha Starr-McCluer, and Brian J. Surette. 2000. "Recent Changes in U.S. Family Finances: Results from the 1998 Survey of Consumer Finances." *Federal Reserve Bulletin* 86(1): 1–29.

Kingsley, G. Thomas, and Kathryn L. S. Pettit. 2003. "Concentrated Poverty: A Change in Course." *Neighborhood Change in Urban America* 2: 1–12. Available at: www.urban.org/uploadedPDF/310790_ncua2.pdf (last accessed August 18, 2003).

Landry, Bart. 1987. *The New Black Middle Class.* Berkeley, Calif.: University of California.

Leibowitz, Arleen. 1974. "Home Investments in Children." *Journal of Political Economy* 82(2): S111–31.

Levy, Frank, and Richard J. Murnane. 1992. "U.S. Earnings Levels and Earnings Inequality: A Review of Recent Trends and Proposed Explanations." *Journal of Economic Literature* 30(3): 1333–81.

Mayer, Susan E. 1997. "Has America's Antipoverty Effort Failed?" *Northwestern University Policy Research* 2(1). Available at: www.northeastern.edu/ipr/publications/nupr/nuprv02n1/mayer.html (last accessed August 18, 2003).

McLanahan, Sara, and Gary Sandefur. 1994. *Growing Up with a Single Parent: What Hurts, What Helps.* Cambridge, Mass.: Harvard University Press.

Pebley, Anne R., and Narayan Sastry. 2002. "Neighborhoods, Poverty, and Children's Well-being: A Review." Working paper DRU-3001-NICHD. Santa Monica, Calif.: Rand Corporation.

Phillips, Meredith, and Tiffani Chin. 2003. "School Inequality: What Do We Know?" Working paper. New

York: Russell Sage Foundation (July). Available at: www.russellsage.org/programs/proj—reviews/si/revphillipschin.pdf (last accessed August 20, 2003).

Primus, Wendell, Lynette Rawlings, Kathy Larin, and Kathryn Porter. 1999. "The Initial Impacts of Welfare Reform on the Incomes of Single Mother Families." Washington: Center on Budget and Policy Priorities.

Scholz, John Karl, and Kara Levine. 2002. "U.S. Black-White Wealth Inequality: A Survey." Working paper. New York: Russell Sage Foundation (February). Available at: www.russellsage.org/programs/proj—reviews/si/revscholzlevine01.pdf (last accessed August 20, 2003).

Smith, James P., F. Thomas Juster, Joseph Lupton, and Frank Stafford. 1999. "Savings and Wealth: Then and Now." Paper presented to the Conference on Health and Retirement. Amsterdam (October).

Summers, Anita A., and Barbara Wolfe. 1977. "Do Schools Make a Difference?" *American Economic Review* 67(4): 639–52.

Topel, Robert H. 1997. "Factor Proportion and Relative Wages: The Supply-Side Determinants of Wage Inequality." *Journal of Economic Perspectives* 11(1): 55–74.

U.S. Department of Commerce. U.S. Census Bureau. 2002a. "Historical Income Tables: Tables F-10, 10A, 10B, and 10C: Families: Presence of Children Under Eighteen Years Old by Type of Family: White, Black, and Hispanic Families by Median and Mean Income: 1974 to 2001." Washington: U.S. Department of Commerce (September 30). Available at: www.census.gov/hhes/income/histinc/incfamdet.html.

———. 2002b. "Historical Poverty Tables: Table 4: Poverty Status of Families, by Type of Family, Presence of Related Children, Race, and Hispanic Origin: 1959 to 2001." Washington: U.S. Department of Commerce (September 30). Available at: www.census.gov/hhes/poverty/histpov/hstpov4.html.

———. 2002c. "Historical Income Tables: Table F-4: Gini Ratios for Families, by Race and Hispanic Origin of Householder: 1947 to 2001." Washington: U.S. Department of Commerce (September 30). Available at: www.census.gov/hhes/income/histinc/f04.html.

———. 2002d. "Historical Income Tables: Table F-5: Race and Hispanic Origin of Householder: Families by Median and Mean Income: 1947 to 2001." Washington: U.S. Department of Commerce (September 30). Available at: www.census.gov/hhes/income/histinc/f05.html.

U.S. Department of Education. National Center for Education Statistics. 2001. "Table 4-1: Percentage Distribution of Six- to Eighteen-Year-Olds According to Parents' Highest Education Level, by Child's Race-Ethnicity: 1974–1999." In *The Condition of Education 2001*. NCES 2001-072. Washington: U.S. Government Printing Office.

U.S. Department of Health and Human Services. 1998. *Trends in the Well-being of America's Children and Youth: 1998*. Washington: Government Printing Office.

———. 2000. *Trends in the Well-being of America's Children and Youth: 2000*. Washington: Government Printing Office.

Vandell, Deborah, and Barbara Wolfe. 2000. "Child Care Quality: Does It Matter and Does It Need to Be Improved?" Special report 78. Madison: University of Wisconsin, Institute for Research on Poverty (November).

Wolff, Edward. 1998. "Recent Trends in the Size and Distribution of Household Wealth." *Journal of Economic Perspectives* 12(3): 131–50.

———. 2001. "The Rich Get Richer and Why the Poor Don't." *The American Prospect*, February 12: 15–17.

Chapter 5

Inequality in Parental Investment in Child-Rearing: Expenditures, Time, and Health

Suzanne Bianchi, Philip N. Cohen, Sara Raley, and Kei Nomaguchi

What parents do for children "matters"—or so it is assumed. Much of the literature on social inequality at the individual or household level in the United States has focused on the role that families play in (re)producing inequality. For example, in the late 1960s and 1970s, the most studied topic in U.S. social stratification was intergenerational occupational mobility (Blau and Duncan 1967; Duncan, Featherman, and Duncan 1972; Jencks 1972). This tradition of research in sociology has had parallel streams within economics (see, for example, Robert Haveman and Barbara Wolfe's 1994 book *Succeeding Generations*). The continued focus on mechanisms through which parents monitor children's educational progress and risk-taking behavior and ensure their adult success is also manifest in the large and influential literature on the supposed harmful effects of growing up in a single-parent family. In the past decade many studies have tried to improve our understanding of what constitutes "successful parenting" and the costs that accrue when the conditions of parenting (for example, poverty or single-parenting or both) are less than optimal for producing salutary child outcomes; examples include Sara McLanahan and Gary Sandefur's widely cited 1994 book *Growing up in a Single-Parent Family: What Hurts? What Helps?* and Susan Mayer's 1997 book *What Money Can't Buy: Family Income and Children's Life Chances.*

Beginning with the early work of James Coleman, an extensive literature developed on education that asked whether schools make a difference. The backdrop for these studies, however, was always implicitly family investment: Does the quality of schools add to the likelihood of later life success, or is variation in student performance largely determined within the family (either through genetic endowment or differential family investments or both in combination)? Recently, the importance of peer influences as determinants of child outcomes have captured the attention of researchers. Yet again, the backdrop remains the relative influence of these factors compared with genetic endowment, family factors, and parenting behaviors that help ensure children's well-being.

The common theme in the large literature on the role of parents in determining children's success and well-being is that inequality in material and other investments that parents make in child-rearing may be one of the "keys" to predicting the inequality in the success of the next generation. Our subject in this chapter is the inequality in investment that occurs by socioeconomic level of the parents, focusing on the variation by college education.

Several changes in U.S. society since the 1970s lead us to speculate that differentials in parents' ability to bestow resources on their children may be widening in recent years. First, as the wage gap between college-educated and less-educated workers widened in the 1980s and 1990s, income growth for children living in families with a college-educated parent outpaced that of children whose parent had less than a college degree. The family income distribution for children became more unequal after 1973. The Gini index for the income of children's families increased from 0.356 to 0.470 between 1973 and 1996 (Levy 1998, 164). Second, the growth in single-parent families shifted many children living only with their mother to the bottom of the income distribution (Cancian and Reed 1999; Chevan and Stokes 2000; Karoly and Burtless 1995; Levy 1998), and the prevalence of single-parenthood has been greater for less-than-college-educated men and women than for those with a college education. It is hypothesized that the decline in men's economic ability to support a family, combined with the availability of public assistance, has eroded the benefits of marriage among less-than-college-educated men and women (Becker 1981; Becker, Landes, and Michael 1977; Murray 1984; Oppenheimer 2000; Wilson 1987, 1996). Finally, there has been a dramatic increase in the employment of married mothers who responded to increased educational and labor force opportunities in recent decades, and that increase has been especially pronounced among more-educated women (Cohen and Bianchi 1999; Juhn, Murphy, and Pierce 1993).

More and more children reside in two-parent families where both parents are employed. Wives' employment reached 80 percent for married-couple families in the top income quintile in 1996, up from 32 percent in 1949 (Levy 1998, table 2.4). Although families at all income levels experienced an increase in wives' employment, the increase is greater for highly educated women than for less-educated women. Moreover, high rates of marital homogamy by educational attainment have also been increasing (see Kalmijn 1991; Mare 1995). Thus, well-educated, dual-earner, two-parent families now typify families at the top of the family income distribution. Children with college-educated parents seem to be in a better position economically compared with children whose parents are not college-educated. As college-educated parents' family income rose relative to that of less-educated parents, the better-educated parents may have also become better able to make large financial investments in their children.

In this chapter, we examine three major ways in which parents invest in their children. First, we focus on child-oriented expenditures. If, as Frank Levy (1998) argues, the family income of children's families by level of parents' education became more unequal, other things being equal, it would follow that expenditures targeted toward children should also have become more unequal. This implies that child-related purchases have increased or decreased at the same rate at which family income has increased or decreased. However, it may well be that parents protect monetary provisions for their children relative to other household expenditures. If this is the case, we would expect such expenditures to be inelastic relative to changes in income over time. By analyzing direct expenditures on children, we can ascertain whether increased income inequality has substantially increased the dispersion of material investments in children.

Second, parents engage in an array of activities with their children that are aimed at promoting the health and well-being of their offspring. Mothers in higher-income households used to stay at home, at least when their children were young, and early time diary studies suggested that highly educated mothers did more enriching activities with their children than less-educated mothers (Leibowitz 1974; Hill and Stafford 1985). The increase in employment among college-educated mothers and the increase in family income for those with a college education suggest two countervailing possibilities in trends in the inequality in parental time investment in children. On the one hand, there may be growing similarity in maternal time investments in child-rearing across the income distribution as employment rates rise among highly educated, married mothers. Moreover, because of the increase in family income, highly educated parents may have encountered disincentives to use parental care for their children because the opportunity costs of time spent parenting, primarily mothers' time, have increased (Becker 1981). On the other hand, if parents wish to spend time with their children regardless of their level of education and family income, then it may be easier for well-educated parents than for less-educated parents to protect time for their children from the demands of paid work because they may have higher status, more flexible jobs, and a greater ability to purchase housekeeping services, prepared meals, and other services that reduce housework other than child care. How these countervailing tendencies have affected overall parental time with children is not immediately obvious, nor is it clear, without empirical investigation, whether these changes served to heighten socioeconomic differences in parental time with children, lessen them, or leave them unchanged.

Finally, from the point of view of children, having healthy parents is an important advantage. Although the link between parental health behaviors and child outcomes is not as direct as that between the time and money spent on children and child outcomes, staying healthy and maintaining a healthy lifestyle is an indirect but important "investment" that parents can make in their children to enhance their children's life chances (see Zill 1999, 2000). Parents' behaviors set examples for children. Healthier parents are in a better position to make the necessary time and money investments that child-rearing requires. Parents are known to be a self-selected group who, on average, have better health behaviors than those who remain childless (Umberson 1987). More-educated adults are also known to be healthier and to have better health behaviors than less-educated adults (Ross and Mirowsky 1999; Ross and Wu, 1995). However, we know less about variation in the health behaviors of parents than of adults in general; nor do we know whether the socioeconomic variation in the health of parents changed between the mid-1970s and the mid-1990s.

For each domain, expenditures, time, and health, we ask three questions. First, what is the differential *level* of investment between college-educated and less-than-college-educated parents? Second, what has been the *trend* in investment for parents at different points on the educational distribution? That is, are trends in investments in children salutary or not, and are trends similar or dissimilar for college-educated and less-than-college-educated parents? Finally, following from this assessment of trends, is there evidence of growing *bifurcation* in expenditures on children, parental time with children, and parental health behaviors between the college-educated and less-than-college-educated parents during the period of rising income inequality?

In the first section, we investigate levels and trends in child-oriented expenditures. Here we use data from the Consumer Expenditure Surveys (CEX) to examine expenditures on goods that directly benefit children. Our assessment covers change between the late 1980s and the late 1990s. In the second section, we focus on (co-residential) parents' time with children. We examine the series of time diary studies to investigate the college-noncollege differential in parental time in child-rearing. These data collections span the period 1965 to 2000, with collections at roughly ten-year intervals beginning in 1965. We are particularly interested in levels and trends in parental time in child-rearing for 1975 to 1995, the period of rising income inequality. In the third section, we track changes in parental health habits, using supplements to the National Health Interview Survey (NHIS) conducted in 1975–76, 1985, and 1995. We examine smoking, doctor visits, obesity, exercise participation, and self-reported illness and health status. In the last section, we summarize our findings by returning to the questions we raised at the outset about levels, trends, and increasing differentials in child-oriented expenditure patterns, parental time, and health behaviors.

CHILD-ORIENTED EXPENDITURES

Researchers have long recognized that consumption may be a better indicator of economic well-being than current income (Lazear and Michael 1988; Mayer and Jencks 1989), for several reasons. Many people, especially the relatively rich, do not spend all the money they have because they choose to or are able to save money. There are also people who have temporarily low incomes but go on consuming by using past savings or the promise of future income (credit). Among the poor, on the other hand, many people consume goods and services purchased with money they do not literally have—or at least, do not report. For example, they may borrow money or goods informally or trade services (such as child care) with family members and friends. The net effect of these patterns is that at any one time there is less inequality in consumption than there is in income.

Previous studies have shown that income does not capture a lot of variability in consumption between the poor and the nonpoor (Federman et al. 1996; Tan 2000) and that differences in consumption across family types also vary in ways that income alone cannot predict (Lino 1994). For children, looking at consumption instead of income may be especially important. By focusing their spending on children's necessities, for example, poor parents may be able to protect their children from some of the effects of poverty. On the other hand, it may be that the multiple burdens of poverty compel the poor to cut corners in ways that make being poor even worse for their children. In this analysis, we ask whether increasing income inequality has affected families' spending on their children.

Consumer Expenditure Survey Data

To assess how spending for children has changed over time, we use data from the 1988 and 1998 Consumer Expenditure Survey (Branch 1994; U.S. Department of Labor 1998). The data represent a sample of the non-institutionalized urban and rural population. Sample sizes were approximately 5,000 households until 1998, and 7,500 thereafter. Expenditure data from each household are collected once per quarter for four quarters, and each interview covers the previous three months. For the analysis, we use all the expenditure data for each of the calendar years 1988 and 1998. Households contribute between one and twelve months of data to the sample. We annualize the data for each household by dividing the expenditures by the number of months each household reports for the calendar year and then multiplying by twelve. The demographic characteristics of the sample are collected at an initial interview, then updated at each additional interview. We use the information reported from the last interview for each household.

The unit of analysis in the Consumer Expenditure Survey is the consumer unit, which includes all members of the household when they are related by blood or legal arrangement. Other individuals and groups who share living expenses, whether alone or in households with others, are considered separate consumer units. Some households therefore include multiple consumer units. We include those consumer units in which there is at least one child age fifteen or younger. The resulting sample size is 3,755 in 1988 and 4,501 in 1998; the analyses are unweighted.

Complete information on spending targeted solely at children is impossible to obtain from the CEX. Some goods—from housing to milk—are shared, and their consumption cannot be attributed to any one household member. Families with children may spend more money on some items, but unlike others who have used these data (Lazear and Michael 1988), we do not try to determine what portion of household expenses is intended for children. However, the CEX includes a number of detailed expenditure categories for goods and services that clearly are intended for consumption by children in the household. (We exclude items purchased as gifts for people outside the household.) We focus only on these spending categories, while acknowledging that they represent an unknown portion of all spending for children. An important caveat is that the CEX does not collect information on how *much* of any particular good or service is purchased, merely the dollar amount spent. For example, we cannot distinguish one hour of child care at eight dollars from two hours at four dollars each.

We use the following spending categories: infant furniture; infant equipment; school bus fees; playground equipment; school books and supplies; elementary and high school tuition; school meals; toys, games, hobbies, and tricycles; day care and related expenses; child care (in own or another home); and clothes and shoes for infants and children. We break these expenses into four groups to represent different types of investment in children. The first includes all the child-related spending categories, the broadest measure. The second includes all categories except day care and child care expenses. We consider a category excluding day care and child care because such spending may reflect less investment of parental time with children and therefore may or may not be an investment in children. That said, we also examine spending on child care, day care, and related expenses as our third group. Finally, the fourth group of expenditures includes only clothing and shoes for infants and children, representing the best indicator we have of child-specific spending on necessities. The dependent variables reflect annualized spending for each group of expenditures, with the 1988 figures adjusted to 1998 dollars.

We construct models for each expenditure group using consumer unit characteristics as predictors. Most variables measure characteristics of the reference person—identified by respondents as "the person or one of the persons who owns or rents the home." These variables include: race (white, black, Latino, other), age, and education level (less than high school, high school only, B.A. or higher degree completed). Consumer unit variables include: total expenditure rank (consumer unit expenditure ranking in the total population, from zero to one), financial assets (the sum of checking and savings account balances, bonds and securities), family type (married couple, single father, single mother, other), number of earners in the household (none, one, two or more), number of children under age two, and number of children age two to fifteen. Descriptive statistics for the sample are presented in table 5A.1.

Results

Descriptive statistics for the expenditure analysis show a change from 1988 to 1998 in the pattern of spending on children, but not much change in the overall level (table 5.1). The only substantial increase was in spending on day care and related expenses, which increased 64 percent from $590 per child in 1988 to $968 per child in 1998. Non-day-care-related spending dropped a corresponding amount, so that the total spending stayed almost the same (increasing from $1,933 to $2,009 in total spending per child).

Using the per-child spending totals for each consumer unit, and weighting each consumer unit by the number of children present, we compute child-level Gini indices for each

TABLE 5.1   *Descriptive Statistics, Expenditure Analysis: Households with Children, 1988 to 1998*

	Dollars (Standard Deviation)		Logged	
	1988	1998	1988	1998
Total all child categories	1,933 (2,676)	2,009 (3,813)	6.67 (1.89)	6.54 (2.02)
Day care and related expenses	590 (1,556)	968 (2,270)	2.26 (3.24)	4.04 (3.21)
Total less day care expenses	1,344 (2,032)	1,041 (2,923)	6.35 (1.84)	5.74 (2.20)
Clothing and shoes only	611 (807)	594 (869)	5.33 (2.18)	5.15 (2.33)
Number of cases	3,755	4,501		

Source: Authors' configuration.
Note: Spending is annual consumer unit spending per child under age fifteen, in 1998 dollars.

group of spending categories. The results, presented in table 5.2, show increases in inequality among children, with the exception of day care and related expenses. This group presumably shows a decrease in inequality principally because there are fewer children with no day-care-related spending. The overall increase in inequality in total expenditures, from .570 to .614, is greater than that shown for clothing and shoes. This expenditure category showed the least mean change and the smallest increase in the standard deviation (consistent with our interpretation of this as an essentials group).

Tables 5.3 and 5.4 show the results from regressions computed separately for each spending group. We use OLS regression for all models except day care and related spending. For this outcome, we use Tobit regression because there are many cases with zero spending (table 5.4). In each analysis the samples from 1988 and 1998 are pooled, with a time interaction for each variable. For presentation, we show coefficients for each variable for each period, and the changes from 1988 to 1998, in separate columns.

We concentrate on the results related to increases in economic inequality: education, total expenditures, and financial assets. Coefficients for each of these variables at both time periods show significant inequality in spending on children. That is, children in households with more educated parents, greater total spending, and greater financial assets consume

TABLE 5.2   *Gini Indices: Spending on Children (per Child), 1988 to 1998*

	1988	1998	Change
Total all child categories	.570	.614	.043
Total less day care expenses	.552	.613	.061
Day care and related expenses	.863	.793	− .070
Clothing and shoes only	.556	.576	.020

Source: Authors' configuration.

TABLE 5.3   *OLS Coefficients: Two Categories of Spending per Child (ln), 1988 to 1998*

	Total All Child Categories (OLS)[a]			Total Less Day-Care Expenses (OLS)[b]		
	1988	1998	Change	1988	1998	Change
Intercept	5.436***	5.355***	−.082	4.890***	3.590***	−1.300***
Expenditure rank	2.654***	2.897***	.243	2.415***	2.483***	.068
Financial assets (ln)	.017+	.014+	−.003	.014*	.028**	.014
High school only	.394***	.187*	−.207+	.346***	.086	−.260*
College degree or more	.465***	.350***	−.116	.404***	.164	−.240
Black	−.259**	−.065	.194	−.319**	.070	.389**
Latino	−.159	−.134	.025	−.156	.098	.253+
Other race/ethnicity	−.409**	−.315**	.094	−.378*	−.181	.196
Age of reference person	−.015***	−.010***	.005	−.002	.013***	.015**
Single father	.394+	−.402*	−.795**	.206	−.464*	−.670*
Single mother	.461***	.377***	−.084	.287**	.329***	.041
Not own children	−.289**	−.208*	.081	−.396***	−.384***	.012
No earners	−.383**	−.551***	−.168	−.211	−.452***	−.241
Two or more earners	.275***	.069	−.206*	.105	.087	−.019
Children under age two	−.113	−.040	.073	−.095	.402***	.496***
Children age two to fifteen	−.144***	−.191***	−.047	−.111***	−.060+	.050

Source: Authors' configuration.
Notes: Excluded categories are white; less then high school; married couple with own children; one earner in household. N = 8,276.
[a]Adjusted R-squared = .185.
[b]Adjusted R-squared = .151.
+ $p < .10$; * $p < .05$; ** $p < .01$; *** $p < .001$

more child-related goods and services than do other children, holding constant other characteristics of the household.

However, the change over time in these effects is either negative or insignificant, a finding that is not consistent with the increasing-inequality hypothesis. The coefficients for expenditure rank show the difference between the lowest- and highest-spending consumer units. In each case the effect of this variable does not change significantly from 1988 to 1998. The education effects show positive effects on spending associated with higher levels of education, but these effects also either decrease or do not significantly change. Finally, the financial-assets effect is positive and significant in each model except day care in 1998, for which it is no longer significant.

To see whether the growing use of day care and related services is taking a toll on spending on other necessities for children, we estimate a separate model (not shown) of spending on clothing and shoes that includes spending on day care as a predictor. We find that, in both 1988 and 1998, households that spent more on day care actually spent more— not less—on clothing and shoes for their children, holding constant other variables in the

TABLE 5.4   *OLS/Tobit Coefficients: Two Categories of Spending per Child (ln), 1988 to 1998*

	Clothing and Shoes Only (OLS)[a]			Day Care and Related Expenses (Tobit)[b]		
	1988	1998	Change	1988	1998	Change
Intercept	3.634***	3.602***	−.031	.717	2.930***	2.214**
Expenditure rank	2.357***	2.274***	−.083	6.005***	5.226***	−.779
Financial assets (ln)	.034**	.033**	−.001	.124***	.033	−.091*
High school only	.213*	−.043	−.256[+]	.921**	.700**	−.221
College degree or more	.221[+]	−.020	−.241	1.897***	1.239***	−.658
Black	−.049	.197*	.246[+]	−.559	−.570*	−.011
Latino	−.136	.268**	.404*	−.623	−1.075***	−.452
Other race/ethnicity	−.223	−.177	.046	−1.201*	−1.251**	−.050
Age of reference person	.000	.003	.003	−.216***	−.095***	.120***
Single father	.308	−.514*	−.822*	1.914*	−1.004[+]	−2.918**
Single mother	.420***	.328**	−.092	1.930***	.317	−1.613**
Not own children	−.264*	−.376***	−.112	.621	.200	−.421
No earners	.007	−.385*	−.392[+]	−3.429***	−1.015*	2.414**
Two or more earners	.085	−.025	−.110	1.245***	−.267	−1.512***
Children under age two	.318***	.631***	.314**	.496*	−.060	−.556[+]
Children age two to fifteen	−.073*	−.067[+]	.006	.289**	.120	−.169

Source: Authors' configuration.
Notes: Excluded categories are white; less then high school; married couple with own children; one earner in household. N = 8,276.
[a]Adjusted R-squared = .085.
[b]Pseudo R-squared = .057.
[+] p < .10; * p < .05; ** p < .01; *** p < .001

model. Therefore, it does not appear that day care is substituting for other necessities in households with children.

PARENTAL INVESTMENT OF TIME IN CHILD-REARING

A number of studies during the past three decades have directly assessed parental time spent with children, though usually for only one point in time. Studies using time diary data from the mid-1970s to the early 1980s focus on maternal time with children, particularly variation by maternal educational attainment. More highly educated mothers are found to spend more time in direct child care (Hill and Stafford 1985; Zick and Bryant 1996), and mothers' time with children declines less steeply with the age of the child among better-educated mothers (Hill and Stafford 1985). Maternal education is also related to the type of child care activities mothers engage in with their children: more highly educated mothers spend more time reading to their children and less time watching television with them (Timmer, Eccles, and O'Brien 1985).

In a recent study using two points in time, 1981 and 1997, John Sandberg and Sandra Hofferth (2001) find that these differences not only persisted through 1997 but may have grown wider. In 1981 children of mothers with some college spent more time in art and reading and less time watching TV than children of mothers with no college. Although the same was true in 1997, further differences had emerged. In 1997 children of mothers with some college also spent more time in market work, sports, outdoor activities, hobbies, household conversations, studying, other passive leisure, and day care relative to 1981. These differences probably reflect both changed values and the ability of more highly educated parents to afford such activities for their children. However, it is not clear to what extent they reflect increasing inequality in maternal time between college-educated mothers and mothers with no college education because, with the exception of television viewing, the overall differences in activities between children of college and non-college-educated mothers were small in both 1981 and 1997 (Sandburg and Hofferth 2001).

The focus of recent research on parental time has shifted to assessments of father's education and time with children. Two studies report that education has no effect on physical care of preschool-age children (Aldous, Mulligan, and Bjarnason 1998; Marsiglio 1991) but that more highly educated fathers spend more time playing with, reading to, or going on outings with preschool-age children (Cooney et al. 1993). Studies that examine the effect of paternal education on time with school-age children have found either no relationship (Barnett and Baruch 1987; Ishii-Kuntz and Coltrane 1992; Pleck 1981; Zick and Bryant 1996) or a positive relationship (Aldous, Mulligan, and Bjornason 1998; Fisher, McCulloch, and Gershuny 1999; Haddad 1994; Marsiglio 1991; Yeung et al. 2001).

For example, married fathers with some postsecondary education spend more time on weekdays with children in achievement-oriented activities and more in social-related activities than fathers with no postsecondary education (Yeung et al. 2001). More specifically, fathers with higher levels of education are more likely to help their children with homework and reading assignments as well as have one-on-one conversations with them (Marsiglio 1991). Fathers with higher levels of education have also been observed stimulating, responding to, and providing care to their nine-month-old infants more frequently than less-educated fathers (Volling and Belsky 1991).

Further, paternal time with children does not appear to substitute for maternal time with children: the more time mothers invest in child care, the more time fathers also spend with their children (Aldous, Mulligan, and Bjornason 1998). When mothers hold a college degree, children spend about four and a half hours more per week with their fathers than children whose mothers do not have a degree (Sandberg and Hofferth 2001). Children in all family types spend more time with either parent when their mother holds a college degree (Sandberg and Hofferth 2001).

Time Diary Data

Time with children often occurs in disjointed segments throughout the day, and it is exceedingly difficult to accurately recall and add up such time in response to a stylized question such as: "How much time do you spend with your child on an average day?" Therefore, the best data for assessing parental time with children in the United States have been collected in periodic time diary studies of representative samples of adults. The time diary mode of data collection "walks" a respondent through his or her day, most often the day previous to the interview, and asks the respondent to recall activities in a sequential order as they occurred during the day.

One of the advantages of the diary mode of data collection is that respondents are forced to adhere to the twenty-four-hour constraint. Especially for unpaid work and family caregiving activities like housework and child care, estimates derived from answers to survey questions often result in hours estimates that exceed the daily twenty-four-hour constraint.

TABLE 5.5   Methodological Features of U.S. National Time Diary Studies

	1965	1975	1985	1995	1998	2000
Location conducted	University of Michigan	University of Michigan	University of Maryland	University of Maryland	University of Maryland	University of Maryland
Funder	National Science Foundation	National Science Foundation	National Science Foundation; AT&T	Electric Power Research Institute	National Science Foundation	Alfred P. Sloan Foundation
Sample	Total = 1,244 Parents = 742	Total = 2,406 Respondents = 1,519 Spouses = 887 Parents = 1,087	Total = 5,358 Parents = 1,612	Total = 1,200 Parents = 493	Total = 1,151 Parents = 496	Total = 1,200 Parents = 1,200
Age range	Eighteen to sixty-five	Eighteen and older	Twelve and older	Twelve and older	Eighteen and older	Eighteen and older
Months	October to November	October to December	January to December	January to December	March to December	June to May (one-day) August to June (weekly)
Mode/response rate	Personal (72%)	Personal (72%)	Mailback (51%) Telephone (67%) Personal (60%)	Telephone (65%)	Telephone (56%)	Telephone (64%) Mailback (23 to 30%)
Diary type	Tomorrow (1,244) Yesterday (130)	Yesterday (2,406)	Tomorrow (3,890) Yesterday (1,468)	Yesterday (1,200)	Yesterday	Yesterday Last week
Sample restrictions	Residents of labor force families in nonfarm, urban locations	Excludes households on military reservations	Households in the contiguous United States (plus D.C.)	Households in the contiguous United States	Households in the contiguous United States	Parents living with children under age eighteen in household in contiguous United States
Identification of parents	"Do you have any children eighteen years of age or younger living in this household?"	Constructed from household roster: the number of children age seventeen or younger in household	Variable indicating children under age eighteen in household	Variable indicating children under age eighteen in household	Flag created by Liana Sayer based on marital status and number of adults in home	Interviewer asks if there are children under age eighteen in the household and asks to speak with parent
Miscellaneous		Spouse interviewed as well as respondent				Weekly diaries went to select parents[a]

Source: Authors' configuration.
[a]Parents who worked at least ten hours a week for pay and at least one of the parents had some college education.

Recent comparisons of housework hours elicited in the diary format with estimates from survey questions suggest that the estimates from survey questions tend to be 50 percent higher, though the relationship of covariates to the estimates under either format tend to be similar (Bianchi et al. 2000).

Table 5.5 provides summary information for each of the time diary data collections in the United States, collected at roughly ten-year intervals beginning in 1965. The National Science Foundation funded data collections in 1965 and 1975, conducted at the University of Michigan, and in 1985 and 1998 to 1999 at the University of Maryland. From all sampled cross-sections of the U.S. adult population, we identified parents as those who were living with children under age eighteen. The 1975 study also included diaries with spouses of married respondents. For comparability with other years, we exclude the spousal diaries from our analysis. We include two other national surveys, both collected at the University of Maryland: a 1995 survey funded by the Electric Power Research Institute (EPRI), and a 2000 survey, funded by the Alfred P. Sloan Foundation's Working Families Program, that used a national probability sample of 1,200 parents living with their children under age eighteen.

A standard methodology for administering the time diary and a comparable set of coding conventions has been used across this time period in the United States. All data collections include reports of "primary activities" during a twenty-four-hour period—that is, the sequential reporting that a respondent gave to the question, "What were you doing?" These activities might be regarded as the most salient activity for a respondent and are collected so as to fix beginning and ending times for each activity. We have primary activity data for each of our time points, and the child care estimates we report include time coded into the following nine activity categories: baby care, child care, helping and/or teaching, talking and/or reading, indoor playing, outdoor playing, medical care for child, other child care, and travel for child care.

In most but not all of the data collections, respondents were also asked to report "what else they were doing," resulting in estimates of secondary activity. Researchers have suggested that child care activities in particular may be substantially underestimated because child care is often done in conjunction with other activities and may go unreported when only primary activity is ascertained. In addition, several of the collections also collect "with whom" data. That is, respondents were asked to report "who was with you" during each activity, providing yet another measure of time "with children."

For the trend analysis in this chapter, we focus on primary child care time of mothers and fathers on the diary day. This results in low estimates of the proportion of parents who engaged in child care, particularly those who had older children and were less likely to be doing direct child care activities such as changing diapers and reading to their children. These differences are illustrated with the 2000 data in table 5.6. For example, whereas the estimate of primary time parents spent in child care activities is 87 minutes a day on average, this estimate rises by almost 50 percent when secondary child care time is added. Time spent "with children" is three times as great as the combination of primary and secondary child care time. The distribution for fathers is affected by the choice as well: when the focus is on primary child care time, the ratio of fathers at the seventy-fifth to the twenty-fifth percentile cannot be calculated because more than one-quarter of fathers of children under age eighteen reported no direct time in the activities coded as child care, whereas fathers at the twenty-fifth percentile reported spending an average of 120 minutes, or two hours, a day "with" their children.

Data limitations compel us to concentrate on primary activity time in child care rather

TABLE 5.6   *Child Care Time (Minutes per Day) in the United States, 2000*

	Primary	Primary or Secondary	Total Time with Children
Total parents			
Mean	87	123	372
(Standard deviation)	115	155	261
Seventy-fifth percentile	127	185	540
Median	45	67	325
Twenty-fifth percentile	0	0	160
Ratio of Seventy-fifth to Twenty-fifth	—	—	3.4
Total mothers			
Mean	108	159	437
(Standard deviation)	112	161	257
Seventy-fifth percentile	165	235	655
Median	70	110	402
Twenty-fifth percentile	11	30	225
Ratio of Seventy-fifth to Twenty-fifth	15.0	7.8	2.9
Total fathers			
Mean	62	80	293
(Standard deviation)	113	130	241
Seventy-fifth percentile	85	115	450
Median	15	30	255
Twenty-fifth percentile	0	0	120
Ratio of Seventy-fifth to Twenty-fifth	—	—	3.8

Source: Authors' configuration.

than a more expansive definition that includes all time with children. The diary data deposited at the Inter-University Consortium for Political and Social Research (ICPSR) for 1965 include only summed minutes of primary and secondary time per day in each coded activity, and we cannot determine what portion of secondary child care time overlaps with primary child care time. To avoid double-counting child care time and violating the twenty-four-hour constraint, we focus on primary time. Similarly, the diary data deposited for 1985 include only primary time. Finally, secondary activities were not ascertained in the 1995 EPRI collection.

A final caveat concerns the 2000 data. All time diary data collections include the diary portion of the questionnaire within a survey that asks demographic information and includes questions on activities that vary from survey to survey. All surveys except the 2000 collection were done with cross-sections of all adults, parents as well as nonparents, and hence the questions surrounding the diary are not particularly child-focused. This is not true of the 2000 collection, which was funded by the Sloan Foundation to collect diary and survey estimates on parents and about parenting. The questions surrounding the 2000 diary collection are hence much more focused on parental activities and parents' feelings about their children.

Figure 5.1 graphs the trend in average (mean) time caring for children for mothers and fathers. Solid lines show the trends for college-educated parents, dotted lines for less-than-college-educated parents. Estimates are reported in minutes per day. The trend in figure 5.1, apparent in all of the lines, is curvilinear: reported child care time dropped from 1965 to 1975 and rose thereafter. The first data point, 1965, was near the end of the postwar

FIGURE 5.1   *Maternal and Paternal Primary Time (Minutes per Day) Caring for Children, by Educational Status, 1965 to 2000*

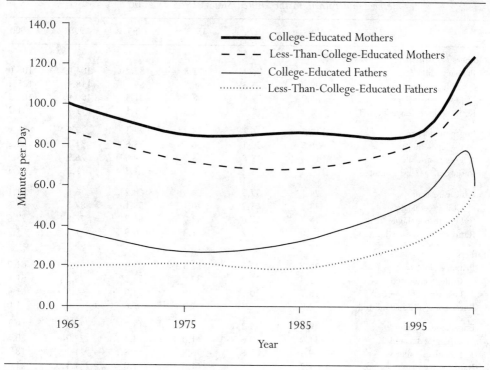

Source: Authors' configuration.

baby boom, when households with children still included relatively large numbers of (young) children. At the next data point, 1975, the baby bust was in full swing, with declining numbers of (young) children per household. If we also take 1975 as a rough marker of the beginning of a period of dramatically rising income inequality, Figure 5.1 suggests that an *increase* in the mean parental child care time coincided with rising inequality. At each point the line for college-educated parents is higher than for less-than-college-educated parents, and not surprisingly, lines for mothers are much higher than for fathers.

Table 5.7 shows the mean child care times by educational attainment. We separate child care time into two components: one we label "engagement," which includes activities such as reading, talking, and playing with children and helping children with homework, and the other component, the bulk of child care time, we label "basic care" time. Shown in the table is the ratio of time for college-educated relative to less-than-college-educated mothers and fathers. For mothers, the ratio at all time points is in the range of 1.1 to 1.3. The ratio for fathers is more variable: in 1965 college-educated fathers have means twice as high as those of less-educated fathers, and this ratio declines and fluctuates between 1.0 and 1.7 at each of the data points between 1975 and 1998. In the 2000 data collection, estimates for college-educated and less-than-college-educated fathers are virtually the same. However, as noted earlier, we suspect that this collection may not be strictly comparable to earlier cross-sections because questions surrounding the diary are more child-focused.

Table 5.8 reports descriptive statistics on the mean and standard deviation of child care

TABLE 5.7   *Differentials in Mean Total Primary Child-Care Time, Engagement Time, and Basic Care Time (Minutes per Day) Between College-Educated and Less-Educated Mothers and Fathers in the United States, 1965 to 2000*

	1965	1975	1985	1995	1998	2000
Mothers						
Primary child care	87.2	74.1	71.8	82.2	104.4	108.0
College-educated	99.7	85.3	86.8	86.6	118.4	125.3
Less than college	86.2	72.4	68.7	81.3	100.8	102.9
Ratio college/less-educated	1.2	1.2	1.3	1.1	1.2	1.2
Engagement time	12.5	16.4	15.3	22.1	27.9	26.9
College-educated	26.5	20.1	16.7	33.8	31.3	32.5
Less than-college	11.4	15.8	15.0	19.6	26.9	25.2
Ratio college/less-educated	2.3	1.3	1.1	1.7	1.2	1.3
Basic care time	74.1	57.7	56.5	60.2	76.6	81.1
College-educated	73.2	65.2	70.1	53.1	87.1	92.8
Less than college	74.8	56.6	53.7	61.7	73.8	77.6
Ratio college/less-educated	1.0	1.2	1.3	0.9	1.2	1.2
Fathers						
Primary child care	21.2	22.2	22.5	37.9	57.3	61.7
College-educated	37.8	27.2	32.8	53.3	78.2	61.8
Less than college	18.7	20.8	18.9	33.0	49.8	61.4
Ratio college/less-educated	2.0	1.3	1.7	1.6	1.6	1.0
Engagement time[a]	9.7	5.2	7.9	13.7	21.5	19.1
College-educated	11.0	10.6	11.0	13.4	22.7	20.8
Less than college	9.5	3.8	6.8	13.8	21.1	18.5
Ratio college/less-educated	1.2	2.8	1.6	1.0	1.1	1.1
Basic care time[b]	11.5	16.9	14.6	24.2	35.8	42.7
College-educated	26.7	16.5	21.8	39.9	55.5	40.7
Less than college	9.2	17.1	12.1	19.2	28.7	43.3
Ratio college/less-educated	2.9	1.0	1.8	2.1	1.9	0.9
Sample size						
Mothers	417	369	913	312	273	728
College-educated	41	39	154	71	84	243
Less than college	376	330	759	241	189	485
Fathers	343	251	699	181	163	472
College-educated	67	57	180	62	64	163
Less than college	276	194	519	119	99	309

Source: Authors' configuration.

[a]Engagement time includes time spent helping and/or teaching child, talking and/or reading to child, and indoor and outdoor play with child.

[b]Basic care time includes caring for infants, arranging social and extracurricular activities of child, medical care of child, and traveling related to child-care activities.

time for parents, mothers, and fathers, and also the median, seventy-fifth, and twenty-fifth percentiles of the distribution of child care time. As the mean rises between 1975 and 2000, the standard deviation of the distribution rises, as do the reported amounts of time at the seventy-fifth percentile of the distribution. However, what is most striking in the table is the relatively high proportions of fathers who, on a given day, reported no time in direct child

TABLE 5.8   *Trends in the Distribution of the Primary Child-Care Time of Parents (Minutes per Day) in the United States, 1965 to 2000*

	1965	1975	1985	1995	1998	2000
Total parents						
Mean	57	51	48	63	85	87
(Standard deviation)	78	76	85	96	106	115
Seventy-fifth percentile	82	78	60	100	140	127
Median	28	15	0	5	50	45
Twenty-fifth percentile	0	0	0	0	0	0
Reporting any primary child-care time in diary day	61.5%	59.5%	49.2%	50.8%	62.9%	66.5%
Total mothers						
Mean	87	74	72	82	104	108
(Standard deviation)	89	82	97	102	110	112
Seventy-fifth percentile	140	105	102	140	180	165
Median	60	52	30	40	70	70
Twenty-fifth percentile	15	0	0	0	0	11
Reporting any primary child-care time in diary day	90.1%	76.0%	63.9%	57.6%	70.6%	76.6%
Total fathers						
Mean	21	22	23	38	57	62
(Standard deviation)	42	53	56	77	94	113
Seventy-fifth percentile	30	25	20	55	90	85
Median	0	0	0	0	15	15
Twenty-fifth percentile	0	0	0	0	0	0
Reporting any primary child-care time in diary day	38.7%	38.2%	33.4%	41.7%	52.1%	54.2%
Sample size						
Total	760	620	1,612	493	436	1,200
Mothers	417	369	913	312	273	728
Fathers	343	251	699	181	163	472

Source: Authors' configuration.

care between 1965 and 1995—hence the medians and twenty-fifth percentiles are zero for the distribution of fathers' time.

The first column of table 5.9 shows the bivariate estimates for time in child care among the college-educated as compared with those with less education: college-educated mothers spent about twenty-six minutes more per day in child care than did less-educated mothers, and college-educated fathers spent over forty minutes more per day in primary child care than less-than-college-educated fathers. The linear relationship between year and time expenditures is shown in model 2, with both mothers and fathers spending significantly more time in child care in 2000 relative to the 1970s.

In models 3 and 4, which include the linear trend (column 3) and show estimates with controls for age, marital status, children, and employment of the parent (column 4), coefficients for college education remain statistically significant. Models 5 and 6 test whether the primary child care time of parents has become increasingly differentiated for college-educated as compared with less-than-college-educated parents. None of the interaction terms for year and education are statistically significant in the models for either the mothers

TABLE 5.9   *Tobit Models Predicting Primary Child-Care Time (Minutes per Day) of Mothers and Fathers, 1965 to 2000 (1975 as Omitted Category)*

	Model 1	Model 2	Model 3	Model 4	Model 5	Model 6
Mothers						
College-educated	26.1***	—	24.1***	29.3***	15.9	41.1*
yr65	—	17.8	19.2*	4.4	18.7*	2.8
yr85	—	−15.1+	−16.1*	20.3**	−18.4*	20.6**
yr95	—	−10.0	−11.1	14.2	−10.6	16.5
yr98	—	27.6	25.7+	43.2***	25.6+	44.1***
yr00	—	36.7***	34.3***	50.3***	32.6**	46.5***
yr65 × college	—	—	—	—	−0.5	−17.2
yr85 × college	—	—	—	—	14.9	−29.0
yr95 × college	—	—	—	—	−0.6	−19.8
yr98 × college	—	—	—	—	3.9	0.8
yr00 × college	—	—	—	—	10.7	−17.5
Controls						
Age	—	—	—	−1.13**	—	−1.15**
Married	—	—	—	17.7*	—	17.8*
Children under age six	—	—	—	95.2***	—	95.5***
Number of children	—	—	—	12.1***	—	12.1***
Employed	—	—	—	−25.3***	—	−25.1***
Weekly hours employed	—	—	—	−0.6***	—	−0.6***
Fathers						
College-educated	43.4***	—	40.8***	38.7***	70.7**	44.7+
yr65	—	−0.4	2.3	0.5	−5.6	−4.6
yr85	—	−8.9	−11.8	9.2	−18.9	5.9
yr95	—	27.3+	25.3	32.1*	16.8	28.4
yr98	—	66.3***	63.1***	62.1***	50.0*	55.6**
yr00	—	74.2***	72.3***	64.6***	76.1***	68.4***
yr65 × college	—	—	—	—	−5.7	7.4
yr85 × college	—	—	—	—	−19.7	−10.7
yr95 × college	—	—	—	—	−13.8	−8.5
yr98 × college	—	—	—	—	−60.2	−36.6
yr00 × college	—	—	—	—	−48.2	−22.5
Controls						
Age	—	—	—	1.4**	—	1.5**
Married	—	—	—	19.5	—	19.5
Children under age six	—	—	—	100.2***	—	99.7***
Number of children	—	—	—	−0.5	—	−0.8
Employed	—	—	—	33.9*	—	34.0*
Weekly hours employed	—	—	—	−1.1***	—	−1.1***

Source: Authors' configuration.

Notes: Year is coded as yr65 = 1, yr75 = 1, yr85 = 1, yr95 = 1, yr98 = 1, yr100 = 1, in this concatenated data. Age of youngest child is coded "1" if the parent has a child under age six in 1965, 1998, and 2000 and coded "1" if the parent has a child under age five in 1985 and 1995. There is no variable for work hours that is consistent across all years, so we sum activity measures of work time based on total work time, not including commuting to work.

+ $p < .10$; * $p < .05$; ** $p < .01$; *** $p < .001$

or the fathers. There is no suggestion that the college-noncollege differential in parental investment of time in children has increased or diminished during the period of increased income inequality.

PARENTAL HEALTH BEHAVIORS

Studies suggest that parental health and health-related behaviors have important influences on children's health, illness, and health behaviors. For example, children with mothers who are healthier and get adequate prenatal checkups are less likely to be born with low birthweight or to die shortly after birth than children with less healthy mothers (Cramer 1987; Hummer 1993). Lower birthweight and illness in childhood have significant long-term influences on health in later years (Barker and Osmond 1986; Wadsworth 1986). Further, children learn healthy lifestyles from their families. Some studies have found a direct association between adolescent children's health-related behavior, such as smoking, drinking, exercise, and eating and sleeping habits, and their parents' health lifestyles (Wickrama et al. 1999).

There is a well-established health gradient by socioeconomic status (Kitagawa and Hauser 1973; Preston and Taubman 1994; Williams 1990). Socioeconomic status can be measured in several ways, including income, occupational status, and education, but many studies have suggested that education is the best indicator, showing the most robust association with mortality and health among U.S. adults (Ross and Mirowsky 1999; Williams 1990). Catherine Ross and Chia-ling Wu (1995) argue that adults with more education are healthier than those with less education because they not only have better jobs and higher income but are also more likely to avoid health-risk behaviors and to engage in more health-enhancing behavior. Those with more education smoke less, exercise more, get regular health checkups, and drink more moderately compared with those with less education.

Determining causality between socioeconomic status and health status is complex. Are individuals less well off because they are in poor health and have poor health behaviors, or does poverty and low income lead to inadequate medical care and less healthy conditions at home and at work? Do poor health habits decrease individuals' ability to pursue educational and occupational achievement, or do individuals with a higher socioeconomic status have better economic resources and social support to achieve healthier lifestyles? Rather than focusing on causality, we are more curious about the extent to which there is a gap in health and health-related behaviors between college-educated and less-educated parents and whether that gap has been growing during a time of growing income inequality.

National Health Interview Survey Data

Data for the analysis of health and health-related behavior are drawn from supplements of the National Health Interview Survey. The NHIS is an ongoing national survey of the civilian non-institutionalized population of the United States annually conducted by the National Center for Health Statistics (NCHS). Information about health-related behavior is obtained in *Current Health Topics*, special supplements in which different topics are included each year. We use four supplements: the 1975 Physical Fitness Supplement (1975 PFS—for exercise participation only), the 1976 Health Habits Supplement (1976 HHS—for other health indicators we examine in this section), the 1985 Health Promotion and Disease Prevention Supplement (1985 HPDP), and the 1995 Year 2000 Objectives Supplement (1995 Year 2000 Objectives). From each supplement, we selected adults who lived with their children under age eighteen. The sample sizes for these parents are 6,302 in 1975, 12,320 in 1976, 12,248 in 1985, and 6,242 in 1995.[1]

We examine six indicators of health and heath-related behavior: current cigarette smokers, doctor visits, obesity, exercise participation, subjective health, and work loss due to illness or injury. Each of these health indicators is measured as follows:

* Current cigarette smokers:

   "Do you now smoke cigarettes every day, some days, or not at all?"

* Doctor visits:

   "About how long has it been since you last saw or talked to a medical doctor or assistant?"

* Obesity:

   Respondents' body mass index (BMI) was calculated to determine presence of obesity

* Exercise participation:

   "In the past two weeks, have you done any of the following exercises, sports, or physically active hobbies?" (1985 HPDP and 1995 Year 2000 Objectives)

   "Do you do any of the following exercises on a regular basis?" (1975 PHS)

* Subjective health:

   "Would you say your health in general is excellent, good, fair, or poor?" (1976 HHS)

   "Would you say your health in general is excellent, very good, good, fair, or poor?" (1985 HPDP and 1995 Year 2000 Objectives)

* Work loss due to illness or injury:

   "During the past two weeks, how many days did you miss more than half of the day from your job or business because of illness or injury?"

Current cigarette smokers include those who smoked cigarettes every day or some days of the week. In measuring the answers to the question about *doctor visits,* we consider no contacts with medical professionals for over two years to be a sign of inadequate health care (see Zill 1999). *Obesity* is defined as a body mass index of 30.0 or more, with BMI calculated using information on weight and height collected in the survey (BMI = [weight in pounds divided by height in inches divided by height in inches] multiplied by 703; National Heart, Lung, and Blood Institute 1998). *Exercise participation* is measured by whether respondents participated in one or more of five listed exercise activities on a regular basis (for the 1975 supplement) or in the previous two weeks (in the 1985 and 1995 supplements): walking for exercise, lifting weights, jogging or running, riding a bicycle, and swimming. The questions on exercise participation in the 1975 survey are not strictly comparable to those in the 1985 and 1995 surveys. Thus, we are cautious about our findings on *trends* in exercise participation rates, although the issue of comparability is less critical for within-year comparisons of college-educated parents and less-than-college-educated parents. We consider answers of "fair" or "poor" in response to the question on *subjective health* to be indicators of negative states of health. *Work loss due to illness or injury* during the previous two weeks is the final health indicator we measured.

Results

Table 5.10 presents the percentage of mothers by educational attainment who were current cigarette smokers, who had no doctor visits during the preceding two years, who were obese, who participated in exercise activities, who were in fair or poor (subjective) health, and who lost work time during the past two weeks owing to illness or injury. College-educated mothers show higher levels of health and health-related behavior than mothers with less than a college education on all indicators in all years except for work loss in 1976 and 1985. For instance, in 1995 college-educated mothers, compared with their less-educated counterparts, were only 40 percent as likely to be smokers; only 56 percent as likely to have had no contact with a doctor for over two years; only 64 percent as likely to be obese; 26 percent *more* likely to exercise; only 32 percent as likely to report that they were in fair or poor health; and only 58 percent as likely to have missed a day of work during the previous two weeks owing to illness or injury.

Trends in health and health-related behaviors among mothers suggest both rises and declines in good health and health-related behaviors, depending on the health indicators. Smoking declined between 1976 and 1995 among all mothers regardless of college education, but the decline seems to have been more dramatic for college-educated mothers. The percentage of current smokers among mothers with a college education declined from 23.3 to 12.4 percent between 1976 and 1985, whereas the decline was only from 37.3 to 34.5 percent during the same period for those with less than a college education. Regardless of college education, the percentage of mothers who reported no doctor contacts over the previous two years changed little between 1976 and 1995, with 5.3 to 6.9 percent of college-educated mothers and 8.7 to 10.3 percent of less-than-college-educated mothers not visiting doctors over that period. There was an increase in obesity, particularly between 1985 and 1995, regardless of the mother's level of education. The percentage of mothers who were obese increased between 1985 and 1995 from 6.8 to 12.1 percent for the college-educated and from 12.3 to 19.0 percent for those with less than a college education. Exercise participation rates increased for both college-educated and less-than-college-educated mothers during the two decades. Between 1975 and 1995 the percentage of mothers who exercised increased from 54.2 to 72.1 percent for college-educated mothers and from 43.4 to 57.0 percent for less-than-college-educated mothers.[2] The percentage of mothers with less than a college education who reported fair or poor health declined dramatically between 1976 and 1985, from 15.1 to 9.4 percent, whereas it changed little during the period for mothers with a college education (from 4.6 to 3.4 percent). The percentage of less-than-college-educated mothers who missed one or more workdays owing to illness or injury increased slightly between 1985 and 1995, from 6.7 to 8.0 percent, whereas for college-educated mothers it declined during the period, from 8.5 to 4.7 percent.

Table 5.11 suggests a similar picture for fathers. College-educated fathers show better levels of health and health-related behaviors than less-than-college-educated fathers on all indicators in all years. In 1995 fathers with a college education, compared with fathers with less than a college education, were only 39 percent as likely to be smokers; only 82 percent as likely to have had no doctor visits in the previous two years; only 68 percent as likely to be obese; 26 percent *more* likely to exercise; only 27 percent as likely to report that they were in fair or poor good health; and only 80 percent as likely to have missed a day of work during the previous two weeks owing to illness or injury.

Trends among fathers from the mid-1970s to the mid-1990s suggest patterns similar to

TABLE 5.10   *Indicators of Health and Health-Related Behaviors for College-Educated Mothers and Less-Than-College-Educated Mothers, 1975 to 1976, 1985, and 1995*

	1975 to 1976	1985	1995
Current smoker			
Total sample	n/a	35.8%	35.0%	26.8%
College-educated	n/a	23.3	12.4	11.2
Less than college	n/a	37.3	34.5	27.8
Ratio college/less than college	n/a	0.62	0.36	0.40
No doctor visits in previous two years			
Total sample	n/a	8.3	9.9	8.9
College-educated	n/a	5.3	6.9	5.5
Less than college	n/a	8.7	10.3	9.7
Ratio college/less than college	n/a	0.61	0.67	0.56
Obese			
Total sample	n/a	9.6	11.0	18.2
College-educated	n/a	3.6	6.8	12.1
Less than college	n/a	10.3	12.3	19.0
Ratio college/less than college	n/a	0.35	0.55	0.64
Participation in leisuretime physical activities[a]			
Total sample	44.4%	n/a	56.7	59.9
College-educated	54.2	n/a	64.3	72.1
Less than college	43.4	n/a	55.5	57.0
Ratio college/less than college	1.25	n/a	1.16	1.26
Fair or poor health			
Total sample	n/a	14.0	7.5	7.0
College-educated	n/a	4.6	3.4	3.4
Less than college	n/a	15.1	9.4	10.7
Ratio college/less than college	n/a	0.30	0.36	0.32
At least one day absent from work due to illness in previous two weeks[b]			
Total sample	n/a	6.5	4.5	6.1
College-educated	n/a	7.2	8.5	4.7
Less than college	n/a	6.4	6.7	8.0
Ratio college/less than college	n/a	1.14	1.27	0.58
College-educated	9.4	10.6	13.4	19.3
Number of cases	3,346	6,478	7,630	3,887

Source: Authors' configuration.
[a]In any of the five activities: walking for exercise, lifting weights, jogging, riding a bicycle, and swimming.
[b]Currently employed mothers only.

those for mothers, with a few exceptions. As for mothers, there was a decline in smoking for both college-educated and less-than-college-educated fathers over the period. Again, the decline seems to have been more dramatic among college-educated fathers. The percentage with no doctor contacts over the previous two years seemed to increase between 1976 and 1985 but declined again between 1985 and 1995 to the 1976 level for both college-educated and less-than-college-educated fathers. Regardless of college education, there was an increase in obesity, particularly between 1985 and 1995. Exercise participation increased between 1975 and 1985 regardless of college education (from 54.9 to 67.1 percent for

TABLE 5.11   *Indicators of Health and Health-Related Behaviors for College-Educated and Less-Than-College-Educated Fathers, 1975 to 1976, 1985, and 1995*

	1975 to 1976		1985	1995
Current smoker				
Total sample	n/a	45.0%	31.5%	24.6%
College-educated	n/a	30.5	19.3	12.5
Less than college	n/a	48.3	39.5	31.9
Ratio college/less than college	n/a	0.63	0.49	0.39
No doctor visits in previous two years				
Total sample	n/a	18.8	25.0	21.6
College-educated	n/a	15.5	20.3	18.5
Less than college	n/a	19.6	26.3	22.7
Ratio college/less than college	n/a	0.79	0.77	0.82
Obese				
Total sample	n/a	8.4	11.6	17.7
College-educated	n/a	5.6	7.6	13.5
Less than college	n/a	9.0	12.0	19.8
Ratio college/less than college	n/a	0.62	0.64	0.68
Participation in leisuretime physical activities[a]				
Total sample	42.6%	n/a	53.5	54.0
College-educated	54.9	n/a	67.1	63.8
Less than college	39.8	n/a	49.6	50.5
Ratio college/less than college	1.38	n/a	1.35	1.26
Fair or poor health				
Total sample	n/a	11.7	8.6	9.3
College-educated	n/a	3.3	1.7	2.3
Less than college	n/a	13.6	9.1	8.6
Ratio college/less than college	n/a	0.24	0.19	0.27
At least one day absent from work due to illness in previous two weeks[b]				
Total sample	n/a	5.8	7.0	7.3
College-educated	n/a	4.0	4.1	5.2
Less than college	n/a	6.2	4.6	6.5
Ratio college/less than college	n/a	0.65	0.89	0.80
College-educated	18.3	18.3	22.0	26.2
Number of cases	2,956	5,842	4,718	2,355

Source: Authors' configuration.

[a]In any of the five activities: walking for exercise, lifting weights, jogging, riding a bicycle, and swimming.
[b]Currently employed fathers only.

college-educated fathers and from 39.8 to 49.6 percent for less-than-college-educated fathers), then declined between 1985 and 1995 among college-educated fathers. There was little change between 1975 and 1995 in reports of fair or poor health among fathers with a college degree (from 3.3 to 2.3 percent), whereas the percentage of those with less than a college education who reported fair or poor health declined between 1976 and 1995 (from 13.6 to 8.6 percent). There was little change in the percentage of fathers who missed workdays because of illness or injury over the period, regardless of educational level.

Tables 5.12 and 5.13 present results from logistic regressions for the six indicators of

TABLE 5.12   Logistic Regression Coefficients Predicting Health and Health-Related Behaviors for Mothers, 1975 to 1976, 1985, and 1995

	Current Smokers		No Doctor Visits During Previous Two Years		Obesity		Exercise Participation[d]		Subjective Health (Fair or Poor)		Work Loss Due to Illness During Previous Two Weeks[e]	
	Model 1	Model 2	Model 1	Model 2	Model 1	Model 2	Model 1	Model 2	Model 1	Model 2	Model 1	Model 2
College-educated	−1.02***	−0.70***	−0.49***	−0.46*	−0.61***	−0.94***	0.54***	0.46***	−0.98***	−1.03***	0.01	0.14
yr76 (reference)[a]	—	—	—	—	—	—	—	—	—	—	—	—
yr85	−0.21***	−0.16***	0.34***	0.34***	0.41***	0.39***	0.45***	0.46***	−0.33***	−0.34***	0.08	0.05
yr95	−0.47***	−0.43***	0.20**	0.22**	0.92***	0.88***	0.62***	0.58***	−0.27***	−0.27***	0.12	0.24
yr76 × college (reference)[b]	—	—	—	—	—	—	—	—	—	—	—	—
yr85 × college	—	−0.59***	—	0.02	—	0.34	—	−0.01	—	0.10	—	0.13
yr95 × college	—	−0.40*	—	−0.16	—	0.46	—	0.29	—	0.02	—	−0.68*
Controls												
Age	−0.01***	−0.01***	0.02***	0.02***	0.02***	0.02***	−0.02***	−0.02***	0.04***	0.04***	−0.003	−0.003
Married	−0.24***	−0.24***	−0.12	−0.11	0.01	0.005	−0.16***	−0.17***	−0.33***	−0.33***	−0.20*	−0.19*
Race[c]												
White (reference)	—	—	—	—	—	—	—	—	—	—	—	—
Black	−0.13*	−0.13*	−0.17	−0.17	0.85***	0.85***	−0.16**	−0.16**	0.93***	0.93***	0.05	0.05
Hispanic	−0.78***	−0.78***	0.34***	0.34***	0.22*	0.21*	n/a	n/a	0.54***	0.54***	−0.10	−0.11
Other race	−0.78***	−0.79***	0.69***	0.69***	−0.11	−0.11	−0.47***	−0.46***	0.50**	0.50**	0.10	0.09
Children under age six	−0.03	−0.03	−0.64***	−0.64***	−0.11*	−0.11*	−0.04	−0.04	−0.07	−0.07	0.14	0.14
Number of children	0.01	0.01	0.13***	0.13***	0.09***	0.09***	−0.03*	−0.03*	0.02	0.02	0.005	0.005
Employed	0.03	0.03	−0.07	−0.07	−0.16**	−0.16**	−0.20***	−0.20***	−0.60***	−0.60***	n/a	n/a
Intercept	0.22*	0.18*	−2.92***	−2.93***	−3.42***	−3.39***	0.75***	0.79***	−3.02***	−3.02***	−2.50***	−2.53***
−2 log likelihood ratio	714.88***	732.54***	312.32***	313.00***	582.29***	585.93***	498.13***	504.73***	1117.01***	1117.16***	11.14	20.66
df	11	13	11	13	11	13	10	12	11	13	10	12
Number of cases	17,614		17,856		17,655		14,656		17,943		9,800	

Source: Authors' configuration.

[a]yr75 for exercise.

[b]yt75 × college for exercise.

[c]In the exercise analysis only (which uses the 1975 survey), Hispanics and "other race" are combined into one category as "other race."

[d]In any of the five activities: walking for exercise, lifting weights, jogging, riding a bicycle, and swimming.

[e]Currently employed mothers only.

* p < 0.05; ** p < 0.01; *** p < 0.001

TABLE 5.13   Logistic Regression Coefficients Predicting Health and Health-Related Behaviors for Fathers, 1975 to 1976, 1985, and 1995

	Current Smokers		No Doctor Visits During Previous Two Years		Obesity		Exercise Participation[d]		Subjective Health (Fair or Poor)		Work Loss Due to Illness During Previous Two Weeks[e]	
	Model 1	Model 2	Model 1	Model 2	Model 1	Model 2	Model 1	Model 2	Model 1	Model 2	Model 1	Model 2
College-educated	−0.95***	−0.79***	−0.28***	−0.28***	−0.51***	−0.49***	0.78***	0.70***	−1.34***	−1.25***	−0.28***	−0.47**
yr76 (reference)[a]	—	—	—	—	—	—	—	—	—	—	—	—
yr85	−0.44***	−0.41***	0.34***	0.35***	0.42***	0.43***	0.38***	0.35***	−0.23***	−0.21**	−0.23*	−0.29**
yr95	−0.77***	−0.71***	0.12**	0.10	1.02***	1.02***	0.42***	0.42***	−0.34***	−0.35***	0.14	0.09
yr76 × college (reference)[b]	—	—	—	—	—	—	—	—	—	—	—	—
yr85 × college	—	−0.21	—	−0.03	—	−0.04	—	0.18	—	−0.34	—	0.35
yr95 × college	—	−0.40**	—	0.07	—	−0.02	—	0.001	—	0.07	—	0.24
Controls												
Age	−0.01***	−0.01***	−0.01**	−0.01**	0.01***	0.01***	−0.02***	−0.02***	0.04***	0.04***	−0.007	−0.007
Married	0.33***	0.33***	−0.17*	−0.17*	0.55***	0.55***	−0.45***	−0.45***	0.18	0.18	0.19	0.19
Race[c]												
White (reference)	—	—	—	—	—	—	—	—	—	—	—	—
Black	0.07	0.07	0.12	0.12	0.22***	0.22***	0.07	0.07*	0.71***	0.71***	0.04	0.04
Hispanic	−0.37***	−0.37***	0.42***	0.43***	0.19*	0.19*	n/a	n/a	0.39***	0.40***	−0.41*	−0.41
Other race	0.10	0.11	0.48***	0.47***	−0.46*	−0.46*	−0.20*	−0.20*	0.25	0.25	−0.52	−0.53
Children under age six	−0.08*	−0.08	0.04	0.04	−0.14*	−0.14*	−0.02	−0.02	−0.11	−0.11	0.02	0.02
Number of children	−0.01	−0.01	0.03	0.03	0.06***	0.06***	−0.01	−0.01	0.02	0.02	0.02	0.02
Employed	−0.15**	−0.15*	0.33***	0.33***	−0.03	−0.03	−0.26***	−0.26***	−1.35***	−1.35***	—	—
Intercept	0.45***	0.40***	−1.48***	−1.48***	−3.39***	−3.39***	0.85***	0.86***	−2.77***	−2.78***	−2.70***	−2.66***
−2 log likelihood ratio	758.13***	766.63***	200.97***	201.54***	330.11***	330.17***	537.03***	540.45***	1300.16***	1302.09***	32.52***	34.69***
df	11	13	11	13	11	13	10	12	11	13	10	12
Number of cases	11,922		12,752		12,751		9,835		12,864		11,294	

Source: Authors' configuration.

[a] yr75 for exercise.

[b] yr75 × college for exercise.

[c] In the exercise analysis only (which uses the 1975 survey), Hispanics and "other race" are combined into one category as "other race."

[d] In any of the five activities: walking for exercise, lifting weights, jogging, riding a bicycle, and swimming.

[e] Currently employed fathers only.

* p < 0.05; ** p < 0.01; *** p < 0.001

health and health-related behaviors for mothers and fathers, respectively. In each analysis, the samples from 1975 (for exercise only) or 1976 (for other health indicators), 1985, and 1995 are pooled. The number of cases varies depending on the indicator because of missing values. Model 1 shows the relationship between college education, the year of interview, and each indicator of health, controlling for age, race (non-Hispanic white, non-Hispanic black, Hispanic, and other race), marital status, presence of children under age six, number of children, and employment status (except for the analysis of work loss days, in which the sample is restricted to those who were employed). This model examines the educational differences and the trend in each health indicator. Model 2 includes interactions between the year of interview and college education. The purpose of this model is to test whether the differentials by college education changed over the period. All regressions are weighted.

The first column of table 5.12 suggests that, controlling for the year of interview and demographic variables (model 1), mothers with a college education were significantly less likely than mothers with less than a college education to be smokers. The effects of the year of interview suggest that there was a decline in smoking among mothers between 1976 and 1985 and between 1976 and 1995. Model 2 suggests that differences in the likelihood of current smoking between college-educated and less-than-college-educated mothers widened over the two-decade period, particularly between 1976 and 1985. There are significant interaction effects between college education and the year of interview for both 1985 and 1995. The coefficients for the interaction between college education and the year of interview are negative and greater for 1985 than for 1995.

The results for doctor visits, obesity, exercise participation, and subjective health show similar patterns. College-educated mothers were significantly less likely than less-educated mothers to have had no physician visits for over two years, less likely to be obese, more likely to participate in exercise activities, and less likely to report fair or poor health. Across time, fewer mothers had seen a doctor in the preceding two years and more mothers were obese, yet more mothers reported participating in exercise activities and fewer mothers reported fair or poor heath. There were no significant interaction effects between college education and year of interview, suggesting that there was no significant change in the differential between college-educated and less-than-college-educated mothers in doctor visits, obesity, exercise participation, and subjective health.

Among employed mothers, the effect of college education on work days lost to illness or injury during the previous two weeks depended on the year of interview. Whereas model 1 shows no significant effects of college education on work loss due to illness or injury, model 2 shows a significant negative interaction effect between college education and the year 1995. This suggests that college-educated mothers in the mid-1990s were less likely than their counterparts in the mid-1970s to miss days from work owing to illness or injury, whereas less-than-college-educated mothers in the mid-1990s showed little change in work loss due to illness or injury compared with their counterparts in the mid-1970s (see the bivariate relationship in table 5.10).[3]

Table 5.13 shows similar results for fathers. As for mothers, less-educated fathers were more likely to be smokers at each point, and the gap widened between college-educated and less-educated fathers. There were no significant interaction effects between year of interview and college education for other indicators, although college-educated fathers reported better health behaviors and health status than less-than-college-educated fathers at each point.

In sum, college-educated mothers and fathers showed better health and health-related behavior than their less-than-college-educated counterparts on all indicators we examine here. Trends in health-related behavior among parents suggest that both American mothers and fathers have developed better health-related behavior over time in terms of smoking and exercise but became less healthy in terms of obesity and physician contact from the mid-1970s to the mid-1990s. Also, fewer mothers and fathers reported fair or poor health in both 1985 and 1995 than in 1976. Fewer fathers missed days from work owing to illness or injury in 1985 than in 1976, although the level returned to the 1976 level in 1995. For mothers, there was little change between 1976 and 1995 in workdays lost to illness. On one health indicator, smoking, the differential between college-educated and less-educated parents widened between 1975 and 1995—the period of increased income inequality.

CONCLUSION

Since 1973, the earnings gap between college-educated and less-educated workers has grown, and family structure has changed dramatically, with more working mothers and more single-parents today than three decades ago. During this period of increased family change and growing income inequality, we speculated that we might find increased differentials in parental inputs to children between college-educated and less-than-college-educated parents. However, we also noted at the outset that some conditions, such as the rapid growth of maternal labor force participation among more highly educated, married mothers, might mitigate these differences.

We document a considerable inequality in parental investment in child-rearing by level of parents' education in each domain of parental investment examined in this chapter: child-oriented expenditures, parental time, and parental health behaviors. Our estimates suggest that in 1998 a child of a college-educated parent could expect 42 percent more in total expenditures and 245 percent higher expenditures on child care. In 1998 college-educated mothers averaged 17 percent more time with their children than less-than-college-educated mothers, and college-educated fathers spent 57 percent more time with their children than fathers without a college degree. In 1995 a child of a college-educated mother was only 40 percent as likely to live with a mother who smoked, only 56 percent as likely to have a mother who had no routine medical checkup during the previous two years, only 64 percent as likely to have a mother who was obese, 26 percent *more* likely to live with a mother who exercised, only 32 percent as likely to have a mother in fair or poor health, and only 58 percent as likely to have a mother who missed a day of work during the previous two weeks because of illness or injury. A child of a college-educated father was only 39 percent as likely to live with a father who smoked, only 82 percent as likely to have a father who had had no contact with a medical doctor for over two years, only 68 percent as likely to have a father who was obese, 26 percent *more* likely to live with a father who exercised, only 27 percent as likely to have a father in fair or poor health, and only 80 percent as likely to have a father who missed work during the previous two weeks owing to illness or injury.

What might we conclude about the trends in each of these indicators of parental investment during the period of growing income inequality? With respect to child-oriented expenditures, there was relatively little change in real dollar terms between 1988 and 1998 except that more was being spent on child care at the later point, when a greater percentage of parents were using some paid child care. Child-oriented expenditures did become more unequal, as measured by the Gini index, but the growth in this inequality was not closely linked to parental educational attainment. In fact, the effect of education on spending for children either decreased or was unchanged during the period, a finding consistent with the suggestion that parents may be able to protect their children from some of the effects of growing income inequality.

Trends in time spent with children were generally salutary (parents spent more time in child care activities) for both educational groups during the period of growing income inequality. We discovered that maternal time with children was relatively high in the 1960s, but then fell in the 1970s, rose in the 1980s, and fluctuated thereafter. College-educated mothers invested more time in child-rearing than less-educated mothers, other things being equal. However, this differential investment in child care did not grow larger during the period. Fathers' time in child care increased significantly after 1985 for both educational groups. Again, although college-educated fathers did more child care, the educational differential among fathers did not increase significantly during the period.

Finally, the changes in parental health were mixed, with positive trends in some indicators (reduced smoking, more exercise, and a decline in self-reported fair or poor health) for both educational groups, but negative trends in other indicators (a decrease in routine doctor visits and more obesity) for both education groups. Here again, although children of college-educated parents are advantaged, there is relatively little evidence that their advantage grew during the period 1975 to 1995, with the exception of smoking. Whereas the percentage of smokers among parents declined for both education groups from 1975 to 1995, the decline was significantly steeper for college-educated than less-educated parents. This finding is especially noteworthy because of the direct child health consequences of exposure to secondhand smoke and warrants further attention.

Overall, we found little evidence that the differences between the investments of college-educated and less-educated parents in their children grew wider over the period of rising income inequality. This suggests that even though some families are being economically squeezed, parents appear to find ways of protecting the resources they devote to their children when the household has fewer resources overall. To maintain the flow of resources to children, parents may scale back on expenditures in other domains of their lives, on time spent in non-child-care activities, and on at least some unhealthy behaviors, such as smoking. Meeting children's needs is probably a major—if not the top—priority of these families.

At the same time, because we examine the three domains of time, money, and health, the cumulative advantages of children of college-educated parents appear to be quite substantial. These children receive significantly greater parental investments in time and expenditures, and their parents are healthier. Therefore, growing inequality may not increasingly disadvantage children, but it does have implications for children. Future research could illuminate the multiplicity of advantages that accrue to children with better-educated, higher-income parents. The flow across generations remains very unequal by parents' educational attainment in the United States.

TABLE 5.A1 Descriptive Statistics, Expenditure Analysis: Households with Children, 1988 to 1998

	1988				1998			
	Mean	Standard Deviation	Minimum	Maximum	Mean	Standard Deviation	Minimum	Maximum
Spending variables								
Total all child categories	1,933.48	2,676.02	0	35,595.29	2,009.34	3,812.73	0	116,856.00
Logged	6.67	1.89	0	10.48	6.54	2.02	0	11.67
Day care and related expenses	589.68	1,555.89	0	24,182.15	968.19	2,270.25	0	26,700.00
Logged	2.26	3.24	0	10.09	4.04	3.21	0	10.19
Total less day care expenses	1,343.80	2,032.47	0	33,115.07	1,041.15	2,922.82	0	116,856.00
Logged	6.35	1.84	0	10.41	5.74	2.20	0	11.67
Clothing and shoes only	611.43	806.57	0	16,534.80	593.61	869.03	0	14,760.00
Logged	5.33	2.18	0	9.71	5.15	2.33	0	9.60
Household characteristics								
Expenditure rank	.58	.25	.00	1	.58	.23	.01	1
Financial assets (ln)	3.31	3.42	.32	12.64	3.04	3.38	.69	14.18
High school only	.58	.49	0	1	.59	.49	0	1
College degree or more	.21	.41	0	1	.24	.43	0	1
Black	.14	.35	0	1	.15	.35	0	1
Latino	.10	.30	0	1	.15	.35	0	1
Other races/ethnicity	.05	.21	0	1	.06	.23	0	1
Age	37.11	9.75	7	87	38.08	9.95	17	87
Single father	.02	.13	0	1	.02	.14	0	1
Single mother	.14	.35	0	1	.16	.37	0	1
Not own children	.10	.30	0	1	.12	.33	0	1
No earners	.07	.25	0	1	.06	.23	0	1
Two or more earners	.62	.48	0	1	.59	.49	0	1
Children under age two	.25	.47	0	2	.22	.44	0	2
Children age two to fifteen	1.60	1.03	0	9	1.63	1.00	0	8

Source: Authors' configuration.

Notes: Spending is annual consumer unit spending per child under fifteen, in 1998 dollars. Number of cases: 1988—3, 775; 1998—4, 501.

TABLE 5.A2   *Means for Variables in Time Diary Analysis for Mothers and Fathers, 1965, 1975, 1985, 1995, 1998, and 2000*

	Mothers	Fathers
College-educated	0.17	0.23
Age	35.65	37.60
Married	0.74	0.87
Children under age six	0.45	0.45
Number of children	2.02	2.02
Employed	0.57	0.89
Weekly hours employed	18.50	37.20
Number of cases	3,012	2,109

Source: Authors' configuration.
Note: Means are weighted.

TABLE 5.A3   *Means for Variables in Health Analysis for Mothers and Fathers, 1975 to 1976, 1985, and 1995*

	1975, 1985, 1995 (Exercise Only)		1976, 1985, 1995 (Other Health Indicators)	
	Mothers	Fathers	Mothers	Fathers
College-educated	0.14	0.22	0.14	0.21
Age	35.48	37.24	35.99	37.77
Married	0.75	0.86	0.75	0.87
Race				
White	0.75	0.78	0.75	0.78
Black	0.14	0.11	0.14	0.11
Hispanic	0.11[a]	0.11[a]	0.09	0.09
Other race			0.03	0.03
Children under age six	0.48	0.48	0.49	0.48
Number of children	2.07	2.07	2.17	2.15
Employed	0.56	0.88	0.55	0.87
Number of cases	14,863	10,029	17,995	12,915

Source: Authors' configuration.
Note: Means are weighted.
[a]Includes "other race."

NOTES

1. The "core" of the 1975 National Health Interview Survey is composed of 41,649 households containing 116,289 persons. The 1975 PFS is drawn from the core person file using a multistage probability sampling of all persons age eighteen or older in the households (n = 11,741). The core of the 1976 NHIS consists of 41,559 households containing 113,178 persons. The 1976 HHS is drawn from the core person file using multistage probability sampling of all persons age nineteen or older in the households (n = 23,088). The core of the 1985 NHIS is composed of 36,399 households containing 91,531 persons with an oversampling of the black population. One adult, age eighteen or older, is selected from each family for the 1985 HPDP supplement (n = 33,630). The core of the 1995 NHIS is composed of 41,824 households containing

102,467 persons with oversampling of black and Hispanic populations. In the 1995 Year 2000 Objectives supplement, one adult in half of the households was interviewed (n = 17,317).

2. We cannot be totally confident about the estimated increase between 1975 and 1985 because of the unknown effect of the change in question wording.

3. We are cautious about these findings because the goodness-of-fit tests suggest that our models do not fit well in predicting whether mothers missed days from work because of illness or injury.

REFERENCES

Aldous, Joan, Gail M. Mulligan, and Thoroddur Bjarnason. 1998. "Fathering over Time: What Makes the Difference?" *Journal of Marriage and the Family* 60: 809–20.

Barker, David J. P., and Charles Osmond. 1986. "Infant Mortality, Childhood Nutrition, and Ischemic Heart Disease in England and Wales." *The Lancet* 1: 1077–81.

Barnett, Rosalind C., and Grace K. Baruch. 1987. "Determinants of Fathers' Participation in Family Work." *Journal of Marriage and the Family* 49: 29–40.

Becker, Gary. 1981. *A Treatise on the Family.* Cambridge, Mass.: Harvard University Press.

Becker, Gary, Elizabeth M. Landes, and Robert T. Michael. 1977. "An Economic Analysis of Marital Instability." *Journal of Political Economy* 85: 1141–87.

Bianchi, Suzanne M., Melissa Milkie, Liana Sayer, and John Robinson. 2000. "Is Anyone Doing the Housework? Trends in the Gender Division of Household Labor." *Social Forces* 79: 191–228.

Blau, Peter M., and Otis D. Duncan. 1967. *The American Occupational Structure.* New York: John Wiley.

Branch, E. Raphael. 1994. "The Consumer Expenditure Survey: A Comparative Analysis." *Monthly Labor Review* 117(12): 47–55.

Cancian, Maria, and Deborah Reed. 1999. "The Impact of Wives' Earnings on Income Inequality: Issues and Estimates." *Demography* 36(May): 173–84.

Chevan, Albert, and Randall Stokes. 2000. "Growth in Family Income Inequality, 1970 to 1990: Industrial Restructuring and Demographic Change." *Demography* 37(August): 365–80.

Cohen, Philip N., and Suzanne M. Bianchi. 1999. "Marriage, Children, and Women's Employment: What Do We Know?" *Monthly Labor Review* 122(12, December): 22–31.

Cooney, Teresa M., Frank A. Pedersen, Samuel Indelicato, and Rob Palkovitz. 1993. "Timing of Fatherhood: Is 'On-Time' Optimal?" *Journal of Marriage and the Family* 55: 205–15.

Cramer, James C. 1987. "Social Factors and Infant Mortality: Identifying High-Risk Groups and Proximate Causes." *Demography* 24: 299–322.

Duncan, Dudley, David Featherman, and Beverly Duncan. 1972. *Socioeconomic Background and Achievement.* New York: Seminar Press.

Federman, Maya, Thesia I. Garner, Kathleen Short, W. Bowman Cutter, John Kiely, David Levine, Duane McDough, and Marilyn McMillen. 1996. "What Does It Mean to Be Poor in America?" *Monthly Labor Review* 119(5): 3–17.

Fisher, Kimberly, Andrew McCulloch, and Jonathan Gershuny. 1999. "British Fathers and Children." Unpublished paper. (December). Institute for Social and Economic Research, University of Essex, UK.

Haddad, Tony. 1994. "Men's Contribution to Family Work: A Reexamination of 'Time Availability.'" *International Journal of Sociology of the Family* 24: 87–111.

Haveman, Robert, and Barbara Wolfe. 1994. *Succeeding Generations: On the Effects of Investments in Children.* New York: Russell Sage Foundation.

Hill, C. Russell, and Frank P. Stafford. 1985. "Parental Care of Children: Time Diary Estimates of Quantity, Predictability, and Variety." In *Time, Goods, and Well-being,* edited by F. Thomas Juster and Frank P. Stafford. Ann Arbor: University of Michigan, Institute for Social Research.

Hummer, Robert A. 1993. "Racial Differentials in Infant Mortality in the U.S.: An Examination of Social and Health Determinants." *Social Forces* 72: 529–54.

Ishii-Kuntz, Masako, and Scott Coltrane. 1992. "Predicting the Sharing of Household Labor: Are Parenting and Housework Distinct?" *Sociological Perspectives* 35: 629–47.

Jencks, Christopher. 1972. *Inequality.* New York: Harper & Row.

Juhn, Chinhui, Kevin Murphy, and Brooks Pierce. 1993. "Wage Inequality and the Rise in Returns to Skill." *Journal of Political Economy* 101(3): 410–42.

Kalmijn, Matthijs. 1991. "Shifting Boundaries: Trends in Religious and Educational Homogamy." *American Sociological Review* 56(6): 786–800.

Karoly, Lynn A., and Gary Burtless. 1995. "Demographic Change, Rising Earnings Inequality, and the Distribution of Personal Well-being, 1959 to 1989." *Demography* 32: 379–406.

Kitagawa, Evelyn M., and Philip M. Hauser. 1973. *Differential Mortality in the United States: A Study in Socioeconomic Epidemiology.* Cambridge, Mass.: Harvard University Press.

Lazear, Edward P., and Robert T. Michael. 1988. *Allocation of Income Within the Household.* Chicago: University of Chicago Press.

Leibowitz, Arleen. 1974. "Home Investments in Children." *Journal of Political Economy* 82(2): S111–31.

Levy, Frank. 1998. *The New Dollars and Dreams.* New York: Russell Sage Foundation.

Lino, Mark. 1994. "Income and Spending Patterns of Single-Mother Families." *Monthly Labor Review* 117(5): 29–37.

Mare, Robert. 1995. "Changes in Educational Attainment and School Enrollment." In *State of the Union,* vol. 1, edited by Reynolds Farley. New York: Russell Sage Foundation.

Marsiglio, William 1991. "Paternal Engagement Activities with Minor Children." *Journal of Marriage and the Family* 53: 973–86.

Mayer, Susan. 1997. *What Money Can't Buy: Family Income and Children's Life Chances.* Cambridge, Mass.: Harvard University Press.

Mayer, Susan, and Christopher Jencks. 1989. "Poverty and the Distribution of Material Hardship." *Journal of Human Resources* 24(1): 88–114.

McLanahan, Sara, and Gary Sandefur. 1994. *Growing Up with a Single Parent: What Hurts? What Helps?* Cambridge, Mass.: Harvard University Press.

Murray, Charles. 1984. *Losing Ground: American Social Policy, 1950 to 1980.* New York: Basic Books.

National Heart, Lung, and Blood Institute. 1998. *Clinical Guidelines on the Identification, Evaluation, and Treatment of Overweight and Obesity in Adults.* Bethesda, Md.: National Heart, Lung, and Blood Institute.

Oppenheimer, Valerie K. 2000. "The Continuing Importance of Men's Economic Position in Marriage Formation." In *The Ties That Bind: Perspectives on Marriage and Cohabitation,* edited by Linda J. Waite, Christine Bachrach, Michelle Hindin, Elizabeth Thomson, and Arland Thornton. New York: Aldine de Gruyter.

Pleck, Joseph H. 1981. *The Myth of Masculinity.* Cambridge, Mass.: MIT Press.

Preston, Samuel H., and Paul Taubman. 1994. "Socioeconomic Differences in Adult Mortality and Health Status." In *Demography of Aging,* edited by Linda D. Margin and Samuel H. Preston. Washington, D.C.: National Academy Press.

Ross, Catherine R., and John Mirowsky. 1999. "Refining the Association Between Education and Health: The Effects of Quality, Credential, and Selectivity." *Demography* 36: 445–60.

Ross, Catherine R., and Chia-ling Wu. 1995. "The Links Between Education and Health." *American Sociological Review* 60(5): 719–45.

Sandberg, John F., and Sandra Hofferth. 2001. "Changes in Children's Time with Parents, United States, 1981 to 1997." *Demography* 38: 423–36.

Tan, Lucilla. 2000. "Spending Patterns of Public Assisted Families." *Monthly Labor Review* 123(5): 29–35.

Timmer, Susan Goff, Jacquelynne Eccles, and Keith O'Brien. 1985. "How Children Use Time." In *Time, Goods, and Well-being,* edited by F. Thomas Juster and Frank P. Stafford. Ann Arbor: University of Michigan, Institute for Social Research.

Umberson, Debra. 1987. "Family Status and Health Behaviors: Social Control as a Dimension of Social Integration." *Journal of Health and Social Behavior* 28: 306–19.

U.S. Department of Labor. 1998. "Consumer Expenditure Survey, Interview Survey." Washington: Bureau of Labor Statistics.

Volling, Brenda, and Jay Belsky. 1991. "Multiple Determinants of Father Involvement During Infancy in Dual-Earner and Single-Earner Families." *Journal of Marriage and the Family* 53: 461–74.

Wadsworth, M. E. 1986. "Serious Illness in Childhood and Its Association with Later-Life Achievement." In *Class and Health,* edited by Richard G. Wilkinson. London: Tavistock.

Wickrama, K. A. S., Rand D. Conger, Lora Ebert Wallace, and Glen H. Elder Jr. 1999. "The Intergenerational Transmission of Health-Risk Behaviors: Adolescent Lifestyles and Gender Moderating Effects." *Journal of Health and Social Behavior* 40: 258–72.

Williams, David R. 1990. "Socioeconomic Differentials in Health: A Review and Redirection." *Social Psychology Quarterly* 53: 81–99.

Wilson, William Julius. 1987. *The Truly Disadvantaged*. Chicago: University of Chicago Press.

———. 1996. *When Work Disappears*. New York: Knopf.

Yeung, W. Jean, John F. Sandberg, Pamela Davis-Kean, and Sandra L. Hofferth. 2001. "Children's Time with Fathers in Intact Families." *Journal of Marriage and the Family* 63(1): 136–54.

Zick, Cathleen D., and W. Keith Bryant. 1996. "A New Look at Parents' Time Spent in Child Care: Primary and Secondary Time Use." *Social Science Research* 25: 260–80.

Zill, Nicholas. 1999. *Setting an Example: The Health, Medical Care, and Health-Related Behavior of American Parents*. Washington, D.C.: Child Trends.

———. 2000. "Parents' Health and Risky Behaviors." In *Research Brief*. Washington, D.C.: Child Trends.

Part III

Inequality in School and Work

Chapter 6

Inequality in Early Childhood Education and Care: What Do We Know?

Marcia K. Meyers, Dan Rosenbaum, Christopher Ruhm, and Jane Waldfogel

The distribution of household income grew more unequal in the United States during the closing decades of the twentieth century. Persistent and growing income inequality is arguably a problem in its own right, but it is also a source of concern if income deficits and inequality exacerbate other social problems. These issues are particularly salient in the case of children, who have the least control over their economic circumstances but may have the most to gain (or lose) from economic resources. A large research literature links poverty with worse child outcomes, in terms of both short-term health and well-being and longer-term accumulation of human capital. There is some evidence that income inequality itself may also be a risk factor for children. Susan Mayer (2000), for example, examines the association between trends in income inequality (at the state level) and the educational attainment of children. She finds that as income inequality increases, the educational attainment of low-income children declines while that of high-income children rises.

Although most inequality research has focused on disparities in income and wealth, other forms of inequality may also contribute to worse child outcomes. Early childhood education and care (ECEC) is one of the most crucial of these domains. As mothers with young children have entered the labor force in record numbers, families have shifted a greater portion of early child care from parents to nonparental babysitters, family child care providers, and centers. Most young children from all income levels now spend a portion of their time in nonparental care. But these care arrangements differ substantially across more- and less-affluent families.

Care arrangements differ by income (and other socioeconomic characteristics) in the financial burden they impose on families of different means. Parents assume the majority of the costs of purchasing child care. Disparities in the resulting "cost burden"—out-of-pocket expenditures relative to income—are both a product of and a potentially exacerbating factor in income inequality. Cost burden may also increase inequality indirectly by discouraging the employment of low-skilled parents.

Care arrangements also differ with socioeconomic characteristics in the type and quality of care that children receive. To the extent that children in less-advantaged families receive less formal or lower-quality care, these differences represent a direct form of social inequality. To the extent that the quality of these arrangements influences development and health, inequalities in children's early care may also have lasting consequences. If children from less-advantaged families receive worse-quality care than their more affluent counterparts, and child care quality is associated with the early development of human capital, then child care inequalities may exacerbate a multigenerational cycle of disadvantage.

Government policies can ameliorate disparities in child care cost burden and quality by subsidizing child care costs for low-income families and offering compensatory early education programs. The opposite can also occur, however, if policies increase the use of nonparental care (for example, through work-related welfare policies) without equalizing cost burdens and quality between more- and less-affluent families. The development of early childhood education and care policies has been uneven both across time and across regions of the country, and our knowledge about their impact on inequality is limited.

This review examines several dimensions of ECEC in relation to the recent growth in income inequality. The first section briefly reviews trends in income inequality and the wage, labor supply, and family composition factors that have interacted to increase inequality in recent decades. Section 2 reviews the current state of knowledge about three potential links between ECEC and inequality: disparities in families' child care cost burdens and employment disincentives; inequalities in children's enrollment in formal and educationally oriented modes of care and in the quality of care; and short- and long-term consequences of ECEC experiences and quality for children's cognitive development, socioemotional adjustment, and health. We use a combination of literature review and original data analyses to summarize the state of knowledge about these relationships and identify key areas for future research. The third section provides an overview of major public policies for financing child care and improving child care quality and comments briefly on what is known about the contribution of government. The last section concludes by summarizing what is known, and what remains to be learned, about the associations between inequalities in ECEC and income.

Although many of the individual issues addressed here have been the subject of considerable research, they have almost never been examined in the context of the relationship between ECEC and inequality. For instance, there is a large literature examining the impact of child care costs on the employment decisions of mothers with young children. To our knowledge, however, no one has previously examined how these labor supply decisions affect either the inequality of family incomes or disparities in school readiness among children. Similarly, patterns of ECEC use have been studied, but research has rarely focused on how differentials in use relate to family incomes (or other dimensions of inequality) or how they contribute to or ameliorate inequality in family or child outcomes. Many aspects of this review are therefore inconclusive or speculative in nature and point to directions for future inquiry.

INCOME INEQUALITY

Income inequality grew substantially toward the end of the twentieth century. Arthur F. Jones and Daniel H. Weinberg (2000) report that between 1975 and 1993 households in the ninetieth percentile saw their incomes rise by 24.5 percent, while those in the tenth percentile experienced decreases of 2.3 percent. To understand how these dramatic changes in the income distribution came about, and the relevance of ECEC, we very briefly consider the trends in wages, household composition, and labor supply that, in combination, represent major sources of household incomes.

The growth of income inequality can be traced in large part to rising wage inequality, particularly during the 1979 to 1995 period (Katz and Autor 1999; Ellwood and Jencks this volume). The consequences of the changing wage structure were partially offset by increases in women's labor force participation. The proportion of women in the labor force rose from 38 percent in 1960 and 52 percent in 1980 to 60 percent in 1999 (U.S. Department of Commerce 2001). Two-adult families in particular responded to declining wages by moving more adults into the workforce (Mishel, Bernstein, and Schmidt 2001).

Growing income inequality from the 1970s through the 1990s can also be partly traced to changes in family composition. Single-motherhood has increased, particularly among less-skilled women (Ellwood and Jencks this volume). In sharp contrast, there was little change in single-motherhood among mothers in the top third of the educational distribution.

Like their married counterparts, single mothers increased their labor supply quite dramatically during the latter half of the century. By the early 1990s the annual hours of work among single and married mothers with children under six were nearly identical (Cohen and Bianchi 1999); by 2000 more single mothers with children under six were in the labor force (70 percent) than married mothers with children of the same age (63 percent) (U.S. Department of Commerce 2001, 373).

INCOME INEQUALITY AND EARLY CHILDHOOD EDUCATION AND CARE

The proportion of pre-school-age children spending some time in nonmaternal care has risen steadily in recent years, closely paralleling the rise in women's labor force participation. Child care is now a fact of life for most children. In 1999, for example, 66 percent of preschool-age children under the age of five were in some type of regular child care arrangement.[1] A large share of nonmaternal care (43 percent) is provided by relatives, but nearly as many children (37 percent) are cared for by nonrelatives in market settings such as child care centers or family day care homes—and 14 percent of preschoolers are cared for by both relatives and nonrelatives.

The distribution of ECEC in the largely market-based U.S. system has historically reflected socioeconomic differences in both parents' demand and parents' ability to pay for various forms of care. The rise in ECEC use and in income inequality at the end of the twentieth century gives these issues new urgency because the factors contributing to income inequality are intimately connected to patterns of child care use. Most obviously, the rise in women's employment was associated with a substantial increase in the use of nonparental child care. The sharp rise in employment among single mothers is particularly notable in this regard. Importantly, this increase in the use of nonparental child care was occurring in tandem with rising wage inequality and falling wages for the least-skilled workers. An unprecedented number of families were placing their young children in nonparental care by the end of the twentieth century, and many were doing so with very limited financial resources.

The implications of these changes for inequalities in income and in child care and the relationships between these inequalities are poorly understood. At least three linkages are plausible.

First, *ECEC costs may impose unequal cost burdens on families that increase income inequality both directly and indirectly.* Until children are old enough to enter kindergarten, most ECEC arrangements are private—privately financed by parents and privately provided by individuals, centers, or preschools. Purchasing these care arrangements imposes a substantial cost burden on many families who use care; if the expenses are relatively similar within modes of care, they will impose an exceptionally high burden on families with low incomes. This unequal cost burden may increase inequality directly. Child care expenses may also contribute indirectly to inequality by depressing maternal labor supply and earnings, particularly among lower-skilled workers for whom child care expenses represent a particularly steep marginal tax.

Second, *disparities in ECEC use related to socioeconomic status may create social inequalities in the type and quality of care received by children in more- and less-advantaged families.* Although the use of ECEC has expanded for all income groups in recent years, patterns of care differ substantially by income, race/ethnicity, location, and other family characteristics. Highly disadvantaged children are less likely than their more-advantaged peers to receive care in formal arrangements, more often receive informal care by relatives and friends, and are less likely to be enrolled in educationally oriented preschool programs during their preschool years. These differentials may reinforce existing economic and social inequalities by segregating lower-income children in less formal types of care. This stratification has more serious implications if the quality of care is lower in less formal arrangements than more formal and highly regulated settings, or if, within modes of care, lower-income families use less expensive and worse-quality arrangements.

Third, *ECEC differentials may contribute to increasing inequality in the long term through their effects on children's early development, learning, and health.* Evidence is growing that children's early experiences matter: a good start in life can promote learning and help children enter primary school with the skills, knowledge, behaviors, and attitudes necessary not only for learning but for meeting normative expectations. School is the arena where children from different backgrounds meet and in principle benefit from equal opportunities, yet many low-income children enter school already at a disadvantage relative to their more-affluent peers, and disparities in educational performance between low- and high-performing children appear to be growing over time. Children's early child care and educational experiences are not the only, or even necessarily the most influential, causes of these gaps. But if the mode of care and its quality do make significant contributions, and if children's access to high-quality arrangements is constrained by their parents' income, then disparities in ECEC may be widening the gap between the most- and least-advantaged children in both short-term school readiness and longer-term human capital development and life chances.

In the rest of this section, we take up each of these three issues in greater depth, reviewing what is known and what remains to be learned about the links between ECEC and inequality.

The Costs of Early Childhood Education and Care and Income Inequality

The direct and indirect impact of child care costs on family income is both the most obvious dimension of ECEC inequality and one of the mechanisms that may be underlying other disparities. If child care costs are similar for families with different incomes, the relative "burden" or share of family resources devoted to child care will be greater for lower-income families. As income inequality has increased and wages and incomes have declined for lower-skilled workers, both the absolute size and relative inequality of this burden may have increased. Indirectly, child care costs may further exacerbate income inequalities by depressing the labor supply of less-skilled parents, for whom child care costs represent a relatively larger marginal tax.

Assessing the inequality in the cost burden of ECEC is difficult because expenses as a share of income result from multiple interrelated factors, including: family structure (single- versus dual-parent households); employment probabilities and earnings potential; the probability of using nonparental care and the mode of care used; and the cost of different modes of care. Information on each of these factors is needed to provide reliable estimates of the cost burden of ECEC, but such data are difficult to obtain and often not comparable over time. Moreover, determining whether public policy exacerbates or mitigates differences in the cost burden of ECEC requires understanding not only cost differences across groups but also variations in the need for nonparental care. Thus, it is important to examine how factors that influence the need for child care, such as family structure and maternal employment, have varied across groups and over time.

Large literatures have developed around each of these factors (see, for example, Katz and Autor 1999; Ellwood and Jencks this volume; Council of Economic Advisers 1998). However, none of this research directly examines the combined impact on the need for child care and the resources available for obtaining it. For instance, a fall in birth rates among single mothers or a rise in marriage probabilities tends to reduce the fraction of young children residing in single-parent households, possibly decreasing the extent to which ECEC costs raise inequality. Conversely, higher maternal employment (particularly if induced by restrictions on welfare) is likely to elevate ECEC costs for low-income women and raise disparities. Similarly, greater wage inequality may increase the share of income devoted to child care expenses by families at the bottom of the distribution and so further increase inequality of net incomes.

In light of these complexities, we employ several alternative methods in our review of the literature on inequality in cost burden. We begin with a review of cross-sectional estimates of ECEC arrangements and expenses by income group and maternal employment. We next suggest an analytic approach for examining changes over time in the cost burden of ECEC by educational group. We conclude by reviewing evidence for an indirect effect of ECEC costs on inequality through maternal labor supply.

ECEC Expenses   We begin with an analysis of the 1990 National Child Care Survey, as summarized by Sandra Hofferth and her colleagues (1991). These data provide the most complete source of published data on how child care arrangements and costs vary by income group at a point in time. Table 6.1 summarizes some of these researchers' key findings by presenting costs of primary care for the youngest child (and these costs as a share of income) by income quintile for families with children under the age of five.[2] The top panel of the table shows that annual costs rise substantially with income.[3] Yet even though high-income families pay more for primary child care, these costs represent a greater share of the incomes of poorer families—accounting for 5 percent of income for the lowest quintile versus just 2 percent for the highest. Costs as a share of income are higher for families with employed mothers than for those without, and again they are disproportionately high at the bottom of the income distribution. For instance, primary child care costs in the lowest quintile, for families with an employed mother who pays for care, are five times as high as for those in the highest quintile (25 percent versus 5 percent).[4]

One reason poorer families spend less (in absolute dollars) on primary child care is because they rely much more heavily on free sources of care. What is particularly striking is that, in 1990, while only one in five poor families paid for primary care for their youngest child, more than half of high-income families did so. One reason for this difference was that mothers in low-income families were less likely to work, although that gap would narrow some in the late 1990s. Still, that is only a part of the story: low-income families were also much more likely to receive free nonparental primary care, particularly from relatives (see table 6.2).

TABLE 6.1   *Estimated Costs of Primary Child Care for the Youngest Child, by Income Quintile for Families with Children Under Age Five, 1990*

Primary Child-Care Expenses	Less Than $20,000	$20,001 to $33,000	$33,001 to $46,000	$46,001 to $66,000	More Than $66,000
Average costs per year					
All families	$527	$866	$1,089	$1,817	$2,458
With employed mothers	1,005	1,350	1,584	2,412	3,025
With employed mothers and paying					
for care	2,514	3,510	3,414	4,556	4,546
Costs relative to income					
All families	5%	3%	3%	3%	2%
With employed mothers	10	5	4	4	3
With employed mothers and paying					
for care	25	13	9	8	5

Source: Numbers are taken from (or extrapolated from) the tables in Hofferth et al. (1991), using data from the 1990 National Child Care Survey.
Notes: All dollar amounts are in 2000 dollars. Each of the income groups represents approximately one-fifth of the overall population of families with children under five.

Conversely, high-income families were much more likely to use expensive (and more formal) primary care. Greater use of expensive care among high-income families was largely due to their higher probability of utilizing center-based or family child care. A notable exception to this pattern was the relatively high use of these arrangements among families with non-employed mothers in the lowest income quintile. These families were more likely to use center-based or family child care than similar families with incomes in the middle quintiles (although not in the highest), probably as a result (as discussed later) of the availability of means-tested compensatory and early education programs (such as Head Start) for the lowest-income families.

The data from the 1990 National Child Care Survey indicate that families with children under five who were paying for care paid an average of $71 per week for primary care for the youngest child. Patricia Anderson and Philip Levine (2000) and Kristin Smith (2002), using different data sources and time periods, provide similar estimates of the average cost of primary care. Thus, estimates across sources and years appear to be reasonably consistent and indicate an average hourly rate of about $2.50 per hour, assuming that about thirty hours of primary care are paid for per week.

Anderson and Levine (2000) show that differences in costs largely depend on the mode of care, with relatively little variation across education groups conditional on mode. Center-based care is the most expensive, followed by family child care, and relative care is by far the least expensive. Overall, this analysis suggests that poor families spend less on child care than their wealthier counterparts in absolute dollars, but much more as a share of income. This suggests that the ECEC system in the United States imposes particularly steep financial costs on low-income families.

Trends in ECEC Cost Burden

To illustrate how combinations of factors that influence the need for child care might be examined, table 6.3 uses data from the 1986 to 2001 March Current Population Survey (CPS) to document how hours worked, earnings, and family structure have changed over time for various groups of mothers with children under

TABLE 6.2   *Employment and Child Care Arrangements for the Youngest Child, by Income Quintile for Families with Children Under Age Five, 1990*

	Less Than $20,000	$20,001 to $33,000	$33,001 to $46,000	$46,001 to $66,000	More Than $66,000
Mothers employed	40%	55%	57%	62%	66%
Primary care for all families					
Parent	49	53	47	48	31
Relative	19	16	19	14	13
Center-based or family day care	26	26	29	34	49
Primary care for families with employed mothers					
Parent	31	30	29	31	21
Relative	24	23	24	15	14
Center-based or family day care	41	43	43	49	60
Primary care for families with non-employed mothers					
Parent	62	80	71	74	50
Relative	15	8	12	12	10
Center-based or family day care	16	7	11	11	28
Cost of primary care for all families					
Parental care	49	53	47	48	31
Free nonparental care	30	23	21	13	15
Under $1.32 per hour	12	10	11	9	11
$1.32 to $2.64 per hour	7	13	15	22	27
More than $2.64 per hour	1	1	6	9	16
Cost of primary care for families with employed mothers					
Parental care	31	30	29	31	21
Free nonparental care	29	32	25	16	12
Under $1.32 per hour	24	16	16	12	13
$1.32 to $2.64 per hour	13	20	22	30	33
More than $2.64 per hour	3	2	8	12	20

Source: Numbers are taken from (or extrapolated from) the tables in Hofferth et al. (1991), using data from the 1990 National Child Care Survey.
Notes: All dollar amounts are in 2000 dollars. Primary care arrangement options do not add up to 100 percent because two additional categories, "in-home provider" and "other," are not shown.

six. The fraction of mothers who were married decreased between 1985 and 1988 and between 1997 and 2000 for high school graduates and those with some college (but no degree), with little change among those with more or less education. Maternal hours of work rose for all groups. Family earnings fell 4 to 10 percent for the three lowest educational groups, while college graduates experienced a 13 percent increase.

Table 6.4 reports a summary measure of the total effect of these various factors, calling it the "child care burden." The child care burden is calculated by multiplying the mother's work hours by the number of children she has under age six and by $2.50 per hour (which approximates the average cost of paid care) and then dividing this amount by total family earnings. Unlike other estimates that include the effects of endogenously determined differences in child care costs, our measure calculates costs as a ratio of incomes assuming all families pay the same price for their child care.[5] Although this represents a useful starting

TABLE 6.3   *Maternal Hours and Family Earnings for Families with Children Under Age Six, by Mother's Education and by Period, 1985 to 2000*

	1985 to 1988	1989 to 1992	1993 to 1996	1997 to 2000
Mothers with less than high school education				
Fraction of all mothers	0.197	0.188	0.180	0.157
Fraction married	0.593	0.556	0.550	0.594
Mother's annual hours of work	487	468	500	656
Family earnings per year	$15,481	$13,933	$13,329	$17,240
Mothers with only a high school education				
Fraction of all mothers	0.408	0.375	0.326	0.313
Fraction married	0.773	0.731	0.695	0.691
Mother's annual hours of work	833	898	943	1,052
Family earnings per year	$33,037	$31,792	$31,241	$34,211
Mothers with some college				
Fraction of all mothers	0.229	0.253	0.284	0.290
Fraction married	0.818	0.791	0.744	0.747
Mother's annual hours of work	910	984	1,059	1,126
Family earnings per year	$44,061	$43,483	$42,162	$46,800
Mothers with a bachelor's degree or more				
Fraction of all mothers	0.166	0.184	0.209	0.241
Fraction married	0.928	0.928	0.926	0.928
Mother's annual hours of work	996	1,107	1,135	1,158
Family earnings per year	$68,940	$72,301	$78,048	$85,247

Source: The data are authors' calculations from the 1986 to 2001 March CPS.
Notes: Data are weighted using CPS weights and by the number of children under age six. All dollar amounts are in 2000 dollars.

point for assessing the relationship between child care costs and inequality, it is incomplete to the extent that it ignores the effects of changes over time in tax or transfer policies (such as increases in child care subsidies for low-income families, child care tax credits for middle- and high-income households, or expansions of the Earned Income Tax Credit [EITC]) and in government child care and early education programs (like Head Start).

Table 6.4 indicates that the child care burden increased between 1985 and 2000 for all groups, except the most highly educated. During the early period, the child care burden was 2.4 (1.8) times as large for high school dropout (graduate) mothers as for those with at least a bachelor's degree. By 1997 through 2000, it had mushroomed to 3.0 (2.2) times as large. The child care burden rose relatively little for married couples, because higher earnings tended to offset increases in maternal hours of work. The situation was different for unmarried mothers. Because the child care burden simply is the ratio of the child care costs per hour for all of a woman's children divided by her wage rate, the lower wage rates of less-educated mothers result in a very high child care burden.

This analysis suggests that inequality in the child care burden may be increasing with time. Once again, this is simply a measure of the potential cost of ECEC across educational groups, since it does not reflect the lower cost (and possibly lower quality) of the child care arrangements typically used by lower-income mothers. Perhaps more important, it does not

TABLE 6.4   *Child Care Burden for Families with Children Under Age Six, by Mother's Education and by Period, 1985 to 2000*

	1985 to 1988	1989 to 1992	1993 to 1996	1997 to 2000
Child care burden for all families				
Mothers with less than a high school education	13.84%	15.23%	16.77%	16.22%
Mothers with only a high school education	10.07	11.15	11.78	11.90
Mothers with some college	8.22	8.99	9.86	9.31
Mothers with a bachelor's degree or more	5.72	6.00	5.84	5.45
Child care burden for married couples				
Mothers with less than a high school education	10.24	10.70	10.72	10.55
Mothers with only a high school education	8.16	8.81	8.93	8.74
Mothers with some college	6.92	7.39	7.82	7.16
Mothers with a bachelor's degree or more	5.26	5.59	5.46	5.08
Child care burden for unmarried mothers				
Mothers with less than a high school education	61.74	67.88	72.69	61.56
Mothers with only a high school education	44.03	43.25	45.05	40.46
Mothers with some college	33.47	36.55	35.53	32.16
Mothers with a bachelor's degree or more	22.00	19.98	19.43	17.20

Source: The data are authors' calculations from the 1986 to 2001 March CPS.
Notes: Data are weighted using CPS weights and by the number of children under age six. All dollar amounts are in 2000 dollars. "Child care burden" is calculated as the annual hours for mothers times the number of children under six times $2.50 per hour divided by the annual earnings for the family.

reflect other sources of income, such as transfer and child support payments or investment income, which may vary dramatically across groups.

ECEC Costs and Maternal Employment

Variation in the relative burden of expenses across families is not the only way in which child care costs contribute to inequality. It also seems likely that these expenses directly reduce the incentive to obtain work. Since such effects are likely to be particularly salient for mothers who would receive low wages, income inequality may be further exacerbated. Anderson and Levine's (2000) review of the extensive literature linking labor supply and child care costs concludes that there is a consistent negative relationship between child care expenses and maternal employment. Estimated employment elasticities (a measure of the sensitivity of one variable to another) with respect to child care costs cluster around −0.3 to −0.4; elasticities in this range indicate fairly strong disincentive effects.

One limitation is that most prior research relies on either individual variation in child care costs (Averett, Peters, and Waldman 1997; Connelly 1992; U.S. General Accounting Office 1994; Kimmel 1995, 1998; Michalopoulos, Robins, and Garfinkel 1992; Ribar 1992, 1995) or geographic variation in these expenses (Blau and Robins 1988; Han and Waldfogel

2002). Using such methods, it is likely to be difficult to disentangle the effects of cost from those of unobserved characteristics that determine employment or the use of paid child care. Therefore, it is reassuring that similar elasticities are obtained by Mark Berger and Dan Black (1992), Jonah Gelbach (2002), and Marcia Meyers, Theresa Heintze, and Doug Wolf (2002), using data from natural experiments on a few selected samples. A third approach, employed by Bruce Meyer and Dan Rosenbaum (2001) and Jay Bainbridge, Marcia Meyers, and Jane Waldfogel (forthcoming), exploits variation over time within and across states to estimate the effect of child care subsidies on employment. Once again, both papers find that single mothers in states with higher subsidies have higher employment rates, with estimated elasticities in most specifications between -0.1 and -0.3.

Some caution is required in concluding that child care costs contribute to income inequality by affecting employment or work hours, since linking ECEC expenses and labor supply does not directly reveal whether child care costs exacerbate income inequality by reducing employment among low-income mothers more than among high-income mothers. Since these costs are generally a larger share of income for disadvantaged families and the literature has generally found that the employment of less-skilled and low-income mothers is more sensitive to child care costs, this seems likely.[6] However, a full answer to this question depends on knowing the employment elasticity with respect to the child care burden (rather than dollar costs).

Summary   Although a number of studies have examined ECEC costs, few have taken up the questions of how child care cost burdens reflect and contribute to income inequality. Our review of the literature suggests that, although poor families spend less in absolute dollars on child care than more-affluent families, this is largely due to differences in their use and mode of care. Differences in costs to families are dwarfed by the disparities in incomes, with the result that ECEC expenses impose particularly steep financial costs on low-income families. We estimate that the child care burden increased during the 1985 to 2000 period for all groups except the most highly educated, increasing the inequality in cost burden over time. The literature also suggests that child care costs make an indirect contribution to inequality by depressing maternal employment, particularly among less-skilled and single mothers.

Despite large literatures on family structure, family labor supply, income inequality, child care policy, and child care arrangements and costs, very little is known about the interrelationships between these forces. Important questions for future research include:

- Did child care burdens become more equal or more unequal as employment increased for married mothers and later for single mothers?

- Have child care policies, such as Head Start, child care subsidies, and child care tax credits kept up with increases in maternal employment? And have the changes in policies ameliorated or exacerbated income inequality?

- Do families with higher child care burdens choose lower-cost (and presumably lower-quality) child care options? Is maternal employment lower among these families with higher child care burdens, which perhaps contribute indirectly to income inequality?

Inequality in the Use, Type, and Quality of ECEC

The preceding section demonstrated that lower-income families are more likely than more-affluent families to rely on less formal forms of nonparental care. These differences may reduce inequalities in cost burden by reducing child care expenses among the lowest-income families, but they may also represent other forms of inequality. Income-related differences in the use and mode of ECEC constitute a direct form of social inequality if the use of ECEC is a normal good (one that people would want to buy more of if they could) and the receipt of any care and the type of care used are constrained by family income. These differences reflect more serious inequalities if they are associated with differences in quality. Income may be associated with quality in at least two ways. Low-income children may receive worse-quality care if formal care is, on average, of higher quality or more develop-mentally enhancing than informal care. Quality may also vary within modes of care. If this variation is related to price, low-income children may receive worse-quality care within modes than those in families with more resources for purchasing care.

In this section, we review what is known about income-related differences in the type and quality of care that children receive. We begin by examining patterns of child care use in greater detail, using recent data on care arrangements for young children and over-time data on preprimary enrollment specifically among children age three to five. We then turn to two questions about ECEC and income inequality: Do differentials in ECEC arrange-ments reflect income constraints? And do they correspond to differences in the quality of care received by children?

Variation in ECEC Arrangements

The previous section documented large differences in the types of care received by more- and less-advantaged children as of 1990. An analysis of more recent data suggests that these disparities persisted through the end of the decade.[7] Table 6.5 describes the ECEC arrangements of children in 1999 using data from the SIPP.[7] Looking first at the top panel, which describes the care arrangements of all children under age six, we can see that no nonparental care (that is, only maternal or parental care) is more common for poor and near-poor children (44 to 45 percent) than for those who are more affluent (36 percent). The primary care arrangement is also more likely to be informal relative care for poorer children (23 to 25 percent) than for children in more-affluent families (19 percent). The relationship between income and the use of center-based care is U-shaped: children under age six in near-poor families are least likely to be in center-based care for their primary arrangement (20 percent), in contrast to 28 percent of those in more-affluent families and 23 percent of those in poor families.[8] This suggests that the availability of means-tested public ECEC programs for the poorest children may partially offset income-related disparities in the use of center arrangements. Nevertheless, both poor and near-poor children lag their more-affluent counterparts in receipt of formal care.

Table 6.5 reveals other associations between ECEC use and families' socioeconomic characteristics. The likelihood that children will experience no nonparental care declines steadily with mothers' income, while the probability of having any center-based care rises. Differences by race-ethnicity are also striking: Hispanic families make notably lower use of center-based arrangements for their children. As noted earlier, differences in rates of mater-nal employment would be expected to explain some of the differences in ECEC use be-tween less- and more-affluent families. The bottom panel of table 6.5 suggests, however, that some of these differences are more extreme if we consider only families in which the mother is employed.

These findings echo those of a number of other studies that have documented socio-economic differences in children's exposure to nonparental, and particularly formal, care arrangements at various points in time (Hofferth et al. 1991; West et al. 1992; Anderson and Levine 2000; NICHD ECCRN 1997; Ehrle, Adams, and Tout 2001; Snyder and Hoff-

TABLE 6.5   *Primary Care Arrangement of Children Under Age Six, by Type of Child Care, 1999*

	Maternal Care	Paternal Care	Relative Care	Other Nonrelative Care	Family Day Care	Center-Based Care and Education	Any Center-Based Care and Education[a]
All children	28%	12%	21%	7%	7%	25%	30%
Ethnicity							
White, non-Hispanic	29	13	18	8	7	26	30
Hispanic	37	10	25	4	6	19	22
African American	17	9	30	5	7	33	40
Other	30	11	32	2	5	20	27
Education							
No degree	40	7	25	3	5	20	24
High school diploma or GED	29	14	25	5	5	23	28
Some college	25	11	22	7	9	26	30
College degree	24	13	14	10	8	30	35
Poverty status							
200 percent or less of poverty line	35	10	24	4	6	21	25
More than 200 percent of poverty line	23	13	19	9	8	28	33

Poverty status							
100 percent or less of poverty line	38	6	23	3	6	23	27
100 to 200 percent of poverty line	33	12	25	4	5	20	24
More than 200 percent of poverty line	23	13	19	9	8	28	33
All children of employed mothers	5	19	27	11	9	29	37
Ethnicity							
White, non-Hispanic	5	21	22	13	9	30	38
Hispanic	5	20	37	7	12	19	25
African American	3	13	34	5	8	38	45
Other	4	19	45	3	7	23	5
Education							
No degree	4	15	41	5	10	26	33
High school diploma or GED	4	23	31	8	7	27	35
Some college	6	17	27	11	10	28	35
College degree	4	19	17	15	9	35	42
Poverty status							
100 percent or less of poverty line	5	16	34	6	10	28	36
100 to 199 percent of poverty line	5	23	34	7	8	23	30
200 percent or more of poverty line	4	19	23	13	9	32	39
Poverty status							
200 percent or less of poverty line	5	20	34	7	9	24	32
200 percent or more of poverty line	4	19	23	13	10	32	40

Source: Authors' calculations of 1999 SIPP data.
Notes: Distribution of children across primary care arrangements may not sum to 100 owing to rounding of numbers.
[a] This includes center-based care or education that was reported as a secondary care arrangement.

FIGURE 6.1　　Pre-Primary Enrollment of Three- and Four-Year-Olds, 1964 to 1998

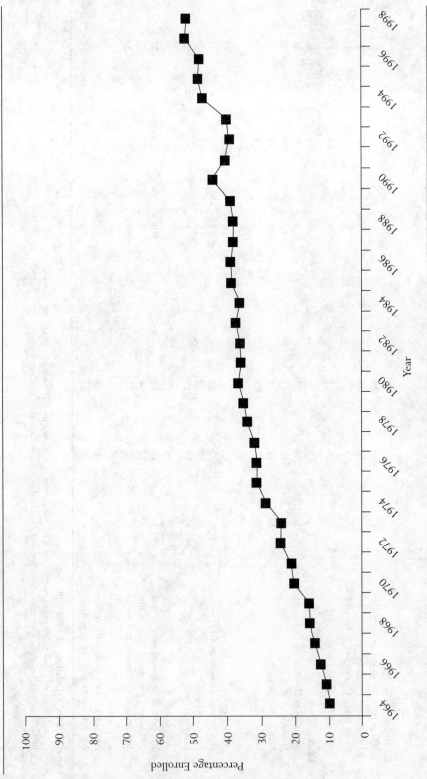

Source: Current Population Reports, U.S. Department of Commerce (October 1994, 1995, 1996, 1997, 1998, and 1999).

man 2003). Together, these studies suggest substantial income and educational stratification in children's experience of early care. Because they rely on data sources that differ in their samples, measures, and coding, however, it is difficult to draw conclusions about whether socioeconomic differences in ECEC have grown or diminished over time.

To compare ECEC disparities over time, we make use of data from the October Current Population Survey from 1964 to 2000. This survey collects data annually on children's school enrollment. Although primarily designed to collect school enrollment data for older children, the survey also collects information on enrollment of children age three to five in pre-primary school programs.[9] Despite minor changes in question wording over the period, the October CPS provides a fairly consistent time series of data on the enrollment of three- to five-year-olds in center- and school-based preschool programs such as Head Start, nursery schools, prekindergarten, and kindergarten.[10]

These measures are particularly relevant to issues of inequality, since educationally oriented preschool experiences have become an increasingly normative part of children's preparation for school entry. The use of pre-primary arrangements has grown steadily in recent decades, with the percentage of three- and four-year-old children enrolled in pre-primary school programs increasing from less than 10 percent in 1964 to 52 percent in 1998 (figure 6.1).

When we disaggregate this trend by the age of the child and by family characteristics (figures 6.2 and 6.3), we see evidence that while enrollment in pre-primary school programs has increased over time for all groups, socioeconomic differences have been remarkably persistent. For both three- and four-year-old children, enrollments have remained somewhat higher for those whose mother is employed. Hispanic children have been less likely to attend schools and centers than their non-Hispanic counterparts. Interestingly, there are no notable differences by mother's marital status. The most striking differences are associated with maternal education and family income. For both three- and four-year-olds, the children of the most highly educated parents have had the highest rates of enrollment and the children of the least-educated parents have had the lowest. In both age groups children in the highest-income families have remained the most likely to attend pre-primary programs, with lower and relatively similar rates of attendance among children in the bottom two quartiles of the income distribution.

Trends in pre-primary school enrollments for five-year-olds, shown in figure 6.4, provide an interesting contrast. By the late 1970s, the enrollment of five-year-olds in some form of school (for the most part public kindergarten) was nearly universal. Differentials associated with race/ethnicity, mother's education, and family income were evident at the start of this data series, in the 1960s, but these differences largely disappeared in the period between 1970 and 1980 as enrollments in public kindergarten rose.

ECEC Differences and Inequality   Observed socioeconomic differences in ECEC use and mode raise the obvious question of whether, and to what extent, these differences result from inequalities in family resources. Does the cost burden associated with more formal modes of care effectively price lower-income families out of more desirable modes of care?

Researchers have considered a number of alternatives to income for explaining socioeconomic differences in ECEC. Disparities in child care use are sometimes credited to problems of supply. There is little evidence of widespread shortages of child care services, as private markets have been quite responsive to increases in parents' demand for child care. David Blau (2001), for example, estimates that the for-profit child care sector expanded by 143 percent, and the nonprofit sector by 77 percent, between 1982 and 1997 as more

(Text continues on p. 244.)

FIGURE 6.2   Pre-Primary Enrollment of Three-Year-Olds, 1968 to 2000

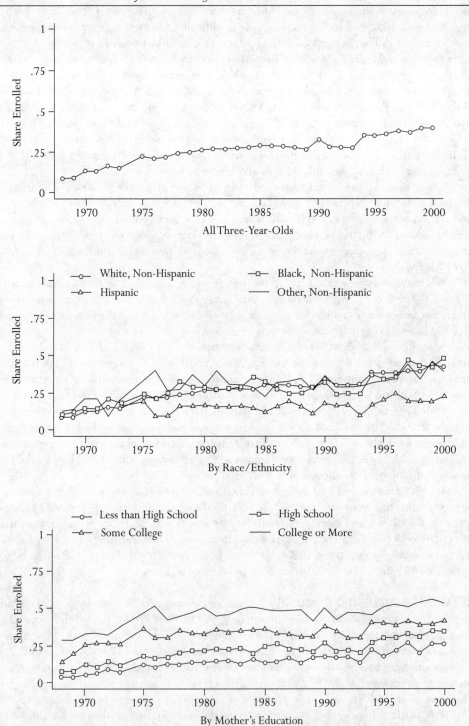

FIGURE 6.2   (*Continued*)

By Mother's Employment

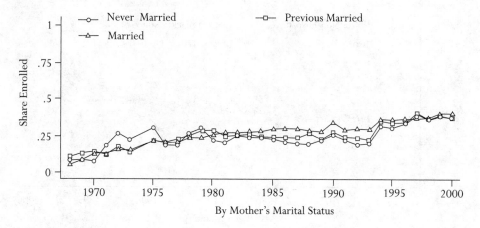

By Mother's Marital Status

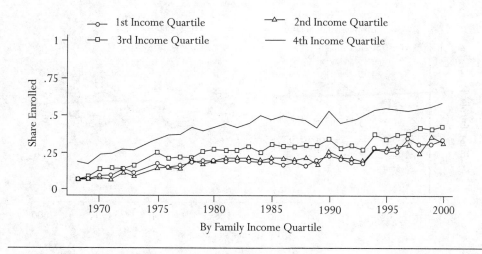

By Family Income Quartile

FIGURE 6.3   *Pre-Primary Enrollment of Four-Year-Olds, 1968 to 2000*

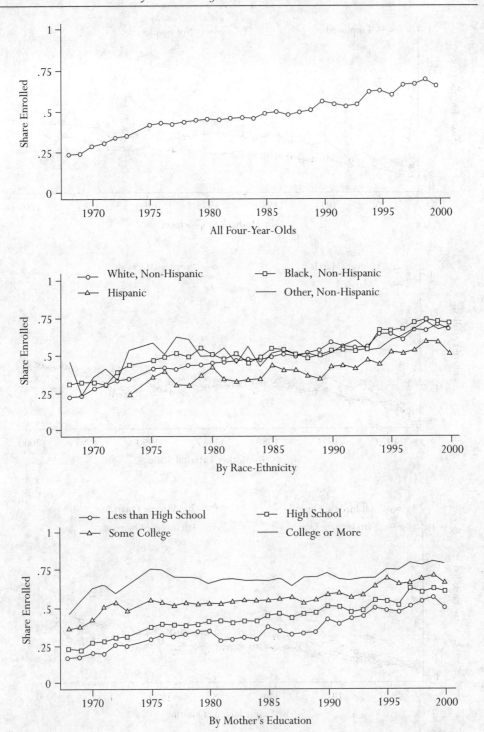

All Four-Year-Olds

By Race-Ethnicity

By Mother's Education

Source: October CPS.

FIGURE 6.3   (*Continued*)

By Mother's Employment

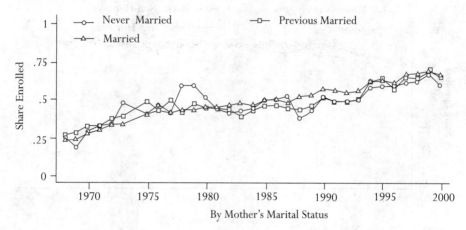

By Mother's Marital Status

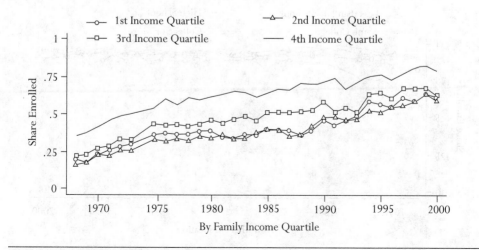

By Family Income Quartile

FIGURE 6.4   *Pre-Primary Enrollment of Five-Year-Olds, 1968 to 2000*

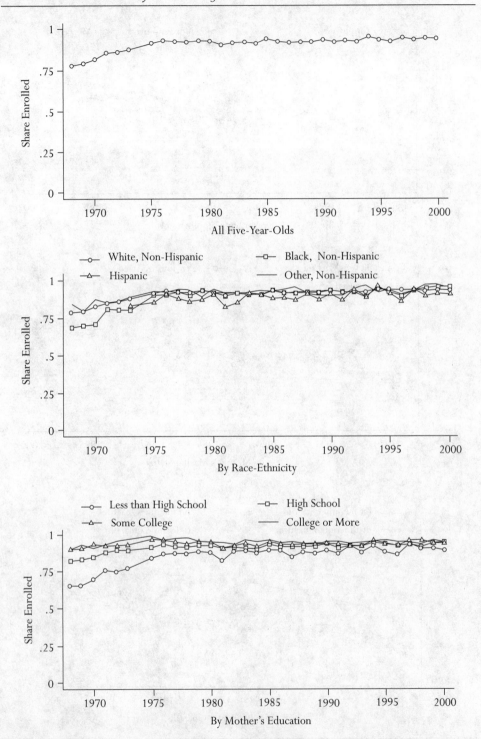

All Five-Year-Olds

By Race-Ethnicity

By Mother's Education

Source: October CPS.

FIGURE 6.4   (*Continued*)

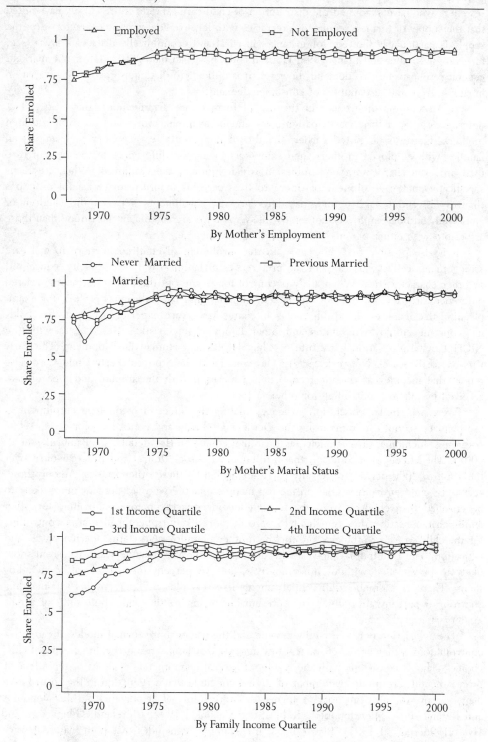

By Mother's Employment

By Mother's Marital Status

By Family Income Quartile

women entered employment and sought substitute child care arrangements. Several researchers who have examined the distribution of child care services more closely have noted that the supply of formal, regulated care varies with local socioeconomic characteristics; the supply is particularly limited, for instance, in rural and economically distressed areas (see, for example, Fuller and Liang 1996; Gordon and Chase-Lansdale 2001). Given the market's general responsiveness to demand, however, it is difficult to distinguish geographic variation in supply from the distribution of consumer demand.

Socioeconomic differences in the use of formal care arrangements may also reflect differences in labor force participation between, for example, more- and less-well-educated mothers. However, as noted earlier, the use of nonparental care is very high among all families with employed mothers, and some socioeconomic differences in the type of care used are even sharper among families in which mothers are employed. When we focus specifically on the enrollment of three- to five-year-olds in pre-primary school programs (figures 6.2 and 6.3), we find that differences in enrollments between the children of employed and non-employed mothers, while persistent, are smaller in magnitude than those associated with either parents' education or family income.

It is also possible that differences in the enrollment of children in more formal care arrangements reflect variations in the preferences of families by race, ethnicity, education, or other characteristics. When analysts control for (some of) these factors, income-related differences are reduced but not eliminated. Hofferth and her colleagues (1993), for example, find that income-related differences in center-based care experience persist after holding constant employment status and other family characteristics. Researchers with the NICHD ECCRN (National Institute of Child Health and Human Development, The Early Child Care Research Network 1997), who conducted the Study of Early Child Care, also report that income has the most consistent association with the amount and type of care received by infants, controlling for other factors.

We reach similar conclusions when estimating the effect of income on enrollment in pre-primary school programs using the October CPS data and controlling for a rich set of covariates, including race, ethnicity, and parental education (for details, see Bainbridge et al. 2002). The effects of income on the enrollment of three-, four-, and five-year-olds, over the 1968 to 2000 period, were only partly explained by these other factors. Among three-year-olds, children from families in the top income quartile were 23 percent more likely to be enrolled than children from the bottom income quartile before controlling for other family characteristics; they remained 15 percent more likely to be enrolled after controlling for the child's race or ethnicity and for the mother's employment status, marital status, and education. The results for four-year-olds are similar: the top quartile was 23 percent more likely to be enrolled without other controls, and 16 percent more likely after including them. There is a smaller differential among five-year-olds—7 percent before including controls, 6 percent after doing so—presumably owing to the wide availability of public kindergarten at that age.

The association between family income and the use of more formal modes of care after controlling for other family characteristics suggests that family resources do constrain ECEC choices. This is consistent with the results of several econometric analyses of the effect of price on child care mode. A number of studies conclude that a reduction in the cost of care leads parents to substitute market forms for more informal arrangements (Michalopoulos and Robins 2002; Michalopoulos, Robins, and Garfinkel 1992; Cleveland, Gunderson, and Hyatt 1996; Powell 1997). Blau (2001), for example, concludes that both maternal wage and family income elasticities are positive for center care and negative for other forms of care, suggesting that as wages and family income rise, families tend to switch from less formal to more formal care arrangements. As he suggests, "parents feel most 'priced out' of center and family day care and would prefer these types over other nonparental care and parental care if they were equally as cheap" (74).

ECEC Quality and Inequality

If lower-income families are priced out of not only formal care but high-quality care, these disparities may result in even more serious forms of social inequality. To evaluate these issues, we would ideally like to know the degree of socioeconomic inequality in the quality of ECEC and whether this dimension of inequality has risen or fallen over time. Unfortunately, the research here is not well developed.

The quality of child care is hard to define, and even harder to measure. Measures of quality generally consider issues of health and safety, adequacy of supervision, developmental appropriateness, and the warmth and responsiveness of the caregiver. These factors are important in the short term (for example, for the safety of children and the satisfaction of their emotional needs). As we discuss later in the chapter, these factors have also been associated with children's cognitive development and school preparation.

Most studies of child care quality rely on the structural characteristics of child care settings, such as group size, staff-to-child ratios, and the educational qualifications of the caregivers. These characteristics are relatively easy to measure and have been associated with both caregiver responsiveness and child outcomes (see, for example, NICHD ECCRN 2002a). But they are unlikely to fully capture the quality of the care actually delivered. The most in-depth studies of quality have gathered data on dimensions of process quality—such as cognitive stimulation and sensitivity to children's needs—by having one or more observers spend time at the child care setting recording the quality of care along various dimensions, using standardized scales developed for this purpose.[11]

A number of observational studies conclude that the quality of most child care in the United States is low. Using data from the Cost Quality and Outcomes Study (CQOS), Suzanne Helburn and her colleagues (1995) conclude that care at most centers is poor to mediocre, with only one of seven judged to be providing a level of quality sufficient to promote healthy development. The youngest children fare the worst: almost half the infant and toddler rooms provide poor quality, and only one in twelve supplies developmentally appropriate care. Ellen Galinsky and her colleagues (1994) had similar results in a study of relative and family child care: only one in ten providers is rated as providing good care, about one-third supply inadequate care, and slightly over half provide care that is adequate or custodial. More recently, the NICHD ECCRN (1997) has assessed the quality of child care experienced by a sample of children born in 1991. Using a specially developed measure (the Observational Record of the Caregiving Environment) that allowed formal and informal providers to be assessed on the same scale, the study found that 61 percent of the ECEC arrangements experienced by these children under age three were of "poor" to "fair" quality.

In relation to inequality, we are primarily interested in the question of whether quality is lower, on average, for children from less-advantaged families. Differences in mode of care may serve as a proxy for quality differences because market forms of care (centers and family child care) are more likely to be regulated for quality than informal care with relatives and friends. Quality standards are highest, and most consistently enforced, in public early education programs such as Head Start. Although public regulation of private arrangements is a less consistent predictor of quality, the dimensions regulated by most states—particularly staff training and education—have been found to predict process quality and better child outcomes (see, for example, Clarke-Stewart et al. 2002; Burchinal et al.

2002; Burchinal, et al. 2000; Blau 1997, 2000; Ghazvini and Mullis 2002; NICHD ECCRN 1999, 2002a). The stringency of state regulations has also been linked to lower rates of accidental injury in child care settings (Currie and Hotz 2001).

Assuming that more formal, highly regulated forms of care provide higher quality of care is problematic for a number of reasons. As noted earlier, observational studies suggest that the majority of care in formal settings may not meet professional standards for developmentally enhancing care. Children also benefit from different types of care at different ages, and the formal modes of care most likely to be regulated (centers) may confer fewer developmental benefits for younger children. And although market forms of care are more likely to be regulated, these regulations are highly variable and weak in many states. (We return to this issue in our discussion of public policy.) More direct evidence would be obtained by comparing quality dimensions across modes of care, but given the measurement difficulties, researchers have rarely made such comparisons. The NICHD Study of Early Child Care, one of the few studies to do so, has assessed "positive caregiving" in both formal and informal settings and finds that it is in general more characteristic of informal settings (NICHD ECCRN 2000). Notably, these researchers conclude that this is particularly true for infants and toddlers, raising the possibility that younger children receive fewer benefits from group care.

Contrary evidence that formal settings provide higher quality is provided by studies that compare children's outcomes by mode of care. As we review in more detail in the next section, high-quality ECEC has been associated with improved developmental outcomes that have particular relevance for the school readiness of older preschool children. A handful of studies suggest that these improved outcomes are more strongly associated with more formal care arrangements. Children who have received center-based care tend to have better pre-academic skills and better language development than those who have not (Clarke-Stewart and Fein 1983; Belsky 1984; Hayes, Palmer, and Zaslow 1990). The same ECCRN researchers who rate informal care more highly on positive caregiving have also concluded that center-based care is more strongly associated than informal care with children's cognitive and language development (NICHD ECCRN 2000). These results have been confirmed in more recent analyses (NICHD ECCRN 2002b).[12] Similarly, a recent study using data from the Infant Health and Development Program (IHDP), which provided high-quality center-based care, finds that the greatest and most lasting cognitive gains accrue for the children who would otherwise have experienced non-center-based care (Hill, Waldfogel, and Brooks-Gunn 2002). This study is important because it suggests that children currently using non-center-based care would benefit if they were moved into high-quality center-based care.

Although far from conclusive, research suggests that the minimally regulated informal arrangements used disproportionately by low-income families may provide less developmentally enhancing care than more formal arrangements. Evidence is less ambiguous that they use poorer quality of care within modes. For children in family or relative care, income is positively associated with quality. In their study of such children, Galinksy and her colleagues (1994) find that families with higher incomes are more than twice as likely (65 percent) to be using regulated family child care as those with incomes below poverty (26 percent), while middle-income families are in between (39 percent). Regulation is not synonymous with high quality, but these authors find that, even after controlling for maternal education, family child care providers serving higher-income families are rated as more sensitive and less restrictive than those serving low-income families. Care arrangements used by more-affluent families are also more likely to be rated as at least "adequate" than those used by lower-income families. The NICHD ECCRN (1997) has also studied quality differentials among children using relative or family child care and found a positive correlation between quality and family income.

Studies of children in child care centers also reveal income-related disparities in quality, but here the U-shaped distribution described earlier for both access and costs is again evident. The highest-quality care is received by children in affluent families, who can afford to purchase good care, and by children in the poorest families, who may be enrolled in public compensatory and early education programs (Phillips et al. 1994). Most recently, the NICHD ECCRN (1997) reports that among children in center-based settings, those from low- and high-income families receive higher-quality care than those from moderate-income families.

Summary   Children in low-income families, and those with less-educated mothers, are less likely than their counterparts to be enrolled in formal care and pre-primary school programs. Over the last twenty years income and other socioeconomic differences in pre-primary enrollments have largely disappeared for five-year-olds, but they have persisted for younger children. The notable exception to this pattern is the somewhat higher enrollments of very poor children (relative to those in near-poor families) in center-based arrangements, probably owing to the availability of means-tested preschool programs.

A number of studies suggest that the cost of formal, market forms of care depresses use by lower-income families. The disproportionate, and possibly increasing, cost burden of ECEC described here may therefore contribute directly to the persistence of inequalities in the type of care children receive. Whether these inequalities have additional implications for children's well-being depends on the quality of care provided in various modes of care. Direct evidence that more highly regulated, formal settings provide higher-quality care is limited because researchers rarely compare quality across types of settings. Indirect evidence is provided by studies linking the regulated features of care to quality and studies documenting better cognitive and school readiness outcomes for children who experience formal care. These advantages are likely to be particularly important for three- to five-year-old children, insofar as child care centers, preschools, and prekindergartens expose them to educationally oriented materials and help them acquire skills and behaviors that they will need in school. Researchers have done more to document income-related disparities of quality within types of care. Unless they are enrolled in high-quality public preschool programs, children from lower-income families appear to receive worse-quality care within care modes.

The available research thus suggests that many low-income children may be triply disadvantaged by being disadvantaged at home, having lower enrollments in educationally oriented center-based or school-based programs, and being exposed to lower-quality care even if they do attend such programs. Data also suggest that public programs may be offsetting some of this disadvantage for the poorest children, who are more likely to be enrolled in formal care and to receive somewhat higher-quality care than near-poor children. We know relatively little yet about how these income-related disparities have changed over time and in relation to changes in income inequality.

A number of important questions need to be answered to more fully understand the relationships between ECEC arrangements, quality, and income inequality:

- To what extent is income a barrier to the use of formal care, controlling for other family-level characteristics that influence child care choices? How have disparities in the use of formal care changed over time, given changes in maternal employment, wages, family composition, and other factors affecting child care needs and resources?

- Has the effect of income on families' ECEC arrangements changed over time? Have government policies strengthened or weakened this association?

- How does the quality of care vary both across and within modes of care? Does this association itself vary with the age of the child and other family characteristics? Has it changed over time, given changes in families' consumption of ECEC and changes in government policy designed to reduce income constraints and improve child care quality?

The Links Between ECEC and Inequality in Child and Adult Outcomes

If ECEC makes a significant contribution to children's early health and development, which in turn shape adult skill development and economic success, ECEC disparities could contribute to perpetuating (or breaking) a cycle of inequality. For this reason, we next review the evidence on how ECEC influences children's outcomes in three areas associated with long-term well-being: cognitive development, socioemotional development, and health.

Cognitive Development   Children's early life experiences—both in the home and in nonfamilial settings such as child care—influence the development of cognitive capacities that help children succeed in school and in later life (Shonkoff and Phillips 2000). Although development continues throughout childhood and into adulthood, the quality of children's very early experiences may be particularly crucial for shaping their later life chances.

Children's cognitive abilities are already very unequal by the time they start school. Baseline data from the Early Childhood Longitudinal Survey, Kindergarten Class of 1998–99, for example, indicate that low-income children score more poorly than higher-income children on all four measured dimensions of school readiness: cognitive skills and knowledge, social skills, physical health and well-being, and approaches to learning (West, Denton, and Germino-Hausken 2000; see also data from the National Household Education Survey's School Readiness modules in Nord et al. 2000). These early disparities are likely to persist into later childhood and adolescence. Thus, Meredith Phillips (1999) finds that at least half the test score gap between black and white children in the twelfth grade was already present in first grade (see also Entwisle and Alexander 1993; Alexander and Entwisle 1996; Phillips et al. 1998).

Sorting out the causes of these disparities is a complex task. Some differences in school readiness between higher- and lower-income children can be traced to the home environment (see, for example, Nord et al. 2000). Even though the influence of the home environment may be paramount, research suggests that nonfamilial experiences during early childhood are also important. A number of randomized and controlled experiments have documented lasting cognitive gains for children who experience high-quality interventions in the years before school (for reviews, see Karoly et al. 1998; Brooks-Gunn 2000; Ramey and Ramey 2000; Vandell and Wolfe 2000; Waldfogel 2002). These gains are particularly large for the most disadvantaged children, who appear to benefit the most dramatically from high-quality early childhood interventions and to be most adversely affected by poor-quality care (Berlin et al. 1998; Ramey and Ramey 1998; Currie 2000). There is related evidence that the cognitive gains are also largest for children whose mothers have the lowest levels of education themselves (see evidence from the IHDP summarized in Karoly et al. 1998; Waldfogel 2002).

Non-experimental studies provide additional evidence about the influence of ECEC experiences. A number of researchers have used naturally occurring variation in families' use of ECEC to assess the impact of ECEC on children's outcomes. These studies have the advantage of including a range of care arrangements that vary in structural and process quality. They have the disadvantage, however, of not being able to control for unobserved factors associated with the selection of different types of children into different types of care or care of different levels of quality. This caveat notwithstanding, the evidence suggests that children attending higher-quality child care in their preschool years have higher levels of cognitive skills (Clarke-Stewart, Gruber, and Fitzgerald 1994; Kontos et al. 1995; Peisner-Feinberg and Burchinal 1997; NICHD ECCRN 1999, 2000, 2002b) and enter school better prepared to learn (Peisner-Feinberg et al. 1999, 2001). The effects of quality also tend to be larger for low-income children than for more-affluent children, and for children with less-educated mothers than for children with more-educated mothers (Vandell and Corasaniti 1990; Baydar and Brooks-Gunn 1991; Bryant et al. 1994; Caughy, DiPietro, and Strobino 1994; Peisner-Feinberg and Burchinal 1997; Burchinal, Peisner-Feinberg, et al. 2000).

Although encouraging, these studies are limited in important respects. Most rely on indirect measures of quality (such as staffing ratios) that, as noted earlier, may not capture important dimensions of quality. Non-experimental studies may also be contaminated by the omission of controls for unobserved differences between families choosing different child care settings. This latter issue is explored at length in NICHD ECCRN and Duncan (2002). They conclude that higher quality is associated with small improvements in child cognitive development, with larger effects for children whose cognitive scores were low to start with.

Socioemotional Development   A large literature has examined the links between early child care experiences and children's socioemotional development (for recent reviews, see Lamb 1998; Shonkoff and Phillips 2000; Belsky 2001; Bornstein et al. 2001). The focus of much study has been on learning whether early and extensive experience of nonmaternal care places a child at risk of insecure attachment to the mother and hence at risk of later behavioral problems.

After extensive research, the issue of insecure attachment seems to have been put to rest. As an authoritative review in *The Handbook of Child Psychology* concludes: "It now seems clear that most infant-mother attachments are not adversely affected by regular nonmaternal care" (Lamb 1998, 92). However, the question of possible links between early and extensive child care and later behavior problems remains. Early maternal employment or use of child care is frequently associated with more problem behaviors for children (Haskins 1985; Belsky 1986, 1990; Vandell and Corasaniti 1990; Baydar and Brooks-Gunn 1991; Belsky and Eggebeen 1991; Bates et al. 1994).[13] Unfortunately, most of the investigations have been limited by small sample sizes and a lack of information on the child's home and ECEC environments. In particular, the results may be biased by the lack of data on the quality of child care, which has been found to be an important contributor to children's behavioral and social competence outcomes (Lamb 1998; Bornstein et al. 2001).

The continuing interest in the possible links between early child care use and poor behavioral outcomes provided one important rationale for the NICHD ECCRN Study of Early Child Care, which since 1991 has been studying the cognitive and socioemotional development of a cohort of children from ten sites nationwide. The NICHD ECCRN collected extensive data on children's early home and child care environments and on their cognitive and socioemotional outcomes. The latest available results indicate that early and extensive experience of nonmaternal child care is associated with an elevated risk of behavior problems among four-and-a-half-year-old children (NICHD ECCRN 2003). However, children attending centers that meet recommended standards for quality have fewer behavioral problems than those experiencing poorer-quality care (NICHD 1999). Marc Bornstein and his colleagues (2001) report similar findings for a small sample of children followed to age seven. These findings are consistent with most earlier research on two main points: early and extensive experience of child care is correlated with higher levels of later behavior problems; and the number of behavior problems is negatively related to the quality of child care.

It is worth noting that participation in high-quality early intervention programs does not appear to adversely affect socioemotional outcomes. Instead, research typically finds either no significant effects or positive impacts. For instance, the Perry Pre-School Program achieved its strongest and most lasting (beneficial) effects on social outcomes such as delinquency and crime (Karoly et al. 1998). Perry Pre-School care may have had these effects because it did not begin early, did not last for long hours, and was of very high quality.

Taken together, the evidence does not suggest one uniform set of effects of ECEC on socioemotional outcomes. Rather, the consequences are likely to depend on the age at which the child enters ECEC, the hours spent in the program, and the quality of the care provided. The effects are also likely to vary depending on the characteristics of the child (Shonkoff and Phillips 2000), but aside from gender differences, this latter issue has received surprisingly little attention to date.

Child Health   An extensive medical literature has examined the potential effects of early nonparental day care on child health. Conversely, information is more limited on the role of early enrichment programs that provide compensatory education to low-income or at-risk children in the years immediately preceding school entry (such as Head Start). There is also only a small literature on ECEC and injuries, prompted by concerns that children in nonparental care might be at elevated risk.

The medical literature indicates that infants and toddlers placed in day care are more likely to contract infectious diseases such as upper and lower respiratory tract infections, gastroenteritis, and infections caused by viruses such as hepatitis A, cytomegalovirus (CMV), and H. influenza type B. Respiratory tract infections (such as asthma and wheezing, allergies, ear infections, colds, bronchitis, and pneumonia) have been most thoroughly researched. The evidence uniformly indicates that child care in the first year or two of life increases the frequency of these ailments, and that higher risks are generally associated with center-based than family day care (Celedón et al. 1999; Rovers et al. 1999; Koopman et al. 2001). Nonparental care also raises the risk of acute diarrhea, particularly center-based care (Reves et al. 1993; Matson 1994; Louhiala et al. 1997). Other infectious diseases have not been as well researched, but most existing studies indicate similar patterns.[14]

The mechanisms by which infectious diseases are transmitted in day care settings are fairly well understood. Key environmental factors are the age of the child and the structure of the facility. Typically, children are at greatest risk during their first two years, both because of immunologic and physiologic factors (for example, eustachian-tube dysfunction is most common among very young children, who are also less likely to have developed protective antibodies for certain diseases) and because risk is compounded by the tendency of pre-toilet-trained children to place their hands and other objects in their mouths. The size of the facility is also important. Most significantly, exposure to infectious agents rises with the number of children cared for. Increased age-mixing may also play a role, particularly if toilet-trained and non-toilet-trained children come into contact with each other (Thacker et al. 1992; Osterholm 1994; Huskin 2000).

Less is known about the severity of the resulting health problems. Isolated infections generally have only transitory effects. However, day care attendance is linked to higher incidence of repeated otitis media (middle-ear infections) and recurrent upper respiratory infections, which sometimes have longer-term consequences (Collet et al. 1994; Hardy and Fowler 1993; Hildesheim, Hoffman, and Overpeck 1999). For example, 5 to 10 percent of children with otitis media develop chronic middle-ear disease, often leading to short- or long-term hearing loss (Schwartz et al. 1994). Center-based care has also been linked to increased risk of pneumococcal disease and cytomegalovirus infection. The first of these is an important cause of serious illnesses, including pneumonia, septicemia, and meningitis (Takala et al. 1995). The second is usually not harmful to the child, but when passed on to child care workers or mothers who then become pregnant, it is the leading cause of viral birth defects and a major cause of severe multiple birth defects (Dobbins et al. 1994). Finally, respiratory tract infections and gastroenteritis impose direct costs in the form of frequent physician and hospital visits (Bell et al. 1989) and often require a parent to take time off from work to care for the child.

Surprisingly, increased early incidence of infectious diseases occurring in day care may also have positive effects. Most important, several recent studies suggest that the higher rates of respiratory illnesses among infants and toddlers may reduce asthma, allergies, and related morbidities at later ages (Ball et al. 2000; Infante-Rivard et al. 2001; Celedón et al. 2002; Krämer et al. 1999; see also Ball et al. 2002). The hypothesized mechanism for this protective effect is that exposure to the microorganisms stimulates the immune system, leading to reductions in asthma and atopy (allergies). This hypothesis seems plausible and receives support from evidence that children in large families (who are also more exposed to infectious diseases) are less likely to be asthmatic. However, the research results are not unequivocal (see, for example, Nystad, Skrondal, and Magnus 1999; Nafstad et al. 1999). Finally, the selection of relatively healthy children into day care may lead to a spurious appearance of health improvements, as discussed later.

Research on non-infectious diseases is more limited. In their meta-analysis on type I diabetes, Brinderjit Kaila and Shayne Taback (2001) conclude that nonparental care may have a weak protective effect but that there is considerable uncertainty about this.[15] Conversely, Rachel Moon, Kantilal Patel, and Sarah Shaefer (2000) find that child care is associated with a higher risk of sudden infant death syndrome (SIDS), possibly owing to infants sleeping more often in a prone position than supine or on their side. These effects are more pronounced for children in family child care (rather than centers), possibly reflecting the poor training of providers in the role of sleep position in SIDS prevention.

Health problems (or benefits) associated with early day care could also affect other aspects of child development. Particularly interesting is evidence by the NICHD ECCRN (2001) confirming the link between child care and infectious diseases but indicating that these illnesses do not reduce future language competence or school readiness.

All of this research generally includes some controls for confounding factors, but these are unlikely to account fully for the selection into day care. In particular, limited information is usually included on children's health status during infancy. This is important because women with unhealthy children are less likely to be employed or to utilize day care (Norberg 1998; Neidell 2000; Ermisch and Francesconi 2001). The disproportionate use of

ECEC by relatively healthy children implies that the related increases in infectious diseases or other health problems are understated. Conversely, at least some of the observed reductions in future asthma and allergies or diabetes might reflect this selection process rather than a true protective effect of nonparental care.

Preschool and early school enrichment programs, such as Head Start, might affect health differently than other early day care experiences.[16] Therefore, it is distressing that, despite the explicit focus of many such programs on providing health-related services to children, few assessments of them have measured health benefits in either the short or long run (Karoly et al. 1998). What limited evidence is available provides no indication that these programs improve health. Janet Currie and Duncan Thomas (1995) exploit sibling differences to hold constant difficult-to-observe components of family backgrounds when analyzing Head Start. They uncover no evidence that participation leads to health improvements as measured by child height-for-age or immunization rates.[17] Similarly, assessments at three, five, and eight years of age for the Infant Health and Development Program (a random assignment intervention for low-birthweight infants) fail to show any gains in health from participation (McCarton et al. 1997). However, this result could be contaminated because both the treatment and control groups received health services.

Unintentional injuries are the leading cause of death among one- to four-year-olds in the United States (Anderson 2001). Therefore, we might be particularly concerned if children placed in day care have higher rates of accidents. The available evidence suggests that this is unlikely. Frederick Rivara and his colleagues (1989) and Branko Kopjar and Thomas Wickizer (1996) uncover lower injury rates in center-based than parental care.[18] One difficulty is in defining the denominator over which the rates are calculated. A careful recent analysis by Janet Currie and Joseph Hotz (2001) confirms that injury rates are lower in center-based care and indicates that accidents decline as the quality of care increases. Particularly interesting is their finding that regulations requiring providers to have at least a high school education are associated with substantial reductions in injuries. Similarly, there is little evidence of differences in the severity of injuries across modes of care. However, the types of injuries do differ: falls and accidents involving other children (such as bites) are more common in day care centers (Rivara and Sacks 1994). Conversely, home accidents more often involve burns, foreign bodies, and poison (Rivera et al. 1989).

Summary   Although researchers have not examined how ECEC disparities in early childhood contribute to social and economic inequality in the long term, a substantial body of research suggests that such a relationship is plausible. Both experimental and non-experimental research provides evidence that children experiencing high-quality, developmentally appropriate care fare better in the domains of cognitive development and school readiness than those receiving poor-quality or only informal (non-center-based) care. Carefully controlled studies suggest that these impacts are modest on average, but also that children from the most-disadvantaged backgrounds benefit (suffer) disproportionately from high (low) quality. ECEC has little effect on children's overall socioemotional development, but early age of entry and long hours of care may heighten the risk of behavior problems; quality of care appears to be an important moderating factor in this association. The health effects also generally appear to be modest and dependent on the age of the child, the mode of care, and the quality of the ECEC provided.

Understanding the long-term associations between inequalities in ECEC and inequalities in child and adult outcomes poses both the most challenging and the most potentially important research questions:

- Do the effects of ECEC on cognitive, socioemotional, or health outcomes differ systematically by type of care? For instance, does center- or school-based care for three- or four-year-olds promote children's school readiness? Is informal care better for younger children? Would policies that promote the use of center- or school-based care improve outcomes for some children?

- Does the quality of care matter for children's outcomes, and if so, what aspects of quality matter, for what children, and for what outcomes? What role can policies play in improving both quality of care and outcomes for children?

THE ROLE OF GOVERNMENT

Federal and state governments intervene in the mostly private ECEC market in two ways. First, they directly supply some forms of care, and provide subsidies and tax benefits that reduce the out-of-pocket costs of purchasing private care. Second, quality regulations, mostly at the state level, set minimum standards for health, safety, and some features of process quality. Public policies governing ECEC have changed substantially in recent years, but whether these changes have reduced or actually exacerbated the various forms of inequality in ECEC remains largely unknown.

Policies to Increase Access and Reduce Costs

Federal and state governments support a three-track system for increasing access to and reducing the costs of child care: compensatory early education programs, means-tested child care assistance, and tax benefits. Over the past three decades, federal commitments to these policies have grown and changed markedly in distribution. As shown in figure 6.5, tax expenditures (for child care tax benefits) constituted the single largest federal ECEC investment throughout the 1970s and 1980s. Conversely, investments in compensatory education dominated federal spending in the early 1990s, but they were soon overtaken by expenditures for means-tested subsidies for welfare and working-poor families. Each of these policy approaches has different implications for ECEC inequalities.

Compensatory Early Education Programs   Compensatory early education programs are most explicitly targeted at reducing inequality. These programs aim to increase the consumption of high-quality care among poor families and to decrease the human capital deficits (or increase the school readiness) of poor children. Head Start remains the single largest compensatory early education effort. As detailed in table 6.6, federal appropriations for Head Start totaled nearly $5.3 billion in 2000 (U.S. Department of Health and Human Services 2002).

In recent years states have taken the lead in expanding early education programs. Public kindergarten for five-year-olds is nearly universal, although only half the states fund full-day programs. Thirty-six states now provide funding for prekindergarten services, totaling almost $2 billion in 2001. Most public prekindergarten programs target children at economic or educational risk, although six states have extended eligibility to all four-year-olds, regardless of risk status.

Means-Tested Child Care Assistance   By subsidizing private, market-based child care arrangements, means-tested child care assistance reduces the cost of nonparental care for low-income families. The federal government currently funds means-tested assistance

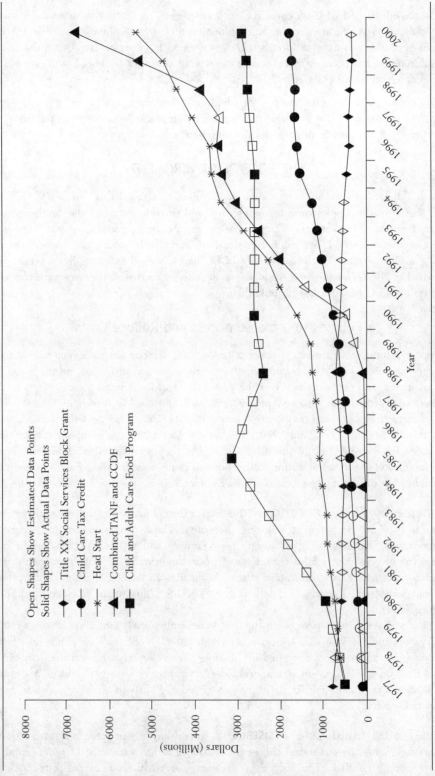

FIGURE 6.5   Federal Spending on Child Care, 1977 to 2000

Open Shapes Show Estimated Data Points
Solid Shapes Show Actual Data Points

◆ Title XX Social Services Block Grant
● Child Care Tax Credit
✳ Head Start
◀ Combined TANF and CCDF
■ Child and Adult Care Food Program

Sources: Title XX Social Services Block Grants: Gish (2002), Robins (1988), and U.S. Department of Health and Human Services (2000); Head Start: Administration for Children and Families (2002); TANF: Gish (2002), Robins (1988); CCDF: Gish (2002); Child and Adult Care Food Program: U.S. Department of Agriculture (2001); Child Care Tax Credit: Internal Revenue Service (2002).

TABLE 6.6   *Annual Federal and State Expenditures, Selected ECEC Programs, 2000*

	Federal Expenditures (Millions of Dollars)	Percentage of All Federal Expenditures	State Expenditures (Millions of Dollars)[a]
Compensatory and early education			
Head Start	$5,267	30%	$177
State prekindgergarten (fiscal years 2001 and 2002)			$1,949
Means-tested subsidy assistance			
Title XX social services block grants	$248	1%	n/a
Temporary Aid to Needy Families	$1,411	8%	$774[b]
Child Care Development Fund	$5,286	30%	$1,936[c]
Tax benefits			
Child and Dependent Care Tax Credit	$2,791	16%	n/a
Flexible spending accounts (1999)	$985	6%	
Other			
Child and Adult Care Food Program	$1,684	10%	n/a
Total	$17,672	100%	$2,710

Sources: Prekindergarten and state Head Start supplements: Doherty (2002): Title XX social services block grants, TANF, and CCDF: Gish (2002); CDCTC: Internal Revenue Service (2002); flexible spending accounts Blau (2001); CACFP: U.S. Department of Agriculture (2002).
[a]Excluding Washington, D.C.
[b]States may double-count child care expenditures for TANF-eligible families for purposes of maintenance of effort (MOE). Only the TANF MOE in excess of CCDF MOE state expenditures is reported in this figure.
[c]This figure reflects all reported CCDF expenditures eligible toward the state MOE.

through three block grants to the states. States supplement federal funds to assist families through direct contracts with private providers or (more commonly) through vouchers or other mechanisms that reimburse private providers and parents for the cost of services. Federal and state funding for means-tested assistance has grown sharply in recent years as a result of welfare reform policies. Federal investments in the three block grants combined approached $7 billion in 2000 (Gish 2002), constituting 42 percent of all Federal ECEC investments (see table 6.5).

The single largest federal block grant is the Child Care and Development Fund (CCDF). States can use CCDF funds to serve working families with incomes up to 85 percent of the state median (although many set a lower threshold). States must offer parents a choice of care types and providers but are free to set parental copayments, provider reimbursements, and procedures for establishing and recertifying eligibility. The second major funding stream for means-tested assistance is the Temporary Assistance to Needy Families (TANF) block grant, which replaced the Aid to Families with Dependent Children (AFDC) program in 1996. States may transfer up to 30 percent of their TANF funds to the CCDF program, and about half the states commit some TANF funds to CCDF (Gish 2002). States can also use TANF funds directly to provide child care (largely through vouchers) for welfare-reliant families who are preparing for work and for current and former welfare recipients who are employed. The Social Services Block Grant (SSBG) is the third and smallest source of federal child care assistance for poor families. In 1999 approximately 13 percent of SSBG funds were used for child care services or vouchers (Gish 2002).

Tax Benefits   Tax benefits, which include both deductions and credits, are the third major form of child care assistance. Under the federal Child and Dependent Care Tax Credit (CDCTC), parents may deduct a portion of out-of-pocket child care expenses from their taxable earnings. Tax expenditures for the federal credit were the single largest federal ECEC investment throughout the 1980s and totaled nearly $3 billion in 2000 (Internal Revenue Service 2002). Over half the states provide additional tax credits, usually calculated as a portion of the federal benefit (National Women's Law Center 2001). Families working for a participating employer may elect to use Dependent Care Assistance Plans (DCAP) instead to deduct child care expenses from their taxable income; DCAP tax expenditures were estimated to total about $1 billion in 1999 (Blau 2001).

Policies to Increase Child Care Quality

Child care quality depends on a variety of factors, including health and safety characteristics (such as the cleanliness of the setting), structural factors (such as the number of children cared for and the staff-to-child ratio), and the characteristics of providers (for example, the type and quality of their interactions with children). Government policies regulate these features directly in only the minority of programs operated under public auspices. For the majority of arrangements, government provides largely post hoc control through the licensing of private providers.

The direct provision of ECEC services provides government the most explicit control over service quality. The Federal Head Start program, in particular, sets national performance standards for curriculum, staff training, and other features of care. Quality standards are more variable in state-level early education and prekindergarten programs. Staffing ratios are generally more stringent for prekindergarten programs than for private child care centers. Nevertheless, only nineteen states require prekindergarten teachers to have the same educational preparation as kindergarten teachers (Doherty 2002).

Public regulation of child care quality in private programs is generally a weaker tool for controlling service quality. There is some evidence that the service dimensions regulated in most states, such as staffing ratios and provider education, are relevant. For example, researchers from the NICHD ECCRN (2002a) conclude that both staff training and caregiver-child ratios influence child outcomes through their effects on process quality. But licensing, quality standards, and enforcement vary substantially from state to state. Although all states require the licensing of some child care centers, many exempt certain settings, such as religious centers (twelve states) and half-day nursery schools (twenty states) (Helburn and Bergmann 2002). The licensing of family child care homes is even more inconsistent. Only eleven states require all family child care homes to be licensed; others exempt providers who care for only a few children or those not receiving public funds (Helburn and Bergmann 2002). Moreover, state resources for enforcing these requirements are generally limited, and an unknown number of family child care homes operate illegally even in states that require licensing.

The stringency of standards also varies across locations. State regulations most commonly address health and safety (such as requirements on minimum square footage, immunization, and smoke detectors). Standards for structural features associated with quality are more variable. For example, only twelve states require child care center teachers to have at least a high school education, and just twenty-nine require family child care providers to have any pre- or in-service training (Children's Foundation 2000). William Gormley (1995, 1999) finds that centers provide higher-quality care when subject to more frequent inspections. But standards are enforced through unannounced inspections for both centers and family child care homes in only seventeen states.

The effect of post hoc regulation on ECEC costs raises other complexities with respect to reducing income-related inequalities in quality. In purely public programs the government absorbs the costs of structural improvements such as higher staff training and compensation. Conversely, in private care these costs are passed on to consumers. Economic theory predicts, and empirical research confirms, that some parents respond to the expense associated with the stringent regulation of private child care arrangements by substituting less expensive forms of care (see, for example, Blau and Hagy 1998; Currie and Hotz 2001; Powell 2002). As Currie and Hotz (2001, 1) observe in their study of accidental injuries in child care: "Regulation creates winners and losers: some children benefit from safer environments while those who are squeezed out of the regulated sector are placed at higher risk of injury."

Implications of Government ECEC Policies for Inequality

Of the three major types of ECEC programs, compensatory education programs have the most direct implications for short-term income inequality. By reducing the cost of care to zero for participating families, they provide access to care that is designed to provide developmentally and educationally enhancing experiences for poor children. The effects are limited, however, by the lack of universal enrollment for those who are income-eligible. Nationwide only about one-half of eligible three- to four-year-old children receive Head Start services (Butler and Gish 2002). Variation across states is also substantial: as of 1999, the share of children under six who were enrolled in some form of early education—including Head Start, kindergarten, and prekindergarten programs—varied from 12 to 33 percent (authors' calculation using data from the National Center for Educational Statistics and the Current Population Survey).

Public compensatory and early education programs may also reduce quality differentials related to socioeconomic status. Public compensatory education programs generally set quality standards that exceed those imposed by state licensing standards (Doherty 2002). The enrollment of low-income children in more highly regulated, compensatory public programs is the most often cited explanation for the finding that child care center quality tends to be relatively high for the poorest families (compared to child care for near-poor families whose incomes may be too high to qualify for such programs).

Means-tested subsidies also target low-income families but may have limited effects, owing to low levels of coverage and benefits. As with compensatory and early education, their total effect also depends on the number of families assisted. At current funding levels, the impact is probably modest. By recent estimates, only about 15 percent of income-eligible families receive assistance nationwide, with the proportion varying from 6 to 25 percent across states (U.S. Department of Health and Human Services 2000; Schumacher, Greenberg, and Duffy 2001). The effect of subsidies on child care use also depends on the structure of the assistance: substantial state-to-state variation has been observed in the types of care subsidized, levels of reimbursement to providers, and family copayments (Meyers et al. 2002; Adams, Snyder, and Sandfort 2002; Collins et al. 2000; Crosby, Huston, and Gennetian 2001).

We know little of the role played by subsidies in reducing socioeconomic differentials in child care quality or children's school readiness. Although increased purchasing power would be expected to raise the quality of care purchased, few studies have examined whether the quality of care obtained by low-income children actually improves. This is salient because child care subsidies generally impose few restrictions on the quality of the care children receive. Although states may provide a portion of child care services through direct contracts with providers (in which quality levels can be specified), they must also make available vouchers that allow families to purchase care from any provider who meets state regulations and licensing standards or is legally exempt from those requirements. The quality of care provided through means-tested benefits is further constrained by low state reimbursements of providers: twenty-two states set reimbursement levels below the federally recommended level of the seventy-fifth percentile of prevailing local rates (Children's Defense Fund 2001). These and other program rules may force subsidy-reliant families into less formal and lower-quality care.

Although child care tax credits, the third major type of child care policy instrument, are often criticized as "middle-class" entitlements that exacerbate rather than reduce inequalities in child care access and cost burden, their actual impact is complex. The benefits are used more heavily by higher-income families who are most likely to pay for their child care (Gentry and Hagy 1996). However, while take-up is tilted toward more-affluent families, the size of the benefit declines steadily with income. This progressivity is limited, nonetheless, because credits are nonrefundable and the lowest earners (with zero tax liability) are eligible for no assistance. William Gentry and Alison Hagy (1996) consider the combined effects of benefit take-up and benefit structures in the CDCTC (Child and Dependent Care Tax Credit). Controlling for employment status and the use of paid care, they find that take-up of the credit is similar among lower- and higher-income families, but that the credits provide no assistance to the bottom 10 percent of the income distribution and are regressive in the bottom quintile of incomes (but slightly progressive for the remainder of the distribution). Moreover, they conclude that overall benefits are too small (averaging about 1.24 percent of family income) "to influence the income distribution dramatically" (2).

Summary

Public funding for ECEC has expanded in recent decades at both the national and state levels. The implicit priorities of public ECEC funding have also changed. Means-tested subsidies now account for about 40 percent of federal ECEC spending, nearly as much as compensatory education (about 30 percent) and tax benefits (about 20 percent) combined. State-to-state variation in ECEC financing and policy has also increased with the devolution of federal policy authority (for example, through the creation of child care block grants) and the growth of state-based programs (such as prekindergarten). States vary in the relative emphasis they put on spending for compensatory education and subsidies, on the rules governing eligibility for and benefits through these programs, and on the rigor and enforcement of quality regulations.

Policy structures, trends, and state-level variation raise a number of questions about how government interventions influence the distributions of ECEC services, quality, and costs:

- How do investments in means-tested child care subsidies, compensatory education, and tax benefits influence socioeconomic disparities in the types and quality of care that children receive? How do they influence variation in the ECEC cost burden for families at different income levels?

- Have changes over time in investments in alternative policy tools strengthened or weakened the equalizing effects of government policy, given concurrent increases in wage and income inequality? Have they offset or exacerbated inequalities resulting from policies (such as welfare reform) that increase the employment of low-skilled mothers?

- How do states vary in their investments in ECEC and quality oversight? Does this variation influence families' use of various modes and quality of care? Does it influence the cost burden for families at different points in the income distribution?

- Has state variation in policy and in policy effects grown or lessened over time? With what implications for both income and geographic disparities?

CONCLUSIONS

The increase in wage and income inequality at the end of the twentieth century has received considerable research attention. Researchers have also described the increase in families' use of substitute care arrangements during these same decades. Despite evidence of persistent income-related disparities in the use of any ECEC, and the type and quality of that care, relatively little attention has been paid to the potential links between income and ECEC inequality. These linkages are particularly interesting given evidence that the experience and quality of ECEC may influence children's well-being in the short term and their cognitive and other development in the longer term.

In this review, we have summarized the current state of knowledge about how ECEC may reflect, exacerbate, and/or reduce income inequality. Given the lack of direct attention to these issues, our review finds that knowledge is incomplete in many areas and inconclusive in others. This leads us to suggest several avenues for further study.

Research on ECEC expenses suggests that while lower-income families spend less in absolute dollars than more-affluent families, this is largely due to their greater reliance on less expensive or even free types of care, such as babysitting by relatives. Even given lower expenses, however, ECEC imposes a disproportionately high cost burden on lower-income families, and this burden may be increasing over time. These costs may also contribute to income inequality by depressing maternal employment disproportionately among lower-skilled women. Estimating the magnitude, trends, and consequences of inequality in cost burden is complicated, however, because this burden results from interactions among resources, need, and choice of care arrangement. Rates of maternal employment, families' use of ECEC, the number of families headed by a single mother, and male and female wages were all changing during the same decades in which we observe growth in income inequality. More research is needed to estimate the combined effects of these changes on inequality in cost burden and on the consequences for inequalities in ECEC use and maternal employment.

Greater reliance on informal and free forms of care may help lower-income families reduce their child care cost burden. It also produces inequalities in children's exposure to formal and market-based forms of care. A number of researchers have documented income, educational, and ethnic disparities in care arrangements for children under six. One of the few data sources that tracks care arrangements over time suggests that disparities in one of the most important forms of care from the standpoint of school readiness—pre-primary programs such as Head Start, nursery schools, prekindergarten, and kindergarten—have largely disappeared for five-year-old children but have persisted for three- and four-year-olds. Analyses of these and other data find evidence of income-related disparities even after controlling for other family characteristics.

Less is known about whether these disparities in care type translate into disparities in quality. More highly regulated forms of care may provide more developmentally enhancing care, particularly for older preschool children, but using mode of care as a proxy for quality is complicated. Some support for this conclusion is provided by econometric research that suggests that families substitute formal for informal care when they can afford it and by several child outcome studies that suggest that receipt of formal care is associated with higher pre-academic and language skills. Within modes of care, several studies have concluded that, unless they are enrolled in high-quality public programs, low-income children receive lower-quality care than children from more-affluent families.

We have suggested that these disparities in type and quality of care may create a "triple disadvantage" for low-income children, who are disadvantaged in the home, less likely to receive formal care, and less likely to receive high-quality care even if they do. But the associations among income, mode of care, and quality of care remain uncertain, and we know little about how inequalities in quality of care have changed over time. Research is needed both to document change over time in ECEC disparities and to disentangle the effects of families' needs, preferences, and resources on their mode of care. More work is also needed to clarify the associations between mode and quality of care and to track changes in ECEC quality disparities over time.

Issues of child care quality are particularly germane to questions about inequality because research suggests that the quality of ECEC influences early childhood outcomes and school readiness. Research suggests at least three avenues through which quality affects child well-being and outcomes. First, both experimental and non-experimental research suggests that ECEC quality is associated with children's cognitive, pre-academic, and language development; some experimental studies suggest that these effects persist throughout later childhood. Importantly, several studies also find that quality effects are strongest for children in low-income, poorly educated families, who gain the most from high-quality care and experience the greatest harm from low-quality care. Second, ECEC quality has been found to moderate the potentially negative effect of early and extensive nonparental care experience on children's socioemotional development. Finally, enrollment in ECEC has been associated with some negative health outcomes (such as increased frequency of infectious diseases and possibly their greater severity), along with some benefits (including lower rates of asthma and accidental injuries). Although research on the role of quality in health outcomes is limited, there is some indication that lower-quality care is associated with greater risk, for example, through large group sizes, poor health practices, and more poorly trained providers.

Evidence that quality of care matters for children's cognitive, socioemotional, and health outcomes gives particular urgency to issues of ECEC inequality. Researchers have demonstrated that more highly disadvantaged children benefit disproportionately from high-quality care but that these same children are less likely to receive nonparental and formal care and are more likely to experience lower-quality care. Additional research is needed to clarify these inequalities and their consequences for children's short-term well-being, children's long-term development, and income inequality in a subsequent generation.

The size, persistence, and potential consequences of ECEC inequalities raise questions about the role of public policy. Government ECEC policies address the availability, affordability, and quality of ECEC through compensatory education programs, means-tested subsidies, tax benefits, and quality regulation. The importance of these policies is suggested by studies documenting a U-shaped distribution in both the use and quality of ECEC by income. Although government policies appear to be playing some role in closing ECEC disparities, there has been surprisingly little research on the magnitude of this effect.

Research is also needed to assess whether the influence of policy has grown or diminished in recent decades. Public expenditures for ECEC have grown steadily for more than three decades, but the emphasis of these investments has shifted over time from compensatory education to middle-class tax relief to means-tested subsidies for the welfare poor and the working poor. The implications of these changes for ECEC inequality are poorly understood. Research is needed on the effect of public policy on inequalities in ECEC cost burden and on whether policies have reduced (or exacerbated) these inequalities during recent decades as employment increased, and income fell, in families headed by lower-skilled adults. Related questions concern differences in the effect of alternative policy instruments on disparities in the use, type, and quality of care. Given the differences in policy effects—for example, between compensatory education and means-tested benefits—research is needed to sort out how these effects may have changed over time given changing economic and demographic conditions. As income inequality grew at the end of the twentieth century, did changes in government policies offset or exacerbate the consequences for poor children through their effects on families' access to high-quality child care?

We would like to thank Eric Wanner and the Russell Sage Foundation for their support, and Jay Bainbridge, Se-Ook Jeong, Katherine Magnuson, and Sakiko Tanaka for their help in preparing this chapter. We are also grateful to David Blau for sharing the 1999 SIPP data.

NOTES

1. Unless otherwise noted, our statistics on child care usage are calculated using data from the 1999 (most recent) release of the Survey of Income and Program Participation (SIPP). The SIPP has been tracking child care usage since 1985. Originally limited to families with employed mothers, its child care module is now administered to all families with children. Its "Who's Minding the Kids?" reports provide a comprehensive overview of child care use in the United States. (For the most recent published report, which uses data from 1997, see Smith 2002.) Some caution must be exercised in using the SIPP to track changes over time because of changes in the survey questions and timing. Most important, the survey was historically administered in the fall but is now administered in the spring and early summer.

2. The numbers for tables 6.1 and 6.2 come from several tables in Hofferth et al. (1991). Additional extrapolations used to fill in the table required assumptions about (1) hours of primary care for the youngest child for non-employed mothers who pay for care; (2) the distribution of hourly expenditures for primary care for non-employed mothers who pay for care; and (3) the mean earnings for each income quintile. In future work, we plan to update these calculations using data from the 1999 SIPP, which have only recently become available.

3. Unless otherwise noted, all dollar amounts in this chapter are in 2000 dollars.

4. Other sources of data are consistent with these results; see, for example, Smith (2002) and Giannarelli and Barsimantov (2000).

5. Hofferth et al. (1991), Smith (2000, 2002), Anderson and Levine (2000), and Giannarelli and Barsimantov (2000) provide estimates of the child care burden that incorporate differences across groups in child care costs.

6. Anderson and Levine (2000), U.S. General Accounting Office (1994), Han and Waldfogel (2002), and

Connelly and Kimmel (1999) find that the employment of less-skilled, unmarried, or low-income mothers is more sensitive to child care costs.

7. Estimates of child care arrangements from various data sources should be compared only with caution, owing to differences in question wording, timing of data collection, and coding categories (see note 10).

8. These figures and the ones that follow refer to the share of children using center-based care as their primary child care arrangement. Since many children are in multiple arrangements, the share of children using any center-based care is higher. This is shown in the final column of table 6.5.

9. The October CPS began collecting data in 1964, but the microdata for 1964 to 1967 are not readily available. The 2000 year data were the most current available at the time the analysis was conducted.

10. From 1968 to 1984, the survey asked: "Is [name of child] attending or enrolled in school?" In 1985 the question was changed to: "Is [name of child] attending or enrolled in regular school?" Then, in 1994, a prompt was added after the question, which now reads, in its entirety: "Is [name of child] attending or enrolled in regular school? (Regular school includes nursery school, kindergarten, or elementary school and schooling which leads to a high school diploma)." The October CPS and the National Household Education Survey (NHES) find a similar share of three- to five-year-old children enrolled in pre-primary school programs. (For instance, both surveys find 68 percent of children in this age group enrolled in 1999.) In contrast, two major child care surveys, the National Survey of America's Families (NSAF) and SIPP, find a lower share of three- to five-year-olds enrolled in center- or school-based programs, probably because these two surveys do not ask explicitly about school programs and also because they interview some families during the summer months, when school programs would be closed.

11. These include the ITERS (Infant-Toddler Environment Rating Scale), used to rate centers serving infants and toddlers, and the ECERS (Early Childhood Environment Rating Scale), used to rate centers serving older preschoolers.

12. However, NICHD ECCRN (2002a) reports preliminary evidence that the effects of center-based care on cognitive and language scores may not be robust to the inclusion of controls for factors associated with selection into care.

13. Other studies have not found this association; see, for example, Howes (1988), Crockenberg and Litman (1991), and Greenstein (1993). There is also a large literature on early maternal employment and child cognitive outcomes. For a review and recent evidence, see Brooks-Gunn, Han, and Waldfogel (2002).

14. See, for example, Chomel et al. (2001) on elevated CMV infection rates and Hurwitz et al. (1994) and Venczel et al. (2001) on increased hepatitis A diagnoses. See Osterholm (1994) for a useful review of earlier research.

15. The hypothesized mechanism for a protective effect is, once again, that early exposure to infections promotes the development of autoimmune responses that reduce the risk of diabetes.

16. For instance, Linda Randolf (1994) details the potential health benefits of child care in the areas of screening assessments (for example, vision, hearing, and dental testing), preventive medicine (for example, immunizations), nutritional assessment and supplementation, the detection of child abuse, and health promotion practices.

17. Immunization rates are slightly higher for Head Start participants than for those not attending preschool but are no different than those for children at other (non–Head Start) preschools. This raises the possibility that preschool has a positive effect on immunizations, or that these differences are due to nonrandom attendance.

18. In other research (Kotch et al. 1997), however, no significant differences were found.

REFERENCES

Adams, Gina, Kathleen Snyder, and Jodi Sandfort. 2002. *Getting and Retaining Child Care Assistance*. Washington, D.C.: Urban Institute Press.

Alexander, Karl L., and Doris R. Entwisle. 1996. "Schools and Children at Risk." In *Family-School Links: How Do They Affect Educational Outcomes?*, edited by Alan Booth and Judy Dunn. Mahwah, N.J.: Lawrence Erlbaum Associates.

Anderson, Patricia, and Philip Levine. 2000. "Child Care and Mother's Employment Decisions." In *Finding Jobs: Work and Welfare Reform,* edited by David Card and Rebecca Blank. New York: Russell Sage Foundation.

Anderson, Robert N. 2001. *Deaths: Leading Causes for 1999.* National Vital Statistics Reports 49(11). Hyattsville, Md.: National Center for Health Statistics.

Averett, Susan L., H. Elizabeth Peters, and D. M. Waldman. 1997. "Tax Credits, Labor Supply, and Child Care." *Review of Economics and Statistics* 81(1): 125–35.

Bainbridge, Jay, Marcia K. Meyers, Sakiko Tanaka, and Jane Waldfogel. 2002. "Who Is Getting Early Education? Family Income and the Gaps in Enrollment of Three- to Five-Year-Olds from 1968 to 2000." Unpublished paper. Columbia University School of Social Work, New York.

Bainbridge, Jay, Marcia K. Meyers, and Jane Waldfogel. Forthcoming. "Child Care Reform and the Employment of Single Mothers." *Social Science Quarterly.*

Ball, Thomas M., Jose A. Castro-Rodriguez, Kent A. Griffith, Catharine J. Holberg, Fernando D. Martinez, and Anne L. Wright. 2000. "Siblings, Day Care Attendance, and the Risk of Asthma and Wheezing During Childhood." *New England Medical Journal* 343(8): 538–43.

Ball, Thomas M., Catharine Holberg, Michael Aldous, Fernando Martinez, and Anne L. Wright. 2002. "Influence of Attendance at Day Care on Common Cold from Birth Through Thirteen Years of Age." *Archives of Pediatric and Adolescent Medicine* 15(2): 121–26.

Bates, John, Denny Marvinney, Timothy Kelly, Kenneth A. Dodge, David S. Bennett, and Gregory S. Petit. 1994. "Child Care History and Kindergarten Adjustment." *Developmental Psychology* 30(5): 690–700.

Baydar, Nazali, and Jeanne Brooks-Gunn. 1991. "The Effects of Maternal Employment and Child Care Arrangements on Preschoolers' Cognitive and Behavioral Outcomes: Evidence from Children of the National Longitudinal Survey of Youth." *Developmental Psychology* 27(6): 932–45.

Bell, David M., Dennis W. Gleiber, Alice Atkins Mercer, Robi Phifer, Robert H. Guinter, A. Jay Cohen, Eugene U. Epstein, and Manoj Narayanan. 1989. "Illness Associated with Day Care: A Study of Incidence and Cost." *American Journal of Public Health* 79(4): 479–83.

Belsky, Jay. 1984. "Two Waves of Day Care Research: Developmental Effects and Conditions of Quality." In *The Child and Day Care Setting,* edited by Ricardo C. Ainslie. New York: Praeger.

———. 1986. "Infant Day Care: A Cause for Concern?" *Zero to Three* 6: 1–9.

———. 1990. "Parental and Nonparental Child Care and Children's Socioemotional Development: A Decade in Review." *Journal of Marriage and the Family* 52: 885–903.

———. 2001. "Developmental Risks (Still) Associated with Early Child Care" (Emanuel Miller Lecture). *Journal of Child Psychology and Psychiatry and Allied Disciplines* 42(7): 845–59.

Belsky, Jay, and David Eggebeen. 1991. "Early and Extensive Maternal Employment and Young Children's Socioemotional Development: Children of the National Longitudinal Survey of Youth." *Journal of Marriage and the Family* 53: 1083–1110.

Berger, Mark C., and Dan A. Black. 1992. "Child Care Subsidies, Quality of Care, and the Labor Supply of Low-Income Single Mothers." *Review of Economics and Statistics* 74(4): 635–42.

Berlin, Lisa J., Jeanne Brooks-Gunn, Cecelia McCarton, and Marie C. McCormick. 1998. "The Effectiveness of Early Intervention: Examining Risk Factors and Pathways to Enhanced Development." *Preventive Medicine* 27: 238–45.

Blau, David. 1997. "The Production of Quality in Child Care Centers." *Journal of Human Resources* 32(2): 354–87.

———. 2000. "Child Care Subsidy Programs." Working paper 7806. Cambridge, Mass.: National Bureau of Economic Research.

———. 2001. *The Child Care Problem.* New York: Russell Sage Foundation.

Blau, David M., and Alice Hagy. 1998. "The Demand for Quality in Child Care." *Journal of Political Economy* 106(1): 104–46.

Blau, David M., and Philip K. Robins. 1988. "Child Care Costs and Family Labor Supply." *Review of Economics and Statistics* 70(3): 297–316.

Bornstein, Marc, Nancy F. Gist, Chun-Shin Hahn, O. Maurice Haynes, and Mary D. Voight. 2001. "Long-term Cumulative Effects of Day Care Experience on Children's Mental and Socioemotional Development." Unpublished paper. National Institute of Child Health and Human Development, Washington, D.C.

Brooks-Gunn, Jeanne. 2000. "Do You Believe in Magic? What We Can Expect from Early Childhood Intervention Programs." Paper presented to a research briefing on "Early Childhood Intervention Programs: Are the Costs Justified?" sponsored by the Subcommittee on Human Resources of the U.S. House of Representatives Committee on Ways and Means and the Joint Center for Poverty Research, Washington, D.C. (May).

Brooks-Gunn, Jeanne, Wen-Jui Han, and Jane Waldfogel. 2002. "Maternal Employment and Child Cognitive Outcomes in the First Three Years of Life: The NICHD Study of Early Child Care." *Child Development* 73(4): 1052–72.

Bryant, Donna M., Margaret Burchinal, Lisa B. Lau, and Joseph J. Sparling. 1994. "Family and Classroom Correlates of Head Start Children's Developmental Outcomes." *Early Childhood Research Quarterly* 9(3–4): 289–309.

Burchinal, Margaret R., Debby Cryer, Richard M. Clifford, and Carollee Howes. 2002. "Caregiver Training and Classroom Quality in Child Care Centers." *Applied Developmental Science* 6(1): 2–11.

Burchinal, Margaret R., Ellen Peisner-Feinberg, Donna M. Bryant, and Richard Clifford. 2000. "Children's Social and Cognitive Development and Child Care Quality: Testing for Differential Associations Related to Poverty, Gender, or Ethnicity." *Applied Developmental Science* 4(3): 149–65.

Burchinal, Margaret R., Joanne E. Roberts, Rhodus Riggins Jr., Susan A. Zeisel, Eloise Neebe, and Donna Bryant. 2000. "Relating Quality of Center-Based Child Care to Early Cognitive and Language Development Longitudinally." *Child Development* 71(2): 338–57.

Butler, Alice, and Melinda Gish. 2002. *Head Start Background and Funding.* Washington: Library of Congress, Congressional Research Service.

Caughy, Margaret O'Brien, Janet A. DiPietro, and Donna Strobino. 1994. "Day Care Participation as a Protective Factor in the Cognitive Development of Low-Income Children." *Child Development* 65: 457–71.

Celedón, Juan C., Augusto A. Litonjua, Louise Ryan, Scott T. Weiss, and Diane R. Gold. 2002. "Day Care Attendance, Respiratory Tract Illness, Wheezing, Asthma, and Total Serum IgE Level in Early Childhood." *Archives of Pediatric and Adolescent Medicine* 15(3): 241–45.

Celedón, Juan C., Augusto A. Litonjua, Scott T. Weiss, and Diane R. Gold. 1999. "Day Care Attendance in the First Year of Life and Illnesses of the Upper and Lower Respiratory Tract in Children with a Familial History of Atopy." *Pediatrics* 104(3): 495–500.

Children's Defense Fund. 2001. *A Fragile Foundation: State Child Care Assistance Policies.* Washington, D.C.: Children's Defense Fund.

Children's Foundation. 2000. *Child Care Licensing Study.* Washington, D.C.: Children's Foundation.

Chomel, J. J., J. P. Allard, D. Floret, D. Honneger, L. David, B. Lina, and M. Aymard. 2001. "Role of Cytomegalovirus Infection in the Incidence of Viral Acute Respiratory Infections in Children Attending Day Care Centers." *European Journal of Clinical Microbiology and Infectious Diseases* 20(3): 167–72.

Clarke-Stewart, K. Alison, and Greta G. Fein. 1983. "Early Childhood Programs." In *Handbook of Child Psychology,* vol. 2, edited by Paul Mussen. New York: John Wiley.

Clarke-Stewart, K. Alison, Christian P. Gruber, and Linda May Fitzgerald. 1994. *Children at Home and in Day Care.* Hillsdale, N.J.: Lawrence Erlbaum Associates.

Clarke-Stewart, K. Alison, Deborah Lowe Vandell, Margaret Burchinal, Marion O'Brien, and Kathleen McCartney. 2002. "Do Regulable Features of Child Care Homes Affect Children's Development?" *Early Childhood Research Quarterly* 17(1, March): 52–86.

Cleveland, Gordon, Morley Gunderson, and Douglas Hyatt. 1996. "Child Care Costs and the Employment Decision of Women: Canadian Evidence." *Canadian Journal of Economics* 29(1): 132–51.

Cohen, Philip, and Suzanne Bianchi. 1999. "Marriage, Children, and Women's Employment: What Do We Know?" *Monthly Labor Review* 122(12): 22–31.

Collet, Jean Paul, P. Burtin, Michael S. Kramer, D. Floret, N. Bossard, and T. Ducruet. 1994. "Type of Day Care Setting and Risk of Repeated Infections." *Pediatrics* 94(6): 997–99.

Collins, Ann, Jean I. Lazer, J. Lee Kreader, Alan Werner, and Fred B. Glantz. 2000. *National Study of Child Care for Low-Income Families: State and Community Substudy Interim Report.* Cambridge, Mass.: Abt Associates.

Connelly, Rachel. 1992. "The Effect of Child Care Costs on Married Women's Labor Force Participation." *Review of Economics and Statistics* 74(1): 83–90.

Connelly, Rachel, and Jean Kimmel. 1999. "Marital Status and Full-time/Part-time Work Status in Child Care

Choices: Changing the Rules of the Game." Paper presented to ASPE/Census Bureau Small Grants Sponsored Research Conference, Washington (May 17–18).

Council of Economic Advisers. 1998. *Economic Report of the President, 1998*. Washington: U.S. Government Printing Office.

Crockenberg, Susan, and Cindy Litman. 1991. "Effects of Maternal Employment on Maternal and Two-Year-Old Child Behavior." *Child Development* 62(5): 930–53.

Crosby, Danielle A., Aletha C. Huston, and Lisa A. Gennetian. 2001. *Does Child Care Assistance Matter? The Effects of Welfare and Employment Programs on Child Care for Preschool- and Young School-Age Children*. New York: Manpower Research Demonstration Corporation.

Currie, Janet. 2000. "Early Childhood Intervention Programs: What Do We Know?" Paper presented to a research briefing on "Early Childhood Intervention Programs: Are the Costs Justified?" sponsored by the Subcommittee on Human Resources of the U.S. House of Representatives Committee on Ways and Means and the Joint Center for Poverty Research, Washington (May).

Currie, Janet, and V. Joseph Hotz. 2001. "Accidents Will Happen? Unintentional Childhood Injuries and Child Care Policy." Unpublished paper. University of California at Los Angeles (June).

Currie, Janet, and Duncan Thomas. 1995. "Does Head Start Make a Difference?" *American Economic Review* 85(3): 341–64.

Dobbins, James G., Stuart P. Adler, Robert F. Pass, James F. Bale, Lena Grillner, John A. Stewart. 1994. "The Risks and Benefits of Cytomegalovirus Transmission in Child Day Care." *Pediatrics* 94(6): 1016–18.

Doherty, Kathryn W. 2002. "Early Learning: Data on State Early-Childhood Policies and Programs Have Large Gaps." *Education Week* XXI(17): 54–67.

Ehrle, Jennifer, Gina Adams, and Kathryn Tout. 2001. *Who's Caring for Our Youngest Children? Child Care Patterns of Infants and Toddlers*. Washington, D.C.: Urban Institute Press.

Entwisle, Doris R., and Karl L. Alexander. 1993. "Entry into School: The Beginning of School Transition and Educational Stratification in the United States." *Annual Review of Sociology* 19: 401–23.

Ermisch, John, and Marco Francesconi. 2001. "The Effects of Parents' Employment on Children's Educational Attainment." Unpublished paper. University of Essex (June).

Fuller, Bruce, and Xiaoyan Liang. 1996. "Market Failure? Estimating Inequality in Preschool Availability." *Educational Evaluation and Policy Analysis* 18(1): 31–49.

Galinsky, Ellen, Carollee Howes, Susan Kontos, and Marybeth Shinn. 1994. *The Study of Children in Family Child Care and Relative Care: Highlights of Findings*. New York: Families and Work Institute.

Gelbach, Jonah. 2002. "Public Schooling for Young Children and Maternal Labor Supply." *American Economic Review* 92(1): 307–23.

Gentry, William, and Alison P. Hagy. 1996. "The Distributional Effects of the Tax Treatment of Child Care Expenses." In *Empirical Foundations of Household Taxation*, edited by Martin S. Feldstein and James M. Poterba. Chicago: University of Chicago Press.

Ghazvini, Alisa, and Ronald L. Mullis. 2002. "Center-Based Care for Young Children: Examining Predictors of Quality." *Journal of Genetic Psychology* 163(1): 112–25.

Giannarelli, Linda, and James Barsimantov. 2000. *Child Care Expenses of American Families*. Assessing the New Federalism occasional paper 40. Washington, D.C.: Urban Institute.

Gish, Melinda. 2002. *Child Care: Funding and Spending Under Federal Block Grants*. Washington: Library of Congress, Congressional Research Service.

Gordon, Rachel A., and P. Lindsay Chase-Lansdale. 2001. "Availability of Child Care in the United States: A Description and Analysis of Data Sources." *Demography* 38(2): 299–316.

Gormley, William T., Jr. 1995. *Everybody's Children: Child Care as a Public Problem*. Washington, D.C.: Brookings Institution.

———. 1999. "Regulating Child Care Quality." *Annals of the American Academy of Political and Social Science* 563: 116–29.

Greenstein, Theodore N. 1993. "Maternal Employment and Child Behavioral Outcomes." *Journal of Family Issues* 14(3): 323–54.

Han, Wenjui, and Jane Waldfogel. 2002. "The Effect of Child Care Costs on the Employment of Single and Married Mothers." *Social Science Quarterly* 82(3): 552–68.

Hardy, Ann M., and Mary Glenn Fowler. 1993. "Child Care Arrangements and Repeated Ear Infections in Young Children." *American Journal of Public Health* 83(9): 1321–25.

Haskins, Ronald. 1985. "Public School Aggression Among Children with Varying Day Care Experiences." *Child Development* 56: 689–703.

Hayes, Cheryl D., John L. Palmer, and Martha J. Zaslow. 1990. *Who Cares for America's Children: Child Care Policy for the 1990s.* Washington, D.C.: National Academy Press.

Helburn, Suzanne W., edited 1995. *Cost, Quality, and Child Outcomes in Child Care Centers: Technical Report.* Denver: University of Colorado, Department of Economics, Center for Research in Economic and Social Policy.

Helburn, Suzanne W., and Barbara Bergmann. 2002. *America's Child Care Problem.* New York: St. Martin's Press.

Hildesheim, Mariana E., Howard J. Hoffman, and Mary D. Overpeck. 1999. "Frequent Ear Infections in Association with Child Care Characteristics, Based on the 1988 Child Interview Supplement to the National Health Interview Survey." *Pediatric and Perinatal Epidemiology* 13(4): 466–72.

Hill, Jennifer, Jane Waldfogel, and Jeanne Brooks-Gunn. 2002. "Differential Effects of High-Quality Care." *Journal of Policy Analysis and Management* 21(4): 601–27.

Hofferth, Sandra L., April Brayfield, Sharon Deich, and Pamela Holcomb. 1991. *National Child Care Survey, 1990.* Washington, D.C.: Urban Institute Press.

Hofferth, Sandra L., Jerry West, Robin Henke, and Phillip Kaufman. 1993. *Access to Early Childhood Programs for Children at Risk.* Washington: U.S. Department of Education, Office of Educational Research and Improvement.

Howes, Carollee. 1988. "Relations Between Early Child Care and Schooling." *Developmental Psychology* 24(1): 53–57.

Hurwitz, Eugene S., Carmen C. Deseda, Craig N. Shapiro, David R. Nalin, M. Jayne Freitg-Koontz, and Jun Hayashi. 1994. "Hepatitis Infections in the Day Care Setting." *Pediatrics* 94(6): 1023–24.

Huskin, W. Charles. 2000. "Transmission and Control of Infections in Out-of-Home Child Care." *Pediatric Infectious Disease Journal* 19(10): 106–10.

Infante-Rivard, Claire, Devendra Amre, Dense Gautrin, and Jean-Luc Malo. 2001. "Family Size, Day Care Attendance, and Breastfeeding in Relation to the Incidence of Childhood Asthma." *American Journal of Epidemiology* 153(7): 653–58.

Internal Revenue Service. 2002. "Statistics of Income Bulletin." vol. 21(4), pub. num. 1136, Winter 2001–2002. Washington: Internal Revenue Service.

Jones, Arthur F., and Daniel H. Weinberg. 2000. "The Changing Shape of the Nation's Income Distribution: 1948–1998." *Current Population Reports, P60-204, June.* Washington: U.S. Government Printing Office.

Kaila, Brinderjit, and Shayne P. Taback. 2001. "The Effect of Day Care Exposure on the Risk of Developing Type 1 Diabetes." *Diabetes Care* 24(8): 1353–58.

Karoly, Lynn A., Peter W. Greenwood, Susan S. Everingham, Jill Houbé, M. Rebecca Kilburn, C. Peter Rydell, Matthew Sanders, and James Chiesa. 1998. *Investing in Our Children: What We Do and Don't Know About the Costs and Benefits of Early Childhood Interventions.* Santa Monica, Calif.: Rand Corporation.

Katz, Lawrence F., and David H. Autor. 1999. "Changes in the Wage Structure and Earnings Inequality." In *Handbook of Labor Economics,* vol. 3A, edited by Orley Ashenfelter and David Card. New York: Elsevier Science, North-Holland.

Kimmel, Jean. 1995. "The Effectiveness of Child Care Subsidies in Encouraging the Welfare-to-Work Transition of Low-Income Single Mothers." *American Economic Review* 85(2): 271–75.

———. 1998. "Child Care Costs as a Barrier to Employment for Single and Married Mothers." *Review of Economics and Statistics* 80(2): 287–99.

Kontos, Susan, Carollee Howes, Marybeth Shinn, and Eleanor Galinsky. 1995. *Quality in Family Child Care and Relative Care.* New York: Teachers College Press.

Koopman, Laurens P., Henriette A. Smit, Marie-Louise A. Heijnen, Alet Wijga, Rob T. van Strien, Marjan Kerkhof, Jorrit Gerritsen, Bert Brunekreef, Johan C. deJongste, and Herman J. Neijens. 2001. "Respiratory Infections in Infants: Interaction of Parental Allergy, Child Care, and Siblings—The PIAMA Study." *Pediatrics* 108(4): 943–48.

Kopjar, Branko, and Thomas Wickizer. 1996. "How Safe Are Day Care Centers? Day Care Versus Home Injuries Among Children in Norway." *Pediatrics* 97(1): 43–48.

Kotch, J. B., V. M. Dufort, P. Stewart, J. Fieberg, M. McMurray, S. O'Brien, M. Ngui, and M. Brennan. 1997. "Injuries Among Children in Home and Out-Of-Home Care." *Injury Prevention* 3(4): 267–71.

Krämer, U., J. Heinrich, M. Wyst, and H.-E. Wichmann. 1999. "Age of Entry to Day Nursery and Allergy in Later Childhood." *The Lancet* 353(9151): 450–54.

Lamb, Michael E. 1998. "Nonparental Child Care: Context, Quality, Correlates, and Consequences." In *Handbook of Child Psychology,* edited by William Damon. New York: John Wiley.

Louhiala, Pekka J., Niina Jaakkola, Risto Ruostalainen, and Jouni J. K. Jaakkola. 1997. "Day Care Centers and Diarrhea: A Public Health Perspective." *Journal of Pediatrics* 131(3): 476–79.

Matson, David O. 1994. "Viral Gastroenteritis in Day Care Settings: Epidemiology and New Developments." *Pediatrics* 94(6): 999–1001.

Mayer, Susan. 2000. "How Did the Increase in Economic Inequality Between 1970 and 1990 Affect Children's Educational Attainment?" Unpublished paper. University of Chicago, Joint Center for Poverty Research.

McCarton, Cecilia, Jeanne Brooks-Gunn, Ina F. Wallace, Charles R. Bauer, Forrest C. Bennett, Judy C. Bernbaum, R. Sue Broyles, Patrick H. Casey, Marie C. McCormick, David T. Scott, Jon Tyson, James Tonascia, and Curtis L. Meinert. 1997. "Results at Age Eight Years of Early Intervention for Low-Birthweight Premature Infants: The Infant Health and Development Program." *Journal of the American Medical Association* 277(2): 126–32.

Meyer, Bruce D., and Dan T. Rosenbaum. 2001. "Welfare, the Earned Income Tax Credit, and the Labor Supply of Single Mothers." *Quarterly Journal of Economics* 116(3): 1063–1114.

Meyers, Marcia K., Laura Peck, Ann Collins, J. Lee Kreader, Annie Georges, Elizabeth E. Davis, Roberta Weber, Deanna Schexnayder, Daniel Schroeder, and Jerry A. Olson. 2002. *The Dynamics of Child Care Subsidy Use: A Collaborative Study of Five States.* New York: National Center for Children in Poverty.

Meyers, Marcia K., Theresa Heintze, and Doug Wolf. 2002. "Child Care Subsidies and the Employment of Welfare Recipients." *Demography* 39(1): 165–79.

Michalopoulos, Charles, and Philip K. Robins. 2000. "Employment and Child Care Choices in Canada and the United States." *Canadian Journal of Economics* 33(2): 435–70.

Michalopoulos, Charles, Philip K. Robins, and Irwin Garfinkel. 1992. "A Structural Model of Labor Supply and Child Care Demand." *Journal of Human Resources* 27(1): 166–203.

Mishel, Lawrence, Jared Bernstein, et al. 2001. *The State of Working America: 2000–2001.* Ithaca, N.Y.: ILR Press/Cornell University Press.

Moon, Rachel, Kantilal M. Patel, and Sarah J. McDermott Shaefer. 2000. "Sudden Infant Death Syndrome in Child Care Settings." *Pediatrics* 106(2): 295–300.

Nafstad, Per, A. Hagen Jørgen, Leif Øie, Per Magnus, and Jouni J. K. Jaakkola. 1999. "Day Care Centers and Respiratory Health." *Pediatrics* 103(4): 753–58.

National Institute of Child Health and Human Development (NICHD). Early Child Care Research Network (ECCRN). 1997. "Child Care in the First Year of Life." *Merrill Palmer Quarterly* 43(3): 340–60.

———. 1999. "Child Outcomes When Child Care Center Classes Meet Recommended Standards for Quality." *American Journal of Public Health* 89: 1072–77.

———. 2000. "The Relation of Child Care to Cognitive and Language Development." *Child Development* 71(4): 958–78.

———. 2001. "Child Care and Common Communicable Illnesses: Results from the NICHD Study of Early Child Care." *Archives of Pediatric and Adolescent Medicine* 155(4): 481–88.

———. 2002a. "Type of Child Care and Children's Development at Fifty-four Months." Unpublished paper. University of North Carolina, Greensboro.

———. 2002b. "Early Child Care and Children's Development Prior to School Entry: Results from the NICHD Study of Early Child Care." *American Educational Research Journal* 39(1, Spring): 133–64.

———. 2003. "Does Amount of Time Spent in Child Care Predict Socioemotional Adjustment During the Transition to Kindergarten?" *Child Development* 74(4, July–August): 976–1005.

National Women's Law Center. 2001. *Recent Changes in State Child and Dependent Care Tax Provisions: Tax Year 2001.* Washington, D.C.: National Women's Law Center.

Neidell, Matthew J. 2000. "Early Parental Time Investments in Children's Human Capital Development: Effects of Time in the First Year on Cognitive and Noncognitive Outcomes." Unpublished paper. University of California at Los Angeles (August).

NICHD Early Child Care Research Network and Greg Duncan. 2002. "Modeling the Impacts of Child Care Quality on Children's Preschool Cognitive Development." Unpublished paper. Northwestern University, Evanston, Ill.

Norberg, Karen. 1998. "The Effects of Day Care Reconsidered." Working paper 6769. Cambridge, Mass.: National Bureau of Economic Research (October).

Nord, Christine Winquist, Jean Lennon, Baiming Liu, and Kathryn Chandler. 2000. "Home Literacy Activities and Signs of Children's Emerging Literacy: 1993 and 1999." *Education Statistics Quarterly* 2(1): 19–27.

Nystad, Wenche, Anders Skrondal, and Per Magnus. 1999. "Day Care Attendance, Recurrent Respiratory Tract Infections, and Asthma." *International Journal of Epidemiology* 28(5): 882–87.

Osterholm, Michael T. 1994. "Infectious Disease in Child Care: An Overview." *Pediatrics* 94(6): 987–90.

Peisner-Feinberg, Ellen, and Margaret Burchinal. 1997. "Concurrent Relations Between Child Care Quality and Child Outcomes: The Study of Cost, Quality, and Outcomes in Child Care Centers." *Merrill-Palmer Quarterly* 43: 451–77.

Peisner-Feinberg, Ellen S., Margaret R. Burchinal, Richard M. Clifford, Mary L. Culkin, Carollee Howes, Sharon L. Kagan, Noreen Yazejian, Patricia Byler, Jean Rustici, and Janice Zelazo. 1999. "The Children of the Cost, Quality, and Outcomes Study Go to School: Executive Summary." Chapel Hill, N.C.: Frank Porter Graham Child Development Center.

Peisner-Feinberg, Ellen S., Margaret R. Burchinal, Richard M. Clifford, Mary L. Culkin, Carollee Howes, Sharon L. Kagan, and Noreen Yazejian. 2001. "The Relation of Preschool Child Care Quality to Children's Cognitive and Social Developmental Trajectories Through Second Grade." *Child Development* 72(5): 1534–53.

Phillips, Deborah, Miriam Voran, Ellen Kisker, Carollee Howes, and Marcy Whitebrook. 1994. "Child Care for Children in Poverty: Opportunity or Inequity?" *Child Development* 65: 472–92.

Phillips, Meredith. 1999. "Early Inequalities: The Development of Ethnic Differences in Academic Achievement During Childhood." Ph.D. diss., Northwestern University.

Phillips, Meredith, Jeanne Brooks-Gunn, Greg Duncan, Pamela K. Klebanov, and Jonathan Crane. 1998. "Family Background, Parenting Practices, and the Black-White Test Score Gap." In *The Black-White Test Score Gap,* edited by Christopher Jencks and Meredith Phillips. Washington, D.C.: Brookings Institution.

Powell, Lisa. 1997. "The Impact of Child Care Cost on the Labor Supply of Married Mothers: Evidence from Canada." *Canadian Journal of Economics* 30(3): 577–94.

———. 2002. "Joint Labor Supply and Child Care Choice Decisions of Married Mothers." *Journal of Human Resources* 37 (1): 106–28.

Ramey, Craig T., and Sharon L. Ramey. 1998. "Prevention of Intellectual Disabilities: Early Interventions to Improve Cognitive Development." *Preventive Medicine* 27: 224–32.

Ramey, Sharon L., and Craig T. Ramey. 2000. "The Effects of Early Childhood Experiences on Developmental Competence." In *Securing the Future: Investing in Children from Birth to College,* edited by Sheldon Danziger and Jane Waldfogel. New York: Russell Sage Foundation.

Randolf, Linda A. 1994. "The Potential Health Benefits of Child Day Care." *Pediatrics* 94(6): 1050–52.

Reves, Randall R., Ardythe L. Morrow, Alfred V. Bartlett, Charles J. Caruso, Richard L. Plumb, Bening T. Lu, and Larry K. Pickering. 1993. "Child Day Care Increases the Risk of Clinic Visits for Acute Diarrhea and Diarrhea Due to Rotavirus." *American Journal of Epidemiology* 137(1): 97–107.

Ribar, David C. 1992. "Child Care and the Labor Supply of Married Women: Reduced Form Evidence." *Journal of Human Resources* 27(1): 134–65.

———. 1995. "A Structural Model of Child Care and the Labor Supply of Married Women." *Journal of Labor Economics* 13(3): 558–97.

Rivara, Frederick P., Carolyn DiGuiseppi, Robert S. Thompson, and Ned Calogne. 1989. "Risk of Injury to Children Less Than Five Years of Age in Day Care Versus Home Care Settings." *Pediatrics* 84(6): 1011–16.

Rivara, Frederick P., and Jeffrey J. Sacks. 1994. "Injuries in Child Day Care: An Overview." *Pediatrics* 94(6): 1031–33.

Robins, Philip K. 1988. "Federal Support for Child Care: Current Policies and a Proposed New System." *Focus* 11: 1–9.

Rovers, Maroeska M., Gerhard A. Zielhuis, Koen Ingels, and Gert-Jan van der Wilt. 1999. "Day Care and Otitis Media in Young Children: A Critical Overview." *European Journal of Pediatrics* 158(1): 1–6.

Schumacher, Rachel, Mark Greenberg, and Janellen Duffy. 2001. *The Impact of TANF Funding on State Child Care Subsidy Programs.* Washington, D.C.: Center for Law and Social Policy.

Schwartz, Benjamin, G. Scott Giebink, Frederick W. Henderson, Mary R. Reichler, John Jereb, and Jean-Paul Collet. 1994. "Respiratory Infections in Day Care." *Pediatrics* 94(6), Part II: 1018–20.

Shonkoff, Jack, and Deborah Phillips, eds. 2000. *From Neurons to Neighborhoods: The Science of Early Childhood Development.* Washington, D.C.: National Academy of Sciences.

Smith, Kristin. 2000. "Who's Minding the Kids? Child Care Arrangements Fall 1995." Washington: U.S. Government Printing Office for U.S. Census Bureau.

———. 2002. "Who's Minding the Kids? Child Care Arrangements." *Current Population Reports,* series P70, no. 86. Washington: U.S. Government Printing Office for U.S. Census Bureau.

Snyder, Thomas D., and Charlene Hoffman. 2003. *Digest of Educational Statistics, 2002.* Washington: U.S. Department of Education, National Center for Education Statistics.

Takala, Aino K., Jussi Jero, Eija Kela, Pirjo-Riitta Ronnberg, Eeva Koskenniemi, and Juhani Eskola. 1995. "Risk Factors for Primary Invasive Pneumococcal Disease Among Children in Finland." *Journal of the American Medical Association* 273(11): 859–65.

Thacker, Stephen B., David G. Addiss, Richard A. Goodman, Barbara R. Holloway, and Harrison B. Spencer. 1992. "Infectious Diseases and Injuries in Child Day Care: Opportunities for Healthier Children." *Journal of the American Medical Association* 268(13): 1720–26.

U.S. Department of Agriculture (USDA). 2001. "Expenditures on Children by Families." In USDA: Center for Nutrition Policy and Promotion, Miscellaneous Publication Number 1528–2000. Washington: U.S. Government Printing Office.

U.S. Department of Commerce. U.S. Census Bureau. 2001. *Statistical Abstract of the United States.* Washington: U.S. Government Printing Office.

———. Various years. "School Enrollment: Social and Economic Characteristics of Students." *Current Population Reports,* series P20. Washington: U.S. Government Printing Office.

U.S. Department of Health and Human Services. Administration for Children and Families. 2000. *Access to Child Care for Low-Income Working Families.* Washington: Department of Health and Human Services.

———. 2002. *Temporary Assistance for Needy Families Program Participants.* Washington: U.S. Department of Health and Human Services.

U.S. General Accounting Office. 1994. *Child Care: Child Care Subsidies Increase Likelihood That Low-Income Mothers Will Work.* Washington: U.S. General Accounting Office.

Vandell, Deborah Lowe, and Barbara Wolfe. 2000. "Child Care Quality: Does It Matter and Does It Need to Be Improved?" Special report. Madison: University of Wisconsin, Madison, Institute for Research on Poverty (November).

Vandell, Deborah Lowe, and Mary A. Corasaniti. 1990. "Child Care and the Family: Complex Contributors to Child Development." *New Directions for Child Development* 49: 23–37.

Venczel, Linda V., Desai M. Mayur, Diane Vertz, Bob England, Yvan J. F. Hutin, Craig Shapiro, and Beth P. Bell. 2001. "The Role of Child Care in a Communitywide Outbreak of Hepatitis A." *Pediatrics* 108(5): E78.

Waldfogel, Jane. 2002. "Child Care, Women's Employment, and Child Outcomes." *Journal of Population Economics* 15: 527–48.

Waldfogel, Jane, Wen-Jui Han, and Jeanne Brooks-Gunn. 2002. "The Effects of Early Maternal Employment on Child Cognitive Development." *Demography* 39: 369–92.

West, Jerry, Kristin Denton, and Elvie Germino-Hausken. 2000. "America's Kindergartners: Findings from the Early Childhood Longitudinal Study, Kindergarten Class of 1998–99: Fall 1998." *Education Statistics Quarterly* 2(1): 7–13.

West, Jerry, and Elvie Germino-Hausken, Kathryn Chandler, and Mary Collins. 1992. *Experiences in Child Care and Early Childhood Programs of First- and Second-Graders Prior to Entering First Grade: Findings from the 1991 National Household Education Survey.* Washington: U.S. Department of Education, National Center for Educational Statistics (NCES).

Chapter 7

Progress in Schooling

Robert M. Hauser

It is far from creditable that in hardly a city in the country can the school authorities tell how many pupils begin each school year, or how fast they advance, or what proportion finish or why they fall out, or where and why they lose time.

—Leonard P. Ayres, *Laggards in Our Schools* (1909, 7)

Much as age-grading changed the definition of a quality school system from one with high rates of failure to one with high rates of promotion, so in the 1940s, educators began to adopt the idea that automatic promotion, or as it would later be called "social promotion," of virtually all students was the sign of true educational quality.

—David Angus, Jeffrey Mirel, and Maris Vinovskis, "Historical Development of Age Stratification in Schooling" (1998)

This chapter reviews measures, trends, and differentials in grade retention and dropout in American elementary and secondary schools from the early 1970s to the late 1990s. Differentials in grade retention and school dropout reflect social and economic inequalities and, for that reason, may have been affected by the rise of income and wealth inequality in and after the 1970s. However, there appears to be more evidence of stability than of change in the effects of social origins on progress through elementary and secondary school. The distribution of progress through school has been altered by changes in the distribution of social origins, but there have been no large changes in the effects of social and economic origins. Grade retention and dropout—and socioeconomic differentials in them—may also be sensitive to changing national and state educational policies, and the following discussion highlights their connections. Even if the rising economic inequality of the past three decades has not led to larger socioeconomic differentials in progress through school, the pace and scope of school reform around the turn of the century may lead to such changes. Thus, it is instructive to review the progress of American students through elementary and secondary school across the past three decades to provide a baseline for an assessment of future trends, as well as to assess the consequences of the past growth of inequality.

The combination of grade retention and dropout in this review may seem artificial. However, their intimate relationship was well understood almost a century ago by Leonard P. Ayres, one of the early social researchers supported by the Russell Sage Foundation:

We may now consider the relation which such low percentages of promotion have to retardation and the evil which is its corollary—elimination. It is apparent

271

that if considerable numbers of the children entering school fail to be advanced regularly, the lower grades will become abnormally swollen by the damming of the stream of pupils through them. Experience teaches us, too, that in the upper grades the pupils who have advanced slowly and so are over-age will drop out before completing the course, thus making these grades abnormally small. . . . Retardation results in elimination. (Ayres 1909, 139–40)

Across the past century, throughout the unprecedented expansion of the American educational system, the inescapable problem of balancing socialization and selection through the schools has played out through increases in age-grading and observable variations in the pace of progress through schools and in rates and patterns of school-leaving.[1] As age at entry to regular schooling declined and age at school-leaving increased, the focus of public concern with trade-offs between socialization and selection gradually shifted from the lower to the higher grades—from completion of the elementary grades to high school completion (Duncan 1968; National Research Council 1989). Although this chapter focuses on the processes leading to high school completion—or its absence—the recent, massive increase in transitions to postsecondary schooling raises the same questions in somewhat altered form.[2] Who should attend college, and what role should society play in influencing college-going decisions? Which students should receive financial help in postsecondary schooling? How should financial support for postsecondary schooling be organized? How—if at all—should colleges accommodate their programs to students with varying levels of educational preparation? What is the appropriate pace for students making their way through the college years?

The language of the contemporary debate about the success or failure of schools substitutes "high standards" for socialization and "dropout" for selection, and there are real differences in their meanings and those of the corresponding terms, "retardation" and "elimination," that accompanied educational debate a century ago (Ayres 1909). Several common themes persist. A larger share of children should complete the course of study. Universal school completion supports democratic values and improves labor market chances. Schooling is a production process that can be improved in all respects by scientific knowledge and businesslike administration. Gender, health, race-ethnic origins, immigrant status, social background, and residential stability all affect progress through schooling. Too many students learn that they are failures in school, and retention in grade leads to early school-leaving. Local school authorities fail to collect data adequate to diagnose or solve the problems of failure and attrition in their schools. Problems of data availability are compounded by erroneous assumptions and poor analyses of available data. A thorough reading of Ayres's (1909) *Laggards in Our Schools*—which is, I think, far more often cited than read—could leave one feeling that contemporaneous research and policy debates exemplify "déja vu all over again."

To be sure, there are real and substantial differences in contemporary distributions and processes of school completion, not least among which are that elementary schooling is essentially universal among persons born in the United States, that high school completion, in some form, is nearly universal, and that postsecondary schooling awaits a large majority of high school graduates. In the case of elementary and secondary schooling, the most visible goal of policymakers and advocates has changed from school completion to academic achievement—that is, from selection to socialization—and much of the educational debate focuses on the use of standardized tests to assess and certify success in schooling. A century ago there was no parallel to the contemporary advocacy of publicly funded alternatives to public common schools. While both economic and political goals for schooling have persisted, there has been a shift in the primary emphasis—from preparation for membership in a democratic society to preparation for work in a globally competitive labor market.

Data and analytic resources are in many respects far superior to those of a century ago. One improvement is the ability to track individual progress through schools across time, both in samples and in whole populations. A second is the availability, across a wide span of years, of comparable and detailed social and economic characteristics of current and former students. Educational goals, policies, and resources, as well as data about the process of schooling, now come increasingly from national sources—including not just the federal government but nationally based advocacy organizations and a few dominant commercial suppliers of educational textbooks and achievement tests. Yet the limits of our present understanding of persistence and success in elementary and secondary schooling are amply illustrated by the fact that there is no consensus about the extent of high school completion among population groups and across localities (Greene 2002), nor even about the desirability or feasibility of universal high school completion (Hayward 2000).[3]

RETENTION IN GRADE

Retention in grade was not a highly visible issue in American education from the late 1940s to the early 1990s. It was a variable local educational practice, not a recognizable tool of educational policy at the district, state, or federal level (American Federation of Teachers 1997). In 1998 President Clinton made high standards for promotion a cornerstone of his educational policy goals for the nation. Clinton combined a demand for high-stakes testing of individual students with a call for "an end to social promotion." In a memorandum to the secretary of education, President Clinton (1998, 1–2) wrote that he had "repeatedly challenged States and school districts to end social promotions—to require students to meet rigorous academic standards at key transition points in their schooling career, and to end the practice of promoting students without regard to how much they have learned. . . . Students should not be promoted past the fourth grade if they cannot read independently and well, and should not enter high school without a solid foundation in math. They should get the help they need to meet the standards before moving on."[4] In his 1999 State of the Union address, the president reiterated the proposal—to sustained applause—by calling for legislation to withhold federal education funds from school districts practicing social promotion. In October 1999, President Clinton told a summit meeting of political and business leaders that "students who are held back because they fail to vault newly raised bars should be treated with tough love. . . . Look dead in the eye some child who has been held back and say, 'This doesn't mean there's something wrong with you, but we'll be hurting you worse if we tell you you're learning something when you're not.'" (Steinberg 1999).

The Clinton administration's proposals for educational reform strongly tied the ending of social promotion to early identification and remediation of learning problems. The president called for smaller classes, well-prepared teachers, specific grade-by-grade standards, challenging curriculum, early identification of students who need help, after-school and summer school programs, and school accountability. He also called for "appropriate use of tests and other indicators of academic performance in determining whether students should be promoted" (Clinton 1998, 3).

The subsequent rush to embrace high-stakes testing for promotion or retention would have been comic at times had it not had serious implications for the future of millions of children and youth. In Atlanta, Georgia, the school board fired its superintendent for refusing to implement a policy of failing any student whose test scores were below average. The state superintendent of schools in Louisiana declared that the state was not failing a large enough share of students early enough in their careers, yet the state of Louisiana was already leading the nation, both in grade retention and high school dropout. When asked about the use of the Iowa Test of Basic Skills to retain students in the Chicago Public Schools, the chief accountability officer told a panel of the National Research Council that, as long as the *Chicago Tribune* backed the testing program, "we are committed to use the Iowa forever and ever" (National Research Council 1999, 31).

In Texas, then-Governor George W. Bush proposed that "3rd graders who do not pass the reading portion of the Texas Assessment of Academic Skills would be required to receive help before moving to regular classrooms in the 4th grade. The same would hold true for 5th graders who failed to pass reading and math exams and 8th graders who did not pass tests in reading, math, and writing. The state would provide funding for locally developed intervention programs" (Johnston 1998). As president, through his support for the No Child Left Behind Act (U.S. Congress 2002), Bush has largely succeeded in initiating—on a large scale—many of the educational policy changes that were denied his predecessor.

The new federal legislation mandates the administration of state-developed achievement tests to every schoolchild from the third through the eighth grades, and there is every likelihood that these tests will be used to retain students in grade as well as to diagnose what they know and can do. While section 1111 of the No Child Left Behind Act specifically does not *require* the use of tests as promotion or graduation criteria (U.S. Congress 2002, 1444), neither does it discourage such use. The recent history of testing suggests that, if tests are given, they will be used to make decisions about students (National Research Council 1999; Linn 2000). Section 1240 includes a requirement that states provide information about children's promotion or retention as an indicator of "program quality" (1566). Section 1503 requires the secretary of education to "conduct an independent study of assessments used for State accountability purposes and for making decisions about the promotion and graduation of students" (1597).

Measurement of Grade Retention

The main federal source of information about education, the National Center for Education Statistics (NCES), provides essentially no statistics about grade retention or social promotion. For example, there are no data on this subject in current editions of its two major statistical compendiums, the *Digest of Education Statistics* (National Center for Education Statistics 2002b) and *The Condition of Education* (National Center for Education Statistics 2002a).[5]

No federal or independent agency monitors social promotion and grade retention. Occasional data on retention are available for some states and localities, but coverage is sparse, and little is known about the comparability of these data (Shepard and Smith 1989). For example, the denominators of retention rates may be based on beginning-of-year or end-of-year enrollment figures. The numerators may include retention as of the end of an academic year or as of the end of the following summer session. Some states include special education students in the data; others exclude them. In the primary grades retention is usually an all-or-nothing matter; in high school retention may imply that a student has completed some requirements but has too few credits to be promoted. Some states do not collect retention data at all or collect very limited data.[6]

There might appear to be a contradiction between high rates of retention in grade and the widespread belief—common among teachers as well as the general public—that poorly performing students regularly pass from one grade to the next. That need not be the case. As Leonard Ayres understood, seemingly modest grade-level retention rates have a large cumulative impact on progress through school (1909, 141–49). For example, each year Texas reports retention rates separately by grade level and race-ethnicity. Retention rates have been stable since 1990, well before the new initiatives to "end social promotion." The retention rate is typically about 6 percent in the first grade and 1 to 3 percent in other elementary grades. Retention rates peak at about 18 percent in the ninth grade but fall off quickly thereafter to 8 percent, 5.5 percent, and 4.5 percent in the tenth to twelfth grades (Texas Education Agency 2001, 72–74). If all Texas students were subject (at random) to the failure rates of 1996 to 1997, 17 percent would fail at least once between the first and eighth grades, and 32 percent would fail at least once between the ninth grade and high school completion (Texas Education Agency 1998). Among African American students, the corresponding rates are 20 percent and 42 percent, and among Hispanic students they are 21 percent and 44 percent.[7]

The recent public discussion of "social promotion" has made little reference to past or current retention practices, and one might easily gain the impression that, until the recent reforms, almost no students had been retained in grade. In fact, while retention practice has varied across time and place, grade retention is and has been pervasive in American schools. Ignorance about the practice of grade retention may be due in part to sporadic data collection and reporting, but far more consistent statistical data are available about the practice of grade retention than, say, about academic tracking. It is possible to describe rates, trends, and differentials in grade retention using data from the U.S. Census Bureau, but these data have not been widely used.

Weak inferences about the extent of grade retention may be obtained from historic data on educational attainment by age. For example, in the census of 1940, 17.6 percent of seven-year-olds had not completed any school, 31.5 percent of eight-year-olds had not completed more than the first grade, and 46.3 percent of twelve-year-olds had not completed more than the fifth grade (U.S. Department of Commerce 1943, table 2). Similar inferences may be drawn from a table based on the U.S. Census Bureau's Current Population Surveys (CPS) of 1964 through 1966 that shows age by year of school in which students are enrolled (U.S. Department of Commerce 1967, table 9). During this period 5.1 percent of six-year-olds had not yet entered the first grade, 11.7 percent of seven-year-olds had not yet entered the second grade, and 20.5 percent of eleven-year-olds had not yet entered the sixth grade. In each of these cases, we infer that the increase with age in grade completion or enrollment below the modal level implies grade retention. However, the inferences are weak because they are based on comparisons of birth cohorts in cross-section and because age at school entry varies across cohorts, especially in the earlier period. All the same, the data appear to show substantial increases in grade retardation as children age, presumably caused by grade retention.

The best source of current information on levels, trends, and differentials in grade retention is the annual October school enrollment supplement to the monthly Current Population Survey.[8] Using published data from the annual October supplements, it is possible to track the distribution of school enrollment by age and grade each year for groups defined by sex and race-ethnicity.[9] These data have the advantage of comparable national coverage from year to year, but they say nothing directly about educational transitions or about the role of specific educational practices, such as high-stakes testing, in grade retention.[10] We can only infer the minimum rate of grade retention by observing changes in the enrollment of children below the modal grade level for their age from one calendar year to the next. Suppose, for example, that 10 percent of six-year-old children were enrolled below the first grade in October 1994. If 15 percent of those children were enrolled below the second grade in October 1995, when they were seven years old, we would infer that at least 5 percent were held back in the first grade between 1994 and 1995. Using this approach, I briefly review trends and differentials in retention, as indicated by age-grade retardation.

Trends and Differentials in Age-Grade Retardation

Extended Kindergarten Attendance   Historically, there has been great variation in age at school entry in the United States.[11] This variation once had more to do with the labor demands of a farm economy and the availability of schooling to disadvantaged groups than with readiness for school. The variability declined as school enrollment completed its diffusion from middle childhood into younger and older ages (Duncan 1968; National Research Council 1989).

The age at entry into graded school has gradually crept upward since the early 1970s, reversing one of the major historic trends contributing to the growth of schooling in the United States. The Census Bureau's statistics on grade enrollment by age show that, from the early 1970s to the late 1980s, entry into first grade gradually came later in the development of many children. However, for the past decade there has been little change in age at school entry. Figure 7.1 shows the percentages of six-year-old children who had not yet entered the first grade as of October of the given year. Among six-year-old boys, only 8 percent had not yet entered the first grade in 1971,[12] but 22 percent were not yet in the first grade in 1987, and 20 percent were not yet in the first grade in 2000. Among six-year-old girls, only 4 percent had not yet entered the first grade in 1971, but 16 percent were not yet in the first grade in 1987 or in 2000. While boys are consistently more likely than girls to enter first grade after age six, there are only small differences between blacks and whites in age at entry into graded school, and these differences consistently favor black children. That is, six-year-old black children are slightly less likely than white children of the same age and sex to be enrolled below the first grade or not enrolled in school. Also, six-year-old Hispanic boys are consistently more likely than white boys to have entered first grade. However, six-year-old Hispanic girls are less likely than white girls to have entered first grade.

It is not clear why age at school entry has increased. One contributing factor has been the influence of state laws on minimum age at school entry. Another factor—suggested by the initially slow school entry of white boys—is that some parents "red shirt" their children at an early age in order to give them an advantage in athletic competition later on. Early school retention is a third potential explanation of the trend.

Over the past two decades attendance in kindergarten has been extended to two years for many children in American schools.[13] There is no single name for this phenomenon. As Lorrie Shepard (1991) reports, the names for such extended kindergarten classrooms include "junior-first," "prefirst," "transition," and "readiness room." There are also no distinct categories for the first and second years of kindergarten in census enrollment data. Fragmentary reports suggest that, in some places, kindergarten retention may have been as high as 50 percent in the late 1980s (Shepard 1989; Shepard 1991). There are also reports of inappropriate use of cognitive tests in such decisions (Shepard 1991, 287; Shepard, Kagan, and Wurtz 1998). The degree to which early retention decisions originate with parents—

FIGURE 7.1   Six-Year-Old Children Who Have Not Entered First Grade, by Race-Ethnicity, 1972 to 1999

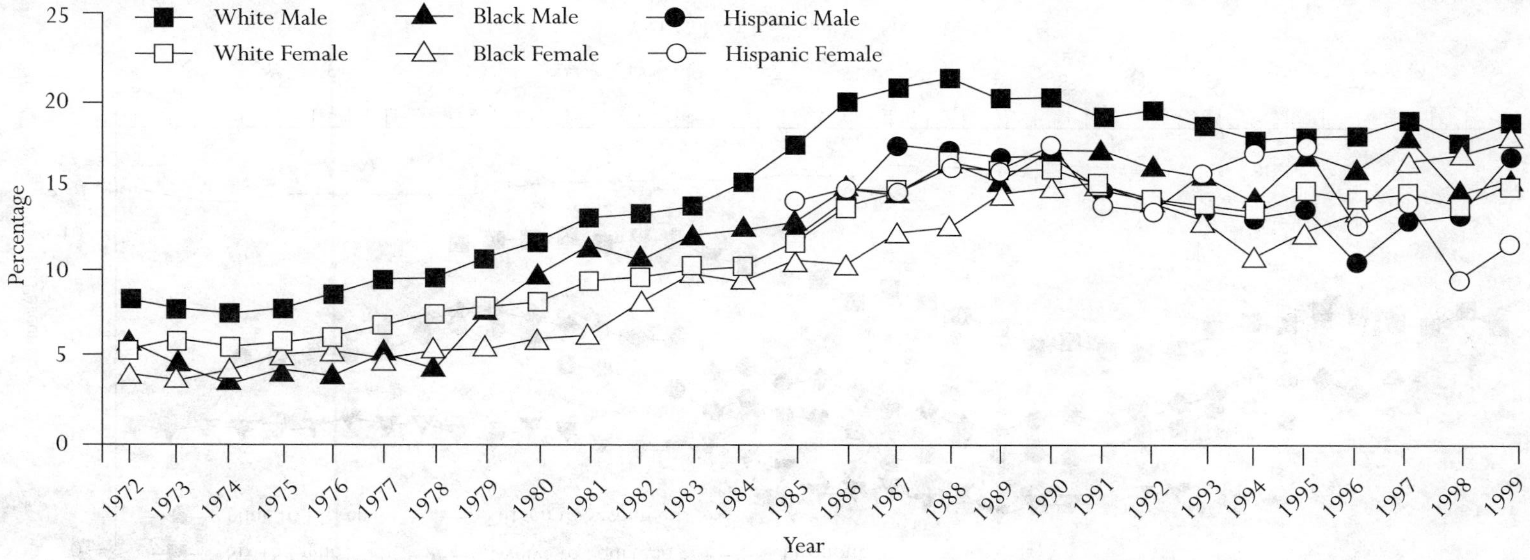

Source: U.S. Department of Commerce, U.S. Census Bureau, "School Enrollment: Social and Economic Characteristics of Students," Current Population Reports, P-20 series, nos. 241, 260, 272, 286, 303, 319, 333, 346, 360, 400, 408, 413, 426, 439, 443, 452, 460, 469, 474, 479, 487, 492, 500, 516, 521, and 533.
Note: Entries are three-year moving averages.

FIGURE 7.2   *Children Enrolled Below Modal Grade for Age, by Age Group and Year in Which Cohort Was Six to Eight Years Old*

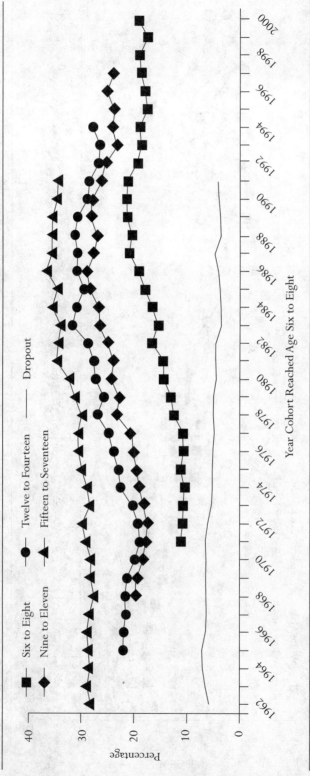

Source: U.S. Department of Commerce, U.S. Census Bureau, table A-3, "The Population Six to Seventeen Years Old Enrolled Below Modal Grade," http://www.census.gov/population/socdemo/school/tabA-3.pdf.

for example, to increase their children's chances for success in athletics—rather than with teachers or other school personnel is not known. Moreover, there are no regular national estimates of the prevalence of kindergarten retention, and none of the available state data indicate exceptionally high kindergarten retention rates. From occasional national surveys, Nancy Karweit (1999) suggests that "by first grade between 7 and 11 percent of children have been retained."

Excepting the ubiquitous tendency for girls to enter (and complete) primary and secondary school at earlier ages than boys, there is little sign of social differentiation in age at school entry. Instead, socially differentiated patterns of grade retention begin to develop after entry into graded school, and they persist through secondary school.

Retention in the Primary and Secondary Grades   Age-grade retardation refers to enrollment below the modal grade level for a child's age. (No broader meaning is either intended or implied.) I have examined national rates of age-grade retardation by age, sex, and race-ethnicity for three-year age groups at ages six to seventeen from 1971 to 2000 and also parallel tabulations for young children by single years of age from 1971 to 2000. In each case, I have organized the data by birth cohort (year of birth) rather than by calendar year, so it is possible to see the evolution of age-grade retardation throughout the schooling of a birth cohort as well as changes in age-grade retardation rates from year to year.[14]

The recent history of age-grade retardation is summarized in figure 7.2. It shows age-grade retardation at ages six to eight, nine to eleven, twelve to fourteen, and fiteen to seventeen among children who reached ages six to eight between 1962 and 2000. The horizontal axis shows the year in which an age group reached ages six to eight, so vertical comparisons among the trend lines at a given year show how age-grade retardation cumulated as a birth cohort grew older.

For example, consider children who were six to eight years old in 1991—the most recent cohort whose history can be traced all the way from ages six to eight up through age fifteen to seventeen. At ages six to eight, 21.2 percent were enrolled below the modal grade for their age. By 1994, when this cohort reached ages nine to eleven, age-grade retardation had grown to 26.2 percent, and it was 28.5 percent in 1997, when the cohort reached ages twelve to fourteen. By 2000, when the cohort had reached ages fifteen to seventeen, the percentage who were either below the modal grade level or had left school was 34.5 percent. Almost all of the growth in retardation after ages twelve to fourteen, however, was due to dropout (4.3 percent) rather than grade retention among the enrolled.

We could read the rate of enrollment below the modal grade at ages six to eight as a baseline measure, that is, as if it does not necessarily indicate that grade retention took place. Relative to that baseline, increases in enrollment below the modal grade at older ages clearly show the net effects of retention in grade. This reading of the data would suggest that, in most birth cohorts, retention occurs mainly between ages six to eight and ages nine to eleven or between ages twelve to fourteen and ages fifteen to seventeen.[15] This way of looking at the data surely understates the prevalence of grade retention, for much of it occurs within ages six to eight and within ages fifteen to seventeen—that is, either early in elementary school or during the high school years.

The series for ages fifteen to seventeen includes early school dropout, which is also shown as a separate series along the bottom of figure 7.2. Dropout, rather than retention, evidently accounts for a substantial but declining component of the increase in age-grade retardation between ages twelve to fourteen and ages fifteen to seventeen.

The trend in age-grade retardation at ages six to eight, nine to eleven, twelve to

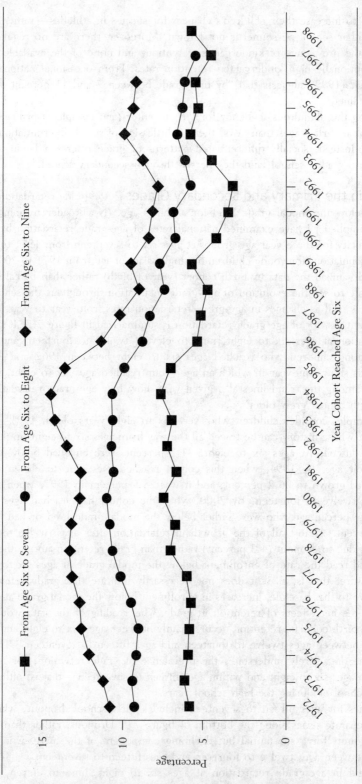

FIGURE 7.3   Change in Age-Grade Retardation from Age Six to Age Seven, Eight, and Nine, by Year When Cohort Was Six Years Old

Percentage

Year Cohort Reached Age Six

■ From Age Six to Seven   ● From Age Six to Eight   ◆ From Age Six to Nine

Source: U.S. Department of Commerce, U.S. Census Bureau, "School Enrollment: Social and Economic Characteristics of Students," Current Population Reports, P-20 series, nos. 241, 260, 272, 286, 303, 319, 333, 346, 360, 400, 408, 413, 426, 439, 443, 452, 460, 469, 474, 479, 487, 492, 500, 516, 521, and 533.
Note: Entries are three-year moving averages.

fourteen, and fifteen to seventeen can be read across figure 7.2 from left to right. Age-grade retardation increased in every age group from the cohorts of the early 1970s through those of the middle to late 1980s. Age-grade retardation increased at ages fifteen to seventeen after the mid-1970s despite the slow decline in the early school dropout component throughout the period. That is, grade retention increased while dropout decreased. Peak rates occurred earlier at older than at younger ages, suggesting that policy changes occurred in specific calendar years rather than consistently throughout the life of successive birth cohorts. Among cohorts entering school after 1970, the percentage enrolled below the modal grade level was never less than 10 percent at ages six to eight, and it exceeded 20 percent for cohorts of the late 1980s. The trend-lines suggest that age-grade retardation has declined slightly for cohorts entering school after the mid-1980s, but rates have not approached the much lower levels of the early 1970s.

Overall, a large share of each birth cohort now experiences grade retention during elementary school. Among children ages six to eight from 1982 to 1997, age-grade retardation had reached 24 to 29 percent by ages nine to eleven.

Retention After School Entry   Enrollment below the first grade at age six is a convenient baseline against which to assess the effects of later grade retention. The comparisons of age-grade retardation at ages seven to nine with that at age six are shown in figure 7.3.[16] There are two main patterns in the series. First, grade retention takes place through the elementary years at each successive age. Retention cumulates rapidly after age six. For example, among children who were six years old in 1991, enrollment below the modal grade increased by 3.4 percentage points between ages six and seven and by 4.7 more percentage points between ages seven and nine. Excepting the cohorts that entered school between 1988 and 1993, age-grade retention increased by 9 percent or more between ages six and nine, and it never increased by less than 7 percent between those two ages. Second, there appears to have been a decline in retention after the early 1980s and a possible reversal of that trend for cohorts entering school in the 1990s. That is, comparing figure 7.1 with figure 7.3, we can infer a shift in elementary school age-grade retardation downward in age from the transition between ages six and seven to somewhere between ages four and six—including the possible effects of legal changes in age at school entry.

How much grade retention is there after ages six to eight? And does the recent growth in grade retardation by ages six to eight account for its observed growth at older ages? Figure 7.4 shows changes in age-grade retardation between ages six to eight and each of the three older age groups.[17] Age-grade retardation grew substantially after ages six to eight as a result of retention in grade. For example, among children who reached ages six to eight between 1972 and 1985, almost 20 percent more were below the modal grade for their age by the time they were fifteen to seventeen years old. Among children who reached ages six to eight between the mid-1970s and the mid-1980s, grade retardation grew by about ten percentage points by ages nine to eleven, and it grew by close to five percentage points more by ages twelve to fourteen. Relative to ages six to eight, age-grade retardation at ages nine to eleven and ages twelve to fourteen increased for cohorts who were six to eight years old in the early 1970s; it was stable from the mid-1970s to the mid-1980s, and it has declined since then. However, the gap between retention at ages fifteen to seventeen and that at ages six to eight has been relatively stable—close to twenty percentage points—possibly excepting a very recent downward turn. Thus, the rise in age at entry into first grade—which is partly due to kindergarten retention—accounts for much of the overall increase in age-grade retardation among teenagers.

FIGURE 7.4   Changes in Age-Grade Retardation from Age Six to Eight to Age Nine to Seventeen, by Year When Cohort Was Six to Eight Years Old

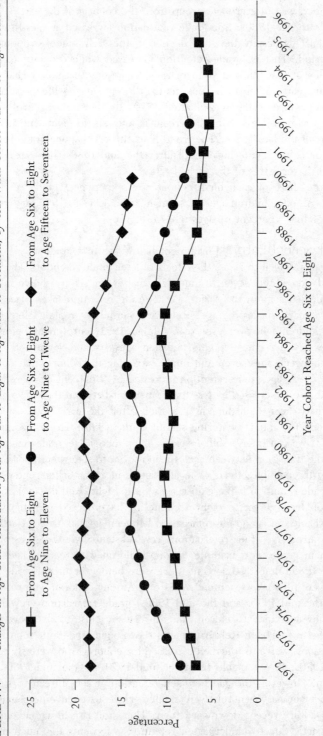

Source: U.S. Department of Commerce, U.S. Census Bureau, table A-3, "The Population Six to Seventeen Years Old Enrolled Below Modal Grade," http://www.census.gov/population/socdemo/school/tabA-3.pdf.
Note: Dropouts are included in the series at age fifteen to seventeen. Entries are three-year moving averages.

In summary, grade retention is pervasive in American schools. It is cautionary to think about the implications of "an end to social promotion" when ages at school entry are increasing and a large share of each new cohort of youth already experiences grade retention. It is especially important to consider the implications of an end to social promotion in light of the social differences in retention rates.

Social Differences in Retention

While there are similarities in the age pattern of grade retardation among major population groups—among boys and girls and among majority and minority groups—there are also substantial differences in rates of grade retardation, many of which develop well after school entry. Figure 7.5 shows rates of age-grade retardation of boys and girls at ages six to eight and ages fifteen to seventeen. Overall, the gender differential gradually increases with age, from five percentage points at ages six to eight to ten percentage points at ages fifteen to seventeen. That is, boys are initially more likely than girls to be placed below the modal grade for their age, and they fall further behind girls as they pass through childhood and adolescence.

The differentiation of age-grade relationships by race and ethnicity is even more striking than that by gender. Figures 7.6 to 7.9 show trends in the development of age-grade retardation by race-ethnicity in each of the four age groups: six to eight years old, nine to eleven years old, twelve to fourteen years old, and fifteen to seventeen years old. Unlike the case of gender differentiation, at ages six to eight the rates of age-grade retardation are very similar among whites, blacks, and Hispanics. By ages nine to eleven, the percentages enrolled below modal grade levels have typically been five to ten percentage points higher among blacks or Hispanics than among whites, but the white and Hispanic rates have converged for cohorts entering school after 1987.

The differentials continue to grow with age, and at ages fifteen to seventeen, rates of grade retardation range from 40 to 50 percent among blacks and Hispanics, while they have gradually drifted up from 25 percent to 35 percent among whites. By this age, there is also a differential between Hispanics and blacks, favoring the latter; this appears to follow from high rates of early school dropout among Hispanics. Figure 7.10 shows the rates of school dropout among fifteen- to seventeen-year-old whites, blacks, and Hispanics. There is almost no difference in early school dropout between whites and blacks, but Hispanics are much more likely to leave school at an early age.[18] Thus, early high school dropout contributes very little to the observed difference in age-grade retardation between blacks and whites, which is mainly due to retention in grade. Early dropout does account in part for the difference in age-grade retardation between Hispanics and whites or blacks.

In recent years, gender and race-ethnic differentials in age-grade retardation, even at young ages, are a consequence of school experience and not primarily of differentials in age at school entry. Social differentials in age-grade relationships are vague at school entry, but a hierarchy is clearly established by age nine, and it persists and grows through the end of secondary schooling. This growth can be explained only by grade retention. By age nine, there are sharp social differentials in age-grade retardation, favoring whites and girls relative to blacks or Hispanics and boys. By ages fifteen to seventeen, close to 50 percent of black males have fallen behind in school—thirty percentage points more than at ages six to eight—but age-grade retardation has never exceeded 30 percent among white girls of the same age. These rates and differentials in age-grade retardation are characteristic of a schooling regime in which social promotion is perceived to be the norm. Both the rates and differentials could become much larger as new policies of achievement testing and accountability are put in place.

(Text continues on p. 290.)

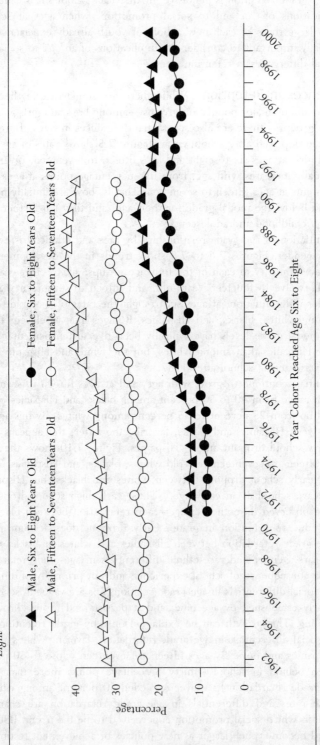

FIGURE 7.5   Children Enrolled Below Modal Grade at Age Six to Eight and at Age Fifteen to Seventeen, by Sex and Year Cohort Reached Age Six to Eight

Legend:
— Male, Six to Eight Years Old
—△— Male, Fifteen to Seventeen Years Old
● Female, Six to Eight Years Old
○ Female, Fifteen to Seventeen Years Old

Y-axis: Percentage
X-axis: Year Cohort Reached Age Six to Eight (1962 to 2000)

Source: U.S. Department of Commerce, U.S. Census Bureau, table A-3, "The Population Six to Seventeen Years Old Enrolled Below Modal Grade," http://www.census.gov/population/socdemo/school/tabA-3.pdf.

Note: Dropout is counted as age-grade retardation at age fifteen to seventeen.

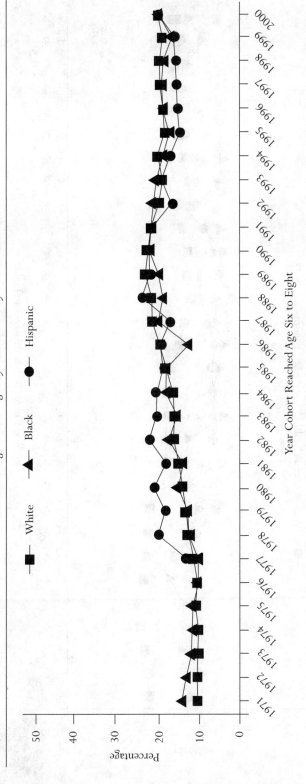

FIGURE 7.6   Children Enrolled Below Modal Grade at Age Six to Eight by Race-Ethnicity and Year

■ White   ▲ Black   ● Hispanic

Year Cohort Reached Age Six to Eight

Source: U.S. Department of Commerce, U.S. Census Bureau, table A-3, "The Population Six to Seventeen Years Old Enrolled Below Modal Grade," http://www.census.gov/population/socdemo/school/tabA-3.pdf.

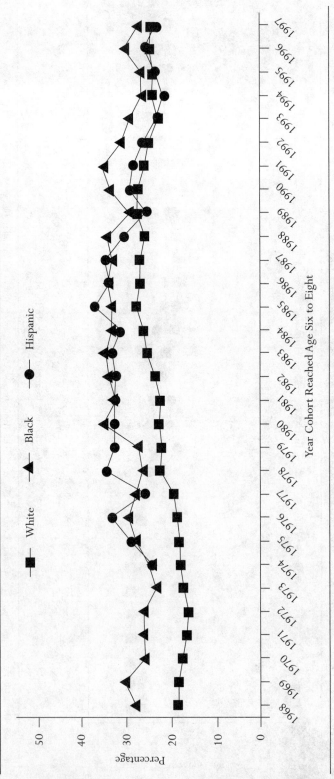

FIGURE 7.7   Children Enrolled Below Modal Grade at Age Nine to Eleven, by Year Cohort Reached Age Six to Eight by Race-Ethnicity

Year Cohort Reached Age Six to Eight

Percentage

White   Black   Hispanic

Source: U.S. Department of Commerce, U.S. Census Bureau, table A-3, "The Population Six to Seventeen Years Old Enrolled Below Modal Grade," http://www.census.gov/population/socdemo/school/tabA-3.pdf.

FIGURE 7.8   Children Enrolled Below Modal Grade at Age Twelve to Fourteen, by Year Cohort Reached Age Six to Eight by Race-Ethnicity

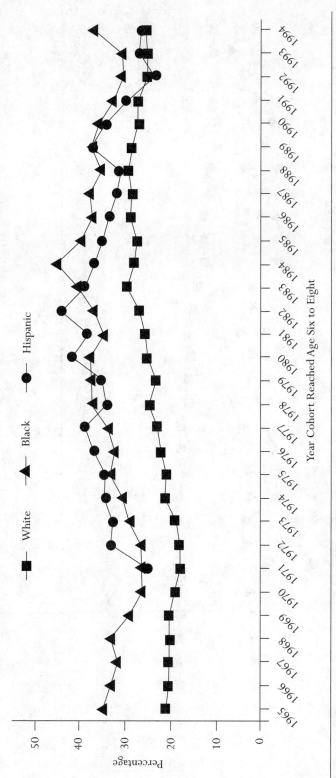

Source: U.S. Department of Commerce, U.S. Census Bureau, table A-3, "The Population Six to Seventeen Years Old Enrolled Below Modal Grade," http://www.census.gov/population/socdemo/school/tabA-3.pdf.

FIGURE 7.9   Children Enrolled Below Modal Grade or Dropping Out by Age Fifteen to Seventeen, by Year Cohort Reached Age Six to Eight by Race-Ethnicity

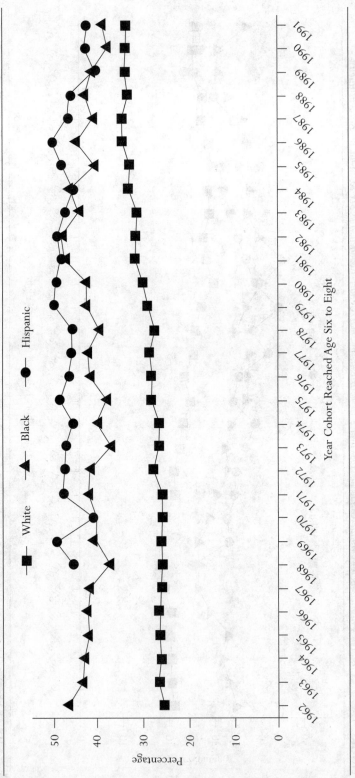

Source: U.S. Department of Commerce, U.S. Census Bureau, table A-3, "The Population Six to Seventeen Years Old Enrolled Below Modal Grade," http://www.census.gov/population/socdemo/school/tabA-3.pdf.

Note: Dropout is counted as age-grade retardation at age fifteen to seventeen.

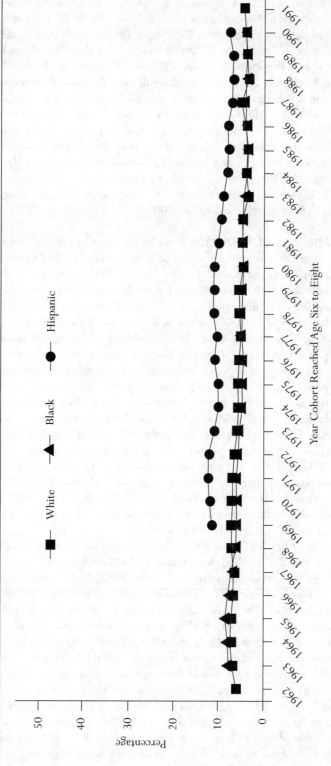

FIGURE 7.10   *Children Dropping Out by Age Fifteen to Seventeen, by Year Cohort Reached Age Six to Eight by Race-Ethnicity*

Source: U.S. Department of Commerce, U.S. Census Bureau, table A-3, "The Population Six to Seventeen Years Old Enrolled Below Modal Grade," http://www.census.gov/population/socdemo/school/tabA-3.pdf.

Figures 7.11 and 7.12 show trends in age-grade retardation in three broad family income groups: the bottom fifth, the top fifth, and the middle 60 percent of the income distributions.[19] Both at ages six to eight and at ages fifteen to seventeen, there have been large differences in grade retardation by family income, and these have been larger at older than at younger ages.[20] For example, from 1972 to 1974 through 1993 to 1995, at ages fifteen to seventeen, roughly 20 percent more youth from families in the bottom fifth of the income distribution fell behind than youth in the middle 60 percent. The differential between the top and bottom fifths of the family income distribution exceeded thirty-five percentage points over the same period. However, with a single recent exception, there has been little indication of increasing inequality in age-grade retardation by family income. On the contrary, at ages six to eight, the income differentials decreased steadily from 1987 to 1989 through 1996 to 1998, and at ages fifteen to seventeen, the differentials decreased after 1993 to 1995. One worrisome exception is the apparent reversal of trend at ages six to eight between 1996 to 1998 and 1999 to 2000.

Multivariate Analyses of Retention   While the disproportionate rates of grade retention among minorities are both large and of long standing (U.S. Department of Commerce 1979; National Research Council 1999; Hauser 2001), relatively little research has focused on the role that socioeconomic and family differences between population groups play in accounting for those differences. At the national level, we can look back only to a few simple tabulations from the 1976 Survey of Income and Education (U.S. Department of Commerce 1979) and to an exploratory—but exemplary—analysis of family background and age-grade retardation in the October Current Population Survey of 1979 (Bianchi 1984). Both of these analyses suggest that social and economic background, rather than minority status per se, accounts for a large share of group differences in retention.

My colleagues and I (Hauser, Pager, and Simmons 2000) have analyzed differentials in age-grade retardation by social and family background among six-, nine-, twelve-, fifteen-, and seventeen-year-olds, using data from the October Current Population Survey from 1972 through 1998. These ages span the period between normative entry into graded school and the later years of high school, but they do not extend to the ages at which a substantial minority of youth no longer live in parental or quasi-parental households. At these ages, the modal October grade levels are first, fourth, seventh, tenth, and twelfth. By looking at several ages across almost three decades, we observed trends in typical developmental patterns of retention and of differentials in retention.

From 1972 to 1998, the October CPS data files include between 57,500 and 63,500 cases at each age. The file attaches characteristics of school-age youth and of their households to enrollment data (Hauser, Jordan, and Dixon 1993; Hauser and Hauser 1993). The individual data include race-ethnicity, enrollment status, grade level, region of residence, and metropolitan location. The linked characteristics of the household and householders include family income, the number of children in the household, whether it is a single-parent household, the education of the household head and the spouse of the head, whether the head or spouse has no occupation, the occupation of the head and of the spouse, and housing tenure. However, the CPS data lack any measure of academic achievement.

In Hauser, Pager, and Simmons (2000), we carried out logistic regression analyses of enrollment below modal grade level versus enrollment at or above modal grade level at each age. Our estimates for six-year-olds are shown in table 7.1. Columns 1, 2, and 3 show the effect of each variable alone, with no other variables controlled, and columns 4, 5, and 6 show effects when all of the variables have been entered in the equation. Estimated effects of race-ethnicity show lower odds of age-grade retardation among African Americans and "others" than among non-Hispanic whites or Hispanics. One strong and expected effect is that of gender: the odds of boys' enrollment below the first grade, other things being equal, are 40 percent higher than those of girls. Also, the odds of age-grade retardation are lower in major central cities than in other areas, and lower in the East than in other regions. Otherwise, the effects of social and economic background characteristics are modest, reflecting the lack of social and economic differentiation in age at school entry.

At each successive age, social and geographic differentials become more pronounced: gross race-ethnic differentials become larger; the effects of socioeconomic background variables increase; central cities become notably more likely to have overage students than suburbs; and regional differences between the South and all other regions become sharper. For example, table 7.2 shows estimates from Hauser, Pager, and Simmons (2000) for seventeen-year-old youth. Students in the South are significantly more likely to be below modal grade for age. The regional differences hold for cities as well as for the whole region: southern cities have the highest rates of age-grade retardation, while northern and western cities have the lowest rates. Also, there is increasing differentiation between central cities and their suburbs with increases in age. By age seventeen, rates of age-grade retardation are roughly one-third higher in the largest central cities than in their suburbs, after controlling social background characteristics.

Perhaps most striking in our findings were the net effects of social background relative to the race-ethnic differentials. The odds of age-grade retardation (or dropout) at age seventeen were about two and a half times larger among African Americans and Hispanics than among white non-Hispanics. However, once the full set of social background and geographic characteristics were controlled, the major differences among the race-ethnic groups disappeared. The most important effects were the structural and socioeconomic characteristics of families, not the geographic characteristics (regional, central city, or suburban location). For example, a one-unit change in the log of family income reduced the odds of age-grade retardation by 20 percent, and homeownership reduced the odds by more than 35 percent. Actually, relative to other age groups, the seventeen-year-olds showed exceptionally large net effects of race-ethnicity. Although most of the very large race-ethnic differential at age seventeen is explained by the other variables in the model, there remain modestly larger odds of age-grade retardation among minorities. At other ages, although the raw odds of falling behind were about twice as great in minority groups as among whites, the race-ethnicity differentials were negligible after social background and geographic location were controlled. These findings also held in separate analyses of data from the 1970s, the 1980s, and the 1990s. Thus, over the past three decades there has been little evidence of direct race-ethnic discrimination in progress through the elementary and secondary grades.

However, these findings do not clearly demonstrate that there is no discrimination against minorities in progression through school. Given the large and ubiquitous race-ethnic differentials in achievement test scores, we should expect that minority students will have substantially *lower* rates of age-grade retardation than whites, if academic achievement as well as social and economic background variables are controlled. Thus, the absence of net differences in age-grade retardation, when social background but not academic achievement is controlled, suggests that minorities are subject to lower academic standards than whites. Some analysts suggest that the appearance of parity in age-grade relationships indicates a different form of discrimination, the absence of high academic standards. A corollary of these observations is that the recent movement toward high-stakes testing for promotion could magnify race-ethnic differentials in retention.

(*Text continues on p. 296.*)

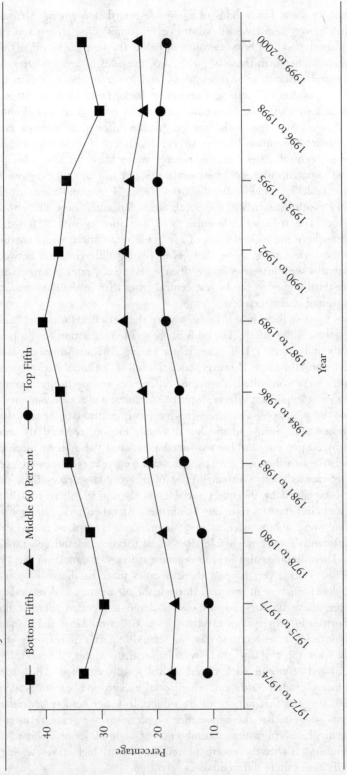

FIGURE 7.11   Children Age Six to Eight Who Were Enrolled Below the Modal Grade Level or Not Enrolled in School, by Family Income Group and Survey Year

Source: U.S. Department of Commerce, U.S. Census Bureau, October Current Population Survey, uniform files, 1972 to 2000.

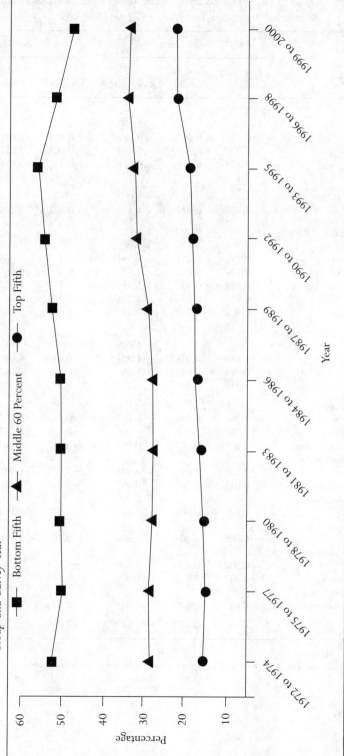

FIGURE 7.12   Children Age Fifteen to Seventeen Who Were Enrolled Below the Modal Grade Level or Had Dropped Out of School, by Family Income Group and Survey Year

Bottom Fifth   Middle 60 Percent   Top Fifth

Percentage

Year

1972 to 1974
1975 to 1977
1978 to 1980
1981 to 1983
1984 to 1986
1987 to 1989
1990 to 1992
1993 to 1995
1996 to 1998
1999 to 2000

Source: U.S. Department of Commerce, U.S. Census Bureau, October Current Population Survey, uniform files, 1972 to 2000.

TABLE 7:1   *Effects of Geographic Location, Social Background, and Year on Age-Grade Retardation Among Six-Year-Olds, 1972 to 1998*

	Gross Effect			Net Effect		
	Coefficient	Standard Error	EXP (Coefficient)	Coefficient	Standard Error	EXP (Coefficient)
Race-ethnicity						
White	—	—	1.000	—	—	1.000
African American	−0.375	0.041	0.687	−0.313	0.048	0.732
Hispanic	0.026	0.044	1.026	0.004	0.052	1.004
Other	−0.209	0.068	0.811	−0.382	0.071	0.682
Gender						
Female	—	—	1.000	—	—	1.000
Male	0.346	0.026	1.414	0.361	0.026	1.435
Metropolitan status						
Major central city	—	—	1.000	—	—	1.000
Major suburb	0.295	0.064	1.344	0.272	0.068	1.313
Smaller central city	0.438	0.062	1.549	0.465	0.064	1.592
Smaller suburb	0.439	0.059	1.551	0.447	0.063	1.564
Nonmetropolitan	0.710	0.056	2.035	0.678	0.061	1.971
Not identifiable	0.806	0.059	2.238	0.685	0.064	1.984
Region						
East	—	—	1.000	—	—	1.000
Midwest	0.684	0.038	1.983	0.688	0.040	1.989
South	0.226	0.040	1.254	0.171	0.042	1.187
West	0.345	0.041	1.411	0.248	0.043	1.281
Family background						
Log (family income)	−0.108	0.014	0.897	−0.086	0.020	0.918
Homeownership	−0.041	0.026	0.960	−0.065	0.032	0.937
Head's K–12 education	−0.003	0.007	0.997	−0.022	0.008	0.979
Head's postsecondary education	−0.002	0.007	0.998	−0.003	0.010	0.997
Spouse's K–12 education	−0.013	0.008	0.987	−0.015	0.010	0.985
Spouse's postsecondary education	0.025	0.008	1.025	0.029	0.011	1.030
Head's occupational status	−0.009	0.007	0.991	0.007	0.009	1.007
Spouse's occupational status	0.000	0.010	1.000	−0.023	0.012	0.977
Non-intact family	−0.012	0.030	0.988	−0.105	0.043	0.900
Total number of children in household	0.017	0.009	1.018	0.048	0.010	1.049
Constant	—	—	—	−2.699	0.246	0.067

Source: Author's compilation.

Note: Analyses also controlled for year and for missing data on some household variables. N = 60,506.

TABLE 7.2   *Effects of Geographic Location, Social Background, and Year on Age-Grade Retardation Among Seventeen-Year-Olds, 1972 to 1998*

	Gross Effect			Net Effect		
	Coefficient	Standard Error	EXP (Coefficient)	Coefficient	Standard Error	EXP (Coefficient)
Race-ethnicity						
White	—	—	1.000	—	—	1.000
African American	0.868	0.026	2.381	0.098	0.032	1.103
Hispanic	0.980	0.034	2.663	0.106	0.042	1.112
Other	0.511	0.049	1.668	0.124	0.055	1.132
Gender						
Female	—	—	—	—	—	1.000
Male	0.537	0.019	1.711	0.611	0.020	1.841
Metropolitan status						
Major central city	—	—	1.000	—	—	1.000
Major suburb	−0.886	0.040	0.412	−0.315	0.044	0.730
Smaller central city	−0.283	0.038	0.753	−0.064	0.042	0.938
Smaller suburb	−0.625	0.035	0.535	−0.136	0.041	0.873
Nonmetropolitan	−0.444	0.033	0.641	−0.195	0.040	0.823
Not identifiable	−0.556	0.037	0.574	−0.123	0.044	0.884
Region						
East	—	—	1.000	—	—	1.000
Midwest	−0.010	0.027	0.990	0.095	0.029	1.100
South	0.351	0.026	1.420	0.224	0.029	1.251
West	0.019	0.029	1.019	−0.027	0.032	0.973
Family background						
Log (family income)	−0.657	0.012	0.518	−0.234	0.016	0.791
Homeownership	−0.952	0.021	0.386	−0.458	0.025	0.633
Head's K–12 education	−0.150	0.004	0.861	−0.073	0.005	0.929
Head's postsecondary education	−0.149	0.006	0.862	−0.051	0.008	0.950
Spouse's K–12 education	−0.205	0.006	0.815	−0.086	0.007	0.917
Spouse's postsecondary education	−0.122	0.008	0.885	−0.013	0.010	0.987
Head's occupational status	−0.202	0.005	0.817	−0.054	0.007	0.947
Spouse's occupational status	−0.203	0.008	0.817	−0.056	0.010	0.945
Non-intact family	0.632	0.021	1.882	0.238	0.032	1.269
Total number of children in household	0.150	0.006	1.162	0.106	0.007	1.112
Constant	—	—	—	3.087	0.182	21.902

Source: Author's compilation.
Note: Analyses also controlled for year and for missing data on some household variables. N = 57,564.

If the large, observed race-ethnic differentials in age-grade retardation over the past three decades can largely be explained by group differences in family structure and social background, it follows that the effects of the latter variables are also large and persistent. Economic and social analysts tend to identify income as the key policy variable in child outcomes, but the estimates in table 7.2 show that each of a larger set of background characteristics has important effects on age-grade retardation. These include parental education and occupation, family structure, number of children in the household, and housing tenure, as well as family income. From existing research, it is not clear whether this array of background characteristics actually affects retention directly or whether its influence is largely or entirely mediated by academic performance. It should be possible to address this question, using data from the National Longitudinal Survey of 1988, by observing grade retention *after* the initial survey and test administration at the eighth-grade level.

Effects of Grade Retention

Retention in grade is not a negative outcome if it benefits the student. Are there positive consequences of being held back in school? Do students do better after repeating a grade, or would they have fared just as well or better if promoted with their peers? Research data indicate that simply repeating a grade does not generally improve achievement (Hauser 2001; Holmes 1989; House 1989; Jimerson 2001; McCoy and Reynolds 1999; Reynolds 1992). Furthermore, there is overwhelming evidence that retention increases school dropout (Gampert and Opperman 1988; Grissom and Shepard 1989; Anderson 1994; Darling-Hammond and Falk 1995; Luppescu et al. 1995; Reardon 1996; Hauser, Simmons, and Pager 2000; Alexander, Entwisle, and Kabbani 2001, 767, 775). Indeed, the latter findings might be traced back to Ayres's (1909, 139–40) seminal observations about the link between promotion, age, and school-leaving. Some recent studies have reported favorable effects of retention on academic achievement, but without exception, these have all been subject to methodological criticism because of poor research design or questionable interpretations of data (Alexander, Entwisle, and Dauber 1994; Shepard, Smith, and Marion 1996; Karweit 1999; Dworkin 1999; Lorence et al. 2002; Shepard 2002; Roderick et al. 1999, 12–13; Moore 1999, 3; Roderick et al. 2000). I have reviewed several of these studies elsewhere (Hauser 2001).

It would perhaps be too much to say that grade retention cannot possibly succeed in raising academic performance more than the obvious alternative—promotion with remediation—but surely there is no compelling evidence that it increases academic achievement on a large scale or in the long term. To be sure, the available evidence is almost all based on typical educational practice, and we might believe that new practices would yield more favorable outcomes. However, if there are effective new practices, why not use valid assessments to identify students with learning difficulties and intervene before retention is the only alternative?

One of the greatest limitations of retention research is that, with the exception of three very early studies, there are no true field experiments. Many educational researchers dismiss this option because, they believe, it would be unethical. But if we truly do not know whether retention helps or hurts low-performing students, why would it be unethical to assign volunteers among low-performing students to either retention or promotion? Would this be any less ethical, say, than creating the variations in class size that have led to new understanding of the value of very small class sizes in the primary grades (Mosteller, Light, and Sachs 1996) ? If there is truly continuing disagreement about the observational evidence on retention and academic achievement, then a large-scale field experiment is a logical choice (Burtless 2002; Krueger 1999). Surely, such an experiment would be preferable to massive interference in the lives of America's most vulnerable children.

HIGH SCHOOL DROPOUT AND HIGH SCHOOL COMPLETION

There is no doubt that failure to complete high school limits social and economic life chances. Noncompleters have poor chances of employment, and those chances grew worse relative to those of high school graduates from the mid-1970s until the economic boom of the late 1990s. At ages twenty-five to thirty-four, the earnings of noncompleters are typically 20 percent less than those of graduates among men and 30 percent less among women. Electoral participation by high school dropouts is less than among high school graduates, and the gap has widened since the mid-1960s (National Center for Education Statistics 1994, 100–1). Illustrative differentials between dropouts and graduates could be elaborated endlessly. Failure to obtain at least a high school diploma looks more and more like the contemporary equivalent of functional illiteracy. High school dropout indicates a failure to pass minimum thresholds of economic, social, or political motivation, access, and competence.

Whether or not a person has completed a high school education would appear to be a simple matter of fact, yet there are diverse indicators of high school dropout and completion and diverse opinions about trends and differentials in them. In this section, I review evidence related to trends and to social and economic differentials in high school dropout and completion.[21] I then connect the two major sections of this chapter by turning to evidence about the relationship between grade retention and high school dropout.

Among the highly publicized "National Educational Goals" (U.S. Department of Education 1990), 90 percent high school completion was cited as one of six primary goals.[22] Since the mid-1980s, there has been a steady stream of new reports about the familial and socioeconomic origins of high school dropout (McLanahan 1985; Ekstrom et al. 1986; Krein and Beller 1988; Astone and McLanahan 1991; Haveman, Wolfe, and Spaulding 1991; Sandefur, McLanahan, and Wojtkiewicz 1992; Rumberger and Larson 1998; Hauser, Simmons, and Pager 2000), and the National Center for Education Statistics has produced a regular series of annual reports on trends and differentials in high school dropout (Frase 1989; Kaufman and Frase 1990; Kaufman, McMillen, and Whitener 1991; Kaufman et al. 1992; McMillen et al. 1993; McMillen, Kaufman, and Whitener 1994; McMillen and Kaufman 1996, 1997; McMillen 1997; Kaufman, Klein, and Frase 1999; Kaufman, Kwon, et al. 1999, 2001; Kaufman, Alt, and Chapman 2001). Thus, the association of high school dropout with educational and economic deprivation, minority status, and family disruption is well documented, as is the global trend in high school dropout, which has generally—but not always—declined since the 1970s.

The possible consequences for high school dropout of higher educational standards—especially test-based promotion and graduation—have stimulated new interest in dropout. Many believe that higher standards—or the expectation of eventual failure—will accelerate decisions to leave school on the part of marginal students (Lillard and DeCicca 2001). Some argue that high standards create pressure on school administrators, as well as on students, to leave school early if they have poor chances of graduation (Haney 2000). Others declare that lower rates of high school completion are acceptable if that is the price of higher demonstrated competence among those who persist to graduation (Hayward 2000). However, there is as yet little evidence about the effects of higher standards on school dropout, on eventual high school completion, or, for that matter, on the academic achievements of high school graduates. That is, we are still poorly equipped to assess the costs and benefits of the trade-offs between the quality and quantity of high school graduates that may be entailed in standards-driven educational reforms.

It is not clear how long we may have to wait to observe the effects of educational policy changes on dropout rates, or whether the effects of visible policy changes may be swamped by other changes—for example, changes in overall economic activity (Duncan 1967). To provide an appropriate baseline to monitor future changes, I outline the recent social and historic context of high school dropout: How much high school dropout is there? Who drops out of high school? What are the major social and economic characteristics affecting high school dropout? What do we know about the connection between age-grade retention and high school dropout?

Measuring High School Dropout and Completion

School-leaving is a process that takes place over time, and it is not an irreversible process. Many students leave and return to high school (Anderson 1994). Thus, the fact that some-one of high school age has not completed high school and is not currently enrolled does not imply that he or she will not eventually return to school and graduate. The problem of measuring dropout is compounded—for both statistical and practical purposes—by the fact that many youth gain high school equivalency credentials, typically by passing the General Educational Development (GED) examination, and often without enrolling in a regular school. Since 1990 the U.S. Census Bureau has confounded high school diplomas with completion of the GED by combining those two forms of certification in its definition of high school graduation, while adding a category of persons who completed twelve years of schooling but do not hold a high school diploma. Immigration creates additional problems in the measurement of dropout and high school completion. Especially in populations of His-panic or Asian origin, many persons of school age, as well as older persons, may have had little exposure to American schools. In these populations, noncompletion of high school is not a valid indicator of high school dropout per se. For these reasons, among others, there is no one preferred measure of high school dropout or completion; the progress of populations through high school must be assessed with multiple measures.[23]

Figure 7.13 shows time series, by gender, of the annual high school dropout rate used in periodic reports of the National Center for Education Statistics (Kaufman, Alt, and Chapman 2001). The rate rose from just over 5 percent to over 6 percent between 1967 and 1974, after which it declined regularly to about 4 percent in 1991. This is a very large decline, implying a cumulative reduction in dropout across grades ten to twelve—assuming no one returns to school—from almost 18 percent to less than 12 percent. For reasons explained later, there is a break in the series between 1991 and 1992, but the data suggest that dropout increased briefly in the early 1990s and then leveled off. Men were more likely to drop out than women between the early 1970s and the late 1980s, but before and since that period there has been little difference in high school dropout rates between women and men.

Annual dropout rates can be ascertained each year from the October Current Popula-tion Survey (Kominski 1990; Kominski and Adams 1993). Among rates that are available annually and for major population subgroups, this measure comes closest to recognizing that high school completion is a process that may involve repeated moves out of and back into school. Another important advantage of the annual dropout rates is that they condition on

FIGURE 7.13   *Annual (Event) Dropout Rate by Gender, 1967 to 2000*

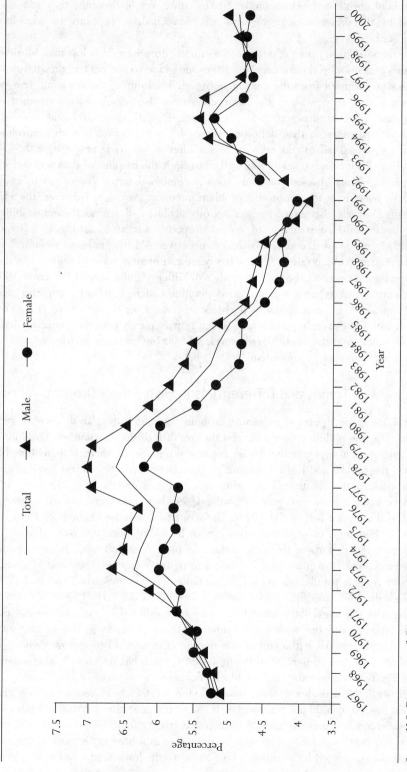

Source: U.S. Department of Commerce, U.S. Census Bureau, October Current Population Survey, as reported by National Center for Education Statistics (2002 table C–3).

Note: Entries are two-year averages at end points and three-year averages elsewhere.

prior school enrollment. Thus, unlike "status" measures of dropout, they are not directly affected by the presence of immigrants who have had no exposure to schooling in the United States.

At the same time, the definition of the annual dropout rate is less than ideal because it combines persons who do not continue from one grade to the next in the survey year with persons who drop out from the next higher grade level during the academic year preceding the survey, as if they were in the same cohort. It also fails to identify return enrollees among each year's students at each grade level. Despite these problems, the concept is useful, perhaps more so than definitions based on grade completion and enrollment by a specific age, which fail to take account of variation in age-grade progression.[24]

Perhaps to increase reliability as well as to limit the number of data series that need to be displayed, annual dropout rates are usually combined across grades ten to twelve. This also partly overcomes the conceptual problem in cohort coverage. However, the aggregation across grade levels also exacerbates a serious problem of temporal comparability in the series. Because the construction of annual dropout rates based on the October CPS has, since 1992, rested on the official distinction between "12th grade no diploma" and "high school graduate (or equivalent)," there has been a substantial upward shift in the annual rate of high school dropout in the twelfth grade (McMillen, Kaufman, and Whitener 1994, 13).[25] We may accept or reject the new census definition of high school completion, but there would appear to be a conceptual inconsistency between the definitions of grade completion at the tenth- and eleventh-grade levels, which remain purely nominal, with the definition of grade completion at the twelfth-grade level, which now excludes persons who did not earn a high school diploma or equivalent.[26]

Trends and Differentials in High School Dropout

Figure 7.14 shows the trend in annual dropout rates for three family income groups: the bottom fifth, the middle 60 percent, and the top fifth of the distribution. Dropout has been consistently much larger in the lowest income group, while there is a smaller differential between the middle and highest income groups. Dropout in the lowest income group converged modestly toward that in the other two groups from the early 1970s to 1992. There may have been a brief divergence through 1994, but movement toward convergence resumed in the second half of the 1990s. Unfortunately, because of the post-1990 changes in census methodology, these observations cannot be taken entirely at face value.

Across the past three decades, annual dropout rates followed different paths among white, black, and Hispanic youth. As shown in figure 7.15, the white and black time series have been roughly parallel but converged partially between the early 1970s and 1990. White and black dropout rates differed by about 4.5 points in the early 1970s, but only by about 2.5 points in the late 1980s. Since 1992 they have differed by only 1.6 to 2.3 percentage points. Hispanic dropout rates were similar to those of blacks in the 1970s, but they diverged sharply upward at the end of that decade. The annual dropout rate among Hispanics peaked at more than 10 percent in the mid-1990s, but it has since declined, remaining a few percentage points above the rate for black youth.

Figure 7.16 provides a very different view of trends in race-ethnic differentials in progress toward high school completion. It shows the educational status of white, black, and Hispanic youth between the ages of sixteen and twenty-four[27]—specifically, the percentage of all youth in the age range who were not enrolled in school in October of the survey year and had not completed high school.[28] There is a steady downward trend in the series among

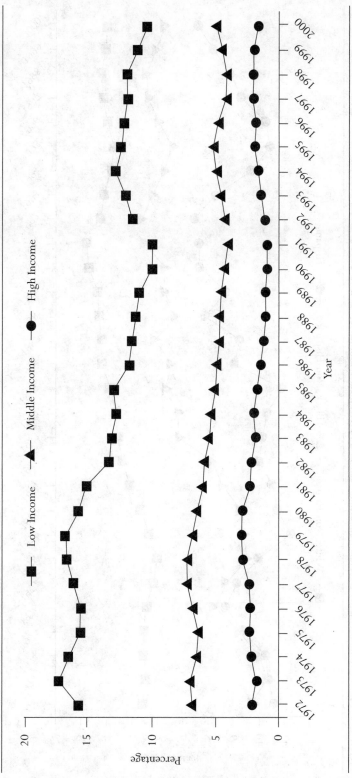

FIGURE 7.14 — Annual (Event) Dropout Rate from Grades Ten to Twelve, by Family Income, 1972 to 2000

■ Low Income ▲ Middle Income ● High Income

Source: U.S. Department of Commerce, U.S. Census Bureau, October Current Population Survey, as reported by National Center for Education Statistics (2002 table B-3).
Note: Entries are two-year averages at end points and three-year averages elsewhere.

FIGURE 7.15   Annual (Event) Dropout from Grades Ten to Twelve, by Race-Ethnicity, 1972 to 2000

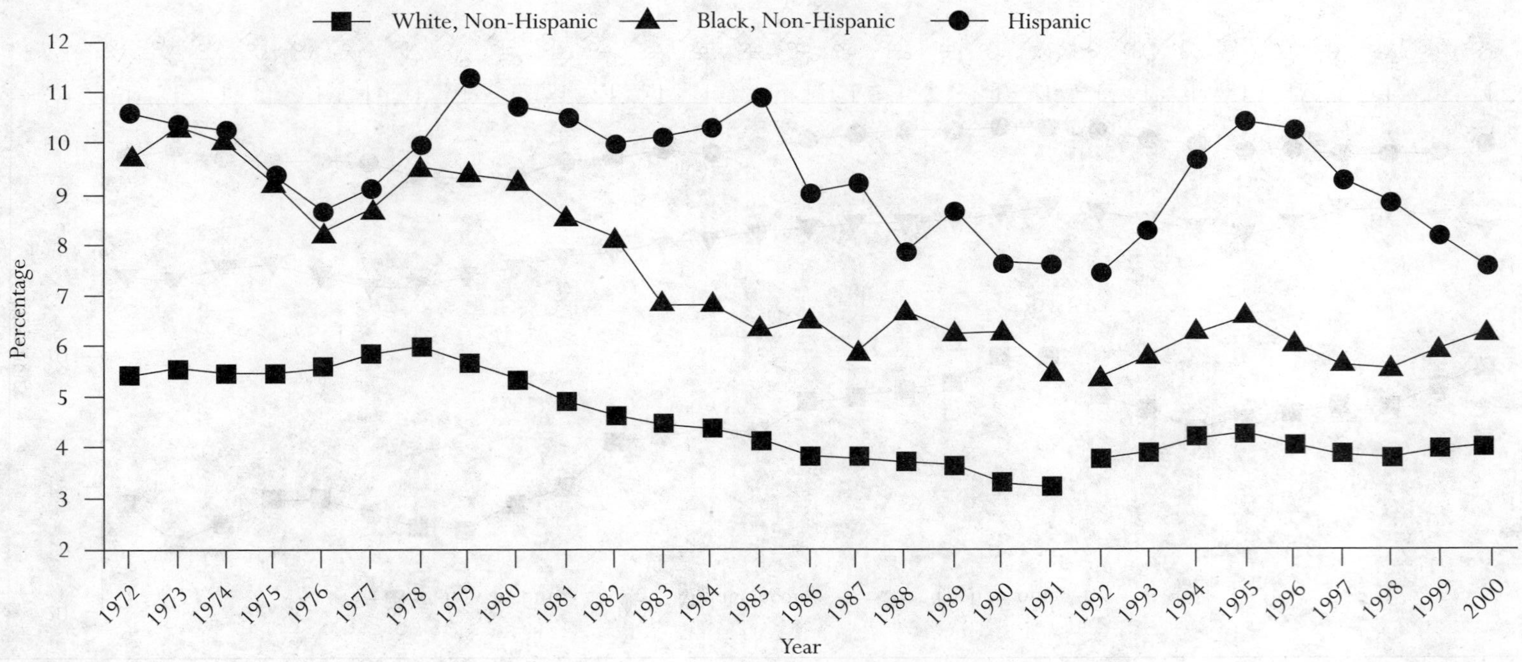

Source: U.S. Department of Commerce, U.S. Census Bureau, October Current Population Survey, as reported by National Center for Education Statistics (2002 table C-3).

Note: Entries are two-year averages at end points and three-year averages elsewhere.

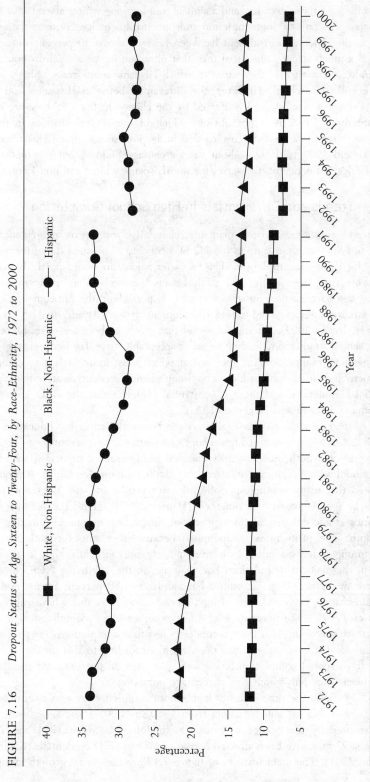

FIGURE 7.16   Dropout Status at Age Sixteen to Twenty-Four, 1972 to 2000

Legend:
- ■ White, Non-Hispanic
- ▲ Black, Non-Hispanic
- ● Hispanic

Percentage (y-axis): 5, 10, 15, 20, 25, 30, 35, 40

Year (x-axis): 1972, 1973, 1974, 1975, 1976, 1977, 1978, 1979, 1980, 1981, 1982, 1983, 1984, 1985, 1986, 1987, 1988, 1989, 1990, 1991, 1992, 1993, 1994, 1995, 1996, 1997, 1998, 1999, 2000

Source: U.S. Department of Commerce, U.S. Census Bureau, October Current Population Survey, as reported by National Center for Education Statistics (2002 table B-5).

Note: Entries are three-year averages.

blacks across the past three decades, and a similar trend among whites after 1980. However, among Hispanics the rate of noncompletion and nonenrollment has consistently been much higher than in the other two groups: it has been near or above 30 percent since the early 1970s. This is a much larger differential than that observed in the annual dropout rate, and it provides indirect evidence of the extent to which Hispanic immigrants of high school age have never enrolled in school. However, the differential between Hispanics and non-Hispanics in this series was substantially affected by the change in the CPS measure of educational attainment in 1992. It is not obvious which of the several changes in the census measure accounts for the abrupt downward shift in dropout status among Hispanics between 1990 to 1991 and 1991 to 1992—about five percentage points—but the methodological change had far less influence on the series for non-Hispanic whites and non-Hispanic blacks.

Trends and Differentials in High School Completion

Because educational attainment is, in principle, cumulative and irreversible (Duncan 1968), it should be possible, at some time in the life of a cohort, to obtain a definitive measure of the cohort's high school completion. This is easier said than done, partly because some credentials are earned later in life, and partly because researchers and policymakers like to know how far a cohort has gone in school as early as possible in the life course. One widely used (and criticized) series is educational attainment at ages twenty-five to twenty-nine (Hauser 1997; Greene 2002). The modal age of that group is about ten years beyond typical ages at high school graduation, leading to an unacceptably large lag between the measurement of high school completion and the time at which most individuals have completed it. Moreover, many individuals obtain high school equivalency credentials after the typical ages of high school completion, and there is substantial evidence that the GED is less valuable than a diploma (Cameron and Heckman 1993).

In this context, for the past several years the National Center for Education Statistics has featured an "early" measure of high school completion: the percentage of eighteen- to twenty-four-year-old youth, not currently enrolled in high school or below, who had completed high school with a diploma (or, after 1991, with a diploma or GED). A problem with this measure is that many youth, especially minority youth, are still "on track" in regular high schools at ages eighteen and nineteen (Hauser 1997). Thus, the measure tends to exaggerate race-ethnic differentials in high school completion by underestimating it among minority youth. The problem is compounded because high school completion is highly contingent among older students, so it may indicate unrealistically high levels of school completion in the majority population. For example, in the 1990s the NCES measure was above 90 percent for non-Hispanic whites but barely over 80 percent among non-Hispanic blacks. An alternative, early measure of high school completion that I have suggested elsewhere (Hauser 1997) is the percentage of *all* persons who have completed high school by ages twenty to twenty-four. This share is modestly less than completions by ages twenty-five to twenty-nine, and it covers the entire population. According to this measure, during the 1990s white high school completion levels were just over 85 percent, and the completion rate among blacks was only about five percentage points less.

Figure 7.17 shows the time series of high school completion by ages twenty to twenty-four among whites, blacks, and Hispanics from 1970 to 2000. These series were not substantially disrupted by the change in census methodology between 1991 and 1992, but growth after 1992 may have been affected by the growth in GED credentials (Kaufman, Alt, and Chapman 2001). The main features of figure 7.17 are the glacial growth in high school completion among whites—about five percentage points over three decades—the rapid growth in high school completion among young African Americans—from barely 60 percent in 1970 to more than 80 percent throughout the 1990s—and the consistently poor showing of Hispanics.[29] In that group the only sustained improvement in high school completion was an increase from 60 to 65 percent during the 1990s. At the end of the twentieth century the gap in high school completion between Hispanics and blacks was about the same as that between blacks and whites thirty years earlier.

National, State, and Local Estimates of Dropout

It is difficult to monitor rates of high school dropout and completion at the national level; it is much harder to do so at the state or local level. The annual NCES dropout reports have for some years included averaged annual rates of high school completion (among persons not enrolled in school) at ages eighteen to twenty-four (Kaufman, Alt, and Chapman 2001). Because of the small number of sample cases in many states, this statistic is not highly reliable, and the defects of excluding enrolled students and including persons at ages eighteen and nineteen remain. The NCES has also reported averaged annual dropout rates for states from a federal-state cooperative program, part of the Common Core of Data (CCD). This program developed estimates of the annual dropout rate from public schools in each state that would be comparable to those in the Current Population Survey (Kaufman, Alt, and Chapman 2001, 59–61). However, only twenty-seven states comply fully with the statistical standards of the CCD, and only nine other states use methods that are similar enough to justify publication of their series in the NCES reports (Winglee et al. 2000). A recently published compendium of these estimates (Young and Hoffman 2002) covers the years 1991 to 1992 through 1997 to 1998 and classifies dropout and completion only by year, locality, gender, and race-ethnicity.

In the fall of 2001 there was national media coverage of a privately funded effort to produce a comparable series of estimates of high school graduation at the national, state, and local levels (Greene 2002).[30] Jay Greene proposes to estimate the high school graduation rate as the ratio of the number of high school diplomas awarded in the spring of 1998 to the number of youth enrolled in the eighth grade in the fall of 1993, after the base enrollment estimate was adjusted for change in the size of the total school population across the four-year period. His scheme yields a national graduation rate of 71 percent, far less than that estimated from CPS data, and he attributes the difference largely to the inclusion of the GED in CPS-based estimates of high school completion.

Greene surely has a valid point in arguing for the exclusion of the GED from the definition of high school completion, but beyond that his scheme has no merit. In fact, it joins the ranks of numerous, equally flawed efforts to estimate high school completion as the ratio of diplomas awarded to school enrollment in a prior year. First, at the state or local level—and even at the national level—there is a problem of population closure: students move across district, state, and national boundaries. Second, and perhaps more important—notwithstanding Greene's (2002, 3) protests to the contrary—the number of students enrolled in a prior year is not an appropriate base population for calculation of a graduation rate in a system where students are retained in grade. The reason—well understood a century ago by Leonard Ayres (1909, chs. 3, 5, and 6)—is that retained students contribute repeatedly to the denominator of such "rates," leading to a downward bias in them.[31] A student can appear in the numerator of Greene's "rate" only once, but he or she may appear in the denominator many times. Another way to see the weakness of Greene's

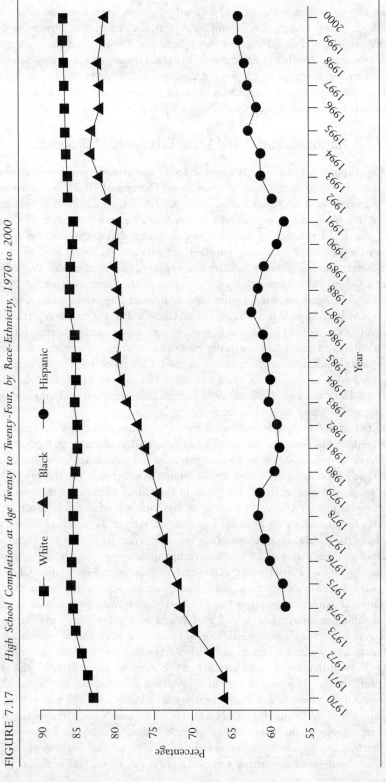

FIGURE 7.17 High School Completion at Age Twenty to Twenty-Four, by Race-Ethnicity, 1970 to 2000

Source: U.S. Department of Commerce, U.S. Census Bureau, October Current Population Survey.
Note: Entries are two-year averages at end points and three-year averages elsewhere.

effort is simply to look at the time series in figure 7.17: however inappropriate, the inclusion of the GED in the post-1991 classification of high school graduates had relatively little impact on the time series.

MULTIVARIATE ANALYSIS OF HIGH SCHOOL DROPOUT

My colleagues and I (Hauser, Simmons, and Pager 2000) have reported a comprehensive analysis of social and economic factors affecting high school dropout over the past three decades, based on annual dropout data from the October Current Population Survey, 1972 to 1998. Our analysis links enrollment data for more than 165,000 persons of school age with the social and economic characteristics of their households, that is, the characteristics of families and parents. Few students in the tenth to twelfth grades live outside a parental or quasi-parental household, so there is little missing data.[32] It is not possible to carry out parallel analyses of dropout status (at ages sixteen to twenty-four) or of high school completion (at ages eighteen to twenty-four or ages twenty to twenty-four) because many children no longer live with their parents by age twenty.[33] As with all analyses based on census-type data, we did not have a measure of academic ability or achievement.

There are problems of population coverage in the Current Population Survey, especially for black males. For example, for Current Population Surveys in 1996, the U.S. Census Bureau reports coverage ratios of 0.83 for black men at ages sixteen to nineteen and 0.66 for black men at ages twenty to twenty-nine.[34] Excepting Hispanic men, for whom coverage is also poor, these are much lower than coverage ratios for other combinations of age, gender, and race-ethnicity, which typically range from 0.85 to 0.95 (U.S. Department of Commerce 2000, table 16.1). The coverage problem is corrected to some degree by the weighting procedures used by the Census Bureau.

For all covered youth, we knew age, sex, race-ethnicity, grade at risk, region of residence, and metropolitan location (Hauser, Simmons, and Pager 2000). We linked several relevant social and economic characteristics of the household and householders to the youth's record: female-headed household, employment status of household head, number of children in household, education of head, education of spouse of head, occupation of head, family income, and housing tenure.

Some believe that school location in cities versus suburbs accounts for a large share of race-ethnic differentials in dropout. For that reason, we examined trends and differentials in school dropout by location during three periods: 1972 to 1980, 1981 to 1989, and 1990 to 1998. Dropout is consistently greater in central cities. For example, during the 1990s the cumulative dropout rate was 18.0 percent in major central cities and 19.2 percent in other central cities, while it was 10.2 percent and 11.9 percent in their respective suburban rings.[35] In addition, the overall decline in school dropout appears in almost all areas. The decline is most consistent in the large central cities, from 23.1 in the 1970s to 21.6 in the 1980s and 18.0 in the 1990s. The largest decrease in dropout occurred in the other (small metropolitan and nonmetropolitan) areas between the 1970s and 1980s—from 19.0 percent to 13.7 percent.

The same differentials and trends by metropolitan status occurred for each major race-ethnic group. For example, clear differences in dropout between central cities and their rings occurred for whites, as for African Americans, along with a decrease in dropout rates across time. In the 1990s the cumulative dropout rate was 12.8 percent among whites and 15.0 percent among African Americans in the major central cities, while it was 8.3 percent among whites and only 7.3 percent among blacks in the suburban rings of those cities. In other metropolitan areas, dropout was 17.0 percent among whites and 19.9 percent among blacks in the central cities, but there was a much larger differential in the suburban ring— 10.3 percent among whites and 17.3 percent among blacks. Thus, neither the differential in dropout between African Americans and whites nor that between central cities and their rings is merely a consequence of racial separation between schools in those two types of areas. However, it should also be kept in mind that minorities are more likely than non-Hispanic whites to be located in the central cities, where dropout rates are higher.

The social and economic characteristics of youth and their families have large effects on school dropout. Table 7.3 shows our estimates of these effects in the 1970s, 1980s, and 1990s. Overall, dropout increases with grade level during the high school years, and the chances of dropout are much larger in the twelfth grade than in the tenth or eleventh grades. Men are consistently more likely to drop out of school than women. Family and socioeconomic characteristics have the expected effects on dropout. For example, higher family income and parental educational attainment reduce the risk of dropout, while living in a single-parent family increases the risk substantially, especially among whites. Youth who live in households with small numbers of other children and in owner-occupied housing are unlikely to drop out.

The effects of social and economic background variables on school dropout have varied modestly over the past three decades, but there has been no global tendency for them either to increase or decrease. For example, the effect of family income was −.290 in the 1970s, −.255 in the 1980s, and −.330 in the 1990s. The only family background variable whose effect even appears to have increased regularly across time is living in a female-headed family. After controlling other variables, residence in a female-headed family increased the odds of school dropout by about 19 percent in the 1970s, by 23 percent in the 1980s, and by almost 46 percent in the 1990s. However, even with more than 165,000 observations, the difference between the effect in the 1970s and that in the 1990s is not statistically significant at even the 5 percent level.

The distributions of many of the social and family background variables have not changed substantially across the past three decades, but there has been a notable increase in single-family households, a decrease in the number of children in households, and a substantial increase in parental levels of education. These changes in social background account for part, but not all, of the decline in high school dropout among blacks and whites from the 1970s to the 1990s.

There are very large differences in social, economic, and family background between white, black, and Hispanic youth. We have seen that observed differences in high school dropout among the groups are quite large, but we find that these are fully explained by intergroup differences in background (Hauser, Simmons, and Pager 2000). The estimated effects of being anything other than white and non-Hispanic are negative in table 7.3. That is, social background rather than race-ethnicity per se accounts for the intergroup differences in high school dropout. Moreover, since our analysis does not control for academic achievement, while blacks and Hispanics perform far below whites, our findings imply that minority dropout levels are much lower than those among whites with similar levels of academic achievement and social background.

We also found that age has *very* large effects on school dropout. For example, independent of all other variables, black youth were 150 percent more likely to drop out at age nineteen than at age seventeen and 300 percent more likely to drop out at age twenty than at age seventeen. The effects of age are similar, but somewhat smaller, among whites and Hispanics. Since grade level is constant in our analyses, by construction, the implication is that students who are over-age for grade are exceptionally likely to drop out of high school. We were scarcely novel in pointing to the role of age-grade retardation in school dropout. Our work simply documented, on a large scale and across several decades, a finding that has appeared in one study after another (Grissom and Shepard 1989; Temple, Reynolds, and Miedel 2000; Roderick 1993; Anderson 1994; Rumberger and Larson 1998; Alexander, Entwisle, and Dauber 1994).

THE POLICY CONTEXT OF GRADE RETENTION AND SCHOOL DROPOUT

The continuing push for higher standards in elementary and secondary education, exemplified by the policy initiatives of the Clinton and Bush administrations, has seemingly obvious implications for high school completion and dropout. As grade retention increases, high school dropout will eventually increase as well, though perhaps with a delay of some years. When a child is retained in the third or fourth grade, with the best of intentions, the stage is set for that child to be over-age for grade some years later during high school. The belief, contrary to most evidence, that retention is helpful to students is sustained in part by the lengthy gap between the retention decision and its effects.

The future course of high school dropout will probably also be affected by the combination of grade retention practices with the use of high-stakes tests, both to retain students and to certify their competence as high school graduates. The direct effect of a high school exit exam is to deny high school diplomas to students who fail the test—usually after repeated administrations of it. In the terms of the educational classification system now used by the U.S. census, exit test failure classifies students as having completed twelve years of school, but with no diploma. Such individuals are classified as dropouts or noncompleters unless they subsequently pass a high school equivalency examination. It is less clear how these people will fare in the labor market—or even in access to postsecondary education. The available evidence, for example, from the Texas Academic Assessment System (TAAS) and the Massachusetts Comprehensive Assessment System (MCAS), suggests much higher failure rates will occur in minority populations than among non-Hispanic whites. A similarly large-scale trial of exit examinations is about to take place in New York State and several other states. It is not clear whether such tests will be modified to increase pass rates, or whether a backlash against their use will occur when very large numbers of students fail.

Exit exams may also have important indirect effects on high school completion. First, there has been widespread speculation that the introduction of high school exit exams will discourage many poorly performing students from continuing in high school. There is as yet little evidence to support or disprove this hypothesis. Second, in Texas, Walter Haney (2000) has argued, there is administrative and political pressure on schools to achieve high pass rates on the TAAS, which is first administered in the tenth grade. This pressure leads to very high retention rates, especially of minority students, in the ninth grade—and to their early departure from high school.[36] This is a highly controversial argument (Toenjes and Dworkin 2002; Haney 2001; Carnoy, Loeb, and Smith 2001), and the evidence for and against it deserves detailed examination. One of the ironies of current debates about the effects of TAAS is that much of the evidence so far proposed is based on ratios of high school completion in a target year to enrollment in the ninth or sixth grade three or six years earlier. Such data bear the same fatal flaw that Leonard Ayres (1909, chs. 3, 5, and 6) identified a century ago in parallel data about the completion of elementary school: cumulative retention invalidates earlier grade-level populations as a base for the graduation rate.

TABLE 7.3   Effects of Social Background and Geographic Location on High School Dropout in the 1970s, 1980s, and 1990s

	1970s (N = 66,762)			1980s (N = 56,567)			1990s (N = 44,064)		
	Coefficient	Standard Error	EXP (Coefficient)	Coefficient	Standard Error	EXP (Coefficient)	Coefficient	Standard Error	EXP (Coefficient)
Race-ethnicity									
White	—	—	1.000	—	—	1.000	—	—	1.000
African-American	−0.654	0.058	0.520	−0.527	0.070	0.590	−0.667	0.086	0.513
Hispanic	−0.593	0.076	0.553	−0.288	0.083	0.750	−0.147	0.091	0.863
Other	−0.741	0.128	0.477	−0.660	0.118	0.517	−0.320	0.115	0.727
Gender, grade, and dependency status									
Male (grade 10 and dependent)	—	—	1.000	—	—	1.000	—	—	1.000
Female (grade 10 and dependent)	−0.425	0.065	0.654	−0.207	0.083	0.813	−0.196	0.105	0.822
Grade 11	0.406	0.067	1.500	0.273	0.084	1.314	0.477	0.108	1.612
Grade 12	1.148	0.075	3.150	0.818	0.092	2.266	2.094	0.116	8.119
Female and grade 11	0.017	0.088	1.017	−0.142	0.109	0.868	−0.025	0.137	0.975
Female and grade 12	−0.219	0.087	0.804	−0.223	0.106	0.800	−0.163	0.127	0.849
Grade 11 and nondependent	−0.214	0.126	0.807	−0.243	0.150	0.784	−0.435	0.178	0.647
Grade 12 and nondependent	−1.453	0.120	0.234	−0.987	0.140	0.373	−1.363	0.165	0.256
Nondependent	1.884	0.122	6.579	1.461	0.141	4.309	1.579	0.165	4.849
Female and nondependent	0.782	0.093	2.185	0.563	0.108	1.755	0.468	0.125	1.596
Age									
Ages fourteen and fifteen	0.871	0.087	2.389	0.326	0.128	1.385	0.464	0.142	1.590
Age sixteen	0.128	0.057	1.136	−0.146	0.076	0.865	0.171	0.089	1.186
Age seventeen	—	—	1.000	—	—	1.000	—	—	1.000
Age eighteen	−0.355	0.053	0.702	0.088	0.064	1.092	−0.324	0.079	0.723
Age nineteen	0.253	0.069	1.288	0.602	0.080	1.826	0.012	0.096	1.012
Age twenty	0.784	0.103	2.191	1.136	0.117	3.113	0.757	0.130	2.133
Ages twenty-one and twenty-two	1.094	0.113	2.987	1.673	0.122	5.326	0.895	0.147	2.447
Ages twenty-three and twenty-four	0.656	0.155	1.927	1.731	0.148	5.645	0.868	0.201	2.382

	Coefficient	SE	Odds ratio	Coefficient	SE	Odds ratio	Coefficient	SE	Odds ratio
Metropolitan status									
Major central city	—	—	1.000	—	—	1.000	—	—	1.000
Major suburb	-0.285	0.074	0.752	-0.257	0.092	0.773	-0.119	0.109	0.888
Other central city	-0.098	0.066	0.906	-0.138	0.081	0.872	0.206	0.097	1.229
Other suburb	-0.260	0.067	0.771	-0.214	0.082	0.808	-0.055	0.097	0.947
Other	-0.263	0.062	0.769	-0.353	0.075	0.703	-0.126	0.091	0.881
Region									
East	—	—	1.000	—	—	1.000	—	—	1.000
Midwest	0.134	0.053	1.143	0.093	0.066	1.098	0.259	0.080	1.295
South	0.344	0.052	1.411	0.377	0.063	1.458	0.457	0.078	1.579
West	0.295	0.056	1.342	0.401	0.066	1.494	0.272	0.080	1.313
Family background									
Log (family income)	-0.290	0.032	0.748	-0.255	0.035	0.775	-0.330	0.040	0.719
Homeownership	-0.559	0.041	0.572	-0.539	0.049	0.583	-0.518	0.059	0.596
Head's K–12 education	-0.059	0.010	0.942	-0.053	0.013	0.949	-0.039	0.017	0.962
Head's postsecondary education	-0.084	0.020	0.919	-0.139	0.024	0.870	-0.129	0.027	0.879
Spouse's K–12 education	-0.110	0.009	0.896	-0.067	0.011	0.935	-0.025	0.014	0.976
Spouse's postsecondary education	-0.116	0.022	0.890	-0.119	0.022	0.888	-0.151	0.025	0.860
Head with no occupation	0.226	0.072	1.254	0.249	0.077	1.282	0.175	0.096	1.192
Head's occupational status	-0.011	0.002	0.989	-0.010	0.002	0.990	-0.005	0.002	0.996
Head in a farm occupation	-0.418	0.097	0.659	-0.663	0.152	0.515	-0.324	0.191	0.724
Spouse's occupational status	0.000	0.010	1.000	-0.023	0.012	0.977	-0.023	0.012	0.977
Female-headed family	0.173	0.074	1.188	0.210	0.086	1.233	0.378	0.104	1.459
Total number of children in household	0.078	0.011	1.081	0.072	0.016	1.075	0.110	0.020	1.116
Constant	2.042	0.329	—	1.279	0.368	—	0.097	0.438	—

Source: Author's compilation.

Note: Analyses also control for year and for missing data on some household variables.

The TAAS system has been in place for several years, and it will soon be replaced by a new test with a higher passing threshold.[37] A definitive analysis of the aggregate and distributional effects of the TAAS could be of great value in the development and assessment of educational policy.

We might have expected high school graduation to have become virtually universal in the United States by the beginning of the twenty-first century. Instead, growth in high school completion has been glacial in most American population groups over the past thirty years. The major exception is the African American population, which made major advances during this period. Is there any reason to expect that high school education will approach universality in the current policy climate? On the contrary, new educational policies are likely to increase retention and encourage dropout in the name of high standards. Nearly a century ago, Leonard Ayres pointed to compulsory school attendance as a key to the successful extension of schooling, and he complained about school regimes that regularly retained students so as to guarantee that they would not complete elementary school before exceeding the age of compulsory student attendance. There is a similar and growing inconsistency today between the emerging school regime and the requirements of school attendance. Absent an increase in the legally permissible age at school-leaving—a policy change that is not on anyone's agenda—it is likely that high school completion will become less prevalent and less equally distributed over the coming decade.

This research was supported by the Russell Sage Foundation through its program of research on social dimensions of inequality and its visiting scholar program, and by the Vilas Estate Trust at the University of Wisconsin-Madison. The opinions expressed herein are those of the author.

NOTES

1. Angus, Mirel, and Vinovskis (1988) review the development of graded schooling in the midnineteenth century and the later introduction of age-grading. In his useful history of school-leaving in the United States, Sherman Dorn (1996) focuses on the invention of the problem of high school dropout in the early 1960s.

2. From 1974 through 1991, about half of high school graduates ages twenty-five to thirty-four had completed at least some college (U.S. Department of Commerce 2001). Beginning in 1992, the percentage with some college rose rapidly to 65 percent in 2000. From 1940 to 1974, the percentage of high school graduates with college experience rose only from 38 to 47 percent at ages thirty-five to forty-four, while the percentage of persons who graduated from high school rose from 35 to 80 percent. Thus, through much of the twentieth century the rise in college attendance and completion was driven by growth in high school completion, not by increased chances of going from high school to college.

3. In the *Boston Herald,* Ed Hayward (2000) quotes author and state school board member, Abigail Thernstrom, as saying, "Suppose the dropout rate goes up slightly, but the skills of the kids who stay become significantly stronger. We'll be better off."

4. For a striking contrast, see the account by Angus, Mirel, and Vinovskis (1988, 227–31) of the development and rationale for social promotion during the 1930s.

5. Full-text searches in these volumes for the strings "retention," "retain," "promote," and "failure" yielded no relevant hits.

6. For some historic data on age-grade retardation at the state level, see Angus, Mirel, and Vinovskis (1988, 226–27).

7. To estimate each rate, I multiplied the complements of the reported failure rates across grade levels to estimate the probability of never having failed. The complement of that probability is the estimated probability of having failed at least once.

8. Since 1990 the annual decennial censuses have been of limited value in tracking retention. The censuses of 1990 and 2000 did not obtain data on grade of current enrollment, and exact grade completed was not ascertained below the ninth grade.

9. Data on school enrollment by single years of age, grade in which enrolled, gender, and race-ethnicity have been published in aggregate form in *Current Population Reports* for all years since 1971, and the data are available in unit record form from 1968 onward.

10. The October supplement did ask specifically about grade retention in 1992 and 1995.

11. This section is based on, but updates, material in Hauser (2001).

12. The percentages include those enrolled below the first-grade level and a small share of six-year-olds who were not enrolled in school. The data are virtually unchanged if non-enrolled children are eliminated from the analysis: neither the trends nor the differences by race-ethnicity and gender are affected.

13. Another relevant factor is change in state or local requirements about the exact age a child must reach before entering kindergarten or first grade.

14. These data have been assembled from U.S. Department of Commerce, U.S. Census Bureau, Table A-3, "Historical Statistics: Persons Six to Seventeen Years Old Enrolled Below Modal Grade, 1971 to 2000," available at www.census.gov/population/socdemo/school/tabA-3.pdf, and from "School Enrollment: Social and Economic Characteristics of Students," *Current Population Reports,* P-20 series, nos. 241, 260, 272, 286, 303, 319, 333, 346, 360, 400, 408, 413, 426, 439, 443, 452, 460, 469, 474, 479, 487, 492, 500, 516, 521, and 533.

15. We ignore the logical possibility that age-retardation at younger ages could be counterbalanced by double-promotion at older ages.

16. Figure 7.3 is substantially revised from Hauser (2001, 162) to correct an error as well as update data through 2000. In the earlier paper, I erroneously arrayed the data to display cross-sectional differences in retention by age at the survey year, rather than arraying them by age at school entry to display intracohort change in age-grade retardation.

17. Again, early school dropout (at ages fifteen to seventeen) is counted as age-grade retardation.

18. Dropout by ages fifteen to seventeen does not indicate ultimate rates of failure to complete high school because large numbers of youth complete regular schooling through age nineteen or, alternatively, pass the GED exam through their late twenties (Hauser 1997).

19. The figures are based on my tabulations of data from the October Current Population Surveys, 1972 to 2000. Income groups are based on price-adjusted family incomes over the entire period, not on year-by-year distributions of family income.

20. Note the difference between the vertical scales of figures 7.11 and 7.12.

21. In part, this review updates Hauser (1997).

22. However, the operational definition of 90 percent high school completion has varied from time to time (Hauser 1997). Early in 2002 Congress dissolved the National Educational Goals Panel.

23. See Hauser (1997) for a more extensive review of the measurement of high school dropout and completion.

24. For further discussion of the conceptualization and measurement of high school dropout, see Kominski (1990), Pallas (1989), and Kaufman (2000). State and local estimates are discussed later in the chapter.

25. There were also minor breaks in the series between 1986 and 1987, when new editing rules were adopted, and in 1994, when the CPS began to use computer-assisted interviewing technology (Kaufman, Alt, and Chapman 2001, app. D).

26. The effect of the changing definition is especially large among overage students covered by the annual dropout concept, that is, persons ages twenty to twenty-four, and there is scarcely a blip in the series below age twenty. Thus, an alternative to revising the definition of high school completion used in the series would be to limit the dropout rate to students ages fifteen to nineteen.

27. Because individuals in the upper half of this age range are unlikely to live with their parents, it is not possible to assess differentials in this dropout measure by social and economic background using the October CPS data.

28. In principle, this measure is also affected by the post-1990 changes in the definition of high school completion, but the shift in the time series after 1991 appears to be very small.

29. Again, the rate of high school completion among Hispanics is undoubtedly lowered by the presence of poorly educated immigrants.

30. Actually, Greene (2002) produced estimates for only one year, 1998. If his estimates were valid, they could be produced for other years.

31. In this context, it is almost amusing to read Greene's (2002, 6–7) effort to explain the inconsistency between his estimate of the high school graduation rate among African Americans of 56 percent and the 73 percent high school completion rate estimated by NCES. Greene fails to consider the effect of grade retention on base enrollment in the black population, and he ends up suggesting that black youth simply lie about whether they have completed high school.

32. Over the past three decades, 3.1 percent of youths have been nondependent at the tenth-grade transition; 5 percent have been nondependent at the eleventh-grade transition; and 11.8 percent have been nondependent at the twelfth-grade transition.

33. However, it would be possible to analyze dropout *status* at a younger age, say, sixteen to nineteen, the age range within which the Annie E. Casey Foundation has recently assessed progress toward high school graduation.

34. The annual dropout measure is based on persons ages fifteen to twenty-four.

35. Cumulative dropout was estimated by projecting the effect of the annual dropout rate over a three-year period (Hauser, Simmons, and Pager 2000, 5).

36. In the *GI Forum* case, a federal judge found that the TAAS exit exam had a disparate impact on minority students, but held that its use was legal because the state of Texas had introduced the test with the intention of improving the quality of education.

37. When it was introduced, the passing standard of the TAAS was at the twenty-fifth percentile.

REFERENCES

Alexander, Karl L., Doris R. Entwisle, and Susan L. Dauber. 1994. *On the Success of Failure: A Reassessment of the Effects of Retention in the Primary Grades.* Cambridge: Cambridge University Press.

Alexander, Karl L., Doris Entwisle, and Nader S. Kabbani. 2001. "The Dropout Process in Life Course Perspective: Early Risk Factors at Home and School." *Teachers College Record* 103(5): 760–822.

American Federation of Teachers. 1997. *Passing on Failure: District Promotion Policies and Practices.* Washington, D.C.: American Federation of Teachers.

Anderson, Douglas K. 1994. "Paths Through Secondary Education: Race-Ethnic and Gender Differences." Ph.D. diss., University of Wisconsin, Madison, Department of Sociology.

Angus, David L., Jeffrey E. Mirel, and Maris A. Vinovskis. 1988. "Historical Development of Age Stratification in Schooling." *Teachers College Record* 90(2): 211–36.

Astone, Nan M., and Sara McLanahan. 1991. "Family Structure, Parental Practices, and High School Completion." *American Sociological Review* 56(3): 309–20.

Ayres, Leonard P. 1909. *Laggards in Our Schools: A Study of Retardation and Elimination in City School Systems.* New York: Charities Publication Committee.

Bianchi, Suzanne M. 1984. "Children's Progress Through School: A Research Note." *Sociology of Education* 57(3): 184–92.

Burtless, Gary. 2002. "Randomized Field Trials for Policy Evaluation: Why Not in Education?" In *Evidence Matters: Randomized Trials in Education Research,* edited by Frederick Mosteller and Robert Boruch. Washington, D.C.: Brookings Institution.

Cameron, Stephen, and James Heckman. 1993. "The Nonequivalence of High School Equivalents." *Journal of Labor Economics* 11(1, pt. 1): 1–47.

Carnoy, Martin, Susanna Loeb, and Tiffany L. Smith. 2001. "Do Higher State Test Scores in Texas Make for Better High School Outcomes?" Paper presented to the conference Dropout Research: Accurate Counts and Positive Interventions, sponsored by Achieve, Inc., and the Civil Rights Project. Harvard University, Cambridge, Mass. (January 12, 2001).

Clinton, William J. 1998. "Memorandum to the Secretary of Education." Press release. Washington: White House (February 23, 1998).

Darling-Hammond, Linda, and Beverly Falk. 1995. *Using Standards and Assessments to Support Student Learning: Alternatives to Grade Retention.* Report to the Chancellor's Committee on Grade Transition Standards, National Center for Restructuring Education, Schools and Teaching. New York: Teachers College, Columbia University.

Dorn, Sherman. 1996. *Creating the Dropout: An Institutional and Social History of School Failure.* Westport, Conn.: Praeger.

Duncan, Beverly. 1967. "Early Work Experience of Graduates and Dropouts." *Demography* 4: 19–29.

———. 1968. "Trends in Output and Distribution of Schooling." In *Indicators of Social Change: Concepts and Measurements,* edited by Eleanor B. Sheldon and Wilbert E. Moore. New York: Russell Sage Foundation.

Dworkin, A. Gary. 1999. "Elementary School Retention and Social Promotion in Texas: An Assessment of Students Who Failed the Reading Section of the TAAS." Report to the Texas Education Agency. Houston, Tx.: University of Houston, Sociology of Education Research Group.

Ekstrom, Ruth B., Margaret E. Goertz, Judith M. Pollack, and Donald A. Rock. 1986. "Who Drops Out of High School and Why? Findings from a National Study." *Teacher's College Record* 87(3): 356–73.

Frase, Mary J. 1989. *Dropout Rates in the United States: 1988.* National Center for Education Statistics analysis report 89-609. Washington: U.S. Government Printing Office.

Gampert, Richard, and Prudence Opperman. 1988. "Longitudinal Study of the 1982–83 Promotional Gates Students." Paper presented to the annual meeting of the American Educational Research Association. New Orleans (April 1988).

Greene, Jay P. 2002. *High School Graduation Rates in the United States.* New York: Manhattan Institute for Policy Research.

Grissom, James B., and Lorrie A. Shepard. 1989. "Repeating and Dropping Out of School." In *Flunking Grades: Research and Policies on Retention,* edited by Lorrie A. Shepard and Mary L. Smith. London: Falmer Press.

Haney, Walter. 2000. "The Myth of the Texas Miracle in Education." *Educational Policy Analysis Archives* 8(41). Available at http://epaa.asu.edu/epaa/v8n41.

———. 2001. "Revisiting the Myth of the Texas Miracle in Education: Lessons About Dropout Research and Prevention." Paper presented to the conference Dropout Research: Accurate Counts and Positive Interventions, sponsored by Achieve, Inc., and the Civil Rights Project. Harvard University, Cambridge, Mass. (January 12, 2001).

Hauser, Robert M. 1997. "Indicators of High School Completion and Dropout." In *Indicators of Children's Well-being,* edited by Robert M. Hauser, Brett V. Brown, and William R. Prosser. New York: Russell Sage Foundation.

———. 2001. "Should We End Social Promotion? Truth and Consequences." In *Raising Standards or Raising Barriers? Inequality and High-Stakes Testing in Public Education,* edited by Gary Orfield and Mindy L. Kornhaber. New York: Century Foundation Press.

Hauser, Robert M., and Taissa S. Hauser. 1993. *Current Population Survey, October Person-Household Files, 1968–90: Cumulative Codebook.* Madison: University of Wisconsin, Center for Demography and Ecology, Department of Sociology.

Hauser, Robert M., Linda Jordan, and James A. Dixon. 1993. *Current Population Survey, October Person-Household Files, 1968–90.* Madison: University of Wisconsin, Center for Demography and Ecology, Department of Sociology.

Hauser, Robert M., Devah I. Pager, and Solon J. Simmons. 2000. "Race-Ethnicity, Social Background, and Grade Retention." Working paper 2000-08. Madison: University of Wisconsin, Center for Demography and Ecology, Department of Sociology.

Hauser, Robert M., Solon J. Simmons, and Devah I. Pager. 2000. "High School Dropout, Race-Ethnicity, and Social Background from the 1970s to the 1990s." Working paper 2000-12. Madison: University of Wisconsin, Center for Demography and Ecology, Department of Sociology.

Haveman, Robert, Barbara L. Wolfe, and James Spaulding. 1991. "Educational Achievement and Childhood Events and Circumstances." *Demography* 28(1): 133–57.

Hayward, Ed. 2000. "MCAS Opponents Link Test to Minority Dropout Rates." *Boston Herald,* September 28, p. 22.

Holmes, C. Thomas. 1989. "Grade-Level Retention Effects: A Meta-analysis of Research Studies." In *Flunking Grades: Research and Policies on Retention,* edited by Lorrie A. Shepard and Mary L. Smith. London: Falmer Press.

House, Ernest R. 1989. "Policy Implications of Retention Research." In *Flunking Grades: Research and Policies on Retention,* edited by Lorrie A. Shepard and Mary L. Smith. London: Falmer Press.

Jimerson, Shane R. 2001. "Meta-analysis of Grade Retention Research: Implications for Practice in the Twenty-first Century." *School Psychology Review* 30(3): 420–37.

Johnston, Robert C. 1998. "Texas Governor Has Social Promotion in His Sights." *Education Week* (February 11, 1998). Available at http://www.edweek.org.

Karweit, Nancy L. 1999. "Grade Retention: Prevalence, Timing, and Effects." Center for Education of Students Placed at Risk(CRESPAR) report 33. Baltimore, Md.: Center for Social Organization of Schools.

Kaufman, Phillip. 2000. "Calculating High School Dropout and Completion Rates: The Complexities of Data and Definitions." Paper presented to the National Academies' workshop, School Completion in Standards-Based Reform: Facts and Strategies. Washington, D.C.(July 17–18, 2000).

Kaufman, Phillip, Martha N. Alt, and Christopher D. Chapman. 2001. *Dropout Rates in the United States: 2000.* National Center for Education Statistics analysis report 2002-114. Washington: U.S. Government Printing Office.

Kaufman, Phillip, and Mary J. Frase. 1990. *Dropout Rates in the United States: 1989.* National Center for Education Statistics analysis report 90-659. Washington: U.S. Government Printing Office.

Kaufman, Phillip, Steve Klein, and Mary Frase. 1999. *Dropout Rates in the United States: 1997.* National Center for Education Statistics analysis report 1999-082. Washington: U.S. Government Printing Office.

Kaufman, Phillip, Jin Y. Kwon, Steve Klein, and Christopher D. Chapman. 1999. *Dropout Rates in the United States: 1998.* National Center for Education Statistics analysis report 2000-022. Washington: U.S. Government Printing Office.

———. 2001. *Dropout Rates in the United States: 1999.* National Center for Education Statistics analysis report 2001-022. Washington: U.S. Government Printing Office.

Kaufman, Phillip, Marilyn M. McMillen, Elvie Germino-Hausken, and Denise Bradby. 1992. *Dropout Rates in the United States: 1991.* National Center for Education Statistics analysis report 92-129. Washington: U.S. Government Printing Office.

Kaufman, Phillip, Marilyn M. McMillen, and Summer Whitener. 1991. *Dropout Rates in the United States: 1990.* National Center for Education Statistics analysis report 91-053. Washington: U.S. Government Printing Office.

Kominski, Robert. 1990. "Estimating the National High School Dropout Rate." *Demography* 27(2): 303–11.

Kominski, Robert, and Andrea Adams. 1993. "School Enrollment—Social and Economic Characteristics of Students: October 1992." *Current Population Reports,* series P-20-474. Washington: U.S. Census Bureau.

Krein, Sheila F., and Andrea H. Beller. 1988. "Educational Attainment of Children from Single-Parent Families: Differences by Exposure, Gender, and Race." *Demography* 25(2): 221–34.

Krueger, Alan B. 1999. "But Does It Work?" *New York Times,* November 7, p. 46.

Lillard, Dean R., and Philip P. DeCicca. 2001. "Higher Standards, More Dropouts? Evidence Within and Across Time." *Economics of Education Review* 20: 459–73.

Linn, Robert L. 2000. "Assessments and Accountability." *Educational Researcher* 29(2): 4–16.

Lorence, Jon, A. Gary Dworkin, Laurence A. Toenjes, and Antwanette N. Hill. 2002. "Grade Retention and Social Promotion in Texas: Academic Achievement Among Elementary School Students." In *Brookings Papers on Educational Policy 2002,* edited by Diane Ravitch. Washington: Brookings Institution.

Luppescu, Stuart, Anthony S. Bryk, Paul Deabster, John Q. Easton, and Yeow M. Thum. 1995. "School Reform, Retention Policy, and Student Achievement Gains." Chicago: Consortium on Chicago School Research.

McCoy, Ann R., and Arthur J. Reynolds. 1999. "Grade Retention and School Performance: An Extended Investigation." *Journal of School Psychology* 37(3): 273–98.

McLanahan, Sara. 1985. "Family Structure and the Reproduction of Poverty." *American Journal of Sociology* 90(4): 873–901.

McMillen, Marilyn M. 1997. *Dropout Rates in the United States: 1996.* National Center for Education Statistics analysis report 98-250. Washington: U.S. Government Printing Office.

McMillen, Marilyn M., and Phillip Kaufman. 1996. *Dropout Rates in the United States: 1994.* National Center for Education Statistics analysis report 96-863. Washington: U.S. Government Printing Office.

———. 1997. *Dropout Rates in the United States: 1995.* National Center for Education Statistics analysis report 97-473. Washington: U.S. Government Printing Office.

McMillen, Marilyn M., Phillip Kaufman, Elvie Germino-Hausken, and Denise Bradby. 1993. *Dropout Rates in the United States: 1992.* National Center for Education Statistics analysis report 93-464. Washington: U.S. Government Printing Office.

McMillen, Marilyn M., Phillip Kaufman, and Summer Whitener. 1994. *Dropout Rates in the United States: 1993.* National Center for Education Statistics analysis report 94-669. Washington: U.S. Government Printing Office.

Moore, Donald R. 1999. *Comment on "Ending Social Promotion: Results from the First Two Years."* Chicago: Designs for Change.

Mosteller, Frederick, Richard J. Light, and Jason A. Sachs. 1996. "Sustained Inquiry in Education: Lessons from Skill Grouping and Class Size." *Harvard Educational Review* 66(4): 797–842.

National Center for Education Statistics. 1994. *The Condition of Education 1994.* Washington: U.S. Government Printing Office.

———. 2002a. *The Condition of Education 2002.* NCES report 2002-025. Washington: U.S. Government Printing Office.

———. 2002b. *Digest of Education Statistics 2001.* NCES report 2002-130. Washington: U.S. Government Printing Office.

National Research Council. 1989. *A Common Destiny: Blacks and American Society.* Edited by Gerald David Jaynes and Robin M. Williams Jr., Committee on the Status of Black Americans, Commission on Behavioral and Social Sciences. Washington, D.C.: National Academy Press.

National Research Council, Committee on Appropriate Test Use. 1999. *High Stakes: Testing for Tracking, Promotion, and Graduation.* Edited by Jay Heubert and Robert M. Hauser. Washington, D.C.: National Academy Press.

Pallas, Aaron M. 1989. "Conceptual and Measurement Issues in the Study of School Dropouts." In *Research in the Sociology of Education and Socialization,* vol. 8, edited by Krishnan Namboodiri and Ronald G. Corwin. Greenwich, Conn.: JAI Press.

Reardon, Sean. 1996. "Eighth-Grade Minimum Competency Testing and Early High School Dropout Patterns." Paper presented to the annual meeting of the American Educational Research Association. New York (April 1996).

Reynolds, Arthur J. 1992. "Grade Retention and School Adjustment: An Explanatory Analysis." *Educational Evaluation and Policy Analysis* 14(2): 101–21.

Roderick, Melissa. 1993. *The Path to Dropping Out: Evidence for Intervention.* Westport, Conn.: Auburn House.

Roderick, Melissa, Anthony S. Bryk, Brian A. Jacob, John Q. Easton, and Elaine Allensworth. 1999. *Ending Social Promotion: Results from the First Two Years.* Chicago: Consortium for Chicago School Research.

Roderick, Melissa, Jenny Nagaoka, Jen Bacon, and John Q. Easton. 2000. *Update: Ending Social Promotion— Passing, Retention, and Achievement Trends Among Promoted and Retained Students, 1995 to 1999.* Chicago: Consortium for Chicago School Research.

Rumberger, Russell W., and Katherine A. Larson. 1998. "Student Mobility and the Increased Risk of High School Dropout." *American Journal of Education* 107(1): 1–35.

Sandefur, Gary D., Sara McLanahan, and Roger A. Wojtkiewicz. 1992. "The Effects of Parental Marital Status During Adolescence on High School Graduation." *Social Forces* 71(1): 103–21.

Shepard, Lorrie A. 1989. "A Review of Research on Kindergarten Retention." In *Flunking Grades: Research and Policies on Retention,* edited by Lorrie A. Shepard and Mary L. Smith. London: Falmer Press.

———. 1991. "Negative Policies for Dealing with Diversity: When Does Assessment and Diagnosis Turn into Sorting and Segregation?" In *Literacy for a Diverse Society: Perspectives, Practices, and Policies,* edited by Elfrieda Hiebert. New York: Teachers College Press.

———. 2002. "Comment on 'Grade Retention and Social Promotion in Texas: Academic Achievement Among Elementary School Students.'" In *Brookings Papers on Educational Policy 2002,* edited by Diane Ravitch. Washington, D.C.: Brookings Institution.

Shepard, Lorrie A., Sharon L. Kagan, and Emily Wurtz. 1998. *Principles and Recommendations for Early Childhood Assessments.* Washington: U.S. Government Printing Office.

Shepard, Lorrie A., and Mary L. Smith. 1989. *Flunking Grades: Research and Policies on Retention*. London: Falmer Press.

Shepard, Lorrie A., Mary L. Smith, and Scott F. Marion. 1996. "Failed Evidence on Grade Retention." *Psychology in the Schools* 33(3): 251–61.

Steinberg, Jacques. 1999. "Clinton Urges Tough Love for Students Who Are Failing." *New York Times*, October 1, p. 18.

Temple, Judy A., Arthur J. Reynolds, and Wendy T. Miedel. 2000. "Can Early Intervention Prevent High School Dropout? Evidence from the Chicago Child-Parent Centers." *Urban Education* 35(1): 31–56.

Texas Education Agency. 1998. *1998 Comprehensive Biennial Report on Texas Schools: A Report to the 76th Texas Legislature*. Austin: Texas Education Agency.

———. 2001. *2001 Comprehensive Biennial Report on Texas Schools: A Report to the Seventy-seventh Texas Legislature*. Austin: Texas Education Agency.

Toenjes, Laurence A., and A. Gary Dworkin. 2002. "Are Increasing Test Scores in Texas Really a Myth, or Is Haney's Myth a Myth?" *Educational Policy Analysis Archives* 10(17). Available at http://epaa.asu.edu/epaa/v10n17.

U.S. Department of Commerce. U.S. Census Bureau. 1943. "Educational Characteristics of the Population of the United States, by Age: 1940." *Current Population Reports*, series P-19-4. Washington: U.S. Department of Commerce.

———. 1967. "School Enrollment: October 1966." *Current Population Reports*, series P-20-167. Washington: U.S. Government Printing Office.

———. 1979. "Relative Progress of Children in School: 1976." *Current Population Reports*, series P-20-337. Washington: U.S. Government Printing Office.

———. 2000. "Educational Attainment in the United States: March 2000." *Current Population Reports*, series P-20-536. Washington: U.S. Government Printing Office.

———. 2001. "Table A-1: Years of School Completed by People Twenty-five Years Old and Over, by Age and Sex: Selected Years 1940 to 2000." *Historical Tables*. Available at: www.census.gov/population/socdemo/education/tableA-1.txt.

U.S. Department of Education. 1990. *National Goals for Education*. Washington: U.S. Government Printing Office.

U.S. Congress. U.S. Senate. 2002. *An Act to Close the Achievement Gap with Accountability, Flexibility, and Choice, So That No Child Is Left Behind*. PL 107-110. Washington: U.S. Government Printing Office.

Winglee, Marianne, David Marker, Allison Henderson, Beth A. Young, and Lee Hoffman. 2000. *A Recommended Approach to Providing High School Dropout and Completion Rates at the State Level*. National Center for Education Statistics analysis report 2000-305. Washington: U.S. Government Printing Office.

Young, Beth A., and Lee Hoffman. 2002. *Public High School Dropouts and Completers from the Common Core of Data: School Years 1991–92 Through 1997–98*. National Center for Education Statistics analysis report 2000-317. Washington: U.S. Government Printing Office.

Chapter 8

College-Going and Inequality

Thomas J. Kane

Since 1973, when Congress undertook the last major structural reform of federal financial aid rules by establishing the Pell Grant program—a school voucher program for low-income undergraduates—very little has changed in the way in which government helps families pay for college. Meanwhile, the environment has changed dramatically. First, the labor market for college graduates is quite different. The percentage difference in earnings between those with and without a college degree has more than doubled since 1980. Second, a supply response seems to be under way. The proportion of eighteen- to twenty-four-year-olds enrolled in college has increased by more than one-third since 1980. This chapter describes some of the characteristics of that supply response: which racial and gender groups are responding and which are not, and what role income inequality may be playing in shaping those responses.

The rise in earnings inequality in the labor market, which has been well documented over the past decade and a half, has important potential implications for social mobility. There were large differences in college entry and completion by parental family income and race in 1980. Moreover, the gaps in college enrollment by family income and by race seem to have widened.

I begin by discussing changes over time in the gaps in college-going by family income and by race. The large gaps in college-going by family income appear to be widening over time. Moreover, despite some closing of the racial gap in high school graduation rates and test scores, the racial gap in the proportion of blacks and whites attending college also appears to be widening.[1] The next section surveys the evidence on the "causal" role of parental income in determining college enrollment rates, citing the results of various attempts to control for any correlation between family income and other parental characteristics, such as a preference for educational investments, that might be generating a correlation between parental income and college-going. The following section presents the evidence on the effect of tuition policies and financial aid on college-going. Included there is a summary of the evidence regarding the existence of any capital market constraints on students' ability to invest in schooling. The next section revisits the question of whether public financing of higher education increases or decreases family income inequality, a long-standing debate that flared up following the publication by Hansen and Weisbrod of an analysis of California higher education in 1968 but that has received much less attention recently. The chapter concludes with an evaluation of the evidence that capacity constraints in higher education during the early 1970s may have contributed to the rise in earnings inequality since the late 1970s.

PERSISTENT AND WIDENING GAPS IN COLLEGE-GOING BY FAMILY INCOME

The large gaps in college-going by family income are evident in the top panel of table 8.1, which reports differences in college-going among seniors from the high school classes of 1980 and 1982, as reported in Ellwood and Kane (2000).[2] Eighty percent of the students from the top income quartile attended some type of postsecondary institution within twenty months of their high school graduation, as compared with 57 percent of those from the lowest income quartiles. The gaps by family income were particularly large in four-year college entrance, with 55 percent of the highest-income youth attending a four-year college at some point and only 29 percent of the lowest-income youth.

Moreover, although the evidence is somewhat sparser, these gaps appear to be widening over time. It is surprisingly difficult to keep track of differences in college-going by family income with the data available in the federal statistical system. The annual October Current Population Survey (CPS), for instance, collects data on the college enrollment of youth but collects income information only for their current household, which is not necessarily their parents' household.[3] Parental income is available only for those who are members of their parents' household. Moreover, the major longitudinal surveys collected by the National Center for Education Statistics (NCES), the High School and Beyond (HS&B) and National Educational Longitudinal Study (NELS) of 1988, which do contain information on the income of parents while their youth are in high school, ask about parental family income in slightly different ways in different years.

As reported in table 8.1, Ellwood and Kane (2000) define parental family income quartiles in consistent ways using the NELS and HS&B, and they report changes in college enrollment over time by family income quartile.[4] Although college entry rates grew for all groups between the high school classes of 1980 through 1982 and 1992, the increases were larger for middle- and higher-income families. For example, there was a ten-percentage-point increase in the proportion of the highest-income youth attending some postsecondary institution between 1980 through 1982 and 1992. Moreover, the increase in four-year attendance was largest for high-income youth attending four-year colleges, rising from 55 percent to 66 percent. In contrast, we estimate that there was only a three-percentage-point rise in postsecondary entry for youth from the lowest-income quartile and a one-percentage-point decline (albeit statistically insignificant) in the proportion of low-income youth attending a four-year college.

In other words, the persistently large gaps in college-going by family income appear to be widening. However, even if the gaps in college-going by family income were not widening, the rising payoff to college since 1980 has magnified the consequences of the preexisting gap in college entry by family income. While the gap in postsecondary training between the highest- and lowest-income quartiles grew by one-third (from twenty-three percentage points to thirty percentage points), the earnings differentials between college entrants and high school graduates more than doubled between 1980 and 1997. Between the two phenomena—the widening gap in college enrollment by family income and the rising payoff to a college education—the latter is likely to have larger implications for social mobility.

Widening Gaps in College Enrollment by Race

While the Current Population Survey makes it difficult to track college-going rates by parental income level, it does allow us to track college-going rates by race. Given the

TABLE 8.1   *Students Who Enroll in Postsecondary Schools Within Twenty Months of High School Graduation, by Income Quartile, 1980 to 1982 and 1992*

Parental Income Quartile	Total	Any Postsecondary Schooling		
		Vocational, Technical	Two-Year College	Four-Year College
Classes of 1980 through 1982				
Bottom quartile	0.57	0.12	0.16	0.29
Third quartile	0.63	0.11	0.19	0.33
Second quartile	0.71	0.10	0.22	0.39
Top quartile	0.80	0.06	0.19	0.55
Total	0.68	0.10	0.19	0.39
Class of 1992				
Bottom quartile	0.60	0.10	0.22	0.28
Third quartile	0.70	0.07	0.25	0.38
Second quartile	0.79	0.06	0.25	0.48
Top quartile	0.90	0.05	0.19	0.66
Total	0.75	0.07	0.23	0.45

Note: Based on tabulations of the High School and Beyond Survey and National Education Longitudinal Study of 1992. Parental income was reported by parents. Figures were reported in Ellwood and Kane (2000).

correlation between race and income, any increase in income gaps ought to be reflected in a widening of the racial gap. Figure 8.1 reports the trend in the percentage of eighteen- to twenty-four-year-olds enrolled in college by race-ethnicity between 1972 and 1998. The panel on the left reports enrollment rates by race; the panel on the right reports the difference in enrollment rates relative to whites for both blacks and Hispanics each year. After remaining flat for most of the 1970s, enrollment rates began to rise during the 1980s for all groups. The proportion of white eighteen- to twenty-four-year-olds enrolled in college increased from 27 percent to 41 percent between 1980 and 1998. Enrollment rates for African American youth also increased over that period—from 19 to 29 percent—but the magnitude of the increase for African Americans (10 percent) was smaller than the magnitude of the increase for white non-Hispanics (14 percent).[5] As a result, as reported in the right panel of figure 8.1, the gaps in college enrollment by race also increased.

The widening racial gaps in college enrollment rates are particularly striking when contrasted with the gradual closing of the racial gaps in high school graduation and test performance over the same period. Figure 8.2 reports the trends in high school status dropout rates (the proportion of youth not enrolled in school who do not have a high school diploma) for sixteen- to twenty-four-year-old youth by race-ethnicity from 1972 through 1998. As in figure 8.1, the left panel of figure 8.2 reports the trends in high school status dropout rates by race-ethnicity; the right panel reports the differences in high school drop-out rates for blacks and Hispanics relative to white non-Hispanics. Throughout much of the period, high school dropout rates were gradually falling for all three groups. However, the decline among African Americans accelerated between the mid-1970s and the mid-1980s, closing somewhat the black-white gap in high school graduation rates. Between 1975 and 1988 the status dropout rate fell from 11.4 to 9.6 percent for white non-Hispanics (a 1.8-percentage-point drop) and from 22.9 to 14.5 percent for black non-Hispanics (a 8.4-percentage-point drop).

FIGURE 8.1   *College Enrollment Rates of Eighteen- to Twenty-Four-Year-Olds, by Race, 1972 to 1999*

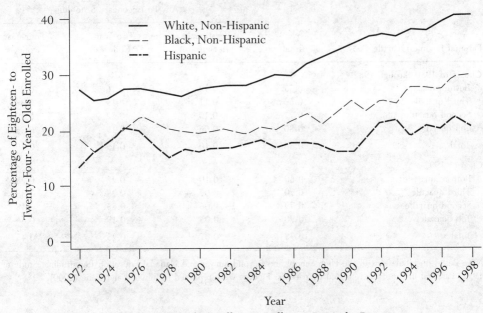

Trend in College Enrollment Rates, by Race

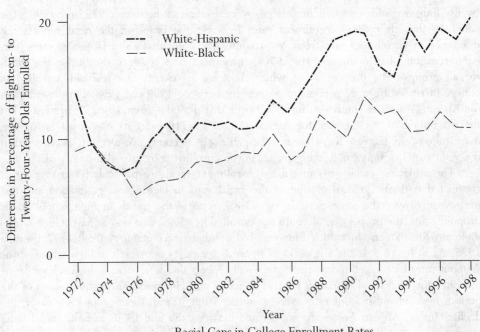

Racial Gaps in College Enrollment Rates

Source: U.S. Department of Education (2000a, table 189).

FIGURE 8.2   *High School Status Dropout Rates Among Sixteen- to Twenty-Four-Year-Olds, by Race, 1972 to 1999*

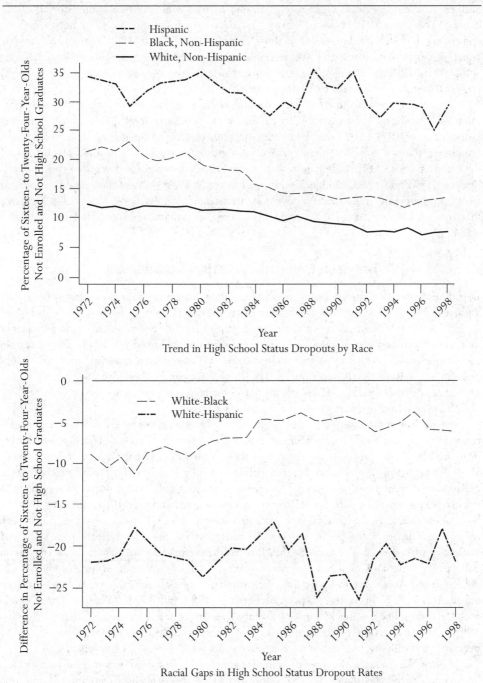

Trend in High School Status Dropouts by Race

Racial Gaps in High School Status Dropout Rates

Source: U.S. Department of Education (2000a), table 108.

Some portion of this closing racial gap in high school dropout rates may be attributable to a rise in GED receipt rather than an increase in high school diplomas. However, it is unlikely that an increase in GED receipt among African Americans accounted for all of the closing. The Current Population Survey first began to distinguish in 1988 between those completing high school diplomas and those completing GEDs. In 1990 a small but roughly equal proportion of black and white eighteen- to twenty-four-year-olds reported having completed a GED or other equivalent rather than a regular high school degree (5 percent) (U.S. Department of Health and Human Services 2000, 311).

Figure 8.3 reports the trend in math and reading test scores on the National Assessment of Educational Progress (NAEP) exams by race-ethnicity for thirteen- and seventeen-year-olds since 1975.[6] For both age groups, in both reading and math, blacks and Hispanics are closing the gap in achievement relative to white non-Hispanics. A student-level standard deviation on the NAEP reading test was approximately forty points over this time period. Between 1975 and 1988, the black-white gap in reading test scores at age seventeen closed from approximately 1.25 standard deviations to .5 standard deviations. Since 1988, it seems that the gap has opened up again slightly, but the gap remains considerably smaller than it was in 1975.

Trends in Eventual Educational Attainment

Enrollment rates, which reflect the stock of eighteen- to twenty-four-year-olds in college at a point in time, do not provide a complete picture. For example, if the time-to-degree were to increase, they would rise even if the proportion of youth ever entering college had not increased. Moreover, an increase in college enrollment rates need not imply an increase in the proportion of youth completing college degrees if completion rates for marginal college entrants are quite low (Rosenbaum 2001). In this section, I therefore also report trends over time in the proportion of twenty-five- to twenty-seven-year-olds ever entering college and the proportion reporting having a bachelor's degree.

Figure 8.4 shows trends in the proportion of twenty-five- to twenty-seven-year-olds reporting any postsecondary enrollment, by race and gender. Three facts are worth noting in figure 8.4. First, the timing of the rise in the proportion of twenty-five- to twenty-seven-year-olds reporting ever having entered college roughly matches the timing of the rise in college enrollment rates of eighteen- to twenty-four-year-olds. The rise for twenty-five- to twenty-seven-year-old white non-Hispanics began in approximately 1987, meaning that the increase began with the cohort who turned eighteen in 1979—the same year in which college enrollment rates began to rise. Second, because this rise reflects the "stock" of students enrolled in college and not the "flow" of new entrants, the magnitude of the rise in college enrollment of eighteen- to twenty-four-year-olds somewhat overstates the rise in college entry. As we saw in figure 8.1, the proportion of eighteen- to twenty-four-year-olds enrolled in college grew by 31 percent between 1983 and 1994. (These cohorts should roughly correspond to the cohorts of twenty-five- to twenty-seven-year-olds in 1988 and 1999.) The proportion of these cohorts *ever* entering college also rose (from 47 to 57 percent), but only by two-thirds as much in proportional terms (21 percent).

Figure 8.5 reports the proportion of twenty-five- to twenty-seven-year-olds with a bachelor's degree. Beginning in 1992, the format of the educational attainment question changed. As a result, we have to be careful in comparing rates of degree completion before and after 1992. Keeping the appropriate caveats in mind, the increases were roughly consistent with the rise in the proportion of those who had ever entered college. Between 1988 and 1999, the proportion of twenty-five- to twenty-seven-year-olds with a B.A. degree or higher rose by 23 percent (from 22.1 to 27.2 percent). On a proportionate basis, the rise in B.A. degree completion roughly matched the rise in college entry; this suggests that there was little decline in college completion rates over the period when college entry rates were rising. Presumably, the larger proportionate rise in the stock of college enrollees than in the flow of college entrants or the flow of college completers reflects an increase in part-time enrollment and a lengthening time-to-degree.

Figure 8.6 reports the racial-ethnic gaps in educational attainment among twenty-five- to twenty-seven-year-olds over time and by gender. The top panel reports the gaps in the proportion of twenty-five- to twenty-seven-year-olds reporting that they have entered college at some point; the bottom panel reports the gaps in B.A. degree completion rates for the same age group. Just as figure 8.1 indicates a widening gap in college enrollment rates among eighteen- to twenty-four-year-olds by race, there appears to have been a widening in the gaps in educational attainment among twenty-five- to twenty-seven-year-olds by race. Moreover, the racial-ethnic gaps widened in the proportion of those who have ever entered college as well as in the proportion completing a B.A. degree.

Gender Differences in Educational Attainment

As reported in figure 8.4, the rise in college entry since 1980 was larger for women than for men. Administrative data published by the U.S. Department of Education confirm that women now account for a disproportionate share of enrollment and for more than half of the associate's, bachelor's, and master's degrees conferred (U.S. Department of Education 1999a, tables 170 and 172).[7] As argued in Kane (1994) and Charles and Luoh (2001), it is difficult to attribute the widening gap by gender to any differences in the rise in the education wage premium since 1980, since the apparent rise in the payoff to schooling was quite similar for men and women through the early 1990s. Peter Gottschalk and Steve Pizer (1999) report similar increases in the experience differential for college-educated men and women. There may be other explanations, such as advantages in nonwage characteristics of jobs for college graduates (for example, flexibility in hours), that could account for the large increases in enrollment by women. However, this important trend is currently not very well understood.

Concentration of Peer Effects and Resources Among B.A. Degree Holders

Of course, college enrollment itself is an imperfect measure of the educational resources to which one has been exposed. Caroline Hoxby and Bridget Terry (1999) decompose the rise in earnings inequality among thirty-two-year-old male college graduates in 1972, 1986, and 1995 (who had graduated from high school in approximately 1958, 1972, and 1981, respectively) into three components: family background (race, parental education, family size, and parental income), college selectivity (using average SAT scores to break schools down into twelve categories), and a measure of expenditures per student at the college the individual attended and interactions between the variance in student SAT scores and college selectivity.

The interpretation of the variance decomposition is somewhat complicated by the fact that the authors did not have any direct measure of an individual's ability (such as an individual test score). As a result, the second component, reflecting the effects of college selectivity, combines any change in the return to individual skill differences as well as any

(Text continues on p. 332.)

FIGURE 8.3   *NAEP Test Scores by Race, 1974 to 1997*

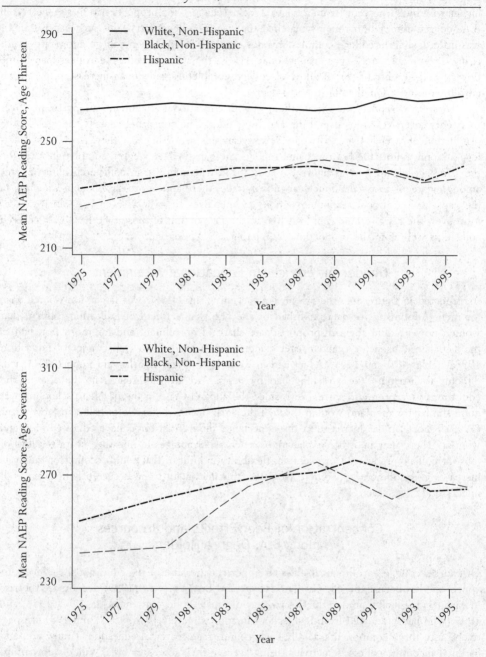

Source: U.S. Department of Education (2000b).
Note: Scale has been adjusted for each graph to be roughly equal to two standard deviations.

FIGURE 8.3   *(Continued)*

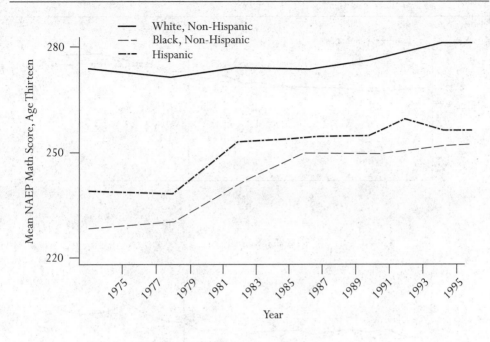

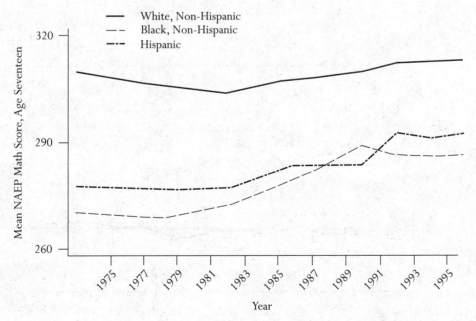

FIGURE 8.4   *Proportion of Twenty-Five- to Twenty-Seven-Year-Olds Reporting Any College, by Race and Gender, 1979 to 1999*

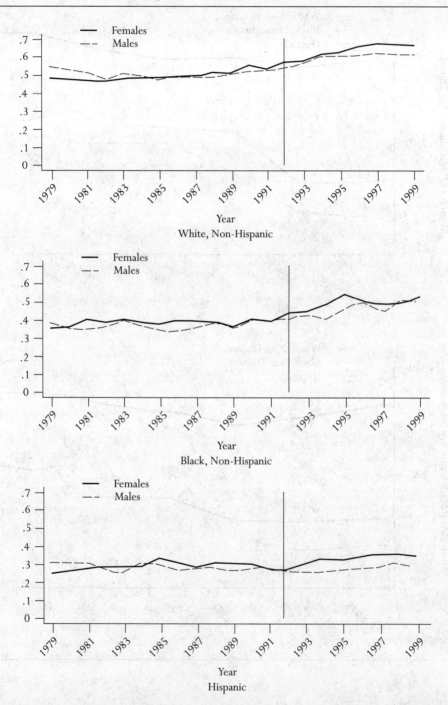

Note: Based on author's tabulation of CPS outgoing rotation groups. The educational attainment question changed format in 1992.

FIGURE 8.5   *Proportion of Twenty-Five- to Twenty-Seven-Year-Olds Reporting a B.A. Degree, by Race and Gender, 1979 to 1999*

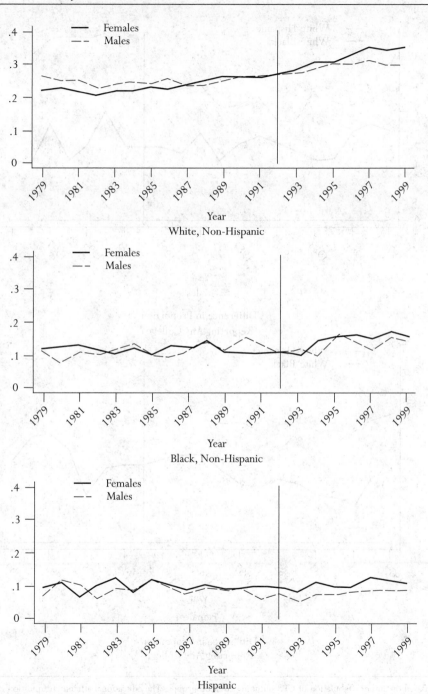

Note: Based on author's tabulation of CPS outgoing rotation groups. The educational attainment question changed format in 1992.

FIGURE 8.6   *Racial Gaps in Reporting Any College and in B.A. Completion Among Twenty-Five- to Twenty-Seven-Year-Olds, by Race and Gender, 1979 to 1999*

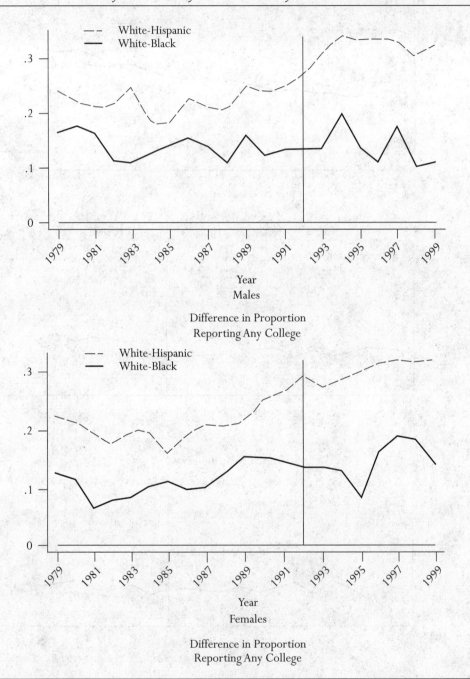

Difference in Proportion
Reporting Any College

Note: Based on author's tabulation of CPS outgoing rotation groups. The educational attainment question changed format in 1992.

FIGURE 8.6   (Continued)

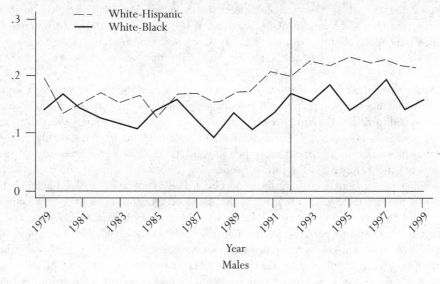

Year

Males

Difference in
B.A. Completion

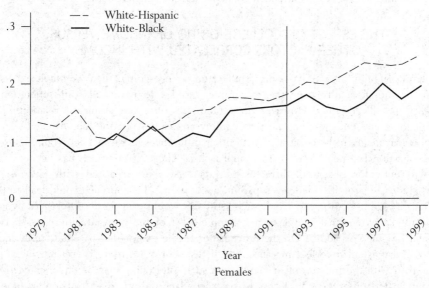

Year

Females

Difference in
B.A. Completion

change in the payoff to attending a more selective institution. The component described by the authors as the "peer effect" from attending a more selective institution is actually the interaction between the variance in student test scores and college selectivity. As expected, they find that the wider the variance in test scores at an elite institution, the less of an advantage the elite institution provides (and the reverse for the bottom institutions). This may not be a "peer effect," however, since it may simply mean that a college's selectivity provides a less accurate proxy of a student's own ability than when a school is more homogeneous.

Much more straightforward to interpret is the fraction of the rise in earnings inequality that is attributable to changes in payoff to college expenditures per student and the variance in the expenditures per student. Roughly one-third of the rise in earnings inequality among college graduates between 1972 and 1995 could be attributed to a rise in the payoff to attending an institution that spent more per student and the rise in the inequality in spending per student.[8] (The rise in the return to spending per student and the rise in the variance in spending per student were equally important.) The importance of this finding is highlighted by the fact that, since 1981, when the youngest cohort studied by Hoxby and Terry entered school, the most selective colleges have become rather more selective and the variance in expenditures per student in colleges has widened even further. Elsewhere (Kane 1999) I have reported that expenditures per student rose by 70 percent in real value at private four-year institutions between 1980 to 1981 and 1994 to 1995, but by only 28 and 30 percent, respectively, at public two-year and four-year colleges. Future work should study not only differences in college entry by family income but also differences in spending per student in the institutions attended by high- and low-income families.

THE EFFECT ON COLLEGE-GOING OF INCOME VERSUS OTHER FACTORS CORRELATED WITH INCOME

If the level of family income has a direct effect on college-going, then we might expect the rise in income inequality over the past three decades to have had some effect on the inequality in college-going. However, the commonly observed empirical relationship between income and college-going need not imply any causal relationship. After all, income differences are likely to be correlated with other differences in family background. Research on this question has taken one of four approaches. The first approach has been to try to control directly for observed characteristics that may be correlated with income—test scores, grades, school attended, even parental education. This approach could lead to biases in either direction. On the one hand, such estimates would exaggerate differences by family income to the extent that they are an incomplete list of the relevant differences between high- and low-income youth. On the other hand, to the extent that parental family income in a given year is an imperfect measure, and if test scores are more correlated with "true" income than with the measurement error, then such differences may be understated. Moreover, anticipated differences in access to postsecondary options may lead low-income students to focus less on their studies in elementary and secondary school and thus to perform more poorly on standardized tests. If so, controlling for test scores would understate the importance of family income.

Using observed differences in family background and test scores, much of the difference in college entry by family income remains, even after we attempt to control for test scores, high school grades, and elementary schools attended by different youth. Table 8.2 reports differences in college-going by family income and by students' scores on a stan-

TABLE 8.2   *Students in the Class of 1992 Who Enrolled in Postsecondary Schools Within Twenty Months, by Parental Income Quartile and Math Test Tertile*

Parental Income Quartile	Bottom	Middle	Top	Overall Average
Any postsecondary enrollment				
Lowest	48%	67%	82%	60%
	(1.6)	(1.8)	(2.1)	(1.1)
Second	50	75	90	71
	(1.9)	(1.6)	(1.2)	(1.0)
Third	64	83	95	82
	(2.1)	(1.3)	(0.8)	(0.8)
Highest	73	89	96	90
	(2.4)	(1.2)	(0.6)	(0.7)
Overall average	55	79	93	76
	(1.0)	(0.8)	(0.6)	(0.5)
Enrollment in a four-year college				
Lowest	15	33	68	30
	(1.1)	(1.8)	(2.5)	(1.0)
Second	14	37	69	39
	(1.3)	(1.8)	(1.8)	(1.1)
Third	21	47	78	52
	(1.8)	(1.8)	(1.5)	(1.1)
Highest	27	59	84	67
	(2.3)	(2.0)	(1.1)	(1.0)
Overall average	17	44	77	47
	(0.7)	(0.9)	(0.8)	(0.5)

Note: Standard errors in parentheses. Based on author's tabulation of 8,313 observations from the National Education Longitudinal Study of 1988. Figures reported in Ellwood and Kane (2000).

dardized test of basic math skills administered when youth were in twelfth grade. Among students with test scores in the bottom third of the class of 1992, the differences in enrollment by family income are particularly large: 73 percent of youth from the highest income category went on to postsecondary schooling despite low test scores, while only 48 percent of low-income students with such test scores went on to college. However, differences remain even among students with test scores in the top third of their class: 96 percent of high-income, high-test-score students went on to postsecondary schooling as compared with 82 percent of low-income, high-test-score youth. The differences are particularly striking in four-year college entry. Only 68 percent of the low-income, high-test-score youth went on to a four-year college within twenty months of high school graduation, as compared with 84 percent of high-income, high-test-score youth.

Although table 8.2 accounts for only one difference between high- and low-income youth (math test scores), Ellwood and Kane (2000) also included a longer list of student characteristics in attempting to control for other differences in academic preparation between high- and low-income students. Table 8.3 reports differences in the proportion of youth receiving any postsecondary training (at a two-year college, four-year college, or vocational school) and attending a four-year college within twenty months of graduating from high school in 1992. The first column reports the simple difference we can observe without controlling for other factors. Youth from the top quartile were twenty-eight percentage points more likely to have attended any postsecondary training and thirty-six per-

TABLE 8.3   *Differences in Postsecondary Training for the High School Class of 1992, by Parental Family Income Quartile*

Parental Income Quartile	None	Other Variables Held Constant		
		Math and Reading Scores; High School Rank	Math and Reading Scores; High School Rank; Same Eighth-Grade School	Math and Reading Scores; High School Rank; Eighth-Grade School; Parents' Education
Difference in proportion entering any postsecondary training within twenty months relative to youth from the bottom quartile:				
Third	.109*	.068*	.058*	.044*
Second	.215*	.145*	.135*	.105*
Top	.278*	.176*	.141*	.098*
Difference in proportion entering a four-year college within twenty months relative to youth from the bottom quartile:				
Third	.090*	.017	.010	− .009
Second	.204*	.081*	.074*	.035*
Top	.357*	.176*	.121*	.061*

Source: Based on author's tabulation of 6,652 observations from the National Educational Longitudinal Study of 1988.
*Difference is statistically different from zero at .05 level.

centage points more likely to have attended a four-year college within twenty months after high school graduation. (The proportion of the lowest quartile receiving any postsecondary training was 63 percent, and the proportion entering a four-year college was 32 percent.) As reported in the second column of table 8.3, large differences remained among youth with similar test scores and similar high school class ranks. For instance, there was an eighteen-percentage-point difference in the proportion entering any postsecondary training and in the proportion entering a four-year college. (Although the difference was largest among youth with test scores in the bottom of the class, differences remained even among youth with test scores in the top quarter of the class.) The third column compares youth with similar test scores and high school class rank who had also attended the same schools in eighth grade. Youth from the top quartile were fourteen percentage points more likely to have had any postsecondary training and twelve percentage points more likely to attend a four-year college.

The last column of table 8.3 compares youth with similar parental education as well as similar test scores and high school class ranks.[9] There are advantages and disadvantages to including parental education as a control variable in such an exercise. On the one hand, part of the difference in college-going by family income may reflect differences in parental "preferences" for education. As a result, we might want to control for such differences. On the other hand, parental education probably measures more than just parental encouragement to pursue higher education in that it is also likely to provide an indirect measure of family wealth. As a result, controlling for differences in parental education may overstate the importance of differences in parental tastes for education and understate the differences attributable to parental ability to pay. Nevertheless, much of the difference in college-going by parental income remains, even after including measures of parental education as regressors.

A second approach is to evaluate the impact of temporary changes in income on college-going, attempting to control for average income. Susan Mayer (1997) measures the educational attainment of children in families who experienced a 35 percent or more decline in income in two adjacent years over a ten-year period, controlling for average income over the period. Although families experiencing large drops in earnings did not differ on many outcomes, such as elementary school test scores, teen childbearing, or high school dropout, youth from families experiencing large declines in income did complete fewer years of schooling after high school.

However, the source of fluctuations in income—one earner leaving the household, an error in reporting income, a marital status change, parental job loss—may have its own direct effect on educational attainment, or it may be related to other factors influencing educational choices. John Shea (2000) takes a related approach, exploring the relationship between parental family income differences associated with specific characteristics—union status, industry of employment, and recent job loss—and various youth outcomes, including educational attainment. His hypothesis is that while union status or job loss has large effects on parental income, it may have no direct effect on youth educational attainment other than through income. When using the nationally representative component of the Panel Study of Income Dynamics (PSID) sample, he finds no relationship between income differences associated with any of these traits and children's educational attainment or earnings. However, when using the low-income sample from the PSID, he finds large, statistically significant effects of such variation in parental income on youth wages and earnings and marginally significant effects on youth educational attainment. He interprets these results as providing mixed evidence on the causal role of income fluctuations in educational attainment. However, it is not at all clear why such factors would not have their own direct effect on college-going other than through family income. For instance, the children of union members may receive preferences for entry into union apprenticeship programs. Children whose parents work in industries with high wages for a given level of educational attainment may also have an edge in applying for jobs in these industries. If so, attending college may make less sense economically for these youth than for others and may explain the fact that children of these parents do not have higher college entry rates.

A third approach involves exploiting changes in the income distribution over time, holding constant percentile ranking, and asking whether changes in levels of family income at different points in the family income distribution are related to changes in children's educational attainment. Suppose that the relationship between an individual's rank in the family income distribution and the non-income family background characteristics that influence his or her likelihood of going to college have remained constant over time. Changes in real family income at different percentiles of the family income distribution would then tell us something about the effect of income itself on college-going. For instance, using the PSID, Mayer (1997) notes that average income for the poorest quintile fell by 21 percent in real terms between the 1972 to 1975 period and the 1980 to 1983 period and increased by 4 percent in the top two quintiles. She then looks at changes in youth outcomes for those from the top and bottom of the income distribution over that time period and compares the changes to what we might have expected from the simple cross-sectional relationship between parental income and those same outcomes. The change in years of schooling for youth who were high school graduates—both the decline for those in the bottom quintile and the rise for those in the top two quintiles—was actually larger than we might have expected based on the simple cross-section.

Daron Acemoglu and Jorn-Steffen Pischke (2001) take a related approach. Using the National Longitudinal Study of the Class of 1972, the High School and Beyond survey of the classes of 1980 through 1982, and the National Educational Longitudinal Study of those graduating from high school in 1992, the authors calculated mean college-going rates and mean parental family income for four income quartiles, in four regions, for each of the three cohorts. They then studied the effect of changes in the absolute level of income within each quartile over time on changes in college enrollment rates. Like Mayer, they find estimates of the effect of income on college-going that are actually larger than the effects in the cross-section.

One problem with this approach is that changes in the income distribution reflect differential changes in the "prices" of parental characteristics, which may themselves be related to college-going. For example, we know that the earnings of more-educated parents grew more than the earnings of less-educated parents. If parental education has a direct effect on children's college-going, conditioning on family income, then we might expect larger increases in college-going for those in the higher family income percentiles.

A fourth approach is to randomly provide additional income to parents and observe the effects on student enrollment. The income maintenance experiments conducted in a number of sites in the mid-1970s essentially did just that. Although the primary purpose of those experiments was to evaluate the effect on parental labor supply of providing a guaranteed income, the experiments also kept track of children's school enrollment and work decisions. Steven Venti (1984) studied the impact of the income maintenance programs in Seattle and Denver on youth's work and schooling decisions between the ages of sixteen and twenty-one. Among eighteen- and nineteen-year-olds, he estimated, being in a family participating in the income maintenance experiment was associated with a fourteen- and nine-percentage-point increase, respectively, in the probability of attending school (relative to an enrollment rate of 28 and 13 percent, respectively, in the control group). Although he did not distinguish between high school and college enrollment, the impacts were largest among those of initial college age (eighteen and nineteen years old). The impacts for sixteen- and seventeen-year-olds were only two and four percentage points, respectively. Youth in the treatment group were also less likely to work.

It is not clear that these were purely income effects. Families in the program also faced the higher tax rates on total household income that accompanied the guaranteed incomes. If parents passed along some of this tax by retrieving from the student at least part of the reduction in family grant assistance attributable to the youth's earnings, then the program lowered the marginal payoff to working for youth and lowered the opportunity cost of going to school. In other words, the negative income tax not only may have increased family income but may also have lowered the opportunity cost of attending college. Without knowing how families passed along any taxes on the earnings of secondary workers, it is difficult to know how much was due to the income effect and how much of the rise in enrollment was due to the change in the cost of schooling. However, these results were at least consistent with a causal role for family income.

THE ROLE OF RISING TUITION LEVELS IN WIDENING
THE GAPS IN ENROLLMENT BY FAMILY INCOME

After growing slowly between 1965 and 1980, tuition levels began rising more rapidly than overall inflation between 1980 and 1999.[10] Figure 8.7 portrays the trend in tuition levels at public and private, two-year and four-year colleges and universities. Between 1965 and 1980, the average tuition at a private four-year institution rose only 22 percent faster than inflation. However, between 1980 and 1999, tuition at private four-year institutions rose 136 percent in real terms. After rising by 17 percent in real value between 1965 and 1980, the average public four-year tuition rose by 114 percent between 1980 and 1999.

Over the years a large literature has developed to study the impact of various types of tuition and financial aid policies on college-going. In their review of the literature on student responsiveness to changes in college cost, Larry Leslie and Paul Brinkman (1988) report a consensus estimate that a $1,000 change in college costs (in 1990 dollars) is associated with an approximately five-percentage-point difference in college enrollment rates. Table 8.4 summarizes the results from three recent sets of studies, published since the Leslie and Brinkman review: those that use differences in public tuition levels between states and over time; those that evaluate the impact of financial aid policies that operate outside the usual need-analysis system; and those evaluating changes in financial aid policy operating through the regular financial aid process.

The second, third, and fourth papers use between-state differences in state tuition policy and essentially compare the college entry rates of otherwise similar youth in high- and low-tuition states. The empirical strategy in this literature uses the assumption that the price that is relevant for the marginal student is the tuition at public institutions in their state and evaluate the effect of tuition on college-going by comparing college-going rates in high- and low-tuition states. Such studies also assume that the supply of college slots is perfectly elastic: given a change in price, it is solely student demand that determines enrollment, not the supply of college slots.

Two characteristics of these studies deserve comment. First, although they use three different datasets—the October Current Population Survey, the National Longitudinal Survey of Youth, and the High School and Beyond survey—each generates similar results. A $1,000 difference in tuition is associated with a six-percentage-point difference in college-going. Indeed, these estimates are quite consistent with the older literature summarized by Leslie and Brinkman (1987).

Second, a weakness of these studies is that they rely on relatively fixed differences in tuition levels between states. For instance, California has been a relatively low-tuition state for the past forty years. California has also built a number of community colleges around the state. We may be attributing to tuition policy the effect of these other policy differences, such as the construction of community colleges. As a result, in Kane (1999), I used administrative data to look at what happens to enrollments within a state when it raises tuition. Interestingly, we see effects of tuition changes within states over time comparable to what we would estimate looking across states.

Despite strong evidence of student and parent responsiveness to tuition costs, the evidence for the impact of the Pell Grant program is much weaker. Lee Hansen (1983) first noted that there had been little evidence of a disproportionate rise in college enrollment by low-income youth during the 1970s, when the Pell Grant program was established. Although that paper was criticized for relying too heavily on two years of data and for including males, whose decisions may have also been affected by the end of the Vietnam War,

FIGURE 8.7   *Trend in Real Tuition Levels at Public and Private Institutions (1999 Dollars)*

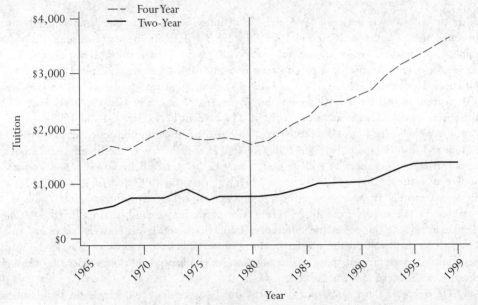

In-State Tuition at Public Two-Year and Four-Year Colleges

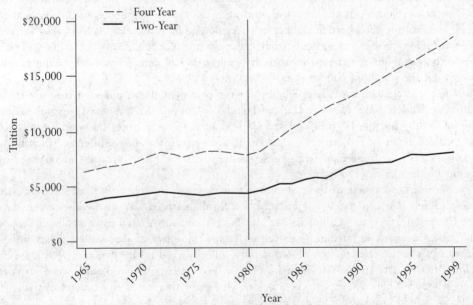

Tuition at Private Two-Year and Four-Year Colleges

Source: U.S. Department of Educational (2000a), table 317. Adjusted for inflation using CPI-U-XI.

TABLE 8.4   *Estimated Impact of a $1,000 (1990 Dollars) Change in Direct Cost of College on College Entry Rates*

Study	Estimate	Brief Description
Literature before 1987		
Leslie and Brinkman (1987)	−.05 (.005)	Literature review of twenty-five articles
Based on between-state differences in tuition		
Cameron and Heckman (2001)	−.07 (.02)	State differences in public tuition charges (NLSY)
Kane (1994)	−.05 (.01)	State differences in public tuition charges (October CPS)
Kane (1999)	−.05 (.01)	State differences in public tuition charges (NELS)
Based on nontraditional financial aid		
Dynarski (1999)	−.04 (.02)	End of Social Security Student Benefit program
Dynarski (2000)	−.03 (.02)	Hope Scholarship program in Georgia
Before-after the Pell Grant program was established in 1973		
Hansen (1983)		No disproportionate growth by low-income (October CPS)
Kane (1994)		No disproportionate growth by low income (October CPS)
Manski (1992–93)		No disproportionate growth in B.A. completion by low income (NLS-72 and HSB)

Source: Author's compilation.

later work (Kane 1994) confirmed that the result was not sensitive to the choice of annual end points or to the inclusion of males. Charles Manski (1992–93) also reported little evidence of a disproportionate growth in B.A. completion by low-income youth graduating from high school between 1972 and 1980.

One hypothesis to reconcile the estimates of tuition impacts with the failure to find an increase in enrollment by low-income youth following the establishment of the Pell Grant program is that students are expected to make a significant up-front investment to apply to college and to apply for financial aid before they learn anything about the amount of aid available, whereas they can read about a tuition increase in the newspaper or see it in a college's application materials. The amount of aid that is available may come as a surprise. Those who are sufficiently committed to fill out the paperwork required to apply for federal financial aid may simply be less price-sensitive than others.

Also cited in table 8.4, Sue Dynarski has recently estimated the impact of two other programs that operated outside of the federal need-analysis framework: one looking at the impact of the cessation of tuition benefits for Social Security survivors, and the other evaluating the effect of the Hope Scholarship program in Georgia. Dynarski (1999) finds that after the discontinuation of the Social Security Student Benefit program, college entry by students with deceased parents declined by 19.4 to 25.6 percentage points relative to other youth. To convert this estimate to a scale similar to those reported here, Dynarski calculates that the value of the benefit program had been roughly $5,300 (in 1990 dollars). This implies an impact of 3.7 to 4.8 percentage points per $1,000 change in price.

In a second paper, Dynarski (2000) reports on her study of enrollment rates for youth in Georgia relative to other southern states, before and after the Hope Scholarship program was initiated in that state. She estimates that the program increased college enrollment rates of eighteen- to nineteen-year-olds by 7.0 to 7.9 percentage points. Given the value of the Hope Scholarship, this estimate converts to an estimate of 3.1 to 3.5 percentage points per $1,000 difference in cost.

Interestingly, because both programs operate outside the typical need-analysis system, eligibility was known a priori and did not require that an individual submit a Free Application for Federal Student Aid (FAFSA) form and wait for an award letter to know whether he or she had qualified for the aid. As such, both financial aid programs operated similarly to a tuition increase, which is relatively costless to anticipate. In contrast, the Pell Grant program requires remarkable foresight. An applicant has to fill out a FAFSA, be assigned an expected family contribution, and receive an award letter from a school simply to learn how much federal aid is on offer. It may not be a coincidence that the estimated impacts of such nontraditional forms of aid and tuition increases are so similar, and larger than the apparent impact of the establishment of the Pell Grant program.

However, there is other evidence that unexpected grant aid awards can have relatively large impacts on enrollment behavior, even among those who have already filled out financial aid forms. In a recent evaluation of the Cal Grant program (Kane 2003), I found large impacts of grant aid on student college enrollment decisions for California residents submitting financial aid applications. The Cal Grant program provides California residents with grants to attend college if their high school grade point average (GPA) exceeds a specific threshold and if their family income and assets fall below program maxima. Before 2001, the GPA threshold was unknown to parents or to program administrators until after the application deadline had passed. The reason was that the legislature funded a fixed number of grant awards, and the minimum GPA was set where the maximum number of grants were awarded. In years when many students were applying to college, the threshold was set high; when fewer students were applying, the threshold was lower. This may have made it difficult for parents to make their financial plans, but it was certainly fortuitous for the purpose of evaluation, since those immediately above or immediately below the threshold might plausibly be considered similar.[11] In 1998 the GPA threshold for the most generous Cal Grants was 3.15. For those with income and assets low enough to qualify, Kane (2003) reports a three- to four-percentage-point difference in college enrollment rates for eligible youth with GPAs immediately above and immediately below the threshold. Interestingly, there is no evidence of a similar discontinuity at the GPA cutoff for those with family income or assets above the eligibility limits.

Interaction Between Tuition and Family Income

Much work has focused on estimating differences in sensitivity to tuition increases for high- and low-income families. Manski and Wise (1983), Radner and Miller (1970), Bishop (1977), and Kohn, Manski, and Mundel (1976) report greater responsiveness to tuition differences among those from lower income quartiles. More recently, McPherson and Schapiro (1991) and Kane (1994, 1996) also find greater impacts of tuition on the enrollment decisions of low-income youth. On the other hand, Ellwood and Kane (2000) report findings with the

NELS data that are somewhat sensitive to specification. In some specifications they find an interaction effect, but not in others. Cameron and Heckman (1998) also fail to find robust evidence of an income interaction effect: although their point estimates show decreasing effects of tuition as parental income rises, they cannot reject the hypothesis that tuition has similar effects at varying income levels.

Comparatively Sluggish Response to Rising Returns to College

Parents and students appear to be extremely sensitive to tuition policies, at least relative to their responsiveness to the rise in the labor market payoffs to college. Recall from table 8.1 that there was a seven-percentage-point increase in college entry by high school graduates between the 1980 to 1982 period and 1992, from 68 percent to 75 percent. This seems large until we compare it to the growth in the payoff to educational attainment over the time period. Using the student responsiveness to tuition cited earlier, the rise in college enrollment witnessed during the 1980s was roughly as large as we might have expected to see in response to a $1,000 to $1,500 increase in annual tuition, based on the empirical estimates cited here. For an individual who was considering being in school for four years, this would have amounted to a $3,700 to $5,500 increase in anticipated expense over those four years (using a discount rate of 6 percent).

Obviously, the actual payoff of a college degree for the cohort of youth graduating from high school in 1992 remains to be seen, since they have yet to enjoy the benefit of a full career. However, it is possible to form a reasonable estimate based on contemporaneous evidence. Any such estimate would probably suggest that the payoffs to college have risen much more than $5,500 in present value. Suppose youth considering college formed an expectation of the payoff to college by looking around at people of varying ages and educational attainment to form an estimate of the value of a college degree. Among twenty-five- to thirty-four-year-old males, high school graduates working full-year, full-time earned $26,984 in 1980 while college graduates earned $34,096.[12] The differential in annual earnings between the two educational groups had grown from $7,112 in 1980 to $14,579 by 1992. The differential in annual income among thirty-five- to forty-four-year-olds grew from $16,486 per year to $24,391; among forty-five- to fifty-four-year-olds from $21,886 to $26,051; and among fifty-five- to sixty-four-year-olds from $22,355 to $24,141. Discounting each of these back to the viewpoint of a twenty-one-year-old considering four years of college, the estimated value of a college degree would have increased by $78,649 over the period 1980 to 1992, using a 6 percent discount rate.

Of course, not everyone could expect to finish a four-year degree, particularly those on the margin of college entry. However, the present value of completing one to three years of college would also have increased by a sizable $47,574, using a similar method.

Although parents and students did seem to respond to the rise in the college wage premium by enrolling in college at higher rates, the increase was only about as large as we would have expected from a much smaller increase in tuition. Either people are hypersensitive to tuition or they are making a much more conservative estimate of the future value of a college degree than a cross-section estimate would suggest. In either case, it is important to attempt to reconcile the large estimates of the impact of tuition differences with the seemingly more muted response to the rise in the value of a college education over time.

Borrowing Constraints?

As pointed out by Gary Becker in his classic volume *Human Capital* (1993), the capital market for college investments is likely to be imperfect. Potential college entrants have little collateral to provide to investors. And as a result, without contracts allowing for indentured labor, there is no way for lenders to force college graduates to earn up to their potential. Families are likely to be in the best position to do so (although as any parent would testify, even their points of leverage are limited). Those with greater family resources are likely to have the greatest access to such capital.

The federal government has attempted to create such a market by providing a federal guarantee on loans made to qualified students attending qualified institutions. However, the solution is incomplete. The most that dependent students can borrow under the federally guaranteed student loan programs is $2,625 their first year in college, $3,500 the second year, and $5,500 for subsequent undergraduate years. With the average tuition at public two-year and four-year institutions and at private four-year institutions being $1,600, $3,200 and $14,500, respectively, in 1998–1999, such loan limits may be sufficient to pay tuition expenses at some institutions, but they generally fall well short of the full cost of attendance, which would include forgone earnings. Beginning in 1993, a student's parents could borrow to cover the combined cost of tuition and room and board costs for a student—but payments on such parental loans begin immediately, limiting their usefulness to those parents with insufficient cash flow. Although parental loans have accounted for much of the growth in loan volume over time, only a small share of parents have taken advantage of such loans.

The large differences in college-going by family income among those with similar test scores and the greater sensitivity of low-income youth to tuition differences would be consistent with borrowing constraints. However, they would be consistent with other explanations as well. For instance, a single test score is likely to be an imperfect measure of a student's academic preparation. Observed differences in college-going by family income among students with similar test scores may simply reflect unmeasured differences in academic preparation between high- and low-income youth. Cameron and Heckman (1998) report that with a sufficiently general allowance for family background selectivity with the NLSY, we could not reject the hypothesis that the estimated effect of parental income is zero. Moreover, Keane and Wolpin (2001) argue that borrowing constraints are not necessary to produce an interaction between tuition sensitivity and parental income.

Recent estimates of the payoff to schooling have suggested that those on the margin, whose decisions about entering college are influenced by such things as proximity to college and college costs, may have higher-than-average payoffs to college. Such results would also be consistent with borrowing constraints, since only those with higher-than-average returns to college would have surmounted the barriers to college attendance presented by borrowing constraints. In the presence of borrowing constraints, Kevin Lang (1993) and David Card (1995a) point out that the estimated payoff to college should be higher for those on the margin, since their cost of borrowing funds is higher. Recent instrumental variable estimates using geographic distance to college to estimate payoff to college (Kane and Rouse 1994; Card 1995b) have found that those on the margin, whose decisions about college are influenced by such factors, do tend to exhibit higher marginal returns. However, recent papers by Pedro Carneiro and James Heckman (2002) and Carneiro, Heckman, and Vytlacil (2001) question the validity of the instruments used in those studies and, using an alternative identification strategy, find below-average returns for those on the margin.

A recent paper by Cameron and Taber (forecoming) takes issue with such an interpretation of the instrumental variable results. They argue that borrowing constraints are more likely to be binding with respect to the direct costs of college—such as tuition and transportation costs—than with respect to forgone earnings. They proceed by comparing the instrumental variable estimates we find using proximity to college and the average earnings of high school graduates in their county as two different sources of variation in college costs. In fact, they do not find higher payoffs to college when using college proximity as an instrument than when they use forgone earnings as an instrument.[13] They cite this as evidence against the presence of borrowing constraints.

However, it is not clear why Cameron and Taber would expect borrowing constraints to apply to direct costs and not to at least some portion of the cost of forgone earnings. Suppose that in the absence of borrowing constraints an individual is consuming at a particular level. (For example, if that individual has a dependent spouse or child, he or she would face substantial costs of feeding and clothing them while in school.) If that individual cannot finance *both* his or her tuition and the desired level of consumption, then he or she is liquidity-constrained. In fact, in *Human Capital*, Becker (1993) discusses the symmetry of direct costs and forgone earnings in families' investment decisions.

A final piece of evidence that may be useful in identifying the potential importance of borrowing constraints is the difference in timing of college entry in high- and low-tuition states. Elsewhere (Kane 1996) I have found that youth graduating from high school in states with higher levels of tuition for state residents at public colleges in the state (presumably the least-cost alternative for most students) tend to enter college later. This too would be consistent with borrowing constraints, because in the absence of borrowing constraints, students would want to complete their educational investments as early in life as possible. The basic reasoning is that, by delaying a year, one is delaying costs as well as benefits. If, for a particular individual, the benefits to college are greater than the costs of college, then the costs of any delay in terms of deferred benefits must exceed the benefits of a delay in terms of any deferred costs. As a result, both delayed entry and part-time enrollment may themselves be prima facie evidence of borrowing constraints. The fact that delayed entry is more common in high-tuition states further corroborates such an interpretation.

However, once again, there may be alternative explanations for the observation of delayed timing in high-tuition states. For example, if labor market experience after high school provides some information regarding opportunity costs and the potential payoff to college, students in high-tuition states may be more eager to collect such information before making an investment in college than those in low-tuition states, since the cost of learning whether or not one is "college material" by entering college first is lower. Such an explanation may also predict delayed entry in high-tuition states.

In summary, even though there are a number of pieces of evidence that would be consistent with borrowing constraints, it is difficult to find a definitive test of the existence of borrowing constraints in the literature. In each case, there are alternative explanations that would not require borrowing constraints to be part of the story. In this regard, the debate over borrowing constraints is similar to the debate over whether the payoff to educational attainment is a payoff to concrete skill or a payoff to the signal provided by that skill. Although the answer is fundamental to any consideration of the social benefits of further investments in training, many pieces of evidence would be consistent with either interpretation.[14]

DOES PUBLIC FINANCING INCREASE OR
DECREASE INEQUALITY?

In 1968, W. Lee Hansen and Burton Weisbrod calculated the value of the subsidies received and taxes paid by families with students attending the University of California and compared those benefits to the subsidies and taxes paid by students attending other institutions in the state—the California state university system and the community college system—as well as those receiving no postsecondary schooling at all. The calculations implied a large net subsidy for families attending the University of California, a more modest subsidy for those attending less selective public institutions in the state, and a net transfer from families with students not attending college. Given the correlation between family income and attendance at the University of California, Hansen and Weisbrod (1969) suggested that the system for financing higher education in California increased rather than decreased inequality.

The original Hansen-Weisbrod paper provoked nearly a decade-long debate, leading the *Journal of Human Resources* to publish seven responses to the original article between 1970 and 1977. The debate raised a number of issues, but perhaps the most important critique came from Joseph Pechman (1970). Rather than calculate net subsidies for different parts of the University of California system and then point to the correlation between attendance and income as evidence for the inequity of higher education finance, as Hansen and Weisbrod had done, Pechman used the same data to directly calculate net subsidies received by family income. When calculated by income class rather than by institution attended, the calculations revealed that higher-income families actually paid more in taxes to support higher education than they received in benefits. In other words, although those attending the University of California received large subsidies, attendance at the university was not sufficiently correlated with income to offset the fact that higher-income families paid a large share of the taxes that supported the system.

Table 8.5 reports similar calculations for a more contemporary sample, using results first reported in Kane (1999). The table employs information on student aid received by students in the National Postsecondary Student Aid Survey of undergraduates in 1992–1993 merged with data from the Integrated Postsecondary Education Data System on state and local appropriations per student at each of the institutions attended. Data on college enrollment rates and years in college by parental family income were calculated using the National Educational Longitudinal Survey sample of those graduating from high school in 1992. Subsidies were calculated by income level. The first column reports information about state and federal grant aid received by undergraduates of various income levels. Given the means-testing for most state and federal grant aid programs, such subsidies are clearly targeted at lower-income families, with students from families with incomes of $13,000 or less receiving $1,848 on average—roughly ten times as much state and federal grant aid as those with parental incomes above $90,000 receive. The second column reports the subsidy value of the state and federal loans received by the same students, using a rough rule of thumb that a dollar in loan aid contains a subsidy equal to roughly one-third of its value. Loan subsidies too are quite unequally distributed. The third column reports state and local appropriations per student at the institutions attended by students of varying parental income levels. Perhaps surprisingly, there is not a strong relationship between the state and local appropriations received by students of varying income levels. On the one hand, high-income students attending public institutions did tend to attend the public institutions with large subsidies. On the other hand, higher-income students were also considerably more likely to attend private universities. The two effects were roughly offsetting. The fourth column reports the

TABLE 8.5   *Public Subsidies to College Students, by Parental Family Income (1992 Dollars)*

Parental Income	State and Federal Grant Aid	State and Federal Loan Aid	State and Local Appropriations	Total Annual Subsidy per Student	Proportion Entering College	Years of Enrollment	Total Subsidy (Column 4 × Column 5 × Column 6)
$0 to 13,000	$1,848	$334	$1,790	$3972	.390	3.11	$4,812
$13,000 to 25,000	1,132	266	1,813	3,211	.535	3.35	5,750
$25,000 to 35,000	719	252	1,929	2,900	.558	3.45	5,573
$35,000 to 45,000	352	164	1,549	2,066	.643	3.44	4,559
$45,000 to 65,000	243	129	2,145	2,517	.720	3.83	6,927
$65,000 to 90,000	172	136	1,965	2,273	.822	4.12	7,647
$90,000 or more	161	50	2,114	2,325	.898	4.41	9,195

Source: Table drawn from Kane (1999).
Notes: These estimates combine data from the National Postsecondary Student Aid Survey in 1992–1993 with data from the Integrated Postsecondary Education Data System on state and local appropriations per student. Students at any public or private, two-year or four-year college or proprietary school were included. Part-time students were allocated one-third of the state and local appropriation per student. Independent students were excluded. Data on college entry rates were drawn from the 1994 follow-up of the NELS sample of eighth-grade students in 1988. The students were two years out of high school. Data on academic years of enrollment were drawn from the High School and Beyond survey of high school sophomores in 1980 when they were followed up in 1992. Years of enrollment do not refer to years of college completed but to the number of years during which a student reported some enrollment.

sum of grant, loan, and direct institutional subsidies for average students from various income levels, revealing a modest progressivity in the targeting of public subsidies to low-income students.

What drives the correlation between family income and public subsidies to college is not the fact that high-income college students attend expensive places like the University of California at Berkeley, but the fact that they are simply more likely to attend any college at all. As reported in columns 5 and 6, higher-income students are more likely both to attend college and to remain in college conditional upon enrolling. The last column in table 8.5 accounts for both of these effects: high school graduates from families earning over $90,000 per year receive nearly double the subsidies received by families with incomes of less than $13,000.

Table 8.5 does not report the taxes paid by students of varying income levels. Usually, it is difficult to identify the marginal source of tax revenue or expenditure used to pay for higher education. However, it is also clear that any tax would have to be extremely regressive to reverse Pechman's conclusion that despite a correlation between income and college-going, public financing of higher education provides larger benefits to low-income students than the taxes paid by low-income families to support them. The reason is that even though families in the highest-income category received subsidies that were *twice* as large as those received by the lowest-income families, their incomes are more than *seven* times as large. If higher education were supported by a proportional income tax, higher-income families would pay more than the value of the subsidies they receive, even though they would be more likely to receive subsidies than lower-income parents. Moreover, average lower-income students would receive greater subsidies than the taxes their parents would have paid. Therefore, while it is true that public funding of higher education is a transfer from those who do not send their children to college to those who do, and that higher-income families are more likely to attend college, it still serves on net to redistribute income from higher- to lower-income families, because the differences in college-going are not nearly as large as the differences in average income between high- and low-income families.

THE DIRECT EFFECT OF THE SUPPLY OF COLLEGE-EDUCATED LABOR ON WAGE INEQUALITY

Most of the discussion of the rising payoff to a college education in the late 1980s and early 1990s looked for explanations by focusing on demand-side factors such as computerization, the changing nature of work, and the rise of the "knowledge economy." However, an important paper by Lawrence Katz and Kevin Murphy (1992) identifies a potential role of supply-side factors as well. They note that we can get surprisingly far in explaining trends in the payoff to educational attainment by positing a constant rate of increase in demand for skilled labor in postwar America, with the fluctuations in the college premium driven by a sharp rise in the educational attainment of the workforce during the 1970s and a sharp slowdown in the supply of skilled labor during the 1980s. Although David Autor, Lawrence Katz, and Alan Krueger (1998) find evidence of some acceleration in the demand for skilled labor beginning in the 1970s, fluctuations in the rate of growth in the supply of college-educated labor also seem to have played an important role. David Card and Thomas Lemieux (2000) also point to the importance of a slowdown in the relative supply of college-educated workers as an important cause of the rising education premium.

The potential importance of supply factors noted by Katz and Murphy (1992) leads immediately to two additional questions: First, what factors accounted for the sharp slowdown in educational attainment? Second, might the current growth in college enrollment eventually surpass the growth in demand for skilled labor and lead to a closing of the wage gap between more- and less-educated workers?

Figure 8.8 reports trends in educational attainment by age and cohort for those turning twenty-six to thirty between 1950 and 2008. Following Autor, Katz, and Krueger (1998), I report the log of the relative supply of college graduates to high school graduates. Specifically, the relative supply is calculated as the log of the ratio of the proportion of college equivalents (the proportion of the cohort with a bachelor's degree plus 1.2 times the proportion with a graduate degree plus 0.5 times the proportion with "some college") to the proportion with the equivalent of a high school degree (the proportion with a high school degree plus .83 times the proportion of high school dropouts). The advantage of this statistic is that it collapses into one dimension any changes in several different levels of educational attainment: B.A. degree completion, high school dropout rates, and so on. One alternative would have been to calculate average number of years of schooling, but changes in the way educational attainment was collected in the CPS in 1993 make that impossible.

The results in figure 8.8 pool information across a number of Current Population Surveys. Estimates are reported by the year in which the cohort was age twenty-six to thirty. The educational attainment of a given cohort was observed at different ages. Cohorts tend to report higher educational attainment as they age, reflected in the vertical discon-

FIGURE 8.8   *Trends in the Relative Supply of College-Educated Men and Women, by the Year in Which Each Cohort Was Age Twenty-Six to Thirty*

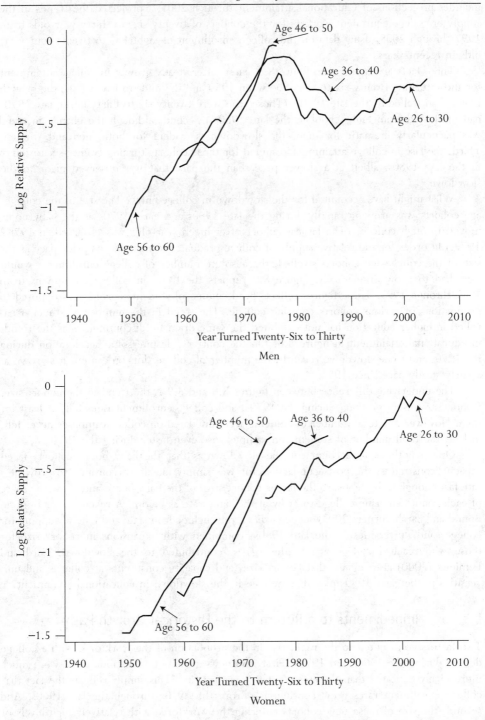

Men

Women

tinuities in the line segments in figure 8.8. (The data were reported for the population in each cohort and were not limited to employed persons, for instance.) Figure 8.8 also includes projections of educational attainment through 2001. I projected the trends in the supply of college-equivalent workers for the cohorts of twenty-six- to thirty-year-olds from 1997 through 2008, using data on the college enrollment of eighteen- to twenty-four-year-olds in recent years.

Three facts are apparent in figure 8.8. First, after steady growth in college attainment for those turning twenty-six to thirty between 1950 and the mid- to late 1970s, the growth largely had stalled by the late 1970s. (Those who were twenty-six to thirty in the late 1970s had graduated from high school in the late 1960s.) Second, although the change in trend was particularly dramatic for men, the slowdown is evident for both men and women. Third, the rise in college attainment resumed for those cohorts turning twenty-six to thirty in the late 1980s, albeit at a slower pace than the pace that was observed prior to the slowdown.

What might have accounted for the slowdown in college entry? The size of the college-age cohorts was growing rapidly during the late 1960s and early 1970s as the baby boom moved through college. (The largest cohort of eighteen-year-olds was observed in 1978–1979.) In order for the relative supply of college graduates to maintain its prior pace as the size of the college-age cohorts swelled, the absolute number of college enrollments would have had to grow dramatically. Figure 8.9 reports the trend in college enrollment from 1947 through 1995. These figures reflect "head counts" of students enrolled, as opposed to proportions of various cohorts entering college. The trend in the number of students enrolled in higher education has not exhibited the same dramatic discontinuities as the trends in educational attainment in figure 8.8. On the contrary, despite some acceleration during the 1970s and some slowdown recently, the number of college slots on campus has grown at a fairly steady pace since 1952.

The underlying difference between figures 8.8 and 8.9 is the trend in the cohort size. Cohort sizes were growing during the 1970s, and college enrollment rates fell, at least for men. However, the total number of students accommodated on college campuses never fell; in fact, the total number of students on campus rose even faster during the 1970s.

One hypothesis to account for the slowdown is that the baby boom cohorts faced capacity constraints: the postsecondary sector was simply unable to continue to grow at a rate fast enough to both absorb the larger cohort sizes of the baby boom and allow the share of each cohort entering college to grow at the same rate as before. A recent paper by John Bound and Sarah Turner (2003) suggests that a retrenchment in state and federal support for colleges and universities in the late 1960s, combined with expansions in cohort size for those who reached college age in the 1970s, contributed to the slowdown. Card and Lemieux (2000) also suggest that cohort sizes and capacity constraints at colleges and universities in the early 1990s played some role in the slowdown in educational attainment.

Impediments to a Return to the Historical Growth Path

Two factors contributed to the rapid rise in the proportion of the workforce with a college degree during the 1960s and 1970s. First, the new entrants to the labor force were much more highly educated than the cohorts who were retiring. This simply reflects the fact that college enrollment rates grew continuously from the 1920s through the late 1960s. And second, the size of these new cohorts entering the workforce with relatively high levels of education was larger than previous cohorts. Neither of these factors is true now. Because of

FIGURE 8.9   *Trend in Total Enrollment in U.S. Higher Education*

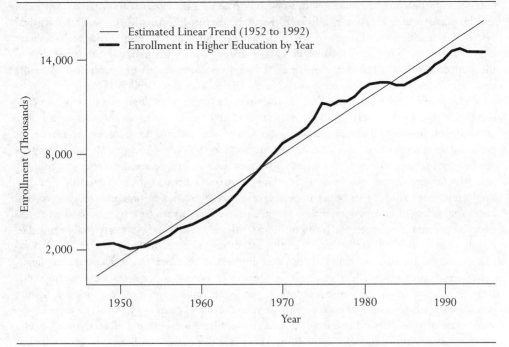

— Estimated Linear Trend (1952 to 1992)
— Enrollment in Higher Education by Year

Source: U.S. Department of Education (2000a), table 175.

the slowdown in the rate of growth in educational attainment for college-age cohorts beginning during the 1970s, the difference in educational attainment between the new entrants
and retirees is not as large as it had been. Moreover, the number of eighteen-year-olds is
only now climbing out of a trough, after declining by roughly one-fifth since the late 1970s.
As Ellwood (2001) notes, both facts imply that growth in the relative supply of college
graduates in the workforce over the next twenty years is likely to be sluggish, despite the
recent rises in college enrollment.

CONCLUSION

As has been well documented over the last decade and a half, the labor market payoff to a
college degree rose between 1980 and the mid-1990s and has remained high. Families' and
students' response has received much less attention. The percentage of twenty-five- to
twenty-seven-year-olds reporting any past college enrollment rose from 47 percent to 57
percent between 1988 and 1999, a 21 percent increase. The timing of the rise in enrollment coincided with the change in labor market rewards: the rise began for those turning
eighteen in 1979—the year the college wage differential began rising. Moreover, the proportion of twenty-five- to twenty-seven-year-olds with a B.A. degree or higher also rose,
from 22.1 to 27.2 percent, over this period. On a proportionate basis, the fact that the rise
in B.A. degree completion (23 percent) roughly matched the rise in college entry (21
percent) implied that there was little decline in the proportion of college entrants completing a bachelor's degree. This is remarkable given that we might have expected the marginal
college entrant to have been less well prepared academically.

Historically, there have been large gaps in college entry by race and by income. However, the evidence suggests that those gaps are widening, not closing. The rise in college entry since 1980 was larger for whites and other non-Hispanics than for African American and Hispanic youth. Moreover, although there are regrettable gaps in the federal statistical system for tracking enrollment of youth by parental income, the rise seems to have been larger for middle- and high-income parents than for those with parental family income in the bottom quartile. (The latter evidence is based on comparisons of enrollment rates for youth graduating from high school in the early 1980s and early 1990s.)

The "causal" role of parental family resources in students' college enrollment decisions remains in question. Family income is clearly related to academic achievement—a major correlate of postsecondary enrollment—but there are differences in college enrollment even among students with similar achievement test scores in high school. (Although the gaps are larger for those with test scores in the bottom quartile, there are differences in college-going by family income even among students with test scores in the top quartile.) Still, a single test score is likely to be an imperfect measure of academic preparation and parental tastes for college. I have reported the evidence derived from various attempts to identify the effect of parental resources. As is often the case, the evidence suggests that family resources do play a role, but it is difficult to find the definitive empirical test.

A second question of immediate policy interest is whether the difference in college-going by family income is the result of imperfect access to capital—"borrowing constraints"—or some other cause related to family income. (For example, higher-income parents may simply enjoy the consumptive value of college entry. Even if family income plays a causal role, it need not imply a need for public intervention.) Here the evidence is also suggestive, but even more irresolute. There is a dispute in the literature over whether the payoffs to college for marginal entrants are higher or lower than the return for the average entrant. Earlier work by Card (1995a, 1995b) and others using instrumental variable estimators suggested that the payoffs for the marginal entrant may indeed be higher—a finding that would be consistent with borrowing constraints. However, recent work by Carneiro, Heckman, and Vytlacil (2001) raises questions about the validity of those strategies using instrumental variables and presents alternative estimates suggesting that marginal entrants enjoy lower returns.

The U.S. system for financing higher education is at least as misunderstood today as the health care finance system was twenty years ago. Not only are parents paying for their child's college education in more ways than they realize—through direct subsidies to institutions, through financial aid programs, through generous new tax benefits—but the impact of each of these subsidies on the decisions of various groups of youth is not well understood by policymakers. In 2003 it will have been three decades since the Pell Grant program was established, yet differences in college-going by family income remain wide and, according to some recent evidence, appear to be widening. The higher education policy debate has become too bogged down with incremental questions involving issues such as changes in the need-analysis formula to notice the bigger questions: Why is it that the establishment of the Pell Grant program seemed to have no impact on the college enrollment rates of low-income youth? What is the "bang for the buck" achieved with different types of public subsidies, from across-the-board subsidies to keep tuition low to Pell Grants to loan subsidies? Why do so few parents save for college, and how are their decisions influenced by state and federal policies? We will not make progress in closing the gaps in college enrollment by family income unless we have some of the answers to such questions.

We usually think about higher education policy as merely responding to the labor market—as if the price of college-educated labor were dictated exogenously by technological factors. However, recent work has suggested that capacity constraints in higher education in the early 1970s may have contributed to the rapid rise in the college differential, by leading to a slowdown in the rate of increase in the supply of college-educated labor. Moreover, if there is to be an eventual reduction in the earnings gap between college and high school graduates, higher education policy may well have a role to play by increasing the supply of college graduates relative to high school graduates. Unfortunately, the prospects for a more robust response are dimmed by demographic trends. Between 1980 and 2000, the share of the labor force with a college degree rose by eight percentage points, from 22 percent to 30 percent. Even under very optimistic assumptions, Ellwood (2001) projects, the percentage of the labor force with a college degree will grow by only five percentage points over the next twenty years.

NOTES

1. This is true if we report college-going rates as a proportion of the population in a particular age group or as a proportion of high school graduates in a population group. Given the rise in high school graduation rates for blacks, the latter fact would be less surprising. It is the former that is discussed later.

2. These data rely on the parent-reported family income data rather than the less reliable student responses. If students attended more than one type of postsecondary institution, they were categorized as four-year college if they ever attended a four-year college and, if not, as two-year college entrants if they ever attended a two-year college.

3. For an analysis using the October CPS, see Hauser (1993). Occasionally, tables reporting college-going by family income are reported in Department of Education publications. For example, *The Condition of Education: 1999* (U.S. Department of Education 1999b, 114) reports college enrollment rates by "family income." The CPS reports household income, not parental family income. Students who have formed their own household may be counted as a "low-income" household. As a result, during a period of rising enrollment rates, we might expect that an increasing share of "low-income" households with young people in college are in fact households formed by college students.

4. Both sets of estimates are based on parent-reported, not student-reported, family income.

5. The increases over the time period were larger for women than for men.

6. For a more detailed discussion of the closing gaps in test performance between blacks and whites, see Jencks and Phillips (1998), particularly chapters 5 and 6.

7. Men still account for the majority of doctorate and first-professional degrees conferred.

8. Hoxby and Terry (1999) do not break out the effect of this subcomponent directly. I calculated the contribution of the component using the coefficients in table 8.1 and the variances in the expenditures per student over time reported in the appendix.

9. Parental education was measured by including dummy variables for the highest level of education of either parent, as measured by an indicator of whether either of an individual's parents graduated from high school, attended college, completed a bachelor's degree, or completed a graduate degree.

10. All series were adjusted for inflation using the CPI-U-X1.

11. Under an entitlement program where the threshold is known beforehand, those with GPAs immediately above the threshold are likely to disproportionately include the college-bound, while those immediately below the threshold would disproportionately contain those who do not need the funding.

12. All figures in this paragraph have been converted to 1990 dollars using the GDP deflator.

13. Cameron and Taber (forthcoming) also report the results from a structural model that also uses the same assumption for identification—that is, that borrowing constraints should apply to direct costs and not to indirect costs.

14. Andrew Weiss (1995) provides explanations for the same set of empirical findings that would involve either education as a skill or education as a job market signal.

REFERENCES

Acemoglu, Daron, and Jorn-Steffen Pischke. 2001. "Changes in the Wage Structure, Family Income, and Children's Education." *European Economic Review* 45: 890–904.

Autor, David, Lawrence F. Katz, and Alan B. Krueger. 1998. "Computing Inequality: Have Computers Changed the Labor Market?" *Quarterly Journal of Economics* 113(4): 1169–1214.

Becker, Gary S. 1993. *Human Capital: A Theoretical and Empirical Analysis, with Special Reference to Education.* 3rd ed. Chicago: University of Chicago Press.

Bishop, John. 1977. "The Effect of Public Policies on the Demand for Higher Education." *Journal of Human Resources* 12: 285–307.

Bound, John, and Sarah Turner. 2003. "Cohort Crowding: How Resources Affect Collegiate Attainment." Unpublished paper. University of Virginia, Charlottesville (March).

Cameron, Stephen V., and James J. Heckman. 1998. "Life Cycle Schooling and Dynamic Selection Bias: Models and Evidence for Five Cohorts of American Males." *Journal of Political Economy* 106(2, April): 262–333.

———. 2001. "The Dynamics of Educational Attainment for Black, Hispanic and White Males." *Journal of Political Economy* 109(3): 455–99.

Cameron, Stephen V., and Christopher Taber. Forthcoming. "Borrowing Constraints and Returns to Schooling." *Journal of Political Economy.*

Card, David. 1995a. "Earnings, Schooling, and Ability Revisited." *Research in Labor Economics* 14: 23–48.

———. 1995b. "Using Geographic Variation in College Proximity to Estimate the Return to Schooling." In *Aspects of Labor Market Behavior: Essays in Honor of John Vanderkamp,* edited by Louis Christofides, E. Kenneth Grant, and Robert Swidinsky. Toronto: University of Toronto Press.

Card, David, and Thomas Lemieux. 2000. "Dropout and Enrollment Trends in the Postwar Period: What Went Wrong in the 1970s." Working paper 7658. Cambridge, Mass.: National Bureau of Economic Research.

Carneiro, Pedro, and James Heckman. 2002. "The Evidence on Credit Constraints in Postsecondary Schooling." *Economic Journal* 112(October): 705–34.

Carneiro, Pedro, James Heckman, and Edward Vytlacil. 2001. "Estimating the Rate of Return to Education When It Varies Among Individuals." Working paper. University of Chicago.

Charles, Kerwin, and Ming-Ching Luoh. 2001. "Gender Differences in Completed Schooling." Working paper. Ann Arbor: University of Michigan, Department of Economics (January).

Dynarski, Susan. 1999. "Does Aid Matter? Measuring the Effect of Student Aid on College Attendance and Completion." Working paper 7422. Cambridge, Mass.: National Bureau of Economic Research (November).

———. 2000. "Hope for Whom? Financial Aid for the Middle Class and Its Impact on College Attendance." Working paper 7756. Cambridge, Mass.: National Bureau of Economic Research (June).

Ellwood, David T. 2001. "The Sputtering Labor Force of the Twenty-first Century: Can Social Policy Help?" Unpublished paper. Harvard University, John F. Kennedy School of Government, Cambridge, Mass. (January).

Ellwood, David, and Thomas J. Kane. 2000. "Who Is Getting a College Education: Family Background and the Growing Gaps in Enrollment." In *Securing the Future,* edited by Sheldon Danziger and Jane Waldfogel. New York: Russell Sage Foundation.

Gottschalk, Peter, and Steve Pizer. 1999. "Changes in Inequality Among Recent Labor Market Entrants: The Role of Rising Skill Intensity of Females." Unpublished paper. Boston College, Department of Economics, and Abt Associates (April).

Hansen, W. Lee. 1983. "Impact of Student Financial Aid on Access." In *The Crisis in Higher Education,* edited by Joseph Froomkin. New York: Academy of Political Science.

Hansen, W. Lee, and Burton A. Weisbrod. 1969. "The Distribution of Costs and Direct Benefits of Public Higher Education: the Case of California." *Journal of Human Resources* 4: 176–91.

Hauser, Robert. 1993. "Trends in College Attendance Among Blacks, Whites, and Hispanics." In *Studies of Supply and Demand in Higher Education,* edited by Charles Clotfelter and Michael Rothschild. Chicago: University of Chicago Press.

Hoxby, Caroline Minter, and Bridget Terry. 1999. "Explaining Rising Income and Wage Inequality Among the College-Educated." Working paper 6873. Cambridge, Mass.: National Bureau of Economic Research (January).

Jencks, Christopher, and Meredith Phillips, eds. 1998. *The Black-White Test Score Gap.* Washington, D.C.: Brookings Institution.

Kane, Thomas J. 1994. "College Attendance by Blacks Since 1970: The Role of College Cost, Family Background, and the Returns to Education." *Journal of Political Economy* 102(5): 878–911.

———. 1996. "College Cost, Borrowing Constraints, and the Timing of College Entry." *Eastern Economic Journal* 22(2): 181–94.

———. 1999. *The Price of Admission: Rethinking How Americans Pay for College.* Washington, D.C., and New York: Brookings Institution and Russell Sage Foundation.

———. 2003. "A Quasi-experimental Estimate of the Impact of Financial Aid on College-Going." Working paper 9703. Cambridge, Mass.: National Bureau of Economic Research (May).

Kane, Thomas J., and Cecilia Rouse. 1994. "Labor Market Returns to Two-Year and Four-Year Colleges." Working paper. Princeton, N.J.: Princeton University, Industrial Relations Section.

Katz, Lawrence F., and Kevin Murphy. 1992. "Changes in Relative Wages, 1963–1987: Supply and Demand Factors." *Quarterly Journal of Economics* 107: 35–78.

Keane, Michael, and Ken Wolpin. 2001. "The Effect of Parental Transfers and Borrowing Constraints on Educational Attainment." *International Economic Review* 42(4): 1051–1103.

Kohn, Meir, Charles Manski, and David Mundel. 1976. "An Empirical Investigation of Factors Which Influence College-Going Behavior." *Annals of Economic and Social Measures* 5: 391–419.

Lang, Kevin. 1993. "Ability Bias, Discount Rate Bias, and the Return to Education." Discussion paper. Boston University Department of Economics (May).

Leslie, Larry, and Paul T. Brinkman. 1987. "Student Price Response in Higher Education: The Student Demand Studies." *Journal of Higher Education* 58(2): 181–204.

———. 1988. *Economic Value of Higher Education.* New York: Macmillan.

Manski, Charles F. 1992–93. "Income and Higher Education." *Focus* (University of Wisconsin, Madison, Institute for Research on Poverty) 14(3, Winter): 14–19.

Manski, Charles F., and David A. Wise. 1983. *College Choice in America.* Cambridge, Mass.: Harvard University Press.

Mayer, Susan. 1997. *What Money Can't Buy: Family Income and Children's Life Chances.* Cambridge, Mass.: Harvard University Press.

McPherson, Michael S., and Morton Owen Schapiro. 1991. "Does Student Aid Affect College Enrollment? New Evidence on a Persistent Controversy." *American Economic Review* 81: 309–18.

Pechman, Joseph A. 1970. "The Distributional Effects of Public Higher Education in California." *Journal of Human Resources* 5(3): 361–70.

Radner, Roy, and L. S. Miller. 1970. "Demand and Supply in U.S. Higher Education: A Progress Report." *American Economic Review* 60: 326–34.

Rosenbaum, James. 2001. *Beyond College for All.* New York: Russell Sage Foundation.

Shea, John. 2000. "Does Parents' Money Matter?" *Journal of Public Economics* 77(2): 155–84.

U.S. Department of Education. National Center for Education Statistics. 1999a. *Digest of Education Statistics: 1998.* Washington: U.S. Government Printing Office.

———. 1999b. *The Condition of Education: 1999.* Washington: U.S. Government Printing Office.

———. 2000a. *Digest of Education Statistics: 1999.* Washington: U.S. Government Printing Office.

———. 2000b. *NAEP 1999 Trends in Academic Progress: Three Decades of Student Performance, NCES 2000–469.* Washington: U.S. Government Printing Office.

U.S. Department of Health and Human Services. 2000. *Trends in the Well-being of America's Children and Youth: 2000.* Washington: U.S. Government Printing Office.

Venti, Steven F. 1984. "The Effects of Income Maintenance on Work, Schooling, and Nonmarket Activities of Youth." *Review of Economics and Statistics* 66(1): 16–25.

Weiss, Andrew. 1995. "Human Capital Versus Signaling Explanations of Wages." *Journal of Economic Perspectives* 9(4): 133–54.

Chapter 9

Digital Inequality: From Unequal Access to Differentiated Use

Paul DiMaggio, Eszter Hargittai, Coral Celeste, and Steven Shafer

The Internet boosts immeasurably our collective capacity to archive information, search through large quantities of it quickly, and retrieve it rapidly. It is said that the Internet will expand access to education, good jobs, and better health and that it will create new deliberative spaces for political discussion and provide citizens with direct access to government. Insofar as such claims are plausible, Internet access is an important resource, and inequality in Internet access is a significant concern for social scientists who study inequality.

This chapter reviews what we know about inequality in access to and use of new digital technologies. Until recently most research has focused on inequality in access (the "digital divide"), measured in a variety of ways. We agree that inequality of access is important, because it is likely to reinforce inequality in opportunities for economic mobility and social participation. At the same time we argue that a more thorough understanding of digital inequality requires placing Internet access in a broader theoretical context and asking a wider range of questions about the impact of information technologies and informational goods on social inequality.

This chapter is structured around five key issues:

1. *The digital divide. Who has access to the Internet, who does not have access, and how has access changed?* This is the topic about which information is currently most abundant.

2. *Is access to and use of the Internet more or less unequal than access to and use of other forms of information technology?* Even if access to and use of the Internet is profoundly unequal, the Internet's spread may represent a net increase in equality over the pre-Web media landscape. The implications of the new digital technologies for inequality in access to information can be understood only in the context of a comparative analysis of the impact of inequality on access to and use of all the major communication media—not just the Internet but broadcast media, newspapers and magazines, telephones, and even word of mouth. If publishers stopped printing newspapers and put all the news online, would inequality in information about politics and world affairs diminish, become greater, or stay the same?

3. *Among the increasing number of Internet users, how do such factors as gender, race, and socio-economic status shape inequality in ease, effectiveness, and quality of use? What mechanisms*

account for links between individual attributes and technological outcomes? We place great importance on understanding socially structured variation in the ability of persons with formal access to the Internet to use it to enhance their access to valuable information resources. In particular, we are interested in the impact of social inequality on where, how easily, and with how much autonomy people can go online; the quality of the hardware and connection that users have at their disposal; how skilled users are at finding information; how effectively they can draw on social support in solving problems that they encounter in their efforts to do so; and how productively they use their Internet access to enhance their economic life chances and capacity for social and political participation.

4. *Does access to and use of the Internet affect people's life chances?* From the standpoint of public policy, the digital divide is only a problem insofar as going online shapes Internet users' life chances and capacity for civic engagement. What do we know about the effects of Internet access and use on such things as educational achievement and attainment, labor force participation, earnings, and voting? To what extent, if at all, do returns vary for different types of users? If there are no effects, or if the benefits for use are restricted to the already advantaged, then the case for government intervention to reduce inequality in access to digital technologies is correspondingly weaker.[1]

5. *How might the changing technology, regulatory environment, and industrial organization of the Internet render obsolete the findings reported here?* Because the Internet is a relatively new technology—browsers have been available for only about a decade and the Web was not fully privatized until the mid-1990s—we cannot assume that the results of research undertaken in past years will be replicated even a few years hence. The Internet is a moving target, with many economic and political interests vying to control its ultimate configuration. How might institutional changes—in economic control, in the codes that drive the technology, or in government regulatory and legislative actions—alter observed patterns of inequality in access and use?

We begin with a brief account of the origins and spread of Internet technology. Next, in order to place this chapter in a broader perspective, we review earlier attempts to address the relationship between technological change and social inequality. Finally, we review the literature on each of the five main questions and, where the research is lacking, develop an agenda for the work that needs to be done.[2]

A BRIEF HISTORY OF THE INTERNET

By "Internet" we mean the electronic network of networks that spans homes and workplaces and that people use to exchange e-mail, participate in interactive spaces of various kinds, and visit sites on the World Wide Web. ("Intranets," by contrast, are dedicated to a particular organization or set of organizations.) Because the Internet blazed into public consciousness with blinding rapidity, it is important to recall how briefly it has been a part of our lives: as early as 1994, just 11 percent of U.S. households had online access (NTIA 1995), and that was used almost exclusively for e-mail or for specialized purposes such as financial trading through dedicated connections. At the same time the Internet has deep roots: a computerized network linked scientists by the late 1960s, and the military devised a similar network a few years later. The various forebears were linked into an Internet in 1982. But only since 1993, after graphical interfaces became available and the scope of commercial activity broadened, did use of the medium begin to extend rapidly outside academic and military circles (Abbate 1999; Castells 2001).

From that point on, access to and use of the Internet spread swiftly. The number of Americans online grew from 2.5 million in 1995 (Pew Center for the People and the Press 1995) to 83 million in 1999 (IntelliQuest 1999), with 55 million Americans using the Internet on a typical day by mid-2000 (Pew Internet and American Life Project 2000, 5). Based on the Current Population Survey (CPS), in December 1998 the Internet had penetrated 26.2 percent of U.S. households. Less than two years later the figure stood at 41.5 percent, and almost 45 percent of individuals age three or older were reported to go online at home, school, work, or elsewhere (NTIA 2000). By September 2001 more than half of U.S. households had Internet service, and almost 54 percent of individuals went online (NTIA 2002).[3] (Many more have "access" in the sense of an available connection, whether or not they choose to use it, at home, work, school, a library, or a community center.) Since the autumn of 2001, growth in Internet use has stalled in the United States as fewer new users have come online and some existing users have gone offline (Lenhart et al. 2003).

Compared to other technologies, the Internet diffused rapidly, its trajectory similar to those of television and radio, each of which reached more than 50 percent of households within a few years of commercial introduction (Schement and Forbes 1999). Unlike those media, however, the Internet's adoption rate has slowed well short of full penetration. The gravity of the digital divide depends on whether slowing adoption after 2000 reflected a short-term effect of economic recession or a durable ceiling. Based on the experience of telephone service and cable television, which, like Internet service, entail monthly payments rather than a one-shot purchase, the latter seems more likely.

TECHNOLOGY AND INEQUALITY: A SELECTIVE TOUR OF SOCIAL-SCIENTIFIC PERSPECTIVES

The Internet is one in a long series of information and communication technologies—from speech to printing, movable type, telegraphy, telephony, radio, and television—that arguably influenced patterns of social inequality by destroying existing competencies and permitting early adopters to interact with more people and acquire more information over greater distances and in a shorter time. Before focusing on the Internet, then, we ask how the work of earlier generations of social analysts might place digital media into a broader context.

The most notable conclusion is that students of social inequality have paid very little attention to changes in communication technology. For the most part, researchers who *have* looked at technology have been more concerned with technologies of production (the factory system and various forms of automation, for example) than with technologies of consumption. Nonetheless, four ways in which technological change may influence social inequality are evident.

1. *Competence destruction increases inequality.* Harry Braverman (1974) argued that capitalist firms seek to develop technologies that "de-skill" workers—that permit firms to substitute unskilled operatives for workers with scarce craft skills in order to reduce wages and exert more effective workplace control. If this were the case, wage inequality would increase as unskilled jobs replace skilled jobs. Research on the de-skilling hypothesis (Spenner 1983) has found substantial support at the occupational level but little for the labor force as a whole. New technologies, it seems, have predictable trajectories, at their inception generating new skilled occupations that are "de-skilled" over time. The continual emergence of new technologies, however, ensures that skill levels in the labor force as a whole are stable

or increasing, even as those for specific occupations decline. More recent research finds less support for the de-skilling hypothesis, even at the firm level. Companies vary substantially in the extent to which they implement versions of technology that locate expertise and control, respectively, in white-collar technicians or shop-floor workers (Kelley 1990). The shift in findings appears to reflect a change in managerial practice, which may reflect the combination of more educated workers, a shift in managerial ideologies, weaker unions, and more capital-intensive labor processes (Fernandez 2001).

2. *New technologies reduce inequality by generating demand for more skilled workers.* In contrast, many students of social change argue that technological advance promotes equality. There are three versions of this argument. First, some claim that technological upgrades that replace workers with machines reduce inequality (at the workplace level) by substituting fewer better-paid and more-skilled workers for larger numbers of unskilled workers. In the short run, whether such a change reduces inequality in the economy at large depends on demographic factors and the speed with which "redundant" workers are retrained. Second, some studies show that management may implement technological change in ways that do not replace operatives but rather make work more complex and workers more autonomous. Indeed, Manuel Castells (1996) argues that the increased use of digital communication technologies to tailor goods and services to smaller markets supports a trend toward more flexible workplaces, more skilled work, and more autonomous workers. Third, some students of inequality believe that, as Peter Blau and Otis Dudley Duncan put it (1967, 428), "technological progress has undoubtedly improved chances of upward mobility and will do so in the future," whether or not it reduces structural inequality. In this view, technological change reshuffles the deck, enabling early movers from modest backgrounds to achieve success in new occupations. Oded Galor and Daniel Tsiddon (1997) contend that technological innovation increases both equality of opportunity and *in*equality of income (because employers pay premiums for new workers relative to the existing labor force).

3. *New technologies influence inequality indirectly by altering the structure of political interests and the capacity of groups to mobilize.* In this view, technology alters the occupational structure, which in turn influences the political sphere, leading to changes in policy as an unanticipated result. Despite its Rube Goldberg–esque indirection, this model's history is venerable. Marx argued that the factory system would lead to capitalism's demise by reducing skilled workers to a proletarianized mass and concentrating them in vast workplaces where they would organize revolt (1867/1887). Veblen (in *Engineers and the Price System* [1921/1983]) and others argued that technological advance created a "new class" of intellectual laborers (engineers, scientists, technicians, researchers) with interests and values opposed to those of management. These new workers, so the story goes, are committed to technical rationality, on the one hand, and to cosmopolitan and egalitarian values on the other (Gouldner 1979). Plausible as this formulation is, firm-level research finds little evidence that technical workers view themselves as a collectivity with distinctive interests (Lewin and Orleans 2000). Moreover, in public opinion research, "new class" members, while socially tolerant, are no more egalitarian or economically liberal than other members of the middle class (Brint 1984).

4. *New technologies enhance social equality by democratizing consumption.* Whereas the first three approaches emphasize the results of technological change at the point of production, another tradition has emphasized that new technologies reduce barriers to consumption and, in so doing, level status distinctions and reduce the impact of social honor, conventional manners, dress, deportment, or taste on economic success. According to Max Weber, "every technological repercussion and economic transformation threatens stratification by

status and pushes the class situation into the foreground" (1956/1978, 938). In particular, new information technologies, from movable type and cheap newsprint to telephone service and the Internet, may democratize the consumption of information by reducing the cost of communication. Scholars who believe such technologies reduce inequality emphasize price effects, whereas naysayers emphasize the advantage of the well-off in putting new information to productive use.

Despite the diversity of views, most students of technology agree on three conclusions, all of which apply to the Internet. First, *the specific forms that new technologies take, and therefore their social implications, are products of human design that reflect the interests of those who invest in them.* For example, the military built the Arpanet as a decentralized network that could withstand the effects of enemy attack; ironically, this very decentralization and redundancy made it attractive to libertarian computer scientists, who developed the Internet in ways that accentuated those features. The Internet's architecture is currently changing to better serve the economic interests of commercial enterprises (Lessig 1999; Castells 2001). Second, *technologies are continually reinvented by their users as well as their designers.* As the Internet's user base has shifted from idealistic young technologists to upscale consumers and government policy has sought to support emerging e-businesses, sites and technologies that enhance commercial uses and easy access to information have displaced more complex technologies that emphasized interaction and technical problem-solving. Third, *it follows from the first two principles that technologies adapt to ongoing social practices and concerns rather than "influencing" society as an external force* (Fischer 1992). Rather than exploit all the possibilities inherent in new technologies, people use them to do what they are already doing more effectively. Technology may contribute to change by influencing actors' opportunities, constraints, and incentives, but its relationship to the social world is co-evolutionary, not causal.

THE DIGITAL DIVIDE

Social scientists and policymakers began worrying about inequality in Internet access as early as 1995 (Anderson et al. 1995), when just 3 percent of Americans had ever used the World Wide Web (Pew Center for the People and the Press 1995). At first most believed that the Internet would enhance equality of access to information by reducing its cost. As techno-euphoria wore off, however, observers noted that some kinds of people used the Internet more than others and that those with higher Internet access also had greater access to education, income, and other resources that help people get ahead (Hoffman and Novak 1998, 1999; Benton Foundation 1998; Strover 1999; Bucy 2000). Concern that the new technology might exacerbate inequality rather than ameliorate it focused on what analysts have called the "digital divide" between the online and the offline.

Since the mid-1990s researchers have found persistent differences in Internet use by social category (NTIA 1995, 1998, 1999, 2000, 2002; Lenhart et al. 2003). Although operational definitions of access vary from study to study, most make a binary distinction between people who use the Web and other Internet services (especially e-mail) and people who do not. At first "access" was used literally to refer to whether a person had the means to connect to the Internet *if she or he so chose* (NTIA 1995). Later "access" became a synonym for use, conflating opportunity and choice. This is unfortunate, because studies that have measured both access *and* the extent of Internet use have found, first, that more people have access than use it (NTIA 1998 and Lenhart et al. 2003 report that 20 percent of residents of Internet households never go online), and second, that whereas resources drive access, demand drives intensity of use among people who have access. Thus, young adults are less likely to have home access than adults between the ages of twenty-five and fifty-four (NTIA 2000), but in Internet households teenagers spend more time online than adults (Kraut et al. 1998).

The view of the "digital divide" as a gap between people with and without Internet access was natural at the onset of diffusion, because the Internet was viewed through the lens of a decades-old policy commitment to the principle of universal telephone service. Thus, the federal agency responsible for achieving universal access to telephone service, the National Telecommunications and Information Administration (NTIA), claimed jurisdiction over policies affecting the distribution of access to the Internet. The goal of universal access, enunciated in the Communications Act of 1934, was echoed in the Telecommunications Act of 1996, which mandated that the Federal Communications Commission (FCC) pursue the same objective for new "advanced telecommunications services" that reached high levels of penetration (Neuman, McKnight, and Solomon 1998; Leighton 2001).

The NTIA's research publications echoed this tradition. The universal-service paradigm was profoundly concerned with household access (defined in binary fashion), with special concern for inequality between rural and urban areas (a salient distinction, owing to both the challenging economics of rural telephone service and the bipartisan appeal of programs that assist rural America) (Hall 1993; Schement and Forbes 1999). The telephone paradigm's influence is evident in the NTIA's (1995, 1) first study of the digital divide, *Falling Through the Net: A Survey of the "Have-nots" in Rural and Urban America*. The report's authors carefully framed their attention to the Internet as continuous with existing policy, noting: "At the core of U.S. telecommunications policy is the goal of 'universal service'—the idea that all Americans should have access to affordable telephone service. The most commonly used measure of the nation's success in achieving universal service is 'telephone penetration.'"

Consistent with tradition, that report included data only on households, emphasized a binary distinction between "haves" and "have-nots," and—most strikingly—presented all data separately for rural, urban, and central-city categories. (The latter typology reflected the grafting of Great Society concerns with racial inequality onto traditional concerns with rural America—a union reflected in references to rural "have-nots" and "disadvantaged" central-city dwellers.) As the NTIA's research program evolved, new categories of "have-nots," based on race, income, education, age, and, most recently, disability status (NTIA 2000), were added. Beginning in 1999, data were reported for individuals as well as for households.

Thanks to the NTIA's research program, we have a series of valuable snapshots (based on the Current Population Survey in 1994, 1997, 1998, 2000, and 2001) of intergroup differences in Internet use by:

1. *Region and place of residence:* Rates of Internet use are highest in the Northeast and far West and lowest in the Southeast. Of Americans age three or older (the NTIA reporting base for most purposes), state-level estimates range from 42 percent online in Mississippi to 69 percent in Alaska (NTIA 2002, 7–8). Suburbanites are most likely to use the Internet (57 percent), followed by rural dwellers (53 percent) and central-city residents (49 percent) (19).

2. *Employment status:* In 2001, 65 percent of employed people age sixteen or older were Internet users, compared to just 37 percent of those who were not working (NTIA 2002, 12).

3. *Income:* Internet use rates rise linearly with family income, from 25 percent for persons with incomes of less than $15,000 to almost 80 percent for those with incomes above $75,000.

4. *Educational attainment:* Among persons age twenty-five or older, educational attainment is strongly associated with rates of Internet use. Proportions online range from fewer than 15 percent of those without a high school diploma to 40 percent of persons with a high school diploma, and more than 80 percent of college graduates (NTIA 2002, 17).

5. *Race-ethnicity:* Rates of Internet use are greater for Asian Americans and non-Hispanic whites (about 60 percent for each) than for non-Hispanic blacks (40 percent) and persons of Hispanic origin (just under 32 percent) (NTIA 2002, 21). Variation among these groups in income and education explains much of the difference, but even among those similar in educational attainment or income level, fewer African Americans than whites use the Internet (Hoffman, Novak, and Schlosser 2001; Lenhart et al. 2003).

6. *Age:* Rates of Internet use rise rapidly from age three to a peak around age fifteen, when nearly 80 percent of Americans are online; decline to around 65 percent at age twenty-five; then descend gently to just below 60 percent by age fifty-five. At that point rates decline rapidly with age (NTIA 2002, 13).

7. *Gender:* In early surveys men used the Internet at higher rates than women, but by 2001 women and men were equally likely to be online (Losh 2003). From the late teens to the late forties, women are *more* likely than men to use the Internet; men acquire an increasing edge after age fifty-five (NTIA 2002, 14).

8. *Family structure:* Families with children in the home are more likely to have computers and the Internet than are families without children (NTIA 2002, 14).

These patterns of inequality are similar to those observed in other countries. In Switzerland, for example, in 2000, 69 percent of university graduates but only 19 percent of high school graduates were online, and similar advantages were found for persons with high incomes, the young, and men (with the gender gap notably greater than in the United States) (Bonfadelli 2002, 75; see also De Haan 2003 on the Netherlands; Heil 2002 on the United Kingdom and Germany; and McLaren and Zappalà 2002 on Australia).

Persistent Disagreement

The availability of high-quality data has failed to dampen a hot debate over whether socio-economic and racial divisions in Internet access warrant government action. During the Clinton administration the Commerce Department advanced an ambitious set of programs aimed at wiring schools, libraries, government offices, and community centers throughout the country. The second Bush administration has alternately treated the digital divide as something that was never a problem (Bush's FCC chair likened it to the "Mercedes divide") and a problem that has been solved. (The NTIA's 2002 report on Internet access is triumphantly titled *A Nation Online.*) Almost everyone agrees that the CPS data are reliable. But disagreement on how to interpret the trends persists. It centers on four questions:

1. *What do we mean by "access"?* If we mean an individual's ability to get online in some fashion at some location, then inequality is much diminished. If "access" means an individual's ability to use graphically complex websites from his or her home, differences among groups remain substantial.

2. *Which "digital divide"?* Some intergroup differences that were large at the onset of the digital revolution have diminished or disappeared. Others have persisted.

3. *How should we measure the difference?* It is simple to find measures that convey whatever impression an advocate prefers. But some measures are better than others.

4. *How should we interpret trends?* Can we count on the market to provide extensive service soon enough in the future (and how extensive and how soon are "extensive" and "soon enough"?), or are current inequalities likely to persist indefinitely?

What Do We Mean by Access?   The original literal sense of "access" has gradually been replaced by a set of more concrete operational definitions. Different definitions yield somewhat different conclusions about inequality. We compare digital divides based on three increasingly demanding definitions of access: using the Internet anywhere; using the Internet at one's place of residence; and using the Internet at home through a high-speed connection. (The second criterion is meaningful because most people can surf more freely and spontaneously at home than at the office or in a public library. High-speed connections enable people to access streaming media or graphically complex websites.) For each criterion, table 9.1 provides access rates for two contrasting groups and a measure of inequality—the ratio of the odds of access for the more- and less-privileged groups.[4]

Three features of this table deserve note. First, different criteria yield different estimates of inequality. For example, the disadvantage of people over age fifty-five relative to that of the young (age eighteen to twenty-five) is greater with respect to using the Internet anywhere than it is with respect to using the Internet at home and, especially, to having a high-speed home connection. (The difference reflects the fact that older people have higher incomes, more stable residences, and fewer other places to go online than the young.) Similarly, in 2001 women surpassed men in rates of Internet use, but men were still ahead in access to the Internet at home, especially through high-speed connections.

Second, different criteria yield different impressions for different intergroup comparisons. Inequality with respect to age and educational attainment (comparing college graduates to high school graduates) is greatest for Internet use anywhere. Racial inequality, however, is greatest for at-home access, and income inequality (people with family incomes of $67,500 or more compared to those with incomes between $20,000 and $30,000) is greatest for high-speed connections at home.

Third, it follows that the size of intergroup "divides" depends on how we define "access." Inequality in Internet access anywhere between college and high school graduates dwarfs inequality between blacks and nonblacks, but racial inequality is slightly greater for access to high-speed connections at home. By the same token, the age and education "divides" exceed inequality between income groups in use of the Internet at all, but income inequality slightly exceeds that associated with age and educational attainment for use of the Internet in one's home.

Which Divide?   In the few years that the Internet has been widely available, it has diffused widely. Some inequalities in access have already closed. Other gaps persist, however (see figures 9.1 through 9.4).[5] Differences in rates of Internet use between men and women essentially disappeared between 1994 and 2001. (This descriptive conclusion is confirmed by Hiroshi Ono and Madeline Zavodny's [2003] logistic regression analyses with controls for income, age, educational attainment, and marital status.) Age remains strongly associated with Internet use, but the disadvantage of persons in their fifties and sixties has diminished.

TABLE 9.1   *Internet Access of Americans Age Eighteen and Older, 2001*

	Use Internet	Use Internet At Home	Use Internet at Home High-Speed
Black	39.09%	26.21%	5.57%
Non-black	57.89	46.54	10.87
Non-black/black			
Odds ratio	2.111	2.451	2.068
Women	56.33	44.23	9.71
Men	55.84	45.03	11.09
Male/female odds ratio	0.970	1.033	1.160
High school degree	54.61	42.71	9.53
College graduate	83.39	68.90	16.69
B.A./high school degree odds ratio	4.173	2.972	1.903
Income $20,000 to $29,999	40.02	28.04	4.79
Income greater than $67,500	68.24	57.01	14.91
Greater/lesser income odds ratio	3.220	2.991	3.484
Age eighteen to twenty-five	67.62	50.00	11.57
Age fifty-five and older	30.96	25.30	5.98
Younger/older odds ratio	4.657	2.952	1.837

Source: 2001 CPS.

Regional differences and urban/rural differences also have declined (on the latter, see Bikson and Panis 1999).

By contrast the absolute gap between Asian Americans and Euro-Americans, on one side, and African Americans and Native Americans, on the other, increased (though the ratio of the more-privileged to the less-privileged groups' rates declined; see also Hoffman, Novak, and Schlosser 2001). Most absolute differences based on educational attainment and income fanned out in the early years of rapid penetration, then remained stable (or in the case of differences among the topmost categories, declined) thereafter. Policy analysts particularly interested in disparities based on gender, age, or place of residence are likely to find reasons for cheer in the Internet's trajectory, whereas analysts especially concerned about racial or socioeconomic inequality will be far less satisfied.

Which Measures?   Interpretation of trend data is complicated by the fact that different measures of inequality yield diametrically different results. Observers measure over-time change in intergroup inequality in Internet use in many ways: absolute percentage differences; the ratio of the proportion online in the advantaged group to the proportion online in the less-advantaged group; the ratio of the proportion offline in the less-advantaged group to the proportion offline in the more-advantaged group; the odds ratios of adoption (or non-adoption) between two groups; and for forms of inequality that can be expressed ordinally, pseudo-gini coefficients expressing deviation from equality in the distribution of Internet users across income (or educational) strata. Some measure relative rates of change: ratios in the rate of increase of the less-advantaged to the more-advantaged group, or ratios of the rate of decrease of non-use of the more-advantaged to the less-advantaged use (both expressed as change in either absolute rates or in odds ratios).

Figures 9.5 and 9.6 use CPS data to illustrate why this proliferation of measures is

FIGURE 9.1   *Internet Users in the United States, by Education (Age Eighteen and Older)*

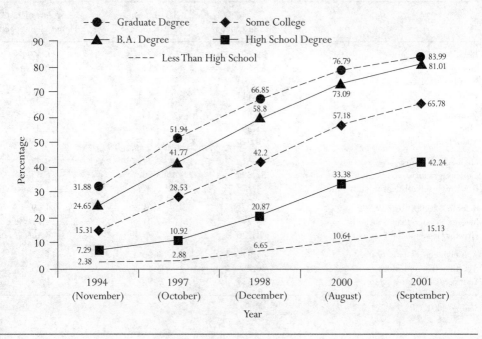

Source: CPS.

FIGURE 9.2   *Internet Users in the United States, by Family Income (Age Eighteen and Older)*

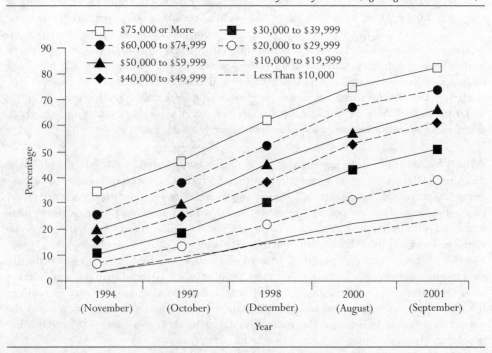

Source: CPS.

FIGURE 9.3   *Internet Users in the United States, by Race (Age Eighteen and Older)*

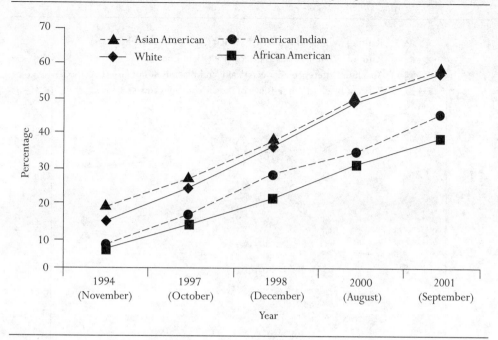

Source: CPS.

FIGURE 9.4   *Internet Users in the United States, by Gender (Age Eighteen and Older)*

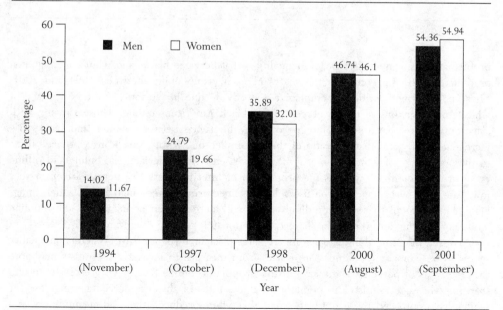

Source: CPS.

FIGURE 9.5   *Measure of Inequality in Black and White Americans' Internet Use (Age Eighteen and Older)*

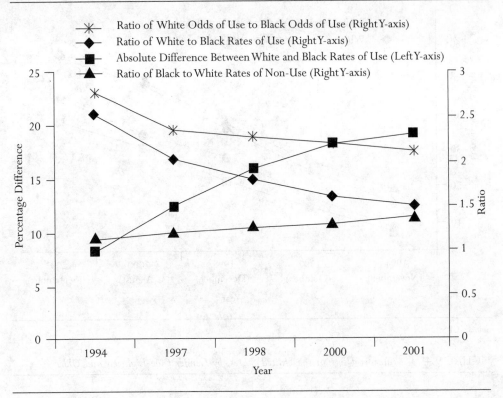

Data Source: CPS.

problematic, using a single type of inequality—that between blacks and whites age eighteen or older. Figure 9.5 compares the shares of each group online between 1994 and 2001. Those pointing with pride can emphasize a steady decline in the ratio of the percentage of white Americans online to the percentage of black Americans online. Those viewing with alarm may note that the absolute percentage difference between whites and blacks has increased slightly and that the ratio of the percentage of African Americans who are offline to the percentage of whites who are offline has risen steadily. In fact, the online and offline ratios are mirror images, for as the proportion of Internet users has increased from a very low base, the percentage of non-users has declined from a very high base. Other things being equal, groups that start at a disadvantage will increase their percentage of those online while constituting an ever-larger share (proportionately) of the disenfranchised.

We see the same thing if we compare rates of change (figure 9.6). Whether inequality seems to be worsening or improving varies from measure to measure. Optimists may note that the rates of percentage increase in the proportion online have been greater for blacks than for whites. Pessimists can point out that the rates of absolute percentage increase for whites have outpaced those for blacks and that whites reduced their offline numbers at a higher rate than blacks throughout this period.

Steven Martin (2003) argues that there is something wrong with measures that yield opposite conclusions depending on whether one measures the proportion of two groups

FIGURE 9.6   *Measures of Inequality in Rate of Change in Black and White Americans'*
              Internet Use (Age Eighteen and Older)

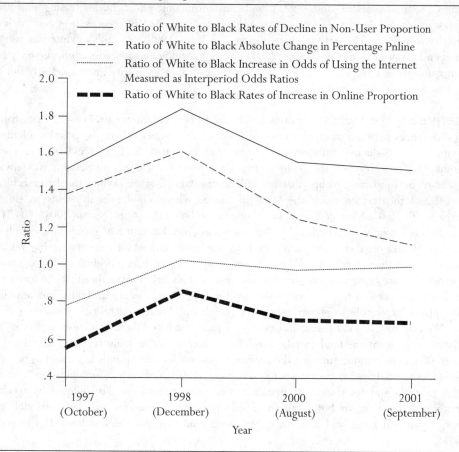

Data Source: CPS.

online or the complement of that proportion (intergroup ratios of use/non-use rates or rates of change in use/non-use, as well as quasi-gini coefficients for forms of inequality that can be represented ordinally), and he offers an attractive solution. Odds ratios do not have this problem, he notes: they are the same whether one focuses on the proportions of two groups who are users or the proportions who have been left behind. We include odds ratios in both figure 9.5 (the ratio of the odds that a white American is online to the odds that a black American is online) and figure 9.6 (the ratio of interperiod changes in odds for whites to changes in odds for blacks). Both demonstrate that the white advantage declined notably between 1994 and 1997 and remained stable or grew slightly from 1997 to 2001.

To understand the mechanisms that produce inequality it is helpful to identify the advantages and disadvantages that accrue to people as a consequence of their race (or gender or income) independent of other salient characteristics that travel in tandem with race (or gender or income). A good measure of a characteristic's net contribution to inequality in Internet use is its coefficient in a logistic regression equation with statistical controls for other factors associated with going online. One study that employed this technique, using

CPS household data from 1994 to 2000, found that the net effects of education, race, and, to a lesser extent, income increased over this period (Leigh and Atkinson 2001). Another, using CPS data from 1993 and 1997, found constant income effects but increasing education effects on use of Internet services, as well as growing net differences between African Americans and non-Hispanic whites (Bikson and Panis 1999). A study of Internet use in fourteen European countries (Norris 2001) found growing effects of education, income, and occupation from 1996 to 1999. Such studies indicate that inequality grew modestly during the first years of diffusion.[6]

Interpreting the Trends   Andrew Leigh and Robert Atkinson (2001) argue that changing differences between groups in rates of Internet use simply reflect the position of those groups on an S-shaped diffusion curve that will culminate in full access for everyone. Groups that have reached the point of rapid ascent at the curve's midsection will always appear to be outpacing groups that are still in the takeoff stage. When the latter achieve takeoff and the former reach the "top" of the S, where rapid growth yields to slower increases, the less-advantaged groups will appear to be catching up (Norris 2001, 30–31).

This is a crucial analytic insight. But *can* we assume that different groups are merely at different points on the same curve? Perhaps the most important question facing policymakers is whether disadvantaged groups are simply a few paces behind or, by contrast, whether they are becoming marooned as the rest of the world moves ahead. If the former is true, we can count on time to bridge the divide; if the *trajectories* are different, public policy must play a larger role to reduce inequality (Leigh and Atkinson 2001).

We can make a good theoretical case for either scenario. Liberals, who set policy in the Clinton administration, tend to take the latter stance, whereas conservatives, like those in the Bush administration, embrace the former. The case for the optimistic scenario goes like this. In its rapid diffusion the Internet is traversing the path of such communication technologies as radio and television. At first access is restricted to an elite defined by wealth, institutional location, or both, but increasing penetration reduces gaps between rich and poor, urban and rural, old and young, the well educated and the unschooled (Compaine 2001).

Peter Blau's (1977) insights explain why purely structural factors may ensure that inequality in access declines with diffusion. The first people to gain access to a new technology usually occupy privileged positions on several dimensions—for example, income, white-collar work, educational level, race, rural residence, and gender. But many fewer people are privileged on all dimensions than on each. For example, there are a lot more white-collar workers than there are high-income, white, male, urban-dwelling, college-educated, white-collar workers. As penetration grows, access cascades beyond multiply privileged groups to people who are privileged in some ways but disadvantaged in others; the latter, in turn, become conduits to others with whom they share less-privileged characteristics. For example, when a rural, Latina, white-collar worker gains Internet access at her workplace, she may use the skills she acquires to help blue-collar family members go online, thus playing a role in reducing inequality between Hispanic and non-Hispanic Americans, and between urban and rural dwellers.[7]

An equally strong case can be made for the opposite scenario. When we examine technology diffusion, a distinction emerges between products and services. Even expensive products often reach high penetration levels when economies of scale reduce their prices (television sets, VCRs, computers) or less expensive secondary markets emerge (automobiles, refrigerators), or both. By contrast, the diffusion of services that entail continuing expense has been slower, bumpier, and less complete (Schement 2003). As critical as telephone service would seem to be (especially to residents of rural areas), telephone penetration grew slowly and actually declined (markedly among farm families) during the Great Depression (Fischer 1992). Despite federal efforts, telephone service did not penetrate 90 percent of households until the 1970s, and the rate remains much lower than 90 percent in inner-city neighborhoods (Schement and Forbes 1999; Mueller and Schement 2001).

Evidence as well as theory can be mustered on behalf of both the optimistic and pessimistic points of view. Four arguments favor the former. First, as we have seen, some "divides" (gender, region, age, rural/urban) have already diminished. The trajectory of other gaps depends on the measures we use, but Internet use has undeniably expanded among all groups, so straight-line extrapolation (until recently at least) has suggested eventual convergence.

Second, surveys indicate that despite slowing growth after 2000, the market for Internet services is far from saturated. A spring 2000 survey by the Pew Center reported that 41 percent of Americans who did *not* use the Internet intended to do so (Lenhart 2000, 2); two years later, 44 percent of non-users predicted they would do so. If they did (and if those who said they probably or definitely would not go online did not), the proportion of Americans who are Internet users would rise above 70 percent.

Third, non-users' expectations are strongly correlated with age. In the Pew survey, 65 percent of non-users age fifty or younger expected to go online, compared to just 36 percent of non-users over age fifty, suggesting that generational succession will send Internet usage rates even higher. Based on these cohort differences, Lenhart (2000, 3) predicts that "in a generation, Internet penetration will reach the levels enjoyed by the telephone . . . and the television." Finally, late adopters come from less-privileged backgrounds than Internet pioneers. In both 1998 and 2000, surveys found that new users had lower incomes and less education than Americans who had been online longer (Horrigan 2000a; Cummings and Kraut 2000; Howard, Rainie, and Jones 2001; Katz, Rice, and Aspden 2001).

Evidence in favor of the pessimistic scenario is equally strong. Inequality by race, income, and educational attainment has diminished little, if at all: Americans with few years of education and low incomes were still less likely to be online in 2001 as Americans with the most education and the highest incomes had been in 1994. Moreover, we can discount those divides that *have* been bridged as special cases: place of residence became less important because networks were built out and the technology became more flexible, and women and the elderly are usually slower technology adopters than men and the young, but both groups ordinarily catch up.

Second, the high diffusion rate of the 1990s did not represent a "natural" trajectory but rather the success of federal and state initiatives to encourage the Internet's rapid evolution and broad availability and the special benefits to the Internet of an extraordinary economic bubble (the eponymous "boom" of the late 1990s). The reversal of both public policy and macroeconomic fortune after 2000 has already belied projections made as recently as 1999 that income inequality in the use of Internet services would vanish by 2001 (Bikson and Panis 1999) and in 2001 that household Internet access would reach 90 percent by 2003 (Leigh and Atkinson 2001, 6). Instead, diffusion slowed as the bubble popped (Lenhart et al. 2003). If curves plateau at or near 2001 rates, existing levels of inequality could be locked in for decades.

Third, although newer adopters are of lower socioeconomic status than longtime users, they may not *stay* online. In particular, loss of income during hard times may make consumers less able to pay monthly connection fees. Many people adopt the technology only to give it up later, and these Internet dropouts come disproportionately from groups with lower probabilities of going online in the first place. In surveys undertaken between 1995 and 2000, James Katz and his colleagues (Katz and Aspden 1997; Katz and Rice 2002) found that approximately 20 percent of those who had ever used the Internet no longer did so. In the fall of 2001, 3.3 percent of CPS households reported that they had discontinued Internet service (NTIA 2002, 77). Analyses prepared for this chapter reveal that about 10 percent of General Social Survey (GSS) respondents who used the Internet in the spring of 2000 no longer did so when they were reinterviewed eighteen months later. A 2002 study (Lenhart et al. 2003, 21) reports that 7 percent of U.S. adults are *former* Internet users and that between 27 and 44 percent of *current users* have gone offline for extended periods after becoming users.[8] This study concludes that "the road to Internet use is so paved with bumps and turnarounds" (3) that the binary division of the population into "online" and "offline" is misleading.

The Digital Divide: A Research Agenda

Because the diffusion process is at a relatively early stage, monitoring change through ongoing data collection remains a critical priority. The NTIA's research program of CPS surveys remains the most important source of information, though studies with richer sets of covariates (like the GSS) or more focused questions (like the Pew Center's surveys) are important complements.

We must also fill significant gaps in the analysis of data already collected. First, as we have seen, trend studies have suffered from a babble of competing measures and definitions of Internet access. Descriptive research employing reliable measures to describe change over time in (several definitions of) access would be a valuable baseline contribution. Second, we know relatively little about differences between predictors of access at work, home, or other locations, or about the extent to which members of less-privileged groups rely either on workplace connections or on community settings to go online. Different factors influence access at different locations (the unemployed, for example, cannot go online at work), with implications for intergroup inequality. We know even less about access through interfaces other than computers or television screens (in the United States at least), like cell phones, personal digital assistants (PDAs), and various hybrids of the two.

Third, we know very little about social network processes that culminate in adoption. Because the Internet is characterized by *network externalities* (its value increases with the number of people using it), an important predictor of adoption should be the number of one's friends, relatives, or business contacts who are already online. Internet users are twice as likely as non-users to report that most people they know use the Internet, and just 4 percent of users, compared to 27 percent of non-users, report that none or very few of their acquaintances go online (Lenhart et al. 2003, 28). Research on computers indicates that families whose friends and neighbors own and use computers are more likely than otherwise similar people to purchase a first computer themselves (Goolsbee and Klenow 2000). Adoption within networks is probably marked by tipping points at which using e-mail or instant messaging becomes essential for full participation. Thus, aggregate diffusion curves may reflect local lumpiness (rapid takeoffs within and cascades across relatively small network regions, along with limited diffusion among other networks), making patterns of intergroup inequality dependent on network dynamics that we understand poorly.

Fourth, the little research on the influence of institutional affiliations in inducing people to go online suggests that the topic warrants more attention. One study reports that 30 percent of Hispanics take up the Internet through school (almost twice the proportion for non-Hispanic whites and blacks), whereas 43 percent of African Americans first go online at work—a substantially higher proportion than among whites or, especially, Hispanics (Spooner and Rainie 2000, 8). The imbrication of school and workplace with information-seeking trajectories and how that differs for different kinds of people are important research priorities.

Fifth, we must learn more about Internet dropouts and about the extent to which differential persistence exacerbates inequality. Understanding the etiology of dis-adoption—the roles of weak network externalities and institutional disaffiliation (job loss, termination of schooling, reduction in discretionary income)—is an important step. And it may be useful to model changes in intergroup inequality as the product of group-specific adoption and abandonment rates.

Finally, how do public policy and macroeconomic conditions affect diffusion rates and equality of access? State-level analyses that explore the relationships between these outcomes and state policies and federal investments, while controlling for macroeconomic conditions and population composition, represent a promising approach.

ONLINE INEQUALITY COMPARED TO INEQUALITY IN THE USE OF OTHER MEDIA

To understand the Internet's implications for equality of access to information, we must examine comparative evidence on access to and use of other communication media. Even if people with lots of money or education have privileged access to information online, whether or not an increasing role for the Internet exacerbates or ameliorates information inequality depends on whether access to and use of other media is more or less equally distributed. Socioeconomic status is ordinarily associated with access to communication media and, among those with access, with getting information (for evidence from the political domain, see Verba, Schlozman, and Brady 1995); it would be headline news if the Internet were an exception. As Pippa Norris (2001, 12) argues: "The interesting question is not whether there will be *absolute* social inequalities in Internet access [but] . . . whether *relative* inequalities in Internet use will be similar to disparities in the penetration rates of older communication technologies."

How might the Internet compare to mundane communication technologies like newspapers, magazines, the daily press, or even face-to-face conversation? Most online information is a free good. Economic theory tells us that if price elasticity is greater than zero, free information will be consumed at a faster rate than costly information, especially by people with little discretionary income. Thus, for those who have access to it, the Internet should make the distribution of information more equal. Yet this argument requires qualification in a number of ways. First, many competing information sources (network television news, interpersonal communication by telephone, daily newspapers) are either free or inexpensive. Second, online information is a "free good" only insofar as the user's time is without value. If lower-status Internet users take longer to find information (because their search skills are poorer, their connections slower, or their domain knowledge less), then the Internet could be a more "expensive" form of information than the newspaper, television, or a phone call to a friend. If going online requires a drive to the library or the risk of getting caught surfing while at work, it may be more expensive still. Third, because of the vast amount of information online, the Internet may be most attractive to those whose demand for information is highest (in many domains, high-SES users). Others may be satisfied by more limited media. Heinz Bonfadelli (2002) argues that the heterogeneity and depth of Internet-based information (in comparison to the relative homogeneity of material in newspapers or news broadcasts) is likely to exacerbate information inequality. In other words, we could plausibly hypothesize that the Internet will lead to a more egalitarian distribution of information, *or* that it will reinforce or even exacerbate the usual inequalities.

We must distinguish analytically between *access* and *use* in this regard. With respect to access, we may ask what would happen (holding constant the way people distribute attention across media) if information *producers* took information currently transmitted by newspaper, television, or word of mouth and began distributing it through the Internet instead. For example, to what extent would low-income parents be hurt or helped if public schools used local newspapers less and websites more to distribute information about class assignments, policy changes, and extracurricular activities? With respect to use, the question is (given the current allocation of information across media), how would inequality be affected if information *consumers* shifted their attention from one medium to another? For example, would low-income parents learn more or less about their kids' schools if they spent more time online and less time reading the newspaper or talking with neighbors?

We know of only four studies that address such questions directly. Norris (2001, 90), using 1999 Eurobarometer data, found remarkably similar predictors of scores on a "new media index" (computer, CD-ROM, modem, and Internet) and an "old media index" (VCR, fax, satellite TV, cable TV, Teletext, and Videotext) in several European countries. Mariko Lin Chang (2003) used data from the 1998 Survey of Consumer Finances to investigate the impact of education, race, and other factors on where people get financial information. Education was more strongly associated with use of the Internet than with use of any other source of information; wealth (but not income) was significantly predictive of Internet use as well (but less so than of contact with financial professionals). African Americans favored financial professionals and advertisements over the Internet. Young people preferred the Internet and eschewed financial professionals; the elderly did the opposite. In a study of health information–seeking, Sanjay Pandey, John Hart, and Sheela Tiwary (2002) found that income and education significantly predicted Internet use. Compared to information sought from a doctor or in the newspaper, the Web was the only medium stratified by socioeconomic status. In a study of the use of media for political news, Bruce Bimber (2003) reported that African Americans were less underrepresented among Internet users than among newspaper readers and that young people were disproportionately likely to seek information online.

For this chapter, we analyzed data from the 2000 and 2002 General Social Surveys, which contained domain-specific questions about information-seeking in the areas of health (2000 and 2002), politics (2000), and jobs (2002). Respondents were first asked if they had "looked for information" at all during the past year; those who replied affirmatively were then asked which of several sources of information they employed.[9] Therefore, we can explore variation in search behaviors among people for whom we know that the knowledge domain is salient.

Here we focus on the association between median family income and the use of each source of information. Comparison of median incomes (reported in dollar ranges, to which we assigned values at the midpoint) indicates that respondents who sought information at all about health care or political candidates were financially better off than those who did not (see table 9.2). No difference was evident for job information. Table 9.3 describes the search behavior of respondents who sought information in each domain. The results are striking: in each case, people who sought information on the Internet had notably higher

TABLE 9.2   *Median Income of Respondents Who Did or Did Not Search for Information*

	Health Information (2000)	Health Information (2002)	Political Information (2000)	Employment Information (2002)
Sought information	$37,500	$45,000	$45,000	$37,500
Did not seek information	32,500	32,500	32,500	37,500

Data Source: 2000 and 2002 GSS.

incomes than people who searched through other means. The difference was least for employment information ($37,500 compared to $32,500), but the Internet was the *only* source for which users had higher incomes than non-users. The income advantage of those who sought political information online was greater than for any other source but general-interest magazines (both $55,000 for users and $37,500 for non-users). The differences were most marked in health care, where the Web users' income advantage was far greater than it was for any other information source.

TABLE 9.3   *Median Family Income of Respondents Who Did or Did Not Use Specific Media for Information (Respondents Who Sought Such Information from Any Source Only)*

	Panel A: Health Information Search (2000)						
	Doctor or Nurse	Friend or Relative	World Wide Web	Magazine (Health)	Magazine (General)	TV/Radio	Newspaper
Yes	$37,500	$45,000	$55,000	$37,500	$37,500	$32,500	$37,500
No	35,000	37,500	27,500	37,500	37,500	45,000	41,250

	Panel B: Health Information Search (2002)						
	Doctor or Nurse	Friend or Relative	World Wide Web	Magazine (Health)	Magazine (General)	TV/Radio	Newspaper
Yes	45,000	45,000	55,000	37,500	37,500	37,500	37,500
No	45,000	37,500	32,500	45,000	45,000	45,000	45,000

	Panel C: Political Information Search (2000)						
	Newspaper	TV/Radio	Magazine (General)	Friend or Relative	Political Campaign	World Wide Web	Magazine (Political)
Yes	45,000	45,000	55,000	45,000	45,000	55,000	45,000
No	37,500	55,000	37,500	37,500	45,000	37,500	45,000

	Panel D: Employment Information Search (2002)							
	Newspaper	Friend or Relative (Non-coworker)	Outside Contact	World Wide Web	Coworker	Publication	Counseling Service	TV/Radio
Yes	37,500	37,500	37,500	37,500	37,500	37,500	32,500	25,625
No	45,000	45,000	37,500	32,500	37,500	37,500	37,500	37,500

Data Source: 2000 and 2002 GSS.

To summarize, the little evidence we have is equivocal with respect to socioeconomic inequality in the use of different media, but it suggests that for some purposes at least information would be more unequally distributed in a world in which the Internet played a greater role and other media a correspondingly smaller one. Insofar as we can judge from available studies, the level of socioeconomic inequality in access to information online is no less, and is probably greater, than the degree of inequality in access to information through other media.

Comparing Media Sources: A Research Agenda

Three issues must be addressed. First, *what is the quality of the information that people get from difference sources?* If the information that people get off of the Internet is markedly inferior to the information they get from other sources, then any advantage that higher-SES users have in employing that medium is a poor advantage indeed. In addition to generic differences in information quality among media, researchers should address differences associated with socioeconomic status in the quality of the information that users actually retrieve. If low-income Internet users obtain less reliable information from more poorly designed sites that their higher-income counterparts, but are getting the same information when they read the newspaper or watch the evening news, the Internet may reinforce information inequality in ways that are not apparent from simple measures of use.

Second, *to what extent do differences in search behaviors reflect limitations on access versus differences among people who already have access?* To what extent do differences like the ones documented here reflect greater inequality in access to the Internet than to other sources of information, and to what extent do they reflect socioeconomic differences in what people do online? If everyone had easy and autonomous access to the Internet, would differences diminish? Or do users of different socioeconomic backgrounds have different patterns of information-seeking behavior independent of medium?

Third, *among people who seek information online, to what extent is their use of the Internet a complement to or substitute for other kinds of information-seeking activities?* If the Internet is used only to complement more conventional information sources, it represents an incremental benefit for users. If it replaces other sources, depending on the quality of the information people find there, it may represent a net decline or increase in utility. Early studies of Internet users (Althaus and Tewksbury 2000; Bromley and Bowles 1995; Stempel, Hargrove, and Bernt 2000) reported that Web use did not limit use of other media, but more recent studies indicate that Internet users watch less broadcast television than others (Waldfogel 2002). Such studies have not yet focused on the use of media to acquire specific types of information, nor have they explored differences in substitution patterns for different kinds of users.

BEYOND THE DIGITAL DIVIDE: INEQUALITY ONLINE

Such questions take us away from the digital divide and call attention to socioeconomic inequality among people who already go online. Research on access is still important because it documents a significant social change and establishes a baseline for evaluating progress toward the policy goal of universal service. At the same time, as Internet access has reached the point where almost every American can find a connection at a public library (Schement 2003), the key research questions about distributional issues have changed.[10] The pressing question now is less "Who can find a network connection from which to log on?"

than "What are people doing, and what are they *able* to do, when they go online?" Moving beyond a binary view of access to a more detailed conception of inequality of technological opportunity involves four steps: identifying critical dimensions of inequality; documenting differences among groups; explaining the antecedents of inequality on these dimensions; and modeling the relationships between different forms of inequality and between these and critical outcomes. In pursuing these questions, students of the Internet can draw both on prior studies of culture, information, and social inequality and on a more directly relevant tradition of research on the "knowledge gap" hypothesis.

Culture and Information in the Stratification Order

Sociologists have long studied inequality in access to cultural and information goods (DiMaggio 2001). Such work has addressed not only formal education, long a staple of research on social inequality, but also command of prestigious types of cultural knowledge (Bourdieu and Passeron 1977), linguistic abilities (Bernstein 1977), cognitive styles (Kohn and Schooler 1982), and access to technology (Attewell and Battle 1999). Lessons from this research tradition are applicable to research on inequality in access to and use of the Internet.

One generalization that emerges from this work is what we call the *differentiation principle*. At first, scarce information services are often relatively undifferentiated. As they become more available, they also become more differentiated in character, as the relatively privileged seek advantage by accumulating kinds that are more richly rewarded in marital or labor markets. The type case here is education: as access to high school became nearly universal, increasing proportions of children from upper- and middle-class families began attending college. With the onset of mass higher education, college training was further differentiated into selective private and public institutions and several tiers of less selective institutions (Brint 1998; Collins 1979; Karabel and Astin 1975).[11] Such differentiation created new forms of inequality within the ranks of the college-educated, alongside the old kind of inequality between those with and without a college education.

Similar patterns are visible in other cultural and informational goods. Pierre Bourdieu (1984) emphasized the ways in which elite groups with high levels of cultural capital but relatively few financial resources develop elaborate forms of cultural distinction, compared to the solidly classical tastes of traditional business elites. In the sphere of information technology, hand-held communication devices have been differentiated, as the old stationary telephone has evolved into cellular telephones, personal digital assistants, wireless Internet devices, and varied combinations thereof. We anticipate that high rates of Internet penetration will increase the salience of new kinds of inequality *among Internet users* that affect the extent to which they reap benefits from going online.

The "Knowledge Gap" Hypothesis

Research on inequality in the use of earlier communication technologies establishes a precedent. According to the "knowledge gap" hypothesis (Tichenor, Donohue, and Olien 1970), people of high socioeconomic status are always advantaged in exploiting new sources of information. Because of their privileged social locations, they find out about them first, and because of their high incomes, they can afford to access them while they are new. Moreover, schooling provides an initial cognitive advantage that enables the well-educated to process new information more effectively, so that their returns to investments in knowledge are higher. As a consequence, not only do the socioeconomically advantaged learn more than others, but the gap is destined to grow ever larger owing to their advantage in access to new sources of information.

Empirical tests of the knowledge gap hypothesis have been generally but not exclusively supportive. A review of more than twenty studies with longitudinal data reports that, consistent with the theory, knowledge gaps on issues often increase when media attention is greatest and narrow when coverage declines (Gaziano 1997). Studies that control for media exposure have also reported that readers or viewers with more prior knowledge of a topic are better able to assimilate new information (Viswanath and Finnegan 1996). Public health studies, however, suggest that information campaigns on salient medical issues initially expand inequality in knowledge but ultimately reduce it (Viswanath and Finnegan 1996). Indeed, there is some evidence that when information is widely available and consumers are strongly motivated to learn, media exposure can *reduce* knowledge gaps over time (Ettema, Brown, and Luepker 1983).

Phillip Tichenor, Donohue, and Olien (1970) hypothesized that knowledge gaps would be smaller for highly salient knowledge domains in relatively small communities, and some studies have supported this view (Viswanath et al. 2000). Insofar as this is the case, the Internet's ability to create compact online communities of interest in which status differences among members are relatively invisible may enable rapid learning among users at all SES levels who find their way to specialized websites, especially sites that include an interactive component. (If high-SES people are more likely to access such resources, however, the Internet's interactivity and anonymity might actually exacerbate inequality.)

The lesson of knowledge gap research for students of the Internet is that "access" is never enough to ensure productive use. Students of the knowledge gap call attention first to individual differences (often associated with education) in motivation, salience, and skill, and second to the social context of information consumption (for example, the availability of opportunities to discuss new information with peers) as explanations of unequal impact. Similar factors probably shape the extent to which different kinds of people benefit from the Internet's availability (Bonfadelli 2002).

Dimensions of Inequality Online

We call attention to five broad forms of inequality. The first is variation in the *technical means* (hardware, software, and connections) by which people access the Internet. The second is variation in the extent to which people exercise *autonomy* in using the Web—for example, whether they access it from work or from home, whether their use is monitored or unmonitored, whether they must compete with other users for time online. The third is inequality in the *skill* that people bring to their use of the medium. The fourth is inequality in the *social support* on which Internet users can draw. The fifth is variation in the *purposes* for which people use the technology. We view each type of inequality as likely to shape significantly the experience that users have online, the uses to which they can put the Internet and the satisfactions they draw from it, and their returns to Internet use in the form of such outcomes as earnings or political efficacy.

Inequality in Technical Apparatus   Rob Kling (1998) distinguishes between technological and social access, calling attention to the importance of "the physical availability of suitable equipment, including computers of adequate speed and equipped with appropriate software for a given activity." How does inequality in the adequacy of hardware, software, and connections limit the ways in which different kinds of users can employ the Internet? As bandwidth increases and more websites require late-model browsers to display java applications, sophisticated graphics, or streaming video, to what extent can users without access to expensive systems access the full range of Internet content?

Among Internet users, the same factors associated with being online in the first place (income, educational attainment, race, and metropolitan residence) predict having high-speed connections (Horrigan and Rainie 2002, 10; Mossberger, Tolbert, and Stansbury 2003). Research suggests that inferior technical apparatus reduces the benefits that users can gain from the Internet directly and indirectly. First, users with slow connections and obsolete software or hardware are simply unable to access many sites. Second, because their online experience is less gratifying, they go online less often and acquire fewer information retrieval skills. John Horrigan and Lee Rainie (2002) report that, after controlling for experience and demographic variation, broadband users search for information more widely, engage in a broader range of activities, and more often produce their own Web content than users without high-speed connections. Similarly, Elizabeth Davison and Shelia Cotton (2003) report that broadband users spend more time online and are more likely to use online business and consumer services and recreational sites.[12]

Inequality in Autonomy of Use   How much control do people exercise over their Internet use? An important aspect of this dimension is location of access (Bimber 2000)—that is, whether people go online at home or at work, in school, or at a library or community center. If access is outside the home, how much flexibility does the user have in determining the hours at which she or he can go online? How far does the user have to travel? To what extent do regulations, time limits, filtering software, or monitoring arrangements limit use? If access is at work, what uses are permitted (and how does this vary with organizational role), what kinds of filtering or monitoring systems are in place, and how stringently are rules enforced (O'Mahoney and Barley 1999)? (In 2001, 63 percent of large employers monitored their employees' Internet connections and 47 percent stored and reviewed their e-mail communications [American Management Association 2001].) If access is at home, to what extent is autonomy limited by the actions of other family members or the policies of the Internet service provider (ISP) (Lessig 1999)? Does in-home access have different effects on educational or occupational outcomes than access from other locations? Among people who have access at work, what predicts the degree of autonomy they possess in determining *how* they use the technology?

We have seen that educational attainment, income, and race are all associated with having Internet access at home. We hypothesize that, where individuals have access to the Internet at work, the autonomy with which they can exercise that access is associated with their organizational rank and functional position. Finally, we expect that among people with access to the Internet, the greater the autonomy of use, the greater the benefits the user derives.

Inequality in Skill   Kling (1998) points to the importance of inequality in users' possession of "know-how, a mix of professional knowledge, economic resources, and technical skills, to use technologies in ways that enhance professional practices and social life." Ernest Wilson (2000) refers to inequality in "cognitive access": the extent to which users are trained to find and evaluate the information they seek. Internet users vary in their possession of at least four kinds of relevant knowledge: recipe knowledge about how to log on, conduct searches, and download information; non-domain-specific background knowledge (such as knowledge of Boolean logic for designing search algorithms); integrative knowledge about the way the Web operates that helps them navigate better; and the technical knowledge about software, hardware, and networks necessary for troubleshooting problems or staying up-to-date (for example, by downloading patches and plug-ins). Taken together, these four kinds of knowledge constitute what we might call—after sociolinguists' notion of "communicative competence" (Hymes 1974)—"digital competence": the capacity to respond pragmatically and intuitively to challenges and opportunities in a manner that exploits the Internet's potential and avoids frustration (Hargittai 2002).

We know very little about what explains inequality in the competence needed to find information online. Evolution in website construction and growth in the volume of information has required new skills for the technology's efficient use. Flashy software implemented with little attention to human factors renders many sites accessible only to sophisticated users with state-of-the-art hardware and software and sophisticated navigation skills (Hargittai 2003b). Moreover, limitations in search technology—most search engines index no more than a small percentage of all content online (Lawrence and Giles 1999)—render it difficult for the average user to find many sites.

Despite a growing literature on website usability issues (much of it from library science and social informatics), we know little about how and why skill is related to personal characteristics. A few researchers have examined self-reports of skill and found that users with less formal education are less confident in their abilities (Bonfadelli 2002). We also know that women are less confident in their online skills than men and that self-assessments predict performance poorly (Hargittai 2003a).

Eszter Hargittai's recent study (2003a) is unique in that the author subjected a random sample of residents of a socially heterogeneous New Jersey county to extensive testing, including surveys, open-ended interviews, and, most important, observations while they attempted to locate several kinds of material online, using computers and browsers similar to those they ordinarily employed. Hargittai finds that skill (defined, first, as the ability to complete a task and, second, as the amount of time spent on the task) is only modestly associated with demographic measures (and associated in different ways for different tasks); relatively weakly associated with offline domain familiarity; and more strongly related to autonomy of use and the amount of time subjects spend online in a typical week.

A study of online sessions of a sample of new users (Neuman, O'Donnell, and Schneider 1996) demonstrated that emotional impact—whether users felt frustrated or gratified at the session's end—was a function of their success in attaining their objectives. We infer from this that Internet competence is related to the satisfaction that users derive from the experience, the extent to which they find it stressful or rewarding, and therefore the extent to which they persist in Internet use and acquire additional skills.

Inequality in the Availability of Social Support

Based on these observations, we might expect inequality in competence to deepen inexorably as skillful users find the Internet rewarding and acquire greater skill and less able users grow frustrated and turn away. Yet we know that most new users do gain competence and persist. We suspect that this is the case because novices draw on *social support* from more experienced users when they need help. Such support has become more important as the technology has penetrated new sectors of the population. Anecdotal evidence suggests that early Web users were embedded in dense networks of technically sophisticated peers. By contrast, more recent recruits are often less sophisticated and more isolated (Kiesler et al. 2000). Y. Kim and Joo-Young Jung

(2002), in a study of East Asian youth, found strong effects of social support (from both family and friends) on the breadth and extent of online activity.

We hypothesize that three kinds of support increase users' motivation to go online and their digital competence: technical assistance from persons employed to provide it (for example, workplace support staff, customer support staff, librarians, and teachers); technical assistance from friends and family members; and emotional reinforcement from friends and family in the form of commiseration when things go wrong and positive interest when things go right. We further hypothesize that social support influences returns to Internet access, however these are measured.

Variation in Use   How do income, education, and other factors influence *the purposes for which one uses the Internet?* From the standpoint of the contribution of technology use to socioeconomic life chances, not all uses are equal. The Internet prophets who foresaw that the Web would empower citizens, increase social capital, and enhance equality of opportunity probably did not have gambling or pornography sites in mind when they made these predictions. We place high priority on examining determinants of different kinds of use, especially distinguishing among uses that increase economic welfare (for example, skill enhancement, learning about employment opportunities, consumer information, or education) or political or social capital (using the Internet to follow the news, gather information relevant to electoral decisionmaking, learn about public issues, engage in civic dialogue, or take part in social movement activities) versus those that are primarily recreational.

The variety of uses to which one puts the Internet is likely to reflect the number of hours one spends online. We have no cumulative data on the latter, but surveys have asked how many hours respondents are online *now* and how many years they have been online, and both measures are associated with variety of use. Moreover, among Internet users, those with more education began to use the Internet earlier and go online more frequently (at least in the early stages of diffusion) than less-educated users (Bonfadelli 2002, 77). In the United States, women with Internet access went online less frequently than otherwise similar men (Bimber 2000).

Evidence that users from more privileged backgrounds are more likely to use the Internet to get ahead and equip themselves to participate in community affairs or politics is beginning to accumulate. DiMaggio and Hargittai (2002) report that among respondents to the 2000 GSS, education, income, and vocabulary test scores have strong effects on "capital-enhancing" uses of the Internet but much weaker (or negative) effects on recreational use. Bonfadelli (2002) finds that, among Swiss Internet users, education is positively associated with using the Web for information and services but negatively associated with using it for entertainment.

DiMaggio and Hargittai (2002) do not find significant effects of race, net controls (see also Alvarez 2003). Tom Spooner and Lee Rainie (2000) find that African American Internet users are more likely than their white counterparts to use the Web for education and job-hunting. The NTIA (1998, 2000) reports that lower-income and less-educated Internet users are more likely than wealthy users to use the Internet to find jobs, a result that may reflect exclusion from the informal social networks through which information about the most desirable jobs is distributed (Lin 2000). Egalitarians should find such results encouraging. Yet relatively early adopters in groups with lower levels of adoption may be atypical in ways that make generalization unwise (see Bourdieu and Passeron 1977 on "overselection").

Note that in distinguishing among uses in this way, we do not suggest that recreational Internet activities are without value—only that both public policy and students of inequality place a higher priority on equality of economic opportunity and civic engagement than on sociability and the pursuit of happiness. Researchers interested in social inequality and social policy should distinguish between online activities that are likely to cultivate the former and those primarily devoted to the latter.

Research Agenda: Modeling Digital Inequality

With well over half of U.S. adults online, we must supplement research on the digital divide with studies of inequality within the online population. The research agenda is long, comprising each form of inequality described earlier, as well as integration of the parts into a comprehensive model.

The most important lesson of this section is that "Internet use" is far less likely to have strong or consistent effects (or antecedents) if we measure it as a single entity than if we distinguish among different types of Internet use and examine their causes and consequences separately. Among the differences that may matter most are how one goes online, what one goes online to do (for example, e-mail versus Web-surfing), and, when one does use the Web, what kinds of sites one tries to access and how one goes about searching for them (Anderson and Tracey 2001; Hargittai 2003a).

Priorities for the study of inequality in access to advanced technology are both methodological and substantive. Many aspects of Internet technology are unfamiliar to less-sophisticated users, who may be unable to answer questions about connection speeds or processing power. Work on question design could improve data quality considerably. Substantively, we need to move beyond cross-sectional research to ensure that differences associated with connection speed or hardware quality do not simply reflect selection effects (that is, the greater likelihood that heavy and sophisticated users will invest in more expensive technology).

With respect to autonomy, the big question is the impact of *where* one goes online on *what* one does there. Within the home, which family members use Internet connections the most, for what purposes, and why? On the job we know that workplace Internet monitoring is widespread, but we know very little about the purposes of surveillance (whether employers aim to enforce broad prohibitions against time-wasting surfing or whether they target only employee behaviors—sexual harassment or fraud, for example—for which they bear vicarious liability); about differences among employees in different job classifications in monitoring or regulation of workplace Web use; or about the effect of monitoring on employee behavior.

Measurement is the most difficult challenge for students of skill. Hargittai's (2003a) observational approach is effective, but most researchers will find the cost prohibitive for large-scale data-gathering. We need survey-ready proxies for search skill, troubleshooting ability, and recipe knowledge, but the quest for such measures is complicated by the fact that the technology generates new forms of skill (or makes old ones obsolete) as fast as researchers can validate their measures. If suitable measures *can* be found, the next step is to understand the mechanisms that produce variations in skill and the consequences of such variation for the persistence and productivity of Internet use.

Better data on social support, especially data that distinguish between problem-solving assistance and affective support, is a high priority. Such data would make it possible to explore how social relationships enhance skill development and reduce frustration and, in so doing, increase the extent and productivity of Internet use.

Surveys increasingly ask Internet users about the kinds of sites they visit and about frequency of behavior. What most surveys do *not* tell us is *why* people fail to use the Internet for particular purposes—for example, whether Internet users who never visit political sites get their political news from other media or simply are indifferent to political information in any form. An important priority, then, is to ask respondents about information-seeking offline to provide context for interpreting their online behavior. A long-term priority is to go beyond self-reports by exploiting "clickstream" data—detailed records (collected by market researchers) of the sites that individual Web users visit (Goldfarb 2002). Employing clickstream data presents many challenges—gathering information about respondents' demographic traits and social attitudes without violating their privacy, classifying sites by topical domain, providing functional codes (for example, shopping, playing games, gathering information) for particular visits based on information about the pages accessed, deducing when multiple users are employing the same account—that will require collaboration between social scientists and computer scientists. At the same time, because clickstream data are both behavioral and extremely detailed, they can answer questions (for example, what kinds of users access the highest-quality information, or the extent to which users avoid or seek out sites that challenge their political views or aesthetic preferences) that survey data can only begin to address.

Taken together, the hypotheses set out in this section aggregate to a model of the influence of technological inequality on individual life chances that applies to the Internet and generalizes beyond it (see figure 9.7). As we conceive the process, demographic and situational factors affect the quality of technical apparatus and autonomy of use, skill, and social support at the individual level. These in turn influence the efficacy with which Web users employ the medium, both directly (by making it easier to achieve their objectives) and indirectly (by enhancing learning and satisfaction, which in turn promote persistence, efficacy, and volume and breadth of use). Ultimately, in this model, increases in human capital (including educational attainment), social capital (including political agency), and earnings are direct functions of the efficacy, intensity, and purposes of use and indirect consequences (through these mediating variables) of apparatus quality, autonomy, skill, and support. These latter relationships are sufficiently important that we devote the next section to them alone.

DOES INTERNET USE MATTER?

In one way, we know that Internet access matters. It matters keenly to the millions of people who rely on the Internet for e-mail, news, and other forms of information and entertainment. The high school and college students for whom instant-messaging has replaced the telephone, the operatives in the Jesse Ventura and Howard Dean campaigns who used the Web to get their dark-horse candidate into the race, the members of dispersed or stigmatized communities who can find one another online, and all the people who report having met spouses online (and the many more who hope to find them there) could not be convinced that the new medium is anything less than transformative.

From the standpoint of both public policy and social science, however, this question has a narrower meaning: Are people who have access to the Internet any better off—especially with respect to economic welfare (education, jobs, earnings) or social participation (political participation, community engagement, or receipt of government services and other public goods)—than they would be without the Internet? If the answer is no, then the case for public intervention is far less compelling than if it is yes.

The knowledge gap hypothesis discussed earlier raises a second question: Do returns to technology vary by socioeconomic status, race, place of residence, or gender? Are higher-

FIGURE 9.7   *The Impact of Internet Access on Life Chances*

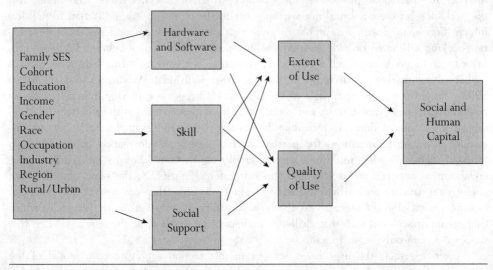

Source: Authors' compilation.

status users more effective at converting access into information and information into occupational advantage or social influence than less-privileged users? Does the low cost of information online level the playing field, or does online inequality reproduce existing patterns of inequality? Few studies have assessed the Internet's impact on individual economic welfare or occupational mobility. But research on the effects of computer use on earnings, quality of work life, and school achievement offers valuable lessons to those who would undertake similar research on the Internet.

Do Technical Skills Enhance Earnings?

Using CPS data from the late 1980s, Alan Krueger (1993) reports that workers who use computers on the job earn 10 to 15 percent more than their otherwise similar peers. Based on these analyses, he argues that the expansion in computer use in the 1980s accounted for one-third to one-half of the increase in the rate of return to education during that time. Using German data, John DiNardo and Jorn-Steffen Pischke (1997) likewise find significant wage differentials associated with computer use—but also with on-the-job use of calculators, telephones, and pencils. They argue that Krueger's results reflect selection effects rather than real returns to computer use, because computers have simply become part of the armamentarium of office work.

   Horst Entorf and Francis Kramarz (1997) and Entorf, Michel Gollac and Kramarz (1999) have replicated the earlier results cross-sectionally in France, but their panel analyses indicate that workers who become computer users experience no immediate wage increase. Rather, the earnings payoff appears to come with experience. Even then it is modest—just 2 percent after two to three years. The authors conclude that the difference between this estimate and the 15 to 20 percent differences found in cross-sectional studies reflects selection effects: when employers implement new technologies, they choose their best workers (who are already the highest paid) to use them. Similarly, Lucy Chennells and John Van

Reenen (1997, 599), assuming that "high wages signal high workforce quality and that this quality enables new technologies to be adopted at lower costs," find in the United Kingdom that although computers were first introduced into high-wage work settings, their introduction had little effect on blue-collar wages (see also Hughes and Lowe 2000).

We found only one study of Internet users' wages—Ernest Goss and Joseph Phillips's (2002) study of the effects of Internet use on workers' wages in the U.S. manufacturing sector. They report significant returns to Internet use: 13.5 percent, with a range by industry from 4.9 to 16.4 percent. Internet users receive greater wage premiums in low-tech industries, a result the authors attribute to the more recent introduction of the technology in the latter and to possible selectivity bias.

It is clear, then, that people who use computers at work earn more, but there is much debate about why this is the case. David Autor, Lawrence Katz, and Alan Krueger (1998) have studied aggregate changes in the relative supply and wages of workers by education from 1940 to 1996. Finding strong and persistent growth in relative demand favoring college graduates, they conclude that rapid skill upgrading within detailed industries has accounted for most of the growth in demand for educated workers since 1970 and that upgrading was most extensive in the most computer-intensive industries (1169). They conclude that such "skill-biased technological change" goes a long way toward explaining growing wage inequality in recent decades. In response, David Card and John DiNardo (2002) contend that most of the rise in wage inequality between 1980 and 2000 occurred between 1980 and 1986, whereas the pace of technological innovation (based on growth in the size of the information technology sector, the pace of Internet development, and aggregate productivity growth) was greatest in the 1990s.[13] They argue that new technologies always entail short-term premiums for workers with the skills to use and maintain them, as long as the latter remain relatively scarce. Consistent with Braverman (1974) and Spenner (1983), as reviewed earlier, once such skilled workers become more plentiful and the work is routinized, wage premiums decline.

A uniquely comprehensive study of the effects of technological change at the establishment level followed a major retooling of a food-processing plant that dramatically increased the skill level of the workforce (Fernandez 2001). Despite increased task complexity, mean and median wages for hourly workers remained unchanged during the three years of the study. Moreover, wage inequality (overall and between white and minority workers) increased markedly, with declining wages for those below the median and more positions for well-paid maintenance mechanics and electricians.

Do Technical Skills Enhance the Quality of Work Life?

Technology may change the qualitative experience of work as well as influence earnings. Manuel Castells (2001) argues that technological change is central to a broader transformation in work for both manual workers and "self-programmable" labor ("which must be able to reprogram itself in skills, knowledge, and thinking, according to changing tasks in an evolving business environment" [91]). Although he rejects technological determinism, Castells argues that "work flexibility, variable employment patterns, diversity of working conditions, and individualization of labor relations are systematic features of e-business. From this core of the new economy, flexible labor practices tend to diffuse into the entire labor market" (96). These hypotheses clearly merit sustained empirical examination as technological change unfolds.

What do we know about the impact of computerization on the quality of work life?

Based on CPS data, Richard Freeman (2002) reports that computerization and use of the Internet are associated with longer hours as well as higher wages. Using the 1992 Employment in Britain Survey, Duncan Gallie (1996) reports that managers in technically advanced work settings adopt more consultative styles of interaction with manual workers (a result that could reflect changes in ideology or worker training as well as technological imperatives). Roberto Fernandez (2001) finds that technological change results in greater task complexity across several skill dimensions. Whereas 17 percent of workers used computers before the renovation, 90.2 percent did afterward. Furthermore, and contrary to the de-skilling thesis, management expects workers to have a more complete knowledge of the production process and to be able to accomplish a wider variety of tasks. Fernandez emphasizes that "organizational and human resources factors were seen as [an] integral part of the plant retooling" from the start: workers were reorganized into teams, and managers were encouraged to view themselves as coaches rather than bosses. It seems likely, then, that changes in the labor process and the quality of work life reflect changes in managerial ideology as well as technology.

Some ethnographic studies suggest that implementation of new technologies makes workers who can use them more autonomous and may lead to a redistribution of power as well. Stephen Barley (1990) finds that the introduction of computerized scanning technologies into hospital radiology units has enhanced the relative standing and power of technicians, whose skills have become indispensable to newly deferential physicians. Studying change in a large insurance firm, Clare Lewin and Myron Orleans (2000) report that managers become less coercive and more consultative in dealing with computer specialists, who operate with considerable autonomy. Such findings support Weber's observation that technological change invariably challenges the viability of status structures based on social honor. One can imagine (although research has not documented it) that during transitional moments, young employees with strong Internet skills may move to the center of informal workplace networks and, in so doing, attain more influence and respect than their job descriptions would imply.

We must avoid broad generalizations about the effects of the Internet or even computerization on organizational design and workers' experience. The most thorough review of the literature on the organizational effects of digital technology finds little support for expectations about network effects and reports that many much-anticipated effects (for example, telecommuting) are still relatively rare (O'Mahoney and Barley 1999). The most notable examples of change reflect the application of specialized computer networks to specific kinds of work, such as the disintermediating impact of cellular communications on relations between central command structures and field-workers in industries as diverse as trucking and the U.S. military (Nagarajan, Bander, and White 2000; Fountain 2001).

Does Technology Improve School Performance?

Paul Attewell and Juan Battle (1999) find that computer use at home is significantly related to children's reading and mathematics test scores. (As with cross-sectional wage studies, it may be that computer use proxies a bundle of unmeasured resources that are available in computerized households.) This study is one of a few that address the question of whether returns to technology vary in a manner that reinforces or challenges existing inequalities. The authors report that the former was the case, with higher returns for boys, whites, and children from families of higher socioeconomic status. Focusing on home use, Attewell, Belkis Suzao-Garcia, and Battle (2003) report that young home computer users derive modest but significant sociocognitive benefits, but that these effects reverse among the heaviest users.

In a review of the literature on computers, schooling, and educational inequality, Attewell (2001) concludes that the context in which technology is introduced makes a big difference. For example, he notes that research has demonstrated positive effects on test scores of home computer use but *negative* effects of school computer use. Other studies from the 1990s find that low-income and minority students use computers at school more than middle-class and white students, but that their teachers are less qualified and their schools use computer labs as a form of baby-sitting. Similarly, David Bolt and Ray Crawford (2000) report that after public schools surged online in the late 1990s, staffing and teacher training lagged far behind, rendering the technologies educationally ineffective. Indeed, only one-third of teachers describe themselves as well prepared to incorporate computers or the Internet into their lesson plans (cited in Goolsbee and Guryan 2002). The only study to investigate the impact of school-level Internet service (as opposed to computer use in general) found no impact of subsidies for Internet adoption on test scores measured at the school level. Because of the focus on subsidies, however, rather than on adoption by both subsidized and unsubsidized districts, the results cannot be generalized (Goolsbee and Guryan 2002).

Does Technology Reduce Inequality in the Sphere of Consumption?

Fiona Scott-Morton, Florian Zettelmeyer, and Jorge Silva-Risso (2001, 2003) report that consumers who buy automobiles over the Internet receive a significant discount, with benefits especially great for African Americans. Similarly, Joel Waldfogel and Lu Chen (2003) report that Internet shoppers who use comparison sites (especially those with reliability ratings) patronize highly branded sellers less frequently—a sure sign that they are paying lower prices. Jeffrey Brown and Austan Goolsbee (2002) find effects on insurance prices but note that when the number of consumers using online price comparison sites reaches critical mass, non-users get a free ride on users' efforts.

The long-term effects of such processes on inequality are unclear. On the one hand, if more well educated and higher-income people are more likely to be online (which they are) and to be more sophisticated in their navigational skills (which they may be), the Internet could increase inequality by elevating the difference between the prices that rich and poor pay for the same goods. On the other hand, price disparities already exist for many goods, so that low-income persons who *do* use the Internet effectively will benefit more than their high-income counterparts. And in markets where many persons compare prices online, costs may decline for everyone.

Does Technology Enhance Political Influence and Community Engagement?

There is extensive evidence on the impact of the Internet on political participation and civic engagement based both on surveys and on quasi-experimental studies in which residential communities are wired and then investigated (Ishida and Isbister 2000). Although much of this work is beyond the scope of this chapter, we can summarize major findings succinctly.

First, despite fears to the contrary, Internet use does not lead to passivity or privatism. Internet users tend to consume more information offline than non-users and to be more active in other ways as well, and their online activities do not diminish their other efforts (Robinson et al. 2000). Dhavan Shah, Jack McLeod, and So-Hyang Yoon (2001) find that informational use of the Internet has a small but significant positive impact on community participation, whereas recreational uses have no effect. (An influential experimental study has found that Internet use leads to social withdrawal, but only in the short term; a follow-up shows that the negative effects dissipate relatively quickly [Kraut et al. 1998, 2002].) Second, Internet use does not *cause* people to become socially or politically involved. Rather, it makes it easier for people who are already engaged in community activities and political affairs to become even more so (Bimber 2003). Third, Internet use simultaneously increases local *and* long-distance communication, serving as a complementary channel to (rather than a substitute for) face-to-face interaction (Hampton and Wellman 2000; Katz, Rice, and Aspden 2001; Kavanaugh and Patterson 2001). Barry Wellman (2001) refers to this phenomenon as "glocalization."

The big question, about which we know rather little, is whether Internet use exacerbates inequality in political engagement and social participation. High-status people are more likely to be online and probably use the Internet to influence the world around them more than others because they were more politically involved *before* they went online. On the other hand, Internet use may have a larger *net* effect on the behavior of socially and politically engaged users with fewer resources, for whom the advantages afforded by the Internet may be correspondingly more important.[14]

Effects of Internet Use: Research Agenda

Scholars and policymakers interested in whether and under what conditions Internet use helps people get ahead stand before a gulf of ignorance, partially concealed by a fog of speculation. Dispelling the fog is essential for policy analysts, for if the Internet has no positive effects (or if the effects are positive only for the already privileged), then egalitarian arguments for public investment are weakened. (Not all are, of course: if government insists on interacting with citizens online, and if citizens must have Internet access to fulfill the obligations of citizenship or to get public services to which they are entitled, this in itself would create a compelling rationale for universal service.)

Research on the impact of computer use on earnings can teach us important lessons. First, panel data are essential. Even with panel data, selection effects are difficult to distinguish from genuine impacts; cross-sectional data in this area defy interpretation. Second, selection effects aside, it is unlikely that Internet use will be associated with positive, individual-level economic outcomes in large national samples. The mechanisms that connect skills to rewards are profoundly local, reflecting specific conditions of labor supply and demand and specific task requirements in particular industries. If there are positive effects of Internet use, we will need to disaggregate to find them.

Third, research on inequality online suggests that we are unlikely to find effects of global (and especially binary) measures of Internet access or use. Variation in how extensively people use the Internet, how skilled they are at finding the resources they need, and why they choose to go online is substantial and likely to be related to the payoffs they receive.

Fourth, research on Internet effects should routinely address the question of differential returns based on users' educational attainment, income, gender, or race—that is, the question of whether the Internet's benefits tend to ameliorate or reinforce existing patterns of inequality. In so doing, we should distinguish between two types of inequality-reinforcing mechanisms: those that reflect differences in how, where, to what extent, how skillfully, and for what purposes different kinds of people go online, and those that reflect discrimination, labor-market position, or other factors that alter returns to people whose Internet use is equivalent in quantity and quality.

Fifth, research on the effects of Internet use on consumption and on political and social participation should likewise explore the extent to which Internet use reinforces or counteracts intergroup inequalities. We also need to learn more about the extent to which the movement of government services online is associated with declines in offline service and about the effects of such shifts on persons in low-income (and low-Internet-use) communities (see Fountain 2001).

THE SOCIAL ORGANIZATION OF TECHNOLOGICAL INEQUALITY

The "Internet" is a protean family of technologies and services that are rapidly being reshaped by the interacting efforts of profit-seeking firms, government agencies, and nongovernmental organizations. Patterns of inequality can be understood as the aggregate consequences of individual choice only if those choices are themselves viewed as functions of decision contexts shaped by the political and strategic decisions of the state and corporations. Digital inequality reflects not just differences in individual resources but also the ways in which economic and political factors make such differences matter. Understanding the relationship between economic inequality and inequality of access to information requires research into the predictors of inequality at the level of communities, organizations, local states, and national societies. There is a growing literature on inequality among nation-states (Hargittai 1999; Norris 2001; Kiiski and Pohjola 2002; Guillén and Suarez 2002) but only suggestive evidence about the factors that influence patterns of inequality over time within the United States and the other advanced industrial societies.

Government Policies and Internet Adoption

The Clinton-Gore administration championed the Internet and used the power of the federal government to encourage its growth. The Internet's rapid diffusion in the United States during the late 1990s was almost certainly influenced by a wide range of federal policies: the privatization of the Internet early in the decade; the decision to exempt online sales from federal tax; Commerce Department grants for projects that brought new communication technologies to low-income communities; and the federal "E-rate" policy of subsidizing investments in Internet technology by public schools and libraries. Internet connectivity in U.S. public schools jumped from 3 percent in 1994 to 63 percent in 1999 (U.S. Department of Education 2000), and library connectivity rose to over 90 percent (Schement 2003). Research suggests that, in California at least, schools in low-income and minority communities were most responsive to the subsidies (Goolsbee and Guryan 2002).

Such policies influence patterns of inequality in access. Public schools appear to be doing much to democratize access to computers, but they have been less successful in ameliorating inequality in access to the Internet. Just over one-third of African Americans between the ages of ten and seventeen report using the Internet in school, compared to almost 58 percent of whites in that age range (NTIA 2002, 49–51). Youth from high-income families are also considerably more likely to use the Internet at school than are their low-income peers. We have no way of knowing whether these differences reflect differences in resources among schools with different student body compositions, differences between schools in their ability to productively employ the resources they have, or variation in access among students within online schools. The authors of one early review (Bikson and Panis 1999, 23) conclude that equalizing Internet resources at school has little effect on inequality in Internet use because students gain skills and experience by having computers available at home. By contrast, the availability of the Internet at public libraries enhances access for less-privileged groups: African Americans and people with low incomes are more likely to use the Internet in libraries than are whites and people with family incomes greater than $50,000 (NTIA 2002, 41).

Government exerts an impact through law as well as subsidy. The importance of financial inequality in limiting Internet access depends, for example, on regulatory and legislative decisions that expand definitions of "intellectual property" (and constrict the definition of "fair use") in ways that enable Internet firms to substitute pay-information services for free-information services. The fact that the government issues accessibility standards for electronic and information technology with which all government websites have to comply (Access Board 2000) also exemplifies how institutional measures can contribute to the degree to which sites are accessible to users with different needs and resources. The government's own use of the Internet is also consequential: the capacity of different kinds of Americans to gain access to information about government services, for example, depends on the extent to which government agencies and political institutions make information available, the form in which they present the information, the strategies they use to promote their sites, and the manner in which they interact with different types of users (Fountain 2001).

Local governments have invested in the Internet to a greater extent in Europe than in the United States. Willem Van Winden (2001) notes that several European cities, including Manchester in the United Kingdom and Rotterdam and The Hague in the Netherlands, view new communication technologies as "a catalyst for new social cohesion" and dedicate significant resources to providing citizens with the infrastructure to create virtual communities and participate more actively in local politics. Van Winden argues that such programs have failed, however, to achieve either social integration (subcultural groups tend to interact online among themselves) or broader political participation (because new opportunities are exploited predominantly by already active and privileged citizens).

The Impact of Business Strategies

Corporate strategies, as modified by government regulation and consumer response, also systematically influence individual-level incentives and constraints that produce inequality of access to technology (Neuman, McKnight, and Solomon 1998). The extent to which differences in the quality of hardware, connections, or software shape one's effective access to the full range of information on the Web, for example, is in part a product of how businesses and other organizations design their websites and whether they provide "low-graphics" or "text-only" options for users with less advanced equipment. Companies that produce browsers and ISPs responsible for the software used to access the Internet also influence people's ability to navigate the Web.

Institutions also shape access through their decisions about investments in network infrastructure. For example, Internet connectivity in rural America was initially limited by weak telecommunications infrastructure investment. As a result, rural areas have had less competition among ISPs, higher rates, and fewer households online (Strover 1999). By contrast, the superior availability of infrastructure in urban areas is responsible for the relatively rapid penetration of high-speed Internet access in inner-city public libraries, a development that has increased access for the low-income and minority communities that many such libraries serve (Bertot and McClure 1998).

Content creators can reach large audiences only if online gatekeepers (Web services that categorize links and search facilities to other sites) channel users to them (Hargittai 2000). During the 1990s entrepreneurs developed comprehensive and strongly branded "portals" (websites containing search engines, category guides, and shopping and information services) to match users and content. Internet traffic is highly concentrated: 80 percent of "hits" (successful efforts to contact a site) go to just 0.5 percent of websites. By 1999 portal sites accounted for one in four of the most visited destinations (Waxman 2000a, 2000b). The search engines that such sites feature are often biased in their rankings of sites in response to user queries (Introna and Nissenbaum 2000). The Web destinations that portal sites display prominently or that search engines rank high are likely to monopolize the attention of all but the most sophisticated Internet users. Most Internet searchers "satisfice"—they trade off comprehensive coverage to minimize search costs. An analysis of almost one billion queries on the Altavista search engine revealed that 77 percent of sessions included only one query and that 85 percent of users viewed only the first screen of search results (Silverstein et al. 1998). If Castells (1996, 371) is right in his prediction that Internet users will soon divide into "two distinct populations, the interacting and the interacted," then understanding the economic and political economic determinants of this process will be essential to understanding and explaining digital inequality.

Indeed, many media companies envision a media convergence in which the Internet essentially becomes a means of transmitting movies, recorded music, and television programming—in effect, cable television on steroids.[15] Insofar as this agenda is realized, the predictors and effects of Internet connectivity are likely to change markedly from what researchers discovered in the late 1990s and early 2000s. For example, if Internet users become more like television viewers, their relatively high levels of social and community engagement may not survive the transition to broadband.

Wilson (2000) has called attention to another dimension of inequality between social and linguistic groups: the availability of suitable content. This in turn is related to barriers to entry, especially the skills and time required to mount a website and the capital necessary to promote it and keep it current. Relatively little empirical research bears on the availability of culturally and linguistically specific Internet content of different kinds (except to document the dominant position of English as the language of the Web [OECD 1997]), and even less has examined the impact of availability on Web use by non-English-speaking or other minority communities.

Institutional Effects on Digital Inequality:
A Research Agenda

In effect, the challenge here is to understand measures of inequality in access to and use of technology as the explananda, and institutional arrangements—both government policies and business practices—as the independent variables. Whereas most of the research proposed in previous sections has focused on individual and household behavior, in this section the goal has been to understand the impact of policy regimes and industrial organization (broadly defined) on *patterns* of inequality. The trick is to navigate between the Scylla of quantitative analyses of policy outcomes one intervention at a time, which are almost certain to demonstrate negligible effects, and the Charybdis of undisciplined case studies, which too often reveal the results for which the author hopes.

We may get some leverage on public-sector policies by exploring variations in Internet use at the state level as a function of differences in state-government subsidies and other policies (and in federal expenditures within states) aimed at encouraging more equal Internet use. A useful first step would be to inventory state-level policies and to identify significant variants thereof.

Cross-national research is useful as well, although understanding the interaction of policy and business strategy in different nation-states is a daunting challenge probably best undertaken by teams of scholars from different countries. The advantage of cross-national designs is that public policies, technological infrastructures, and industrial organization vary so markedly across national borders, with dramatic consequences for the ways in which people access the Internet (for example, the balance between PCs and hand-held devices, which is often related to investments in cable and telephone infrastructures). Historical factors, like France's early attempt to create a subsidized national Teletext system through its postal service, and details of telephone service charges (for example, whether local calls are cross-subsidized by business and long-distance charges, as in the United States, or relatively expensive, as in the United Kingdom) may also be consequential.

With respect to private-sector strategies, perhaps the initial priority is simply to map the terrain and identify those strategic decisions (and interactions among them) that are most likely to influence inequality in access to the Internet in the future. Given the rapidity of change, monitoring the strategies of and relationships among ISPs, content providers, and other participants in the Internet industry would represent a useful step.

CONCLUSION

The digital divide paradigm served researchers and policymakers well during the opening years of Internet diffusion. Even though we know relatively little about the net effects of Internet access on educational attainment, labor market success, and life-course outcomes, the fact that public services and government information are increasingly migrating to the Internet makes access an important topic from the standpoint of public policy. Now that more than half of Americans go online, we should pursue a more differentiated approach to understanding the Internet's implications for social and economic inequality—one that focuses on the extent and causes of different returns to Internet use for different kinds of users. In particular, it is crucial to move beyond description and projection to understand the mechanisms, consequences, and institutional context of inequality in access to the Internet and use of the services it offers.

This chapter sets out the following research agenda:

1. Expand the focus of research from the digital divide between haves and have-nots (or between users and non-users) to the full range of *digital inequality* in equipment, autonomy, skill, support, and scope of use among people who are already online.

2. Compare inequality in access to and use of the Internet for significant purposes to inequality in access to and use of other media for the same purposes.

3. Develop and test models of the social processes that engender or ameliorate inequality by mediating the relationship between individuals' social identities and their access to and use of new technologies.

4. Extend such models to the relationship between the use of these technologies and valued individual-level outcomes, and investigate variations in rates of return to technology use for different subgroups within the population.

5. Supplement individual-level research with analysis of the institutional factors that shape and modify the relationships between individual characteristics and individual outcomes.

This agenda requires more intensive analyses of existing resources, more surveys of Internet users and non-users to address an expanded menu of topics, and improvements in survey design. Students of digital inequality also need to expand their methodological armory to include observational designs, analyses of clickstream data, analyses of link patterns between websites, ethnographies of use, cross-national comparisons, experimental survey designs, and political-economic research on industrial organization and regulatory issues.

This is a large agenda, but not impossibly so. The digital revolution is the first major technological change that has occurred *after* the emergence of federal social science funding and the expansion of research universities in the 1960s. As such, it represents a challenge to the social sciences (in collaboration with colleagues in computer science and engineering) to demonstrate their ability to understand and anticipate the consequences of technological changes as they are taking place. Properly conducted, such work can serve as an example for social scientists concerned with the effects of biotechnology and other technological revolutions that are sure to come.

Indeed, the research we call for here is one front in what should be a larger effort to understand the causes and impacts of inequality in access to and use of information of many kinds. Information figures crucially in the generation of inequality in advanced industrial societies in myriad ways: it shapes our children's ability to succeed in school and compete for access to higher education; its quality determines the returns on our financial investments; it even influences our ability to avoid illness and extend our lives. Currently, research on informational inequality is severely balkanized: educational researchers study the determinants and influence of test scores; a few economists and economic sociologists investigate where people get information about investment opportunities and labor markets; public health researchers analyze the determinants of knowledge about wellness and the health care system; and political scientists study sources of political information. We suggest, at the very least, that:

1. Information is a centrally important determinant of life chances; inequality in access to and use of information is a systematic source of social inequality; and cumulative patterns of disadvantage in access to different types of information may have cumulative consequences.

2. Scholars working in currently autarchic research areas that share a focus on the relationship between information and inequality in life-course outcomes may have a lot to learn from one another.

3. Similar questions and analytic strategies—for example, a focus on information ecologies rather than single sources of information; the study of information-seeking careers, with attention both to changes in information-gathering behavior over the life course and to the implications of such behavior in one domain on later behavior in others; and analyses of variation not simply in knowledge but in returns to investment in strategies of knowledge acquisition—may be useful across domains.

These considerations constitute not the conclusion of this chapter, however, but the introduction to a different chapter, the production of which is a collective project for another day.

Support from the Russell Sage Foundation, the National Science Foundation (grant IIS0086143), and the Markle Foundation is gratefully acknowledged, as is institutional support from the Princeton Center for Arts and Cultural Policy Studies and the Office of Population Research. This chapter reflects the impact on the first author's thinking of several helpful and provocative comments by participants at the Russell Sage Foundation Inequality Project's Harvard meeting in the summer of 2001.

NOTES

1. There may be a case for government action to increase equality in *returns to* Internet use; if such programs succeeded, the case for action to increase equality of access would be strengthened. Even if Internet use does not help people get ahead economically, the case for government intervention would still be very strong if access to the Internet were to become necessary to gain access to government services and sustain a minimal level of social and political participation.

2. Our focus throughout this chapter is on the United States, although we believe that the general framework is applicable to other economically advanced industrial societies.

3. CPS estimates tend to be more conservative than those from other studies. For example, a November–December 2000 survey by the Pew Internet and American Life Project found 58 percent of a national sample online (Horrigan 2000b, 7).

4. The odds ratio, r_{jk}, equals $(p_j/[1 - p_j])/(p_k/[1 - p_k])$, where p_j is the probability that the more-advantaged group has access and p_k is the probability that the less-advantaged group has access.

5. Figures 9.1 to 9.4 were produced by Hargittai using CPS data. Comparable graphs for region, metropolitan residence, gender, and Hispanic ethnicity are available at http://www.eszter.com/netuse.html. Data for 1994 are on the presence of modems in the household. Data for subsequent years are on use of the Internet for any purpose.

6. Unfortunately, it is difficult to interpret these results with much confidence. The authors of the U.S. study chose a method (linear as opposed to logistic regression) that would tend to lead coefficients to become larger (other things being equal) as the Internet's penetration increased. The author of the European study describes her method as linear (OLS) regression in the text but as logistic regression in the notes to the table reporting results, complicating interpretation (Norris 2001, 86, 88).

7. This line of reasoning must make two assumptions, for both of which there is much empirical support. First, the parameters with respect to which advantage is accorded must be only moderately correlated with one another (Blau 1977); second, personal relationships must be characterized by bias toward homophily—that is, people must tend to have friends who are similar to themselves (Marsden 1987).

8. Lenhart and her colleagues (2003) state that 58 percent of adults are Internet users and that 17 percent of non-users have been users in the past. We derive the 7 percent figure by multiplying the proportion of adults who are non-users $(1 - .58)$ by .17.

9. The text of the health item was: "In the past year . . . have you looked for information about a health concern or medical problem? If yes, please tell me if you tried to find such health information from [articles in a daily newspaper; articles in a general-interest magazine; special health or medical magazine or newsletter; a doctor, nurse, or other medical professional; friends or relatives; radio or television programs; the Internet or World Wide Web]." The text for the political item was: "In the past two years . . . have you looked for information about the views or background of a candidate for political office? If yes, please tell me if you tried to find such political information from [articles in a daily newspaper; articles in general newsmagazines like *Time, Newsweek,* or *U.S. News & World Report;* special magazine or newsletter

with particular policy interest or perspective; radio or television programs; friends or relatives; campaign materials from campaign worker or candidate; the Internet or World Wide Web]." The text for the jobs item was: "In the past year . . . have you searched for information about a new job or explored career opportunities? Please tell me how many times you tried to find such information from [classified ads in a daily newspaper; classified ads in an industry or professional publication; a fellow worker or human resources staff member at your workplace—that is, where you were working when you were searching; business or work contacts outside your workplace—that is, outside where you were then working; friends outside of work or relatives; any job placement or career counseling service; radio or television program; information posted on the Internet]." (The job responses were binarized as yes or no.) Note that respondents were asked these questions *before* being asked the series of items about their use of the Internet, so that they were *not* primed to think about the latter.

10. Some policy analysts have argued that once most members of a society are able to log on to the Internet, the digital divide will have been overcome and equality of access to the benefits of the Internet, at least for those who want them, will have been achieved. Drawing on the history of telephone access, Benjamin Compaine (2000) argues against legislation to ensure universal access because, he maintains, the combination of market forces and government programs currently in place are achieving that goal already. We question whether the telephone is the right analogy. For one thing, the view of telephone access as a binary good—a good for which the critical distinction is simply whether one has it or not—is appropriate only to the last quarter of the twentieth century. In the early and middle years of telephony, service varied in quality, some Americans connected through party lines (and were thus unable to use the technology for confidential communication) whereas others had individual connections, and long-distance service rates were discriminatory (Fischer 1992). In the first part of the twenty-first century the rise of cell phones, Palm Pilots, and other devices that blur the distinction between telephones and computers are redifferentiating telephone access. By the same token, the ability to log on to the Internet differs from the ability to pick up a receiver and find a dial tone in that the range of uses to which one can put the Internet and the extent to which many of these uses depend on the quality of the connections and equipment, user knowhow, and social support are far greater than was the case for the telephone even a decade ago.

11. The precise nature of the hierarchy varied from country to country. For example, in the United Kingdom, the contrast between the elite universities and the newer "red brick" universities was particularly striking. In the United States distinctions were graduated, with elite public research universities rivaling elite privates, but with much of the growth channeled to the less selective public institutions, especially two-year colleges.

12. Horrigan and Rainie (2002) note that causality is probably reciprocal in that investing in broadband is most attractive to users who use the Internet for a diverse set of purposes, a supposition strengthened by a subsequent report (Horrigan 2003) on users who plan to switch to broadband. Although Davison and Cotton (2003) do not explore the possibility, their findings suggest that broadband adopters may constitute two groups, one business-oriented and one driven by recreational enthusiasms.

13. Card and DiNardo's (2002) critique of the skill-biased technological change (SBTC) hypothesis rests in part on a comparison of changes in intergroup inequality among groups with varying degrees of technology use. They note that the racial wage gap declined sharply during the 1970s and remained stable during the 1980s while overall earnings inequality was rising, even though the SBTC hypothesis would predict that a group that was less likely to use computers at work (like African Americans) would see its relative position decline substantially during this period. They also contend that the SBTC hypothesis cannot explain "the fall in the relative wages of younger versus older workers, the fall in the relative wages of computer science and engineering graduates, the greater widening of wage inequality among FTFY (full-time, full-year employment) men than among broader groups of workers, and the failure of industry wage differences to expand over the 1980s" (772).

14. Shah, McLeod, and Yoon (2001) report that the positive effects of Internet use on community engagement are stronger for young users, for whom the medium is a central part of life, a difference that would tend to increase equality of participation.

15. On October 4, 2002, CBS Marketwatch (a financial news subscription service) ran an item headed "AOL Takes New Cue from Cable TV." AOL, the reader may recall, purchased the media conglomerate Time

Warner during the Internet stock boom, but synergy eluded its management, AOL lost subscribers, and the share price of the merged company (AOL Time Warner) fell precipitously. In the fall of 2002, AOL CEO Jonathan Miller announced a new strategy. AOL, he promised, "will offer a regular schedule of day-parted programming" (that is, different offerings available at different times of the day) appealing to subscriber interests, with more than 40 "shows" on such topics as finance, health, and education. According to Marketwatch, Miller also promised "more entertainment programming, and more and better live chats." In other words, having failed to commercialize successfully the Internet as it developed before 2002, AOL's business strategy would be to turn the Internet into cable television.

REFERENCES

Abbate, Janet. 1999. *Inventing the Internet.* Cambridge, Mass.: MIT Press.

Access Board. Architectural and Transportation Barriers Compliance Board. 2000. "Electronic and Information Technology Accessibility Standards." *Federal Register* (December 21). Available at: www.access-board.gov/ Technology Accessibility Standards." *Federal Register* (December 21). Available at: www.access-board.gov/ sec508/508standards.htm.

Althaus, Scott L., and David Tewksbury. 2000. "Patterns of Internet and Traditional News Media Use in a Networked Community." *Political Communication* 17: 21–45.

Alvarez, Anthony Steven. 2003. "Behavioral and Environmental Correlates of Digital Inequality." *IT and Society* 1(5): 97–140. Available at: www.stanford.edu/group/siqss/itandsociety/v01i05/v01i05a06.pdf.

American Management Association. 2001. "2001 AMA Survey: Workplace Monitoring and Surveillance: Summary of Key Findings." Available at: www.amanet.org/research/summ.htm (last accessed August 8, 2003).

Anderson, Ben, and Karina Tracey. 2001. "Digital Living: The Impact (or Otherwise) of the Internet on Everyday Life." *American Behavioral Scientist* 45: 456–75.

Anderson Robert H., Tora K. Bikson, Sally Ann Law, Bridger M. Mitchell, et al. 1995. *Universal Access to E-mail: Feasibility and Societal Implications.* Santa Monica, Calif.: Rand Corporation.

Attewell, Paul. 2001. "The First and Second Digital Divides." *Sociology of Education* 74: 252–59.

Attewell, Paul, and Juan Battle. 1999. "Home Computers and School Performance." *The Information Society* 15: 1–10.

Attewell, Paul, Belkis Suzao-Garcia, and Juan Battle. 2003. "Computers and Young Children: Social Benefit or Social Problem?" *Social Forces* 82: 275–94.

Autor, David H., Lawrence F. Katz, and Alan B. Krueger. 1998. "Computing Inequality: Have Computers Changed the Labor Market?" *Quarterly Journal of Economics* 113: 1169–1213.

Barley, Stephen R. 1990. "The Alignment of Technology and Structure Through Roles and Networks." *Administrative Science Quarterly* 35: 61–103.

Benton Foundation. 1998. *Losing Ground Bit by Bit: Low-Income Communities in the Information Age.* Washington, D.C.: Benton Foundation and National Urban League.

Bernstein, Basil. 1977. *Class, Codes, and Control,* vol. 3. London: Routledge & Kegan Paul.

Bertot, John Carlo, and Charles R. McClure. 1998. *The 1998 National Survey of U.S. Public Library Outlet Internet Connectivity: Final Report.* Washington, D.C.: American Library Association and National Commission on Libraries and Information Science.

Bikson, Tora K., and Constantijn W. A. Panis. 1999. *Citizens, Computers, and Connectivity: A Review of Trends.* Santa Monica, Calif.: Rand Corporation. Available at: www.rand.org/publications/MR/MR1109/ (last accessed August 26, 2003).

Bimber, Bruce. 2000. "The Gender Gap on the Internet." *Social Science Quarterly* 81: 868–76.

————. 2003. *Information and American Democracy: Technology in the Evolution of Political Power.* New York: Cambridge University Press.

Blau, Peter M. 1977. *Inequality and Heterogeneity: A Primitive Theory of Social Structure.* New York: Free Press.

Blau, Peter M., and Otis Dudley Duncan. 1967. *The American Occupational Structure.* New York: John Wiley.

Bolt, David, and Ray Crawford. 2000. *Digital Divide: Computers and Our Children's Future.* New York: TV Books.

Bonfadelli, Heinz. 2002. "The Internet and Knowledge Gaps: A Theoretical and Empirical Investigation." *European Journal of Communication* 17: 65–84.

Bourdieu, Pierre. 1984. *Distinction*. Cambridge, Mass.: Harvard University Press.

Bourdieu, Pierre, and Jean-Claude Passeron. 1977. *Reproduction in Education, Society, and Culture*. Beverly Hills, Calif.: Sage Publications.

Braverman, Harry. 1974. *Labor and Monopoly Capital*. New York: Monthly Review Press.

Brint, Steven. 1984. "'New Class' and Cumulative Trend Explanations of Liberal Political Attitudes of Professionals." *American Journal of Sociology* 90: 30–71.

———. 1998. *Schools and Societies*. Thousand Oaks, Calif.: Pine Forge Press.

Bromley, Rebekah V., and Dorothy Bowles. 1995. "Impact of Internet on Use of Traditional News Media." *Newspaper Research Journal* 16.

Brown, Jeffrey R., and Austan Goolsbee. 2002. "Does the Internet Make Markets More Competitive? Evidence from the Life Insurance Industry." *Journal of Political Economy* 110: 481–507.

Bucy, Erik P. 2000. "Social Access to the Internet." *Press/Politics* 5: 50–61.

Card, David, and John E. DiNardo. 2002. "Skill-Biased Technological Change and Rising Wage Inequality: Some Problems and Puzzles." *Journal of Labor Economics* 20: 733–83.

Castells, Manuel. 1996. *The Rise of the Network Society*, vol. 1, *The Information Age: Economy, Society, and Culture*. Boston: Blackwell.

———. 2001. *Internet Galaxy: Reflections on the Internet, Business, and Society*. New York: Oxford University Press.

Chang, Mariko Lin. 2003. "With a Little Help from My Friends (and My Financial Planner): How Socioeconomic Status and Race Influence the Search for Financial Information." Paper presented to the session on culture and economy at the 2003 annual meeting of the American Sociological Association, Atlanta (August 16–18, 2003).

Chennells, Lucy, and John Van Reenen. 1997. "Technical Change and Earnings in British Establishments." *Economica* 64: 587–604.

Collins, Randall. 1979. *The Credential Society: An Historical Sociology of Education*. New York: Academic Press.

Compaine, Benjamin M. 2000. "Re-examining the Digital Divide." Paper presented to the twenty-eighth Telecommunications Policy Research Conference, Alexandria, Va. (September 23–25).

———. 2001. "Information Gaps: Myth or Reality?" In *The Digital Divide: Facing a Crisis or Creating a Myth?*, edited by Benjamin M. Compaine. Cambridge, Mass.: MIT Press.

Cummings, Jonathon N., and Robert Kraut. 2000. "Domesticating Computers and the Internet." Unpublished paper. Carnegie-Mellon University, Pittsburgh.

Davison, Elizabeth, and Shelia R. Cotton. 2003. "Connection Discrepancies: Unmasking Further Layers of the Digital Divide." *First Monday* 8(3). Available at: firstmonday.org/issues/issue8—3/davison/index.html (last accessed September 1, 2003).

De Haan, Jos. 2003. "IT and Social Inequality in the Netherlands." *IT and Society* 1 (4, Spring): 27–45. Available at: www.stanford.edu/group/siqss/itandsociety/v01i04/v01i04a04.pdf.

DiMaggio, Paul. 2001. "Social Stratification, Lifestyle, Social Cognition, and Social Participation." In *Social Stratification in Sociological Perspective*, 2nd ed., edited by David Grusky. Boulder, Colo.: Westview Press.

DiMaggio, Paul, and Eszter Hargittai. 2002. "From the Digital Divide to Digital Inequality." Paper presented to the annual meeting of the American Sociological Association, Chicago (August).

DiNardo, John E., and Jorn-Steffen Pischke. 1997. "The Returns to Computer Use Revisited: Have Pencils Changed the Wage Structure Too?" *Quarterly Journal of Economics* 20: 291–303.

Entorf, Horst, Michel Gollac, and Francis Kramarz. 1999. "New Technologies, Wages, and Worker Selection." *Journal of Labor Economics* 17: 464–91.

Entorf, Horst, and Francis Kramarz. 1997. "Does Unmeasured Ability Explain the Higher Wages of New Technology Workers?" *European Economic Review* 41: 1489–1509.

Ettema, James S., James W. Brown, and Russell V. Luepker. 1983. "Knowledge Gap Effects in a Health Information Campaign." *Public Opinion Quarterly* 47: 516–27.

Fernandez, Roberto M. 2001. "Skill-Based Technological Change and Wage Inequality: Evidence from a Plant Retooling." *American Journal of Sociology* 107: 273–320.

Fischer, Claude S. 1992. *America Calling: A Social History of the Telephone to 1940*. Berkeley: University of California Press.

Fountain, Jane. 2001. *The Virtual State: The Politics of Digital Government*. Washington, D.C.: Brookings Institution.

Freeman, Richard B. 2002. "The Labor Market in the New Information Economy." *Oxford Review of Economic Policy* 18: 288–305.

Gallie, Duncan. 1996. "New Technology and the Class Structure: The Blue-Collar/White-Collar Divide Revisited." *British Journal of Sociology* 47: 447–73.

Galor, Oded, and Daniel Tsiddon. 1997. "Technological Progress, Mobility, and Economic Growth." *American Economic Review* 87: 363–82.

Gaziano, Cecilie. 1997. "Forecast 2000: Widening Knowledge Gaps." *Journalism and Mass Communications* 74: 237–64.

Goldfarb, Avi. 2002. "Analyzing Web Site Choice Using Clickstream Data." In *Advances in Applied Microeconomics*, vol. 11, *The Economics of the Internet and E-Commerce*, edited by Michael R. Baye. London: Elsevier Science.

Goolsbee, Austan, and Jonathan Guryan. 2002. "The Impact of Internet Subsidies on Public Schools." Working paper. Cambridge, Mass.: National Bureau of Economic Research.

Goolsbee, Austan, and Peter J. Klenow. 2002. "Evidence on Learning and Network Externalities in the Diffusion of Home Computers." *Journal of Law and Economics* 45: 317–44. Available at: gsbwww.uchicago.edu/fac/austan.goolsbee/research/computer.pdf (last accessed August 29, 2003).

Goss, Ernest P., and Joseph M. Phillips. 2002. "How Information Technology Affects Wages: Evidence Using Internet Usage as a Proxy for IT Skills." *Journal of Labor Research* 23: 463–74.

Gouldner, Alvin. 1979. *The Future of Intellectuals and the Rise of the New Class*. New York: Seabury Press.

Guillén, Mauro, and Sandra Suarez. 2002. "The Political Economy of Internet Development: A Cross-national Time-series Analysis." Working paper. Philadelphia: Wharton School, University of Pennsylvania.

Hall, Peter A. 1993. "Policy Paradigms, Social Learning, and the State: The Case of Economic Policymaking in Britain." *Comparative Politics* 27: 275–96.

Hampton, Keith, and Barry Wellman. 2000. "Examining Community in the Digital Neighborhood: Early Results from Canada's Wired Suburb." In *Digital Cities: Experiences, Technologies, and Future Perspectives*, edited by Toru Ishida and Katherine Isbister. New York: Springer-Verlag.

Hargittai, Eszter. 1999. "Weaving the Western Web: Explaining Differences in Internet Connectivity Among OECD Countries." *Telecommunications Policy* 23: 701–18.

———. 2000. "Open Portals or Closed Gates? Channeling Content on the World Wide Web." *Poetics* 27: 233–53.

———. 2002. "Second-level Digital Divide: Differences in People's Online Skills." *First Monday* 7(4). Available at: www.firstmonday.dk/issues/issue7_4/hargittai (last accessed September 1, 2003).

———. 2003a. "How Wide a Web: Inequalities in Access to Information Online." Ph.D. diss., Sociology Department, Princeton University.

———. 2003b. "Serving Citizens' Needs: Minimizing Online Hurdles to Accessing Government Information." *IT and Society* 1: 27–41.

Heil, Alexander. 2002. "The Information Society in the United Kingdom and Germany: Chances, Risks, and Challenges." Master's thesis, University of Leipzig. Available at: www.falling-through-the-net.de/analysis.pdf (last accessed September 1, 2003).

Hoffman, Donna L., and Thomas P. Novak. 1998. "Bridging the Racial Divide on the Internet." *Science* 280: 390–96.

———. 1999. "Examining the Relationship of Race to Internet Access and Usage over Time." Working paper. Nashville: eLab Manuscripts, Vanderbilt University.

Hoffman, Donna L., Thomas P. Novak, and Ann E. Schlosser. 2001. "The Evolution of the Digital Divide: Examining the Relationship of Race to Internet Access and Usage over Time." In *The Digital Divide: Facing a Crisis or Creating a Myth?*, edited by Benjamin M. Compaine. Cambridge, Mass.: MIT Press.

Horrigan, John. 2000a. *New Internet Users: What They Do Online, What They Don't, and Implications for the Net's Future*. Washington, D.C.: Pew Internet and American Life Project (September 25).

———. 2000b. *The Holidays Online: E-mails and E-greetings Outpace E-commerce*. Washington, D.C.: Pew Internet and American Life Project (December 31).

———. 2003. "Adoption of Broadband to the Home." Pew Internet Project Data Memo. Washington, D.C.: Pew Internet and American Life Project (May).

Horrigan, John, and Lee Rainie. 2002. "The Broadband Difference: How Online Americans' Behavior Changes with High-Speed Internet Connections at Home." Washington, D.C.: Pew Internet and American Life Project (June 23).

Howard, Philip, Lee Rainie, and Steve Jones. 2001. "Days and Nights on the Internet: The Impact of a Diffusing Technology." *American Behavioral Scientist* 45: 383–404.

Hughes, Karen D., and Graham S. Lowe. 2000. "Surveying the 'Post-industrial' Landscape: Information Technologies and Labor Market Polarization in Canada." *Canadian Review of Sociology and Anthropology* 37: 29–53.

Hymes, Dell. 1974. *Foundations in Sociolinguistics: An Ethnographic Approach.* Philadelphia: University of Pennsylvania Press.

IntelliQuest. 1999. "Intelliquest Study Shows 83 Million U.S. Internet Users and 56 Million Online Shoppers." Press release (April 19,1999). http://www.intelliquest.com/press/archive/release78.asp. (Last accessed October 21, 2003.)

Introna, Luc, and Helen Nissenbaum. 2000. "Shaping the Web: Why the Politics of Search Engines Matters." *The Information Society* 16: 1–17.

Ishida, Toru, and Katherine Isbister, eds. 2000. *Digital Cities: Experiences, Technologies, and Future Perspectives.* New York: Springer-Verlag.

Karabel, Jerome, and Alexander Astin. 1975. "Social Class, Academic Ability, and College 'Quality.'" *Social Forces* 53: 381–98.

Katz, James E., and Philip Aspden. 1997. "Motives, Hurdles, and Dropouts." *Communications of the ACM* 40: 97–102.

Katz, James E., and Ronald Rice. 2002. *Social Consequences of Internet Use: Access, Involvement, and Interaction.* Cambridge Mass.: MIT.

Katz, James E., Ronald Rice, and Philip Aspden. 2001. "The Internet, 1995–2000: Access, Civic Involvement, and Social Interaction." *American Behavioral Scientist* 45(3): 405–19.

Kavanaugh, Andrea L., and Scott J. Patterson. 2001. "The Impact of Community Computer Networks on Social Capital and Community Involvement." *American Behavioral Scientist* 45(3): 496–509.

Kelley, Maryellen R. 1990. "New Process Technology, Job Design, and Work Organization: A Contingency Model." *American Sociological Review* 55: 191–208.

Kiesler, Sara, Bozena Adaniuk, Vicki Lundmark, and Robert Kraut. 2001. "Troubles with the Internet: The Dynamics of Help at Home." *Human Computer Interaction* 15: 323–51.

Kiiski, Sampska, and Matti Pohjola. 2002. "Cross-country Diffusion of the Internet." *Information Economics and Policy* 14: 297–310.

Kim, Yong-Chan, and Joo-Young Jung. 2002. "Digital Divide in 90 Percent Access: Multidimensional Examination of Adolescents' Internet Connectedness in Seoul, Singapore, and Taipei." In *A Study on the Digital Divide of the Youth,* edited by J. Hwang, J. Yu, and J. Lee. Seoul: Korea Institute for Youth Development.

Kling, Rob. 1998. "Technological and Social Access to Computing, Information, and Communication Technologies." White paper for Presidential Advisory Committee on High-performance Computing and Communications, Information Technology, and the Next Generation Internet. Available at: www.slis.indiana.edu/faculty/kling/pubs/NGI.htm.

Kohn, Melvin L., and Carmi Schooler. 1982. "Job Conditions and Personality: A Longitudinal Assessment of Their Reciprocal Effects." *American Journal of Sociology* 87: 1257–86.

Kraut, Robert, Sara Kiesler, Bonka Boneva, Jonathon Cummings, Vicki Helgeson, and Anne Crawford. 2002. "Internet Paradox Revisited." *Journal of Social Issues* 58: 49–74.

Kraut, Robert, Michael Patterson, Vicki Lundmark, Sara Kiesler, Tridas Mukophadhyay, and William Scherlis. 1998. "Internet Paradox: A Social Technology That Reduces Social Involvement and Psychological Well-being?" *American Psychologist* 53: 1011–31.

Krueger, Alan B. 1993. "How Computers Have Changed the Wage Structure: Evidence from Micro Data." *Quarterly Journal of Economics* 108: 33–60.

Lawrence, Steve, and Lee Giles. 1999. "Accessibility of Information On the Web." *Nature* (400): 107–9.

Leigh, Andrew, and Robert Atkinson. 2001. "Clear Thinking on the Digital Divide." Washington, D.C.: Progressive Policy Institute (June 26,1999). Available at: www.NDOL.org?Documents/DigitalDivide.PDF. (Last accessed October 21, 2003.)

Leighton, Wayne A. 2001. "Broadband Deployment and the Digital Divide: A Primer." *Policy Analysis* (Cato Institute) 410(August 7). Available at: www.cato.org/pubs/pas/pa410.pdf. (Last accessed August 26, 2003.)

Lenhart, Amanda. 2000. "Who's Not Online: 57 Percent of Those Without Internet Access Say They Do Not Plan to Log On." Washington, D.C.: Pew Internet and American Life Project (September 21).

Lenhart, Amanda, John Horrigan, Lee Rainie, Katherine Allen, Angie Boyce, Mary Madden, and Erin O'Grady. 2003. "The Ever-Shifting Internet Population: A New Look at Internet Access and the Digital Divide." Washington, D.C.: Pew Internet and American Life Project (April 16).

Lessig, Lawrence 1999. *Code and Other Laws of Cyberspace.* New York: Basic Books.

Lewin, Clare, and Myron Orleans. 2000. "The Class Situation of Information Specialists: A Case Analysis." *Sociological Research Online* 5. Available at: www.socresonline/org.uk/5/3/lewin.html.

Lin, Nan. 2000. *Social Capital.* New York: Cambridge University Press.

Losh, Susan Carol. 2003. "Gender and Educational Digital Chasms in Computer and Internet Access and Use over Time: 1983–2000." *IT and Society* 1(4, Spring): 73–86. Available at: www.stanford.edu/group/siqss/itandsociety/v01i04/v01i04a06.pdf.

Marsden, Peter V. 1987. "Core Discussion Networks of Americans." *American Sociological Review* 52: 122–31.

Martin, Steven P. 2003. "Is the Digital Divide Really Closing? A Critique of Inequality Measurement in *A Nation Online.*" *IT and Society* 1(4, Spring): 1–13. Available at: www.stanford.edu/group/siqss/itandsociety/v01i04/html. (Last accessed June 12, 2003.)

Marx, Karl. 1867/1887. *Capital: A Critical Analysis of Capitalist Production.* Translated by Samuel Moore and Edward Aveling. London: Sonnenschein, Lowrey.

McLaren, Jennifer, and Gianni Zappalà. 2002. "The 'Digital Divide' Among Financially Disadvantaged Families in Australia." *First Monday* 7(11). Available at: firstmonday.org/issues/issue7_11/mclaren/index.html. (Last accessed September 1, 2003.)

Mossberger, Karen, Caroline J. Tolbert, and Mary Stansbury. 2003. *Virtual Inequality: Beyond the Digital Divide.* Washington, D.C.: Georgetown University Press.

Mueller, Milton L., and Jorge Reina Schement. 2001. "Universal Service from the Bottom Up: A Study of Telephone Penetration in Camden, New Jersey." In *The Digital Divide: Facing a Crisis or Creating a Myth?,* edited by Benjamin M. Compaine. Cambridge, Mass.: MIT Press.

Nagarajan, Anu, James L. Bander, and Chelsea C. White. 2000. "Trucking." In *U.S. Industry in 2000: Studies in Competitive Performance,* edited by Board on Science, Technology and Economic Policy, National Research Council. Washington, D.C.: National Academy Press.

National Telecommunications and Information Administration (NTIA). 1995. *Falling Through the Net: A Survey of the "Have-nots" in Rural and Urban America.* Washington: U.S. Department of Commerce (July).

———. 1998. *Falling Through the Net II: New Data on the Digital Divide.* Washington: U.S. Department of Commerce (July).

———. 1999. *Falling Through the Net: Defining the Digital Divide.* Washington: U.S. Department of Commerce (November).

———. 2000. *Falling Through the Net: Toward Digital Inclusion.* Washington: U.S. Department of Commerce (October).

———. 2002. *A Nation Online: How Americans Are Expanding Their Use of the Internet.* Washington: U.S. Department of Commerce (February).

Neuman, W. Russell, Lee McKnight, and Richard Jay Solomon. 1998. *The Gordian Knot: Political Gridlock on the Information Highway.* Cambridge, Mass.: MIT Press.

Neuman, W. Russell, Shawn R. O'Donnell, and Steven M. Schneider. 1996. "The Web's Next Wave: A Field Study of Internet Diffusion and Use Patterns." Unpublished paper. MIT Media Laboratory, Cambridge, Mass.

Norris, Pippa. 2001. *Digital Divide? Civic Engagement, Information Poverty, and the Internet in Democratic Societies.* New York: Cambridge University Press.

O'Mahoney, Siobhan, and Steven R. Barley. 1999. "Do Digital Telecommunications Affect Work and Organization? The State of Our Knowledge." *Research in Organizational Behavior* 21: 125–61.

Ono, Hiroshi, and Madeline Zavodny. 2003. "Gender and the Internet." *Social Science Quarterly* 84: 111–21.

Organization for Economic Cooperation and Development (OECD). 1997. *Webcasting and Convergence: Policy Implications.* Paris: OECD. Available at: www.oecd.org/dsti/sti/it/cm/prod/e_97-221.htm.

Pandey, Sanjay K., John J. Hart, and Sheela Tiwary. 2002. "Women's Health and the Internet: Understanding Emerging Trends and Implications." *Social Science and Medicine* 56: 179–91.

Pew Center for the People and the Press. 1995. *Technology in the American Household*. Washington, D.C.: Pew Center for the People and the Press.

Pew Internet and American Life Project. 2000. *Tracking Online Life: How Women Use the Internet to Cultivate Relationships with Family and Friends*. Washington, D.C.: Pew Internet and American Life Project (May 10).

Robinson, John P., Meyer Kestnbaum, Alan Neustadtl, and Anthony Alvarez. 2000. "Mass Media Use and Social Life Among Internet Users." *Social Science Computer Review* 18: 490–501.

Schement, Jorge Reina. 2003. "Measuring What Jefferson Knew and Tocqueville Saw: Libraries as Bridges Across the Digital Divide." *IT and Society* 1(4, Spring): 118–25. Available at: www.stanford.edu/group/siqss/itandsociety/v01i04/v01i04a10.pdf.

Schement, Jorge Reina, and Scott C. Forbes. 1999. "Approaching the Net: Toward Global Principles of Universal Service." Available at: www.benton.org/policy/schement/ptc99/home.html. (Last accessed November 16, 2001.)

Scott-Morton, Fiona, Florian Zettelmeyer, and Jorge Silva-Risso. 2001. "Internet Car Retailing." *Journal of Industrial Economics* 49: 501–19.

———. 2003. "Consumer Information and Discrimination: Does the Internet Affect the Pricing of New Cars to Women and Minorities?" *Quantitative Marketing Economics* 1: 65–92.

Shah, Dhavan V., Jack M. McLeod, and So-Hyang Yoon. 2001. "Communication, Context, and Community: An Exploration of Print, Broadcast, and Internet Influences." *Communication Research* 28: 464–506.

Silverstein, Craig, Monica Henzinger, Hannes Marais, and Michael Moricz. 1998. "Analysis of a Very Large AltaVista Query Log." *SRC Technical Note* (October 26,1998): 6–12.

Spenner, Kenneth. 1983. "Deciphering Prometheus: Temporal Change in the Skill Level of Work." *American Sociological Review* 48: 824–37.

Spooner, Tom, and Lee Rainie. 2000. *African Americans and the Internet*. Washington, D.C.: Pew Internet and American Life Project (October 22).

Stempel, Guido H., III, Thomas Hargrove, and Joseph P. Bernt. 2000. "Relation of Growth of Use of the Internet to Changes in Media Use from 1995 to 1999." *Journalism and Mass Communication Quarterly* 77: 71–79.

Strover, Sharon. 1999. *Rural Internet Connectivity*. Columbia, Mo.: Rural Policy Research Institute.

Tichenor, Phillip, George Donohue, and Clarice Olien. 1970. "Mass Media Flow and Differential Growth of Knowledge." *Public Opinion Quarterly* 34: 159–70.

U.S. Department of Education. 2000. *Internet Access in U.S. Public Schools and Classrooms: 1994–1999: Statistics in Brief*. Washington: U.S. Department of Education, National Center for Educational Statistics (February).

Van Winden, Willem. 2001. "The End of Social Exclusion? On Information Technology Policy as a Key to Social Inclusion in Large European Cities." *Regional Studies* 35: 861–77.

Veblen, Thorstein. 1921/1983. *Engineers and the Price System*. New Brunswick, N.J.: Transaction Books.

Verba, Sidney, Kay Schlozman, and Henry E. Brady. 1995. *Voice and Equality: Civic Voluntarism in American Politics*. Cambridge, Mass.: Harvard University Press.

Viswanath, Kasisomayajula, and John Finnegan. 1996. "The Knowledge Gap Hypothesis: Twenty-five Years Later." In *Communication Yearbook*, vol. 19, edited by Brant R. Burleson. Thousand Oaks, Calif.: Sage Publications.

Viswanath, Kasisomayajula, Gerald M. Kosicki, Eric S. Fredin, and Eunkyung Park. 2000. "Local Community Ties, Community Boundedness, and Local Public Affairs Knowledge Gaps." *Communication Research* 27: 27–50.

Waldfogel, Joel. 2002. "Consumer Substitution Among Media." Working paper. Federal Communications Commission Media Ownership Working Group (September). Available at: hraunfoss.fcc.gov/edocs—public/attachmatch/DOC-226838A8.pdf. (Last accessed August 29, 2003.)

Waldfogel, Joel, and Lu Chen. 2003. "Does Information Undermine Brand? Information Intermediary Use and Preference for Branded Web Retailers." Working paper. Wharton School, University of Pennsylvania (August 21). Available at: bpp.wharton.upenn.edu/waldfogj/pdfs/Infoint.pdf. (Last accessed August 29, 2003.)

Waxman, Jared. 2000a. *The Old 80/20 Rule Takes One on the Jaw: Internet Trends Report 1999 Review*. San Francisco: Alexa Research.

———. 2000b. *Leading the Pack . . . Internet Trends Report 1999 Review*. San Francisco: Alexa Research.

Weber, Max. 1956/1978. "The Distribution of Power Within the Political Community: Class, Status, and Party." In *Economy and Society,* edited by Guenther Roth and Claus Wittich. Berkeley: University of California Press.

Wellman, Barry. 2001. "Physical Place and Cyber Place: The Rise of Personalized Networking." *International Journal of Urban and Regional Research* 25: 227–52.

Wilson, Ernest J. 2000. *Closing the Digital Divide: An Initial Review: Briefing the President.* Washington, D.C.: Internet Policy Institute (May).

Chapter 10

The Shareholder Value Society:
A Review of the Changes in Working Conditions and
Inequality in the United States, 1976 to 2000

Neil Fligstein and Taek-Jin Shin

Increases in income inequality in the United States over the past quarter-century have been well documented (Murphy and Welch 1992; Karoly 1992; Freeman 1997; Levy and Murnane 1992; Katz and Autor 1999). Everyone has agreed to three main facts: income and wage inequality increased in the 1980s, stabilized in the late 1980s and early 1990s, then began to increase until the late 1990s, when it once again stabilized (Freeman 1997; Lee 1999). Generally, the workers who fared the worst in these changes were those who did not finish high school. They saw their wages relative to those of college graduates slip by at least 30 percent (Freeman 1997, Lee 1999; Mishel, Bernstein, and Schmitt 2001). Finally, women generally saw their situation improve relative to men over the period (Karoly 1992; Freeman 1997). From the data, it appears as if low-skilled men suffered the brunt of these changes (Lee 1999).

There has been a lively theoretical and empirical debate over the causes of these changes (for some review articles, see Topel 1990; Fortin and Lemieux 1997). Some observers have concluded that most of the change stemmed from the increase in demand for skilled labor caused by technological change (Katz and Murphy 1992; Bresnahan, Brynjolfsson, and Hitt 2000; Krueger 1993). Others have focused attention on institutional factors, such as the decline in unions and the lack of any increase in the minimum wage (Lee 1999; Freeman 1997; Card 1992). Still others have tried to examine how the continuing shift from manufacturing to services and the increased exposure to world markets has helped skilled workers and hurt unskilled workers (Freeman 1997; Bluestone and Harrison 1982). Finally, some researchers have focused on the depressive effect of immigration patterns on the wages of low-skilled workers (Borjas 1999). This debate turns very much on how we measure these factors and their effects.

A related debate concerns how work and jobs have changed in the past twenty-five years. Many observers argue that during the 1980s the employment relation in the United States began to change for all workers (see, for example, Osterman 1999; Gordon 2000; Pfeffer and Baron 1988; Blair and Kochan 2000). Firms began to redefine their core workers and to downsize, outsource, and employ more contract workers. This made workers generally more insecure, and as we show, dissatisfied with work. This chapter reviews the literature on this subject and tries to link these changes to shifts in income inequality.

401

We provide descriptive evidence consistent with the view that work changed over this period as income became more unequally distributed. The literature shows very clearly that not only did workers on the bottom of the skill distribution fare poorly by losing ground on wages, but they also encountered less safe working conditions, found themselves working less regular shifts, received fewer benefits such as pensions and health care, and experienced lower job security and job satisfaction. In essence, the increases in wage inequality were accompanied by a growing insecuritization of work for those at the bottom. The evidence is somewhat different for those at the top of the income distribution. While they experienced more insecurity at work as well, they also benefited from the changes in employment relations. Their benefits remained more stable. For those whose incomes went up the most, job satisfaction increased as well as their sense of efficacy at work. Hours of work also increased for those with the highest incomes, but most appear to enjoy their work.

In this review, we first consider more carefully the argument about what has changed in the employment relations of various groups of workers in the past twenty-five years. Then we look at the evidence that measures those changes. We make an explicit attempt to link these changes to changes in income inequality wherever possible. Finally, we discuss the further research implied by our review.

THE RISE OF A SHAREHOLDER VALUE SOCIETY, CHANGES IN WORK, AND INCOME INEQUALITY

There are several remarkable facts that have not been noticed by most of those who have worked on the problem of income inequality. First, all of the changes in working conditions have gone in one direction: they have benefited those with skill who tend to occupy managerial or professional occupations, and not those who hold other kinds of jobs. Second, these changes have occurred across every sector of the economy. Although they may have begun in the hollowing out of the manufacturing sector in the early 1980s, the employment relation and the structure of work were eventually changed everywhere in the economy. Third, it is not just that high-skilled workers, managers, and professionals are doing better relative to other workers, but that other workers are systematically being treated worse. Indeed, it is clear that not only are high-skilled workers benefiting financially, but that they are enjoying better working conditions relative to those of lower-skilled workers, who are finding themselves with lower wages *and* worse working conditions.

This suggests that there is another story to tell about the past twenty years in the United States that would be consistent with these facts. The changes in employment relations were responses to the economic crisis of the 1970s. The prevailing analysis of the high inflation and slow economic growth of the 1970s was that these problems were caused by a federal government being too intrusive, firms growing fat and lazy, and workers enjoying too many protections in the labor market (Fligstein 2001). Federal policies starting in the Carter administration began to deregulate industries like trucking and airlines to increase competition. They also began to unravel the social safety net in order to decrease labor market "rigidities." Federal policies in the past twenty-five years have consistently curtailed government benefits, like unemployment insurance, welfare, and food stamps. They have made it more difficult for workers to organize and allowed firms to pay lower benefits to workers and engage in mass layoffs. Because the minimum wage was never indexed to inflation, it fell steadily over time.

During the 1980s changes in the market for corporate control promoted "shareholder value" over stakeholder rights. It was thought that management was not focused enough on profits and too focused on growth and size. With this change in perspective, management culture began to view employees not so much as partners as costs to be minimized. Plants were closed, some economic activities were moved offshore, others were outsourced to lower cost operations (often with low-wage workers working part-time with few benefits), and technology was generally used to make workers less essential (Harrison and Bluestone 1988). As a result, lower-skilled workers experienced less security in the workplace in the form of higher threats of job loss, fewer pay increases, and fewer benefits. The clear beneficiaries of the "shareholder value" solution to the economic crisis of the 1970s were shareholders and the managers and professionals who controlled the restructuring of firms. The stakeholders in firms, particularly workers and communities, lost out (for different versions of this same story, see Appelbaum and Berg 1996; Gordon 2000; Harrison and Bluestone 1988; Osterman 1999).

There is one main ambiguity in our story: the degree to which managers and professionals were made more insecure as well as other workers. In a shareholder value society all workers in all sectors of the economy are potentially subject to the new labor market regime. One way to tell the story is to see middle managers and professionals who had focused on working for a single firm for their entire career as victims of shareholder value (Blair and Kochan 2000; Osterman 1999). In this version of the story, because managers and professionals had more skills, it was not so much that they benefited in the labor market as that they were better able than less-skilled workers to prevent their situation from deteriorating (Bernhardt et al. 2001). Another way to tell the story is to note that the most highly skilled workers were able to take control over their careers and parlay their skills into higher and higher incomes. By changing their loyalty to firms and shifting jobs more frequently, skilled workers were able to benefit from the more flexible labor markets of the 1980s and 1990s and thus raise their wages (DiPrete 1993; Osterman 1999).

Paradoxically, our review of the empirical literature shows support for both perspectives. All workers, including managers and professionals, experienced less job security and tougher work conditions over time. With downsizing, managers and professionals were asked to work more hours at a more intense pace. But they were highly rewarded for this extra work in several ways. We show that managers and professionals who worked overtime came to make disproportionately more than their counterparts who did not work long hours. On the whole, managers and professionals reported higher job satisfaction and a great deal of fulfillment from work. The intensification of work was rewarded by a greater feeling of efficacy at work.

Our review of the literature has brought us to the conclusion that the changes in the workplace from 1980 until the late 1990s came in two waves. The first wave occurred during the recession of the early 1980s. Large corporations closed plants, laid off blue-collar workers, and moved plants offshore. This deindustrialization process, coupled with the recession and the lack of any increase in the minimum wage, depressed wages for people at the bottom of the skill distribution, thus causing the largest increase in income inequality to appear (Card and DiNardo 2002). Wages for this group have never really improved.

The second wave occurred in and around the recession in the early 1990s, when downsizing hit middle managers, professionals, and other white-collar workers and the service sector more generally (Farber 1997a; Schmidt 1999; Appelbaum and Berg 1996). The effect of downsizing was to intensify work for managers and professionals and make them more insecure. Those who were not laid off found themselves expected to work more hours in order to replace the labor of those who used to work for them. As a reward, their income was substantially increased. This created the idea of working "24/7" (twenty-four hours a day, seven days a week). For those who got this work, the rewards were very high. We also have evidence, however, that today many managers and professionals would prefer to work fewer hours, not more.

Our strategy in this review is to present the evidence for changes in work in six parts. First, we describe what we know about changes in job tenure and job displacement over the period. Second, we consider changes in part-time and temporary work as they relate to work insecurity. In the third section, we take up the conditions of work and discuss changes in benefits and the health and safety conditions of work. The fourth section analyzes changes in hours and overtime and their relationship to changes in income inequality. The fifth section looks at more subjective results on changes in job satisfaction, personal fulfillment, and financial security. The sixth section explores the themes raised in the other sections by analyzing some recent data on changes in working conditions in California.

The most difficult evidence to gather concerns the link between the actions of firms and the response of workers. We have little direct evidence of what exactly firms did. Instead, we (and others) use the available large-scale datasets to look for results that plausibly fit what we know about firms that tended to reorganize themselves during the 1980s and 1990s.

CHANGES IN TENURE AND JOB DISPLACEMENT, 1975 TO 2001

One of the main themes in the literature on new forms of work is the growing insecurity of work. There are a number of ways to index the changing insecurity at work. If labor relations regimes have changed, then we would expect job tenure (defined as the time that an individual has been employed with the current employer) to decrease for all workers. More important, if our hypothesis on the bifurcation of work is correct, the decline of job tenure would be greater for blue-collar and service workers. Second, and relatedly, we would expect to see more job displacement for workers over time owing to plant closings and downsizing. This, again, should be particularly true for blue-collar and service workers. Finally, we would expect to see increases in part-time employment, temporary employment, and contract employment. Such increases in nonstandard employment would reflect the reluctance of firms to make commitments to employees and their desire to avoid paying benefits. This section presents evidence on the changes in tenure and job displacement; the increase in nonstandard employment, another indication of insecuritization, is discussed in the next section.

There are several ways in which changes in insecurity could be related to increased income inequality. First, less tenure on the job and more frequent job shifting imply that workers are getting less on-the-job experience and hence have less firm-specific human capital. Over time this decrease in human capital would also make workers' income trajectories flatter, translating into lower overall wages and salaries for all workers if they are equally affected. Moreover, if job turnover is higher among workers with fewer skills (low-skilled or blue-collar and service workers), this could cause increases in income inequality. Finally, the fact that part-time or temporary workers typically do not receive paid benefits such as health care or pensions increases inequality because full-time employees get even more income than their temporary counterparts. We examine this effect in the next section.

A change over time in job tenure—the number of years an individual is employed by the same employer—could reflect the choices of either workers or employers. It is not the same as job displacement due to employers weakening the labor contract. Moreover, overall changes in tenure on the job could reflect changes in the age structure. Young people, for example, change jobs more frequently than older workers. If the percentage of young workers were on the rise, then we would expect that tenure on the job in the population would be decreasing.

There have also been problems in the measurement of job tenure over time. The most extensive series of data that we have on job tenure comes from the Current Population Survey (CPS) done by the U.S. Census Bureau. Unfortunately, the wording of the job tenure question changed in 1983. Before 1983 people were asked how long they had held their current job. After 1983 they were asked how long they had worked for their current employer. The problem here is that, as a result of the change in the question, people who had changed jobs within their same employer were probably underreporting their job tenure.

Charles Schultze (1999, 33) gathers the data on job tenure from the CPS and makes an adjustment for the discontinuities in the data. According to his calculation, job tenure dropped about 20 percent for male workers age twenty-five to forty-four from 1963 until 1981. It changed little for workers age forty-five to sixty-four. During 1983 until 1998, job tenure dropped substantially for all age groups. Tenure for workers age thirty-five to forty-four dropped from 6.6 years in 1983 to 4.8 years in 1998. For workers age forty-five to fifty-four, it drooped from 11.0 years to 7.6 years, and for workers age fifty-five to sixty-four, it dropped from 14.8 years to 10.7 years. The largest drops occurred after 1987. Schultze shows that this drop was the most severe for men, while tenure for women remained constant from 1983 to 1998 (37).

Paul Osterman (1999, 41–43) presents similar data based on the CPS. He shows that between 1983 and 1998 the mean tenure on the job dropped for men age thirty-five to forty-four from 7.3 years to 5.5 years. The mean tenure on the job for men age forty-five to fifty-four dropped from 12.8 years to 9.4 years, and for men age fifty-five to sixty-four it dropped from 15.3 years to 11.2 years. Although Osterman's numbers are different in magnitude from those presented in Schultze (1999), the drops in tenure are similar, in the magnitude of 25 to 30 percent. In the data used by Osterman, women experienced little change in average job tenure. Thus, the two studies show substantial drops in job tenure over time.

There is some controversy about whether these "raw" data actually show a decline over time in tenure. Francis Diebold, David Neumark, and Daniel Polsky (1997) make the most forceful argument that what they call "retention rates" of various types of workers have not changed in the overall population from the 1970s to the 1990s. Their work is based on earlier work by Robert Hall (1982) and Manuelita Ureta (1992). These scholars argue that average tenure on the job is the wrong measure to use to understand tenure because the distribution is censored (that is, we do not know how long people will continue to hold their jobs). Using a synthetic cohort approach, they calculate the retention rate for various classes of workers over time. Using this technique, Diebold and his colleagues argue that the overall retention rate for employees has not been going down over time. Henry Farber (1998), using the CPS data, corroborates this result for 1973 to 1993.

But there is also dissension here. David Neumark, Daniel Polsky, and Daniel Hansen (1999) show that overall rates of retention did decrease during the 1990s. Farber (1997b, 2) extends his analysis to 1996 and concludes that "the fraction of workers reporting more than 10 and more than 20 years of tenure fell substantially after 1993 to its lowest level since 1979." The debate reflects the difference in the methods these researchers used and the periods they examined. Whether or not overall rates of retention are decreasing over time, there is ample evidence that these rates did change over time for different educational, occupational, and age groups. Younger workers have experienced decreases in their retention rates over time relative to those of older workers. Less-educated workers have lower retention rates over time than more-educated workers. Blue-collar and service workers have lower retention rates than managers and professionals, and their rates have decreased over time.

Another strategy to get at this question is to analyze longitudinal data to assess whether changes are occurring for the same individuals over time. The Panel Study of Income Dynamics (PSID) is one source for this analysis. Unfortunately, the problem with these data is not being able to tell whether a person has actually changed employers or has only changed jobs within the same employer. Several studies (Rose 1995; Boisjoly, Duncan, and Smeeding 1998) argue that there has been a decrease in job tenure over time in the PSID. Other scholars (Polsky 1999; Jaeger and Stevens 1999), using different measures, have concluded that overall rates of changing employers have not increased over time. But as with the other studies of retention, these studies agree that within groups there have been changes. Lower-educated, younger, black, and male workers have tended to have higher job turnover over time, thereby supporting the insecuritization hypothesis.

Annette Bernhardt and her colleagues (2001) use the National Longitudinal Survey of Young Men (NLSYM) (first interviewed in 1966 and followed up until 1981) and compare it with the National Longitudinal Survey of Youth (NLSY) (first interviewed in 1979 and followed up yearly through 1994). These surveys have several advantages. First, they use unique employer identifiers to ensure that workers changed employers in the measures of tenure. Second, they allow comparisons of two cohorts as they entered the labor market. The first cohort entered the labor market in 1966 and were able to establish themselves during a period of both economic expansion and contraction. The second cohort entered the labor market at the beginning of the turbulent 1980s, when insecurity was supposed to have increased. By studying the same young men over time, it is possible to compare cohort experiences in the likelihood of establishing careers in a particular firm in two different periods. Finally, by studying young men, scholars can see whether the changes going on in the labor market had a particular impact on that group.

Bernhardt and her colleagues (2001, 84–85) show that 35 percent of the earlier cohort had tenure on the job of less than two years while 45 percent of the latter cohort did the same—a change of almost 30 percent. Higher-educated workers and managers and professionals tended toward longer tenure. But even in those groups, tenure decreased across the two cohorts. For example, high school graduates in the first survey with three years of tenure had a 34 percent lower chance of switching jobs than similar men in the later sample (86). Taken together, these results imply that overall retention rates probably fell somewhat for all workers over time.

A more direct way to assess the insecurity hypothesis is to examine more closely the reasons why workers lose their jobs. The insecuritization hypothesis can be framed more narrowly around the issue of involuntary job loss. If firms changed their internal labor market practices by closing plants and downsizing, then we should observe higher rates of dismissal for these reasons over time. A second part of this hypothesis is that this change in labor market practices affected blue-collar workers during the 1980s more frequently and managerial and professional employees more frequently in the 1990s.

Probably the most careful study of this was done by Farber (1997a), using the Displaced Worker Surveys (DWS) conducted every two years by the CPS from 1984 to 1996. Displacement is defined as involuntary separation owing to the operating decision of the employer. Events such as a plant closing, a layoff without recall, or an employer going out of business count as displacement, while those who quit or are fired for any other reason are not considered to have been displaced. Farber looks at job loss in the past three years as his measure of displacement. There have been several changes in the survey and questionnaire design that affect the ability of the analyst to compare survey results. Still, these are the most systematic datasets available on job displacement for all workers.

Not surprisingly, job displacement was related to the general state of the economy. During the recessions of 1981 to 1983 and 1991 to 1993, there were higher rates of job displacement than during the period 1983 to 1991, when the economy was better. There was one important piece of evidence for an increase in job insecurity. During the 1993 to 1995 period, a period of relative growth in the economy, job loss due to displacement was the highest over the whole period (Farber 1997a, 72). During all of the periods, younger and less-educated workers were more likely than older and more-educated workers to lose their jobs.

Farber (1997a) also showed some interesting differences by occupation and industry. Managers were more likely to lose their jobs during the 1991 to 1993 recession than during the earlier recession of 1981 to 1983. The opposite was true for crafts, operatives, and labor. This evidence is consistent with the observation that in the 1981 to 1983 recession the most vulnerable workers were those in blue-collar occupations, while managers were a more likely target during the 1991 to 1993 recession. Professional, technical, and sales workers also appeared to have higher rates of job loss during the 1991 to 1993 recession. Farber concludes (1997a, 77) that the data seem consistent with the interpretation that the first wave of corporate reorganization involved the permanent closure and downsizing of production facilities and the second wave involved downsizing more white-collar corporate functions. There were industrial differences in job loss during the two recessions. Manufacturing had higher losses in the earlier recession. Finance, real estate, insurance, nonprofessional services, and professional services all had higher job loss rates in the later recession. Thus, the earlier recession was centered more on manufacturing firms and workers and the later recession on white-collar and service firms.

There is other evidence that white-collar employment declined more during the corporate restructurings of the late 1980s and 1990s. Johanne Boisjoly, Greg Duncan, and Timothy Smeeding (1998) show that involuntary job loss increased during the 1980s and 1990s relative to the 1970s for managerial-professional and highly educated workers, using the PSID longitudinal dataset. Their results are similar to Farber's (1997a). Daniel Aaronson and Daniel Sullivan (1998) analyze the Displaced Worker Survey and the General Social Survey (GSS) data to explore this issue. They show that the displacement rates of college-educated workers came close to those of non-college-educated workers during the 1990s. They also show that blue-collar and white-collar displacement rates began to close as well. There is some convergence for these groups in whether people thought they would lose their job in the next twelve months and whether they would have difficulty finding a comparable job. They conclude that during the 1990s educated and white-collar workers became more insecure at work both objectively and subjectively.

It is useful to summarize these results before considering their effects on inequality. There is some evidence that over the past twenty years all types of workers experienced job insecurity, defined as decreases in tenure and increases in job displacement. There is some debate over whether overall tenure rates have decreased. The raw data seem to show that tenure rates decreased substantially for men but not for women. There is agreement that tenure rates declined more for younger, less-educated, and blue-collar or service workers than for older, more-educated, and professional or managerial workers over time. This points to a new kind of inequality in the workplace.

An important question is how these patterns of change in job tenure and job displacement affect wage inequality. Here the literature is more consistent. Studies that use the DWS show that workers who lose their jobs through displacement suffer substantial periods of unemployment and that earnings on new jobs are well below earnings on previous jobs (Podgursky and Swaim 1987; Kletzer 1989; Topel 1990). Farber (1993) demonstrates that these effects were relatively constant during the 1981 to 1983 and 1991 to 1993 recessions. In a later paper, Farber (1997a) shows that job loss increased during the mid-1990s and that its costs were substantial for all workers. Over time highly educated and white-collar workers have become more vulnerable to job loss and their pay losses have increased. They still have an advantage over other workers and experience less of a pay loss when they are displaced. Since the rates of job displacement and the loss associated with job displacement are quite different for educated and white-collar workers than for less-educated and blue-collar and service workers, job insecurity is a source of earnings inequality. Daniel Polsky (1999) confirms these results using the PSID.

Bernhardt and her colleagues (2001, 130) produce similar results using the NLS studies. They show that displacement has both a short-term and long-term effect on earnings. They also show that workers without a college degree in the recent cohort are more likely to have less tenure and experience and to encounter more job displacement than their counterparts in the earlier survey, and therefore to experience much less earnings growth. Generally, the winners in the recent cohorts were workers with a college degree, employed in a managerial or professional occupation in a high-end service industry. They did better than their counterparts in the first survey because they experienced less job displacement and more tenure and, of course, received higher returns to their schooling (145).

CHANGES IN INVOLUNTARY PART-TIME, TEMPORARY, AND CONTRACT WORK

One other way to measure insecurity on the job is to look at the increase in involuntary part-time and temporary or contract work. Reviews of this literature appear in Pfeffer and Baron (1988) and Kalleberg (2000). There are two dimensions of work that structure our ways of classifying employment relations. First, scholars typically distinguish full-time from voluntary and involuntary part-time work. Full-time work has usually been defined as working thirty-five hours a week or more, while part-time work is defined as working less than thirty-five hours a week. Many part-time workers choose to work part-time because of schooling, age, or family constraints. Workers who want to work only part-time hours are called voluntarily part-time. Those who want to work more than thirty-four hours a week but cannot find the work are called involuntarily part-time.

The second dimension of work that describes employment relations is the nature of the labor contract with the employer. Most workers are employed and paid by a particular employer. There are three classes of other types of work arrangements: contract, other self-employed, and temporary. Contract employees are independent contractors, consultants, and freelance workers. Many of these workers are highly educated and well paid. "Other self-employed" is a residual census category that refers to workers who claim to be self-employed but do not identify themselves as a contractor. Many of these people own small businesses. Temporary workers identify themselves as working in a temporary job. They may work for an employment agency, operate as an on-call worker, or be a day laborer. If we cross-classify the two dimensions, we can see, for example, that a worker could be part-time but a regular employee.

Most analysts argue that firms began to use more part-time and temporary workers in the 1980s. It turns out that this is not entirely true. Part-time workers in the United States grew from about 13 percent of the labor force in 1970 to 19 percent in 1993, with most of the growth occurring during the 1970s. Citing CPS data, Osterman (1999, 197) shows that in 1979, 13.8 percent of men and 21.4 percent of women worked part-time. In 1983 the figures were 13.8 percent of men and 22.8 percent of women, and in 1993 they were 13.3 percent and 20.0 percent. There was a change in the definition of part-time work in 1993, and subsequent CPS figures are not directly comparable. In 1997 the overall part-time rate was 17.7 percent (Stinson 1997). Thus, part-time employment has not changed very much since 1979, for either men or women.

What has changed is involuntary part-time employment (Blank 1990, 125). In 1979 the rate was 3.7 percent of all male workers and 4.9 percent of all female workers. By 1993 these percentages had risen to 5.5 percent for men and 6.4 percent for women (Osterman 1999, 197). Thomas Nardone (1995, 286) shows that the greatest rise in involuntary part-time employment occurred during the recession of 1981 to 1983. Although involuntary part-time employment dropped a little during the 1980s, it remained substantially higher than during the 1970s and continued to remain at a high level during the recession of 1991 to 1993. To summarize, the data support the insecurity story that more part-time workers wish they were working full-time, not that more are working part-time.

Increases in contract, other self-employment, and temporary work over time are harder to track. We know that the fraction of workers who reported in the CPS that they were self-employed has not changed much in the past twenty years (Kalleberg 2000). There has been some increase over time in the percentage of people who work as contractors (Clinton 1997). There is more information about the growth of workers in the temporary category. In 1956 there were only twenty thousand employees in the temporary help industry (Gannon 1984). In 1972 the industry had 0.3 percent of the labor force, and in 1998 nearly 2.5 percent (Kalleberg 2000, 346). Temporary work fluctuates with the business cycle. When the economy is growing, temporary work grows, and when the economy shrinks, temporary workers are laid off. Temporary workers operate as a kind of "reserve army of the proletariat" (Appelbaum 1987). Lonnie Golden (1996) shows that the use of temporary workers tripled from 1982 to 1992, primarily because firms preferred temporary over permanent workers.

The CPS undertook a direct study of employment arrangements in 1995 and 1997. In Osterman's (1999, 58) analysis, the surveys show little change in the number of contingent work arrangements between 1995 and 1997. In his extensive analysis of these data, Farber (1999) shows that 15.3 percent of workers were working part-time, 4.5 percent of whom were involuntary. Among all workers, 82.5 percent had regular employment relations, and 5.9 percent identified as contractors, 5.4 percent as "other self-employed," and 6.2 percent as temporary. Not surprisingly, people who were contractors, other self-employed, or temporary were three to four times more likely to report being employed part-time involuntarily. Temporary workers were most frequently employed part-time, but a large number of them worked voluntarily part-time. The main purpose of Farber's paper is to examine whether people who have become temporary workers are more likely to have taken those jobs because they were laid off.

The data on the role of part-time and temporary work present a mixed picture for the growth of job insecurity in the labor force. There has been no large increase in the number of people who work part-time since 1980. There has been some growth in the number of workers who are involuntarily part-time, many of whom are temporary workers. But during the 1990s temporary work and the percentage of workers who worked involuntarily part-time seemed to stabilize. Temporary workers now make up about 2.5 percent of the labor force, and involuntarily part-time workers about 4.5 percent.

GROWING INEQUALITY IN BENEFITS AND HEALTH AND SAFETY AT WORK

Changes in job security have been mirrored by changes in benefits and health and safety at work. Over time health and pension benefits have decreased for all workers. But temporary and part-time workers and blue-collar and service workers have seen their access to benefits decrease the most. Further, health and safety issues at work have also been related to growing inequality.

We begin by considering health insurance and pensions. The strongest relationship between being offered these benefits at work and other work-related measures is whether a person works full- or part-time. So, for example, Rebecca Blank (1990) reports (using the CPS) that in 1987 only 16.7 percent of part-time workers were included in pension plans, while 54.3 percent of full-time workers were included. Only 22.6 percent of part-time workers had health care benefits, compared with 76.1 percent of full-time workers. Full-time workers were at least three times more likely to have health and pension benefits as their part-time counterparts.

Barbara Wolfe, Amy Wolaver, and Timothy McBride (1998) use various data sources to piece together changes in health benefits from 1980 to 1994. They show that in 1980, 78.8 percent of families had private health insurance. This had dropped to 70.1 percent by 1994. More important are figures that relate health benefits to income. They show that 38.6 percent of low-income families had health insurance in 1980 and that this had decreased to 24.7 percent by 1994. This change compares with 93.7 percent of high-income families in 1980 who had health insurance and 92.7 percent who had health insurance in 1994. Thus, during the period of greatest change in insecurity, the lowest-income group saw its ability to be covered by health insurance erode significantly, while the highest-income group saw only a slight drop in coverage. This is evidence for an increase in inequality.

Henry Farber and Helen Levy (1998) have updated the trends on health insurance coverage to 1997. Using CPS data, they show that overall private insurance coverage decreased from 73.4 percent in 1979 to 67.4 percent in 1997. The largest drop in insurance coverage appeared between 1988 and 1993. The drop was almost entirely a product of the private sector lowering the rate at which it offered insurance, from 69.1 percent in 1988 to 64.7 percent in 1993. Farber and Levy show that most of these declines occurred among workers who were in either new full-time jobs (of durations less than a year) or part-time jobs. For new full-time workers, the rate decreased from 84.1 percent of workers in 1988 to 78.1 percent in 1997. The rate of health insurance offered in part-time jobs in 1988 was 58.6 percent, while in 1997 it had fallen to 35.5 percent. Farber and Levy show that 80.6 percent of college graduates in 1979 had health insurance and that this percentage had dropped to 76.0 percent by 1997. The largest drop was from 1988 to 1993. Rates of health insurance for workers with only a high school education dropped from 71.4 percent in 1979 to 61.6 percent in 1997. In the past twenty years, we can conclude, health insurance coverage declined for everyone but especially for lower-income or part-time workers. The largest drop occurred between 1989 and 1993, and the workers who took the brunt of the changes were part-time and newly hired workers.

Alan Gustman and Thomas Steinmeier (1999) consider pension benefits at three points in time—1969, 1980, and 1992—using the Health and Retirement Study, a panel study of a nationally representative sample of households, sponsored by the National Institute on Aging. They present a "good news–bad news scenario." The good news is that all classes of workers received more pension benefits over time. The bad news is that the top half of the wealth distribution received more and larger increases in both absolute and relative terms than the bottom half of the distribution. So, for example, the top 10 percent of the wealth distribution saw its real pension benefits double between 1969 and 1992, while the bottom 10 percent saw its benefits increase by less than 10 percent. For the wealthiest households, pension benefits increased substantially during both the 1970s and the 1980s. But for the bottom 10 percent, all of the gains occurred during the 1970s and there were almost no gains during the 1980s. Thus, inequality in pension benefits increased over time and increased the most during the 1980s.

Daniel Hamermesh (1999) examines evidence associated with changes over time in what he calls "workplace amenities." He is interested in two types of change: increases in rates of accidents and increases in working evening and night shifts. Using CPS and Bureau of Labor Statistics (BLS) data, he constructs a time series on lost days due to workplace injury over time. He shows that workers in the top half of the earnings distribution experience lower rates of accident than workers in the bottom half and that the difference between the groups becomes more pronounced over time. As earnings inequality has increased, the safety of working has decreased for those at the bottom. Using the NLSY, Hamermesh shows that the number of lost workdays due to injury on the job was about four times higher in the period 1994 to 1996 for the lowest quartile of the earnings distribution than for the highest quartile (1108).

Hamermesh next considers the issue of workers having to work night shifts. Using CPS data, he shows that from 1973 until 1991, the incidence of evening and night work changed substantially for the workers with the lowest as opposed to the highest earnings. Hamermesh also calculates the income value of these disamenities. He demonstrates that they contributed to the growing inequality between workers at the top and the bottom of the earnings distribution.

Harriet Presser (1995) explores the issue of nonstandard work hours more thoroughly using the 1991 CPS data. Of all U.S. workers in 1991, 40.1 percent did not work a standard eight-to-five schedule, Monday through Friday. She shows that 62.3 percent of part-time workers worked a nonstandard schedule (weekends or evenings or nights), while only 33.6 percent of full-time workers did. Of those working nonstandard schedules, 36.1 percent did so voluntarily, while 58.7 percent were required to do so by their employer. Not surprisingly, those in blue-collar and service occupations were more likely to work nonstandard work schedules than those in white-collar occupations.

HOURS OF WORK AND INCOME INEQUALITY

The issue of how work hours have changed in the past twenty years is a matter of some controversy. Juliet Schor (1996, 29), using CPS data, argues that men increased their work hours only slightly but increased the number of weeks they worked substantially. Women increased both hours and weeks worked. Lawrence Mishel, Jared Bernstein, and John

Schmitt (2001) also show that hours of work per year increased during the 1980s and 1990s, mostly as a function of an increase in weeks worked.

Mary Coleman and John Pencavel (1993a) use the decennial census and the CPS to show that median work hours for men were virtually constant, contradicting Schor's results. Elsewhere, however, they do document the rise of hours of work for women (Coleman and Pencavel 1993b). John Robinson and Geoffrey Godbey (1997) argue that the hours reported in the CPS overestimate real work hours, supporting Coleman and Pencavel's criticism. Michael Hout and Caroline Hanley (2002), however, reanalyze the CPS data and show that one of the differences between Schor's and Coleman and Pencavel's results is that hours increased mainly because of the increase in weeks worked. Arguing that the relevant unit of analysis is the household, they convincingly show that most of the action is in the increase in the hours of working women over time.

More important for our argument is the role of hours worked in processes of inequality. Here the research is more consistent. It supports the view that during the 1980s and the 1990s hours of work increased the most for educated workers and those in professional and managerial occupations. This finding is consistent with our hypothesis that these employees faced pressures to increase their hours of work as firms downsized. Pencavel (1998) uses the PSID to estimate work hours over time for women and shows that the number of hours worked is highly related to education. During the 1970s women with a college degree worked virtually identical hours to women with just a high school degree. But by the mid-1990s this had changed. College-educated women worked 1,758 hours a year in the 1970s, but by the mid-1990s they were working 1,925 hours a year. Their counterparts with just a high school degree were working 1,727 hours in the 1970s and 1,740 hours in the mid-1990s.

Coleman and Pencavel (1993a, 1993b) confirm these results using decennial census data and the CPS. They show that for men with less than a high school degree, hours of work decreased from 2,033 in 1980 to 1,909 in 1988, while hours of work for men with a college degree increased from 2,114 in 1980 to 2,243 in 1988. Women with less than a high school degree compared with women with a college degree showed a similar pattern. These patterns reversed historical patterns: hours of work were lowest in the 1940 to 1970 period for college-educated workers and higher for workers with less education.

Dora Costa (2000) uses various state-level sources of data to compare work hours between workers of different income levels. She shows that in 1973 the top 10 percent of the wage distribution worked only 93 percent of the hours that the bottom 10 percent worked (162). By 1991 this had reversed, so that the top 10 percent worked 108 percent of the hours the bottom 10 percent worked. The same result holds for women (163).

Philip Rones, Randy Ilg, and Jennifer Gardner (1997) examine data on the percentage of people working forty-nine hours or more a week on average in 1985 and 1993. These levels and increases were highly related to occupation, with managers and professionals registering the longest hours and the largest increase in long workweeks. Forty-five percent of managers claimed to be working forty-nine or more hours a week in 1985, and this rose to 50 percent in 1993. Thirty-three percent of professionals worked forty-nine or more hours a week in 1985, and this rose to 37 percent in 1993. These figures contrast to those for other workers: only 15 percent of service workers worked forty-nine or more hours a week in 1985, and about 16 percent worked this many hours in 1993. Twenty-one percent of skilled blue-collar workers were working forty-nine or more hours a week in 1985, and this increased to 24 percent in 1993. Overall, long hours increased substantially from 1985

FIGURE 10.1   *Number of Hours Worked in the Previous Week by Full-Time Workers, by Hourly Wage Percentiles, 1976 to 2001*

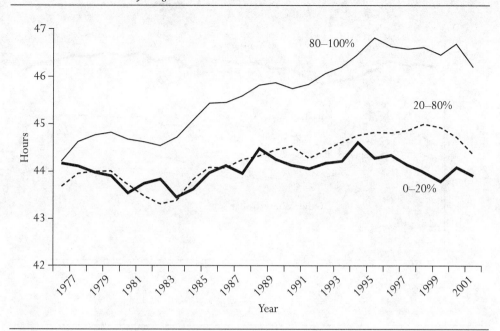

Source: Authors' calculations from the March CPS.

to 1993. But they were already highest for managers and professionals, and these groups experienced the largest gains in hours from 1985 until 1993.

We have produced a similar table for the March CPS. Full-time workers age twenty-four to sixty-four were selected and asked: "How many hours did you work last week?" Figure 10.1 shows that in 1976 the top 20 percent of the wage distribution worked 44.2 hours a week on average. By 1995 this had increased to 46.8 hours a week. For someone working 50 weeks a year, this implies an additional 130 hours, or more than three additional weeks of 40 hours each. The bottom 20 percent of the wage distribution and the middle 60 percent saw their hours fluctuate over the same period between 43.5 and 45 hours a week, without any substantial increases over 45 hours.

These results suggest that the highest-paid employees worked more and more hours during the 1980s and 1990s. It is interesting to ask which occupational groups were being rewarded for their extra efforts. Figure 10.2 shows the percentage of employees who worked overtime for the four main occupational groups. Our results show that around half of managers usually worked over forty hours a week, around 35 percent of professionals, and fewer than 30 percent of service, blue-collar, and other white-collar workers. From 1976 until 1991, these patterns did not change much.

Figure 10.3 shows the average yearly earnings for managers who worked overtime versus those who worked part-time and full-time. Since most managers are salaried, this table gives a good feel for whether managers working more hours earned more. From 1976 until 1981, there was a small gap between those who worked full-time and those who worked overtime. Beginning in 1985, this gap began to widen. Managers who just worked

FIGURE 10.2   *Percentage of Workers who Worked Overtime, by Occupational Groups, 1976 to 2001*

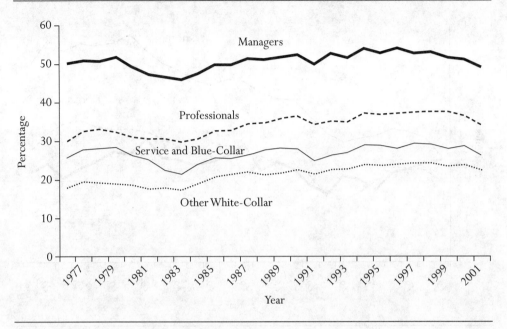

Source: Authors' calculations from the March CPS.

full-time saw their incomes fall between 1980 and 1991, from about $50,000 to $43,500. Their average incomes rose thereafter to a little over $50,000 in 2001. At the same time, managers who worked overtime saw their incomes climb. In 1981 their average income was $54,500. By 2001 it was over $67,700. The gap between managers who worked full-time and those who worked overtime increased from close to 17 percent in 1976 to about 35 percent in 2001.

A similar pattern appeared for professionals (see figure 10.4). During the 1976 to 1981 period, there was a gap of 14 to 20 percent between professionals who worked full-time and those who worked overtime. It should be noted that some professionals, like doctors, lawyers, and accountants, do bill their time hourly. So we would expect that there would be a larger income gap between those who worked full-time and those who worked extra hours. After 1981 this gap began to widen, and in 1996 it widened even more substantially. In 2001 full-time professionals earned $46,600 a year on average, while those who worked overtime earned $63,400—a gap of about 36 percent.

Taken together, these results support our general story. Hours of work increased the most between 1976 and 2001 for those with the highest wages. Hours of work remained stable for the rest of the wage distribution. These changes in hours show the bifurcation of work that occurred during the reorganization of work in the 1980s and 1990s. The most interesting result is the widening from 1986 to 2001 of earnings differences between managers and professionals who did and did not work overtime hours. Average yearly earnings for managers and professionals who worked additional hours increased from 20 percent more than those of their counterparts working full-time to about 36 percent more.

FIGURE 10.3   *Average Yearly Earnings of Managers Who Worked Part-Time, Full-Time, and Overtime, 1976 to 2001*

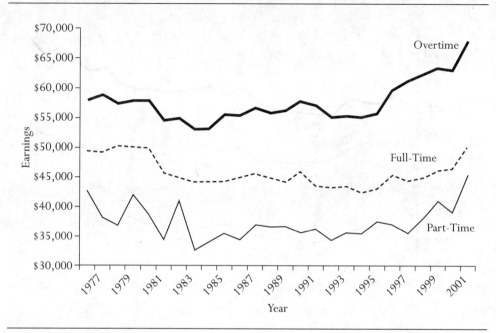

Source: Authors' calculations from the March CPS.

CHANGES IN THE PERCEPTION OF WORK

There has been much less research into how workers have experienced the changes in work. The results presented so far suggest that work became more onerous and less rewarding for those at the bottom of the income, skill, and occupational distributions. It paints a more mixed picture for those at the top. Although those at the top experienced more job turn-over, acquired less tenure, and worked more hours, those managers and professionals who took on the longer hours received increased rewards. We can hypothesize that workers in the 1990s notice these changes and subjectively come to view their situation differently than workers in the 1980s.

Stephanie Schmidt (1999) analyzes General Social Survey data that track whether work-ers think they will lose their job in the next twelve months. She shows not only that this perception is highly related to general economic conditions but that over the past twenty years this fear has increased net of general economic conditions. Finally, she demonstrates that blue-collar workers feared job loss more in the 1980s, while managerial and profes-sional workers feared job loss more during the 1990s.

Figure 10.5 presents data on job satisfaction over time that comes from the General Social Survey. Potential answers to the question "How satisfied are you with your job?" are "very satisfied," "somewhat satisfied," "somewhat dissatisfied," and "very dissatisfied." The "very satisfied" responses—the most evident indication of job satisfaction—were calculated. Here we present data on the top 20 percent of the income distribution, the middle 60 percent, and the bottom 20 percent. In 1978 about 57 percent of the people in the top 20

FIGURE 10.4   *Average Yearly Earnings of Professionals Who Worked Part-Time, Full-Time, and Overtime, 1976 to 2001*

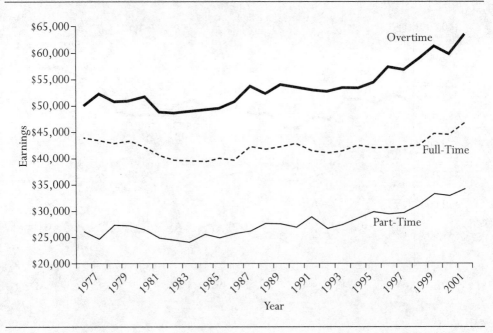

Source: Authors' calculations from the March CPS.

percent of the distribution said they were very satisfied with their job, and this increased to 62 percent in 1998. The rest of the income distribution actually experienced less job satisfaction over time. The middle 60 percent of the income distribution dropped from about 48.0 percent being very satisfied in 1978 to 45.0 percent being very satisfied in 1998, while the bottom 20 percent dropped during the same period from 46.3 percent being very satisfied to 39.0 percent. Clearly, job conditions for those at the bottom were less satisfying after the reorganization of work from 1980 until 2000. For those at the top, jobs became more satisfying.

We also tracked a variable based on the question: "How satisfied are you with your current financial situation?" We coded the answers according to the percentage of those who were very satisfied with their financial situation. Figure 10.6 presents the results. In 1978 only 30.1 percent of the bottom 20 percent of the income distribution were satisfied with their financial situation, and this had dropped to 18.2 percent by 1998. The situation was reversed for those at the top of the income distribution: 47.7 percent reported such satisfaction in 1978, and this had increased to 52.7 percent by 1998. These results thus parallel the changes in job satisfaction. People at the top of the income distribution in 2000 were more satisfied with their jobs and more financially secure than people in that position in 1980. People in the bottom of the income distribution were less happy with their jobs and less financially secure in 2000 than in 1980. From a subjective point of view, this suggests that the reorganization of work that occurred over the twenty-year period had worse effects on those at the bottom of the income distribution than on those at the top.

FIGURE 10.5   *Percentage of Respondents Who Were Very Satisfied with Work, by Family Income Percentiles, 1978 to 1998*

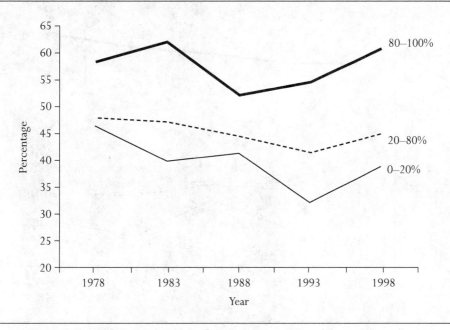

Source: Authors' calculations from the General Social Survey.

THE CONTEMPORARY SITUATION IN CALIFORNIA

We have suggested that the experiences of managerial and professional workers present a more mixed view of the changes in work over the past twenty years. These workers were not immune from the corporate reorganizations, particularly those that began in the late 1980s and early 1990s. Indeed, their job tenure decreased, their involuntary job loss increased, and they became more fearful of losing their jobs. But at the same time, they worked more hours and the rewards for those who worked those hours increased substantially. For these most successful people, their satisfaction with work grew dramatically, as did their financial situation. The growing income inequality that began with the dramatic drop in earnings for less-skilled blue-collar and service workers in the 1980s was accompanied by a growing insecurity, fewer benefits, and fewer work hours for those workers. In spite of being subject to some of the same pressures, those at the top found their work lives improving if they managed to be in positions where hours increased. They earned more than their peers and increased their financial security and job satisfaction.

It is useful to explore this theme in more details. The results reported in the next section come from a survey on working conditions in California conducted by the Survey Research Center at the University of California in the fall of 2001 and sponsored by the university's Institute for Labor and Employment. Although the California Workforce Survey is only a one-shot view of working conditions and covers only California, it asked a number of questions that elaborate how work is differently experienced by managers, professionals and other white-collar workers and by blue-collar and service workers. Details on the survey are in the appendix to this chapter. The data presented here contain results that were

FIGURE 10.6   *Percentage of Workers Who Were Very Satisfied with Their Financial Situation, by Family Income Percentiles, 1978 to 1998*

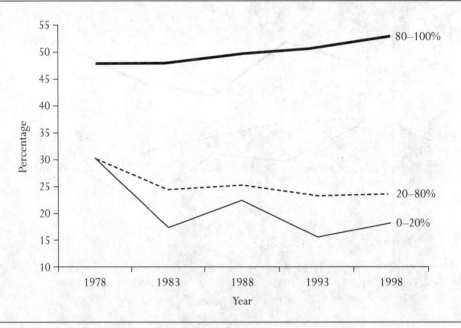

Source: Authors' calculations from the General Social Survey.

consistent with many of the patterns already described here. California is the source of one-sixth of the American economy. It is also home to some cutting-edge American firms and, presumably, labor market practices.

Table 10.1 presents average weekly hours across different occupational categories in California. Managers put in the longest hours, fifty hours a week, followed by professionals with forty-four hours, service and blue-collar workers with forty-one, and finally, other white-collar workers, who work an average of thirty-eight hours a week. These numbers are close to those reported in the CPS for these groups in the entire U.S. labor force.

The significant work-hour differences across occupations can also been seen in the answers to the question: "How often do you work overtime?" Overall, 42.8 percent of California workers reported that they usually worked overtime, while 29.8 percent sometimes did and only 27.3 percent reported that they never did. Although these answers suggest that a huge proportion (72.7 percent) of working Californians work overtime at least some of the time, there are great differences among occupational categories. Eighty percent of managers reported that they usually worked overtime, while 52.7 percent of professionals reported that they did. This contrasts with only 26.1 percent of other white-collar workers and 39.9 percent of service and blue-collar workers. Although managers and professionals were earning the most money, they were also putting in the most hours.

Workers were asked if they were given enough time to do the work assigned to them. A large majority, 83 percent, reported that they were given enough time, but both managers and professionals reported that they were less likely to be given enough time to do their work than other white-collar or service and blue-collar workers. Further evidence of the greater time pressures experienced by managers and professionals can be gleaned from

TABLE 10.1   *Work Hours for Full-Time Workers in California, 2001*

	Average Weekly Work Hours	"How Often Do You Work Overtime?"			"Do You Have Enough Time to Do Work?"	"Does Your Job Involve a Tight Deadline?"
		Usually	Sometimes	Never		
Total sample	41.7	42.8%	29.8%	27.3%	83.0%	53.8%
Managers	50.0	80.0	13.2	6.9	74.0	60.6
Professionals	44.1	52.7	33.0	14.2	78.4	66.8
Other white-collar	38.0	26.1	29.6	44.4	83.5	50.8
Service and blue-collar	41.0	39.9	31.0	29.1	87.3	45.9

Source: Authors' calculations from the 2001 California Workforce Survey.

their answers to a question about whether their jobs involved tight deadlines: 60.6 percent of managers and 66.8 percent of professionals reported having tight deadlines, compared with 50.8 percent of other white-collar workers and 45.9 percent of service and blue-collar workers. These data suggest that managers and professionals were usually working overtime at least partly because they were facing tight deadlines and did not have enough time to complete their work.

One of the most interesting questions in the survey concerned the use of pagers and cell phones in the workplace. One of the defining characteristics of our economy of the last ten years has been the telecommunications revolution, which has made it possible for people to be more closely wired into their workplaces. The California Workforce Survey provides evidence that, indeed, new telecommunications devices have spread across the world of work to an astounding degree (table 10.2). More than one-third of all workers (37.7 percent) reported using a cell phone or pager on the job. Managers were the most likely (65.4 percent) to have a cell phone or pager. Relatively high levels of other workers also had cell phones and pagers: 44.0 percent of professionals, 27.3 percent of other white-collar workers, and 35.0 percent of service and blue-collar workers. Respondents were also asked whether cell phones and pagers were used to keep them in touch after working hours. An astonishing 87.8 percent of managers who had a cell phone or a pager reported that these devices were used to keep them in touch after-hours. Very high percentages of other workers who had a cell phone or pager were also technologically tethered to work: 68.2 percent of professionals, 56.9 percent of other white-collar workers, and 62.3 percent of service and blue-collar workers. These results confirm the view that in the new economy, telecommunications devices are being extensively used to keep workers connected to their offices not only during working hours but after-hours as well. The perception that people work 24/7 is not an exaggeration, particularly for managers.

The California Workforce Survey also asked questions about who determines overtime, and whether workers want more or fewer hours. When asked who determined whether a respondent worked overtime, 61.0 percent said that they themselves determined overtime, while 34.7 percent said their boss did; 4.3 percent said both did. We think that the high voluntary response is due to the fact that workers often formally have the discretion to turn down overtime hours, even if their boss wants them to work them. This number is also highly affected by occupational position: 75.6 percent of managers and 80.9 percent of professionals reported that they determined their overtime hours, while 60.7 percent of

TABLE 10.2   *Cell Phone and Pager Use and Overtime Decisions for Full-Time Workers in California, 2001*

| | "Do You Use a Cell Phone or Pager on the Job?" | "Do You Use a Cell Phone or Pager for Work After-Hours?" | "Who Determines Whether You Work Overtime?" | | |
			Respondent	Boss	Both
Total sample	37.7%	66.5%	61.0%	34.7%	4.3%
Managers	65.4	87.8	75.6	22.7	1.7
Professionals	44.0	68.2	80.9	15.3	3.8
Other white-collar	27.3	56.9	60.7	35.0	4.3
Service and blue-collar	35.0	62.3	42.0	52.6	5.4

Source: Authors' calculations from the 2001 California Workforce Survey.

other white-collar workers and 42.0 percent of service and blue-collar workers had this discretion.

Another indicator of the degree to which people feel overworked is the question "If you could, would you work more hours for more pay, the same hours for the same pay, or fewer hours for less pay?" Overall, 32.1 percent of respondents said that they would work more hours, while 50.1 percent said they would work the same hours and only 8.7 percent said they would work fewer hours (see table 10.3). The breakdown of this variable across occupational groups is quite revealing. Only 17.4 percent of managers and 18.4 percent of professionals reported that they would like to work more hours for more pay, while 32.2 percent of other white-collar workers and 43.5 percent of service and blue-collar workers indicated this preference. These data suggest that while a substantial percentage of other white-collar and service and blue-collar workers are not getting enough hours, most managers and professionals are at their limit. About twice as many managers and professionals wished they could work fewer hours for less pay than service and blue-collar workers (10.7 and 13.2 percent versus 6.4 percent). Not surprisingly, managers and professionals were more likely than the other occupational groups to report having difficulties finding time for

TABLE 10.3   *Work Hours Preferences Among Full-Time Workers in California, 2001*

| | "If You Could, Would You . . ."[a] | | | "Do You Have a Problem Finding Time for Both Work and Family?" |
	"Work More Hours"	"Work Same Hours"	"Work Fewer Hours"	Yes[b]
Total sample	32.1%	50.1%	8.7%	35.4%
Managers	17.4	70.9	11.7	47.7
Professionals	18.4	68.5	13.2	40.2
Other white-collar	32.2	60.7	7.1	35.4
Service and blue-collar	43.5	50.1	6.4	34.6

Source: Authors' calculations from the 2001 California Workforce Survey.
[a]Categories are (1) work more hours for more pay; (2) work same hours for same pay; (3) work fewer hours for less pay.
[b]Percentages reflect full-time workers who answer "very serious problem" or "moderately serious problem."

TABLE 10.4   *Reasons for Working Overtime Among California Workers, 2001*

	Required to[a]	Unofficially Expected to	Enjoy Work	Enjoy Workplace and Colleagues
Total sample	47.7%	46.7%	81.0%	70.8%
Managers	40.2	41.8	80.0	80.0
Professionals	39.1	46.5	85.2	67.5
Other white-collar	43.9	40.6	71.4	64.3
Service and blue-collar	58.2	51.0	72.6	63.3

Source: Authors' calculations from the 2001 California Labor Survey.
[a]Percentage who answered "very important" or "somewhat important."

both work and family: 47.7 percent of managers and 40.2 percent of professionals had a problem balancing work and family, compared with 35.4 percent of other white-collar workers and 34.6 percent of service and blue-collar workers.

It is interesting to consider why various groups of workers work overtime. Table 10.4 presents data on this issue. The respondents' answers were coded into four categories: "very important," "somewhat important," "not very important," and "not important at all." We report the percentage of respondents who answered "very important" or "somewhat important" for the various reasons. In the overall sample, 47.7 percent reported working overtime because they were required to, 46.7 percent because they were unofficially expected to, 81.0 percent because they enjoyed work, and 70.8 percent because they enjoyed the workplace and their colleagues.

These results suggest that the vast majority of California workers in managerial and professional occupations like to work because of the intrinsic character of their work and the opportunity to be with their colleagues in the workplace. Our findings that enjoyment of colleagues and the workplace are important reasons for working overtime supports Arlie Hochschild's thesis (1997). In a study of an office of a large firm, she shows that some workers actually prefer work life to home life.

Service and blue-collar workers were most likely to report that they were required to work overtime (58.2 percent), while the other three groups reported being required to work overtime as their reason only about 40 percent of the time. Service and blue-collar workers were also more likely to report that they were unofficially expected to work such hours. This finding reinforces our earlier discussion regarding the high degree of discretion that workers report having over working overtime. Managers and professionals reported higher levels of working overtime because they enjoyed work. Eighty percent of managers reported enjoying the workplace and colleagues as a reason to work overtime. The other occupational groups gave this reason less frequently.

Table 10.5 presents evidence on how rewards are distributed across occupational categories at different levels of work hours. We use three categories of work hours: less than thirty-five hours (part-time work), thirty-five to forty (full-time work), and forty-one or more (overtime). Work hours have a large and direct effect on yearly earnings. Part-time workers make substantially less than full-time workers. Interestingly, full-time workers in each of the occupational categories display less variation than workers who work more than forty hours a week. The most interesting part of the table is the degree to which overtime affects the annual earnings of managers and professionals. Managers who worked more than forty hours a week made $71,102, while professionals who worked overtime made

TABLE 10.5 *Mean Yearly Earnings of California Workers, by Occupation and Hours Worked, 2001*

Hours Worked	Manager	Professional	Other White-Collar	Service and Blue-Collar
Less than thirty-five	$20,282	$32,428	$16,225	$13,208
Thirty-five to forty	42,998	47,860	29,275	35,922
Forty-one or more	71,102	75,039	45,414	35,908

Source: Authors' calculations from the 2001 California Labor Survey.

$75,039. Recalling table 10.1, 80.0 percent of managers and 52.7 percent of professionals reported that they usually worked overtime, while only 26.1 percent of other white-collar workers and 39.9 percent of service and blue-collar workers reported usually working overtime. Thus, managers and professionals both worked overtime and were amply rewarded for working overtime. One other interesting fact from table 10.5 is that service and blue-collar workers who worked overtime did not appear to benefit much for it in their yearly earnings. This result probably reflects the fact that the kinds of jobs that tend to involve working overtime in this large category are more likely to pay low wages. These results are consistent with the results presented earlier from the CPS data.

These results imply a bifurcation of work. Managers and professionals work long hours and usually work overtime. They are likely to do so because they enjoy the work and the workplace and because they are subject to tight deadlines. Although they are highly paid for working overtime, managers and professionals report being tied to work by cell phones and pagers and having problems finding time for both work and family. They are highly rewarded, but they are at their limit in terms of work hours. Workers in other white-collar and service and blue-collar occupations also enjoy work and the workplace and choose to work overtime because for this reason. But they also have less discretion over working overtime and feel more informal pressure to do so when asked. They are also more likely to report that they do not have enough hours of work. Finally, service and blue-collar workers who do get overtime do not appear to get a large benefit from doing so.

CONCLUSION

This chapter considered changes in working conditions as a source of new inequalities in American society. We began by arguing that the economic crises of the 1970s produced the reorganizations of U.S. firms during the 1980s and 1990s. These reorganizations greatly affected the work and earnings of American workers. In the first wave of reorganization, the focus was on blue-collar and service workers. Firms closed plants and offices and laid off workers. During the second wave managerial and professional staff lost their positions.

The main issues we considered were the changes in working conditions. There is evidence that work changed for all workers. Tenure dropped for all workers, involuntary job loss increased, and general fear over losing jobs increased. Involuntary part-time and temporary employment increased, while pension and health benefits decreased. For people who lost their jobs involuntarily, lifetime earnings decreased.

Many of these changes were distributed unequally. Declines in pension and health benefits primarily affected the most vulnerable workers: those who were employed part-time, temporary workers, those who were less-educated, and those in other white-collar, service, and blue-collar jobs. For those at the top of the income distribution, managers and professionals, hours of work increased and work intensified. Some of their incomes increased substantially over the incomes of their colleagues who worked just full-time. Workers at the top of the income and skill distributions came over time to also have higher job satisfaction and become more financially secure.

We explored this last theme—the relative position of those at the top and the bottom—in a recent survey of working conditions in California. We confirmed that managers and professionals are working more hours and making much more money than their counterparts who are only working full-time. Service and blue-collar workers wish they were working more hours, and managers and professionals are either happy with their hours or wish they could work fewer hours. Managers and to a lesser extent professionals say that they are forced to work overtime because they are not being given enough hours in which to do their work. But because managers and professionals also appear to like to work and to like being with their coworkers, they are compensated for their long hours with these intrinsic rewards.

Our results suggest a bifurcation of work. Work has become more insecure for all Americans. But there are also great opportunities for those at the top of the skill distribution to work more hours and increase their pay as much as 36 percent over that of those working only full-time. These workers have also gained in job satisfaction and life rewards. Ironically, the intensification of work has given these workers opportunities for increasing their personal efficacy. For those at the other end of the occupational distribution, however, the story is quite different. There are not enough work hours, benefits have declined, working conditions have grown more unsafe, and job and financial satisfaction have decreased.

Given that work plays a central role in American life, it is important to consider what might be done to increase opportunities to have work be more satisfying and rewarding. Some obvious policy changes could be to guarantee access to health care and pension benefits for all workers. Others might take up issues of occupational health and safety standards. It seems obvious that workers in more dangerous occupations ought to be protected by measures that would ensure their safety.

The most difficult issue to tackle is the general downgrading of employment for service, blue-collar, and other white-collar workers. Firms have decided that they can make more money by squeezing less-skilled workers and persuading managers and professionals to put in longer hours (albeit at higher pay) in order to hire fewer of them. The changes in the workplace during the 1980s and 1990s reflect the transformation of the market for corporate control characterized by "shareholder value." The consequence of the transformation was the bifurcation of work. The shareholders who controlled the restructuring of firms reaped most of the benefits of the "shareholder value" solution to the economic crisis of the 1970s. Managers and professionals who worked long hours under intense working conditions were highly rewarded by their salaries, benefits, job security, and job satisfaction. By contrast, the stakeholders in the firms—employees—lost out and were systematically treated worse. From uniformly consistent evidence, we draw the conclusion that the changes in working conditions in the United States reflect a fundamental transformation in the labor market regime and the emergence of a "shareholder value" society.

There is remarkably little evidence that links firms' tactics oriented toward "increasing shareholder value" to actual changes in either their financial position or their competitive position (but see Osterman 1999). We know that firms can advance their share price in the short term by announcing layoffs. But we do not know whether the changes that have produced this new work order have also increased the competitiveness or financial health of firms. There is controversy in the literature on work about whether firms do better financially by trying to build worker loyalty through empowering them on the job or rewarding them with job security. Firms seem to have empowered some managerial and professional workers, asked them to work long hours, and given them high pay. They have made others more insecure and reduced their health and pension benefits and safety on the job. Whether or not this is a tactic that improves competitiveness is a frontier issue in research.

APPENDIX: DATA AND METHODS

The March Current Population Survey

A series of analyses on earnings and working hours came from the March supplements to the Current Population Survey from 1976 to 2001, which were prepared by the U.S. Census Bureau for the Bureau of Labor Statistics. We used the sample of the respondents who were employed and age twenty-four to sixty-four, excluding those who had a job but were not at work, were unemployed, were not in the labor force, were in the armed forces, or were unincorporated self-employed. The number of respondents who met the selection criteria ranged from 35,715 for 1976 to 52,940 for 1981—approximately 48,000.

A respondent's average hourly wage was annual earnings divided by the product of weeks worked and usual weekly hours. We constructed quintile variable for every twentieth percentile of hourly wage, 0 to 20 percent being the lowest wage group and 80 to 100 percent the highest. All dollar values in this chapter were corrected for inflation using a price deflator based on the official consumer price index (CPI) for all urban consumers. This was necessary in examining changes over time.

Work hours in the analyses refer to the number of hours the respondent worked in the week before the survey. The March CPS uses two reference periods for work hours questions: how many hours the respondent worked in the week before the survey (the week including the twelfth of the month), and how many hours he or she worked in the previous year. It should be noted that the choice of reference period could result in a difference in hours worked. We chose to use the reference period of the previous week because the reference period of the previous year tends to suffer greater errors owing to the longer recall period. Part-time workers were defined as those who worked less than thirty-five hours a week in the previous year. Employees who worked thirty-five or more hours were divided into two groups: full-time workers who worked thirty-five or more but less than forty-one hours, and overtime workers who worked forty-one or more hours a week in the previous year. The definition of part-time workers follows the official definition used by the Bureau of Labor Statistics, and the concept of overtime corresponds to the legal definition.

Owing to the confidentiality of respondents, the public-use files of the CPS report income and earnings that are limited to a certain maximum, or top-code. Values above the top-code are suppressed and imputed as the top-code. During the last twenty-five years the top-coding procedure has changed several times; for example, the top-code for income from wages and salary was $50,000 for 1976 to 1981, $75,000 for 1982 to 1984, and $99,999 for 1985 to 1988. Since a relatively small fraction of workers have their wage top-coded, top-coding does not affect our calculation of quintile variables as presented in figure 10.1. The top-code is much higher than the cutoff value of the top quintile. However, top-coding can affect our calculation of earnings as presented in figures 10.3 and 10.4. If we ignore top-coding and use the censored data in our calculations of wages and salary, the result will be understated. We adjusted for the top-coding problem of the CPS earnings data by multiplying all top-coded values by 1.4. Previously, Lawrence Katz and Kevin Murphy (1992) assigned 1.45T to any value that was top-coded at T, and Chinhui Juhn, Kevin Murphy, and Brooks Pierce (1993) assigned 1.33T, but we followed a recent method used by David Card and John DiNardo (2002).

Since 1996, however, the Census Bureau has lowered the top-codes and replaced all top-coded values with the average values of twelve socioeconomic groups defined on the bases of gender, race, and worker status. Instead of imputing earnings values top-coded at T as 1.4T, as we did for 1976 to 1995, we used the averages provided by the Census Bureau for 1996 to 2001.

In all calculations of the CPS data presented in this chapter, the CPS final weights were used to yield nationally representative estimates. The CPS data used here came from Unicon Research Corporation (producer and distributor of CPS Utilities) in Santa Monica, California.

The General Social Survey

Measures of subjective attitudes come from the General Social Survey. The GSS is a nationally representative annual survey conducted by the National Opinion Research Center (NORC). In this chapter, we analyzed twenty-three surveys between 1972 and 2000, but in some years (1979, 1981, 1992, 1995, 1997, and 1999) the GSS was not conducted, and in others some of the questions included in this study were not asked. The sample used here includes all respondents who were employed and age twenty-four to sixty-four, excluding those who had a job but were not at work, were unemployed, were not in the labor force, or were in the armed forces.

Two questions in the GSS were used in exploring respondents' perceptions and attitudes regarding conditions of work and living. First, job satisfaction was measured by the question: "On the whole, how satisfied are you with the work you do? Would you say you are very satisfied, moderately satisfied, a little dissatisfied, or very dissatisfied?" Similarly, to measure respondents' satisfaction with their financial situation, another question asked was: "So far as you and your family are concerned, would you say that you are pretty well satisfied with your present financial situation, more or less satisfied, or not satisfied at all?" In the two questions on satisfaction, "very satisfied" responses, the most evident indication of job satisfaction, were calculated. The graphical representation of the trends in perceived job security and satisfaction (figures 10.5 and 10.6) indicates the fraction of respondents who showed the most obvious and unambiguous responses to a given question.

The 2001 California Workforce Survey

The fall 2001 California Workforce Survey was designed to assess the state of the California workforce. The survey collected data on California workers' attitudes toward a range of issues as well as on the status, conditions, and practices of their employment. The survey was sponsored by the Institute for Labor and Employment at the University of California and done by the Survey Research Center at the University of California. There were two California samples for this study: a cross-section sample and a union-member oversample. The survey had 1,404 cases, including an oversample of 342 union members. We weighted the sample to compensate for the oversample.

Both samples covered all telephone exchanges in the state of California. A total of twenty-two replicates were created to facilitate sample management—twelve of the twenty-two replicates were allocated to the cross-section sample in which all adults in residential households were eligible, and the other ten replicates were allocated to the union-member oversample in which only adult union members currently working full- or part-time were eligible. Note that those not currently working were asked most of the attitudinal questions, but of course the questions about their current jobs were skipped.

Both samples of telephone numbers for this survey were generated using a procedure called list-assisted random-digit sampling. This method preserves the characteristics of a simple random sample but takes advantage of the availability of large computer databases of telephone directory information to make the sample more efficient. It allows us to reduce the number of unproductive calls to nonworking telephone numbers and to obtain a higher proportion of households in our sample than we would achieve by simple random-digit dialing.

Briefly, the method worked like this: all possible telephone numbers in the state of California were divided into two strata—telephone numbers from series of one hundred numbers with zero or one residential listing in the telephone directories, and telephone numbers from series with at least two such listings. The sample of telephone numbers used for this project was then generated with random numbers, in order to include unlisted numbers, from the stratum containing series of telephone numbers with at least two residential listings. The stratum containing series of telephone numbers with zero or one residential listing was unlikely to contain many residential numbers and therefore was excluded from the sampling frame. For a detailed description of this sampling method, see Casady and Lepkowski (1993). This procedure resulted in the following sample. The survey had a response rate of 50.8 percent (1,255 respondents out of 2,471 calls).

The following two-digit census occupation codes were coded into the four occupation groups for the CPS, GSS, and California Survey analyses.

Managerial

1. Managers, administrators, and public officials

3. Management analysts

32. Retail and other sales supervisors

51. Supervisors, protective services

52. Supervisors, food services

53. Supervisors, cleaning and building services

54. Supervisors, personal services

61. Farmers, farm managers and supervisors, and other supervisors of agricultural and forestry work

62. Captains and other officers of fishing vessels

71. Supervisors, mechanics and repairers

72. Supervisors, construction trades

73. Supervisors, extractive occupations (oil drilling, mining)

74. Supervisors, production occupations

81. Supervisors, motor vehicle operators

83. Ship captains and mates

84. Supervisors, material moving equipment operators

92. Supervisors of handlers, equipment cleaners, and laborers

Professionals

2. Accountants, auditors, underwriters, and other financial officers

4. Personnel, training, and labor relations specialists

5. Purchasing agents and buyers

6. Business and promotion agents

7. Inspectors and compliance officers

11. Doctors and dentists

12. Veterinarians

13. Optometrists

14. Other health diagnosing occupations: podiatrists, chiropractors, acupuncturists, and so on

15. Nurses (RNs, LVNs, LPNs)

16. Physician's assistants

17. Pharmacists and dietitians

18. Therapists: physical therapists, speech therapists, inhalation therapists, and so on

19. Health techs (hospital lab techs, dental hygienists, and so on)

20. Elementary and high school teachers

21. College and university teachers

22. Counselors, educational and vocational

23. Librarians, archivists, and curators

24. Lawyers and judges

25. Social scientists and urban planners: economists, psychologists, sociologists, and urban planners

26. Clergy, social, recreation, and religious workers

27. Writers, artists, entertainers, and athletes

28. Engineers, scientists, architects

29. Computer programmers

30. Other technicians (draftsmen, other lab techs, airline pilots, air traffic controllers, legal assistants, and so on)

Other White-Collar

8. Administrative assistants

33. Retail sales workers and cashiers

34. Real estate and insurance agents

35. Stock brokers and related sales occupations

36. Advertising and related sales occupations

37. Sales representatives—manufacturing and wholesale

38. Street and door-to-door sales workers, news vendors, and auctioneers

39. Other sales occupations

40. Office and clerical supervisors and managers

41. Secretaries, typists, stenographers, word processors, receptionists, and general office clerks

42. Records processing clerks: bookkeepers, payroll clerks, billing clerks, file and records clerks

43. Shipping and receiving clerks, stock clerks

44. Data-entry keyers

45. Computer operators

46. Telephone operators and other communications equipment operators

48. Bank tellers

49. Teacher's aides

50. Other clerical workers

Service and Blue-Collar Workers

47. Postal clerks, mail carriers, messengers, and so on

55. Cooks, waiters, and related restaurant and bar occupations

56. Health service (dental assistants, nursing aides, attendants)

57. Personal service (barbers, hairdressers, public transportation attendants, welfare service aides)

58. Cleaning and building service (maids, janitors, housekeepers, elevator operators, pest control)

59. Child care workers

60. Firemen, policemen, and other protective service occupations

63. Farm workers

64. Graders, sorters, and inspectors of agricultural products

65. Animal caretakers

66. Nursery workers

67. Groundskeepers and gardeners

68. Forestry and logging workers

69. Fishermen, hunters, and trappers

70. Other farming, forestry, and fishing occupations

77. Extractive occupations (oil drillers, miners)

78. Precision production occupations (tool and die makers, cabinetmakers, jewelers, butchers, bakers, and so on)

79. Precision inspectors, testers, and related workers

80. Plant and system operators (water and sewage treatment plant operators, power plant operators)

82. Railroad conductors and yardmasters

85. Machine operators

86. Motor vehicle operators (truck, bus, and taxi drivers)

87. Railroad (engineers, conductors, other operators)

88. Ships (fishing boat captains, sailors, merchant marine)

89. Bulldozer and forklift operators, longshoremen, and other material movers

90. Fabricators, assemblers and handworking occupations: welders, solderers, hand grinders and polishers, and so on

91. Production inspectors, testers, samplers, and weighers

93. Construction helpers and laborers

94. Factory and other production helpers

95. Service station attendants, car mechanic's helpers, tire changers, and so on

96. Garbage collectors, stock handlers and baggers, and other movers of materials by hand

97. Helpers of surveyors and extractive occupations

We would like to thank Henry Brady, David Card, Mike Hout, and Steve Raphael for their comments on an earlier version of this paper.

REFERENCES

Aaronson, Daniel, and Daniel Sullivan. 1998. "The Decline of Job Security in the 1990s: Displacement, Anxiety, and Their Effect on Wage Growth." *Economic Perspectives* (Federal Reserve Bank of Chicago) 22(1): 17–43.

Appelbaum, Eileen. 1987. "Restructuring Work: Temporary, Part-time, and At-Home Employment." In *Technology and Women's Employment*, edited by Heidi Hartman. Washington, D.C.: National Academy Press.

Appelbaum, Eileen, and Peter Berg. 1996. "Financial Market Constraints and Business Strategy in the U.S." In *Creating Industrial Capacity: Towards Full Employment*, edited by Jonathan Michie and John Grieve Smith. New York: Oxford University Press.

Bernhardt, Annette, Martina Morris, Mark S. Handcock, and Marc A. Scott. 2001. *Divergent Paths: Economic Mobility in the U.S. Labor Market*. New York: Russell Sage Foundation.

Blair, Margaret M., and Thomas A. Kochan. 2000. *The New Relationship: Human Capital in the American Corporation*. Washington, D.C.: Brookings Institution.

Blank, Rebecca. 1990. "Are Part-time Jobs Bad Jobs?" In *A Future of Lousy Jobs? The Changing Structure of U.S. Wages*, edited by Gary Burtless. Washington, D.C.: Brookings Institution.

Bluestone, Barry, and Bennett Harrison. 1982. *The Deindustrialization of America*. New York: Basic Books.

Boisjoly, Johanne, Greg J. Duncan, and Timothy Smeeding. 1998. "The Shifting Incidence of Involuntary Job Loss from 1968 to 1992." *Industrial Relations* 37: 207–31.

Borjas, George. 1999. *Heaven's Door: Immigration Policy and the American Economy*. Princeton, N.J.: Princeton University Press.

Bresnahan, Timothy, Eric Brynjolfsson, and Lorin Hitt. 2000. "Technology, Organization, and the Demand for Skilled Labor." In *The New Relationship: Human Capital in the American Corporation*, edited by Margaret M. Blair and Thomas A. Kochan. Washington, D.C.: Brookings Institution.

Card, David. 1992. "The Effects of Unions on the Distribution of Wages." Working paper 4195. Cambridge, Mass.: National Bureau of Economic Research.

Card, David, and John E. DiNardo. 2002. "Skill-Based Technological Change and Rising Wage Inequality: Some Problems and Puzzles." Working paper 8769. Cambridge, Mass.: National Bureau of Economic Research.

Casady, Robert J., and James. M. Lepkowski. 1993. "Stratified Telephone Survey Designs." *Survey Methodology* 19: 103–13.

Clinton, Angela. 1997. "Flexible Labor: Restructuring the American Workforce." *Monthly Labor Review* 120: 3–17.

Cohany, Sharon R. 1998. "Workers in Alternative Employment Arrangements: A Second Look." *Monthly Labor Review* 121: 3–21.

Coleman, Mary T., and John Pencavel. 1993a. "Changes in Hours of Male Employees, 1940 to 1988." *Industrial and Labor Relations Review* 46: 262–83.

———. 1993b. "Trends in the Market Work Behavior of Women Since 1940." *Industrial and Labor Relations Review* 46: 653–76.

Costa, Dora. 2000. "The Wage and the Length of the Workday: From the 1890s to 1991." *Journal of Labor Economics* 18(1): 156–84.

Diebold, Francis X., David Neumark, and Daniel Polsky. 1997. "Job Stability in the United States." *Journal of Labor Economics* 15(2): 206–33.

DiPrete, Thomas. 1993. "Industrial Restructuring and the Mobility Response of American Workers." *American Sociological Review* 58(1): 74–96.

Farber, Henry S. 1993. "The Incidence and Costs of Job Loss: 1981 to 1991." *Brookings Papers on Economic Activity: Microeconomics*: 73–132.

———. 1997a. "The Changing Face of Job Loss in the U.S., 1981 to 1995." *Brookings Paper on Economic Activity: Microeconomics*: 55–142.

———. 1997b. "Trends in Long-term Employment in the U.S., 1979 to 1996." Working paper no. 384. Princeton,N.J.: Princeton University, Industrial Relations Section.

———. 1998. "Are Lifetime Jobs Disappearing?" In *Labor Statistics Measurement Issues*, edited by John Haltiwanger, Marilyn Manser, and Robert Topel. Chicago: University of Chicago Press.

———. 1999. "Alternative and Part-time Employment Arrangements as a Response to Job Loss." *Journal of Labor Economics* 17: S142–69.

Farber, Henry, and Helen Levy. 1998. "Recent Trends in Employer-Sponsored Health Insurance Coverage: Are Bad Jobs Getting Worse?" Working paper 6709. Cambridge, Mass.: National Bureau of Economic Research.

Fligstein, Neil. 2001. *The Architecture of Markets.* Princeton, N.J.: Princeton University Press.

Fortin, Nicole, and Thomas Lemieux. 1997. "Institutional Changes and Rising Wage Inequality: Is There a Linkage?" *Journal of Economic Perspectives* 11(2): 75–96.

Freeman, Richard B. 1997. *When Earnings Diverge.* Report 284. Washington, D.C.: National Planning Association.

Gannon, M. J. 1984. "Preferences of Temporary Workers: Time, Variety, and Flexibility." *Monthly Labor Review* 107: 26–28.

Golden, Lonnie. 1996. "The Expansion of Temporary Help Employment in the U.S., 1982 to 1992: A Test of Alternative Economic Explanations." *Applied Economics* 28: 1127–41.

Gordon, David. 2000. *Fat and Mean: The Corporate Squeeze of Working Americans and the Myth of Downsizing.* New York: Free Press.

Gustman, Alan L. and Thomas L. Steinmeier. 1999. "Pensions and Retiree Health Benefits in Household Wealth: Changes from 1969 to 1992." Working paper 7320. Cambridge, Mass.: National Bureau of Economic Research.

Hall, Robert. 1982. "The Importance of Lifetime Jobs in the U.S. Economy." *American Economic Review* 72(4): 716–24.

Hamermesh, Daniel. 1999. "Changing Inequality in Markets for Workplace Amenities." *Quarterly Journal of Economics* 114: 1085–1123.

Harrison, Bennett, and Barry Bluestone. 1988. *The Great U-Turn: Corporate Restructuring and the Polarizing of America.* New York: Basic Books.

Hochschild, Arlie Russell. 1997. *The Time Bind: When Work Becomes Home and Home Becomes Work.* New York: Metropolitan Books.

Hout, Michael, and Caroline Hanley. 2002. "Working Hours: A Family-Based Perspective on Trends and Nontrends." Working paper. Berkeley: University of California, Survey Research Center.

Jaeger, David A., and Ann Huff Stevens. 1999. "Is Job Stability in the United States Falling? Reconciling Trends in the Current Population Survey and Panel Study of Income Dynamics." *Journal of Labor Economics* 17(4): S1–28.

Juhn, Chinhui, Kevin M. Murphy, and Brooks Pierce. 1993. "Wage Inequality and the Rise in Returns to Skill." *Journal of Political Economy* 101(3): 410–42.

Kalleberg, Arne. 2000. "Nonstandard Employment Relations: Part-time, Temporary, and Contract Work." *Annual Review of Sociology* 26: 341–65.

Karoly, Lynn. 1992. "The Trend in Inequality Among Families, Individuals, and Workers in the U.S." In *Uneven Tides: Rising Inequality in America,* edited by Peter Gottschalk and Sheldon Danziger. New York: Russell Sage Foundation.

Katz, Lawrence, and David Autor. 1999. "Changes in the Wage Structure and Earnings Inequality." In *Handbook of Labor Economics,* vol. 3, edited by Orley Ashenfelter and David Card. New York: North-Holland.

Katz, Lawrence, and Kevin Murphy. 1992. "Changes in Relative Wages, 1963 to 1987: Supply and Demand Factors." *Quarterly Journal of Economics* 107(1): 35–78.

Kletzer, Lori. 1989. "Returns to Seniority After Permanent Job Loss." *American Economic Review* 79(3): 536–43.

Krueger, Alan. 1993. "How Computers Changed the Wage Structure." *Quarterly Journal of Economics* 108(1): 33–60.

Lee, David S. 1999. "Wage Inequality in the U.S. During the 1980s: Rising Dispersion or Falling Minimum Wage?" *Quarterly Journal of Economics* 114: 977–1023.

Levy, Frank, and Robert J. Murnane. 1992. "U.S. Earnings Levels and Earnings Inequality: A Review of Recent Trends and Proposed Explanations." *Journal of Economic Literature* 30(3): 1333–81.

Mishel, Lawrence R., Jared Bernstein, and John Schmitt. 2001. *The State of Working America 2000/2001.* Ithaca, N.Y.: Cornell University Press.

Murphy, Kevin, and Finis Welch. 1992. "The Structure of Wages." *Quarterly Journal of Economics* 107(1): 285–306.

Nardone, Thomas. 1995. "Part-time Employment: Reasons, Demographics, and Trends." *Journal of Labor Research* 3: 276–92.

Neumark, David, Daniel Polsky, and Daniel Hansen. 1999. "Has Job Stability Declined Yet?" *Journal of Labor Economics* 17(4): S29–64.

Osterman, Paul. 1999. *Securing Prosperity: The American Labor Market: How It Has Changed and What to Do About It.* Princeton, N.J.: Princeton University Press.

Pencavel, John. 1998. "The Market Work Behavior and Wages of Women, 1975 to 1994." *Journal of Human Resources* 33: 779–804.

Pfeffer, Jeffrey, and James N. Baron. 1988. "Taking the Workers Back Out: Recent Trends in the Structuring of Employment." *Research in Organizational Behavior* 10: 257–303.

Podgursky, Michael, and Paul Swaim. 1987. "Job Displacement and Earnings Loss: Evidence for the Displaced Worker Survey." *Industrial and Labor Relations Review* 41: 17–29.

Polsky, Daniel. 1999. "Changing Consequences of Job Separation in the U.S." *Industrial and Labor Relations Review* 52: 565–95.

Presser, Harriet. 1995. "Job, Family, and Gender: Determinants of Nonstandard Work Schedules." *Demography* 32(4): 577–98.

Presser, Harriet B., and Amy G. Cox. 1997. "The Work Schedules of Low-Educated American Women and Welfare Reform." *Monthly Labor Review* 120: 25–34.

Robinson, John, and Geoffrey Godbey. 1997. "Changes in Hours Worked Since 1950." *Federal Reserve Bank of Minneapolis Quarterly Review* (Winter): 2–19.

Rones, Philip, Randy E. Ilg, and Jennifer M. Gardner. 1997. "Trends in Hours of Work Since the Mid-1970s." *Monthly Labor Review* 120: 3–14.

Rose, Stephen. 1995. "Declining Job Security and the Professionalization of Opportunity." Research report 95-04. Washington, D.C.: National Commission for Employment Policy.

Schmidt, Stephanie R. 1999. "Long-term Trends in Workers' Belief About Their Own Security." *Journal of Labor Economics* 17: 127–41.

Schor, Juliet. 1996. *The Overworked American.* New York: HarperCollins.

Schultze, Charles. 1999. "Has Job Security Eroded for American Workers?" In *The New Relationship: Human Capital in the American Corporation,* edited by Margaret M. Blair and Thomas A. Kochan. Washington, D.C.: Brookings Institution.

Stinson, John F., Jr. 1997. "New Data on Multiple Jobholding Available from the CPS." *Monthly Labor Review* 120: 3–8.

Topel, Robert. 1990. "Specific Capital and Unemployment: Measuring the Costs and Consequences of Job Loss." *Carnegie Rochester Conference Series on Public Policy* 33: 181–214.

Ureta, Manuelita. 1992. "The Importance of Lifetime Jobs in the U.S. Economy, Revisited." *American Economic Review* 82(1): 322–35.

Wolfe, Barbara, Amy Wolaver, and Timothy McBride. 1998. "Government Mandates, Health Insurance, and the Deterioration of the Low-Wage Labor Market: Are They Connected?" In *The State of Social Welfare, 1997,* edited by Peter Flora. Brookfield, Mass.: Ashgate.

Chapter 11

The Changing Distribution of Education Finance, 1972 to 1997

Sean Corcoran, William N. Evans, Jennifer Godwin,
Sheila E. Murray, and Robert M. Schwab

Jonathan Kozol's *Savage Inequalities* (1991) is a searing indictment of the American system of public education. It paints a bleak picture of inner-city students struggling in over-crowded classrooms and dilapidated buildings. Kozol compares these children to suburban students at well-funded schools with large campuses, modern scientific equipment, and highly paid and well-trained faculty. While inner-city students, Kozol tells us, are often fortunate to graduate from high school, students from suburban schools are not asked if they will attend college, but where.

These extremes, according to Kozol, are a result of the decentralized structure of education in the United States. As we show later in this chapter, the federal government provides only 7 percent of all of the funds devoted to K–12 education. The states and the nearly sixteen thousand school districts each provide roughly one-half of the rest. Local districts rely heavily on the property tax, a cornerstone of the U.S. education system. Kozol argues persuasively that funding local schools through local property taxes is inherently unfair because large disparities in tax bases across school districts lead inevitably to large differences in spending.

In this chapter, we focus on many of the issues that are central to Kozol's work and present four main results. First, we show that while significant inequality remains, we have in fact made a great deal of progress in reducing some of the glaring disparities Kozol described in 1991. Depending how we measure inequality in school spending, we find that inequality fell by 20 to 35 percent between 1972 and 1997.

Second, we show that the states have played an essential role in reducing inequality in school spending. The states have assumed much greater responsibility for funding schools, and we show that state aid for schools effectively offsets some of the differences in local spending.

Third, we argue that the courts have also played an important role in reducing inequality in school spending. A long string of court cases, beginning with *Serrano v. Priest* in 1971, have challenged the constitutionality of local funding of public schools. Opponents of local funding for primary and secondary schools have now brought cases in forty-three states. In this chapter, we argue that court-mandated education-finance reform often achieves its main objective. Court-ordered reform reduced inequality by raising district spending at the bottom of the distribution while leaving spending at the top unchanged.

Fourth, we argue that while the gap in spending between rich and poor schools has shrunk, important differences in certain education inputs persist. We show, for example, that the qualifications of teachers, access to computers, and class size vary systematically across socioeconomic groups.

In the second and third sections of the chapter, we look at the changing distribution of education spending. This focus on dollars makes sense in many ways. Dollars have been the measuring rod of education inequality during much of the long debate over education opportunity. As we show in the third section, for example, differences in spending across school districts were the key issue in *Serrano* and much of the subsequent litigation. This focus on dollars, however, is in some ways limited; the debate over inequality in education is also a debate over the distribution of the education resources those dollars can purchase. In the last section, we summarize what is known about the distribution of teacher characteristics, technology in the classroom, and the physical condition of schools.

THE LEVEL AND DISTRIBUTION OF EDUCATION FINANCE AND SPENDING

In this section, we look at trends in aggregate spending, the changing role of the states in education finance, and inequality in resources across districts over the last thirty years. Here and in much of the rest of the chapter we define education resources as current education expenditures (or the education revenues received by school districts) deflated by a broad measure of prices, the national consumer price index (CPI). Although this is the standard measure in the education literature, it does have several limitations, some of which we discuss in appendix A.

Aggregate Education Spending

We begin by looking at changes in aggregate education revenues. Figure 11.1 presents real per pupil revenues for K–12 education from the 1970 to 1971 through the 1998 to 1999 school years. The data are aggregated from all school districts in the country, and amounts are reported in real 1992 dollars. These data are taken from the National Center for Education Statistics *Digest of Education Statistics*. The top line of the graph represents total revenues from all sources; the lower lines report the cumulative revenues from federal, state, and local governments.

A number of important trends are illustrated in figure 11.1. First, per pupil spending rose from just over $3,400 in 1970 to just over $6,200 in 1998, and thus real revenues per student nearly doubled during this twenty-eight-year period (U.S. Department of Education 2001a).[1]

Eric Hanushek and Steven Rivkin (1997) offer some interesting insights on the growth in per student revenues in the post-1970 period. They show that as a result of the baby bust, enrollment in public schools fell from roughly 45.5 million students in 1970 to 40.4 million in 1990 (U.S. Department of Education 2001a). Even though the number of students fell 11 percent during this period, the number of teachers actually rose by about 16 percent (U.S. Department of Education 2001a). In the 1980 to 1990 period, they show, the average teacher salary rose by about 27 percent. Hanushek and Rivkin go on to note that much of the change in the size of the instructional staff is related to a growing special education population.

Second, the source of education revenues also changed over the last thirty years. The

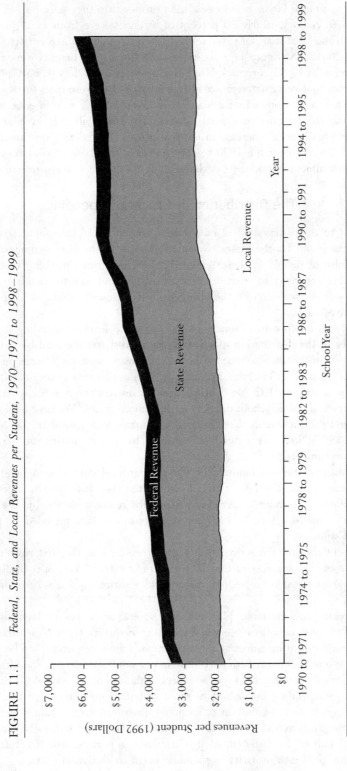

FIGURE 11.1   Federal, State, and Local Revenues per Student, 1970–1971 to 1998–1999

Source: U.S. Department of Education (1997a).

states now play a much larger role in education finance than they once did. In the early part of the twentieth century, nearly 80 percent of revenues were from local governments. By the mid-1940s the local share of revenues had fallen to about 60 percent (U.S. Department of Education 2001a). As figure 11.1 shows, in 1970 local governments were responsible for about 53 percent of K–12 revenues, while the state share was less than 40 percent. By the 1998 to 1999 school year, states provided roughly half of all resources for K–12 education. We discuss later the reasons why the states have taken a larger role in education finance.

Third, the federal government has always played a small role in education finance. Although there has been an increase in the real dollars the federal government provides to education (57 percent over the 1970 to 1998 period), the share of resources coming from the federal government has actually declined from 8.4 to 6.8 percent over this period.

The Distribution of Education Spending

We now turn to the distribution of education spending. There are about sixteen thousand school districts in the United States. Given the variety in the size, demographic composition, and wealth of people in these school districts, it is not surprising that there is also considerable heterogeneity in what districts are willing and able to spend on K–12 education. In this section, we describe the changing distribution of education spending over the past twenty-five years.

Although we can obtain estimates of the aggregate level of spending for each school year, estimates of the distribution of spending across districts are available only for limited periods. Our primary data source is the U.S. Census Bureau's Census of Government School System Finance (F33) File. The Census of Governments is conducted in years that end in a 2 or 7, and the F33 file contains data on district revenue, expenditures, and fall enrollment from all public school districts in the United States. We have used data from the 1972 through 1992 surveys in the past (Evans, Murray, and Schwab 1997; Murray, Evans, and Schwab 1998); here we extend our analysis to include information from the 1997 Census of Governments.

We summarize the development of our district-level dataset in appendix B. As discussed in that appendix, the dataset includes about ten thousand districts in forty-six states. (We drop Montana, Vermont, Hawaii, and Alaska for reasons discussed in the appendix.) It excludes many small districts; in 1997 the districts in our data included 91 percent of all public school students.

We present data on the source of per pupil revenues in the first rows of table 11.1. The results from this analysis mirror the numbers in figure 11.1. Specifically, our sample shows rapidly rising real revenues per student and a shrinking share of revenue from local governments.

The second panel in table 11.1 presents several measures of inequality in district spending. All of these measures rise when spending inequality rises. (For a thorough discussion of the properties of measures of equity in public school resources, see Berne and Stiefel 1984.) The ratio of the ninety-fifth percentile in per pupil spending to the fifth percentile in spending is a simple ranking that treats transfers to the top or bottom of the distribution the same; changes in spending in the rest of the distribution do not change the 95-to-5 ratio. Changes throughout the distribution of spending contribute to the values of the coefficient of variation, the Theil index, and the Gini coefficient. The Theil index gives more weight to changes in the tails of the distribution; it is attractive in part because it is relatively easy to decompose the Theil into disparity in spending between and within states.

TABLE 11.1   *Current U.S. Education Expenditures, 1972 to 1997*

	1972	1977	1982	1987	1992	1997
Funding per student (1992 dollars)						
Local	$1,857	$1,915	$1,867	$2,268	$2,540	$2,595
State and Federal	1,469	1,841	2,061	2,598	2,767	3,221
Total	3,327	3,756	3,928	4,866	5,307	5,816
Measures of inequality						
Gini coefficient (×100)	16.3	15.0	13.8	15.8	15.5	13.0
95-to-5 ratio	2.72	2.37	2.22	2.53	2.40	2.10
Coefficient of variation	30.8	28.1	25.6	29.6	29.9	26.0
Theil index (×1,000)	43.7	37.1	31.0	40.7	40.5	30.6
Theil index decomposition						
Within states	13.7	14.4	14.0	12.6	13.4	9.9
Between states	30.0	22.8	17.0	28.2	27.1	20.7
National	43.7	37.1	31.0	40.7	40.5	30.6
Household income						
Median (1992 dollars)	$32,548	$31,422	$29,326	$32,186	$30,636	$32,348
Gini coefficient (×100)	40.1	40.2	41.2	42.6	43.4	45.9

Source: Authors' calculations from U.S. Department of Commerce (1972–1977–1982–1987–1992–1997).

All of the inequality measures in table 11.1 follow a similar pattern. They show a sharp decline in inequality through 1982. Inequality increased between 1982 and 1987 as the recession of the early 1980s reduced state revenues. Inequality stayed fairly constant between 1987 and 1992; two measures show slight declines, and two measures show small increases in inequality. Since 1992, however, all measures show a dramatic drop in inequality. In aggregate, school spending in the United States is now distributed much more equally than in the early 1970s. The Gini, 95-to-5 ratio, coefficient of variation, and Theil index fell by 20, 23, 35, and 30 percent, respectively.

The third panel of table 11.1 breaks spending inequality into two components: inequality due to differences in spending within states and inequality due to differences across states. The results shown here make a number of interesting points. We find that between-state inequality is much larger than within-state inequality. In nearly all years, variation across the states represents about two-thirds of the total variance in per pupil spending whereas within-state inequality accounts for the remaining third. Declines in between-state inequality have been the source of much of the decline in national inequality in spending. Between 1972 and 1997, declining between-state differences in spending accounted for about 70 percent of the reduction in the Theil index over this period. The time-series patterns of the between- and within-state Theil index are quite different. The within-state Theil index was roughly flat from 1972 to 1992 and then dropped sharply between 1992 and 1997.

Table 11.2 offers further evidence on the dramatic decline in between-state inequality

TABLE 11.2   *Growth Rate in Education Spending per Student in Selected States,*
              1992 to 1997

State	Per Pupil Spending (1992 Dollars)	Rank in Per Pupil Spending, 1992	Rank in Per Pupil Spending Growth Rate, 1992 to 1997
Utah	$2,972	46	10
Alabama	3,008	45	1
Mississippi	3,070	44	7
Tennessee	3,157	43	2
Idaho	3,170	42	3
Arizona	3,201	41	4
Arkansas	3,479	40	8
Oklahoma	3,530	39	16
Kentucky	3,655	38	5
New Mexico	3,743	37	18

Source: Authors' calculation U.S. Department of Commerce (1972–1977–1982–1987–1992–1997).

in the 1990s. This table lists the ten states (in our sample of forty-six states) with the lowest per student revenues in 1992. The last column of this table ranks each of those states in terms of the growth rate in revenues over the 1992 to 1997 period. Table 11.2 shows that spending in initially low-spending states rose sharply. In particular, it shows that eight of the ten lowest-spending states were among the ten states with the largest increases in spending. Given those patterns, it is not surprising that between-state inequality has fallen as dramatically as it has.[2]

This decline in education spending inequality occurred during a period when income inequality rose sharply. In the final rows of table 11.1, we report real median household income and the national Gini coefficient for household income. Income inequality at the national level, as measured by the Gini, rose by about 15 percent from 1972 through 1997. It would be reasonable to expect that if everything else had remained equal, this increase in income inequality would have led to an *increase* in inequality in school spending. Thus, the 20 to 30 percent *decrease* in inequality in school spending we in fact see over this period is even more dramatic than it might first appear.

Variation in the Cost of Education Across Districts

We would have liked to account for differences in costs across districts. (Recall that our measure of education resources is current education expenditures deflated by the national consumer price index.) There are several alternative district-level deflators, but unfortunately none are available for the period before 1987. We have done some work with those deflators, and we summarize that work in appendix C.

School Spending Inequality and the Socioeconomic Characteristics of Students

To this point, we have focused on the magnitude of differences in spending across school districts. So, for example, we have looked at differences in spending between a district in the ninety-fifth percentile of the spending distribution and a district in the fifth percentile.

We now turn to a closely related issue. Here we are concerned with inequality in school spending across districts with different socioeconomic characteristics.

To implement this analysis, we need a detailed dataset with both district-level education finance and demographic characteristics. Amy Harris, William Evans, and Robert Schwab (2001) have developed just such a dataset, and we utilize that sample here. Their dataset is a national panel of public school districts for 1972, 1982, and 1992. The panel was created by merging six national school districts datasets: the 1970 Census of Population and Housing Special Fifth-Count Tallies (U.S. Department of Commerce 1970), the 1980 Census of Population and Housing Summary Tape File 3F (U.S. Department of Commerce 1980), the 1990 Census School District Special Tabulation, School District Data Book (U.S. Department of Education 1990a), and the 1972, 1982, and 1992 Census of Governments: School Districts (U.S. Department of Commerce 1972-1982-1992). (For a complete discussion of the construction of the data used in this research and a detailed description of the merging procedure, see Harris 1999.) Our sample is similar in spirit to the one used by Caroline Hoxby (2001), who was the first researcher to construct a panel of school districts from these data. Our balanced panel consists of about nine thousand of the sixteen thousand unified, elementary and secondary school districts in the forty-eight continental states and the District of Columbia.

Using our district-level dataset, we weight district observations by the number of enrolled students in a certain demographic group and then calculate the means. This procedure generates a mean for an average student picked randomly from the population. So, for example, in the first row of table 11.3, we report the mean expenditures per student for white and nonwhite students. It is clear that differences in expenditures across race are very small; in 1992 average spending was actually lower for whites than for nonwhites.

In the next two panels of table 11.3, we report similar calculations but use district characteristics to define groups. In the second panel, we divide districts by quartiles of district median household income. Notice that in 1972 districts in the highest quartile of median household income spent about 40 percent more than districts in the lowest quartile—a difference of almost $900 per pupil. Between 1972 and 1992, spending in both groups increased rapidly, but the increase was much larger in poorer districts. In 1992 the districts in the highest quartile were still spending over $800 per pupil more than in the lowest quartile, but the relative difference had fallen to 20 percent.

Differences in the average pupil-teacher ratio are very small. In columns 4, 5, and 6 of table 11.3, we generate estimates of the pupil-teacher ratio by merging information from the employment section of the Census of Governments with our balanced panel of districts for 1972, 1982, and 1992. Notice that when we weight the data by the number of white and nonwhite students in the district, there is virtually no difference in the pupil-teacher ratios between these groups in any year.[3]

The convergence of pupil-teacher ratios between white and black students was first noted by Michael Boozer, Alan Krueger, and Shari Wolkon (1992). Using a number of new data sources to track the changing level of education resources in black schools since the *Brown v. Board of Education* decision, they report pupil-teacher ratios from 1915 through 1989 for seventeen states and the District of Columbia that had legally segregated schools before the *Brown* decision. In 1953–1954, just prior to the *Brown* decision, the pupil-teacher ratio for white students was 27.6 but 31.6 for blacks, a difference of 4.0 students. By 1966, the authors note, the average difference in pupil-teacher ratios for blacks and whites had fallen to just 2.1. Using data from the Common Core of Data in 1989 (U.S. Department of Education 1990b), the authors report average pupil-teacher ratios of 18.1 for blacks and 18.3 for whites.

TABLE 11.3   *Schooling Inputs, by Demographic Characteristics, 1972 to 1992*

	Expenditures Per Pupil (1992 Dollars)			Pupils Per Teacher		
	1972	1982	1992	1972	1982	1992
By average white and nonwhite student in the district						
White	$2,856	$3,414	$4,661	19.32	15.13	13.09
Nonwhite	2,800	3,460	4,796	19.58	14.58	12.52
Ratio of white to nonwhite	1.02	0.99	0.97	0.99	1.04	1.05
By median household income in the district						
First quartile	2,212	3,040	4,214	19.22	14.24	11.93
Second quartile	2,388	3,381	4,324	19.24	14.56	12.56
Third quartile	2,970	3,359	4,686	18.82	15.25	13.20
Fourth quartile	3,095	3,667	5,047	19.82	15.70	13.53
Ratio of fourth to first quartile	1.40	1.21	1.20	1.03	1.10	1.13
By poverty status						
Out of poverty	2,881	3,432	4,700	19.34	15.11	13.06
In poverty	2,660	3,331	4,531	19.42	14.81	12.81
Ratio of out of poverty to in poverty	1.08	1.03	1.04	1.00	1.02	1.02

Source: Authors' calculations from U.S. Department of Commerce (1970–1972–1980–1982–1992); U.S. Department of Education (1990a).

In contrast to the variation in expenditures that exists between wealthier and poorer school districts in all years, there are actually more students per teacher in wealthier districts than in poorer districts. This difference was one-half of a student in 1972 and rose to six-tenths of a student in 1992.

The Role of the States

All state governments provide aid to local school districts, and as we showed in the previous section, the share of total education revenues coming from the states has increased over time. Depending on how these resources are distributed, state revenues can either increase or decrease inequality across districts. In this section, we show that state aid to education reduces inequality and that it can explain much of the change in within-state inequality that has occurred over the past twenty-five years.

Initially, we approach this problem by comparing actual inequality in school spending to inequality under a counterfactual where states leave the total amount they provide to school districts unchanged but distribute these funds equally on a per student basis. This approach is thus equivalent to asking what would happen to inequality if we converted all state education aid programs to a system of flat-grants. Table 11.4 sets out a hypothetical example intended to clarify this comparison. Consider a state that has three districts. All three have the same number of students. The first column shows actual local spending for each district. The next two columns show actual state and total spending. In our example, the state spends an average of $3,000 per student. It provides the highest aid to the lowest-spending district (district 1) and the smallest aid to the highest-spending district (district 3). The last two columns show state and total spending under our counterfactual. Here the

TABLE 11.4   *The Impact of State Aid on Spending Inequality: Hypothetical Example*

District	Local	Actual			Counterfactual	
		State	Total		State	Total
District 1	$2,000	$3,500	$5,500		$3,000	$5,000
District 2	3,000	3,000	6,000		3,000	6,000
District 3	4,000	2,500	6,500		3,000	7,000
Gini coefficient (×100)			3.7			7.4

Source: Authors' calcualtions.

state continues to spend $3,000 per student but now gives each district the same amount of aid.

The last row of table 11.4 sets out the Gini coefficient (multiplied by 100) for total spending. The Gini given actual spending is 3.7; if the state had distributed aid equally to all districts, the Gini would have been 7.4. Thus, in this example we would say that state aid reduced inequality in school spending by one-half.

We begin by calculating the actual and counterfactual Ginis for each state in 1972. In figure 11.2, we graph the actual within-state Gini coefficient on the vertical axis and the flat-grant counterfactual on the horizontal axis. All points that lie below the forty-five-degree line are states that would have had higher measures of inequality had they distributed resources evenly on a per student basis. The fact that nearly all points lie below the forty-five-degree line indicates that on average states actively redistributed resources to lower-spending districts.

We next show that the states have increased their efforts to reduce inequality in school spending. In figure 11.3, we redo the analysis from figure 11.2 using 1997 data. As in the previous figure, the vertical axis is the actual Gini coefficient in within-state student revenues while the horizontal axis is the counterfactual Gini that would arise if local spending stayed the same but states distributed aid equally to all districts on a per student basis. Notice that more states now lie below the forty-five-degree line than in 1972. Notice also that the vertical distances between the points below the forty-five-degree line and the line itself are now much larger than before, indicating more redistribution.

Figure 11.4 makes this point in a slightly different way. Consider the difference between the actual Gini coefficient for a state and the counterfactual Gini; for the hypothetical state summarized in table 11.4, this statistic would equal $7.4 - 3.7 = 3.7$. This difference is a measure of the degree of redistribution in education resources. In figure 11.4, we graph the degree of redistribution in 1997 on the horizontal axis and the degree of redistribution in 1972 on the vertical axis. Points below the forty-five-degree line represent states that have become more redistributive over time. The bulk of the points lie below the forty-five-degree line.

An Econometric Analysis of State Education Spending Inequality

We can summarize the extent to which state aid reduces education spending inequality more formally in a regression context. Specifically, if we regress local revenues on district demographic characteristics, we should find that wealthier, better-educated districts spend

FIGURE 11.2   *Comparison of Actual and Synthetic State Gini Coefficients for Total Revenue per Pupil in 1972*

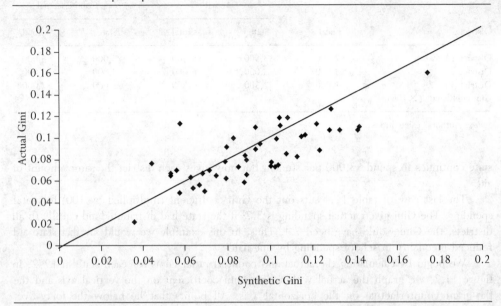

Source: Authors' calculations.

FIGURE 11.3   *Comparison of Actual and Synthetic State Gini Coefficients for Total Revenue per Pupil in 1997*

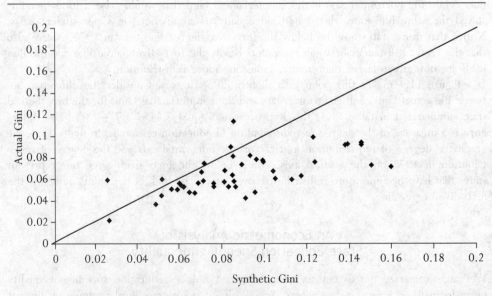

Source: Authors' calculations.

FIGURE 11.4   *Comparison of the Degree of Redistribution in 1972 Versus 1997*

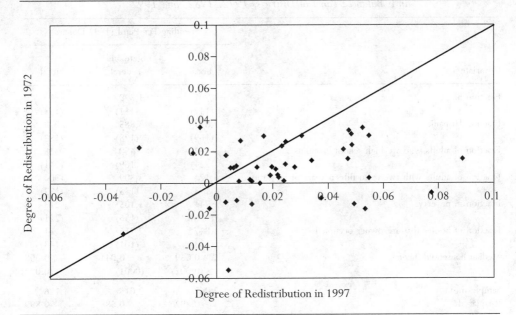

Source: Authors' calculations.

more from local sources on education (for example, by raising more money from the property tax). Given the redistributive nature of state aid for education, we should see the opposite relationship when we turn to state revenue.

We use the balanced panel of nine thousand unified school districts that includes both school finance and socioeconomic data for 1972, 1982, and 1992 that we described earlier. With that dataset, we estimate a model that examines the correlates of local, state, and total revenues per pupil at the district level. The dependent variable is district level per pupil revenues in a particular year (1972, 1982, or 1992) for each revenue source. The demographic covariates in the model include characteristics of the population who live in a school district, such as the fraction nonwhite, the fraction Hispanic, the fraction of adults with less than twelve years of education, the fraction of adults with twelve to fifteen years of education, the fraction in poverty, the fraction who own homes, and median household income. In each model, we include district fixed effects to account for any unobserved, permanent differences in preferences for education services or costs between school districts that alter per pupil revenues. We include state-specific year effects to account for changes in school finances that are correlated at the state level over time (such as the finance reform movement we discuss in a later section).

Table 11.5 sets out the estimates of these models. In the first column, we report results for *local* revenues per pupil. Because most of the variation in per pupil local revenues is between districts, our use of district fixed effects generates a high R-squared. We replicate most of the stylized facts from previous work; per pupil local revenues were lower in districts with a higher fractions of blacks, Hispanics, poorly educated adults, renters, and poor people. All of these coefficients are precisely estimated, and the estimated magnitudes are qualitatively important. Using the distribution of the covariates across districts in 1992,

TABLE 11.5   *Determinants of Local, State, and Total Per Pupil Revenues on K–12 Education in a Balanced Panel of Districts, 1972, 1982, and 1992*

| Covariate | Spending Per Pupil (1992 Dollars) | | |
	Local	State and Federal	Total
Fraction black	−1,701	1,829	−79
	(147)	(111)	(158)
Fraction Hispanic	−2,837	3,885	278
	(169)	(128)	(182)
Fraction of adults who are high school dropouts	−852	450	328
	(224)	(169)	(241)
Fraction of adults with twelve to fifteen years of education	−6,124	3,809	−1904
	(178)	(135)	(192)
Fraction in poverty	−744	1,105	213
	(206)	(156)	(221)
Fraction of homes that are owner occupied	−1,847	2,216	14
	(133)	(101)	(143)
Median household income	0.059	−0.044	0.008
	(0.002)	(0001)	(0.002)
Sample mean	2,067	2,015	4,126
R-squared	0.892	0.888	0.899

Source: Authors' calculations.
Notes: All models include district fixed effects and state-specific year effects. Standard errors are given in parentheses.

a two-standard-deviation increase in the fraction black, Hispanic, in poverty, and owner-occupied homes is estimated to reduce per pupil local revenues by $408, $624, $199, and $369, respectively.[4] The change in local revenues generated by income changes is even more dramatic. The standard deviation in household income across districts in 1992 is $11,000. A one-standard-deviation increase in median household income would raise local spending by about $650.

In the second column of table 11.5, we use the same specification but change the dependent variable to per pupil state revenues. In all cases, the signs on the demographic characteristics in this model are the opposite of what they are in the local revenues regression. Thus, the states redistribute resources to local districts that, a priori, we would expect to raise fewer funds locally. For many of the variables the coefficient on the demographic variable in the state revenue model is roughly the negative of the coefficient in the local revenue model. It is no surprise then that when we reestimate the model using total revenues per pupil (the third column of table 11.5), we find that in five of seven cases the coefficients on the demographic variables are statistically insignificant and quantitatively unimportant. Although the coefficient on median household income is statistically significant, the coefficient is small. In 1992 there is a $35,000 difference in the district with the fifth to the ninety-fifth percentile in median household income, but this movement would generate a change in total per pupil revenues of only about $280.

EDUCATION-FINANCE REFORM

We showed in the previous section that within-state inequality in education spending fell sharply between 1972 and 1997. We also showed that the states played an important role in reducing differences in spending. Here we argue that state efforts to reduce inequality in education resources were in part a response to a string of successful school finance legal cases. This section thus draws a link between the schoolhouse, the courthouse, and the statehouse.

The property tax was the key issue in these cases. The property tax is a cornerstone of the U.S. education system, accounting for more than 96 percent of total tax revenue in independent school districts.[5] This share is below 90 percent in only three states (Kentucky, Louisiana, and Pennsylvania). Critics have often argued that the property tax is inherently unfair because large disparities in tax bases across school districts lead inevitably to large differences in spending. In the landmark 1971 case *Serrano v. Priest,* the California State Supreme Court declared the state's public school finance system unconstitutional. In the *Serrano* case, the plaintiffs' attorneys showed that Beverly Hills spent more than twice as much per student as Baldwin Park, a low-income community twenty-five miles east of Los Angeles. Because of Beverly Hills' larger tax base, however, its school property tax rate was less than half of Baldwin Park's (Fischel 1996). The court ordered the state to develop a system in which school support did not depend on district wealth—in other words, a system of fiscal neutrality.

Litigation in other states soon followed. California is one of forty-three states where opponents of local funding for primary and secondary schools have challenged the constitutionality of the public school finance system. By 1999 the courts had overturned systems in nineteen states. In response to court orders, state legislatures implemented or revised equalization formulas and increased their state's share of educational spending. In this section, we review the history of education-finance reform litigation and summarize some of the empirical work that describes the impact of finance reform.

A Short History of Education-Finance Litigation

In the 1960s a number of critics began to formulate an attack on the system of local funding for public schools.[6] There was broad agreement on the source of the problem: local control of key education decisions had led to significant differences in education spending. The best legal strategy, however, was open to debate. One strategy portrayed education as a "fundamental interest" for equal protection purposes and thus argued that it could not be distributed unequally within a state in the absence of a compelling state interest for doing so. This legal strategy drew an analogy with reapportionment cases, arguing that if courts were willing to insist on a one-man, one-vote standard, perhaps they could be persuaded to see the logic of a one-scholar, one-dollar standard for education. Thus, this strategy argued for an end to unequal spending based on the equal protection clause.

A second strategy argued that because some children may have different educational needs, equal protection might require the state to spend more on the education of low-achieving, low-income students than on students from affluent, well-educated families. The courts were not sympathetic to this line of argument (Minorini and Sugarman 1999, 37). Federal courts in a 1968 Illinois case, *McInnis v. Shapiro,* and a 1969 Virginia case, *Burris v. Wilkerson,* concluded that a needs-based theory left too many questions unanswered. As the

Burris decision put it, the "courts have neither the knowledge, nor the means, nor the power to tailor the public moneys to fit the varying needs of these students throughout the State." As we will see, the courts in the last decade have been much more receptive to this interpretation of equal protection. Both *McInnis* and *Burris* were appealed to the U.S. Supreme Court, where the lower court rulings were affirmed without comment.

A third strategy did prove to be successful. John Coons, William Clune, and Stephen Sugarman (1970) argued that unequal spending itself was not the key issue. Instead, in their view, the basic problem was that poor school districts had little property wealth that they could tax (Minorini and Sugarman 1999, 37). It was evident that poor districts were trying: they often set higher tax rates than did wealthy districts. But despite their efforts, these districts spent far less per student. Coons, Clune, and Sugarman argued that it was this link between wealth and school spending that was the fundamental constitutional issue. They put forth what became known as the principle of fiscal neutrality: the quality of public education, most commonly measured as dollar inputs, may not be a function of wealth other than the wealth of the state itself.

Fiscal neutrality has a number of interesting implications. It allows, for example, for the possibility that some communities would wish to spend more on education than other communities, as long as those differences were unrelated to differences in wealth. Thus, a community would be free to set a higher tax rate than another if the two communities raised the same tax revenue after choosing the same rate. Fiscal neutrality had little to offer high-property-wealth, low-income districts. Low wealth is often associated with poverty, but the two are far from synonymous. For example, the elderly often have lower than average incomes but higher than average wealth. Similarly, large cities with a significant nonresidential tax base might have a large stock of taxable commercial property but a high fraction of low-income students. Money would not be redistributed to these areas since their property tax base is large. Coons, Clune, and Sugarman were willing to accept these anomalies because they believed that fiscal neutrality was a viable legal strategy in the battle over school finance.

It is probably best to view fiscal neutrality as a legal strategy that might be successful in court rather than as a description of an optimal way to fund education. Coons, Clune, and Sugarman knew from the *McInnis* and *Burris* decisions that the courts were unwilling to become embroiled in difficult problems such as defining the needs of individual students. The test here was straightforward: Is school spending independent of wealth? Clearly, this is an easier question for the courts to answer than the questions that the public interest lawyers were asking the courts to broach.

Federal courts, however, were unreceptive to Coons, Clune, and Sugarman's argument. A lower federal court ruled in *Rodriguez v. San Antonio Independent School District* in favor of the plaintiffs based on the principle of fiscal neutrality (Minorini and Sugarman 1999, 39). The decision was appealed to the Supreme Court. In a 1973 decision, by a 5–4 majority, the U.S. Supreme Court overturned the lower court's decision and ruled against the plaintiffs. The Court saw this as a federalism issue: "It would be difficult to imagine a case having a greater potential impact on the federal system than the one now before us, in which we are urged to abrogate systems of financing public education presently in existence in virtually every state." As a result of *Rodriguez,* the federal courts were no longer an option for anyone seeking legal reform of education finance.

Reformers were far more successful in state courts. Table 11.6 lists the nineteen states identified by Paul Minorini and Stephen Sugarman (1999) in which plaintiffs have successfully challenged a state's system of school finance. In another twelve states the plaintiffs

TABLE 11.6   *Successful Education Finance Cases Argued in State Courts, 1971 to 1998*

State	Decision	Year(s)
Alabama	*Harper v. Hunt*	1993, 1997
Arizona	*Roosevelt Elementary School District 66 v. Bishop*	1994, 1997
Arkansas	*Dupree v. Alma School District*	1983
	Lake View v. Arkansas	Filed 1994
California	*Serrano v. Priest*	1971, 1977
Connecticut	*Horton v. Meskill*	1977
	Sheff v. O'Neill	1996
Kentucky	*Rose v. The Council*	1989
Massachusetts	*McDuffy v. Secretary of Education*	1993
Missouri	*The Committee v. Missouri and Lee's Summit P.S.U. v. Missouri*	1996
Montana	*Helena School District v. Montana*	1989
	Montana Rural Education Association v. Montana	Filed 1993
New Hampshire	*Claremont v. Gregg*	1997
New Jersey	*Robinson v. Cahill*	1973, 1976
	Abbott v. Burke	1990, 1994, 1997, 1998
North Carolina	*Leandro v. North Carolina*	1997
Ohio	*DeRolph v. Ohio*	1997
Tennessee	*Tennessee Small School Systems v. McWherter*	1993, 1995
Texas	*Edgewood v. Kirby*	1989, 1991, 1992, 1995
Vermont	*Lamoile Co. v. Vermont*	1997
	Brigham v. Vermont	1997
Washington	*Seattle v. Washington*	1978
	Tronson v. Washington	1991
West Virginia	*Pauley v. Kelly*	1979, 1984
	Pauley v. Bailey	File 1994
Wyoming	*Washakie v. Herschler*	1980
	Campbell v. Wyoming	1995

Source: Minorini and Sugarman (1999).

lost and the cases are over. Finally, there is ongoing litigation in twelve states. (Either a case that has been decided at the lower level has not yet been decided at a higher level, or no lower court ruling has been issued as yet.) There has been no litigation in only seven states.

These cases have been decided on a range of legal grounds. Interestingly, the 1971 *Serrano* decision relied primarily on the U.S. Constitution's equal protection clause, a line of argument that made little sense following *Rodriguez*. Later, in the 1976 *Serrano II* decision, the California Supreme Court emphasized the state constitution's equal protection provisions. Other cases relied in whole or in part on state constitutional provisions specific to education. These provisions are often ambiguous and ambitious. The New Jersey constitution (art. 8, sect. 4), for example, calls for a "thorough and efficient system of free public schools."

Plaintiffs in a traditional school finance equity case often argued that a state's method for funding public schools was inequitable because it violated the principle of fiscal neutrality. Alternatively, they might have argued that differences in spending, regardless of their source, violated the state constitution. In either event, plaintiffs would present evidence on disparities in inputs and resources across the state.

A number of more recent cases have taken a very different approach. These cases focus on ensuring that all students in a state have equitable access to adequate educational opportunities (Minorini and Sugarman 1999, 47). The argument here is that at least some districts do not provide students with an adequate education and that it is the state's responsibility to see that they receive the funding to allow them to do so. The remedy might require some districts to spend more (perhaps significantly more) than other districts; if districts with many students from low-income families and families where English is not the first language need to spend more to provide an adequate education, so be it. Clearly, these new adequacy cases are a rebirth of the "needs-based" claims of the late 1960s.

An adequacy claim would place more emphasis on outcomes than would a wealth-neutrality or spending-equalization claim. But there is a second important strand to this adequacy stance. Adequacy typically emphasizes absolute rather than relative standards. In the past, debates over equity focused on comparisons among children and districts and how well they fared relative to each other. Adequacy demands the setting of absolute standards rather than defining equity in terms of the relative performance of school finance systems.

Adequacy began to emerge in the 1976 New Jersey decision in *Robinson v. Cahill,* the 1978 Washington decision in *Seattle v. State of Washington,* and the 1979 West Virginia decision *Pauly v. Kelly.* But the key adequacy decision came in the 1989 Kentucky case *Rose v. Council for Better Education.* In *Rose,* the Kentucky court ruled that not only was the disparity in resources between rich and poor districts unconstitutional, but the entire state education system—financing, governance, and curriculum—was unconstitutional as well. The court stopped short of demanding specific changes, but it did provide specific guidelines for the legislature to follow. Those guidelines defined an adequate education as one that provides students with the opportunity to develop at least the following seven capabilities:

1. Sufficient oral and written communication skills to function in a complex and rapidly changing civilization

2. Sufficient knowledge of economic, social, and political systems to make informed choices

3. Sufficient understanding of governmental processes to understand the issues that affect his or her community, state, and nation

4. Sufficient self-knowledge and knowledge of his or her mental and physical wellness

5. Sufficient grounding in the arts to appreciate his or her cultural and historic heritage

6. Sufficient training or preparation for advanced training in either an academic or vocational field to be able to choose and pursue life work intelligently

7. Sufficient levels of academic or vocational skills to compete favorably with counterparts in surrounding states, in academics, or in the job market

The state responded to the ruling on the finance system by raising the state's foundation grant, adjusting equalization grants and property assessments so that poorer districts received a larger share of state aid, and changing the aid formula so that state funding would be calculated on a per pupil basis. The state also changed governance and curriculum. It reorganized the Department of Education, introduced site-based management councils that make decisions previously made by principals, and established a reward system tied to a performance-based assessment system.

Rose has turned out to be a very influential case. Since 1989, courts in New Hampshire, Alabama, and Massachusetts have declared their education systems to be constitutionally inadequate, relying specifically on the Kentucky court's definition of an adequate education. We return to some of these issues in a later section.

The Impact of Finance Reform

We now turn to a more systematic review of the evidence concerning the impact of finance reform. Since California is the largest state and the first to experience court-ordered finance reform, it is no surprise that much of the work in this area has focused on this state. We therefore begin with a summary of the California experience in the wake of *Serrano*. We then turn to broader empirical studies that use more nationally representative datasets.

The general consensus from the California work is that the shift toward state financing of education has led to a significant decrease in spending on education. Fabio Silva and Jon Sonstelie (1995) try to estimate what proportion of this decline should be attributed to *Serrano* and ensuing policy changes, such as Proposition 13, and how much should be attributed to other factors, such as changes in income and number of students.[7] They begin by estimating the determinants of education spending using data from all states other than California. Using this equation, they show that prior to *Serrano* spending in California was similar to spending in other states during the same period after adjusting for differences in family income and the tax price of an additional dollar of education. They find a very different story in 1989–1990. Spending was significantly lower in California than they would have predicted. They conclude that roughly one-half of the decline in spending in California can be attributed to the *Serrano* decision.

Broader empirical work attempts to go beyond the California experience by looking at data from many states. Robert Manwaring and Steven Sheffrin (1997) use a panel dataset from 1970 through 1990 to examine the role of equalization litigation and reform in determining the level of education funding in a dynamic model. They find that, on average, successful litigation or legislative education reform raises education spending significantly. In a similar paper, Thomas Downes and Mona Shah (1995) show that the stringency of constraints on local discretion determines the effects of reforms on the level and growth of spending. Further, for any particular type of reform, the characteristics of a state's schools determine the direction and magnitude of the postreform changes in spending.

As noted earlier, we have looked at this question ourselves in several papers. In Murray, Evans, and Schwab (1998), we estimate a series of econometric models to explain state-level inequality between 1972 and 1992.[8] We come to three main conclusions. First, court-mandated education-finance reform reduced within-state inequality significantly. Depending on the way we measure inequality, our results imply that reform in the wake of a court decision reduced spending inequality within a state by anywhere from 16 to 38 percent. Second, we find that, as a result of court-ordered reform, spending rose by an estimated 11 percent in the lowest-spending school districts, rose by 7 percent in the median district, and remained roughly constant in the highest-spending districts. Therefore, court-ordered reform reduced inequality by raising spending at the bottom of the distribution while leaving spending at the top unchanged. Third, finance reform caused states to increase spending for education and leave spending in other areas unchanged, and thus by implication states have funded the additional spending on education through higher taxes. As a consequence, the state's share of total spending has risen as a result of court-ordered reform.

For this project, we have extended the basic econometric models from our previous work to include newly released data from the 1997 Census of Governments. Extending this data is important for two reasons. First, as table 11.6 shows, the finance systems of a number of states were overturned by the courts in the early 1990s, and these states were not a part of our earlier work. It is therefore of interest to see how the results hold up to these new court rulings. Second, many states that faced finance reform in the late 1980s and early 1990s had fully implemented their reforms by 1997.

Initially, we examine the impact of finance reform on the within-state distribution of resources in a state. As in our previous work, we utilize state-level observations from the six Censuses of Governments from 1972 through 1997 for our forty-six-state sample. Our basic econometric model is a fixed-effects specification, where we regress a measure of within-state inequality for a state in a particular year on state and year effects plus some measure of finance reform. The state fixed effects capture the permanent differences between states in spending inequality, whereas the year fixed effects capture those factors that affect all states equally (such as recessions) but vary across time. As in our earlier work, we include two indicators to capture the effects of finance reform. The first equals one in the first five years after finance reform. The second variable is also an indicator that equals one six years or more after court-ordered reform. These two indicators allow us to capture any growth in the effect of the finance reform over time. In essence, this fixed-effects specification is a "difference in difference" model where we compare the outcome of interest before and after a state is ordered to reform education finance with the same differences in states that were not subject to reform. This second group of states identifies the secular change in the outcome of interest that would have occurred in the absence of reform.

In table 11.7, we report basic results using various measures of within-state inequality as an outcome. These measures of inequality are based on variation across districts in a state in per pupil current expenditures. Expenditures are weighted by enrollment so that the dispersion measure represents the amount of inequality across students. We use three inequality measures: the Gini coefficient, the Theil index, and the log of the ratio of per pupil expenditures at the ninety-fifth and fifth percentiles of spending in the state. All regressions use data from 276 (forty-six states multiplied by six years) observations.

The results indicate that six years after court-ordered finance reform, there was a statistically significant drop in all measures of inequality. The Gini dropped by an estimated 0.016, the Theil by 0.004, and the ln(95th/5th) by 0.083. These values represent 25, 37, and 19 percent of their sample means, which are very large changes in within-state inequality. Much of the decline in inequality was generated by changes in spending in the lower half of the expenditure distribution. Six years after court-ordered reform, we find, spending in the bottom half of the distribution had increased by a statistically precise fourteen percentage points, whereas there was a six-percentage-point increase at the ninety-fifth percentile.[9]

In Evans, Murray, and Schwab (1997) we try to separate the responses of state and local governments to court mandates. In that work, we find that state revenues increased as a result of reform and that the state share of education spending increased dramatically. In table 11.8, we update this work by including data through 1997, maintaining the same specification that was used in the previous table.

In table 11.8, we find that six years after reform total per pupil revenues from all sources had increased an average of $620, 14 percent of the sample mean value. Nearly all of this money, $578, can be attributed to higher state spending. Six years after court-ordered reform, the state share of revenues had increased by 5.6 percentage points. Overall, our results suggest that court-ordered reform has encouraged a much larger role for states in K–12 education finance.

Hoxby (2001) considers the role of the school finance equalization formulas (and thus indirectly the impact of school finance litigation, since successful litigation often leads to a

TABLE 11.7   *Impact of Education Finance Reform on the Level and Distribution of Education Spending, 1972 to 1997*

| Dependent Variable | Coefficient (Standard Error) | | R-squared |
	One to Five Years After Reform	Six or More Years After Reform	
Gini coefficient	−0.0052	−0.0162	
	(0.0034)	(0.0036)	0.799
Theil index	−0.0017	−0.0040	
	(0.0010)	(0.0010)	0.750
ln(95th/5th percentile)	−0.0485	−0.0826	
	(0.0241)	(0.0262)	0.707
ln(95th percentile)	0.0391	0.0605	
	(0.0281)	(0.0305)	0.924
ln(50th percentile)	0.0754	0.1140	
	(0.0252)	(0.0273)	0.932
ln(5th percentile)	0.0877	0.1430	
	(0.0291)	(0.0377)	0.919

Source: Authors' calculations.
Notes: The data cover forty-six states in six time periods. All models include state and year effects.

change in state aid for education) on the level of spending over time and the productivity of schools. She shows that some equalization formulas may induce a "leveling down" in which greater spending equality is accompanied by lower average spending. Depending on the level of funding specified in the minimum level of funding for a foundation grant, average total spending in a state could rise or fall. If the funding level is set according to the preferences of a district with unusually low tastes for school spending and spending is equalized, then average spending falls. If funding levels are set according to the preferences of districts with high tastes for school inputs, then average spending increases. In a power equalization scheme, if tax rates were set according to the preference of districts

TABLE 11.8   *Impact of Court-Mandated Finance Reform on State, Local, and Total Revenue, 1972 to 1997 (1992 Dollars)*

| Dependent Variable | Mean of Dependent Variable | Coefficient (Standard Error) | | R-squared |
		One to Five Years After Reform	Six or More Years After Reform	
Per pupil total revenues		225	620	
	4,314	(142)	(154)	0.884
Per pupil revenues from state sources		128	578	
	2,192	(102)	(111)	0.856
Per pupil revenues from local sources		97	42	
	2,122	(119)	(129)	0.873
State share of total revenues		0.008	0.056	
	0.52	(0.017)	(0.018)	0.891

Source: Authors' calculations.
Note: All models include state and year effects.

with low demand for education, school spending would decrease under the equalization plan.

Hoxby (2001) empirically investigates the influence of types of school finance formulas on the growth in district spending between 1972 and 1992. To show the effect of the schemes on mean state spending, she compares the predicted average spending and measures of inequality under her econometric model to what mean spending would have been if no equalization program had been in place. Her results suggest that in some states a highly equalizing finance formula has been associated with leveling down. For example, in California mean per pupil spending was 15 percent lower under the state's equalization scheme than it would have been if no school finance equalization had been in effect. Hoxby finds, however, that in practice leveling up occurs because most states impose less dramatic equalization schemes.

OTHER MEASURES OF INEQUALITY IN EDUCATION

To this point, we have focused on the distribution of education revenues and spending. But as we argued at the beginning of this chapter, a focus on dollars is in some ways limited. The debate over inequality in education is also a debate over the distribution of the education resources that those dollars in fact purchase. The link between dollars and education resources might differ from district to district. For example, inner-city school districts might have to pay higher salaries to attract well-qualified teachers. Some districts might have inefficiently large bureaucracies.

In this section, we shift gears and look at several measures of education resources other than dollars. Specifically, we have collected five different measures of the school environment: school safety, quality of physical capital, teacher quality, advanced placement courses, and computer use. We report data from several nationally representative surveys.[10] In many cases we have information over time, but in some cases we have only information at a point in time.

Violence in U.S. Schools, 1996

Tragic events such as the Columbine High School shootings in Littleton, Colorado, in 1999 have brought to the forefront the problem of violence in schools. Violence in schools is more prevalent in communities with particular characteristics, such as higher fractions of poor and minority students. In table 11.9, we show the fraction of schools reporting serious violent incidents and the number of these violent incidents per one thousand students.[11] The data are drawn from the National Center for Education Statistics (NCES) survey *Principal/School Disciplinarian Survey on School Violence* (1997b), and the table reports data from the 1996 to 1997 school year.

As table 11.9 shows, schools with the largest fraction of minority students were two and a half times more likely to report a violent incident and had five times the incidence rate as schools with the lowest fraction minority. The differences based on the fraction of students receiving free or reduced-price lunches show similar patterns, though the differences are smaller. Schools with a poverty rate above 75 percent were 25 percent more likely to have a violent incident during the school year compared with schools with a poverty rate below 20 percent. The incidence rate in the schools with the highest poverty rates was two and a half times that in schools with the lowest poverty rates.

TABLE 11.9   *Reported Incidents of Serious Violent Criminal Incidents in Public Schools, 1996 to 1997*

	Schools Reporting Serious Violent Incidents	Incidents Per 1,000 Students
By minority enrollment of school		
0 to 5 percent	5.8%	0.2
5 to 19 percent	10.9	0.4
20 to 49 percent	11.1	0.5
>50 percent	14.7	1.0
By percentage of students participating in the free or reduced-price lunch program		
0 to 20 percent	8.6	0.3
21 to 34 percent	11.7	0.6
35 to 49 percent	11.6	0.5
50 to 75 percent	8.9	0.7
75 to 100 percent	10.2	0.8

Source: U.S. Department of Education (1997b).
Note: Serious violent crimes include murder, rape or other type of sexual battery, suicide, physical attack or fight with a weapon, or robbery.

The Quality of Physical Capital in U.S. Schools, 1998

Over the past decade, the physical condition of public schools has received considerable attention. Arguably the single most dramatic feature of Kozol's (1991) indictment of public school systems was his vivid description of the dilapidated condition of urban and high-poverty schools compared with pristine suburban, low-poverty schools. Many of the lawsuits challenging school funding, such as *Roosevelt Elementary School No. 66 v. Bishop,* have drawn attention to the poor conditions of school facilities. In table 11.10, we report selected characteristics of the quality of school facilities (overcrowding, age and adequacy of the physical structure) by the school's poverty status (as defined by the percentage of students eligible for the free or reduced-price lunch program in 1999). The data are from the NCES fast-response survey *Conditions of America's Public School Facilities: 1999* (1999).

As table 11.10 shows, in the highest-poverty schools—those where more than 70 percent of the students are eligible for the free and reduced-price lunch program—overcrowding is particularly severe. Twelve percent of these schools reported being more than 25 percent over capacity compared with 8 percent of low-poverty schools. Similarly, 21 percent of the highest-poverty schools were located in buildings that were more than thirty-five years old compared with 15 percent of the low-poverty schools. Principals in high-poverty schools were far more likely to report problems with the roof, plumbing, or heating/AC system than were principals in low-poverty schools. Thus, overall the schools in the highest-poverty settings tend to have the worst physical capital.

The Quality of Teachers in U.S. Schools, 1993

Table 11.11 looks at a cross-section of schools from the 1993–1994 Schools and Staffing Survey (SASS) to see how the characteristics of newly hired teachers differ across schools.[12] SASS is a periodic survey conducted by the NCES that collects data from a nationally

TABLE 11.10   *Characteristics of the Capital Quality of U.S. Public Schools, 1999*

	Students Eligible for the Free or Reduced-Price Lunch Program			
Percentage of Schools That Are:	Fewer than 20 Percent	20 to 39 Percent	40 to 69 Percent	More than 70 Percent
6 to 25 percent over capacity	16%	13%	16%	12%
More than 25 percent over capacity	6	8	7	12
More than thirty-five years old	11	15	11	21
Have less than adequate:				
Roofs	18	21	22	32
Plumbing	23	23	23	32
Heating, ventilation/AC	28	26	29	35

Source: U.S. Department of Education (1999).

representative sample of public and private schools on the characteristics and views of school personnel.[13]

In this analysis, we focus on new teachers, defined as those with two years of experience or less. Table 11.11 shows that while average base year salaries vary little between schools with different concentrations of minority students (top panel) or poor students (bottom panel), the qualifications and job satisfaction of new teachers across these schools vary greatly.[14] For example, in 1993–1994 new teachers in schools where 90 percent or more of the students were minority were less likely to be certified in their primary teaching field than new teachers in schools that had 10 percent or fewer minority students. When asked whether they would teach again if given the chance to return to college, only 60.7 percent answered in the affirmative among new teachers in primarily minority schools, compared with 81.3 percent in primarily white schools. Similarly, teachers in primarily minority schools were more than five times as likely to state that they "definitely plan to leave teaching as soon as possible" when asked how long they expected to teach.

Differences in the qualifications of new teachers are even more striking when comparing across schools with different proportions of students in poverty. New teachers in the highest-poverty schools (defined as schools where more than 90 percent of the students qualify for free or reduced-price lunch) were 15 percent less likely to be certified and 36 percent less likely to hold an advanced degree than new teachers in low-poverty schools. The fraction of students in poverty in a school does not appear, however, to have as large an impact on the job satisfaction of new teachers as does the fraction of minority students in the school. While new teachers in the highest-poverty schools were more likely to state that they planned to leave teaching as soon as possible, or that they regretted the decision to become a teacher, the differences across types of schools are small and statistically insignificant.

The Quality of School Curricula, 1971 to 1991

Table 11.12 uses three large longitudinal surveys conducted by the NCES to examine the availability of advanced placement (AP) courses.[15] The datasets we use are the National Longitudinal Survey of 1972 (U.S. Department of Education 1972), the 1982 follow-up to the NCES survey High School and Beyond (HS&B)(U.S. Department of Education 1995),

TABLE 11.11   *Characteristics of Newly Hired Teachers, by Race and Income Composition of School, 1993 to 1994*

Teacher Characteristics	All	Percentage of Students Who Are Black			
		0 to 10 percent	10 to 50 percent	50 to 90 percent	More than 90 percent
Number of cases	3,643	2,656	696	181	110
Mean years of experience	1.48	1.48	1.49	1.49	1.51
Certified in primary teaching field	91.4%	93.8%	88.8%	87.3%	86.8%
Have bachelor's degree or higher	99.5	99.4	99.7	99.8	99.7
Have master's degree or higher	16.7	15.6	15.1	26.2	28.4
Teach full-time	86.0	83.6	88.1	94.7	94.2
Say they would teach again	77.3	81.3	73.1	66.3	60.7
Plan to exit teaching as soon as possible	2.5	1.6	2.2	8.2	9.1
Plan to exit teaching at first opportunity	14.3	13.1	12.9	27.2	21.7
Mean academic base year salary	$23,083	$22,741	$23,509	$23,943	$24,209
		Percentage of Students Who Qualify for Free or Reduced-Price Lunch Program			
Number of cases	3,643	834	1,878	729	202
Mean years of experience	—	1.47	1.47	1.49	1.58
Certified in primary teaching field	—	95.6%	93.1%	86.7%	80.9%
Have bachelor's degree or higher	—	99.3	99.6	99.5	99.6
Have master's degree or higher	—	22.9	14.3	16.3	14.7
Teach full-time	—	82.6	84.4	91.1	90.5
Say they would teach again	—	79.9	78.1	74.5	72.5
Plan to exit teaching as soon as possible	—	1.6	1.5	5.0	3.9
Plan to exit teaching at first opportunity	—	13.1	13.5	17.8	11.2
Mean academic base year salary	—	$24,282	$22,331	$23,232	$24,268

Source: Authors' calculations from U.S. Department of Education (1994).
Note: SASS teacher weights are used in all cases. We define "newly hired teachers" as teachers with two or fewer years of experience.

and the 1992 National Educational Longitudinal Survey (NELS)(U.S. Department of Education 1992).

The entries in table 11.12 represent the fraction of schools that offer one or more advanced placement courses.[16] Although significant gains were made among all schools in AP offerings, schools with majority black and majority disadvantaged student populations were almost always much less likely to offer these courses than largely nonblack or nonpoor schools. For example, in 1972 students in schools where at least 90 percent of the students were black were 30 percent less likely to have the opportunity to take AP courses than students in schools where less than 10 percent of the students were black. By 1990, however, these schools had made large strides in course offerings, and mostly black schools were about as likely to have AP courses as mostly nonblack schools. Stark differences remained,

TABLE 11.12   *U.S. Schools Offering Advanced Placement Courses, by Race and Income Composition of School, 1972, 1982, 1992*

Category	High School Class of		
	1972	1982	1992
All schools	31.0%	48.3%	76.4%
By percentage black			
0 to 10 percent	30.0	45.6	72.8
10 to 50 percent	36.0	57.6	84.0
50 to 90 percent	23.9	50.0	77.9
90 to 100 percent	21.4	41.9	76.7
By percentage qualified for free or reduced-price lunch			
0 to 10 percent	38.9	52.0	84.2
10 to 50 percent	20.6	46.0	74.2
50 to 90 percent	8.3	34.4	69.0
90 to 100 percent	0.0	26.7	38.5

Source: Authors' calculations from U.S. Department of Education (1972–1982–1992).
Notes: Calculations apply only to public high schools participating in these three surveys. Schools were counted as having an AP program if they offered one or more advanced placement courses.

however, between rich and poor schools in 1990. As table 11.12 shows, in 1990, 39 percent of the schools where at least 90 percent of the students were eligible for free or reduced-price lunch offered AP courses; in contrast, 84 percent of the schools where no more than 10 percent of the students were poor offered such classes.

The Distribution of Internet Access and Computer Use, 1984 to 2000

Computers have become an essential part of K–12 education. The drop in computer prices and the rise of the Internet have led schools to reevaluate computer use in the classroom. Almost all education groups recognize the important role that technology will play in the future economy, yet most groups are still struggling with how best to integrate computers into the classroom. Even with these uncertainties, schools and the federal government have invested considerable resources to buy computers and wire classrooms for Internet access.

Not surprisingly, computers became common first in wealthier districts. This disparity in computer access in all segments of society is known as the digital divide, and it is of particular concern in education. In this section, we provide some evidence on differences in computer resources across schools with different characteristics. We draw on a series of recent NCES annual surveys on computer equipment and Internet access in U.S. public schools.

In table 11.13, we report the fraction of schools with Internet access. In the first row of that table, we find that although only one-third of schools had some Internet access in 1994, that number had risen to 98 percent by 2000. Given the high fraction of schools with access to the Internet, it should come as no surprise that there is little variation in access to the Internet across schools with different characteristics. For example, schools with a high fraction of minority students or a high fraction of students receiving free or reduced-price lunch still had Internet access rates in excess of 94 percent in 2000.

TABLE 11.13   *Schools with Internet Access, 1994 to 2000*

	1994	1995	1996	1997	1998	1999	2000
All schools	35%	50%	65%	78%	89%	95%	98%
By percentage minority enrollment							
(1) 0 to 6 percent	38	52	65	84	91	95	98
(2) 6 to 20 percent	38	58	72	87	93	97	100
(3) 21 to 49 percent	38	55	65	73	91	96	98
(4) 50 to 100 percent	27	39	56	63	82	92	96
Difference (1) − (4)	11	13	9	21	9	3	2
By percentage students eligible for free or reduced-price lunch							
(1) 0 to 35 percent	39	60	74	86	92	95	99
(2) 35 to 49 percent	36	48	59	81	93	98	99
(3) 50 to 74 percent	31	41	53	71	88	96	97
(4) 75 to 100 percent	20	31	53	62	79	89	94
Difference (1) − (4)	19	29	21	24	13	6	5

Source: U.S. Department of Education (2001b).

In table 11.14, we report the fraction of *classrooms* wired for the Internet by the same school characteristics as in table 11.13. There is good news and bad news in this table. First the good news: the fraction of classrooms with Internet access has increased dramatically in all schools. In schools where more than 75 percent of students receive free or reduced-price lunch, the fraction of classrooms wired for the Internet had increased to 60 percent by 2000. Now the bad news: this number is 22 percent below the rate for students with a smaller fraction of students receiving reduced-price lunches. The NCES document that reports these statistics notes a number of other quality differences between schools with different socioeconomic characteristics, including differences in the speed of the Internet connection, the training of the teachers, and the number of computers.

TABLE 11.14   *Classrooms with Internet Access, 1994 to 2000*

	1994	1995	1996	1997	1998	1999	2000
All schools	3%	8%	14%	27%	51%	64%	77%
By percentage minority enrollment							
(1) 0 to 6 percent	4	9	18	37	57	74	85
(2) 6 to 20 percent	4	10	18	35	59	78	83
(3) 21 to 49 percent	4	9	12	22	52	64	79
(4) 50 to 100 percent	2	3	5	13	37	43	64
Difference (1) − (4)	2	6	13	24	20	31	21
By percentage students eligible for free or reduced-price lunch							
(1) 0 to 35 percent	3	9	17	33	57	73	82
(2) 35 to 49 percent	2	6	12	33	60	69	81
(3) 50 to 74 percent	4	6	11	20	60	69	81
(4) 75 to 100 percent	2	3	5	14	38	38	60
Difference (1) − (4)	1	6	12	19	19	35	22

Source: U.S. Department of Education (2001b).

The rapid pace at which schools and classrooms have become wired has been aided in part by the federal E-rate program. Created as part of the Telecommunications Act of 1996, this program provides subsidies for low-income schools and certain libraries to pay for Internet access. The program is funded by a tax on long-distance service, and schools may use the proceeds to pay for investments in Internet and communications technology. The E-rate program spends up to $2.25 billion per year; to put this in perspective, note that other school expenditures on hardware, software, and training average roughly $4 billion annually.

The E-rate program subsidizes school spending by 20 to 90 percent, depending on school characteristics. For example, schools with 75 to 100 percent students receiving reduced-price or free lunch were subsidized at a 90 percent rate, whereas urban schools with less than a 1 percent free or reduced-price lunch population received the 20 percent subsidy. Using data for California schools, Austan Goolsbee and Jonathan Guryan (2002) examine the impact of the E-rate program on the speed with which schools obtain Internet access. They estimate that by 2000 there were 6 percent more schools with Internet access than there would have been without the E-rate program. They argue that this is equivalent to accelerating Internet access by about four years.

The NCES data provide information on the *availability* of computers in schools; they do not, however, tell us anything about actual usage. Fortunately, data on computer use has been collected in the October School Enrollment Supplement of the Current Population Survey (CPS). The CPS is a monthly survey of approximately fifty thousand households conducted by the Census Bureau. Its primary purpose is to collect information on the size and characteristics of the labor force. Each October the CPS administers the school enroll-ment supplement that collects educational attainment and enrollment information for both adults and children in the household. In 1984, 1987, 1993, and 1997, this supplement also included questions about computer use at home, school, and work.[17]

Table 11.15 shows the fraction of students in each category who use a computer in school (among students for whom the computer use information was not missing). As with tables 11.13 and 11.14, the numbers in table 11.15 show that although computer use in school has increased considerably for all groups, significant differences remain. In 1984 usage of computers by white, non-Hispanic students was eighteen percentage points higher than for blacks and almost 20 percent higher than for Hispanics. Over the next thirteen years, computer use in school by these minority groups has more than tripled, with the difference in use rates being cut in half for blacks, but showing little progress for Hispanics. Looking at children by household income, we see again sharp increases in use among all students. The raw difference in use between children from high- and low-income house-holds was cut in half over the 1984 to 1997 period.

CONCLUSION

In this chapter, we have documented the changing level and distribution of education spend-ing and revenues over the past thirty years. Over time the level of spending on K–12 education has increased considerably, and overall inequality in spending has declined dramat-ically. Much of the decline in spending inequality can be traced to various state policies. States have historically redistributed education resources from richer to poorer commu-nities, but these redistributive policies have been more aggressive in recent years. In some cases redistributive policies were put into place only after states were instructed by courts to reform their education-finance rules. Even with these changes in state school finance

TABLE 11.15   *K–12 Students Who Use a Computer in School*

Category	1984	1987	1993	1997
By race				
(1) White, non-Hispanic	36.20%	56.27%	70.58%	80.91%
(2) Black, non-Hispanic	18.18	39.03	56.29	71.52
(3) Other race, non-Hispanic	31.67	51.97	66.17	73.75
(4) Hispanic	19.73	41.66	56.72	66.59
Difference (1) − (2)	18.02	17.24	14.29	9.39
Difference (1) − (4)	16.47	14.61	13.86	14.32
By incomes of households with children				
(1) Top third	39.51	58.62	71.10	81.02
(2) Middle third	33.31	54.89	67.90	79.38
(3) Bottom third	24.14	45.73	62.27	72.49
Difference (1) − (3)	15.37	12.89	8.83	8.53
By highest education within household				
(1) College degree	42.04	59.90	72.87	81.54
(2) High school degree	31.35	51.90	66.11	77.64
(3) Less than High school degree	20.01	38.53	56.57	63.86
Difference (1) − (3)	22.03	21.37	16.30	17.68

Source: Authors' calculations from Current Population Surveys (1984–1987–1993–1997).

rules, much of the variation in school spending is between states, not within states over time. In recent years some states that historically spent relatively little on K–12 education have redirected more resources to schools, helping to reduce between-state inequalities.

We also investigated changes in the distribution of specific resources in schools: safety, the quality of physical capital, teacher quality, curriculum quality, and computer use. Although dollars have become much more equal across districts over time, many nonmonetary inputs into the education process are not distributed as equally. Schools serving larger percentages of poor or minority students are more likely to report a violent incident, lower-quality physical structures, less-experienced teachers, fewer AP course offerings, and lesser levels of Internet connection. However, for the two measures of school environment for which we have consistent data over time, curriculum quality and Internet access, we find that differences by the poverty and minority status of schools have also declined.

Many of the changes that have encouraged higher state support for K–12 education were instituted during the 1990s—a period of rapid economic growth and flush state budgets. In recent years the economic slowdown has been particularly hard on state budgets. A recent report by the National Governors' Association notes that since state 2002 budgets were enacted, forty states have had to fight budget shortfalls totaling $40 billion— about 4 percent of aggregate state budgets. Because state budget growth tends to lag recessions, the association is predicting more lean years ahead. It will be interesting to see whether these budget problems will alter the states' role in education finance.

APPENDIX A

Some analysts argue that commonly used general price indices, such as the CPI or the gross domestic product (GDP) deflator, understate the rising costs of educational inputs. This understatement occurs because the indices do not take into account the fact that education and other service sectors must raise salaries to compete successfully with other sectors for workers. But education and other labor-intensive sectors, as William Baumol (1993) explains, do not benefit as much as the rest of the economy from technological change. Because the CPI understates the rise in costs, adjusting spending by the CPI leads to an overestimate of the growth of real resources. The resulting error can be very large. Richard Rothstein and Karen Miles (1995), for example, have developed an index that measures inflation in the service sectors in their study of the growth of school spending. They find that real education spending defined according to their measure rose roughly 40 percent less than real expenditures based on the CPI.

Although we are sympathetic to these concerns, given the goals of this chapter, we do not think the limitations should substantively change our research methodology. The goal here is to find the appropriate deflator to measure the growth of inputs. The Baumol argument therefore seems to be irrelevant here. The following example makes this point clear. Compare two sectors of the economy, A and B. Both produce output with a single input, labor. Suppose the wage rate doubles and the labor force remains unchanged in both sectors. Labor productivity (and therefore total factor productivity, since labor is the only input) doubles in A but is unchanged in B. As a consequence, output doubles in A but remains constant in B. The cost index doubles in both industries. The appropriate index to measure output is halved in A and remains constant in B, but this is irrelevant if we are trying to measure inputs.

We would agree, however, that the CPI is far from the perfect measure. A better measure would look specifically at input prices in education. Labor costs represent roughly 55 percent of the total cost of education, and a better measure would incorporate changes in the necessary wage to attract "constant-quality" teachers. This is a difficult problem to tackle. There have been profound changes in the market for teachers. The vast majority of K–12 teachers are women, and labor market opportunities for women have expanded dramatically over the last forty years. As a consequence, as we have found elsewhere (Corcoran, Evans, and Schwab 2002), the most capable women are now far less likely to enter teaching; almost certainly, schools will have to offer significantly higher wages to attract teachers of the same quality as in the past.

APPENDIX B

Combining data from more than sixteen thousand school districts from fifty states over a twenty-five-year time period required a significant amount of editing in order to obtain consistent measures of school resources. In this section, we define the sample used in our study. The data edits are described in detail in our previous papers and are only briefly outlined here.

Given the differences in the costs of operating primary and secondary schools, we have limited our analysis to unified school districts, which are districts that provide K–12 education. More than 90 percent of all public school students are enrolled in a unified school district.[18] Similarly, only regular operating districts are included in the sample.

School districts raise part of the money they spend by levying their own taxes. They rely heavily on the local property tax but also generate revenues from other sources such as income and sales taxes and fees. In addition, virtually all districts receive at least some funds from the state government and the federal government. Because the treatment of those funds in the Census of Governments has changed over time, we do not try to separate federal and state funds. Thus, what we call money from the states is actually the sum of money from the state and the federal government. It is unlikely that this decision seriously distorts our results since, as we argued earlier, the federal government's contribution to public education has always been small.

In analyzing per pupil revenue data at the district level, we detected some extremely large and small values. These values could be valid, but it is more likely that some districts incorrectly reported enrollments or revenues.[19] Finally, we deleted all districts in some states. We dropped data from Montana and Vermont from the sample because these states have virtually no unified districts.[20] We deleted data from Hawaii because it has a state-based system and from the District of Columbia because it is the sole system in the jurisdiction. Data for Alaska were also dropped. The final sample has data for over ten thousand districts from forty-six states for six years. In 1997 these districts represented 91 percent of the pupils in the United States.

APPENDIX C

We use three indices to adjust for differences in the cost of real education resources: the Barro (1992) index, the Chambers (1995) Teachers' Cost Index (TCI), and the McMahon and Chang (1991) Cost of Living (COL) index. All three have developed separate cost indices for urban and non-urban districts in each state; in some states, separate indices for the largest urban areas are also available. The Barro measure is an index of average teacher salaries that adjusts for teachers' education level and experience. Because a given district can influence teachers' wages by hiring only candidates with graduate degrees, this measure would overstate the adjustment necessary for purchasing power parity among districts. The TCI measure adjusts for regional variations in the cost of living and amenities. This measure removes the impact of within-state differences by adjusting for district-level characteristics that, unlike average teachers' educational attainment or tenure, are not subject to district control. Finally, the McMahon and Chang index is a geographic index that controls only for the differences in housing values, income, and population growth across districts; this index yields the smallest inflation adjustment.[21]

Table 11A.1 summarizes our attempts to adjust for cost differences between metropolitan and nonmetropolitan school districts in 1992. The first column gives the unadjusted estimates and the remaining columns give the estimates using the Barro, TCI, and COL indices. After controlling for the higher costs associated with urban school districts, we find a noticeable decline in our measures of inequality. For example, the 95-to-5 ratio and the coefficient of variation decrease between 10 to 20 percent, respectively; the Theil index falls by 16 percent (COL) to 37 percent (Barro).

The second panel of table 11A.1 breaks revenue inequality into inequality due to differences in revenue within states and inequality due to differences across states, and thus it parallels our decomposition of expenditure inequality in table 11.1. The cost-of-living adjustments change our view of the magnitude of the differences in revenue between states, but within-state Theils do not change appreciably. The cost-adjusted between-state Theils are 20 to 40 percent lower than the unadjusted Theils. Once we account for differences in costs, we find that differences in revenue between states account for 53 to 60 percent of the total disparity in per pupil resources in the United States; when we do not adjust for cost differences, between-state inequality accounts for 66 percent of total inequality.[22]

TABLE 11A.1   *Summary of Resources Adjusted for Cost-of-Living Differences, 1992*

		Cost-of-Living Adjustment		
	Unadjusted	Barro Index	Chambers (1995) TCI	McMahon and Chang (1991) COL Index
Measures of inequality				
95-to-5 ratio	2.47	2.07	2.08	2.19
Theil index	37.9	26.4	29.2	32.4
Coefficient of variation	30.1	24.4	25.7	27.1
Theil index decomposition				
Within states	12.9	12.2	12.2	12.9
Between states	25.0	14.2	17.0	19.5
National	37.9	26.4	29.2	32.4

Source: Authors' compilation.

The authors wish to thank their colleagues in the Department of Economics and the Maryland Population Research Center for their help. The opinions expressed are solely the authors' and do not represent those of RAND or any of its sponsors.

NOTES

1. The rise in spending over the past thirty years continues a trend established late in the nineteenth century. Eric Hanushek and Steven Rivkin (1997) examine the growth in school spending over the last one hundred years and show that real expenditures per student (in 1990 dollars) quintupled every fifty years, from $164 in 1890 to $772 in 1940, to $4,622 in 1990.

2. Table 11.2 should be interpreted cautiously because of the possibility that it reflects, in part, a "reversion to the mean." That is, if part of education spending is random, and random events are uncorrelated over time, then on average large increases in spending will follow low spending.

3. We should note that these estimates use district-level measures of teachers and students and abstract from any within-district and within-school variation in class assignment.

4. In 1992 the standard deviation of the fraction black, Hispanic, in poverty, and owner-occupied homes across districts in our sample was 0.12, 0.11, 0.08, and 0.10, respectively.

5. Independent districts are not part of a municipality or county government.

6. This section draws heavily from Minorini and Sugarman (1999).

7. Proposition 13 was an amendment to the California state constitution that limited property tax rates and property valuations, thereby limiting local governments' access to the main source of funding for education (see Fischel 1989, 1996).

8. Reform states in our previous econometric work include: Arkansas, California, Connecticut, Kansas, Kentucky, Texas, Wisconsin, Washington, West Virginia, and Wyoming. This list differs from Minorini and Sugarman (1999) because we do not consider the reforms after 1989 that would not have affected spending in the 1991–1992 school year, the last year in which we have complete data; we include Kansas and Wisconsin; and we exclude Montana because that state has no unified K–12 districts.

9. The results for the one- to five-year dummy variable suggest that the impact of court-ordered finance reform on spending is larger in the long run than in the short run. For example, table 11.7 shows that spending at the fifth percentile of the distribution rises by an estimated 5 percent in the first five years after successful litigation and 9 percent in the sixth year and later.

10. In some cases we summarize the work of other researchers. As a result, we cannot always use consistent definitions. So, for example, at times in this section we implicitly define a poor school district as one in which more than 75 percent of the students are eligible for free or reduced-price lunch; at other times we implicitly define a poor school district as one in which more than 90 percent of the students are eligible for free or reduced-price lunch.

11. Violent incidents are defined as murder, rape or other type of sexual battery, suicide, physical attack or fight with a weapon, and robbery.

12. The SASS provided sample weights to account for differences in teachers' sampling probabilities and survey nonresponse. We use the SASS final teacher weights in computing all statistics in table 11.

13. Many of the same survey questions have been used in each cross-sectional cycle of the survey, allowing researchers to investigate trends over time. The questionnaires for each round of SASS are available online and can be downloaded from the "Questionnaires and Items" page. When data from the 2000 survey are released, it will be possible to update these tables.

14. Base year salaries are not adjusted for cost-of-living differences across school districts.

15. Two surveys—the National Longitudinal Study of the High School Class of 1972 (NLS-72) and High School and Beyond (HS&B)—indicate the poverty status of schools using the percentage of students qualifying for free lunch, while the NELS uses percentage "disadvantaged."

16. Our calculations from these surveys of the overall fraction of schools offering AP courses are much larger (in all years) than those reported by the College Board, the organization that administers AP exams. Although these surveys specifically asked whether the school offered "College Board advanced placement courses," the responses may reflect some confusion among survey respondents as to what the survey meant by "advanced placement course." To the extent that survey respondents' definitions of advanced placement courses were consistent across schools and across time, our calculations should be representative of differences in AP offerings across schools. However, these numbers should be interpreted with appropriate caution.

    The NLS-72 and HS&B asked whether the school offered College Board AP courses; the NELS asked what fraction of the student body took AP courses and the number of twelfth-graders in AP courses. For the NELS, we assumed the school offered AP if either of these numbers was not zero. The NLS-72 sample consists of the public high schools that participated in the base year (1972) administrator survey. The HS&B sample consists of the public high schools that participated in the first follow-up (1982). The NELS sample consists of the public high schools that participated in the first follow-up (1990).

17. For this chapter, we use the data about computer use at school. Our sample includes children age five to eighteen who attend first through twelfth grade. Computer use at school is based on the following question asked of the adult respondent for each child in the household: "Does ——— directly use a computer at school?" One limitation of the survey is that parents are responding for their children, and there may be substantial measurement error in the outcome of interest. We construct means of computer use at school for all students and subgroups of students based on race, income, and parents' education. The race classifications are based on the students' characteristics; however, household income, the educational attainment of the most educated member of the household, and community categories are based on household-level data. The income classifications are constructed for each year by dividing all households in the sample into three income groups. Each group contains roughly one-third of the households. Each child within a household was assigned to that income group.

18. This definition of a unified district encompasses districts that offer kindergarten, prekindergarten, and some vocational programs in addition to elementary and secondary education.

19. For example, because of differences in the way districts count regional vocational high school students, some Pennsylvania districts underreport enrollments (McLoone, Golladay, and Sonnenberg 1979, 165).

20. There are some unified districts in Vermont, although most districts are composed entirely of either elementary or secondary grades. In addition, the Vermont communities bordering New Hampshire send some of their public school students to Vermont private schools.

21. Although these cost indices are the best available, it is not clear that they successfully capture the full difference in the costs of education across districts. Ideally, a cost index would account for the difference in wages that a central-city school district would have to offer to attract teachers with the same qualifica-

tions, ability, and training that wealthy suburban districts attract. We suspect that these indices do not capture those differences and that it is therefore likely that they overstate the resources available to central-city students. The available indices look at differences in the cost of inputs but do not address variation in student needs; see Duncombe, Ruggiero, and Yinger (1996) for an important discussion of this issue.

22. We were also able to reestimate our decomposition using the individual-district TCI available from the NCES. The results of that decomposition are very similar to the estimates in table 11A.1: 57 percent of the overall inequality as measured by the Theil index is due to differences in resources between states.

REFERENCES

Barro, Steven M. 1992. *Cost-of-Education Differentials Across the States.* Washington, D.C.: SMB Economic Research.

Baumol, William J. 1993. "Social Wants and Dismal Science: The Curious Case of the Climbing Costs of Health and Teaching." Working paper RR 93-20. New York: New York University, C. V. Starr Center for Applied Economics.

Berne, Robert, and Leanna Stiefel. 1984. *The Measurement of Equity in School Finance: Conceptual, Methodological, and Empirical Dimensions.* Baltimore: Johns Hopkins University Press.

Boozer, Michael A., Alan B. Krueger, and Shari Wolkon. 1992. "Race and School Quality Since *Brown v. Board of Education.*" *Brookings Papers on Economic Activity—Microeconomics* (1): 269–326.

Chambers, Jay G. 1995. "Public School Teacher Cost Differences Across the United States: Introduction to a Teacher Cost Index (TCI)." In *Developments in School Finance, 1995,* edited by Willliam J. Fowler Jr. Washington: U.S. Department of Education, National Center for Education Statistics.

Coons, John E., William H. Clune, and Stephen D. Sugarman. 1970. *Private Wealth and Public Education.* Cambridge, Mass.: Harvard University Press.

Corcoran, Sean, William N. Evans, and Robert Schwab. 2002. "Changing Labor Market Opportunities for Women and the Quality of Teachers 1957 to 1992." Working paper 9180. Cambridge, Mass.: National Bureau of Economic Research.

Downes, Thomas A., and Mona P. Shah. 1995. "The Effect of School Finance Reforms on the Level and Growth of Per Pupil Expenditures." Unpublished paper. Northwestern University, Evanston, Ill.

Duncombe, William, John Ruggiero, and John Yinger. 1996. "Alternative Approaches to Measuring the Cost of Education." In *Holding Schools Accountable: Performance-Based Reform in Education,* edited by Helen F. Ladd. Washington, D.C.: Brookings Institution.

Evans, William N., Sheila E. Murray, and Robert M. Schwab. 1997. "School Houses, Court Houses, and State Houses After *Serrano.*" *Journal of Policy Analysis and Management* 16(1): 10–31.

Fischel, William A. 1989. "Did *Serrano* Cause Proposition 13?" *National Tax Journal* 42(4): 465–74.

———. 1996. "How *Serrano* Caused Proposition 13." *Journal of Law and Politics* 12(4): 607–36.

Goolsbee, Austan, and Jonathan Guryan. 2002. "The Impact of Internet Subsidies on Public Schools." Working paper 9090. Cambridge, Mass.: National Bureau of Economic Research.

Hanushek, Eric A., and Steven G. Rivkin. 1997. "Understanding the Twentieth-Century Growth in U.S. School Spending." *Journal of Human Resources* 32(1): 35–68.

Harris, Amy Rehder. 1999. "Data Chapter: The Construction of a National School District Panel." Unpublished paper, University of Maryland, College Park (November). Available at: www.bsos.umd.edu/econ/evans/wkpap.htm.

Harris, Amy, William N. Evans, and Robert M. Schwab. 2001. "Public Education Finance in an Aging America." *Journal of Public Economics* 81(3): 449–72.

Hoxby, Caroline M. 2001. "All School Finance Equalizations Are Not Created Equal." *Quarterly Journal of Economics* 116(4): 1149–1525.

Kozol, Jonathan. 1991. *Savage Inequalities: Children in America's Schools.* New York: Crown.

Manwaring, Robert L., and Steven M. Sheffrin. 1997. "Litigation, School Finance Reform, and Aggregate Educational Spending." *International Tax and Public Finance* 4(2): 107–27.

McLoone, Eugene P., Mary A. Golladay, and William Sonnenberg. 1979. *Public School Finance: Profiles of the States.* 1979 ed. Washington: U.S. Department of Education, National Center for Education Statistics.

McMahon, Walter W., and Shao-Chung Chang. 1991. *Geographical Cost-of-Living Differences: Interstate and Intrastate, Update 1991.* MacArthur/Spencer Working paper series 20. Normal: Illinois State University, Center for the Study of Educational Finance.

Minorini, Paul, and Stephen Sugarman. 1999. "School Finance Litigation in the Name of Educational Equity: Its Evolution, Impact, and Future." In *Equity and Adequacy in School Finance,* edited by Helen Ladd and Rosemary Chalk. Washington, D.C.: National Academy Press.

Murray, Sheila E., William N. Evans, and Robert M. Schwab. 1998. "Education-Finance Reform and the Distribution of Education Resources." *American Economic Review* 88(4): 789–812.

Rothstein, Richard, and Karen Hawley Miles. 1995. *Where's the Money Gone? Changes in the Level and Composition of Education Spending.* Washington, D.C.: Economic Policy Institute.

Silva, Fabio, and Jon Sonstelie. 1995. "Did *Serrano* Cause a Decline in School Spending?" *National Tax Journal* 48(2): 199–215.

U.S. Department of Commerce. U.S. Census Bureau. 1970. *1970 Census of Population and Housing Special Fifth-Count Tallies.* Ann Arbor: University of Michigan, Interuniversity Consortium for Political and Social Research.

———. 1972–1977–1982–1987–1992–1997. *Census of Government School System Finance (F33).* Ann Arbor: University of Michigan, ICPSR.

———. 1980. *1980 Census of Population and Housing Summary Tape File 3F.* Ann Arbor: University of Michigan, ICPSR.

———. 1984–1987–1993–1997. *October School Enrollment Supplement of the Current Population Survey.* Washington: U.S. Government Printing Office for U.S. Census Bureau. Available at: www.census.gov.

U.S. Department of Education. National Center for Education Statistics. 1972. *National Longitudinal Survey of 1972.* Washington: U.S. Government Printing Office. Available at: www.ed.gov.

———. 1990a. *1990 Census School District Special Tabulation, School District Data Book.* Data file. Available at http://nces.ed.gov/surveys/sdds/c1990d.asp.

———. 1990b. *Common Core of Data, 1989, School District Data Book.* Washington: U.S. Government Printing Office. Available at: www.ed.gov.

———. 1992. *National Educational Longitudinal Survey.* Washington: U.S. Government Printing Office. Available at: www.ed.gov.

———. 1994. *Schools and Staffing Survey, 1993 to 1994.* Washington: U.S. Government Printing Office. Available at: www.ed.gov.

———. 1995. *CD-ROM: High School and Beyond: 1992 (Restricted) Data File.* Washington: U.S. Department of Education. National Center for Education Statistics. NCES pub. no. 95361.

———. 1997a. *Digest of Education Statistics.* Washington: U.S. Government Printing Office.

———. 1997b. *Principal/School Disciplinarian Survey on School Violence.* Washington: U.S. Government Printing Office. Available at: www.ed.gov.

———. 1999. *Conditions of America's Public School Facilities: 1999.* Washington: U.S. Government Printing Office.

———. 2001a. *Digest of Education Statistics.* Available at: www.nces.ed.gov/pubsearch/pubsinfo. asp?pubid=2002130.

———. 2001b. *Internet Access in U.S. Public Schools and Classrooms, 1994 to 2000.* Washington: U.S. Government Printing Office. Available at: www.ed.gov.

Chapter 12

School Inequality: What Do We Know?

Meredith Phillips and Tiffani Chin

As we enter the twenty-first century, poor and non-Asian minority students lag considerably behind their nonpoor, Asian, and white counterparts on many dimensions of academic performance. Although scholars have long known that these academic disparities stem from many causes, commentators on both sides of the political spectrum often attribute these gaps to disparities in school quality. Thus, President George W. Bush has promoted his "No Child Left Behind" education reform legislation as a crusade against low-quality schools. "We don't want schools languishing in mediocrity and excuse-making," Bush said in 2002. "We want the best for every child. . . . And that starts with making sure that every child gets a good education."

But just how unequal is the U.S. educational system? Do schools that serve disadvantaged students "languish in mediocrity"? It is certainly true that dilapidated facilities staffed by inexperienced teachers haunt journalists' depictions of the schools that serve disadvantaged students (see, for example, Kozol 1991). But to what extent do these portraits accurately describe the *typical* schools that disadvantaged students attend? This chapter uses national data to examine the prevalence of "savage inequalities" at the turn of the twenty-first century. We assess not only the extent to which poor and nonwhite students attend "worse" schools than their nonpoor and white counterparts, but also whether these inequalities have widened or narrowed since the late 1980s. In addition, we discuss whether reducing disparities in any particular dimension of school quality is likely to reduce disparities in students' academic achievement.

We begin by describing trends in academic performance among students from different ethnic and socioeconomic backgrounds. In the next section, we briefly examine the extent of ethnic and socioeconomic segregation across schools. The third and most important section describes ethnic and socioeconomic disparities in public school quality and, when possible, whether these disparities widened or narrowed over the 1990s. We first examine inequities in teacher quality, including differential access to well-educated, credentialed, experienced, and academically skilled teachers. Then we describe disparities in access to instructional attention, as reflected both in the amount of time students spend in school and in class sizes. Next we look at inequalities in instructional resources, as measured by the availability of "gifted" or "advanced placement" programs, instructional materials, computer technology, visual and performing arts offerings, and exposure to academically oriented peers. We conclude this section by describing disparities in access to school services, comfortable facilities, and a safe school environment. The next section briefly discusses whether our focus on public schools understates the extent of education inequality in the United States, and finally, we summarize our main conclusions and offer suggestions for future research.

ETHNIC AND SOCIOECONOMIC DISPARITIES IN ACADEMIC PERFORMANCE

Because questions about school inequality often stem from concerns about ethnic and socio-economic "gaps" in academic performance, we begin by reviewing the evidence on disparities in test scores and grades. The best data for describing trends in test scores come from the National Assessment of Educational Progress (NAEP). Since the mid-1970s, NAEP has tested nine-, thirteen-, and seventeen-year-olds in reading and math using the same sampling procedures and many of the same test questions.[1] We show trends for thirteen-year-olds because these data are the most complete and consistent over time.[2] We describe disparities in "standard deviations units" because this metric allows readers to compare gaps across different types of tests. For readers who would like a benchmark for understanding the magnitude of a standardized gap, a gap of .80 standard deviations, the size of the reading gap between African American and white thirteen-year-olds in 1999, indicates that the typical African American student scored lower than 75 percent of white students. Readers can also think of a .80 standard deviation gap as equivalent to an eighty-point gap on the verbal section of the SAT.

Test Score Trends

Test score gaps among ethnic and socioeconomic groups narrowed during the 1970s and 1980s. The gaps then stopped narrowing and, in some instances, widened. Figures 12.1 and 12.2 show reading and math trends for white, African American, and Latino thirteen-year-olds. Between the mid-1970s and late 1980s, the reading gap between African Americans and whites narrowed by about half and the math gap narrowed by over one-third.[3] Over this same time period the Latino-white reading gap may have narrowed by almost one-third and the math gap by almost half.[4] During the 1990s, however, the Latino-white math and reading gaps stopped narrowing and the black-white reading and math gaps widened.[5]

Compared with changes in the black-white gap over the 1970s and 1980s, changes in the test score gap between children from different educational backgrounds were more moderate (see figures 12.3 and 12.4). Although socioeconomic disparities seem to have narrowed somewhat during the 1970s and 1980s, by the end of the 1990s the gap between children whose parents did not graduate from high school and those whose parents attended college was as large as it had been in the early 1980s.

Current Test Score Gaps

Most studies indicate that moderate to large ethnic and socioeconomic test score gaps exist by the time children enter kindergarten or first grade (Jencks and Phillips 1998; Lee and Burkham 2002; Phillips, Crouse, and Ralph 1998). These gaps persist through the school years. The most current test score data for a nationally representative sample of children come from the NAEP.[6] Figure 12.5 shows that the average black fourth-grader scores about .80 standard deviations below the average white fourth-grader in reading and over .90

FIGURE 12.1   *NAEP Reading Trends for Thirteen-Year-Olds, by Ethnicity, 1975 to 1999*

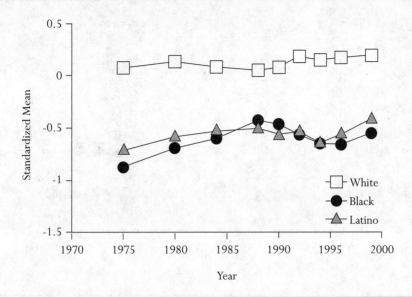

Source: Overall and subgroup means, standard deviations, and standard errors were obtained from percentile tables in U.S. Department of Education (2000). Means and standard errors are also reported in Campbell et al. (2000).

Note: NAEP data were gathered by the U.S. Department of Education for reading in 1971, 1975, 1980, 1984, 1988, 1990, 1992, 1994, 1996, and 1999 and for math in 1978, 1982, 1986, 1990, 1992, 1994, 1996, and 1999. Standardized means were calculated by subtracting the overall mean in 1999 from the mean for each group for each year and dividing the difference by the overall standard deviation in 1999.

standard deviations below the average white fourth-grader in math. Latino-white gaps are slightly smaller than black-white gaps and, contrary to popular wisdom, are slightly larger in math than in reading. These gaps change little between fourth and eighth grade or between eighth and twelfth grade.[7]

Figure 12.6 shows math and reading disparities for children from different educational backgrounds. Gaps between children of high school dropouts and children of college graduates average around .90 standard deviations. Gaps between children of high school graduates and children of college graduates average around .60 standard deviations.[8]

Test scores become particularly consequential when students apply to selective colleges. Even though college applicants are more academically homogeneous than all twelfth-graders, test score gaps among college-bound students are as large as those in the general population. In 2002 black-white gaps on the verbal and math sections of the SAT I were .87 and .93 standard deviations, respectively (College Board 2002). The analogous Latino-white gaps were .68 and .65 standard deviations.[9] Verbal and math gaps between students with family incomes below $30,000 and those with family incomes above $100,000 were 1.01 standard deviations and .96 standard deviations, respectively.[10]

FIGURE 12.2   *NAEP Math Trends for Thirteen-Year-Olds, by Ethnicity, 1978 to 1999*

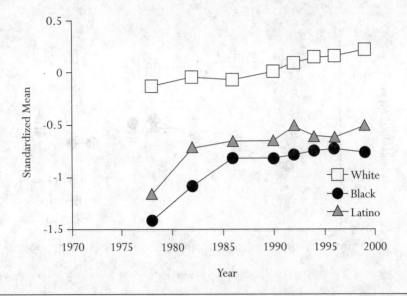

Source: Overall and subgroup means, standard deviations, and standard errors were obtained from percentile tables in U.S. Department of Education (2000). Means and standard errors are also reported in Campbell, Hombo, and Mazzeo (2000).

Note: NAEP data were gathered by the U.S. Department of Education for reading in 1971, 1975, 1980, 1984, 1988, 1990, 1992, 1994, 1996, and 1999 and for math in 1978, 1982, 1986, 1990, 1992, 1994, 1996, and 1999. Standardized means were calculated by subtracting the overall mean in 1999 from the mean for each group for each year and dividing the difference by the overall standard deviation in 1999.

Grade Gaps

Although scholarly descriptions of academic performance tend to focus on test scores, families frequently use grades to gauge students' school performance, and colleges rely heavily on students' grades in their admissions decisions. Although no data source provides consistent evidence on grade gaps over the past few decades, evidence from the 1990s suggests that ethnic disparities in grades are somewhat smaller than ethnic disparities in test scores (at least among high school students). For example, in the early 1990s the black-white grade gap was about .60 standard deviations in high school (about half a grade point on a 4.0 scale) and about .75 standard deviations in elementary school.[11] The Latino-white grade gap was .43 standard deviations in high school and .52 standard deviations in elementary school.[12]

In contrast, socioeconomic disparities in grades are similar to socioeconomic disparities in test scores. For example, in 1990 the gap between high school students whose mothers did not graduate from high school and those whose mothers completed a B.A. degree was 1.06 standard deviations (or 0.9 grade points on a 4.0 scale).

FIGURE 12.3   *NAEP Reading Trends for Thirteen-Year-Olds, by Parents' Education, 1971 to 1999*

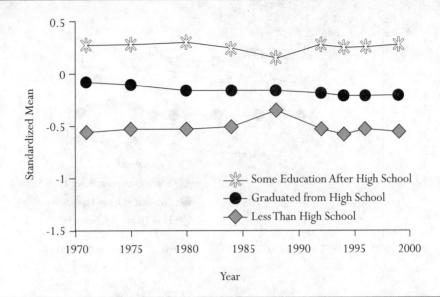

Source: Overall and subgroup means, standard deviations, and standard errors were obtained from percentile tables in U.S. Department of Education (2000). Means and standard errors are also reported in Campbell, Hombo, and Mazzeo (2000).

Note: NAEP data were gathered by the U.S. Department of Education for reading in 1971, 1975, 1980, 1984, 1988, 1990, 1992, 1994, 1996, and 1999 and for math in 1978, 1982, 1986, 1990, 1992, 1994, 1996, and 1999. Standardized means were calculated by subtracting the overall mean in 1999 from the mean for each group for each year and dividing the difference by the overall standard deviation in 1999. Math tests ask whether students' parents graduated from college, but reading tests ask only whether parents attended school beyond high school.

Consequences of Disparities in Academic Performance

Reducing these ethnic and socioeconomic disparities in academic performance would go a long way toward reducing ethnic and socioeconomic disparities in adults' educational attainment and earnings. Academic skills have become more strongly associated with economic success over the past few decades, and black-white differences in test scores currently account for about two-thirds of the black-white wage gap among men and the entire black-white wage gap among women (Johnson and Neal 1998).[13]

Disparities in academic skills also help explain disparities in educational attainment (Jencks and Phillips 1998). The most recent data on the consequences of academic skills for adult success come from the National Education Longitudinal Study (NELS), which surveyed and tested a nationally representative sample of eighth-graders in 1988 and surveyed them again in 2000, when they were approximately twenty-six years old. By 2000, 46 percent of Asian Americans and 34 percent of whites had completed a B.A. degree, compared with only 17 percent of African Americans and 15 percent of Latinos. However, when we compare NELS students who had the same test scores and grades in eighth grade, the black-white B.A.-completion gap disappears entirely, the Latino-white B.A.-completion gap

FIGURE 12.4   *NAEP Math Trends for Thirteen-Year-Olds, by Parents' Education, 1978 to 1999*

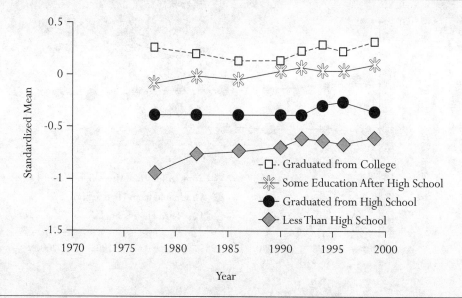

Source: Overall and subgroup means, standard deviations, and standard errors were obtained from percentile tables in U.S. Department of Education (2000). Means and standard errors are also reported in Campbell, Hombo, and Mazzeo (2000).

Note: NAEP data were gathered by the U.S. Department of Education for reading in 1971, 1975, 1980, 1984, 1988, 1990, 1992, 1994, 1996, and 1999 and for math in 1978, 1982, 1986, 1990, 1992, 1994, 1996, and 1999. Standardized means were calculated by subtracting the overall mean in 1999 from the mean for each group for each year and dividing the difference by the overall standard deviation in 1999. Math tests ask whether students' parents graduated from college, but reading tests ask only whether parents attended school beyond high school.

shrinks by half, and the B.A.-completion gap between the children of college graduates and the children of high school dropouts shrinks by one-third.[14]

Because policymakers and citizens increasingly expect *schools* to reduce the disparities in grades and test scores that contribute to adult inequalities, the remainder of this review examines disparities in students' access to high-quality public schools. We limit our review to public schools both because of space constraints and because public schools serve the vast majority of U.S. schoolchildren—48 million compared with the 5.5 million served by private schools (Wirt et al. 2002).[15]

Although this review focuses on quality differences among schools, we urge readers to remember that disparities in children's academic skills emerge *before* children enter school and are strongly associated with children's environments *outside* of school. Thus, our focus on school quality disparities should not be taken to imply that equalizing school inputs would be the most effective or least costly way to remedy inequalities in academic performance. Likewise, readers should note that our review ignores quality differences *within* schools. Because many schools (especially middle schools and high schools) offer different courses to students based on their academic performance, students who attend the same school may spend much of their time with different teachers and a different peer group.[16] Our description of disparities in *average* school characteristics understates ethnic and socio-

FIGURE 12.5   *Recent NAEP Reading and Math Scores, by Grade Level and Ethnicity*

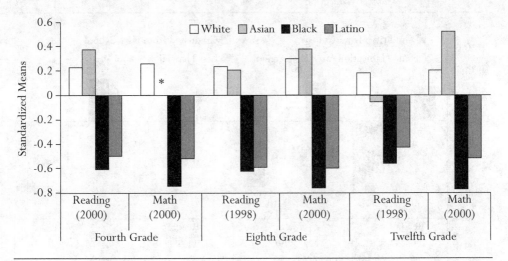

Source: U.S. Department of Education, National Center for Education Statistics, "The Nation's Report Card," NAEP main sample data for reading (1998, 2000) and math (2000) retrieved through Data Tool: http://nces.gov/nationsreportcard/naepdata/search.asp. Means and standard errors are also available in Donahue et al. (2001).

Note: Standardized means were calculated by subtracting the overall mean from the mean for each group and dividing the difference by the overall standard deviation. We do not show fourth-graders' scores by parents' education because 34 percent of fourth-graders do not know their parents' education.

* In 2000 there were too few Asian fourth-graders in the sample to estimate an average math score.

economic disparities in school quality if, within any particular school, poor or minority students disproportionately sit in the largest classrooms, learn with the least-motivated peers, or are taught by the least-qualified teachers.

THE ETHNIC AND SOCIOECONOMIC COMPOSITION OF PUBLIC SCHOOLS

The main purpose of this chapter is to describe how school quality differs among schools attended by students from various ethnic and social class backgrounds. If students from different backgrounds were randomly distributed among schools, however, ethnic or socioeconomic disparities in school quality would not exist. Yet almost a half-century after the landmark *Brown v. Board of Education* decision, U.S. schools remain remarkably segregated by ethnicity and social class.

During the 2000–2001 school year the typical white student attended a school that was 80 percent white. The typical African American student, in contrast, attended a school that was 31 percent white, and the typical Latino attended a school that was only 29 percent white.[17] (The typical Asian American student attended a school that was 46 percent white.) Likewise, in 2000–2001 only 11 percent of whites attended predominantly minority schools, compared with 55 percent of Asian Americans, 71 percent of African Americans, and 76 percent of Latinos. And fewer than 1 percent of white students attended schools that were over 90 percent minority, whereas over one-third of all African American and Latino students attended such schools.[18]

FIGURE 12.6   *Recent NAEP Reading and Math Scores for Eighth- and Twelfth-Graders, by Parents' Education*

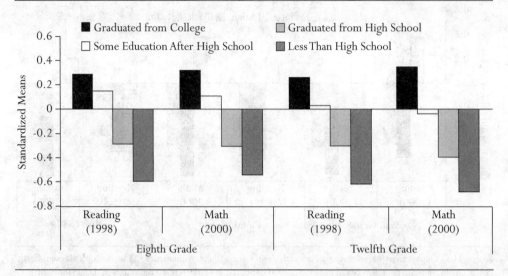

Source: U.S. Department of Education, National Center for Education Statistics, "The Nation's Report Card," NAEP main sample data for reading (1998, 2000) and math (2000) retrieved through Data Tool: http://nces.gov/nationsreportcard/naepdata/search.asp. Means and standard errors are also available in Donahue et al. (1999).

Note: Standardized means were calculated by subtracting the overall mean from the mean for each group and dividing the difference by the overall standard deviation. We do not show fourth-graders' scores by parents' education because 34 percent of fourth-graders do not know their parents' education.

Schools are also socioeconomically segregated. The only measure of socioeconomic status typically reported by schools is the percentage of students who are eligible for subsidized (either free or reduced-price) meals.[19] Throughout this chapter, we refer to students who qualify for subsidized meals as "poor." During the 2000 to 2001 school year the typical nonpoor student attended a school in which 25 percent of the students were poor, whereas the typical poor student attended a school in which 58 percent of the students were poor. Likewise, whereas nearly half (47 percent) of all nonpoor students attended schools in which fewer than one-fifth of the students were poor, a mere 8 percent of poor students attended such low-poverty schools.[20]

Moreover, because poverty and ethnicity are correlated, African American and Latino students are more likely than white and Asian American students to attend poor schools.[21] For example, whereas only 2 percent of white students and 10 percent of Asian American students attended schools that were over 80 percent poor in 2000 to 2001, over 25 percent of African American students and 28 percent of Latino students attended such high-poverty schools.

Defining Ethnic Composition

Most previous research has measured a school's ethnic composition using the percentage of nonwhite or "minority" students at the school. For comparability, we do the same in this chapter. Yet schools that have equal percentages of "minority" students often have very different ethnic compositions. Some serve mainly African American students, others serve mainly Latino students, and others serve a combination. In fact, "percentage minority" correlates only .66 with "percentage African American" and only .60 with "percentage Latino." And the percentage of African American students at a school is uncorrelated with the percentage of Latino students ($r = -.10$). Yet the one thing that schools with the same percentage of "minority" students have in common is, by definition, the percentage of white students. Thus, readers may find it helpful to think of "percentage minority" as the opposite of "percentage white." And although we emphasize the percentage of minority students in our discussion of school quality, we also note when analyzing the percentages of African American or Latino students separately tells a markedly different story.

Categorizing Schools by Their Ethnic and Socioeconomic Composition

Our review of the existing literature on school quality disparities revealed no consensus about what constitutes a so-called low- or high-poverty (or low- or high-minority) school. Rather than developing hypotheses about the thresholds of poor or minority students that might produce differences in school quality, researchers have typically taken a purely statistical approach to categorizing schools—dividing them into four categories, each of which includes approximately 25 percent of schools in the nation. Because this "quartile" approach ensures approximately equal sample sizes of schools within categories, it facilitates the detection of statistically significant differences among categories. Other researchers seem to have chosen categories that either minimize or exaggerate disparities in school quality. For consistency, we rely on categories used in previous work throughout this review (see table 12.1). Because many of our tables suggest a nonlinear association between school composition and quality, however, future research should focus on describing more precisely the association between composition and quality, as well as assessing statistical interactions between ethnic and socioeconomic composition.

Table 12.1 shows how students from different ethnic and socioeconomic groups are distributed among frequently used school categories—and thus in the tables and figures that follow. This table highlights two facts that will help readers understand the kind of students who attend the schools we describe in this chapter. First, nearly two-thirds of white students attend schools with fewer than 20 percent minority students (that is, schools in the lowest two "minority" categories), yet fewer than 10 percent of African American and Latino students attend those types of schools. Second, 50 percent of poor students attend schools that are more than 59 percent poor, but fewer than 10 percent of nonpoor students attend such high-poverty schools.

DISPARITIES IN PUBLIC SCHOOL QUALITY

Although policymakers often link disparities in school quality to disparities in academic performance, we do not limit this review to inputs that affect children's academic skills. We include educational and non-educational inputs both because parents and children judge schools based on academic quality *and* atmosphere (Lee, Croninger, and Smith 1996; Peterson, Myers, and Howell 1998; Goldring and Hausman 1999) and because we suspect that disparities in school environments cause disparities in children's and teachers' day-to-day well-being. As Christopher Jencks put it more than thirty years ago:

TABLE 12.1   Distribution of Schools and Students in Minority and Poverty Enrollment Categories Used in This Chapter, by Student Ethnicity and Poverty

	All Schools	All Students	White Students	African-American Students	Latino Students	Asian American Students	Poor Students	Nonpoor Students
School minority enrollment								
5 percent or less	25.3%	18.4%	29.5%	0.9%	0.9%	2.9%	11.4%	23.9%
6 to 20 percent	23.4	23.5	33.9	6.0	5.8	14.7	12.3	28.9
21 to 50 percent	22.0	24.1	26.1	22.1	17.4	28.3	20.5	26.2
More than 50 percent	29.3	34.0	10.6	71.1	75.9	54.2	55.9	21.2
Free/reduced-price-lunch-eligible enrollment (categories used for teacher quality measures)								
Less than 15 percent	21.5	24.0	32.9	7.4	8.6	28.5	4.3	36.3
15 to 32 percent	23.9	25.1	31.2	15.4	13.6	24.0	15.1	31.4
33 to 59 percent	28.5	26.2	26.1	27.6	25.5	23.9	30.4	23.5
More than 59 percent	26.1	24.7	9.9	49.6	52.4	23.5	50.2	8.7
Free/reduced-price-lunch-eligible enrollment (categories used for technology, arts instruction, and some safety measures)								
Less than 35 percent	48.0	51.5	66.9	24.8	23.9	54.5	21.5	70.4
35 to 49 percent	16.7	15.5	16.1	15.1	13.8	14.0	16.7	14.7
50 to 74 percent	20.3	18.5	13.4	27.9	27.1	17.9	29.3	11.7
75 percent or more	15.0	14.5	3.6	32.3	35.3	13.5	32.5	3.2
Free/reduced-price-lunch-eligible enrollment (categories used for school facilities measures)								
Less than 20 percent	28.7	32.1	43.5	11.2	12.2	36.7	8.0	47.3
20 to 39 percent	25.9	25.6	30.1	19.1	16.6	23.3	19.5	29.4
40 to 69 percent	27.5	25.1	21.3	32.8	30.6	23.8	35.0	18.9
70 percent or more	18.0	17.2	5.0	37.0	40.6	16.2	37.5	4.4

Source: Authors' tabulations of the Common Core of Data (CCD) school-level file for 2000 to 2001.

Some schools are dull, depressing, even terrifying places, while others are lively, comfortable, and reassuring. If we think of school life as an end in itself rather than a means to some other end, such differences are enormously important. Eliminating these differences . . . would do a great deal to make the quality of children's (and teachers') lives more equal. Since children are in school for a fifth of their lives, this would be a significant accomplishment. (Jencks 1972, 256)

In addition, while many school characteristics may not affect how much any particular child learns during a particular school year, all school inputs and outcomes tend to become interrelated over time. For example, although high-quality computers probably do not dramatically improve children's achievement (nor do falling ceiling tiles likely reduce achievement), the most educationally oriented parents and students—and the most highly qualified teachers—tend to gravitate toward schools with state-of-the-art technology and to avoid schools with unsightly infrastructure. These parents, students, and teachers, in turn, help to enhance the academic climate of the school, which in turn probably improves students' skills. Because so many aspects of a school's environment may, over the long term, influence its academic climate, we define "school quality" broadly and examine disparities in its many dimensions.

Teacher Quality

The United States spends over $347 billion on public elementary and secondary education each year (Snyder and Hoffman 2002). And as Sean Corcoran and his colleagues show elsewhere in this volume, state and federal revenue streams have largely equalized per pupil revenues across districts within the same state. Although districts with identical revenues can spend their money in different ways, teachers' salaries and benefits typically constitute the bulk of their expenditures. And because students spend most of their time in classrooms, teachers also represent the aspect of school quality that is most closely linked to gains in students' academic achievement (Goldhaber and Brewer 1997; Rivkin, Hanushek, and Kain 1998).

Even though scholars agree that good teachers improve students' achievement, researchers have yet to figure out what makes a teacher "good" (Goldhaber 2002).[22] Simply put, the characteristics of teachers that are easiest to measure, such as whether they have a credential or a master's degree, do not account for their success in the classroom.[23] Improving our understanding of teacher quality probably requires moving beyond administrative and survey datasets. Future research should focus on developing methods for collecting reliable, large-scale, observational information about what teachers actually do in their classrooms.

Degrees and Certification   Table 12.2 shows how the percentages of teachers with a master's degree or a teaching certificate changed over the 1990s. It suggests that disparities in the percentage of teachers who have a master's degree increased slightly, with the difference between schools with the fewest minority students and those with the most growing to 7.6 percent by 2000. The gap in the percentage of teachers with full certification also widened between low- and high-minority elementary schools.

Table 12.2 also shows that disparities in teacher education and certification between high- and low-poverty schools remained relatively constant throughout the 1990s, although relatively small certification gaps and somewhat larger education gaps (14 percent) persisted

TABLE 12.2 Public School Teachers with a Master's Degree or Full Certification, by Minority and Poverty Enrollment, 1987–1988 to 1999–2000

	1987 to 1988			1993 to 1994			1998			1999 to 2000		
	Master's Degree	Certified (Elementary)	Certified (Secondary)	Master's Degree	Certified (Elementary)	Certified (Secondary)	Master's Degree	Certified (Elementary)	Certified (Secondary)	Master's Degree	Certified (Elementary)	Certified (Secondary)
Minority enrollment												
5 percent or less	45.3%	90.5%	91.6%	47%	95%	91%	49%	96%	92%	47.9%	92.9%	86.5%
	(0.7)	(0.7)	(0.4)	(1.0)	(0.8)	(0.5)	(1.9)	(0.8)	(1.4)	(1.0)	(0.8)	(0.8)
6 to 20 percent	47.0	90.4	91.1	48	95	90	51	95	94	48.8	92.8	88.8
	(1.0)	(0.8)	(0.6)	(1.1)	(0.8)	(0.8)	(2.1)	(1.1)	(0.9)	(1.1)	(0.7)	(0.7)
21 to 50 percent	45.1	90.2	90.5	44	94	91	43	93	93	42.7	93.4	86.6
	(0.8)	(1.2)	(0.8)	(1.0)	(0.9)	(0.7)	(2.1)	(1.6)	(1.0)	(1.0)	(0.9)	(1.1)
More than 50 percent	43.7	87.6	86.7	43	90	87	38	88	87	40.3	85.6	82.1
	(0.9)	(1.3)	(0.9)	(1.3)	(1.5)	(1.1)	(2.2)	(1.7)	(1.2)	(1.1)	(1.4)	(1.0)
Free/reduced-price-lunch-eligible enrollment												
Less than 15 percent	51.6	90.4	91.5	53	93	91	57	94	92	53.1	92.2	87.6
	(0.8)	(0.8)	(0.5)	(1.0)	(0.7)	(0.6)	(1.8)	(1.3)	(1.2)	(1.0)	(1.0)	(0.7)
15 to 32 percent	43.8	90.5	91.4	46	96	91	46	95	93	45.0	93.9	86.4
	(0.7)	(0.8)	(0.6)	(0.9)	(0.7)	(0.6)	(2.0)	(1.5)	(1.0)	(1.1)	(0.8)	(0.8)
33 to 59 percent	40.5	90.5	88.5	41	93	89	41	95	94	41.0	91.6	84.2
	(1.1)	(0.9)	(0.9)	(1.0)	(0.8)	(0.7)	(2.4)	(0.9)	(1.0)	(1.1)	(0.9)	(0.9)
More than 59 percent	41.3	87.0	85.7	41	91	86	37	90	87	39.5	87.0	83.3
	(1.1)	(1.3)	(1.5)	(1.2)	(1.3)	(1.5)	(2.3)	(1.3)	(1.5)	(1.3)	(1.3)	(1.5)

Sources: U.S. Department of Education, NCES, Schools and Staffing Survey (SASS): 1987 to 1988 (authors' calculations), 1993 to 1994 (as reported in Lewis et al. 1999), and 1999 to 2000 (authors' calculations); Fast Response Survey (FRSS): 1998 (as reported in Lewis et al. 1999).

Note: See data appendix for description of school and teacher sample.

between the richest and poorest schools. However, because most high-quality studies indicate that students do not perform better on achievement tests when their teacher has a master's degree or a credential, remedying gaps in teacher education is unlikely to narrow the achievement gap (Goldhaber and Brewer 1997; Greenwald, Hedges, and Laine 1996; Rivkin, Hanushek, and Kain 1998).

Experience and Stability   Some studies indicate that more experienced teachers are better than newer teachers at improving students' academic skills, while other studies find that the association is nonlinear or nonexistent (for reviews, see Hanushek 1997; Greenwald, Hedges, and Laine 1996). Evidence from Texas suggests that elementary school students learn about .10 standard deviations less per year in math and reading when they are assigned to a first- or second-year teacher (Rivkin, Hanushek, and Kain 1998). Meta-analytic evidence based on longitudinal studies suggests that students gain around .07 standard deviations in achievement for each standard deviation increase in their teacher's experience (Greenwald, Hedges, and Laine 1996).

Table 12.3 shows that teachers in predominantly minority schools average about two and a half fewer years of experience than teachers in the whitest schools—a gap of about one-quarter of a standard deviation. Teachers in predominantly minority schools have also taught at their current school for three and a half fewer years than teachers in the whitest schools. Both of these gaps seem to have widened since the late 1980s. Gaps in overall experience and "current school" experience between the richest and poorest schools average about two years and did not change significantly over the past decade. These gaps in teacher experience imply that disadvantaged schools have greater teacher turnover and a higher percentage of novice teachers, implications confirmed in table 12.4. If estimates of the negative effects of inexperienced teachers are correct, creating incentives for teachers with at least several years of teaching experience to remain in schools with high concentrations of minority or poor students could help narrow test score gaps.

Subject Matter Knowledge   In the late 1980s, scholars began to argue that teachers are more effective when they know their subject well. Some studies have found that middle and high school students learn more math from teachers who majored in math in college or graduate school (Goldhaber and Brewer 1997, 2001; Monk 1994; Rowan, Chiang, and Miller 1997). Little research exists on the importance of teachers' subject matter knowledge for students' English or social studies achievement, however. Nor do we know how teachers' subject matter knowledge affects elementary school students' achievement. Nonetheless, several recent reports have emphasized the extent of students' exposure to "out-of-field" teachers (see, for example, Darling-Hammond 1997; Ingersoll 1998, 2001).

Table 12.5 shows disparities across different types of schools in the percentages of middle and high school teachers who majored or minored in their main assignment field.[24] These estimates suggest that the percentage of out-of-field teachers increased slightly over the 1990s. Gaps among different types of schools did not change much, however, although the estimates are too imprecise to tell for sure. The current gap between low-minority and high-minority schools in the percentage of in-field English or social studies teachers is neither large nor statistically significant. However, nearly 80 percent of math teachers in the whitest schools have majors or minors in math, compared with only 71 percent of math teachers in high-minority schools. In-field teaching varies even more by school poverty. Whereas 78 percent of math teachers in the richest schools have a major or minor in math, only 64 percent in the poorest schools do. English and science show similar gaps.[25]

TABLE 12.3   *Public School Teachers' Years of Experience and Years at Current School, by Minority and Poverty Enrollment, 1987–1988 to 1999–2000*

	1987 to 1988		1993 to 1994		1998		1999 to 2000	
	Average Years Teaching	Average Years at Current School	Average Years Teaching	Average Years at Current School	Average Years Teaching	Average Years at Current School	Average Years Teaching	Average Years at Current School
Minority enrollment								
5 percent or less	15.34	10.66	16	12	17	13	15.95	11.68
	(0.08)	(0.09)	(0.2)	(0.2)	(0.4)	(0.3)	(0.18)	(0.20)
6 to 20 percent	15.34	9.59	16	10	16	10	15.57	9.86
	(0.11)	(0.13)	(0.2)	(0.2)	(0.4)	(0.3)	(0.25)	(0.21)
21 to 50 percent	15.04	8.94	16	9	15	9	14.62	8.83
	(0.19)	(0.15)	(0.2)	(0.2)	(0.4)	(0.3)	(0.22)	(0.19)
More than 50 percent	14.98	8.53	14	9	13	8	13.42	8.17
	(0.19)	(0.15)	(0.2)	(0.2)	(0.5)	(0.3)	(0.23)	(0.18)
Free/reduced-price-lunch-eligible enrollment								
Less than 15 percent	15.86	10.35	17	11	16	11	15.54	10.27
	(0.10)	(0.11)	(0.2)	(0.2)	(0.3)	(0.3)	(0.19)	(0.17)
15 to 32 percent	15.02	9.66	16	10	17	11	15.26	9.90
	(0.16)	(0.13)	(0.2)	(0.2)	(0.4)	(0.4)	(0.21)	(0.21)
33 to 59 percent	14.88	9.23	15	10	16	10	14.88	9.68
	(0.14)	(0.11)	(0.2)	(0.2)	(0.4)	(0.4)	(0.20)	(0.21)
More than 59 percent	14.58	8.71	14	9	13	8	13.55	8.36
	(0.21)	(0.18)	(0.2)	(0.2)	(0.4)	(0.3)	(0.25)	(0.19)

Sources: U.S. Department of Education, NCES, SASS: 1987 to 1988 (authors' calculations), 1993 to 1994 (as reported in Lewis et al. 1999), and 1999 to 2000 (authors' calculations); Fast Response Survey (FRSS): 1998 (as reported in Lewis et al. 1999).

Math and Verbal Skills   One of the more consistent findings in the teacher quality literature is that children learn more when they have teachers with strong math and verbal skills, either as measured by standardized tests or as proxied by the selectivity of their undergraduate college (Ehrenberg and Brewer 1995; Ferguson 1991, 1998; Ferguson and Ladd 1996; Greenwald, Hedges, and Laine 1996; Hanushek 1972; Rowan, Chiang, and Miller 1997; Strauss and Sawyer 1986). Yet college students with strong cognitive skills are less likely than students with weaker skills to become teachers, and those who do are more likely to leave the profession (Murnane et al. 1991). In addition, teachers with stronger cognitive skills tend to teach in schools with fewer disadvantaged children (Ballou 1996; Ferguson 1998; Kain and Singleton 1996; Lankford, Loeb, and Wyckoff 2002; Podgursky, Monroe, and Watson 2002).

Nationally representative data on teachers' math and verbal skills and the types of schools in which they teach are not available. However, we can use a proxy for teachers' skills—the average SAT or ACT (American College Test) scores of the college from which they graduated—to provide a tentative estimate of the extent to which teachers' skills vary across types of schools.[26] Table 12.6 suggests that the average verbal and math skills of teachers declined slightly over the 1990s and that the teacher skill gap between advantaged

TABLE 12.4   *Teachers Who Remained in the Same School Between Spring 1999 and Fall 2000 and New Teachers, by Minority and Poverty Enrollment, 1999 to 2000*

	Teachers in Same School	Teachers with One Year of Experience or Less
Minority enrollment		
5 percent or less	89.2%	4.4%
	(0.53)	(0.30)
6 to 20 percent	87.0	5.2
	(0.68)	(0.39)
21 to 50 percent	85.5	5.2
	(0.75)	(0.41)
More than 50 percent	83.8	7.8
	(0.73)	(0.59)
Free/reduced-price-lunch-eligible enrollment		
Less than 15 percent	88.3	5.5
	(0.53)	(0.38)
15 to 32 percent	87.4	4.9
	(0.70)	(0.43)
33 to 59 percent	86.2	5.2
	(0.63)	(0.39)
More than 59 percent	83.1	7.5
	(0.92)	(0.62)

Source: Authors' calculations using U.S. Department of Education, NCES, SASS: 1999 to 2000 (which includes some data from 2001 Teacher Follow-up Survey [TFS]).

and disadvantaged schools may have narrowed somewhat. Nonetheless, by the turn of the century the typical teacher in a low-poverty school had graduated from a more selective college (by nearly forty SAT points) than had the typical teacher in a high-poverty school. The teacher skill gap between white and predominantly minority schools, however, is smaller.[27]

Given the consistent association between teachers' and students' academic skills, policymakers would be wise to invest in policies designed to ensure the academic competencies of teachers. However, policies that simply require prospective teachers to pass tests will probably not help reduce the achievement gap unless districts provide strong incentives for bright students from selective colleges to consider teaching as a career, require potential teachers to pass relatively difficult exams, and then provide incentives for high-scoring teachers to teach (and ideally, remain) in high-poverty schools.[28]

Professional Development   Because the task of recruiting and retaining "smarter" and more "subject-wise" teachers is so daunting, especially in disadvantaged schools, some scholars suggest focusing instead on providing first-rate professional development to increase the effectiveness of existing teachers (see Ladd and Hansen 1999). Although scholars have conducted relatively little high-quality research on the effectiveness of professional development in raising student achievement, current evidence suggests that professional development that is intense, highly structured, and closely aligned with curriculum may help raise students' scores (Angrist and Lavy 2001; Cohen and Hill 2000; Jacob and Lefgren 2002; for a review, see Kennedy 1999).

Table 12.7 shows the intensity of teachers' exposure to "in-depth, subject-specific" professional development—the type most likely to be associated with improved student learning.[29] This table reveals that teachers in high-minority and high-poverty schools are *more* likely than teachers in low-minority and low-poverty schools to receive in-depth, subject-

TABLE 12.5 Secondary School (Grades Seven Through Twelve) Teachers with a Major or Minor in Their Main Teaching Field, by Minority and Poverty Enrollment: 1987–1988 to 1999–2000

	1987 to 1988				1993 to 1994				1998				1999 to 2000			
	English	Math	Science	Social Studies	English	Math	Science	Social Studies	English	Math	Science	Social Studies	English	Math	Science	Social Studies
Minority enrollment																
5 percent or less	82.6%	82.1%	79.4%	90.6%	78%	79%	82%	88%	87%	85%	93%	88%	77.8%	79.7%	84.7%	84.2%
	(1.6)	(1.6)	(1.7)	(1.3)	(1.6)	(1.6)	(1.8)	(1.3)	(3.0)	(4.4)	(2.2)	(3.8)	(1.8)	(1.9)	(2.2)	(2.0)
6 to 20 percent	84.6	81.8	83.2	88.1	78	79	89	87	89	81	89	88	81.5	77.8	85.4	86.1
	(1.7)	(1.9)	(1.8)	(1.7)	(1.6)	(2.7)	(1.4)	(1.9)	(2.6)	(3.7)	(3.1)	(3.6)	(1.7)	(2.4)	(2.0)	(2.1)
21 to 50 percent	78.0	78.8	74.8	87.4	81	77	79	85	86	87	88	93	73.5	78.7	75.3	85.8
	(1.7)	(2.0)	(2.7)	(1.6)	(1.6)	(2.6)	(2.2)	(2.3)	(2.6)	(3.9)	(3.4)	(2.7)	(2.4)	(2.2)	(2.8)	(2.0)
More than 50 percent	76.8	73.0	83.7	89.3	74	71	77	88	83	76	81	86	74.3	70.7	78.3	88.1
	(1.8)	(2.7)	(2.7)	(1.8)	(2.6)	(2.8)	(2.8)	(1.8)	(3.7)	(5.6)	(4.7)	(3.6)	(2.2)	(2.8)	(2.7)	(1.7)
Free/reduced-price-lunch-eligible enrollment																
Less than 15 percent	86.0	85.5	85.7	90.7	84	81	86	89	90	87	93	91	81.2	78.4	88.9	88.6
	(1.1)	(1.4)	(1.3)	(1.2)	(1.3)	(1.9)	(1.4)	(1.4)	(2.0)	(3.4)	(2.1)	(2.6)	(1.6)	(2.2)	(1.4)	(1.6)
15 to 32 percent	81.4	78.7	79.0	89.8	78	79	84	89	89	89	92	87	80.8	85.8	81.3	83.4
	(1.5)	(1.7)	(2.1)	(1.5)	(1.6)	(2.2)	(1.2)	(1.5)	(2.7)	(3.1)	(2.8)	(3.6)	(1.8)	(1.4)	(2.0)	(2.4)
33 to 59 percent	78.0	76.6	71.1	85.1	73	70	76	84	86	81	81	89	71.5	72.3	72.0	85.1
	(2.0)	(2.6)	(3.1)	(2.1)	(2.1)	(2.6)	(2.6)	(2.6)	(3.1)	(4.1)	(4.9)	(3.2)	(2.2)	(2.3)	(3.1)	(1.9)
More than 59 percent	64.0	61.6	73.5	87.5	70	70	75	81	76	69	83	86	67.9	63.7	76.4	85.2
	(3.2)	(5.2)	(4.6)	(3.1)	(2.9)	(3.8)	(3.9)	(3.2)	(5.0)	(6.4)	(6.0)	(4.4)	(3.1)	(3.9)	(3.3)	(3.1)

Sources: U.S. Department of Education, NCES, SASS: 1987 to 1988 (authors' calculations), 1993 to 1994 (as reported in Lewis et al. 1999), and 1999 to 2000 (authors' calculations); FRSS: 1998 (as reported in Lewis et al. 1999).

TABLE 12.6   *Average SAT Scores of Students Admitted to Teachers' Alma Mater, by Minority and Poverty Enrollment, 1987 to 1988 and 1999 to 2000*

	1987 to 1988	1999 to 2000
Overall	955.7	943.4
	(1.1)	(1.0)
Minority enrollment		
5 percent or less	962.2	947.2
	(1.4)	(1.9)
6 to 20 percent	961.7	952.7
	(2.4)	(1.8)
21 to 50 percent	944.3	937.8
	(2.2)	(2.6)
More than 50 percent	944.5	936.0
	(3.3)	(2.9)
Free/reduced-price-lunch-eligible enrollment		
Less than 15 percent	981.5	959.6
	(1.5)	(1.4)
15 to 32 percent	954.4	930.5
	(1.8)	(3.3)
33 to 59 percent	933.8	920.9
	(2.2)	(3.0)
More than 59 percent	926.1	921.9
	(3.6)	(3.4)

Source: Authors' calculations using teachers' reports of college attended and year graduated from SASS 1987 to 1988 and 1999 to 2000 and HERI selectivity file.

specific professional development. Given that student achievement is so much lower in high-minority and high-poverty schools, it is both fortunate and logical that professional development is targeted at teachers in those schools.

Instructional Attention

In addition to teacher quality, the other obvious, school-based influence on academic success is students' exposure to instruction. School-based strategies for increasing "time on task" range from lengthening the school day and school year to reducing class sizes (for a review of the literature on time and learning, see Aronson, Zimmerman, and Carlos 1999).

Length of School Day and Year   The typical school day increased by 13.8 minutes over the 1990s, while the average length of the school year (179 days) stayed virtually the same (see table 12.8). This implies that the typical student attended school for about forty-one more hours per year in 2000 than in 1988. While predominantly minority schools averaged about eighteen fewer hours of school per year in 1988 than the whitest schools, this gap had disappeared by 2000. High- and low-poverty schools did not differ in average school day or school year length in 1988 or 2000.

Although students' time in school hardly varies across different types of schools, it is possible that extending the school day or year in disadvantaged schools would narrow the achievement gap. This hypothesis stems, in part, from evidence that disadvantaged children lose more academic ground than advantaged children over summer vacation—when they are

TABLE 12.7   *Hours of In-depth, Subject-Specific Professional Development Received by Public School Teachers Within the Past Twelve Months, by Minority and Poverty Enrollment, 1999 to 2000*

	None	One to Eight Hours	Nine to Fifteen Hours	Sixteen to Thirty-Two Hours	Thirty-Three Hours or More
Minority enrollment					
5 percent or less	45.6%	10.8%	16.0%	12.0%	15.7%
	(0.85)	(0.62)	(0.76)	(0.62)	(0.63)
6 to 20 percent	41.2	11.3	15.1	13.6	18.9
	(1.03)	(0.61)	(0.69)	(0.61)	(0.90)
21 to 50 percent	39.7	10.9	14.7	14.6	20.2
	(0.94)	(0.70)	(0.69)	(0.91)	(0.87)
More than 50 percent	33.0	12.0	17.6	15.4	21.9
	(1.01)	(0.65)	(0.76)	(0.76)	(0.88)
Free/reduced-price-lunch-eligible enrollment					
Less than 15 percent	44.0	12.3	15.6	12.1	16.0
	(0.94)	(0.64)	(0.69)	(0.60)	(0.65)
15 to 32 percent	41.4	10.1	15.4	13.0	20.0
	(1.11)	(0.57)	(0.65)	(0.71)	(0.94)
33 to 59 percent	39.6	11.0	15.9	14.8	18.7
	(0.96)	(0.56)	(0.61)	(0.73)	(0.94)
More than 59 percent	33.0	11.3	17.0	16.0	22.7
	(1.23)	(0.83)	(0.87)	(0.83)	(0.93)

Source: U.S. Department of Education, NCES, SASS: 1999 to 2000 (authors' calculations).

not in school (Entwisle, Alexander, and Olson 1997; Heyns 1978; Phillips and Chin, forthcoming). Extending time in school may be too blunt a policy, however, to have a large payoff, since any increase in school time would raise achievement only if students used the extra time for academics. And considering the likely expense, it would probably be more efficient to provide after-school and summer tutoring to the neediest or most motivated students in a "learning center" setting. Given the lack of longitudinal or experimental studies, one can only guess about the effects of additional instruction—either in- or out-of-school—on achievement. Yet, these effects may be large, especially if they accumulate over twelve years of schooling.

Class Size   Reducing class size is another way to increase the amount of instructional attention students receive. Not only does research indicate that students learn more in smaller classes, at least in the early grades, but it also suggests that minority students benefit from smaller classes twice as much as white students do, thereby narrowing achievement gaps (for reviews, see Ferguson 1998; Ehrenberg et al. 2001). Class size reduction policies became popular in the 1990s, and consequently average class sizes declined, especially in elementary schools (see table 12.9).[30] Whereas elementary school classes had an average of over 25.0 students in the late 1980s, by the end of the decade they averaged closer to 22.0 students. Although class size disparities changed little over the decade, predominantly minority elementary schools currently average 1.6 more students in their classes than the whitest schools. Classes in predominantly minority secondary schools are especially large, averaging nearly 25.0 students, compared with an average of 22.5 in the whitest secondary

TABLE 12.8   *Average Hours in the School Day and Days in the School Year, by Minority and Poverty Enrollment, 1987 to 1988 and 1999 to 2000*

	1987 to 1988		1999 to 2000	
	Hours/Day	Days/Year	Hours/Day	Days/Year
Overall	6.41	179.02	6.64	179.01
	(0.01)	(0.05)	(0.01)	(0.12)
Minority enrollment				
5 percent or less	6.46	178.83	6.67	178.78
	(0.01)	(0.06)	(0.01)	(0.09)
6 to 20 percent	6.37	179.02	6.62	178.46
	(0.02)	(0.07)	(0.01)	(0.47)
21 to 50 percent	6.42	179.08	6.63	178.97
	(0.02)	(0.19)	(0.02)	(0.11)
More than 50 percent	6.34	179.39	6.62	179.76
	(0.02)	(0.22)	(0.02)	(0.08)
Free/reduced-price-lunch-eligible enrollment				
Less than 15 percent	6.41	179.40	6.61	178.93
	(0.01)	(0.09)	(0.01)	(0.54)
15 to 32 percent	6.42	178.76	6.64	179.10
	(0.01)	(0.14)	(0.01)	(0.10)
33 to 59 percent	6.44	178.98	6.66	178.84
	(0.02)	(0.14)	(0.02)	(0.12)
More than 59 percent	6.38	178.86	6.63	179.24
	(0.02)	(0.29)	(0.02)	(0.10)

Sources: U.S. Department of Education, NCES, SASS: 1987 to 1988 and 1999 to 2000 (authors' calculations).

schools. In contrast, however, poorer secondary schools tend to have *smaller* classes than richer schools (23.1 versus 24.4).

Unfortunately, scholars have not yet determined the ideal class size for improving student achievement. The STAR experiment in Tennessee, which provides the most convincing evidence on the benefits of small classes, shrank classes to between 13 and 17 students (Mosteller 1995; Finn and Achilles 1999; Krueger 1999). Given that typical classes, even in the most advantaged schools, average over 21 students, classes may need to get much smaller to produce notable academic benefits. And because class size reduction is so expensive (it requires hiring more teachers and building additional classrooms), it may be less cost-effective than hiring *better* teachers. Moreover, when class size reduction is implemented on a large scale, as it was in California, it can have the unintended consequences of reducing teacher quality, especially in poor schools, and increasing class sizes in grades not covered by the class size reduction policy (Bohrnstedt and Stecher 2002; Jepsen and Rivkin 2002).

Challenging Coursework

No matter how "smart" their teachers are or how much instruction time they receive, children still need challenging, pertinent curricula to achieve academic success. Several studies have shown that students learn more when exposed to more challenging coursework (Jencks and Phillips 1999; Meyer 1999; Shouse 1996; Phillips 1997). We found little na-

TABLE 12.9 Average Class Sizes in Public Elementary and Secondary Schools, by School Type, Minority Enrollment, and Poverty Enrollment, 1987–1988 to 1999–2000

	1987 to 1988		1993 to 1994		1998		1999 to 2000	
	Elementary	Secondary	Elementary	Secondary	Elementary	Secondary	Elementary	Secondary
Overall	25.3	24.1	24	24	23	24	22.1	23.9
	(0.12)	(0.12)	(0.1)	(0.1)	(0.2)	(0.1)	(0.11)	(0.10)
Minority enrollment								
5 percent or less	24.8	22.9	23	23	22	23	21.2	22.5
	(0.24)	(0.21)	(0.2)	(0.1)	(0.4)	(0.2)	(0.16)	(0.17)
6 to 20 percent	25.8	24.1	24	24	23	24	22.0	24.4
	(0.36)	(0.22)	(0.2)	(0.1)	(0.3)	(0.2)	(0.17)	(0.20)
21 to 50 percent	25.5	24.9	24	25	23	24	22.0	24.2
	(0.33)	(0.36)	(0.2)	(0.2)	(0.3)	(0.3)	(0.21)	(0.19)
More than 50 percent	25.7	25.7	24	25	23	25	22.8	24.7
	(0.25)	(0.34)	(0.3)	(0.3)	(0.3)	(0.3)	(0.26)	(0.21)
Free/reduced-price-lunch-eligible enrollment								
Less than 15 percent	26.3	24.2	24	24	23	24	22.6	24.4
	(0.31)	(0.17)	(0.2)	(0.1)	(0.3)	(0.3)	(0.20)	(0.17)
15 to 32 percent	25.2	23.9	24	23	22	24	22.0	24.1
	(0.24)	(0.21)	(0.2)	(0.1)	(0.4)	(0.3)	(0.18)	(0.16)
33 to 59 percent	24.7	23.8	24	24	22	24	21.9	23.6
	(0.23)	(0.31)	(0.2)	(0.2)	(0.2)	(0.3)	(0.19)	(0.25)
More than 59 percent	24.8	24.7	24	24	23	24	22.0	23.1
	(0.27)	(0.48)	(0.2)	(0.3)	(0.3)	(0.4)	(0.26)	(0.27)

Sources: U.S. Department of Education, NCES, SASS: 1987 to 1988 (authors' calculations), 1993 to 1994 (as reported in Lewis et al. 1999), and 1999 to 2000 (authors' calculations); FRSS: 1998 (as reported in Lewis et al. 1999).

TABLE 12.10   *Number of Classes That Public High Schools Require for Graduation, by Subject, Minority Enrollment, and Poverty Enrollment, 1987 to 1988 and 1999 to 2000*

	1987 to 1988				1999 to 2000			
	English	Math/Computer Science	Science	Social Studies	English	Math	Science	Social Studies
Overall	3.79	2.37	2.02	2.78	3.86	2.60	2.32	3.00
	(0.02)	(0.02)	(0.02)	(0.03)	(0.02)	(0.01)	(0.01)	(0.01)
Minority enrollment								
5 percent or less	3.69	2.30	1.98	2.71	3.79	2.50	2.23	2.94
	(0.03)	(0.04)	(0.03)	(0.04)	(0.03)	(0.02)	(0.03)	(0.02)
6 to 20 percent	3.87	2.35	2.00	2.81	3.85	2.61	2.30	3.06
	(0.02)	(0.04)	(0.04)	(0.05)	(0.03)	(0.03)	(0.03)	(0.03)
21 to 50 percent	3.84	2.44	2.08	2.79	3.98	2.71	2.47	3.11
	(0.04)	(0.05)	(0.05)	(0.04)	(0.01)	(0.02)	(0.03)	(0.03)
More than 50 percent	3.92	2.50	2.07	2.92	3.90	2.63	2.33	2.93
	(0.03)	(0.04)	(0.04)	(0.04)	(0.02)	(0.03)	(0.03)	(0.04)
Free/reduced-price-lunch-eligible enrollment								
Less than 15 percent	3.76	2.31	1.95	2.75	3.85	2.58	2.31	3.09
	(0.02)	(0.03)	(0.03)	(0.03)	(0.02)	(0.03)	(0.03)	(0.02)
15 to 32 percent	3.83	2.39	2.02	2.79	3.83	2.59	2.31	2.95
	(0.03)	(0.03)	(0.03)	(0.04)	(0.03)	(0.03)	(0.03)	(0.03)
33 to 59 percent	3.77	2.42	2.13	2.79	3.91	2.67	2.36	2.98
	(0.08)	(0.05)	(0.04)	(0.05)	(0.02)	(0.03)	(0.04)	(0.03)
More than 59 percent	3.98	2.58	2.22	2.86	3.88	2.58	2.32	2.94
	(0.02)	(0.07)	(0.09)	(0.09)	(0.03)	(0.05)	(0.05)	(0.06)

Sources: U.S. Department of Education, NCES, SASS: 1987 to 1988 and 1999 to 2000 (authors' calculations).
Note: Sample is limited to "regular" (not special education or vocational) schools that have grades nine through twelve and reported based on a four-year high school program. In 1987 to 1988 districts reported math and computer science together. In 1999 to 2000 they reported math and computer science requirements separately. We chose to report the math scores alone for 1999 to 2000. If anything, increases from the "math/computer science" category in 1987 to 1988 to the "math" category in 1999 to 2000 underestimate increases in math requirements since both math and computer science requirements increased during that time period.

tional data, however, on how schools institutionally encourage students to challenge themselves. Data on ethnic and socioeconomic differences in course enrollments exist, but such data are not accurate indicators of inequalities in educational *opportunity* because course enrollments reflect not only course offerings but also differences in students' course-taking decisions and prior academic preparation. The number of courses that schools require students to take in order to graduate does, however, provide some indication of how much schools demand of their students.

Table 12.10 shows that district graduation requirements increased, on average, in all subjects over the 1990s. For example, while the class of 1988 had to take two science classes in order to graduate, the class of 2000 had to take an average of two and one-third science classes. The data in table 12.10 provide no evidence, however, that predominantly minority or predominantly poor schools are more likely to be located in districts with weaker graduation requirements. If anything, minority schools tend to be located in districts

TABLE 12.11   *Public Elementary and High Schools That Offer Gifted or AP Programs, by Minority and Poverty Enrollment, 1999 to 2000*

	Elementary Schools: Gifted Program	High Schools: AP Program
Minority enrollment		
5 percent or less	72.81%	61.45%
	(1.21)	(1.42)
6 to 20 percent	72.02	76.32
	(1.90)	(1.55)
21 to 50 percent	73.70	81.23
	(1.94)	(1.83)
More than 50 percent	64.81	75.68
	(1.95)	(2.01)
Free/reduced-price-lunch-eligible enrollment		
Less than 15 percent	76.37	82.35
	(1.84)	(1.53)
15 to 32 percent	75.37	71.25
	(1.66)	(1.72)
33 to 59 percent	71.73	64.24
	(1.65)	(1.70)
More than 59 percent	62.97	61.56
	(1.60)	(2.42)

Source: U.S. Department of Education, NCES, SASS: 1999 to 2000 (authors' calculations).

with heavier graduation requirements, though this pattern varies across regions.[31] In fact, these data suggest that the whitest and least-poor schools have *raised* their requirements over the past decade, narrowing the gap in graduation requirements between them and their more disadvantaged counterparts.

Of course, graduation requirements provide only minimum standards for the lowest-achieving students and do not reflect the extent to which schools challenge their high-achieving students. Many schools do, however, offer gifted and talented (GATE) programs (in elementary school) and advanced placement (AP) programs (in high school) to provide more rigorous curricula to high-achieving students (see Mayer, Mullens, and Moore 2000). Recently, an ACLU lawsuit brought media and policy attention to the problem of disparities in access to AP courses, arguing that California students who attend poor, minority schools have access to far fewer AP courses than students who attend richer, whiter schools (ACLU 1999; Hill 2000).[32] Although we lack national data on the number of AP courses schools offer, table 12.11 displays data on whether schools offer an AP (or GATE) program at all. Almost 72 percent of all high schools offer an AP program, but this percentage varies across types of schools. Surprisingly, the whitest schools are least likely to offer an AP program (61 percent). In contrast, 76 percent of predominantly minority schools offer an AP program. Eighty-two percent of nonpoor schools offer an AP program, compared with 62 percent of the poorest schools. Among predominantly minority schools, schools with larger percentages of African American students are less likely to have AP programs than schools with larger percentages of Latino students (results not shown).

The availability of gifted programs follows a more predictable pattern. Poor schools are less likely to have gifted programs (63 percent) than nonpoor schools (76 percent). High-minority schools are less likely to have gifted programs (65 percent) than white schools (73

TABLE 12.12   *Public School Teachers Who Report That They Lack Sufficient Materials to Teach, by Minority and Poverty Enrollment, 1987 to 1988 and 1999 to 2000*

	1987 to 1988		1999 to 2000	
	Inadequate	Grossly Inadequate	Inadequate	Grossly Inadequate
Overall	23.0%	7.4%	25.5%	8.9%
	(0.4)	(0.2)	(0.5)	(0.3)
Minority enrollment				
5 percent or less	20.3	6.0	19.4	5.0
	(0.7)	(0.4)	(0.8)	(0.4)
6 to 20 percent	21.6	6.3	20.1	6.1
	(0.7)	(0.4)	(0.9)	(0.5)
21 to 50 percent	21.5	7.0	23.9	8.7
	(0.8)	(0.5)	(0.9)	(0.6)
More than 50 percent	31.7	12.2	36.5	14.6
	(1.0)	(0.8)	(1.1)	(0.8)
Free/reduced-price-lunch-eligible enrollment				
Less than 15 percent	20.2	6.4	19.7	6.1
	(0.7)	(0.4)	(0.7)	(0.5)
15 to 32 percent	22.2	6.7	22.7	7.3
	(0.7)	(0.4)	(0.8)	(0.5)
33 to 59 percent	23.3	7.2	26.1	8.8
	(0.7)	(0.5)	(1.1)	(0.6)
More than 59 percent	31.0	11.7	34.4	13.8
	(1.1)	(0.8)	(1.2)	(0.9)

Sources: U.S. Department of Education, NCES, SASS: 1987 to 1988 (authors' calculations) and 1999 to 2000 (authors' calculations).

percent). Because gifted programs range considerably in content and quality, however, we suspect that simply requiring poor and minority schools to offer "some kind of gifted program" would do little to improve the achievement of these schools' best students.

Instructional Resources

Journalists' portraits of school inequality often focus on some schools' severe lack of instructional resources, such as textbooks. Although we could not find national data on textbook availability per se, we did find statistics on teachers' perceptions of the availability of instructional resources (including textbooks), the number of books in school libraries, school administrators' perceptions of the adequacy of their libraries and science labs, schools' access to computer and Internet technology, and schools' investment in arts education.

Teaching Materials   The Schools and Staffing Survey (SASS) asks teachers how much they agree or disagree with the statement: "Necessary materials (e.g., textbooks, supplies, copy machine) are available as needed by the staff." When teachers disagree or strongly disagree with that statement, we characterize them as having inadequate materials; we show these percentages in the first and third columns of table 12.12. The second and fourth

TABLE 12.13   *Number of Books in Public Elementary and High School Libraries, by Minority and Poverty Enrollment, 1999 to 2000*

	Elementary Schools		High Schools	
	Total	Per Student	Total	Per Student
Minority enrollment				
5 percent or less	9,084	34.5	11,268	33.6
	(374)	(1.7)	(370)	(1.0)
6 to 20 percent	9,634	24.1	14,534	23.8
	(325)	(0.7)	(588)	(1.7)
21 to 50 percent	9,460	21.9	15,101	18.1
	(236)	(0.6)	(450)	(0.8)
More than 50 percent	8,533	17.9	16,247	21.8
	(327)	(0.6)	(842)	(1.6)
Free/reduced-price-lunch-eligible enrollment				
Less than 15 percent	9,826	22.1	15,675	19.2
	(209)	(0.6)	(505)	(0.9)
15 to 32 percent	2,614	28.0	13,119	26.7
	(235)	(1.2)	(449)	(1.3)
33 to 59 percent	9,323	24.0	12,552	31.6
	(429)	(0.9)	(652)	(1.5)
More than 59 percent	8,224	21.6	12,154	29.9
	(307)	(0.9)	(488)	(1.7)

Source: U.S. Department of Education, NCES, SASS: 1999 to 2000 (authors' calculations).

columns show just the percentages who strongly disagree, whom we characterize as having grossly inadequate materials.

Readers can perhaps take comfort in the fact that only 9 percent of teachers feel that their materials are grossly inadequate. Yet this percentage varies in the expected direction with the demographic composition of schools. More than one-third of the teachers in predominantly minority or predominantly poor schools feel that their teaching materials are inadequate, compared with 20 percent of teachers in the whitest and least-poor schools. And nearly 15 percent of teachers in predominantly minority schools feel that their teaching materials are grossly inadequate, compared with only 5 percent of teachers in mostly white schools. Moreover, these gaps have widened a little over time, with perceived inadequacy increasing in predominantly minority and poor schools but remaining constant in the whitest and least-poor schools.

Libraries and Science Labs   Well-stocked libraries probably affect academic achievement only to the extent that teachers and librarians succeed at convincing students to use them. However, high-quality libraries do serve as symbols that probably attract educationally involved parents and convey the importance of reading to children. Table 12.13 shows disparities in the total number of books in school libraries and the number of books per student. Neither measure is ideal. The first is not adjusted for school size and the second ignores thresholds below which students no longer have access to a diverse selection of books. And obviously, neither measure accounts for the age of the collection nor its distribution across topics or genres (much less whether libraries have "comfy" beanbags for children to sit on while they read!).

TABLE 12.14   *Schools Reporting That Their Library and/or Media Centers and Science Laboratories Meet Functional Requirements "Not at All Well," by Minority and Poverty Enrollment, 1995*

	Library/Media Centers	Science Laboratories
Minority enrollment		
Less than 5.5 percent	13.6%	39.3%
5.5 to 20.4 percent	11.0	38.9
20.4 to 50.4 percent	12.7	42.8
50.5 percent or more	15.5	49.1
Poverty enrollment		
Less than 20 percent	9.7	33.0
20 to 39 percent	10.7	38.0
41 to 69 percent	15.2	48.5
70 percent or more	15.0	50.3

Source: U.S. GAO (1995, tables 4.6 and 4.8).

These two measures tell quite different stories, however, about library inequality. In terms of overall volumes, the whitest elementary schools and predominantly minority elementary schools average about the same number of books, while the whitest high schools average nearly 5,000 fewer books than their predominantly minority counterparts.[33] But because whiter schools also tend to be smaller, disparities in the number of books per student follow the opposite pattern. White elementary schools have nearly twice as many books per student as their predominantly minority counterparts.

The association between library quality and socioeconomic composition follows a different pattern. High-poverty elementary schools have an average of 1,600 fewer books in their school libraries than low-poverty elementary schools, and that gap is even larger—over 3,500 books—among high schools. Yet, when considered in terms of books per student, the richest and poorest elementary schools do not differ at all, and rich high schools have fewer books per student than their poorer counterparts.

Over the past decade libraries have evolved to provide electronic as well as print references and are now called "library and/or media centers." In the mid-1990s, the U.S. General Accounting Office (GAO) (1995) asked schools how well their library and/or media center met their school's functional requirements. About 15 percent of poor schools reported that their library and/or media center met their functional requirements "not at all well," compared with 10 percent of the least-poor schools (see table 12.14). Disparities were even smaller between white and minority schools. Yet when the General Accounting Office asked schools the same question about their science labs, a very large percentage of schools reported that their labs did not meet functional requirements "at all well." Indeed, one-third of the lowest-poverty schools—and half of the highest-poverty schools—reported that their labs did not meet functional requirements. We do not know how these percentages have changed over the past eight years, but they suggest that many schools, and especially schools that serve minority and poor children, are poorly equipped to teach laboratory science.

Computer Technology
Schools' access to wired computer technology increased dramatically over the past decade (Kleiner and Farris 2002). Figures 12.7 and 12.8 show that

FIGURE 12.7   *Schools and Instructional Classrooms with Internet Access, by School Minority Enrollment, 1994 to 2001*

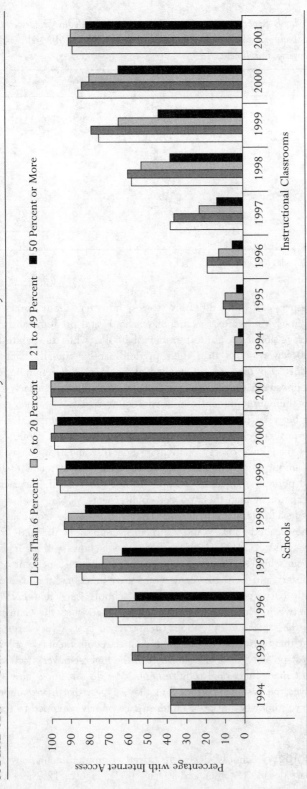

Source: Snyder and Hoffman (2002, table 421) use data from the U.S. Department of Education, NCES, FRSS, "Internet Access in U.S. Public Schools and Classrooms: 1994–2000", and unpublished data.

Notes: Estimates for school-level connectivity include computers for instructional or administrative use. Instructional classrooms include all classrooms, computer labs, and library/media centers.

FIGURE 12.8   Schools and Instructional Classrooms with Internet Access, by School Poverty Enrollment, 1994 to 2001

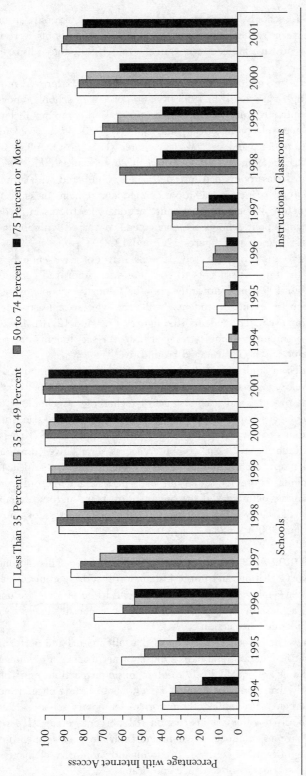

Source: Snyder and Hoffman (2002, table 421) use data from the U.S. Department of Education, NCES, FRSS, "Internet Access in U.S. Public Schools and Classrooms: 1994–2000", and unpublished data.
Notes: Estimates for school-level connectivity include computers for instructional or administrative use. Instructional classrooms include all classrooms, computer labs, and library/media centers.

by 2001 nearly all U.S. schools had Internet access, compared with only around 35 percent of schools just seven years earlier. Moreover, while the richest schools were twice as likely as the poorest schools to have Internet access in the mid-1990s, these disparities had disappeared by 2001.

Connecting every instructional classroom to the Internet has proved more challenging than simply connecting each school. In 1995 over 60 percent of schools reported not having adequate technology infrastructure to support computers and computer technology (such as phone lines, cable lines, electrical power, and outlets), and these problems were more pronounced in older, poorer, and central-city schools (U.S. GAO 1995).[34] Despite these obstacles, gains in classroom Internet access have been substantial. In 1994 fewer than 5 percent of instructional classrooms had Internet access, compared with around 85 percent by 2001. And although disparities in classroom connections remain, these disparities are not egregious—approximately 80 percent of the instructional classrooms in predominantly minority and predominantly poor schools are connected, compared with about 90 percent in the whitest and richest schools (see figures 12.7 and 12.8).

Even when classrooms are connected, schools may not have enough computers for students to use. Yet the ratio of students to computers has improved considerably, even in the poorest schools. In 1998 predominantly poor or minority schools averaged one computer for every sixteen to seventeen students, while the whitest or least-poor schools averaged one computer for every ten students (see figures 12.9 and 12.10). By 2001, however, predominantly poor or minority schools averaged just over six students per computer while the whitest and least-poor schools averaged around five.[35]

Because disparities in students' access to Internet-connected computers have declined so rapidly in recent years, journalists and scholars now argue that the newest "digital divide" reflects disparities in students' and teachers' *use* of technology (Technology Counts 2001). Evidence from 1997 suggests that African American, Latino, and Asian students are less likely than white students to use computers and the Internet at school (Krueger 2000). But given the speed at which disparities in computer access shrank over time, usage gaps are probably much smaller now than in the late 1990s. Nonetheless, we suspect that disparities in teachers' and students' computer savvy and skills persist, and these disparities probably create disparities in any academic payoff that might result from increased computer usage at school (for a review of the existing literature on the effectiveness of computer-assisted instruction, see Krueger 2000).

Visual and Performing Arts   In this era of test-based "basic skills" accountability, educators and parents worry that art and music instruction may be getting short shrift. Moreover, because lower-performing schools (which also tend to be poorer) are under the greatest pressure to raise achievement, such schools may be especially likely to forgo art and music in favor of "academic" instruction.

Table 12.15 shows the percentage of schools that offer visual and performing arts, have specific rooms for that instruction, and have a music or art teacher. Predominantly minority schools and white schools are equally likely to offer music instruction, but white elementary schools are more likely than minority elementary schools to have a music room (71 percent compared with 53 percent). Predominantly minority elementary schools are less likely than white elementary schools to offer art instruction (81 percent versus 92 percent) and may also be less likely to have an equipped art room and an art teacher, though those differences are not statistically significant. In contrast, predominantly minority elementary schools are *more* likely than white schools to offer dance and drama.

FIGURE 12.9   *Ratio of Students to Instructional Computers with Internet Access, by School Minority Enrollment, 1998 to 2001*

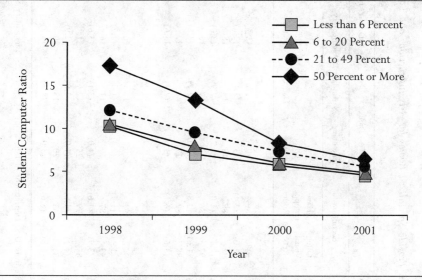

Source: Kleiner and Farris (2002), which uses data from U.S. Department of Education, NCES, FRSS, "Internet Access in U.S. Public Schools and Classrooms: 1994–2001", and unpublished data.

FIGURE 12.10   *Ratio of Students to Instructional Computers with Internet Access, by School Poverty Enrollment, 1998 to 2001*

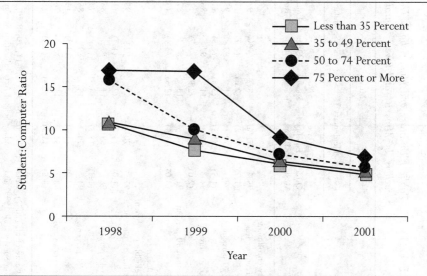

Source: Kleiner and Farris (2002), which uses data from U.S. Department of Education, NCES, FRSS, "Internet Access in U.S. Public Schools and Classrooms: 1994–2001", and unpublished data.

TABLE 12.15   Public Elementary and High Schools That Offer Instruction in the Arts, Provide Specialized Rooms for Arts Instruction, and Lack Arts Teachers, by Minority and Poverty Enrollment of Schools, 1999

| | Music | | | | | Visual Arts | | | | | Dance | | Drama/Theater | |
| | Elementary | | | Secondary | | Elementary | | | Secondary | | Elementary | Secondary | Elementary | Secondary |
	Offer Music	Have Equipped Room	No Special Teacher	Offer Music	Have Equipped Room	Offer Visual Arts	Have Equipped Room	No Special Teacher	Offer Visual Arts	Have Equipped Room	Offer Dance	Offer Dance	Offer Drama	Offer Drama
Minority enrollment														
5 percent or less	95% (1.7)	71% (4.2)	8% (2.6)	90% (2.7)	93% (1.9)	92% (2.2)	58% (4.9)	23% (4.2)	94% (2.0)	89% (2.4)	17% (3.2)	9% (2.1)	15% (2.8)	39% (3.6)
6 to 20 percent	97 (1.5)	70 (4.5)	11 (3.3)	93 (2.5)	95 (1.9)	89 (2.8)	59 (4.9)	20 (3.8)	92 (2.7)	89 (3.0)	18 (2.7)	13 (2.7)	18 (3.0)	57 (4.5)
21 to 50 percent	94 (2.0)	72 (3.5)	11 (2.9)	92 (2.7)	86 (3.5)	86 (3.6)	57 (5.1)	31 (4.6)	97 (1.6)	86 (3.8)	17 (3.0)	17 (2.7)	18 (3.5)	56 (4.1)
More than 50 percent	91 (3.0)	53 (4.4)	13 (2.5)	87 (3.4)	87 (3.5)	81 (2.9)	48 (4.5)	32 (4.2)	88 (3.6)	82 (4.1)	27 (3.6)	21 (2.4)	27 (3.6)	46 (4.8)
Free/reduced-price-lunch-eligible enrollment														
Less than 35 percent	97 (1.0)	70 (3.6)	9 (2.4)	92 (1.7)	95 (1.1)	94 (1.5)	65 (3.7)	18 (2.4)	96 (1.4)	92 (1.7)	20 (2.4)	16 (1.5)	20 (2.7)	53 (2.7)
35 to 49 percent	98 (1.3)	69 (5.3)	11 (3.7)	92 (3.2)	88 (3.4)	74 (4.6)	51 (6.9)	27 (6.1)	93 (3.9)	87 (4.6)	17 (4.0)	11 (3.1)	16 (3.6)	48 (6.3)
50 to 74 percent	94 (2.0)	70 (4.8)	15 (3.5)	89 (3.3)	85 (4.1)	89 (2.8)	48 (4.8)	36 (3.9)	85 (4.1)	79 (4.6)	25 (4.0)	12 (2.8)	21 (3.9)	38 (4.5)
75 percent or more	88 (3.5)	51 (5.3)	11 (2.4)	89 (5.3)	76 (8.1)	79 (3.6)	42 (4.5)	35 (4.2)	85 (6.8)	65 (8.6)	20 (3.0)	13 (4.4)	20 (3.2)	36 (8.9)

Source: Carey et al. (2002), tables 1, B-1, 10, B-10, 11, B-11, 20, B-20, 23, B-23, 27, and B-27. They use data from U.S. Department of Education, NCES, FRSS: "Elementary School Arts Education Survey: Fall 1999" and "Secondary School Arts Education Survey: Fall 1999."

Disparities in the visual and performing arts are more strongly associated with school poverty composition than with minority composition. Whereas nearly all low-poverty elementary schools offer music instruction, 88 percent of high-poverty elementary schools do. Moreover, only about half of high-poverty elementary schools have a room equipped for music, compared with 70 percent of low-poverty schools. This problem persists at the secondary level, where about one-quarter of high-poverty high schools lack a music room compared with only 5 percent of low-poverty schools. Similar gaps exist for art rooms and drama offerings.

Academically Oriented Peers   Because students interact with one another throughout the school day, both in and out of class, the academic achievement and ambitions of a school's student body may influence students' academic performance as much as the other instructional resources described in this chapter. Yet it is very difficult to estimate how much peers influence other students because students typically choose their friends from among their schoolmates (for recent attempts, see Hanushek, Kain, Markman, and Rivkin 2001; Hoxby 2000). Moreover, the academic quality of a school's student body also influences other aspects of school quality. For example, schools with stronger students tend to attract higher-quality teachers and offer more challenging courses. Consequently, many school quality disparities result, at least in part, from differences among schools in the types of students they attract.

Because student achievement differs so dramatically by ethnicity and socioeconomic status, and because students from different ethnic and socioeconomic backgrounds often attend different schools, schools differ considerably in their average levels of academic achievement. To take just one example, the average reading performance of fourth-graders in low-poverty schools is over one standard deviation higher than the average reading performance of fourth-graders in high-poverty schools.[36] Likewise, as table 12.16 shows, only 33 percent of twelfth-graders from high-poverty high schools go on to four-year colleges, compared with 51 percent of twelfth-graders from low-poverty high schools.

Comfort and Safety

While current educational policymaking focuses on raising students' achievement, many non-instructional aspects of schools, such as the availability of support staff, the upkeep of the physical plant, and school safety, affect students' and teachers' well-being. Students turn to nonteaching staff for medical attention when they feel ill at school, for assistance with social problems, and for advice on courses and colleges. The effectiveness of these adults depends heavily on how many students they are supposed to serve. Well-kept buildings and yards not only improve students' aesthetic experience but also provide a positive signal about academic quality to prospective parents. And though most parents hope for a strong academic program, they seem more concerned about overcrowding, discipline, and safety (Snyder and Hoffman 2001). Some evidence even suggests that reducing serious violence at school might improve high school graduation and college attendance rates (Grogger 1997).

Support Staff   Unreasonably high student-counselor ratios—often more than 500 students per counselor—garner fairly regular media attention in urban newspapers (see, for example, Spielvogel 2002). Table 12.17, which describes the number of full-time support staff per 100 students, shows that these numbers are only somewhat exaggerated—the average high school student shares a counselor with over 250 other students. And while

TABLE 12.16   *Twelfth-Graders Who Went to Two- or Four-Year Colleges, by Minority and Poverty Enrollment, 1987 to 1988 and 1999 to 2000*

	1987 to 1988	1999 to 2000	
	Two- or Four-Year College	Two- or Four-Year College[a]	Four-Year College
Minority enrollment			
5 percent or less	53.35%	65.91%	44.68%
	(0.62)	(0.62)	(0.61)
6 to 20 percent	56.85	66.82	43.87
	(0.85)	(0.77)	(0.90)
21 to 50 percent	52.45	65.49	41.29
	(1.16)	(0.93)	(0.93)
More then 50 percent	48.26	62.05	37.84
	(1.24)	(1.02)	(1.07)
Free/reduced-price-lunch-eligible enrollment			
Less than 15 percent	57.91	72.00	50.81
	(0.74)	(0.67)	(0.71)
15 to 32 percent	50.67	64.83	41.52
	(0.86)	(0.67)	(0.63)
33 to 59 percent	48.58	62.39	38.02
	(1.17)	(0.74)	(0.78)
More than 59 percent	43.22	55.73	33.29
	(2.34)	(1.21)	(1.07)

Sources: U.S. Department of Education, NCES, SASS: 1987 to 1988 and 1999 to 2000 (authors' calculations).
Notes: In 1987 to 1888 the question about college asked the percentage of students who "applied" to two- or four-year colleges. In 1999 to 2000 the questionnaire asked the percentage of students who "went to college." In the 1987 to 1988 questionnaire, a single question asked about two- and four-year college-going. In 1999 to 2000 two separate questions were asked. For comparability, we created a "two- or four-year" variable for 1999 to 2000, which we report here, but we also show four-year college-going separately.

most U.S. students get little attention from school support staff, students who attend predominantly minority schools have even less access to counselors, nurses, psychologists, and speech therapists than do students in white schools. Although many of these disparities do not seem large at first glance, they can translate into large gaps. For example, while the whitest elementary schools have one full-time speech therapist for every 333 children, predominantly minority elementary schools have one for every 526 children. Likewise, the whitest high schools have a full-time psychologist for every 833 students, while predominantly minority high schools have one for every 1,667 students. These disparities are surprising given the greater prevalence of speech and learning disabilities in predominantly minority schools.

In contrast, poor and nonpoor elementary schools have similar support staff-to-student ratios. And poor high schools have *more* counselors, nurses, psychologists, social workers, and speech therapists per capita than their richer counterparts. Note, however, that our data do not allow us to distinguish between college counselors, grief counselors, therapists, and disciplinarians. And because social and psychological problems tend to be more prevalent in poor schools, higher support staff-to-student ratios need not imply that children in poor schools receive sufficient attention relative to their needs.

TABLE 12.17 *Average Staff-Member-to-100-Pupils Ratios, for Different Types of Staff Members, by Minority and Poverty Enrollment, 1999 to 2000*

	Elementary Schools					High Schools			
	Nurses	Psychologists	Social Workers	Speech Therapists	Counselors	Nurses	Psychologists	Social Workers	Speech Therapists
Minority enrollment									
5 percent or less	0.21	0.17	0.07	0.30	0.39	0.17	0.12	0.07	0.17
	(0.014)	(0.017)	(0.004)	(0.018)	(0.006)	(0.007)	(0.005)	(0.005)	(0.006)
6 to 20 percent	0.16	0.13	0.08	0.22	0.35	0.11	0.08	0.05	0.10
	(0.006)	(0.009)	(0.005)	(0.008)	(0.010)	(0.006)	(0.006)	(0.003)	(0.007)
21 to 50 percent	0.15	0.12	0.08	0.21	0.33	0.11	0.06	0.04	0.08
	(0.006)	(0.006)	(0.006)	(0.008)	(0.005)	(0.006)	(0.004)	(0.003)	(0.005)
More than 50 percent	0.16	0.12	0.08	0.19	0.35	0.11	0.06	0.07	0.12
	(0.013)	(0.013)	(0.004)	(0.012)	(0.011)	(0.006)	(0.005)	(0.005)	(0.009)
Free/reduced-price-lunch-eligible enrollment									
Less than 15 percent	0.15	0.14	0.08	0.20	0.34	0.10	0.08	0.05	0.07
	(0.006)	(0.010)	(0.004)	(0.010)	(0.005)	(0.003)	(0.003)	(0.003)	(0.003)
15 to 32 percent	0.17	0.13	0.08	0.22	0.35	0.13	0.09	0.06	0.12
	(0.007)	(0.007)	(0.006)	(0.008)	(0.007)	(0.006)	(0.006)	(0.004)	(0.007)
33 to 59 percent	0.16	0.16	0.07	0.24	0.39	0.14	0.10	0.06	0.17
	(0.005)	(0.010)	(0.004)	(0.012)	(0.011)	(0.007)	(0.006)	(0.005)	(0.010)
More than 59 percent	0.18	0.12	0.08	0.22	0.40	0.18	0.10	0.07	0.19
	(0.013)	(0.013)	(0.004)	(0.012)	(0.015)	(0.014)	(0.009)	(0.009)	(0.013)

Source: U.S. Department of Education, NCES, SASS: 1999 to 2000 (authors' calculations).

Facilities   Journalists' portraits of dilapidated schools have justifiably garnered public sympathy (see, for example, Kozol 1991). Even seemingly mundane problems such as poorly maintained bathrooms have embarrassed school districts and prompted repairs (Associated Press 2003; Niesse 2002). Well-maintained school facilities certainly make teaching and learning more pleasant for teachers and students and may help attract qualified teachers and involved parents (Murnane 1981). Yet because schools tend to devote few resources to capital improvement, almost three-fifths of U.S. schools need structural maintenance (U.S. GAO 1995). Tables 12.18 and 12.19 show the percentage of public schools that rate their buildings and facilities as inadequate. Regardless of their poverty or minority concentration, around 20 percent of schools report that their original buildings are in less than adequate condition. However, high-minority and poor schools are almost twice as likely as white and nonpoor schools to report that their non-original buildings need maintenance. Predominantly minority schools report more problems with their interior finishes and electric power than do their white counterparts, and poor schools report more problems with their roofs, electric power, and life safety features than their rich counterparts.

When the General Accounting Office (2002) compared suburban and inner-city schools in the same metropolitan areas, they found that the inner-city schools tended to have smaller playgrounds and less playground equipment than their suburban counterparts. Inner-city schools were also more likely than the suburban schools to have all-asphalt yards instead of grass fields.

Overcrowding   From Westchester County, New York, to inner-city Los Angeles, overcrowding, brought on by the so-called baby boomlet, has forced some schools to raise class sizes and others to convert storage closets to classrooms (Rubenstein 2003; Rothstein 2002). More often, schools have built portable classrooms on what used to be playgrounds. Table 12.20 shows the distribution of overcrowding nationally. In 1999 about 15 percent of all schools were somewhat overcrowded (6 to 25 percent over capacity). Another 15 percent of predominantly minority schools and 12 percent of the poorest schools were extremely overcrowded (more than 25 percent over capacity), compared with only 4 percent of the whitest and 6 percent of the richest schools.

Crime and Safety   Concern about violence in schools—and the bullying that may provoke it—surged in the wake of the 1999 shootings at Columbine High School in Littleton, Colorado. Yet over the course of the 1990s the incidence of serious violent crime at schools remained relatively constant (or even declined slightly), and the incidence of less serious crime—such as theft—declined considerably (see figures 12.11 and 12.12). Ethnic and socioeconomic gaps in less serious crime shrank over the 1990s, mainly because white children and children from more affluent families reported fewer crime incidents as the decade progressed.

Figure 12.13 shows that African American and Latino students are twice as likely as white students to fear being attacked at school or going to or from school, and they are more likely than white students to say that they avoid places at school. In contrast, white students are the most likely to report being bullied at school. These data also reveal, however, that the vast majority of students from all ethnic groups say that they are not afraid at school.

Because students' decisions about what counts as a crime, as well as whether to report it, probably influence the data shown thus far, we also present data on the percentage of schools that reported at least one crime incident to the police during the 1996 to 1997 school

TABLE 12.18   *Public Schools That Rate Their Buildings as Less Than Adequate, by Minority and Poverty Enrollment, 1999*

	School Has Original Buildings	Original Buildings in Less Than Adequate Condition	School Has Permanent Additions	Permanent Additions in Less Than Adequate Condition	School Has Temporary Buildings	Temporary Buildings in Less Than Adequate Condition
Minority enrollment						
5 percent or less	99%	19%	68%	11%	25%	12%
	(0.5)	(3.2)	(3.0)	(3.4)	(3.1)	(4.3)
6 to 20 percent	100	18	70	14	39	22
	(0.2)	(3.5)	(3.5)	(3.2)	(4.0)	(5.3)
21 to 50 percent	100	16	62	16	44	14
	n.a.	(2.7)	(3.8)	(4.6)	(3.8)	(3.7)
More than 50 percent	100	23	67	24	51	24
	n.a.	(3.0)	(3.4)	(3.5)	(4.2)	(4.1)
Free/reduced-price-lunch-eligible enrollment						
Less than 20 percent	99	20	63	8	35	17
	(0.6)	(3.1)	(3.3)	(2.3)	(3.3)	(4.4)
20 to 39 percent	100	18	64	13	36	16
	n.a.	(2.4)	(3.7)	(3.3)	(3.0)	(3.9)
40 to 69 percent	100	16	74	16	42	19
	n.a.	(2.5)	(3.5)	(3.2)	(2.7)	(3.3)
70 percent or more	100	25	65	30	43	25
	n.a.	(4.2)	(4.4)	(5.1)	(4.6)	(5.3)

Source: Lewis et al. (2000, tables 2 and 2a). They use data from the U.S. Department of Education, NCES, FRSS: "Survey of the Condition of Public School Facilities, 1999."
Note: "Less than adequate" includes ratings of "fair," "poor," and "needs to be replaced."

TABLE 12.19   *Public Schools That Rate Their Buildings as Less Than Adequate, by Minority and Poverty Enrollment, 1999*

	At Least One Feature	Roofs	Framing, Doors, Foundations	Exterior Walls, Finishes, Windows, Doors	Interior Finishes, Trim	Plumbing	Heat, Ventilation, Air Conditioning	Electric Power	Electrical Lighting	Life Safety Features
Minority enrollment										
5 percent or less	48%	21%	15%	26%	14%	22%	28%	18%	16%	18%
	(3.3)	(2.8)	(2.9)	(3.2)	(2.4)	(2.8)	(2.9)	(2.6)	(2.1)	(2.8)
6 to 20 percent	49	25	15	23	17	26	29	18	16	22
	(4.1)	(3.8)	(3.0)	(3.4)	(2.7)	(3.8)	(3.5)	(2.9)	(2.8)	(3.5)
21 to 50 percent	46	17	12	17	14	23	25	19	15	18
	(3.9)	(3.0)	(2.4)	(2.7)	(3.0)	(3.7)	(3.7)	(3.3)	(3.3)	(3.5)
More than 50 percent	59	28	14	29	24	29	34	32	23	24
	(3.4)	(3.7)	(2.5)	(3.2)	(3.2)	(3.3)	(3.4)	(3.8)	(4.0)	(2.9)
Free/reduced-price-lunch-eligible enrollment										
Less than 20 percent	45	18	14	21	17	23	28	18	14	16
	(3.4)	(2.9)	(2.4)	(2.6)	(2.5)	(3.1)	(3.0)	(2.5)	(2.1)	(2.6)
20 to 39 percent	45	21	11	21	14	23	26	20	15	18
	(3.7)	(2.8)	(2.3)	(2.8)	(2.4)	(2.8)	(2.7)	(2.4)	(2.3)	(2.1)
40 to 69 percent	53	22	16	25	14	23	29	21	18	22
	(3.3)	(2.9)	(2.3)	(2.6)	(2.6)	(3.4)	(2.8)	(2.6)	(2.7)	(3.3)
70 percent or more	63	32	17	30	26	32	35	30	24	27
	(4.5)	(4.6)	(3.9)	(4.4)	(4.2)	(4.3)	(4.2)	(4.6)	(5.2)	(3.5)

Source: Lewis et al. (2000, tables 4 and 4a).

TABLE 12.20   *Overcrowding in Schools, by Minority and Poverty Enrollment, 1999*

	6 to 25 Percent Over Capacity	More Than 25 Percent Over Capacity
Minority enrollment		
5 percent or less	12%	4%
	(3.0)	(1.2)
6 to 20 percent	16	8
	(3.1)	(2.1)
21 to 50 percent	18	6
	(2.4)	(1.5)
More than 50 percent	13	15
	(2.4)	(2.7)
Free/reduced-price-lunch-eligible enrollment		
Less than 20 percent	16	6
	(2.8)	(1.6)
20 to 39 percent	13	8
	(2.4)	(1.8)
40 to 69 percent	16	7
	(2.6)	(2.0)
70 percent or more	12	12
	(2.6)	(2.9)

Source: Lewis et al. (2000, tables 19 and 19a).

Note: Respondents reported how many students the school was designed to serve (permanent buildings only, not including portables or other temporary space) and how many students were currently enrolled in the school. The extent of overcrowding was estimated by subtracting total enrollment from the capacity of the school's permanent buildings and dividing the difference by the capacity of the permanent buildings.

year (figure 12.14). These data reinforce the pattern in figures 12.11 and 12.12 showing that serious crime is far less common than theft. These data also reveal that predominantly minority schools were more likely to report at least one incident of theft or larceny to the police (41 percent) than the whitest schools (24 percent). And 15 percent of predominantly minority schools reported at least one serious violent incident to the police, compared with only 6 percent of the whitest schools.

Associations between crime and school poverty are weaker. Reports of theft, fights, and violent crime differ only slightly between high- and low-poverty schools. However, about 25 percent of schools from every socioeconomic bracket considered at least one attack or fight serious enough to merit a police report.

Of course, students are not the only victims of school violence. Table 12.21 reveals that 18 percent of teachers have been threatened by a student and that 8 percent have been attacked. And teachers at predominantly minority and predominantly poor schools are the most likely to have been threatened or attacked. Although most teachers have been neither threatened nor attacked, teachers at the poorest schools are twice as likely as those at the richest schools to have been attacked. These data reinforce the argument that policymakers must provide especially strong incentives to attract good teachers to poor schools (Ladd and Hansen 1999).

In response to crime, many schools implement safety measures. As table 12.22 shows,

(Text continues on p. 507.)

FIGURE 12.11 Crime Incidents at School or Going to or from School Per 1,000 Students, by Type of Crime and Student Ethnicity, 1992 to 2000

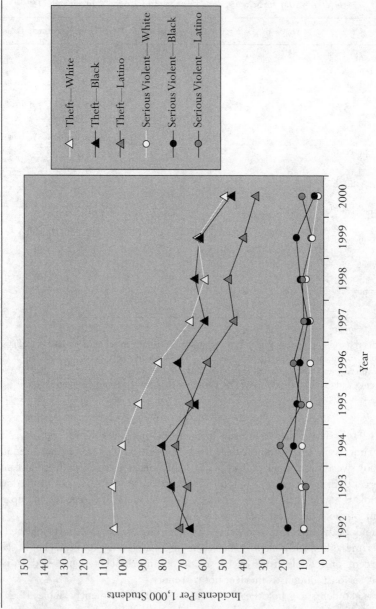

Source: DeVoe et al. (2002, tables 2.2 and S2.2). They use data from the U.S. Department of Justice, Bureau of Justice Statistics (BJS), National Crime Victimization Study, 1992 to 2000.

FIGURE 12.12   Crime Incidents at School or Going to or from School, by Type of Crime and Students' Family Income, 1992 to 2000

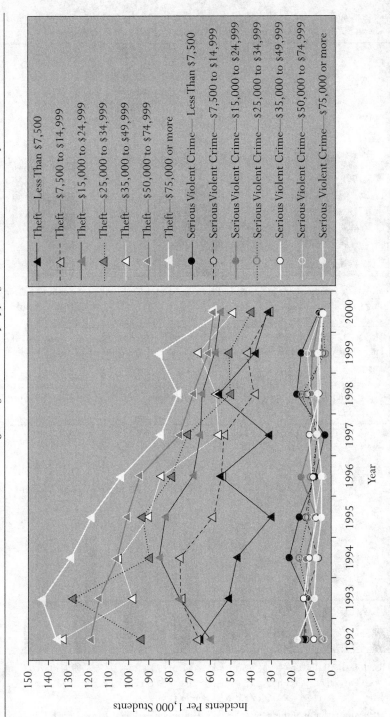

Source: DeVoe et al. (2002, tables 2.2 and S2.2). They use data from the U.S. Department of Justice, Bureau of Justice Statistics (BJS), National Crime Victimization Study, 1992 to 2000.

FIGURE 12.13   *Students Age Twelve to Eighteen Who Report Fear, Avoidance, or Being Bullied at School, by Student Ethnicity, 2001*

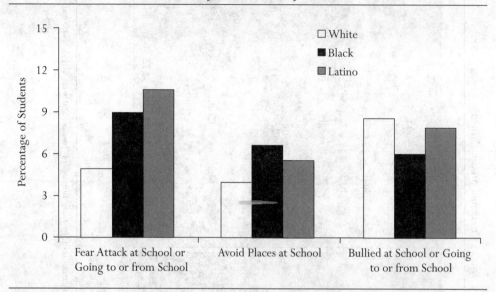

Source: DeVoe et al. (2002, tables 6.1, S6.1, 12.1, S12.1, 13.1, and S13.1). They use data from the U.S. Department of Justice, Bureau of Justice Statistics (BJS), National Crime Victimization Study, School Crime Supplement 2001.

FIGURE 12.14   *Schools Reporting Crimes to the Police, by Type of Crime, Minority Enrollment, and Poverty Enrollment, 1996 to 1997*

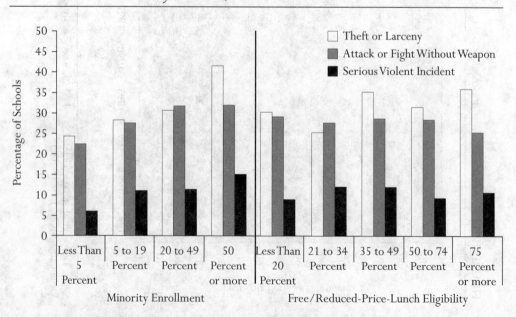

Source: DeVoe et al. (2002, tables 7.1 S7.1, 8.2, and S8.2). They use U.S. Department of Education, NCES, FRSS, School Principal/Disciplinarian Survey on School Violence, 1997.

TABLE 12.21   *Teachers Who Have Never Been Attacked or Threatened by a Student, by Minority and Poverty Enrollment, 1999 to 2000*

	Never Threatened	Never Attacked
Overall	82.1%	92.2%
	(0.38)	(0.26)
Minority enrollment		
5 percent or less	84.8	94.3
	(0.60)	(0.38)
6 to 20 percent	85.9	94.1
	(0.71)	(0.45)
21 to 50 percent	81.8	91.9
	(0.76)	(0.58)
More than 50 percent	76.8	89.0
	(1.10)	(0.63)
Free/reduced-price-lunch-eligible enrollment		
Less than 15 percent	86.0	95.5
	(0.61)	(0.39)
15 to 32 percent	83.2	92.0
	(0.75)	(0.54)
33 to 59 percent	81.0	92.2
	(0.80)	(0.51)
More than 59 percent	77.6	88.5
	(0.98)	(0.66)

Source: U.S. Department of Education, NCES, SASS: 1999 to 2000 (authors' calculations).

about 12 percent of predominantly minority high schools and 10 percent of poor high schools have metal detectors, compared with fewer than 1 percent of white or rich high schools. About one-third of predominantly minority and poor high schools use random metal detector checks of students, compared with less than 10 percent of white and rich high schools. Predominantly minority high schools are also much more likely (79 percent) than white high schools (25 percent) to have a daily police presence, although poor and nonpoor high schools are equally likely to have police. Although metal detectors and police probably help students feel less afraid, these same safety measures also signal to students (and prospective parents and teachers) that crime must be a problem.

PRIVATE AND "CHOICE" SCHOOL ENROLLMENT TRENDS

Our description of public school quality begs the question of whether we have understated ethnic and socioeconomic inequalities in children's access to high-quality schools by ignoring private schools. Inequality increases at the margin every time a high-achieving student, a very involved parent, or a highly qualified teacher moves from a poor or predominantly minority school into a whiter or richer school (whether public or private). It is possible that pro-choice advocates' growing push for private school vouchers over the 1990s forced states and school districts to increase public school choice and that these new options led to greater "creaming off" of good students and parents (and subsequently, good teachers) from disadvantaged schools. Likewise, it is also possible that growing income inequality allowed more affluent parents to choose private schools.

However, the aggregate trends we describe in this review include public schools of

TABLE 12.22   *Public High Schools (Including Charter Schools) Employing Safety Measures, by Minority and Poverty Enrollment, 1999 to 2000*

	Metal Detectors at Entrances	Random Metal Detector Checks of Students	Daily Police Presence
Minority enrollment			
5 percent or less	0.3%	4.0%	25.2%
	(0.1)	(0.6)	(1.3)
6 to 20 percent	0.5	7.7	53.5
	(0.3)	(0.9)	(1.8)
21 to 50 percent	0.8	18.8	66.8
	(0.3)	(1.5)	(2.0)
More than 50 percent	12.0	35.7	79.4
	(1.2)	(2.1)	(1.5)
Free/reduced-price-lunch-eligible enrollment			
Less than 15 percent	0.1	6.9	57.3
	(0.1)	(0.9)	(1.8)
15 to 32 percent	1.1	11.1	45.6
	(0.2)	(1.0)	(1.6)
33 to 59 percent	4.4	17.7	46.6
	(0.8)	(1.4)	(1.9)
More than 59 percent	9.5	29.0	54.2
	(1.2)	(2.0)	(2.5)

Source: U.S. Department of Education, NCES, SASS: 1999 to 2000 (authors' calculations).

choice—namely, charter schools and magnet schools—so any systematic movement of affluent or white children into those types of schools over the 1990s would appear in our tables as an increase in the quality of richer or whiter schools. And although the length of this chapter precludes us from presenting details about private school quality, the percentage of children enrolled in private schools (10 percent) is about the same as it was in 1970 (Reardon and Yun 2002).

Student enrollment in public "choice" schools did increase, however, over the 1990s (see table 12.23). By 1999, 12 percent of white students, 18 percent of Latino students, and 23 percent of African American students attended public schools that were not their assigned schools. Given that many parents exercise school choice before they even move into a home, these relatively high rates of attendance at public schools of choice suggest that a large fraction of parents, particularly African American and Latino parents, are exercising school choice *within* the public school system.

CONCLUSION

Nonwhite and poor students often attend different schools than their white and nonpoor counterparts and lag behind them academically. The purpose of this chapter was to review what we know about the extent of school inequality nationwide and how it has changed in recent decades.

Some aspects of school quality grew more unequal between the late 1980s and the late 1990s, especially between white and predominantly minority schools. Gaps in teachers' education and experience widened somewhat. And teachers in predominantly minority and

TABLE 12.23   *Students Who Attend Assigned Public Schools and Public and Private Schools of Choice, by Ethnicity and Family Income, 1993, 1996, 1999*

	1993				1996				1999			
	Public, Assigned	Public, Chosen	Private, Religious	Private, Secular	Public, Assigned	Public, Chosen	Private, Religious	Private, Secular	Public, Assigned	Public, Chosen	Private, Religious	Private, Secular
Race-ethnicity												
White	81.0%	8.6%	8.6%	1.8%	77.1%	11.1%	9.2%	2.7%	77.1%	11.5%	8.7%	2.7%
	(0.5)	(0.4)	(0.4)	(0.2)	(0.6)	(0.4)	(0.4)	(0.2)	(0.5)	(0.4)	(0.4)	(0.2)
African American	77.2	18.6	3.4	0.8	72.9	21.5	4.2	1.4	71.5	22.6	4.4	1.6
	(1.0)	(0.8)	(0.4)	(0.2)	(1.4)	(1.3)	(0.4)	(0.3)	(1.2)	(1.2)	(0.5)	(0.3)
Latino	79.2	13.7	6.4	0.7	76.4	16.1	6.3	1.3	77.0	18.0	3.9	1.1
	(1.1)	(1.0)	(0.5)	(0.2)	(1.1)	(0.9)	(0.7)	(0.3)	(1.0)	(1.0)	(0.4)	(0.2)
Family income												
$10,000 or less	82.5	14.3	2.8	0.4	76.5	19.4	2.5	1.7	73.9	21.9	2.7	1.4
	(1.1)	(0.9)	(0.5)	(0.2)	(1.5)	(1.4)	(0.5)	(0.5)	(1.6)	(1.5)	(0.6)	(0.4)
$10,001 to 20,000	82.4	13.7	3.4	0.5	78.8	16.3	3.6	1.3	78.1	17.4	3.2	1.4
	(1.6)	(1.7)	(0.4)	(0.2)	(1.1)	(1.1)	(0.6)	(0.3)	(1.1)	(1.0)	(0.5)	(0.4)
$20,001 to 35,000	81.6	10.6	6.9	0.9	78.3	13.9	6.4	1.4	78.4	15.7	4.4	1.5
	(0.6)	(0.6)	(0.6)	(0.1)	(0.9)	(0.8)	(0.5)	(0.2)	(0.8)	(0.7)	(0.4)	(0.4)
$35,001 to 50,000	79.7	10.0	8.9	1.5	77.2	12.4	8.8	1.7	76.6	13.6	8.0	1.9
	(1.0)	(0.6)	(0.7)	(0.2)	(0.9)	(0.8)	(0.6)	(0.2)	(0.9)	(0.7)	(0.6)	(0.3)
$50,001 to 75,000	77.1	9.1	11.4	2.4	76.0	9.9	11.8	2.4	78.3	11.0	8.7	2.1
	(0.9)	(0.6)	(0.7)	(0.3)	(0.9)	(0.6)	(0.8)	(0.3)	(0.9)	(0.6)	(0.7)	(0.3)
More than $75,000	72.2	7.6	14.4	5.8	67.7	11.2	15.1	6.0	70.3	10.4	14.2	5.1
	(1.4)	(0.6)	(0.1)	(0.9)	(1.1)	(0.7)	(0.9)	(0.5)	(0.9)	(0.6)	(0.7)	(0.5)

Source: U.S. Department of Education, NCES, "The Condition of Education Indicator 29: Parental Choice of Schools," tables 29–2 and S29–2. The data for those tables come from the National Household Education Survey Program (NHES), School Readiness Survey, 1993; School Safety and Discipline Survey, 1993; Parent and Family Involvement Survey, 1996; and Parent Interview Survey, 1999.

very poor schools became even more likely than their counterparts in whiter and richer schools to feel that their teaching materials were inadequate. Other aspects of school quality seem to have declined in general. Teachers became slightly more likely to teach subjects outside their main assignment field, and the selectivity of the colleges from which teachers graduated may have declined as well.

Yet over the same time period other aspects of school quality became more equal. In particular, school Internet access became ubiquitous, gaps in classroom Internet access decreased, and gaps in computer availability shrank considerably. Other aspects of school quality improved across the board. The school day got longer, graduation requirements increased, class sizes shrank, and the incidence of nonserious crimes committed at school— such as theft—declined.

Nonetheless, at the beginning of the twenty-first century disparities in teachers' education, credentials, experience, subject matter knowledge, and cognitive skills continue to favor white and nonpoor schools. Poor schools also offer less music and visual arts instruction than their nonpoor counterparts, and they have more buildings in need of repair. Minority schools have fewer support staff, such as counselors, than whiter schools, and they are more likely to be extremely overcrowded. African American and Latino students are also more likely than white students to avoid certain places at school and to fear being attacked.

Our tabulations of these disparities in school quality help to update James Coleman and his colleagues' (1966) tabulations in their famous *Equality of Educational Opportunity* report, which described the extent of school inequality in 1965. Although our chapter covers much less ground, it merits the same wise caveats Coleman raised years ago.

First, in this chapter we present only averages, which necessarily obscure considerable variation within each type of school. Thus, when tables show apparent ethnic and socioeconomic equality in school characteristics, these similarities should not be taken to imply that *all* schools are equal. Indeed, even when school quality is not associated with ethnic or socioeconomic composition, it often varies quite substantially along other dimensions (such as, size and location).

Second, this chapter uses what social scientists refer to as a variable-based analytic approach to describe school inequality. Each table examines a separate aspect of school quality and asks whether it differs between poor and nonpoor schools or between predominantly minority and white schools. Although most of the tables show disparities that favor whiter and richer schools, many of these disparities, as Coleman found nearly forty years ago, are not that large.

As anyone who has attended school knows, however, children do not experience variables in isolation. To the extent that the inequalities shown in separate tables are correlated with one another, some students are likely to experience considerably "worse" schools than others. Children who attend "bad" schools sit in classrooms that lack enough materials to go around and are too crowded for the teacher to move a "problem" child away from the group. These children's teachers lack experience, classroom management skills, and the knowledge and talent needed to communicate their subject matter accurately and joyfully. These same students attend schools that offer neither gifted programs nor art instruction. As these disparities add up, the effects of slightly larger classes, slightly less knowledgeable teachers, and slightly fewer perks begin to accumulate. And since many students attend middle schools and high schools that are similar to their elementary schools, some students experience a long string—maybe even twelve consecutive years—of "bad" schools, while others may get a long string of "good" schools. We suspect that if future research employs a more holistic "case-based" approach to studying school inequality it may be more successful at identifying the sets of schools that provide students with the worst *overall* educational experience and for which policy intervention could have the largest payoff.

DATA APPENDIX

The data we analyze in this chapter come from two main sources, the Common Core of Data (CCD): 2000 to 2001 and the Schools and Staffing Survey (SASS): 1987 to 1988 and 1999 to 2000.

We restrict the SASS samples to make them comparable with the Fast Response Survey System (FRSS) samples to which we compare them in some tables. Our SASS samples include charter and magnet schools but exclude special education schools, vocational-technical schools, alternative schools, and schools that do not offer any grades between first and twelfth. Our sample sizes of elementary and secondary schools, taken together, range from 7,325 to 8,368. Our teacher samples include only full-time teachers of grades one through twelve who taught general elementary, math, science, English and/or language arts, social studies, or foreign languages. Our sample sizes of elementary and secondary teachers, taken together, range from 18,790 to 22,150. We weight all SASS estimates with the appropriate school or teacher weights and use the SASS-provided replicate weights and the BRR replication method in WesVar 4.0 to correct the standard errors for stratification and clustering. We show these standard errors in parentheses. See Broene and Rust (2000) for a comparison of variance estimation in the SASS using different types of software packages.

For comparability with the FRSS, we define elementary teachers as those who teach self-contained classes. (Ninety-five percent of teachers of self-contained classes teach in elementary schools.) We define secondary teachers as those who teach in departmentalized settings. Certification refers to a "regular or standard state certificate, or advanced professional certificate" (as opposed to a provisional, probationary, temporary, or emergency certificate, or no certificate). We define elementary schools as schools in which the lowest grade is any of grades prekindergarten through four and the highest grade is any of grades one through eight. High schools are schools in which the lowest grade is any of grades seven through twelve and the highest grade is any of grades nine through twelve.

When tables show the SASS and FRSS data side by side, the standard errors are larger for the FRSS because its samples are smaller. Estimates from the SASS (1993 to 1994) and FRSS (1998) have fewer decimal places because these numbers come from a published report (Lewis et al. 1999).

We are grateful to Dan McGrath of the National Center for Education Statistics for sharing his SAS and Wesvar code on out-of-field teaching; the Higher Education Research Institute at the University of California at Los Angeles for sharing its college selectivity data; Kathryn Neckerman for her helpful comments on this chapter; and the Russell Sage Foundation for its generous financial support.

NOTES

1. NAEP reported reading scores by parental education beginning in 1971 but did not provide separate data for Latinos until 1975. Math scores are available by ethnicity and parental education beginning in 1973, but we excluded the 1973 assessment because it had very few items in common with later assessments.

2. Thirteen-year-olds' reports of their parents' education are more complete, and probably more reliable, than those of nine-year-olds. In 1999, for example, 11 percent of thirteen-year-olds in the reading sample reported that they did not know their parents' education, compared with 34 percent of nine-year-olds (Campbell, Hombo, and Mazzeo 2000). Trends for thirteen-year-olds are also less likely than those for seventeen-year-olds to have been influenced by changing ethnic or socioeconomic differentials in high school dropout rates.

3. Many researchers have shown that black-white gaps narrowed during this period; see, for example, Jaynes and Williams (1989), Grissmer, Flanagan, and Williamson (1998), Hauser and Huang (1996), Hedges and Nowell (1998), and Phillips, Crouse, and Ralph (1998). For evidence on why the gaps narrowed, see Cook and Evans (2000), Grissmer, Flanagan, and Williamson (1998), and Hedges and Nowell (1998).

4. Small Latino samples in NAEP produce large standard errors. Thus, while the decline in the Latino-white math gap is statistically significant, the decline in the Latino-white reading gap is not statistically significant at the .05 level (see standard errors in the appendices of Campbell, Hombo, and Mazzeo 2000).

5. Phillips, Crouse, and Ralph (1998) find that the reading gap widened but that the math gap did not. Their analyses did not, however, include post-1996 data. Campbell, Hombo, and Mazzeo (2000) show that the 1999 black-white math gap was statistically significantly larger than the 1986 math gap.

6. NAEP administers two different achievement tests to two samples of U.S. students. Trend data come from students in the trend sample, who take tests that contain many of the same items year after year. The NAEP main sample takes tests that are aligned to changing curricular standards and are not comparable over time. (Nor are they comparable to the data from trend samples displayed in figures 12.1 through 12.4.)

7. Phillips, Crouse, and Ralph (1998) argue, however, that although cross-sectional test score gaps remain constant over the school years, this need not imply that gaps among similarly prepared students do not widen.

8. Many people assume that ethnic differences in test scores simply reflect socioeconomic differences. However, the test score gap between African American and white students whose parents have the same income and education is nearly as large as the overall gap (Jencks and Phillips 1998). Studies that have tried to equate the "family environment" of ethnic groups—by considering traditional measures of socioeconomic status as well as parenting practices—have explained between half and all of the gap, depending on the dataset and the size of the gap (see, for example, Fryer and Levitt 2002; Phillips et al. 1998).

9. The College Board (2002) reports separate scores for students of Mexican, Puerto Rican, and other Latino origin. We report a weighted average that combines scores for these groups. The denominator for the gaps is the verbal or math standard deviation for all SAT I test-takers in 2002.

10. These income cutoffs correspond roughly to the bottom and top quintiles of the income distribution of students who took the SAT I in 2002. The average score for the bottom quintile represents the weighted average of scores for the lowest three income categories.

11. Estimates in this paragraph come from the authors' analyses of National Education Longitudinal Study (NELS) high school transcript data and school records data for third-graders in the congressionally mandated study of educational growth and opportunity (PROSPECTS). For NELS, we averaged transcript reports of math, science, English, and social studies grades and recoded the average to reflect a 4.0 scale. We weighted our estimates with the transcript panel weight for grades eight through twelve because our estimates of mothers' education come from students' and parents' reports beginning in eighth grade. For PROSPECTS, we used the methods reported in Phillips (2000), but our estimates differ slightly because we do not hold gender constant.

12. In high school Asian Americans' grades are 0.3 grade points higher than those of whites. Thus, if Asians are the comparison group, grade disparities among ethnic groups are much larger (.94 standard deviations for the Asian-black gap and .77 standard deviations for the Asian-Latino gap).

13. See Grogger and Eide (1995) and Murnane, Willett, and Levy (1995) for evidence on increasing returns to cognitive skills. See Jencks and Phillips (1998) for suggestive evidence that the economic returns to cognitive skills rose more for African Americans than for whites between the 1960s and 1990s.

14. The adjusted difference between the B.A.-completion rates of African Americans and whites is 1.52 percent, which is not statistically significant. Also, Asian Americans complete college at a higher rate than any other ethnic group, even conditioning on eighth-grade test scores and grades. Our estimates are based on logit models that include NELS respondents with scores on all eighth-grade tests and self-reported eighth-grade grades (N = 10,693 in the ethnicity model; N = 10,636 in the parents' education model). Adjusted models include math, reading, science, and social studies test scores (and their squares) and self-reported grade point averages (and their squares), and they are weighted with the f4bypnwt; standard errors are adjusted for clustering. The predicted probability calculations hold test scores and grades at their mean.

15. These enrollment statistics come from supplemental tables 2.1 and 2.3 of the *Condition of Education 2002* (Wirt et al. 2002). Stacey Bielick, Kathryn Chandler, and Stephen Broughman (2001) estimate that another 850,000 U.S. students are home-schooled. We compare the quality of public and private schools overall, as well as those located in similar neighborhoods, in a separate paper.

16. In fact, Michael Cook and William Evans's (2000) analysis of why the black-white test score gap narrowed during the 1970s and 1980s finds that 75 percent of the convergence can be attributed to narrowing *within* schools, whereas only 25 percent of the reduction resulted from changes in parental background and changes in quality differences among schools. See Lucas (1998) for evidence on the effects of tracking on inequality. See Ferguson (1998) for an excellent review of the tracking and ability-grouping literature.

17. These tabulations differ slightly from those reported in Frankenberg, Lee, and Orfield (2003) because we do not impute missing ethnic enrollment data in the CCD for Tennessee.

18. For more information on trends in school segregation, see Frankenberg, Lee, and Orfield (2003). They show that the percentage of black students attending predominantly minority schools fell during the late 1960s and early 1970s, held constant during the 1980s, and then increased. In contrast, the percentage of Latino students attending predominantly minority schools increased between the late 1960s and the early 1980s. We do not show those trends here, however, because we do not trust the comparability of the data over time. Prior to 1987, data on schools' ethnic enrollments were gathered by the U.S. Department of Education's Office of Civil Rights. Because the data were collected explicitly for civil rights enforcement purposes, the Office of Civil Rights often did not gather data from suburbs, particularly suburbs with few minority students. According to Gary Orfield (1983, 37): "The data are particularly inadequate for metropolitan areas with highly fragmented educational systems that include many small suburban districts. This pattern characterizes the older urban centers of the East and Midwest—areas that are often the centers of segregation in what are now the nation's most segregated states." Also, surveys before 1980 rarely collected separate data for Latinos, and although we cannot find any specific documentation about the ethnicity definitions used in pre-1980 data, we suspect that the definitions changed over time. Frankenberg, Lee, and Orfield (2003) also use data from the earliest CCDs to examine segregation trends. However, CCD data from the late 1980s and early 1990s are incomplete. For example, in the first year that the CCD collected data on ethnic enrollments (1987 to 1988), seventeen states (enrolling 27.8 percent of U.S. students) did not report these numbers.

19. Children qualify for free (reduced-price) meals if their family income falls below 130 percent (185 percent) of the poverty line (U.S. Department of Agriculture 2002).

20. The CCD (2000–2001) from which we tabulated these percentages lacks subsidized meal data from Arizona, Connecticut, Illinois, Tennessee, and Washington. We do not report historical trends for subsidized meal eligibility because different states report lunch data on the CCD from one year to the next.

21. The correlation between the percentage minority and percentage poor was .62 in 2000 to 2001.

22. Teachers also influence children's social and psychological development, but scholars know even less about what makes a teacher "good" in those domains.

23. For reviews on teacher quality, especially certification, see Darling-Hammond (2002), Darling-Hammond, Berry, and Thoreson (2001), Goldhaber and Brewer (2000, 2001), and Walsh (2001a, 2001b).

24. Researchers have developed several measures of out-of-field teaching (Ingersoll 1998, 2001; Seastrom et al. 2002). Although the percentage of teachers with majors or minors in their main assignment field underestimates the extent of the out-of-field teaching problem, we report this measure because our teacher sample is limited to teachers with main assignments in regular subjects. Consequently, our sample would severely understate out-of-field teaching if we used measures based on the percentages of courses or students taught by teachers lacking a degree in a particular subject. We defined teachers as having a major or minor in a field if they majored or minored in that field during undergraduate, graduate, or professional training. Although we restricted our sample more than Seastrom and her colleagues (2002) did, we used their procedures for matching teachers' degrees with school subjects. For simplicity, we used the broadest fields for "science" and "social studies." For instance, we considered biology, physics, and chemistry teachers to be science teachers and called them "in-field" if they had a degree in any of the sciences. (Thus, a physics teacher was in-field if he or she majored in biology, chemistry, or physics.) Obviously, estimates of out-of-field teaching would be much larger if fields were more narrowly defined.

25. The percentages in table 12.5 overstate the extent of out-of-field teaching in high schools because they include middle schools. Out-of-field teaching tends to be more common in middle schools (Seastrom et al. 2002), possibly because some middle schools use "block classes" in which the same teacher teaches both math and science or both English and social studies, thus forcing teachers to be out-of-field for half of their classes. We have not yet seen evidence on whether subject-specific expertise is less important for student learning in middle school than in high school.

26. The estimates we report are approximate. The college selectivity data come from the Higher Education Research Institute (HERI) selectivity file, which is based on public reports of institutions' mean SAT and/or ACT scores. Because we lacked selectivity data for the precise year in which many teachers entered college (the HERI file contains data for 1973, 1977, 1982, and 1999), we used the closest year for which we had data. Fortunately, college selectivity is highly correlated from year to year—estimates from 1973, 1977, and 1982 correlate over .90; the 1999 estimate correlates between .78 and .82 with the other estimates. However, we chose to exclude the 1999 selectivity data. Because the 1999 scores reflect recentering of the SAT in 1995, and because only teachers in the 1999 to 2000 sample could have entered college closer to 1999 than to 1982, using the 1999 selectivity scores would have reduced the comparability of the two time periods. Note, however, that analyses using the 1999 selectivity scores showed overall averages in 1999 to 2000 that were about ten points higher than in 1987 to 1988, a smaller gap (seven points) between high- and low-minority schools, and a larger gap (forty-six points) between high- and low-poverty schools.

27. Note, however, that when we categorize schools according to their percentages of African American students, the selectivity gap between the bottom and top quartile is forty-six points. The gap between quartiles of schools based on the percentage of Latino students is thirty-one points.

28. Most schools are already located in districts that require teacher applicants to pass a basic skills or professional knowledge test, although the content and difficulty of these tests vary widely across districts and states. Disadvantaged schools are, if anything, more likely than other types of schools to be located in districts that require such tests (table available from the authors).

29. We intended to examine changes in participation in professional development, hypothesizing that participation may have increased, and inequality decreased, due to the pressures of accountability reform. However, questions on previous SASS questionnaires refer to a different time frame ("since the end of the last school year" instead of "in the last 12 months"), making the data incomparable over time.

30. Michael Boozer, Alan Krueger, and Shari Wolkon (1992) show that pupil-teacher ratios (a proxy for class size) and inequalities between African American and white students declined dramatically over the twentieth century.

31. In the Midwest, predominantly minority and predominantly poor schools are more likely than other schools to be located in districts with heavier graduation requirements, and this pattern drives the results in table 12.10. In other regions, however, predominantly minority and predominantly poor schools tend to be located in districts that have neither much higher nor much lower graduation requirements than other schools.

32. In California, Julian Betts, Kim Rueben, and Anne Danenberg (2000) find that 2.0 percent of courses at the median school in the bottom SES quintile are AP, compared with 3.2 percent of courses at the median

school in the top SES quintile. Betts and his colleagues also show large within-quintile variance in AP offerings: 7.1 percent of the courses offered by schools at the ninetieth percentile of the top SES quintile are AP, compared with 0.6 percent of courses at schools at the tenth percentile of the bottom SES quintile. According to the American Civil Liberties Union (1999), California is at the "forefront nationally" in offering AP courses, but does not offer all students the same AP opportunities. The exemplar schools they compared in their lawsuit were Beverly Hills High School, which offers forty-five AP classes, and Arvin High School (near Bakersfield, California), which offers two.

33. Some of this difference is driven by schools with very large collections. Nonetheless, when we compare the holdings of the median white school and the median predominantly minority school, the white school still has 3,900 fewer books than its predominantly minority counterpart.

34. Schools often had more instructional computers than they could use efficiently given their structural deficiencies. In the GAO (1995) survey, 61.2 percent reported inadequate phone lines for instructional use, 60.6 percent reported inadequate conduits, raceways, and computer network cables, 57.5 percent reported inadequate modems, 46.1 percent reported inadequate electrical wiring, and 34.6 percent reported inadequate electrical power. Only 25.2 percent reported inadequate instructional computers. In site visits, GAO observers found brand-new computers still in boxes because schools did not have enough electrical power to use them.

35. A major cause of the rapid reduction in technology disparities seems to be the E-Rate program, which subsidized low-income schools' acquisition of Internet access (see Goolsbee and Guryan 2002).

36. Wirt and his colleagues (2002) report NAEP reading scores in 2000 by the percentage of students eligible for subsidized meals. Based on Wirt and his colleagues' categories, in low-poverty schools fewer than 11 percent of students are eligible for subsidized meals and the mean NAEP score is 236. In high-poverty schools over 75 percent of students are eligible for subsidized meals, and the mean NAEP score for this group is 191. The student-level fourth-grade standard deviation for reading scores is forty points.

REFERENCES

American Civil Liberties Union. 1999. "In Class-Action Lawsuit, ACLU Says CA Students Are Denied Access to Advanced Placement Course." Press release. New York: ACLU.

Angrist, Joshua D., and Victor Lavy. 2001. "Does Teacher Training Affect Pupil Learning? Evidence from Matched Comparisons in Jerusalem Public Schools." *Journal of Labor Economics* 19: 343–69.

Aronson, Julie, Joy Zimmerman, and Lisa Carlos. 1999. "Improving Student Achievement by Extending School: Is It Just a Matter of Time?" San Francisco: WestEd.

Associated Press. 2003. "Los Angeles to Hire 125 Janitors and Spend $10 Million a Year to Fix School Restrooms." Newswire. Los Angeles.

Ballou, Dale. 1996. "Do Public Schools Hire the Best Applicants?" *Quarterly Journal of Economics* 111: 97–133.

Betts, Julian, Kim S. Rueben, and Anne Danenberg. 2000. "Equal Resources, Equal Outcomes? The Distribution of School Resources and Student Achievement in California." San Francisco: Public Policy Institute of California.

Bielick, Stacey, Kathryn Chandler, and Stephen P. Broughman. 2001. "Home-schooling in the United States: 1999." *Education Statistics Quarterly* 3: 25–32.

Bohrnstedt, George W., and Brian M. Stecher. 2002. *What We Have Learned About Class Size Reduction in California*. Palo Alto, Calif.: American Institutes for Research.

Boozer, Michael A., Alan B. Krueger, and Shari Wolkon. 1992. "Race and School Quality Since *Brown v. Board of Education*." *Brookings Papers on Economic Activity—Microeconomics* (1): 269–326.

Broene, Pam, and Keith Rust. 2000. *Strengths and Limitations of Using SUDAAN, Stata, and WesVarPC for Computing Variances from NCES Datasets*. Washington: U.S. Department of Education.

Campbell, Jay R., Catherine M. Hombo, and John Mazzeo. 2000. *NAEP 1999 Trends in Academic Progress: Three Decades of Student Performance*. Washington: U.S. Department of Education.

Carey, Nancy, Brian Kleiner, Rebecca Porch, and Elizabeth Farris. 2002. *Arts Education in Public Elementary and Secondary Schools: 1999–2000*. Washington: U.S. Department of Education, National Center for Education Statistics.

Cohen, David K., and H. C. Hill. 2000. "Instructional Policy and Classroom Performance: The Mathematics Reform in California." *Teachers College Record* 102: 294–343.

Coleman, James S., Ernest Q. Campbell, Charles J. Hobson, James McPartland, Alexander Mood, F. D. Wienfeld, and R. L. York. 1966. *Equality of Educational Opportunity.* Washington: U.S. Government Printing Office.

College Board. 2002. "2002 College-Bound Seniors: A Profile of SAT Program Test-Takers." New York: College Board.

Cook, Michael D., and William N. Evans. 2000. "Families or Schools? Explaining the Convergence in White and Black Academic Performance." *Journal of Labor Economics* 18: 729–54.

Darling-Hammond, Linda. 1997. *Doing What Matters Most: Investing in Quality Teaching.* New York: National Commission on Teaching and America's Future.

———. 2002. "Research and Rhetoric on Teacher Certification: A Response to 'Teacher Certification Reconsidered.'" *Education Policy Analysis Archives* 10 (36, September 6), available at: http://epaa.asu.edu/epaa/v10n36.html.http://epaa.asu.edu/epaa/v10n36.html.

Darling-Hammond, Linda, Barnett Berry, and Amy Thoreson. 2001. "Does Teacher Certification Matter? Evaluating the Evidence." *Educational Evaluation and Policy Analysis* 23: 57–77.

DeVoe, Jill F., Katherin Peter, Phillip Kaufman, Sally A. Ruddy, Amanda K. Miller, Mike Planty, Thomas D. Snyder, Detis T. Duhart, and Michael R. Rand. 2002. *Indicators of School Crime and Safety: 2002.* Washington: U.S. Department of Education and U.S. Department of Justice.

Donahue, Patricia L., Robert J. Finnegan, Anthony D. Lutkus, Nancy L. Allen, and Jay R. Campbell. 2001. *The Nation's Report Card: Fourth-Grade Reading 2000.* Washington: U.S. Department of Education, National Center for Education Statistics.

Donahue, Patricia L., Kristin E. Voelkl, Jay R. Campbell, and John Mazzeo. 1999. *NAEP 1998 Reading Report Card for the Nations and States.* Washington: U.S. Department of Education.

Ehrenberg, Ronald G., and Dominic J. Brewer. 1995. "Did Teachers' Verbal Ability and Race Matter in the 1960s? Coleman Revisited." *Economics of Education Review* 14: 1–21.

Ehrenberg, Ronald G., Dominic J. Brewer, Adam Gamoran, and J. Douglas Willms. 2001. "Class Size and Student Achievement." *Scientific American* 285(5, November 1): 78–85.

Entwisle, Doris R., Karl L. Alexander, and Linda S. Olson. 1997. *Children, Schools, and Inequality.* Boulder, Colo.: Westview Press.

Ferguson, Ronald F. 1991. "Paying for Public Education: New Evidence on How and Why Money Matters." *Harvard Journal on Legislation* 28: 465–97.

———. 1998. "Can Schools Narrow the Black-White Test Score Gap?" In *The Black-White Test Score Gap,* edited by Christopher Jencks and Meredith Phillips. Washington, D.C.: Brookings Institution.

Ferguson, Ronald F., and Helen F. Ladd. 1996. "How and Why Money Matters: An Analysis of Alabama Schools." In *Holding Schools Accountable,* edited by Helen F. Ladd. Washington, D.C.: Brookings Institution.

Finn, Jeremy D., and Charles M. Achilles. 1999. "Tennessee's Class Size Study: Findings, Implications, Misconceptions." *Educational Evaluation and Policy Analysis* 21: 97–109.

Frankenberg, Erica, Chungmei Lee, and Gary Orfield. 2003. "A Multiracial Society with Segregated Schools: Are We Losing the Dream?" Cambridge, Mass.: Civil Rights Project.

Fryer, Roland G., and Steven D. Levitt. 2002. *Understanding the Black-White Test Score Gap in the First Two Years of School.* Working paper. Cambridge, Mass.: National Bureau of Economic Research.

Goldhaber, Dan. 2002. "The Mystery of Good Teaching." *Education Next* 2: 50–55.

Goldhaber, Dan D., and Dominic J. Brewer. 1997. "Why Don't Schools and Teachers Seem to Matter? Assessing the Impact of Unobservables on Educational Productivity." *Journal of Human Resources* 32: 505–23.

———. 2000. "Does Teacher Certification Matter? High School Teacher Certification Status and Student Achievement." *Educational Evaluation and Policy Analysis* 22: 129–45.

———. 2001. "Evaluating the Evidence on Teacher Certification: A Rejoinder." *Educational Evaluation and Policy Analysis* 23: 79–86.

Goldring, Ellen B., and Charles S. Hausman. 1999. "Reasons for Parental Choice of Urban Schools." *Journal of Educational Policy* 14: 469–90.

Goolsbee, Austan, and Jonathan Guryan. 2002. "The Impact of Internet Subsidies in Public Schools." Working paper. Cambridge, Mass.: National Bureau of Economic Research.

Greenwald, Rob, Larry V. Hedges, and Richard D. Laine. 1996. "The Effect of School Resources on Student Achievement." *Review of Educational Research* 66: 361–96.

Grissmer, David, Ann Flanagan, and Stephanie Williamson. 1998. "Why Did the Black-White Test Score Gap Narrow in the 1970s and 1980s?" In *The Black-White Test Score Gap,* edited by Christopher Jencks and Meredith Phillips. Washington, D.C.: Brookings Institution.

Grogger, Jeff. 1997. "Local Violence and Educational Attainment." *Journal of Human Resources* 32: 659–82.

Grogger, Jeff, and Eric Eide. 1995. "Changes in College Skills and the Rise in the College Wage Premium." *Journal of Human Resources* 30: 280.

Hanushek, Eric A. 1972. *Education and Race: An Analysis of the Educational Production Process.* Lexington, Mass.: Lexington Books.

————. 1997. "Assessing the Effects of School Resources on Student Performance: An Update." *Educational Evaluation and Policy Analysis* 19: 141–64.

Hanushek, Eric A., John F. Kain, Jacob M. Markman, and Steven G. Rivkin. 2001. "Does Peer Ability Affect Student Achievement?" Working paper. Cambridge, Mass.: National Bureau of Economic Research.

Hanushek, Eric A., John F. Kain, and Steven G. Rivkin. 2001. "Why Public Schools Lose Teachers." Working paper. Cambridge, Mass.: National Bureau of Economic Research.

Hauser, Robert M., and Min-Hsiung Huang. 1996. *Trends in Black-White Test-Score Differentials.* Madison: University of Wisconsin, Institute for Research on Poverty.

Hedges, Larry V., and Amy Nowell. 1998. "Black-White Test Score Convergence Since 1965." In *The Black-White Test Score Gap,* edited by Christopher Jencks and Meredith Phillips. Washington, D.C.: Brookings Institution.

Heyns, Barbara. 1978. *Summer Learning and the Effects of Schooling.* New York: Academic Press.

Hill, David. 2000. "Test Case." *Education Week* 19: 34–38.

Hoxby, Caroline. 2000. "Peer Effects in the Classroom: Learning from Race and Gender Variation." Working paper. Cambridge, Mass.: National Bureau of Economic Research.

Ingersoll, Richard M. 1998. "The Problem of Out-of-Field Teaching." *Phi Delta Kappan* 79: 773–76.

————. 2001. "The Realities of Out-of-Field Teaching." *Educational Leadership* 58: 42–45.

Jacob, Brian A., and Lars Lefgren. 2002. "The Impact of Teacher Training on Student Achievement: Quasi-experimental Evidence from School Reform Efforts in Chicago." Working paper. Cambridge, Mass.: National Bureau of Economic Research.

Jaynes, Gerald David, and Robin Murphy Williams. 1989. *A Common Destiny: Blacks and American Society.* Washington, D.C.: National Academy Press.

Jencks, Christopher. 1972. *Inequality: A Reassessment of the Effect of Family and Schooling in America.* New York: Harper & Row.

Jencks, Christopher, and Meredith Phillips. 1998. "Introduction." In *The Black-White Test Score Gap,* edited by Christopher Jencks and Meredith Phillips. Washington, D.C.: Brookings Institution.

————. 1999. "Aptitude or Achievement: Why Do Test Scores Predict Educational Attainment and Earnings?" In *Earning and Learning: How Schools Matter,* edited by Susan E. Mayer and Paul E. Peterson. Washington, D.C. and New York: Brookings Institution and Russell Sage Foundation.

Jepsen, Christopher, and Steven G. Rivkin. 2002. "What Is the Trade-off Between Smaller Classes and Teacher Quality?" Working paper. Cambridge, Mass.: National Bureau of Economic Research.

Johnson, William R., and Derek Neal. 1998. "Basic Skills and the Black-White Earnings Gap." In *The Black-White Test Score Gap,* edited by Christopher Jencks and Meredith Phillips. Washington, D.C.: Brookings Institution.

Kain, John F., and Kraig Singleton. 1996. "Equality of Educational Opportunity Revisited." *New England Economic Review* May/June: 87–111.

Kennedy, Mary. 1999. "Form and Substance in Mathematics and Science Professional Development." Arlington, Va.: National Science Foundation.

Kleiner, Anne, and Elizabeth Farris. 2002. *Internet Access in U.S. Public Schools and Classrooms: 1994 to 2001.* Washington: U.S. Department of Education, National Center for Education Statistics.

Kozol, Jonathan. 1991. *Savage Inequalities: Children in America's Schools.* New York: Crown.

Krueger, Alan B. 1999. "Experimental Estimates of Education Production Functions." *Quarterly Journal of Economics* 114: 497–532.

————. 2000. "The Digital Divide in Educating African American Students and Workers." In *Education and Training for the Black Worker in the Twenty-first Century,* edited by Cecilia Conrad and Margaret Simms. Washington, D.C.: Joint Center for Political and Economic Studies.

Ladd, Helen F., and Janet S. Hansen. 1999. *Making Money Matter: Financing America's Schools.* Washington, D.C.: National Academy Press.

Lankford, Hamilton, Susanna Loeb, and James Wyckoff. 2002. "Teacher Sorting and the Plight of Urban Schools: A Descriptive Analysis." *Educational Evaluation and Policy Analysis* 24: 37–62.

Lee, Valerie E., and David T. Burkam. 2002. *Inequality at the Starting Gate: Social Background Differences in Achievement as Children Begin School.* Washington, D.C.: Economic Policy Institute.

Lee, Valerie E., Robert G. Croninger, and Julia B. Smith. 1996. "Equity and Choice in Detroit." In *Who Chooses? Who Loses? Culture, Institutions, and the Unequal Effects of School Choice,* edited by Bruce Fuller and Richard Elmore. New York: Teachers College Press.

Lewis, Laurie, Basmat Parsad, Nancy Carey, Nicole Bartfai, Elizabeth Farris, and Becky Smerdon. 1999. *Teacher Quality: A Report on the Preparation and Qualifications of Public School Teachers.* Washington: U.S. Department of Education.

Lewis, Laurie, Kyle Snow, Elizabeth Farris, Becky Smerdon, Stephanie Cronen, Jessica Kaplan, and Bernie Greene. 2000. *Condition of America's Public School Facilities: 1999.* Washington: U.S. Department of Education.

Lucas, Samuel R. 1998. *Tracking Inequality: Stratification and Mobility in American High Schools.* New York: Teachers College Press.

Mayer, Daniel P., John E. Mullens, and Mary T. Moore. 2000. *Monitoring School Quality: An Indicators Report.* NCES 2001-030. Washington: U.S Department of Education.

Meyer, Robert H. 1999. "The Effects of Math and Math-Related Courses in High School." In *Earning and Learning: How Schools Matter,* edited by Susan E. Mayer and Paul E. Peterson. Washington, D.C. and New York: Brookings Institution and Russell Sage Foundation.

Monk, David H. 1994. "Subject-Area Preparation of Secondary Mathematics and Science Teachers and Student Achievement." *Economics of Education Review* 13: 125–45.

Mosteller, Frederick. 1995. "The Tennessee Study of Class Size in the Early School Grades." *Future of Children* 5: 113–27.

Murnane, Richard. 1981. "Interpreting the Evidence on School Effectiveness." *Teachers College Record* 83(1): 19–35.

Murnane, Richard, Judith D. Singer, John B. Willett, James J. Kemple, and Randall J. Olsen. 1991. *Who Will Teach? Policies That Matter.* Cambridge, Mass.: Harvard University Press.

Murnane, Richard J., John B. Willett, and Frank Levy. 1995. *The Growing Importance of Cognitive Skills in Wage Determination.* Cambridge, Mass.: National Bureau of Economic Research.

Niesse, Mark. 2002. "School Bathrooms Undergo Transformation." *Chattanooga Times–Free Press,* August 21, 2000.

Orfield, Gary. 1983. *Public School Desegregation in the United States: 1968–1980.* Washington, D.C.: Joint Center for Political Studies.

Peterson, Paul E., David Myers, and William G. Howell. 1998. "An Evaluation of the New York City School Choice Scholarships Program: The First Year." Harvard University, Cambridge, Mass.

Phillips, Meredith. 1997. "What Makes Schools Effective? A Comparison of the Relationships of Communitarian Climate and Academic Climate to Mathematics Achievement and Attendance During Middle School." *American Educational Research Journal* 34: 633–62.

————. 1998. "Do African American and Latino Children Learn More in Predominantly White Schools?" Paper presented to the 1998 meeting of the American Sociological Association. San Francisco, Calif. (August 21–25, 1998).

————. 2000. "Grades Versus Standardized Tests: Which Is a Better Measure of Student Achievement?" Paper presented to the meeting of the American Sociological Association. Washington, D.C. (August 12–16, 2000).

Phillips, Meredith, Jeanne Brooks-Gunn, Greg J. Duncan, Pamela Klebanov, and Jonathan Crane. 1998. "Family Background, Parenting Practices, and the Black-White Test Score Gap." In *The Black-White Test Score Gap,* edited by Christopher Jencks and Meredith Phillips. Washington, D.C.: Brookings Institution.

Phillips, Meredith, and Tiffani Chin. Forthcoming. "Summer Learning: How Do Teacher and Student Characteristics Matter?" In *Summer Learning: Research, Policies, and Programs,* edited by Geoffrey Borman and Matthew Boulay. Mahwah, N.J.: Lawrence Erlbaum.

Phillips, Meredith, James Crouse, and John Ralph. 1998. "Does the Black-White Test Score Gap Widen After Children Enter School?" In *The Black-White Test Score Gap,* edited by Christopher Jencks and Meredith Phillips. Washington, D.C.: Brookings Institution.

Podgursky, Michael, Ryan Monroe, and Donald Watson. 2002. "Teacher Mobility, Pay, and Academic Quality." Paper presented to the annual meeting of the Society of Labor Economists. Baltimore, Md.(May 4–5, 2002).

Reardon, Sean, and John T. Yun. 2002. "Private School Racial Enrollments and Segregation." Cambridge, Mass.: Civil Rights Project.

Rivkin, Steven G., Eric A. Hanushek, and John F. Kain. 1998. "Teachers, Schools, and Academic Achievement." Working paper. Cambridge, Mass.: National Bureau of Economic Research.

Rothstein, Richard. 2002. "Lessons: A Crowding Quandry Meets a Quake Code." *New York Times,* sec. B, p.7, col.1, Metro Desk, Education, April 13, 2002.

Rowan, Brian, Fang-Shen Chiang, and Robert J. Miller. 1997. "Using Research on Employees' Performance to Study the Effects of Teachers on Students' Achievement." *Sociology of Education* 70: 256–84.

Rubenstein, Karin. 2003. "Multiplication Problem." *New York Times,* Sec. 14WC, p. 1, col. 2, Weschester Weekly Desk, February 16, 2003.

Seastrom, Marilyn McMillen, Kerry J. Gruber, Robin Henke, Daniel J. McGrath, and Benjamin A. Cohen. 2002. *Qualifications of the Public School Teacher Workforce: Prevalence of Out-of-Field Teaching 1987–88 to 1999–2000.* Washington: U.S. Department of Education.

Shouse, Roger C. 1996. "Academic Press and Sense of Community: Conflict, Congruence, and Implications for Student Achievement." *Social Psychology of Education* 1: 47–68.

Snyder, Thomas D., and Charlene M. Hoffman. 2001. *Digest of Education Statistics 2001.* Washington: U.S. Department of Education.

Spielvogel, Jill. 2002. "High School Guidance Counselors Overworked." *San Diego Union-Tribune,* June 1, 2002.

Strauss, Robert P., and Elizabeth A. Sawyer. 1986. "Some New Evidence on Teacher and Student Competencies." *Economics of Education Review* 5: 41–48.

Technology Counts. 2001. "The New Divides: Looking Beneath the Numbers to Reveal Digital Inequities." *Education Week* 20: 10–11.

U.S. Department of Agriculture. Food and Nutrition Services. 2002. "Child Nutrition Programs: Income Eligibility Guidelines." *Federal Register* 67: 8933–34.

U.S. Department of Education. National Center for Education Statistics. 2000. "Results over Time: NAEP 1999 Long-term Trend Summary Data Tables" (August). Available at: nces.ed.gov/nationsreportcard/tables/Ltt1999.

———. 2002. *Common Core of Data (CCD) School Years 1987–88 through 1999–2000.* Washington: U.S. Department of Education.

———. 2003. *Restricted-Use Data SASS, 1987–88, 1990–91, 1993–94, 1999–2000; TFS, 1988–89, 1991–92, 1994–95.* Washington: U.S. Department of Education.

U.S. Department of Health and Human Services. 2000. "The 2000 HHS Poverty Guidelines." *Federal Register* 65: 7555–57.

U.S. General Accounting Office. 1995. *School Facilities: America's Schools Not Designed or Equipped for Twenty-first Century: Report to Congressional Requesters.* Washington: U.S. GAO.

———. 2002. "Per-Pupil Spending Differences Between Selected Inner-City and Suburban Schools Varied by Metropolitan Area." Washington: U.S. GAO.

Walsh, Kate. 2001a. "Teacher Certification Reconsidered: Stumbling for Quality." Baltimore: Abell Foundation.

———. 2001b. "Teacher Certification Reconsidered: Stumbling for Quality—A Rejoinder." Baltimore: Abell Foundation.

Wirt, John, Susan Choy, Debra Gerald, Stephan Provasnik, Patrick Rooney, Satoshi Watanabe, and Richard Tobin. 2002. *The Condition of Education 2002.* Washington: U.S. Department of Education.

Part IV

Inequality in Health

Chapter 13

Health, Income, and Inequality

John Mullahy, Stephanie Robert, and Barbara Wolfe

Increases in income and earnings inequality over the past twenty-five years have been well documented. What we do not know is whether there have been associated increases in inequality in other dimensions, such as health status. Health status may have a reciprocal relationship with income inequality. Health can affect human capital and hence the ability to earn, to engage more productively in nonmarket activities, and to enjoy consumption more or less fully. In turn, health can be affected by income inequality through a number of potential pathways.

Both analysts and policymakers are devoting increasing attention to various "disparities" in health and health care (Miller and Paxson 2001). One of the two main goals of the federal government's *Healthy People 2010* initiative is to reduce inequalities in health. The role of economic inequality in causing these disparities is not well understood, although a growing literature is exploring ties between income, income inequality, and health.

What do we mean by "health"? While mortality is the "health" measure most commonly discussed—and arguably the one most precisely measured—in this literature other measures of health may clearly be more important to consider in order to inform particular questions about the relationships between income (inequality) and health. Nonmortality measures of health may be of many types: cellular or molecular (for example, LDL cholesterol levels, measles antibody titres); subclinical (for example, systolic blood pressure); clinical (for example, body mass index, birthweight, forced expiratory volume [FEV] scores); functional (for example, activities of daily living [ADL] or instrumental activities of daily living [IADL] scores, restricted activity days); self-rated (for example, excellent, very good, fair, poor [EVGFP] and health-related quality of life [HRQOL]); and others. The manner in which income influences such measures of health is likely to vary enormously in the population. For instance, some measures of health may be largely determined by genetic factors (such as a risk for schizophrenia), while others may depend quite directly on factors that are closely related to income (such as access to medical care or risks for immunizable communicable diseases). The point here is to recognize that the focus on any particular health measure should stem from the nature of the health-income question being posed; mortality may be an appropriate measure in some instances, while in others it may not.

In this chapter, we synthesize the empirical and review literature in this area and point to some of the directions in which we believe researchers should turn next. In the first section, we review the recently burgeoning empirical and review literature on income

523

inequality and health. We start by differentiating between several hypotheses that attempt to link income inequality to health inequality: the absolute income hypothesis, the absolute deprivation hypothesis (or poverty hypothesis), the relative income or relative position hypothesis, and an income inequality hypothesis. We conclude that the strongest evidence suggests that those with low levels of income have poorer health than those with more income. This evidence predicts that if the increase in inequality has led to a decrease in the income of those at the bottom end of the income distribution, then we would expect some decline in their health and hence an increase in inequality in health. The evidence that income inequality directly decreases health is far weaker. We critique the existing literature on the health effects of income inequality per se, raising a number of issues that need to be addressed further.

In the second section, we pay particular attention to several measurement issues that we think will be crucial to explore in future work on income inequality and health. We set up a simple model that is designed to assist us in thinking about the links between health, income, and income inequality.

INCOME INEQUALITY AND HEALTH: REVIEW AND REDIRECTION

The question of whether income inequality is related to health, and hence to health inequality, has received a good deal of attention, and there has been considerable debate about the nature of the ties between income, income inequality, health, and health inequality. A number of recent reviews of the literature have been published by researchers in a variety of disciplines, including economics, sociology, and epidemiology (see, for example, Wagstaff and van Doorslaer 2000; Deaton 2001; Robert and House 2000a, 2000b; Lynch et al. 2000), and we build on them in our own literature review. We begin with a brief summary differentiating the various hypotheses that link income and income inequality to health, then review the evidence for these hypotheses.

The idea that income is associated with health goes back a long way in the literature. Perhaps the most influential work affecting contemporary work in this area was by Samuel Preston (1975), who observed, in comparing mortality rates across countries, that the impact of additional income on health (as measured by mortality) is greater on those with low income than on those with higher income. This effect is illustrated in figure 13.1, which shows the health of individuals on the vertical axis, plotted against the income of the individual's family group on the horizontal axis. The concave shape of the curve conveys the idea that because a dollar transferred from the rich to the poor improves the health of the poor person more than it decreases the health of the rich person, this transfer increases the average level of health of the members of a community.

This is called the *absolute income hypothesis,* and in its simplest form it argues that if all that matters to health at the level of an individual is income, a community with more equal income will tend to have better average health than a community with more inequality when comparing two communities with equal average income. In an international context, Angus Deaton (2001) points out that, according to the absolute income hypothesis, redistribution could improve health even if average income was not increased, and that redistribution from rich to poor countries would in principle improve worldwide average health.

A related concept is the *absolute deprivation* or *poverty hypothesis.* According to this hypothesis, those with the lowest incomes face poorer health and a greater risk of mortality owing to a variety of factors associated with extreme poverty, such as inadequate nutrition,

FIGURE 13.1   *Implications of the Concavity of the Health-Income Relationship*

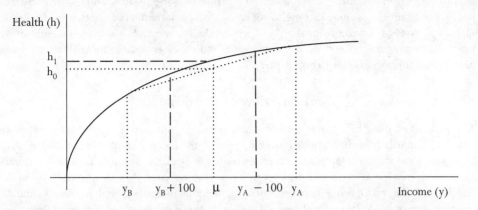

Source: Wagstaff and Van Doorslaer (2000, 546, fig. 2).

lack of quality health care, exposure to a variety of physical hazards, and heightened stress. In this hypothesis, a dollar redistributed from rich to poor would improve the health of the poor and improve the average health of the entire population. The difference between the absolute income hypothesis and the absolute deprivation or poverty hypothesis is that in the former greater income improves the health of all persons, although in a nonlinear way, while in the latter only those who have low incomes are expected to see health improvements as a result of an increase in income.

The *relative income hypothesis* focuses on an individual's income relative to that of others in that individual's "group" rather than on his or her absolute income. According to this hypothesis, if the income of everyone but one in a group increases, that one person's health is expected to deteriorate. A related hypothesis is the *relative position* or *relative deprivation hypothesis*. According to this hypothesis, it is an individual's relative rank in society that is tied to health outcomes. This hypothesis encompasses the relative income hypothesis, but it extends the concept of relative position to measures of rank other than income, such as occupational rank or educational rank. These hypotheses are consistent with some research in the United States and the United Kingdom that demonstrates that the association between socioeconomic position and health occurs at all levels of the socioeconomic hierarchy, with even those in the highest socioeconomic groups having better health than those just below them in the socioeconomic hierarchy, which is referred to as a "gradient effect" of socioeconomic position on health (Adler et al. 1994; Marmot et al. 1991).

The relative income and relative position hypotheses imply that it is not just the conditions experienced by those in absolute poverty that lead to poor health. Rather, there are psychosocial and other factors that remain unevenly distributed all the way up the income scale that perpetuate income inequalities in health. Perceptions of being relatively deprived ("keeping up with the Joneses"), stress, and other more psychosocial and behavioral than material factors may play a role in perpetuating income inequalities in health at the upper income levels. Health effects at the upper end of the income distribution may reflect relative position, whereas health effects at the lower end may reflect absolute deprivation (Adler and Newman 2002).

The hypothesis that focuses most directly on the tie between health inequality and income inequality is the *income inequality hypothesis.* According to the strong version of this hypothesis, societies with greater inequality produce worse health among their citizens, holding constant the average income of societies. Although these arguments were first made in comparisons of income inequality between countries, research has more recently examined whether regions, states, counties, and cities with greater income inequality have worse health than their more equal counterparts.

A Brief Review of the Evidence

Although all of these hypotheses initially seem testable, controversy arises because they are not always mutually exclusive. For example, tests of the income inequality hypothesis at the aggregate level may be empirically consistent with tests of the absolute poverty or relative income hypotheses at the individual level. Such overlap continues to obscure our understanding of the relationship between income, income inequality, and health. Without a clearer conceptual and empirical understanding of these relationships, program and policy recommendations about how to reduce income-related inequalities in health remain elusive and hotly debated.

In general, two empirical approaches have been taken to examine these hypotheses. Research examining the absolute deprivation, relative income, and relative position hypotheses has usually examined individual-level data on income and health or mortality to examine the existence and shape of the income-health relationship among individuals. Recent research has extended examination of these hypotheses by including aggregate measures of *community* socioeconomic level, such as the percentage of persons in poverty or community median family income, along with individual-level income data. In contrast, research examining the income inequality hypothesis has employed aggregate data either exclusively or at least at the level of measuring income inequality. We divide our brief review of the literature into these two general types of studies, focusing particularly on the recent research testing the income inequality hypothesis.

Income and Health   Voluminous empirical studies and reviews demonstrate a robust association between income and morbidity and mortality, using various measures of both income and health across samples and at various time points (Adler et al. 1993, 1994; Antonovsky 1967; Feinstein 1993; Williams and Collins 1995; Robert and House 2000a). To date, most of the evidence demonstrates a nonlinear rather than linear gradient relationship between income and mortality (Backlund, Sorlie, and Johnson 1996; McDonough et al. 1997; Ettner 1996) and between income and morbidity (House et al. 1990, 1994; Mirowsky and Hu 1996).

Although most research on income and health is cross-sectional, there is some evidence that there may be widening socioeconomic inequalities in health in the United Kingdom (Black et al. 1982), the United States (Pappas et al. 1993), and other developed countries (Evans, Barer, and Marmor 1994; Marmot, Kogevinas, and Elston 1987). However, Deaton (2001,60) suggests that the rapid increases in income inequality in the 1970s and 1980s in Britain and the United States "have not been associated with any slowdown in the rate of mortality decline." To date, datasets have been of insufficiently long duration or too incomplete in terms of longitudinal information on both income and health to explore the relationship between income, income inequality, and health over time.

Figure 13.2 reports on trends in family income from 1974 to 1996. It illustrates the growing share of income received by the top 5 percent of families and shows the proportion

FIGURE 13.2   *Trends in Income of U.S. Families, 1974 to 1996*

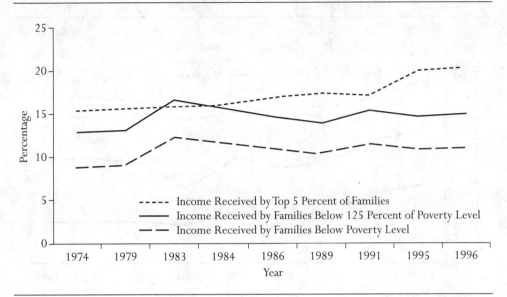

Source: U.S. Department of Commerce (2000, tables 745, 760).

of U.S. families below the official poverty line and the proportion who are near-poor (those below 125 percent of the poverty line). The growing share of the top 5 percent is indicative of growing inequality; the proportion poor and near-poor shows a more complicated picture—an increase from 1974 to 1983, a decline through 1989, followed by a smaller increase to 1991, with little change in the next few years.

Figure 13.3 reports the proportion of the population who reported poor or fair health by income group over these same years. Consistent with both the absolute income and deprivation hypotheses and the relative income and deprivation hypotheses, the health of the poor is always worse than that of the nonpoor, and the health of the near-poor is between the two. The trends over time show a continual improvement in the health of the nonpoor, but not among the poor and near-poor: in both cases, after some improvement over the period 1974 to 1989, there was some deterioration in health from 1991 to 1996. Caution should be used in viewing these trends, however, since the way in which these health statistics are reported changed over this time period; hence the "jump" may be due to the reporting change. The increase after 1991, however, cannot be explained by the change in reporting, since there were no further changes.[1]

Health status also differs systematically by race, and increasing attention is being paid to racial inequalities in health in the United States. There is a strong but far from complete overlap between racial and income inequalities in health (Williams 2002; Hayward et al. 2000; Williams and Collins 1995; Sorlie, Backlund, and Keller 1995; Ren and Amick 1996). Although this overlap is often acknowledged, it is not explicitly examined in much research on income and health.

Figures 13.4 and 13.5 present the trend in poverty and in poor and fair health for white and African American respondents. Figure 13.5 highlights the well-known higher poverty rates among African Americans and the higher proportion of African Americans with poor or fair health relative to the white population. The trends in health are of

FIGURE 13.3   *Trends in Self-Reported Health of U.S. Families, by Family Income,*
1974 to 1996

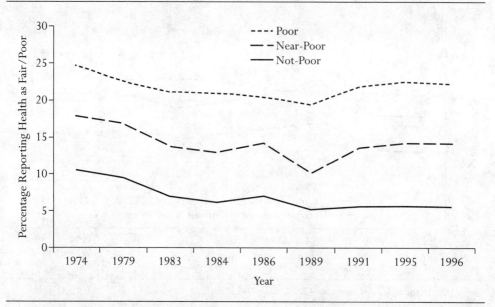

Source: National Center for Health Statistics (198 to 1999).

interest, for they are consistent with a tie between poverty and overall health for whites but not for African Americans. After 1983, the two lines track closely for whites. For African Americans, figure 13.5 shows generally improving health, while the poverty rate fluctuates more. In this case, the figure does not illustrate or suggest a link between the two, although if the trend lines began in 1983, both would show some steady decline and hence improvement in health and reduction of poverty. Clearly, more attention should be paid to measuring trends in the relationship between income, race, and health and mortality over time in the United States.

Some recent research examines not only the relationship between individual or family income and health but also the impact of the neighborhood or community income level on individual health (see reviews in Robert 1999; Bond Huie 2001; Pickett and Pearl 2001; Robert and House 2000b; Diez-Roux 2000, 2001). This research finds evidence that living in communities with a higher proportion of poverty households, or with overall lower income (for example, low median family income), is associated with poor health and mortality over and above the effects of individual or family income in the United States (Haan, Kaplan, and Camacho 1987; Waitzman and Smith 1998a; Robert 1998; Diez-Roux et al. 1997; Anderson et al. 1997; Blakely, Lochner, and Kawachi 2002). Living in poorer communities may be detrimental to the health of all residents, regardless of their own income.

Most of this multilevel research, however, finds that individual- or family-level socioeconomic characteristics are more significant correlates of health than are community variables (Robert 1998; Brooks-Gunn, Duncan, and Aber 1997; Elliott et al. 1996).

Combining multilevel research on the individual and community socioeconomic context and health with research on race, income, and health may be particularly important. For example, because the United States is residentially segregated by race (Jargowsky 1997;

FIGURE 13.4   *Comparing Self-Reported Health and Poverty Status of U.S. Families: White Families, 1974 to 1996*

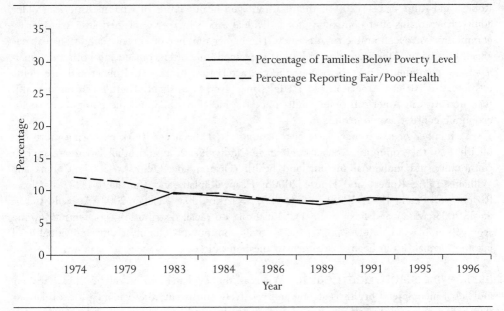

Sources: U.S. Department of Commerce (2000); National Center for Health Statistics (1981 to 1999).

FIGURE 13.5   *Comparing Self-Reported Health and Poverty Status of U.S. Families: African American Families, 1974 to 1996*

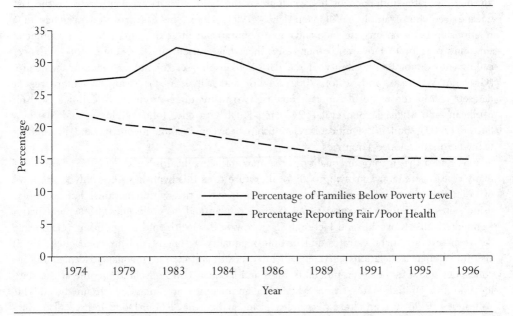

Sources: U.S. Department of Commerce (2000); National Center for Health Statistics (1981 to 1999).

Massey and Denton 1993; Wilson 1987), African American and non-Hispanic white people of the same family income level live in very different neighborhoods. In a study by Stephanie Robert and Kum Yi Lee (2002), the disadvantaged health status of African American older adults that remains after controlling for individual SES is further explained after considering community socioeconomic characteristics. The higher number of chronic conditions experienced by African American older adults is explained only after considering both individual-level and community-level socioeconomic characteristics. Moreover, Robert and Lee demonstrate that African American older adults may even have slightly better self-rated health than non-African American older adults once the individual SES and the community socioeconomic context are controlled.

A number of researchers have also demonstrated the necessity of exploring more explicitly how the community racial context and individual race and ethnicity are related to community and individual income and health (Deaton and Lubotsky 2003; Collins and Williams 1999; Robert and House 2000b; Haan, Kaplan, and Camacho 1987; LeClere, Rogers, and Peters 1997, 1998; Robert 2002; Nazroo 2003; Krieger 2003; Acevedo-Garcia et al. 2003; Miller and Paxson 2001). What role do racial distribution, concentration, and segregation play in determining or explaining community-, family-, and individual-level income inequalities in health? We turn to these questions.

Income Inequality and Health   Whereas the evidence for a relationship between individual income and health is strong and relatively consistent, the evidence for a relationship between aggregate measures of income inequality and health is weak and controversial. There has been much focus in recent years on the latter research, with heated and excited debate about the importance to health and well-being of living in more or less unequal places. Ironically, the focus on this latter, more speculative, research may have unwittingly diverted attention from the former, more consistent, research.

The literature regarding the income inequality hypothesis must refer to Richard Wilkinson, given the influence of his writings on the field. In various writings over the last decade (see, for example, Wilkinson 1992, 1994, 1996), he has provided evidence of a relationship between income inequality in a country and life expectancy, both at a point in time and over time. However, other researchers have raised questions about this evidence, calling into doubt the reliability of the data Wilkinson uses to measure income inequality (Gravelle, Wildman, and Sutton 2002; Mellor and Milyo 2001). Using two more recent datasets considered to be of superior quality, two teams of researchers, Ken Judge, Jo-Ann Mulligan, and Michaela Benzeval (1998) and Hugh Gravelle, John Wildman, and Matthew Sutton (2002), find no significant relationship between income inequality and life expectancy across developed countries.[2]

The idea that income inequality per se may influence health has caught the attention of many researchers, and a growing body of literature tests this hypothesis not only at the level of countries but across regions, states, counties, and cities within nations. For example, using states as the unit of comparison, George Kaplan and his colleagues (1996) and Bruce Kennedy, Ichiro Kawachi, and Deborah Prothrow-Stith (1996) find a significant relationship between several mortality rates and income inequality. Kennedy and his colleagues (1998) also find similar associations between self-rated health and income inequality. Kaplan and his colleagues find a tie between mortality rates and inequality in household income at the state level in the United States, even when median incomes are included. Kennedy and his colleagues (1996) use an alternative index of inequality, the "Robin Hood Index," also using state data for the United States. In their analysis of a variety of mortality rates, inequality is a statistically significant predictor. A follow-up study by Kawachi and Kennedy (1997) explores additional measures of inequality and mortality with similar results: a statistically significant link between measures of income inequality at the state level and health as measured by mortality rates. Examining 283 metropolitan areas as units of analysis rather than states, John Lynch, George Kaplan, and Elsie Pamuk (1998) similarly look at the relationships between multiple measures of inequality and mortality. The inequality measures predict mortality over and above other community-level factors, such as per capita income and the proportion of the population with incomes under 200 percent of the poverty level. Using county and tract-level data, Felicia LeClere and Mah-Jabeen Soobader (2000) find independent income inequality effects primarily at the county level, but only for some specific subgroups by age, race, and gender. In these studies, various controls were added for median income, for proportion below the poverty line or near poverty, per capita income, and average household size.

Although most researchers accept this raw association between income inequality and health, even after controlling for median income levels or poverty, debate arises primarily over potential *explanations* for this relationship. Lynch and his colleagues (2000) describe three types of explanations for the association between income inequality and health: the individual income interpretation, the psychosocial environment interpretation, and the neomaterial interpretation. According to the *individual income interpretation,* aggregate associations between income inequality and health simply reflect the nonlinear (concave) relation between income and health at the individual level. According to the *psychosocial environment interpretation,* perceptions of inequality produce instabilities in social capital—perceived mistrust, lack of social cohesion, and so on—that work through behaviors and psychosocial responses that affect an individual's biological responses and ultimate health. The *neomaterial interpretation* suggests that places with the greatest income inequality are places that also have inequalities in human, physical, health, and social infrastructure that ultimately affect health.

The individual income interpretation suggests that, theoretically, if the relationship between individual income and health is nonlinear, then there should be an aggregate-level association between income inequality and health (Ecob and Davey Smith 1999; Gravelle 1998; Preston 1975; Rodgers 1979). Empirically, this has been tested in several studies that control for individual income while examining the association between income inequality and health. The association between income inequality and health or mortality sometimes remains after controlling for individual SES (Waitzman and Smith 1998b; Soobader and LeClere 1999; Fiscella and Franks 2000; Kennedy et al. 1998; LeClere and Soobader 2000; Lochner et al. 2001), and sometimes it does not (Fiscella and Franks 1997, 2000; Mellor and Milyo 1999; LeClere and Soobader 2000; Blakely, Lochner, and Kawachi 2002; Daly et al. 1998). For example, Tony Blakely, Kimberly Lochner, and Ichiro Kawachi (2002) use individual-level data from the 1996 and 1998 Current Population Survey in conjunction with 1990 Gini coefficient measures at the metropolitan area (MA) levels to look at self-rated health. They find no significant association between MA-level income inequality and health self-rated as poor or fair after controlling for sex, age, race, individual-level household income, and MA-level household income. In a recent review, Subramanian, Blakely, and Kawachi (2003) suggest that the only consistent associations between income inequality and health in multilevel studies may be seen at the state level in the United States, rather than at either smaller levels of aggregation within the United States or between or within other countries.

It seems crucial to explore further the extent to which the relationship between measures of inequality at the aggregate level and health reflects the nonlinear association between individual income and health. However, even if the aggregate relationship were fully explained by the individual-level relationship, the interpretation of this finding would still be open for debate. Should the aggregate relationship then be seen as an artifact of the individual-level data, and therefore not meaningful, or does income inequality at more macro levels play a more causal role in producing or reproducing income inequalities in health?

Much of the heated debate in the literature on income inequality and health seems to stem from reactions to the so-called psychosocial environment interpretation. A number of researchers have explored the possibility that inequality per se produces a social environment that ultimately affects an individual's health (see, for example, Wilkinson 1996). For example, Kawachi and his colleagues (1997) suggest that high income inequality within states is associated with low social cohesion and disinvestment in social capital, which then affect mortality. Examples of this would be the relative income and deprivation hypotheses, which suggest that an individual's perceived relative income or position may affect health through psychosocial pathways (Adler et al. 1994).

Proponents of the neomaterial interpretation believe that more consideration should be given to factors that exist outside of, or as precursors to, psychosocial pathways. For example, Lynch and his colleagues (2000) point out that there are structural, political, and economic processes that generate inequality, and that these processes exist before individuals experience or perceive their effects. Therefore, focusing on the structural, political, and economic processes that both produce and result from inequality may be more appropriate than attending primarily to individual perceptions or experiences that occur downstream from these processes.

Examples of research exploring neomaterial interpretations of the link between income inequality and health include research that explores the potential intermediating role of public investment in, for instance, health care, public safety, education, and environmental quality. To the extent that such investments are concentrated in higher-income areas, or in less unequal areas, then an individual living in such areas gains more access to such goods and services (Kaplan et al. 1996; Lynch, Kaplan, and Pamuk 1998; Davey Smith 1996). The neomaterial interpretation implies that greater income inequality in society leads to greater differences in resources across communities that are associated with greater differences in health across communities. This finding highlights deprivation, but in this view deprivation at the individual level is compounded by deprivation at the community level as socioeconomic segregation and greater income inequality make the indirect costs of acquisition of health care and a healthy lifestyle more expensive to those with the lowest incomes. This suggests interaction effects between income inequality and individual income level. A number of studies suggest that income inequality may be a significant determinant of health, but only for those with the lowest incomes (Mellor and Milyo 1999; Soobader and LeClere 1999).

Critiquing the Literature on Income Inequality and Health

To summarize our primary understanding of the literature on income, income inequality, and health: there is a strong relationship between individual income and health that persists, and perhaps strengthens, over time. The shape of the relationship between income and health appears to be nonlinear, such that increases in income among those at the low end of the distribution should have greater positive consequences for their health than similar increases in income would have for the health of those at the top end of the income distribution. Much attention has been paid recently to the possibility that income inequality per se is related to health. The results of this research are still tenuous, though deserving of further study. However, it appears that the focus on this more tenuous research has unwittingly diverted attention from the former research on individual income and health. We conclude that (1) more research is needed to examine the relationship between income inequality and health, although (2) the greater advances in our understanding of the relationship between income and health will come from research that refocuses attention on the relationship between individual income level and health. Nevertheless, even if the primary relationship between income and health should be examined at the individual level, mediators of this relationship may very well operate at more aggregate levels such as households or neighborhoods.

Further Research on the Relationship Between Income Inequality and Health

Much of the recent focus of research on income inequality and health has centered on the question of whether there are "independent effects" of income inequality on health. Is living in an area with greater income inequality associated with poor health over and above other individual- and area-level factors? If the answer to this question is yes, and if such associations can be demonstrated to run causally from income inequality to health, then there are certainly interesting implications for efforts to reduce disparities in health—these interventions may need to be entirely different from those that have traditionally been considered. For instance, cost-benefit evaluations of interventions targeted at inequality reduction would properly have to assess health improvements as part of the benefit estimation. Therefore, this question is important to address, and even more crucial to address *well*. As others point out, multiple limitations of the existing data have prevented us from having definitive evidence regarding independent effects of income inequality on health and mortality. Future research needs to examine better multilevel data—particularly on income, health, race, racial concentration and segregation, and community boundaries—and all of this information needs to be examined over time.

However, perhaps an even greater limitation of current work in the area of income inequality and health has been this narrow focus on testing for independent effects of income inequality on health. The literature conveys the message that if there are no "independent effects" of income inequality on health, then there is no need to think about income inequality at these more macro levels—the relationship between income inequality and health is simply spurious and has no meaning in and of itself. Surprisingly inadequate attention has been paid to either conceptualizing or examining the *indirect* effect that income inequality may have on health. Moreover, even if income inequality has no independent effect on health and only small indirect effects, understanding income inequality and its links to the factors that more directly affect health may provide important clues about how to improve the health of the poor, reduce health disparities, or reduce the link between income and health. Therefore, we agree with Lynch and his colleagues (2000) that the direction to head in is one that more clearly examines whether and how the individual income and neomaterial interpretations combine to explain links between income inequality and health. As they summarize:

> An unequal income distribution is one result of historical, cultural, and political-economic processes. These processes influence the private resources available to individuals and shape the nature of public infrastructure—education, health services, transportation, environmental controls, availability of food, quality of

housing, occupational health regulations—that form the "neo-material" matrix of contemporary life. . . . Thus income inequality per se is but one manifestation of a cluster of neo-material conditions that affect population health. This implies that an aggregate relation between income inequality and health is not necessary— associations are contingent on the level and distribution of other aspects of social resources. If income inequality is less linked to investments in health-related public infrastructure, the aggregate level association between income inequality and health may break down. (1202)

In this scenario, reducing health disparities may not require a reduction in income inequality if the distribution of resources in society is decoupled from the income inequality of an area. Not that income inequality itself would thus become insignificant. A number of authors (Mellor and Milyo, Wagstaff and van Doorslaer) raise the issue of whether income inequality is associated with public policies (toward the poor, in particular) that then affect health. What is curious is that some of these authors then imply that income inequality is not important to understand if its relationship to health is mediated by these policies—it is only the policies that must be understood and changed. In reality, however, it may be impossible to understand and change these policies without understanding and considering how the context of income inequality has shaped or maintains the policies. For example, if health care providers are not willing to practice in low-income areas, simply providing more coverage to the lower-income population may do little to improve access to health care for residents of low-income areas. The U.S. policy to encourage such reallocation seems to have come face to face with this reality.

The point here is that even if the relationship between state-level income inequality and health is "explained" by state-level policy generosity, it might be imperative to understand whether or how income inequality affects or reflects this policy generosity. Greater contributions from political science on these subjects, such as research on interstate competition in health and welfare programs (for example, Bailey and Rom 2001) and David Coburn's (2000) recent work on neoliberalism as a cause of income inequality, may extend our understanding of whether and how income inequality and racial distribution and composition contribute to regional variations in access to resources that ultimately affect health.

Although new research on income inequality and health is needed, we believe that such new research will be more useful to the extent that it explicitly integrates issues of race and ethnicity. A fuller consideration of the association between racial composition, racial segregation, and health and mortality is likely to help us understand the link between income inequality and health specifically, the link between income and health more generally, and patterns of health inequality most importantly. Several researchers (Deaton and Lubotsky 2003; LeClere and Soobader 2000; Robert and House 2000b) point out that places with the greatest income inequality are the same places with the greatest percentage of black people in the population. Income inequality and percentage of black people in a state or county are so highly correlated that it seems odd that the literature on income inequality and health has considered income inequality quite separate from the racial composition of a state or county. A recent study by Angus Deaton and Darren Lubotsky (2003) demonstrates that, conditional on the percentage of black residents, mortality rates at the city and state levels are not associated with income inequality. However, both black and white mortality rates are higher in places with a greater percentage of black residents. This work redirects attention to the important intersection of income inequality and neighborhood or geographic racial distribution and their joint effects on health.

Moreover, little research has explored the role of *racial residential segregation*, income inequality, and health using multilevel data (Robert 2002; Krieger 2003; Nazroo 2003; Acevedo-Garcia et al. 2003). Whereas *racial concentration* focuses on the percentage of a population that is black, for example, racial residential segregation refers to the differential distribution of black individuals across smaller residential units (such as census tracts) within a larger geographical unit (such as a city or county) (Massey and Denton 1988a). In the United States, research has examined how racial segregation produces and reinforces the economic segregation of black people (Massey 1990; Massey and Denton 1988b, 1989; Alba and Logan 1993; Wilson 1987; Jargowsky 1997). However, little research examines the *health* consequences of living in a racially segregated community.

There is aggregate-level evidence that racially segregated communities have higher adult and infant mortality rates (McCord and Freeman 1990; LaVeist 1992, 1993; Collins and Williams 1999; Polednak 1993, 1996; Guest, Almgren, and Hussey 1998; Shihadeh and Flynn 1996; Bird 1995). Most of this research examines whether racial segregation is associated with mortality rates over and above the community socioeconomic context. For example, Chiquita Collins and David Williams (1999) examine black and nonblack mortality rates for people age fifteen to sixty-four in 107 cities with a black population of 10 percent or greater. Using the Dissimilarity Index and the Isolation Index (Massey and Denton 1988a), they test whether high racial segregation is associated with mortality rates (from all causes and from heart disease, cancer, and homicide), controlling for the proportion of the population in poverty, the proportion not employed in managerial or professional positions, and city population size. They find independent associations between high racial segregation and both black and white adult mortality, though the association is stronger and more consistent across different types of black mortality, particularly for black males. Other aggregate-level studies similarly have found that high racial segregation predicts mortality rates over and above the community socioeconomic context (Polednak 1991; Guest, Almgren, and Hussey 1998; Shihadeh and Flynn 1996; LaVeist 1989; Bird 1995; Bird and Bauman 1998).

Combining the literature on income inequality and health with the literature on racial concentration and segregation and health seems crucial in order to move forward our understanding of income and racial inequalities in health in the United States. Some first-order research questions would include: How does state-level inequality relate to policy generosity? If we actually wanted to make changes to the policies, might it make sense to understand how social and political processes work differently in more unequal states? Are there more competing interests in more unequal states? If so, is it a "competition" that ultimately can never be won by those representing the poorest in society? Is it politics based on racial conflict that results in less generous policies? Why is it that the most unequal places also tend to have the highest concentrations of racial-ethnic minorities?

In sum, we agree with others that income inequality per se is not the main factor affecting health status in the United States or other countries. We agree that other factors at either the individual or aggregate level appear to account for the relationship between income inequality and health. We do not then conclude, however, that variations in income inequality provide no useful information about how and why health is unequally distributed within the United States and between the United States and other countries. We suspect that there are complex causal links between income inequality, income level, racial distribution, residential segregation, and social and political decisionmaking that provide the more complete picture of how and why income and income inequality are related to health.

The Most Promising Research: Looking at the Links Between Individual Income and Health

Individual or family income dominates aggregate income inequality or aggregate income level as a direct determinant of individual health. The recent focus on income inequality at aggregate levels is useful in that it may demonstrate economic factors beyond individual income that affect health, highlight macrosocial processes that indirectly affect health by shaping individual income, highlight political and economic processes that distribute resources unequally, and shift our attention to potential macrosocial interventions that might have microsocial benefits. However, it still remains most important that we understand and attend to the strong direct link between income level and health.

In particular, we need to focus on understanding how and why *low* income produces and reproduces poor health. Because people with high income, on average, may be approaching the biological limits of improvement in health and longevity, increases in their income have diminishing returns for individual and population health. Therefore, the greatest determinant of individual and population health is the absolute and relative income and position of those in the lower range of the income distribution, and it is here that we need to focus attention.

What are the factors that link low income to health in consistent, reciprocal relationships? The mediators in this relationship may exist on several levels, not just at the individual level. The link between income and health should be explored by investigating potential mediating individual-level, family-level, community-level, and state- or system-level factors. This focuses our attention on explaining *why* poor people have poor health but does not limit explanatory factors to those that characterize only the individual. A poor individual may have characteristics that "explain" his or her poor health, such as health-related behaviors like smoking or not getting exercise. These individual characteristics may be determined in part, however, by "exogenous" factors such as the availability and marketing of cigarettes or the lack of a safe venue for exercise. Additional extra-individual factors, such as local policies, programs, and resources, affect multiple individuals' access to health-promoting resources. Understanding both the individual- and community-level mediators of the relationship between income and health, and their interactions, will be important in helping us determine our most effective policy or program options. Finally, attention needs to be paid to the various dimensions of health that are likely to be tied to income and income inequality.

EMPIRICAL APPROACHES TO UNDERSTANDING HEALTH INEQUALITIES

To guide our future work, we propose a simple model that we believe will help us explore more completely the links between income, income inequality, and a variety of dimensions of health. We recognize various empirical obstacles and list here just a few such considerations: Does the model apply to individuals or to a group? What measure of income is relevant? Personal income? Family income adjusted for needs? Family income? Permanent income? How should a comparison group be defined? At what level of aggregation? A population that is somehow similar to the individual? If so, how should "similar" be defined? What time span is relevant for testing the hypotheses? What other factors should be taken into account (controlled for) in testing the hypotheses? What measure of health do the hypotheses include? All of them? Mortality and life expectancy only? Acute health problems only? Chronic health problems only?

A simple model of health and income is useful to consider in addressing such issues. In such a model, we might postulate that health and income have the following distributional properties: they are in some manner jointly distributed, and in general there will be temporal relationships involved in this joint distribution. The joint probability model describing such relationships would then provide the basic foundation for inferences about health, health inequality, how health or health inequality relates to income or income inequality, and how the relationship between health (inequality) and income (inequality) may entail a lagged structure.

From such a model concepts such as mean health at time t and the variance of health at time t can be meaningfully and precisely described, and discussions about health inequality might then concretely begin. Analogously, considerations of the role of income and/or income inequality would logically require reference to the population income distribution at time t in order to make statements about mean income, income inequality, and so on.

So, for instance, if our objective is estimation of a model that sets out to describe time trends (denoted by τ) in the contemporaneous relationship between income inequality and health outcomes, we can appeal to this statistical framework to specify a model such as:

$$h_{it} = \alpha + (\beta + \gamma \times \tau) \times \text{var}(m_t) + \ldots + u_t$$

where β would capture the main effect and γ the time trend. Such conceptual clarity, we feel, is of considerable importance, since it is our experience that some confusion can easily creep into discussions about these topics.

One feature of the health inequality phenomenon we have considered is its intertemporal character. In the context of the earlier formulation, we might be concerned with not just how a concept like mean health evolves over time, but also with how variations in health change over time. We may also be concerned with the intertemporal covariance structure between health and income (Abowd and Card 1989; Staiger 1998). For example, we might find interesting covariances between contemporaneous health status and lagged income, suggesting (although obviously not proving) a lagged causal dependence of h on m.

If we could build a coherent and representative longitudinal dataset containing information on health and income (along with other salient covariates, such as age and gender), then we could begin to explore the covariance structure of health and income (or health and wealth, and so on). Some of our effort up to this point has been devoted to determining the best data sources for achieving such an objective or, if not practical, asking whether alternative methods, like repeated cross-sections suitably aggregated (for example, the National Health Interview Survey for nonmortality measures, or the Behavioral Risk Factors Surveillance System for years of healthy life), could be informative along these lines.

In assessing time trends in health inequality using survey-based data, our research to date suggests the importance of accommodating survivor bias over time if health measures other than mortality are of concern. Specifically, surveys of *living* individuals fail to account for the fact of differential mortality patterns over time. To be concrete, suppose the health status measure is a health-related quality-of-life indicator measured (as is common) on a zero-one scale, with one indicating an individual is in perfect health and zero indicating an individual is dead. Suppose further that there is an intervention or shock at time t$'$ that, owing perhaps to a redistribution of resources, increases mortality probabilities for some segments of the population but simultaneously increases health-related quality of life for other population segments.

A survey of the surviving members of this population at a date after t′ may then reveal an *increase* in mean health-related quality of life (as is well known from the demographic literature), and a *decrease* in health inequality as more individuals in the surviving population are compressed toward the higher end of the zero-one scale (a result not so commonly appreciated in the demographic literature). Yet for many interesting purposes, our intuition is that health inequality should have been viewed as *increasing* from before t′ to after t′ (since such intuitions may often be based more on cohort-related questions than on period-related ones). As such, as part of our effort to measure time trends in nonmortality measures of health and health inequality, we are considering various approaches to correct for such "biases."

Conceptualizing Health

As noted earlier, an important limitation of the existing literature is the lack of systematic examination of how income and income inequality are associated with *multiple* dimensions of individual health and well-being. Most multilevel studies have focused on mortality; fewer have examined measures of morbidity (number of chronic conditions, self-rated health, functional health). Moreover, illness or the *lack* of health has been the focus of most "health" research, with mortality and morbidity used as physical outcomes and depression as a mental health outcome; few researchers have viewed and examined health as the presence of something *positive* (Ryff and Singer 1998a, 1998b; Singer and Ryff 2000).[3] Studying the determinants of positive health and well-being may provide added insight into the link between income inequality and health (Ryff et al. 1999; Singer and Ryff 2000).

We are convinced of the importance of examining properties of health outcomes other than mortality. For one thing, mortality outcomes may be relatively sluggish indicators of the underlying health of a population at any one point in time. Moreover, there is increasing appreciation of the fact that health-related quality of life is in some sense as important as longevity when summarizing the health of a population at a point in time (for example, the *Healthy People 2010* initiative). Of course, measurement issues tend to be more problematic when we are dealing with outcomes other than mortality (which is generally measured very accurately). Measures of central tendencies or inequalities may require particular attention, given their sometimes noncardinal metrics (for example, self-reported health status is often reported as excellent, very good, good, and so on; see Allison and Foster 1999). Nonetheless, measures like self-reported health status, self-rated disability status, and healthy days (Centers for Disease Control and Prevention 2000) are likely to be of considerable interest and to occupy much of our attention during the next phase of the project.

There are additional reasons to differentiate health. Certain types of health may be genetically determined and, as of a point in time, not treatable. These are not likely to be influenced by a change in income inequality or improved access to health care. Acute illnesses and contagious illnesses may be influenced by exposure and by prevention activities. We would expect these to be far more likely to respond to decreases in income inequality or, more directly, to improved access to care that includes preventive services. A third category is treatable, noncontagious illness; again, we might expect some improvement in health if income inequality or access to care is improved. The incidence of accidents and suicides may also be responsive to changes in income inequality, as may certain types of mental illness. In sum, the tie between income, income inequality, and health is likely to differ for different dimensions of health and ill health, of health outcomes versus health care, and so on.

CONCLUSION

As we reflect on some of the heated exchanges that occur in this field, we believe that some of the debate attending the roles played by income and income inequality as determinants of health and health inequality stems from conflicting goals. Researchers may want to understand, for instance, whether, why, and how income inequality is related to health. Policy makers may want to reduce income related disparities in health. Only by understanding the complex relationships between income, income inequality, and health will we be able to fully understand our choices for best addressing disparities in health in the United States.

NOTES

1. Since 1991, poor has been defined as family income below the poverty threshold, near-poor as income between 100 and 200 percent of the poverty threshold, and not-poor as income 200 percent of or greater than the poverty threshold. For the years before 1991, the income categories were defined as follows: 1974: poor—family income less than $5,000, near-poor—family income from $5,000 to $6,999, not-poor—family income from $10,000 to $14,999; 1979: poor—family income less than $7,000, near-poor—family income from $7,000 to $9,999, not-poor—family income from $15,000 to $24,999; 1983 to 1986: poor—family income less than $10,000, near-poor—family income from $10,000 to $14,999, not-poor—family income from $20,000 to $34,999; 1989: poor—family income less than $14,000, near-poor—family income from $14,000 to $34,999, not-poor—family income from $35,000 to $49,999.

2. Only for infant mortality do Judge, Mulligan, and Benzeval (1998) find any evidence of a significant tie between income inequality and health.

3. This idea is also consistent with the recent National Academy of Sciences report by the Committee on Future Directions for Behavioral and Social Sciences Research at the National Institutes of Health, which suggests: "As a much needed counterpoint to long-standing focus on illness and disease, we urge the NIH to invest significant new resources in advancing knowledge of positive health" (Singer and Ryff 2000, 45).

REFERENCES

Abowd, John, and David Card. 1989. "On the Covariance Structure of Earnings and Hours Changes." *Econometrica* 57: 411–45.

Acevedo-Garcia, Dolores, Kimberly A. Lochner, Theresa L. Osypuk, and Sukanya V. Subramanian. 2003. "Future Directions in Residential Segregation and Health Research: A Multilevel Approach." *American Journal of Public Health* 93(2): 215–21.

Adler, Nancy E., Thomas Boyce, Margaret A. Chesney, Sheldon Cohen, Susan Folkman, Robert L. Kahn, and S. Leonard Syme. 1994. "Socioeconomic Status and Health: The Challenge of the Gradient." *American Psychologist* 49(1): 15–24.

Adler, Nancy E., W. Thomas Boyce, Margaret A. Chesney, Susan Folkman, and S. Leonard Syme. 1993. "Socioeconomic Inequalities in Health: No Easy Solution." *Journal of the American Medical Association* 269: 3140–45.

Adler, Nancy E., and Katherine Newman. 2002. "Socioeconomic Disparities in Health: Pathways and Policies." *Health Affairs* 21(2): 60–76.

Alba, Richard D., and John R. Logan. 1993. "Minority Proximity to Whites in Suburbs: An Individual-Level Analysis of Segregation." *American Journal of Sociology* 98(6): 1388–1427.

Allison, R. Andrew, and James E. Foster. 1999. "Measuring Health Inequality Using Qualitative Data." Working paper 99-W04. Nashville, Tenn.: Vanderbilt University, Department of Economics and Business Administration.

Anderson, Roger T., Paul Sorlie, Eric Backlund, Norman Johnson, and George A. Kaplan. 1997. "Mortality Effects of Community Socioeconomic Status." *Epidemiology* 8: 42–47.

Antonovsky, Aaron. 1967. "Social Class, Life Expectancy, and Overall Mortality." *Milbank Memorial Fund Quarterly* 45: 31–73.

Backlund, Eric, Paul D. Sorlie, and Norman J. Johnson. 1996. "The Shape of the Relationship Between Income and Mortality in the United States: Evidence from the National Longitudinal Mortality Study." *Annals of Epidemiology* 6(1): 12–20.

Bailey, Michael A., and Mark Carl Rom. 2001. "Interstate Competition in Health and Welfare Programs." Working paper WP-19. Boston: Robert Wood Johnson Foundation Scholars in Health Policy Research Program.

Bird, Sheryl T. 1995. "Separate Black and White Infant Mortality Models: Differences in the Importance of Structural Variables." *Social Science and Medicine* 41(11): 1507–12.

Bird, Sheryl T., and Karl E. Bauman. 1998. "State-Level Infant, Neonatal, and Postneonatal Mortality: The Contribution of Selected Structural Socioeconomic Variables." *International Journal of Health Services* 28(1): 13–27.

Black, Douglas, J. N. Morris, Cyril Smith, and Peter Townsend. 1982. *Inequalities in Health: The Black Report.* New York: Penguin.

Blakely, Tony A., Kimberly Lochner, and Ichiro Kawachi. 2002. "Metropolitan-Area Income Inequality and Self-Rated Health: A Multilevel Study." *Social Science and Medicine* 54(1): 65–77.

Bond Huie, Stephanie A. 2001. "The Concept of Neighborhood in Health and Mortality Research." *Sociological Spectrum* 21: 341–58.

Brooks-Gunn, Jeanne, Greg J. Duncan, and J. Lawrence Aber, eds. 1997. *Neighborhood Poverty: Context and Consequences for Children,* vol. 1. New York: Russell Sage Foundation.

Centers for Disease Control and Prevention. 2000. *Measuring Healthy Days.* Atlanta: Centers for Disease Control and Prevention.

Coburn, David. 2000. "Income Inequality, Social Cohesion, and Health Status of Populations: The Role of Neoliberalism." *Social Science and Medicine* 51(1): 135–46.

Collins, Chiquita A., and David R. Williams. 1999. "Segregation and Mortality: The Deadly Effects of Racism?" *Sociological Forum* 14(3): 495–523.

Daly, Mary C., Greg J. Duncan, George A. Kaplan, and John W. Lynch. 1998. "Macro-to-Micro Links in the Relation Between Income Inequality and Mortality." *Milbank Memorial Fund Quarterly* 76(3): 303–4, 315–39.

Davey Smith, George. 1996. "Income Inequality and Mortality: Why Are They Related?" *British Medical Journal* 313: 987–88.

Deaton, Angus. 2001. "Health, Inequality, and Economic Development." Working paper 8318. Cambridge, Mass.: National Bureau of Economic Research (June).

Deaton, Angus, and Darren Lubotsky. 2003. "Mortality, Inequality, and Race in American Cities and States." *Social Science and Medicine* 56(6): 1139–53.

Diez-Roux, Ana V. 2000. "Multilevel Analysis in Public Health Research." *Annual Review of Public Health* 21: 171–92.

———. 2001. "Investigating Neighborhood and Area Effects on Health." *American Journal of Public Health* 91: 1783–89.

Diez-Roux, Ana V., F. Javier Nieto, Carles Muntaner, Herman A. Tyroler, George W. Comstock, Elad Shahar, Leslie S. Cooper, Robert L. Watson, and Moyses Szklo. 1997. "Neighborhood Environments and Coronary Heart Disease: A Multilevel Analysis." *American Journal of Epidemiology* 146(1): 48–63.

Ecob, Russell, and George Davey Smith. 1999. "Income and Health: What Is the Nature of the Relationship?" *Social Science and Medicine* 48(5): 693–705.

Elliott, Delbert S., William J. Wilson, David Huizinga, Robert J. Sampson, Amanda Elliott, and Bruce Rankin. 1996. "The Effects of Neighborhood Disadvantage on Adolescent Development." *Journal of Research in Crime and Delinquency* 33: 389–426.

Ettner, Susan L. 1996. "New Evidence on the Relationship Between Income and Health." *Journal of Health Economics* 15(1): 67–86.

Evans, Robert G., Morris L. Barer, and Theodore R. Marmor, eds. 1994. *Why Are Some People Healthy and Others Not? The Determinants of Health of Populations.* New York: Aldine de Gruyter.

Feinstein, Jonathan S. 1993. "The Relationship Between Socioeconomic Status and Health: A Review of the Literature." *Milbank Memorial Fund Quarterly* 71: 279–322.

Fiscella, Kevin, and Peter Franks. 1997. "Poverty or Income Inequality as a Predictor of Mortality: Longitudinal Cohort Study." *British Medical Journal* 314: 1724–27.

———. 2000. "Individual Income, Income Inequality, Health, and Mortality: What Are the Relationships?" *Health Services Research* 35(1): 307–18.

Gravelle, Hugh. 1998. "How Much of the Relationship Between Population Mortality and Unequal Distribution of Income Is a Statistical Artifact?" *British Medical Journal* 316: 382–85.

Gravelle, Hugh, John Wildman, and Matthew Sutton. 2002. "Income, Income Inequality, and Health: What Can We Learn from the Aggregate Data?" *Social Science and Medicine* 54: 577–89.

Guest, Avery M., Gunnar Almgren, and Jon M. Hussey. 1998. "The Ecology of Race and Socioeconomic Distress: Infant and Working-Age Mortality in Chicago." *Demography* 35(1): 23–34.

Haan, Mary, George A. Kaplan, and Terry Camacho. 1987. "Poverty and Health: Prospective Evidence from the Alameda County Study." *American Journal of Epidemiology* 125(6): 989–98.

Hayward, Mark D., Toni P. Miles, Eileen M. Crimmins, and Yu Yang. 2000. "The Significance of Socioeconomic Status in Explaining the Racial Gap in Chronic Health Conditions." *American Sociological Review* 65: 910–30.

House, James S., Ronald C. Kessler, A. Regula Herzog, Richard P. Mero, Ann M. Kinney, and Martha J. Breslow. 1990. "Age, Socioeconomic Status, and Health." *Milbank Memorial Fund Quarterly* 68(3): 383–411.

House, James S., James M. Lepkowski, Ann M. Kinney, Richard P. Mero, Ronald C. Kessler, and A. Regula Herzog. 1994. "The Social Stratification of Aging and Health." *Journal of Health and Social Behavior* 35: 213–34.

Jargowsky, Paul A. 1997. *Poverty and Place: Ghettos, Barrios, and the American City.* New York: Russell Sage Foundation.

Judge, Ken, Jo-Ann Mulligan, and Michaela Benzeval. 1998. "Income Inequality and Population Health." *Social Science and Medicine* 46(4–5): 567–79.

Kaplan, George A., Elsie R. Pamuk, John W. Lynch, Richard D. Cohen, and Jennifer L. Balfour. 1996. "Inequality in Income and Mortality in the United States: Analysis of Mortality and Potential Pathways." *British Medical Journal* 312: 999–1003.

Kawachi, Ichiro, and Bruce P. Kennedy. 1997. "The Relationship of Income Inequality to Mortality: Does the Choice of Indicator Matter?" *Social Science and Medicine* 45: 1121–27.

Kawachi, Ichiro, Bruce P. Kennedy, Kimberly Lochner, and Deborah Prothrow-Stith. 1997. "Social Capital, Income Inequality, and Mortality." *American Journal of Public Health* 87(9): 1491–98.

Kennedy, Bruce P., Ichiro Kawachi, Roberta Glass, and Deborah Prothrow-Stith. 1998. "Income Distribution, Socioeconomic Status, and Self-rated Health in the United States: Multilevel Analysis." *British Medical Journal* 317: 917–21.

Kennedy, Bruce P., Ichiro Kawachi, and Deborah Prothrow-Stith. 1996. "Income Distribution and Mortality: Cross-sectional Ecological Study of the Robin Hood Index in the United States." *British Medical Journal* 312: 1004–7.

Krieger, Nancy. 2003. "Does Racism Harm Health? Did Child Abuse Exist Before 1962? On Explicit Questions, Critical Science, and Current Controversies: An Ecosocial Perspective." *American Journal of Public Health* 93(2): 194–99.

LaVeist, Thomas A. 1989. "Linking Residential Segregation to the Infant-Mortality Race Disparity in U.S. Cities." *Sociology and Social Research* 73(2): 90–94.

———. 1992. "The Political Empowerment and Health Status of African Americans: Mapping a New Territory." *American Journal of Sociology* 97: 1080–95.

———. 1993. "Segregation, Poverty, and Empowerment: Health Consequences for African Americans." *Milbank Memorial Fund Quarterly* 71(1): 41–64.

LeClere, Felicia B., Richard G. Rogers, and Kimberley D. Peters. 1997. "Ethnicity and Mortality in the United States: Individual and Community Correlates." *Social Forces* 76(1): 169–98.

———. 1998. "Neighborhood Social Context and Racial Differences in Women's Heart Disease Mortality." *Journal of Health and Social Behavior* 39: 91–107.

LeClere, Felicia B., and Mah-Jabeen Soobader. 2000. "The Effect of Income Inequality on the Health of Selected U.S. Demographic Groups." *American Journal of Public Health* 90(12): 1892–97.

Lochner, Kimberly, Elsie Pamuk, Diane Makuc, Bruce P. Kennedy, and Ichiro Kawachi. 2001. "State-Level Income Inequality and Individual Mortality Risk: A Prospective, Multilevel Study." *American Journal of Public Health* 91(3): 385–91.

Lynch, John W., George Davey Smith, George A. Kaplan, and James S. House. 2000. "Income Inequality and Mortality: Importance to Health of Individual Income, Psychosocial Environment, or Material Conditions." *British Medical Journal* 320(7243): 1200–4.

Lynch, John W., George A. Kaplan, and Elsie R. Pamuk. 1998. "Income Inequality and Mortality in Metropolitan Areas of the United States." *American Journal of Public Health* 88: 1074–80.

Mackenbach, Johan. 2002. "Income Inequality and Population Health." *British Medical Journal* 324: 1–2.

Marmot, Michael G., Manolis Kogevinas, and Mary Ann Elston. 1987. "Social/Economic Status and Disease." *Annual Review of Public Health* 8: 111–35.

Marmot, Michael G., G. Davey Smith, Stephen A. Stansfeld, C. Patel, F. North, J. Head, I. White, E. J. Brunner, and A. Feeney. 1991. "Health Inequalities Among British Civil Servants: The Whitehall II Study." *Lancet* 337(8754):1387–93.

Massey, Douglas S. 1990. "American Apartheid: Segregation and the Making of the Underclass." *American Journal of Sociology* 96: 329–58.

Massey, Douglas S., and Nancy A. Denton. 1988a. "The Dimensions of Residential Segregation." *Social Forces* 60(2): 281–315.

———. 1988b. "Suburbanization and Segregation in U.S. Metropolitan Areas." *American Journal of Sociology* 84: 592–626.

———. 1989. "Hypersegregation in U.S. Metropolitan Areas: Black and Hispanic Segregation Along Five Dimensions." *Demography* 26(3): 373–91.

———. 1993. *American Apartheid: Segregation and the Making of the Underclass.* Cambridge, Mass.: Harvard University Press.

McCord, Colin, and Harold P. Freeman. 1990. "Excess Mortality in Harlem." *New England Journal of Medicine* 322(3): 173–77.

McDonough, Peggy, Greg J. Duncan, David Williams, and James House. 1997. "Income Dynamics and Adult Mortality in the United States, 1972 Through 1989." *American Journal of Public Health* 87(9): 1476–83.

Mellor, Jennifer M., and Jeffrey D. Milyo. 1999. "Income Inequality and Individual Health: Evidence from the Current Population Survey." Working paper 8. Boston: Robert Wood Johnson Foundation Scholars in Health Policy Research Program.

———. 2001. "Reexamining the Evidence of an Ecological Association Between Income Inequality and Health." *Journal of Health Politics, Policy, and Law* 26(3): 487–522.

Miller, Douglas, and Christina Paxson. 2001. "Relative Income, Race, and Mortality." Working paper. Princeton, N.J.: Princeton University, Center for Health and Wellbeing.

Mirowsky, John, and Paul Nongzhuang Hu. 1996. "Physical Impairment and the Diminishing Effects of Income." *Social Forces* 74: 1073–96.

National Center for Health Statistics. Various years. *Health, United States.* Washington: U.S. Government Printing Office.

Nazroo, James Y. 2003. "The Structuring of Ethnic Inequalities in Health: Economic Position, Racial Discrimination, and Racism." *American Journal of Public Health* 93(2): 277–84.

Pappas, Gregory, Susan Queen, Wilbur Hadden, and Gail Fisher. 1993. "The Increasing Disparity in Mortality Between Socioeconomic Groups in the United States, 1960 and 1986." *New England Journal of Medicine* 329: 103–9.

Pickett, Kate E., and Michelle Pearl. 2001. "Multilevel Analyses of Neighborhood Socioeconomic Context and Health Outcomes: A Critical Review." *Journal of Epidemiology and Community Health* 55: 111–22.

Polednak, Anthony P. 1991. "Black-White Differences in Infant Mortality in Thirty-eight Standard Metropolitan Statistical Areas." *American Journal of Public Health* 81(11): 1480–82.

———. 1993. "Poverty, Residential Segregation, and Black-White Mortality Ratios in Urban Areas." *Journal of Health Care for the Poor and Underserved* 4(4): 363–73.

————. 1996. "Trends in U.S. Urban Black Infant Mortality, by Degree of Residential Segregation." *American Journal of Public Health* 86(5): 723–26.

Preston, Samuel. 1975. "The Changing Relation Between Mortality and Level of Development." *Population Studies* 29: 231–48.

Ren, Xinhua S., and Benjamin Amick. 1996. "Race and Self-assessed Health Status: The Role of Socioeconomic Factors in the United States." *Journal of Epidemiology and Community Health* 50: 269–73.

Robert, Stephanie A. 1998. "Community-Level Socioeconomic Status Effects on Adult Health." *Journal of Health and Social Behavior* 39: 18–37.

————. 1999. "Socioeconomic Position and Health: The Independent Contribution of Community Context." *Annual Review of Sociology* 25: 489–516.

————. 2002. "Community Context and Aging: Future Research Issues." *Research on Aging* 24(6): 579–99.

Robert, Stephanie A., and James S. House. 2000a. "Socioeconomic Inequalities in Health: An Enduring Sociological Problem." In *Handbook of Medical Sociology,* edited by Chloe E. Bird, Peter Conrad, and Allen M. Fremont. New York: Prentice-Hall.

————. 2000b. "Socioeconomic Inequalities in Health: Integrating Individual-, Community-, and Societal-Level Theory and Research." In *Handbook of Social Studies in Health and Medicine,* edited by Gary L. Albrecht, Ray Fitzpatrick, and Susan C. Scrimshaw. London: Sage Publications.

Robert, Stephanie A., and Kum Yi Lee. 2002. "Explaining Race Differences in Health Among Older Adults: The Contribution of Community Socioeconomic Context." *Research on Aging* 24(6): 654–83.

Rodgers, Gerry B. 1979. "Income and Inequality as Determinants of Mortality: An International Cross-section Analysis." *Population Studies* 33: 343–51.

Ryff, Carol D., William J. Magee, K. C. Kling, and E. H. Wing. 1999. "Forging Macro-Micro Linkages in the Study of Psychological Well-being." In *The Self and Society in Aging Processes,* edited by Carol D. Ryff and Victor W. Marshall. New York: Springer-Verlag.

Ryff, Carol D., and Burton Singer. 1998a. "The Contours of Positive Human Health." *Psychological Inquiry* 9: 1–28.

————. 1998b. "Human Health: New Directions for the Next Millennium." *Psychological Inquiry* 9: 69–85.

Shihadeh, Edward S., and Nicole Flynn. 1996. "Segregation and Crime: The Effect of Black Social Isolation on the Rates of Black Urban Violence." *Social Forces* 74(4): 1325–52.

Singer, Burton H., and Carol D. Ryff, eds. 2000. *New Horizons in Health: An Integrative Approach.* Washington, D.C.: National Academy Press.

Soobader, Mah-Jabeen, and Felicia B. LeClere. 1999. "Aggregation and the Measurement of Income Inequality: Effects on Morbidity." *Social Science and Medicine* 48: 733–44.

Sorlie, Paul D., Eric Backlund, and Jacob B. Keller. 1995. "U.S. Mortality by Economic, Demographic, and Social Characteristics: The National Longitudinal Mortality Study." *American Journal of Public Health* 85: 949–56.

Staiger, Douglas. 1998. "The Covariance Structure of Mortality Rates in Hospitals." In *Inquiries in the Economics of Aging,* edited by David A. Wise. Chicago: University of Chicago Press/National Bureau of Economic Research.

Subramanian, Sukanya V., Tony Blakely, and Ichiro Kawachi. 2003. "Income Inequality as a Public Health Concern: Where Do We Stand?" *Health Services Research* 38: 153–67.

U.S. Department of Commerce. U.S. Census Bureau. 2000. *Statistical Abstract of the United States: 2000.* Washington: U.S. Government Printing Office.

Wagstaff, Adam, and Eddy van Doorslaer. 2000. "Income Inequality and Health: What Does the Literature Tell Us?" *Annual Review of Public Health* 21: 543–67.

Waitzman, Norman J., and Ken R. Smith. 1998a. "Phantom of the Area: Poverty-Area Residence and Mortality in the United States." *American Journal of Public Health* 88(6): 973–76.

————. 1998b. "Separate but Lethal: The Effects of Economic Segregation on Mortality in Metropolitan America." *Milbank Memorial Fund Quarterly* 76(3): 341–73.

Wilkinson, Richard G. 1992. "Income Distribution and Life Expectancy." *British Medical Journal* 304: 165–68.

————. 1994. "The Epidemiological Transition: From Material Scarcity to Social Disadvantage?" *Daedalus* 123: 61–77.

————. 1996. *Unhealthy Societies: The Affliction of Inequality.* London: Routledge.

Williams, David R. 2002. "Racial/Ethnic Variations in Women's Health: The Social Embeddedness of Health." *American Journal of Public Health* 92(4): 588–97.

Williams, David R., and Chiquita Collins. 1995. "U.S. Socioeconomic and Racial Differences in Health: Patterns and Explanations." *Annual Review of Sociology* 21: 349–86.

Wilson, William Julius. 1987. *The Truly Disadvantaged: The Inner City, the Underclass, and Public Policy.* Chicago: University of Chicago Press.

Chapter 14

The Income-Health Relationship and the Role of Relative Deprivation

Christine E. Eibner and William N. Evans

While there is a strong, positive relationship between individual income and individual health, there is less evidence of a relationship between aggregate income and aggregate health. Several recent papers argue that increases in individual income affect health and well-being not just through increases in absolute material standards but also through a relative deprivation effect (Åberg-Yngwe et al. 2003; Luttmer 2003; Eibner and Evans, forthcoming). Low relative income may cause stress and depression, conditions that could raise the probability of contracting a disease or increase the tendency to engage in risky behavior. We argue that if relative deprivation matters, then an increase in an individual's income could have a negative impact on the health of the population at large. This insight could help explain the ambiguous relationship between national income and national health.

In this chapter, we summarize the results of our earlier work linking relative deprivation to poor health (Eibner and Evans, forthcoming) and extend the analysis in a number of important ways. First, we demonstrate the persistence of the result by performing a number of specification tests. We examine the relationship using a variety of definitions of "health" and "health habits," for several different subsamples, and using a number of different definitions of "reference group." The impact of relative deprivation is statistically precise and quantitatively important across a variety of specifications. After establishing the basic empirical relationship between relative deprivation and mortality, we examine whether this hypothesis can explain the disparity in results for the income-mortality relationship at the individual and aggregate levels. Our models suggest that 50 percent of the impact of income on mortality found in previous work may be capturing the impact of relative deprivation. We should be clear that we are not saying income has a limited role in predicting mortality. On the contrary, our results simply suggest that as individual incomes rise, much of the decline in mortality may be due to a reduction in relative deprivation rather than a straightforward income effect.

Finally, we perform some simple simulations to determine what happens to aggregate mortality when incomes change for particular groups of people. As individual income rises, individual mortality should fall. However, as the income of *others* rises, individual mortality should increase. Interestingly, our simulations suggest that with a uniform increase in income of 10 percent, the relative deprivation effect will dominate the pure income effect and aggregate mortality will increase. Our results therefore may explain the weak relationship between income and health at the aggregate level.

545

We want to be cautious about our results. In a cross-section, we find that people with poor economic performance relative to their peers have poorer health habits and higher mortality. Although our results are consistent with the relative deprivation hypothesis, we do not have enough evidence to indicate that this relationship is causal. It is possible that some omitted factor explains both a person's poor economic performance relative to his peers and his poorer health outcomes. Our results are intriguing, however, and certainly suggest that the relative deprivation hypothesis may explain the disparity in the income-health relationship between individual and aggregate studies.

BACKGROUND

A large body of literature, spanning many disciplines, has established that individuals with lower incomes have poorer health outcomes and higher mortality rates (Kitigawa and Hauser 1973; Duleep 1986; Wolfson et al. 1993; Chapman and Hariharan 1994; McDonough et al. 1997; Ettner 1996; Lantz et al. 1998; Deaton and Paxson 1998, 2001a, 2001b). A relationship between health and income has been documented for virtually all measures of health and health habits, within many countries and over time, and recent research suggests that the statistical correlation between income and health may have actually increased over the past forty years (Feldman et al. 1989; Pappas et al. 1993; Preston and Elo 1995; Deaton and Paxson 1998; Evans, Ringel, and Stech 1999).

In contrast to the persistent correlation between income and health at the individual level, there is much weaker evidence of a link between income and health in aggregate data for developed countries. Samuel Preston's (1975) famous paper on national per capita income and life expectancy demonstrated that increases in real per capita national income produce smaller and smaller increments to life expectancy. Andrew Clarkwest and Christopher Jencks (2003) use Preston's estimates to argue that by 1960 life expectancy was unrelated to income for countries with incomes about one-quarter of U.S. aggregate income. Richard Wilkinson (1996) finds little correlation between life expectancy and per capita gross domestic product across OECD countries. Using a panel of state-level mortality data from 1972 to 1991, Christopher Ruhm (2000) finds that higher state per capita incomes are associated with higher mortality. Angus Deaton and Christina Paxson (2001b) note that since 1950, in both Britain and the United States, mortality rates have fallen for almost all age groups and for both sexes, yet the authors cannot find much of a role for income growth in explaining mortality declines. These authors give us the best summary of the disparity in this literature between results with individual and aggregate data when they note: "Why there should be such a contrast between individual and national effects of income is a topic that requires a good deal of further thought and analysis" (31).

In the 1990s a number of researchers suggested that the impact of income inequality on health may explain this empirical puzzle. In a 1992 paper and subsequent book, Wilkinson (1996) argues that there is a negative correlation between income inequality and average life expectancies across countries and that this relationship cannot be attributed to omitted country-specific factors such as diet and exercise. Subsequent studies show a similar correlation between income inequality and health across different countries, the U.S. states, and smaller geographic regions such as metropolitan statistical areas (MSAs) (Waldmann 1992; Kaplan et al. 1996; Kennedy, Kawachi, and Prothrow-Stith 1996, to name just a few).

The literature linking health and inequality has ballooned over the past decade, with dozens of articles investigating this question. Much of the growing literature is highly critical, however, of these initial papers. A number of papers have demonstrated that the statistical relationship between inequality and health in these initial papers is diminished greatly or even erased when the basic models are altered by changing the countries in the sample (Lynch et al. 2001), using higher-quality data (Judge, Mulligan, and Benzeval 1997), adding additional covariates to the regression (Deaton 2001; Deaton and Lubotsky 2003; Mellor and Milyo 2001), using individual-level data (Gravelle 1998; Friscella and Franks 1997; Lochner et al. 2001; Mellor and Milyo 2002; Deaton 2001; Gravelle, Wildman, and Sutton 2002), or using within-group estimation techniques (Mellor and Milyo 2001; Clarkwest and Jencks 2003). The state of the literature is summarized in detail in a number of recent reviews. Clarkwest and Jencks (2003) argue that the income inequality–health link is difficult to detect and modest at best. Deaton's (2003, 151) summary of the literature is even more negative. "It is not true," he writes, "that income inequality itself is a major determinant of population health. There is no robust correlation between life expectancy and income inequality among the rich countries, and the correlation across the states and cities of the United States is almost certainly the result of something that is correlated with income inequality."

The starting point for this chapter is the apparent inability of the inequality-health relationship to explain the disparity between the individual-level and aggregate-level income-health relationship. Initially, the literature in the income inequality–health nexus focused on establishing the statistical correlation between these two variables. But as the initial "positive" results increased, so did the suggested pathways through which inequality might have an impact on health. A number of authors hypothesized that income inequality reduces spending on health-improving public health programs, while others suggested that income inequality reduces social capital. One explanation for the inequality–health relationship made popular by Wilkinson is the "relative deprivation" hypothesis, which argues that individuals are adversely affected when they perceive themselves to be economically deprived relative to their peers. It's typically assumed that a person's health is negatively related to the income of people in his or her reference group, so that as person j becomes richer, person i's health deteriorates.

What is interesting about the appeals to relative deprivation in this context is that income inequality and relative deprivation are measuring fundamentally different things. Clearly these two variables are related—areas with high income inequality have higher average relative deprivation. For example, using a definition of relative deprivation based on Runciman (1966), Shlomo Yitzhaki (1979) shows that average relative deprivation in a reference group is simply mean income times the Gini coefficient. However, income inequality is a group measure, while relative deprivation is specific to the individual. Two people living in the same state or country are "exposed" to the same measure of group inequality, yet these two people can have vastly different measures of relative deprivation. Unfortunately, a number of authors have used income inequality and relative deprivation interchangeably, blurring the meaning of the two variables. Wilkinson (1997) argues that "income inequality summarizes the health burden of individual relative deprivation." Although aggregate measures of income inequality may proxy for relative deprivation, they are at best an indirect test of the relative deprivation hypothesis.

There is biological evidence to support the notion that relative status plays a role in both psychological and physical health. Studies indicate that socially subordinate monkeys have lower levels of serotonin, higher basal cortisol concentrations, and greater susceptibility to viral infections than dominant animals (Shively, Laber-Laird, and Anton 1997; Sapolsky, Alberts, and Altmann 1997; Cohen et al. 1997; McGuire and Raleigh 1985). Low serotonin levels and high basal cortisol concentrations are associated with numerous adverse health outcomes, including affective disorders, anorexia nervosa, sleep disorders, and Alzheimer's disease. The relationship between social status and health persists even when the social hierarchy of the monkey troop is manipulated scientifically. Although human social hierarchies are more complicated and more difficult to study than those of monkeys, social scientists draw parallels between research on primates and the potential relationship between relative income and health in humans (Frank 1985; Wilkinson 1996; Cohen et al. 1997). The nature of causality in some of these studies has not been conclusively established, but they are still suggestive of a potential link between relative status and individual-level health outcomes.

Further evidence of the harmful effects of relative deprivation is found in the famous Whitehall study that tracked the mortality outcomes of members of the British Civil Service. Evaluation of ten-year, age-adjusted mortality rates revealed that the lowest-ranking civil servants were three times more likely to die than the highest-ranking civil servants (Marmot, Shipley, and Rose 1984; Marmot 1986). Moreover, the greatest discrepancies in mortality rates occurred for coronary heart disease and lung cancer, two types of death that are greatly influenced by behavioral factors. Though these results are not adjusted for income or education levels, even the lowest-ranking civil servants were employed and had access to nationalized health care. One conclusion often made from the Whitehall Study is that at least part of the mortality difference between the highest and lowest civil service grades was driven by relative deprivation.

Several recent studies using individual-level data find that relative deprivation is related to lower self-reported health status (Åberg-Yngwe et al. 2003), lower self-reported happiness (Luttmer 2003), and increased probability of death (Eibner and Evans, forthcoming). Monica Åberg-Yngwe and her colleagues (2003) find that relative deprivation is a binary variable equal to one if the individual's income is less than 70 percent of the mean income in his or her age, social class, and region. Using mean income within an individual's locality as his measure of relative deprivation, Erzo Luttmer (2003) posits that, as mean income increases, people feel more deprived and are therefore less happy. In Eibner and Evans (forthcoming), we use data from the National Health Interview Survey Multiple Cause of Death (NHIS/MCOD) file and the Behavioral Risk Factor Surveillance System (BRFSS) to examine the impact on health of relative deprivation within a reference group. We define reference groups using combinations of state, race, education, and age. Those with high relative deprivation as described in Yitzhaki (1979) have a higher probability of death, are more likely to self-report poor health, have higher body mass indexes, are more likely to report disabilities, and are more likely to engage in poor health habits.

In the remainder of this chapter, we summarize our earlier work and elaborate on the results. Our chapter contributes to the existing literature in several different ways. First, we focus specifically on the relative deprivation hypothesis. Second, we define reference groups using not only state of residence but also other demographic characteristics, such as age, race, and education. Third, while we are able to use mortality as one of our key outcomes, we also examine a number of other health outcomes and health-related behaviors, such as smoking. Fourth, we experiment with several definitions of relative deprivation and numerous definitions of reference group. Fifth, we examine directly the within-group and between-group disparity in results for the income-health link and find that this difference can be explained by the impact of relative deprivation.

After discussing our results and running specification checks, we then conduct simulations to determine how increases in individual income affect population health under the assumption that relative deprivation matters. We find that relative deprivation is an intriguing explanation for the ambiguous relationship between aggregate income and aggregate health.

REFERENCE GROUPS

To address the relative deprivation hypothesis, we must consider how individuals define "reference group." The social psychology literature argues that members of one's reference group are typically selected based on either geographic proximity or demographic similarity (Singer 1981). However, it is well acknowledged that there is no perfect formula for determining reference groups. Critics assert that the Achilles' heel of social evaluation theory is the "failure to explain adequately how the relevant comparisons are selected in the first place" (Pettigrew 1978, 36). Most studies dealing with health and inequality define reference groups within the context of geographical location, such as state or MSA of residence. Restricting inequality measures to geographic boundaries makes sense if inequality affects health through its impact on public investment in human and social capital. However, if social comparison is one of the mechanisms through which low income affects health, demographic characteristics may be an important part of reference group determination. Individuals may compare themselves to others of similar demographic backgrounds, regardless of geographical location (Frank 1985). Deaton (1999) addresses the issue of "similar circumstances" by using birth cohorts to define reference groups. While he finds no relationship between income inequality and mortality at the cohort level, he demonstrates that the gradient between income and mortality is steeper when income inequality is higher.

Deaton acknowledges that birth cohorts provide an imperfect measure of an individual's true reference group. However, he claims that birth cohorts should contain a high ratio of "relevant to irrelevant reference people" as compared to the general population. Thus, birth cohorts can act as a rough proxy for true reference groups. In this study, we construct reference groups based on observable demographic characteristics such as state of residence, race, education, and age. Groups defined using such characteristics do not necessarily constitute the unobservable true reference groups. Yet members of such groups have a high degree of similarity and are likely to contain a high proportion of relevant reference people. Following Deaton (1999), we assume that reference groups with a high "relevant-irrelevant" ratio are reasonable proxies for the unobservable true reference groups. In our work, we use information for four racial groups (white, black, Hispanic, and other) and four education groups (less than high school, high school graduate, some college, and college graduate). Age groups are defined in five-year intervals.

MEASURING RELATIVE DEPRIVATION

Our starting point for measuring relative deprivation (RD) is based on Runciman (1966) and subsequent theory developed by Yitzhaki (1979). For a person i with income y_i who is part of a reference group with N people, Yitzhaki's measure is defined as:

$$RD_i = \frac{1}{N} \sum_j (y_j - y_i) \qquad \forall y_j > y_i \qquad (14.1)$$

This measure posits that relative deprivation for person i is driven by the incomes of people who earn more than y_i.[1] The summation in equation 14.1 is divided by the size of the reference group to make the measure invariant to the size of the reference group. Dividing by N can also be interpreted as adjusting for the probability of making a comparison. If person i and person j are alone on a desert island, N is low and the probability of making a comparison is high. In contrast, if person i and person j live in New York City, N is high and the probability of making a comparison is low. If income for person i is thought of as a draw from a distribution, the relative deprivation measure in equation 14.1 can be rewritten as:

$$RD_i = [E(y \mid y > y_i) - y_i] \times prob(y > y_i) \tag{14.2}$$

Intuitively, Yitzhaki's relative deprivation measure is equal to the expected difference between i's income and the expected income of those with incomes greater than y_i, times the probability that income is greater than i's income. In the results that we report, we scale the Yitzhaki measure by dividing by 10,000.

To get a better sense of what relative deprivation is measuring, in table 14.1 we calculate relative deprivation for individuals of various incomes and demographic characteristics. Reference groups are defined using state, age, race, and education. As we discuss in more detail later, we calculate measures of relative deprivation using data from the U.S. Census 5 Percent Public Use Micro Samples (PUMS) for males age twenty-one to sixty-four. Table 14.1 shows that, as income increases, relative deprivation falls. But table 14.1 also demonstrates that, for any given income, relative deprivation varies depending on the characteristics of the reference group. A white college graduate with an income of $10,000 has a relative deprivation score of 6.57, whereas a black high school graduate with the same income has a relative deprivation score of only 2.58. The black high school graduate is less relatively deprived than the white college graduate because, on average, the income of black high school graduates is lower than that of white college graduates. Table 14.1 illustrates that, while relative deprivation and income are correlated, the variation between the two measures can be substantial. For instance, in relative terms, a black high school graduate with $10,000 is less relatively deprived than a white college graduate with $50,000.

In addition to Yitzhaki's measure, we experiment with other measures of relative deprivation, including centile rank, z-score, and Yitzhaki's index based on the logarithm of income as opposed to income levels. A more detailed account of these additional measures is provided in Eibner and Evans (forthcoming).

DATA

Our primary sample is a restricted-use version of the National Health Interview Survey (NHIS) Multiple Cause of Death files. The NHIS is an annual survey of the U.S. civilian non-institutionalized population conducted by the National Center for Health Statistics. Individual information from the NHIS person file contains about 120,000 observations each year. The person file includes a wide variety of demographic data (age, sex, race, family income, and so on), as well as health-related information such as height, weight, and self-reported health status. Respondents from the 1986 through 1994 NHIS were tracked using the National Death Index through the end of 1997. As a result, for each year of the NHIS a corresponding Multiple Cause of Death (MCOD) file is available that contains year of death, month of death, and cause of death for NHIS respondents who were deceased by the end of 1997. Data from the MCOD can be merged with the NHIS persons file to form the linked file that we refer to as the NHIS/MCOD. Using date of death information from the MCOD, we can calculate a binary indicator variable for whether or not the individual died

TABLE 14.1   *Relative Deprivation for Forty-Year-Old California Males, 1990*

Income:	White High School Graduate	Black High School Graduate	White College Graduate	Black College Graduate
$10,000	3.70	2.58	6.57	5.61
$25,000	2.36	1.43	5.14	4.21
$50,000	0.92	0.35	3.11	2.31
$75,000	0.38	0.06	1.83	1.23

Source: U.S. Census Bureau, 5 Percent PUMS.
Note: RD is measured using Yitzhaki's (1979) index multiplied by 10,000. Reference groups are defined over state, age, race, and education.

in five years, which we use to measure mortality.[2] The restricted-use version of the NHIS contains data on state of residence. This access gives us an advantage in that we can use individual-level income data, we can use mortality as our outcome of interest, and we can include geography as part of our reference-group definition.

To construct the relative deprivation measure outlined here, we need data on the individual's own income and information about the income distribution for the reference group. The own-income measure used to construct relative deprivation is set at the midpoint of the individual's family income interval from the NHIS—for example, for the $0 to $1,000 category, income is set at $500. For the top-coded category in the NHIS (income of $50,000 or more), family income is set at the reference-group conditional mean income given that income is greater than or equal to $50,000. This conditional mean is taken from the 5 Percent Public Use Microdata Sample of the 1990 census. Rather than rely on data from the NHIS to construct measures of relative deprivation, we instead match income variables from the NHIS to household income data from the PUMS.[3] The 1990 PUMS is the best available source of income data because it has extremely large sample sizes and the income variable is continuous. While household income is top-coded at a level that varies by state, top-coded individuals are assigned household income equal to the median household income in their state given that income is greater than the top-code value.[4] We restrict our sample from the PUMS to male householders and male spouses over the age of twenty, which gives us 3,316,833 observations.[5] We then use this information to calculate relative deprivation measures for each individual in the NHIS dataset. Reference groups are defined using various combinations of state, age group, race, and education.[6] Our final dataset contains 122,427 NHIS/MCOD observations for the years 1988 to 1991 linked to measures of relative deprivation taken from the 1990 PUMS.[7] For our baseline results, we restrict the sample to men between the ages of twenty-one and sixty-four, which leaves us with 104,320 observations. Further, we use only NHIS respondents for whom the PUMS reference group contained at least fifty observations, which causes the sample size to diminish slightly in models where we use more stratified reference groups.

Mortality is a convenient measure of health because it is easily observable and precisely measured. However, there are some drawbacks to using mortality as our primary outcome. Death is a rare event for younger people. Further, it is possible that relative deprivation has an adverse impact on morbidity without directly affecting mortality. To explore this issue, we look at two additional outcomes from the NHIS: self-reported health status and limited-activity status.

Both self-reported health status and limited-activity status are measures that can be taken from the NHIS. Self-reported health status is a categorical variable with five possible outcomes: excellent, very good, good, fair, and poor. As in Mellor and Milyo (2002), we construct a binary variable that equals one if the individual reports fair or poor health. Studies have shown that self-reported health status is highly correlated with mortality (Idler and Benyamini 1997). Limited-activity status measures whether the individual is physically restricted or unable to perform activities, which include work, school, and other pastimes. The question has four possible responses: unable to perform major activity; limited in the kind or amount of major activity; limited in other activities, and not limited. We create a binary variable that is equal to one if respondents report any limitation. In total, 13.2 percent of our sample reports being limited in some capacity.

As an additional source of data, we use information from the Behavioral Risk Factor Surveillance System for the years 1989 to 1991 to examine health-compromising behaviors. The BRFSS is an ongoing telephone survey conducted by the states and supported by the Centers for Disease Control (CDC). Households are telephoned at random, and a series of questions are asked of a randomly selected adult member of the household. BRFSS data are available for the years 1984 to the present. Initially only fifteen states conducted BRFSS surveys, but by 1990 forty-four states and the District of Columbia were participating.[8] Together the 1989 to 1991 BRFSS surveys contain 236,270 observations, but after limiting our sample to men between the ages of twenty-one and sixty-four, we have 73,085 records. In addition to basic demographic data, the BRFSS contains measures of exercise habits, body mass index (BMI), and current and former smoking status. The BRFSS also contains data on household income, which is reported as a seven-level categorical variable with a top-coded value of $50,000; we impute individual incomes with this information using the same strategy discussed earlier for the NHIS.[9] To calculate the income distribution for the reference group, we use data from the 1990 PUMS.

Table 14.2 shows the underlying characteristics of both the NHIS and BRFSS samples. Average relative deprivation is highest and the variance is lowest when reference groups are defined over states only. This result is predictable; as reference groups become more similar, income differences become less pronounced. To get a sense of the magnitude of relative deprivation, if reference groups are defined using state of residence, Connecticut has the highest average relative deprivation at 2.3, and South Dakota has the lowest at 1.1. The descriptive statistics from the NHIS are comparable to those of the BRFSS. For example, average annual income in the NHIS is $38,237, while average income in the BRFSS is $40,369. Both samples are nearly 80 percent white, and the average age is roughly thirty-nine.

A SIMPLE ECONOMETRIC MODEL

For our baseline results, we estimate the following equation:[10]

$$\text{Outcome}_{ir} = \beta_o + \beta_1 \text{RD}_{ir} + \sum_{k=1}^{26} \text{income}_{kir}\Theta_k + \delta_r + X_{ir}\Gamma + \varepsilon_{ir} \qquad (14.3)$$

where Outcome_{ir} is a binary variable representing one of several health-related outcomes, such as whether the individual died in five years or whether the individual smokes. The subscripts i and r represent individual and reference group, respectively. All regressions are estimated using ordinary least squares. RD_{ir} is the Yitzhaki-based relative deprivation mea-

TABLE 14.2   *Descriptive Statistics, NHIS and BRFSS Samples*

| Variable | Reference Group Defined Over: | | | |
	State	State and Age	State, Age, and Race	State, Age, Race, and Education
NHIS				
RD/10,000	1.679	1.649	1.579	1.454
	(1.108)	(1.227)	(1.181)	(1.180)
Died in five years	2.44%	2.44%	2.44%	2.45%
Income	$38,237	$38,237	$38,272	$38,432
	(21,659)	(21,659)	(21,657)	(21,645)
Age	39.1	39.1	39.1	39.2
	(11.8)	(11.8)	(11.8)	(11.8)
White	78.8%	78.8%	79.1%	80.8%
Observations	104,320	104,320	103,834	101,577
BRFSS				
RD/10,000	1.740	1.656	1.615	1.613
	(1.119)	(1.219)	(1.193)	(1.263)
Income	$40,369	$40,369	$40,427	$40,584
	(27,249)	(27,249)	(27,260)	(27,308)
Age	38.9	38.9	38.9	39.0
	(11.9)	(11.9)	(11.9)	(11.9)
White	79.6%	79.6%	80.2%	81.8%
Observations	73,085	73,085	71,936	69,606

Source: Authors' compilations.
Note: Sample size diminishes as reference groups are more specifically defined, since we drop reference groups with fewer than fifty observations in the PUMS.

sure, divided by 10,000. To control for income independently of the relative deprivation effect, we add a complete set of dummy variables for the twenty-seven income categories in the NHIS. The independent income effect is captured in the term income$_{kir}$, which equals one if the individual's income is in group k, zero otherwise.

The term δ_r is a reference-group fixed effect meant to capture persistent differences across reference groups. Finally, X_{ir} is a vector of dummy variables that control for individual-specific characteristics such as age, education, and marital status. The set of variables that enter δ_r and X_{ir} change depending on how reference groups are defined. In the first model, where reference groups are defined by state alone, δ_r is a state fixed effect and X_{ir} contains all of the other demographic dummy variables, including age group, race, and education. As reference groups become more narrowly defined, the relevant variables are moved out of X_{ir} and entered into δ_r as interaction terms. For instance, when reference groups are defined using state and age group, δ_r becomes a state $\times$ age-group interaction term and age effects are no longer included in X_{ir}.

RESULTS

In the first row of table 14.3, we report the baseline results estimated from equation 14.3 for men age twenty-one to sixty-four. Even after controlling for individual income and a number of covariates, Yitzhaki-based relative deprivation appears to be strongly related to the probability of dying. The relative deprivation effect varies depending on the measure and how reference groups are defined, and the weakest effect is found where reference groups are broadly defined using only state of residence. The coefficients are largest in the state and age group models (column 4), where the effect of a one-standard-deviation (1.2 point) increase in relative deprivation appears to increase mortality by 1.4 percentage points (57 percent). These results seem sizable, but they are consistent with other literature on socio-economic status and mortality. For instance, Michael Marmot (1986) found that British civil servants from the lowest socioeconomic class were three times more likely to die than their high-status counterparts. Alternatively, in a linear probability model where relative deprivation is not included as a covariate, moving from $40,000 to $10,000 doubles the probability of death.[11] It is also true that a 1.2 point (one-standard-deviation) decline in relative deprivation is a large change. Using table 14.1 as a guide, we see that for forty-year-old men in California, moving from $25,000 to $50,000 in annual income for a black college graduate, increasing annual income from $10,000 to $25,000 for a white high school graduate, or increasing income from $50,000 to $75,000 for a white college graduate, all decrease relative deprivation by about 1.2 points.

The additional rows in the first panel of table 14.3 look at cause-specific mortality. Relative deprivation is positively related to mortality from coronary heart disease (CHD) and smoking-related cancers. However, there is no relationship between relative deprivation and mortality due to other types of cancer and accidents or adverse events. One possible explanation for this finding is that individuals who feel deprived may be particularly likely to engage in health-compromising behaviors, such as smoking. Positing that health-compromising behavior may be a key mechanism in linking relative income, stress, and health, Wilkinson (1996, 185–86) argues: "Among the many ways people respond to stress, unhappiness, and unmet emotional needs, one is to increase their consumption of various comforting foods—which usually have a higher sugar and fat content—and of various drugs including alcohol and of course tobacco." Since CHD and lung cancer are highly related to the comforting behaviors that Wilkinson describes, it is perhaps unsurprising that relative deprivation has a stronger effect on mortality due to these causes.

In the second panel of table 14.3, we look at two additional measures of health status: whether the individual reports being poor or fair health, and whether the individual is limited in his ability to perform activities. In both cases, we find that relative deprivation is positively related to poor health in all but the state-only models. A one-standard-deviation increase in relative deprivation (reference groups defined using state, age, race, and education) is associated with a 0.8-percentage-point (10 percent) increase in the probability of reporting fair or poor health, and a 1.8-percentage-point (13.6 percent) increase in the probability of reporting activity limitations.

We further test the relationship between relative deprivation and health-compromising behavior in the third panel, where we look specifically at health-related behavior. Here we find that relative deprivation is positively linked to current smoking and body mass index.[12] Further, relative deprivation is negatively linked to the probability that an individual exercises or consistently wears a seat belt in all but the state-only models. As with the mortality results, the link between relative deprivation and health-related behavior is sizable in magnitude. For instance, a one-standard-deviation increase in relative deprivation where reference groups are defined using state, age, race, and education is associated with a 2.3-percentage-point (8.3 percent) increase in the probability of being a current smoker.

These results suggest that relative deprivation may lead to adverse behavior, which in turn translates into poor health outcomes. However, it is also possible that the type of individuals who smoke, overeat, and take health risks tend to be myopic, lazy, reckless, or

TABLE 14.3   *Impact of Relative Deprivation on Health Outcomes Among Males Age Twenty-One to Sixty-Four*

| | | | Coefficient (Robust Standard Error) on RD/10,000 Defining Reference Groups by: | | | |
	Number of Cases	Mean	State Only	State and Age	State, Age, and Race	State, Age, Race, and Education
Cause-specific mortality (from NHIS/MCOD)						
All cause mortality	104,247	0.0244	0.0041	0.0120	0.0106	0.0069
			(0.0023)	(0.0014)	(0.0014)	(0.0011)
Coronary heart disease	101,530	0.0067	0.0035	0.0050	0.0049	0.0027
			(0.0012)	(0.0008)	(0.0007)	(0.0006)
Smoking-related cancers	101,530	0.0029	0.0000	0.0018	0.0023	0.0014
			(0.0008)	(0.0005)	(0.0005)	(0.0004)
All other cancers	101,530	0.0042	−0.0006	0.0008	0.0005	0.0009
			(0.0010)	(0.0006)	(0.0006)	(0.0005)
Accidents and adverse events	101,530	0.0037	−0.0006	0.0008	0.0005	0.0009
			(0.0010)	(0.0006)	(0.0006)	(0.0005)
Health status (from NHIS)						
Self-reports poor health?	101,305	0.0826	−0.0178	0.0357	0.0309	0.0068
			(0.0038)	(0.0025)	(0.0024)	(0.0018)
Limited in activity?	101,503	0.1320	−0.0095	0.0403	0.0445	0.0150
			(0.0050)	(0.0032)	(0.0031)	(0.0025)
Health-related behaviors (from BRFSS)						
Current smoker?	69,353	0.2860	0.0170	0.0141	0.0165	0.0199
			(0.0116)	(0.0083)	(0.0075)	(0.0058)
Ever smoked?	69,476	0.5656	0.0089	−0.0308	−0.0240	0.0033
			(0.0138)	(0.0095)	(0.0087)	(0.0071)
BMI	69,091	25.79	0.1596	0.1632	0.1542	0.1543
			(0.0988)	(0.0727)	(0.0689)	(0.0530)
Exercises?	69,533	0.7317	0.0032	−0.0447	−0.0380	−0.0249
			(0.0113)	(0.0080)	(0.0076)	(0.0061)
Wears seat belt?	69,410	0.5390	0.0093	−0.0138	−0.0207	−0.0234
			(0.0133)	(0.0094)	(0.0088)	(0.0070)

Source: Authors' compilation.
Note: Robust standard errors in parentheses. Unreported control variables are a reference-group (state × age-group × race × education) fixed effect, year, marital status. Controls for family size are included in NHIS data only.

otherwise different from those who do not take health risks. If unobservable qualities such as myopia are related to having a low income relative to one's peers (Fuchs 1982), then the relationship between relative deprivation and health may be driven by omitted variables bias.

Although we cannot rule out the omitted variables hypothesis with our data, we can provide some evidence to the contrary. If people who have ever smoked are more myopic or otherwise different from those who have never smoked, and if myopia (or laziness or other factors) is driving the relationship between relative deprivation and health, then we would expect to see a correlation between relative deprivation and having ever smoked. Since the decision to smoke is made early in one's life, a contemporaneous correlation between relative deprivation (say at age fifty) and whether a person ever smoked (a decision made before age twenty-one) would certainly suggest that the models are subject to an omitted variables bias. However, if relative deprivation affects health-related behaviors through stress, we would not expect current relative deprivation to have any relationship to whether the individual smoked in the past. Row 2 of the third panel shows no systematic relationship between relative deprivation and whether the individual ever smoked. The lack of a consistent correlation between relative deprivation and whether a person ever smoked gives us some comfort that our models are not subject to this criticism.

To summarize, our baseline results suggest that relative deprivation is related to five-year mortality (especially from causes of death that are linked to behavior), poor self-reported health status, and a host of poor health habits. One interesting finding that emerges from table 14.3 is that our results are generally the weakest when reference groups are defined using state only. In fact, for seat belt use, exercise, and the health status measures, the relative deprivation effect is counterintuitive in sign when reference groups are defined using state alone. This result is consistent with the argument that state alone is too broad to be considered the appropriate reference group.

SENSITIVITY TESTING

In table 14.4, we test to see whether our basic mortality results differ when we alter the model by changing the age of the respondents or dropping the 26,661 NHIS respondents in our sample whose incomes were top-coded. In general, the point estimates on the relative deprivation coefficients are larger for senior citizens than they are for younger people; however, they are not precisely estimated. Moreover, since the probability of death is much higher for seniors, even the larger point estimates translate into smaller effects in percentage terms. Overall, we interpret these results as suggesting that relative deprivation has a stronger effect on young people than it does on senior citizens. This may be due in part to the fact that wealth and assets are a more important component of both social class and social rank among the elderly than they are among younger, working-age people.

Since men are more likely to be the primary income earners in a family, we do not estimate these results for women. To the extent that relative deprivation is capturing self-esteem issues related to earnings, we imagine that the effect will be stronger for men. Åberg-Yngwe and her colleagues (2003) provide evidence to support the idea that relative deprivation matters more for males.

In the last row of table 14.4, we drop the 25.6 percent of the NHIS/MCOD sample who had top-coded incomes. Since such a large proportion of the sample was top-coded, we want to make sure that our results are not sensitive to our income imputations for these individuals. When we drop top-coded people, the findings become considerably more pronounced. A one-standard-deviation increase in relative deprivation in the state, age, race, and education model is now associated with a 2.1-percentage-point (90 percent) increase in the probability that the individual will die within five years after the survey. The increase in magnitude might reflect the fact that relative deprivation has a larger effect on those with low incomes than it does on those with higher incomes.

Much of the literature to date that has examined the link between inequality and health has restricted the definition of reference groups to geographic boundaries. This is consistent with studies from the social psychology literature that argue that members of one's reference group are typically selected based on either geographic proximity or demographic similarity (Singer 1981). As we noted earlier, if Wilkinson's (1997) psychosocial pathways

TABLE 14.4   *Impact of Relative Deprivation on Five-Year Mortality, NHIS/MCOD Data*

Samples	Number of Cases	Died in Five years	Coefficient (Robust Standard Error) on RD/10,000 Defining Reference Groups by:			
			State Only	State and Age	State, Age, and Race	State, Age, Race, and Education
Males, twenty-one to sixty-four	104,247	2.4%	0.0041 (0.0023)	0.0120 (0.0014)	0.0106 (0.0014)	0.0069 (0.0011)
Males, sixty-five or older	18,180	23.4	0.0112 (0.0187)	0.0149 (0.0170)	0.0142 (0.0162)	0.0017 (0.0107)
Males, twenty-one to sixty-four without top-coded incomes	77,586	2.8	0.0158 (0.067)	0.0248 (0.0039)	0.0247 (0.003)	0.0179 (0.0034)

Source: Authors' compilation.
Note: Robust standard errors in parentheses.

are the more probable culprits, then it is not clear that reference groups should be limited to geographical proximity. Individuals may compare themselves to others of similar demographic backgrounds regardless of geographical location. Robert Frank makes this point in his 1985 book *Choosing the Right Pond:*

> To be sure, people in similar circumstances, even though located far away, can be even more important than people nearby whose circumstances are markedly different. For example, a 35-year-old vice president in a bank branch in San Francisco may take a much greater interest in the salary of her counterpart at the Los Angeles branch than in the salary of the 50-year-old dentist in her own neighborhood. (33–34)

In table 14.5, we check to see whether the baseline results are sensitive to the choice of the demographic variables that we use to define reference groups. Here we show the initial results from the state, age, race, and education model, and then we add columns where reference groups are defined using age only, age and race, and age, race, and education. Regardless of how we define reference groups, the fundamental results are unchanged. Increases in relative deprivation are positively associated with mortality, poor health, smoking, and body mass index and are negatively related to the probability of exercise.

Two concerns arise surrounding the Yitzhaki-based relative deprivation measure that we use in our analyses. First, it does not take into account differences in the scale of the income distribution across reference groups. In other words, if everyone's income doubles, relative deprivation doubles as well. This would certainly be a problem if we were looking at relative deprivation over time and incomes were unadjusted for inflation. Since we deal with cross-sectional data, it is not clear whether we should be concerned about the scale of the reference-group income distribution. If people view within-reference-group income differences in proportional terms, then Yitzhaki's measure overstates the relative deprivation of individuals in high-income reference groups. If absolute differences within reference groups matter, then Yitzhaki's measure is appropriate. The latter scenario would make sense if everyone uses a common yardstick to measure relative deprivation (say, average U.S. income) but comparisons are made only within reference groups. Since it is plausible that

TABLE 14.5   *Impact of Relative Deprivation on Health Outcomes in Males Age Twenty-One to Sixty-Four, Using Alternative Reference-Group Measures*

	Number of Cases[a]	Mean	Coefficient (Robust Standard Error) on RD/10,000 Defining Reference Groups by:			
			State, Age, Race, and Education	Age Only	Age and Race	Age, Race, and Education
Cause-specific mortality (from NHIS/ MCOD)						
All cause mortality	104,247	2.4	0.0069 (0.0011)	0.0041 (0.0023)	0.0106 (0.0014)	0.0051 (0.0013)
Health status (from NHIS)						
Self-reports poor health?	101,305	0.0826	0.0068 (0.0018)	0.0735 (0.0029)	0.0628 (0.0028)	0.0092 (0.0018)
Health-related behaviors (from BRFSS)						
Current smoker?	69,353	0.2860	0.0189 (0.0055)	0.0156 (0.0102)	0.0189 (0.0092)	0.0201 (0.0056)
Body mass index	69,091	25.79	0.1317 (0.0514)	0.0702 (0.0898)	0.0613 (0.0834)	0.1456 (0.0531)
Exercises?	69,533	0.7317	−0.0241 (0.0058)	−0.0749 (0.0095)	−0.0621 (0.0088)	−0.0276 (0.0055)

Source: Authors' compilation.
Note: Robust standard errors in parentheses.
[a]Varies depending on how references groups are constructed (since we dropped observations where there were fewer than fifty people in the PUMS reference group).

people measure relative deprivation in proportional terms, we have constructed two additional measures of relative deprivation that do not vary with the scale of the reference-group income distribution. First, we calculate Yitzhaki's measures using log income, which is equivalent to substituting $\ln(y)$ for y in equations 14.1 and 14.2.[13] Second, we divide Yitzhaki's measure by individual income.

A second concern about the Yitzhaki-based relative deprivation measure is that it assumes that the distance between y_i and y_j matters. Yet the animal studies discussed earlier emphasize rank over distance. To test whether rank matters, we investigate whether the individual's centile rank within the reference-group income distribution (where income is sorted in ascending order) is related to health outcomes. Since centile rank is inversely correlated with relative deprivation, we refer to centile rank as a measure of relative performance. A second measure of relative performance is the individual's z-score, which measures the number of standard deviations the individual's own income is above (or below) the mean. Formally,

$$z-\text{score} = \frac{(y_i - \mu_r)}{\sigma_r} = \left(\frac{y_i}{\sigma_r}\right) - \left(\frac{\mu_r}{\sigma_r}\right) \qquad (14.4)$$

TABLE 14.6   *Other Outcomes with Reference Groups Defined Using State, Age, Race, and Education*

	Number of Cases	Mean	Coefficient (Robust Standard Error) on Relative Deprivation				
			RD/10,000	RD of Logs	RD/Income	Centile Rank	Z-Score
Cause-specific mortality (from NHIS/ MCOD)							
All cause mortality	101,530	0.0244	0.0069 (0.0013)	0.0359 (0.0066)	0.00037 (0.00029)	0.0002 (0.0001)	0.0244 (0.0030)
Health status (from NHIS)							
Self-reports poor health?	101,305	0.0826	0.0068 (0.0018)	0.0268 (0.0100)	0.00009 (0.0006)	0.0005 (0.0001)	0.0549 (0.0048)
Health-related behaviors (from BRFSS)							
Current smoker?	69,353	0.2860	0.0199 (0.0058)	0.1059 (0.0275)	0.0140 (0.0046)	0.0001 (0.0004)	0.0467 (0.0108)
Body mass index	69,091	25.79	0.1543 (0.0530)	0.6605 (0.2473)	0.0600 (0.0387)	0.0017 (0.0033)	0.1868 (0.0949)
Exercises?	69,533	0.7317	−0.0249 (0.0061)	−0.1060 (0.0283)	−0.0103 (0.0049)	0.0006 (0.0004)	−0.0503 (0.0106)

Source: Authors' compilation.
Note: Robust standard errors in parentheses. Unreported control variables are a reference-group (state × age-group × race × education) fixed effect, year, marital status. Controls for family size are included in NHIS data only.

where μ_r and σ_r are the reference-group mean and standard deviation. On average, this measure is insensitive to distances between y_i and y_j, since by definition the mean of z-score is equal to zero and the standard deviation is equal to one. Using the z-score alters the properties of the relative deprivation measure because a change in income below y_i affects μ_r and σ_r. Given the properties of the z-score and the centile rank, we prefer to think of these variables as measures of relative performance rather than relative deprivation.

Table 14.6 shows results from estimating equation 14.3 using the various relative deprivation measures discussed here. All of the Yitzhaki-based measures are positively correlated with poor health outcomes. For example, a one-standard-deviation (0.5) increase in relative deprivation of the logarithms is associated with a 1.8-percentage-point (74 percent) increase in the probability of death.

The other measures of relative deprivation do not paint a consistent picture of its impact on health. Both measures of relative performance (centile rank and z-score) are *positively* associated with poor health outcomes. Since z-score and centile rank are inversely related to relative deprivation, these results appear to be in conflict with the other results reported in this chapter. We should stress, however, that these additional variables do not necessarily measure relative deprivation. For instance, the original Yitzhaki measure is insensitive to changes in income below y_i, but z-score is not. Although there is a large literature describing desirable and undesirable properties in income inequality measures (Cowell 1977), there are no established guidelines for measuring relative deprivation. We believe that a rigorous investigation of the pros and cons of various measures of relative deprivation would be a fruitful avenue for future research.

The results for z-score illustrate the point that some measures of "relative deprivation" may be picking up much more than Runciman's relative deprivation effect. Looking at equation 14.4, note that the measure of z-score for person i in a reference group r can be written as two different components: y_i/σ_r and μ_r/σ_r. This last term is a constant for all members of the reference group and as a result is captured by the group fixed effects in equation 14.3. Therefore, the z-score model is actually identified by including only one term in the regression: y_i/σ_r. This term is essentially y_i divided by some measure of income inequality. The positive coefficient on z-score suggests that the basic income-mortality relationship is larger in absolute value in areas with higher income inequality. This result is replicated in other studies. Deaton (2001), for example, finds that the coefficient on income in a mortality regression is larger in areas with more income inequality. To verify this coefficient directly in our analysis, we run a separate model—one with income and an interaction between income and the Gini coefficient for income inequality. In this regression, we find that the coefficient on the income-inequality interaction is negative, suggesting, again, that the income-health gradient is larger in absolute value in areas with more inequality. Given the specific characteristics of our model (we add reference-group fixed effects) and the definition of z-score, it is not clear that this variable is measuring relative deprivation. Instead, we believe that this variable is simply measuring the strength of the income-health relationship across different groups, rather than measuring a within-group income effect.

SIMULATIONS: CHANGING WITHIN-GROUP AND BETWEEN-GROUP INCOME

Relative deprivation is closely related to income, in that, holding all else constant, an increase in an individual's income will always lead to a decrease in his relative deprivation. The variation between income and relative deprivation comes from the fact that, unlike income, relative deprivation is sensitive to the income of others in one's reference group. Because of the close link between income and relative deprivation, it is interesting to see how the relationship between income and health changes depending on whether we control for relative deprivation. This is more difficult to do with our initial results because we have a series of twenty-six dummy variables plus the relative deprivation measure.

In table 14.7, we provide a more simplified analysis where we regress various health outcomes on log income and a vector of control variables.[14] We then reestimate the same equation adding relative deprivation as an additional control. We see in this table that an increase in log income is associated with a decrease in the probability of death, regardless of whether we control for relative deprivation. However, the point estimate on the log-income coefficient falls substantially when relative deprivation is included as a control. When we do not include relative deprivation in the model (first panel, column 1), a 1 percent increase in log income is associated with a 1.2-percentage-point decline in the probability of death. After controlling for relative deprivation, the coefficient on log income falls by more than 50 percent, so that a 1 percent increase in log income is associated with a 0.5-percentage-point decline in the probability of death. Similarly, in the second panel we find that the relationship between income and CHD is mitigated after controlling for relative deprivation.

TABLE 14.7   *Linear Probability Models, Various Outcomes with Reference Groups Defined over State, Age, Race, and Education*

	(1)	(2)
All cause mortality (NHIS)		
Log(income)	−0.0120	−0.0054
	(0.0009)	(0.0018)
Yitzhaki RD/10,000		0.0049
		(0.0012)
Coronary heart disease mortality (NHIS)		
Log(income)	−0.0037	−0.0009
	(0.0005)	(0.0009)
RD		0.0021
		(0.0006)
Current smoker (BRFSS)		
Log(income)	−0.0511	−0.0223
	(0.0042)	(0.0098)
RD		0.0187
		(0.0055)

Source: Authors' compilation.
Note: Robust standard errors in parentheses. Unreported control variables are marital status, year, reference-group fixed effect, and family size (NHIS only).

In fact, after controlling for relative deprivation, the relationship between log income and CHD is no longer statistically precise. Finally, in the third panel we find that the relationship between log income and smoking falls by more than 50 percent after we control for relative deprivation.

Although the coefficient on log income drops considerably in all cases when we add relative deprivation to the model, the model still predicts that higher incomes are protective for health. The benefits of higher income, however, are spread over two variables: more income and a lower relative deprivation. Interestingly, both models predict roughly the same change in mortality for a given change in income. This result can be demonstrated with a simple simulation. First, we take the sample of men age twenty-one to sixty-four from the 5 Percent PUMS sample we used earlier, and we round income to the nearest $1,000. Next, we calculate the Yitzhaki measure of relative deprivation defined in equation 14.1 assuming reference groups are defined across state, age, race, and education groups. Third, we calculate average relative deprivation for people at all income levels. Finally, we simulate the benefits of an additional $1,000 in income for a person in this sample. We graph these benefits under two scenarios. First, we assume the reduction in five-year mortality comes only from an increase in income, as suggested by model 1 in table 14.7. So, for example, an additional $1,000 in income reduces five-year mortality rates by −0.00114.[15] The impact of an additional $1,000 for all people up through $60,000 in income is illustrated as the dotted line in figure 14.1. Second, we graph the predicted reduction in mortality that would occur from model 2, where higher incomes also reduce relative deprivation. In the PUMS data, the average value of relative deprivation for someone with $10,000 is 1.69, and 1.64 for someone with $11,000 in income, so according to model 2, a $1,000 increase in income should reduce the probability of five-year mortality by −0.00115.[16] These values are repre-

FIGURE 14.1   *Impact of an Additional $1,000 on the Five-Year Mortality Rate*

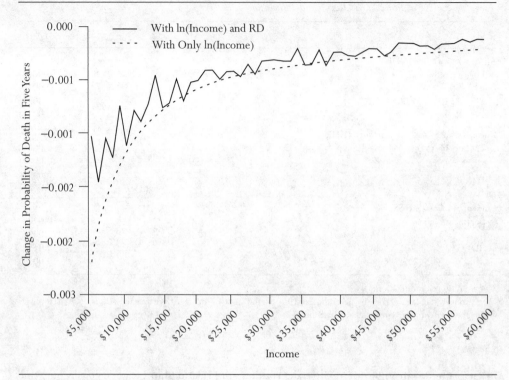

Source: Authors' compilation.

sented by the solid line in figure 14.1. Notice that in the figure both models predict nearly the same impact of an increase in income on five-year mortality.

Since relative deprivation increases when reference-group income increases, it follows that an increase in an individual's income will have two effects. First, it makes that individual better off, through both the decrease in his relative deprivation and the independent effect of income on health. Second, it contributes to a decrease in health for others in the individual's reference group, owing to the fact that an increase in y_i leads to an increase in relative deprivation for all individuals with incomes less than y_i. Therefore, while an increase in i's income unambiguously leads to an improvement in i's health, it is not clear whether an increase in y_i leads to an aggregate improvement in the health of society. In fact, it is possible that an increase in y_i causes average health to decline at the population level. This insight may help to reconcile a paradox in the income and health literature: income is positively related to health at the individual level (Kitigawa and Hauser 1973; Sorlie, Backlund, and Keller 1995; Smith 1999; Rogers, Hummer, and Nam 2000), but there is less evidence of a relationship between national GDP and mean population health (Wilkinson 1996; Ruhm 2000).

To simulate this, we use the PUMS dataset constructed earlier, where incomes are rounded to the nearest $1,000 and a measure of relative deprivation is constructed using reference groups defined across state, age, race, and education groups. This dataset has information for 2,705,748 people. We know from the NHIS/MCOD data file that roughly 2.5 percent of these people, about 65,000 of them, will die over the next five years. Next,

TABLE 14.8   *Impact of a Change in Income on Five-Year Mortality Among Black and White Males, Age Twenty-One to Sixty-Four, 1990*

Sample	Change in Total Deaths (Percent of Total Deaths) in Each Subgroup	
	Increase All Incomes by 10 percent	Increase Income Above Median by 10 percent
All people (2,705,748 people, 2.5 percent will die in five years, or 64,936 people)		
Model 1, table 15.5: ln(Income) only	−3,073	−1,548
	(−4.7%)	(−2.3%)
Model 2, table 15.5: ln(Income) and RD	614	1,697
	(0.9%)	(2.6%)
People below median (1,352,587 people, 3.3 percent will die in five years, or 44,639 people)		
Model 1, table 15.5: ln(Income) only	−1,525	0
	(−3.4%)	(0%)
Model 2, table 15.5: ln(Income) and RD	610	1,693
	(1.4%)	(3.8%)
People above median (1,353,161 people, 1.5 percent will die in five years, or 20,297 people)		
Model 1, table 15.5: ln(Income) only	−1,548	−1,548
	(−7.6%)	(−7.6%)
Model 2, table 15.5: ln(Income) and RD	4	4
	(0.02%)	(0.02%)

Source: Authors' compilation based on U.S. Census Bureau, 5 Percent PUMS.

we perform some simulations similar to those we used for figure 14.1, but instead of just changing one person's income, we change income for a whole group of people. We report the predicted changes in mortality for these simulations for two models: one with only log income in the equation (model 1 of table 14.7) and one with both log income and relative deprivation (model 2 of table 14.7). The results from these simulations are reported in table 14.8.

In column 1, we examine what would happen to aggregate mortality if everyone were given 10 percent more income. In models that include only log income as a covariate, the prediction is clear: all people would face a lower probability of death and aggregate mortality would fall. We calculate that an additional 10 percent of income would reduce aggregate mortality by 4.7 percent, preventing 3,073 deaths. The predicted change in mortality, however, is very different when we consider models that contain both log income and relative deprivation as covariates. Because a 10 percent increase in income gives more dollars to someone with higher income compared to those with lower income, almost all people in the sample now face an increase in relative deprivation. The increase in deprivation is in fact so large that the benefits of higher individual incomes are wiped out and our models predict that in this scenario a 10 percent increase in income would raise aggregate mortality by 0.9 percent, or 614 deaths. When we compare what is happening to people below and above the median income, we find that aggregate deaths have increased for people below the median income and that there is no change in mortality at all for people above the median income.

We explore this result in a little more detail in the second column of table 14.8, where we simulate the impact of increasing incomes by 10 percent for men above the median income. In models with only log income as the covariate, there is no change in mortality for people below the median income (their income has not changed). But when we add relative deprivation as a covariate, people below the median income experience an increase in relative deprivation when incomes above the median rise. As a result, deaths below the median increase by 3.8 percent and aggregate mortality increases by 2.6 percent.

The results in figure 14.1 and tables 14.7 and 14.8 provide suggestive evidence that the relative deprivation hypothesis may in fact explain the disparity in results for the income-health link for within-group and between-group studies. In table 14.7, we see that once we add relative deprivation to a standard model with some measure of health as the outcome, the coefficient on income falls by half. In figure 14.1, we note that models with and without relative deprivation as covariates predict the same change in mortality from an increase in individual income. However, in the case where we include relative deprivation as a covariate, mortality falls when individual income rises, owing to both a direct income effect and an indirect effect of the fall in relative deprivation. Focusing on between-group comparisons, the simulations in table 14.8 indicate that when the incomes of all people rise, aggregate mortality may actually increase. In this case, if everyone's income increases by a fixed percentage, the benefits of higher income are counteracted by a rise in relative deprivation.

CONCLUSION

In this chapter, we use unique data from the NHIS/MCOD restricted-access files that allow us to observe income, mortality, and state of residence at the individual level. With these data, we can examine the relationship between relative deprivation and mortality while simultaneously controlling for individual income and reference-group fixed effects. We find that there is a strong, positive, and statistically significant link between relative deprivation and the probability that an individual will die within five years of the NHIS survey. These results are robust across a wide variety of models, including changes in the definition of the outcome (mortality, morbidity, and health habits), reference groups, or the measure of relative deprivation.

From a theoretical standpoint, relative deprivation is thought to affect health through risky behavior. We find that for heart disease mortality and tobacco-related cancers, the relative deprivation effect is proportionately stronger than it is in the models for mortality from all causes. Likewise, in our examination of relative deprivation's impact on various health habits using data from the BRFSS, we find that relative deprivation is related to increases in the probability that an individual will smoke and decreases in the probability that an individual will wear a seat belt. Further, we find that relative deprivation is positively associated with body mass index and negatively associated with the probability of exercise.

Although our results paint a consistent picture of the impact of relative deprivation on health, we should stress that these results are only suggestive of a causal link between relative deprivation and poor health. It is possible that our results simply reflect a statistical correlation. Results from the "ever smoked" models provide some evidence to refute the Fuchs hypothesis; however, more research is needed to distinguish causation from correlation.

We began this chapter by noting some paradoxical results in the income-health relationship. Studies that look at individuals within a group find a strong positive correlation between health and income. In contrast, when researchers view the correlation in health across groups (such as across states or countries, or within a country over time), the evidence of a link between income and health is much weaker. The simulations that end this report indicate that the impact of relative deprivation on health may explain these paradoxical results. As group incomes rise, some may be negatively affected in that the change in relative deprivation may mitigate the benefits of more income. In fact, our results suggest that a 10 percent increase in aggregate income may in fact raise aggregate mortality for men between the ages of twenty-one and sixty-four by about 0.9 percent. These results hint at a relationship between economic conditions, psychological factors, and individual behavior that is only beginning to be investigated by researchers.

The relationship we investigate may provide insights into other observed correlations in the data. For example, the fact that relative income affects health may help explain why the gradient between income and health persists even at high levels of income (Adler et al. 1994; Deaton 2001), or why mortality appears to be pro-cyclic (Ruhm 2000). Likewise, there may be a link between rising income inequality over the past twenty-five years and rising inequality in health outcomes (Preston and Elo 1995) and in health habits (Evans, Ringel, and Stech 1999).

The authors wish to thank Angus Deaton, Jonah Gelbach, Judy Hellerstein, Sandy Jencks, Larry Katz, Andrew Lyon, Ed Montgomery, Seth Sanders, and Bob Schwab for a number of helpful comments. We also wish to thank Negasi Beyene, Bob Krasowski, and the staff at the National Center for Health Statistics Research Data Center for providing restricted-access data from the National Health Interview Survey.

NOTES

1. Yitzhaki (1979) proposes an analogous relative satisfaction metric that is equal to $\mu - RD$. Since we are using reference-group fixed effects, this measure is a linear combination of the fixed effect and the relative deprivation measure. A second potential measure of relative satisfaction, $\{y_i - E(y \mid y < y_i)\} \times \text{prob}(y < \ln y_i)$, is a linear combination of RD, y_i, and μ.
2. We impute month of interview using quarter and week of interview.
3. Although family income is recorded in the NHIS, the survey does not give guidelines as to what constitutes a family. In the PUMS, families are defined as two or more related individuals living together. Single people without children in the PUMS are assigned family income equal to zero because technically they are not part of a family. Respondents in the NHIS clearly interpret family income differently, because single people in the NHIS report positive family income. Since family income is the only income variable available in the NHIS and family income in the PUMS is not applicable for single people, we construct relative deprivation using the household income variable in the PUMS and the family income variable in the NHIS.
4. Information on top-code imputations for each state can be found on the Integrated Public Use Microdata Series (IPUMS) website; go to www.ipums.org/usa/volii/topcode_odd.html.
5. The sample is restricted to householders and spouses to avoid counting two observations from the same household.
6. Age groups are recorded in five-year increments: twenty-one to twenty-five, twenty-six to thirty, and so on. The final age group, eighty-six and over, is open-ended. Race is defined as white non-Hispanic, black non-Hispanic, other non-Hispanic, or Hispanic. Education is high school dropout, high school graduate, some college, or college graduate.
7. In the interest of confidentiality, a randomized state indicator replaces state identification codes after the merge.
8. States that did not participate were Alaska, Nevada, Wyoming, Kansas, Arkansas, and New Jersey.

9. The income categories in the BRFSS are: $10,000 or less, $10,000 to $14,999, $15,000 to $19,999, $20,000 to $24,999, $25,000 to $34,999, $35,000 to $50,000, $50,000 or more.

10. Eibner (2001) shows that the basic results are unchanged when we use logit models as opposed to linear probability models.

11. Authors' own calculations, available on request.

12. Body mass index $=$ (weight in kilograms)/(height in meters)^2. BMIs greater than 24.9 are considered unhealthy.

13. We assume that income is log-normally distributed within the reference group and calculate the log-income relative deprivation measure using a closed-form solution. For further discussion, see Eibner and Evans (forthcoming).

14. We impute income from the categorical variables in the NHIS using the procedure described earlier.

15. $-0.012[\ln(11,000) - \ln(\$10,000)] = -0.00114$.

16. $-0.0054[\ln(\$11,000) - \ln(\$10,000)] + 0.0049[1.64 - 1.69] = -0.00115$.

REFERENCES

Åberg-Yngwe, Monica, Johan Fritzell, Olle Lundberg, Finn Diderichsen, and Bo Burström. 2003. "Exploring Relative Deprivation: Is Social Comparison a Mechanism in the Relation Between Income and Health?" *Social Science and Medicine* 57(8): 1463–73.

Adler, Nancy E., Thomas Boyce, Margaret A. Chesney, S. Cohen, S. Folkman, R. Kahn, S. L. Syme. 1994. "Socioeconomic Status and Health: The Challenge of the Gradient." *American Psychologist* 49(1): 15–24.

Chapman, Kenneth S., and Gouind Hariharan. 1994. "Controlling for Causality in the Link from Income to Mortality." *Journal of Risk and Uncertainty* 8(1): 85–93.

Clarkwest, Andrew, and Christopher Jencks, 2003. "Inequality and Mortality in Rich Countries: Who Owns the Null Hypothesis?" Working paper. Cambridge, Mass.: John F. Kennedy School of Government, Harvard University.

Cohen, Sheldon, S. Line, Stephen B. Manuck, Bruce S. Rabin, Eugene R. Heise, and Jay R. Kaplan. 1997. "Chronic Social Stress, Social Status, and Susceptibility to Upper Respiratory Infections in Nonhuman Primates." *Psychosomatic Medicine* 59(3): 213–21.

Cowell, Frank A. 1977. *Measuring Inequality.* Oxford: Philip Allan.

Deaton, Angus. 1999. "Inequalities in Income and Inequalities in Health." Working paper 7141. Cambridge, Mass.: National Bureau of Economic Research.

———. 2001. "Relative Deprivation, Inequality, and Mortality." Working paper 8099. Cambridge, Mass.: National Bureau of Economic Research.

———. 2003. "Health, Inequality, and Economic Development." *Journal of Economic Literature* 41(1): 113–58.

Deaton, Angus, and Darren Lubotsky. 2003. "Mortality, Inequality, and Race in American Cities and States." *Social Science and Medicine* 56(6, March): 1139–53.

Deaton, Angus, and Christina Paxson. 1998. "Aging and Inequality in Income and Health." *American Economic Review* 88(2): 248–53.

———. 2001a. "Mortality, Education, Income, and Inequality Among American Cohorts." In *Themes in the Economics of Aging,* edited by David Wise. Chicago: University of Chicago Press for National Bureau of Economic Research.

———. 2001b. "Mortality, Income, and Income Inequality Among British and American Cohorts." Princeton, N.J.: Princeton University, Center for Health and Well-being.

Duleep, Harriet Orcutt. 1986. "Measuring the Effect of Income on Adult Mortality Using Longitudinal Administrative Record Data." *Journal of Human Resources* 21(2, Spring): 238–51.

Eibner, Christine E. 2001. "Income, Relative Deprivation, Behavior, and Mortality: Evidence from Individual-Level Data." Ph.D. diss., University of Maryland.

Eibner, Christine E., and William N. Evans. Forthcoming. "Relative Deprivation, Poor Heath Habits, and Mortality." *Journal of Human Resources.*

Ettner, Susan L. 1996. "New Evidence on the Relationship Between Income and Health." *Journal of Health Economics* 15(1): 67–85.

Evans, William N., Jeanne S. Ringel, and Diana Stech. 1999. "Tobacco Taxes and Public Policy to Discourage Smoking." *Tax Policy and the Economy* 13: 1–55.

Feldman, J. J., Diane M. Makuc, J. C. Kleinman, and Joan Cornoni-Huntley. 1989. "National Trends in Educational Differentials in Mortality." *American Journal of Epidemiology* 129(5): 919–33.

Fiscella, Kevin, and Peter Franks. 1997. "Poverty or Income Inequality as a Predictor of Mortality: Longitudinal Cohort Study." *British Medical Journal* 314: 1724–28.

Frank, Robert H. 1985. *Choosing the Right Pond: Human Behavior and the Quest for Status.* New York: Oxford University Press.

Fuchs, Victor R. 1982. "Time Preference and Health: An Exploratory Study." In *Economic Aspects of Health,* edited by Victor R. Fuchs. Chicago: University of Chicago Press.

Gravelle, Hugh. 1998. "How Much of the Relation Between Population Mortality and Unequal Distribution of Income Is a Statistical Artifact?" *British Medical Journal* 316(7128): 382–85.

Gravelle, Hugh, John Wildman, and Matthew Sutton. 2002. "Income, Income Inequality, and Health: What Can We Learn from Aggregate Data?" *Social Sciences and Medicine* 54(4): 577–89.

Idler, Ellen L., and Yael Benyamini. 1997. "Self-rated Health and Mortality: A Review of Twenty-seven Community Studies." *Journal of Health and Social Behavior* 38(1): 21–37.

Judge, Ken, Jo-Ann Mulligan, and Michaela Benzeval. 1997. "Income Inequality and Population Health." *Social Science and Medicine* 46(4–5): 567–79.

Kaplan, George A., Elsie R. Pamuk, John W. Lynch, Richard D. Cohen, and Jennifer L. Balfour. 1996. "Inequality in Income and Mortality in the United States: Analysis of Mortality and Potential Pathways." *British Medical Journal* 312(7037): 999–1003.

Kennedy, Bruce P., Ichiro Kawachi, and Deborah Prothrow-Stith. 1996. "Income Distribution and Mortality: Cross-sectional Ecological Study of the Robin Hood Index in the United States." *British Medical Journal* 312(7037): 1004–7.

Kitagawa, Evelyn M., and Philip M. Hauser. 1973. *Differential Mortality in the United States: A Study in Socio-economic Epidemiology.* Cambridge, Mass.: Harvard University Press.

Lantz, Paula M., J. S. House, James M. Lepkowski, David R. Williams, Richard P. Mero, and Jieming Chen. 1998. "Socioeconomic Factors, Health Behaviors, and Mortality: Results from a Nationally Representative Prospective Study of the United States." *Journal of the American Medical Association* 279(21): 1703–8.

Lochner, Kimberly, Elsie R. Pamuk, D. Makuc, Bruce P. Kennedy, and Ichiro Kawachi. 2001. "State-level Income Inequality and Individual Mortality Risk: A Prospective Multilevel Study." *American Journal of Public Health* 91(3): 385–91.

Luttmer, Erzo F.P. 2003. "Do People Care How Much Their Neighbors Earn? How Relative Earnings Affect Well-being." Working paper. Cambridge, Mass.: John F. Kennedy School of Government, Harvard University.

Lynch, John, George Davey-Smith, Marianne Hillemeier, Mary Shaw, Trivellore Raghunathan, and George Kaplan. 2001. "Income Inequality, Psychosocial Environment, and Health: Comparisons Across Wealthy Nations." *The Lancet* 358: 194–200.

Marmot, Michael G. 1986. "Social Inequalities in Mortality: The Social Environment." In *Class and Health,* edited by Richard Wilkinson. London: Tavistock.

Marmot, Michael G., Martin J. Shipley, and Geoffrey Rose. 1984. "Inequalities in Death—Specific Explanations of a General Pattern?" *The Lancet*: 1: 1003–6.

McDonough, Peggy, Greg J. Duncan, David Williams, and James House. 1997. "Income Dynamics and Adult Mortality in the United States, 1972 Through 1989." *American Journal of Public Health* 87(9): 1476–83.

McGuire, Mark T., and Michael J. Raleigh. 1985. "Serotonin-Behavior Interactions in Vervet Monkeys." *Psychopharmacology Bulletin* 21(3): 458–63.

Mellor, Jennifer, and Jeffrey Milyo. 2001. "Reexamining the Evidence of an Ecological Association Between Income Inequality and Health." *Journal of Health Politics, Policy, and Law* 26(3): 487–522.

———. 2002. "Income Inequality and Individual Health: Evidence from the Current Population Survey." *Journal of Human Resources* 37(3): 510–39.

Pappas, Gregory, Susan Queen, Wilbur Hadden, and Gail Fisher. 1993. "The Increasing Disparity in Mortality Between Socioeconomic Groups in the United States, 1960 and 1986." *New England Journal of Medicine* 329(2): 103–9.

Pettigrew, Thomas F. 1978. "Three Issues in Ethnicity: Boundaries, Deprivations, and Perceptions." in *Major Social Issues,* edited by J. Milton Yinger and Stephen J. Cutler. New York: Free Press.

Preston, Samuel H. 1975. "The Changing Relation Between Mortality and Level of Economics Development." *Population Studies* 29(2): 231–48.

Preston, Samuel H., and Irma T. Elo. 1995. "Are Educational Differentials in Adult Mortality Increasing in the United States?" *Journal of Aging and Health* 7(4): 476–96.

Rogers, Richard G., Robert A. Hummer, and Charles B. Nam. 2000. *Living and Dying in the USA: Behavioral, Health, and Social Differentials in Adult Mortality.* New York: Academic Press.

Runciman, Walter G. 1966. *Relative Deprivation and Social Justice.* London: Routledge & Kegan Paul.

Ruhm, Christopher. 2000. "Are Recessions Good for Your Health?" *Quarterly Journal of Economics* 115(2): 617–50.

Sapolsky, Robert M., Susan C. Alberts, and Jeanne Altmann. 1997. "Hypercortisolism Associated with Social Subordinance or Social Isolation Among Wild Baboons." In *The Society and Population Health Reader: Income Inequality and Health,* edited by Ichiro Kawachi, Bruce P. Kennedy, and Richard G. Wilkinson. New York: New Press.

Shively, Carol A., Kathy Laber-Laird, and Raymond F. Anton. 1997. "Behavior and Physiology of Social Stress and Depression in Female Cynomolgus Monkeys." *Biological Psychiatry* 41(8): 871–82.

Singer, Eleanor. 1981. "Reference Groups and Social Evaluations." in *Social Psychology: Sociological Perspectives,* edited by Morris Rosenberg and Ralph H. Turner. New York: Basic Books.

Smith, James P. 1999. "Healthy Bodies and Thick Wallets: The Dual Relation Between Health and Economic Status." *Journal of Economic Perspectives* 13(2): 145–66.

Sorlie, Paul D., Eric Backlund, and Jacob B. Keller. 1995. "U.S. Mortality by Economic, Demographic, and Social Characteristics: The National Longitudinal Mortality Study." *American Journal of Public Health* 85(7): 949–56.

Waldmann, Robert J. 1992. "Income Distribution and Infant Mortality." *Quarterly Journal of Economics* 107(4): 1283–1302.

Wilkinson, Richard G. 1996. *Unhealthy Societies: The Afflictions of Inequality.* London: Routledge.

———. 1997. "Health Inequalities: Relative or Absolute Material Standards?" *British Medical Journal* 314(7080): 591–95.

Wolfson, Michael C., Goeff. Rowe, Jane F. Gentlemen, and Monica Tomiak. 1993. "Career Earnings and Death: A Longitudinal Analysis of Older Canadian Men." *Journal of Gerontology* 48(4): S167–79.

Yitzhaki, Shlomo. 1979. "Relative Deprivation and the Gini Coefficient." *Quarterly Journal of Economics* 93(2): 321–24.

Chapter 15

Inequality in Life and Death:
What Drives Racial Trends in U.S. Child Death Rates?

Janet Currie and V. Joseph Hotz

This chapter examines the trends in and determinants of child death rates in the United States over the period 1980 to 1998. The annual death rate (number of deaths per 100,000 population) of children age zero to nineteen declined by 39.6 percent over this period, from 117.6 deaths per 100,000 in 1980 to 71.0 in 1998. Several explanations have been offered for this marked decline in the child death rate. For example, David Cutler and Ellen Meara (2000) focus on the role that innovations in medical technology played in the declines in infant mortality. Sherry Glied (2001) draws attention to the dramatic declines in child death rates due to unintentional injuries, or accidents, and the importance of information about public safety and better-educated parents.

We extend the previous literature on childhood death rates in three ways. First, we look at how trends differ across causes of death, ages of children, and race. As we document in this chapter, the overall decline in childhood death rates masks important differences along these dimensions. We show that while the overall death rates between black and nonblack children narrowed over the final two decades of the twentieth century, the gap was still sizable in 1998. For example, as of 1998 black children were still twice as likely to die from unintentional injuries as white children. Furthermore, this pattern of narrowing gaps did not hold across all causes of death. Among young children, the black-white gap in death rates due to auto accidents actually increased, and for almost all ages the racial gap in deaths due to intentional injuries, including those involving firearms, increased over this period.

Second, our chapter examines a variety of different determinants of these trends that have been identified in the literature and assesses the robustness of their estimated effects to the inclusion of various controls, including state fixed effects and state time trends. We examine the influence of three broad sets of factors: income and inequality as measured by state-level median household income, as well as the differences between the ninetieth and fiftieth percentiles and between the fiftieth and tenth percentiles of the income distribution; other indicators of socioeconomic status (SES), such as maternal education, maternal employment, and the incidence of single-headed households; and indicators of access to medical and trauma care.

However, there are many general improvements in factors affecting health and safety that are difficult to measure. Our third innovation is to ask whether child mortality rates are primarily affected by innovations in the factors just mentioned, or whether these trends can be explained by improvements that also drive death rates among adults. For example, safer cars might be expected to benefit both adults and children, while the use of car seats would primarily affect young children. To address this question, we construct regression-adjusted death rates for twenty-four- to forty-four-year-old men, where the regression adjustments net out the effects of our measures of income, socioeconomic status, and medical access. Presumably, these "residual" measures of adult male death rates capture changes in factors that are not readily measured and that affect both adults and children within a state, year, and race group, including changes in medical technology, product safety and regulation, and health care practices.

Our models generally do a good job of explaining the level of death rates and the gap in death rates between blacks and whites. Income, inequality, and measures of socio-economic status such as maternal education are often important predictors of death rates, and gaps in black and nonblack incomes can explain gaps in death rates for some ages and causes of death. However, it is more difficult to explain trends in death rates over time or to explain the narrowing or broadening of the gap between black and nonblack death rates. For example, the gap between black and nonblack median incomes increased slightly over the period, while the gap in death rates narrowed. Moreover, our measures of medical access typically have little explanatory power, though this may be because they are relatively crude. It is possible that year effects, state effects, state time trends, and the male residuals are capturing a good deal of the improvements in medical access and medical technology that took place over the period.

In contrast, our estimates indicate that the "male residuals" can explain much of the change in the gaps between black and nonblack death rates. This finding suggests that the gap between black and nonblack overall death rates narrowed because of factors that affected adults as well as children rather than solely because of factors affecting children.

In the next section, we discuss the previous literature concerning childhood death rates and their potential causes. The third section describes the data sources we use and the variables we have constructed. In the following sections, we lay out the trends in childhood death rates by cause, age, and race; we also describe the trends in our explanatory variables. Next, we present the results from our regression analysis and discuss our findings. We conclude with a short summary of our findings and their implications.

BACKGROUND

Death rates among children in the United States declined markedly over the final two decades of the twentieth century. At the same time, as highlighted in the literature, important differences in child death rates by race, socioeconomic status, and residential location persisted. For example, children from low-income households are twice as likely to die in a motor vehicle accident, four times more likely to drown, and five times more likely to die in a fire than nonpoor children (National SAFE KIDS Campaign 1998). A variety of explanations and hypotheses have been offered to account for the reductions in death rates as well as for the disparities in these rates across segments of the population.

The Relationship Between Socioeconomic Status and Health

One common explanation for the differences in death rates by race is that the socio-economic status (SES) of the household or neighborhood in which children are raised has direct effects on their health status and, ultimately, their mortality. There is a vast literature documenting the relationship between median income, other features of the distribution of income—including inequality—and overall mortality rates (for surveys of this work, see Marmot and Wilkinson 1999; Deaton 2001), accidental deaths among adults (Miller and Paxson 2001), and infant mortality (see Flegg 1982; Judge, Mulligan, and Benzeval 1997; Mellow and Milyo 2000). For example, William Collins and Melissa Thomasson (2002) examine the racial gap in infant mortality rates over the period 1920 to 1970 and conclude that much of the gap before 1945 can be explained by differences in the income, education, and location of whites and blacks. They are less successful in explaining racial differences in the postwar period. Susan Mayer and Ankur Sarin (2002) examine infant mortality in 1985, 1987, and 1991 and find that it is linked to a measure of economic segregation. However, they note, this finding is not robust to the inclusion of state fixed effects.

A central question in much of this literature is whether these associations reflect the causal effect of unequal distributions of income, at the community or societal level, on health and mortality or simply nonlinear effects of *individual* and *family* income on mortality. The income inequality explanation is most often associated with the work of Richard Wilkinson (1992, 1996, 2000); the latter explanation of the role of income is often referred to as the absolute income hypothesis, or the poverty hypothesis. Angus Deaton and Christina Paxson (1999) emphasize the difficulty of distinguishing between these two explanations using aggregate cross-country or cross-state data, as many previous studies have attempted to do. They show, through examples, that a relationship between low income and poor health in individual-level data may look like a relationship between inequality and health when the data are aggregated.

There have been fewer investigations of the relationship between socioeconomic status and health outcomes among children over a year old.[1] Anne Case, Darren Lubotsky, and Christina Paxson (2002) show that a relationship between family income and health status does exist during childhood, and that it becomes more pronounced as children age. In a related study, Janet Currie and Rosemary Hyson (1999) ask whether the long-run impact of low birthweight differs with socioeconomic status in a cohort of British children born in 1958. They find that while low birthweight has a persistent negative impact on a range of outcomes, there is little evidence that its effects vary with socioeconomic status, although low-SES children are more likely to suffer from low birthweight to begin with. Similarly, Currie and Mark Stabile (forthcoming) examine a panel of Canadian children and show that although the cross-sectional relationship between income and health is similar to that found in the United States by Case, Lubotsky, and Paxson, health shocks have persistently negative effects among both rich and poor children, and both rich and poor children appear to recover from such shocks to a similar extent. They conclude that the fact that the health gap between rich and poor increases as children age must reflect the fact that poor children receive more health shocks rather than that they recover more slowly to a given shock.

There is also a good deal of evidence that low-SES children are more likely to suffer negative health shocks than high-SES children. For example, Paul Newacheck and his colleagues (1994) show that poor children are more likely than better-off children to suffer from a wide array of chronic conditions, while the Institute of Medicine (1999) reports that low-SES children are more likely than higher-SES children to suffer from virtually all types of accidental injuries, which are the leading cause of morbidity and death among children over a year old.

In what follows, we consider a range of measures of socioeconomic status, including family income, measures of income inequality, maternal education, the incidence of single-parenthood, and maternal employment. Although income and education are common measures of SES, the latter two measures may require some explanation. Maternal employment increases family income, while single-parenthood tends to decrease it, and so, given imperfect measurement of income, they may be associated with health through this mechanism. At the same time, the rise in the labor force attachment of mothers has led to mothers spending less time directly supervising children and a greater reliance on nonparental child care. The potential risk to children associated with this lack of maternal supervision is especially acute in female-headed and disadvantaged households, where working mothers may not be able to afford high-quality child care. Elsewhere (Currie and Hotz, forthcoming) we argue that higher-quality child care can reduce the probability of injury, though regulation to increase quality may have the perverse effect of driving some children into unregulated care.

Increased maternal employment can also be viewed as a manifestation of the increased opportunity costs associated with raising children as the wages and employment opportunities of women have improved. Gary Becker (1991) and Becker and Nigel Tomes (1976) argue that this increase has led parents to invest more in child "quality" at the expense of the "quantity" of children. In other words, as parents invest more in each child, they also become more averse to losing a child through illness or injury and correspondingly more willing to invest in the child's health and safety.

Changes in Medical Technology and Access to Care

A second prominent explanation for declining death rates focuses on technological change in medicine, access to health care, and innovations in health care delivery systems. Douglas Almond, Kenneth Chay, and Michael Greenstone (2001) examine postwar reductions in the black-white gap in infant mortality and find a large reduction relative to trends between 1965 and 1971. They show that the decline was concentrated in the South and argue that it reflects greater access to hospitals among black mothers giving birth, which in turn was due to the civil rights movement. Their paper illustrates the potential importance of racial differences in access to medical care. However, since the vast majority of both white and black births now occur in hospitals, it is unlikely that movement in this particular measure of access has contributed a great deal to changes in black and white infant mortality over the past twenty years.

The frontier in terms of medical and health care access has moved to other life-saving developments, such as the development and diffusion of neonatal intensive-care units, the development of surfactant therapy (which prevents respiratory failure in premature infants), and the availability of new vaccines against diseases such as meningitis. Cutler and Meara (2000) and Cutler and Mark McClellan (2001) argue that these developments have had a tremendously positive impact on life expectancy and overall social welfare. In work in progress, Cutler and Meara (2003) point out that reductions in black-white gaps in infant mortality since 1970 have occurred against a backdrop of increases in preterm birth and the incidence of low birthweight among blacks, suggesting that the gap would have been much larger without the increased use of medical interventions to save these babies.

Expansions of public health insurance programs over the past twenty years have made these life-saving developments more accessible to poor children. Currie (1995) and Currie and Gruber (1996a, 1996b) show that expansions in programs such as Medicaid to cover previously ineligible children narrowed socioeconomic gaps in the utilization of medical care and health among infants and children, though it did not eliminate them.[2] With respect to health care delivery, it is argued that efforts by states to organize trauma care networks that direct seriously injured patients to the hospitals best able to care for them has reduced the likelihood that injuries will result in death among children and adults (Bonnie, Fulco, and Liverman 1999; Nathens et al. 2000, 2001).

If improvements in medical care are an important cause of reductions in overall child death rates, then improvements in access to care are also likely to play an important role, particularly among groups such as African American children, who may continue to suffer poorer access to care than white children. For example, C. H. Pui and his colleagues (1995) report that higher mortality rates among black pediatric cancer patients reflect inferior care, while James Fossett and John Peterson (1989) show that "black" areas of the city of Chicago have many fewer physicians in private practice than "white" areas.

Currie and Thomas (1995) use data from the National Longitudinal Survey of Youth Child (NLSY-C) file, which has followed the children of the initial respondents since 1986, to examine whether Medicaid coverage has differential effects on white and black children. The longitudinal nature of the data allows them to include child-specific fixed effects, thereby controlling for any unmeasured, constant characteristics of the child and the home environment that might be correlated with Medicaid status. Their estimates indicate that private insurance and Medicaid coverage are associated with a higher number of visits for preventive care among both white and black children, while increases in the number of visits for illness is seen only in white children with private insurance coverage. The study does not resolve the question of whether these racial disparities can be attributed to a shortage of providers, other barriers to care, or differing attitudes toward care by race.

Improvements in Product Safety, Regulation, and Information

Deaths due to accidents, or unintentional injuries, represent an important cause of death among children, especially children over the age of one. Furthermore, as we document in this chapter, death rates associated with accidents have fallen dramatically over the last twenty years. It has been argued that improvements in the safety of the products that families use and/or to which children are exposed have played an important role in this decline. For example, cars have become much safer over the past thirty years, and innovations such as childproof caps on medicines, fall bars on windows, and fencing around swimming pools are credited with saving many lives. Many safety advocates argue that these improvements are the result of increased consumer safety regulation and that the declines in accidental deaths to children demonstrate their effectiveness.

Glied (2001) discusses many important regulations affecting product safety, including the Poison Prevention Packaging Act of 1970 and laws mandating the use of infant and child safety seats in cars, which were first introduced in 1977 and had been adopted by all states by 1984. She argues that these regulations cannot explain declining trends in accident rates, and it is certainly clear that the measures she discusses are unlikely to account for declining death rates in recent years.

It is extremely difficult to directly test the hypothesis that regulation is responsible for declines in accident rates, given the myriad regulations at the federal, state, and even local level. Glied's test is based on the argument that younger children should benefit most from new product regulation, or conversely, that children with older siblings may be more at risk from dangerous older products. However, the Vital Statistics data that she uses—and that we use—do not allow one to identify siblings, so Glied's test is based on data merged in from the Current Population Surveys (CPS) about the average characteristics of households in the state, including average number of children in two age groups.

In addition to regulation, efforts by epidemiologists, public health agencies, and safety advocacy groups have increased the supply of information about the possible hazards confronting children in everyday life and about strategies for preventing illness and accidents. This information is disseminated to the public through public service announcements, product labeling (which is generally regulated, so that there is an overlap between regulation and information dissemination), school safety education programs, and parenting books. These efforts may account for some of the decline in accidental deaths to children (National SAFE KIDS Campaign 1998). Glied (2001) discusses the increased overall public awareness of safety issues (including a comparison of old and new editions of Dr. Spock's famous book on infant and child care). She argues that this information hypothesis can be tested by interacting maternal education with time. The idea is that as knowledge about prevention becomes more important, the gap between the death rates of children of more- and less-educated mothers should increase over time. However, she finds little evidence of significant maternal education effects in her data.

We might expect that improvements in products, regulations, and information would benefit everyone eventually. However, groups that are better educated may be better informed, and groups that are richer may have access to superior products sooner. Thus, it is possible that rapid improvements in products and information could benefit white children sooner than black children, leading to temporary expansions of gaps in black and white death rates.

DATA

In this chapter, we use aggregated, time-series, and cross-sectional data on annual rates of death due to various causes that are constructed from the Vital Statistics Detail Mortality (VSDM) data for 1980 to 1998. The VSDM is a census of all deaths, and so while deaths are an extreme (and thankfully rare) example of a negative health outcome, the data have the advantage of being large and comprehensive enough to allow us to examine trends for different groups of children over time. We use the individual vital statistics records to construct state- and year-level "cells" for death rates, where separate cells are constructed for different racial and age groups. With respect to race, we defined three groups: black, white, and "other," which includes Asian Americans, Pacific Islanders, American Indians, and any other race not included in white or black.[3] In the regression analyses presented here, we aggregate the white and other categories into a "nonblack" category, which we compare with blacks. With respect to age, we grouped our data into four age groups—zero to four, five to nine, ten to fourteen, and fifteen to nineteen.[4]

We examine four broad causes of death: medical causes, auto-related accidental injuries, other non-intentional injuries (or accidents), and intentional injuries. One remaining category of causes of death, which includes deaths due to war and some deaths of unknown cause, were not analyzed in the regression analysis to be discussed here but were included in the death rates due to all causes that are considered in our discussion of trends in the next section. A detailed description of how we constructed our mortality rate cells and the socioeconomic and state-level characteristics used in our analysis is found in the data appendix.

With respect to our categorization of causes of death, there are potential problems of misclassification. For example, it is possible that there is systematic misreporting of intentional injuries as non-intentional injuries, or that the likelihood of correctly identifying an intentional injury differs across states and over time. In our regression analyses, we partially account for the latter type of misreporting by including state and year effects as well as state-multiplied-by-five-year-period time dummy variables in our models. However, we will be sensitive to the possibility of misreporting in the interpretation of models of intentional injury rates. Given that unintentional injuries are much more common than intentional injuries, reporting error is likely to be more of a problem for models of the latter than models of the former.

We also construct death rates for twenty-five- to forty-four-year-old men by state, year, and race, and the same four causes of death. As described later, we use these rates as a benchmark against which to compare death rates of children in the same year, state, and racial groups.

The use of this aggregated data on mortality has advantages as well as disadvantages. Given that it is derived from death certificates, it provides very accurate information on both the incidence and causes of death by location and over time. At the same time, the data measure only one dimension of health. For each death that results from childhood injury, it is estimated that there are more than 1,000 emergency room visits and an unknown number of injuries that receive no medical treatment (Children's Safety Network 1991). It is estimated that between 1987 and 1995, while 6,600 American children died annually from preventable injuries, 246,000 children per year were hospitalized owing to injuries and that injuries resulted in almost 9 million emergency room visits and 12 million physician visits each year (National SAFE KIDS Campaign 1998). Similarly, even most children who are ill enough to be hospitalized eventually recover. Hence, it would be very interesting to conduct a similar analysis of the incidence of disease and injury were accurate, comprehensive data to become available.

We also constructed a number of different indicators of the socioeconomic status of households, measures of income inequality, and access to health care and medical facilities from other data sources that we merged with our data on death rates. We used the March Current Population Surveys to construct state-, race-, and year-level measures of average years of maternal education, the fraction of mothers who were employed, and median family income in the state. Our other measures of socioeconomic status were constructed at the state-year level (and therefore do not vary by race within states and years). These include the fraction of single mothers and two state-specific indicators of income inequality, namely, the difference in family income between households in the ninetieth and fiftieth percentiles and the corresponding difference between the fiftieth and tenth percentiles.

To measure the accessibility of medical care, we constructed several measures. First, we constructed an index of the generosity of the Medicaid program in each state. After selecting a national sample of children of each age group in 1990, we used information about the Medicaid eligibility age and income thresholds to calculate the fraction of these children who would have been eligible in each state, year, and race group. This procedure, which is similar to that used in Currie and Gruber (1996a, 1996b), abstracts from demographic changes within the state by using a fixed group of children—that is, variation in the measure reflects only changes in state rules governing Medicaid eligibility. The number of hospitals per 100,000 people and the number of trauma units per 100,000 people were calculated using data gathered by the American Hospital Association (AHA).[5]

TRENDS IN CHILDHOOD DEATH RATES

In this section, we describe the trends in death rates for children as well as the socioeconomic, inequality, and health care access indicators described in the previous section

FIGURE 15.1   *Death Rates by Cause, Age Zero to Nineteen, 1980 to 1998*

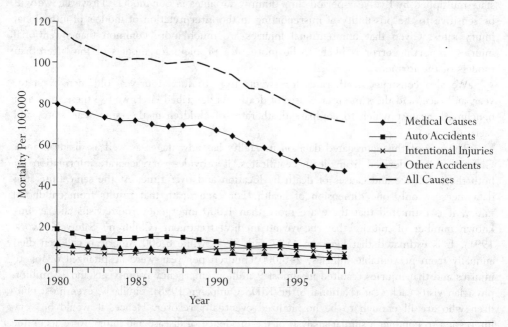

Source: Authors' compilation.

over the period 1980 and 1998. Figures 15.1 through 15.15 display trends in death rates of children (age zero to nineteen) in the United States over the last two decades of the twentieth century. (Detailed tabulations of mean death rates by cause, race, and age groups are found in table 15A.1 in the Appendix.)

As can be seen in figure 15.1, overall child death rates declined by 39.6 percent between 1980 and 1998, at an average annual rate of decline of 2.9 percent. The decline in death rates among children was relatively steady over this period, although the rates remained relatively constant over the period 1985 to 1990. With respect to deaths due to various causes, we can see that medical-related factors were the leading cause of death for children as a group, with death rates from this set of causes three to four times higher than those from any other cause of death. Most of these deaths were among infants, and much of the mortality among infants occurs in the first month of life.

Among the various causes, death rates associated with accidental deaths (injuries associated with auto accidents and other accidents) showed the most rapid rates of decline over this period, falling by 47 percent over the period, or an annual rate of decline of 3.4 percent. Deaths due to medical causes declined by 40 percent over the period for an average annual rate of 2.8 percent. Death rates due to intentional injuries, while occurring at relatively low rates, actually increased slightly over the period 1980 to 1998 (by 0.5 percent) and were notably higher from 1985 to 1994.

The trends in children's death rates by cause are even more differentiated when we examine how they vary by race and age. Consider the trends by race displayed in figures 15.2 through 15.5. Overall death rates were much higher among black children than whites or other racial groups over the last two decades of the twentieth century (figure 15.2). This difference in death rates among children across racial groups, especially for blacks compared

FIGURE 15.2   *Death Rates by Race, All Causes, Age Zero to Nineteen, 1980 to 1998*

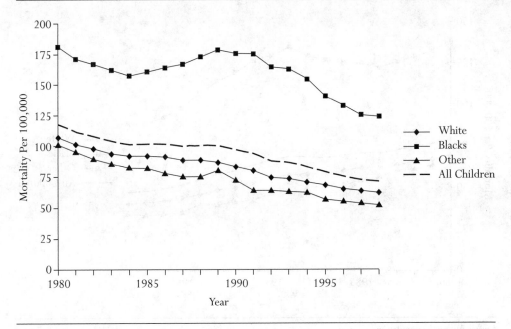

Source: Authors' compilation.

with whites, has been well documented and is true for adult death rates as well. Moreover, while the average *gap* in death rates between black and white children was slightly smaller in 1998 (61.7) than it was in 1980 (73.8), the average annual declines in death rates among black children was 2 percent, compared with 3 percent for white children and 3.5 percent for children from other racial groups. As a result, the *ratio* of black to white death rates among children increased from 1.7 to 2.0 from 1980 to 1998. Finally, one of the most notable features of the trends in racial differences was the substantial rise in black death rates from 1985 to 1990, which did not occur among white children or children from other racial groups.

Death rates associated with different causes also varied substantially by race over this period. Deaths due to medical causes were substantially higher for black children than for other children over the entire period, and there was a noticeable increase in deaths due to this set of causes among black children from 1985 to 1990 that did not occur for the other racial groups (figure 15.3). Death rates due to auto accidents were highest among white children at the beginning of the 1980s, occurring at rates almost twice as high as those for blacks or children of other race (figure 15.4). But over the period death rates associated with automobiles declined by 3.3 percent among whites and 4.4 percent among other racial groups but by only 0.5 percent for blacks, resulting in a notable narrowing in the gap between whites and blacks by 1998. Finally, we note that the gap in death rates due to intentional injuries between blacks and all others widened markedly between 1980 and 1998, owing to the rapid increase in deaths due to this set of causes among blacks from 1985 to 1995. (The corresponding rates for white children and those of other races also rose over the latter period, but not nearly as rapidly as they did for blacks.)

Figures 15.7 through 15.11 show trends in cause of death by age. As figure 15.7

(*Text continues on p. 584.*)

FIGURE 15.3   *Deaths Due to Medical Causes, by Race, Age Zero to Nineteen, 1980 to 1998*

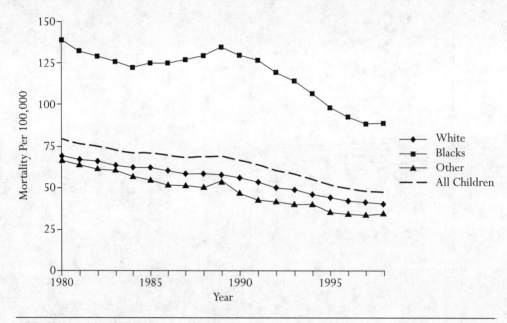

Source: Authors' compilation.

FIGURE 15.4   *Deaths Due to Auto Accidents, by Race, Age Zero to Nineteen, 1980 to 1998*

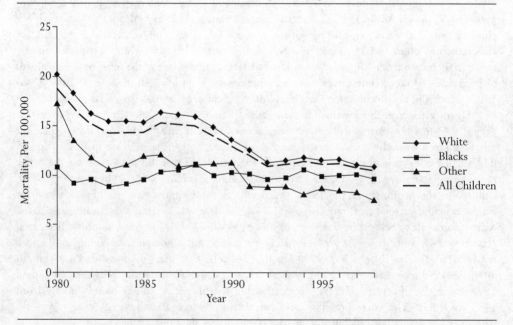

Source: Authors' compilation.

FIGURE 15.5   *Deaths Due to Other Accidental Injuries, by Race, Age Zero to Nineteen,*
1980 to 1998

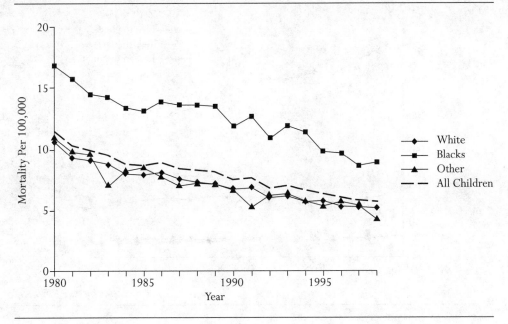

Source: Authors' compilation.

FIGURE 15.6   *Deaths Due to Intentional Injuries, by Race, Age Zero to Nineteen,*
1980 to 1998

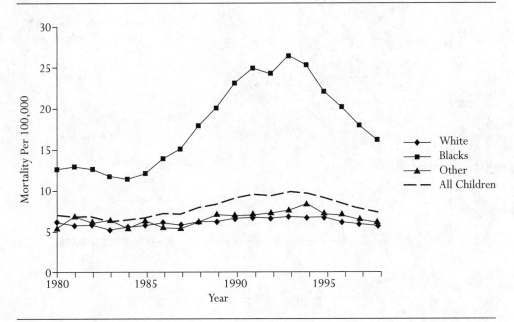

Source: Authors' compilation.

FIGURE 15.7   *Death Rates by Age, All Causes, 1980 to 1998*

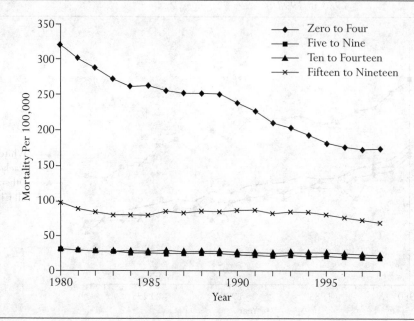

Source: Authors' compilation.

FIGURE 15.8   *Death Rates by Cause, Age Zero to Four, 1980 to 1998*

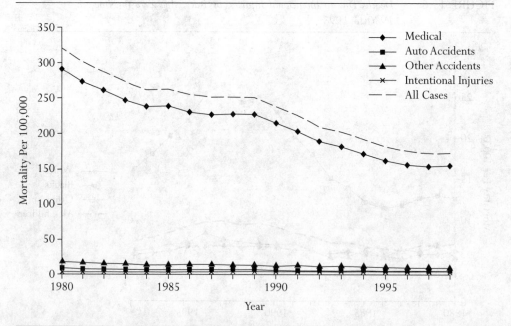

Source: Authors' compilation.

FIGURE 15.9   *Death Rates by Cause, Age Five to Nine, 1980 to 1998*

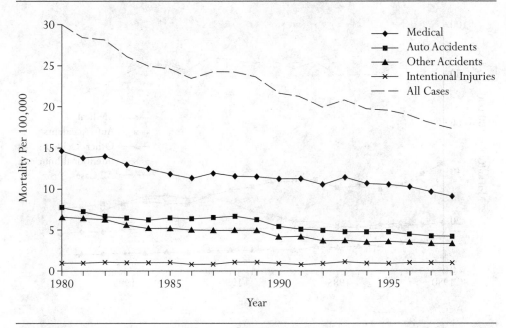

FIGURE 15.10   *Death Rates by Cause, Age Ten to Fourteen, 1980 to 1998*

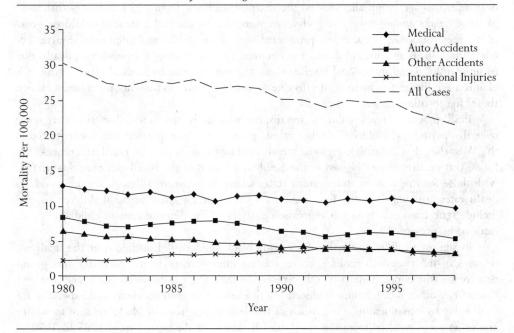

FIGURE 15.11   *Death Rates by Cause, Age Fifteen to Nineteen, 1980 to 1998*

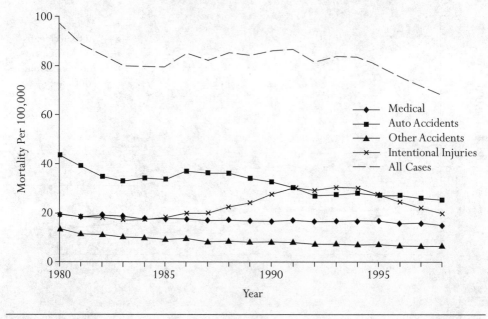

Source: Authors' compilation.

shows, most child deaths occurred among the youngest children (age zero to four), and deaths for this age group also showed the sharpest declines. Figure 15.8 indicates that most of these deaths among very young children were due to medical causes. As children grow older, medical causes become less prominent and unintentional and intentional injuries become more likely as causes of death. For children age five to nine, the number of deaths due to unintentional and intentional injuries rivals the number due to medical causes, while for children age fifteen to nineteen, deaths due to auto accidents and intentional injuries exceed those due to other causes.

Finally, because black children are disproportionately concentrated in southern states over this period and children of other ethnic groups are disproportionately concentrated in the West (largely California), regional trends could have an impact on racial differences. We found that death rates are highest in the South and lowest in the Northeast over this period, with those for midwestern and western states falling in between, although secular trends in death rates are similar in the four regions. To account for these regional differences, we include state fixed effects in our regression analyses of the determinants of childhood death rates to be presented here.

In summary, although death rates among black children did decline over the final two decades of the twentieth century, there was no improvement in mortality for this group relative to whites or children of other races. In fact, the gap between black children and those from other racial groups widened for deaths due to auto accidents and especially for deaths due to intentional injuries. Much of this lack of progress for blacks relative to whites and other races resulted from the rise in death rates over the period from 1985 to 1990 or 1995, depending on the cause. The factors that might account for these racial disparities will be taken up in the next section.

TRENDS IN FACTORS THAT MAY
INFLUENCE CHILDHOOD DEATH RATES

It is well known that income inequality increased greatly over our sample period. The distribution of family income widened from 1980 to 1998, with the gap between the ninetieth and tenth percentiles growing by almost 40 percent (see table 15A.4). Thus, children in the United States were increasingly being raised in a more (income) unequal environment over this period. Moreover, this widening in the distribution of income was skewed, in that the differential between the ninetieth and fiftieth percentiles grew by almost 50 percent over this period while the corresponding gap between the fiftieth and tenth percentiles grew by only 23 percent.

To the extent that black children tend to be at the bottom of the income distribution, we might expect this trend toward increasing inequality to be reflected in larger gaps between black and white incomes. Over this period blacks had substantially lower family incomes compared with either whites or other racial groups, averaging only 51 percent of white family income and 61 percent of the median income of other racial groups. Furthermore, the gap between blacks and whites grew by 24 percent over this period, starting in 1985 and continuing to grow until the late 1990s, when there was a slight narrowing in the differential in income.

Our other indicators of socioeconomic status show differing trends. While the educational attainment of mothers, maternal employment, and the fraction of mothers who were single trended upwards between 1980 to 1998, the gap in educational attainment between black and white mothers declined by about 6 percent over this period and black-white differences in employment rates grew. The incidence of single-motherhood in each state could not be calculated accurately for blacks and whites, so this variable is included at the state-year rather than at the state-year-race level.

As discussed earlier, a potentially important factor influencing childhood death rates is access to medical care. Previous research has shown that the access of poor children to health care and the disparities in access between blacks and other groups dramatically improved with the expansions of the Medicaid program. At the same time, the number of hospitals and trauma centers per 100,000 fell markedly, as shown in table 15A.4. However, to the extent that technological change has allowed patients to be treated on an out-patient rather than an in-patient basis, the number of hospitals may be a misleading indicator of access to care. Similarly, even though the number of trauma units has declined, the organization of trauma care networks may allow the remaining facilities to be used more effectively and to become more specialized. These trends are not captured by our crude measures.

The set of measurable indicators is rather limited and does not capture trends and differences in such things as general improvements in medical technology, automobile safety, and other risk factors. We attempt to measure these influences in an indirect way by using data on the racial and temporal patterns in death rates for adult males age twenty-five to forty-four. The overall trends in death rates for this group, broken out by race and cause of death, are displayed in table 15A.2. In an attempt to use these data to isolate other factors that might influence childhood death rates, we estimated the residuals from cause-specific regressions of the death rates of these men, where the regressors used were the income, socioeconomic status, and medical access measures just described. We then matched these residuals to our childhood death rate data by year, state, and race groups.

The estimates for the regressions used to form these residuals are presented in table 15A.3, and we plot the trends by causes of death for blacks and nonblacks in figures 15.12 through 15.15. There appears to be little information that might account for racial and

FIGURE 15.12   *Residuals from Adult Male Deaths Due to Medical Causes, by Race, 1980 to 1998*

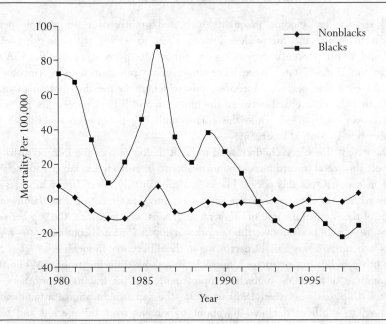

Source: Authors' compilation.

FIGURE 15.13   *Residuals from Adult Male Deaths Due to Auto Accidents, by Race, 1980 to 1998*

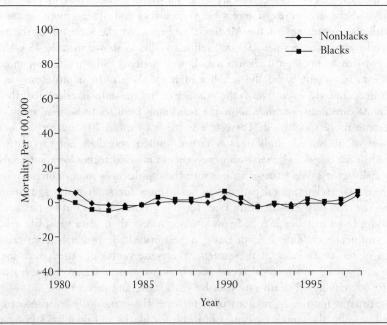

Source: Authors' compilation.

FIGURE 15.14   *Residuals from Adult Male Deaths Due to Other Accidents, by Race, 1980 to 1998*

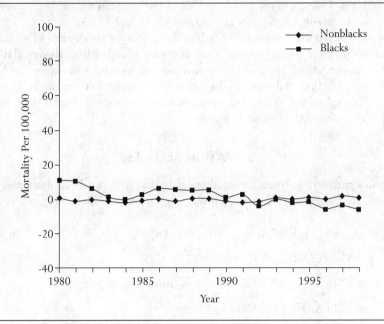

Source: Authors' compilation.

FIGURE 15.15   *Residuals from Adult Male Deaths Due to Intentional Injuries, by Race, 1980 to 1998*

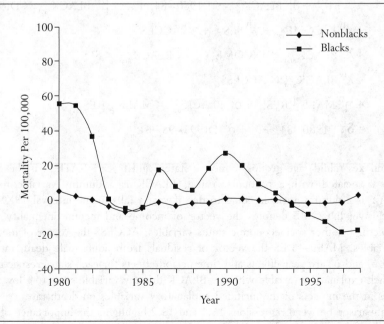

Source: Authors' compilation.

temporal differences in childhood death rates in the adult male death rate residuals for either auto or other accidents (see figures 15.13 and 15.14). In contrast, there are much more noticeable differences in the trends by race in the residuals for medical causes of death and deaths due to intentional injuries (see figures 15.12 and 15.15).

These residuals capture unmeasured factors that affect the death rates of adults and may affect those of children within a state, year, and race group. Although our ability to say exactly what these residuals represent is limited, we can use them to explore the extent to which general rather than child-specific factors may be responsible for the declines in child death rates. We explore the extent and nature of the correlations between these factors and childhood death rates in the following section.

ESTIMATION RESULTS

We estimate separate regressions for death rates by the four causes of death and four age groups noted earlier. For each cause-age group, we estimate the following two regressions:

$$
\begin{aligned}
\text{RATE}_{arst} = {} & \alpha_0^{III} + \theta_t^{III} + \beta_1^{III}\text{BLACK}_{arst} \times \text{D1980-84}_t + \ldots + \beta_4^{III}\text{BLACK}_{arst} \times \text{D1980-84}_t \\
& + \gamma_0^{III}\text{INCOME}_{rst} + \gamma_2^{III}\text{SES}_{rst} + \gamma_3^{III}\text{ACCESS}_{st} \\
& + \lambda_1^{III}\text{BLACK}_{arst} \times \text{INCOME}_{rst} + \lambda_2^{III}\text{BLACK}_{arst} \times \text{SES}_{rst} \qquad (15.1) \\
& + \lambda_3^{III}\text{BLACK}_{arst} \times \text{ACCESS}_{st} \\
& + \delta_{s1}^{III}\text{D1980-84}_t + \delta_{s2}^{III}\text{D1985-89}_t + \delta_{s3}^{III}\text{D1990-94}_t + \delta_{s4}^{III}\text{D1995-98}_t + \varepsilon_{arst}^{III}
\end{aligned}
$$

and

$$
\begin{aligned}
\text{RATE}_{arst} = {} & \alpha_0^{IV} + \theta_t^{IV} + \beta_1^{IV}\text{BLACK}_{arst} \times \text{D1980-84}_t + \ldots + \beta_4^{IV}\text{BLACK}_{arst} \times \text{D1995-98}_t \\
& + \gamma_1^{IV}\text{INCOME}_{rst} + \gamma_2^{IV}\text{SES}_{rst} + \gamma_3^{IV}\text{ACCESS}_{st} \\
& + \lambda_1^{IV}\text{BLACK}_{arst} \times \text{INCOME}_{rst} + \lambda_2^{IV}\text{BLACK}_{arst} \times \text{SES}_{rst} \qquad (15.2) \\
& + \lambda_3^{IV}\text{BLACK}_{arst} \times \text{ACCESS}_{st} \\
& + \eta^{IV}\text{MALE\_RES}_{rst} + \phi^{IV}\text{BLACK}_{arst} \times \text{MALE\_RES}_{rst} \\
& + \delta_{s1}^{IV}\text{D1980-84}_t + \ldots + \delta_{s4}^{IV}\text{D1995-98}_t + \varepsilon_{arst}^{IV}
\end{aligned}
$$

where a indexes (child) age groups, r race, s states, and t year; RATE_{arst} is the childhood death rate associated with a particular cause; BLACK is a dummy variable for blacks; D19XX–YY is a dummy variable equal to one if year t falls in the interval 19XX through 19YY, inclusive; INCOME denotes the vector of income and income inequality variables; SES the vector of other socioeconomic status variables; ACCESS the vector of medical care access variables; MALE—RES the vector of residuals from adult male death rate regressions; and θ_j^k and δ_{sj}^k are year effects and time period effects for each state, respectively.[6] We interact each explanatory variable with the BLACK dummy variable so as to allow for racial differences in the impacts of the included explanatory variables on death rates.

A comparison between regressions 15.1 and 15.2 highlights the importance of the male residuals as explanatory variables. We have also estimated regressions without state fixed effects in order to examine the sensitivity of the results to this change in specification. Although these estimates are not shown, we discuss later the comparison between models with and without state fixed effects.

Estimates of regressions 15.1 and 15.2 for the four causes of death and four age groups are presented in tables 15.1 through 15.4. Before discussing the results for specific causes and age groups, we note the following overall patterns in these regressions.

1. We find some evidence that income and maternal education and employment are important determinants of childhood death rates. However, some point estimates are sensitive to the inclusion of time trends for each state.

2. The adult male death rate residuals are often statistically significant, even when no other explanatory variables are, suggesting that factors influencing the death rates of adults other than those controlled for in our regressions also are important predictors of childhood death rates. Moreover, trends in these residuals frequently explain a good deal of the trend in the black versus nonblack gap in mortality.

3. With the exception of intentional injuries, the estimated models for children age zero to four appear to be more informative than those for older children. Although we might be tempted to speculate that this is due to higher (and more accurately calculated) death rates among young children, death rates for zero- to four-year-old children are actually comparable to those for older children when we consider deaths due to unintentional or intentional injuries.

4. Although greater numbers of hospitals per capita are often predictive of lower death rates for black children, our measure of access to trauma care is generally either statistically insignificant or "wrong signed." Increases in the fraction of children who are eligible for Medicaid in a given race-state-year cell are generally not significant once all of the variables are included in the model.

Table 15.1 shows determinants of death rates among zero- to four-year-olds. Consider the estimates for deaths due to medical causes, which are by far the most important cause of death in this age group. It appears that much of the narrowing of the racial gap in death rates over time can be accounted for by the variables included in our models. That is, the variables that measure the trend are statistically insignificant when other variables are included. Income becomes an increasingly important determinant of child mortality as more factors are included in the model. This same pattern holds for the effect of the average years of education of mothers.

We also find in table 15.1 that there are differences in the effects of the explanatory variables on death rates due to medical causes between black and nonblack children age zero to four. For example, increases in the gap between the ninetieth and fiftieth percentiles of a state's income distribution appear to increase the death rates among nonblack children but actually lower the corresponding rates for black children. The employment of mothers has a marginally significant negative effect on death rates among nonblacks but is estimated to increase black death rates due to this cause for very young children. As noted earlier, the medical access variables are generally either insignificant or have counterintuitive signs. The exception to this is that larger numbers of hospitals are estimated to decrease black death rates.

The residuals from adult male death rates due to medical causes have significant effects on the nonblack death rates due to this same cause for children age zero to four but much

TABLE 15.1   Determinants of Death Rates of Children Age Zero to Four, 1980 to 1998

	Due to Medical Causes		Due to Auto Accidents		Due to Other Accidents		Due to Intentional Injuries	
	(1)	(2)	(1)	(2)	(1)	(2)	(1)	(2)
Black × 1980 to 1984	156.24	187.57	2.12	−0.91	9.36	−46.13	−13.43	−6.19
	(241.47)	(224.25)	(16.83)	(20.16)	(34.59)	(35.58)	(20.02)	(19.88)
Black × 1985 to 1989	165.11	203.00	1.90	−1.18	10.53	−45.42	−13.86	−6.01
	(244.10)	(226.35)	(16.98)	(20.30)	(35.06)	(36.09)	(20.29)	(20.14)
Black × 1990 to 1994	134.67	178.84	3.41	0.28	10.90	−43.95	−14.85	−7.02
	(241.11)	(224.10)	(16.89)	(20.17)	(34.65)	(35.63)	(20.19)	(19.97)
Black × 1995 to 1998	86.22	153.54	3.13	−0.06	10.16	−43.85	−15.52	−6.39
	(241.95)	(225.29)	(16.95)	(20.28)	(34.94)	(35.92)	(20.29)	(20.12)
Log of median family income	−29.84***	−108.50***	−0.75	−2.37	−5.86**	−21.38***	−1.67	−4.70**
	(14.53)	(23.03)	(1.38)	(2.33)	(2.39)	(3.67)	(1.25)	(2.01)
Black × log of median family income	9.15	11.97	1.05	1.56	2.02	11.56***	−1.52	−2.10
	(17.16)	(24.89)	(1.51)	(2.50)	(2.77)	(3.89)	(1.48)	(2.24)
Log of gap between 90th and 50th percentile of family income	14.33**	16.29***	0.33	0.03	0.10	0.38	−0.08	0.11
	(6.06)	(6.02)	(0.70)	(0.73)	(1.09)	(1.15)	(0.50)	(0.56)
Black × log of gap between 90th and 50th percentile of family income	−68.45***	−44.84***	0.03	0.99	−3.99	−1.13	−0.25	0.34
	(15.81)	(14.37)	(1.17)	(1.20)	(2.55)	(2.60)	(1.40)	(1.42)
Log of gap between 50th and 10th percentile of family income	16.65	67.50***	3.14***	3.23***	2.86	9.03***	1.04	2.26*
	(10.90)	(15.53)	(1.12)	(1.58)	(1.84)	(2.54)	(0.93)	(1.31)
Black × log of gap between 50th and 10th percentile of family income	56.34***	21.46	−1.15	−2.15	2.64	−4.80	2.63	1.72
	(21.23)	(22.34)	(1.59)	(1.89)	(3.18)	(3.51)	(1.73)	(2.02)

Average years of schooling of mothers	−11.13**	−19.65***	0.11	−0.21	−0.15	−0.70	0.63*	0.04
	(4.71)	(4.49)	(0.40)	(0.40)	(0.71)	(0.69)	(0.38)	(0.37)
Black × average years of schooling of mothers	9.32	3.87	−0.39	−0.48	−0.36	−0.90	1.04	0.73
	(8.45)	(7.52)	(0.63)	(0.64)	(1.29)	(1.24)	(0.76)	(0.72)
Fraction of mothers employed	−21.60	−38.22*	−1.83	−0.60	0.53	−3.91	−4.43**	−3.51*
	(21.97)	(20.32)	(2.16)	(2.25)	(3.64)	(3.69)	(1.89)	(1.83)
Black × fraction of mothers employed	−7.04	91.67***	6.93**	5.64*	−8.20	2.06	1.18	5.84***
	(36.75)	(31.32)	(2.88)	(2.98)	(5.63)	(5.55)	(2.84)	(2.81)
Fraction of mothers who are single	−12.99	57.82**	−0.94	1.94	−7.63*	2.40	1.53	3.14
	(22.78)	(25.67)	(2.64)	(3.01)	(4.16)	(4.80)	(2.05)	(2.30)
Black × fraction of mothers who are single	15.19	−31.50	11.54***	8.87*	−17.86***	−22.20***	−9.20**	−9.95**
	(62.16)	(52.81)	(4.41)	(4.74)	(8.06)	(8.11)	(4.99)	(4.97)
Fraction of children eligible for Medicaid	28.73*	52.65***	0.42	0.59	−2.69	0.12	−2.38*	−1.67
	(15.26)	(15.04)	(1.56)	(1.68)	(2.62)	(2.65)	(1.30)	(1.28)
Black × fraction of children eligible for Medicaid	39.81	18.97	−3.51	−3.66	2.69	−0.37	5.61**	4.99**
	(31.14)	(27.55)	(2.21)	(2.22)	(5.17)	(4.81)	(2.42)	(2.32)
Number of trauma centers per 100,000 population in state	4.01	10.33**	0.02	0.06	1.10	1.77**	−0.16	−0.01
	(4.76)	(4.31)	(0.49)	(0.51)	(0.87)	(0.88)	(0.42)	(0.42)
Black × number of trauma centers per 100,000 population in state	43.89***	31.54***	−0.60	−0.34	4.58***	3.06***	1.78**	1.37**
	(7.96)	(6.56)	(0.51)	(0.55)	(1.15)	(1.09)	(0.71)	(0.67)
Number of hospitals per 100,000 population in state	−0.60	2.34	0.02	0.27	−0.36	0.06	−0.48	−0.29
	(4.87)	(4.61)	(0.55)	(0.55)	(0.85)	(0.83)	(0.40)	(0.39)
Black × number of hospitals per 100,000 population in state	−13.05***	−13.92***	0.05	−0.12	0.40	0.72*	−0.64***	−0.79***
	(2.47)	(2.47)	(0.20)	(0.23)	(0.39)	(0.41)	(0.21)	(0.22)

(Table continues on p. 590.)

TABLE 15.1 (Continued)

	Due to Medical Causes		Due to Auto Accidents		Due to Other Accidents		Due to Intentional Injuries	
	(1)	(2)	(1)	(2)	(1)	(2)	(1)	(2)
Residuals for men's death rates, medical causes		0.37***		0.01		0.04***		0.01
		(0.09)		(0.01)		(0.01)		(0.01)
Black × residuals for men's death rates, medical causes		−0.22***		−0.01		−0.02*		−0.01
		(0.08)		(0.01)		(0.01)		(0.01)
Residuals for men's death rates, auto accidents		−0.05		0.04*		0.05		0.02
		(0.16)		(0.02)		(0.03)		(0.01)
Black × residuals for men's death rates, auto accidents		0.13		0.04*		0.02		−0.02
		(0.23)		(0.02)		(0.04)		(0.02)
Residuals for men's death rates, other accidental injuries		−0.11		0.00		−0.02		0.01
		(0.17)		(0.02)		(0.03)		(0.02)
Black × residuals for men's death rates, other accidental injuries		0.95***		0.02		0.12***		0.04*
		(0.23)		(0.02)		(0.04)		(0.02)
Residuals for men's death rates, intentional injuries		0.66***		0.01		0.16***		0.02*
		(0.17)		(0.02)		(0.03)		(0.01)
Black × residuals for men's death rates, intentional injuries		0.01		−0.01		−0.13***		0.02
		(0.18)		(0.02)		(0.03)		(0.02)
Constant	331.76***	681.03***	−20.18	−0.33	45.15**	143.66***	6.77	29.04**
	(127.87)	(158.61)	(14.28)	(18.94)	(22.00)	(27.00)	(10.86)	(14.00)
Observations	1,456	1,456	1,456	1,456	1,456	1,456	1,456	1,456
R-squared	0.96	0.97	0.73	0.74	0.79	0.81	0.74	0.76

Source: Authors' compilation.
Notes: Robust standard errors are in parentheses. Estimates are weighted by number of children in age group × race group × state group, using data from 1990 U.S. Census of Population. Regressions also include year-specific time dummy variables and state-specific-by-five-year-interval dummy variables.
*p < .10; **p < .05; ***p < .01

smaller effects on black death rates, while residuals for men's death rates due to other accidental injuries have a significant effect for blacks but not nonblacks; the residuals associated with intentional injuries have similar significant effects for both groups. Thus, taken as a group, the residuals in male death rates are quite significant, suggesting that factors not accounted for in our regression analysis that affect death rates among adults also can explain death rates among children.

As discussed, rates of deaths due to other causes of death are much lower than for those due to medical causes among zero- to four-year-old children. Nonetheless, the estimates in table 15.1 indicate that higher median family income reduces deaths due to "other accidents" in this age group, while increases in inequality raise them. In this age group, the fraction of mothers who are single is estimated to increase deaths due to intentional injuries among nonblacks but to decrease deaths due to intentional injuries and other accidents among blacks. Among blacks, having more hospitals is associated with higher death rates due to other accidents but with lower death rates due to intentional injuries, while the number of trauma centers has wrong-signed effects in both cases. As with deaths due to medical causes, we find that the residuals from male death rates are highly significant in the regressions for other accidents among children age zero to four.

The estimates in tables 15.2 and 15.3 suggest that it is much more difficult to explain death rates among children age five to nine and ten to fourteen than among children age zero to four. Furthermore, although we find that many of the explanatory variables are significant in regressions without state specific controls for time periods, once these controls are included, many coefficients become statistically insignificant. We do find, however, that increases in the income differential between the tenth and fiftieth percentiles raise death rates for medical causes and auto accidents among five- to nine-year-old children, while higher levels of maternal education appear to reduce death rates due to other (non-automobile) accidents among children in this age group, though they contribute to higher death rates due to auto accidents among children age ten to fourteen. And as with our findings for young children, we find that the residuals from adult male death rates are significant determinants of death rates among children age five to nine and ten to fourteen.

Finally, table 15.4 displays the coefficient estimates of the determinants of death rates among fifteen- to nineteen-year-olds for the four causes of death. Based on these estimates, it appears that the variables we analyze have little effect on deaths due to medical causes for this age group. Only median family income is significant at the 95 percent level of confidence. However, the variables have much more explanatory power for deaths due to intentional and unintentional injuries among older children. For example, we find that median family income has a sizable and statistically significant negative effect on deaths due to intentional injuries, while increases in the gap between the ninetieth and fiftieth percentiles of a state's income distribution appear to increase death rates due to this cause, especially among blacks.

In contrast to the results for younger children, in which the estimates suggest that maternal education has a "protective" effect for children, higher levels of maternal education appear to increase death rates due to intentional injuries among older black children, although this indicator is found to significantly reduce death rates due to auto accidents among nonblacks. With respect to our medical access variables, we find that the number of hospitals per capita in a state has a consistently negative effect on death rates due to all types of injuries for blacks, while the number of trauma units is either insignificant or wrong-signed (in the model for intentional injuries).

(Text continues on p. 601.)

TABLE 15.2   Determinants of Death Rates of Children Age Five to Nine, 1980 to 1998

	Due to Medical Causes		Due to Auto Accidents		Due to Other Accidents		Due to Intentional Injuries	
	(1)	(2)	(1)	(2)	(1)	(2)	(1)	(2)
Black × 1980 to 1984	−31.01	−25.40	−1.90	1.78	14.46	17.35	3.96	6.18
	(26.84)	(28.06)	(18.41)	(20.04)	(19.71)	(21.88)	(8.29)	(9.12)
Black × 1985 to 1989	−30.76	−25.05	−2.12	1.92	14.12	16.86	4.09	6.43
	(27.25)	(28.49)	(18.59)	(20.18)	(19.94)	(22.15)	(8.40)	(9.23)
Black × 1990 to 1994	−28.73	−22.93	−2.87	0.83	13.51	16.41	3.96	6.36
	(26.95)	(28.18)	(18.49)	(20.07)	(19.81)	(22.02)	(8.40)	(9.23)
Black × 1995 to 1998	−27.91	−22.13	−3.57	0.40	13.62	16.91	3.72	6.52
	(27.01)	(28.27)	(18.58)	(20.21)	(19.84)	(22.12)	(8.45)	(9.31)
Log of median family income	2.50	3.96	−0.66	−2.22	0.15	−0.93	0.88	−0.35
	(1.86)	(2.83)	(1.39)	(2.24)	(1.47)	(2.40)	(0.61)	(1.00)
Black × log of median family income	−2.30	−3.40	−0.33	0.41	−1.57	−2.33	−2.28***	−2.47**
	(2.25)	(3.27)	(1.56)	(2.47)	(1.64)	(2.55)	(0.70)	(1.11)
Log of gap between 90th and 50th percentile of family income	0.77	1.19	−0.21	−0.81	0.16	−0.01	−0.20	−0.38
	(0.85)	(0.91)	(0.65)	(0.71)	(0.61)	(0.67)	(0.25)	(0.28)
Black × log of gap between 90th and 50th percentile of family income	2.27	1.88	0.81	1.00	−2.21	−1.00	−0.06	0.42
	(1.77)	(1.88)	(1.27)	(1.28)	(1.41)	(1.48)	(0.62)	(0.64)
Log of gap between 50th and 10th percentile of family income	−0.70	−1.26	1.31	2.93*	0.53	1.64	−0.19	0.86
	(1.53)	(2.16)	(1.08)	(1.54)	(1.05)	(1.52)	(0.46)	(0.70)
Black × log of gap between 50th and 10th percentile of family income	4.42*	5.57**	−0.23	−1.71	2.76	1.78	1.58**	0.91
	(2.27)	(2.78)	(1.55)	(1.94)	(1.74)	(2.10)	(0.80)	(0.96)

Average years of schooling of mothers	−0.72 (0.49)	−0.50 (0.52)	0.16 (0.38)	−0.27 (0.40)	−0.67* (0.39)	−0.88*** (0.41)	−0.09 (0.17)	−0.20 (0.17)
Black × average years of schooling of mothers	−0.49 (0.89)	−0.65 (0.89)	−0.18 (0.65)	−0.13 (0.66)	0.19 (0.73)	0.24 (0.72)	0.54* (0.30)	0.49 (0.31)
Fraction of mothers employed	1.47 (2.83)	1.59 (2.96)	−1.99 (2.06)	−1.19 (2.23)	−0.12 (2.13)	−0.89 (2.22)	0.57 (0.85)	−0.09 (0.86)
Black × fraction of mothers employed	−3.37 (3.90)	−3.09 (4.05)	5.89** (2.99)	6.66** (3.13)	1.06 (3.22)	1.53 (3.37)	−1.48 (1.26)	0.38 (1.31)
Fraction of mothers who are single	0.89 (3.56)	−1.63 (4.02)	0.87 (2.57)	3.90 (2.95)	−1.84 (2.47)	1.38 (2.76)	−0.22 (1.04)	1.33 (1.16)
Black × fraction of mothers who are single	11.47* (6.56)	14.00** (6.81)	3.29 (4.43)	1.42 (4.59)	−4.54 (5.34)	−7.99 (5.47)	−4.15* (2.37)	−5.86** (2.42)
Fraction of children eligible for Medicaid	2.00 (4.75)	3.41 (5.16)	1.34 (3.28)	1.65 (3.69)	1.90 (3.43)	2.30 (3.70)	−1.35 (1.56)	−1.23 (1.68)
Black × fraction of children eligible for Medicaid	−7.14 (4.65)	−8.32* (4.89)	0.95 (3.36)	1.22 (3.64)	−4.54 (3.41)	−3.71 (3.55)	1.51 (1.59)	1.48 (1.66)
Number of trauma centers per 100,000 population in state	−0.56 (0.63)	−0.54 (0.66)	−0.57 (0.47)	−0.42 (0.48)	1.35** (0.54)	1.48*** (0.54)	−0.20 (0.24)	−0.11 (0.24)
Black × number of trauma centers per 100,000 population in state	−0.56 (0.68)	−0.45 (0.72)	−0.27 (0.54)	−0.35 (0.56)	−0.24 (0.70)	−0.53 (0.77)	0.70** (0.31)	0.52* (0.30)
Number of hospitals per 100,000 population in state	−0.55 (0.63)	−0.77 (0.64)	0.02 (0.55)	0.24 (0.54)	−0.38 (0.53)	−0.21 (0.54)	0.16 (0.20)	0.23 (0.20)
Black × number of hospitals per 100,000 population in state	−0.37 (0.27)	−0.49* (0.29)	−0.28 (0.21)	−0.33 (0.23)	0.09 (0.24)	0.16 (0.27)	−0.22** (0.09)	−0.18* (0.10)

(Table continues on p. 594.)

TABLE 15.2   (Continued)

	Due to Medical Causes		Due to Auto Accidents		Due to Other Accidents		Due to Intentional Injuries	
	(1)	(2)	(1)	(2)	(1)	(2)	(1)	(2)
Residuals for men's death rates, medical causes		−0.01		0.02**		0.02*		0.01**
		(0.01)		(0.01)		(0.01)		(0.00)
Black × residuals for men's death rates, medical causes		0.01		−0.02**		−0.01		−0.00
		(0.01)		(0.01)		(0.01)		(0.00)
Residuals for men's death rates, auto accidents		−0.05**		0.04**		0.02		0.01
		(0.03)		(0.02)		(0.02)		(0.01)
Black × residuals for men's death rates, auto accidents		0.03		−0.03		0.01		−0.01
		(0.03)		(0.02)		(0.02)		(0.01)
Residuals for men's death rates, other accidental injuries		−0.03		−0.02		0.04*		−0.01
		(0.03)		(0.02)		(0.02)		(0.01)
Black × residuals for men's death rates, other accidental injuries		0.03		0.03		−0.01		−0.00
		(0.03)		(0.02)		(0.02)		(0.01)
Residuals for men's death rates, intentional injuries		0.01		−0.01		−0.01		0.00
		(0.02)		(0.02)		(0.02)		(0.01)
Black × residuals for men's death rates, intentional injuries		−0.01		0.03		0.02		0.01
		(0.02)		(0.02)		(0.02)		(0.01)
Constant	−4.19	−18.95	1.24	10.06	5.07	8.20	−3.80	1.22
	(17.07)	(21.63)	(13.14)	(16.73)	(13.09)	(17.55)	(5.36)	(7.05)
Observations	1,447	1,447	1,447	1,447	1,447	1,447	1,447	1,447
R-squared	0.57	0.58	0.59	0.59	0.64	0.64	0.41	0.44

Source: Authors' compilation.

Notes: Robust standard errors are in parentheses. Estimates are weighted by number of children in age group × race group × state group, using data from 1990 U.S. Census of Population. Regressions also include year-specific time dummy variables and state-specific-by-five-year-interval dummy variables.

*p < .10; **p < .05; ***p < .01

TABLE 15.3   Determinants of Death Rates of Children Age Ten to Fourteen, 1980 to 1998

	Due to Medical Causes		Due to Auto Accidents		Due to Other Accidents		Due to Intentional Injuries	
	(1)	(2)	(1)	(2)	(1)	(2)	(1)	(2)
Black × 1980 to 1984	2.91	−9.87	−33.91**	−45.80***	20.06	32.94*	−43.27***	−48.99***
	(25.97)	(27.37)	(15.02)	(17.25)	(19.11)	(19.49)	(16.04)	(16.26)
Black × 1985 to 1989	3.68	−9.18	−34.25**	−46.36***	19.88	32.55*	−43.47***	−48.60***
	(26.18)	(27.64)	(15.18)	(17.40)	(19.35)	(19.66)	(16.24)	(16.47)
Black × 1990 to 1994	3.32	−9.47	−32.61**	−44.68**	18.90	31.97	−41.27**	−46.62***
	(26.09)	(27.54)	(15.11)	(17.33)	(19.28)	(19.63)	(16.19)	(16.43)
Black × 1995 to 1998	5.47	−7.21	−33.12**	−45.36***	18.91	32.32	−43.85***	−48.09***
	(26.17)	(27.65)	(15.14)	(17.38)	(19.35)	(19.73)	(16.22)	(16.47)
Log of median family income	−2.97	−5.88*	−0.66	−4.05*	−0.27	1.26	1.29	−5.72***
	(1.93)	(3.13)	(1.63)	(2.34)	(1.40)	(2.11)	(1.19)	(1.79)
Black × log of median family income	2.32	5.04	0.10	3.36	−1.98	−5.27**	−3.10**	0.39
	(2.13)	(3.39)	(1.63)	(2.44)	(1.55)	(2.30)	(1.45)	(1.94)
Log of gap between 90th and 50th percentile of family income	0.22	0.93	−1.47**	−1.98***	0.72	0.91	−0.33	−0.06
	(0.87)	(0.93)	(0.70)	(0.75)	(0.60)	(0.64)	(0.50)	(0.52)
Black × log of gap between 90th and 50th percentile of family income	−0.40	−0.55	1.94*	2.73**	0.01	1.34	0.67	1.30
	(1.79)	(1.92)	(1.12)	(1.16)	(1.34)	(1.33)	(1.04)	(1.02)
Log of gap between 50th and 10th percentile of family income	1.95	3.00	0.16	3.55**	0.66	0.38	−0.48	3.71***
	(1.44)	(2.26)	(1.29)	(1.72)	(0.99)	(1.39)	(0.91)	(1.27)
Black × log of gap between 50th and 10th percentile of family income	−3.41	−4.90*	1.77	−1.42	0.37	1.12	4.88***	0.93
	(2.31)	(2.92)	(1.53)	(1.84)	(1.82)	(2.10)	(1.55)	(1.66)

(Table continues on p. 596.)

TABLE 15.3   (Continued)

	Due to Medical Causes		Due to Auto Accidents		Due to Other Accidents		Due to Intentional Injuries	
	(1)	(2)	(1)	(2)	(1)	(2)	(1)	(2)
Average years of schooling of mothers	-0.37	-0.34	0.75*	0.61	-0.10	-0.12	0.18	-0.20
	(0.57)	(0.59)	(0.40)	(0.42)	(0.36)	(0.37)	(0.35)	(0.34)
Black × average years of schooling of mothers	1.37	1.28	-0.25	-0.03	-0.51	-0.55	2.02***	1.64***
	(0.89)	(0.91)	(0.60)	(0.61)	(0.61)	(0.61)	(0.61)	(0.58)
Fraction of mothers employed	-1.32	-2.62	-1.84	-3.91*	-3.82*	-3.99*	-3.26*	-5.49**
	(2.67)	(2.97)	(2.24)	(2.36)	(2.02)	(2.10)	(1.69)	(1.78)
Black × fraction of mothers employed	-2.74	-0.44	3.86	3.76	11.03***	9.90***	-5.86***	1.38
	(3.88)	(4.07)	(2.49)	(2.63)	(2.82)	(3.01)	(2.57)	(2.59)
Fraction of mothers who are single	-1.03	-1.50	-0.88	4.86	1.18	2.43	0.43	3.69
	(3.47)	(3.92)	(2.79)	(3.07)	(2.53)	(2.80)	(2.14)	(2.29)
Black × fraction of mothers who are single	-3.31	-0.75	-3.65	-7.87*	-2.99	-5.50	1.34	0.00
	(6.20)	(6.46)	(3.94)	(4.10)	(4.95)	(4.96)	(4.54)	(4.21)
Fraction of children eligible for medicaid	11.25**	13.82**	-6.48	-3.93	-1.22	-0.06	-2.74	2.04
	(5.28)	(5.75)	(4.74)	(4.77)	(3.66)	(3.91)	(3.64)	(3.57)
Black × fraction of children eligible for medicaid	-11.06**	-12.33***	1.12	-0.62	-2.58	-2.87	2.69	-0.91
	(5.21)	(5.55)	(4.13)	(4.21)	(3.56)	(3.73)	(3.80)	(3.67)
Number of trauma centers per 100,000 population in state	-0.53	-0.44	-0.29	0.04	-0.03	0.06	0.13	0.47
	(0.57)	(0.59)	(0.70)	(0.70)	(0.48)	(0.48)	(0.45)	(0.45)
Black × number of trauma centers per 100,000 population in state	0.64	0.19	0.47	0.04	-0.16	-0.17	1.42**	0.76
	(0.76)	(0.82)	(0.46)	(0.48)	(0.55)	(0.58)	(0.56)	(0.53)
Number of hospitals per 100,000 population in state	0.45	0.39	-0.90	-0.73	-0.35	-0.33	-0.08	-0.01
	(0.69)	(0.69)	(0.57)	(0.56)	(0.50)	(0.51)	(0.37)	(0.37)
Black × number of hospitals per 100,000 population in state	-0.14	0.01	-0.91***	-0.71***	0.02	-0.12	-0.26	-0.19
	(0.28)	(0.32)	(0.17)	(0.20)	(0.19)	(0.21)	(0.18)	(0.21)

	(1)	(2)	(3)	(4)	(5)	(6)	(7)	(8)
Residuals for men's death rates, medical causes		0.00		0.03***		0.00		0.02***
		(0.01)		(0.01)		(0.01)		(0.01)
Black × residuals for men's death rates, medical causes		−0.00		−0.02***		0.00		−0.01***
		(0.01)		(0.01)		(0.01)		(0.01)
Residuals for men's death rates, auto accidents		−0.02		0.02		−0.03		−0.00
		(0.03)		(0.02)		(0.02)		(0.01)
Black × residuals for men's death rates, auto accidents		−0.01		0.00		0.07***		−0.01
		(0.03)		(0.02)		(0.02)		(0.01)
Residuals for men's death rates, other accidental injuries		0.04		0.00		0.04*		0.00
		(0.03)		(0.02)		(0.02)		(0.02)
Black × residuals for men's death rates, other accidental injuries		0.00		−0.01		0.00		−0.01
		(0.03)		(0.02)		(0.02)		(0.02)
Residuals for men's death rates, intentional injuries		0.03		−0.01		−0.01		0.05***
		(0.02)		(0.02)		(0.02)		(0.01)
Black × residuals for men's death rates, intentional injuries		−0.03		−0.00		0.01		−0.01
		(0.02)		(0.02)		(0.02)		(0.01)
Constant	23.11	35.57	23.70*	30.45*	−1.69	−16.56	−2.40	29.26**
	(18.11)	(22.99)	(13.61)	(16.50)	(12.12)	(15.47)	(10.49)	(13.61)
Observations	1,446	1,446	1,446	1,446	1,446	1,446	1,446	1,446
R-squared	0.48	0.49	0.62	0.62	0.67	0.68	0.56	0.61

Source: Authors' compilation.

Notes: Robust standard errors are in parentheses. Estimates are weighted by number of children in age group × race group × state group, using data from 1990 U.S. Census of Population. Regressions also include year-specific time dummy variables and state-specific-by-five-year-interval dummy variables.

*p < .10; **p < .05; ***p < .01

TABLE 15.4   Determinants of Death Rates of Children Age Fifteen to Nineteen, 1980 to 1998

	Due to Medical Causes		Due to Auto Accidents		Due to Other Accidents		Due to Intentional Injuries	
	(1)	(2)	(1)	(2)	(1)	(2)	(1)	(2)
Black × 1980 to 1984	−5.94	−8.06	−186.26***	−277.86***	13.60	40.29*	−617.62***	−519.43***
	(30.01)	(32.58)	(36.13)	(38.16)	(20.72)	(21.94)	(108.36)	(92.90)
Black × 1985 to 1989	−4.27	−6.16	−184.18***	−276.20***	14.82	41.50*	−617.61***	−513.21***
	(30.39)	(33.00)	(36.50)	(38.54)	(20.91)	(22.12)	(109.72)	(93.97)
Black × 1990 to 1994	−5.07	−6.99	−180.38***	−272.55***	15.81	42.73*	−590.36***	−485.70***
	(30.38)	(32.94)	(36.37)	(38.41)	(20.84)	(22.04)	(109.54)	(93.87)
Black × 1995 to 1998	−5.27	−6.69	−178.68***	−270.91***	13.49	41.20*	−613.54***	−494.17***
	(30.54)	(33.14)	(36.55)	(38.70)	(20.93)	(22.16)	(110.12)	(94.25)
Log of median family income	−4.65*	−7.22**	3.57	−13.59***	0.93	4.76*	−28.00***	−60.74***
	(2.40)	(3.66)	(4.17)	(5.08)	(1.90)	(2.63)	(10.37)	(12.02)
Black × log of median family income	1.20	2.47	0.33	17.10***	−0.91	−6.25**	22.55*	13.81
	(2.68)	(4.00)	(4.14)	(5.29)	(2.06)	(2.84)	(11.64)	(12.56)
Log of gap between 90th and 50th percentile of family income	−1.23	−1.17	−2.28	−5.44***	0.30	1.13	−5.67**	−4.85**
	(1.07)	(1.18)	(1.80)	(1.85)	(0.82)	(0.92)	(2.50)	(2.20)
Black × log of gap between 90th and 50th percentile of family income	−1.87	−1.81	16.23***	15.57***	0.04	1.08	27.27***	30.60***
	(2.17)	(2.30)	(2.58)	(2.50)	(1.46)	(1.48)	(7.66)	(6.22)
Log of gap between 50th and 10th percentile of family income	2.15	3.77	−3.29	1.67	0.37	−0.92	9.82	23.90***
	(1.69)	(2.53)	(3.23)	(4.01)	(1.54)	(2.07)	(6.26)	(6.93)
Black × log of gap between 50th and 10th percentile of family income	0.45	−0.88	0.01	−8.80**	−0.28	1.37	−6.90	−13.69
	(2.61)	(3.19)	(3.93)	(4.24)	(1.94)	(2.28)	(12.55)	(11.73)

	(1)	(2)	(3)	(4)	(5)	(6)	(7)	(8)
Average years of schooling of mothers	-0.01 (0.62)	-0.23 (0.66)	-1.21 (1.04)	-2.42** (1.06)	0.11 (0.49)	-0.03 (0.50)	2.19 (2.04)	-2.18 (1.70)
Black × average years of schooling of mothers	1.31 (1.09)	1.21 (1.11)	1.82 (1.46)	2.52* (1.40)	-0.50 (0.81)	-0.37 (0.80)	16.68*** (3.42)	12.78*** (2.79)
Fraction of mothers employed	0.81 (3.24)	0.29 (3.52)	3.91 (5.53)	2.48 (5.60)	-5.83** (2.68)	-5.20* (2.75)	-35.25*** (9.86)	-38.47*** (8.19)
Black × fraction of mothers employed	-1.05 (4.62)	1.84 (5.01)	-20.89*** (6.15)	-13.19** (6.20)	6.73** (3.37)	3.86 (3.47)	-61.15*** (15.91)	6.40 (13.50)
Fraction of mothers who are single	-10.43** (4.20)	-8.77** (4.69)	7.29 (7.25)	21.88*** (7.66)	-3.27 (3.32)	-4.36 (3.75)	-23.66* (12.79)	-5.65 (10.85)
Black × fraction of mothers who are single	10.22 (7.26)	9.70 (7.66)	14.80 (9.28)	4.64 (8.95)	7.03 (5.14)	6.07 (5.24)	136.98*** (30.61)	105.23*** (23.07)
Fraction of children eligible for Medicaid	0.99 (9.14)	3.42 (9.67)	7.74 (13.00)	3.96 (13.30)	-4.05 (6.08)	-0.27 (6.42)	8.24 (23.08)	32.52* (18.78)
Black × fraction of children eligible for Medicaid	-9.46 (8.56)	-10.76 (9.03)	-13.31 (11.23)	-7.43 (11.50)	1.42 (5.48)	-1.68 (5.77)	-15.35 (23.51)	-31.19* (18.72)
Number of trauma centers per 100,000 population in state	-0.82 (0.83)	-0.65 (0.85)	0.07 (1.49)	0.16 (1.37)	0.89 (0.65)	0.85 (0.66)	-2.49 (1.97)	-1.11 (1.57)
Black × number of trauma centers per 100,000 population in state	-0.04 (0.94)	-0.51 (1.03)	1.26 (1.12)	-0.93 (1.08)	-0.01 (0.62)	0.13 (0.65)	14.36*** (3.95)	7.39** (2.98)
Number of hospitals per 100,000 population in state	-0.56 (0.84)	-0.48 (0.84)	0.90 (1.56)	2.28 (1.43)	-0.76 (0.75)	-0.80 (0.72)	0.95 (2.08)	2.45 (1.74)
Black × number of hospitals per 100,000 population in state	-0.56* (0.32)	-0.48 (0.38)	-4.36*** (0.41)	-2.76*** (0.44)	-0.31 (0.24)	-0.56** (0.26)	-2.42** (1.09)	-2.09** (0.97)

(Table continues on p. 600.)

TABLE 15.4   (Continued)

	Due to Medical Causes		Due to Auto Accidents		Due to Other Accidents		Due to Intentional Injuries	
	(1)	(2)	(1)	(2)	(1)	(2)	(1)	(2)
Residuals for men's death rates, medical causes		0.01		0.07***		0.00		0.07**
		(0.01)		(0.02)		(0.01)		(0.03)
Black × residuals for men's death rates, medical causes		−0.01		−0.05***		0.00		−0.01
		(0.01)		(0.02)		(0.01)		(0.03)
Residuals for men's death rates, auto accidents		0.01		0.41***		−0.05*		0.23***
		(0.03)		(0.05)		(0.03)		(0.06)
Black × residuals for men's death rates, auto accidents		−0.02		−0.43***		0.08***		−0.42***
		(0.03)		(0.05)		(0.03)		(0.09)
Residuals for men's death rates, other accidental injuries		−0.00		−0.03		0.13***		−0.03
		(0.03)		(0.05)		(0.03)		(0.06)
Black × residuals for men's death rates, other accidental injuries		0.02		0.02		−0.09***		0.04
		(0.04)		(0.05)		(0.03)		(0.10)
Residuals for men's death rates, intentional injuries		0.02		0.03		−0.05**		0.30***
		(0.03)		(0.04)		(0.02)		(0.06)
Black × residuals for men's death rates, intentional injuries		−0.00		−0.03		0.05**		0.19***
		(0.03)		(0.04)		(0.02)		(0.06)
Constant	59.46***	71.19***	62.91*	226.23***	−1.07	−33.69*	256.22***	484.28***
	(21.02)	(26.95)	(36.17)	(39.06)	(17.50)	(20.43)	(73.35)	(81.67)
Observations	1,455	1,455	1,455	1,455	1,455	1,455	1,455	1,455
R-squared	0.66	0.66	0.89	0.91	0.73	0.74	0.82	0.88

Source: Authors' compilation.

Notes: Robust standard errors are in parentheses. Estimates are weighted by number of children in age group × race group × state group, using data from 1990 U.S. Census of Population. Regressions also include year-specific time dummy variables and state-specific-by-five-year-interval dummy variables.

*p < .10; **p < .05; ***p < .01

The residuals from adult male death rates have statistically significant effects on deaths due to injuries among children age fifteen to nineteen, although their importance differs by race. For nonblacks, the adult male residuals for auto accidents are predictive of death rates due to auto accidents for this age group, although this is not the case for blacks. Similarly, the male residuals for deaths due to other accidents have a larger effect on such deaths for nonblacks than for blacks. However, when we look at death rates due to intentional injuries, which is one of the more important causes of death in this age group, the male residuals are highly significant for both nonblacks and blacks and are more important for blacks than for nonblacks. Thus, factors that lead to more violent deaths among adult males also are linked to violent deaths among children in their late teens.

Given that our primary interest is in understanding the determinants of racial differences in childhood death rates and their trends over the last two decades of the twentieth century, we are particularly interested in answering two different sets of questions. First, to what extent do the specific explanatory variables, such as median family income, account for the black versus nonblack gaps in childhood mortality at any point in time? Second, to what extent do the changes in these variables account for the trends in the observed racial gaps in childhood mortality over the period 1980 to 1998?

To address both of these questions, we decompose the black versus nonblack gaps in mortality into the portions that can be "accounted for" by differences in the values of the explanatory variables and their estimated impacts recorded in tables 15.1 through 15.4. These decompositions are presented in tables 15.5 through 15.8, which are organized by age groups and causes of death to parallel tables 15.1 through 15.4. Mean differences by race in the explanatory variables for different age groups and time periods are provided in table 15A.4. (Detailed descriptions of how the entries in tables 15.5 through 15.8 are constructed are found in the appendix.)

In the first row, we reproduce the unadjusted estimates of the black versus nonblack death rates for the five-year (four-year) periods from 1980 to 1998. In the first columns of these panels, we display the "normed" predicted black versus nonblack differentials in death rates attributable to a particular explanatory variable (or set of variables) over the period 1980 to 1998, where these predicted values are normalized by the unadjusted black versus nonblack death rate differential for the period 1980 to 1984. As the notes to these tables make clear, these predicted differentials depend on the racial differentials in the explanatory variables and the racial differences in the estimated impacts of these variables on the childhood death rates recorded in tables 15.1 through 15.4. The second column in each panel of these tables presents an estimate of the average annual percentage change in the predicted racial differentials attributable to the various explanatory variables in order to assess the extent to which these explanatory variables account for the trends in the black versus nonblack gaps in childhood death rates.

Consider the contribution of median family income to the racial gap in deaths due to medical causes for children age zero to four in table 15.5. Given the normalization used, the entry in column 1 indicates that differences in the (log) of median income would predict a black versus nonblack gap of 0.8097. That is, based on the black versus nonblack gap in log median income of -0.664 (see table 15.A.4) and the estimated effects of median income from table 15.1, the black versus nonblack gap in childhood death rates due to medical causes based on income alone would have been about 20 percent smaller than it was. At the same time, we find that relatively little of the (declining) trend gap in death rates due to this cause for children age zero to four is accounted for by the changes in median income. In particular, changes in the racial gap in the (log of) median family income alone are predicted to generate an average annual *increase* in the death rate gap of .03 percent when in fact the actual black versus nonblack gap in death rates due to this cause actually *declined* by 0.49 percent per year on average. Similarly, although maternal education is an important determinant of child mortality due to medical causes in this age group, changes in the gap in educational attainment between black and nonblack women explain almost none of the closure of the gap in black versus nonblack mortality rates due to medical causes.

The calculations presented in table 15.5 do indicate that changes in the residuals from male death rates played a major role in accounting for the declining gap in death rates for young children due to medical causes, even though these variables account for only a fraction of the average gap in death rates between black and nonblack children over this period. For example, racial differences in these residuals account for only 4.7 percent of the racial gap in death rates due to medical causes among children age zero to four. But changes in these residuals predict an average annual decline in the gap in death rates of 0.38 percent, which is 73 percent of the actual average annual decline of 0.49 percent in this cause of death for this age group. In short, this finding suggests that much of the convergence in black and nonblack death rates for this age and cause was driven by those factors that affected adult death rates other than income, inequality, socioeconomic status, and measures of health care availability and access used in our regression analyses.

The estimates shown in table 15.5 indicate that changes in the male residuals are also predictive of changes in the racial gaps in deaths due to auto accidents and other accidents. For example, the changes in the residuals would predict an average annual increase in the gap in black relative to nonblack death rates due to auto accidents of 0.40 percent, which is 27 percent of the actual increase of 1.50 percent for this cause of death among this age group. Similarly, changes in the residuals predict a 0.42 percent decline in the gap in deaths due to other accidents, compared with an actual decline of 0.72 percent. However, trends in the male residuals go in the wrong direction when it comes to explaining actual changes in the racial gap in intentional injuries in this age group.

The male residuals are less predictive of changes in racial gaps for five- to nine-year-olds, as shown in table 15.6. They predict a decline of 0.29 percent compared with a decline of 0.68 percent per year in gaps in deaths due to non-automobile accidents; they predict a decline in the gap in death rates due to auto accidents when there was actually an increase, and they overpredict the actual decline in the black-nonblack gap in deaths due to unintentional injuries.

Table 15.7 suggests that the temporal changes in the residuals for male death rates due to intentional injuries account for a sizable share of the changes in the black versus nonblack gap in death rates due to non-automobile accidents among ten- to fourteen-year-olds over our sample period, although changes in the residuals for intentional injuries again move in the wrong direction for explaining the increasing racial gap in intentional injuries in this age group.

Finally, the estimates in table 15.8 imply that trends in the racial differentials in these adult male residuals should have led to a closing of the gap in death rates due to intentional injuries between black and nonblack fifteen- to nineteen-year-olds rather than the observed widening in the racial gap for this cause of death. Given the table 15.4 finding that the residuals from male death rates play an important role in explaining the level death rates of fifteen- to nineteen-year-old children, this is a surprising finding. It is possible that declines in intentional injuries among black youths are lagging declines among adults.

(Text continues on p. 612.)

TABLE 15.5　Accounting for the Effects of Explanatory Variables on Black-Nonblack Differences in Childhood Death Rates, Age Zero to Four, 1980 to 1998

	Due to Medical Causes		Due to Automobile Accidents		Due to Other Accidental Injuries		Due to Intentional Injuries	
	Average Difference, 1980 to 1998	Average Annual Percentage Change, 1980 to 1998	Average Difference, 1980 to 1998	Average Annual Percentage Change, 1980 to 1998	Average Difference, 1980 to 1998	Average Annual Percentage Change, 1980 to 1998	Average Difference, 1980 to 1998	Average Annual Percentage Change, 1980 to 1998
Unadjusted black-nonblack death rate differences	232.83***	−0.49%	2.33***	1.50%	11.15***	−0.72%	7.08***	0.15%
Normed predicted black-nonblack differences in death rates by variable:								
Black × 19XX—YY	0.7830	−0.25	−0.2121	0.94	−4.0269	0.32	−0.9037	−0.06
Log of median family income	0.8097	0.03	6.9204	0.18	10.9937***	0.18	−2.2757	0.00
Log of gap between 90th and 50th percentiles of family income	−1.9470***	−0.10	4.2953	0.36	−1.0203	−0.05	0.4868	0.03
Log of gap between 50th and 10th percentiles of family income	0.8892	0.03	−8.8965	−0.18	−4.1478	−0.05	2.3380	0.07
Average years of schooling of mothers	0.2406	0.00	−2.4633	−0.51	−0.9590	−0.13%	1.2495	0.18
Fraction of mothers employed	0.2210***	0.09	1.3315*	0.80	0.1137	0.04	0.4686**	0.21
Fraction of mothers who are single	−0.0308	−0.01	1.0419*	0.64	−0.5304***	−0.20	−0.3679**	−0.17

(Table continues on p. 604.)

TABLE 15.5 (Continued)

	Due to Medical Causes		Due to Automobile Accidents		Due to Other Accidental Injuries		Due to Intentional Injuries	
	Average Difference, 1980 to 1998	Average Annual Percentage Change, 1980 to 1998	Average Difference, 1980 to 1998	Average Annual Percentage Change, 1980 to 1998	Average Difference, 1980 to 1998	Average Annual Percentage Change, 1980 to 1998	Average Difference, 1980 to 1998	Average Annual Percentage Change, 1980 to 1998
Fraction of children eligible for medicaid	0.1058*	0.11	−0.6859*	−1.59	−0.0127	−0.02	0.2718*	0.52
Number of trauma centers per 100,000 population in state	0.1177***	−0.13	−0.1339	0.22	0.2327***	−0.24	0.1729**	−0.22
Number of hospitals per 100,000 population in state	−0.2460***	0.13	−0.2439	0.22	0.2618*	−0.13	−0.4471***	0.27
Sum of residuals from male death rate regressions	0.0470***	−0.38	0.0795**	0.40	0.0965***	−0.42	0.0684***	−0.71
Residuals from men's death rates, medical causes	0.0137***	−0.08	−0.0011	0.14	0.0354***	−0.19	0.0023	0.01
Residuals from men's death rates, auto accidents	0.0005	0.00	0.0539***	0.71	0.0097**	0.08	0.0009	0.02
Residuals from men's death rates, other accidental injuries	0.0039***	−0.07	0.0124*	−0.35	0.0101***	−0.17	0.0079 ***	−0.17
Residuals from men's death rates, intentional injuries	0.0288***	−0.23	0.0143	−0.09	0.0412***	−0.15	0.0574***	−0.57
State × five-year period fixed effects[a]	0.0103	0.01	−0.0309	0.03	−0.0008	−0.02	−0.0616	0.03
Year dummy variables	−0.0005***	0.00	−0.0021***	0.00	−0.0004**	0.00	0.0000	0.00

Source: Authors' compilation.

Notes:

Unadjusted black-nonblack death rate differences This entry is defined as:

$$(\overline{\text{RATE}}_{B,a} - \overline{\text{RATE}}_{\sim B,a}),$$ (15.3)

where a = 0–4, 5–9, . . . , where the means are averaged over the interval 1980 to 1999.

Normed Predicted Black-Nonblack Differences in Death Rates by Variable This entry for a particular explanatory variable, X_i, is calculated as follows:

$$\frac{(\overline{RATE}_{B,a} - \overline{RATE}_{\sim B,a} \mid \overline{X}_{i,B,a}, \overline{X}_{i,B,a})}{Abs(\overline{RATE}_{B,a,t=1980-84} - \overline{RATE}_{\sim B,\neq t\ 1980\ 84})} \qquad (15.4)$$

where a $= 0-4, 5-9, \ldots$ and where the numerator in (15.4) is given by:

$$(\overline{RATE}_{B,a} - \overline{RATE}_{\sim B,a} \mid \overline{X}_{i,B,a}, \overline{X}_{i,\sim B,a})$$

$$= (\hat{\gamma}_{l,i}^{IV} + \hat{\lambda}_{l,i}^{IV})\overline{X}_{i,B,a} - \hat{\gamma}_{l,i}^{IV}\ \overline{X}_{i,\sim B,a}$$

$$= \underbrace{\hat{\gamma}_{l,i}^{IV} (\overline{X}_{i,B,a} - \overline{X}_{i,\sim B,a})}_{\text{differential due to changes in } X_i} + \underbrace{\hat{\lambda}_{l,i}^{IV}\ \overline{X}_{i,B,a}}_{\substack{\text{differential due to differences in impacts of } X_i \text{ between blacks and nonblacks}}} \qquad (15.5)$$

Thus, the normalized differential associated with a particular explanatory variable amounts to normalizing the total black-nonblack differential in (15.3), predicted for using $\overline{X}_{i,r,a,t}$ for blacks (a = B) and nonblacks (a = $\sim$B) that are found in table 15A.4, where the normalizing factor is the unadjusted mean black-nonblack difference for 1980 to 1984.

For each of the normalized black-nonblack differentials associated with X_i, we calculated the standard errors of these statistics, where we take account of the estimation error only in the estimated coefficients, and $\hat{\gamma}_{l,i}^{IV}$ and $\hat{\lambda}_{l,i}^{IV}$ in forming these statistics. We then determine the statistical significance associated with the differentials, with the latter reported in tables 15.5 through 15.8.

Average Annual Percentage These entries are calculated by taking the average annual changes over the period 1980 to 1999 and dividing them by "18" (number of years) (the norming value)). Note that the sum of the average annual changes under the "Normed predicted . . ." heading is equal to the average annual change in the corresponding "Unadjusted black-nonblack death rate differences" row, that is, −0.490 percent in the first rows of table 15.5.

^{a}Significance levels were not calculated for black-nonblack differences attributable to state × period fixed effects.

*p < .10; **p < .05; ***p < .01

TABLE 15.6   Accounting for the Effects of Explanatory Variables on Black-Nonblack Differences in Childhood Death Rates, Age Five to Nine, 1980 to 1998

	Due to Medical Causes		Due to Automobile Accidents		Due to Other Accidental Injuries		Due to Intentional Injuries	
	Average Difference, 1980 to 1998	Average Annual Percentage Change, 1980 to 1998	Average Difference, 1980 to 1998	Average Annual Percentage Change, 1980 to 1998	Average Difference, 1980 to 1998	Average Annual Percentage Change, 1980 to 1998	Average Difference, 1980 to 1998	Average Annual Percentage Change, 1980 to 1998
Unadjusted black-nonblack death rate differences	4.49***	1.82%	2.23***	0.23%	4.70***	−0.68%	1.40***	−0.22%
Normed predicted black-nonblack differences in death rates by variable:								
Black × 19XX–YY	−5.3362	2.02	0.5767	−1.26	3.5933	−0.15	4.5603	0.47
Log of median family income	−7.6595	−0.20	2.4123	0.08	−4.4633	−0.04	−16.2504**	−0.21
Log of gap between 90th and 50th percentiles of family income	4.2407	0.39	4.5213	0.27	−2.1514	−0.11	3.0113	0.17
Log of gap between. 50th and 10th percentiles of family income	11.9386**	0.38	−7.4193	−0.12	3.6431	0.08	6.3069	0.18
Average years of schooling of mothers	−1.7165	−0.42	−0.6685	−0.15	0.7132	0.01	4.3155	0.54
Fraction of mothers employed	−0.3887	−0.24	1.6543**	0.77	0.1849	0.06	0.1499	0.07
Fraction of mothers who are single	0.8299**	0.55	0.2130	0.11	−0.4508	−0.17	−1.1071**	−0.52
Fraction of children eligible for Medicaid	−0.4145**	−1.05	0.3508	0.55	−0.1374	−0.21	0.1319	0.28
Number of trauma centers per 100,000 population in state	−0.0787	0.15	−0.1254	0.18	−0.1303	0.11	0.3422*	−0.43
Number of hospitals per 100,000 population in state	−0.4085	0.32	−0.6320	0.40	0.1537	−0.08	−0.5654*	0.36

Sum of residuals from male death rate regressions	−0.0184	−0.15	0.0642*	−0.37	0.0536***	−0.29	0.1383***	−1.12
Residuals from men's death rates, medical causes	−0.0179	0.14	0.0138	0.06	0.0357**	−0.19	0.0703***	−0.51
Residuals from men's death rates, auto accidents	−0.0114	−0.19	0.0097	0.16	0.0113	0.08	0.0007	0.03
Residuals from men's death rates, other accidental injuries	0.0015	−0.03	0.0015	−0.02	0.0088**	−0.15	−0.0093	0.19
Residuals from men's death rates, intentional injuries	0.0094	−0.06	0.0391	−0.58	−0.0021	−0.03	0.0766***	−0.83
State × five-year period fixed effects[a]	0.0132	0.05	0.0546	−0.23	−0.0079	0.08	−0.0345	−0.02
Year dummy variables	−0.0015***	0.00	−0.0020***	0.00	−0.0007**	0.00	0.0012***	0.00

Source: Authors' compilation.

Note: See table 16.5 note for explanation of how entries were constructed.

[a]Significance levels were not calculated for black-nonblack differences attributable to state × period fixed effects.

*p < .10; **p < .05; ***p < .01

TABLE 15.7   Accounting for the Effects of Explanatory Variables on Black-Nonblack Differences in Childhood Death Rates, Age Ten to Fourteen, 1980 to 1998

	Due to Medical Causes		Due to Automobile Accidents		Due to Other Accidental Injuries		Due to Intentional Injuries	
	Average Difference, 1980 to 1998	Average Annual Percentage Change, 1980 to 1998	Average Difference, 1980 to 1998	Average Annual Percentage Change, 1980 to 1998	Average Difference, 1980 to 1998	Average Annual Percentage Change, 1980 to 1998	Average Difference, 1980 to 1998	Average Annual Percentage Change, 1980 to 1998
Unadjusted black-nonblack death rate differences	4.86***	1.01%	−1.17	1.61%	3.59***	−0.55%	3.05***	0.73%
Normed predicted black-nonblack differences in death rates by variable:								
Black × 19XX–YY	−1.8568	1.23	−39.0779***	0.33	9.0467*	−0.28	−15.7758***	0.91
Log of median family income	10.4727	0.22	29.2206	0.24	−13.8891**	−0.17	2.5301	0.18
Log of gap between 90th and 50th percentiles of family income	−1.1299	−0.07	23.6740**	0.61	3.7681	0.21	4.3260	0.42
Log of gap between 50th and 10th percentiles of family income	−9.7056*	−0.23	−11.7346	−0.06	3.0182	0.07	2.9261	0.20
Average years of schooling of mothers	3.2448	0.49	−0.5768	0.07	−1.8378	−0.23	6.5702***	1.42
Fraction of mothers employed	−0.0291	−0.03	1.8865	0.36	1.5465***	0.59	0.3167	0.18
Fraction of mothers who are single	−0.0491	−0.03	−1.7193*	−0.36	−0.3963	−0.16	0.0289	0.03

Fraction of children eligible for Medicaid	−0.0761	−0.21	−0.5950*	−0.43	−0.1572	−0.23	0.0398	0.09
Number of trauma centers per 100,000 population in state	0.0427	−0.05	0.0240	−0.01	−0.0442	0.05	0.2079	−0.43
Number of hospitals per 100,000 population in state	−0.0119	0.02	−2.3464***	0.60	−0.1201	0.05	−0.2522	0.24
Sum of residuals from male death rate regressions	0.0130	−0.39	0.1119*	0.16	0.0567***	−0.36	0.1777***	−2.49
Residuals from men's death rates, medical causes	0.0031	−0.02	0.1962***	−0.52	0.0282	−0.19	0.0559***	−0.54
Residuals from men's death rates, auto accidents	−0.0118	−0.11	0.0301	0.12	0.0204**	0.09	−0.0108	−0.13
Residuals from men's death rates, other accidental injuries	0.0128**	−0.28	−0.0119	0.10	0.0167***	−0.27	−0.0058	0.17
Residuals from men's death rates, intentional injuries	0.0090	0.03	−0.1023**	0.47	−0.0086	0.02	0.1385***	−2.00
State × five-year period fixed effects[a]	0.0867	0.07	0.1359	0.09	0.0095	−0.09	−0.0956	0.00
Year dummy variables	−0.0015***	0.00	−0.0027*	0.00	−0.0010***	0.00	0.0003	0.00

Source: Authors' compilation.

Note: See table 15.5 for explanation of how entries were constructed.

[a]Significance levels were not calculated for black-nonblack differences attributable to state × period fixed effects.

*p< .10; **p < .05; ***p < .01

TABLE 15.8   Accounting for the Effects of Explanatory Variables on Black-Nonblack Differences in Childhood Death Rates, Age Fifteen to Nineteen, 1980 to 1998

	Due to Medical Causes		Due to Automobile Accidents		Due to Other Accidental Injuries		Due to Intentional Injuries	
	Average Difference, 1980 to 1998	Average Annual Percentage Change, 1980 to 1998	Average Difference, 1980 to 1998	Average Annual Percentage Change, 1980 to 1998	Average Difference, 1980 to 1998	Average Annual Percentage Change, 1980 to 1998	Average Difference, 1980 to 1998	Average Annual Percentage Change, 1980 to 1998
Unadjusted black-nonblack death rate differences	9.46***	0.69%	−18.62***	1.21%	1.47*	19.91%	36.53***	3.04%
Normed predicted black-nonblack differences in death rates by variable:								
Black × 19XX–YY	−0.7394	0.34	−14.7494***	0.47	28.2703*	20.09	−13.7902***	2.94
Log of median family income	2.9700	0.09	9.0458***	0.10	−41.8950**	−11.88	4.7057	0.31
Log of gap between 90th and 50th percentiles of family income	−1.9317	−0.15	8.4494***	0.33	7.4769	8.40	8.4671***	1.13
Log of gap between 50th and 10th percentiles of family income	−0.9004	0.00	−4.5560**	−0.07	9.0381	3.18	−3.6120	−0.12
Average years of schooling of mothers	1.5696	0.25	1.7088*	0.12	−3.0937	−7.46	4.2817***	1.26
Fraction of mothers employed	0.1051	0.06	−0.3911**	−0.12	1.5685	11.00	0.1355	0.09
Fraction of mothers who are single	0.2553	0.14	0.0939	0.03	1.0486	8.09	0.7728***	0.79

Fraction of children eligible for Medicaid	−0.1314*	−0.11	−0.0365	−0.02	−0.1933	−2.26	−0.0294	−0.06
Number of trauma centers per 100,000 population in state	−0.0435	0.07	−0.0456	0.04	0.0301	−1.14	0.1851**	−0.50
Number of hospitals per 100,000 population in state	−0.1975	0.14	−0.6406***	0.25	−1.4577*	13.63	−0.2515**	0.34
Sum of residuals from male death rate regressions	0.0204	−0.30	0.0208**	0.04	0.0695	−22.63	0.1421***	−3.26
Residuals from men's death rates, medical causes	0.0064	−0.04	0.0196**	−0.07	0.0312	−4.40	0.0307***	−0.49
Residuals from men's death rates, auto accidents	−0.0037	−0.03	0.0026	0.07	0.0339	1.97	−0.0086**	−0.08
Residuals from men's death rates, other accidental injuries	0.0029	−0.06	−0.0014	0.02	0.0545***	−17.30	0.0004	−0.02
Residuals from men's death rates, intentional injuries	0.0148	−0.17	−0.0001	0.02	−0.0502	−2.90	0.1197***	−2.68
State × five-year period fixed effects[a]	0.0241	0.16	0.1021	0.04	0.1464	1.09	−0.0066	0.12
Year dummy variables	−0.0004*	0.00	−0.0015***	0.00	−0.0087***	−0.21	−0.0002	0.00

Source: Authors' compilation.

Note: See table 15.5 for explanation of how entries were constructed.

[a] Significance levels were not calculated for black-nonblack differences attributable to state × period fixed effects.

*p < .10; **p < .05; ***p < .01

DISCUSSION AND CONCLUSIONS

For all ages, blacks tend to have higher death rates than nonblacks.[7] As we have shown, this pattern certainly holds for children. However, it has proven surprisingly difficult to identify the reasons for these gaps or to explain why they change over time. We have demonstrated that racial inequalities in child death rates vary considerably by cause of death and by age of children. While race is often interpreted as a marker for socioeconomic status, our estimates suggest that the reasons for "excess mortality" among blacks, and for changes in racial gaps in mortality over time, are more complex. For example, while black families have half the income of nonblack families on average, and while higher income is generally predictive of lower death rates, changes in family income can explain little of the change in the gaps over time and often go in the "wrong" direction.

Our strategy of measuring a richer set of factors that may influence childhood death rates by using the residuals from regression models of adult male death rates suggests that future research aimed at explaining the evolution of the gap in black versus nonblack child death rates should widen the focus beyond searching for child-specific factors and look for factors that have affected both child and adult death rates within state, year, and racial groups. Our analysis suggests that whatever these factors are, they have played a major role in influencing childhood death rates and that they often accounted for many of the trends in the gaps in death rates between black and nonblack children over the last two decades of the twentieth century.

Description of Data and Variable Construction

Mortality Data   The mortality data are from the Vital Statistics Mortality: Multiple Cause-of-Death Summary files compiled yearly by the U.S. National Center for Health Statistics. We first aggregated the ICD-9 codes of death in the mortality data files into the following thirty-seven categories:

1. Infectious and Parasitic diseases (ICD 1–139)

2. Cancer (ICD 140–239)

3. Metabolic disorders (ICD 240–259, 270–279, 282–289)

4. Nutrition (ICD 260–269, 280–281)

5. Mental disorder (ICD 290–319)

6. Nervous and sense organs (ICD 320–389)

7. Circulatory problems (ICD 390–459)

8. Respiratory problems (ICD 460–519)

9. Digestive/urogenital (ICD 520–629)

10. Complication of pregnancy (ICD 630–676)

11. Skin problem (ICD 680–709)

12. Skeletal problem (ICD 710–739)

13. Congenital or perinatal problem (ICD 740–779)

14. Ill-defined conditions (ICD 780–799)

15. Motor vehicle collision with pedestrian (ICD 814)

16. Other motor vehicle accident (ICD 810–813, 815–819)

17. Other type vehicle accident (ICD 800–807, 820–829, 840–849)

18. Boating accident (ICD 830–838)

19. Accidental poisoning (ICD 850–869)

20. Medical mishap (ICD 870–879)

21. Falls (ICD 880–888)

22. Conflagration (ICD 890–892)

23. Injury by controlled fire (ICD 893–899)

24. Injury by nature (ICD 900–909)

25. Drowning (ICD 910)

26. Accidental suffocation (ICD 911–913)

27. Accidental injury with firearm missile (ICD 922)

28. Accident with hot or caustic materials (ICD 924)

29. Accident with electric current (ICD 925)

30. Other accident (ICD 923, 914–921, 926–928)

31. Late effects accidental injury (ICD 929)

32. Drug reactions (ICD 930–949)

33. Suicide (ICD 950–959)

34. Homicide or assault (ICD 960–969)

35. Legal intervention (ICD 970–978)

36. War (ICD 990–999)

37. Undetermined if accidental or purposeful (ICD 980–989)

We further aggregated these categories into the following five causes of death:

1. Deaths due to medical causes: categories 1 through 14

2. Deaths due to auto-related accidental injuries: categories 15 through 17

3. Deaths due to other accidental injuries: categories 18 through 31

4. Deaths due to intentional injuries: categories 32 through 34

5. Deaths due to other causes: categories 35 through 37

The fifth category of causes of death was used to compile estimates of deaths due to *all causes* but was omitted from the regression analysis presented in the text. As noted in the text, we also separated out deaths due to AIDS and those due to all other medical causes when analyzing death rates for men ages twenty-five to forty-four.

We aggregated deaths for children into four age categories: ages zero to four, five to nine, ten to fourteen, and fifteen to nineteen, and for our regression analyses we divided our data into two race categories, nonblack and black. (In our descriptive analyses of trends, we analyzed three racial categories, white, black and other [which includes Asians] but resorted to the black versus nonblack categorization in our regression analysis owing to small cell sizes.) Finally, all data on deaths were aggregated by state and by year. Thus, our data on death rates consist of cause × age × race × state × year cells. Finally, all death data were expressed as *rates*, where the denominator is the number of all children in the cell. The latter data were obtained from U.S. Census Bureau population estimates.

CPS Variables

All CPS variables were constructed using the March annual demographic supplements, which contain family income information.

For the median family income variable, we restricted the sample to families with at least one child under the age of eighteen and constructed median family income for blacks and nonblacks by state and year. (All income variables were expressed in 1980 dollars.) The CPS added more categories to the race variable in 1989 and so for 1980 to 1988 nonblack is defined as white plus other and for 1989 to 1998 nonblack is defined as white plus American-Indian plus Asian/Pacific Islander plus other. We also used these income data to construct state-by-year estimates of the difference in family income between the ninetieth and fiftieth percentiles and between the fiftieth and tenth percentiles.

We constructed several variables for mothers in households. We used data for mothers between the ages of fourteen and sixty-five in families with at least one child under the age of eighteen. To identify such mothers in the data, we used the household recode variable (HHR 1) from 1980 to 1988, and a similar variable, detailed household and family status (HHDFMX), from 1989 to 1998. Both these variables identify the relationship and status of the person in the household and in the family.

The mothers' education variable is constructed as the average number of completed years of education of mothers by state, year, and race (nonblack and black). Beginning in 1992, the CPS changed the focus of the education question to be more specific as to degree completion. We used the recommendations in Jaeger (1997) for reconciling the education questions before and after 1992.

To construct the fraction of single mothers by state and year, we simply divided the total number of single mothers by the total number of mothers in each state and year. We identified single mothers using the variable PARENT, which asks if both parents are present in the household as opposed to only mother or only father or neither. To ensure that this identified single mothers correctly, we also looked at the family type variable (husband-wife, male reference head, or female reference head) for these single mothers.

For the variable fraction of mothers employed by state, year, and race, we identifed mothers as employed if the mother reported working any positive hours in the last week (HOURSWO changed to A__LFSR in 1989). We also used the employment status recode variable for 1980 to 1988 and the labor force status recode variable for 1989 to 1998 (unavailable for 1994) to double-check, and the two time series were similar.

We also constructed three measures of health care access. Using CPS data and information on Medicaid eligibility rules by year, we constructed estimates of what fraction of a fixed national sample of children were eligible for Medicaid in each state, year, and race group. We used the 1990 population of all children under age nineteen in the CPS as our fixed national sample. For 1980 to 1985, the income cutoff for Medicaid was the same as the cutoff for AFDC, so we calculated what fraction of the fixed sample of children lived in households with single heads and income less than the AFDC yearly payment standards.

Starting with OBRA 1986, the government started to break the link between AFDC and Medicaid, initially for younger children and then for older children. We used the income eligibility cutoffs for Medicaid as set by these laws (OBRA 1986–1987, Medicare Catastrophic Coverage Act, 1988, OBRA 1989–1990) to determine eligibility after 1985.[8] For children (generally the oldest ones) who were not explicitly covered by the Medicaid expansions, we used the AFDC income cutoffs to determine eligibility. The data for AFDC payment standards for different years were obtained from the *Green Book*, a welfare rules dataset obtained from Robert Moffitt's website and the Welfare Rules Database compiled by the Urban Institute. Since SCHIP (State Child Health Insurance Program) began in 1998, we used the income cutoffs for the SCHIP program to determine eligibility in 1998. These income cutoffs were obtained from the maternal and child health section of the National Governors' Association (NGA) Center for Best Practices website (www.nga.org/center/ topics/1,1188,D—3782,00.html). This methodology for constructing the Medicaid eligibility index follows that of Currie and Gruber (1996a).

We also constructed a measure of hospitals and trauma centers available to the population in a state for each year of our data. To construct the hospital index, we used data from the American Hospital Association's (AHA) annual surveys of all hospitals and medical networks. We constructed a measure of the number of hospitals in each state and year per 100,000 of the population in that state and year. We also used these data to construct a similar measure of the number of certified trauma centers per 100,000 of the population. We had access to AHA data only for 1982, 1984, 1985, 1991, 1995, and 1997, so we merged data on the number of hospitals by state from the Area Resource File (ARF) for 1980 and 1985 to 1995. For years where we had both AHA and ARF data, we compared the number of hospitals in each state, and measures using both datasets were the same. So we used AHA data for 1982, 1984, and 1997 and ARF data for the remaining years. For years where we had neither AHA nor ARF data, we imputed the value linearly. For the trauma variable, we used the AHA data exclusively.

TABLE 15A.1   *Trends in Child Death Rates, by Race and Age, 1980 to 1998*

Panel A: Death Rates for

	Due to Medical Causes					Due to Auto Accidents				
Year	White	Black	Other	All Racial Groups	Black-White Gap	White	Black	Other	All Racial Groups	Black-White Gap
1980	254.0	531.7	228.7	290.4	277.7	8.4	10.5	11.5	8.5	2.1
1981	239.7	491.6	214.9	272.8	251.9	7.3	8.8	9.4	7.3	1.4
1982	228.7	468.4	199.0	260.6	239.7	7.2	9.2	9.5	7.2	2.0
1983	215.4	448.8	191.1	246.5	233.3	6.9	8.5	6.9	6.7	1.5
1984	208.2	432.5	181.9	237.8	224.3	6.2	8.0	8.9	6.2	1.8
1985	207.5	439.3	174.1	238.7	231.8	6.4	8.6	9.6	6.5	2.2
1986	197.9	438.5	165.6	230.4	240.7	6.3	8.5	9.1	6.4	2.3
1987	191.9	443.1	166.1	226.8	251.2	6.5	8.5	5.8	6.5	2.1
1988	192.2	446.2	160.6	227.5	254.0	6.6	8.1	7.0	6.4	1.5
1989	187.9	455.2	175.4	227.0	267.3	6.3	7.8	10.2	6.4	1.5
1990	178.9	433.3	149.2	215.4	254.4	5.5	8.3	7.5	5.8	2.8
1991	168.0	416.5	132.6	203.6	248.5	5.4	7.5	5.2	5.3	2.2
1992	155.8	387.7	128.9	189.3	231.9	4.9	7.6	5.0	5.1	2.7
1993	150.3	370.3	120.4	181.6	220.0	5.0	8.2	6.1	5.2	3.2
1994	142.8	346.4	121.4	171.7	203.6	5.3	8.9	5.9	5.5	3.7
1995	137.2	321.1	104.4	162.3	183.9	4.8	7.3	4.7	4.9	2.5
1996	132.5	313.5	105.0	156.5	181.1	5.0	7.7	5.5	5.1	2.7
1997	131.9	308.9	102.7	154.3	177.0	4.4	7.6	5.0	4.6	3.2
1998	131.5	321.2	108.8	155.4	189.7	4.4	8.1	3.8	4.5	3.7
Percentage change for:										
1980 to 1984	−18.0%	−18.7%	−20.4%	−18.1%	−19.2%	−26.2%	−23.4%	−22.3%	−26.7%	−12.1%
1985 to 1989	−9.4	3.6	0.8	−4.9	15.3	−0.8	−8.9	5.7	−1.9	−32.3
1990 to 1994	−20.1	−20.1	−18.6	−20.2	−20.0	−4.5	7.6	−21.2	−4.8	31.6
1995 to 1998	−4.1	0.0	4.2	−4.3	3.1	−9.7	10.8	−19.9	−9.0	51.1
1980 to 1998	−48.2	−39.6	−52.4	−46.5	−31.7	−48.3	−23.0	−67.1	−47.6	80.6

Children Age Zero to Four

	Due to Other Accidental Injuries					Due to Intentional Injuries				
	White	Black	Other	All Racial Groups	Black-White Gap	White	Black	Other	All Racial Groups	Black-White Gap
	16.2	31.0	15.8	17.9	14.9	2.3	8.8	1.6	3.2	6.5
	14.4	30.0	14.4	16.4	15.6	2.2	9.0	3.0	3.2	6.8
	13.8	27.5	13.4	15.2	13.8	2.3	9.5	4.0	3.5	7.2
	13.7	27.0	9.4	14.9	13.3	1.9	8.5	3.2	3.0	6.6
	12.2	24.0	13.9	13.5	11.8	2.4	8.5	1.7	3.3	6.1
	12.7	22.5	13.1	13.6	9.8	2.3	7.9	1.7	3.0	5.7
	13.0	24.7	12.0	14.1	11.8	2.4	10.7	2.6	3.6	8.2
	12.9	25.3	10.7	14.1	12.4	2.4	8.8	2.3	3.3	6.4
	12.0	26.1	9.7	13.4	14.1	2.8	10.1	2.0	3.8	7.3
	11.5	25.2	11.5	13.1	13.6	2.6	10.9	4.2	3.9	8.4
	10.9	21.4	9.3	12.1	10.5	2.5	10.5	3.2	3.8	8.0
	11.5	22.7	8.9	12.9	11.1	2.9	11.3	3.5	4.1	8.5
	10.1	19.0	9.0	11.0	8.9	2.7	10.2	3.1	3.8	7.5
	10.5	21.2	9.0	11.7	10.7	2.7	11.3	3.8	4.1	8.6
	9.7	21.0	8.4	10.9	11.3	2.8	10.2	3.6	3.9	7.4
	9.2	17.5	9.0	10.1	8.3	2.8	10.3	2.4	3.9	7.5
	8.5	17.8	7.5	9.4	9.4	2.8	10.0	3.0	3.9	7.2
	8.4	15.8	8.2	9.2	7.4	2.7	8.9	3.2	3.5	6.2
	8.2	16.4	5.2	8.9	8.2	2.6	11.0	2.2	3.7	8.4
	−24.5%	−22.6%	−11.9%	−24.3%	−20.6%	5.3 %	−2.5%	1.4%	1.9%	−5.3%
	−9.0	11.9	−12.0	−3.0	38.9	13.3	37.9	146.0	28.9	47.8
	−11.3	−2.2	−9.4	−9.5	7.3	13.5	−3.2	12.7	5.0	−8.3
	−10.6	−6.1	−42.9	−11.3	−1.1	−6.8	6.7	−8.1	−4.4	11.7
	−49.0	−47.1	−67.3	−50.0	−44.9	12.7	24.9	34.8	14.9	29.2

(Table continues on p. 618.)

TABLE 15A.1   (*Continued*)

Panel B: Death Rates for

	Due to Medical Causes					Due to Auto Accidents				
Year	White	Black	Other	All Racial Groups	Black-White Gap	White	Black	Other	All Racial Groups	Black-White Gap
1980	14.6	16.4	10.8	14.6	1.9	7.5	10.0	8.3	7.7	2.6
1981	13.5	16.5	8.1	13.8	3.0	7.2	8.8	7.6	7.2	1.6
1982	13.6	16.8	9.5	14.0	3.2	6.6	8.9	4.4	6.6	2.3
1983	12.7	15.2	10.3	12.9	2.5	6.2	8.2	8.3	6.5	2.0
1984	12.0	15.7	8.2	12.4	3.7	6.2	7.9	5.1	6.2	1.7
1985	11.4	15.4	9.5	11.8	4.0	6.3	7.7	7.7	6.5	1.4
1986	11.0	14.1	9.8	11.2	3.2	5.9	8.9	8.5	6.3	3.1
1987	11.5	14.6	10.0	11.9	3.2	6.5	8.5	5.4	6.5	2.1
1988	10.7	15.9	10.9	11.5	5.1	6.5	8.8	5.1	6.6	2.3
1989	10.9	14.7	10.7	11.4	3.8	6.1	8.5	4.9	6.2	2.4
1990	10.7	15.0	9.7	11.2	4.3	5.2	7.0	6.2	5.4	1.8
1991	10.6	15.2	8.7	11.2	4.6	5.0	7.0	4.1	5.0	2.0
1992	9.8	15.7	7.9	10.5	5.9	4.7	7.4	5.1	4.9	2.7
1993	10.7	15.8	8.4	11.3	5.1	4.5	6.8	4.5	4.7	2.3
1994	9.7	15.4	8.5	10.6	5.7	4.5	7.2	4.1	4.7	2.7
1995	9.4	16.2	8.2	10.5	6.8	4.6	6.4	4.4	4.7	1.8
1996	9.4	15.0	7.3	10.2	5.6	4.3	6.3	3.9	4.4	2.0
1997	8.8	14.9	7.9	9.6	6.2	4.1	6.3	3.7	4.1	2.3
1998	8.3	13.5	6.1	9.0	5.2	3.8	6.9	3.6	4.1	3.0
Percentage change for:										
1980 to 1984	−17.2%	−4.2%	−24.1%	−15.0%	97.5%	−16.9%	−21.3%	−39.1%	−19.8%	−34.4%
1985 to 1989	−3.9	−4.4	13.1	−3.1	−5.9	−2.7	9.9	−36.0	−3.9	65.9
1990 to 1994	−9.8	2.3	−12.4	−5.6	32.3	−13.4	3.3	−34.0	−13.1	52.3
1995 to 1998	−11.9	−17.1	−25.3	−14.3	−24.3	−16.5	7.4	−18.0	−12.8	69.0
1980 to 1998	−43.0	−18.0	−43.4	−38.7	176.5	−48.6	−31.5	−57.0	−47.2	18.6

Children Age Five to Nine

	Due to Other Accidental Injuries					Due to Intentional Injuries				
White	Black	Other	All Racial Groups	Black-White Gap		White	Black	Other	All Racial Groups	Black-White Gap
5.7	12.6	7.5	6.5	6.9		0.8	2.0	0.8	1.0	1.3
5.6	10.8	6.6	6.4	5.2		0.7	1.9	1.2	0.9	1.2
5.5	11.7	6.5	6.3	6.2		0.8	2.2	0.6	1.0	1.4
5.0	9.9	5.5	5.6	4.9		0.8	1.8	1.3	1.0	1.0
4.5	9.9	4.4	5.2	5.4		0.7	2.8	1.0	1.0	2.1
4.4	10.3	6.9	5.2	6.0		0.7	2.4	2.0	1.0	1.6
4.3	10.0	4.1	5.0	5.7		0.5	2.4	1.1	0.8	1.9
4.5	8.7	5.1	4.9	4.2		0.6	1.8	0.9	0.8	1.2
4.1	9.6	5.2	4.9	5.5		0.8	2.4	0.9	1.0	1.6
4.3	9.4	3.9	4.9	5.1		0.7	2.5	2.3	1.0	1.8
3.7	7.6	4.0	4.1	4.0		0.6	2.4	0.7	0.9	1.7
3.6	7.8	3.3	4.2	4.1		0.6	1.9	0.8	0.7	1.3
3.2	6.7	3.1	3.6	3.5		0.6	2.1	1.7	0.9	1.5
3.0	7.7	4.6	3.6	4.8		0.8	2.5	0.9	1.0	1.6
2.8	7.0	4.6	3.4	4.1		0.6	1.9	1.2	0.9	1.3
3.1	5.7	3.9	3.5	2.6		0.7	1.9	1.0	0.8	1.2
2.9	6.7	3.6	3.4	3.8		0.8	1.9	0.7	0.9	1.2
2.6	6.5	4.4	3.2	3.9		0.7	2.1	1.3	0.9	1.4
2.8	6.7	3.5	3.2	3.9		0.7	1.9	1.3	0.9	1.2
−21.4%	−21.7%	−41.7%	−20.8%	−21.9%		−15.0%	36.3%	26.0%	3.4%	67.5%
−0.9	−9.1	−43.1	−5.4	−15.1		−7.3	4.9	15.7	−1.0	10.5
−22.4	−8.8	15.9	−16.3	3.8		0.5	−19.0	66.9	−1.4	−26.3
−10.5	17.2	−11.5	−6.9	50.4		−0.6	0.1	37.7	4.5	0.5
−51.2	−46.9	−53.5	−50.9	−43.3		−14.9	−7.2	58.4	−10.3	−2.5

(Table continues on p. 620.)

TABLE 15A.1   (*Continued*)

Panel C: Death Rates for

	Due to Medical Causes					Due to Auto Accidents				
Year	White	Black	Other	All Racial Groups	Black-White Gap	White	Black	Other	All Racial Groups	Black-White Gap
1980	12.6	16.2	10.0	13.0	3.6	8.9	6.4	10.2	8.4	−2.5
1981	12.1	15.7	10.0	12.5	3.6	8.4	5.2	7.3	7.8	−3.2
1982	11.8	15.5	8.5	12.3	3.7	7.7	5.3	4.5	7.1	−2.4
1983	11.0	15.7	11.0	11.7	4.7	7.5	5.2	5.8	7.0	−2.3
1984	11.6	15.1	10.3	12.1	3.6	8.0	5.7	3.6	7.4	−2.3
1985	10.8	15.8	8.1	11.3	5.0	8.2	6.3	5.4	7.6	−1.9
1986	11.3	15.0	7.5	11.8	3.7	8.5	6.2	7.4	7.8	6.7
1987	10.0	14.8	9.3	10.7	4.7	8.5	6.1	6.9	7.9	−2.4
1988	10.8	15.4	8.8	11.4	4.5	8.1	7.1	6.2	7.5	−1.0
1989	11.0	16.1	9.2	11.6	5.1	7.6	5.6	5.8	7.0	−1.9
1990	10.5	15.4	8.3	11.0	5.0	6.8	6.1	5.7	6.4	−0.7
1991	10.5	14.5	7.5	10.9	4.0	6.4	6.7	5.2	6.2	0.3
1992	10.1	14.1	7.8	10.5	4.0	5.9	6.0	3.8	5.6	0.1
1993	10.6	14.8	8.2	11.1	4.2	6.1	6.7	4.9	5.9	0.6
1994	9.9	15.7	9.5	10.8	5.8	6.5	6.5	4.1	6.2	0.0
1995	10.2	17.1	9.1	11.1	6.9	6.5	6.1	5.4	6.1	−0.3
1996	9.8	16.9	7.7	10.7	7.1	6.4	5.1	4.6	5.8	−1.3
1997	9.6	14.8	7.1	10.2	5.2	6.1	6.3	4.8	5.8	0.2
1998	9.1	13.9	8.6	9.7	4.8	5.6	5.6	5.2	5.3	0.0
Percentage change for:										
1980 to 1984	−8.2%	−6.5%	2.9%	−7.1%	−0.3%	−9.9%	−10.4%	−64.8%	−12.5%	−8.6%
1985 to 1989	2.4	2.3	14.5	2.5	2.1	−8.0	−10.3	7.7	−7.5	−0.4
1990 to 1994	−5.0	2.0	14.9	−2.2	16.7	−3.6	7.1	−28.4	−3.3	−95.3
1995 to 1998	−10.7	−18.9	−5.7	−13.1	−31.0	−13.0	−7.9	−3.9	−13 .0	−106.0
1980 to 1998	−27.6	−14.1	−14.3	−25.5	33.0	−36.7	−12.0	−49.6	−37.3	−100.8

Children Age Ten to Fourteen

	Due to Other Accidental Injuries					Due to Intentional Injuries			
White	Black	Other	All Racial Groups	Black-White Gap	White	Black	Other	All Racial Groups	Black-White Gap
6.1	10.2	5.8	6.4	4.1	2.0	3.5	1.1	2.2	1.5
5.5	9.9	8.2	6.0	4.5	1.9	4.5	2.7	2.3	2.7
5.4	8.5	4.0	5.6	3.0	2.0	3.5	3.4	2.2	1.5
5.4	9.4	3.4	5.7	4.0	2.0	3.7	1.9	2.3	1.7
5.0	9.2	3.8	5.3	4.3	2.6	4.4	2.8	2.9	1.8
4.8	8.7	4.7	5.2	3.8	3.0	3.8	3.0	3.1	0.8
4.8	9.2	5.7	5.2	4.4	2.8	4.5	2.6	3.0	1.7
4.2	8.9	4.9	4.7	4.7	2.7	5.8	2.8	3.1	3.1
4.3	8.2	5.1	4.7	3.9	2.5	6.4	3.2	3.1	3.9
4.2	8.6	4.8	4.6	4.5	2.7	7.0	2.8	3.3	4.3
3.8	7.0	3.9	4.0	3.2	2.9	7.5	2.2	3.6	4.6
4.0	7.2	2.9	4.2	3.1	3.0	7.6	1.8	3.5	4.6
3.4	6.3	5.2	3.8	2.9	3.3	8.5	3.0	4.0	5.2
3.5	6.1	3.9	3.8	2.6	3.3	9.3	3.5	4.1	6.0
3.2	6.9	3.3	3.7	3.7	3.1	8.2	3.0	3.8	5.1
3.4	6.6	2.8	3.7	3.2	3.4	6.6	3.8	3.8	3.3
3.0	6.2	4.8	3.5	3.1	2.8	5.9	3.5	3.2	3.0
3.1	5.5	3.6	3.4	2.3	2.7	5.3	2.8	3.0	2.7
2.9	5.4	2.7	3.1	2.5	2.9	4.4	3.3	3.1	1.5
−19.0%	−9.2%	−34.6%	−17.4%	5.6%	29.7%	24.8%	160.9%	28.4%	18.2%
−14.3	−0.1	1.7	−10.9	18.0	−9.4	83.3	−8.3	5.5	420.5
−14.8	−1.3	−13.8	−7.6	14.7	8.7	9.4	37.8	5.7	9.8
−15.2	−18.2	−5.7	−15.6	−21.4	−14.9	−33.7	−13.1	−17.8	−53.3
−52.7	−46.8	−53.6	−50.8	−37.9	44.3	25.8	213.3	37.7	1.2

(Table continues on p. 622.)

TABLE 15A.1   (*Continued*)

Panel D: Death Rates for

	Due to Medical Causes					Due to Auto Accidents				
Year	White	Black	Other	All Racial Groups	Black-White Gap	White	Black	Other	All Racial Groups	Black-White Gap
1980	18.7	26.8	14.8	19.6	8.1	48.9	15.9	38.4	43.6	−33.0
1981	17.3	24.5	17.3	18.2	7.2	44.5	13.6	29.4	38.9	−31.0
1982	18.1	25.1	17.9	19.1	6.9	39.4	14.4	28.3	34.7	−25.0
1983	17.9	24.7	16.5	18.8	6.8	37.7	13.3	21.7	32.9	−24.5
1984	16.7	24.1	12.6	17.5	7.4	38.7	14.4	26.8	34.2	−24.3
1985	16.3	25.2	13.0	17.6	8.9	38.1	15.3	25.1	33.6	−22.8
1986	16.6	25.2	12.5	17.6	8.6	42.2	17.2	23.2	37.0	−25.0
1987	15.9	25.3	10.5	16.9	9.4	41.1	18.3	25.2	36.3	−22.8
1988	15.8	26.3	12.3	17.2	10.5	41.0	20.1	25.6	36.1	−21.0
1989	15.5	26.5	13.3	16.9	11.0	38.9	17.8	23.4	34.1	−21.1
1990	15.8	24.5	11.6	16.7	8.8	37.1	19.7	25.8	32.7	−17.4
1991	15.9	25.3	12.9	17.1	9.5	34.7	19.8	21.6	30.6	−14.9
1992	15.6	25.1	11.0	16.6	9.6	31.0	17.9	22.4	27.2	−13.1
1993	15.7	24.8	13.3	16.9	9.2	31.7	17.8	21.0	27.7	−13.9
1994	15.4	27.3	11.2	16.9	11.9	32.1	20.0	19.1	28.2	−12.1
1995	15.6	27.1	12.1	16.9	11.6	31.0	20.2	21.4	27.3	−10.9
1996	14.6	25.1	10.3	15.8	10.4	31.2	20.9	20.4	27.4	−10.3
1997	15.0	23.5	12.6	16.1	8.5	29.6	20.0	20.2	26.3	−9.6
1998	14.1	23.6	10.7	15.1	9.4	29.2	17.8	17.5	25.5	−11.4
Percentage change for:										
1980 to 1984	−10.9%	−10.4%	−15.3%	−10.8%	−9.1%	−20.7%	−9.3%	−30.2%	−21.4%	−26.2%
1985 to 1989	−5.1	5.2	1.9	−4.0	24.1	2.1	16.1	−6.8	1.3	−7.3
1990 to 1994	−2.2	11.4	−3.5	1.0	35.9	−13.4	1.6	−25.8	−13.7	−30.4
1995 to 1998	−9.2	−13.1	−12.0	−11.1	−18.3	−5.9	−11.8	−18.3	−6.6	5.0
1980 to 1998	−24.5	−12.2	−28.1	−23.2	16.1	−40.2	11.9	−54.4	−41.4	−65.3

Source: Authors' compilation.

Children Age Fifteen to Nineteen

	Due to Other Accidental Injuries					Due to Intentional Injuries			
White	Black	Other	All Racial Groups	Black-White Gap	White	Black	Other	All Racial Groups	Black-White Gap
14.0	14.5	14.4	13.6	0.4	16.8	33.0	17.7	19.4	16.2
11.6	12.8	9.7	11.6	1.2	15.9	33.1	20.4	18.7	17.2
11.3	10.5	14.1	11.1	−0.8	16.0	32.6	16.0	18.2	16.6
10.6	10.5	9.3	10.2	−0.1	14.5	30.7	19.5	17.1	16.2
9.9	10.1	10.2	9.8	0.2	15.1	28.4	15.9	17.2	13.3
9.3	10.5	8.9	9.2	1.2	15.7	33.1	18.7	18.3	17.4
9.8	10.9	8.8	9.7	1.1	17.1	36.4	15.5	19.9	19.3
8.2	10.7	6.9	8.2	2.5	16.1	42.2	15.1	19.9	26.1
8.5	9.6	8.6	8.5	1.1	17.6	51.0	18.0	22.6	33.4
8.3	9.6	8.0	8.2	1.3	18.2	59.2	18.5	24.3	40.9
8.3	10.0	9.2	8.2	1.6	20.1	72.6	21.1	27.8	52.5
8.0	11.7	5.4	8.1	3.8	21.0	82.0	22.2	30.2	61.1
7.2	10.2	7.3	7.4	3.0	20.6	79.8	22.0	29.5	59.1
7.4	11.2	7.7	7.6	3.9	20.9	87.3	23.2	30.8	66.4
6.9	9.8	6.4	7.1	2.9	20.6	84.9	27.1	30.3	64.3
7.3	9.1	5.3	7.2	1.9	20.3	71.5	22.1	27.7	51.3
6.9	7.9	7.0	6.7	1.0	17.9	63.7	21.3	24.7	45.8
6.9	6.9	5.2	6.5	0.1	17.0	55.5	18.6	22.3	38.5
6.8	7.6	5.8	6.7	0.8	15.7	46.7	16.9	20.1	31.0
−29.5%	−30.2%	−29.2%	−28.0%	−51.2%	−10.0%	−13.9%	−10.0%	−11.2%	−17.9%
−10.4	−8.1	−10.4	−11.1	10.2	16.5	79.1	−1.5	33.0	135.5
−16.4	−1.6	−30.0	−13.2	73.5	2.7	17.0	28.1	9.0	22.5
−6.5	−16.9	9.4	−8.0	−57.3	−22.4	−34.6	−23.4	−27.5	−39.5
−51.5	−47.4	−60.0	−51.2	82.9	−6.2	41.9	−4.3	3.6	91.5

TABLE 15A.2　　*Trends in Death Rates of Adult Males, Age Twenty-Five to Forty-Four, by Race, 1980 to 1998*

Year	Medical Causes, Excluding AIDS				AIDS			
	White	Black	Other	All	White	Black	Other	All
1980	94.5	263.1	79.5	111.6	0.0	0.0	0.0	0.0
1981	93.2	251.3	77.1	109.3	0.0	0.0	0.0	0.0
1982	91.6	239.0	69.2	106.5	0.0	0.0	0.0	0.0
1983	91.5	238.7	69.7	106.5	0.0	0.0	0.0	0.0
1984	94.8	252.3	69.1	110.8	0.0	0.0	0.0	0.0
1985	101.1	273.0	66.5	118.5	0.0	0.0	0.0	0.0
1986	109.3	295.9	68.0	128.2	0.0	0.0	0.0	0.0
1987	94.3	255.0	64.7	110.9	19.2	60.2	4.3	23.2
1988	94.8	258.6	61.4	111.8	23.0	74.3	6.6	28.1
1989	93.5	251.6	66.2	110.2	30.8	94.1	7.9	37.0
1990	91.2	237.8	65.3	106.8	35.0	101.8	8.0	41.5
1991	92.6	231.1	62.7	107.3	39.3	117.6	10.4	47.1
1992	94.0	221.6	62.4	107.6	42.9	137.3	10.2	52.5
1993	95.4	222.7	68.6	109.3	45.5	155.4	12.6	57.1
1994	95.3	217.0	66.7	108.5	48.5	178.1	15.5	62.5
1995	97.5	213.2	66.9	110.0	47.1	181.9	16.0	61.9
1996	93.9	198.9	67.1	105.3	29.8	139.1	10.0	42.1
1997	92.2	189.2	65.1	102.8	13.3	76.7	4.9	20.6
1998	92.1	184.5	66.2	102.3	9.9	59.4	3.7	15.7
Percentage change 1980 to 1984	0.3%	−4.1%	−13.1%	−0.7%	—	—	—	—
Percentage change 1985 to 1989	−7.6	−7.8	−0.4	−7.0	—	—	—	—
Percentage change 1990 to 1994	4.5	−8.8	2.1	1.6	38.5	74.8	93.8	50.5
Percentage change 1995 to 1998	−5.6	−13.4	−1.2	−7.1	−79.0	−67.4	−77.1	−74.5
Percentage change 1980 to 1998	−2.5	−29.9	−16.8	−8.3	—	—	—	—

Source: Authors' compilation.

Auto Accidents				Other Accidental Injuries				Intentional Injuries			
White	Black	Other	All	White	Black	Other	All	White	Black	Other	All
43.1	44.9	37.9	43.1	22.5	44.7	23.3	24.9	41.7	147.7	33.2	52.4
43.1	42.0	34.0	42.7	21.3	43.1	18.2	23.5	41.6	142.6	30.7	51.9
36.5	38.0	27.5	36.4	21.5	40.7	19.7	23.5	40.1	131.5	29.4	49.4
34.2	36.6	28.7	34.3	21.2	38.7	17.6	23.0	38.5	110.2	28.8	45.9
34.2	37.5	27.2	34.3	20.6	37.3	15.3	22.2	38.0	106.9	26.2	45.1
33.3	38.0	29.1	33.7	20.7	38.9	14.3	22.4	37.5	104.1	26.9	44.3
33.8	40.6	28.8	34.4	21.0	39.4	15.9	22.8	38.8	115.4	27.9	46.8
34.0	38.9	28.7	34.3	19.5	39.8	16.5	21.6	36.9	109.1	25.6	44.5
33.3	39.2	26.7	33.7	20.7	40.5	15.1	22.7	37.2	115.9	27.1	45.6
32.1	39.1	25.9	32.6	20.9	38.8	13.8	22.6	36.9	117.4	27.4	45.6
31.7	38.5	27.1	32.3	19.6	34.6	14.1	21.1	38.4	124.3	27.1	47.7
28.5	34.7	25.0	29.0	19.3	37.8	14.1	21.2	38.6	120.8	28.6	47.7
27.0	30.7	22.1	27.2	20.3	32.7	14.1	21.5	37.9	113.5	25.1	46.2
26.9	31.5	18.6	27.1	22.7	37.8	14.3	24.1	37.8	113.9	28.8	46.4
26.5	28.9	19.8	26.4	22.5	36.4	14.5	23.8	38.1	108.7	30.3	46.2
26.4	32.7	22.3	27.0	23.0	33.5	14.6	23.9	37.1	95.5	26.3	43.6
25.9	30.7	21.5	26.2	22.1	29.3	11.9	22.5	35.5	88.0	26.8	41.4
25.0	31.3	21.7	25.6	23.0	30.6	14.2	23.5	34.6	80.7	24.7	39.8
24.7	31.5	19.5	25.3	23.5	28.5	12.4	23.5	33.6	73.1	24.7	38.0
−20.6%	−16.6%	−28.2%	−20.4%	−8.7%	−16.6%	−34.2%	−10.7%	−8.7%	−27.6%	−20.9%	−14.1%
−3.7	2.7	−11.0	−3.1	1.0	−0.2	−3.5	0.9	−1.6	12.8	1.8	2.8
−16.6	−24.9	−26.7	−18.1	15.0	5.2	2.6	13.0	−0.6	−12.6	12.2	−3.2
−6.5	−3.8	−12.3	−6.3	2.1	−15.0	−15.3	−1.4	−9.5	−23.4	−6.1	−12.8
−42.6	−30.0	−48.4	−41.3	4.2	−36.2	−46.8	−5.3	−19.5	−50.5	−25.7	−27.5

TABLE 15A.3   *Regressions of Death Rates by Cause for Adult Males, Age Twenty-Five to Forty-Four, Used to Form Residuals for Child Death Rate Regressions*

	Deaths Due to Medical Causes, Excluding AIDS	Deaths Due to Auto Accidents	Deaths Due to Other Accidental Injuries	Deaths Due to Intentional Causes
Log of median family income	−133.546***	−12.396***	−13.516***	−79.907***
	(5.735)	(1.784)	(1.511)	(3.675)
Log of gap between 90th and 50th percentiles of family income	−6.850	−9.369***	8.182***	8.613***
	(5.423)	(2.134)	(1.259)	(3.125)
Log of gap between 50th and 10th percentiles of family income	116.481***	−8.830***	−1.140	20.057***
	(7.537)	(2.513)	(1.650)	(4.135)
Average number of years of schooling of mothers	−9.872***	−4.875***	−2.513***	−3.140*
	(2.928)	(1.026)	(0.613)	(1.706)
Fraction of mothers employed	−70.681***	15.708***	−14.045***	−11.100
	(15.046)	(4.304)	(3.639)	(8.634)
Fraction of mothers who are single	140.360***	11.961**	−12.755***	0.256
	(21.806)	(5.693)	(3.970)	(10.210)
Fraction of children in state eligible for Medicaid	119.549***	−30.368***	21.017***	34.249***
	(17.839)	(4.375)	(3.635)	(10.694)
Number of trauma centers per 100,000 population in state	10.758***	−2.522***	−0.732	0.979
	(1.982)	(0.524)	(0.446)	(0.858)
Number of hospitals per 100,000 population in state	−1.852***	1.868***	0.768***	−0.066
	(0.419)	(0.201)	(0.148)	(0.263)
Constant	494.730***	382.200***	123.252***	599.623***
	(62.854)	(21.188)	(19.291)	(32.520)
Observations	1,456	1,456	1,456	1,456
R-squared	0.70	0.50	0.41	0.68

Source: Authors' compilation.

Notes: Robust standard errors are in parentheses. Estimates are weighted by number of men, age twenty-five to forty-four, in race group × state group, using data from 1990 U.S. Census of Population.

*p < .10; **p < .05; ***p < .01

TABLE 15A.4   Means of Explanatory Variables in Childhood Death Rate Regressions, by Race, Age Group, and Year Group

Age Group	Blacks				Nonblacks				Black-Nonblack Difference				Average Annual Percentage Change
	1980 to 1984	1985 to 1989	1990 to 1994	1995 to 1998	1980 to 1984	1985 to 1989	1990 to 1994	1995 to 1998	1980 to 1984	1985 to 1989	1990 to 1994	1995 to 1998	
Log of median family income													
Zero to four	9.283	9.292	9.238	9.344	9.947	10.015	10.007	10.035	−0.664	−0.723	−0.769	−0.691	−0.07%
Five to nine	9.278	9.284	9.231	9.341	9.944	10.012	10.004	10.034	−0.666	−0.728	−0.773	−0.693	−0.07
Ten to fourteen	9.274	9.277	9.229	9.337	9.943	10.010	10.003	10.033	−0.669	−0.733	−0.774	−0.696	−0.07
Fifteen to nineteen	9.274	9.277	9.231	9.337	9.943	10.012	10.005	10.036	−0.669	−0.735	−0.774	−0.699	−0.08
Log of gap between 90th and 50th percentiles of family income													
Zero to four	9.955	10.104	10.166	10.277	9.951	10.085	10.143	10.245	0.004	0.019	0.023	0.032	2.66
Five to nine	9.952	10.100	10.161	10.271	9.946	10.078	10.136	10.238	0.006	0.022	0.025	0.033	2.33
Ten to fourteen	9.949	10.097	10.159	10.268	9.942	10.075	10.133	10.235	0.007	0.022	0.026	0.033	2.19
Fifteen to nineteen	9.948	10.098	10.160	10.270	9.942	10.077	10.136	10.238	0.006	0.021	0.024	0.032	2.32
Log of gap between 50th and 10th percentiles of family income													
Zero to four	9.562	9.682	9.649	9.677	9.573	9.677	9.645	9.663	−0.011	0.005	0.004	0.014	15.43
Five to nine	9.559	9.678	9.645	9.675	9.571	9.674	9.644	9.662	−0.012	0.004	0.001	0.013	30.86
Ten to fourteen	9.558	9.678	9.645	9.676	9.569	9.672	9.644	9.663	−0.011	0.006	0.001	0.013	19.75
Fifteen to nineteen	9.559	9.680	9.648	9.679	9.569	9.674	9.646	9.665	−0.010	0.006	0.002	0.014	14.81
Average years of schooling of mothers													
Zero to four	11.699	12.120	12.410	12.563	12.270	12.558	12.807	12.937	−0.571	−0.438	−0.397	−0.374	0.82
Five to nine	11.684	12.109	12.405	12.559	12.271	12.561	12.814	12.944	−0.587	−0.452	−0.409	−0.385	0.82
Ten to fourteen	11.676	12.103	12.403	12.558	12.269	12.561	12.817	12.950	−0.593	−0.458	−0.414	−0.392	0.80
Fifteen to nineteen	11.677	12.102	12.404	12.560	12.265	12.560	12.817	12.955	−0.588	−0.458	−0.413	−0.395	0.77

(Table continues on p. 628.)

TABLE 15A.4 (Continued)

Age Group	Blacks				Nonblacks				Black-Nonblack Difference				Average Annual Percentage Change
	1980 to 1984	1985 to 1989	1990 to 1994	1995 to 1998	1980 to 1984	1985 to 1989	1990 to 1994	1995 to 1998	1980 to 1984	1985 to 1989	1990 to 1994	1995 to 1998	
Fraction of mothers employed													
Zero to four	0.493	0.534	0.552	0.621	0.517	0.576	0.607	0.642	−0.024	−0.042	−0.055	−0.021	0.16
Five to nine	0.493	0.534	0.553	0.621	0.517	0.577	0.609	0.644	−0.024	−0.043	−0.056	−0.023	0.05
Ten to fourteen	0.492	0.533	0.553	0.621	0.516	0.576	0.609	0.645	−0.024	−0.043	−0.056	−0.024	0.00
Fifteen to nineteen	0.491	0.533	0.553	0.621	0.516	0.576	0.608	0.644	−0.025	−0.043	−0.055	−0.023	0.10
Fraction of mothers who are single													
Zero to four	0.236	0.263	0.285	0.299	0.217	0.239	0.261	0.274	0.019	0.024	0.024	0.025	0.48
Five to nine	0.235	0.264	0.285	0.300	0.216	0.238	0.260	0.273	0.019	0.026	0.025	0.027	0.61
Ten to fourteen	0.235	0.264	0.285	0.300	0.215	0.238	0.260	0.273	0.020	0.026	0.025	0.027	0.53
Fifteen to nineteen	0.235	0.264	0.285	0.300	0.217	0.240	0.262	0.275	0.018	0.024	0.023	0.025	0.58
Fraction of children eligible for Medicaid													
Zero to four	0.291	0.342	0.657	0.699	0.066	0.087	0.296	0.349	0.225	0.255	0.361	0.350	0.78
Five to nine	0.214	0.228	0.392	0.485	0.044	0.044	0.114	0.150	0.170	0.184	0.278	0.335	1.26
Ten to fourteen	0.150	0.159	0.172	0.320	0.036	0.036	0.040	0.087	0.114	0.123	0.132	0.233	1.46
Fifteen to nineteen	0.140	0.129	0.150	0.195	0.035	0.032	0.039	0.053	0.105	0.097	0.111	0.142	0.60
Number of trauma centers per 100,000 population in state													
Zero to four	1.212	1.004	0.670	0.634	1.329	1.087	0.719	0.725	−0.117	−0.083	−0.049	−0.091	0.57
Five to nine	1.213	1.003	0.669	0.636	1.338	1.096	0.727	0.738	−0.125	−0.093	−0.058	−0.102	0.45
Ten to fourteen	1.214	1.004	0.670	0.637	1.340	1.100	0.730	0.741	−0.126	−0.096	−0.060	−0.104	0.42
Fifteen to nineteen	1.221	1.011	0.675	0.641	1.335	1.095	0.724	0.730	−0.114	−0.084	−0.049	−0.089	0.55

Number of hospitals per 100,000 population in state												
Zero to four	4.652	4.464	3.642	3.384	4.964	4.720	3.842	3.563	−0.312	−0.256	−0.200	−0.179	1.04
Five to nine	4.704	4.522	3.696	3.435	5.032	4.794	3.912	3.631	−0.328	−0.272	−0.216	−0.196	0.97
Ten to fourteen	4.714	4.536	3.708	3.448	5.045	4.814	3.933	3.653	−0.331	−0.278	−0.225	−0.205	0.90
Fifteen to nineteen	4.694	4.517	3.691	3.434	5.000	4.769	3.894	3.617	−0.306	−0.252	−0.203	−0.183	0.97
Residuals from men's death rates, medical causes												
Zero to four	39.184	49.216	−6.653	−30.256	−4.895	3.410	−4.095	−4.783	44.079	45.806	−2.558	−25.473	−8.33
Five to nine	38.263	46.999	−6.913	−29.600	−4.909	2.971	−4.097	−4.585	43.172	44.028	−2.816	−25.015	−8.51
Ten to fourteen	38.613	46.911	−6.410	−29.482	−4.795	2.973	−3.982	−4.346	43.408	43.938	−2.428	−25.136	−8.49
Fifteen to nineteen	39.519	48.309	−5.383	−29.519	−4.551	3.391	−3.822	−4.175	44.070	44.918	−1.561	−25.344	−8.28
Residuals from men's death rates, auto accidents												
Zero to four	−1.553	2.182	1.317	4.846	1.978	−0.005	−1.585	−1.128	−3.531	2.187	2.902	5.974	9.35
Five to nine	−1.279	2.445	1.666	5.287	1.989	−0.108	−1.572	−1.023	−3.268	2.553	3.238	6.310	8.03
Ten to fourteen	−1.252	2.522	1.870	5.497	1.898	−0.150	−1.528	−0.930	−3.150	2.672	3.398	6.427	7.59
Fifteen to nineteen	−1.342	2.449	1.821	5.459	1.682	−0.145	−1.523	−0.935	−3.024	2.594	3.344	6.394	7.49
Residuals from men's death rates, other accidental injuries												
Zero to four	5.597	4.929	−1.372	−6.415	−0.825	−0.114	−0.490	1.188	6.422	5.043	−0.882	−7.603	−34.86
Five to nine	5.799	5.009	−1.380	−6.392	−0.789	−0.158	−0.518	1.193	6.588	5.167	−0.862	−7.585	−31.74
Ten to fourteen	5.778	5.086	−1.192	−6.281	−0.801	−0.206	−0.533	1.209	6.579	5.292	−0.659	−7.490	−28.00
Fifteen to nineteen	5.624	5.057	−1.143	−6.240	−0.872	−0.243	−0.584	1.170	6.496	5.300	−0.559	−7.410	−26.92
Residuals from men's death rates, intentional injuries												
Zero to four	29.085	12.039	8.133	−20.085	−0.483	0.335	−1.078	−3.758	29.568	11.704	9.211	−16.327	−9.95
Five to nine	28.682	11.346	7.686	−20.165	−0.695	0.185	−1.163	−3.645	29.377	11.161	8.849	−16.520	−10.34
Ten to fourteen	28.212	10.813	7.440	−20.342	−0.892	0.031	−1.220	−3.613	29.104	10.782	8.660	−16.729	−10.67
Fifteen to nineteen	28.029	10.763	7.586	−20.427	−0.921	0.008	−1.210	−3.655	28.950	10.755	8.796	−16.772	−10.67

Source: Authors' compilation.

The authors are grateful to the Russell Sage Foundation for financial support. Latika Chaudary and Eduardo Fajnzylber provided excellent research assistance.

NOTES

1. James P. Smith (1999) suggests that socioeconomic status affects health in childhood, while the direction of causality may run the other way among adults. Angus Deaton and Christina Paxson (2001) present some evidence regarding the relationship between income inequality and health among U.S. adolescents, while Chris Power and Sharon Matthews (1997) and G. R. Ford and his colleagues (1994) have investigated the relationship between health and inequality among adolescents in the United Kingdom and in Scotland, respectively. All but Ford and his colleagues find the expected positive relationship between income and health.

2. The available evidence suggests that further expansions of public health insurance are unlikely to ever entirely eliminate the relationship between SES and health. The famous Black report in Great Britain concluded that the relationship between SES and health became more pronounced following the introduction of national health insurance, but it is possible that the differential would have widened even further in the absence of national health (Townsend, Davidson, and Whitehead 1988). Similarly, research using Canadian data indicates that there is a significant relationship between health and household income even though Canadians have universal health insurance (Curtis et al. 2001).

3. We use the racial designations found in the U.S. Census of Population, the CPS, and the VSMD to form these race categories. We note that these race categories are not synonymous with ethnicity. For example, a person of Hispanic origin may be classified in any of the three racial categories, white, black, or other.

4. It might be preferable to break out infants and children age one to four separately, but the population estimates we use to calculate death rates are not available separately for these groups by state over the entire period.

5. We had AHA data for 1984, 1991, 1994, 1995, and 1997. The AHA surveys all hospitals and asks whether each one has an associated certified trauma center. Values for other years were interpolated linearly. Data on the number of hospitals came from the AHA and also from the Area Resource File (ARF), which had information about the number of hospitals per county for 1980 and 1985 through 1995.

6. The cell data used in these regressions are weighted in proportion to the *population* of children in the specific age group multiplied by race group multiplied by state group, where we use the population values for 1990 (since there is little variation across time in these population figures).

7. Because this is not true for the "oldest old," however, some have speculated in the literature that blacks who survive to old age may be inherently healthier than those who do not.

8. Several states exercised options under federal law to cover children of different ages over this period. The ages used by states and the timing of their changes were taken from the *Green Book 2000*.

REFERENCES

Almond, Douglas, Kenneth Chay, and Michael Greenstone. 2001. "Civil Rights, the War on Poverty, and Black-White Convergence in Infant Mortality in Mississippi." Unpublished paper. University of California, Department of Economics, Berkeley (September).

Becker, Gary. 1991. *A Treatise on the Family.* Enlarged ed. Cambridge, Mass.: Harvard University Press.

Becker, Gary, and Nigel Tomes. 1976. "Child Endowments and the Quantity and Quality of Children." *Journal of Political Economy* 84: 143–62.

Bonnie, Richard J., Carolyn E. Fulco, and Catharyn T. Liverman, eds. 1999. *Reducing the Burden of Injury.* Washington, D.C.: National Academy Press.

Case, Anne, Darren Lubotsky, and Christina Paxson. 2002. "Economic Status and Health in Childhood: The Origins of the Gradient." *American Economic Review* 92(5, December): 1308–34.

Children's Safety Network. 1991. *A Data Book on Child and Adolescent Injury.* Washington, D.C.: National Center for Education in Maternal and Child Health.

Collins, William, and Melissa Thomasson. 2002. "Exploring the Racial Gap in Infant Mortality Rates, 1920 to 1970." Working paper 8836. Cambridge, Mass.: National Bureau of Economic Research (March).

Currie, Janet. 1995. "Socioeconomic Status and Child Health: Does Public Health Insurance Narrow the Gap?" *Scandinavian Journal of Economics* 97(4): 603–20.

Currie, Janet, and Jon Gruber. 1996a. "Health Insurance Eligibility, Utilization of Medical Care, and Child Health." *Quarterly Journal of Economics* 111(2, May): 431–66.

———. 1996b. "Saving Babies: The Efficacy and Cost of Recent Expansions of Medicaid Eligibility for Pregnant Women." *Journal of Political Economy* 104(6, December): 1263–96.

Currie, Janet, and V. Joseph Hotz. Forthcoming. "Accidents Will Happen? Childhood Injuries and the Effect of Child Care Regulation." *Journal of Health Economics.*

Currie, Janet, and Rosemary Hyson. 1999. "Is the Impact of Health Shocks Cushioned by Socioeconomic Status? The Case of Low Birthweight." *American Economic Review* 89(2, May): 245–50.

Currie, Janet, and Mark Stabile. Forthcoming. "Socioeconomic Status and Health: Why is the Relationship Stronger for Older Children?" *American Economic Review.*

Currie, Janet, and Duncan Thomas. 1995. "Medical Care for Children: Public Insurance, Private Insurance, and Racial Differences in Utilization." *Journal of Human Resources* 30(1, Winter): 135–62.

Curtis, Lori J., Martin D. Dooley, Ellen L. Lipman, and D. H. Feeny. 2001. "The Role of Permanent Income and Family Structure in the Determination of Child Health in Canada." *Health Economics* 10(4, June): 287–302.

Cutler, David, and Mark McClellan. 2001. "Is Technology Change in Medicine Worth It?" *Health Affairs* 20(5, September/October): 11–29.

Cutler, David, and Ellen Meara. 2000. "The Technology of Birth: Is It Worth It?" In *Frontiers in Health Policy Research,* vol. 3, edited by Alan M. Garber. Cambridge, Mass.: MIT Press for National Bureau of Economic Research.

———. 2003. "The Determinants of Trends in Racial Disparities in Infant Mortality Since 1970." Paper presented to the meeting of the American Economic Association. Washington, D.C. (January).

Deaton, Angus. 2001. "Health, Inequality, and Economic Development." Working paper 8318. Cambridge, Mass.: National Bureau of Economic Research (June).

Deaton, Angus, and Darren Lubotsky. 2001. "Mortality, Inequality, and Race in American Cities and States." Working paper 8370. Cambridge, Mass.: National Bureau of Economic Research (July).

Deaton, Angus, and Christina Paxson. 1999. "Mortality, Education, Income, and Inequality Among American Cohorts." Working paper 7140. Cambridge, Mass.: National Bureau of Economic Research.

———. 2001. "Mortality, Education, Income, and Inequality Among American Cohorts." In *Themes in the Economics of Aging,* edited by David Wise. Chicago: University of Chicago Press.

Flegg, A. T. 1982. "Inequality of Income, Illiteracy, and Medical Care as Determinants of Infant Mortality in Developing Countries." *Population Studies* 36: 441–58.

Ford, G. R., Russell Ecob, K. Hunt, S. Macintyre, et al. 1994. "Patterns of Class Inequality in Health Through the Life Span: Class Gradients at Fifteen, Thirty-five, and Fifty-five Years in the West of Scotland." *Social Science and Medicine* 39(8, October): 1037–50.

Fossett, James, and John Peterson. 1989. "Physician Supply and Medicaid Participation: The Causes of Market Failure." *Medical Care* 27: 386–96.

Glied, Sherry. 2001. "The Value of Reductions in Child Injury Mortality in the United States." In *Medical Care Output and Productivity,* edited by David M. Cutler and Ernst R. Berndt. Chicago: University of Chicago Press.

Institute of Medicine. 1999. *Reducing the Burden of Injury.* Edited by Richard Bonnie. Washington, D.C.: National Academy Press.

Jaeger, David. 1997. "Estimating the Returns to Education Using the Newest Current Population Survey Education Questions." Discussion paper 500. Bonn, Germany: IZA.

Judge, Ken, Jo-Ann Mulligan, and Michaela Benzeval. 1997. "Income Inequality and Population Health." *Social Science and Medicine* 46: 567–79.

Marmot, Michael, and Richard G. Wilkinson. 1999. *Social Determinants of Health.* Oxford: Oxford University Press.

Mayer, Susan E., and Ankur Sarin. 2002. "An Assessment of Some Mechanisms Linking Economic Inequality and Infant Mortality." Working paper 02.12. Chicago: University of Chicago, Harris School.

Mellow, Jennifer, and Jeffrey Milyo. 2000. "Reexamining the Evidence of an Ecological Association Between Income Inequality and Health." Working paper. Chicago: University of Chicago, Harris School (August).

Miller, Douglas, and Christina Paxson. 2001. "Relative Income, Race and Mortality." Unpublished paper. Princeton University, Princeton, N.J. (July).

Nathens, Avery B., Gregory J. Jurkovich, Peter Cummings, Frederick P. Rivara, and Ronald V. Maier. 2000. "The Effect of Organized Systems of Trauma Care on Motor Vehicle Crash Mortality." *Journal of the American Medical Association* 283(15): 1990–94.

Nathens, Avery B., Gregory J. Jurkovich, Ronald V. Maier, David C. Grossman, Ellen J. MacKenzie, Maria Moore, and Frederick P. Rivara. 2001. "Relationship Between Trauma Center Volume and Outcomes." *Journal of the American Medical Association* 285(9): 1164–74.

National SAFE KIDS Campaign. 1998. *Fact Sheet*. Washington, D.C.: National SAFE KIDS Campaign (December).

Newacheck, Paul W., et al. 1994. "Poverty and Childhood Chronic Illness." *Archives of Pediatric and Adolescent Medicine* 148(November): 1143–49.

Power, Chris, and Sharon Matthews. 1997. "Origins of Health Inequalities in a National Sample." *Lancet* 350(9091, November 29): 1584–89.

Pui, C. H., et al. 1995. "Outcome of Treatment for Childhood Cancer in Black as Compared with White Children." *Journal of the American Medical Association* (February 22): 633–37.

Smith, James P. 1999. "Healthy Bodies and Thick Wallets: The Dual Relation Between Health and Economic Status." *Journal of Economic Perspectives* 13(2, Spring): 145–67.

Townsend, Peter, Nick Davidson, and Margaret Whitehead. 1988. *Inequalities in Health*. London: Penguin.

Wilkinson, Richard G. 1992. "Income Distribution and Life Expectancy." *British Medical Journal* 304: 165–68.

———. 1996. *Unhealthy Societies: The Affliction of Inequality*. London: Routledge.

———. 2000. *Mind the Gap: Hierarchies, Health, and Human Evolution*. London: Weidenfeld and Nicolson.

Part V

Inequality in
Political Participation

Chapter 16

Political Equality: What Do We Know About It?

Sidney Verba, Kay Lehman Schlozman, and Henry E. Brady

Among the bedrock principles in a democracy is equal consideration of the preferences and interests of all citizens, a commitment that is expressed in such principles as one-person, one-vote, equality before the law, and equal rights of free speech, press, and assembly. Equal consideration of the preferences and needs of all citizens is fostered by equal political activity among citizens, not only in voting turnout but also in other forms of political activity that include working in political campaigns, making campaign contributions, taking part in local community efforts, contacting officials directly, and engaging in protest. Through their activity, citizens in a democracy seek to control who will hold public office and to influence what the government does. Because political activity is the vehicle by which citizens inform governing elites of their needs and preferences and induce them to be responsive, equal citizen participation goes to the heart of political equality. Equal political participation thus matters both for its own sake and for its role in bringing about equality in the other valued goods—life, liberty, and property—that are affected by government policies.[1]

THINKING ABOUT POLITICAL PARTICIPATION AND POLITICAL EQUALITY

Because equality in political participation can have many meanings, let us begin by defining and delimiting the scope of our concern.[2]

We are concerned with *voluntary, political participation*. By "political" participation we refer simply to activity that has the intent or effect of influencing government action—either directly by affecting the making or implementing of public policy or indirectly by influencing the selection of people who make those policies. By "voluntary" participation we mean participation that is not obligatory—no one is forced to volunteer—and that receives no pay or only token financial compensation. Thus, a paid position on a big city school board or a senator's reelection campaign staff does not qualify as voluntary under our definition.

Much of the literature on political equality focuses on *participatory rights,* in particular on equal voting rights. Our discussion assumes equality of rights and deals with the equal use of such rights, as well as with the equal capacity to use participatory rights.

Studies of political participation often focus exclusively on the vote. Although voting is perhaps the most important mode of citizen involvement in political life, it is but one of *many forms of political participation.* We consider a wider range of political acts, including working in and contributing to electoral campaigns; contacting government officials; attending protests, marches or demonstrations; working informally with others to solve some community problem; serving without pay on local elected and appointed boards; being active politically through the intermediation of voluntary associations; and contributing money to political causes.

Political acts differ along a variety of dimensions. We mentioned that citizen participation influences political elites by communicating information about activists' circumstances, preferences, and needs and by generating pressure—whether the promise of support or the threat of opposition—to pay attention. Political acts vary in the amount of information they convey and in the amount of pressure they bring to bear on elites. Participatory acts also differ in the amount and mix of the resources of time, money, and skills they require. The combination of what an act can produce and what it demands is basic to how participation achieves, or fails to achieve, its intended effect.

Political acts also vary in the extent to which it is possible, or even legal, to multiply *the volume of participatory input.* When it comes to the volume of political input, the vote is at one extreme. Each citizen has one and only one vote. In contrast, other kinds of participation can vary in volume: a citizen may contact many public officials, few, or none at all; devote many hours to working in campaigns, few, or none at all; donate many dollars to political campaigns and causes, few, or none at all; and so on. In considering political equality it is important to consider both whether or not citizens are active and how much they participate.

Our concern extends beyond inequalities among individuals to *inequalities among groups.* As the data we present make clear, there are participatory differences among individuals in activity: some citizens are much more active than others. Although these differences are important, what may really count are the differences in political voice across "politically relevant" categories of citizens—that is, categories of citizens who differ in terms of preferences, needs, and priorities for government action. Class differences, gender differences, and racial and ethnic differences are clearly politically relevant in contemporary American politics. This chapter focuses largely on class—especially income—differences.[3]

MEASURING PARTICIPATORY EQUALITY

Because participatory acts mobilize different kinds of political input and because those acts vary in the extent to which the volume of activity can be multiplied, it is impossible to measure with precision participatory disparities between individuals or groups. The task of making comparisons is easiest when it comes to voting. Each individual gets only one vote, and it does not matter how vigorously or skillfully the lever is pulled. However, votes may vary in value if constituencies differ in size (as they do for Senate elections) or in degree of competitiveness if the voting machines are faulty or the registration lists inaccurate. The situation becomes more complex for activities other than the vote. For letters, contributions, and protest marches, all of which are part of a participatory repertory, the volume of activity can vary: the number of letters or protests; the amount of time devoted to a campaign; the size of a contribution. And an activist can engage in these activities with more or less skill. There is therefore no single metric for making comparisons across diverse activities.

WHAT DO WE KNOW ABOUT POLITICAL EQUALITY?

In the following sections, we present data on various aspects of political equality and consider a number of questions:

- What is the degree of inequality for various forms of political activity?

- How substantial are the political inequalities across groups distinguished by social class characteristics (principally income and education) as well as by race or ethnicity and by gender?

- How does the extent of political inequality in the contemporary United States compare with the circumstance in the past? The circumstance in other countries?

- What are the sources of political inequalities in the nonpolitical domains of life and in politics itself?

- What are the consequences of political inequalities with respect to what the government hears and what the government does?

- What, if anything, can be done about political inequality?

Unfortunately, because we have set an ambitious agenda, we must discuss some of the data in a rather cursory fashion.

HOW MUCH INEQUALITY?

As has been made clear, we cannot discuss the amount of political inequality without first answering: "Inequality in what?" and "Among whom?" Discussions of political inequality in the media or in public life often—and quite appropriately—focus on differences in voting turnout between groups differentiated on the basis of, say, income or race. And there is, of course, much discussion of the role of money in American politics where the mode of activity is contributions and the group difference is between rich and poor. These discussions highlight an important aspect of American politics. We live in an era that has witnessed a lowering of the barriers to limitations on universal suffrage and enhanced protection of the right to take part (see Keyssar 2000, esp. pt. 3). Despite the fact that all are more or less equally free to participate, however, there are sharp disparities in the rates of activity across groups defined by their income or education, disparities that obtain for many different kinds of political acts. In short, the story is straightforward and clear: the advantaged are more active than the disadvantaged.

Income and Activity

Figure 16.1 presents differences by income on an overall additive scale of political activity.[4] The scale, a summary measure of the number of political activities in which the individual has engaged, counts each of the following as one act: voting in the 1988 election, working in a campaign, contributing money to a campaign, contacting an official, taking part in a protest, working informally with others in the community on a local issue, being a member of a local governing board or attending the meetings of such a board on a regular basis, and being involved in an organization that takes political stands. The increase in political activity with income is clear: those in the lowest level of income averaged one act (usually voting); those at the top of the income scale averaged more than three acts.

FIGURE 16.1   *Mean Number of Political Acts, by Family Income*

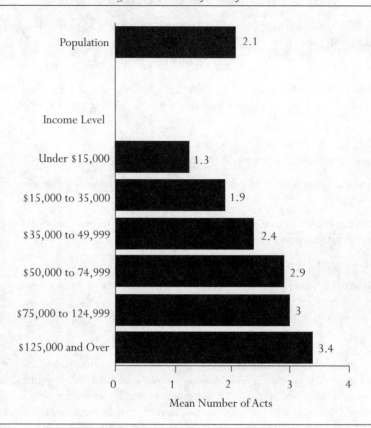

Mean Number of Acts

Source: Citizen Participation Study.

Because the summary measure obscures differences among acts, we can decompose it into its components. Figure 16.2 compares two income groups at the extremes with respect to the proportion who take part in various political activities: those with a family income below $15,000—that is, below or very close to the poverty line—and those with a family income of $75,000 or higher. For each kind of participation, affluence and activity go together. Of the various acts, voting is perhaps the most egalitarian. Turnout is much higher among the wealthy than the poor, but voting is the act for which the ratio of the proportion of the affluent who take part to the proportion of the poor who take part is lowest. The participation gap between income groups is more pronounced among those who take a more active role in electoral politics by working in a campaign or making a campaign contribution. There is also a participation gap between income groups with respect to contacting (a mode of activity that might be of special relevance to the disadvantaged who depend on government programs), participating in informal community activities, and especially, serving on a local governing board. Moreover, although the disparity is somewhat smaller than for other modes of activity, the poor are less likely to attend protests, a form of activity that is often described as the "weapon of the weak" because it is available to those with few economic resources. Thus, the affluent are overrepresented among activists to an extent that varies from act to act: this overrepresentation is least pronounced when it comes

FIGURE 16.2   *Participation in Various Activities, by High- and Low-Income Groups*

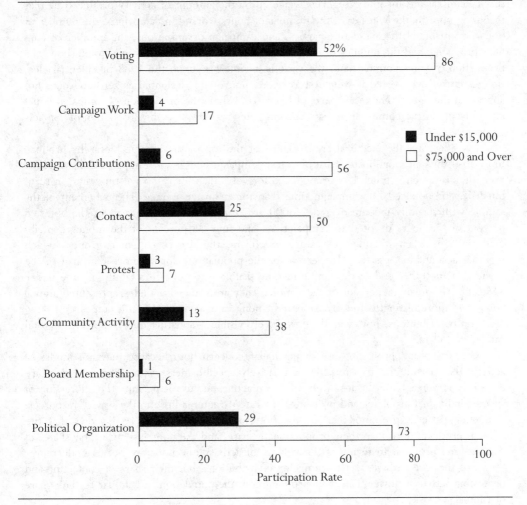

Source: Citizen Participation Study.

to voting and, not unexpectedly, most pronounced when it comes to making campaign contributions (for similar data across a large number of political acts, see Rosenstone and Hansen 1993).

The Volume of Activity

Voting is unique among political acts in that the volume of input from any individual cannot be varied: we are limited to one and only one vote each. For other activities, those who take part can be more or less active. We can learn more about the representation of income groups through various forms of political activity by considering the volume of activity they produce. Figure 16.3 gives us a politician's-eye view of what the citizenry would look like if each income group's visibility depended on the amount of its political activity. The upper-left section of figure 16.3 presents as a baseline the distribution of various family income groupings within the population. The other graphs show the proportion of the population that falls in various income categories weighted by the amount of activity produced by that income group: by the votes cast; the number of hours worked in campaigns; the number of dollars contributed to candidates, parties, and campaign organizations; the number of contacts produced; and the number of protests attended. Thus, the upper-right graph shows the proportion of votes coming from the various income groups in the 1988 presidential election. A citizen who voted is weighted as one; a nonvoter is weighted as zero and does not appear on the figure. The other parts of figure 16.3 show the proportion of campaign hours or campaign dollars coming from each income category as well as the proportion of contacts or protests.

Consider first the electoral arena. Those at the top of the income hierarchy produce more than their proportionate share of votes, campaign hours, and campaign dollars. However, the distortion is much less pronounced for votes than for campaign time and, in turn, much less pronounced for campaign time than for campaign money. The 3 percent of the sample with a family income over $125,000 are responsible for 4 percent of the votes, 8 percent of the hours devoted to campaigning, and fully 35 percent of the money contributed. Indeed, when it comes to campaign dollars, the top two income groups, which together account for less than 10 percent of the population, donate more than half of the money. At the other end of the family income scale are those with a family income under $15,000, who form 19 percent of the sample. They are somewhat underrepresented among voters and more distinctly underrepresented among campaigners. When it comes to making electoral contributions, however, they are barely visible—donating only 2 percent of total campaign dollars.

Contacting and protesting are of particular concern both because they are modes of activity that permit the transmission of relatively specific messages and because they are especially important for the less well off—contacting because it permits the addressing of specific individual problems and protesting because it requires little in the way of resources. Reflecting patterns presented earlier, the bottom section of figure 16.3 shows that the affluent produce more than their proportionate share, and the poor less than their share, of contacts and protests. In terms of the volume of activity, the poor are not as underrepresented as they are with respect to campaign contributions, but their share of contacting and protesting activity is lower than their proportion in the population and similar to their share of campaign work.

We have focused on a comparison of the affluent and the poor. It is important to note, however, that the differences among the modes of activity affect the representation of the middle class as well. Consider the roughly one-fifth of the respondents with a family income between $35,000 and $50,000. They are somewhat overrepresented in terms of votes, campaign hours, and contacts, but substantially underrepresented when it comes to campaign dollars. The pattern of underrepresentation when it comes to giving money is even stronger for the large group one step further down on the economic ladder, those with a family income between $15,000 and $35,000. The special inequality associated with monetary contributions affects the poor most strongly, but it also has an impact on most of the lower middle class as well.

Time and Money

In a certain sense, these data merely underline the obvious: as Hemingway observed, the rich have more money. Nonetheless, the distinctions among votes, time, and money matter

FIGURE 16.3   *Volume of Political Activity (Percentage of Activity from Each Income Level)*

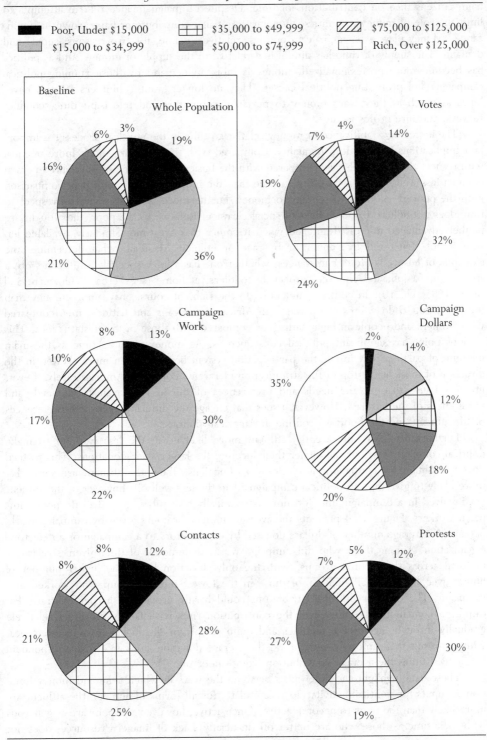

Poor, Under $15,000 $35,000 to $49,999 $75,000 to $125,000

$15,000 to $34,999 $50,000 to $74,999   Rich, Over $125,000

Source: Citizen Participation Study.

for politics. Political campaigns have come to rely more heavily on contributions of money from citizens than on contributions of time. Despite campaign finance reform attempts to limit the role of money in politics, monetary campaign contributions have grown in significance.[5] Money plays a bigger role in politics, relative to time, for two reasons: supply and demand. The supply of time has diminished relative to the supply of money. And as politics has become more professionalized, money is more in demand by those running political campaigns and promoting political causes. They no longer want volunteers to stuff envelopes as much as they want money to purchase computers and television time, conduct surveys, and hire professionals.

The increasing significance of money relative to time in the political process has important implications for political inequality. Compared with time, we are much more unequal with respect to money. That is, compared with the busiest person, the most leisured person is much less well off when it comes to time than the most affluent person is in comparison with the poorest one when it comes to money. Furthermore, stratification with respect to time does not adhere to other lines of social cleavage. Relative to the poor, the affluent are neither advantaged nor disadvantaged when it comes to spare time. Similarly, available leisure is not structured by gender or by race or ethnicity. Instead, what determines the stockpile of leisure is life circumstances: whether one has a job, especially a full-time job; a spouse with a job; and children, especially toddlers, at home (see Verba, Schlozman, and Brady 1995, ch. 10). In contrast, not only do the rich, of course, have more money than the poor, but so do whites compared with African Americans and Latinos, men compared with women, and people in high-status jobs compared with those in lower-status jobs. This obvious point has significant political consequences. As money replaces time as the main medium of participatory input, the participation system becomes even more skewed in the direction of those at the top of the stratification hierarchy. Politics in America rarely, if ever, involves issues that pit the needs and preferences of the harried against the needs and preferences of the leisured. However, issues that engage the differing needs and preferences of the affluent and the poor are routine in American politics.

Furthermore, not only are the affluent more likely than the less well off to make political contributions, but the higher their income, the larger their donations. This pattern does not obtain for contributions of time to campaigns. True, the affluent are somewhat more likely to give time to political campaigns than the less well off; however, if the affluent get involved in a campaign, they do not systematically give more time than do poor campaign workers. Figure 16.4 presents the average number of hours given by campaign workers and the average number of dollars donated by contributors to a campaign or an electoral organization. Among those who did campaign work, the amount of time given is relatively uniform across the income groups, with the only deviation being the higher number of hours given by the small number of those in the lowest income group who worked in a campaign. The data for dollar contributions could hardly provide a sharper contrast. For campaign contributions, the size of the contribution rises with family income—relatively gradually through the middle incomes and quite steeply in the higher-income categories, with the result that, among contributors, the average donation from an affluent respondent is fourteen times the average contribution from a poor one.

These data highlight the differences between the ways in which time and money function as inputs for political activity. To recapitulate, for all forms of activity, the affluent are more likely than the poor to become active. Once active, however, the poor are as generous with their time as those who are better off financially. Lack of financial resources does not

FIGURE 16.4   *Mean Hours and Dollars Given to Political Campaigns (Among Those Who Give Some Hours or Dollars)*

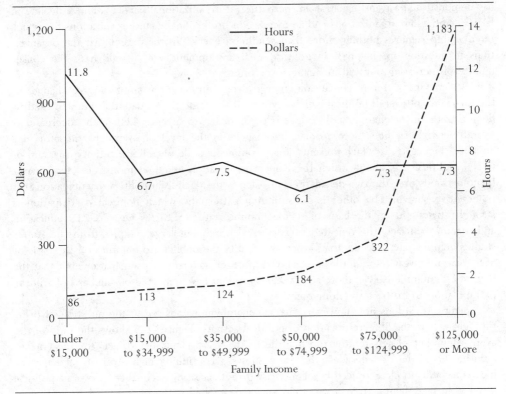

Source: Citizen Participation Study.

seem to be an impediment to the investment of sweat equity. Since nobody's day contains more than twenty-four hours, the well-heeled can give only so much time—apparently not more, on average, than the poor. No such leveling occurs when it comes to money. Not only are those with higher family incomes more likely to be donors, but they write larger checks when they contribute. If time becomes less important in politics, the voice of the less affluent may be drowned out.

Political Inequality: Increasing or Decreasing?

Robert Putnam's (2000) *Bowling Alone* has focused attention recently on the decline of social activity in the United States. Although the discussion of the erosion in civic engagement in America has centered on organized and unorganized social activities in the nonpolitical domain, Putnam (2000) and Rosenstone and Hansen (1993) present evidence that political activity—especially voting—has also decreased since the 1960s.

Interestingly, in the conversation about the contraction in civic activity, very little attention has been paid to changing levels of inequality in participation. We have already seen that the increase in the relative importance of campaign giving gives us reason to presume that, when it comes to campaign finance, the socioeconomic stratification of participatory input has been exacerbated in recent decades. In addition, Theda Skocpol (2003) has demonstrated a transformation in the nature of organizational participation: a decline in large membership organizations and an increase in professionally run organizations for which membership requires nothing more than sending a check. To the extent that the organizations in question are involved in politics, this development, too, would have the consequence of increasing political inequality over time.

A somewhat different conclusion emerges from our recent attempt to trace changes in the inequality of overall political activity. We used the same Roper data that Putnam used to demonstrate the decline in political activity in order to assess whether the decrease in overall activity has been accompanied by changes in the level of overall participatory inequality.[6] Figure 16.5, which presents, for a composite scale of political activity, the sum of twelve political acts about which the Roper organization asked, demonstrates two unambiguous trends over the two-decade period. One is the decline in political participation that others have shown. The other is a continuing pattern by which political participation is strongly structured on the basis of socioeconomic status (SES) (as measured by education and income). In fact, the repeated surveys and consequent large samples from the Roper studies demonstrate not only that, when we stratify the public into quintiles on the basis of SES, year after year the quintiles are arrayed in order in terms of participation, but that the highest SES quintile is even more active than we might have expected on the basis of a linear extrapolation from the lower four quintiles.

Figure 16.5 does not, however, give an unambiguous answer to the question of over-time changes in the SES stratification of political activity. Figure 16.5 shows the ratio of the average number of acts for the top quintile to the average number of acts for the bottom quintile. Over the two decades, that ratio shows a continuing high level of participatory inequality and no clear trajectory of increasing or decreasing inequality in overall political activity. In fact, figure 16.5 shows a circumstance such that the degree of stratification in activity in the mid-1990s was more or less the same as it was in the mid-1970s.

Political Equality in Comparative Perspective

If measuring the extent of income inequality in a cross-national perspective is complex, measuring participatory inequality is even more difficult still—because citizens can be active in many different ways, requiring different kinds of inputs, and because there is a dearth of comparable data. As is well known, voting turnout in the United States is, for several reasons, lower than it is elsewhere. One reason is that it is more difficult to register to vote in the United States: indeed, turnout among registered voters in the United States is closer to that in the European countries with which the United States is usually compared. In addition, American political parties are weaker than their counterparts elsewhere (Powell 1986; Teixeira 1992).

What is less well known is that the United States does not lag behind—indeed, it tends to be ahead—in the frequency of many other forms of political activity. When it comes to the equality of political activity, however, the best evidence is that participatory inequalities are sharper in the United States than in other comparable democracies (Verba, Nie, and Kim 1979). Table 16.1 presents data from the 1970s showing the correlation between three scales (a scale of voting, campaign activity, and political interest) and a measure of socioeconomic status for Austria, the Netherlands, and the United States. In each case, the socioeconomic stratification is stronger in the United States than elsewhere.[7]

FIGURE 16.5   *Equality of Political Activity: Mean Number of Political Activities by Socioeconomic Quintiles, 1973 to 1995*

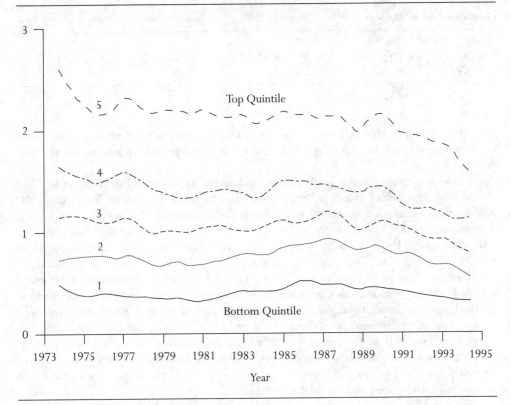

Source: Roper Social and Political Trends.
Note: Lowess Smoothing: f = .10, t = 2

THE SOURCES OF POLITICAL INEQUALITY

Students of political participation point to a large number of individual and contextual factors that influence who takes part politically. The most powerful are summarized in the SES model of participation, which stresses the strong association between political activity and an individual's income, occupation, and, especially, education. The SES model, which was introduced in Sidney Verba and Norman Nie's (1972) *Participation in America* and figures importantly in Raymond Wolfinger and Steven Rosenstone's (1980) *Who Votes?,* has greater empirical than explanatory power. That is, although the SES model has great utility in clarifying the nature and extent of stratification in American political participation, it does not explain how and why higher status fosters activity.

Although it is common to deride the SES model as simplistic, apolitical, and atheoretical, it shows no signs of early demise.[8] Its endurance can be attributed in part to its considerable empirical power in predicting political participation. In contrast to other variables often discussed as being central to the understanding of participation—for example, characteristics of political and social context—in any multivariate analysis socioeconomic status is invariably positively associated with political activity. Even critics of the SES model

TABLE 16.1   *Correlation Between Political Activity and Political Interest Scales and SES in the United States and Three Other Industrialized Democracies in the 1970s*

Correlation Between SES Scale and . . .	Voting Scale	Campaigning Scale	Political Interest Scale
Austria	− .06	.13	.36
Netherlands	.10	.11	.35
United States	.24	.29	.40

Source: Verba, Nie, and Kim (1979).

never fail to include socioeconomic variables in their analyses when they probe the consequences for participation of such political variables as registration laws and the competitiveness of elections.

Moreover, recent scholarship has begun to address its theoretical deficiencies by elaborating the causal links between political activity and high levels of income, occupation, and education. Norman Nie, Jane Junn, and Kenneth Stehlik-Barry (1996) address one puzzling discontinuity: within any cross-sectional sample, high-SES individuals are the most politically active, but rising levels of education within the public have not produced commensurate returns in participation. They stress the primacy of relative rather than absolute education. According to their analysis, what matters for political activity is the positional advantage accruing to those who are well educated relative to their age cohort rather than any particular level of educational attainment. Thus, they construe educational attainment more as a sorting mechanism that allocates "scarce social and political ranks that place citizens either closer to or further from the center of critical social and political networks" (6). In particular, they demonstrate the relationship between educational level and what they call "network centrality"—being personally acquainted with or known to people in important positions in local or national politics and the media (ch. 3).

As presented in Verba, Schlozman, and Brady (1995) and elaborated in Burns, Schlozman, and Verba (2001), the civic voluntarism model helps to explain how the components of socioeconomic status function to produce participation and demonstrate why education is so central to this process. The civic voluntarism model groups the variety of characteristics that predispose an individual to be politically active into three sets of participatory factors: resources, orientations to politics, and recruitment.[9] Not only does education have a direct impact on political activity, but more important, education has indirect effects through its consequences for the acquisition of nearly every other participatory factor. Let us elaborate.

When individuals command the *resources* that make it possible to do so, they are more likely to participate. Important among these resources are civic skills—those organizational and communications capacities that make it easier to get involved and enhance an individual's effectiveness as a participant. These skills are acquired throughout the life cycle, beginning at home and in school and later on, during adulthood, on the job, at church, in nonpolitical organizations, and in politics itself. Another crucial resource is money to make contributions to campaigns and other political causes. These resources are strongly associated with SES. Income is not only simultaneously a component of SES but a central resource for participation. Moreover, those with high levels of educational attainment are more likely to command the kinds of jobs that yield high incomes and to be in a position to develop civic skills in the various domains of adult life.[10]

In addition, several psychological *orientations*—all of which are associated with educational attainment—facilitate political activity. All else being equal, individuals are more likely to participate if they are politically informed, interested, and efficacious—that is, if they know and care about politics and if they think that their participation would make a difference. Although political efficacy has generated particular attention among participation scholars, knowledge about politics is equally strongly related to participation, and interest in and attentiveness to politics are even more tightly connected to political activity. As would be expected, those who identify with a political party also have higher rates of participation, especially in electoral politics.[11]

It is not simply general political predispositions that figure among the factors associated with participation. Political participation is, after all, about politics, and thus the content of political preferences matters as well. Not surprisingly, those who have intense issue commitments—for example, those who take a strong pro-life or pro-choice position on abortion—are more politically active (see Verba, Schlozman, and Brady 1995, ch. 14). In contrast to general political predispositions, which are clearly linked to level of education, the consequence of these issue commitments for political equality is contingent on the particular issue. The political mobilization attendant to strong pro-life views, for instance, tends to reduce the social stratification of political activity, while the activity that results from environmental concerns may increase participatory inequalities. The relationship of group consciousness to political activity is more problematic. Of course, the Marxian concept of group consciousness—the belief that group members have common problems requiring joint political action—originally grew out of class analysis. However, contemporary discussions of group consciousness are more likely to focus on a sense of political solidarity and shared political fate anchored in race, ethnicity, or gender. In contrast to the results for other politically relevant orientations, the findings about the participatory consequences of group consciousness have been decidedly mixed.[12]

Another aspect of politics has the potential to affect participatory inequalities on the basis of gender or race. There is some evidence that the substantial overrepresentation of white males among visible political leaders conveys implicit messages to citizens about who should be playing in the game of politics. African Americans are more politically efficacious and more active in cities with elected black officials, although there is some issue as to which comes first, political activity among black Americans or the stimulating effect of black officials (Bobo and Gilliam 1990). African Americans are also more likely to contact political officials if the officials are African American (Verba and Nie 1972; Gay 1997), and women are more likely to be interested in and informed about politics when they live in states where women hold, or contest for, visible public offices (Burns, Schlozman, and Verba 2001, ch. 13).

The catalyst for political participation is *recruitment:* those who have the wherewithal and the desire to take part in politics are more likely to do so if they are asked. Systematic inquiries confirm the well-known role of parties in mobilizing turnout and electoral activity.[13] Rosenstone and Hansen (1993, ch. 6) emphasize the extent to which it is not simply the characteristics of individuals but the operations of mobilizing institutions that determine participation. They make a more general argument about the implications for participation of the attempts at political mobilization that come at the behest of politically motivated strategic elites—not only party activists but also those who run electoral campaigns or lead political organizations or movements. Beyond the efforts of political elites, processes of recruitment to citizen participation inhere in day-to-day life outside of politics: requests for political activity may come from those we know—relatives, friends, neighbors, work colleagues, fellow organization or church members—as well as from the managers, leaders, and staff of nonpolitical institutions. Whether the request comes in a mass mailing, a phone call, or over the backyard fence, those who seek to get others involved choose as their targets people who would be likely to participate if asked. Thus, while the request may generate activity, those who are asked usually have characteristics that make them inclined to take part, a fact that has the effect of further exacerbating the SES stratification of political participation.[14]

In sum, the single most important source of participatory inequality is the cumulative effect of educational differences. In fact, the participatory consequences of education stretch across the generations. Children whose parents are well educated are more likely to be politically active as adults, both because well-educated parents are likely to be politically active themselves—and thus to create politically rich home environments and to act as role models for their children—and because well-educated parents are likely to produce well-educated children. As our discussion has made clear, those with high levels of education are likely to be in a position to acquire all of the other factors that facilitate participation: to have jobs that generate high levels of income; to be able to develop civic skills in church, in nonpolitical organizations, and, especially, at work; to be politically interested, informed, and efficacious; and to receive requests for political activity.

DOES IT MATTER?

Although the existence of participatory inequalities is unambiguous, it is less clear what difference they make. If the objective of political activity is a particularistic benefit—a Christmas turkey or a city job from an old-style party machine, a government contract or a favorable tax ruling, or any of the many varieties of pork for the local district—then political activity or inactivity has obvious potential effects. However, when the concerns that animate participation are general policies, then the implications are less clear. If those who take part are not distinctive in their *politically relevant characteristics*—that is, in characteristics whose visibility to a public official might make a difference in their responses to citizen participation—then the fact that some people are active while others are not would matter little for political outcomes (for discussion of the nature of politically relevant characteristics, see Verba, Schlozman, and Brady 1995, ch. 6). The list of politically relevant characteristics is long and mutable. At any time, such characteristics can include differences in objective needs for government policy as well as differences in policy preferences in relation to both existing policy controversies and the issues that should be on the political agenda.

In their study of voting turnout, Wolfinger and Rosenstone (1980) made an important point that is now part of the received wisdom in political science: although voters differ from nonvoters in such demographic characteristics as education and income, they are not distinctive in their policy preferences as indicated by their responses to a series of survey questions measuring attitudes toward government policies. As shown in table 16.2, when we replicated the Wolfinger and Rosenstone analysis, we confirmed that there is little attitudinal difference between voters and nonvoters. Others who have investigated the issue have found, at most, small differences (see Verba, Schlozman, and Brady 1995, chs. 6 and 7, as well as DeNardo 1980; Shaffer 1982; Bennett and Resnick 1990). Those who consider electoral outcomes rather than policy attitudes find more or less the same thing: who wins or loses would rarely be overturned by the elimination of turnout differentials among groups (Teixeira 1992).[15] Thus, massive vote mobilization might disappoint those who believe that an equalization of voting turnout across groups would produce a major change in the electoral mandate (see, for instance, Piven and Cloward 1988). However, since the

TABLE 16.2   *Attitudes of Voters and the Whole Population in the United States*

	(1) Percentage of Sample	(2) Percentage of Voters	Difference (2) − (1)	Ratio (2)/(1)
Government provision of jobs				
Liberal	27.7	23.6	−4.1	.85
Moderate	25.7	25.9	.2	1.01
Conservative	46.6	50.6	4.0	1.09
Government spending for services				
Liberal	38.6	36.1	−2.5	.94
Moderate	29.7	29.3	−.4	.99
Conservative	31.7	34.6	2.9	1.09

Source: Citizen Participation Study.

existence of politically relevant differences between active and inactive citizens is at the heart of the issue of the significance of participatory inequality, it is useful to examine the issue more closely.

Voters and Nonvoters—Activists and Inactives

The similarity between voters and nonvoters in their responses to standard American National Election Studies questions on a set of preselected political issues is an important point, but its significance can be overstated. Expanding the inquiry in two ways casts the issue in a different light. First, we must take a broader view of participation, moving beyond electoral turnout to include various kinds of political activity that can convey more precise messages to policymakers and be multiplied beyond the enforced equality of the single vote. In addition, we must take a broader view of politically relevant attributes in order to encompass not only demographics and policy positions as expressed in response to survey questions but also policy-relevant circumstances and the actual content of participatory input.

We can begin by comparing groups defined in terms of their socioeconomic characteristics and their policy preferences—the same pair of attributes Wolfinger and Rosenstone (1980) use to compare voters and nonvoters—with respect to their overall level of political activity as measured by the additive scale of political acts. Figure 16.6, which considers several demographic characteristics and several indicators of political preferences as measured by standard survey questions, shows the overall activity rates of demographic and attitudinal groups. Even when we enlarge our understanding of political activity, the distinction that Wolfinger and Rosenstone make between demography and attitudes holds up. Disparities in activity across socioeconomic groups—whether defined by income, education, or occupation—are much more substantial than across attitudinal groups. Those with high family incomes score much higher in overall participation than those with incomes at the poverty line, and professional and managerial workers score higher than unskilled and service workers. The gap in overall participation between college graduates and those who never finished high school is especially wide. In contrast, attitudinal differences on public issues are associated with less variation in political activity.

FIGURE 16.6   *Mean Number of Political Acts, by Demographics and Political Attitudes*

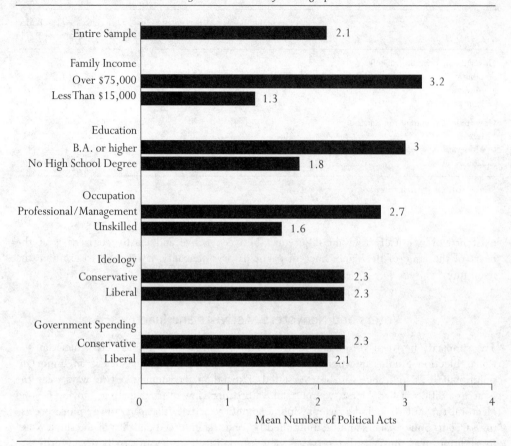

Source: Citizen Participation Study.

Economic Circumstances and Needs

The contrast between the similarity in the amount of activity among groups defined in terms of attitudes and ideological positions and the difference in activity among groups defined in demographic terms might suggest that participatory distortion in descriptive demographic terms is not matched by distortion in substantive representation. The activists who carry the voice of the people into the political process may not look like the rest of the public, but they do not differ much in what they want. However, policy preferences are not the only politically relevant characteristics. Figure 16.7 presents data on the activity of respondents who have varying economic needs and life circumstances. We concentrate on two dimensions—efforts to get by financially and receipt of various government benefits by respondents or immediate members of their families living with them. Our Citizen Partici- pation Survey asked whether, in order to make ends meet, the respondent or any immediate family member living in the household had to "put off medical or dental treatment," "cut back on the amount or quality of food," or "delay paying the rent or making house pay- ments." In addition, we asked whether the respondent or a member of the immediate family living in the household received means-tested government benefits (food stamps, subsidized

FIGURE 16.7   *Mean Number of Political Acts, by Needs and Receipt of Benefits*

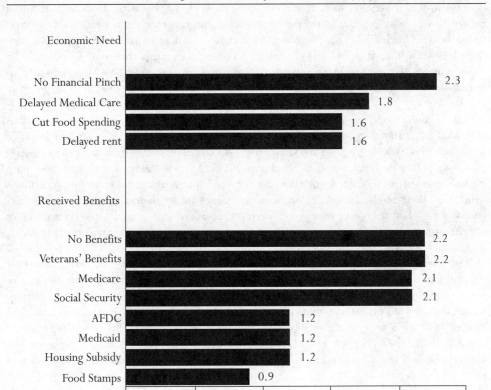

Source: Citizen Participation Study.

housing, Medicaid, or AFDC) or non-means-tested benefits (Social Security, veterans' benefits, Medicare, or educational loans).[16] We were thus able to identify those who have real financial needs or depend on government programs. These measures are, of course, closely related to income, but they give additional indications of respondents' potential interests with respect to government support.

As shown in figure 16.7, there are substantial differences in rates of political activity across groups distinguished by financial need or by the receipt of government benefits. Consider the activity of those who report some financial pinch. They are slightly less active than the population as a whole, with the divergence from the average for all citizens increasing with the severity of the financial squeeze. Those who report the relatively mild—and quite widespread—need to cut back on recreation do not differ from the population as a whole very much. Those who have had to cut back on spending for food or delay paying the rent, however, are substantially less active. Clearly, those with especially pressing needs are less visible in the participatory system.

This pattern is even more pronounced if we consider those who report that they or a member of the immediate family receives one of a number of government benefits.

The receipt of benefits per se does not imply a low level of activity. Those who receive non-means-tested benefits such as student loans or veterans' benefits, Medicare, or Social Security are at least as active as the public as a whole. In contrast, those who receive means-tested benefits such as AFDC, Medicaid, food stamps, and subsidized housing are substantially less active than the public as a whole. The differences imply that those who would be in most need of government response—because they are dependent on government programs—are the least likely to make themselves visible to the government through their activity.

It is useful to decompose the data in figures 16.6 and 16.7, in which activity is measured by a summary of several participatory acts, in order to consider the kinds of participation separately. As we have seen, voters do not differ much from nonvoters when it comes to policy preferences. Table 16.3 reports for various kinds of activity scores on a logged representation scale, a measure of over- or underrepresentation among individuals defined by their political attitudes on economic issues or by their objective economic circumstances.[17] The degree of over- or underrepresentation is measured for several different activist groups: voters, campaign workers, campaign contributors, contacters, protesters, community activists, and members of local boards. By varying both the characteristics of activists and the activities through which they can be over- or underrepresented, table 16.3 thus tells us something about both parts of our puzzle: the citizen characteristics that are better represented through activity and the activities that better represent citizen characteristics. It also indicates the extent of under- and overrepresentation. For instance, the first row of table 16.3 tells us that, among voters, liberals are very slightly underrepresented compared with their proportion in the population as a whole; those with income below the poverty line and those who receive means-tested benefits are underrepresented to a substantially greater degree.

Across all types of activities, those who take part represent more accurately the attitudes of individuals, as measured by the standard survey questions on economic policy, than individuals' actual needs, as measured by income or by receipt of means-tested benefits. Economic liberals are, in general, represented roughly proportionately among activists across the various activities. When we consider the representation index for differences based on the income of citizens and, even more so, for differences based on their receipt of means-tested benefits, we find that the disparities are much greater.

There are also significant variations in terms of types of activity. Considering activities associated with elections, the voting population and the population of campaign workers are, as mentioned, fairly representative of the population at large with respect to attitudes, but the poor and welfare recipients are substantially underrepresented among voters and, especially, campaign workers. Not surprisingly, the underrepresentation of the poor and needy is most pronounced among campaign contributors. Those beset by severe economic problems are not expected to be campaign contributors. Nevertheless, the substantive implication is unchanged: the messages received through participatory channels—in this case, one of the most effective channels—are skewed toward the economically advantaged. Compared with campaign contributors, the underrepresentation of the poor and needy in other activist populations is more moderate. The differences, however, are still substantial compared with the representation of policy attitudes.

For three modes of activity that might be particularly relevant for needy citizens—getting in touch with public officials, attending protests and demonstrations, and being active in the community—the underrepresentation of those who receive means-tested benefits and those in poverty is fairly severe. Presumably, contacting is especially important for

TABLE 16.3   *Over- and Underrepresentation of Economic Liberals, the Poor, and Welfare Recipients Among Activists*

Representation Ratios Among Activists for . . .	Economic Liberals[a]	Poor[b]	Welfare Recipients
Voters	− .04	− .12	− .15
Campaign workers	.00	− .34	− .26
Campaign contributors	.00	− .58	− .56
Contacters	.00	− .15	− .15
Protesters	+ .01	− .22	− .21
Community activists	− .04	− .29	− .30
Local board members	− .09	− .47	− .91

Source: Citizen Participation Study.
[a]Scale of attitudes on economic policy.
[b]Under $15,000 family income.

citizens who receive government benefits, since ensuring the flow of benefits may entail the need to deal with officials. Nonetheless, recipients of means-tested benefits are substantially underrepresented among those who get in touch with public officials. Although protest should be particularly important for disadvantaged groups that lack financial resources or connections, those receiving means-tested benefits are underrepresented in that participant population as well. And the recipients of means-tested benefits are about half as likely to be community activists as their proportion in the population would warrant.

Sending a Message

Participatory acts differ not only in the extent to which their volume can be multiplied but also in the extent to which they can convey to policymakers detailed information about citizen concerns. The Citizen Participation Study data allow us to investigate in several ways this largely uncharted, but crucial, aspect of citizen activity. For one thing, we can consider the characteristics of those activists who combine a substantial participatory investment with a specific message—that is, who combine a significant amount of activity with information about what they want in response. In addition, we can look at those who are active in relation to particular government benefit programs. And finally, we can consider the actual messages sent by activists who engage in modes of participation that permit the communication of information. These data greatly enrich our understanding of the nature of participatory representation.

Let us begin by considering one group of activists who join an activity of substantial dimensions with an explicit message: those who have contributed $250 or more to a political campaign and who report that they "communicated to the candidate or to someone involved in running the campaign [their] views on an issue of public policy—for example, about what [they] wanted the candidate to do when in office." Table 16.4 indicates how well various subgroups defined by their attitudes and economic circumstances are represented within this group of participants whose activity is high in its potential both for generating pressure and conveying information to candidates. As expected, those who make major campaign donations are more representative in terms of their attitudes on economic issues than in terms of their actual economic needs. The affluent are substantially more likely— and those who have had to cut back on necessities are considerably less likely—to appear in

TABLE 16.4   *Representation of Big Campaign Givers Who Communicate an Explicit Message*

Groups Over- or Underrepresented	Representation Rate
People with income over $75,000	+ .69
People with no need to cut necessities	+ .24
Economic liberals	+ .20
Economic conservatives	− .12
People who needed to cut necessities	− .35
People with income under $15,000	− .73
People who received means-tested benefits	− .95

Source: Citizen Participation Study.
Note: For definition of group categories see Verba, Schlozman, and Brady (1995, 216).

this politically potent group than is suggested by their proportion of the population. The most marked underrepresentation is found among the poor and those in households where a family member receives a means-tested benefit. These data echo the results reported earlier as to who is and who is not represented, but the relationships are even more pronounced. When it comes to an act that communicates a good deal of information and has potential clout, the less well off are especially underrepresented.

Political Activity and Program Participation

We have seen that those receiving such means-tested benefits as AFDC, Medicaid, food stamps, and subsidized housing are much less active than those receiving such non-means-tested benefits as Social Security, veterans' benefits, and Medicare. We can take the analysis one step further by probing whether their activity is in any way directly connected to these benefit programs and whether the government therefore receives more messages about benefits programs from recipients of non-means-tested benefits than from recipients of means-tested benefits.

The Citizen Participation Study inquired whether recipients of various government benefits had been active in relation to that benefit. For each government program for which the respondent (or a family member living in the household) was a recipient, we asked about the following activities: Had they taken that program into account in deciding how to vote? Had they given a campaign contribution based, at least in part, on concern about it? Had they contacted an official to complain about the program? Did they belong to an organization concerned about that program? The data on the proportion of the recipients of each benefit who report an activity related to the benefit program are consistent with what we know about the overall activity levels of the recipients of government benefits. For each kind of activity—voting, contributing, contacting, and being a member of an organization—recipients of non-means-tested benefits are more likely to have been active than recipients of means-tested benefits (see figure 16.8).

The differences are especially striking with respect to membership in an organization associated with the benefit—with the AARP and veterans' organizations presumably playing a major role—and to campaign donations. However, they apply as well to the considerations that enter into voting decisions. The data on contacting are interesting. We might expect that inclusion in the non-means-tested programs would be more or less automatic and thus would require fewer contacts. Nevertheless, Medicare recipients are more likely than Medicaid recipients to contact a public official about their medical benefits, and Social Security

FIGURE 16.8   *Political Activities Directly Related to Program*

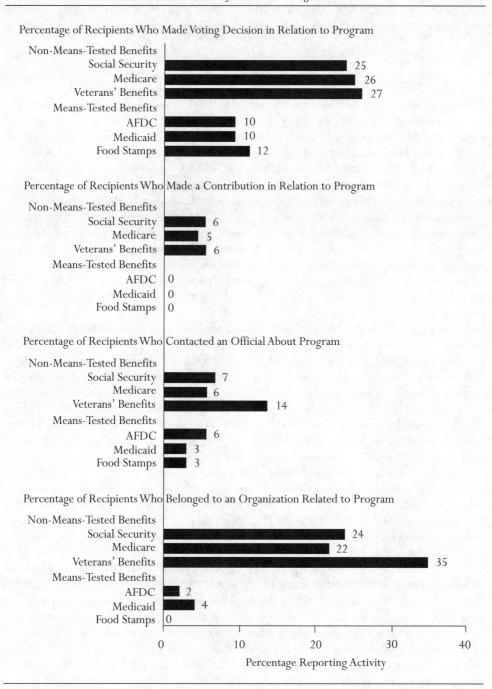

Percentage of Recipients Who Made Voting Decision in Relation to Program

Non-Means-Tested Benefits
Social Security — 25
Medicare — 26
Veterans' Benefits — 27
Means-Tested Benefits
AFDC — 10
Medicaid — 10
Food Stamps — 12

Percentage of Recipients Who Made a Contribution in Relation to Program

Non-Means-Tested Benefits
Social Security — 6
Medicare — 5
Veterans' Benefits — 6
Means-Tested Benefits
AFDC — 0
Medicaid — 0
Food Stamps — 0

Percentage of Recipients Who Contacted an Official About Program

Non-Means-Tested Benefits
Social Security — 7
Medicare — 6
Veterans' Benefits — 14
Means-Tested Benefits
AFDC — 6
Medicaid — 3
Food Stamps — 3

Percentage of Recipients Who Belonged to an Organization Related to Program

Non-Means-Tested Benefits
Social Security — 24
Medicare — 22
Veterans' Benefits — 35
Means-Tested Benefits
AFDC — 2
Medicaid — 4
Food Stamps — 0

0   10   20   30   40
Percentage Reporting Activity

Source: Citizen Participation Study.

recipients are more likely than AFDC recipients to contact an official about their benefits. Clearly, the government hears more from those on some programs than on others, and the ones it hears from are the less-disadvantaged citizens.

What Do They Say?

Political activities differ in their capacity to convey explicit messages to policymakers. The vote is limited in its ability to transmit precise information about citizen priorities and preferences, but a contact can convey detailed instructions. Whenever a respondent reported having been active in a particular way, we asked about the issue or problem that animated their activity. Table 16.5 summarizes the subject matter behind the political activity in which a codable issue concern was expressed and compares advantaged and disadvantaged respondents with respect to the issue concerns that animate their participation. To ensure that what was on people's minds was actually communicated to public officials, we focus solely on those information-rich activities in which an explicit message can be sent: contacting, protesting, campaign work or contributions accompanied by a communication, informal community activity, and voluntary service on a local board. The issue-based political act is the unit of analysis, and the figures represent the proportion of all issue-based activities for which the respondent mentioned, among other things, a particular set of policy concerns.

Although the advantaged and disadvantaged are similar in having wide-ranging policy concerns, they differ in the distribution of their concerns. Compared with the issue-based activity of the advantaged, the activity of the disadvantaged is more than twice as likely—and the activity of respondents in families receiving means-tested benefits four times as likely—to have been animated by concerns about basic human needs: poverty, jobs, housing, health, and the like. Moreover, the activity of the disadvantaged is more likely to have been motivated by concern about drugs or crime. The activity of the advantaged, in contrast, is more likely to have been inspired by abortion, the environment, or economic issues such as taxes, government spending, and the budget.

When we consider the actual number of communications, however, a very different story emerges. Because the disadvantaged are so much less active than the advantaged, public officials actually hear less about issues of basic human need from the disadvantaged than about these issues from the slightly smaller group of advantaged respondents—even though references to basic human needs occupy relatively greater space in the bundle of communications emanating from the disadvantaged.

These findings might be interpreted to suggest that, although the disadvantaged are underrepresented with respect to participatory input, their concerns and needs are nonetheless being expressed by others. When the disadvantaged speak for themselves on issues of basic human need, however, their communications differ in two fundamental ways from those sent by others. First, when the disadvantaged communicate with public officials about basic human needs, they are much more likely than the advantaged to be concerned about problems that affect them personally. Even affluent citizens may need government assistance with respect to basic human needs: they may have health problems or a handicapped child in school; if elderly, they receive Medicare and Social Security. Still, a much larger proportion of the messages about basic human needs from the disadvantaged involve particularized communications about problems specific to themselves or their families—such as a question about eligibility for Social Security, a complaint about the conditions in a housing project, or

TABLE 16.5   *What Respondents Say: Issue-Based Political Activity (Information-Rich Activities Only)*

Proportion of Issue-Based Activity Animated by Concern About . . .	All	Advantaged[a]	Disadvantaged[b]	Receives Means-Tested Benefits
Basic human needs	10%	8%	21%	32%
Taxes	6	6	4	8
Economic issues (except taxes)	5	7	1	1
Abortion	8	11	0	4
Social issues (except abortion)	2	1	5	6
Education	12	15	10	18
Environment	9	8	2	2
Crime or drugs	9	6	10	8
Foreign policy	3	3	0	0
Number of respondents	2,517	425	480	228
Number of issue-based acts	1,556	432	123	73

Source: Citizen Participation Study.
Note: For definition of categories, see Verba, Schlozman, and Brady (1995, 221).
[a]At least some college and family income of $50,000 or more.
[b]No education beyond high school and family income below $15,000.

a request by a disabled respondent for special transportation, to cite some actual examples from our data.

Such particularized concerns are behind 56 percent of the issue-based activity in which human needs issues are mentioned by the disadvantaged, but only 8 percent of that in which human needs issues are mentioned by the advantaged. Even when the human needs issue is framed as a policy issue rather than a particularized concern, the disadvantaged are much more likely to report that the problem is one that affects themselves or their families as well as others in the community. All in all, of those who communicate with public officials about issues of basic human needs, 71 percent of the disadvantaged, but only 29 percent of the advantaged, are discussing something with an immediate impact on themselves or their families. Thus, if the disadvantaged were active in proportion to their numbers, policy-makers would be hearing a different set of messages.

HOW THE GOVERNMENT RESPONDS

Linkage between public preferences and governmental response is, of course, at the core of our concerns, but the matter is not a simple one. The large literature on the correspondence between public opinion and the actions of public officials raises many questions and reaches no consensus about this fundamental question of democratic theory.[18] When public opinion and government actions are of a piece, are we sure we know who is influencing whom? The direction of causality may not be clear. Elected officials may monitor and respond to public opinion, but citizen preferences can be shaped by policy elites and the media. And when public opinion and government actions are not in accord, is the interpretation that policymakers are ignoring citizen preferences? Or is it that policymakers are acting as trustees—responding to what are deemed to be the long-term needs, rather than the expressed preferences, of the public?

In *Politicians Don't Pander*, Lawrence Jacobs and Robert Shapiro (2000) present an interesting mixed picture. Politicians pay attention to the public—by following polls, monitoring the mail, and reading other tea-leaf indications of public opinion—but not so as to be able to follow the public. Rather, they do so to figure out how—through what the authors call "crafted talk"—to bring the public around to favor the policies they want to pursue. The process has affinities to the elite manipulation that others discern but is not completely devoid of citizen control. Since politicians need to convince the citizenry, they have to craft communications that appeal. Thus, they cannot simply ignore the public, and there is necessarily some kind of upward flow of influence.

Turning to the more specific question of the relationship between the inequality of political activity and governmental response, there are relatively few studies, and causal links between participation and policy are difficult to prove. Is the change in the status of African Americans in southern politics since the Voting Rights Act of 1965 unrelated to their enfranchisement and the other activities that have followed from it? It is hard to imagine that there is no connection. Studies show that the mobilization of lower-class voters in a state is related to the generosity of state welfare benefits (see Hill and Leighley 1992; Hill, Leighley, and Hinton-Andersson 1995, as corrected in Ringquist et al. 1997; and Allen and Campbell 1994). In her study of the links between activity by senior citizens and policy on Social Security, Andrea Campbell (2003) uses systematic evidence to demonstrate that threats to Social Security produced upsurges in activity by senior citizens and policy response by Congress.

Comparative analysis also suggests a link between participatory inequality and governmental policies. It is well known that, among advanced industrial democracies, the United States is characterized by high levels of income inequality. Moreover, Verba, Nie, and Kim (1979) demonstrate that, as measured by the relationship of income or education to political activity, political inequality is also greater in the United States than in the countries it most resembles. There is also evidence (Solow 2000) that government policy plays a role in creating the levels of income inequality across these nations, which are relatively similar in the degree of inequality of income before government intervention and quite different after governmental taxes and transfers are taken into account. Tax and transfer policies in the United States produce much less equalization than in other comparable countries. Many factors—ranging from the ideology of the American Dream to the racial and ethnic diversity of the American public—are adduced to explain the distinctive character of politics and policy in the United States. However, it seems likely that one factor in explaining the weakness of redistributive policy is the absence of political clout of those lower on the socioeconomic scale—which is related, in turn, to an institutional configuration in which unions are weak and there is no social democratic or labor party.

EQUALIZING PARTICIPATION

Can disparities in political participation be overcome? Our discussion of the sources of participatory inequalities contains an implicit agenda for achieving something closer to equal political voice, one that involves changes to the rules of politics, to political institutions and processes, and to underlying social structures. Nevertheless, we are not optimistic. Since the inequalities in participation we have discussed result from the interplay of so many factors, each of which makes a significant but small contribution to the outcome, no single magic bullet would do the trick. Moreover, many of the factors that contribute to political inequality are themselves the result of a complex interaction of political, economic, and social factors and cannot be addressed simply by changes in public policy. In addition, even where the circumstances responsible for political equality are amenable to amelioration through public policy, the realities of American politics render it extremely unlikely that certain of those policies would be enacted and implemented.

The laws that establish the rules of politics—especially policies mandating who can vote under what circumstances—have consequences for participatory inequalities. One way to raise participation is to make it easier to take part. In recent decades the states have undertaken a variety of electoral reforms, a number of which have been shown to have a positive impact on turnout: among these reforms are easing restrictions on casting absentee ballots and permitting mail-in ballots.[19] The extent to which registration requirements act as a deterrent to turnout has long been a focus of concern not only among scholars but also among policymakers (see Wolfinger and Rosenstone 1980; Powell 1986). In fact, that concern was the impetus behind the National Voter Registration Act (NVRA) of 1993. The NVRA contains several provisions designed to lower barriers to registration: registration by mail; restrictions on the purging of voter registration lists; agency-based registration at public assistance and unemployment compensation offices; and, most notably, the "motor voter" provision for registration at state motor vehicle bureaus. The numerous studies assessing these and other measures aimed at easing registration requirements suggest that provisions for motor voter and agency registration, as well as extensions of the registration period closer to the election, including same-day registration, all raise voter registration, while provisions for mail registration and restrictions on purging have no impact.[20] There is less agreement, however, about the magnitude of the changes occasioned by these reforms.[21] Furthermore, the findings are quite inconsistent when it comes to the representational impact—that is, does liberalizing registration requirements alter the composition of the electorate with respect either to partisanship or to demographic characteristics of voters, especially race and SES?[22]

More drastic governmental interventions might involve equalizing by making participation compulsory or by limiting participation. Since requiring attendance at meetings or rallies smacks more of authoritarian systems than democratic ones, placing a floor under participation by making it compulsory is probably feasible only in relation to voting. Compulsory voting, which would have its greatest impact on those who would otherwise be least likely to vote, would have equalizing effects. However, the American tradition of voluntarism makes such a policy politically unlikely; moreover, it might be unconstitutional (on compulsory voting, see Lijphart 1997, 8–11, and Franklin 1999).

The other approach to mandated political equality, a ceiling on participation, already exists in relation to voting: each voter has one and only one vote. Campaign finance laws also ameliorate political inequalities by placing a ceiling on inequality—even though the ceilings established by state and federal campaign finance laws are sufficiently high so as not to constrain the activity of most citizens. Without attempting even a superficial accounting of the debates surrounding campaign finance legislation, we should mention the political and constitutional realities that limit the effectiveness of campaign finance law as a vehicle for mandating political equality. First, procedural reforms in American politics inevitably have unintended consequences; it is difficult to draft watertight policy. In addition, incumbents, who benefit from the policy status quo, are on balance not especially enthusiastic about enacting effective campaign finance reform. Finally, since the courts have ruled that some contributions are a form of protected political expression, the First Amendment places boundaries on campaign finance legislation.

Political patterns in other advanced democracies demonstrate that changes to political institutions and processes might diminish political inequality. An important part of the story of political inequality in America is the traditional weakness of both organized labor and the political parties and the absence of a labor or social democratic party. This institutional configuration has dual implications: in many democracies these institutions function both to mobilize those lower on the socioeconomic scale into politics (Verba, Nie, and Kim 1979; Powell 1986; Jackman 1987) and to advocate for policies beneficial for the less advantaged. Not only are the American parties and unions relatively weak in comparative terms, but their power has become further attenuated in recent years, with potential consequences for political inequality. There is evidence that declining voter turnout can be attributed in part to the decreasing effectiveness of the parties as mobilizers (Rosenstone and Hansen 1993) and to the contraction in union membership (Radcliff and Davis 2000).

This uniquely American set of institutional circumstances and processes has complex origins. There is therefore no simple recipe for change and no obvious public policy solution. Nevertheless, stronger institutions to represent the interests of working people and the disadvantaged would have repercussions for political inequality. Similarly, we mentioned that the underrepresentation of women and blacks among visible political figures sends signals about who belongs in politics and thus has implications for participatory inequalities on the basis of gender and race—though not necessarily socioeconomic status. While other democracies have rules mandating the nomination of women for public office and schemes for the representation of religious or linguistic groups within the government, such arrangements run against the grain of American individualism. Still, if the patterns of representation among political leaders were to change, the extent of political inequality might diminish.

Our analysis makes it clear that the origins of political inequality are deeply embedded in the American social structure. Inequalities in participation reflect inequalities in education, occupation, and income. Reducing these social and economic inequalities would have the effect of reducing political inequalities. One way to change the vast political inequalities attendant to the use of money in politics is not by restricting the use of money but by equalizing the capacity to be a campaign donor through income redistribution. Or, since education is the key to many forms of political activity, bringing about greater educational equality should lead to greater participatory equality. Nonetheless, we must note in conclusion that the very inequality in political activity that is the subject of this chapter militates against the implementation of policies designed to bring about greater educational, social, or economic equality.

NOTES

1. This chapter draws on previous work by the authors and their collaborators, in particular Verba and Nie (1972), Verba, Nie, and Kim (1979), Verba, Schlozman, and Brady (1995), and Burns, Schlozman, and Verba (2001).

2. A number of helpful sources contain general discussions of political participation and reviews of the literature: Milbrath and Goel (1977), Bennett and Bennett (1986), Leighley (1995), Brady (1999), Conway (2000), and Schlozman (2002).

3. For a fuller discussion of politically relevant differences with extensive data on racial and ethnic differences, see Verba, Schlozman, and Brady (1995, chs. 6 and 8). For an extended discussion of gender differences, see Burns, Schlozman, and Verba (2001).

4. Data sources are listed on the tables and figures. A description of the data from the Citizen Participation Study used in many of the tables and figures is found in Verba, Schlozman, and Brady (1995, app. A).

5. See, among others, Ackerman and Ayres (2002), Baker (2002), and Magleby (2003). The specific data on the proportions working in campaigns versus the proportion giving money to campaigns are not unam-

biguous. Sidney Verba, Kay Schlozman, and Henry Brady (1995) show a rise in campaign giving and a decline in campaign work between 1967 and 1987; Steven Rosenstone and John Mark Hansen (1993), using National Election Study data from 1952 to 1988, show a clear decline in campaign work. They also show no decline, but no particular increase, in campaign contributions over that period (ch. 6), a pattern that continues in more recent election studies. Perhaps we can resolve the discrepancy by noting that, while there may or may not have been changes in the proportion of citizens who make donations, the aggregate sums contributed have surely risen.

6.   For our results and extensive discussion of the strengths and liabilities of the Roper data and the techniques used to construct the SES quintiles, see Brady, et al. (2002).

7.   The fact that, in all three countries, the relationship of SES to political interest is stronger than the relationship of SES to political activity deserves mention. Compared with political interest, political activity is more dependent on the institutional context in which it takes place. Although political parties can mobilize individuals to political activity and, conversely, "lock out" individuals and groups who find no party for which to vote or work, they cannot as easily create political interest or prevent people from being interested in politics. Thus, the data suggest that political interest is more dependent on socio-economic status, while political activity in the electoral arena may have more to do with institutional structures. As Sidney Verba, Norman Nie, and Jae-on Kim (1979) show, equality of political activity is fostered in nations with strong parties that mobilize to political activity citizens who, on the basis of their individual socioeconomic characteristics, would otherwise have been less likely to be active. In the United States, such strong parties do not exist.

8.   For a trenchant summary of the criticisms of the SES model, see Leighley (1995, 183–88).

9.   The various factors that shape participation are not equally relevant for various participatory acts. For example, strength of partisanship has a more substantial effect on voting than on getting involved in a community problem-solving effort; income is much more strongly related to campaign giving—and in particular, to the size of the gift—than to protesting; civic skills matter more for time-based political activities such as contacting a public official than for voting; and so on (see Verba, Schlozman, and Brady 1995, 356–64). Hence, in generalizing about the roots of political activity it is important to bear in mind the differential relevance of various participatory factors for different political acts.

10.   Available time—which is related to life circumstances, not to SES—would also seem to be an essential resource for political activity. Interestingly, when other participatory factors are taken into consideration, the number of hours left over after accounting for time devoted to school, paid work, and the care of home and children has no impact on participation—the busy are as politically active as the leisured (see Verba, Schlozman, and Brady 1995, chs. 12–13).

11.   There is a great deal of variation in the ways in which these psychological orientations to politics are measured. Further variation is introduced by the differences in the ways in which individual measures are combined into scales. For descriptions of the various measures, discussions of their use in the literature, and extensive data, see the essays on political alienation and efficacy by Mary Jo Reef and David Knoke (1999), on trust in government by Jack Citrin and Christopher Muste (1999), on political information by Vincent Price (1999), and on partisanship by Herbert Weisberg (1999), and in Robinson, Shaver, and Wrightsman (1999); see also Abramson (1983), Bennett (1986), Iyengar (1990), Zaller (1992), and Delli Carpini and Keeter (1996).

12.   In their analysis of the roots of participation among African Americans, Verba and Nie (1972) demonstrated links between group consciousness and political participation. The findings about the impact of group consciousness on activity in subsequent analyses are not especially consistent; see, for example, Schlozman and Verba (1979, ch. 10), Shingles (1981), Miller et al. (1981), Klein (1984, 136), Tate (1991), Tolleson-Rinehart (1992), Ardrey (1994), Wilcox (1997), and Leighley and Vedlitz (1999), as well as the discussions in Walton (1985) and Flammang (1997, 116–19). One regularity underlying what would seem to be discrepant results is that an association between group consciousness and political activity is more likely to emerge in studies conducted during the 1960s and 1970s—when the temperature of American politics was elevated—than in studies based on data collected later. In their 1990 data, Nancy Burns, Kay Schlozman, and Sidney Verba (2001, chs. 10–11) find that group consciousness does not generate participation but instead channels participation. That is, group consciousness does not act as an

independent participatory factor for blacks, Latinos, and women. However, if active, group-conscious members of all three groups are more likely to participate on issues having relevance to the group identity.

13. Recent studies demonstrating the participatory payoff of party efforts at mobilizing citizens include Southwell (1991), Huckfeldt and Sprague (1992; 1995, ch. 12), Wielhouwer and Lockerbie (1994), and Wielhouwer (1999). On the basis of a randomized field experiment, Alan Gerber and Donald Green (2000a, 2000b) show the impact of nonpartisan get-out-the-vote messages. When delivered through personal canvassing, the consequences for participation of these mobilizing messages were substantial. In contrast, telephone calls with similar messages made no difference.

14. On informal processes of recruitment to citizen activity as well as the significance of institutionally based mobilization efforts by employers and leaders of nonpolitical organizations or religious institutions, see Verba, Schlozman, and Brady (1995, chs. 5 and 13). On group-specific processes of political mobilization for racial and ethnic minorities, see Leighley (2001). For analysis of the attempts by rational recruiters to locate potential activists and discussion of the problems of causal direction raised by these processes of targeting, see Brady, Schlozman, and Verba (1999). Rosenstone and Hansen (1993, 166–69) make a parallel argument with respect to the attempts by political parties to mobilize likely and sympathetic voters.

15. John Petrocik (1987), however, finds that differential turnout might have made a difference in 1980 and 1984. On the implications of differences in voter turnout, see Hill and Leighley (1992).

16. Although educational loans are indeed means-tested, because the beneficiaries of student loans are overwhelmingly not among the poor, we group educational loans with the non-means-tested benefits.

17. The scale is defined in Verba, Schlozman, and Brady (1995, ch. 4, and app. C). A generalization of the index developed by Wolfinger and Rosenstone (1980), it is based on the ratio of the percentage of activists with a particular characteristic—a particular policy position or a particular set of needs—to the percentage of people with that characteristic in the population as a whole.

18. Considering the public as a whole, Benjamin Page and Robert Shapiro (1992) and James Stimson, Michael MacKuen, and Robert Erickson (1995) find evidence of similarity between public preferences and governmental response. In contrast, Benjamin Ginsberg (1986) and John Zaller (1992) describe a situation in which elites either dominate or, at least, manipulate citizens. (More recently, however, Zaller [1998] found a good deal of public autonomy when it came to views on Clinton's relationship with Monica Lewinsky.) In their discussions of this literature, Jeff Manza, Fay Cook, and Benjamin Page (2002) and Manza and Cook (2002) make the point that the relationship between the attitudes of the public and the comportment of policymakers is contingent and that the challenge is to discern the circumstances under which various patterns obtain.

19. With respect to absentee eligibility, Eric Oliver (1996) makes clear that reducing the hurdles to absentee voting is not sufficient on its own but is effective only in combination with efforts by parties to mobilize voters. On all-mail elections, see Southwell and Burchett (2000). Oliver and Wolfinger (1999) consider another possible deterrent to voter registration, the fact that in some states jury lists are constructed from registered voters, but find no evidence that jury aversion depresses voter registration.

20. Ruy Teixeira (1992), Glenn Mitchell and Christopher Wlezien (1995), Staci Rhine (1995), Stephen Knack (1995), Stephen Knack and James White (1998), and Michael Martinez and David Hill (1999) all consider several of these reforms together. Daniel Franklin and Eric Grier (1997) concentrate on motor voter registration, and Benjamin Highton (1997) focuses on same-day registration. A number of analysts point out that, because states require renewal of driver's licenses only at several-year intervals, the effects of motor voter provisions would not be expected to be immediate. Knack (1995, 809) discusses the necessity of paying attention to the ways in which particular reforms interact. Thus, mail-in registration may have no effect because it becomes less needed when coupled with more powerful programs like motor voter or same-day registration.

21. Part of the issue is whether higher rates of registration translate into higher rates of turnout. Modeling registration and voting as separate selection processes makes it clear that the less-motivated voters who were deterred from registering by high barriers may be less likely to vote if their registration results from the lowering of the registration hurdle. On this logic, see Knack (1995), Timpone (1998), and Martinez and Hill (1999).

22. With respect to whether facilitating registration ameliorates the socioeconomic bias in the electorate, see the conflicting findings in Nagler (1991), Highton (1997), Timpone (1998), and Martinez and Hill (1999).

REFERENCES

Abramson, Paul R. 1983. *Political Attitudes in America: Formation and Change.* San Francisco: W. H. Freeman.

Ackerman, Bruce A., and Ian Ayres. 2002. *Voting with Dollars: A New Paradigm for Campaign Finance.* New Haven, Conn.: Yale University Press.

Allen, M. P., and John L. Campbell. 1994. "State Revenue Extraction from Different Income Groups: Variations in Tax Progressivity in the United States, 1916 to 1986." *American Sociological Review* 59: 169–86.

Ardrey, Saundra. 1994. "The Political Behavior of Black Women: Contextual, Structural, and Psychological Factors." In *Black Politics and Black Political Behavior: A Linkage Analysis,* edited by Hanes Walton. Westport, Conn.: Praeger.

Baker, Paula, ed. 2002. *Money and Politics.* University Park: Pennsylvania State University Press.

Bennett, Linda, and Stephen Earl Bennett. 1986. "Political Participation: Meaning and Measurement." In *Annual Review of Political Science,* edited by Samuel Long. Norwood, N.J.: Ablex Publishing.

Bennett, Stephen Earl. 1986. *Apathy in America, 1960 to 1984: Causes and Consequences of Citizen Political Indifference.* Dobbs Ferry, N.Y.: Transnational Publishers.

Bennett, Stephen Earl, and David Resnick. 1990. "The Implications of Nonvoting for Democracy in the United States." *American Journal of Political Science* 34(3, August): 771–802.

Bobo, Lawrence, and Franklin D. Gilliam Jr. 1990. "Race, Sociopolitical Participation, and Black Empowerment." *American Political Science Review* 84: 377–93.

Brady, Henry E. 1999. "Political Participation." In *Measures of Political Attitudes,* edited by John P. Robinson, Phillip R. Shaver, and Lawrence Wrightsman. San Diego: Academic Press.

Brady, Henry E., Kay Lehman Schlozman, and Sidney Verba. 1999. "Prospecting for Participants: Rational Expectations and the Recruitment of Political Activists." *American Political Science Review* 93(1, March): 153–68.

Brady, Henry E., Kay Lehman Schlozman, Sidney Verba, and Laurel Elms. 2002. "Who Bowls? The (Un)Changing Stratification of Participation." In *Understanding Public Opinion,* edited by Barbara Norrander and Clyde Wilcox. Washington, D.C.: CQ Press.

Burns, Nancy, Kay Lehman Schlozman, and Sidney Verba. 2001. *The Private Roots of Public Action: Gender, Equality, and Political Participation.* Cambridge, Mass.: Harvard University Press.

Campbell, Andrea Louise. 2003. *How Policies Make Citizens: Senior Political Activism and the American Welfare State.* Princeton, N.J.: Princeton University Press.

Citrin, Jack, and Christopher Muste. 1999. "Trust in Government." In *Measures of Political Attitudes,* edited by John P. Robinson, Phillip R. Shaver, and Lawrence Wrightsman. San Diego: Academic Press.

Conway, M. Margaret. 2000. *Political Participation in the United States.* 3rd ed. Washington, D.C.: CQ Press.

Delli Carpini, Michael X., and Scott Keeter. 1996. *What Americans Know About Politics and Why It Matters.* New Haven, Conn.: Yale University Press.

DeNardo, James. 1980. "Turnout and the Vote: The Joke's on the Democrats." *American Political Science Review* 74(2, June): 406–20.

Flammang, Janet. 1997. *Women's Political Voice.* Philadelphia: Temple University Press.

Franklin, Daniel P., and Eric E. Grier. 1997. "Effects of Motor Voter Legislation: Voter Turnout, Registration, and Partisan Advantage in the 1992 Presidential Election." *American Politics Quarterly* 25: 104–17.

Franklin, Mark N. 1999. "Electoral Engineering and Cross-National Turnout Differences: What Role for Compulsory Voting?" *British Journal of Political Science* 29: 205–24.

Gay, Claudine. 1997. "Taking Charge: Black Electoral Success and the Redefinition of American Politics." Ph.D. diss., Harvard University.

Gerber, Alan S., and Donald P. Green. 2000a. "The Effect of a Nonpartisan Get-out-the-Vote Drive: An Experimental Study of Leafleting." *Journal of Politics* 62: 846–57.

———. 2000b. "Effects of Canvassing, Telephone Calls, and Direct Mail on Voter Turnout: A Field Experiment." *American Political Science Review* 94: 653–63.

Ginsberg, Benjamin. 1986. *The Captive Public: How Mass Opinion Promotes State Power.* New York: Basic Books.

Highton, Benjamin. 1997. "Early Registration and Voter Turnout." *Journal of Politics* 59: 565–75.

Hill, Kim Quaile, and Jan E. Leighley. 1992. "The Policy Consequences of Class Bias in State Elections." *American Journal of Political Science* 36: 351–65.

Hill, Kim Quaile, Jan E. Leighley, and Angela Hinton-Andersson. 1995. "Lower-Class Mobilization and Policy Linkage in the U.S. States." *American Journal of Political Science* 39: 75–86.

Huckfeldt, Robert, and John Sprague. 1992. "Political Parties and Electoral Mobilization: Political Structure, Social Structure, and the Party Canvass." *American Political Science Review* 86: 70–86.

———. 1995. *Citizens, Politics, and Social Communications.* Cambridge: Cambridge University Press.

Iyengar, Shanto. 1990. "Shortcuts to Political Knowledge: The Role of Selective Attention and Accessibility." In *Information and Democratic Processes,* edited by John A. Ferejohn and James H. Kuklinski. Chicago: University of Illinois Press.

Jackman, Robert W. 1987. "Democratic Institutions and Voter Turnout in the Industrialized Democracies." *American Political Science Review* 81: 405–34.

Jacobs, Lawrence R., and Robert Y. Shapiro. 2000. *Politicians Don't Pander: Political Manipulation and the Loss of Democratic Responsiveness.* Chicago: University of Chicago Press.

Keyssar, Alexander. 2000. *The Right to Vote.* New York: Basic Books.

Klein, Ethel. 1984. *Gender Politics.* Cambridge, Mass.: Harvard University Press.

Knack, Stephen. 1995. "Does 'Motor Voter' Work? Evidence from State-Level Data." *Journal of Politics* 57: 796–811.

Knack, Stephen, and James White. 1998. "Did States' Motor Voter Programs Help the Democrats?" *American Politics Quarterly* 26: 344–65.

Leighley, Jan E. 1995. "Attitudes, Opportunities, and Incentives: A Field Essay on Political Participation." *Political Research Quarterly* 48(1, March): 181–209.

———. 2001. *Strength in Numbers? The Political Mobilization of Racial and Ethnic Minorities.* Princeton, N.J.: Princeton University Press.

Leighley, Jan E., and Arnold Vedlitz. 1999. "Race, Ethnicity, and Political Participation: Competing Models and Contrasting Expectations." *Journal of Politics* 61: 1092–1114.

Lijphart, Arend. 1997. "Unequal Participation: Democracy's Unresolved Dilemma." *American Political Science Review* 91(1, March): 1–14.

Magleby, David B., ed. 2003. *The Other Campaign: Soft Money and Issue Advocacy in the 2000 Congressional Elections.* Lanham, Md.: Rowman & Littlefield.

Manza, Jeff, and Fay Lomax Cook. 2002. "A Democratic Polity? Three Views of Policy Responsiveness to Public Opinion in the United States." *American Politics Research* 30(November): 630–67.

Manza, Jeff, Fay Lomax Cook, and Benjamin I. Page. 2002. "Navigating Public Opinion: An Introduction." In *Navigating Public Opinion,* edited by Jeff Manza, Fay Lomax Cook, and Benjamin I. Page. New York: Oxford University Press.

Martinez, Michael D., and David Hill. 1999. "Did Motor Voter Work?" *American Politics Quarterly* 27: 296–315.

Milbrath, Lester W., and M. L. Goel. 1977. *Political Participation: How and Why Do People Get Involved in Politics?* 2nd ed. Chicago: Rand McNally.

Miller, Arthur H., Patricia Gurin, Gerald Gurin, and Oksana Malanchuk. 1981. "Group Consciousness and Political Participation." *American Journal of Political Science* 25(3, August): 494–511.

Mitchell, Glenn E., and Christopher Wlezien. 1995. "The Impact of Legal Constraints on Voter Registration, Turnout, and the Composition of the American Electorate." *Political Behavior* 17(2, June): 179–202.

Nagler, Jonathan. 1991. "The Effect of Registration Laws and Education on Voter Turnout." *American Political Science Review* 85: 1393–1405.

Nie, Norman, Jane Junn, and Kenneth Stehlik-Barry. 1996. *Education and Democratic Citizenship in America.* Chicago: University of Chicago Press.

Oliver, J. Eric. 1996. "The Effects of Eligibility Restrictions and Party Activity on Absentee Voting and Overall Turnout." *American Journal of Political Science* 40(2, May): 498–513.

Oliver, J. Eric, and Raymond E. Wolfinger. 1999. "Jury Aversion and Voter Registration." *American Political Science Review* 93(1, March): 147–52.

Page, Benjamin I., and Robert Y. Shapiro. 1992. *The Rational Public.* Chicago: University of Chicago Press.

Petrocik, John. 1987. "Voter Turnout and Electoral Preferences: The Anomalous Reagan Elections." In *Elections in America,* edited by Kay L. Schlozman. New York: Allen and Unwin.

Piven, Frances F., and Richard Cloward. 1988. *Why Americans Don't Vote.* New York: Pantheon.

Powell, G. Bingham. 1986. "American Voter Turnout in Comparative Perspective." *American Political Science Review* 80(1, March): 17–43.

Price, Vincent. 1999. "Political Information." In *Measures of Political Attitudes,* edited by John P. Robinson, Phillip R. Shaver, and Lawrence Wrightsman. San Diego: Academic Press.

Putnam, Robert D. 2000. *Bowling Alone: The Collapse and Revival of American Community.* New York: Simon & Schuster.

Radcliff, Benjamin, and Patricia Davis. 2000. "Labor Organization and Electoral Participation in Industrial Democracies." *American Journal of Politics* 44(1, January): 132–41.

Reef, Mary Jo, and David Knoke. 1999. "Political Alienation and Efficacy." In *Measures of Political Attitudes,* edited by John P. Robinson, Phillip R. Shaver, and Lawrence Wrightsman. San Diego: Academic Press.

Rhine, Staci L. 1995. "Registration Reform and Turnout Change in the American States." *American Politics Quarterly* 23: 409–26.

Ringquist, Evan J., Kim Quaile Hill, Jan E. Leighley, and Angela Hinton-Andersson. 1997. "Lower-Class Mobilization and Policy Linkage in the U.S. States: A Correction." *American Journal of Political Science* 41(1, January): 339–44.

Robinson, John P., Phillip R. Shaver, and Lawrence Wrightsman, eds. 1999. *Measures of Political Attitudes.* San Diego: Academic Press.

Rosenstone, Steven J., and John Mark Hansen. 1993. *Mobilization, Participation, and Democracy in America.* New York: Macmillan.

Schlozman, Kay Lehman. 2002. "Citizen Participation in America: What Do We Know? Why Do We Care?" In *Political Science: The State of the Discipline,* edited by Ira Katznelson and Helen V. Milner. New York: W. W. Norton.

Schlozman, Kay Lehman, and Sidney Verba. 1979. *Injury to Insult: Unemployment, Class, and Political Response.* Cambridge, Mass.: Harvard University Press.

Shaffer, Stephen. 1982. "Policy Differences Between Voters and Nonvoters in American Elections." *Western Political Quarterly* 35: 396–410.

Shingles, Richard D. 1981. "Black Consciousness and Political Participation: The Missing Link." *American Political Science Review* 75: 76–91.

Skocpol, Theda. 2003. *From Membership to Management in American Civic Life.* Norman: University of Oklahoma Press.

Solow, Robert. 2000. "Welfare: The Cheapest Nation." *New York Review of Books* (March 28, 2000): 20–23.

Southwell, Priscilla L. 1991. "Voter Turnout in the 1986 Congressional Elections: The Media as a Demobilizer?" *American Politics Quarterly* 19: 96–108.

Southwell, Priscilla L., and Justin I. Burchett. 2000. "The Effect of All-Mail Elections on Voter Turnout." *American Politics Quarterly* 28: 72–79.

Stimson, James A., Michael B. MacKuen, and Robert S. Erikson. 1995. "Dynamic Representation." *American Political Science Review* 89(3, September): 543–65.

Tate, Katherine. 1991. "Black Political Participation in the 1984 and 1988 Presidential Elections." *American Political Science Review* 85(4, December): 1159–76.

Teixeira, Ruy A. 1992. *The Disappearing American Voter.* Washington, D.C.: Brookings Institution.

Timpone, Richard J. 1998. "Structure, Behavior, and Voter Turnout in the United States." *American Political Science Review* 92(1, March): 145–58.

Tolleson-Rinehart, Sue. 1992. *Gender Consciousness and Politics.* New York: Routledge.

Verba, Sidney, and Norman H. Nie. 1972. *Participation in America.* New York: Harper & Row.

Verba, Sidney, Norman H. Nie, and Jae-on Kim. 1979. *Participation and Political Equality: A Seven-Nation Comparison.* New York: Cambridge University Press.

Verba, Sidney, Kay Lehman Schlozman, and Henry E. Brady. 1995. *Voice and Equality: Civic Voluntarism in American Politics.* Cambridge, Mass.: Harvard University Press.

Walton, Hanes, Jr. 1985. *Invisible Politics: Black Political Behavior.* Albany: State University of New York Press.

Weisberg, Herbert F. 1999. "Political Partisanship." In *Measures of Political Attitudes,* edited by John P. Robinson, Phillip R. Shaver, and Lawrence Wrightsman. San Diego: Academic Press.

Wielhouwer, Peter W. 1999. "The Mobilization of Campaign Activists by the Party Canvass." *American Politics Quarterly* 27: 177–200.

Wielhouwer, Peter W., and Brad Lockerbie. 1994. "Party Contacting and Political Participation: 1952 to 1990." *American Journal of Political Science* 38: 211–33.

Wilcox, Clyde. 1997. "Racial and Gender Consciousness Among African American Women: Sources and Consequences." *Women and Politics* 17: 73–94.

Wolfinger, Raymond E., and Steven J. Rosenstone. 1980. *Who Votes?* New Haven, Conn.: Yale University Press.

Zaller, John R. 1992. *The Nature and Origins of Mass Opinion.* Cambridge: Cambridge University Press.

———. 1998. "Monica Lewinsky's Contribution to Political Science." *PS: Political Science and Politics* 31(2, June): 182–89.

Chapter 17

An Analytical Perspective on Participatory Inequality and Income Inequality

Henry E. Brady

At least since the sans culottes—literally, "those without breeches"—streamed through the streets of Paris in 1789 to overthrow the ostentatious and corrupt ancien régime, modern social theorists have grappled with the relationship between poverty and political participation. Connections between people's economic resources and their political activities date back to antiquity, but the appearance in the late eighteenth century of democratic nations with novel forms of mass participation and the onslaught in the nineteenth century of the industrial revolution, with its starkly unequal social classes, led to new speculations about how income inequality produces political activity. Alexis de Tocqueville worried that democratic participation would allow the lower classes to use their political power to level society, erasing all differences (including income inequality) and creating uninspired homogeneity. Karl Marx predicted that capitalism's extreme income inequality would generate working-class consciousness and the revolution of the proletariat, ending in communism. In both formulations, economic inequality would spawn political participation that would transform society.

The rapid increase in income inequality in the United States from 1979 to 1994 raises anew the classic concerns of social theorists. Modern social scientists have explored the relationship between income inequality and revolutionary activity across many countries (see, for example, Hibbs 1973; Gurr 1970), and they have investigated the relationship between income and conventional political activities such as voting, campaign work, and campaign contributions by individuals (Verba and Nie 1972; Wolfinger and Rosenstone 1980). Neither of these strains of research, however, adequately addresses the questions raised by the changes in the past thirty years in America. In a stable democratic society such as the United States, income inequality seems less likely to foster revolutionary activity than to erode the conventional activities of some groups and to stimulate the conventional activities of others, leading to changes in who gets what, when, and how. The finding from cross-sectional surveys that political activity increases with higher income captures just part of the story. It says nothing about how over-time increases in income inequality affect political participation.

This chapter offers an analytical perspective on income, income inequality, and participation, and it presents new empirical work that goes beyond existing research. The analytical perspective draws on political science and economics to consider how income and income inequality affect participation. The most important contribution of the chapter is the demonstration that changes in income and changes in economic inequality have very different implications for political participation.

Income is an individual characteristic stemming from personal capabilities, opportunities, decisions, and luck. Income affects individual behaviors such as political participation because it provides a resource for participation. Nowhere is this more obvious than in political giving. It is not surprising that those with more income make greater contributions to politics and that those with less income make smaller contributions (Verba, Schlozman, and Brady 1995). It also seems reasonable to suppose that when a family moves from a higher income level to a lower one, its contributions to politics will be reduced. But does this necessarily mean that political activity by the lower classes will decrease and that the upper classes' political activity will increase when inequality widens?

It does not. Income inequality is a property of society, a social fact about the distribution of incomes. An increase in inequality will not only reduce the incomes of lower-class families but also change that group's political circumstances. With this distressing change in social facts, lower-income people might decide to increase their political activity to redress the situation. They might decide that government should be used to adjust the degree of inequality by adjusting people's capacities, opportunities, luck, or decisionmaking. It seems possible that lower-class activity might increase in these circumstances. It also seems possible that upper-class participation might increase in response.

This chapter investigates mechanisms that can explain how income and income inequality affect political activity. There are two goals here. One is to show how changes in income and income inequality can affect political activity in different, and sometimes opposite, ways. The arguments just cited suggest that they should operate differently, but the well-known positive cross-sectional correlation of contributions and income only suggests that participation should increase with income. The second goal is to specify the empirical tests that might distinguish the impacts of income and income inequality. Thus, the aim is to determine the proper specification of a *political activity equation* such as:

Political Activity $= a + b$ (Income) $+ c$ (Inequality) $+ d$ (Controls) $+$ omitted variables,

where a, b, c, and d are parameters. This chapter provides insights about how to measure income and inequality, the expected signs of b and c, whether to add an interaction term of income and inequality, and the identity of other variables that affect political activity.

The empirical research reported here reveals the seemingly paradoxical result that from the 1970s through the 1990s, participatory inequality *decreased* for at least some forms of political participation and in some places as income inequality *increased*. The analytical perspective suggests various reasons why this might be so, and it provides avenues for future research. Although we append an extensive bibliography of articles that we have consulted, this chapter does not provide an article-by-article review of this literature, partly because there are several other excellent literature reviews (Leighley 1995; Schlozman 2002; Verba, Schlozman, and Brady this volume; Freeman this volume), but primarily because the greatest need is for an analytical perspective on this literature that considers the objectives of the Russell Sage Foundation's project on the "social dimensions of inequality." Without such a perspective, the empirical findings are obtuse, recondite, and confusing.

BASIC CONCEPTS
Political Participation

Political activities are complex human performances (Brady 1999, 768–70) that typically involve actions by ordinary citizens to influence politics. Every society has its own repertoire of allowable, marginal, and illegal acts. Although Europeans no longer engage in illuminations in which protesters light candles at night, they are far more likely to block traffic or occupy buildings than Americans, who favor petitions, lawful demonstrations, and boycotts (see Brady 1999). Europeans also turn out to vote at higher rates than Americans. In America the standard repertoire includes giving money (such as campaign contributions), giving time (through campaign work, protests, or organizational memberships), giving a speech or organizing a meeting (at campaign events or before local boards), writing a letter (for example, to contact governmental officials or the newspaper), and simply going to vote.

For those activities that are meant to influence politics directly, the major distinction is between *electoral* and *non-electoral* activities. Electoral activities include voting, campaign contributions or campaign work, and party membership, activities that are organized and even scheduled by the electoral system. Non-electoral activities are organized outside the electoral system. *Conventional* non-electoral activities consist of contacting government officials, belonging to organizations, or working in the community. *Unconventional* non-electoral activities include legal methods such as petitioning and lawful demonstrations and unlawful methods such as occupying buildings, blocking traffic, destroying property, or even terrorism and assassination.

Because political activity is multifarious, there are good reasons to expect that the impact on political participation of any change in society, such as an increase in income inequality, will depend on the political act. Voting, for example, costs relatively little (Aldrich 1993), so that it seems likely that the impact of income changes on voting will be through routes other than increases or decreases in the relative cost of voting. Campaign contributions, however, cost money by definition, and it seems very likely that a change in income will directly affect the level of campaign contributions. One of the goals of this chapter is to suggest that there are different ways in which income inequality affects different forms of participation.

Income Inequality

Many factors explain political participation, but the focal point of this chapter is income inequality. One of the easiest ways to measure income inequality is to split the population into income percentiles, such as deciles, and to take the difference between the average income of the top decile and the average income of the bottom decile. If incomes are fairly equal, this difference is close to zero; otherwise, it is some positive number. The size of this number indicates the disparity in incomes between the top and bottom deciles, and the number can be considered a measure of *absolute income inequality*. If the number increases within a society, then the top and bottom deciles have become more unequal in absolute terms.

Unfortunately, the size of the top and bottom decile difference also depends on the units in which income is measured, and a comparison across societies requires converting incomes into a common currency. Consequently, economists often take the natural logarithms of these average incomes before taking their difference, which amounts to taking the logarithm of the ratio of the averages.[1] This procedure produces a dimensionless quantity that does not depend on the units in which income is measured and that focuses on *relative income inequality* instead of absolute income inequality. The drawback of a relative income inequality measure is that it treats two societies as the same if the ratio of the top to the bottom income is the same even if in one society the bottom decile gets $100 a year and the top one $1,000 a year and in the other society the bottom decile gets $50,000 a year and the top decile gets $500,000 a year. An absolute measure would reveal that the second society, with a difference of $450,000 between the top and bottom deciles, has much greater absolute income inequality than the first, which has a difference of only $900, although an absolute measure would typically not reveal that there is much more poverty in the first society than in the second one.[2] A very large literature on measuring inequality suggests that, for many purposes, relative income inequality is the most useful concept, although it should be supplemented by poverty measures (Cowell 1977; Champernowne and Cowell 1998).

Figure 17.1 (from Katz and Autor 1999) reports changes in the U.S. 90 percent–10 percent log weekly wage differential over time. Note that the value of this quantity for men and women was between about 1.1 and 1.2 (indicating a ratio in average wages of the highest to the lowest decile of about 3.0 to 3.3) from 1963 until around 1980, when it began to rise, until 1994, when it was between 1.4 and 1.6 (indicating a ratio in average wages between 4 and 5.) Figure 17.2 reports percentage changes in the Gini coefficient, another measure of relative inequality, for families from 1947 to 1998. In this figure, the percentage change remained between plus and minus 5 percent for over thirty years—with increases approximately canceled out by decreases—until the early 1980s, when the percentage change in income inequality began a steady rise beyond 5 percent a year to 10 percent and even perhaps 20 percent a year (although a change in the mode of data collection makes it hard to compare the figures for 1993 onward with the earlier figures). Our goal in this chapter is to understand how these changes in income inequality during the 1980s and the 1990s affected participatory inequality.

POLITICAL SCIENCE MODELS OF PARTICIPATION

Social theorists have made large claims about how economic inequality might lead to political participation, but they have seldom described the specific mechanisms linking economics and politics. In the following sections, we try to characterize in detail the mechanisms that might link income, economic inequality, and political participation. Rather than simply proposing one mechanism, we investigate a number of different prototype mechanisms and their applicability to the problem at hand. We begin with a discussion of political science models, and then we turn to models drawn from economics. The net result is a rich set of tools for thinking about inequality and participation and some useful guidance for specifying political activity equations.

Stylized Facts About Political Participation and the Socioeconomic Model

With any research area, some stylized facts shape research questions. Early empirical research pointed out the many types of political participation (Verba and Nie 1972; Barnes,

FIGURE 17.1   *Overall U.S. Wage Inequality, 1963 to 1995*

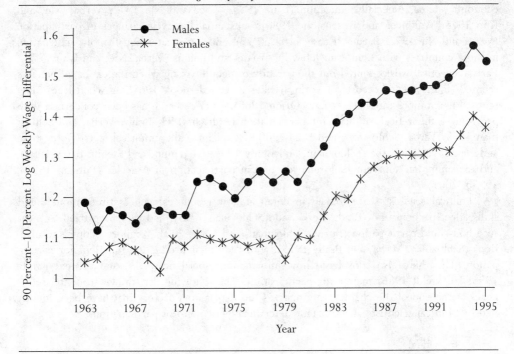

Source: Katz and Autor (1999).

FIGURE 17.2   *Change in Income Inequality for Families, 1947 to 1998*

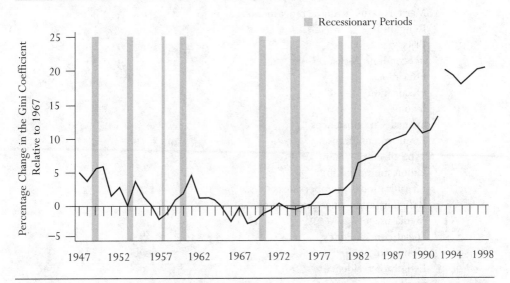

Source: March Current Population Survey. Compiled by U.S. Census Bureau, 2000, *The Changing Shape of the Nation's Income Distribution 1947–1998* (report P60–204).
Note: Change in data collection methodology suggests pre-1993 and post-1992 estimates are not comparable.

Kaase, et al. 1979), the strong positive relationship between participation and socio-economic status, especially education (Lane 1959; Verba and Nie 1972; Verba, Nie, and Kim 1978; Wolfinger and Rosenstone 1980), substantial life-cycle changes in participation (Verba and Nie 1972; Barnes, Kaase, et al. 1979), and the greater equality of participation in those countries with significant left-wing parties and unions (Verba, Nie, and Kim 1978). Early theoretical work pointed out the paradox of people voting when the expected benefits seemed slight given the costs of voting (Riker and Ordeshook 1968) or when free-riding seemed like a more rational strategy (Olson 1965). Later research has been concerned with providing a theoretical rationale for participation (Aldrich 1993; Brady, Verba, and Schloz-man 1995; Verba, Schlozman, and Brady 2000), explaining the empirical facts (Rosenstone and Hansen 1993; Verba, Schlozman, and Brady 1995; Nie, Junn, and Stehlik-Barry 1996), and explaining an apparent long-term decline in participation in America (Putnam 1995a, 1995b, 2001).

Political scientists have looked in detail at how resources such as time, money, and skills affect participation (Brady, Verba, and Schlozman 1995), and they have tried to mea-sure household participation (Burns, Schlozman, and Verba 2001), explore people's motiva-tions (Schlozman, Verba, and Brady 1995), and study their production functions for partici-pation. They have also considered how information, social networks, and context (Mutz 1998; Huckfeldt 1986) matter for participation. The following list (drawn from the refer-ences at the end of the chapter) summarizes the explanatory factors that have been identi-fied by political scientists as important determinants of political participation.

Individual
    Demographic
        Sex
        Age
        Race
        Ethnicity
        Marital status/living arrangements
        Religion
        Place of residence
    Socioeconomic Measures
        Education
        Occupation
        Income
    Individual Circumstances
        Employment status
        Type of employment
        Union membership
        Organizational memberships
        Religious attendance and membership
        Media usage
        Social connectedness
        Homeownership
        Length of residence
    Attitudes
        Interest in politics
        Efficacy

           Personal effectiveness
           Government responsiveness
           Trust in government
           Political cynicism
           Social trust
           Partisan strength
           Candidate preference strength
           Ideology
           Knowledge
       Political Factors
           Registered to vote
           Contact attempts
           Discuss politics
           Influencing others
    State, County, Electoral Unit
       Demographic
       Socioeconomic
       Economic
       Political Factors
           Registration laws
           Party competitiveness
           Political expenditures
           Party control
           Union or interest-group strength
       Political Offices
       Top of ticket
       Contested races
       Incumbency
       Region
           Region/South
    Time Period
       Type of Election
           Presidential/midterm
       Period

    The heart of the traditional models of political participation has been *socioeconomic measures* of education, occupation, and income supplemented with some demographic variables. Early work did not differentiate between education, occupation, and income, but recent work (Wolfinger and Rosenstone 1980; Verba, Schlozman, and Brady 1995; Leighley and Nagler 1992a; Nie, Junn, and Stehlik-Barry 1996) has tried to identify the separate impacts of education, occupation, and income. Almost all research tries to control for *demographic characteristics* such as sex, age, race, ethnicity, marital status, living arrangements, religion, and place of residence. Recent work has explored in detail the impacts of sex and marital status (Kingston and Finkel 1987; Burns, Schlozman, and Verba 2001), race and ethnicity (Ellison and Gay 1989; Tate 1991; Portney and Berry 1997; Leighley and Vedlitz 1999), and place of residence (Oliver 1999, 2000, 2001). Recent work by Campbell (2002) has started to take age seriously.

    The problem with the socioeconomic model of political participation is that it does not distinguish between preference, resource, and opportunity explanations for participation because socioeconomic and demographic characteristics can be proxies for all three factors. In economic models, for example, a correlation between income and the ownership of large houses undoubtedly reveals more about resource constraints than about preferences. But a correlation between gender and ownership of purses reveals more about preferences (and culture) than about resource constraints. Finally, a correlation between education and college teaching indicates more about opportunities, and perhaps individual resources, than about preferences. At best, the socioeconomic model is a "reduced-form" explanation of participation that does not separate out the structural conditions that affect participation. We cannot know whether more highly educated people prefer to participate more, have the resources (such as skills) to participate more, or have the opportunities to participate more. We explore these issues in more detail in the next section, where we take up economic models of political participation.

Attitudinal and Motivational Models

In the 1960s through the 1990s, a great deal of research focused on *attitudinal measures* such as interest in politics, political efficacy, personal effectiveness, sense of governmental responsiveness, trust in government, and political cynicism, but much of this work is subject to the criticism that these variables are very close to the dependent variable—so close that they might be the result of participation as much as its cause. Survey questions about political efficacy, for example, ask people whether they believe that the opinions of people like themselves are taken seriously, and it seems likely that those who participate are more likely to think that their opinions matter (Finkel 1985, 1987). Hence, explaining participation with these variables is somewhat dangerous unless care is taken to determine whether they really cause participation. More recently (Putnam 2001; Uslaner and Brown 2002) there has been an upsurge of interest in social trust as a determinant of participation, but social trust suffers from the same problems of being very similar to the phenomenon that is being explained.

Strong political beliefs, as measured by strength of partisanship, candidate preference strength, and ideology, are somewhat more removed from participation itself, and they have significant impacts on participation. As we would expect, those with stronger political beliefs are more likely to participate, presumably because they care more about the issues at stake and are more connected with the institutions that mobilize participants. One interpretation of political beliefs is that they measure preferences, but they may also reflect greater knowledge and information or even resources. *Political factors* such as being contacted (Rosenstone and Hansen 1993; Wielhouwer and Lockerbie 1994) or registered to vote (Wolfinger and Rosenstone 1980; Nagler 1992) also have an important impact on political participation. These may measure political opportunities, but there are reasons to believe that they also measure political preferences and resources (see, for example, Brady, Schlozman, and Verba 1999).

Contextual, Regional, and Temporal Factors

Researchers have also looked for contextual effects for the state or electoral unit that might affect participation. *Political factors* such as the legal framework for voting, the competitiveness of political parties (Brown, Jackson, and Wright 1999; Hill and Leighley 1993), political expenditures, and the strength of unions and other organizations appear to matter for political participation in some circumstances (Jackson 1993, 1996; Hill and Leighley 1994).

Presumably they help to shape the political opportunity structure. The *offices at the top of the ticket* (presidential, senatorial, or gubernatorial) and the degree to which they are contested matter for electoral participation (Boyd 1989). Some research has also found that the *region,* especially the South, can have an impact on participation. Finally, there are certainly *cycles* in participation, and there may be *time period* effects as well. Electoral activity is reduced in midterm elections, and it increases significantly in presidential races.

The Civic Voluntarism Model

Perhaps the most complete model of political participation is the civic voluntarism model of Sidney Verba, Kay Schlozman, and Henry Brady (1995), which was partly inspired by economic models of labor supply and consumer choice. This model starts from SES and demographic variables and shows how they work through individual circumstances to produce political participation. The model emphasizes how institutions such as jobs, organizations, and churches shape political participation. It also distinguishes between *resources* (Brady, Verba, and Schlozman 1995), such as time, money, and civic skills, *opportunities,* such as social networks (Brady, Schlozman, and Verba 1999), and *motivations* for participation (Schlozman, Verba, and Brady 1995), such as interest in politics and specific issue concerns. Even though the model was partly inspired by economic thinking, it still has no obvious place for the impact of income inequality apart from income. To understand the role of income inequality, we must consider some economic models in more detail.

ECONOMIC MODELS OF PARTICIPATION

In standard economic models, income inequality in a capitalist system is largely the result of individuals exercising their preferences through exchanges in markets that are often shaped by government action. Political participation involves people expressing their preferences to government through political activities fabricated from time, money, skills, and other inputs. Exercising preferences in markets and expressing (or forming) them in politics are clearly two different things, and it is not clear how they might be linked, although the role of government seems important. One possible linkage is that economic inequality affects the *resources,* especially income, available to people for participation, so that richer people have more resources and poorer people have fewer. Another possible connection is that income inequality *motivates* participation, so that poor people are more motivated than rich people to agitate in favor of redistributive policies. The first mechanism relies on income as a personal capacity that supports the ability to participate, while the second involves economic inequality as a social fact, a characteristic of the society as a whole that animates reactions from those whose interests are at stake. Both mechanisms involve trying to influence government action.

We consider four economic models in this section. The first three models provide insights into why income might provide a resource for political participation and how income inequality could indirectly affect participation by changing the distribution of this resource. But these models provide no insight into how income inequality might directly affect participation. In the first model, we think of political participation as similar to labor force participation. Just as people allocate hours to work because of the benefits it provides in the form of wages (but not because of any intrinsic benefits of work itself), people might allocate time to political participation because of the benefits it provides in the form of better public policies. This analogy suggests some interesting distinctions, but it does not seem to capture the fact that participation itself yields utility for some people. In the second model, we assume that people might also gain utility from participation itself, and we treat participation like a consumption decision. This model captures some additional truths about political participation, but it still seems to ignore the fact that some people are better at turning participation into something useful. The third model, the household production model of participation, offers insight into this possibility, and it connects with the civic voluntarism model. Still, none of these models provide a rationale for how income inequality might directly affect participation. The fourth model, a simple model of legislative vote buying by groups, provides some sense of how income inequality might matter by providing a motivation for participation.

Labor Force Participation as the Model of Political Participation

Income and income inequality result from participation in the labor force and in the marketplace. In their models of labor force and marketplace participation, economists have worked out in great detail the relationship between income and economic participation. Because political activity is also a form of participation, it seems sensible to suppose that models of economic participation might provide some insights into the relationships between income, income inequality, and political participation.

For both labor force and marketplace participation, there are good reasons to believe that a change in income affects the amount of participation. Common sense suggests that people work more when their wages increase, but the story told by economists is more complicated than that, and it suggests that the relationship between income and political participation might be quite complicated as well.

In the standard labor force participation model (Blundell and Macurdy 1999), for example, the hours H of labor force participation are chosen by maximizing the utility $U(X,L)$ of consumption X and hours of leisure L, subject to a budget constraint that purchases—defined as the price of one unit of consumption p times the amount of consumption X—must equal total income Y: $pX = wH + V = Y$, where total income is composed of nonlabor income V and of wage income wH, defined as wages w times the number of hours worked H. The hours worked H plus the amount of leisure L must sum to the total number of hours T that are available ($T = H + L$). With some assumptions about the functional form of the utility function, we can write a simple hours-of-work equation—essentially a participation equation for work—as:

$$H = H(w,p,V,Q,\alpha,\varepsilon) = \alpha_0 + \alpha_1 \, w/p + \alpha_2 \, V/p + \alpha_3 Q + \varepsilon, \quad (17.1)$$

where α_0, α_1, α_2, and α_3 are parameters, ε is an error term representing unobserved heterogeneity, and Q is a vector of observable qualities such as age, sex, and education often called "taste shifters," although they may represent "capabilities" or "opportunities" as well.[3] This equation implies that hours of work (H) are determined by wages relative to the price of goods (w/p), nonlabor income relative to the price of goods (V/p), and other factors (Q).

Economic theory provides only an ambiguous prediction about the impact of an increase in wages, because of "income" and "substitution" effects that can work against one another,[4] but at least in the short run α_1 will be positive, indicating that an increase in wages will lead to an increase in hours worked. If, as seems very likely, leisure is a normal good (so that more of it is wanted as income increases), then an increase in nonlabor income V will decrease hours worked (α_2 will be negative) as people use their extra income to buy some leisure. Consequently, even if α_1 is positive, increases in income are not necessarily positively related to hours of work, and the consequences of an increase in income depend on its source.

Furthermore, equation 17.1 refers to changes in a particular labor market; it does not refer to the relationship between hours of work and wages across a set of different labor markets. It is possible, for example, that increases in wages would lead to more hours worked for individuals in a number of different markets—say, those for day laborers, air-craft mechanics, accountants, and doctors. The correlation between the average wages in these occupations and the average hours worked could still be negative, however, with those making more working less because the factors determining hours worked are different for each occupation. Income, in this case, could be a proxy for the nonwage factors that determine work hours in each occupation. The vector of characteristics Q is supposed to control for these factors, but it is hard to know what Q should be, and it is asking a lot for this vector to control completely for other factors. The problem of appropriate controls is a general problem with econometric work—where an independent variable such as income acts as a proxy for other factors that lead to the outcome, in this case participation—and the problem is acute when studying political participation.

Although the commonsense notion that people devote time to working in order to obtain income is sustained by this analysis, the relationship between hours worked and income is complicated, suggesting that an equally complicated relationship holds for political participation. If political participation involves giving time to activities, and if the benefits (like wages from work) are related to the amount of time contributed, then participation will be like hours devoted to work. Thus, equation 17.1 could be used to estimate the relationship between hours devoted to participation (H), benefits obtained per unit of politi-cal participation (w), and income from activities other than political participation (V). The economic model suggests that the relationship between hours of participation and benefits should be positive, but this mechanism does not seem powerful enough to account for the oft-noted positive relationship between *overall* individual income and participation, because the benefits from political participation (Hw) are at most only a small part of total individ-ual income (Hw + V). The problem is that most income (V) for participants will be from activities other than political participation, so that an increase in nonparticipation income should, according to this model, decrease political participation as people substitute leisure for participation. In short, because almost everybody gets more income from sources other than political participation, an increase in these other sources of income causes them to choose leisure instead of putting time into political participation. Hence, this model sug-gests that, contrary to the well-known empirical finding, the correlation between overall income and political participation should be negative.

One adjustment to the economic model that avoids this result is the assumption that participation is a pleasurable hobby for some people, something that provides utility even if there are no benefits beyond the act itself. Then, if the only cost of participation is the time spent doing it, increased income might free up some work time and provide more hours for political participation, which would be traded off against the requirements to work enough to afford other consumption items and to get some leisure as well.[5] This observation sug-gests that we think of participation as consumption that gives pleasure to people.

Consumption Decisions as
the Model of Political Participation

The standard model of consumption assumes that people maximize utility for two commodities $U(X_1, X_2)$, subject to a budget constraint $p_1 X_1 + p_2 X_2 = Y$, where X_1 is the amount of the first commodity and p_1 its price, X_2 the amount of the second and p_2 its price, and Y the person's income. The amount of X_1 demanded (that is, the amount of the person's participation in the market for X_1) is:

$$X_1 = f(p_1, p_2, Y, Q, \alpha, \varepsilon) = \alpha_0 + \alpha_1 (p_2/p_1) + \alpha_2 (Y/p_1) + \alpha_3 Q + \varepsilon, \quad (17.2)$$

where as before, α_0, α_1, α_2, and α_3 are parameters, ε is an error term representing unobserved heterogeneity, and Q is a vector of observable qualities such as age, sex, and education, often called "taste shifters." Economic theory makes some predictions about the signs of the parameters in this equation, depending on the nature of the goods. In most cases, both α_1 and α_2 are positive, so that higher prices for the first commodity lead to less demand for it, while higher prices for the other commodity lead to more demand for the first commodity.[6] The impact of higher income depends on the type of good, with demand for inferior goods decreasing with income (α_3 is negative) and the demand for normal goods increasing with income (α_3 is positive). Most goods, certainly most broad classes of goods, tend to be normal goods, but the theory provides no way, independent of the empirical sign of Y, to distinguish inferior and normal goods.

As with equation 17.1, equation 17.2 refers to ceteris paribus changes; it does not necessarily explain simple correlations across people in a cross-sectional sample. Thus, in a cross-sectional sample we might find that spending on country and western music goes down with income (suggesting that country and western music is an inferior good), but in a time-series sample an increase in the income of a country and western music fan increases spending on this music. In this case, cross-sectional increases in income probably proxy changes in tastes (with higher-income people having less desire for country and western music), which are supposed to be controlled by Q but might not be. Once again, we encounter the problem that income may be a proxy for some other factor that determines tastes.

The consumption model seems readily applicable to participation involving money such as political contributions C where X_1 is the number of political favors purchased for the price p_1 for each favor (and $C = p_1 X_1$). Since political favors are most likely a normal good, an increase in the price of the favors would diminish demand for them, and an increase in income would increase it. But both the number of favors purchased and the price of favors are usually unknown, so most studies of political contributions simply treat the amount of money contributed C as an indicator of X_1. That amounts to assuming that the price p_1 is fixed, which may or may not be true for the case at hand.

The consumption model could also be applied to a case where utility is gained simply from the act of participation itself, and the number of acts of participation X_1 for contributions would be equal to the contribution C. In this case, p_1 would be equal to one. Equation 17.2 still holds, but only the impact of p_2 and Y matter. Increases in the price of all other goods p_2 decrease contributions, and increases in income increase contributions.

Conclusions from the First Two Models

These models suggest that income figures prominently in explaining political participation, and they suggest a positive relationship between overall income and participation under some conditions. For activities that involve the investment of time, it is not enough for political participation to provide benefits, like wages for work, in return for the hours spent doing it. Participation probably also has to provide intrinsic pleasure for there to be a positive relationship between income and political activity. For activities that involve the investment of money but not time, the assumption that political contributions are a normal good yields the desired result, although more by definition than anything else. There is no intrinsic reason why political activity has to be a normal good, but most of the things produced by political contributions, such as policy outcomes and the election of favored politicians, are probably normal goods, if not luxury goods.

These economic models provide some justification for the notion that income helps to explain the level of political participation, although they provide no justification for the impact of income inequality apart from its effects through changes in income. But these models also suggest that income is a proxy for other factors, such as people's circumstances or their preferences. And because most forms of participation are not traded in a market, it is hard, if not impossible, to get information on some of the basic features of the models, such as the prices or benefits of political participation.

This observation suggests a basic problem with applying these economic models to political participation. The economic models of labor force participation and consumption have explanatory power because prices, wages, and income provide people with substantial motivation and significant information about the consequences of economic participation. The empirical reach of the models follows because analysts have access to plentiful data on prices, quantities, and income. Very little of this kind of information seems available and maybe even pertinent for political participation. Moreover, although economists have exhibited great confidence in the theoretical power and tractability of the labor supply and consumer demand models as theories of economic participation, empirical results are sometimes mixed. John Pencaval (1986, 95) ended his review of labor supply research by lamenting that "only a relatively small proportion of the variation in hours of work of prime-age men in the population is removed by the set of variables on which information is collected in most surveys [and] we need to know more about what this 'unobserved heterogeneity' represents."

The limitations of the models may go even deeper than that. They say nothing about how goods are combined with leisure to create activity, nothing about how people choose among activities, and nothing about how people learn about wages and prices. Although the wage of a job or the price of a commodity is important, so too are job security, the organization of the workplace, social connections, fashion, trust, habit, motivations, and many other factors. And these factors might be the ones that must be included in the other factors Q in order to control for changes in tastes or opportunities. Similarly, the importance of the monetary costs of participation may pale in comparison to the many other factors that affect participation.

Household Production Models of Participation

The home production model (Becker 1965; Lancaster 1966) responds to some of these criticisms by taking activities as the basic unit of analysis.[7] It assumes that people get utility from activities and that each activity is produced according to a production function from a vector of commodities and from time. One of these activities is work, which produces income. Another could be political participation. The only constraint is that the sum of hours allocated to the activities must equal the total number of available hours. The model makes predictions about trade-offs of time and goods depending on their prices, the form of the utility function, and the form of the production function. The model's emphasis on time and production seems better suited to studying political participation, where monetary costs may often be trivial in comparison to other factors such as the time required or the need to have skills to run a meeting, write a letter, or make a speech. This theory has many advantages. Thinking about the production of activities by combining commodities and time is much more conducive to understanding participation than thinking about choosing commodities. And the theory has been applied to many areas of participation, including crime (Ehrlich 1973), religion (Azzi and Ehrenberg 1975; Iannaccone 1998), travel (Gronau 1970), and family production (Michael 1973).

There are some problems with the theory in the economic context. Because activities are typically not observed or measured, Reuben Gronau (1986, 279) notes, "any empirical investigation based on this theory is . . . confined to the study of inputs," but "the study of inputs is hampered by the fact that data on inputs are not readily available . . . and prices (specifically the price of time) are unknown." Two types of surveys, consumption expenditure surveys and time budget surveys, do provide some information about commodities and time, although there is almost no data on the allocation of both goods and time. These data make it possible to learn something about variation in inputs, and most important, they have focused attention on the use of time (Juster and Stafford 1991).

The situation is much better in the study of political participation where the activities themselves are observed, and recent surveys have asked about the inputs to participation such as time, money, and skills. In fact, the civic voluntarism model of Verba, Schlozman, and Brady (1995) can be considered a household production theory in which time, money, and civic skills are combined to produce political participation (Brady, Verba, and Schlozman 1995). Although the theory provides no rationale beyond the ones already discussed for why income is positively related to political participation, it does make researchers think about the different ways in which activities such as working for campaigns or giving money to politics are produced and the variations in individual resources and capabilities for undertaking these activities. It still leaves open, however, the question of how income inequality might affect participation apart from its indirect impact through income.

A Favor-Buying Model of Political Participation

The major problem with these models applied to political participation is that they focus more on the resources that go into participation than on the benefits of participation. Legislative vote-buying models (see, for example, Snyder 1991; Groseclose 1996; Groseclose and Snyder 1996) solve this problem by assuming that people trade resources such as money for favors provided by a legislature. None of the models in the literature say much about income or income inequality, but they do suggest that one of the features of a successful model of political participation is that it incorporates a purpose for participation such as garnering favors. One purpose of participation, of course, could be pure consumption, in which case participation would be a commodity like food or clothing, but although participation may sometimes be a pure consumption good, it seems likely that it is also something more than that.

The following simple model suggests how income and income inequality might both affect participation in a model of governmental policymaking. Consider a model with two groups, called zero and one, with different gross incomes, $Y_0 < Y_1$, so that group zero is the "low-income" group and group one is the "high-income" group. Assume that there are M people in group zero and N people in group one. Also assume that the government imposes a proportional tax t on all income above Y_0. The government then takes these tax receipts ($Nt[Y_1 - Y_0]$) and gives them back to each member of a group in proportion to the amount of political contributions given by that member. Each group chooses a common political contribution rate for members—c_0 for group zero and c_1 for group one. The crucial features of this model are that members of each group act together to choose a common contribution rate and that group contributions are exchanged for government subsidies for the group. With these assumptions, the model is easy to set up and solve.[8]

The model yields the following participation equation for political contributions c_j for a person with income Y_j:

$$c_j = -[(M - N)/4M] t Y_0 + [(M - N)/4M] t Y_j$$
$$+ [N/4M] t (Y_1 - Y_0) = \alpha_0 + \alpha_1 Y_j + \alpha_2(Y_1 - Y_0). \quad (17.3)$$

Note that contributions c_j increase with income in this model if α_1 (which equals $[(M - N)/4M]t$) is positive, and α_1 is positive if there are more low-income people (M) than high-income people (N). Somewhat surprisingly, contributions increase with income because there are so few high-income people that they must contribute more than low-income people to get their share of government benefits. In any society with more low-income people than high-income people, we should observe, as we do empirically, a positive correlation between income and political contributions.

In a particular society at a moment in time, the incomes Y_1 and Y_0, the number of people in each income bracket M and N, and the tax rate t are fixed. Consequently, the first term in equation 17.3, which is $[-(M - N)/4M t Y_0]$, and the last term in equation 17.3, which is $[N/4M] t (Y_1 - Y_0)$, do not vary. But any of these quantities, $(Y_1 - Y_0)$, M and N, or t, could change from one period to another or from one place to another. Hence, if data are available from one period to another or across societies, then equation 17.3 can be used to determine the impact of changes in the tax system or inequality.

If M and N are fixed, then $(Y_1 - Y_0)$ is a good measure of absolute income inequality for comparing the average income of the top income group with that of the bottom income group. The model then predicts that contributions c_j for any specific income group j will increase when we compare one period or one society to another with more inequality. Thus, increases in absolute income inequality $(Y_1 - Y_0)$ from one circumstance to another cause each c_j to increase because the quantity being taxed $(Y_1 - Y_0)$ gets bigger and government taxes produce more resources to be "bought" by political contributions.

It does matter, however, how $(Y_1 - Y_0)$ increases. If absolute income inequality increases through an increase in Y_1 while Y_0 stays constant, then both average income and relative income inequality increase.[9] Contributions from the lower class increase because $(Y_1 - Y_0)$ is bigger, even though Y_0 stays the same. Contributions from the upper class increase both because $(Y_1 - Y_0)$ is bigger and because Y_1 is bigger.

It is also possible for absolute income inequality $(Y_1 - Y_0)$ to increase while average income stays constant if Y_0 goes down some amount and Y_1 goes up just enough to keep the average income constant. In this case, relative income inequality also increases.[10] Contributions by the lower class increase because $(Y_1 - Y_0)$ increases, and contributions by the upper class increase because $(Y_1 - Y_0)$ increases and because their income Y_1 increases. Once again, contributions increase because government taxes produce more resources to be bought by political contributors.

Another way in which income inequality could change is if M or N changes but Y_1 and Y_0 stay the same. An increase in the number of low-income people M or in the number of high-income people N leads to an increase in most measures of absolute and relative income inequality.[11] Increases in M and N have complicated impacts because of their effects on the total amount of taxes raised and the total contributions from each group. An increase in the number of low-income people M does not affect the total taxes raised (because low-income people are not taxed), but some simple comparative statistics with equation 17.3 indicate that the contributions of low-income people decline and the contributions of high-income people stay the same if M increases. If the number of high-income people N increases, then the total amount of tax money collected increases, the contributions of high-income people stay the same, and the contributions of low-income people increase to compete for some of the new resources.

Thus, equation 3 has a number of important implications. It suggests that both individual income and income inequality should affect contributions. Political contributions increase with income level because there are fewer rich people than low-income people. This reason differs from those suggested earlier—that participation provides intrinsic gratification and that participation is a normal good so that its consumption increases with income. Political contributions also change with changes in income inequality, whether it is absolute or relative, because of the interaction of the tax system with changes in the income structure, but the results depend on whether incomes Y_0 and Y_1 change or the number of people in each income level M and N change. The model developed here describes a specific way in which this happens, but other models could be developed that would lead to different conclusions. The results from a more elaborate model are described later in the chapter.

Before describing that more elaborate model, it is worth discussing some of the strengths and limitations of this model. Perhaps the most unrealistic feature is that it completely ignores the free-rider problem, and as a result it leads to unreasonable predictions about the size of contributions. It predicts, for example, that the upper-income group will make political contributions equal to one-quarter of its tax bill. In the real world, of course, there are incentives for individuals to forgo their contributions c_j and to free-ride on the contributions of others. There is also uncertainty as to whether contributions will lead to the desired result. But free-riding is a problem with almost all participation models, and in this case it has the desired effect of reducing the amount that is contributed—although preliminary work suggests that, as with voting models (Aldrich 1993), it leads to reductions that are too large.

Another unrealistic feature of this model is that gross income is assigned to people and they cannot choose the number of hours they work in order to substitute leisure for taxed work. A more complex model that incorporated some of the ideas discussed earlier could take this into account. It might also be useful to expand the model to think of political participation as the contribution of time as well as money.

On the plus side, however, the model provides an indication of how both income and income inequality could enter into a participation equation. It also suggests the importance of having income classes that differentially benefit from governmental programs and whose members act together because of the social fact of their membership in that class. These assumptions seem to capture some of the basic elements of classical theories of the role of social class.

I have described a more detailed version of this model, with more than two income classes and a more sophisticated tax system, in Brady (2003). As with the preceding model, this one demonstrates that two kinds of change in income distributions are possible. One kind occurs when income levels remain the same but people move from one level to another, so that the number of people on each level changes. If income follows a Pareto distribution and the size of income classes decreases with income, then when income brackets remain the same but a movement of people leads to increased inequality, the lower classes will provide more political contributions and the upper classes will provide fewer. The other kind of change occurs when the incomes attached to classes change. When income increases proportionately for all classes, then political contributions increase, but only because mean income has increased. In this situation, relative inequality remains the same. When the ratio of the lowest income to the income step between classes increases, then political contributions increase because mean income increases as well.

The political contributions equation that follows from this model has this basic form:

$$\text{Political Contributions} = a + b \text{ (Income)} + c \text{ (Inequality)} \\ + d \text{ (Income} \times \text{Inequality)} + e \text{ (Tax Revenues)} + \text{Other.} \tag{17.4}$$

Note that income, income inequality, and the interaction of income and income inequality have direct impacts on political contributions. More generally, it seems likely that any political participation equation should include these terms, although tax revenues might be replaced with other measures.

EMPIRICAL MODELS OF POLITICAL PARTICIPATION AND INEQUALITY

Empirical Work on Political Participation and Income Inequality

In studies of political participation, the impacts of income have been given far less attention than the impacts of education and occupation, and even less attention has been paid to how income inequality affects participatory inequality. One of the reasons why the effect of income inequality has been neglected is that most of the work on political participation is cross-sectional, so that the degree of income inequality is fixed. Even when the impact of income on participation over time has been studied, much of the work has considered aggregate data, such as national turnout over time or how participation has changed over time by occupational, educational, or income groups. As a result, very little thought has gone into the ways in which income inequality might affect participatory inequality.

A General Empirical Model of Participation

The theoretical models discussed earlier suggest some ways in which income and income inequality might matter for political participation. All the models imply that income should be included in any participation equation, and the favor-buying model indicates that income inequality, its interaction with income, and the tax rate should also be included to explain how political contributions vary with income class. The challenge for empirical work is to develop a specification that can encompass these theoretical notions.[12]

It is useful to begin with a simple empirical model. Assume that data on political activity A_{ist} are available for a sample of individuals i in state (or unit) s at time t. Individuals are the obvious unit of analysis because they decide to participate or not to participate, and there are good reasons to assume that the participation of an individual will change over time. Furthermore, by having observations over time or places, changes in income inequality and other contextual factors can be observed.

A Simple Model of Participation and Income

The simplest model of participation and income treats income as input into the act of participation, as in the household production model. In this model, income represents resources and social connections:

$$A_{ist} = a + f(Y_{ist})\, b_1 + e_{ist}, \tag{17.5}$$

where Y_{ist} is the individual's income and f is some functional form. Two questions immediately present themselves: How should Y_{ist} be measured? And what functional form should f be?

Measurement   We can consider the measurement question first. Because many surveys simply measure total family income, we put aside such complicated questions as whether income should be individual or family income and whether it should be just wage income or wage plus nonlabor income. Instead, we focus on whether income should be:

- Current, *nominal income,* Y_{ist}.

- Inflation-adjusted *real income,* $y_{ist} = Y_{ist}/I_{st}$, where I_{st} is some consumer price index.

- *Relative income,* which can defined as a ratio or a difference relative to some reference group. The ratio definition is: $R_{ist} = Y_{ist}/Y_{+st} = y_{ist}/y_{+st}$, where Y_{+st} is the average nominal income and y_{+st} is the average real income over relevant individuals to which person i compares himself or herself. Note that for this definition the results for nominal and real income are the same. The difference definition is: $r_{ist} = (y_{ist} - y_{+st})$. In this case, it does matter whether nominal or real income is used, and I have chosen real income.

It seems unlikely that current, nominal income Y_{ist} is the right measure. Although some economists, especially Keynesian economists and those writing on the Phillips's curve, have made much of nominal income increases and wage illusion, most economic effects and certainly all long-term economic effects are driven by real income. If income affects participation, it seems likely that real income is what (mostly) matters.

If real income $y_{ist} = Y_{ist}/I_{st}$ matters, then Y_{ist} must be adjusted by some price index I_{st}, which could vary just by time or by state as well. There are many possible choices, and more thought should be given to the best one. In most cases discussed here, we use a national price index, but statewide indices could also be used.

The most important issue, however, is whether real or relative income matters. If participation is a commodity, then real income should matter, and participation's relationship with income should depend on whether participation is an inferior, a normal, or even a luxury good. Political contributions may be the form of participation that is most like a "participatory commodity," so that for contributions we might expect real income to matter. Yet there are good reasons to think that the monetary costs of many other forms of participation are relatively slight and that income affects participation through social processes that have more to do with social standing (Nie, Junn, and Stehlik-Berry 1996) than with the purchasing power of money. In this case, relative income matters.

If relative income matters, then the question arises: relative to what? A general answer is that an individual's income is relative to some average Y_{+st} over relevant individuals who affect the person's behavior or to whom the person compares himself or herself. We call this the reference group, and the effect is an interaction of context and individual characteristics. Without knowing more about the social processes involved, it is hard to know what this reference group should be. One simple assumption is that what matters is the mean income for some unit in which the person is embedded, such as a county or state.

Functional Form   Now we consider the question about functional form. Economists often take the logarithm of income, and there are theoretical reasons to believe that this measure is more basic than income itself. Taking the logarithm yields a more symmetrical distribution of income, and the logarithm of income appears in studies of how education affects income. Moreover, as figure 17.3 shows, for an eight-act measure of participation on the 1990 Citizen Participation Study, the fit of participation to log income is nearly linear. The correlation between participation and family income is only .299, while the correlation between participation and the log of family income is .359. This result suggests that there are good reasons to take the logarithm of income when trying to explain the number of participatory acts that people undertake.

This assumption may not work so well when trying to explain political contributions or the amount of time devoted to politics. Figure 17.4 shows that total political contributions are not even linearly related to family income, and that those at the upper end of the income distribution give much more heavily to politics than those in the middle or at the bottom. Figure 17.5 shows that the relationship between total number of hours devoted to politics and family income is approximately linear.

Because all the empirical results discussed later are either for voting or for the number of participatory acts, we use a logarithmic functional form. This approach also simplifies the mathematical presentation. If a logarithmic form is used along with a ratio definition of relative income, then there is a simple relationship between relative income, individual real income, and mean income for the reference group:

$$\text{Log}(R_{ist}) = \text{Log}(y_{ist}/y_{+st}) = \text{Log}(y_{ist}) - \text{Log}(y_{+st}). \tag{17.6}$$

If a linear form is used along with a difference definition of relative income, then there is a corresponding relationship between relative income, individual real income, and mean income for the reference group:

$$r_{ist} = (y_{ist} - y_{+st}). \tag{17.7}$$

For either of these situations, we can write down a model that includes both the relative and real or absolute income situations as subcases. Consider the logarithmic model:

$$\begin{aligned} A_{ist} &= a + b_{11}\,\text{Log}(R_{ist}) + b_{12}\,\text{Log}(y_{+st}) + e_{ist}, \\ &= a + b_{11}\,[\text{Log}(y_{ist}) - \text{Log}(y_{+st})] + b_{12}\,\text{Log}(y_{+st}) + e_{ist}. \end{aligned} \tag{17.8}$$

FIGURE 17.3   *Participation by Log of Household Income, 1990*

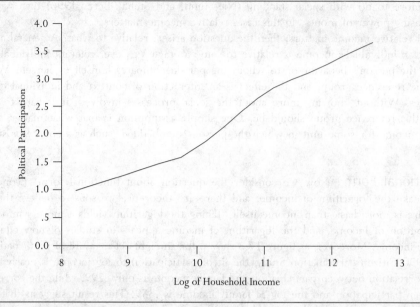

Source: Citizen Participation Study, 1990.
Note: Political participation is an eight-point scale with one point for participating in each of the following activities: working on a campaign, giving money to a campaign, contacting a government official, protesting, attending a governmental board meeting, engaging in informal political activity, voting in 1988, or being involved with a political organization.

FIGURE 17.4   *Political Contributions by Family Income, 1989*

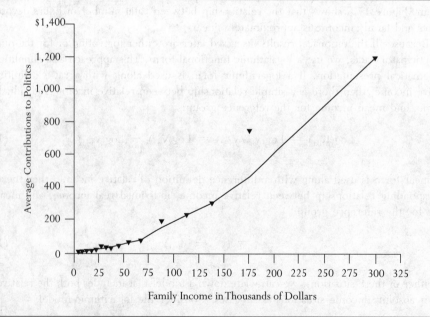

Source: Citizen Participation Study, 1990.
Note: Lowess fit; only thirty-two, nineteen, and forty-one respondents for three highest incomes. Reprinted with permission from Elsevier © 1999 from Katz and Auton (1999).

FIGURE 17.5   *Political Hours by Family Income, 1989*

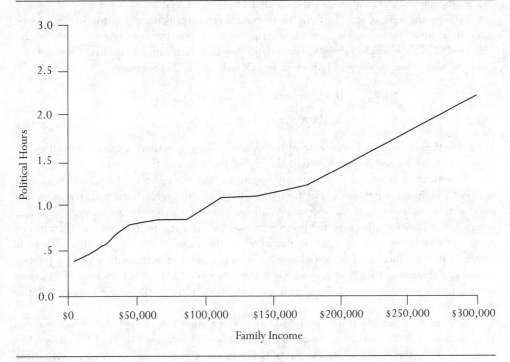

Source: Citizen Participation Study, 1990.
Note: Political hours = Hours given to political meetings, governmental boards, informal political activity, and political campaigns.

Clearly if b_{11} is significant (and presumably positive) and $b_{11} = b_{12}$, then only real or absolute income matters, because the terms involving the reference group drop out. The favor-buying model, for example, suggests that only real or absolute income should matter.

Relative income matters if income is a surrogate for social standing or if people turn to political participation when their income has reached some target fraction of the income of everyone around them. In equation 17.8, if b_{11} is significant but b_{12} equals zero, then only relative income matters.

Average income alone might matter (in which case, b_{11} is zero, but b_{12} is significant) if those states with higher average state incomes have more participation (if b_{12} is positive) because some infrastructure has been developed that makes participation easier. Average income might also be a proxy for the tax revenues that are available in a favor-buying model. Other cases, of course, are also possible, and they might be the result of some combination of contextual and individual-level effects, although without better theories about the mechanisms linking income to participation, they might be hard to interpret.[13]

Impacts of Increased Inequality on Participation Through Income Alone

Although the activity model in equation 17.8 does not include any measure of income inequality, political activity can be affected indirectly by income inequality through income.

Not surprisingly, the impacts on participation depend on how income inequality increases and on the significance and size of the coefficients b_{11} and b_{12}.

Perhaps the easiest way to think of income inequality increasing is for income to be taken from someone below the mean in a state and to be given to someone above the mean. This kind of change would increase all standard measures of income inequality. Consider, for example, the following logarithmic variance (Cowell 1977, 25) measure:

$$LV_{st} = (\text{Log Variance})_{st} = \Sigma_i \left[\text{Log}(y_{ist}/y_{+st})\right]^2/I$$
$$= \Sigma_i \left[\text{Log}(y_{ist}) - \text{Log}(y_{+st})\right]^2/I. \tag{17.9}$$

Note that this measure is the average of the square of logged relative incomes as well as the variation of the logged incomes around the log of the mean of the incomes.

This measure is zero if everyone in the state has the same income (if $y_{ist} = y_{+st}$), and it is positive in all other cases. Furthermore, it has the desirable feature that it stays the same if there is a proportional increase in all incomes (if the new incomes $y_{ist}* = h\, y_{ist}$, where h is a constant), because the mean increases by the same proportion and the ratio of each $y_{ist}*$ to the new mean $y_{+st}*$ is the same as the ratio of y_{ist} to y_{+st}. But clearly it increases if some income d is moved from a person i below the mean to a person j above the mean.[14] Equation 17.9 is also generally highly correlated with other measures of income inequality, such as the ratio of the average income of the top quintile to the bottom quintile or the Gini index.[15]

Now moving income from one person to another does not change the average income y_{+st}, so that $\text{Log}(y_{+st})$ would be unchanged, but it would increase $\text{Log}(R_{ist})$ for the person who was above the mean whose income was increased, and it would decrease $\text{Log}(R_{ist})$ for the person below the mean whose income was diminished.

If b_{11} is significantly positive, then the average of A_{ist} would increase for those above the mean, and it would decrease for those below the mean. Participatory inequality would increase because of the way in which income inequality affects income.

The Direct Impact of Income Inequality on Participation

Equation 17.8 is perhaps the simplest model of the impact of income on participation, and it clearly shows that with this model increases in income inequality can have an impact on participatory inequality. But the impact is entirely through income—with increased income inequality, there are more poor people who participate less because they are poorer and more rich people who participate more because they are richer. There is no direct impact of income inequality. Income inequality has an impact only because income is a resource for participation.

As we saw earlier with the favor-buying model, inequality can also enter directly, as a motivation for participation, although it seems unlikely that it would just enter alone, as in the following model with LV on the right-hand side:

$$A_{ist} = a + b_{13}\,(LV)_{st} + e_{ist}. \tag{17.10}$$

This model implies that increases in inequality in a state have a direct impact—of the same magnitude—on everyone in that state. As a complete picture of how income affects participation, this model seems implausible for two reasons. First, it implies that income has no cross-sectional impact on participation within a state, even though there is abundant cross-sectional evidence that income matters, as in equation 17.9. Second, the model implies that as inequality increases, the impact is the same on everyone. This result might be true if there were some statewide mechanism that affected everyone equally, but it is hard to identify a way in which increasing income inequality could have this kind of impact. One possibility, however, is that b_{13} is positive and more income inequality mobilizes all groups because of the increasingly fractious politics regarding income distribution. It is harder to think of mechanisms that would lead to b_{13} being negative.

A better model that is more in keeping with the favor-buying model of equation 17.4 is that income, income inequality, and their interaction all enter along with the average income:

$$A_{ist} = a + b_{11} \, \text{Log}(R_{ist}) + b_{12} \, \text{Log}(y_{+st}) + b_{13} \, (LV)_{st} \\ + b_{14} \, (LV)_{st} R_{ist} + e_{ist}. \tag{17.11}$$

If b_{14} is negative, this model implies that an increase in inequality mobilizes the lower classes relative to the upper classes. If b_{14} is positive, then an increase in inequality mobilizes the upper classes. This model is appealing because it suggests that income distribution might have an impact on participation not only because of the resources and social structural advantages it provides but also because it represents an issue that matters for participants. In addition, if average income in the state is considered a proxy for tax revenues, then equation 17.11 is very similar to the favor-buying model in equation 17.4.

Estimates of this model could lead to opposing impacts of income distribution. If, for example, b_{11} is significantly positive and b_{14} is significantly negative (and b_{12} and b_{13} are assumed to be zero for simplicity), then the impacts of income inequality through income and the direct impacts of income inequality would run in opposite directions. An increase in income inequality would reduce the degree to which lower-income people participate because resources and social connections as indexed by their relative income $\text{Log}(R_{ist})$ would decrease for some of them, but the participation of upper-income people would increase because relative income would increase for some of them. At the same time, the increase in income inequality would increase the participation of lower-income people because their indignation as measured by $b_{14} \, (LV)_{st} \, R_{ist}$ would be greater than the indignation of upper-income people. Needless to say, these conflicting tendencies might make it difficult to assess the impact of income inequality.

Aggregating the Model

We know of no studies of the impact of income distribution on participation that have tried to estimate equation 17.11 directly. To the extent that there have been studies, they have tended to look at participation over time by aggregate income group (see, for example, Leighley and Nagler 1992a), and we report a great deal of that kind of data here as well.

But aggregate studies have their dangers, for the simple reason that they tend to look at the relationship between some measure of inequality across time or states (or both) and some measure of participatory inequality. This approach would get at the net effects of equation 17.11, but it would not sort out the two major ways in which income inequality might affect participation—by affecting the distribution of resources and connections and by motivating people to participate.

Specification Problems

To simplify matters, we have not included control variables in equation 17.11, but based on our literature review, it is obvious that income variables do not exhaust the determinants of political participation. It seems highly unlikely that sensible results will be obtained without including demographic, other socioeconomic, and many of the other explanatory outlined earlier. Certainly education, age, sex, marital circumstances, and other variables should be included. Omitting education, for example, would clearly bias the coefficient for income upward, because education has a strong positive impact on participation and it is positively correlated with income. If education is omitted, then income would "take up" and proxy its effects.

The empirical work reported here is essentially bivariate, and it is meant to do no more than suggest the complexity of the relationship between income inequality and participatory inequality. Much more work is needed using the kinds of specifications described earlier in order to sort out the meaning of these bivariate relationships. But it seems preferable at this point to report results that are clearly incomplete than to control only partially for important factors and to give a false impression of completeness.

EMPIRICAL RESULTS

The empirical results reported in this section deal with voting turnout and participation in twelve political acts, such as contacting, attending rallies, petitioning, or writing a letter. For simplicity, we refer to these as "voting turnout" and "participation," respectively. The data on turnout come from the November supplement to the Current Population Survey, and they are available for every biennial election from 1972 to 2000 and for every midterm election from 1974 to 1998. Approximately 150,000 respondents were asked in each survey whether they voted or not and whether they were registered to vote or not. The data on participation come from the Roper Social and Political Trends Dataset, which extended from September 1973 to June 1994, with ten studies every year except 1973 (two studies), 1991 (eight studies), and 1994 (six studies). In each survey, approximately two thousand respondents were asked whether they had participated in any of twelve political acts: writing to one's representative or senator; attending a political rally or speech; attending a public meeting on town or school affairs; holding or running for political office; serving on a committee for a local organization; serving as an officer of a club or organization; writing a letter to a newspaper; signing a petition; working for a political party; making a speech; writing an article for a magazine or newspaper; and being a member of a group like the League of Women Voters or another group interested in better government.

Unfortunately, none of these studies measure political contributions in any way. The American National Election Studies (ANES) do ask about contributions, but these studies are only biennial, have relatively small samples (around two thousand), and ask only whether contributions were made. Omitting contributions is a major omission if, as some (including this author) have claimed, politics is moving away from "time-based" activity toward "contribution-based" activity. Furthermore, based on figure 17.4, it seems likely that the greatest impact of growing income inequality would be to increase the inequality in political giving.

Aggregate Results on Turnout

There is a very large literature on turnout (for example, Brody 1978; Reiter 1979; Wolfinger and Rosenstone 1980; Shaffer 1981; Abramson and Aldrich 1982; Powell 1986; Bennett 1990; Rosenstone and Hansen 1993). But there is surprisingly little work on inequality in turnout and income inequality (however, see Leighley and Nagler 1992). We used the Current Population Survey data from 1972 to 2000 to study inequality and turnout.

Figure 17.6 shows the percentage voting by household income quintile by year.[16] The top, solid line is the turnout rate for the top quintile. The bottom, dashed line is the turnout rate for the bottom quintile. The middle, dotted line is the turnout rate for the three middle quintiles. All these turnout rates are somewhat too high because of the well-known problem of overreporting, and this may create some problems for our interpretations (Brady 1999). Two features of this picture stand out. First, the sawtooth pattern vividly depicts the standard pattern of turnout being highest during presidential elections and then falling at midterm elections. Second, there is a significant gap between the turnout of the highest and lowest quintiles. Inequality in turnout is certainly related to inequality in income.

Figure 17.7 computes the ratio of average turnout in the top income quintile to the bottom income quintile. The calculation is made separately for presidential and midterm elections. If we ignore 1976, the line for presidential elections seems to indicate increased inequality in turnout after 1980 (which is when income inequality started to increase), but the evidence is not overwhelming, especially if 1976 is considered. The line for midterm elections is also hard to interpret: it decreases until 1986, when it turns around and increases in 1990 and 1994. All in all, there is not much evidence for a linkage between income inequality and turnout inequality in this figure.

Perhaps the problem is that the data are too aggregated. Using data from the Census Bureau on inequality in the fifty states plus the District of Columbia since 1977, figure 17.8 plots the ratio of turnout for the top to the bottom quintile in each state in each year versus the corresponding ratio of the average income of the top to the bottom quintile.[17] The line is a Lowess nonparametric regression that suggests that there is absolutely no relationship between income inequality and turnout inequality.

There are two ways to interpret these results. On the one hand, given what we know about voting turnout and its relatively weak relationship to income (Wolfinger and Rosenstone 1980), not to mention the theoretical literature's conclusion that the cost of voting is not the major determinant of turnout decisions, the results seem unsurprising. On the other hand, this bivariate analysis may miss important factors (a specification problem), and it may conflate the way in which increasing inequality both demobilizes voters (through individual income effects) and mobilizes them (through contextual inequality effects). That is, in equation 17.11, the impacts of the first two income effects may be canceled out by the impacts of the second two contextual inequality effects.

Aggregate Results on Participation

The Roper data come from in-person clustered samples of about two thousand respondents in each of ten surveys conducted almost every year. These data were not designed to carefully measure income, and they have a number of peculiarities (see the codebook in

FIGURE 17.6   *Voting by Quintile by Year, 1972 to 2000*

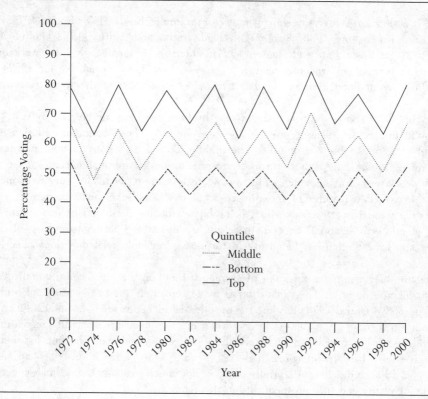

Source: Current Population Surveys.

Brady et al. 2001), but various checks suggest that they capture the major features of changes in income over the period when they were collected.

Figure 17.9 gets at the basic question of how participatory inequality changed from the 1970s to the 1990s. The average number of the twelve acts for the top and bottom income quintiles, and the bottom decile, are plotted for each survey over time.[18] As we would expect, the top quintile is much higher than the bottom quintile, and the bottom decile is the lowest of all. In addition, following a pattern made famous by Robert Putnam (2001), there is a clear over-time decline in participation, at least in the top quintile. Figure 17.10 shows the ratio of the participation index for the top and bottom income quintiles over time. Upside down this curve follows the changes in income inequality (see figures 17.1 and 17.2) very closely, but right side up it is just the opposite. In the middle of the 1970s, when income inequality was down, participatory inequality was up; in the middle of the 1980s, when income inequality was up, participatory inequality was down.[19]

This result is surprising, and it makes sense to seek additional confirmation of it. Does it hold up, for example, across the states? Answering this question runs up against one of the limitations of the Roper data. Unlike the CPS data, which are designed to be representative of the states, the Roper data were not designed to be representative of each state. In fact, not every state is represented in the sample for the entire time period, but information

FIGURE 17.7   *Ratio of Turnout for Top to Bottom Quintile, by Presidential and Midterm Elections, 1972 to 2000*

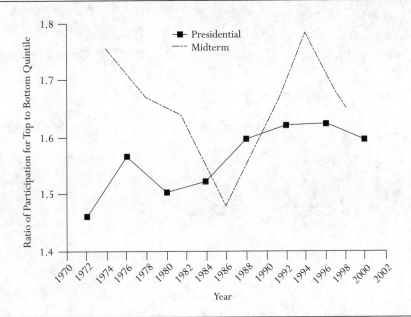

Source: Current Population Surveys.

FIGURE 17.8   *Inequality in Turnout for Presidential Elections, 1980 to 2000, Versus Inequality in Income for Fifty States and the District of Columbia*

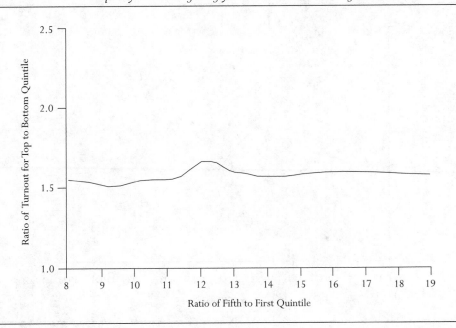

Source: Current Population Surveys.

FIGURE 17.9   *Political Participation by Top Quintile, Bottom Quintile, and Bottom Decile, 1973 to 1994*

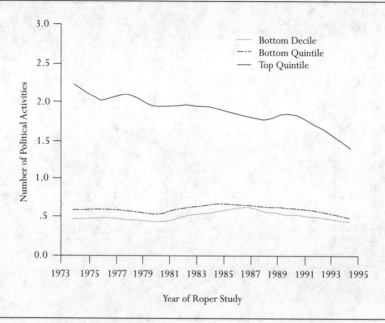

Source: Roper Social and Political Trends Data 1973 to 1994.

FIGURE 17.10   *Ratio of Participation Index for Top to Bottom Quintile*

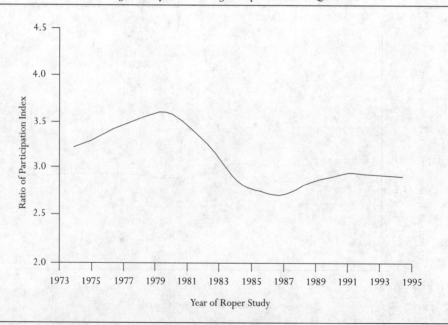

Source: Roper Social and Political Trends Data 1973 to 1994.

FIGURE 17.11   *Log of Participation for Twenty-Nine States, by State Ratios of Fifth to First Quintile, 1985*

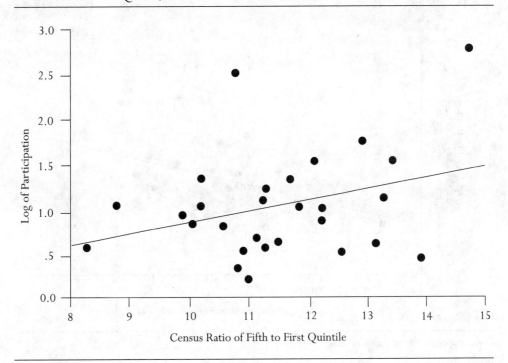

Source: Roper Social and Political Trends Data 1973 to 1994.

on twenty-nine states is available from 1973 to 1994. It is a bit heroic to treat these data as representative of the states, but it is worth a try.

Figure 17.11 plots the log of the ratio of the participation indices for the top and bottom quintiles for each of the twenty-nine states in 1985 versus the census ratio of average incomes in the top and bottom quintiles in the same year. We use the logarithm of the participation ratio because there are substantial differences across the states and the logarithm makes the results tractable. Using an ordinary least squares fit of the data points, we see, somewhat surprisingly, participatory inequality *increasing* with increasing income inequality across the states. Figure 17.12 confirms this result by plotting the average from 1978 to 1994 of the log participation ratio for each state versus the average of the census ratios of the average income for the top to bottom quintiles over the same period. The result is a strong positive relationship between increases in income inequality and increases in participatory inequality.

Thus, we are faced with a cross-sectional *increase* of participatory inequality with increases in income inequality and a time-series *decrease* of participatory inequality with increases in income inequality. Moreover, the cross-sectional result dominates the time-series result, as shown in figure 17.13, where we plot the log of the participation ratios for each state for each year versus the census ratio of the average income for the top to bottom quintiles. The result is a strongly positive relationship.

How can we sort this out? The obvious answer is to appeal to the microlevel models

FIGURE 17.12   *Average of Log of Participation for Twenty-Nine States, by Average of Income Ratios of Fifth to First Quintile, 1978 to 1994*

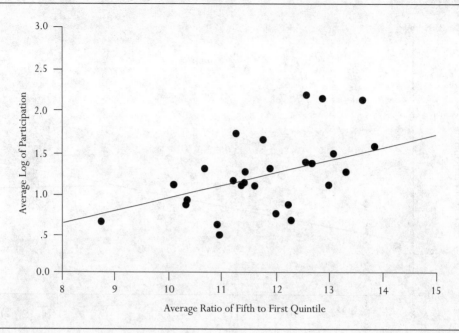

Source: Roper Social and Political Trends Data 1974 to 1994.

FIGURE 17.13   *Log of Participation Ratio by Yearly Ratio of Fifth to First Quintile for Twenty-Nine States, 1978 to 1994*

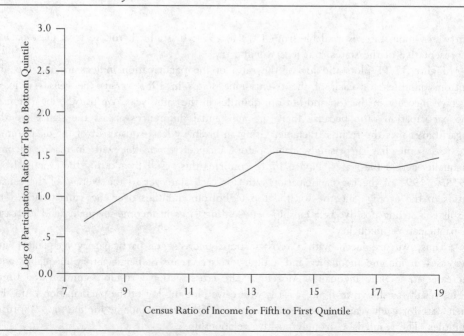

Source: Roper Social and Political Trends Data 1974 to 1994.

like the ones described in this chapter that take into account time-series and cross-sectional variation. We leave that to future work.

CONCLUSIONS

This chapter has shown that changes in income and changes in economic inequality are not the same thing and that they operate on political participation in different ways. *Income* is an individual characteristic stemming from personal capabilities, opportunities, decisions, and luck. Income provides a resource for participation, and changes in this resource as income becomes more or less equally distributed can affect participation. *Income inequality* is a property of society, a social fact about the distribution of incomes. An increase in inequality not only reduces the incomes of lower-class families but also changes that group's political circumstances. As a result, increases in income inequality can provide motivations for political participation.

Models developed in political science and economics show how income directly affects participation. These models also show how income inequality could affect participation indirectly by working through people's incomes. There has been much less theoretical work on how income inequality directly affects participation. The civic voluntarism model of Verba, Schlozman, and Brady (1995) and the household production model of economics both treat income as a resource that can be combined with other resources to produce participation. Neither of these models provides a clear-cut way in which income inequality could directly affect participation, although the civic voluntarism model does consider participatory motivations, and income inequality could be considered such a motivation.

A simple favor-buying model with income groups that compete for government tax revenues through political contributions provides a coherent picture of how income inequality could directly affect political contributions. In this model, the motivation for making political contributions is to maximize one's income given the existing income distribution. The model also provides a rationale for why income should be included in a participation equation and why it should be positively correlated with participation. This model suggests that participation equations should include income, income inequality, their interaction, and the characteristics of the governmental processes (such as taxing) that affect income distribution. Among other things, the model shows that an increase in income inequality could have the contradictory effects of depressing participation among the lower classes by reducing their resources while encouraging their participation by motivating them to overcome income inequality. Similarly, an increase in income inequality could increase participation among the upper classes by increasing their resources while discouraging participation by reducing their need to protect their privileged status.

Preliminary empirical work in this chapter using bivariate analysis demonstrates that there is no simple relationship between income inequality and political participation. Indeed, depending on the analysis and the data, there is evidence for no relationship between increased income inequality and increased participatory inequality; for increases in income inequality decreasing participatory inequality; and for increases in income inequality increasing participatory inequality. These contradictory results might be the result of the limitations of bivariate analysis, or they may indicate actual differences across political acts, places, or times. Certainly the lesson of the theoretical perspectives developed in this chapter is that unraveling the relationships between income inequality, income, and participation is difficult, not only because of the empirical challenges but also because income inequality might operate in contradictory ways by reducing the wherewithal for lower-income people to participate while simultaneously increasing their motivation to become engaged. The net result can be determined only by sorting out, in future empirical work, the possible paths by which income and income inequality operate.

My thanks to Iris Hui who performed invaluable research assistance. Michael Hout, Neil Fligstein, Sidney Verba, Kay Schlozman, and Gene Smolensky made helpful comments at a presentation of this paper. Kathryn Neckerman provided exceptionally useful comments.

NOTES

1. That is, they take ln(Average Income of Top Decile)—ln(Average of Bottom Decile) = ln(Average Income of Top Decile/Average Income of Bottom Decile), where ln is the natural logarithm. A ratio of average incomes of 2.78 to 1 produces a logged value of 1.0; a ratio of 3 to 1 produces a value of 1.1; a ratio of 3.5 to 1 produces a value of 1.25; a ratio of 4 to 1 produces a value of about 1.4; and a ratio of 5 to 1 produces a value of 1.6.

2. Consider a third society with a bottom decile with an average income of $50,000 and a top decile with an average income of $50,900. This society has the same absolute inequality as the poverty-stricken society with incomes of $100 in the bottom decile and $1,000 in the top decile, but it clearly does not have much poverty.

3. Mark Killingsworth and James Heckman (1986, 140), for example, discuss the problem of interpretation when job characteristics are added to a supply equation, but the addition of education or the number of dependents in a household is also problematic (Pencaval 1986, 67).

4. An increase in wages has two effects. The increase in wages means that an hour of leisure "costs" more in terms of wages forgone; this tends to increase work effort as a household *substitutes* other goods for leisure. At the same time, however, an increase in wages means that a person earns more income with the same hours of work; if leisure is a normal good, so that people want more of it with increasing income, then some of this *income* will be used to buy more leisure and to work less. Most empirical work finds that the substitution effect outweighs the income effect in the short run, but the income effect probably outweighs the substitution effect in the long run.

5. If A is hours of political activity, then the model in this case would be the same as before, except that the utility function would include a third argument for political activity, $U(C,L,A)$, and the hours constraint would be $T = H + L + A$. In this case, increases in wages would typically decrease political activity, and increases in nonlabor income would increase it. The model could be elaborated by assuming that participation returns some benefits, but it should be obvious that as soon as an hour of participation provides benefits equal to or greater than wages from work, then the person stops working and just engages in political activity, which is both pleasurable and remunerative, unlike work. The model could be elaborated still further if participation cost money as well as time, in which case the budget constraint would have to include the cost of participation as an expenditure item.

6. This assumes that the first commodity is not an unusual type of good called a Giffen good.

7. "Activities" is the term used by Reuben Gronau (1986).

8. The net income Y_0^* for a member of group zero is:

$$Y_0^* = Y_0 + (c_0/[Mc_0 + Nc_1]) Nt(Y_1 - Y_0) - c_0.$$

This amounts to the member's gross income Y_0 plus the proportion of the tax receipts that the member receives $(c_0/[Mc_0 + Nc_1])Nt(Y_1 - Y_0)$, minus the political contribution c_0 that is spent to get this share of taxed income. The formula for a typical member of the higher-income group is:

$$Y_1{}^* = Y_0 + (1 - t)(Y_1 - Y_0) + (c_1/[Mc_0 + Nc_1]) \, Nt(Y_1 - Y_0) - c_1,$$

which is similar to the formula for group zero except for the fact that the higher-income group has $t(Y_1 - Y_0)$ of its gross income of Y_1 taxed away, leaving it with $Y_0 + (1 - t)(Y_1 - Y_0)$ of its gross income after taxes. Both formulas can be summarized as follows for $j = 0$ or 1:

$$Y_j{}^* = Y_0 + (1 - t)(Y_j - Y_0) + (c_j/[Mc_0 + Nc_1]) \, Nt(Y_1 - Y_0) - c_j.$$

Each group has to choose its contribution c_j to maximize its net income $Y_j{}^*$. The first-order condition for this maximum leads to:

$$c_0 = (N/4M) \, t(Y_1 - Y_0) \text{ and } c_1 = (1/4) \, t(Y_1 - Y_0).$$

If, as is typically the case, $N \ll M$, so that the higher-income group is much smaller than the lower-income group, then the typical contribution of a member of the lower-income group is smaller by a factor of (N/M) than the typical contribution of a member of the higher-income group. Note that even with $N \ll M$, it is possible that c_0 could be bigger than the amount of money available to a person in the zero group. If, for example, $t = \frac{1}{2}$, $N = (1/4)M$, $Y_0 = \$10,000$, and $Y_1 = \$330,000$, then $c_0 = \$10,000$, which is everything that a member of the zero group has. But these are rather extreme numbers.

9. The proof is simple. Average income is $[(MY_0 + NY_1)/(M + N)]$, which increases if Y_1 increases while Y_0 stays constant. A good measure of relative income inequality is simply the ratio of the total income of the top class to the bottom class, which is $[NY_1/MY_0]$, and that clearly increases when only Y_1 changes.

10. Initially, we have the average income $[(MY_0 + NY_1)/(M + N)]$ equal to some constant c, so that we can solve for Y_1 as $[c(M + N)/NMY_0]$. Hence, we can write the relative inequality as $c(M + N)/(MY_0)^2$. When Y_0 goes down to $Y_0{}^*$ but $[(MY_0 + NY_1)/(M + N)]$ is equal to a constant c, the new top income is $Y_1{}^* = c(M + N)/NMY_0{}^*$. Therefore, the ratio of the total income of the top class to the bottom class is now $c(M + N)/(MY_0{}^*)^2$, which is clearly larger than before, because $Y_0{}^*$ is smaller than Y_0. Therefore, relative income inequality increases.

11. Although it might not lead to an increase in measures that look only at the ratio of the average income of the top decile to the bottom decile if all the movement in people's incomes occurs in the intermediate deciles.

12. The following model owes a great deal to comments at the Russell Sage Foundation social inequality seminar held at Berkeley, California, on January 23, 2003. Comments by Michael Hout, Gene Smolensky, and Sidney Verba were especially helpful, although the entire discussion was very useful.

13. The difference definition of relative income is:

$$A_{ist} = a + b_{11} \, (r_{ist}) + b_{12} \, y_{+st} + e_{ist} = a + b_{11} \, [y_{ist} - y_{+st}] + b_{12} \, y_{+st} + e_{ist}.$$

Precisely the same conditions apply for the coefficients b_{11} and b_{12}.

14. For the former person $[Log(y_{ist} - d) - Log(y_{+st})]$ is clearly more negative than $[Log(y_{ist}) - Log(y_{+st})]$, and for the latter person $[Log(y_{jst} + d) - Log(y_{+st})]$ is more positive than $[Log(y_{jst}) - Log(y_{+st})]$. Hence, the square of both terms is larger when d is moved from the lower-income person to the higher-income person and the LV increases.

15. There are exceptions. For example, if income is taken from someone with below-average income in the second quintile and given to someone with above-average income in the fourth quintile, then LV increases but the ratio of the average income of the top quintile to the bottom quintile does not change at all.

16. Along with the decennial census, the CPS provides the data of record for income in the United States. Consequently, we can feel very confident in the CPS income quintile data. However, there are some complexities: income is categorized on the available dataset, and these categories do not always yield equal-sized quintiles. Nevertheless, it is possible to get most quintiles within 1 to 2 percent of the mark.

17. We obtained these data in spreadsheet format directly from the U.S. Census Bureau. Data are available only from 1978 onwards.

18. Even more than with the CPS data, the Roper data presented problems in creating consistent quintiles and deciles. The quintiles are typically within a few percentage points of the mark, but the decile averages about 6 percent of the sample and varies by a few percentage points as well. One of our goals for future work is to create better quintiles and deciles through statistically reasonable imputation and sorting methods.

19. This result is confirmed by plotting for each study the ratio of the participation indices for the top and bottom income quintiles to the ratio of the average incomes for the top and bottom quintiles. There is a clear negative relationship: as income inequality goes up, participatory inequality goes down. The same result is obtained if we compare the ratio of the participation indices to the census ratio of average incomes for the top and bottom quintiles instead of the Roper ratio of average incomes.

REFERENCES

Abramson, Paul R., and John H. Aldrich. 1982. "The Decline of Electoral Participation in America." *American Political Science Review* 76: 502–21.

Aldrich, John H. 1993. "Rational Choice and Turnout." *American Journal of Political Science* 37: 246–78.

Azzi, Corry, and Ronald Ehrenberg. 1975. "Household Allocation of Time and Church Attendance." *Journal of Political Economy* 83: 27–56.

Barnes, Samuel H., Max Kaase, et al. 1979. *Political Action: Mass Participation in Five Western Democracies.* Beverly Hills, Calif.: Sage Publications.

Becker, Gary S. 1965. "A Theory of the Allocation of Time." *Economic Journal* 75: 493–517.

Bennett, Stephen Earl. 1990. "The Uses and Abuses of Registration and Turnout Data: An Analysis of Piven and Cloward's Studies of Nonvoting in America." *PS: Political Science and Politics* 23: 166–71.

Blundell, Richard, and Thomas Macurdy. 1999. "Labor Supply: A Review of Alternative Approaches." In *Handbook of Labor Economics,* vol. 3A, edited by Orley Ashenfelter and David Card. Amsterdam: North-Holland.

Boyd, Richard W. 1989. "The Effects of Primaries and Statewide Races on Voter Turnout." *Journal of Politics* 51: 730–39.

Brady, Henry E. 1999. "Political Participation." In *Measures of Political Attitudes,* edited by John P. Robinson, Phillip R. Shaver, and Lawrence S. Wrightsman. San Diego: Academic Press.

———. 2003. "Why Do Rich People Make Political Contributions? Some Surprising Results from a Formal Model." Working paper.

Brady, Henry E., Robert D. Putnam, Andrea L. Campbell, Laurel Elms, Steven Yonish, and Dorie Apollonio. 2001. *Roper Social and Political Trends Data, 1973–1994.* Individual surveys from Roper Starch Worldwide (computer file) conducted by Roper Organization and Roper Starch Worldwide (producers), 1973 to 1994. Storrs, Conn.: Roper Center for Public Opinion Research, University of Connecticut (distributor).

Brady, Henry E., Kay Lehman Schlozman, and Sidney Verba. 1999. "Prospecting for Participants: Rational Expectations and the Recruitment of Political Activists." *American Political Science Review* 93: 153–68.

Brady, Henry E., Sidney Verba, and Kay Lehman Schlozman. 1995. "Beyond SES: A Resource Model of Political Participation." *American Political Science Review* 89: 271–94.

Brody, Richard A. 1978. "The Puzzle of Political Participation in America." In *The New American Political System,* edited by Anthony King. Washington, D.C.: American Enterprise Institute.

Brown, Robert D., Robert A. Jackson, and Gerald C. Wright. 1999. "Registration, Turnout, and State Party Systems." *Political Research Quarterly* 52: 463–79.

Burns, Nancy, Kay Lehman Schlozman, and Sidney Verba. 2001. *The Private Roots of Public Action.* Cambridge, Mass.: Harvard University Press.

Campbell, Andrea Louise. 2002. "Self-interest, Social Security, and the Distinctive Participation Patterns of Senior Citizens." *American Political Science Review* 96: 565–74.

Champernowne, David Gawen, and Frank A. Cowell. 1998. *Economic Inequality and Income Distribution.* Cambridge: Cambridge University Press.

Cowell, Frank A. 1977. *Measuring Inequality.* London: Prentice-Hall/Harvester Wheatsheaf.

Ehrlich, Isaac. 1973. "Participation in Illegitimate Activities: A Theoretical and Empirical Investigation." *Journal of Political Economy* 81: 521–65.

Ellison, Christopher G., and David A. Gay. 1989. "Black Political Participation Revisited: A Test of Compensatory Ethnic Community and Public Arena Models." *Social Science Quarterly* 70: 101–19.

Finkel, Steven E. 1985. "Reciprocal Effects of Participation and Political Efficacy: A Panel Analysis." *American Journal of Political Science* 29: 891–913.

———. 1987. "The Effects of Participation on Political Efficacy and Political Support: Evidence from a West German Panel." *Journal of Politics* 49: 441–64.

Gronau, Reuben. 1970. "The Effect of Traveling Time on the Demand for Passenger Transportation." *Journal of Political Economy* 78: 377–94.

———. 1986. "Home Production: A Survey." In *Handbook of Labor Economics,* vol. 1, edited by Orley Ashenfelter and Richard Layard. Amsterdam: North-Holland.

Groseclose, Timothy. 1996. "An Examination of the Market for Favors and Votes in Congress." *Economic Inquiry* 34: 320–40.

Groseclose, Timothy, and James M. Snyder Jr. 1996. "Buying Supermajorities." *American Political Science Review* 90(2): 303–15.

Gurr, Ted Robert. 1970. *Why Men Rebel.* Princeton, N.J.: Princeton University Press.

Hibbs, Douglas A. 1973. *Mass Political Violence: A Cross-National Causal Analysis.* New York: John Wiley.

Hill, Kim Quaile, and Jan E. Leighley. 1993. "Party Ideology, Organization, and Competitiveness as Mobilizing Forces in Gubernatorial Elections." *American Journal of Political Science* 37: 1158–78.

———. 1994. "Mobilizing Institutions and Class Representation in U.S. State Electorates." *Political Research Quarterly* 47: 137–50.

Huckfeldt, Robert. 1986. *Politics in Context: Assimilation and Conflict in Urban Neighborhoods.* New York: Agathon Press.

Iannaccone, Laurence R. 1998. "Introduction to the Economics of Religion." *Journal of Economic Literature* 36: 1465–95.

Jackson, Robert A. 1993. "Voter Mobilization in the 1986 Midterm Elections." *Journal of Politics* 55: 1081–99.

———. 1996. "A Reassessment of Voter Mobilization." *Political Research Quarterly* 49: 331–49.

Juster, F. Thomas, and Frank P. Stafford. 1991. "The Allocation of Time: Empirical Findings, Behavioral Models, and Problems of Measurement." *Journal of Economic Literature* 29: 471–522.

Katz, Lawrence F., and David H. Autor. 1999. "Changes in the Wage Structure and Earnings Inequality." In *Handbook of Labor Economics,* vol. 3A, edited by Orley Ashenfelter and David Card. Amsterdam: North-Holland.

Killingsworth, Mark R., and James J. Heckman. 1986. "Female Labor Supply: A Survey." In *Handbook of Labor Economics,* vol. 1, edited by Orley Ashenfelter and Richard Layard. Amsterdam: North-Holland.

Kingston, Paul William, and Steven E. Finkel. 1987. "Is There a Marriage Gap in Politics?" *Journal of Marriage and Family* 49: 57–64.

Lancaster, Kelvin. 1966. "A New Approach to Consumer Theory." *Journal of Political Economy* 74: 132–57.

Lane, Robert E. 1959. *Political Life: Why People Get Involved in Politics.* Glencoe, Ill.: Free Press.

Leighley, Jan E. 1995. "Attitudes, Opportunities, and Incentives: A Field Essay on Political Participation." *Political Research Quarterly* 48: 181–209.

Leighley, Jan E., and Jonathan Nagler. 1992a. "Socioeconomic Class Bias in Turnout, 1964–1988: The Voters Remain the Same." *American Political Science Review* 86: 725–36.

———. 1992b. "Individual and Systematic Influences on Turnout: Who Votes? 1984." *Journal of Politics* 54: 718–40.

Leighley, Jan E., and Arnold Vedlitz. 1999. "Race, Ethnicity, and Political Participation: Competing Models and Contrasting Explanations." *Journal of Politics* 61: 1092–1114.

Michael, Robert T. 1973. "Education in Nonmarket Production." *Journal of Political Economy* 81: 306–27.

Mutz, Diana. 1998. *Impersonal Influence.* Cambridge: Cambridge University Press.

Nagler, Jonathan. 1992. "The Effect of Registration Laws and Education on U.S. Voter Turnout." *American Political Science Review* 85: 1319–1405.

Nie, Norman H., Jane Junn, and Kenneth Stehlik-Barry. 1996. *Education and Democratic Citizenship in America.* Chicago: University of Chicago Press.

Oliver, J. Eric. 1999. "The Effects of Metropolitan Economic Segregation on Local Civic Participation." *American Journal of Political Science* 43: 186–212.

———. 2000. "City Size and Civic Involvement in Metropolitan America." *American Political Science Review* 94: 361–73.

———. 2001. *Democracy in Suburbia.* Princeton, N.J.: Princeton University Press.

Olson, Mancur, Jr. 1965. *The Logic of Collective Action: Public Goods and the Theory of Groups.* Cambridge, Mass.: Harvard University Press.

Pencaval, John. 1986. "Labor Supply of Men: A Survey." In *Handbook of Labor Economics,* vol. 1, edited by Orley Ashenfelter and Richard Layard. Amsterdam: North-Holland.

Portney, Kent E., and Jeffery M. Berry. 1997. "Mobilizing Minority Communities: Social Capital and Participation in Urban Neighborhoods (Social Capital, Civil Society, and Contemporary Democracy)." *American Behaviorist Scientist* 40: 632–38.

Powell, G. Bingham, Jr. 1986. "American Voter Turnout in Comparative Perspective." *American Political Science Review* 80: 17–43.

Putnam, Robert D. 1995a. "Bowling Alone: America's Declining Social Capital." *Journal of Democracy* 6: 65–78.

———. 1995b. "Tuning In, Tuning Out: The Strange Disappearance of Social Capital in America." *PS: Political Science and Politics* 28: 664–83.

———. 2001. *Bowling Alone.* New York: Touchstone Books.

Reiter, Howard. 1979. "Why Is Turnout Down?" *Public Opinion Quarterly* 43: 297–311.

Riker, William H., and Peter Ordeshook. 1968. "A Theory of the Calculus of Voting." *American Political Science Review* 62: 25–42.

Rosenstone, Steven J., and John Mark Hansen. 1993. *Mobilization, Participation, and Democracy in America.* New York: Macmillan.

Schlozman, Kay Lehman. 2002. "Citizen Participation in America: What Do We Know? Why do We Care?" In *Political Science: The State of the Discipline,* edited by Ira Katznelson and Helen Milner. New York: W.W. Norton.

Schlozman, Kay Lehman, Sidney Verba, and Henry E. Brady. 1995. "Participation's Not a Paradox: The View from American Activists." *British Journal of Political Science* 25: 1–36.

Shaffer, Stephen D. 1981. "A Multivariate Explanation of Decreasing Turnout in Presidential Elections, 1960–1976." *American Journal of Political Science* 25: 68–95.

Snyder, James M. 1991. "On Buying Legislatures." *Economics and Politics* 3: 93–109.

Tate, Katherine. 1991. "Black Political Participation in the 1984 and 1988 Presidential Elections." *American Political Science Review* 85: 1159–76.

U.S. Department of Commerce, Bureau of the Census. Various years. *Current Population Reports.* Washington: U.S. Government Printing Office.

Uslaner, Eric, and M. Mitchell Brown. 2002. "Inequality, Trust, and Civic Engagement." Review paper. New York: Russell Sage Foundation.

Verba, Sidney, and Norman H. Nie. 1972. *Participation in America: Political Democracy and Social Equality.* New York: Harper & Row.

Verba, Sidney, Norman H. Nie, and Jae-On Kim. 1978. *A Seven-Nation Comparison: Participation and Political Equality.* Cambridge, Mass.: Harvard University Press.

Verba, Sidney, Kay Lehman Schlozman, and Henry E. Brady. 1995. *Voice and Equality: Civic Voluntarism in American Politics.* Cambridge, Mass.: Harvard University Press.

———. 2000. "Rational Action and Political Activity." *Journal of Theoretical Politics* 12: 243–68.

Wielhouwer, Peter W., and Brad Lockerbie. 1994. "Party Contacting and Political Participation, 1952–1990." *American Journal of Political Science* 38: 211–29.

Wolfinger, Raymond E., and Steven J. Rosenstone. 1980. *Who Votes?* New Haven, Conn.: Yale University Press.

Chapter 18

What, Me Vote?

Richard B. Freeman

Voting turnout, measured by the number of persons voting relative to the population of voting age, is lower in the United States than in other advanced democracies, including the United States' nearest neighbor, Canada. From 1945 to the late 1990s, the United States averaged a 48.3 percent turnout of the voting age population while Canada averaged a 68.4 percent turnout relative to the voting age population. In the 2000 presidential election, 51.4 percent of the voting age population in the United States cast ballots. On a world scale, the United States ranks 138th in turnout among countries that hold elections—far below every other advanced democracy save for Switzerland (in 137th position) (IDEA 1997, 21).[1] Turnout in 2000 was eight percentage points lower than it was in 1960, when President Kennedy appointed a commission to study the "low" turnout of that election.

What explains low and declining turnout? Does low turnout skew the voting population toward more advantaged social groups, defined by education, income, age, or occupation? What institutional features of the electoral process affect turnout?

In this chapter, I examine what social science knows about these questions. Most studies that examine voting rely on the National Election Studies (NES), which conducts surveys of the American electorate in presidential and midterm election years, before and after elections; the November voting supplement to the Current Population Survey (CPS), which asks respondents their registration and voting status in national elections; and administrative counts of votes divided by the voting age population, as published by the U.S. Census Bureau and the *Congressional Quarterly*.[2] Some of the studies rely on other sources as well: tabulations of votes in particular areas, experiments with get-out-the-vote campaigns, exit polls, and so on.

The NES and CPS record the answers of individuals to questions about whether they voted in the most recent election. Both datasets record higher turnout than do the administrative vote counts. One reason for the discrepancy between the self-reported and administrative data is that some people report casting a ballot when they did not do so (Silver, Anderson, and Abramson 1986). Another reason is that the surveys, particularly the NES, disproportionately undercount low-turnout groups. Barry Burden (2000, fig. 2) reports that this problem has grown over time in the NES for presidential elections, in part owing to declining response rates of those surveyed. The level and trend in the discrepancy between the NES and administrative counts is also affected by differences in the populations covered: the administrative turnout figures are based on voting age population, while the NES sample is limited to eligible voters, and to the greater impact of measurement error at lower levels of turnout (McDonald 2001). But rates of turnout based on administrative data are themselves imperfect. The number of votes counted differs from votes cast because of technical difficulties relating to voting machines, voter errors in recording their vote, and so on (Caltech-MIT Voting Technology Project 2001). Most important for assessing turnout, administrative turnout figures relate the number of votes to the voting age population, which exceeds the population eligible to vote. Given available data, it is difficult to estimate the proportion of eligible voters in the voting age population over time.

This review has four major findings regarding turnout and the level and trend in inequality in turnout in the United States:

1. No single factor explains why Americans vote in such low proportions. Turnout in the United States is low in part because the country has a large population of noncitizen immigrants who cannot legally vote; in part because many states disenfranchise ex-felons from voting; in part because increased family and time demands deter some potential voters from going to the polls; and in part because of changes in political mobilization.

2. The level and trend in turnout is related to socioeconomic status. Persons who are older and have higher income, occupational standing, and education are more likely to vote than otherwise comparable persons who are younger and have lower income, occupational standing, and education. From the 1960s to the present, inequality in the rate of voting by socioeconomic group has increased.

3. Policies that make it easier to register to vote—such as increasing the number of venues for registering, reducing the time between registration and voting, and allowing voters to register on voting day—and policies that make it easier to vote—such as mail balloting and opening polling booths for more hours or for more days—have modest positive impacts on turnout. Get-out-the-vote campaigns, particularly face-to-face canvassing, have a somewhat larger impact on turnout.

4. In contrast to the United States proper, one part of the country, Puerto Rico, has an extremely high rate of turnout. In the 1990s, Puerto Rico had a seventy-eight-percentage-point turnout in presidential election years, compared with just over 50 percent turnout in the fifty states. An important reason for this high turnout is that the island makes Tuesday elections a holiday and the political parties mobilize voters extensively on that day.

MAGNITUDE OF TURNOUT

As noted, turnout in the United States for elections is low by international standards. Advanced democracies average a 73 percent rate of turnout, so that even the highest turnout rates in the United States in the post–World War II years, on the order of 60 percent, fall short of the rates in comparable countries (IDEA 1997, fig. 36). As in other countries, turnout in the United States varies by socioeconomic group. Better-educated, higher-paid, and older citizens invariably have higher turnout rates than others (Wolfinger and Rosenstone 1980; Leighley and Nagler 1992). This means that differences in turnout rates across countries and changes in turnout in the same country over time occur largely because of variation in the voting rates of the less-advantaged part of the population. Because of the low turnout of lower-income persons in the United States compared with other democracies, the median voter is higher in the social strata in the United States than else-where.[3]

Cross-country comparisons suggest three reasons for low turnout in the bottom parts of the U.S. distribution. The first is the weakness of trade unions in the United States compared with other countries; unions usually organize lower-income workers to vote, often for labor-oriented parties, so that countries with greater union density tend to have higher turnouts (Radcliff and Davis 2000). The second reason is that the United States has a first-past-the-post two-party system, which elicits smaller turnouts than proportional representation systems of voting, in which minority opinions vote so that they can have a voice in legislatures. The third reason is the congressional-presidential system, which elicits smaller turnouts than parliamentary systems (IDEA 1997).

Historically, institutional features of the U.S. voting process have made it harder for Americans to vote than it is for citizens in most other democracies. The United States is almost alone among major democracies in requiring citizen-initiated registration to vote. In most countries, citizens have the right to vote without going through a special registration system (Highton and Wolfinger 1995). The United States has never mandated voting, say, by fining those who fail to vote, as some countries do (Lijphart 1997). The United States has never introduced voting on weekends or made weekday voting days holidays, as some countries (and Puerto Rico) do. Finally, rather than having a national voting procedure, each of the U.S. states determines its own regulations, which creates variation in registration rules and in the determination of eligible voters. The close 2000 presidential election highlighted the differences in state regulations of voting by ex-felons, as well as the ability of local officials to bend rules in ways that affect turnout.

Turnout in the United States relative to the voting age population fell noticeably in the latter part of the twentieth century, despite diverse policy and regulatory changes that have made it easier for citizens to vote. Figure 18.1 shows that since the 1950s the turnout rate based on administrative data has declined in both congressional and presidential election years. The numerator in this statistic is the number of persons who vote for the highest office in each year, and the denominator is the voting age population—the population age twenty-one and older, until 1972, when the franchise was extended to eighteen- to twenty-year-olds. The drop in turnout in 1972 was partially due to the change in the voting age population in that year. Because a larger proportion of the population votes in years when the nation selects a president than in years when it does not, figure 18.1 differentiates between presidential-year and nonpresidential-year elections. Because more people vote for president than for a representative in the same election, it also differentiates between the voting rate for the two types of offices.

The proportion of the population that votes varies from election to election. It was low in the 1948 election, when presumably everyone thought Thomas Dewey was a sure winner. It was higher in the 1992 campaign, when Ross Perot ran as a third-party candidate, than in surrounding years and was a bit higher in 2000 than in 1996. But these variations have occurred around a general downward trend. From the 1950s to the 1990s, the proportion of Americans who vote has declined. Marvin Wattenberg's (2002) analysis of turnout in other advanced democracies shows a similar pattern throughout the West: falls in voter density in the United Kingdom, continental Europe, and other advanced OECD countries. Country-specific factors might explain the reduction in turnout country by country, but the broad pattern suggests the operation of similar factors across all advanced countries.

The downward trend in voter density in the United States has occurred despite government efforts to make it easier for citizens to register and vote. The most important fran-

FIGURE 18.1   *Voting Age Population Participation in Presidential and Congressional Elections,*
1932 to 2000

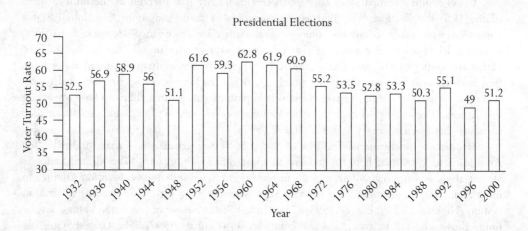

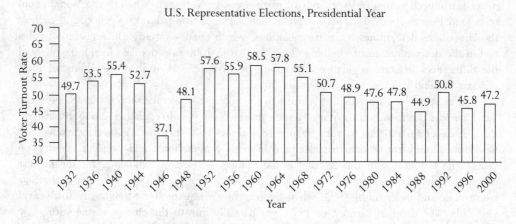

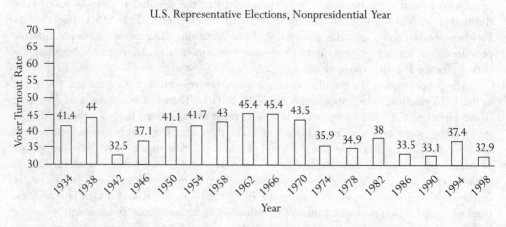

Source: U.S. Department of Commerce (2002, table 395).

chise-increasing law was the 1965 Voting Rights Act, which helped reenfranchise blacks in the South, many of whom had effectively lost the ballot owing to the actions of politically dominant whites. Another important act was the National Voter Registration Act of 1993 (the so-called Motor Voter Act), which increased the venues through which citizens could register, including state car registration offices. Many states enacted other laws or regulations that reduced the burden of registering and voting. That turnout fell during a period when the country was making it easier for citizens to vote rules out any institutional or legal explanation of the trend.

Analysts have examined the impact on turnout of a variety of factors: changes in the proportion of the voting age population eligible to vote; changes in family status; changes in mobilization by political groups; and changes in legal and administrative regulations that influence the burden of voting. Although research has greatly illuminated the factors that affect voting, it has not turned up a simple clear reason for the decline in turnout.

The Role of Demography

The fact that Americans have become more educated, work in higher-status occupations, and have higher family income than in the past operates to raise turnout. One important demographic factor, however, works in the opposite direction: the rising proportion of the adult population who cannot legally vote. The vast majority of this group consists of immigrant noncitizens. In the 1950s noncitizens made up about 2 percent of the voting age population. In 2000 they made up about 8 percent of the voting age population. In addition, the number of incarcerated persons, who generally cannot vote, and ex-felons, who cannot vote in many states, has risen sharply enough to become a political issue. On the order of 1 percent of the voting age population cannot vote owing to their ex-felon status.[4]

In an important study, Michael McDonald and Samuel Popkin (2001) calculate the turnout rate for eligible citizens by replacing the population of voting age by an estimate of the number of citizens with the franchise. Their turnout rate of voters divided by eligible voters in the 1990s is some four percentage points higher than the reported turnout. Lynne Casper and Loretta Bass (1998) and Barry Burden (2000) provide comparable estimates for 1996.[5] Since 1972 (when eighteen- to twenty-year-olds became eligible to vote), McDonald and Popkin estimate that the number of voters divided by the number of eligible voters barely fell in presidential years and increased modestly in congressional elections.

If data on the noncitizen population were perfect, these calculations would go a long way to resolving the question of why turnout fell after 1972, while still leaving a pre-1972 decline in turnout to be explained by other factors. But estimates of the noncitizen population are highly imperfect. One reason is that from 1966 to 1993 the Current Population Survey did not ask respondents directly whether they were citizens, but allowed for the response "not a citizen" to a question about why they were not registered to vote. From 1994 on, the CPS asked directly: "What is your citizenship status?" Thus, we do not have the same data over time to calculate the number of noncitizens and citizens in the adult population. Equally important, the CPS figures show considerable year-to-year variability in the estimated number of noncitizens—the signature of considerable measurement error. Table 1 of McDonald and Popkin (2001), which records their adjustments for turnout, shows a surprising drop of 4.6 million persons in the number of noncitizens from 1992 to 1994. (See table 18A.1 for the key noncitizens series.) This drop presumably reflects changes in the way the CPS posed the question about citizen status between the two years, not a genuine fall in the number of noncitizens. The data also show large jumps in the numbers of noncitizens between 1980 and 1984 and between 1998 and 1990. In addition, there are measurement problems in estimating the number of citizens who lack the franchise because of criminal behavior. We have accurate counts of the prison and jail populations, but because we do not have survey data on the number of ex-felons who are legally ineligible to vote, we must make various assumptions to make this adjustment.

To see how well the rising proportion of noncitizens in the voting age population can explain declining turnout, I estimate a small time-series model that links the number of voters and the population of voting age to the estimated number of persons eligible to vote for the period 1948 to 1998. My analysis shows that the measurement problem with noncitizens of voting age makes it difficult to determine their contribution to the trend decline in turnout.

Model of the Trend in Turnout

Let P be the population of voting age, V the number of voters, E the estimated population eligible to vote, and D a dummy variable for whether the election is in a presidential year; let T be a trend counter. Then V/P is the standard turnout rate, V/E is the turnout rate relative to eligible voters, and E/P is the proportion of the voting age population eligible to vote. To estimate the trend in turnout for the voting age population, I regress the log of the ratio of the number of voters to the voting age population on a trend term and whether the election is a presidential contest or not. The coefficient b on the trend term measures the magnitude of the drop in turnout:

$$(1)\ \ln (V/P) = a + b\,T + c\,D. \tag{18.1}$$

Row 1 of table 18.1 presents estimates of this equation for the period 1948 to 2000. The estimated coefficient (multiplied by 100) on trend is -0.81, which translates roughly into 0.8 percentage points in turnout per year (that is, a drop in turnout from a 0.500 to 0.492 in the next year). This implies a four-percentage-point drop in turnout per decade, given five elections in a decade.

Next, I estimate a turnout equation using the estimated population legally eligible to vote as the denominator (V/E). The coefficient b' on the trend term in this equation measures the magnitude of the drop in turnout relative to the new population base, E. To the extent that the drop in turnout is due to the changing proportion of the voting age population eligible to vote, the coefficient b' should be smaller in absolute terms than the coefficient b.

$$\ln (V/E) = a' + b'D + c'T \tag{18.2}$$

Row 2 of table 18.1 gives the estimate of this equation. Adjusting for the eligible population in the denominator produces a coefficient on trend (multiplied by 100) of -0.48. Changing the base for the turnout statistic to persons eligible to vote thus reduces the downward trend in turnout from 0.81 to 0.48, a reduction of 41 percent ($= .81 - .48/.81$). By this calculation, 41 percent of the trend decline in turnout appears to be due to the rising proportion of persons without the franchise.

But there is an alternative, less restrictive way to examine the effect of the proportion of the voting age population eligible to vote on the trend. Rather than replacing the voting age population P with the estimated population eligible to vote E in the denominator of the

TABLE 18.1   *Regression Coefficients and Standard Errors for Alternative Models of the Impact of Ineligible Voters on Turnout, 1948 to 2000*

	Constant	Trend (× 100)	Presidential Year	Ln Eligible/Voting Age Population	N	R^2
1948 to 2000						
1. Ln (voters / voting age population)	−0.78	−0.81 (0.18)	0.30 (0.03)	—	27	0.86
2. Ln (voters / eligible population)	−0.79	−0.48 (0.09)	0.30 (0.03)	—	27	0.86
3. Ln voters / voting age population	−0.79	−0.27 (0.30)	0.30 (0.03)	1.66 (0.93)	27	0.87
1972 to 1988						
4. Ln voters / voting age population	−0.88	−0.45 (0.21)	0.33 (0.02)	—	15	0.96
5. Ln voters / eligible population	−0.93	0.07 (0.25)	0.33 (0.02)	—	15	0.95
6. Ln voters / voting age population	−0.85	−0.85 (0.45)	0.33 (0.02)	−0.78 (0.77)	15	0.97

Source: Based on data from McDonald and Popkin (2001); see table 18A.1. Reprinted with the permission of Cambridge University Press.
Notes: Eligible population is defined as voting age population minus the number of noncitizens of voting age, minus the number of ineligible felons, plus the estimated overseas voting eligible population. Presidential year is dummy 1 for every presidential-year election.

measure of turnout, I add a new term to equation 18.1: the ratio of eligible voters to the voting age population (E/P). This gives the equation:

$$\ln (V/P) = a'\,{}^{\backprime} + b'\,{}^{\backprime}D + c'\,{}^{\backprime}T + d \ln (E/P) \qquad (18.3)$$

If the number of eligible voters is measured accurately and the model 2 regression is correct, the coefficient d on ln E/P will be 1. This effectively turns the dependent variable in equation 18.3 into ln V/E as in equation 18.2 (since we can move ln E/P to the left-hand side of the equation, where the ln Ps cancel). But if E/P is poorly measured, or if it is related to other factors that affect turnout, the coefficient d may vary from 1. This will give a different estimate of the impact of the rising proportion of ineligible voters on the trend. Row 3 of table 18.1 shows that the trend in the turnout drops to −0.27 and is insignificant. But the estimated coefficient on the ln E/P term is considerably above the coefficient of 1 that we would expect from a correctly specified and measured model, which raises some doubt about the correction procedure.

The strongest claim by McDonald and Popkin (2001) is that the rising proportion of noncitizens explains *all* of the drop in turnout from 1972 on. Adjusted for the number of non-eligible persons of voting age, they find that the drop in turnout was small and statistically insignificant for presidential-year elections and positive in congressional-year elections. To examine this claim, I estimated equations 18.1 through 18.3 for the period 1972 to 2000. These results are given in rows 4, 5, and 6 of table 18.1. The coefficient on trend in row 4 is smaller than the trend coefficient in row 1. The drop in the turnout after 1972 was half as large as that over the 1950 to 1998 period. Consistent with McDonald and Popkin's analysis, when I replace the voting age population with the estimated number of citizens eligible to vote in the denominator of the turnout measure in row 5, the negative trend disappears completely. When I enter the ratio of eligible persons to persons of voting age in row 6, however, the coefficient on the eligible proportion of the voting age population is negative, and significantly different from unity, and the coefficient on trend jumps to -0.85. The problem is that the estimated number of noncitizens fluctuates oddly both before and after the census change in definition, as can be seen in table 18A.1, with odd effects in this small time series.

From these calculations, I conclude that measurement error in estimating the proportion of the voting age population eligible to vote weakens the claim that the rising proportion of ineligibles accounts for the entire drop in turnout since 1972 and makes it unclear what proportion of the longer-term downward trend can in fact be attributed to the changing proportion of eligibles. The rising proportion of ineligible persons of voting age must have reduced the turnout rate, but the measurement problem does not allow us to determine its contribution to the trend with any confidence. That depends on the model we use, with the more flexible model giving the worst results for the 1972 to 2000 period. But even if we choose to ignore the measurement problem and accept regressions 2 and 5 as the appropriate ones, the turnout puzzle would not disappear. The increased education, occupational status, and income of citizens operated to increase turnout, but instead it fell. The puzzle becomes more severe when we recognize that throughout the period the United States made it easier for citizens to register to vote and to vote, exclusive of ex-felons.

Changing Institutional Determinants

Both the federal government and the individual states have adopted policies to make it easier for persons to vote. In 1965 the federal government enacted the Voting Rights Act to help black citizens overcome discriminatory practices in access to voting in the South. In 1993 the National Voter Registration Act enabled citizens to register simultaneously with driver's license application or renewal, to register at diverse government offices that provide public assistance and services, and to register by mail (U.S. Department of Justice 2000). Going further, many states have reduced the time before elections when citizens must register, with seven states (Idaho, Maine, Minnesota, New Hampshire, Wisconsin, Wyoming, and North Dakota) allowing voters to register on election day. Most states have made absentee ballots easier to obtain, particularly for elderly citizens, and Oregon has created a mail-only ballot. Some states open polling stations before elections so that there is an election week rather than only one election day. Because different states have initiated policies at various times, researchers are able to infer the institutional determinants of turnout by comparing turnout in states with different policies in a given year and comparing changes in turnout between states that changed policies and states that did not change policies.

Studies of the effect of legal and administrative policies show that easing registration regulations affects turnout, but only modestly. While early cross-section comparisons found that states with easier forms of registration had considerably higher turnout than other states (Crocker 1990; Wolfinger and Rosenstone 1980; Teixeira 1992; Calvert and Gilchrist 1993), analyses that relate changes in state laws and changes in turnout show much smaller positive effects of the form of registration on turnout. Stephen Knack's (1995, tables 2 and 3) analysis of differences in state registration laws prior to the Motor Voter Act suggests an impact of perhaps twenty-one to twenty-two percentage points, staggered over time. The larger cross-section difference in turnout between states with harder/easier forms of registration presumably reflects omitted characteristics of the state that determine both the policy and the turnout.

The Motor Voter Act changed the way people register to vote. Thirty-five percent of persons who registered to vote after January 1, 1995, registered through motor vehicle offices, 2 percent at a public assistance office, 6 percent at a school, hospital, or campus, 11 percent by mail, and 6 percent at the polls on election day (CPS 2002, table 14). Some experts (Piven and Cloward 1988) anticipated that this would greatly raise registration and turnout. Other experts thought it would have no effect; they predicted that motor voter registrants would register but not show up on election day. Overall, the Motor Voter Act seems to have raised turnout modestly. Raymond Wolfinger and Jonathan Hoffman (2001, 4) find that people who register at motor vehicle offices are about 14 percent less likely to vote than people who register in other ways, but that they still vote in a sizable number that "greatly exceeds the expectations of scholars who thought that motor voter registrants would be largely abstainers."

Another important change in state voting regulations has been the liberalization of rules for absentee balloting. Making it easier for persons to cast absentee ballots has increased the proportion of the electorate choosing that way to vote. In 2000 some 14 percent of voters either cast an absentee ballot or voted at a polling station before election day. Many of the absentee voters would have voted in any case, but some presumably would not have voted without the absentee option. The use of absentee ballots varies considerably among states, depending on each state's election law. California, Texas, and other western states rely extensively on the postal ballot. In 2000 approximately 25 percent of Californians voted absentee. In his study of the effect of absentee ballots on turnout, Eric Oliver (1996) notes that both the use of the absentee ballot and its effect on overall turnout vary with the policies of the state political parties, some of which seek to mobilize absentee voters while others do not. He uses a logistic model to relate voting to the individual characteristics of the respondent and various measures of state laws and the activity of the political parties in the state. The results show that voting is more likely in states that have more open primaries, that expanded eligibility for absentee ballots, and that have final registration dates close to the voting day. His bottom-line estimate is that provisions that make absentee balloting easier increase turnout by one to two percentage points.

Local jurisdictions throughout the United States have conducted thousands of elections by mail rather than by polling booth. This is done largely in small areas, special districts, and school districts. Randy Hamilton's (1988) review of mail-only balloting shows that this innovation has raised turnout and lowered the cost of holding elections. After experimenting with voting by mail, Oregon became the first state to adopt this method of voting as its sole way to conduct elections. Surveys of Oregon voters show that they strongly prefer all-mail voting to voting at polling places, while the state saves millions of dollars in costs. Adam Berinsky, Nancy Burns, and Michael Traugott (2001) estimate that voting by mail increased turnout in Oregon's 1996 election by four to six percentage points compared with previous elections in the state. They also found that voting by mail worked by keeping existing voters in the group that voted rather than by attracting new voters. Michael Traugott and Michael Hammer (2001) find that the high turnout persisted through 2000.

But not all of the evidence supports the claim that mail balloting raises turnout in larger elections. Comparing Oregon elections that used polling place voting with elections under the mail-only voting procedure, Susan Banducci and Jeffrey Karp (2002, table 1) find that higher turnout from mail balloting is slight in major elections, far below the effect of postal balloting on turnout in local races. Analyzing voting data in three California counties, Megan Mullin and Thad Kousser (2002) report little difference between turnout in precincts that use mail-only ballots because they are too small to have polling places and precincts that have voting by poll and absentee ballot.

Finally, comparing turnout in the 2000 election in states that opened their polling booths earlier and kept them open longer with other states, Raymond Wolfinger, Benjamin Highton, and Megan Mullin (2002b) find modest effects on the turnout of registered voters.

In sum, diverse analyses show that easing administrative requirements to vote raises turnout in sensible but modest ways. If these analyses are right, turnout has been increased by three to four percentage points as a result of the diverse changes in registration and voting laws and procedures. This adds to the mystery of why turnout has fallen.

Time and Family Commitments

The increased time constraints on people as a result of work and family commitments may also be a factor in reducing voter turnout. In contrast to the 1950s, when most families had two adults, one a full-time caretaker in the household and the other a full-time worker, in the 1990s the majority of married families had two earners and upward of 25 percent of families were lone-parent families. The result is that the average American devotes more time to work than in the past, and it is harder to find time for nonmarket activities. The time cost of voting has presumably risen most for persons with children, since they now have both time constraints and work commitments.

There is some evidence supporting a "rising time cost" hypothesis. In 1980, 1996, 1998, and 2000, the Census Bureau asked the nonvoting registered population why they had not voted. Table 18.2 summarizes what nonvoters told the CPS in these years. In 1980, 7.6 percent volunteered that the reason was that they had "no time off from work or school or were too busy." In 1998, 34.9 percent gave this as their reason for not voting. In 2000, 20.9 percent gave the "too busy because of school or work" answer. Contrast these responses to the proportion of persons who reported lack of interest as the reason for not voting. In 1980, 11.2 percent said they were not interested or did not care about elections, which is 3.6 percentage points more than the 7.6 percent who said they were too busy. In 2000, 12.2 percent said they were not interested, a modest one percentage point rise. The increase in the proportion of registrants who cited a time constraint for not voting dwarfs the increase in the proportion of registrants not voting who gave the "lack of interest" answer.

If people are giving their true reason for not voting, one would expect groups facing especially heavy demands on their time to disproportionately report that they did not vote because they had no time off or were too busy. Parents—particularly lone parents—are more likely to cite this reason than others, and persons with children are less likely to be registered and to vote than others. NES data analyzed by Ruy Teixeira (1999) and summarized in table 18.3 shows that the difference in turnout rates by parents and nonparents has risen from 1956 through 1996 (exclusive of 1992). His analysis of the CPS files for 1992 further suggests that the parent/nonparent gap differs greatly by the position of parents: the gap is huge among the least-educated and low-income families while nonexistent among college graduates and higher-income families. Wolfinger, Highton, and Mullin (2002b) report, however, that the voting rates of employed persons do not vary with the time that polling booths are open or with state laws that require employers to give workers time off

TABLE 18.2   *Reported Reasons for Not Voting Among Persons Registered to Vote, 1980 to 2000*

	1980	1996	1998	2000
Too busy	7.6%	21.5%	34.9%	20.9%
Not interested	11.2	16.6	12.7	12.2
Ill or disabled	17.1	14.9	11.1	14.8
Dislike candidates	16.0	13.0	5.5	7.7
Out of town	12.6	11.1	8.3	10.2
No transportation	4.1	4.3	1.8	2.4
All else	17.2	15.9	18.5	23.7
Don't know or refused	14.1	2.7	7.1	7.5

Source: U.S. Department of Commerce (1998, 2000, 2002).

to vote. Since employed persons are more likely to be time-constrained than others, these results are inconsistent with the hypothesis that time costs have a large impact on turnout.

Overall, I conclude that rising time costs and family commitments explain at most a minor part of the trend in turnout. If time commitments were a major factor, voters in states such as Texas and Tennessee, which allow voters to cast their ballot before election day or by absentee ballot, would have exceptionally high rates of voting from registered voters, as would Oregon, which has voting by mail. But the rate of voting by registered voters in these states did not diverge greatly from the U.S. average in the 2000 election.

Mobilization

Analysts have examined how factors endogenous to the political process affect voting, including political mobilization, partisan attitudes, campaign spending, prospective voters' views of political efficacy, and the expected closeness of elections. Since politicians determine some of these factors in response to how a campaign is progressing, it is hard to infer their causal impact on turnout. If candidate X thinks she can win an election by mobilizing

TABLE 18.3   *Voter Turnout Rates of Parents and Nonparents, 1956 to 1996*

	Parents	Nonparents	Difference
1956	69%	78%	−9%
1960	78	81	−3
1964	77	78	−1
1968	75	76	−1
1978	52	57	−5
1980	67	74	−7
1982	57	63	−6
1984	70	76	−6
1986	45	58	−13
1988	64	74	−10
1990	37	53	−16
1992	75	78	−3
1996	64	76	−12

Source: Teixeira (1999).

voters through canvassing or media expenditures, she will do so and possibly increase the turnout of her supporters. If candidate Y thinks that campaign mobilization will not work in his race because voters are too turned off, he will canvass or spend less. In the 2000 presidential election, both Bush and Gore spent much of their budgets on a set of "battle-ground states" that each felt he had to win to gain an electoral college majority. Seth McKee (2002, table 6) estimates that turnout was one to two percentage points higher in the battleground states than in other states. But mobilizing in some states and ignoring others could just as easily have reduced national turnout as increased it. Why bother to vote in Massachusetts or Texas when neither candidate was seeking votes there on the assumption that the results were impervious to his efforts? To infer the effects of spending and other campaign policy variables broadly, we need a good instrument for the policy or random assignment of policies.

Alan Gerber and Donald Green (2000), and Green, Gerber, and David Nickerson (2003) have used an experimental design to examine the effect of get-out-the-vote campaigns on turnout. They organized nonpartisan student and community organizations to canvass a randomly assigned group of registered voters in several cities to induce them to vote in local elections. The results of these experiments show that face-to-face canvassing significantly increased turnout: voting rates for persons contacted by the organizations were about seven percentage points higher than for persons not contacted by the groups. However, because the canvassers could not contact two-thirds of those assigned to the treatment groups, the effect of the mobilization campaign on aggregate turnout was more modest. In a related study, Melissa Michelson (2002) reports larger increases in voting and high rates of contacting the treatment group in a mobilization drive focused on Latino Democrats in California. Focusing on young voters, whose turnout falls short of that of other voters, Nickerson (2002) has found that get-out-the-vote drives raise the turnout of contacted youths as much as similar campaigns raise the turnout of contacted adults, but that youths are much harder to reach. The implication is that political parties and nonpartisan organizations can mobilize young persons (and speculatively, other low-turnout groups) to vote if they can locate and speak with them. Examining another mode of galvanizing voters, Wolfinger, Highton, and Mullin (2002b) have found that states that send sample ballots to registered voters—a relatively inexpensive way to provide information—had higher rates of voting than other states in the 2000 election, and that the effect was largely on less-educated persons. Their analysis, however, is not an experimental design; it is possible that some or all of the effect reflects other unmeasured differences among states. Absent before-and-after evidence on voting in states that changed policies, or an actual experiment, we cannot be sure that this relation is causal or as large as estimated in the cross-section comparison.

CPS and NES datasets show that unionization affects voter turnout in the United States. Union members have about a four-percentage-point higher probability of voting than non-members (Freeman 2003), presumably in part because of union efforts to mobilize their members (see also Leighley and Nagler 1992). This suggests that the decline of union density has contributed to the downward trend in density. Benjamin Radcliff and Patricia Davis (2000) report that higher levels of union density are associated with higher turnout across countries and among U.S. states. They link this to attitudes and party ideologies. Kim Hill and Jan Leighley (1992) find modest support for the proposition that the competitiveness of political races and the policies of the Democratic Party in a state affect lower-class voter turnout, but they do not have unionization in their regressions. Higher union density in a state may both induce voters toward liberal Democratic views and produce more competitive races.

That mobilization can increase turnout does not mean that the decline in turnout is due to a decline in mobilization. The NES reports a rise in political contacts in the 2000 election, in which turnout was low for a close election (Banducci and Karp 2001). Since much of the contact occurred through direct marketing rather than door-to-door canvassing and was targeted at likely voters, this evidence could be consistent with an explanation of falling turnout in terms of less face-to-face canvassing of voters. Still, it "questions the conclusion that the lack of party mobilization is to blame [for the fall in turnout]" (Banducci and Karp 2001, 24).

High Turnout the Puerto Rican Way

There is an important but little known anomaly to the pattern of low turnout in the United States. One part of the country votes at high rates. This is Puerto Rico. On the mainland United States, Puerto Ricans have a low rate of voting, consistent with their being a disadvantaged minority group. In 1996, 47 percent of persons who were born in Puerto Rico but resided in the United States reported to the CPS that they voted in the presidential election—a figure noticeably below the 64 percent of all Americans who reported voting in that election. Given self-reporting bias, perhaps 40 to 42 percent of Puerto Ricans in the United States actually voted in the presidential election.[6] But on the island, Puerto Ricans have a high rate of voting. Throughout the 1990s Puerto Rican turnout rates exceeded those for the United States and for most other democracies.

Official Puerto Rican voting data show turnout rates that averaged 84 percent in the three general elections held from 1992 to 2000 and rates that were equally high in earlier years (Álvarez-Rivera 2003). But these rates compare the numbers of persons voting with the numbers of persons registered rather than with the voting age population. To obtain valid comparison rates, I estimated the population of voting age in the 1990 and 2000 Censuses of Population for Puerto Rico and then adjusted the turnout rates to be on a comparable basis with the United States. Figure 18.2 records my adjusted voter turnout rates for the six commonwealth-wide elections held in Puerto Rico between 1992 and 2000. Because an average of 92 percent of persons of voting age were registered in 1990 and 2000, my adjustment still leaves Puerto Rico with an extremely high voting rate: 77 percent in general elections—some twenty-five points above rates in U.S. presidential elections over the same period and nearly double the voting rate for Puerto Ricans residing in the United States.[7] In addition, Puerto Rico has held various plebiscites and referenda on Sundays in non-general-election years. Figure 18.2 shows that turnout in these elections has also been high, though it falls short of the turnout in the general elections.

Why is voter turnout so much higher in Puerto Rico than in the United States? One reason is that Puerto Rico makes its general election day a holiday and treats the day as a special political event, with political parties mobilizing their supporters throughout the day. Since Puerto Ricans can register at the polling place, parties try to bring every single supporter to the polls, including those who may have let their registration lapse. Votes on referenda and plebiscites in the off-presidential and non-general-election years are held on Sundays, another nonworking day. In the 1990s the average turnout rate on Sundays in Puerto Rico was 64 percent—thirteen percentage points less than on Tuesdays. This difference could mean that making voting day a dedicated holiday rather than a normal weekend

FIGURE 18.2   *Change in the Percentages of Voter Turnout in Puerto Rico, 1992 to 2000*

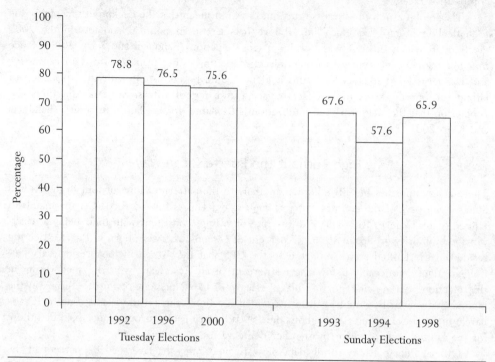

Source: Author's compilation.
Notes: These estimates are obtained by adjusting the reported turnout figures, based on registered voters, into turnouts based on voting age population by multiplying the figures by 92 percent, the average of the registration rates for 1990 and 2000.

day increases turnout. But it could also mean that Puerto Ricans are more involved in the gubernatorial races than in special plebiscites and referenda, even those that may affect the political status of the island.

In any case, turnout is much higher in Puerto Rico than in the United States. Given that differences in the cost of voting have modest impacts on turnout in the United States, I interpret the high turnout in Puerto Rico as a reflection of more than the ease of voting on a holiday or a weekend. The high turnout also reflects the intense mobilization of voters, which is itself easier to accomplish on weekends or holidays when party activists are available to get out the vote and when citizens may find it difficult to say that they are too busy to vote. The combination of mobilization and holiday voting offers the best explanation of the otherwise anomalously high turnout in Puerto Rico.

INEQUALITY AND CHANGES IN INEQUALITY IN TURNOUT

By inequality in turnout I mean differences in rates of turnout between groups of voters from different socioeconomic groups. Virtually every study finds that persons with higher income, higher occupational standing, greater age, and more years of education have higher turnout rates than persons from lower-status groups. The magnitude of the difference in voting by socioeconomic group, however, is more difficult to determine. This is because the survey data that link turnout to individual characteristics are subject to measurement error. Many persons report that they vote on the NES and CPS surveys when they do not. Overreporting of voting differs, moreover, by demographic characteristics. The NES validates survey reports of voting by checking whether the respondent's name is on a list of registered voters. Silver, Anderson, and Abramson (1986) find that the respondents most inclined to overreport voting are highly educated persons—those for whom the norm of voting is most salient. This biases upward the difference in voting by education and presumably has a similar impact on other measures of socioeconomic status. As the gap between NES turnout and official turnout has risen over time, analyses of the trend in inequality in voting based on NES-reported votes could be erroneous. Self-reported voting on the CPS November supplements differs less from official turnout figures, making the overreporting problem less severe. But self-reports of voting on the CPS have not been validated, so there is no simple way to estimate the bias in that dataset.

By changes in inequality in voting I mean differential changes in turnout among identified socioeconomic groups. Given that groups have markedly different rates of voting, the metric by which we measure these changes can be important in determining whether inequality has risen. In assessing trends in inequality of voting, I rely largely on percentage-point changes in turnout rates among groups rather than on percentage changes in those rates or on the level of logistic or probit parameters.[8] With groups having equal rates of turnout, equal percentage-point changes in turnout have no effect on the median voter on the relevant socioeconomic scale, whereas greater falls in turnout by one group will shift the distribution of voters, and thus the median, against that group. But with groups having different rates of turnout, even equal percentage-point changes in turnout can affect the position of the median voter. A ten-percentage-point drop in turnout for a group with a small turnout removes relatively more persons from that group from the electorate than a ten-percentage-point drop in turnout from a group with a high turnout. This shifts the electorate toward the high turnout group, which means toward the more advantaged given their higher turnout rate.[9]

Metric aside, the fact that higher socioeconomic groups have higher turnout than lower socioeconomic groups implies that *large* increases in turnout necessarily reduce inequality in turnout, while large decreases in turnout raise inequality. If 90 percent of the upper half of the population vote and 50 percent of the lower half of the population vote, giving an aggregate turnout of 70 percent, an increase in aggregate turnout of twenty points would have to come disproportionately from the lower half since the upper half cannot increase its turnout beyond 100 percent. A twenty-point increase in aggregate turnout would decrease the gap in turnout for the two groups from forty percentage points to a minimum of twenty percentage points.[10] That large increases in turnout asymptotically reduce inequality in voting does not, however, mean that modest increases in turnout will do the same. With turnout on the order of 50 to 60 percent, modest changes in turnout, say five to ten points, could either have no effect on inequality in voting or increase it.

There is considerable disagreement about whether inequality in voting by socioeconomic group has changed over time. Analysts using different datasets, covering different time periods, and using different metrics or methodologies have reached different conclusions. Howard Reiter (1979) and Steven Rosenstone and John Hansen (1993) find a trend in inequality in NES data. They use income and education to measure socioeconomic status. Walter Burnham (1987) finds a similar trend in CPS data using occupations to measure status. But Teixeira (1992) argues that any trend in the CPS is modest. Leighley and Nagler (1992, 734) make the strongest case that inequality of voting by socioeconomic group has not increased. Analyzing CPS and NES data for elections from the 1960s through the 1980s, they conclude that "class bias has not increased since 1964."

My reading of the evidence is that inequality in voting has increased. Since Leighley and Nagler's (1992) study is the most substantive on the other side of this debate, I examine carefully the CPS and NES data that led them to their conclusion. In addition, I assess the link between various measures of socioeconomic status and voting in the CPS in the 1990s. I find that Leighley and Nagler's evidence supports the claim that inequality in voting has increased, contrary to their interpretation of it. The drop in turnout has occurred largely among less-educated, lower-income, less-skilled, and younger persons, increasing the inequality in voting among those groups.

For starters, table 18.4 records the rate of voting by persons in different age and education groups, as tabulated by the Census Bureau. The age data show a huge rise in inequality of voting by age from 1972 (when eighteen- to twenty-year-olds could first vote) to 2000. Turnout for eighteen- to twenty-year-olds and twenty-one- to twenty-four-year-olds fell from 48 percent and 51 percent, respectively, in 1972 to just 28 percent and 24 percent in 2000. The third group with a large drop in turnout were twenty-five- to thirty-four-year-olds, whose turnout dropped by sixteen percentage points. By contrast, the turnout rate of persons age sixty-five and older rose in this period, and the turnout rate of forty-five- to sixty-four-year-olds fell relatively modestly. Since older persons had higher voting rates in the beginning, the table shows that inequality in turnout grew massively along this dimension.

Table 18.4 also records turnout rates by education from 1964 to 2000. Turnout rates fell for all education groups, but the percentage-point drops were larger for the less-educated groups: a thirty-two-point drop for persons with less than nine years of schooling versus a sixteen-point drop for persons with four years of college or more. But this is a less meaningful comparison than might at first appear to be the case. The problem is that the proportion of people in specific education groups has changed as the population has become more educated. In 1964 approximately 30 percent of persons of voting age had less than nine years of schooling, and just 8 percent had four or more years of college. In 2000 just 12 percent of persons of voting age had less than nine years of schooling, and 23 percent had four or more years of college (for estimates of the distribution of the population by education, see U.S. Department of Commerce 1964, 2000). The greater decline in turnout among persons with less than nine years of schooling could reflect the fact that in 2000 that education group fell lower in the distribution of the population by education. Perhaps the bottom 30 percent of the voting age population had a much smaller fall in turnout. Similarly, perhaps the changing proportion of the population in the college graduate group underlies some of the change in turnout there.

To see whether voting by persons in similar positions in the percentile distribution of education also reveals rising inequality, I estimated the voting rate for the bottom 30 percent of the voting age population in 2000 by taking a weighted average of the rates for persons with less than nine years of education, those with nine to twelve years of education, and high school graduates. The weights reflected the contribution of each group to the bottom 30 percent, and these were multiplied by each group's reported turnout rate. By my calculation, the lower 30 percent of persons by years of schooling in 2000 had an average turnout of 39.2 percent. Thus, I estimate that at the bottom of the education distribution, turnout fell from 59.0 percent to 39.2 percent—a 19.8-percentage-point drop. This is markedly lower than the 32.2-percentage-point drop among persons with less than nine years of schooling shown in table 18.4, but it is still huge. I did a comparable calculation for

TABLE 18.4   *Change in Voter Turnout, by Age, 1972 to 2000, and by Education, 1964 to 2000*

Age	1972	2000	Change
18 to 20-year-olds	48.3%	28.4%	−19.9%
21 to 24-year-olds	50.7	24.2	−26.5
25 to 34-year-olds	59.7	43.7	−16.0
35 to 44-year-olds	66.3	56.0	−10.3
45 to 64-year-olds	70.8	64.1	−6.7
65 years and older	63.5	67.6	4.1
Education	1964	2000	Change
Less than nine years	59.0	26.8	−32.2
Nine to eleven years	65.4	33.6	−21.8
High school graduate	76.1	49.4	−26.7
One to three years of college	82.3	60.3	−22.0
College degree or higher	87.5	72.0	−15.5

Source: U.S. Department of Commerce (1989, table 432; 2002, table 401); see also historical time-series table on voting and registration at: http://www.census.gov/population/socdemo/voting/tabA-2.pdf (*Current Population Report*, November 2000 and earlier reports).

persons with college degrees. Since college graduates made up 23 percent of the voting age population in 2000, I estimated the turnout rate of persons in the upper 23 percent of the education distribution in 1964. By my calculation, 82.5 percent of persons in the upper 23 percent of the education distribution voted in 1964. The decline in voting of persons at the top of the education distribution is thus 10.5 percentage points (from 72.0 to 82.5 percent), which is smaller than the 15.5-percentage-point drop shown in table 18.4. Thus, looking at the voting rate of persons at similar points in the distribution by years of schooling, I estimate that there was a 10.5-percentage-point drop for highly educated persons compared with a 19.8-percentage-point drop for less-educated persons. The rise in inequality among persons at comparable positions in the education distribution was thus huge, though smaller than the rise in inequality among persons with a fixed number of years of schooling.

I turn next to the Leighley and Nagler (1992) analysis of the CPS turnout statistics. Table 18.5, which is taken from their main table, measures socioeconomic status by quintile of income, by three occupation groupings, and by level of education from 1964 to 1988. The top row shows that turnout was stable between 1964 and 1968, fell noticeably from 1968 to 1972 (a drop of 5.4 points), fell moderately from 1972 to 1976 (2.3 points), was stable from 1976 to 1984, and then dropped from 1984 to 1988. Overall, turnout trended downward over the period by 10.4 points. Each measure of socioeconomic status shows greater falls in turnout for lower-status than for higher-status groups. The smallest increase in inequality occurs among income classes, where turnout for the highest-income group dropped by 8.3 percentage points compared with an 11.0-percentage-point drop for the lowest income group—a 2.7-percentage-point difference that they note is "only a slight increase in socioeconomic class bias" (728). The occupation and education measures show much greater increases in inequality, consistent with the other studies cited earlier. The gap between white-collar workers, who have the highest voting rate, and blue-collar workers,

TABLE 18.5   *Voter Turnout by Demographic Characteristics: Current Population Surveys, 1964 to 1988*

Demographic Group	1964	1968	1972	1976	1980	1984	1988
Total	70.5%	70.3%	64.9%	62.6%	62.3%	63.1%	60.1%
Income							
First quintile (low)	53.7	57.5	50.7	47.4	47.7	47.8	42.7
Second quintile	63.1	67	55.9	55.1	54.2	57.5	52.2
Third quintile	72.8	74.2	63.3	62.4	60.5	63.5	58.9
Fourth quintile	78.7	79.7	71.6	69.9	68.9	70.3	67.5
Fifth quintile (high)	85.2	85.4	80.7	78.4	76.1	77.6	76.9
Gini coefficient	−0.09	−0.08	0.094	0.098	0.1	0.099	0.111
Occupation							
Service worker	65.9	62.7	58.6	52.8	51.3	52.9	47.2
Blue-collar	65.6	62.3	54.2	49.8	48	49.4	44.5
White-collar	82.1	79.8	76.4	72.1	70.9	70.8	68.5
Education							
No high school	59.4	56.4	48.9	46.8	44.5	45.1	38.4
Some high school	65.9	63.1	53.7	50.1	48.4	47	43.3
High school graduate	76.5	74.2	66.1	62	61	61	56.6
Some college	82.6	80.2	76	70.1	69.5	69.9	66.4
College graduate	—[a]	84.7	83.6	81.1	80.1	79.3	75.8
Post-college	88.2[a]	86.9	87.4	85.2	84.9	84.4	83.9

Source: Leighley and Nagler (1992, table 1 and endnote 10). Reprinted with the permission of Cambridge University Press.
Note: Table entries are the reported turnout rates for each demographic category.
[a]Available only in combined form.

who have the lowest rate, trends upward from 16.5 percentage points in 1964 to 24.0 percentage points in 1988. The differential between college graduates and high school graduates rises from 10.5 points in 1968 to 19.2 points in 1988. All of this evidence shows that there has been a change in class bias in the electorate since 1964.

Leighley and Nagler (1992) stress the pattern of voting among persons differentiated by income quintile. If the CPS data gave sufficiently accurate income information to sort the population into income quintiles correctly, this would indeed be a highly desirable way to measure inequality in turnout. Unfortunately, however, as table 18.6 shows, the proportion of persons in the CPS income quintiles has varied substantially over the years, rather than being 20 percent in each year. It is difficult to know what to make of changes in turnout by quintiles when in 1964 28 percent of the sample was in the third income quintile and in 1988 just 19 percent was in that quintile. The reason for the varying proportion of persons in the "quintiles" is that the CPS does not ask for actual income but instead categorizes families into a few income classes. Leighley and Nagler also calculate a Gini coefficient for inequality in voters by income. Their Ginis show an increase in voting inequality from 1972 to 1988. In a footnote they report Gini coefficients for 1964 and 1968 but exclude them from their main analysis because they are based on fewer categories. But this excludes the 1968 to 1972 period, when turnout fell the most. Adding their computed Gini coefficients to table 18.5 shows a large trend increase in the Gini coefficient for voters from 0.0856 to 0.1112.[11] Given the problem of varying shares of eligible voters in income quintiles, these

TABLE 18.6   *Eligible Voters in Each Income Quintile: Current Population Surveys, 1964 to 1988*

Income	1964	1968	1972	1976	1980	1984	1988
First quintile (low)	19%	27%	18%	17%	20%	22%	17%
Second quintile	20	24	22	23	15	21	22
Third quintile	28	19	15	24	25	16	19
Fourth quintile	16	20	25	15	14	24	25
Fifth quintile (high)	18	10	19	21	26	17	18

Source: Leighley and Nagler (1992, table A-1). Reprinted with the permission of Cambridge University Press.

data are weak indicators of actual changes in turnout by income, but they show rising class bias in voting.

The NES does not suffer from the problem of varying sizes of quintiles, and the voting data for the NES show a strong rise in inequality by income class. Leighley and Nagler (1992) point out that this could be due to trends in misreporting of voting by income and occupation.[12] Since the NES contains estimates of validated votes, I use Leighley and Nagler's data to see whether this problem invalidates the finding that inequality in voting increased. Their multivariate probit analysis of voting in the NES uses validated voting data (Leighley and Nagler 1992, table 5). They estimate how education and income quintile (and other factors) affected turnout in the elections of 1964, 1976, 1980, 1984, and 1988. They obtain coefficients on education and income that vary quite a bit among the years but show no strong trend; they conclude that there is no increase in inequality. But similar coefficients in a nonlinear form of this type do not imply that a variable has the same *percentage-point* effect for groups in years when voting turnout changes. The impact of a change in a variable is largest when the voting rate is around 50 percent and smaller when the voting rate is very high or very low. To illustrate this point, consider the following logistic model (written in log odds ratio form):

$$\ln P/(1 - P) = a + b\,X, \tag{18.4}$$

where P is the probability of voting and X is some measure of socioeconomic status. Differentiating to find the impact of a change in socioeconomic status, we see that

$$dP/dX = b(P)(1 - P), \text{ or, in percentage terms, } (dP/dX)/P = b\,(1 - P). \tag{18.5}$$

TABLE 18.7   *Voter Turnout and Changes in Turnout in NES-Validated Data, by Income Quintile, 1964 to 1988*

Income Quintile	1964	1976	1980	1984	1988	Turnout Change 1964 to 1988
First quintile (low)	53.7%	47%	45.8%	45.8%	39.7%	− 14%
Second quintile	56.4	60.6	53.8	61.8	49.4	− 7
Third quintile	62	63.4	57.7	63.2	58.6	− 3.4
Fourth quintile	76.4	66.7	68.4	68.4	68.1	− 8.3
Fifth quintile (high)	78.5	79.8	67.6	80	73.7	− 4.8

Source: Darmofal (1999).

TABLE 18.8   *Turnout and Changes in Turnout in NES-Validated Data, by Education Level, 1964 to 1988*

Years of Education	1964	1976	1980	1984	1988	Turnout Change 1964 to 1988
Less than twelve years	57.4%	52.2%	45%	49.6%	43%	−14.4%
Twelve years	68.1	63.8	54.8	58.6	52.7	−15.4
More than twelve years	76.9	73.9	70.1	74.2	72.1	−4.8

Source: Darmofal (1999).

The impact of X on the inequality of voting necessarily varies with turnout. Indeed, stable coefficients in a nonlinear form of this type imply increasing inequality as turnout falls. Thus, I interpret their stable coefficients in a period when turnout was falling as evidence for greater inequality in voting among the relevant groups rather than as evidence for no change in inequality.[13]

Consistent with my reading of the data, David Darmofal (1999)'s analysis of the NES-validated voting sample, summarized in tables 18.7 and 18.8, shows that inequality in voting increased in that sample, as it does in the total sample from 1964 to 1988. Table 18.7 shows a 14.0-point drop in turnout among low-income groups compared with a 4.8-point drop in turnout among high-income groups. The decline in turnout is not monotonic across the income groups, but the pattern moves the median voter up the income distribution. Table 18.8 shows a similar pattern of greater drops in validated turnout among persons with twelve years of schooling and those with twelve or less years of schooling than for those with some college or more.

Since the decline in turnout has varied over time, I have also contrasted changes in the inequality of voting in periods when turnout fell substantially to the inequality of voting in periods when turnout was roughly stable. If turnout affects inequality in voting, then inequality in turnout should rise most when turnout falls. Table 18.9 tabulates data from Leighley and Nagler (1992), who organize the periods by the change in turnout, shows such a relation between changes in turnout and changes in their measures of inequality.

Finally, using data from the NES, 1948 to 1998, Daniel Devroye (2001) has found that in states with low registration levels, income has a greater positive effect on voting than in states with high registration levels. This implies that lower registration and (presumably) turnout are associated with greater income bias in the electorate. He finds similar results in

TABLE 18.9   *Change in Voter Turnout, 1968 to 1988*

Period	Change in Turnout	Change in Gini
1968 to 1972	−5.4	.0164
1984 to 1988	−3.0	.0127
1972 to 1976	−2.3	.0043
1976 to 1980	−0.3	.0013
1964 to 1968	−0.2	−.0086

Source: Calculated from Leighly and Nagler (1992, table 1 and endnote 10).

an analysis of the link between voting and income and voter registration and turnout in CPS files for 1994 to 1998.

In sum, the debate over the trend in inequality in voting and its relation to aggregate turnout and other factors has illuminated the complexities in making inferences from the relevant data, but the evidence supports the proposition that inequality among voters has risen.

CONCLUSION

A rational man decides to vote just as he makes all other decisions: if the return outweighs the cost, he votes: if not, he abstains.

—Anthony Downs, *An Economic Theory of Government* (1957, 260)

Economists are surprised that anyone votes at all. Since no individual vote changes any election, why should a rational man vote? The cost of voting may be slight for many people—a few minutes spent at the polling place early in the morning, after work, or during the day, or even less time in states with absentee ballots, voting by mail, or voting at polling places before election day. But if there are no benefits, why bother? That many people vote implies that people do see benefits, perhaps nonpecuniary benefits, but benefits nonetheless.[14] If we accept this, economic analysis has a more sensible message than "What, me vote?" Per the Downs quotation, it suggests that the decision to vote depends on weighing voting's potential benefits, whatever their form, and costs. In the context of the median voter model, moreover, an individual's vote could shift the median by enough to justify the small time cost of voting. In a world where politicians respond to the median voter, the question isn't, "Will my vote determine the winner?" but, "Will my vote move the winner enough closer to my position to justify my casting the ballot?"

Since the administrative cost of voting has declined in the United States, the downward trend in turnout would seem to suggest that citizens see fewer benefits from voting. They may see fewer benefits because the parties have moved sufficiently close to the median voter to leave little space between them, or because events have made campaign promises irrelevant, or because governments have only a limited range of variation in policies. If this were the case, and if voters were right, low and unequal turnout would have little impact on policies.

But increases in the inequality of voting can shift the socioeconomic position of the median voter. If the voting distribution is skewed in favor of upper-income persons, the median voter will be higher in the distribution, with policy more favorable to them. I estimate that the increased inequality in U.S. voting from 1964 to 2000 raised the family income of the median voter from the fifty-third percentile of the income distribution in 1964 to the fifty-ninth percentile of the income distribution in 2000. Some analysts argue that the lower voting rate and higher income status of the median voter in the United States than in EU countries explains why the United States has a smaller welfare state and does less income redistribution than the EU countries. Consistent with this, Hill and Leighley (1992) show that U.S. states with greater inequality in voting spend less on welfare than states with less inequality in voting.[15] On the other hand, several studies suggest that there is little attitudinal difference between voters and nonvoters (Wolfinger and Rosenstone 1980; Verba, Schlozman, and Brady 1996), so that increases in turnout would not have great effects on policy outcomes. While there is evidence in Europe that high turnouts improve the electoral chances of left parties (Pacek and Radcliff 1985), the impact of turnout on party performance in the United States is less clear, presumably because there are so many nonvoters that higher turnout could come from almost any group. At best, higher turnout seems to favor marginally the Democrats.[16] Over the long run, however, the level of turnout is unlikely to affect party performance, since both parties will adjust their policies toward the new median.

To sum up, my review of what we know about voter turnout shows that the bulk of the evidence supports the claims that turnout has fallen in the United States—albeit by a magnitude that varies depending on how one adjusts for the rising number of ineligible voters—and that inequality in voting among social groups has increased. More likely than not, these changes have had some impact on government decisions and activities, though research has not conclusively demonstrated the magnitude and nature of that impact.

APPENDIX

TABLE 18A.1   *Numbers of Persons in Groups Associated with National Turnout Rates, 1948 to 2000*

Year	Vote for Highest Office (Thousands)	Voting Age Population (VAP) (Thousands)	Turnout Rate (VAP)	Noncitizens (Hundreds)	Ineligible Felons (Thousands)	Overseas Voting-Eligible Population (VEP) (Thousands)	Turnout Rate (VEP)
1948	48,833	95,573	51.1%	2,198	348	440	52.2%
1950	41,984	98,134	42.8	1,880	372	391	43.6
1952	61,552	99,929	61.6	1,899	379	1,131	62.3
1954	43,854	102,075	43.0	1,939	411	987	43.5
1956	62,027	104,515	59.3	1,986	428	981	60.2
1958	47,203	106,447	44.3	2,129	464	951	45.0
1960	68,838	109,672	62.8	2,193	481	912	63.8
1962	53,141	112,952	47.0	2,259	491	1,113	47.7
1964	70,645	114,090	61.9	2,282	478	1,212	62.8
1966	56,188	116,638	48.2	2,363	448	1,621	48.7
1968	73,213	120,285	60.9	2,766	421	1,856	61.5
1970	58,014	124,498	46.6	3,148	443	1,765	47.3
1972	77,719	140,777	55.2	3,640	443	1,581	56.2
1974	55,944	146,338	38.2	4,148	496	1,510	39.1
1976	81,556	152,308	53.5	4,558	588	1,562	54.8
1978	58,918	155,609	37.9	5,780	629	1,753	39.0
1980	86,515	163,945	52.8	6,827	803	1,803	54.7
1982	67,616	166,724	40.6	10,554	932	1,982	43.0
1984	92,653	173,995	53.3	13,252	1,153	2,361	57.2
1986	64,991	177,922	36.5	12,223	1,308	2,216	39.0
1988	91,595	181,956	50.3	13,942	1,533	2,527	54.2
1990	67,859	185,888	36.5	16,297	1,845	2,659	39.8
1992	104,405	189,687	55.0	17,826	2,117	2,418	60.6
1994	75,106	193,163	38.9	13,205	2,365	2,229	41.8
1996	96,263	196,928	48.9	13,948	2,545	2,499	52.6
1998	72,537	200,929	36.1	15,070	2,822	2,937	39.0
2000	105,326	205,813	51.2	16,500	2,851	3,008	55.6

Source: McDonald and Popkin (2001, table 1). Reprinted with the permission of Cambridge University Press.

I have benefited from discussion with Dan Devroye and from comments by Christopher Jencks, Lawrence Mead, and Larry Bartel.

NOTES

1. The U.S. and Canadian comparisons are for 1945 to 1997, as reported by the International Institute for Democracy and Electoral Assistance (IDEA 1997).

2. The NES website is: www.umich.edu/~nes; the CPS data are available at: www.census.gov/population/ www/socdemo/voting.html. In addition to these sources, there are diverse irregular surveys—exit polls, focus group interviews, and general surveys such as the National Opinion Research Center's (NORC) General Social Survey—that provide information on who votes.

3. The median voter model is the simplest model of democratic decisionmaking. According to this model, politicians who seek election pay close attention to the preferences of the person in the middle of the distribution of preferences—the median. With voters arrayed by their attitudes toward government poli-cies on a right-to-left scale, candidates from the right and candidates from the left will move to the middle to gain votes. To win, they need 50 percent or more of the votes and thus must appeal to the median voter (Riker 1962).

4. In addition, some potential citizen voters live abroad. But their number is dwarfed by the number of noncitizens and persons incarcerated or deprived of the franchise because of past incarceration. McDonald and Popkin (2001) deal with this group as well.

5. The range of estimates for 1996 across several studies is about three percentage points. Burden (2000) notes that taking account of this bias explains only a small proportion of the difference in turnout in the NES and in official counts.

6. This calculation multiplies the ratio of the turnout rate in administrative data to the turnout ratio on the CPS for all voters by the turnout rate on the CPS for Puerto Ricans.

7. In 2000 there were approximately 2.73 million persons of voting age in Puerto Rico (see "IDB Summary Demographic Data for Puerto Rico," available at www.census.gov/cgi-bin/ipc/idsum?cty=RQ). In 1990 Puerto Rico had approximately 2.33 million persons of voting age (see welcome.to puertorico.org/censo, "Summary Population and Housing Characteristics," table 1: welcome.topuertorico.org/censo/age/shtml). In 2000, 2.447 million persons were registered to vote, giving a registration rate of 89.6 percent; Puerto Rico had no elections in 1990, so I average the numbers registered in 1988 and 2002 to obtain an estimate of 2.19 million registrants for comparison with the 1990 population—a rate of 93.9 percent. Averaging the 1990 and 2000 estimates, I come up with a 91.8 percent registration rate for Puerto Rico.

8. A ten-percentage-point drop in voting by a group with a low rate of voting is a larger percentage drop than a ten-percentage-point drop in voting by a group with a high rate of voting. In a model of voting using individual data that makes the probability of voting depend on independent variables with a logistic or probit form, changes in a variable will have a bigger impact on the proportion voting depending on groups with a voting rate around 50 percent than on groups with a voting rate much lower or higher than that.

9. Say the population has ten wealthy people and one hundred poor people. Initially all the wealthy vote (ten voters) and half of the poor vote (fifty voters). Then one-sixth of the electorate are wealthy people. A fifty-percentage-point reduction in the turnout of both groups leaves five wealthy voters and no poor voters. The example is extreme but the principle holds.

10. Assume that 100 percent of the upper group voted. Then to get the twenty-point increase, the lower group would have to vote at a rate of 80 percent—a huge thirty-point rise for them.

11. The problem of limited and inaccurate quintile groupings in the NES suggests the value of estimating incomes from detailed occupation codes for working people in the November CPS files and using this to compute inequality measures with thicker income measures. I have not yet done this.

12. Leighley and Nagler's (1992) table 3 shows a large drop in misreporting for both high and low occupation and income groups.

13. I read Todd Shields and Robert Goidel's (1997) "cross-validation" of Leighley and Nagler (1992) as suffering from similar problems. Their estimated logit coefficients on education show strongly rising inequality in voting in both their NES and CPS calculations. Since Shields and Goidel do not record the proportion of people in their income quintiles, I do not know whether that is a problem with their income calculations.

14. There are many other areas in which people participate despite only a minuscule chance of making a gain, such as lotteries. And people root for sports teams, presumably gaining greater pleasure from their team's victory than if they simply watched the sport.

15. Hill, Leighley, and Hinton-Anderson's (1995) extension of this analysis shows similar results; see also Ringquist et al. (1997).

16. Nagel and McNulty (1986) argue that any relation that existed historically has disappeared.

REFERENCES

Álvarez-Rivera, Manuel. 2003. "Elections in Puerto Rico." Official election statistics available at: http://eleccionespuertorico.org/home_en.html.

Banducci, Susan, and Jeffrey Karp, 2001. "Mobilizing American Voters: A Reassessment." Paper presented to the annual meeting of the American Political Science Association. San Francisco (August 30–September 2).

————. 2002. "Going Postal: How All-Mail Elections Influence Turnout." *Political Behavior* 22(3): 223–39.

Berinsky, Adam, Nancy Burns, and Michael Traugott. 2001. "Who Votes by Mail? A Dynamic Model of the Individual-Level Consequences of Vote-by-Mail Systems." *Public Opinion Quarterly* 65: 178–87.

Burden, Barry. 2000. "Voter Turnout and the National Election Studies." *Political Analysis* 8(4): 389–98.

Burnham, Walter. 1987. "The Turnout Problem." In *Elections American Style,* edited by James A. Reichley. Washington, D.C.: Brookings Institution.

Caltech-MIT Voting Technology Project. 2001. "Voting—What Is, What Could Be." Report of the Caltech-MIT Voting Technology Project (July). Available at: www.vote.caltech.edu/Reports.

Calvert, Jerry W., and Jack Gilchrist. 1993. "Suppose They Held an Election and Almost Everybody Came?" *Political Science and Politics* 26(4, December): 695–700.

Casper, Lynne, and Loretta Bass. 1998. "Voting and Registration in the Election of November 1996." *Current Population Reports,* series P20, no. 504 (July). Washington: U.S. Government Printing House for U.S. Census Bureau.

Crocker, Royce. 1990. "Voter Registration and Turnout in States with Mail and Motor Voter Registration Systems." Washington: Library of Congress, Congressional Research Service Report (February 23, 1990).

Darmofal, David. 1999. "Socioeconomic Bias in Turnout Decline: Do the Voters Remain the Same?" Paper presented at the American Political Science Association Meetings. Atlanta, Ga. (September 1999).

————. 2003 submission. "Socioeconomic Bias, Turnout Decline, and the Puzzle of Participation." *American Journal of Political Science.*

Day, Jennifer, and Avalaura Gaither. 2000. "Voting and Registration in the Election of November 1998." *Current Population Reports,* series P20, no. 523RV (August). Washington: U.S. Government Printing House for U.S. Census Bureau.

Devroye, Daniel. 2001. "Does Low Registration Increase Class Bias in Voting? Evidence from the Fifty States." Unpublished paper. Harvard University, Cambridge, Mass. (April).

Downs, Anthony. 1957. *An Economic Theory of Government.* New York: Harper & Row.

Freeman, Richard. 2003. "What Do Unions Do to Voting?" NBER working paper #9992. Cambridge, Mass.: NBER.

Gerber, Alan, and Donald Green. 2000. "The Effects of Canvassing, Telephone Calls, and Direct Mail on Voter Turnout: a Field Experiment." *American Political Science Review* 94: 653–63.

Green, Donald, Alan Gerber, and David Nickerson. 2002. "Getting Out the Youth Vote in Local Elections: Results from Six Door-to-Door Canvassing Experiments." New Haven: Yale University, May 18, 2003.

————. 2003. "Getting Out the Vote in Local Elections: Results from Six Door-to-Door Canvassing Experiments." *Journal of Politics* 65(4, November): 1–29.

Hamilton, Randy. 1988. "American All-Mail Balloting: A Decade's Experience." *Public Administration Review* 48(5, September–October): 860–66.

Highton, Benjamin, and Raymond Wolfinger. 1995. "Anticipating the Effects of the National Voter Registration Act of 1993." Paper presented to the annual meeting of the American Political Science Association. Chicago (August 31–September 3).

Hill, Kim, and Jan Leighley. 1992. "The Policy Consequences of Class Bias in State Electorates." *American Journal of Political Science* 36(2, May): 351–65.

Hill, Kim, Jan Leighley, and Angela Hinton-Anderson. 1995. "Lower-Class Mobilization and Policy Linkage in the U.S. States." *American Journal of Political Science* 39(1, February): 75–86.

International Institute for Democracy and Electoral Assistance (IDEA). 1997. *Voter Turnout from 1945 to 1997: A Global Report.* Stockholm: IDEA.

Jamieson, Amis, Hyon B. Shin, and Jennifer Day. 2002. "Voting and Registration in the Election of November 2000." *Current Population Reports,* series P20, no. 542. Washington: U.S. Government Printing Office for U.S. Census Bureau.

Knack, Stephen. 1995. "Does Motor Voter Work? Evidence from State-Level Data." *Journal of Politics* 57(3, August): 796–811.

Leighley, Jan, and Jonathan Nagler. 1992. "Socioeconomic Class Bias in Turnout, 1964–1988: The Voters Remain the Same." *American Political Science Review* 86(3, September): 725–36.

Lijphart, Arend. 1997. "Unequal Participation: Democracy's Unresolved Dilemma." *American Political Science Review* 91(1): 1–14.

Luttberg, Norman. 1984. "Differential Voting Turnout Decline in the American States." *Social Science Quarterly* 65: 60–74.

McDonald, Michael. 2001. "An External Validity Check of the National Election Study's Turnout Rate." Unpublished manuscript, June 20, 2001, George Mason University.

———. 2003. "On the Overreport Bias of the National Election Study Turnout Rate." *Political Analysis* 11(2): 180–6.

McDonald, Michael P., and Samuel L. Popkin. 2001. "The Myth of the Vanishing Voter." *American Political Science Review* 95(4, December): 963–74. Also available at: http://elections.gmu.edu/APSR%20McDonald%20and_Popkin_2001.pdf.

McKee, Seth. 2002. "Was Turnout Significantly Higher in the Battleground States in the 2000 Presidential Election?" Paper presented to the annual meeting of the American Political Science Association. Boston (September 24–28).

Michelson, Melissa. 2002. "Turning out Latino Voters." Paper presented to the annual meeting of the American Political Science Association. Boston (September 24–28).

Mullin, Megan, and Thad Kousser. 2002. "Separating Selection and Treatment Effects in the Study of Absentee Voting." Paper presented to the annual meeting of the American Political Science Association. Boston (September 24–28).

Nagel, Jack Henry, and John McNulty. 1996. "Partisan Effects of Voter Turnout in Senatorial and Gubernatorial Elections." *American Political Science Review* 90(4, December): 780–93.

Nagler, Jonathan. 1991. "The Effect of Registration Laws and Education on U.S. Voter Turnout." *American Political Science Review* 85: 1393–1405.

Nickerson, David. 2002. "Hunting the Elusive Young Voter." Paper presented to the annual meeting of the American Political Science Association. Boston (September 24–28).

Oliver, J. Eric. 1996. "The Effects of Eligibility Restrictions and Party Activity on Absentee Voting and Overall Turnout." *American Journal of Political Science* 40(2, May): 498–513.

Pacek, Alexander, and Benjamin Radcliff. 1985. "Turnout and the Vote for Left-of Center Parties: A Cross-National Analysis." *British Journal of Political Science* 25(1, January): 137–43.

Piven, Francis, and Richard A. Cloward. 1988. *Why Americans Don't Vote.* New York: Pantheon Books.

Radcliff, Benjamin, and Patricia Davis. 2000. "Labor Organization and Electoral Participation in Industrial Democracies." *American Journal of Political Science* 44(1, January): 132–41.

Reiter, Howard. 1979. "Why Is Turnout Down?" *Public Opinion Quarterly* 43: 297–311.

Riker, William. 1962. *The Theory of Political Coalitions.* New Haven, Conn.: Yale University Press.

Ringquist, Evan, Kim Hill, Jan Leighley, and Angela Hinton-Anderson. 1997. "Lower-Class Mobilization and Policy Linkage in the U.S. States: A Correction." *American Journal of Political Science* 41(1, January): 339–44.

Rosenstone, Steven, and John Hansen. 1993. *Mobilization, Participation, and Democracy in America*. New York: Macmillan.

Shields, Todd, and Robert Goidel. 1997. "Participation Rates, Socioeconomic Class Biases, and Congressional Elections: A Cross-Validation." *American Journal of Political Science* 41(2, April): 683–91.

Silver, Brian, Barbara Anderson, and Paul Abramson. 1986. "Who Overreports Voting?" *American Political Science Review* 80(2, June): 613–24.

Squire, Peverill, Raymond Wolfinger, and David Glass. 1987. "Residential Mobility and Voter Turnout." *American Political Science Review* 81(1, March): 45–66.

Teixeira, Ruy A. 1992. *The Disappearing American Voter*. Washington, D.C.: Brookings Institution.

———. 1999. "Turnout Patterns and Trends and Parental Power." Calculations from National Election Studies survey data (May 24).

Traugott, Michael. 2000. "Why Electoral Reform Has Failed: If You Build It, Will They Come?" Paper presented to the Conference on Political Participation: Building a Research Agenda. Princeton University, Princeton, N.J. (October 12–14).

Traugott, Michael J., and Michael J. Hammer. 2001. "Oregon Vote-by-Mail Project: Report to the League of Conservation Voters Education Fund." Available at: www.voteenvironment.org/pdf/OR%20Vote-By-Mail%20Research.PDF.

U.S. Department of Commerce. U.S. Census Bureau. 1964. "Educational Attainment." *Current Population Reports*, series P20, no. 536 (March). Available at: www.census.gov/population/www/socdemo/educ-attn.html.

———. 1989. *Statistical Abstract of the United States 1989*. Washington: U.S. Government Printing Office.

———. 1998. "Voting and Registration in the Election of November 1996." *Current Population Reports*, series P20, no. 504. Washington: U.S. Government Printing Office (July).

———. 1999. *Statistical Abstract of the United States 1999*. Washington: U.S. Government Printing Office.

———. 2000. "Educational Attainment." *Current Population Reports*, series P20, no. 138 (March). Available at: www.census.gov/population/www/socdemo/educ-attn.html.

———. 2000. "Voting and Registration in the Election of November 1998." *Current Population Reports*, series P20, no. 523RV. Washington: U.S. Government Printing Office (August).

———. 2002. *Statistical Abstract of the United States 2002*. Washington: U.S. Government Printing Office.

———. 2002. "Voting and Registration in the Election of November 2000." *Current Population Reports*, series P20, no. 542. Available at: http://www.census.gov/population/www/socdemo/voting/p20-542.html.

U.S. Department of Justice. Civil Rights Division. 2000. "The National Voter Registration Act (NVRA)." Available at: www.usdoj.gov/crt/voting/nvra/activ__nvra.htm (last revised February 11, 2000).

Verba, Sidney, Kay Schlozman, and Henry Brady. 1996. *Voice and Equality: Civic Voluntarism in American Politics*. Cambridge, Mass.: Harvard University Press.

Wattenberg, Marvin. 2002. *Where Have All the Voters Gone?* Cambridge, Mass.: Harvard University Press.

Wolfinger, Raymond, Benjamin Highton, and Megan Mullin. 2002a. "Between Registering and Voting: How State Laws Affect the Turnout of Young Registrants." Paper presented to the annual meeting of the American Political Science Association. Boston (September 24–28).

Wolfinger, Raymond, Benjamin Highton, and Megan Mullin. 2002b. "State Laws and the Turnout of the Registered." Paper presented to the annual meeting of the Midwest Political Science Association. Chicago (April 2002).

Wolfinger, Raymond, and Jonathan Hoffman. 2001. "Registering and Voting with Motor Voter." *Political Science and Politics*, PS Online, 35(1, March).

Wolfinger, Raymond, and Steven Rosenstone. 1980. *Who Votes?* New Haven, Conn.: Yale University Press.

Chapter 19

Civic Transformation and Inequality in the Contemporary United States

Theda Skocpol

Has civic life in the United States become more or less equal over the past half-century? Even to pose this question in an intelligent way requires us to explore the interrelations of two sets of momentous transformations. We must consider the interactions between shifting inequalities in American society and a sharply transformed universe of voluntary organizations and participation.

In broad terms, America has become both more and less equal in recent decades. Following the civil rights revolution of the 1950s and 1960s, racial segregation and exclusion were no longer legal or socially acceptable, so whites and African Americans could thenceforth participate together in schools and colleges, the job market, and all manner of civic institutions. Gender barriers have also been breached since the 1960s, with women now able to pursue much the same range of economic and civic opportunities as men. But as U.S. society has become more integrated along lines of gender and race, it has simultaneously experienced growing gaps of income and wealth. Economic gaps have grown not just between the poor and nonpoor, but also between privileged professionals, managers, and business owners, on the one hand, and the middle strata of ordinary white-collar employees and better-off blue-collar workers, on the other. Indeed, the very richest 1 percent of Americans have pulled away even from the rest of the privileged. The rich and the super-rich have gotten much more so, especially since the 1970s.

As this contradictory mix of new social inclusions combined with heightened economic disparities took shape, U.S. civic life also changed in seemingly contradictory ways. From nineteenth-century European visitors (Tocqueville 1835–1840/1969; Bryce 1895) to mid-twentieth-century academics (Schlesinger 1944; Almond and Verba 1963, ch. 11), leading observers have celebrated American civic voluntarism, touting the United States as a nation of organizers and joiners. The established wisdom implies that American civic organizers form membership associations that their fellow citizens join. This was never the whole story, for there have always been voluntary associations and institutions without any individual members, or with only a small number of members. But since the 1960s, civic organizing and joining have diverged more sharply than ever before in U.S. history. To characterize recent transformations with stark simplicity, *Americans are organizing more, but joining less.*

An extraordinary burst of voluntary organizing transformed late-twentieth-century civic America. Considering only nationally visible organizations, the *Encyclopedia of Associations* (1959–1999) listed just under six thousand groups in 1959; this total rose to just over ten thousand groups by 1970, to nearly fifteen thousand by 1980, and to nearly twenty-three thousand by 1990, with the totals thereafter remaining around the same level throughout the 1990s. Given that a certain proportion of groups die each year, these heightened totals could only have been attained because even more associations were launched between the 1960s and the 1990s than the net increase of nearly 300 percent shows. Even in relation to an expanding national population, the ranks of associations swelled markedly in the 1970s and 1980s (see Putnam 2000, 49–50, including fig. 7).

Yet even as associations proliferated, Americans in the aggregate became less likely to join associations or to take group responsibility. "The organizational eruption between the 1960s and the 1990s represented a proliferation of letterheads, not a boom of grassroots participation," concludes Robert D. Putnam (2000, 49), who focuses on "social capital" understood as local, face-to-face engagement. Reporting trends from Roper surveys (see table 19.1), Putnam documents declines between 1973–1974 and 1993–1994 in twelve kinds of political and community participation. Individualistic activities, like writing a letter to the newspaper, declined less sharply than civic activities involving group participation, such as serving as a club or association officer or serving on a local committee. Additional survey data analyzed by Putnam reveal that "in 1975–76, American men and women attended twelve club meetings on average each year" and "64 percent of all Americans . . . attended at least *one* . . . meeting in the previous year." But by 1999 the average was five meetings per year, and nearly two-thirds of Americans never attended a meeting (60–61). Putnam also cites time diary data suggesting that "the average American's investment in organizational life (apart from religious groups . . .) fell from 3.7 hours per month in 1965 to 2.9 in 1975 to 2.3 in 1985 and 1995" (62). All told, Putnam concludes that, while nominal affiliation with voluntary groups in general declined only modestly between the 1970s and the 1990s, "active involvement in local clubs and organizations of all sorts fell by more than half in the last several decades of the twentieth century. . . . By comparison with other countries, we may still seem a nation of joiners," he concludes, "but by comparison with our own recent past, we are not—at least if 'joining' means more than nominal affiliation" (61).

If contemporary Americans are organizing more while joining and participating less, how have shifts in racial, socioeconomic, and gender inequalities interacted with these civic transformations? What effects, if any, have shifts in civic organization and participation had on societal inequalities? Have new trends in organizing or joining ameliorated or exacerbated inequalities of class, race, and gender? In the broadest terms, have recent civic transformations made the United States more or less democratic?

These questions turn out to be difficult to answer with the social science research ready at hand, for two reasons. Much research on civic life is done by self-conscious "communitarians" (for example, Joyce and Schambra 1996; Sandel 1996), who pay much more attention to trends in local social connectedness than to matters of inequality or public engagement (for a wide-ranging review of the literature, see Beem 1999). Beyond this, however, it is difficult to synthesize research results, because scholarly investigations of contemporary American civic changes have proceeded along two separate tracks—behavioralist versus organizational—with surprisingly little effort to integrate and combine findings.

Behavioralists focus almost exclusively on mass individual behavior, usually as measured in national sample surveys of attitudes and self-reported characteristics and activities. The

TABLE 19.1   *Civic Activities in Roper Social and Political Trends Surveys, 1973 to 1994*

	Relative Change 1973–1974 to 1993–1994
Served as an officer of a club or organization	−42%
Worked for a political party	−42
Served on a committee for a local organization	−39
Attended a public meeting on town or school affairs	−35
Attended a political rally or speech	−34
Participated in at least one of these twelve activities	−25
Made a speech	−24
Wrote representative or senator	−23
Signed a petition	−22
Was a member of a "better government" group	−19
Held or ran for political office	−16
Wrote a letter to the paper	−14
Wrote an article for a magazine or newspaper	−10

Source: Putnam (2000, 45, table 1) © Simon & Schuster. Reprinted with permission.

best surveys of civic activities are usually onetime cross-sectional studies (for example, Verba, Schlozman, and Brady 1995), and only a few survey research efforts have repeatedly asked similar questions of comparable national samples of respondents. To the degree that behavioralists explore issues of inequality, they usually focus on establishing descriptive similarities or differences in individual-level civic affiliations and activities between men and women, between blacks and whites, and across social strata defined by income or (more commonly) educational attainment. A few survey researchers have also fashioned statistical models to consider the possible impact of macrotrends or community contexts on aggregate patterns of individual civic behavior.

Organizational analysts, meanwhile, have been much more interested in the emergence and growth or decline of voluntary associations and broad social movements. To the degree that studies become systematic, they usually rely on data about the timing of emergence of different types of associations, perhaps supplemented by data on membership trajectories or on trends affecting associational staffs or budgets. For the most part, these studies focus on one type of association or movement at a time; to the degree that issues of equality are considered, organizational analysts usually try to assess whether an emerging movement or type of association has a positive or negative impact on political balances of power in the society as a whole. Only rarely do these analysts attempt to describe and measure the changing shape of the entire universe of voluntary associations through time.

Not only do behavioralists and organizational analysts use different kinds of empirical data and focus on different aspects of civic life, but they make quite distinct, normatively tinged assumptions about equality and democracy. Behavioralists hold out a vision of democracy in which, ideally, every citizen would have equal capacities and opportunities to participate, should he or she be motivated to do so, while organizational analysts care much more about balances of power and collective clout. Behavioralists tend to think of democratic politics and government as being responsive to aggregate individual opinion and to the overall pattern of voting and other individual political acts. Social capital theorists (inspired by Putnam 1993, 2000) modify this picture a bit by looking at local-level collective activity, but they too generally think in terms of aggregate individual behavior. In contrast, because organization theorists envisage clashes of interest groups with different purposes and degrees of clout, they place much more stress on the rise and fall of various types of associations and on what the leaders of resourceful organizations do on behalf of members or constituents.

Because the answers we get depend a lot on how we frame the questions, it may not be surprising that different approaches have led to sometimes opposite conclusions about whether contemporary civic America is becoming more or less equal. On the whole, researchers focusing on recent organizational developments believe that the United States has become more egalitarian and democratic—because new "public interest" associations have proliferated at the relative expense of business associations—while behavioralists focusing on individual-level participation and local social capital are less optimistic—because Americans are joining groups and attending gatherings less often. But neither set of researchers has investigated issues of inequality as thoroughly as possible, even in its own terms. Moreover, neither approach has taken sufficient account of the findings and hypotheses offered by the other.

In this review of selected highlights from the recent literature, I examine behavioralist and organizational studies of contemporary American civic life, focusing on studies that describe and analyze *trends over time*. At various points along the way, and at the end, I suggest how we can extend and integrate previous research to arrive at clearer findings about the egalitarian and inegalitarian aspects of ongoing civic transformations. The civic implications of changing race and gender relations are occasionally mentioned in the pages to come, but the principal focus is on the interrelations of socioeconomic inequality and civic trends.

Because available longitudinal data severely limit what we can learn from national surveys, behavioralist studies alone, I argue, cannot shed sufficient light on contemporary civic trends. Studies of organizational changes have greater promise, but they need to be integrated with each other and with behavioralist findings. I can only start that process here, but as I do, we will see that recent changes in the U.S. associational universe have many more inegalitarian consequences for American democracy than most organizational scholars have noticed or acknowledged. Proliferating professionally managed associations offer fewer opportunities for broad citizen participation than traditional chapter-based federations once did. Contemporary associations are less likely to bring citizens together across class lines. And contemporary associations represent narrower, more specialized values and may over-represent the interests and values of the privileged in public policymaking.

BEHAVIORIALIST FINDINGS ON CIVIC TRENDS

As suggested earlier, behavioralist investigations of long-term trends are rare, because only a small number of questions about associational memberships and participation have been repeatedly posed to comparable national samples of respondents. National surveys of associational memberships stretch, at best, back to isolated dates in the 1950s (see, for example, Hausknecht 1962). Early community studies by sociologists were extraordinarily rich and insightful, especially on issues of social stratification (Babchuk and Booth 1969; Bushee 1945; Minnis 1953; Scott 1957; Tompkins 1955; see also the many early articles and books reviewed in Smith and Freedman 1972), but the early studies tend not to be integrated into today's discussions because they are not nationally representative.

Despite sparse data for tracing and analyzing secular trends, the currently hot debate over what has happened to U.S. "social capital" since the middle of the twentieth century has spurred Putnam and others to squeeze insights out of social surveys with repeated questions about associational affiliations and participation. Available survey archives include, most prominently, the Roper Social and Political Trends surveys of 1973 to 1994, which included questions about serving as associational officers or committee members (see table 19.1), and the General Social Surveys (GSS) of 1974 to 1994, which included questions about membership and participation in sixteen kinds of voluntary associations (fraternal groups; service clubs; veterans' groups; political clubs; labor unions; sports groups; youth groups; school service groups; hobby or garden clubs; school fraternities or sororities; nationality groups; farm organizations; literary, art, discussion, or study groups; professional or academic societies; church-affiliated groups; and "any other groups"). These archives have been used by many investigators. In addition, Putnam (2000) introduced the DDB Needham Lifestyle Surveys of 1975 to 1999 as a rich source of data on informal social life. Some national surveys from the 1950s have also been used to establish early baselines on basic types of associational membership (for use of the 1952 American National Election Study, see Costa and Kahn 2003b; for use of questions repeated in 1957 and 1975, see Putnam 2000, 58, referring to Veroff, Douvan, and Kulka 1981). Time diary data also appear in the Putnam (2000) and Costa and Kahn (2003b) studies at specific points. But most of the long-term trends analyzed in studies of civic participation and social capital necessarily depend on survey questions frequently repeated from the 1970s to the 1990s. As Robert Wuthnow (2002) explains, small sample sizes (especially for the GSS questions about memberships in specific types of associations) lead to a lot of data fluctuations and greatly reduce our confidence that we can discern valid trends. From even the most chronologically wide-ranging behavioralist studies, we learn only modest amounts about societal inequalities and civic trends. And as we are about to see, available studies reach different conclusions.

Has Civic Decline Happened Equally?

In *Bowling Alone* (2000), Robert Putnam documents sharp participatory declines over the last third of the twentieth century using an amalgam of individual-level, survey-based indicators of "social capital." Political acts, membership and participation in voluntary associations, various kinds of informal socializing with friends and family, and attitudes of social trust all figure in Putnam's conception of social capital. Despite nuances here and there, he finds that declines in all sorts of social capital have proceeded across the board among Americans, with no major differences by gender, race, or class. "Civic disengagement appears to be an equal opportunity affliction," he concludes. "The sharp, steady declines in club meetings, visits with friends, committee service, church attendance, philanthropic generosity, card games, and electoral turnout have hit virtually all sectors of American society over the last several decades in roughly equal measure" (185).

To be sure, Putnam believes that high levels of social capital and greater equality go together. With cross-sectional data, this correlation has been established across metropolitan areas within the United States (Alesina and La Ferrara 2000) and also cross-nationally (Costa and Kahn 2003b, n. 15). Extending the cross-sectional picture, Putnam (2000, 360, fig. 92) uses data collected for the various U.S. states around 1990 to establish a correlation between high levels of social capital and economic equality, as well as between high social capital and positive attitudes toward gender and racial equality (354, fig. 90). But because Putnam's analysis is not dynamic, we cannot tell whether long-term declines in state-level social capital have accompanied, followed from, or even helped to cause recent increases in (for example) income inequality. Furthermore, social capital is not measured in the same way in the various major parts of *Bowling Alone*. In parts 1 and 2, social capital prominently includes church membership and participation, but the measures of state-level social capital omit church membership or attendance, thereby setting aside the kind of social capital that has always been the most prominent in the United States. Equally worrisome, the omission of religious memberships and attendance sets aside precisely the sort of associational participation most likely to have recently increased (or held steady) for ordinary Americans, especially in the South (Putnam 2000, ch. 4; Wuthnow 1999). Putnam's state-level correlations among indices of social capital, and his posited correlation between measures of social capital and measures of equality would surely have weakened if indicators of church participation had been included in his state-level index.[1]

Putnam does *not* stress inequality in his explanation of why U.S. social capital in general is declining. Although he presents no full-blown explanatory model (see Putnam 2000, 486, n. 11), Putnam offers a rough pie chart of factors contributing to "guesstimated explanation for civic engagement, 1965–2000" (283–84). Exact percentages for all of the factors in this pie chart are not given, but Putnam writes that "my best guess is that no more than 10 percent of the total decline" in all forms of U.S. social capital considered together is attributable to "pressures of time and money" on the less-privileged and "the special pressures on two-career families." These are the only factors in Putnam's explanatory picture that seem to refer to increased class inequalities and to changed relationships between men and women (changes that might be interpreted as increased equality or at least greater role similarities). Beyond this, Putnam assigns an equally large explanatory weight (roughly 10 percent) to "suburbanization, commuting, and sprawl" and much larger explanatory weight (roughly 65 percent) to increased television watching plus "generational changes." Putnam believes that "generational changes" are by far the most important factors at work, but he does not specify what these factors are. Some of the negative impact of television-watching on social connectedness, Putnam suggests, is due to higher levels of viewing among younger generations. The weighty factor of generational changes also includes the "fading effects of World War II" and other shifts affecting later-born rather than earlier-born age cohorts. Thus, Putnam makes a good case that generationally shifting factors need to be further explored to explain declines in American civic participation over the last third of the twentieth century, but he does not carry this exploration very far. And judging from *Bowling Alone,* it is fair to say that he does not consider inequalities to be very important, either in describing or in accounting for declines in civic participation and social connectedness in late-twentieth-century America.

Putnam's deemphasis of inequality receives partial support in an additional survey-based study called "Who Bowls? The (Un)Changing Stratification of Participation." In this research, Henry Brady, Kay Schlozman, Sidney Verba, and Laurel Elms (2002) create an index of the twelve kinds of political and civic participation measured in the 1973 to 1994 Roper polls (see table 19.1); they also measure church attendance and claims of membership in sixteen types of associations measured in the General Social Surveys between 1972 and 1994. Using education and income variables, these researchers divide American respondents into quintiles and examine ratios of participation by the top to the bottom quintiles from the 1970s to the 1990s. As many other studies have done, this one documents downward trends in various kinds of civic participation. This study also documents a strong correlation between socioeconomic status and levels of participation, with an unusually large gap separating the highly participatory top quintile from the remaining four—except in the area of religious attendance, where there is remarkable equality across class lines. But the study does not reveal any heightened inequality in civic participation or organizational memberships between the mid-1970s and the mid-1990s. Comparing the top socioeconomic quintile of Americans to the bottom quintile, the ratio of participation in the twelve activities measured by the index of Roper items shows increased inequality in the late 1970s and then reduced inequality in the 1980s, but ends up roughly where it started, with a five-to-one participatory advantage for the highest versus the lowest quintile (Brady et al. 2002, 229, fig. 10.2). And the ratio of memberships in types of organizations remains roughly constant at a three-to-one ratio for the highest versus the lowest quintile (231, fig. 10.4).

In an earlier, unpublished draft, Brady and his colleagues (2000) also found that ratios of white to black participation as measured by the index of Roper items end up roughly the same at the end of the data series as at the start. For race, this overall finding may not be surprising, because other research (for example, Rosenstone and Hansen 1993, 244) suggests that postwar gains in racial equality occurred promptly following the civil rights achievements of 1955 to 1964, with remaining disparities remaining stable thereafter. But income gaps in the United States have escalated since the mid-1970s, so the analysis of Brady and his colleagues (2002) might have been expected to find recently growing disparities in civic participation along socioeconomic lines.

Sorting people into income quintiles and contrasting the extremes, however, may actually mask some trends. The bottom quintile of Brady and his colleagues (2002) includes many older Americans, but other research (Campbell 2003) shows that as national policy battles over Social Security heated up in the 1980s, elders—including those with low incomes—got more involved in politics. Civic inequalities may have grown more among working-age adults than among the elderly. Furthermore, available survey questions may be too blunt a measuring instrument. The Roper questions reveal nothing about specific types of voluntary groups, emphasize local forms of participation, and do not measure monetary contributions to politics or associations. These questions would not register possible shifts such as moves by upper-quintile individuals toward participation in more elitist or national groups or shifts toward giving money rather than time. There are also problems with the GSS measures of organizational membership. Brady and his colleagues treat all types of organizational membership as equivalent, but what if elite Americans have become more likely to participate in professional associations and less likely to join cross-class fraternal and veterans' groups, while less-privileged Americans are now less likely to join trade unions and more likely to participate in sports clubs? Such changes would have important consequences for our understanding of social stratification (for evidence, see Skocpol 2003, 186–89, 215–17, figs. 5.1, 5.2, and 5.10). The GSS questions are also problematic in that they register only whether respondents participate in *one or more associations* of a given type, not whether they belong to multiple groups within a type. These questions also stress traditional types of groups, relegating all others to a residual "any other groups" category. If privileged Americans joined more and more professional associations between the 1970s and the 1990s—or affiliated with multiple new-style advocacy groups—the GSS questions would not pick up these multiple memberships and thus could understate a growing class gap in associational affiliations.[2]

If Brady and his colleagues (2002) support Putnam's emphasis on increasing disconnection rather than inequality, the sociologist Robert D. Wuthnow (2002) concludes that overall declines in social capital in the post-1960s United States have been modest yet unequal. In general, Wuthnow cautions against the conclusion that U.S. civil society is collapsing. Various traditional "social capital" indicators have declined only modestly, he points out. Americans' civic involvement remains high by international standards. And there are clear indications of increasing participation in intimate "support groups" and new kinds of associations, movements, and volunteer venues not named in traditional social surveys (for more empirical findings, see Wuthnow 1994, 1998). What is more, even using the GSS results on long-standing kinds of group affiliations, reported memberships have apparently declined only modestly, from 75 percent of all Americans claiming one or more kinds of voluntary group memberships in 1974 to a low of 68 percent claiming such membership in 1991, followed by an increase back to 71 percent in 1994.

After making various statistical probes, Wuthnow concludes that the slight overall recovery in group affiliations reported on GSS surveys during the 1990s may represent a genuine development. So he concentrates on the 1974 to 1991 period to analyze social correlates of membership declines during the period of steepest decline. He hypothesizes that more socially marginal people were especially prone to drop out of associations during the most obvious period of membership decline (Wuthnow 2002, 79–83). He operationalizes marginality in terms of family income during a respondent's youth, father's education, respondent's education, race, and the number of children the respondent is raising. He examines each variable separately, then combines them into a "marginalization index." Patterns for each variable, Wuthnow writes, and for the index as a whole, are "clear, consistent, and striking. . . . In each case, those with fewer socioeconomic privileges were more similar . . . to those with greater socioeconomic privileges in 1974 than they were in 1991. The decline in association membership was always more pronounced among those with fewer socioeconomic privileges to begin with than it was with people who already had greater privileges" (80). Widening gaps between 1974 and 1991 were especially great between whites and nonwhites (who had been virtually equal in associational participation at the start) and between Americans with a college education, who lost little ground, and those educated at the high school level or less, who dropped eleven to twelve percentage points in affiliation levels over this period (81, table 2.6). Without providing systematic statistical tests, Wuthnow hypothesizes that less-privileged Americans tended to withdraw from associations because their life circumstances became more difficult in the late 1970s and 1980s.

Elsewhere in this paper, Wuthnow offers additional pieces of data about differentially decreasing civic trust and participation among the less marginal. Disagreeing with communitarians and social capital theorists who stress disconnection as the most problematic contemporary trend, Wuthnow writes: "As the United States has undergone a significant expansion in the educational levels of its citizens, new forms of social capital have emerged that make it easier for people to participate who may have moved from one community to another, or who have demanding jobs" (2002, 101). Declining involvements have been concentrated among the less privileged, while newer kinds of groups and affiliations disproportionately attract and serve the personal needs of the privileged, without drawing them into politics or larger community affairs. New civic forms "have not been fully successful in bridging socioeconomic levels or in drawing in marginalized people." "*How much* social capital exists" may thus not be the most normatively pressing issue for American democracy today. "With association levels and volunteering at comparatively high levels by cross-cultural standards, the United States may well have enough social capital left to function as a democracy with little loss of effectiveness. *What kind* of social capital . . . is probably a more important question. At present, significant attention in the United States needs to be devoted to creating social capital that does a better job of bridging between the privileged and the marginalized" (102, emphasis added).

Growing Inequality and Ethnic Heterogeneity as Causes of Civic Decline

As we have seen, survey analysts seeking to describe recent trends in aggregate civic involvements have not agreed on whether increasing inequalities are central to the civic trends everyone is trying to explain. Societal inequalities enter into the analysis in a powerful way, however, in a new analysis of the long-term causes of civic disengagement among non-elderly adult Americans completed by a pair of scholars who use *all* of the sources of survey and time-diary data assessed in Putnam (2000) and other recent studies. In "Understanding the American Decline in Social Capital, 1952 to 1998," the economists Dora L. Costa and Matthew E. Kahn (2003b) start by using all available surveys, including one taken in 1952, to document trends in *three distinct kinds* of social capital: volunteering and membership in voluntary organizations—both of which the authors define as social capital produced in the community—and entertaining friends and relatives, which Costa and Kahn label social capital produced inside the home. In agreement with Wuthnow, Costa and Kahn find that the decline in social capital has been modest and in any event is sharper for private socializing than for volunteering and organizational memberships (for trends in the different spheres, see Costa and Kahn 2003b, 26–29, figs. 1 through 4). Note that Costa and Kahn largely restrict their analysis to adults in their prime working years, from twenty-five to fifty-four years old. To explain such declines in social capital as have occurred among these working-age Americans, Costa and Kahn test individual-level variables and also examine contextual variables measured at the metropolitan level, including income differentials, racial heterogeneity, and "birthplace fragmentation" (which measures migration and international immigration).

Results in this tightly focused study underline the civic impact of increasing female labor force participation and heightened levels of metropolitan income inequality and ethnic heterogeneity. Controlling for individual demographic and socioeconomic characteristics, declines in volunteering are well explained and largely attributable (especially among men) to rising metropolitan-area wage inequality (Costa and Kahn 2003b, 30–32, 37). Again controlling for individual-level characteristics, Costa and Kahn conclude that almost one-third of the decline in reported associational membership is due to rising metropolitan wage disparities, and that another 18 percent is due to the increasing heterogeneity of the birthplaces of residents of various metropolitan areas (38, table 7). Three-fifths of the decline in membership measured in social surveys remains unexplained in this study—probably because the basic trend being measured, membership in *any type* of association, is very general. Time diary data show declines in the time spent by women in associations from 1965 to 1985, with participation in the labor force emerging as a significant negative predictor (33–34). As for social capital produced inside the home, community characteristics are not predictors, yet the decline "has been especially large among women, explaining all of the decline in time spent visiting family or friends in the 1990s, suggesting that women's greater labor force attachment may play a role" (37).

Because they examine specific types of social capital, disaggregate data sources, measure trends over as long a stretch as possible, and explore a greater range of explanatory variables than other researchers have done, Costa and Kahn's conclusions are convincing. They have moved macrosocietal contextual trends—rising income inequality, growing racial and ethnic heterogeneity, and increasing female labor force participation—to center stage in our understanding of declines in American civic participation and socializing. They acknowledge some role for the sorts of age-cohort effects stressed by Putnam, but they broadly contrast their argument to his. As they put it (Costa and Kahn 2003b, 18): "Putnam (2000) argued that television and the aging of the 'civic' generations born between 1910 and 1940 are the primary culprits [in declining social capital]. We argue that the decline in participation is more pronounced among women, contemporaneous with the rise in women's labor force participation, and that rising community heterogeneity, particularly income inequality, is one of the primary explanations for the decline in social capital."

In "Civic Engagement and Community Heterogeneity: An Economist's Perspective," Costa and Kahn (2003a) connect their findings to other studies by economists that document negative impacts of income inequality and racial and ethnic heterogeneity on social capital and civic engagement.[3] Apart from Costa and Kahn's own work, much of this research is cross-sectional, not dynamic, and most studies focus on the late-twentieth-century United States, during the recent era of rising income inequalities and the post-1965 era of rapid "new immigration" from Latin America, Asia, Africa, and the Caribbean. When theoretical hypotheses are presented, they are framed ahistorically and in micro terms: they posit that inequality or racial/ethnic heterogeneity inherently dampens civic engagement because (a) different kinds of people may not trust one another or join shared associations or (b) people who find themselves in an ethnic or racial minority may lack critical mass to organize. I very much doubt the generality of the latter mechanism, because U.S. voluntary membership associations, including those formed by racial and ethnic minorities, formed at an extraordinarily rapid rate during a previous era of rapid immigration and increasing ethnic heterogeneity between 1870 and 1920 (see Skocpol 2003, ch. 2). Furthermore, one study completed by my research group (Skocpol and Oser, forthcoming) shows that African Americans seem to have organized more fraternal groups (and churches) per capita than white Americans in the late nineteenth and early twentieth centuries. Facing exclusion from major types of groups run by whites, African Americans organized extraordinary numbers of their own groups in competitive response.

Depending on the context, in short, ethnic and racial heterogeneity can spur competitive counterorganization, not just lead to the suppression of voluntary group formation. The negative relationships between heterogeneity and voluntary group memberships found by various scholars for the post-1965 period in the United States pertain to an era in which many recently formed voluntary entities are *not* membership groups, and during which preexisting cross-class and popular membership associations have been in decline. In an era in which professionally managed associations and nonprofit institutions are proliferating, newly arrived immigrants and other marginal people may find fewer opportunities to organize or join membership associations than was true in previous eras (Skerry 1997).

Dynamic Implications of the Verba Civic Voluntarism Model

So far, we have reviewed important studies of trends in U.S. civic participation, yet the most theoretically powerful survey-based research on civic participation is cross-sectional. Again and again since the 1960s, Sidney Verba and his associates have addressed issues of inequality and civic participation (see especially Almond and Verba 1963; Verba and Nie 1972; Verba, Schlozman, and Brady 1995; Burns, Schlozman, and Verba 2001). These massive studies use different national samples and explore new hypotheses with innovative measures of various dimensions of civic behavior and reconceptualizations of the causal mechanisms at work. Such changes from study to study undercut possibilities for assessing real-world civic transformations, but the silver lining lies in the steady theoretical improvements. By now, Verba and his associates have arrived at a fully elaborated "civic voluntarism model" that offers precise hypotheses about the roots of individual-level participatory inequalities by race, class, and gender. (For this model, see especially the 1995 and 2001 books.) The model considers three clusters of explanatory variables. Individuals may vary in their degrees and kinds of participation because of differences in *resources,* such as time, money, or skills that can be learned at home, on the job, or in associations and institutions. They may also vary in their *engagement,* or motivation to participate, because of different concerns with public issues, knowledge, and beliefs about whether they can make a difference. Finally, individuals may also be *mobilized* or recruited into public life to sharply varying degrees.

Verba and his collaborators use this basic model, enriched by knowledge of the changing institutional contexts of American life, to suggest why gender inequalities may have recently declined but still not disappeared (for this analysis, see Burns, Schlozman, and Verba 2001). They focus even more attention on explaining why "in the United States the skew introduced by the relationship between high levels of education or income and high levels of political activity . . . is especially pronounced" (Schlozman, Verba, and Brady 1999, 431). Stratification-related differences in motivation to participate and in the requests that people receive to give time or money help to explain this class skew in civic participation. But the Verba-ites focus especially on the differential resources people have, or attain, to participate in public life. Although the availability of time for participatory activities is relatively evenly distributed across class lines, money is very unequally distributed, and civic skills are unequal too—especially given that skill differentials originating in families of origin and at school are often further magnified at work. Higher-status jobs require people to speak, run meetings, and write, while others provide little scope for such attainments.

Voluntary associations or institutions outside of government and the economy can either reinforce or counter the inequalities of motivation, resources, and mobilization that Americans otherwise experience. Verba and his collaborators have always been interested in these processes. Some time ago, Verba and Nie (1972) demonstrated that political parties and voluntary associations have a special potential to enhance the political participation of lower- and middle-class citizens. Much of Verba's work since the 1970s fleshes out this basic point, which is also central to the model of civic participation developed by Steven Rosenstone and John Mark Hansen (1993). People with high incomes and education are likely to participate on their own as individuals because they have resources, are interested, and are often contacted by mobilizers who want their money or their special skills. But lower- and middle-class people may need extra skills, network contacts, or sustained encouragement to participate. Strongly organized, mass-mobilizing political parties can reduce class differences in participation. Social movements that mobilize African Americans, women, Christian fundamentalists, or other marginalized or disadvantaged groups can also make a difference. And so can massive nonpolitical voluntary associations, such as unions and churches. Verba and his associates show that unions and churches currently involve non-elites much more fully than other associations seem to do. They also point out that Protestant church denominations stress lay participation in congregational and associated group activities and thus impart extra skills to church members. But not all popularly-rooted associations are the same; as Schlozman, Verba, and Brady (1999) point out, unions convey messages stressing the needs, values, and engagement of less-privileged Americans, while many evangelical churches and related voluntary associations may stress opposition to abortion rights or homosexual rights.

The Verba model and data analyses probe survey results for single points in time, rather than attempting assessments of change over the postwar decades. Nevertheless, suppositions about recent U.S. civic changes are presented (and succinctly summarized in Schlozman, Verba, and Brady 1999). Raising money has become ever more important in electoral politics and associational life, the Verba researchers point out, and this is bound to exacerbate inequality. In addition, churches involve far larger numbers of Americans than unions, and that has consequences not just for the skills people gain but also for the messages they are likely to hear and the attempts at recruitment into public life to which they are likely to be exposed.

Moving beyond illustrative points about churches and unions, we can see that Verba's model for explaining variations in individual-level participation implies some powerful hypotheses about the probable impact of different kinds of voluntary associations—and by extension, about the probable impact of changes during recent decades in the societal mix of associations. Key hypotheses relevant to assessing long-term institutional and associational changes include:

- Associations may have a greater equalizing impact on civic participation to the degree that they involve less-privileged people (instead of, or along with, the more privileged). Almost by definition, this means that the very largest associations are more likely to have an equalizing impact than those of more modest proportions, unless the latter have non-elite constituencies. Among very large associations, in turn, those with non-elite constituencies—such as unions or popular farmers' associations—have the greatest potential equalizing impact.

- Associations will have a greater class-equalizing impact to the degree that they ask supporters to give time as well as money—because time is a more equally distributed resource than money.

- Associations will have a greater equalizing impact to the degree that they offer high proportions of their supporters chances to learn generalizable civic skills. Thus, associations that hold meetings and have large numbers of officer and committee positions are more likely to have an equalizing impact—especially if they also include nonprivileged people and invite them to take leadership positions.

- Associations may have a greater equalizing impact, especially in politics, to the degree that they convey messages about the relevance of democracy and the equal worth of citizens, or of all members of the group regardless of class or other differences. Associations are also more likely to have an equalizing impact to the degree that they focus on shared community needs and values or on assisting the less privileged. This last proposition actually stretches beyond the civic voluntarism model in that it directs our attention toward influences that various types of associations might have not only on their own members or supporters but on larger public debates.

Given the ease with which we can derive hypotheses such as these from the Verba researchers' theoretical model and anecdotal illustrations, the *dynamic* explanatory potential becomes clear. The civic voluntarism model cries out to be connected to a much more systematic, macroscopic analysis of the changing universe of organizations, associations, and social movements active in the United States over the past half-century. In principle, the kind of dynamic analysis done by Rosenstone and Hansen (1993) to explain class and racial shifts in directly political forms of aggregate-individual participation could also be done to bring associations more directly into our understanding of additional dimensions of civic activity. But to make progress in this way requires that we know much more about how voluntary organizing and the overall universe of civic organizations have changed in recent times. We must, in short, learn what we can from scholars who have studied associations and organizations directly.

ORGANIZATIONAL STUDIES OF THE TRANSFORMED ASSOCIATIONAL UNIVERSE

As survey researchers have probed and tried to explain aggregate trends in individual civic participation, other scholars have largely ignored individual-level activities in order to examine social movements and shifting populations of voluntary organizations. Until recently, most of this scholarship has been executed by sociologists and political scientists who celebrate post-1960s increases in pluralism and participation in U.S. democracy. These scholars focus on contemporary Americans as organizers rather than joiners, and they document the civic associations proliferating out of the social movements of "the sixties" (an era that actually stretched from the mid-1950s to the mid-1970s). We will hear first from researchers who have investigated emergent types of civic associations before turning to scholars—especially Putnam (2000) and Skocpol (1999, 2003)—who have looked more broadly at declining as well as emergent groups. My own work in particular finds that recent changes in the national mix of U.S. voluntary associations have inegalitarian as well as equalizing consequences.

The Advocacy Explosion

At the centers of national power, thousands of new advocacy organizations were launched from the 1970s through the 1990s (for overviews, see Berry 1997; Hayes 1986; Judis 1992; Loomis and Cigler 1998; Paget 1990; Schlozman and Tierney 1986; Walker 1991). The ranks of newly launched associations included not just business and professional groups furthering long-standing kinds of claims but hundreds of new civil rights groups, dozens of antipoverty groups, and thousands of professionally led advocacy groups articulating new understandings of the public interest. Putnam and other social capital analysts set aside most recently launched associations on the grounds that the vast majority are nationally centralized, mailing-list groups without firm local roots. Such "tertiary" associations demand little from individual adherents and fail to bring people together in regular meetings. But analysts of recent associational changes have a more optimistic reading. They see advantages not just in the broad variety of contemporary advocacy efforts but in their national focus and expert leadership as well.

National advocacy groups, asserts the sociologist Debra Minkoff (1997, 606–7), reflect "a significant change in how collective identities are constructed and collective action is implemented. Local communities are no longer the sine qua non of mobilization precisely because identity groups transcend parochial boundaries." Minkoff is particularly impressed with the role that new national advocacy groups play in legitimating shared identities, furthering policy goals, and enlarging public discussions on behalf of fragmented, dispersed, or marginalized groups. "For isolated and marginalized constituencies—the disabled, gay men and lesbians, the poor, and others—this sense of collective identity, or 'we,' may literally be life-saving," she points out. National advocacy organizations can help people in dispersed settings and weak networks link up with one another and sustain morale and capacity for collective action over time. Using data on organizational births *and deaths* from the national volumes of the *Encyclopedia of Associations,* Minkoff (1995, 61–62) has done

FIGURE 19.1   *Groups Testifying Before Congress in 1963, 1979, and 1991*

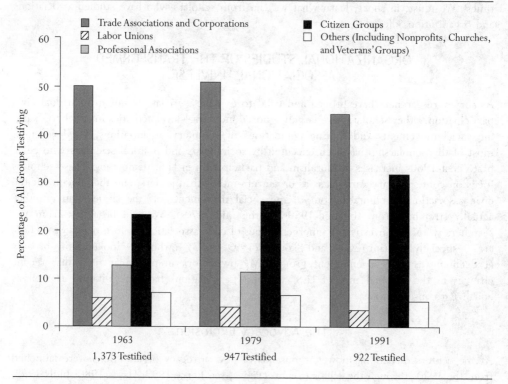

Source: Berry (1999, 20, table 2.1).

empirical research on the proliferation (though not the putative effects) of "rights" associations that address the needs and rights of women, African Americans, and other formerly marginalized ethnic groups in the United States. She finds that there were only 98 such associations listed in 1955, and that the number rose sixfold to 688 by 1985. Groups speaking for African Americans proliferated sharply from the mid-1960s, and women's rights groups, the most numerous category, experienced especially sharp proliferation during the 1970s.

The political scientist Jeffrey M. Berry (1999, 2) adds to our understanding of contemporary associational innovations by exploring the emergence and activities of "citizen groups," which he defines as "lobbying organizations that mobilize members, donors, and activists around interests other than their vocation or profession." As the American population has become more highly educated and prosperous, argues Berry (1999; see also Berry 1977), people want expert-led organizations to speak for "quality of life" concerns—ranging from the quest for a healthy environment to the eradication of injustices, to the advancement of cultural or moral principles. Taking on such concerns, professionally managed advocacy groups do research, monitor and lobby Congress, and develop ties to the national media. As Berry (1999, 3) sees it, this has been a democratizing development. "If we want someone in Washington to stand up for us, to speak passionately, and to aggressively advocate the policies that matter most to us, then a citizen lobby is the most obvious vehicle to serve as our representative in the policy-making process." In *The New Liberalism: The Rising*

FIGURE 19.2   *Press Coverage of Interest Groups in 1963, 1979, and 1991*

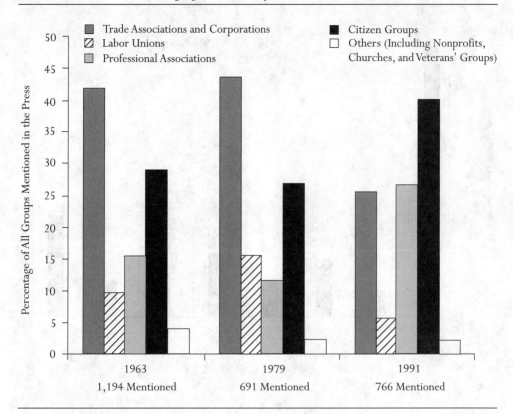

Source: Berry (1999, 24, table 2.2).

Power of Citizen Groups, Berry gathers data on lobbying and media exposure for new citizens' associations compared with older-line business groups and trade unions. Figures 19.1 and 19.2, which summarize some of his results, show that citizen's associations have been increasingly able to gain hearings before Congress and in the media, while business and labor groups have received relatively less attention. Figure 19.2 also shows that professional associations have gained relatively greater attention from the press since 1980.

In *Agendas and Instability in American Politics* (1993), Frank Baumgartner and Bryan D. Jones provide a broader perspective on the changing associational universe partially analyzed by Minkoff and Berry, and they likewise stress the changing balance between business groups, which once predominated among U.S. national associations, and all other groups, including many nonprofit public affairs associations. Using founding dates for "profit" versus nonprofit "citizens'" groups in data gathered by Jack Walker in 1985 on Washington-based associations, Baumgartner and Jones (1993, 181) show that foundings of profit groups exceeded foundings of citizens' groups by around a three-to-one ratio from the 1930s through the 1950s, while between 1960 and 1980 the ratio of profit to citizens' group foundings plummeted to one and a half to one. Baumgartner and Jones also do counts of existing types of U.S. associations from the national *Encyclopedia of Associations,* and I have supplemented

FIGURE 19.3   *National Associations of the United States, 1959 and 1999*

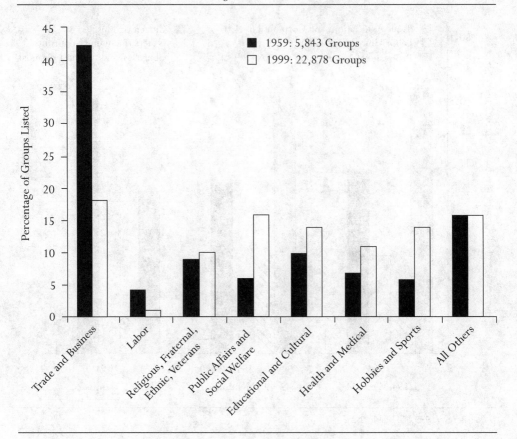

Source: Skocpol (2003, 146–47, table 4.2), updating Baumgartner and Jones (1993, 103, table 6.1).

one of their tables with very recent data to produce the comparisons of 1959 and 1999 presented in figure 19.3. Clearly, "trade and business" associations have sharply declined as a proportion of all national U.S. associations, while relatively nonpolitical groups devoted to "sports and hobbies" have sharply increased, as have other categories of associations that are likely to include active advocacy associations and various nonprofit institutions. Such recently expanded categories encompass "public affairs and social welfare" groups, "educational and cultural" groups, and "health and medical" groups.

A specific area of recent civic innovation and vitality has been the modern environmental movement, which took off in the late 1960s and 1970s (Dunlap and Mertig 1992; Shaiko 1999). Baumgartner and Jones (1993, 187, tables 9.2 and 9.3) have amassed data on that realm of associational proliferation, analyzing founding dates and other information from the *Encyclopedia of Associations.* New foundings of environmental associations sharply accelerated in the 1960s, 1970s, and 1980s, and most groups were still active as of 1990. What is more, old-line as well as recently founded environmental associations sharply increased their membership rolls during the same decades, from the 1960s to the 1990s, when hundreds of new environmental groups were launched (Mitchell, Mertig, and Dunlap 1992, 13, table 1).

American civic life has become not only more pluralistic in recent times but more

FIGURE 19.4   *Organizations Wielding Money and Ideas in Public Affairs, 1960 to 1997*

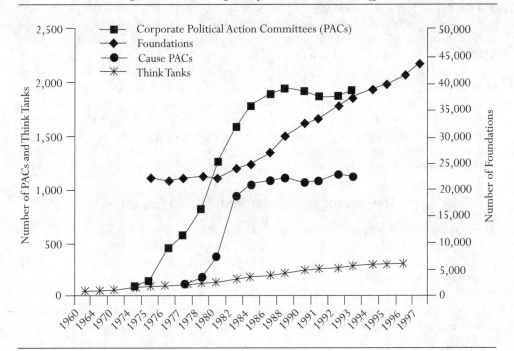

Sources: Think tank data: Andrew Rich (Rich and Weaver 1998); foundation data: Foundation Center 2002; PAC data: Conway and Green (1998, 157, table 7.1).

professionalized. Civic groups regularly work through headquarters—more likely than not in Washington or New York—where lobbyists, lawyers, researchers, and media people act on behalf of causes or constituencies. Indeed, one massive advocacy association, the American Association of Retired Persons (AARP) has its own zip code in the nation's capital (Morris 1996). Entirely directed by trustees and professionals, groups that specialize in deploying money or ideas in public life have proliferated along with constituency-oriented associations, as displayed in figure 19.4, which draws from recent information about fast-multiplying political action committees (PACs), private foundations, and think tanks (on the last, see Ricci 1993; Rich and Weaver 1998). What is more, along with all other civic associations and institutions, citizens' groups and rights associations have become increasingly professionalized—a development facilitated by expanded national funding from foundations (Jenkins 1998) and other institutional patrons (Walker 1991). After the 1950s, many new citizens' associations raised such foundation or patron resources to expand their expert staffs. Today many have combined contributions from mailing-list members with sources of institutional support to sustain national offices devoted to professionally run activities (Shaiko 1999, ch. 1).

Debra Minkoff (1995, 62, fig. 13.3) shows that as groups speaking for women and racial minorities sharply increased in numbers, the mix of such associations recorded in the *Encyclopedia of Associations* shifted away from movement and protest groups toward professionally run types of groups engaged in advocacy and the delivery of social services to target constituencies. Other scholars have also documented the movement of feminist associations toward Washington-focused lobbying (Costain 1981; Schlozman 1990). As already noted, Berry (1977, 1999) stresses the role of professional and expert staffs in directing all sorts of public interest–oriented citizens' associations. And as a prominent case in point for the increasing role of professionals in citizens' groups, Baumgartner and Jones (1993, 187) highlight developments for environmental associations. According to their data, in 1960 there were 119 nationally visible environmental associations employing 316 staff members; by 1990 there were 396 groups employing 2,917 staff members. Clearly, the rapid accumulation of sheer numbers of environmental associations between the 1960s and the 1990s was accompanied by an even more explosive growth of paid professional staff. Functioning as powerful and skilled advocates, such higher-educated employees have taken an increasing role in all sorts of environmental groups, including those with networks of chapters or large mailing-list memberships (Bosso 1991; Mitchell, Mertig, and Dunlap 1992; Shaiko 1999).

The Waning of Popular Membership Groups

At this point in the discussion, consideration of the full range of major types of membership and constituency associations in U.S. civic life can help us situate the findings and arguments of various strands of scholarship. Figure 19.5 presents a chart of such associations, classifying groups under combinations of two rubrics (suggesting real-world referents for each of the resulting eight types). On the horizontal dimension, the chart sorts groups according to their constituencies—ranging from those that represent elites and elites serving the community to those that speak for the public at large or for the less advantaged (for example, the Children's Defense Fund). On the vertical dimension, the chart sorts groups according to how they are directed and how they raise their resources. This dimension differentiates between, on the top row, professionally directed advocacy associations that raise resources through a combination of patron grants, contributions from other organizations, and mass mailings and, on the bottom row, groups of the more traditional membership variety that rely on recurrent membership dues and elect active members as their leaders. Obviously, this chart refers to broad ideal types and does not sort groups along all possible dimensions. Even so, the chart allows us to locate the major dimensions along which contemporary civic transformations have proceeded. And it suggests why leading analysts disagree about the democratic implications of contemporary changes.

Focusing on the types of associations arrayed across the top of figure 19.5, Minkoff (1995, 1997), Berry (1977, 1999), Walker (1991), and Baumgartner and Jones (1993, ch. 9) regard the associational innovations of the 1960s to the 1990s as on the whole equalizing. Other observers (such as Pettinico 1996 and Schudson 1996, 1998) also share this relatively optimistic assessment. Equalization and democratization are understood by these researchers to mean a shift in the balance of organized voice from business associations, whose predominance among all U.S. associations has dwindled, toward various sorts of citizens' associations, including more than ever before organizations that defend individual rights, speak for the general public interest, or advocate on behalf of the less advantaged.

But the other dimension on which contemporary associational change has occurred directs our attention toward overall shifts from membership associations and dues-based groups toward professionally directed entities that derive only small proportions of their funding, if any, from dues-paying members. From this perspective, the most noticeable civic transformation in post-1960s America has been the shift away from classic membership-based associations, with especially sharp declines in popular and cross-class membership groups. Both Putnam (2000) and Skocpol (1999, 2003) acknowledge the innovative associa-

FIGURE 19.5   *Membership and Constituency Associations in U.S. Civic Life*

		Group Speaks for:		
Governance and Resource Base:	Elites	Elites Serving the Community	Public or Cross-Class Constituency	Less Advantaged
Professionally run; money from patrons, other organizations, and/or mass mailings	Business associations	Foundations and other institutions that gather money for community purposes	Public interest advocacy groups (environmental, consumers,' and good government groups)	Advocates for the poor, disabled, children, marginalized minorities, and other vulnerable groups
Elected leaders; high proportion of money from membership dues	Professional associations College alumni/ae groups; fraternities and sororities	Elite service clubs (such as Rotary, Soroptimists, and the Junior League)	Large fraternals (such as the Elks, Masons, Moose, Eagles, and their female partners) Ethnic fraternals Women's federations (such as the WCTU, GFWC, PTA) Religious associations (such as Knights of Columbus and Woman's Missionary Union) Veterans' associations and auxiliaries Inclusive farm groups (such as the Farm Bureau)	Unions Populist farmers' associations

Source: Author's compilation.

tional trends documented by the scholars who focus on new citizen and advocacy groups. But they offer a broader picture of associational change, examining groups that are in decline as well as those in the ascendance. And in different ways, both Putnam and Skocpol ponder the downsides for American society and democracy of the radically changed balance between membership associations and professionally directed civic entities.

Although *Bowling Alone* relies mainly on survey data about individual attitudes and reported participation, Putnam also includes data on organizational populations and membership trends. Because he is interested in localized, face-to-face interaction, Putnam (2000, 51) decries the fact that "membership" in most recently proliferating U.S. voluntary associations "means moving a pen, not making a meeting." Contemporary citizens' groups are very unlikely to have extensive chapter structures, Putnam reports, and the trend away from interactive chapters is accentuated among the most recently founded associations. The few contemporary citizens' groups that do have chapters have relatively sparse networks compared with older-style membership federations. As Putnam points out, there were only nine citizens' associations among the eighty-three in Jeff Berry's 1977 study that "had as many as one hundred local chapters nationwide. By way of comparison, there are seven thousand local Rotary chapters in America, to take a typical 'old-fashioned' chapter-based civic organization."[4]

Most long-standing chapter-based associations have experienced huge membership losses since the 1960s and 1970s. Examining thirty-four large and small chapter-based associations that he feels have been important in the twentieth-century United States, Putnam (2000, 54, fig. 8, and appendix 3) traces membership levels normalized as a proportion of the size of the U.S. population that might be recruited to each group (for example, Knights of Columbus members as a proportion of Catholic men). Putnam clearly shows precipitous decline for chapter-based groups that fit into the middle two categories on the bottom row of figure 19.5. Virtually all of them are associations with elected leaders and membership dues, and their memberships are either recruited across class lines or else consist of elites aiming to serve the larger community (as with the Rotary, Lions, Soroptimists, and other "service clubs" of the type chronicled by Charles 1993).

Just as he does in his analysis of trends in individual-level participation, Putnam downplays issues of class inequality in his analysis of declining membership associations. One critical issue, for example, is whether professional societies have done better at recruiting or retaining members than unions or cross-class membership federations, which are more likely to enroll non-elite Americans. In *Bowling Alone*, Putnam uses differently scaled figures to suggest that membership decreases have occurred across the board (see Putnam 2000, 54, 81–84, figs. 8, 14, and 15). "While the absolute number of Americans who belong to professional associations has grown significantly over the last thirty years—and in that sense, this domain is a singular exception to the general pattern we have seen of declining membership—this is the exception that proves the rule," Putnam concludes, "since even in this area of apparent growth, we see the same pattern of growth in sociability during the first two-thirds of the century, followed by sudden stagnation and then decline during the last third" (85).

But when examined in detail, Putnam's own data on membership losses for various types of associations reveal much more class inequality within overall trends of membership decline. Associations may be contracting across the board, but losses in relation to potential memberships are much more dramatic for blue-collar and cross-class associations than for professional groups. Using data provided by Putnam beyond those published in *Bowling Alone,* I have prepared figure 19.6 to compare the percentage declines that Putnam reports for the

FIGURE 19.6   *Membership Declines in Cross-Class Chapter Groups and Blue-Collar Unions Compared with Elite Professional Societies*

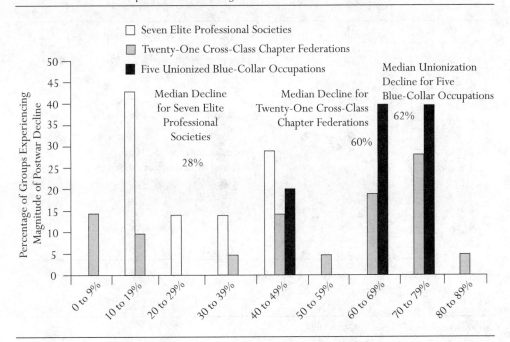

Source: Unions: Putnam (2000, 82); larger cross-class associations: Putnam (2000, 438–39); additional data on elite professional societies: Robert Putnam, personal communication.

adult membership shares for associations that clearly fall into different categories in figure 19.5. One cluster of groups consists of seven national professional societies with highly educated members—doctors, lawyers, dentists, accountants, architects, electrical engineers, and mechanical engineers. Another cluster consists of twenty-one voluntary membership federations with large cross-class memberships and networks of local chapters. The final cluster includes five largely blue-collar occupations in the manufacturing, mining, construction, transportation, and service sectors that were historically heavily unionized. All data refer to associations discussed in *Bowling Alone* and indicate losses in proportions of eligible adults enrolled from the post–World War II peak years to 1997. The findings in my figure are dramatic: *unionized blue-collar occupations and cross-class chapter federations experienced, overall, twice as much membership decline as elite professional societies.* Membership in groups that actually meet and elect officers has become much more of an elite experience in the United States.

Were these results perhaps skewed by the selection of some associations rather than others in the categories tracked by Putnam? National social surveys can be used to check on this to the degree that they ask Americans about individual memberships in any (one or more) associations of particular types. Unfortunately, many of the categories used in the General Social Survey from the mid-1970s to the mid-1990s were too vaguely defined to line up with specific types of voluntary associations (and their eligible membership bases). Nevertheless, two of the GSS categories, "unions" and "professional" groups, do have relatively clear-cut referents. Moreover, the professional category has the added advantage of

FIGURE 19.7   *The Growing Gap Between College-Educated Americans Belonging to Professional Societies and Non-College-Educated Americans Enrolled in Unions, 1970 to 1995*

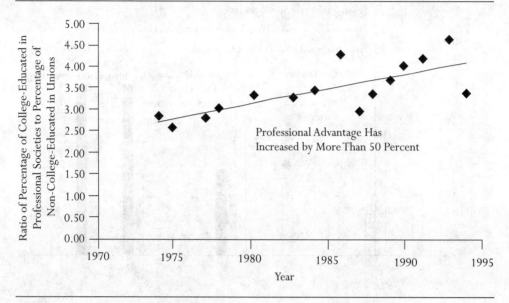

Source: General Social Survey, 1974 to 1994.

capturing reported individual affiliations with smaller and often more specialized professional societies—a type of professional group that has proliferated of late, possibly at the partial expense of the big professional "peak" associations that Putnam investigates. Using the GSS data, I have prepared figure 19.7 to track the ratio of the percentage of Americans with any years of college who report belonging to one or more professional societies to the percentage of Americans educated at the high school level or less who report union membership.[5] This figure tells the same story as the data in figure 19.6 about differentially declining associational membership shares. For occupationally related membership associations, affiliation is increasingly skewed toward the more educated who belong to (one or more) professional societies. Even as the ranks of higher-educated Americans have swelled, the upward gradient of associational change has been extraordinary: the professional membership–share advantage over blue-collar unions has increased by more than 50 percent over just two decades.

Returning to the broader issue of decline in chapter-based membership associations, extensive networks of local chapters may be important as generators of local, face-to-face "social capital," in Putnam's sense, or we may see them as avenues for broad and active participation in ways highlighted by Verba's civic voluntarism model. From the latter perspective, what matters is the sheer number of locally present *and translocally connected* groups that offer large numbers of Americans chances to attend meetings, participate on committees, learn skills as local officers, and climb ladders into state or national leadership. This is the perspective on chapter-based associations stressed by the Harvard Civic Engagement Project (CEP), which has traced the long-term development of very large voluntary membership associations across all of U.S. history, from 1790 to the present (see Skocpol et al.

1999; Skocpol 1999; Skocpol, Ganz, and Munson 2000; Skocpol et al. 2002; Skocpol 2003). The Skocpol project has identified fifty-eight very large voluntary membership groups, apart from churches and political parties, that at some point in U.S. history have enrolled at least 1 percent of U.S. adult men and/or women as members. (The benchmark is 1 percent of men *or* women for gender-specific groups, and 1 percent of both genders for mixed groups.) The fifty-eight very large associations discovered by the Skocpol project are surveyed in figure 19.8, which shows when these associations were founded and displays how many groups had memberships exceeding 1 percent of the adult population during each five-year interval in U.S. history up to 1970. Empirical details about these fifty-eight large membership associations appear in table 19.2.

Almost all of the large associations studied by the CEP fit into columns 3 and 4 of figure 19.5. They are (or were) popular associations of workers or farmers or cross-class associations involving hundreds of thousands to millions of Americans from many occupational strata. Significantly, at least until very recently, the vast majority of very large U.S. voluntary associations have been representatively governed federations with dues-paying members, elected officers, and regular group meetings at the local, state (or regional), and national levels. Each of the two dozen or so very large chapter-based membership federations that flourished in U.S. society from the late-nineteenth through the mid-twentieth century included not just supralocal bodies but thousands of local units, each of which needed to recruit new members and yearly contingents of officers. At the core of U.S. civil society in 1955 were the twenty-three very large membership associations listed in table 19.3. Taken together, these groups, most of which were chapter-based federations, may have required from 3 to 5 percent of the adult population to serve as officers in that year alone. Classic large voluntary membership federations were massive engines for encouraging popular participation in civic life. These federations also maintained elaborate leadership ladders stretching from localities and states to national associational centers; elected national officers had almost always "worked their way up" from widely appreciated performances as local and state (or regional) officers.

Three-quarters of the very large U.S. membership associations of the 1950s have since experienced sharp to catastrophic membership losses (for the details, see Skocpol 2003, 153–56). This is not to say, however, that associations exceeding 1 percent of the U.S. adult population have disappeared. In fact, their ranks have remained roughly steady over the decades (see figure 19.8), although the numbers of very large associations have not kept up with population increases in the United States. Still, very large membership associations have continued to exist, even as thousands of much smaller associations and even some memberless associations have proliferated. But the Skocpol CEP data show that the mix of very large associations has changed, partly because of group turnover and partly because surviving older groups have changed their membership criteria and/or purposes.

At the tail end of the list of very large U.S. membership associations presented in table 19.2, we see the specific associations that have attained peak membership (measured as a percentage of the U.S. adult population) in recent decades, compared with those that attained peaks in earlier eras. Skocpol (2003, 156–61) discusses the changing features of the twenty largest at each decade midpoint from 1945 through 1995. As late as the 1960s, more than 50 percent of the largest U.S. voluntary associations were (juridically or de facto) gender-segregated, but that situation changed abruptly in the 1970s; now only one-fifth of the largest associations are gender-specific. As recently as the midtwentieth century, the largest associations were mostly cross-class fraternal, veterans', church-connected, or community-serving associations devoted to furthering the goals, and proclaiming the values, of

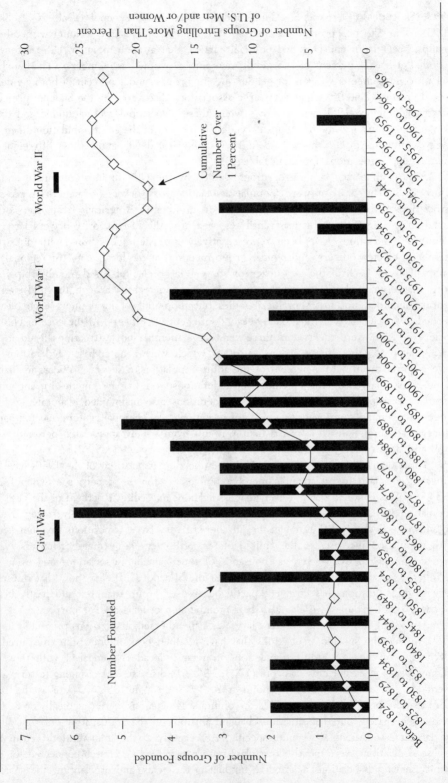

FIGURE 19.8   Foundings and Accumulation of Large U.S. Membership Associations, Precolonial Era to 1969

Source: Skocpol Civic Engagement Project.

brotherhood, sisterhood, fellow citizenship, and national and community service. But today the purpose of large associations is much more likely to be recreation, the provision of economic representation or services, or advocacy about a specific public policy cause. Finally, very large associations today are less likely than their earlier counterparts to recruit their members through nationwide networks of local chapters. Ninety percent of the twenty largest U.S. associations recruited through local chapters in 1945, but this percentage had declined to 60 percent by 1995, when 40 percent of the twenty largest associations used mailing lists or other methods to recruit high and growing proportions of their members individually apart from local chapters. Among the ten largest associations in 1995, moreover, half used the individualistic modes of recruitment.

Looking over the long haul of U.S. associational history, an interesting reversal comes into view. The late nineteenth century witnessed bursts of associational organizing on an unprecedented scale (Gamm and Putnam 1999; Schlesinger 1944; Skocpol et al. 1999), and in that era large and small associations often converged on the model of the representatively governed, federally organized, dues-based membership association. In the late twentieth century, another huge burst of U.S. civic organizing occurred, but this time professionally run groups with more centralized modes of recruitment and funding became normative. Smaller groups have predominated in the recent waves, and surviving or newly founded large "membership" associations are imitating the professional techniques of funding and recruitment used by their smaller cousins. Large as well as smaller contemporary associations are also becoming more specialized in their purposes, and they are much less likely than classic U.S. membership associations to depend on gender-segregated constituencies or to espouse goals of fellowship among brothers, sisters, or fellow citizens.

What Is the Bottom Line for Democracy?

As the overall mix of U.S. civic associations shifts away from chapter-based federations toward professionally run groups without interacting members, scholars debate the consequences for democratic representation and responsiveness. Such consequences are challenging to conceptualize, let alone investigate empirically. But there have been attempts: some have looked at the impact of associational changes on participation, and others have probed the possible consequences for public agendas and public policymaking.

A few investigators have pondered whether associations with mailing-list constituencies have the potential to be more inclusive than old-fashioned chapter-based groups. At first glance, it might seem so. Modern advocacy groups are free from local networks that might be dominated by entrenched oligarchies. Presumably, any American, no matter how marginal in his or her community or workplace, could send in a bit of money and follow the activities of an advocacy group. As Minkoff (1997) argues, because mailing-list groups can speak for widely shared but not necessarily locally important values or interests, in theory they have great potential to be popularly representative or empowering.

With or without mass affiliates recruited through the mail, modern advocacy groups often represent important values with wide public sympathy (Berry 1999; Inglehart 1997). When it comes to direct affiliation with advocacy groups, however, available evidence suggests that mailing-list "members" are disproportionately highly educated and economically privileged. For instance, in a 1982 survey of the mailing-list adherents of the public interest advocacy group Common Cause (McFarland 1984, 48–49), 42.6 percent reported having completed a graduate or professional degree; 14.5 percent had attained some graduate or professional education short of a degree; and another 18.7 percent had attained a college

TABLE 19.2   *Large Membership Associations in U.S. History*

Organization	Founding	Ending	National, State, and Local Units?	Involved in Politics?	Decades Above 1 Percent of Men, Women, or Adults
Ancient and Accepted Free Masons	1733, Boston				1810s to present
Independent Order of Odd Fellows	1819, Baltimore		Yes		1840s to 1950s
American Temperance Society	1826, Boston	1865	Yes	Yes	1830s to 1840s
General Union . . . Observance of Christian Sabbath	1828, New York	1832		Yes	1830s
American Anti-Slavery Society	1833, Boston	1870	Yes	Yes	1830s
Improved Order of Red Men	1834, Baltimore		Yes		1900s to 1920s
Washington Temperance Societies	1840, Baltimore	c. 1848		Yes	1840s
The Order of the Sons of Temperance	1842, New York	c. 1970	Yes	Yes	1840s to 1850s
Independent Order of Good Templars	1851, Utica, New York		Yes	Yes	1860s to 1870s
Young Men's Christian Association (YMCA)	1851, Boston		Yes	War partner	1890s to present
Junior Order of United American Mechanics	1853, Philadelphia	c. 1970	Yes	Yes	1920s to 1930s
National Education Association	1857, Philadelphia		Yes	Yes	1970s to present
Knights of Pythias	1864, Washington, D.C.		Yes		1870s to 1930s
Grand Army of the Republic (GAR)	1866, Decatur, Illinois	1956	Yes	Yes	1860s to 1900s
Benevolent and Protective Order of Elks	1867, New York				1900s to present
Patrons of Husbandry (National Grange)	1867, Washington, D.C.		Yes	Yes	1870s, 1910s to 1920s
Order of the Eastern Star	1868, New York		Yes		1910s to present
Ancient Order of United Workmen (AOUW)	1868, Meadville, Pennsylvania		Yes		1880s to 1900s
Knights of Labor	1869, Philadelphia	1917		Yes	1880s
National Rifle Association (NRA)	1871, New York		Yes	Yes	1980s to present
Nobles of the Mystic Shrine	1872, New York				1910s to 1980s
Woman's Christian Temperance Union	1874, Cleveland		Yes	Yes	1910s to 1930s
Royal Arcanum	1877, Boston		Yes		1900s
Farmers' Alliance	1877, Lampasas, Texas	1900	Yes	Yes	1880s to 1890s
Maccabees	1878, Port Huron, Michigan		Yes		1900s to 1910s
Christian Endeavor	1881, Portland, Maine		Yes		1880s to about 1920s
American Red Cross	1881, Washington, D.C.			War partner	1910s to present

Association	Founded				Years as large association
Knights of Columbus	1882, New Haven, Connecticut		War partner		1910s to present
Modern Woodmen of America	1883, Lyons, Iowa		Yes		1890s to 1930s
Colored Farmers' Alliance	1886, Houston, Texas	1892	Yes		1880s to 1890s
American Federation of Labor (AFL)	1886, Columbus, Ohio		Yes		1880s to present
American Protective Association	1887, Clinton, Iowa	c. 1911	Yes		1890s
Woman's Missionary Union	1888, Richmond, Virginia		Yes		1920s to present
Loyal Order of Moose	1888, Louisville, Kentucky		Yes		1910s to present
National American Woman Suffrage Association	1890, Washington, D.C.	1920	Yes		1910s
Woodmen of the World	1890, Omaha, Nebraska		Yes		1900 to 1930s
General Federation of Women's Clubs	1890, New York		Yes		1900s to 1970s
American Bowling Congress	1895, New York		Yes		1930s to present
National Congress of Mothers (PTA)	1897, Washington, D.C.		Yes		1920s to present
Fraternal Order of Eagles	1898, Seattle, Washington		Yes		1900s to 1980s
German American National Alliance	1901, Philadelphia	1918	Yes		1910s
Aid Association for Lutherans	1902, Appleton, Wisconsin		Yes		1970s
American Automobile Association (AAA)	1902, Chicago		Yes		1920s to present
Boy Scouts of America	1910, Washington, D.C.		War partner		1930s to present
Veterans of Foreign Wars	1913, Denver		Yes		1940s to present
Ku Klux Klan (Second)	1915, Atlanta	1944	Yes		1920s
Women's International Bowling Congress	1916, St. Louis		Yes		1950s to present
American Legion	1919, Minneapolis		Yes		1920s to present
American Farm Bureau Federation	1919, Chicago		Yes		1920s, 1940s to present
Old Age Revolving Pensions, Ltd. (Townsend)	1934, Long Beach, California	1953			1930s
Congress of Industrial Organizations (CIO)	1938, Pittsburgh	1955			1930s to 1950s
March of Dimes	1938, New York				1950s
United Methodist Women	1939, Atlanta				1940s to present
American Association of Retired Persons (AARP)	1958, Washington, D.C.			Yes	1970s to present
National Right to Life Committee	1973, Detroit			Yes	1970s to present
Mothers Against Drunk Driving	1980, Sacramento, California			Yes	1980s to present
Greenpeace USA	1988, Washington, D.C.			Yes	1990s
Christian Coalition	1989, Washington, D.C.			Yes	1990s to present

Source: Author's compilation, Harvard Civic Engagement Project.

TABLE 19.3   *U.S. Membership Associations Enrolling at Least 1 Percent of U.S. Adults in 1955*

Name (Year Founded)	Membership	Percentage of Adults Who Belong	Number of Local Units
AFL-CIO (1886)	12,622,000	12.05	n/a
National Congress of Parents and Teachers (1897)	9,409,282	8.99	40,396 local PTAs
American Automobile Association (1902)	5,009,346	4.78	464 clubs
Ancient and Accepted Free Masons (1733)	4,009,925	7.86 (m)	15,662 lodges
American Legion (1919)	2,795,990	5.48 (m)	16,937 posts
Order of the Eastern Star (1868)	2,365,778	2.26	12,277 chapters
Young Men's Christian Association (1851)	2,222,618	2.12	1,502 local YMCAs
United Methodist Women (1939)	1,811,600	3.37 (w)	n/a
American Bowling Congress (1895)	1,741,000	3.41 (m)	43,090 leagues
American Farm Bureau Federation (1919)	1,623,222	1.55	3,000 local farm bureaus (est.)
Boy Scouts of America (1910)	1,353,370 (est.)	1.29	53,804 local troops
Woman's Missionary Union (1888)	1,245,358	2.32 (w)	65,132 church WMU organizations
Benevolent and Protective Order of Elks (1867)	1,149,613	2.25 (m)	1,720 lodges
Veterans of Foreign Wars (1913)	1,086,859	2.13 (m)	7,000 posts (est.)
Loyal Order of Moose (1888)	843,697	1.65 (m)	1,767 lodges
General Federation of Women's Clubs (1890)	857,915	1.6 (w)	15,168 clubs
Knights of Columbus (1882)	832,601	1.63 (m)	3,083 councils
Nobles of the Mystic Shrine (1872)	761,179	1.49 (m)	166 temples
Fraternal Order of Eagles (1898)	760,007	1.49 (m)	1,566 aeries
Women's International Bowling Congress (1916)	706,193	1.31 (w)	22,842 leagues
Independent Order of Odd Fellows (1819)	543,171	1.07 (m)	7,572 lodges
American Red Cross (1881)[a]	—	—	3,713 chapters
March of Dimes (1938)[a]	—	—	3,090 chapters

Source: Author's compilation, Harvard Civic Engagement Project.

Notes: (m) indicates men only; (w) indicates women only; (est.) indicates a best available estimate; n/a indicates data not available at this time.

[a]Membership data are not given for the Red Cross and March of Dimes because they include contributors as well as participants.

degree. The median Common Cause member reported a family income 85 percent above the national median of that time. Similarly, according to a 1978 survey, more than half the members of the National Abortion Rights Action League (NARAL) had "at least some graduate training" (McCarthy 1987, 60). And an early 1980s study of recruitment to the environmental movement took advantage of the fact that some environmental associations recruited adherents through the mail, while others had chapters and attracted members through social networks. Exploring the possibility that mailing-list recruitment might enlarge civic participation, Kenneth Godwin and Robert Cameron Mitchell (1984) expected that mailing-list recruits might reach more marginal and less-privileged people. But instead, direct-mail recruits to environmentalism were more likely to enjoy high incomes and be longer-term residents of established communities than people recruited through social networks.

Although more research needs to be done, it is safe to hypothesize that modern information technologies allow the managers of professional advocacy groups to be "rational prospectors" who "hunt where the ducks are" (as argued by Schlozman, Verba, and Brady 1999, 446–50; see also McCarthy 1987, 59–61; Schier 2000; Crenson and Ginsberg 2002). Highly educated Americans are the citizens most likely to understand the specialized causes or issues that contemporary professional advocacy associations pursue. And of course, well-established Americans with high incomes are the folks who can write big checks. Such checks are sought not just as "membership dues." Indeed, references to "members" and "dues" are largely symbolic, because modern advocacy groups churn out huge volumes of mail and expect only tiny response rates from adherents who are constantly in flux (Bosso 1995; Godwin 1992; Johnson 1998). In addition, advocacy groups use issue-oriented mailings and phone calls to take advantage of visible public developments—especially those that can be portrayed as threats to the favorite cause. Notified of a threatening occurrence, adherents are sometimes asked to contact public officials, and they are almost always requested to send extra contributions to the national advocacy office. According to the 1970s survey of NARAL members (McCarthy 1987, 60), some 30 percent of the association's mailing-list adherents responded to such appeals by giving more than the standard "membership fee." Obviously, privileged and attentive people are exactly the sorts the national advocacy groups want on their contact lists if they are to succeed at fund-raising through such repeated "emergency appeals"—exquisitely timed to take advantage of crises and legislative struggles.

Leaving aside the immediate participatory effects of new advocacy associations, what about their broader impact on public policymaking? Have recent associational changes improved the democratic responsiveness of U.S. public policymaking? As associations with popular reach atrophy and professionally run groups with relatively privileged constituencies multiply, what difference has it made for public debates and legislative developments? Systematic evidence is virtually nonexistent, but there are some hypotheses and empirical hints.

In a conceptually very interesting example, a comparison of "pro-life" and "pro-choice" mobilizations in the U.S. abortion controversy, the sociologist John McCarthy (1987) first measures public "sentiments" as reflected in national opinion surveys. At the time he wrote, these results showed that pro-choice sentiments were considerably stronger among the U.S. public, yet organized mobilization magnified the pro-life impact on public agendas and legislation far beyond what was achieved by the more popular pro-choice efforts. To see why, McCarthy argues, we must notice the gap between social movements that can build on already existing social institutions and social networks, on the one hand, and "thin infrastructure" movements run by "professional social movement organizations" that use direct-mail techniques, on the other. Although McCarthy does not deny that thin infrastructure movements can make some headway in translating widespread mass sentiment into publicity and legislative results, he sees them as far less effective, relative to the proportion of citizens who may hold a given position, than movements that can build on already organized, network-rich institutions and associations. The clear implication of this argument for our overview of the changing U.S. associational universe is that the advocacy explosion may not have generated as much new democratic leverage as some of its enthusiasts (for example, Berry 1999) believe.

America's capacity to use government for socioeconomically redistributive purposes has almost certainly been diminished in some part because of recent civic transformations—changes that, on the whole, have enhanced the role of professional societies and professionally run advocacy groups while diminishing the resources and clout of unions and cross-class associations. In a very general sense, membership-oriented associations are much more likely to maintain grassroots organizational infrastructures that can invite people personally into electoral as well as associational participation.[6] But there is also the question of *what types* of membership associations are expanding and contracting. In recent times evangelical Protestant churches have expanded their memberships and organizing activities both in community life and in national politics (Schlozman, Verba, and Brady 1999; Wilcox 1996; Wuthnow 1999), while trade unions and many other kinds of popular membership groups have contracted. Since the 1960s especially, U.S. white evangelical churches have been opposed to socioeconomic redistribution and very critical of a strong governmental role in social provision.

Unions, by contrast, more often mobilize popular constituencies electorally as well as in workplaces to demand an active government role in social redistribution. A recent study investigating variations among nations and across the states of the United States argues that union decline helps to explain shrinking electorates. Institutional procedures affect voter turnout, argue Benjamin Radcliff and Patricia Davis (2000, 140), but so does union strength. "Rates of unionization are important determinants of the size of the electorate," they explain, "and, thus, the extent to which the full citizenry is engaged in collective decisions. . . . Declines in labor organization . . . mean that the electorate will increasingly over-represent higher-status individuals. The result, presuming that elected officials are more responsive to those who vote than those who do not, will be public policies less consistent with the interests of the working class." Furthermore, "given that unions also contribute to the maintenance of left party ideology, a declining labor movement implies that left parties may move toward the center. Shrinking union memberships . . . thus contribute to a further narrowing of ideological space."

The dwindling of once-huge cross-class membership federations may have had similar effects. Ideologically, many classic voluntary federations downplayed partisan causes and trumpeted ideals of fellowship and community service, so their decline has left the way clear for alternative modes of public discourse that are less likely to facilitate social inclusion or transpartisan compromises. Modern movements and advocacy associations often use "rights talk" and champion highly specialized identities, issues, and causes. Individuals and previously marginal people have sometimes been newly empowered, as Michael Schudson (1998) and Debra Minkoff (1997) eloquently argue. But modern advocacy tactics, stressing differences between groups and the activation of strong sentiments shared by relatively homogeneous followings, may also have furthered the artificial polarization in American public life (as suggested by Fiorina 1999; McCarthy 1987; and Skerry 1997). Modern advocacy proliferations may also have led to "many movements" but "no majority," in the words of Karen Paget (1990), and the "twilight of common dreams," in the eloquent phrasing of Todd Gitlin (1995).

Historically, popular and cross-class voluntary membership federations championed inclusive public social provision, but contemporary advocacy groups are much less likely to do so, as Skocpol (1999, 502–3) dramatizes in her contrast of the associational politics surrounding the enactment of the GI Bill of 1944 and the defeat of the Clinton proposal for universal health insurance coverage in 1993–1994. Back in the 1940s, a large national membership federation, the (otherwise conservative) American Legion, drafted, lobbied for, and helped to implement the GI Bill, which was one of the most generous and inclusive federal social programs ever enacted (Bennett 1996; Skocpol 1997). By contrast, in the early 1990s, when the Clinton administration tried to devise and enact universal health insurance coverage, specialized professional and advocacy associations influenced the drafting of legislation in ways that defied broad public preferences. Then hundreds of lobbying groups mobilized to stymie and defeat the resulting legislative proposal (for the full story, see Skocpol 1996).

Perhaps the most intriguing empirical hints on the distributive effects of contemporary civic changes appear in Jeffrey Berry's recent book *The New Liberalism* (1999). As noted earlier, Berry is very appreciative of the democratizing impact of new public interest advocacy groups; he stresses the ways in which they champion middle-class "postmaterial" values. As Berry's longitudinal research shows, professionally run public interest groups have increasingly made postmaterial quality-of-life causes such as environmentalism more visible, and they have been prevailing more often after going head to head with business interests in national legislative battles. But Berry also offers some more discouraging evidence about the democratic effects of advocacy efforts (55–57). Recent gains by citizens' associations have not just come at the expense of business; they may also have crowded out advocacy by unions and other groups speaking for the interests and values of blue-collar and/or poor Americans. As professionally run citizens' associations achieved heightened media coverage and legislative victories for "postmaterial" issues from the 1960s to the late 1980s, coverage of and legislative victories for redistributive "social justice" issues were on the wane. Furthermore, Berry shows that liberal-leaning citizen advocacy groups have become *less* likely over time to ally with traditional liberal groups on behalf of redistributive social programs.

Advocacy groups oriented toward upper-middle-class values, interests, and identities may, in short, be increasingly willing to go it alone, shaping public agendas and legislation in ways that may diminish the impact of for-profit business interests in regulatory battles but may also reinforce a general upward tilt in socioeconomically relevant public policymaking. "Liberal citizen groups have concentrated on issues that appeal to their middle-class supporters," writes Berry (1999, 57). "The data collected indicate unequivocally that as the new left grew and grew, the old left was left increasingly isolated."

Interestingly, a similar conclusion emerges from a study by the sociologists Craig Jenkins and Abigail Halcli (1999, 230) of the up to 1 percent of all private foundation grants that channel resources to "previously unorganized or politically excluded" groups. In 1953 there were 4 grants of this sort totaling $85,700 (all figures in current dollars); by 1960 the number had grown modestly to 21 grants totaling just over $250,000. After the 1960s, as professional advocacy groups proliferated, social movement philanthropy also swelled; by 1990, 3,418 grants channeled over $88 million in aid to various causes. From this we might conclude that memberless private foundations did much to democratize U.S. civic life—and this is certainly partly true. Nevertheless, as figure 19.9 suggests, civic priorities changed as the volume of social movement philanthropy increased. According to data collected by Jenkins and Halcli (1999, 240), the overall philanthropic effort shifted from the 1950s and 1960s to the 1990s away from programs intended to further minority rights and economic justice toward more middle-class causes such as environmentalism, consumer rights, peace and world order, and women's rights.

In short, the empirical hints in both Berry (1999, 55–57) and Jenkins and Halcli (1999) point toward a transformed American civic universe that may do more to enhance the voice and leverage of the broad middle class than it does to promote redistribution of participation and leverage toward the working class and the least privileged. This fits the

FIGURE 19.9   *The Changing Priorities of Social Movement Philanthropy, 1953 to 1990*

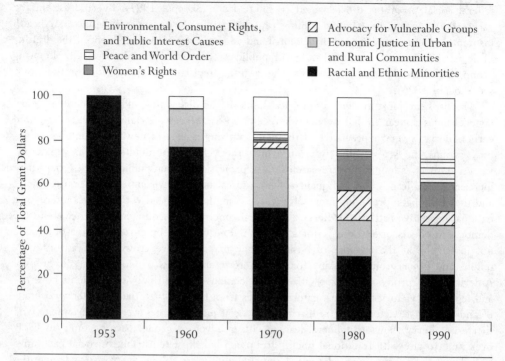

Source: Jenkins and Halcli (1999, 240, table 10.4).

overall picture of associational change we have pieced together from all of the organizational studies reviewed in this section. Professional membership societies have held their own to a greater degree than membership groups that work for the less privileged or are open to Americans across class lines. At the same time, membership groups in general have faded, while professionally run groups, aiming to "speak for" people who may or may not be "thinly" involved as monetary contributors, have proliferated. Variety and voice have certainly been enhanced in this new associational universe forged by the organizing upsurges of the 1960s to the 1990s. But the gains in voice and public leverage have probably accrued mainly to the top third of American society, while the rest have relatively fewer associations representing their values and interests and enjoy dwindling opportunities for active associational participation.

CONCLUSION

As I wrap up this review of the literatures on civic participation and associational changes, it is worth underlining that any insights this chapter has achieved come from *synthesizing* findings that are usually kept separate in scholarly debates. Behavioralists and organizational analysts rarely take note of each other's findings, let alone combine the survey techniques preferred by the former with the historical investigations and organizational data favored by the latter. But it is impossible to grasp the meanings of recent American civic transformations—including the observation that Americans are participating less while organizing more—without synthesizing findings and combining methods. The best opportunity for theoretical advance, moreover, lies in using data on the changing U.S. associational universe to explore the hypotheses I presented in the first section. Revisiting these hypotheses largely derived from the behavioralist civic voluntarism model developed by Sidney Verba and his assorted collaborators suggests that recent changes in the mix of nationally active U.S. voluntary associations may have quite *inegalitarian consequences* for civic engagement and democratic possibilities. Smaller rather than larger associations have proliferated, and groups involving popular or cross-class memberships have lost greater ground than elite membership groups. Whether they are nominally membership groups or not, newly prevalent civic entities are more reliant on contributions of money by patrons or constituents than on contributions of time by participating members. And recently proliferating associations of all sorts are less likely than older chapter-based membership federations to stress values of shared citizenship and to extend opportunities for participation or leadership to ordinary Americans.

Despite the length of this chapter, we have learned that available data are often too general or short-term to pin down the nature, causes, and consequences of long-term shifts in associational involvements and civic participation. This is especially true for individual-level studies; I doubt that it will be possible to go much beyond Costa and Kahn (2003b) in squeezing out insights about participatory decline in general. Future progress with available surveys can primarily be made by looking at trends for major types of voluntary groups— such as professional societies, fraternal groups, and church-connected groups—and by collating trends in reported individual affiliations with what we can learn about trends in organizational populations. It may also be possible to do more with differences in group affiliations by gender, race, and college-educated versus non-college-educated. In the large scheme of things, however, the mid-1970s to mid-1990s period for which General Social Survey trends are available for specific kinds of associational affiliations is a very short stretch of time. To better understand long-term civic changes, their causes and consequences, researchers will need to cool their romance with individual-level data and national sample surveys. If the data were not collected in the past, they cannot be now. We must figure out other ways to get at relevant trends and transformations.

Possibilities for more rigorous measurements and analyses of changes in the universe of U.S. voluntary associations qua organizations are actually brighter than possibilities for squeezing many more insights out of survey archives. Two kinds of further data collection are especially likely to help a variety of researchers. In one project, researchers at the University of Pennsylvania, led by the political scientist Frank Baumgartner and the sociologist John McCarthy, plan to computerize all the information in the *Encyclopedia of Associations,* 1955 to the present, on types, foundings, and incidence of various kinds of national associations. Once these data are available, it will be possible to explore the changing mix of associations in much greater detail.

Another project is one that I have launched in collaboration with Kristin Goss. It will allow exploration of the interaction of socioeconomic and gender transformations in American civic life. Goss and I have discovered a sufficient temporal range and informational richness of directories and other sources to enable us to assemble a relatively complete timeline of all the female-led and women-serving voluntary associations (including religious groups and female auxiliaries) throughout U.S. history, from early colonial times to the present. We expect to be able to identify groups by founding dates, structures, purposes, and constituencies, and we will do our best to document rough membership trends for as many associations as possible. This dataset will allow us to probe exactly how women's civic activities as organizers and joiners have changed over the long run, and especially during and after the feminist and labor force revolutions of the late twentieth century. We will be able to collate such organizational data with survey data about women's participation and attitudes, as well as explore relationships between changes in female voluntary associations and shifts in the agendas of issues publicly debated and addressed in U.S. politics. Given that women traditionally organized and joined membership federations that stressed cross-class fellowship and non-market-oriented public values, it will be fascinating to learn how all this changed during the recent era, marked by the proliferation of professionally led feminist advocacy groups. Are American women's voluntary federations today addressing the issues that most women care about? What has been the role of U.S. women's associations in various periods in shaping the changing agendas of public debate and legislation?

Finally, new kinds of data can also be discovered and marshaled, especially to explore the critical and changing roles of relatively privileged elites in U.S. civic life. To the degree that new civic inequalities have emerged in our time, they may have followed rather abrupt shifts in elite joining as well as organizing behavior, especially from the 1970s on. Tracing patterns of associational emergence may make it possible to see what kinds of people took the lead in launching new kinds of associations in late-twentieth-century America. In addition, we have more to learn about the new kinds of memberships and affiliations favored by relatively privileged Americans. Mass survey data can give us some idea of when college-educated Americans (compared with the non-college-educated) withdrew from certain broad types of associations and joined others (see Skocpol 2003, 186–88, figs. 5.1 and 5.2). But we really need to know much more about specific groups and types of groups—such as advocacy versus membership associations, cross-class versus elite-only groups—than we are likely to learn from broad national surveys. Done with care, retrospective interviews might offer rich data on people's changing affiliations and activities. The political scientist Suzanne Mettler (2002) has successfully conducted such interviews with World War II military veterans, showing that users of the educational provisions of the GI Bill ended up joining more voluntary associations than non-users. She is currently examining trends in the various kinds of associations that World War II veterans joined during the postwar era.

Another possibility is to use repeatedly published elite self-portraits to get at long-term civic trends. To make this work, researchers must discover sources in which recognizable kinds of leaders have been asked to record their associational memberships and other kinds of civic affiliations in roughly the same format over many decades. Such data turn out to be few and far between, but some are certainly to be found. Thus, in one such project, intended to discover how much can be done, my collaborators and I have found rich associational data and personal information in the biographical compendia repeatedly published since the early and mid-twentieth century for state legislators in Massachusetts, Maine, Illinois, and North Carolina, most of whom were businesspeople or professionals before assuming public office. Once these data are computerized for office-holders in specific years, the full range of specific associations to which representatives claimed affiliations can be classified in various ways, setting the stage for longitudinally sensitive statistical and qualitative explorations. When did elites switch from membership groups to other sorts of civic affiliations, or from cross-class to elite-led or elite-exclusive groups? Such questions can be explored for individuals of different ages and other characteristics, and they can be explored for entire sets of legislators who held office at different points in time. Preliminary findings (see Skocpol 2003, 186–96, figs. 5.3 through 5.8) suggest that between 1960 and 1980 state senators abruptly stopped affiliating with cross-class membership associations and instead started claiming memberships on the boards of nonprofit social service and cultural institutions. Results also suggest that state senators abandoned cross-class membership groups *sooner* than citizens in general. Elites were leading rather than following popular civic trends.

Ultimately, it may be possible to explore the relative timing of the elite-level trends documented in these ways with national trends measured through surveys and characterizations of shifting organizational populations. In social science, it is often the case that the most convincing findings emerge from triangulation among diverse data sources, at the intersection of studies using various kinds of data and analytic methodologies. Nowhere is this more the case than in studies of America's changing civic democracy. We see the changing forest as well as the individual trees most clearly when we combine behavioralist and organizational approaches. Such triangulation is certainly essential if we are to grasp the ways in which contemporary U.S. civic life has become more and less equal.

NOTES

1. For quiet acknowledgment of this omission, see Putnam (2000, 487, n. 9).

2. For insightful discussions of these and other problems with traditional surveys about types of group memberships, see Baumgartner and Walker (1988, 1990) and Smith (1990).

3. Interestingly, cross-sectional studies by political scientists take a more skeptical view of the value of social homogeneity in promoting civic engagement. Rodney Hero (1998, 2003) finds that high social capital states within the United States often have relatively poor outcomes on various measures of racial and ethnic equity. And Eric Oliver (2001) finds that homogeneous U.S. suburbs tend to dampen civic engagement. With racial and income groups increasingly segregated into different governmental jurisdictions, he suggests, many issues that once enlivened the politics of smaller towns are now played out as battles among governments, discouraging citizen activity.

4. Putnam actually understates the contrast, because Rotary is a relatively small and elitist "old-fashioned" chapter association. As table 19.3 suggests, larger, more popularly rooted chapter federations have often had even more extensive national networks of chapters.

5. To be sure, college-educated women and men have also joined unions, especially public-sector unions, in substantial numbers during recent decades. As once-massive and predominant industrial unions have declined, modest unionization has occurred in the service and public sectors.

6. On the greater reach and efficacy of personal invitations to voters, compared with the more impersonal methods favored by centralized associations, see Gerber and Green (2000).

REFERENCES

Alesina, Alberto, and Eliana La Ferrara. 2000. "Participation in Heterogeneous Communities." *Quarterly Journal of Economics* 115(3): 847–904.

Almond, Gabriel A., and Sidney Verba. 1963. *The Civic Culture: Political Attitudes and Democracy in Five Nations.* Princeton, N.J.: Princeton University Press.

Babchuk, Nicholas, and Alan Booth. 1969. "Voluntary Association Membership: A Longitudinal Analysis." *American Sociological Review* 34(February): 31–45.

Baumgartner, Frank R., and Bryan D. Jones. 1993. *Agendas and Instability in American Politics.* Chicago: University of Chicago Press.

Baumgartner, Frank R., and Jack L. Walker. 1988. "Survey Research and Membership in Voluntary Associations." *American Journal of Political Science* 32(4): 908–28.

———. 1990. "Response to Smith's 'Trends in Voluntary Group Membership: Comments on Baumgartner and Walker': Measurement Validity and the Continuity of Results in Survey Research." *American Journal of Political Science* 34(3): 662–70.

Beem, Christopher. 1999. *The Necessity of Politics: Reclaiming American Public Life.* Chicago: University of Chicago Press.

Bennett, Michael J. 1996. *When Dreams Came True: The GI Bill and the Making of Modern America.* Washington, D.C.: Brassey's.

Berry, Jeffrey M. 1977. *Lobbying for the People: The Political Behavior of Public Interest Groups.* Princeton, N.J.: Princeton University Press.

———. 1997. *The Interest Group Society,* 3rd ed. New York: Longman.

———. 1999. *The New Liberalism and the Rising Power of Citizen Groups.* Washington, D.C.: Brookings Institution.

Bosso, Christopher J. 1991. "Adaptation and Change in the Environmental Movement." In *Interest Group Politics,* 3rd ed., edited by Allen J. Cigler and Burdett A. Loomis. Washington, D.C.: CQ Press.

———. 1995. "The Color of Money: Environmental Groups and the Pathologies of Fund Raising." In *Interest Group Politics,* 4th ed., edited by Allen J. Cigler and Burdett A. Loomis. Washington, D.C.: CQ Press.

Brady, Henry E., Kay Lehman Schlozman, Sidney Verba, and Laurel Elms. 2000. "Who Bowls? Class, Race, and Participatory Inequality—1973–1994." Unpublished draft. University of California, Berkeley.

———. 2002. "Who Bowls? The (Un)Changing Stratification of Participation." In *Understanding Public Opinion,* 2nd ed., edited by Barbara Norrander and Clyde Wilcox. Washington, D.C.: CQ Press.

Bryce, James. 1895. *The American Commonwealth,* 3rd ed., vol. 2. New York: Macmillan.

Burns, Nancy, Kay Lehman Schlozman, and Sidney Verba. 2001. *The Private Roots of Public Action: Gender, Equality, and Political Participation.* Cambridge, Mass.: Harvard University Press.

Bushee, Frederick A. 1945. "Social Organization in a Small City." *American Journal of Sociology* 51(3): 217–26.

Campbell, Andrea Louise. 2003. *How Policies Make Citizens: Senior Political Activism and the American Welfare State.* Princeton, N.J.: Princeton University Press.

Charles, Jeffrey A. 1993. *Service Clubs in American Society: Rotary, Kiwanis, and Lions.* Urbana: University of Illinois Press.

Conway, M. Margaret, and Joanne Connor Green. 1998. "Political Action Committees and Campaign Finance." In *Interest Group Politics,* 5th ed., edited by Allan J. Cigler and Burdett A. Loomis. Washington, D.C.: CQ Press.

Costa, Dora L., and Matthew E. Kahn. 2003a. "Civic Engagement and Community Heterogeneity: An Economist's Perspective." *Perspectives on Politics* 1(1): 103–11.

———. 2003b. "Understanding the American Decline in Social Capital, 1952 to 1998." *Kyklos* 56(1): 17–46.

Costain, Ann N. 1981. "Representing Women: The Transition from Social Movement to Interest Group." *Western Political Quarterly* 34(March): 100–13.

Crenson, Matthew A., and Benjamin Ginsberg. 2002. *Downsizing Democracy: How America Sidelined Its Citizens and Privatized Its Public.* Baltimore: Johns Hopkins University Press.

Dunlap, Riley E., and Angela G. Mertig, eds. 1992. *American Environmentalism: The U.S. Environmental Movement, 1970 to 1990.* New York: Taylor and Francis.

Encyclopedia of Associations, vol. 1, *National Associations.* 1959–1999. Detroit: Gale Research Co.

Fiorina, Morris P. 1999. "Extreme Voices: A Dark Side of Civic Engagement." In *Civic Engagement in American Democracy,* edited by Theda Skocpol and Morris P. Fiorina. Washington, D.C., and New York: Brookings Institution and Russell Sage Foundation.

Foundation Center. 2002. *Statistics on Foundations.* Available at: http://fdcenter.org/fc__stats.

Gamm, Gerald, and Robert D. Putnam. 1999. "The Growth of Voluntary Associations in America, 1840 to 1940," *Journal of Interdisciplinary History* 29(4): 511–57.

Gerber, Alan S., and Donald P. Green. 2000. "The Effects of Canvassing, Telephone Calls, and Direct Mail on Voter Turnout: A Field Experiment." *American Political Science Review* 94 (3): 653–63.

Gitlin, Todd. 1995. *The Twilight of Common Dreams: Why America Is Wracked by Culture Wars.* New York: Metropolitan Books/Henry Holt.

Godwin, R. Kenneth. 1992. "Money, Technology, and Political Interests: The Direct Marketing of Politics." In *The Politics of Interests: Interest Groups Transformed,* edited by Mark P. Petracca. Boulder, Colo.: Westview Press.

Godwin, R. Kenneth, and Robert Cameron Mitchell. 1984. "The Implications of Direct Mail for Political Organizations." *Social Science Quarterly* 65(3): 829–39.

Hausknecht, Murray. 1962. *The Joiners: A Sociological Description of Voluntary Association Membership in the United States.* New York: Bedminster Press.

Hayes, Michael T. 1986. "The New Group Universe." In *Interest Group Politics,* 2nd ed., edited by Allan J. Cigler and Burdett A. Loomis. Washington, D.C.: CQ Press.

Hero, Rodney E. 1998. *Faces of Inequality: Social Diversity in American Politics*. New York: Oxford University Press.

———. 2003. "Social Capital and Racial Inequality in America." *Perspectives on Politics* 1(1): 113–22.

Inglehart, Ronald. 1997. *Modernization and Postmodernization: Cultural, Economic, and Political Change in Forty-three Societies*. Princeton, N.J.: Princeton University Press.

Jenkins, J. Craig. 1998. "Channeling Social Protest: Foundation Patronage of Contemporary Social Movements." In *Private Action and the Public Good,* edited by Walter W. Powell and Elisabeth S. Clemens. New Haven, Conn.: Yale University Press.

Jenkins, J. Craig, and Abigail Halcli. 1999. "Grassrooting the System? The Development and Impact of Social Movement Philanthropy, 1953 to 1990." In *Philanthropic Foundations: New Scholarship, New Possibilities.* Bloomington: Indiana University Press.

Johnson, Paul E. 1998. "Interest Group Recruiting: Finding Members and Keeping Them." In *Interest Group Politics,* 5th ed., edited by Allen J. Cigler and Burdett A. Loomis. Washington, D.C.: CQ Press.

Joyce, Michael S., and William A. Schambra. 1996. "A New Civic Life." In *To Empower People,* 2nd ed., edited by Michael Novak. Washington, D.C.: AEI Press.

Judis, John B. 1992. "The Pressure Elite: Inside the Narrow World of Advocacy Group Politics." *The American Prospect* 9(Spring): 15–29.

Loomis, Burdett A., and Allan J. Cigler. 1998. "Introduction: The Changing Nature of Interest Group Politics." In *Interest Group Politics,* 5th ed., edited by Allan J. Cigler and Burdett A. Loomis. Washington, D.C.: CQ Press.

McCarthy, John D. 1987. "Pro-Life and Pro-Choice Mobilization: Infrastructure Deficits and New Technologies." In *Social Movements in an Organizational Society,* edited by Mayer N. Zald and John D. McCarthy. New Brunswick, N.J.: Transaction Books.

McFarland, Andrew S. 1984. *Common Cause: Lobbying in the Public Interest*. Chatham, N.J.: Chatham House Publishers.

Mettler, Suzanne. 2002. "Bringing the State Back into Civic Engagement: Policy Feedback Effects of the GI Bill for World War II Veterans." *American Political Science Review* 96(2): 351–65.

Minkoff, Debra C. 1995. *Organizing for Equality: The Evolution of Women's and Racial-Ethnic Organizations in America, 1955 to 1985*. New Brunswick, N.J.: Temple University Press.

———. 1997. "Producing Social Capital: National Social Movements and Civil Society." *American Behavioral Scientist* 40(5): 606–19.

Minnis, Myhra S. 1953. "Cleavage in Women's Organizations: A Reflection of the Social Structure of a City." *American Sociological Review* 18(1): 47–53.

Mitchell, Robert Cameron, Angela C. Mertig, and Riley E. Dunlap. 1992. "Twenty Years of Environmental Mobilization: Trends Among National Environmental Organizations." In *American Environmentalism: The U.S. Environmental Movement, 1970 to 1990,* edited by Riley E. Dunlap and Angela E. Mertig. New York: Taylor and Francis.

Morris, Charles R. 1996. *The AARP: America's Most Powerful Lobby and the Clash of Generations*. New York: Times Books.

Oliver, J. Eric. 2001. *Democracy in Suburbia*. Princeton, N.J.: Princeton University Press.

Paget, Karen. 1990. "Citizen Organizing: Many Movements, No Majority." *The American Prospect* 2(Summer): 115–28.

Pettinico, George. 1996. "Civic Participation Is Alive and Well in Today's Environmental Groups." *The Public Perspective* 7(4): 27–30.

Putnam, Robert D. 1993. *Making Democracy Work: Civic Traditions in Modern Italy*. Princeton, N.J.: Princeton University Press.

———. 2000. *Bowling Alone: The Collapse and Revival of American Community*. New York: Simon & Schuster.

Radcliff, Benjamin, and Patricia Davis. 2000. "Labor Organization and Electoral Participation in the Industrial Democracies." *American Journal of Political Science* 44(1): 132–41.

Ricci, David M. 1993. *The Transformation of American Politics: The New Washington and the Rise of Think Tanks*. New Haven, Conn.: Yale University Press.

Rich, Andrew, and R. Kent Weaver. 1998. "Advocates and Analysts: Think Tanks and the Politicization of Expertise." In *Interest Group Politics,* 5th ed., edited by Allan J. Cigler and Burdett A. Loomis. Washington, D.C.: CQ Press.

Rosenstone, Steven J., and John Mark Hansen. 1993. *Mobilization, Participation, and Democracy in America.* New York: Macmillan.

Sandel, Michael J. 1996. *Democracy's Discontent: America in Search of a Public Philosophy.* Cambridge, Mass.: Harvard University Press.

Schier, Steven. 2000. *By Invitation Only: The Rise of Exclusive Politics in the United States.* Pittsburgh: University of Pittsburgh Press.

Schlesinger, Arthur M., Sr. 1944. "Biography of a Nation of Joiners." *American Historical Review* 50(1): 1–25.

Schlozman, Kay Lehman. 1990. "Representing Women in Washington: Sisterhood and Pressure Politics." In *Women, Politics, and Change,* edited by Louise A. Tilly and Patricia Gurin. New York: Russell Sage Foundation.

Schlozman, Kay Lehman, and John C. Tierney. 1986. *Organized Interests and American Democracy.* New York: Harper & Row.

Schlozman, Kay Lehman, Sidney Verba, and Henry E. Brady. 1999. "Civic Participation and the Equality Problem." In *Civic Engagement in American Democracy,* edited by Theda Skocpol and Morris P. Fiorina. Washington, D.C., and New York: Brookings Institution and Russell Sage Foundation.

Schudson, Michael. 1996. "What If Civic Life Didn't Die?" *The American Prospect* 25(March–April): 17–20.

———. 1998. *The Good Citizen: A History of American Civic Life.* Cambridge, Mass.: Harvard University Press.

Scott, John C., Jr. 1957. "Membership and Participation in Voluntary Associations." *American Sociological Review* 22(3): 315–26.

Shaiko, Ronald G. 1999. *Voices and Echoes for the Environment.* New York: Columbia University Press.

Skerry, Peter. 1997. "The Strange Politics of Affirmative Action." *Wilson Quarterly* (Winter): 39–46.

Skocpol, Theda. 1996. *Boomerang: Clinton's Health Security Effort and the Turn Against Government in U.S. Politics.* New York: W. W. Norton.

———. 1997. "The GI Bill and U.S. Social Policy, Past and Future." *Social Philosophy and Policy* 14(2): 95–115.

———. 1999. "Advocates Without Members: The Recent Transformation of American Civic Life." In *Civic Engagement in American Democracy,* edited by Theda Skocpol and Morris P. Fiorina. Washington, D.C., and New York: Brookings Institution and Russell Sage Foundation.

———. 2003. *Diminished Democracy: From Membership to Management in American Civic Life.* Norman: University of Oklahoma Press.

Skocpol, Theda, Marshall Ganz, and Ziad Munson. 2000. "A Nation of Organizers: The Institutional Origins of Civic Voluntarism in the United States." *American Political Science Review* 94(3): 527–46.

Skocpol, Theda, with the assistance of Marshall Ganz, Ziad Munson, Bayliss Camp, Michele Swers, and Jennifer Oser. 1999. "How Americans Became Civic." In *Civic Engagement in American Democracy,* edited by Theda Skocpol and Morris P. Fiorina. Washington, D.C., and New York: Brookings Institution Press and Russell Sage Foundation.

Skocpol, Theda, Ziad Munson, Andrew Karch, and Bayliss Camp. 2002. "Patriotic Partnerships: Why Great Wars Nourished American Civic Voluntarism." In *Shaped by War and Trade: International Influences on American Political Development,* edited by Ira Katznelsona and Martin Shefter. Princeton, N.J.: Princeton University Press.

Skocpol, Theda, and Jennifer Lynn Oser. Forthcoming. "Organization Despite Adversity: The Origins and Development of African American Fraternal Associations." *Social Science History.*

Smith, Constance, and Anne Freedman. 1972. *Voluntary Associations: Perspectives on the Literature.* Cambridge, Mass.: Harvard University Press.

Smith, Tom W. 1990. "Trends in Voluntary Group Membership: Comments on Baumgartner and Walker." *American Journal of Political Science* 34(3): 646–61.

Tocqueville, Alexis de. 1835–40/1969. *Democracy in America,* edited by J. P. Mayer and translated by George Lawrence. Garden City, N.Y.: Doubleday/Anchor Books.

Tompkins, Jean Beattie. 1955. "Reference Groups and Status Values as Determinants of Behavior: A Study of Women's Voluntary Association Behavior." Ph.D. diss., State University of Iowa.

Verba, Sidney, and Norman H. Nie. 1972. *Participation in America: Political Democracy and Social Equality.* New York: Harper & Row.

Verba, Sidney, Kay Lehman Schlozman, and Henry E. Brady. 1995. *Voice and Equality: Civic Voluntarism in American Politics.* Cambridge, Mass.: Harvard University Press.

Veroff, Joseph, Elizabeth Douvan, and Richard A. Kulka. 1981. *The Inner American: A Self-Portrait from 1957 to 1975.* New York: Basic Books.

Walker, Jack L., Jr. 1991. *Mobilizing Interest Groups in America: Patrons, Professions, and Social Movements.* Ann Arbor: University of Michigan Press.

Wilcox, Clyde. 1996. *Onward Christian Soldiers? The Religious Right in American Politics.* Boulder, Colo.: Westview Press.

Wuthnow, Robert. 1994. *Sharing the Journey: Support Groups and America's New Quest for Community.* New York: Free Press.

————. 1998. *Loose Connections: Joining Together in America's Fragmented Communities.* Cambridge, Mass.: Harvard University Press.

————. 1999. "Mobilizing Civic Engagement: The Changing Impact of Religious Involvement." In *Civic Engagement in American Democracy,* edited by Theda Skocpol and Morris P. Fiorina. Washington, D.C., and New York: Brookings Institution and Russell Sage Foundation.

————. 2002. "United States: Bridging the Privileged and the Marginalized?" In *Democracies in Flux: The Evolution of Social Capital in Contemporary Society,* edited by Robert D. Putnam. New York: Oxford University Press.

Part VI

Inequality and Public Policy

Chapter 20

Crime, Punishment, and American Inequality

Bruce Western, Meredith Kleykamp, and Jake Rosenfeld

Two major social trends steadily reduced the living standards of young American men with little education over the last thirty years. The earnings of men with just a high school education were eroded by the tide of rising U.S. income inequality. While wages fell, growth in the American penal system turned prison and jail time into common life events for low-skill and minority men. The new inequality and the prison boom both date from the mid-1970s, and both trends continued through the end of the 1990s. Given this covariation, a causal interpretation would be tempting, but only weakly supported. To explain the link between imprisonment in the United States and the level of economic inequality, we report new estimates of incarceration among men and review research relating economic conditions to the extent of carceral punishment.

Economic inequality might influence the scale of punishment in two main ways. Rising inequality may increase crime at the bottom of the social hierarchy, generating more arrests, convictions, and prison admissions. Sociologists and economists commonly maintain that the disadvantaged are more involved in crime, so increased inequality can be expected to have aggregate affects on imprisonment. From an economic perspective, Richard Freeman (1996) argues that young black men in the 1980s and 1990s turned to crime in response to declining job opportunities. As a result, contact with the criminal justice system became a regular feature of ghetto life. Troy Duster (1997) similarly claims that the collapse of legitimate employment in poor urban neighborhoods drew young black men into the illegal drug trade, steeply increasing their risks of arrest and incarceration. Both analyses trace the size of the criminal justice system to rising crime rates among disadvantaged men in inner cities.

Alternatively, sociologists of social control argue that rising inequality directly enlarges the penal population, independently of trends in crime. For social control theories, criminal law functions not just to control crime but also to contain marginal populations that are perceived as threatening by elites and voters. The direct link between contemporary patterns of inequality and punishment was forcefully claimed by Loïc Wacquant (2000). Like Freeman and Duster, Wacquant sees the recent growth of the penal system as intimately connected with the decline of urban economies in the later postwar period. In Wacquant's analysis, however, growth in prison populations and city police forces is not driven chiefly by the rise in crime, but by the demise of the ghetto as an economically viable, yet controlling, institution in the lives of African Americans. The "prisonization of the ghetto" represents just the latest form of institutionalized white supremacy.

Has economic inequality boosted the prison population? If so, has the prison population expanded because of crime rates swelled by growth in ghetto poverty or because of increases in the severity of criminal punishment? We begin to answer these questions by first examining trends in prison and jail incarceration over the last two decades. Next, we discuss research linking rising inequality to an increase in crime rates. Then we turn to the social control thesis, in which imprisonment trends respond to economic pressures but are relatively independent of trends in crime.

RECENT TRENDS IN INCARCERATION

The scale of the penal system is often measured by an incarceration rate that expresses the size of the penal population as a fraction of the total population. The U.S. penal system consists of state and federal prisons that hold felons serving sentences of a year or more and local jails holding inmates for short sentences and defendants awaiting trial. State prison inmates make up about two-thirds of the penal population. Between 1920 and 1970, the prison incarceration rate hovered around 100 per 100,000 of the U.S. population. Figure 20.1 shows the imprisonment rate since 1970. At the beginning of this period the imprisonment rate, at 96 per 100,000, stood near its historic average. By 2001 the rate of prison incarceration had increased fivefold to 470 per 100,000. The increase in the incarceration rate was driven by sevenfold growth in the number of prisoners, who numbered 1.34 million by 2001. At the beginning of the new century jail inmates added another 631,000 people to the total penal population, yielding an incarceration rate of 0.7 percent of the U.S. population.

How does the imprisonment trend compare with shifts in crime and inequality? Figure 20.1 measures income inequality with the ratio of the ninetieth to the tenth percentile of the distribution of annual income for male workers. As is well known, male income inequality grew significantly, although far less than the incarceration rate. Figure 20.1 describes changes in crime with a measure of violent crime. U.S. crime rates are usually measured by reports to police compiled by the FBI (the Uniform Crime Reports) and by a biannual household survey (the National Crime Victimization Survey) fielded by the U.S. Census Bureau. We calculate a violent crime rate that sums the total number of violent crimes estimated by the victimization survey and the total number of homicides recorded by the FBI. The number of criminal incidents is expressed per 10,000 of the U.S. population. We focus on violent crime because 50 to 60 percent of prison inmates are violent offenders. Between 1973 and 1994, the violent crime rate fluctuated without any clear trend and then fell through the second half of the 1990s.

The lower panels of figure 20.1 show the relationships between inequality and imprisonment, on the one hand, and crime and imprisonment, on the other. With few reversals, the imprisonment rate climbed steadily with rising inequality. The crime-imprisonment relationship is less clear-cut. Between 1973 and 1995, imprisonment rates rose through small increases and declines in violent crime. From 1995 to 2000, incarceration increased steeply as the violent crime rate plummeted. These simple aggregate trends lend at least superficial plausibility to the idea that inequality, not crime, is behind the prison boom.

The weak aggregate relationship between crime and imprisonment suggests that criminal offenders were treated more harshly in the late 1990s than twenty years earlier (Blumstein and Beck 1999; Boggess and Bound 1997). Indeed, the prison population was most directly fed by an increase in court commitments to prison among those arrested and an increase in time served among those admitted. Although the probability of incarceration

FIGURE 20.1   *Crime, Imprisonment, and Inequality Trends Among Male, Full-Time, Year-Round Workers, 1970 to 2000*

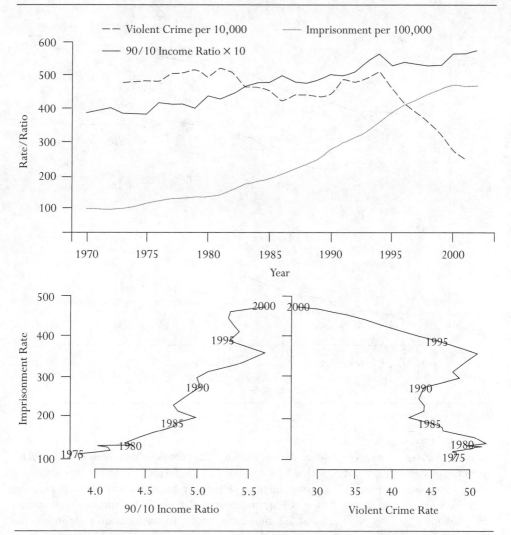

Source: U.S. Office of Justice Programs (2002a, 2002b); U.S. Department of Commerce (2002).

grew for all categories of arrestees, the imprisonment risk grew most for drug offenders. Growth in time served, however, was largest for violent offenders. While murderers served only five years on average in 1980, they were spending more than eleven years in prison by the mid-1990s (Blumstein and Beck 1999, 36). The criminal justice system has certainly become more punitive, but the role of inequality and the intervening role of crime remain unclear without more detailed information about how incarceration is distributed across the population.

Evidence for the inequality-incarceration connection would be stronger if the risks of incarceration had grown most among those who suffered the largest declines in earnings. Because earnings for low-education men deteriorated most (Bernhardt et al. 2001), we

FIGURE 20.2   *Incarceration Rates for White, Hispanic, and Black Men, Age Eighteen to Sixty-Five, 1980 to 2000*

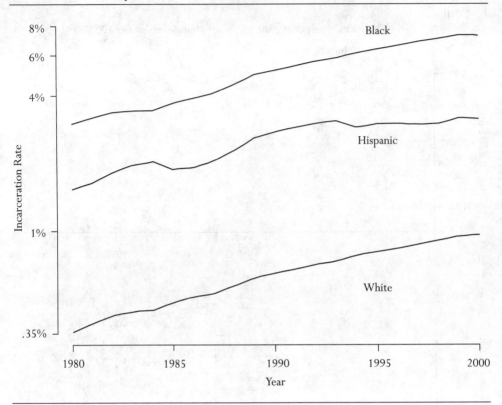

Source: Authors' compilation.

examine changes in incarceration rates for men at different levels of education. Official correctional statistics are not reported by education, so we formed estimates by combining survey data on prison and jail inmates, counts of the non-institutional civilian population from the Current Population Survey (CPS), and counts of those in the military (see appendix). About 93 percent of prison and jail inmates are male, so we focus on male incarceration rates. Figure 20.2 shows incarceration trends for white, Hispanic, and black men from 1980 to 2000. The risk of going to prison or jail grew strongly for all three groups over the last two decades, and by 2000 the incarceration rate among black men had reached nearly 8 percent. Because the incarceration rate is drawn on the log scale, the parallel rise in white and black rates indicates that the white-black ratio in incarceration rates remained roughly constant. Over most of the time series, black men were about seven to eight times more likely to be in prison or jail than white men.

Figure 20.3 reports incarceration rates for young men at three levels of schooling: those who have failed to complete high school, those who have finished high school or a GED, and those who have obtained at least some college education. For blacks, whites, and Hispanics, the risk of incarceration falls quickly with rising education. Young high school dropouts are five to twenty times more likely to be in prison or jail than young men who have been to college. For all three race and ethnic groups, incarceration rates increased

FIGURE 20.3 *Incarceration Rates for Men, Age Twenty-Two to Thirty, by Race and Ethnicity, 1980 to 2000*

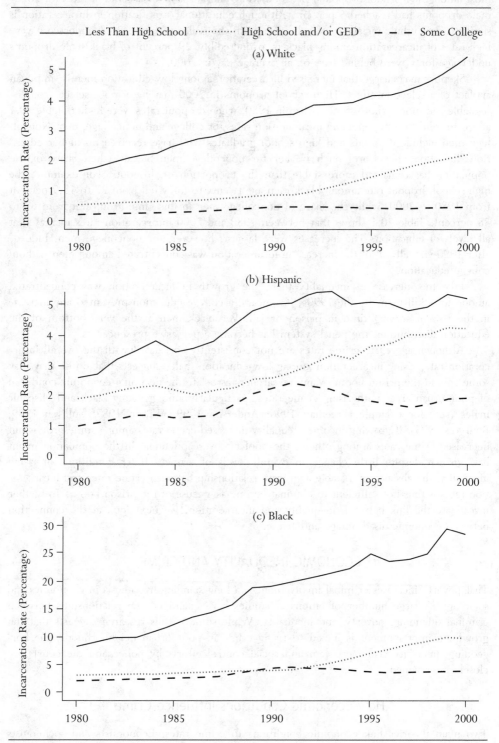

Source: Authors' compilation.

most among high school dropouts. By 2000 white and Hispanic incarceration rates for young male dropouts had reached 5 percent. Although educational stratification in incarceration is similar across ethnic-racial groups, differences in the scales of figure 20.3 underscore very high rates of incarceration among black men. Incredibly, 29 percent of black male dropouts under age forty were behind bars on an average day in 2000.

Skeptics may charge that increased incarceration among low-education men is simply an artifact of a selection effect. High school dropouts in 2000 may be a more select group—less able and more crime-prone—than in 1980, when dropout rates were higher. Table 20.1 addresses selection by reporting incarceration rates for college and noncollege men. Noncollege men include dropouts and high school graduates who have received no higher education. Selection effects are much weaker for noncollege men because their share of the population has remained more stable than the proportion of dropouts. For example, the high school dropout rate among black men age twenty to forty fell from 27 to 15.7 percent from 1980 to 2000, while the share of noncollege men in this same group fell from 67 to 58 percent. Table 20.1 shows that between 1980 and 2000 incarceration rates increased at all levels of education. The increases were largest, however, for noncollege men. Indeed, after 1990 virtually all of the increase in incarceration was concentrated among men without college education.

Like the increase in inequality then, the growth in incarceration was concentrated among low-skill men. By the 1990s, it appears, a college education prevented any increase in the risk of serving time in prison or jail. For black men at the very bottom of the education distribution, the penal system has become a pervasive presence.

Although aggregate crime rates are not consistently correlated with the overall incarceration rate, rising incarceration among low-education males suggests that crime may play some role in the prison boom. Many researchers associate the declining economic condition of poor urban areas with rising crime rates, particularly among young black and Hispanic males (see, for example, Freeman 1996; Anderson 1999; Wilson 1987; Sullivan 1989; Bourgois 1995). If growing income inequality increased crime rates among some groups but decreased crime rates among others, the pool of severe offenders in the population might have grown despite little change in overall levels of crime. Under conditions of rising inequality, the absence of a stable aggregate relationship between crime rates and incarceration rates is thus not sufficient to eliminate crime as a cause of the prison boom. To further investigate the link between inequality and incarceration, we next look at the connection between economic disadvantage and crime.

ECONOMIC INEQUALITY AND CRIME

That poverty increases criminal involvement is a long-standing hypothesis in economics and sociology. A large number of empirical studies have examined the relationships between criminal offending, poverty, and inequality. While some of this research suggests that the growth in imprisonment is linked to rising crime in poor urban neighborhoods, the burgeoning inner-city crime problem and social control efforts by police and the courts are closely intertwined.

How Economic Conditions Influence Crime

Two main theories link economic conditions to crime rates. Economists and sociologists have argued in different ways that those with few economic opportunities turn to crime to

TABLE 20.1   *Incarceration Rates Among Non-College-Educated and College-Educated Men,
Age Twenty to Forty, by Race and Ethnicity, 1980 to 2000*

	All	White	Black	Hispanic
Non-college-educated men				
1980	1.6%	0.8%	5.2%	2.3%
1990	2.9	1.4	8.6	4.0
2000	5.4	2.9	15.2	4.8
College-educated men				
1980	0.4	0.2	2.1	1.0
1990	0.9	0.5	4.5	2.3
2000	1.0	0.5	4.2	2.0

Source: Authors' compilation.

supplement their legitimate incomes. Criminologists, on the other hand, have examined the informal controls on behavior imposed by the social contexts of employment, family, and neighborhood. For these two perspectives, economic inequality is implicated indirectly; low economic status is seen as the chief cause of crime. In the current context of declining earnings among low-skill workers, however, the growth in inequality emerges as an important possible cause of rising crime in poor areas.

The dominant explanation of lower-class criminality observes that all people share similar goals of material success, but legitimate opportunities to attain those goals are unequally distributed. Robert Merton (1968, 223) makes the seminal argument in *Social Theory and Social Structure:* "The moral mandate to achieve success . . . exerts pressure to succeed by fair means if possible and by foul means if necessary." Frustration at blocked opportunities drives the poor to crime so that they might gain access to the material success enjoyed legally by the middle class. Judith Blau and Peter Blau (1982) go further, arguing that ascriptive inequality (like racial inequality), more than inequality based on achievement, appears particularly illegitimate. High levels of racial inequality, rather than economic disadvantage, may fan the frustrations that trigger crime.

Although Gary Becker (1968) eschews the language of norms, blocked opportunities, and ascription, his explicitly utilitarian account of crime is similar to Merton's. For Becker, an individual's choice to engage in crime is produced by calculations of relative cost and benefit. Crime's cost is given by the severity and certainty of punishment and by the legitimate economic opportunities that are forgone if crime is chosen. Although most economic research focuses on the capacity of punishment to deter crime, Freeman (1996) argues that people increasingly engage in crime as their position in the legitimate labor market deteriorates. In his analysis, the high rate of involvement in the penal system among low-education black men is closely linked to their growing involvement in crime and the steep decline in their economic opportunities through the 1980s.

While strain theory and its utilitarian variant highlight the economic forces that push people into crime, social control theories emphasize the constraints that prevent offending. The routines of steady employment, independent of its economic attractions, reduce opportunities for offending. Adopting the language of segmented labor markets, these researchers find that men in primary-sector jobs—where work is consistent, routinized, and monitored—commit less crime than men in the secondary labor market, where employment is irregular (Sullivan 1989; Crutchfield and Pitchford 1997). Research on criminal desistance similarly shows that continuity of employment provides a pathway out of crime for men with criminal histories (Sampson and Laub 1993; Uggen 2000).

Economic disadvantage may also erode informal social control indirectly, through its association with family disruption and neighborhood poverty. Stable families with two parents present in the household can monitor children's activities and divert them from the peer networks that provide a familiar context for delinquency (Sampson 1987). Poor families—which are more likely to be headed by a single parent—have fewer resources to restrain crime (Hagan 1993). Although juvenile crime is often seen to result from family disruption, stable marriages, like steady jobs, are found to be a key source of criminal desistance among adult men with a history of offending (Sampson and Laub 1993; Laub, Nagin, and Sampson 1998). Given that marriage rates are lower among poor (particularly minority) men (Ellwood and Jencks 2001), economic disadvantage may also work indirectly to foster crime among adults.

Like family ties, the social relationships of one's neighborhood may also constrain or enable criminal behavior. Analysis of the criminogenic character of poor neighborhoods can be traced at least to the classic account of Clifford Shaw and Henry McKay (1942). In their analysis, low economic status, ethnic heterogeneity, and residential turnover were destabilizing influences on local communities. Delinquency flourished under these conditions of social disorganization. Modern criminology has adapted these ideas to argue that communities are densely woven webs of social networks that offer both economic opportunities and informal social control. Communities lacking these social connections—where families are only weakly tied to employers, voluntary organizations, and friends—risk high rates of violence and other crime (Wilson 1987; Sullivan 1989; Hagan 1993; Sampson 1987). Here the effect is distinctly contextual: even middle-class citizens are more likely to be involved in crime in poor neighborhoods lacking social capital.

Theories of strain, rational action, and informal social control suggest several hypotheses. Strain may be produced when the poor compare themselves unfavorably with the rich. In this case, relative deprivation (measured by inequality) influences criminal behavior. If people commit crime to fulfill basic needs or because social ties are inadequate to constrain criminal behavior, absolute deprivation (measured by economic level) drives crime. The causal force of relative or absolute deprivation ties an individual's economic status to individual offending, but economic conditions may also have contextual effects. Neighborhood poverty may increase the risk of offending, regardless of an individual's class background.

Empirical Evidence for the Inequality-Crime Relationship

Analysts have used three main research designs to study the empirical links between economic conditions and crime. Studies of survey data and official criminal justice data find high rates of criminal offending among lower-class men. Aggregate studies examine national time series and panels of states and cities. Finally, ethnographers provide detailed field reports of criminal activity in poor neighborhoods.

Consistent with the economic account of crime, many empirical studies find high rates of offending at the bottom of the social ladder. John Braithwaite's (1979) review of 131 studies finds near-unanimous support for individual-level and contextual effects in research prior to 1980. Official records from police and courts indicate that lower-class men and male youth are more involved in crime and delinquency compared with those from a middle-class background. Studies of self-reported crime using survey data are more equivocal (Tittle, Villemez, and Smith 1978). Still, Robert Crutchfield and Susan Pitchford's

(1997) study of the National Longitudinal Survey of Youth (NLSY) offers strong support for the link between crime and economic disadvantage in a national-level survey. Similarly, survey data on criminal victimization show that the poor were at increasing risk of property crime as inequality increased from the mid-1970s to the mid-1990s (Levitt 1999). There is also strong evidence of contextual effects in which individuals in poor and minority neighborhoods commit crime at relatively high rates, regardless of their social class. Consistent with this earlier research on contextual effects, recent studies using detailed data on finely defined neighborhoods also find high rates of homicide in areas of concentrated poverty, controlling for past levels of violence, population turnover, density, and measures of social capital (Sampson and Raudenbush 1999; Morenoff, Sampson, and Raudenbush 2001). The microlevel building block of the inequality hypothesis—high levels of crime among the poor—thus obtains strong empirical support.

Given these microlevel findings, is there evidence that changes in economic inequality affect crime rates in the aggregate? A few time-series analyses claim that rising inequality since the 1970s increased U.S. crime rates. Gary LaFree and Kriss Drass (1996) report that measures of both absolute deprivation (measured by median incomes and unemployment rates) and relative deprivation (measured by family income inequality) are positively associated with black and white arrest rates for robbery, burglary, and homicide in the period 1957 to 1990. Steven Messner, Lawrence Raffolovich, and Richard Millan (2001) perform a similar analysis of black and white youth arrest rates for 1967 to 1998 using a wide array of inequality measures, including the Gini index, the interquartile range, and income shares of the top 5 percent. Although the consistent effect of child poverty rates indicate the influence of absolute deprivation on crime, conclusions about relative deprivation are highly sensitive to the choice of inequality measure. For example, lagged Gini indexes and income shares for the black income distribution are significantly associated with black youth homicide arrest rates, but contemporaneous effects of these variables and the effects of the interquartile range are insignificant. The results of Messner and his colleagues illustrate the fragility of estimates from short time series. When twenty or thirty time points are analyzed, results can depend strongly on the choice of measures and the time period. Freeman (1995, 180) draws a similar conclusion in his review of time-series research on crime and unemployment: "The safest conclusion is that the time series are not a robust way to determine the job market–crime link."

More promising are studies of states or metropolitan areas, which enlist relatively large datasets to estimate the economic sources of crime. In a highly influential paper, Blau and Blau (1982) analyze a sample of 125 metropolitan areas and find that black-white inequality in socioeconomic status is positively associated with violent crime rates, controlling for racial composition, the level of divorce, and population size. Areas with high levels of economic inequality in general also tend to have higher levels of violence. A number of researchers have subsequently revisited the problem of explaining high rates of violence among African Americans in urban areas. Both absolute deprivation (measured by average income) and relative deprivation (measured by income inequality) have been found to influence black homicide rates, though often through the intervening agency of family structure (Sampson 1987; Shihadeh and Steffensmeier 1994). Although these results are suggestive, the cross-sectional design reveals little about the effects of rising income inequality since the 1970s. The research design is also vulnerable to biases due to unmeasured characteristics of localities that may be correlated with crime and economic conditions.

A few studies have extended the cross-sectional design by observing cities or states at several points in time. With this panel design, a number of researchers follow the time-series analysts in claiming that rising inequality has propelled U.S. crime rates. Richard Fowles and Mary Merva (1996) have studied a large number of statistical models in an analysis of violent and property crime rates in large metropolitan areas between 1975 and 1990. These panel data yield consistently signed effects for wage inequality and poverty rates on violent crime rates. They conclude that "increases in the level of wage inequality that have been characteristic of the U.S. economy since the 1970s have significantly increased the violent crimes of murder/non-negligent manslaughter and aggravated assault" (179). Despite this conclusion and a relatively large sample size (N = 728), their estimated inequality effects are often insignificant at conventional levels. We would also expect inequality measures capturing the lower tail of the income distribution to best describe variation in crime. However, Fowles and Merva find that inequality measures that give greatest weight to the bottom of the distribution have the weakest effects (173). In short, the consistency of coefficient signs across models provides only modest support for the inequality hypothesis.

Other analyses of panel data have not provided strong evidence for the effects of absolute or relative deprivation. Kenneth Land, Patricia McCall, and Lawrence Cohen's (1990) study of violent and property crime rates in forty-eight states between 1984 and 1993 finds insignificant effects of a Gini index on wages in all of the twenty-eight models reported. Slightly stronger results were found for the effects of absolute deprivation (average wages) on property crime rates. These researchers studied homicide rates for states, cities, and standard metropolitan statistical areas (SMSAs) between 1960 and 1980. They find no consistent effect of inequality at these three levels of aggregation. Still, an omnibus measure of economic deprivation that combines information about absolute and relative deprivation is significantly associated with higher rates of homicide at the state, city, and SMSA levels.

Although quantitative evidence provides only uneven support for the effects of economic conditions on aggregate crime rates, the connection is strongly drawn by urban ethnographers (for a review, see Hagan 1993). Several ethnographers report that the inner-city drug trade provides a key source of economic opportunity for young men in poor neighborhoods with high rates of joblessness. Philippe Bourgois's (1995, 73) ethnographic research on the views of Hispanic drug gangs fuses the effects of relative and absolute deprivation as "the insult of working for entry-level wages amidst extraordinary opulence [that] is especially painful for Spanish Harlem youths." This inequality drives young Puerto Rican men "deeper into the confines of their segregated neighborhood and the underground economy." The economic significance of drug dealing has also been studied by Sudhir Venkatesh and Steven Levitt (2000), whose research on Chicago's "outlaw capitalism" shows that drug gangs have a well-defined organizational hierarchy in which incomes are graduated from the street sellers at the bottom to the managers at the top. Outside of the context of drug gangs, Mercer Sullivan's (1989) account of three New York neighborhoods shows that young black men, unlike their white counterparts, remain involved in crime after leaving school because African American communities offer fewer local employment opportunities and fewer social connections to entry-level jobs. Much more than the quantitative research, urban ethnographers draw a strong connection between unemployment in the legitimate economy and criminal activity among young minority men.

Discussion of Research on Crime

While ethnographic research studies just a slice in time, urban crime is often linked to long-term structural changes in urban economies. Sullivan (1989, 230) observes that "the concentration of poverty increased during the 1970s, along with persisting high crime rates. . . . The link between un- and underemployment and high rates of street crime in inner-city neighborhoods is pervasive." Moreover, the drug trade replaces the economic opportunity formerly provided by urban manufacturing industry: "Faced with fewer regular jobs, some inner-city black youth find work in the underground economy—notably in street-level drug sales" (Duster 1997, 261). "As the wider regular economy fails them, many young people, particularly men, seek the underground and adopt its ways" (Anderson 1990, 244). This pattern in turn increases the supply of poor urban minority youth to the penal system. Freeman (1996, 25) makes the case most clearly: "Participation in crime and involvement with the criminal justice system has reached such levels as to become part of normal economic life for many young men." Can we square this account of declining public safety in inner cities with quantitative research on the economic sources of crime?

The best evidence for the crime-inequality relationship is found in microlevel quantitative studies and ethnographic research. This research shows that economically disadvantaged youth and men are more involved in delinquency and crime than the affluent. High crime rates are also found in poor neighborhoods, even controlling for local patterns of population turnover, density, and racial composition. There is much weaker evidence that aggregate trends in the economy influence aggregate crime rates. Absolute measures of economic status like average incomes and poverty rates provide somewhat stronger results than relative measures like Gini indexes and wage gaps. Because measures of absolute and relative deprivation tend to be highly correlated, however, we cannot distinguish their effects with confidence (Land, McCall, and Cohen 1990; Levitt 1999). Weak results in the macrolevel research and the cross-sectional character of the microlevel research thus leave important questions unanswered. We simply do not have good quantitative indications that poor young men are more involved in crime now than in the past.

How can we reconcile the modest quantitative findings with claims that crime is increasing in poor urban areas? Freeman's (1995, 1996) account of rising crime among the ghetto poor provides one possible answer. He finds that the criminal propensity of the population increased in the 1980s despite declining rates of criminal victimization. Criminal propensity increased because crime rates fell by less than we would expect given the rise in imprisonment. Most studies reviewed here do not account for increased policing and incarceration, so people's tendency to commit crime may be increasingly underestimated as social control efforts expand. Levitt (1996, 1997) also suggests that criminal activity depends on the efforts of the criminal justice system. He reports two analyses in which crime rates are reduced by formal social control—imprisonment in one study, policing in another. These analyses suggest that the absence of a clear aggregate relationship between crime and the economy may be obscured by the criminal justice system's reduction of crime over a period when economic conditions deteriorated. Against this possibility, however, evidence for economic effects is not strong even when we account for the relationship between criminal processing and crime rates. Levitt estimates the effects of unemployment and median incomes on violent and property crime rates in a panel study of states and finds consistent effects only for unemployment on property crime. In an unusual step for research on the effects of inequality, Morgan Kelly (2000) and Joanne Doyle, Ehsan Ahmed, and Robert Horn (1999) also allow for the mutual dependence of policing and crime. Their results, however, offer little evidence for the effects of economic inequality on offending.

The influence of policing and incarceration on crime rates is not just a technical issue for statistical estimation. It highlights the difficulty of conceptualizing and measuring crime in a way that is independent of its official recognition by criminal justice authorities. While statistical analysis focuses on how the expanding criminal system might suppress the crime rate, a reverse effect may also operate. The appearance of increased criminality in the population may be due to broader definitions of crime and more punitive approaches to criminals. Trends in criminal processing can illuminate how the police, the courts, and corrections dispense the official stamp of criminality. Further analysis of the link between economic inequality and the growth of the penal system thus leads us to look at trends in the system of punishment.

ECONOMIC INEQUALITY AND THE SEVERITY OF PUNISHMENT

In contrast to claims that the new inequality fed the prison boom by increasing crime among the poor, inequality may directly affect the scale of punishment without the intervening influence of rising crime. According to this perspective, institutions of criminal punishment have their own logic that is distinct from criminal behavior in the population. A direct association between inequality and punishment is suggested by aggregate trends. Why would the scale of punishment increase with inequality, however, independent of the level of crime?

Explaining the Effect of Inequality on Punishment

The Frankfurt School social scientist Georg Rusche (1933/1978; Rusche and Kirchheimer 1939/2003) famously pioneered an account of the relationship between criminal punishment and the labor market. He viewed crime as a product of economic necessity that is deterred only when the severity of punishment exceeds the ravages of poverty. Quoting George Bernard Shaw, Rusche (1933/1980, 12) observed that "if the prison does not underbid the slum in human misery, the slum will empty and the prison will fill." Historic forms of punishment—fines, torture, imprisonment—were thus shaped by historic variation in the economic situation of the dispossessed. The unemployed, representing the most desperate and crime-prone workers, occupy a special place in this theory. Elites would stem the threat of rising crime by intensifying punishment as the surplus population expanded; the level of punishment would contract under conditions of labor scarcity.

For the contemporary descendants of Rusche, the criminal justice system embodies a social conflict between authorities and marginal populations. While Rusche viewed punishment chiefly as a means to deter crime, modern proponents see punishment as controlling a broad array of threats to social order posed by troublesome populations. The level of punishment is expected to vary with the size of the troublesome group. In empirical studies, threatening populations have been defined in terms of their employment status, (see, for example, Box and Hale 1982), their race or ethnicity (Hall 1978), or some combination of the two (Melossi 1989; Spohn and Holleran 2000). If not crime, what threat is posed by these marginal groups? Some have claimed that authorities view troublesome populations as endangering not just public safety but the economic order in general (Quinney 1974; Spitzer 1975). Those at the bottom of the social hierarchy may refuse to work, steal from the rich, reject the dominant values of hard work and achievement, and advocate revolutionary change (Spitzer 1975). The destabilizing potential of young men at the bottom of the social structure is well captured by Steven Spitzer's (1975, 645) term "social dynamite," evoking volatility more than chronic disadvantage. While the economic distance between rich and poor drives one conflict theory of punishment, another claims that cultural distance intensifies the punishment of the disadvantaged. Charles Tittle (1994) argues that authorities are often unable to identify with disadvantaged populations; they may also be fearful that those populations are generally dangerous. Under these conditions, marginal populations attract the full force of the social control apparatus.

Framed in the abstract, social threat accounts of punishment sound conspiratorial. By what concrete process do dominant groups actively use the state's legitimate violence against those who are relatively powerless? Three specific mechanisms might link social and economic disadvantage to criminal justice supervision. First, legislators perceiving poor and marginal populations as dangerous or unruly may write criminal law to contain the threat. Second, police may surveil and arrest the poor more frequently than the affluent. Third, once in the court system, poor defendants may receive harsh treatment from judges.

Criminal law embodies a class bias in the sense that it regulates the activities of the poor more than those of the rich. If criminal sentences are increased, the scale of punishment will increase, even if the level of offending is unchanged. In addition to the severity of sentences, the extent of class bias also varies with the kinds of class-related behaviors that are criminalized. Historically, the criminalization of poverty was most transparent in laws against vagrancy. The class bias of vagrancy statutes has been widely observed, not least by Anatole France, who archly questioned the "majestic equality" of the law for "forbid[ding] the rich as well as the poor to sleep under bridges" (*The Red Lily,* 1894). Marcus Dubber (2001) suggests that criminal possession has replaced vagrancy as the main statutory control on the poor. Like vagrancy, possession offenses—covering not just drugs but drug paraphernalia, weapons, stolen property, and a host of other items—punish just the possibility of, rather than actual, criminal victimization. The abstract notion of social threat is thus concretely expressed in laws of possession.

Although the possession offenses listed in the state penal codes proliferated over the last twenty-five years, drug possession and related drug control policy are most widely associated with the growth in U.S. imprisonment rates. In the current period, sentencing enhancements for drug offenses and the expansion of laws of possession appear to have disproportionately affected poor African Americans in urban areas (Tonry 1995; Dubber 2001). Over the past three decades Congress and most state legislatures have adopted mandatory prison sentences for drug possession or trafficking (U.S. Office of Justice Programs 1998, 7). Mandatory minimum sentences provide a plausible explanation for the increased risk of incarceration, given arrest, among drug offenders (Blumstein and Beck 1999). The proportion of drug offenders in state prisons increased fivefold between 1974 and 1997; drug offenders now account for about 30 percent of all state prisoners. Growth in federal imprisonment of drug offenders has been even more dramatic. In the early 1970s there were virtually no drug offenders under federal supervision, but today around 60 percent of federal prison inmates are serving time for drug convictions.

In addition to setting stiffer penalties for drug crimes, state legislatures have supported a variety of sentencing innovations that toughen laws for other offense categories. This statutory front in the war on crime has expanded the use of mandatory minimum prison sentences, habitual offender laws, and truth-in-sentencing provisions, while reducing the possibility of early release through parole. By 1996 all fifty states had some kind of mandatory minimum sentence, most commonly for repeat offenders or for crimes involving firearms (U.S. Office of Justice Programs 1998; Tonry 1994). Mandatory minimums seem most likely to influence prison admission rates, while time served in prison may be lengthened by habitual offender laws that lengthen sentences for offenders with prior records. Truth-in-sentencing laws that mandate incarceration for 70 percent or more of a given sentence may also extend time served. The truth-in-sentencing movement was given additional impetus in 1994 when the federal government provided financial incentives for legislation requiring incarceration for 85 percent of a sentence. By 2000, forty states had adopted truth-in-sentencing measures (Ditton and Wilson 1999). Historically, states provided for early release through parole hearings. By 1996 the discretionary authority of parole boards had been replaced in fourteen states by determinate sentencing schemes that imposed fixed terms reduced by "good time" on a regulated schedule. Although some sentencing reforms were intended to limit the arbitrary treatment of offenders, reduced discretion was often purchased at the price of presumptive imprisonment and longer sentences. A few studies attempt to assess the effects of sentencing policy on prison admissions, although a strong empirical test still awaits the use of longitudinal data for a large number of states (compare Marvell and Moody 1996 and Sorensen and Stemen 2002). In short, a variety of specific changes in the law of criminal sentencing may explain the increase in admission rates and time served that characterizes the prison boom, but so far there are few systematic empirical tests.

Formal social control efforts are reflected not just in the criminal law but also in policing that may disproportionately burden poor and minority communities. In part, police may intensively monitor poor communities, given their levels of crime, because more of daily life, and illegal activity, transpires in public space. Ethnographic research suggests that the purchase and consumption of drugs, drunkenness, and domestic disturbances are more likely to take place in public in urban areas than in private homes in the suburbs. Consequently, poor urban residents are exposed to police scrutiny to a greater degree, and run a greater risk of arrest, than their suburban counterparts (see, for example, Anderson 1999; Duneier 1999; Bourgois 1995). In addition, the police often view poor minorities as more involved in crime. Consequently, ghetto residents are treated with greater suspicion and as threatening to public order (Wilson 1968, ch. 2; Chambliss 1999). The threat of crime often inheres not just in individuals but in poor neighborhoods as a whole; thus, police often proactively maintain order in well-defined "dangerous areas" where poor residents are highly concentrated (Herbert 1997; Bass 2001). Just as the police are distrustful of ghetto residents, the residents often doubt the legitimacy of the police. In these cases, the poor not only are policed more intensively but are also more likely to disobey police directives (Huo and Tyler 2000), increasing their risk of arrest. The association of policing effort with the threat perceived from troublesome populations explains the research finding that the size of the police force and police expenditures increase with the size of a city's black population, even controlling for urban crime rates (Liska, Lawrence, and Benson 1981; Jackson 1989). Closer to our focus on inequality effects, cross-sectional data from 170 cities show that, controlling for the size of the police force and the homicide rate, the use of deadly force by police is more common where the black-white income gap is large (Jacobs and Helms 1998). In short, urban ecology and relations of mutual suspicion arouse the social control efforts of police. As a result, poor urban populations are exposed to relatively high risks of police arrest even given their relatively high rate of criminal involvement.

Finally, judges and prosecutors may treat poor and minority defendants more harshly than others. Research on the sentencing behavior of judges can be traced back at least to Thorsten Sellin (1935, 213) who observed: "The prisoner who stands before [the judge] is not merely an offender who must be dealt with according to the rules laid down by lawmakers, but he is a person who represents a class or a group in society toward which the judge may have certain feelings, perhaps of disapproval or approval."

In the modern context, researchers argue that nonlegal factors affect sentencing through judges' assessments of a defendant's culpability and potential for reform. Low-status defendants may be viewed as more blameworthy than high-status defendants. Although counterintuitive in light of economic theories of crime, judges may follow public opinion in viewing an individual's checkered job history as the product of a lack of effort, particularly if the individual is black (Kluegel 1990; see also Gilens 1999). Such judgments may also affect assessments of defendant culpability (Steffensmeier, Ulmer, and Kramer 1998, 770). Thus, a study of pre-sentence investigation reports in New Haven finds that unemployed defendants were considered more blameworthy and less open to rehabilitation (Daly 1994, 230). Researchers also argue that judges view low-status defendants, especially the unemployed, as more likely to return to crime (Greenberg 1977; Albonetti 1991). Darrell Steffensmeier, Jeffrey Ulmer, and John Kramer (1998, 767) suggest that judges may use the employment and education status of a defendant to predict dangerousness. Celesta Albonetti (1991) argues that predictions of recidivism are especially likely where crime is attributed to the defendant's enduring dispositions rather than seen as the product of temporary circumstance. Consistent with this idea, sentencing research finds that, controlling for offense characteristics and criminal history, particularly severe risks of incarceration are imposed on low-status, unemployed defendants—either minorities or those living in high-unemployment areas (Spohn and Holleran 2000; D'Alessio and Stolzenberg 2002).

In sum, theories of formal social control suggest that rising economic inequality may drive an increase in penal severity, independent of trends in crime. Rising inequality expands problem populations and increases their distance from the mainstream. Lawmakers may respond by writing tough-on-crime penal codes. We would expect to see the effects of tougher sentences reflected in state incarceration rates. Police may respond with aggressive law enforcement aimed at preventing crime among groups that appear threatening. The effects of policing may be evident at lower levels of aggregation, closer to police jurisdictions within cities and counties. Finally, judges may respond to rising inequality by increasing penal severity for the disadvantaged. In this case, the criminal justice system may encourage increasingly punitive sentencing outcomes.

Empirical Evidence for the Inequality-Incarceration Relationship

There is far less research that estimates the effects of economic inequality on punishment than on crime. Quantitative studies of incarceration rely on one of three kinds of research designs. First, some researchers analyze time series of incarceration rates or prison admission rates for a single country, usually the United States. The second variety of macrolevel studies examines variation across states or counties, or a few waves of observations on these aggregates. Common dependent variables for this cross-sectional research include state or county prison admission rates and state imprisonment rates. Finally, researchers study how local economic conditions, generally in counties, influence the sentencing of individual defendants. Sentencing studies have predicted sentence length and the probability that a convicted defendant will receive a prison sentence (the "in/out decision"). In trying to assess the social control effects of economic conditions, all three research designs also introduce statistical controls for criminal offending.

Most research on the economic determinants of incarceration follow Georg Rusche and Otto Kirchheimer (1939/2003) by estimating the effects of unemployment and other measures of surplus population. In their review of results from forty-four published studies, Theodore Chiricos and Miriam Delone (1992) find that analyses of prison admission rates in national time series provide strong and consistent evidence for the hypothesis that higher levels of incarceration are found under conditions of high unemployment. Macrolevel studies of prison populations also support the labor surplus theory of punishment. Results are weaker for individual-level studies of sentencing, in which the defendant's employment status is a key predictor. In sentencing research, employment status coefficients are typically signed consistently with theory, but statistically significant results are found only a quarter of the time. Chiricos and Delone conclude that there is stronger and more consistent evidence for the labor surplus hypothesis than was previously acknowledged.

Despite this conclusion, it is likely that Chiricos and Delone (1992) overestimate support for the effects of unemployment on incarceration. Although the aggregate time-series studies provide the strongest evidence for unemployment effects, such studies often analyze overlapping or highly correlated time series of U.S. incarceration figures. Consequently, different studies yield similar results because similar data are analyzed, not because the labor surplus hypothesis survives multiple independent tests. The individual-level studies are collectively more informative because sentencing data come from a variety of jurisdictions. Each individual-level sentencing analysis independently updates evidence for the hypothesis. The individual-level design is also more powerful because sample sizes are relatively large; evidence against the unemployment effects are more compelling as a result. Because sentencing studies yield positive and significant employment effects in just one-fourth of all analyses, other contextual factors may be driving the variability in results across jurisdictions. Indeed, a second generation of research has found that adverse sentencing outcomes are most likely for offenders with several deficits. For example, recent research finds that a defendant who is young and black, unemployed and black, or unemployed and living in a poor area is more likely to be incarcerated, controlling for criminal history and offense characteristics (D'Alessio and Stolzenberg 2002; Steffensmeier, Ulmer, and Kramer 1998; Spohn and Holleran 2000; Nobiling, Spohn, and Delone 1998).

Although sentencing research provides a stronger test of the social control effects of unemployment than macrolevel studies, the sentencing studies are conservative in at least one important respect. In most cases, sentencing research focuses on the disposition of convicted defendants. (A few studies analyze pre-trial incarceration, but most examine the in/out decision or sentence length.) By the time a defendant is convicted, most of the social control process has already transpired. All the defendants in the sentencing sample—whether they receive probation or prison—have been policed, arrested, charged, and convicted. The economic status of the offender pool at this stage may be very low compared with that of the offender pool in the population. Relatively modest results for economic effects in sentencing decisions should be interpreted as applying to this highly select population, not as general evidence for the weakness of the economic sources of punishment.

Although employment status is the main focus of research on criminal justice outcomes, several studies have investigated the effects of economic inequality. Like research on unemployment effects, analyses of the links between inequality and incarceration have examined national time series, cross-sectional data on states and counties, and individual-level sentencing data. In many cases, researchers were not chiefly interested in the effects of inequality. Such studies, however, give us a usefully disinterested picture of the sensitivity of inequality effects to different model specifications. Thomas Dye (1969, 1091) provides one of the first quantitative studies. In a cross-section of fifty states, using data from 1959, he reports a correlation of .35 between the Gini index on family incomes and the rate of imprisonment. Interestingly, the black-white difference in educational attainment correlates with imprisonment at .43. Measurement strategies are quite similar in current research. Inequality is usually measured with a Gini index or a black-white difference in incomes.

Table 20.2 summarizes the results of eleven studies published between 1978 and 2001 analyzing U.S. data. In general, evidence for the effects of inequality on imprisonment is quite weak. Across the three main research designs, the strongest results are reported in two time-series analyses by David Jacobs and Ronald Helms (1996, 2001). When an annual measure of income inequality is used, these authors report several positive and significant effects of inequality on both the prison incarceration rate and the prison admission rate. Stronger results are reported for the effects of the variance of incomes than for Gini coefficients. This result may have a substantive basis. The variance is far more sensitive than the Gini index to the spread of a distribution. The variance may better capture the nonlinear functional form of the inequality-incarceration relationship. Alternatively, the variance is more volatile and the observed results may be driven by a few extreme observations. More generally, short time series such as these provide little information about the effects of inequality. The empirical base of the time-series research could be enlarged by disaggregating the measures of inequality. Modest evidence for the impact of inequality on imprisonment in a time-series analysis may also be due to the highly aggregated dependent variables. We would expect the effects of rising inequality to fall on those in the lower tail of the income distribution. The time-series design might usefully distinguish between the imprisonment rates of those at different levels of income or education. Sharper measurement may yield stronger results.

Inequality effects are much weaker in macrolevel studies of states or counties. In these studies, where cross-sectional variation predominates, Gini indexes on family income are only weakly related to prison incarceration rates. U.S. states with high levels of inequality do not generally have the highest incarceration rates, once adjustments are made for crime rates and the racial composition of the population. The panel study reported by David Jacobs and Jason Carmichael (2001) goes furthest, showing that states with the largest increases in inequality between 1970 and 1990 did not experience the largest increases in incarceration rates. The design of the cross-sectional studies is rather weak. Relatively little data are brought to bear on the problem, and specification errors may well be large. Analysis of panel data provides a more encouraging approach, but so far research has relied on just two or three waves of data. As for time-series analysis, virtually all these studies use highly aggregated measures of incarceration, like state-level imprisonment. This level of aggregation ignores perhaps the main implication of theories of inequality effects—that the risks of punishment will be highest for those at the edges of the income distribution.

Sentencing studies represent the most disaggregated approach to the analysis of incarceration. Most research on inequality in sentencing has focused on racial, rather than economic, inequality. Summarizing research up to the early 1980s, John Hagan and Kristen Bumiller (1983) and Gary Kleck (1981) conclude that there is little evidence for broad race differences in sentencing once a defendant's prior record and offense are taken into account. However, analyses of large jurisdictions, like states, may conceal discrimination in local areas (Crutchfield, Bridges, and Pitchford 1994). Race may also have indirect effects—for example, on the accumulation of a criminal history.

A few studies examine the effects of local patterns of inequality on sentencing outcomes. The effects of inequality on individual sentencing decisions are typically estimated in a contextual analysis where local levels of inequality are related to a defendant's sentence length or probability of imprisonment. As for the macrolevel research, the results are modest or mixed. There is evidence that blacks are punished relatively harshly in counties with high levels of black-white income inequality (Britt 2000; Myers 1987). Against these results, the standard deviation of the county income distribution had a negative effect on

TABLE 20.2 *Published Research on the Effects of Economic Inequality on Incarceration and Sentencing*

Study	Data	Dependent Variable	Results
Macrolevel time-series analysis			
1. Jacobs and Helms (2001)	U.S. series, 1946 to 1997	PIR	Gini positive and significant in three of three models, controlling for 1992 to 1997 period; positive and significant in two of six other models.
2. Jacobs and Helms (1996)	U.S. series, 1950 to 1990	State PAR	Gini (census) insignificant; variance of incomes (CPS) positive and significant in five of five models.
Macrolevel cross-sectional or pooled cross-sectional analysis			
3. Jacobs and Carmichael (2001)	Fifty states, 1970, 1980, 1990	Log PIR	Gini insignificant in six of six models.
4. Greenberg and West (2001)	Forty-nine states, 1971, 1981, 1991	PIR	Gini insignificant in five of five models.
5. Arvanites and Asher (1998)	Fifty states plus the District of Columbia, 1993	PIR, JIR, PIR + JIR	Gini positive and significant for JIR and JIR + PIR; not significant for four other models.
6. Hochstetler and Shover (1997)	269 urban counties, 1980, 1990	Change in PAR	County poverty rate and mean income insignificant in one model.
7. Bridges and Crutchfield (1988)	Forty-eight states, 1982	Black PIR, white PIR	Black-white relative risk of poverty negative and significant for white PIR; insignificant for black PIR.
8. Jacobs (1978)	Forty-seven states, 1960	Imprisonments per arrest, burglary and larceny	Gini coefficient has positive significant effect on burglary and larceny imprisonment ratios in four out of four models.
Microlevel cross-sectional analysis			
9. Britt (2000)	Pennsylvania felony sentences, 1991 to 1994	Imprisonment, sentence length	County black-white income difference significant and positive for white imprisonment, not significant for black imprisonment and sentence length.
10. Crawford, Chiricos, and Kleck (1998)	Florida felony sentences, 1992 to 1993	Habitual offender sentence	County white-black income difference insignificant in three of three models.
11. Myers (1987)	Georgia felony sentences, 1976 to 1982	Imprisonment, split sentence, sentence length	County income standard deviation negative and significant for sentence length; county black-white income difference positive and significant for split sentence, negative and significant for sentence length. Significant interactions indicate defendants are punished more severely within demographic and offense categories in high-inequality counties.

Source: Authors' compilation.
Note: PIR = prison incarceration rate; PAR = prison admission rate; JIR = jail incarceration rate. Citation key is reported in the appendix.

sentence length among felony defendants in Georgia (Myers 1987), and black-white income differentials were unassociated with sentencing under a habitual offender statute in Florida (Crawford, Chiricos, and Kleck 1998).

Discussion of Research on Punishment

Research in the sociology of punishment sheds some light on the direct link between economic inequality and criminal justice punishment, but theory and empirical research could both be strengthened. The weakest versions of the inequality-incarceration theory explain the modern penal system in terms of its functionality for capitalism by maintaining a reserve army of labor. Ivan Jankovic (1977, 20) appears to take this position, arguing that "imprisonment can be used to regulate the size of the surplus labor force." More commonly, the penal system is viewed as functional for capitalism by eliminating threats to social order posed by problem populations (Quinney 1974; Spitzer 1975; Box and Hale 1982). Few researchers today would explain incarceration in terms of its possible effects; instead, a stronger theory emphasizes the association made by lawmakers, police, and court officials between criminality and poverty or other kinds of social marginality.

The empirical evidence linking economic disadvantage to criminal punishment is uneven. There is reasonable evidence that the scale of punishment in the United States over the last fifty years has increased in periods of rising unemployment. The incarceration-unemployment relation is unstable, however, and over the last ten years imprisonment rates increased as joblessness declined (Michalowksi and Carlson 1999). Microlevel data also provide little support for a consistent relationship between the sentence received by a convict and his employment status. Evidence for the effects of economic inequality is weaker than for the effects of unemployment. Still, some analyses of aggregate time series yield positive results, and a few sentencing studies find harsher punishment in counties with high levels of inequality.

CONCLUSIONS AND FUTURE DIRECTIONS

What, then, do we know about the relationship between the parallel increases in American economic inequality and imprisonment? Supporting the inequality explanation of the prison boom, incarceration rates increased most among those whose economic losses were largest—among men without college education. By 2000 about 3 percent of young non-college-educated white men and 15 percent of non-college-educated black men were in prison or jail. Roughly double these fractions had acquired prison records at some point by their midthirties (Pettit and Western 2004). Sociological and economic theory help explain why increased economic inequality would raise the level of crime among the disadvantaged, and why formal social control efforts would intensify against the poor. Empirical evidence for these theories, however, is not compelling so far. At any given point in time in the recent past, we can be quite sure that poor men and residents of poor neighborhoods were more involved in street crime than the affluent, but we are much less certain that criminal activity increased among the poor as inequality rose over the last twenty years. Similarly, there is evidence that police patrol poor and minority neighborhoods more intensively than crime rates would lead us to expect, and that judges in some jurisdictions treat young, jobless, and minority defendants relatively harshly. There is much less evidence that these efforts have expanded with the sliding economic position of those with little education.

Trends in the law of criminal sentencing are strongly suggestive of an increasingly punitive attitude toward the poor, but even in this case we lack a large-scale empirical test.

Our review suggests that the understanding of the link between economic inequality and punishment might be extended in two main ways. First, a sharper empirical test enlisting much more data could be obtained by disaggregating the key dependent and independent variables. Right now, our confidence in the inequality-incarceration relationship is mostly sustained by a time-series regression on forty or fifty data points. The main empirical insight of social control theories—that punishment risks are concentrated in marginal groups—is largely ignored with this highly aggregated design. By combining macro- and microlevel data, we could calculate incarceration risks for specific birth cohorts and race and education groups. Measurement could thus focus on those groups contemplated by social control theory. An example of this approach is provided by the detailed incarceration rates reported in figure 20.2.

This disaggregated research design also leads us to reconsider how our key predictors are measured. Unemployment rates or population Gini indexes are blunt instruments for measuring the size or economic status of marginal populations. Consider unemployment first: unemployment is generally interpreted to measure the size of a problem population that triggers punitive treatment by the courts or police. However, with rising unemployment, the newly laid-off workers joining the ranks of the unemployed will tend to be more able and at relatively low risk of crime. In contrast to a modern version of the Rusche-Kirchheimer hypothesis, we might expect that attributions of criminality to the unemployed will weaken in times when unemployment is relatively common. Sentencing research and work by Loïc Wacquant (2000), Michael Tonry (1995), and Troy Duster (1997) similarly suggest that it is not cyclical unemployment but more permanent forms of economic disadvantage that elicit social control efforts. Because spells of joblessness tend to be longer for minorities and those with little schooling, disaggregated measures may capture social control processes better than the usual unemployment rate. From this perspective, joblessness among specific race and education groups would provide a better measure of persistent disadvantage.

A similar approach could be taken to study the effects of inequality. Instead of associating Gini coefficients with aggregate incarceration rates, attributions of criminality might be better measured by the distance between a group and some reference point. This approach tries to capture the intuition that the incarceration rate of low-skill blacks, for example, has increased because their economic position has declined relative to other groups. From this perspective, attributions of criminality stem from marginality or the relative position of troublesome populations. Angus Deaton and Christina Paxson (2001) take this approach to studying the effects of inequality on mortality. In their study of criminal punishment, George Bridges and Robert Crutchfield (1988) move in this direction by examining the effects of black-white income differentials on state imprisonment rates for blacks and whites. The analysis could go further by focusing on men at different levels of education.

The purpose of these suggestions for the utility of disaggregation is to achieve a tighter mapping between a group's place in the social hierarchy and its risk of incarceration. Although this link between economic status and punishment is the engine of social control theories, macrolevel research rests on the hopeful assumption that subgroup variation dominates the data at the aggregate level.

The second main branch of research on inequality and punishment is concerned with elaborating the intervening role of crime. Research on social control typically treats crime as a confounding source of variation. Crime rates must be controlled to identify the uncontaminated effect of economically motivated social control. Thus, virtually all of the studies estimating the effects of unemployment or inequality include some adjustment for the level of criminal offending. Although this approach is standard, there are several difficulties. If the measured crime rate is based on police reports, then the observed level of crime is also a product of social control efforts. These social control efforts affect some offenses (drugs, assault, and public order offenses) more than others (homicide). Estimating the effects of inequality controlling for the Uniform Crime Reports rate of index crimes leads us to underestimate the impact of social control processes. Crime rates based on victimization data may thus be more useful when estimating the effects of economic conditions on incarceration.

The link between crime and incarceration may also be a source of bias when estimating the social control effects of inequality on imprisonment. Although studies of deterrence and incapacitation find that increased policing and imprisonment reduce crime (Levitt 1996, 1997; Nagin 1998), this research is largely ignored in studies of formal social control. Indeed, our review found no study that took account of this dependence (or endogeneity) in estimating the effects of unemployment or inequality on imprisonment. The endogeneity bias, at least in the recent period, may be of reasonable size; several researchers argue that the crime drop of the 1990s is partly due to the rising rate of imprisonment (Rosenfeld 2000; Spelman 2000). If the deterrence research is correct, and incarceration nontrivially reduces crime, this endogeneity may also bias our estimate of the effects of inequality. If unemployment or inequality is positively related to crime, we will tend to overestimate the effect of economic conditions on incarceration.

Because formal social control processes affect official crime rates and the dependence of crime rates on incarceration rates may bias estimates of economic effects, it is useful to estimate the effects of economic conditions on incarceration without controlling for crime. Models of this kind are rarely estimated. A reduced form specification that includes only exogenous variables as predictors would estimate the total effect of incarceration through crime and formal social control processes. From our perspective, this total effect is intrinsically interesting. If rising inequality sends large numbers of men to prison, this remains an important social fact whether the causal pathway is through crime or state responses to the threat of crime. The total effect estimate also provides a benchmark that can be compared with the social control effect obtained by controlling for crime. Such an analysis would offer an approximate assessment of the relative importance of formal social control in linking inequality to incarceration.

These methodological challenges should not obscure the main point that imprisonment trends and theory are highly suggestive of a close link between the growth in American income inequality and the growth of the penal population. Prior empirical research is intermittently supportive, but a strong empirical test has not yet been conducted. Such a test must compare the relative risks of incarceration among those who lost ground economically in the 1980s and 1990s with the risks among those who advanced. A compelling test must also take crime more seriously. More than just a confounding source of variation that biases estimates of the social control effect, the level and distribution of crime suffuses the social control process. Crime and social control are mutually determining, and economic conditions may boost prison populations through their effects on the level of criminal offending. A detailed analysis of imprisonment with a richer model of crime thus promises valuable new knowledge about the links between inequality and punishment in the United States.

APPENDIX: CALCULATING THE INCARCERATION RATES

The disaggregated incarceration rate for age-education-race group i in year t (t = 1980, . . . , 2000) is estimated by:

$$\hat{r}_{it} = \frac{\hat{I}_{it}}{\hat{I}_{it} + \hat{N}_{it} + M_{it}}$$

where $\hat{I}_{it}$ is the estimated prison and jail inmate count, $\hat{N}_{it}$ is the estimated count for the civilian non-institutional population, and M_{it} is the observed count of active-duty military personnel. This approach follows Western and Pettit (2000), although the current estimates provide incarceration rates for Hispanics and include military personnel in estimates of the total population. The inmate count is estimated from the Survey of Inmates of State and Federal Correctional Facilities, 1979 to 1997, and the Survey of Local Jails, 1978 to 1996. Because the surveys are conducted only about every five years, they are used to calculate proportions of the annual aggregate counts of inmates published by the Bureau of Justice Statistics. Proportions for intersurvey years are interpolated. Separate series of inmate counts are calculated for jail, state prison, and federal prison. The civilian non-institutional population is estimated using annual data from the merged outgoing rotation group files of the Current Population Survey, 1980 to 2000. The military counts are directly observed and reported in the Defense Manpower Data Center's officer and enlisted master files, maintained by the Department of Defense.

This research was supported by a grant from the Russell Sage Foundation. We gratefully acknowledge the research assistance of Traci Schlesinger and Marylynne Hunt-Dorta. We thank Mike Dove and MSG Pam Bridges-Lewis (U.S. Army) for data from the Defense Manpower Data Center, and Kathy Neckerman for comments on an earlier draft.

REFERENCES

Albonetti, Celesta A. 1991. "An Integration of Theories to Explain Judicial Discretion." *Social Problems* 38: 247–66.

Anderson, Elijah. 1990. *Streetwise: Race, Class, and Change in an Urban Community.* Chicago: University of Chicago Press.

———. 1999. *Code of the Street: Decency, Violence, and the Moral Life of the Inner City.* New York: W. W. Norton.

Arvanites, Thomas M., and Martin A. Asher. 1998. "State and County Incarceration Rates: The Direct and Indirect Effects of Race and Inequality." *American Journal of Economics and Sociology* 57: 207–21.

Bass, Sandra. 2001. "Policing Space, Policing Rate: Social Control Imperatives and Police Discretionary Decisions." *Social Justice* 28: 156–76.

Becker, Gary S. 1968. "Crime and Punishment: An Economic Approach." *Journal of Political Economy* 76(2): 169–217.

Bernhardt, Annette, Martina Morris, Mark Handcock, and Mark Scott. 2001. *Divergent Paths: Economic Mobility in the U.S. Labor Market.* New York: Russell Sage Foundation.

Blau, Judith R., and Peter M. Blau. 1982. "The Cost of Inequality: Metropolitan Structure and Violent Crime." *American Sociological Review* 47(1): 114–29.

Blumstein, Alfred, and Allen J. Beck. 1999. "Population Growth in U.S. Prisons, 1980 to 1996." In *Crime and Justice: Prisons,* vol. 26, edited by Michael Tonry and Joan Petersilia. Chicago: University of Chicago Press.

Boggess, Scott, and John Bound. 1997. "Did Criminal Activity Increase During the 1980s? Comparisons Across Data Sources." *Social Science Quarterly* 78: 725–39.

Bourgois, Philippe I. 1995. *In Search of Respect: Selling Crack in El Barrio.* New York: Cambridge University Press.

Box, Steven, and Chris Hale. 1982. "Economic Crisis and the Rising Prison Population in England and Wales." *Crime and Social Justice* 17: 20–35.

Braithwaite, John. 1979. *Inequality, Crime, and Public Policy.* London: Routledge.

Bridges, George S., and Robert D. Crutchfield. 1988. "Law, Social Standing, and Racial Disparities in Imprisonment." *Social Forces* 66: 699–724.

Britt, Chester L. 2000. "Social Context and Racial Disparities in Punishment Decisions." *Justice Quarterly* 17: 707–32.

Chambliss, William J. 1999. *Power, Politics, and Crime.* Boulder, Colo.: Westview Press.

Chiricos, Theodore G., and Miriam A. Delone. 1992. "Labor Surplus and Punishment: A Review and Assessment of Theory and Evidence." *Social Problems* 39: 421–46.

Crawford, Charles, Theodore G. Chiricos, and Gary Kleck. 1998. "Race, Racial Threat, and Sentencing of Habitual Offenders." *Criminology* 36: 481–511.

Crutchfield, Robert D., George S. Bridges, and Susan R. Pitchford. 1994. "Analytical and Aggregation Biases in Analyses of Imprisonment: Reconciling Discrepancies in Studies of Racial Disparity." *Journal of Research in Crime and Delinquency* 31: 166–82.

Crutchfield, Robert D., and Susan R. Pitchford. 1997. "Work and Crime: The Effects of Labor Stratification." *Social Forces* 76(1): 93–118.

D'Alessio, Stewart J., and Lisa A. Stolzenberg. 2002. "A Multilevel Analysis of the Relationship Between Labor Surplus and Pre-trial Incarceration." *Social Problems* 49: 178–93.

Daly, Kathleen. 1994. *Gender, Crime, and Punishment.* New Haven, Conn.: Yale University Press.

Deaton, Angus, and Christina Paxson. 2001. "Mortality and Income Inequality over Time in Britain and the United States." Working paper 8534. Cambridge, Mass.: National Bureau of Economic Research.

Ditton, Paula M., and Doris James Wilson. 1999. *Truth in Sentencing in State Prisons.* Bureau of Justice Statistics Special Report. Washington: U.S. Department of Justice.

Doyle, Joanne M., Ehsan Ahmed, and Robert N. Horn. 1999. "The Effects of Labor Markets and Income Inequality on Crime: Evidence for Panel Data." *Southern Journal of Economics* 65: 717–38.

Dubber, Markus Dirk. 2001. "Policing Possession: The War on Crime and the End of Criminal Law." *Journal of Criminal Law and Criminology* 91: 829–996.

Duneier, Mitchell. 1999. *Sidewalk.* New York: Farrar, Straus and Giroux.

Duster, Troy. 1997. "Pattern, Purpose, and Race in the Drug War: The Crisis of Credibility in Criminal Justice." In *Crack in America: Demon Drugs and Social Justice,* edited by Craig Reinarman and Harry G. Levine. Berkeley: University of California Press.

Dye, Thomas. 1969. "Income Inequality and American State Politics." *The Journal of Politics* 31(1): 1080–97.

Ellwood, David T., and Christopher Jencks. 2001. "The Growing Difference in Family Structure: What Do We Know? Where Do We Look for Answers?" Unpublished paper. Harvard University, Cambridge, Mass.

Fowles, Richard, and Mary Merva. 1996. "Wage Inequality and Criminal Activity: An Extreme Bounds Analysis for the United States, 1975 to 1990." *Criminology* 34: 163–82.

France, Anatole. 1894. *The Red Lily.* New York: Dodd-Mead.

Freeman, Richard B. 1995. "The Labor Market." In *Crime,* edited by James Q. Wilson and Joan Petersilia. San Francisco: Institute for Contemporary Studies Press.

———. 1996. "Why Do So Many Young American Men Commit Crimes and What Might We Do About It?" *Journal of Economic Perspectives* 10(1): 22–45.

Gilens, Martin. 1999. *Why Americans Hate Welfare: Race, Media, and the Politics of Antipoverty Policy.* Chicago: University of Chicago Press.

Greenberg, David. 1977. "The Dynamics of Oscillatory Punishment Processes." *Journal of Criminal Law and Criminology* 68: 643–51.

Greenberg, David F., and Valerie West. 2001. "State Prison Populations and Their Growth, 1971 to 1991." *Criminology* 39: 615–54.

Hagan, John. 1993. "The Social Embeddedness of Crime and Unemployment." *Criminology* 31: 465–91.

Hagan, John, and Kristen Bumiller. 1983. "Making Sense of Sentencing: A Review and Critique of Sentencing Research." In *Research on Sentencing: The Search for Reform,* edited by Alfred Blumstein, Jacqueline Cohen, Susan Martin, and Michael Tonry. Washington, D.C.: National Academy Press.

Hall, Stuart. 1978. *Policing the Crisis: Mugging, the State, and Law and Order.* London: Macmillan.

Herbert, Steve. 1997. *Policing Space: Territoriality and the Los Angeles Police Department.* Minneapolis: University of Minnesota Press.

Hochstetler, Andrew L., and Neal Shover. 1997. "Street Crime, Labor Surplus, and Criminal Punishment, 1980 to 1990." *Social Problems* 44: 358–67.

Huo, Yuen, and Tom R. Tyler. 2000. *How Different Ethnic Groups React to Legal Authority.* San Francisco: Public Policy Institute of California.

Jackson, Pamela I. 1989. *Minority Group Threat, Crime, and Policing: Social Context and Social Control.* New York: Praeger.

Jacobs, David. 1978. "Inequality and the Legal Order: An Ecological Test of the Conflict Model." *Social Problems* 25: 515–25.

Jacobs, David, and Jason D. Carmichael. 2001. "The Politics of Punishment Across Time and Space: A Pooled Time-Series Analysis of Imprisonment Rates." *Social Forces* 80: 61–91.

Jacobs, David, and Ronald E. Helms. 1996. "Toward a Political Model of Incarceration: A Time-Series Examination of Multiple Explanations for Prison Admission Rates." *American Journal of Sociology* 102(2): 323–57.

———. 1998. "The Determinants of Deadly Force: A Structural Analysis of Police Violence." *American Journal of Sociology* 103(4): 837–62.

———. 2001. "Towards a Political Sociology of Punishment: Politics and Changes in the Incarcerated Population." *Social Science Research* 30: 171–94.

Jankovic, Ivan. 1977. "Labor Market and Imprisonment." *Crime and Social Justice* 8: 17–31.

Kelly, Morgan. 2000. "Inequality and Crime." *Review of Economics and Statistics* 82: 530–39.

Kleck, Gary. 1981. "Racial Discrimination in Criminal Sentencing: A Critical Evaluation of the Evidence with Additional Factors on the Death Penalty." *American Sociological Review* 46: 783–804.

Kluegel, James R. 1990. "Trends in Whites' Explanations of the Black-White Gap in SES." *American Sociological Review* 55: 512–25.

LaFree, Gary, and Kriss A. Drass. 1996. "The Effect of Changes in Intraracial Income Inequality and Educational Attainment on Changes in Arrest Rates for African Americans and Whites, 1957 to 1990." *American Sociological Review* 61: 614–34.

Land, Kenneth C., Patricia McCall, and Lawrence E. Cohen. 1990. "Structural Covariates of Homicide Rates: Are There Any Invariances Across Time and Space?" *American Journal of Sociology* 95: 922–63.

Laub, John H., Daniel S. Nagin, and Robert J. Sampson. 1998. "Trajectories of Change in Criminal Offending: Good Marriages and the Desistance Process." *American Sociological Review* 63(2): 225–38.

Levitt, Steven D. 1996. "The Effect of Prison Population Size on Crime Rates: Evidence from Prison Overcrowding Litigation." *Quarterly Journal of Economics* 111: 319–51.

———. 1997. "Using Electoral Cycles in Police Hiring to Estimate the Effect of Police on Crime." *American Economic Review* 87(3): 270–90.

———. 1999. "The Changing Relationship Between Income and Crime Victimization." *Economic Policy Review* 5: 87–98.

Liska, Allen, Joseph Lawrence, and Michael L. Benson. 1981. "Perspectives on the Legal Order." *American Journal of Sociology* 87(2): 412–26.

Marvell, Thomas B., and Carlisle E. Moody. 1996. "Determinate Sentencing and Abolishing Parole: The Long-term Impacts on Prisons and Crime." *Criminology* 34: 107–28.

Melossi, Dario. 1989. "An Introduction: Fifty Years Later, Punishment and Social Structure in Contemporary Analysis." *Contemporary Crises* 13: 311–26.

Merton, Robert K. 1968. *Social Theory and Social Structure.* Enlarged ed. New York: Free Press.

Messner, Steven F., Lawrence Raffolovich, and Richard McMillan. 2001. "Economic Deprivation and Changes in Homicide Arrest Rates for White and Black Youths, 1967 to 1998." *Criminology* 39: 591–613.

Michalowski, Raymond J., and Susan M. Carlson. 1999. "Unemployment, Imprisonment, and Social Structures of Accumulation: Historical Contingency in the Rusche-Kirchheimer Hypothesis." *Criminology* 37: 217–49.

Morenoff, Jeffrey D., Robert J. Sampson, and Stephen W. Raudenbush. 2001. "Neighborhood Inequality, Collective Efficacy, and the Spatial Dynamics of Urban Violence." *Criminology* 39: 517–59.

Myers, Martha A. 1987. "Economic Inequality and Discrimination in Sentencing." *Social Forces* 65: 746–66.

Nagin, Daniel S. 1998. "Criminal Deterrence Research at the Outset of the Twenty-first Century." *Crime and Justice: A Review of Research* 23: 1–42.

Nobiling, Tracy, Cassia Spohn, and Miriam Delone. 1998. "A Tale of Two Counties: Unemployment and Sentence Severity." *Justice Quarterly* 15: 459–85.

Pettit, Becky, and Bruce Western. Forthcoming. "Inequality in Lifetime Risks of Incarceration." *American Sociological Review*.

Quinney, Richard. 1974. *Criminal Justice in America: A Critical Understanding.* Boston: Little, Brown.

Rosenfeld, Richard. 2000. "Patterns in Adult Homicide, 1980 to 1995." In *The Crime Drop in America,* edited by Alfred Blumstein and Joel Wallman. New York: Cambridge University Press.

Rusche, Georg. 1933/1978. "Labor Market and Penal Sanction." *Crime and Justice* 10: 2–8.

———. 1933/1980. "Labor Market and Penal Sanction: Thoughts on the Sociology of Punishment." In *Punishment and Penal Discipline,* edited by Tony Platt and Paul Takagi. Berkeley, Calif.: Crime and Justice Associates.

Rusche, Georg, and Otto Kirchheimer. 1939/2003. *Punishment and Social Structure.* New Brunswick, N.J.: Transaction Books.

Sampson, Robert. 1987. "Urban Black Violence: The Effect of Male Joblessness and Family Disruption." *American Journal of Sociology* 93(2): 348–82.

Sampson, Robert J., and John H. Laub. 1993. *Crime in the Making: Pathways and Turning Points Through Life.* Cambridge, Mass.: Harvard University Press.

Sampson, Robert J., and Stephen W. Raudenbush. 1999. "Systematic Social Observation of Public Spaces: A New Look at Disorder in Urban Neighborhoods." *American Journal of Sociology* 105(3): 603–51.

Sellin, Thorsten. 1935. "Race Prejudice in the Administration of Justice." *American Journal of Sociology* 41: 212–17.

Shaw, Clifford, and Henry McKay. 1942. *Juvenile Delinquency and Urban Areas.* Chicago: University of Chicago Press.

Shihadeh, Edwin S., and Darrell J. Steffensmeier. 1994. "Economic Inequality, Family Disruption, and Urban Black Violence: Cities as Units of Stratification and Social Control." *Social Forces* 73(2): 729–51.

Sorensen, Jon, and Don Stemen. 2002. "The Effects of State Sentencing Policies on Incarceration Rates." *Crime and Delinquency* 48: 256–75.

Spelman, William. 2000. "The Limited Importance of Prison Expansion." In *The Crime Drop in America,* edited by Alfred Blumstein and Joel Wallman. New York: Cambridge University Press.

Spitzer, Steven. 1975. "Toward a Marxian Theory of Deviance." *Social Problems* 22: 638–51.

Spohn, Cassia, and David Holleran. 2000. "The Imprisonment Penalty Paid by Young, Unemployed Black and Hispanic Male Offenders." *Criminology* 38: 281–306.

Steffensmeier, Darrell, Jeffery Ulmer, and John Kramer. 1998. "The Interaction of Race, Gender, and Age in Criminal Sentencing: The Punishment Cost of Being Young, Black, and Male." *Criminology* 36: 763–97.

Sullivan, Mercer. 1989. *"Getting Paid": Youth Crime and Work in the Inner City.* Ithaca, N.Y.: Cornell University Press.

Tittle, Charles R. 1994. "Theoretical Bases for Inequality in Formal Social Control." In *Inequality, Crime, and Social Control,* edited by George S. Bridges and Martha A. Myers. Boulder, Colo.: Westview Press.

Tittle, Charles R., Wayne J. Villemez, and Douglas A. Smith. 1978. "The Myth of Social Class and Criminality: An Empirical Assessment of the Empirical Evidence." *American Sociological Review* 43(5): 643–56.

Tonry, Michael. 1994. *Sentencing Matters.* New York: Oxford University Press.

———. 1995. *Malign Neglect: Race, Crime, and Punishment in America.* New York: Oxford University Press.

Uggen, Christopher. 2000. "Work as a Turning Point in the Life Course of Criminals: A Duration Model of Age, Employment, and Recidivism." *American Sociological Review* 65(4): 529–46.

U.S. Department of Commerce. U.S. Census Bureau. 2002. "Table IE-2 Measures of Individual Earnings Inequality for Full-time, Year-round Workers by Sex: 1967 to 2000." Washington: U.S. Government Printing Office for U.S. Census Bureau.

U.S. Office of Justice Programs. U.S. Bureau of Justice Assistance. 1998. *1996 National Survey of State Sentencing Structures*. Washington: Bureau of Justice Assistance.

———. 2002. "National Crime Victimization Survey of Violent Crime Trends, 1973 to 2001." Washington: Bureau of Justice Statistics.

———. 2002. *Sourcebook of Justice Statistics*. Washington: Bureau of Justice Statistics.

Venkatesh, Sudhir A., and Steven D. Levitt. 2000. "'Are We a Family or a Business?': History and Disjuncture in the Urban American Street Gang." *Theory and Society* 29: 427–62.

Wacquant, Loïc. 2000. "The New 'Peculiar Institution': On the Prison as Surrogate Ghetto." *Theoretical Criminology* 4: 377–89.

Western, Bruce, and Becky Pettit. 2000. "Incarceration and Racial Inequality In Men's Employment." *Industrial and Labor Relations Review* 54: 3–16.

———. 2002. "Beyond Crime and Punishment: Prisons and Inequality." *Contexts* 1: 37–43.

Wilson, James Q. 1968. *Varieties of Police Behavior: The Management of Law and Order in Eight Communities*. Cambridge, Mass.: Harvard University Press.

Wilson, William Julius. 1987. *The Truly Disadvantaged: The Inner City, the Underclass, and Public Policy*. Chicago: University of Chicago Press.

Chapter 21

The Consequences of Income Inequality for Redistributive Policy in the United States

Gabriel S. Lenz

Although the United States has one of the highest levels of income inequality among developed countries, pre-tax-and-transfer income inequality is only 7 percent higher than the average for twelve other advanced industrial nations (Hacker et al. 2003, 4–5).[1] In other words, market income inequality is not much higher in the United States than in these countries. What differentiates the United States is that taxes and transfers do not redistribute income to the same degree. Although average pre-tax-and-transfer inequality is only 7 percent higher, inequality after taxes and transfers is almost 30 percent higher. Since the early 1980s the degree to which taxes and transfers reduce inequality increased 10 percent among these other nations. By contrast, taxes and transfers now reduce inequality less in the United States than they did in the mid-1980s. Much of this decrease probably results from lower welfare benefits, which, by some measures, declined by more than 40 percent between 1972 and 1991 (Danziger and Gottschalk 1995).

Why has the United States adopted less effective redistributive programs compared with similar nations, and why have these programs decreased while wage inequality increased—the reverse of what occurred in other countries? In the United States, state governments control many of the programs that redistribute income. A rapidly expanding cross-national literature has investigated the determinants of redistribution, focusing in particular on the effect of income inequality, but very little recent research has investigated these relationships at the U.S. state level. To some extent, this is surprising and bound to change. Much of the cross-national research uses small samples of developed countries. The United States presents a remarkable laboratory for research with its fifty states, which have similar cultures and institutions, and better and more comparable data are available for U.S. states than for developed countries. To begin to investigate these questions, I review the literature on the determinants of redistributive public policy, focusing on the potential role of inequality in explaining these policies. I supplement this review with preliminary analysis.

THEORY

Why might inequality affect public policy? Scholars have developed a number of theories about inequality's influence on redistribution, and they have often led to contradictory predictions. The most common prediction about inequality and redistribution is that greater inequality leads to greater redistribution. A number of very different theories make this prediction. The most frequently cited suggests that increased inequality in pretax earnings leads to greater political demands for redistributive policies (Meltzer and Richard 1981; Roberts 1977; Romer 1975). The median voter model provides the logic behind this theory (Black 1958). Candidates for political office can maximize their chances of election victory by adopting the issue position of the median voter—the voter with the middle position on a particular issue.[2] The individual with the median income will be relatively poorer in more unequal societies. The more unequal the income distribution, the more the median voter has to gain through redistribution if net transfers, measured as government-provided benefits minus taxes, are progressive. Thus, the median voter should increasingly prefer greater redistribution as his or her income declines relative to the mean. To increase the odds of victory, candidates for political office should adopt an increasingly redistributive issue position as the median voter's income falls below the mean. If candidates follow this strategy, and if the winning candidate enacts policies that reflect his or her issue positions, then increased income inequality should result in increased redistribution.

In part, the median-voter-model prediction is popular among researchers because it is robust to a number of assumptions, assumptions that might seem problematic. For instance, one assumption to which this prediction is robust is that the median voter increasingly benefits from redistribution as his or her income falls below the mean. This is problematic because many redistributive programs benefit only those with low incomes. However, Thomas Husted (1989) has developed a model of redistributive policy that directly benefits only the poor, such as welfare programs, but results in the same prediction—that is, that greater inequality leads to greater redistribution. For those with low incomes, he suggests, the desire for income redistribution is high and the cost in terms of taxes is low. Among wealthier individuals, the cost in terms of the taxes associated with such programs increases because of tax progressivity, and they have access to alternative safety nets, such as private savings and unemployment insurance. However, at high levels of income the demand for redistribution because of altruism or as a method to alleviate the potential for crime or social unrest may exceed the higher cost in terms of taxes and lower social insurance requirements. Thus, the poor and the rich may desire redistribution while those in the middle oppose it. Using public opinion data to test this hypothesis, Husted finds that the poorest and the wealthiest individuals express a greater desire for spending on welfare programs compared with those in the middle of the income distribution. Since wider income distributions have more individuals in the tails, support for redistribution will increase, according to this theory, as inequality increases. This prediction arises out of a median voter framework, but the median voter is no longer pivotal because the preference for redistribution is concave with respect to income. Thus, the median voter framework can lead to this prediction without assuming that redistribution necessarily benefits the median voter.

The prediction that greater inequality leads to greater redistribution is also robust to relaxing the assumption that candidates concern themselves only with election victory. An alternative view holds that, in addition to winning, the political parties and their candidates care about policy outcomes and represent the interests and values of different constituencies (Alesina and Rosenthal 1995; Calvert 1985; Wittman 1977, 1983). In this approach, parties want to win elections in order to enact their preferred policies. Thus, the parties may not converge to the position of the median voter. However, even though competing parties may not converge, growing inequality may increase the probability that those representing lower-income individuals will win elections. Consequently, models that relax the assumption that the parties converge to the median voter can also predict that greater inequality will lead to greater redistribution.[3]

Other researchers have explained redistribution not through the median voter model but through special-interest-group or pork-barrel models of politics, and they have often resulted in the same prediction (Becker 1983; Cox and McCubbins 1986; Lidbeck and Weibull 1993; Peltzman 1976). In these models, vote-maximizing politicians balance the votes gained from the poor against the votes lost from other groups because of the higher taxes required to fund higher benefits. A number of researchers have applied this model to redistributive policy in the United States but have not considered the potential role of income inequality (Baumgardner 1993; Plotnick and Winters 1985). Different assumptions in these models lead to different predictions, but some are consistent with the theory that greater inequality leads to greater redistribution because it may provide more votes for pro-redistribution candidates. Avinash Dixit and John Londregan (1996, 1143) note that, other things being equal, the poor do well in these models because their votes are relatively cheap. Politicians can more easily purchase the votes of lower-income individuals because the incremental dollar matters much more to them than it does to the wealthy.

Although much theory results in the prediction that greater inequality leads to greater redistribution, cross-national evidence on it is mixed. While Branko Milanovic (2000), for example, finds that greater inequality in market incomes corresponds with greater redistribution, most other cross-national studies find no relationship or a negative one (Benabou 1996; Moene and Wallerstein 2001; Perotti 1994, 1996). Even though this prediction is robust to relaxing some assumptions, these contradictory results may arise because the theories rely on a number of other more unrealistic assumptions about voters, institutions, candidates, and parties. In reviewing the literature on redistribution in the United States, I focus on two problematic assumptions.

First, many of these theories assume that with greater inequality there will be more lower-income voters compared with wealthier voters (those below the mean income compared with those above). However, lower-income voters are less likely to vote and participate in politics generally (Verba, Schlozman, and Brady 1995). Thus, greater inequality may lead to relatively more lower-income individuals, but not relatively more lower-income voters.

The second problematic assumption on which I focus is that elections are fought over a single issue—in this case, redistribution. If voters consider more than one issue during elections, which they most certainly do, then there exists no best position for the candidates (McKelvey 1976; Plott 1976; Riker 1980). As a result, the candidates' platforms on redistribution will not necessarily converge to that of the median voter nor will pro-redistribution parties necessarily benefit from greater numbers of poor voters. Thus, the prediction that redistribution will increase as inequality increases holds only when people cast votes based on this issue. The poor and other groups may often vote on issues other than redistribution. Examples of such issues among the poor in the United States include race (see Key 1949) and anticommunism. Thus, one of the many potential explanations for the mixed cross-national results is that the political parties do not converge to the median voter's position on redistribution because elections and party systems involve many issues, not simply the distribution of wealth.

Some evidence suggests that the parties have become increasingly polarized by income in the United States, making this assumption potentially less problematic. Nolan McCarty, Keith Poole, and Howard Rosenthal (2003, 5) find that in the period following World War II respondents from the highest income quintile were only slightly more likely to identify as

Republicans than were respondents from the lowest quintile. In the 1990s, however, respondents in the highest quintile were more than twice as likely to identify as Republican as were those in the lowest.

Income inequality could have caused this polarization. Given a constant relationship between income and partisanship, an increase in the width of the income distribution would result in greater polarization by income. However, McCarty and his colleagues (2003) find that growing inequality has not caused the polarization. Instead, the effect of income has itself increased. Analysis of congressional roll call votes suggests that the parties' positions have also diverged since the 1970s, though not necessarily on the issue of redistribution (Poole and Rosenthal 1997).

Although I do not examine it in the context of the United States, another important assumption of these theories worthy of mention is that candidates will enact their platforms after winning an election. Greater inequality may lead to the election of more Democrats or more candidates who stand for greater redistribution, but they may not implement higher levels of redistribution while in office. Concern for future elections or for the reputation of their party may create incentives for candidates to enact their platforms, but we know little about the strength of these incentives.

In an analysis of U.S. senators' roll call votes and their constituents' opinions, Bartels (2002) provides an example of voting behavior that does not reflect the median voter's opinion. He finds that senators appear to be much more responsive to the opinions of affluent constituents than to the opinions of constituents with modest incomes. On average, his estimates suggest that constituents at the seventy-fifth percentile of the income distribution have almost three times as much influence on senators' general voting patterns as those at the twenty-fifth percentile. These trends are evident among both Democratic and Republican senators, but especially among Republicans. Bartels's findings suggest that senators do not vote the preferences of the median voter in their constituencies but those of wealthier voters.

Scholars have developed a number of other theories about the relationship between inequality and redistribution that lead to very different predictions. Although this review of public policy and inequality in the United States focuses on the prediction that greater inequality leads to greater redistribution, it is worth briefly reviewing these alternatives.

In contrast to the thesis that greater inequality leads to greater redistribution, another line of reasoning leads to the opposite prediction. Like Husted (1989), a number of scholars have developed theories that do not assume that redistribution directly benefits the median voter; their theorizing leads to the opposite prediction—that greater inequality results in less redistribution (Grogan 1994, 593; Moffitt, Ribar, and Wilhelm 1998). Voters, these theories suggest, prefer to tie welfare benefits to low-skilled wages for a number of reasons. For instance, falling wages may induce greater caseloads, driving up the cost of a marginal increase in benefits. As low-income wages fall, welfare benefits must also fall to avoid creating work disincentives. Finally, falling wages may create a gap between welfare and nonwelfare working poor that voters may wish to reduce with benefit reductions. Thus, falling wages among low-skilled workers may lead to lower welfare benefits. If mean income rises or remains unchanged, then a fall in low-skilled workers' wages will correspond to an increase in inequality. Thus, rising inequality in the lower tail of the income distribution should lead to less redistribution, at least through welfare programs.

Finally, one theory makes different predictions depending on the degree of inequality in different parts of the income distribution. Using a pork-barrel politics framework, Lorenzo Kristov, Peter Lindert, and Robert McClelland (1992) suggest that the extent of redistribution depends not on how much voters will benefit immediately from redistribution but on voters' affinity with those wealthier and poorer than themselves and their perceptions of the likelihood that they will need future transfers. The authors contend that the shape of the income distribution determines in large part these perceptions of affinity and mobility. In countries with a wide gap between those in the middle and those at the bottom, middle-class individuals have less social affinity for, and perceive themselves as less likely to find themselves among, those with lower incomes. Consequently, the middle class wants less redistribution as the income gap between the middle and the bottom increases. Similarly, the wider the income gap between the middle and the top, the less social affinity those in the middle have for those at the top, and the less likely they are to think that they will soon reach the top. Thus, the middle class wants more redistribution as the income gap between the middle and the top increases. Kristov and his colleagues test their theory on thirteen OECD countries between 1960 and 1981 and find support for their hypotheses: wider income gaps between the middle and the bottom are associated with less redistribution; wider income gaps between the middle and the top are associated with more redistribution.

EVIDENCE

To what extent do these theories explain variation in policies regarding redistribution in United States, both across time and across states? Very little research has investigated this question, and most focuses on specific policies, like welfare or Medicaid, and, with notable exceptions, generally does not address theory about redistribution.

The theories reviewed here make predictions that depend on the level of income inequality. Researchers can test these theories only if income inequality varies across states or across time. To what extent does income inequality vary across states and across time? Since its low in 1968, the Gini coefficient of family income, a standard measure of inequality, has risen by more than 20 percent (U.S. Department of Commerce 2002). Figure 21.1 plots Gini coefficients for household income from 1976 to 1995 for each state and includes 95 percent confidence intervals.[4] This figure suggests that most states have experienced a considerable rise in income inequality and that states vary considerably in their initial level of inequality. New York experienced the largest increase in inequality, 0.091, and a number of states experienced little or no increase in inequality, including Utah, Arkansas, and Alaska. Figure 21.2 plots states' Gini coefficients for 1995 by their coefficients for 1976. If inequality had remained stable over time, then states should fall on a forty-five-degree line, which is drawn as a solid line in this figure. However, the figure suggests large increases and, to some extent, a regression to the mean. The dashed line plots predicted values from a linear regression. Its slope suggests that inequality increased somewhat less among the most unequal states and somewhat more among the least unequal. Depending on the theory, this rise in inequality can lead to either greater or lesser redistribution.

Testing theories about the relationship between inequality and redistribution is problematic for a number of reasons, the most important of which is probably endogeneity. Redistribution most likely influences income inequality and income inequality most likely influences redistribution. Researchers attempt to measure pre-tax-and-transfer income inequality, but these measures are imperfect, and government policy may also influence market incomes. Consequently, finding that increases in inequality result in increases in redistribution may be difficult because the redistribution may mask measurements of increased inequality biasing estimates.

Given these problems, there has been little research to test these theories in the

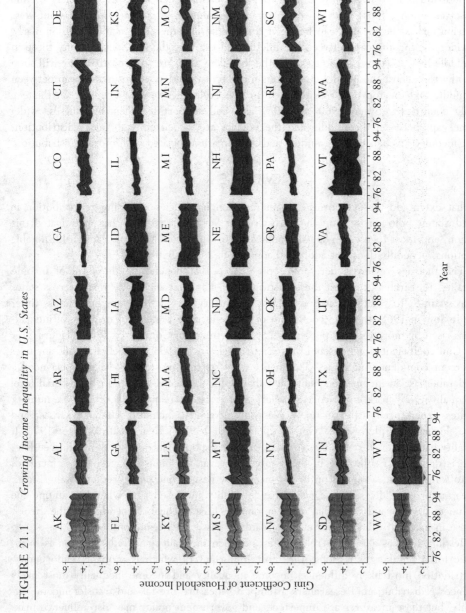

FIGURE 21.1   Growing Income Inequality in U.S. States

Note: The Gini coefficients for family income are from Langer (1999) and are available from www.u.arizona.edu/~llanger/replication _datasets.htm. The shaded region reports 95 percent confidence intervals.

FIGURE 21.2   *The Relationship Between Household Income Inequality in 1976 and 1995*

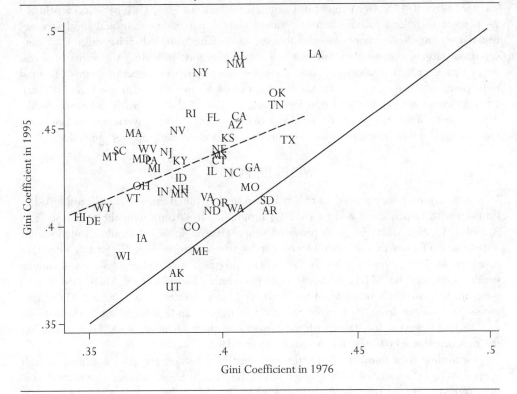

Note: See figure 21.1 for Gini coefficients source.

United States. In fact, the only time-series study that addresses redistribution generally is by Kathy J. Hayes, Daniel J. Slottje, and Susan Porter-Hudak (1991), who explicitly investigate the impact of inequality on federal redistributive spending.[5] Using census data on income inequality, these authors examine the effect of inequality on U.S. federal tax progressivity and federal public assistance expenditures, such as welfare, and on the share of total income held by each quintile of the income distribution. Using data from 1952 to 1982, they find that the share of income held by the middle and top quintiles corresponds with levels of public assistance. As the income share of the third and fourth quintiles rises, federal expenditures on public assistance appear to increase. However, the authors measure policy through expenditures, which can be problematic. More important, states, not the federal government, control many of these policies. Given the variation in income inequality across states, it seems likely that state-level inequality, not federal, drives state policy, though research must eventually test both alternatives.

Other than this paper by Hayes and her colleagues (1991), most research on redistribution in the United States focuses on particular policies. Federal, state, and local governments provide a number of income-tested benefits that redistribute income, including welfare, medical benefits, food stamps, and housing benefits, to name a few. Almost all of the research that investigates the determinants of the generosity of these programs focuses on welfare or Medicaid, which make up the bulk of spending on means-tested programs. Out of total spending on income-tested benefits in 2000, the federal government spent 43 percent on medical benefits, primarily through Medicaid, and state and local governments spent 72 percent (U.S. Department of Commerce 2002, no. 515). Cash benefits constituted 24 percent of federal income-tested spending and 15 percent of state and local income-tested spending. Researchers have also focused on welfare and Medicaid because state governments largely control the generosity of such programs, providing the variance across states that is critical to analysis. Thus, I review the research on these programs. To fund redistributive policies, states must tax their populations, and states can use taxes to redistribute income independently of transfer programs. Thus, I also review the literature on the determinants of tax progressivity. Finally, I briefly discuss other government policies that can influence the distribution of income but that researchers have not yet studied.

WELFARE POLICY

Most research on policy related to redistribution in the United States focuses on the Aid to Families with Dependent Children (AFDC) program. Originating with the Social Security Act of 1935, the AFDC program provided support to single-parent families and, in some states, to families with one unemployed parent whose income met the state's eligibility standard. In 1994, not long before the AFDC program was replaced, almost 4 million families depended on AFDC. Although state governments administered AFDC, the federal government provided a majority of its funds. Federal reimbursement rates for AFDC payments have ranged from 50 percent for states with per capita income above the national median to 83 percent for states with the lowest per capita incomes. State governments set the maximum benefit levels and the eligibility standards (Tweedie 1994).

According to a number of the theories discussed earlier, we should expect greater inequality to be associated with greater redistribution. Although scholars have conducted little research into the relationship between inequality and welfare policy, a few early papers used cross-sectional data from the 1960s to test for such a relationship. For instance, Thomas Dye (1969) found that greater income inequality is associated with less spending on welfare and education, the opposite of the expected relationship. In one of the few papers to focus primarily on inequality and state-level public expenditures, David Jacobs (1980) found that this unexpected relationship holds with other measures of income inequality and controlling for a state's capacity to afford redistribution.[6] Reviewing this literature, Jacobs and Waldman (1983) concluded that in states with the most pronounced income differences, expenditures are likely to be lower not only on AFDC but for other redistributive programs (Jacobs 1980).[7] More recently, Charles Barrilleaux and Belinda C. Davis (2003) find a similar relationship using data from 1980 and 1990. Thus, these findings apparently contradict the prediction that greater inequality leads to greater redistribution. Inequality is associated with less, not more, redistribution.

However, inferences from associations across states in a given year are problematic because correlation does not necessarily mean causation. Other factors that this research does not take into account, including endogeneity, could explain this relationship. Analyzing changes over time permits stronger conclusions about causation. In addition, these papers are part of a large literature in political science that reports cross-sectional analyses of state welfare expenditures. Unfortunately, much of this literature measures welfare benefits with data on expenditures. Expenditures do not necessarily measure policy because unemployment and other factors, including public policy, drive welfare expenditures (Hanson 1984, 313–15; Plotnick 1986, 598). Recent research often measures AFDC policy with the income guarantee, which also frequently serves as the eligibility requirement. Some scholars continue to use expenditure measures because of their availability, but more research is needed to determine the degree to which expenditures reflect policy.

More recently, economists and political scientists have conducted a number of pooled time-series analyses with better measures of state welfare policy, though many focus on nonpolitical determinants of welfare policy, with some notable exceptions (Albritton 1989; Hill, Leighley, and Hinton-Andersson 1995; Moffitt 1990; Peterson and Rom 1989; Soss et al. 2001; Tweedie 1994). Most of these recent studies have failed to include income inequality. In his review of the literature on the determinants of AFDC policy, Jack Tweedie (1994, 655–56) makes no mention of inequality.

Only two papers have tested the hypothesis that greater inequality leads to greater redistribution on AFDC policy across time. Using data from four years in the late 1970s and early 1980s, Husted (1989) estimates a random-effects model, measuring income inequality with the log of the variance of income. To measure AFDC policy, he uses the real effective state AFDC guarantee to a family of four. Husted finds a positive relationship between his measure of income inequality and the real effective welfare benefit guarantee. Based on a number of assumptions and holding all else equal, his results suggest that the state with the highest level of inequality would have an expected welfare benefit $20 higher than that of the state with the least income inequality—a reasonably small effect given that the mean benefit was $127, with a standard deviation of $49.

In another paper, Husted and Kenny (1997) examine the effects of eliminating poll taxes and other barriers to voting on state and local government spending, and they include a measure of income inequality as a control. Using data from 1950 to 1988, they estimate a model that includes fixed effects for years and states and measures inequality as the difference between the first- and third-quartile family incomes, divided by median family income. As their dependent variable, they use total welfare expenditures, which includes AFDC as well as Old-Age Assistance, Aid to the Blind and to the Disabled, and other programs. Unfortunately, better measures of AFDC policy are unavailable back to 1950. Their results suggest that the state with the highest level of inequality would have an expected welfare benefit $65 (in 1982 dollars) higher than that of the state with the least income inequality— a large effect given that the mean benefit was $140, with a standard deviation of $83.

These results provide some mixed support for the theories suggesting that greater inequality leads to greater redistribution. They also contradict the majority of the cross-national findings, which tend to find no relationship or the opposite relationship. Scholars will need to replicate these results with longer time series, better measures of welfare policy, and other measures of income inequality. In addition, these findings contradict evident national trends in both inequality and AFDC spending. Given that inequality has increased dramatically in the United States, the hypothesis that greater inequality leads to greater redistribution suggests that redistribution should increase. However, AFDC benefits dropped considerably during the same period when inequality was increasing, prima facie evidence against this hypothesis. The fact of increasing inequality with decreasing benefits appears to contradict the hypothesis that greater inequality leads to greater redistribution.

Of course, states vary considerably in the degree to which inequality increased and in the degree to which their welfare policy became less generous, as illustrated in figure 21.1. According to one measure of state AFDC policy, the maximum amount that state governments pay per month for a family of four, in 1996 dollars, decreased from $723 to $474 between 1976 and 1995.[8] Oregon decreased its benefit the most, lowering it by more than $500, although Alaska actually increased its welfare benefit by about $50.

Although the national trends contradict the prediction that inequality leads to greater

TABLE 21.1   *Explaining the Decrease in Welfare Benefits Between 1976 and 1995*

	AFDC Benefit: 1995 Minus 1976
Real maximum AFDC 1976	−0.398
	(0.054)
Gini 1995 minus 1976	−130.97
	(526.68)
SER	96.00
Constant	44.80
	(48.69)
R-squared	0.54
Number of cases	50

Note: The dependent variable is the difference between the 1976 and 1995 maximum welfare guarantee for a family of four in 1996 dollars and is available from www.econ.jhu.edu/People/Moffitt/DataSets.html. See figure 21.1 for Gini coefficients source.

redistribution, states that experienced the greatest increase in inequality may have experienced a smaller decrease in welfare generosity. To conduct a simple and preliminary test of this possibility, I regressed the difference between states' maximum welfare benefit to a family of four in 1976 and 1995 on the difference in their Gini coefficients for the same period. Table 21.1 presents this result. I include the maximum AFDC benefit in 1976 as the only control. Its coefficient suggests that states with the most generous programs in 1976 experienced the greatest decrease in generosity. Since higher values of the AFDC benefit difference suggest a smaller drop in welfare spending, the coefficient for the Gini difference suggests that greater increases in inequality are associated with greater decreases in AFDC benefits, the opposite of the expected result, but the coefficient is substantively small and far from statistically significant.[9] Thus, neither the cross-sectional relationship, the decline in welfare benefits, nor variation in that decline is consistent with the hypothesis that greater inequality leads to greater redistribution. Only Husted (1989) and Husted and Kenny (1997) find support for it.

There are alternative explanations for the decline in AFDC benefits. For instance, since the federal government fully funds food stamp benefits but only partially funded AFDC, states could increase total benefits while reducing the cost of providing them by cutting AFDC benefits, making people more eligible for food stamps (Plotnick 1986, 597). The extent to which the AFDC decline resulted from its replacement with fully federally funded programs like food stamps remains controversial (Moffitt 1990; Moffitt, Ribar, and Wilhelm 1998).

Although these results provide mixed support for the prediction that greater inequality leads to greater redistribution when it comes to welfare spending in the United States, one paper's conclusions support precisely the opposite result: higher inequality corresponds with lower welfare generosity. Robert Moffitt, David Ribar, and Mark Wilhelm (1998) test their hypothesis that declining wages among low-skilled workers have led voters to prefer lower welfare benefits.[10] Voters, they suggest, prefer to tie benefits to low-skilled wages because falling wages relative to welfare benefits may decrease incentives to work, increase costs because of greater caseloads, and create a gap between the working poor and welfare recipients. They test this hypothesis using both a 1969 to 1992 panel of state-level data with General Social Survey (GSS) data on voter preferences and Current Population Survey (CPS) data to determine the voter in each state with the median preferred welfare benefit. To measure state decisions about welfare benefits, they use the log of the real monthly

AFDC benefit per recipient. As their measure of low-skilled wages, they use the weekly wage at the twenty-fifth percentile of the state wage distribution and find similar results with a variety of other measures of low-skilled wages. Their analysis suggests that state governments cut AFDC benefits as the log of real wages among unskilled workers declines. Although their measures of low-skilled wages do not necessarily correspond with overall inequality, these measures most likely correspond at least with the spread in the bottom half of the income distribution. Thus, their results appear to contradict Husted's findings and to correspond more closely with the cross-sectional relationships found in earlier research. We can raise questions about Moffitt, Ribar, and Wilhelm's analysis, but their intriguing result is nevertheless worthy of further research.[11]

Explaining the Mixed Results

Theories about the influence of inequality on redistribution rely on a chain of assumptions: that greater inequality leads to more lower-income voters; that voters cast their ballots on the issue of redistribution; and that the presence of more lower-income voters results in more redistributive policy because either the parties shift toward the new position of the median voter on redistribution or the parties representing lower-income voters tend to have more election success. If any of these assumptions are false, then rising inequality will not lead to greater redistribution. Which seem most problematic?

Research has tested the assumption that having more lower-income voters leads to more redistribution, and the evidence appears to support it. For instance, Hill, Leighley, and Hinton-Andersson (1995) find a positive relationship between lower-class voting and the generosity of welfare policy between 1978 and 1990. They measure welfare policy benefits with two variables: the mean AFDC welfare grant and a measure of the relative equity of AFDC payments (total AFDC benefits per recipient divided by the state's per capita income). As a measure of lower-class voter turnout, they use CPS self-reports on turnout, income, and occupation.[12] Based on data provided in a replication dataset, their results suggest that a one-point increase in lower-class voter turnout is associated with a 24 percent increase in the mean welfare payment, a very small effect.[13] The expected difference in mean welfare payments from the state with the lowest to the highest turnout is about $14. According to their measure, mean monthly welfare payments ranged from $39 to $228. While lower-income voter turnout appears to have some influence, the effect is quite small.

Another paper finds similar results. Using the welfare measure already described, Husted and Kenny (1997) also test for an effect of lower-income voter turnout on state welfare expenditures. They use the ratio of lower-income voter turnout to voter turnout at the county level.[14] Holding all else equal, they find that a fall in this ratio of .2 would result in a 5 to 12 percent rise in welfare spending.

These findings provide reasonably strong support for the assumption that when there are more lower-income voters there is greater redistribution. Thus, we must look to one of the other assumptions to help explain the contradictory evidence on the relationship between inequality and redistribution.

Research has not yet tested the first assumption—that greater inequality leads to more lower-income voters. However, some evidence suggests that it might be problematic, since those with lower incomes are much less likely to participate in politics (Verba, Schlozman, and Brady 1995). In fact, an early paper found that higher income inequality is associated cross-sectionally with lower voter turnout in U.S. elections (Dye 1969). Even though increased lower-income voter turnout may lead to more redistribution, income inequality may lead only to more lower-income individuals, not to more lower-income voters. Therefore, the failure of this first assumption may explain the contradictory results on inequality and redistribution.

Although we need research that directly tests this assumption, we can test it indirectly by looking at the relationship between inequality and the success of Democratic candidates. As discussed earlier, some models do not assume that parties converge to the median voter's position, but that the candidates and their parties represent particular constituencies. In these models, rising inequality can lead to greater redistribution because it increases the chances that the party or parties representing the less well-off will win elections. Therefore, rising inequality should in theory lead to greater success by the party that traditionally represents poorer individuals in the United States—the Democrats. However, if growing inequality does not lead to more lower-income voters, then it may not lead to greater Democratic success. Is there any evidence that rising inequality has led to greater Democratic success?

Unfortunately, research has not investigated this hypothesis. Figure 21.3 presents a simple test of whether greater inequality leads to greater success among Democrats in state legislatures. It plots the change in inequality over five-year periods against the change in the proportion of Democrats in the lower house of the state legislatures. The figure pools all five-year differences between 1976 and 1995. If growing inequality leads to greater Democratic success, we would expect an increasing trend to these data points. However, the figure suggests no evidence that increases in inequality are associated with increases in the percentage of Democratic legislators. I have replicated this result, calculating the changes across varying number of years.[15] Although preliminary, this result suggests that greater inequality has not led to greater success by Democratic candidates and, indirectly, that growing inequality does not lead to more lower-income voters relative to wealthier voters. If further analysis confirms this negative result, it will pose serious problems for many of the theories about the relationship between inequality and redistribution, and it may explain the contradictory results on their relationship.

Another important and potentially problematic assumption that may explain the contradictory results concerns the diversity of issues in elections. As discussed earlier, much of the theory on this topic assumes that elections are fought only over the issue of redistribution. However, elections vary in the number of policy issues that enter into campaigns, and wealth inequality may be only one of these issues. Consequently, even if rising inequality produces more lower-income voters relative to wealthier voters, it may be that very few individuals cast their vote on the issue of redistribution. Unfortunately, relaxing this assumption or determining the salience of redistribution in the election proves remarkably difficult.

One approach is to look not at particular elections but rather at the makeup of the parties and their supporters. A number of papers have found that U.S. states vary in the degree to which parties organize around the issue of income (Brown 1995; Jennings 1979). Wealthy individuals are much more likely to be Republican in some states but are not at all more likely to be Republican in others. In states polarized by income, elections may more frequently focus on inequality and redistribution. Thus, one explanation for these contradictory results is that research has tested these theories across all states rather than across polarized states.

To my knowledge, researchers have not investigated this possibility. I have replicated the analysis testing whether growing inequality fosters Democratic electoral success in income-polarized states, but I find no evidence of a relationship. In other words, inequality fails to favor Democrats in states that are polarized by income. Although this preliminary

FIGURE 21.3   *Changes in the Percentage of Democrats by Changes in Inequality over Five-Year Periods from 1976 and 1995*

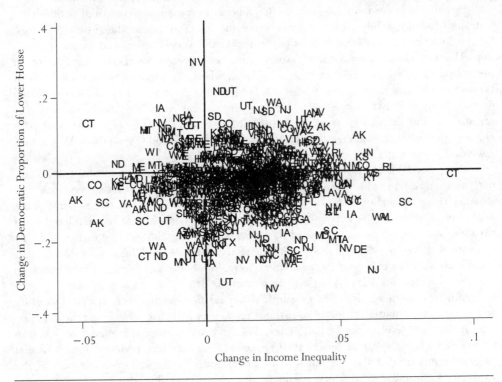

Note: See figure 21.1 for Gini coefficients source. Proportion Democrat is from Burnham (1992) and Council of State Governments (various years).

finding fails to support the argument that these theories are more applicable to states polarized by income, other research is more supportive.

For instance, in one of the more interesting U.S. state-level analyses of welfare policies, Edward T. Jennings (1979) investigates the influence of income polarization on the parties' redistributive policies. Instead of assuming that electoral competition forces parties to converge to the median voter, he argues that the generosity of welfare programs depends on the parties' respective constituencies, the degree to which the parties are polarized by income, and which party controls government. Within states with class-based electoral systems, redistribution tends to increase when the party or faction with lower- and working-class support gains control of government. To test his theory, he categorizes selected states between 1938 and 1970 as divided along class lines or not so divided. While earlier research found that Democratic versus Republican control of government has little influence on welfare spending (Dye 1966; Hofferbert 1966; Winters 1976), he finds that, in states that clearly have a party that represents lower-income individuals, welfare generosity increases to the extent that that party gains power, confirming his hypothesis.[16]

A few recent papers have employed data on the party systems across states, and their results tend to confirm Jennings's theory, suggesting that further research into polarization may help resolve some of the contradictory findings on inequality and redistribution (Brown

1995; Brown and Wright 1992; Paddock 1998; Stonecash 1999). Using CBS News/*New York Times* national polls aggregated from 1976 to 1988, Robert D. Brown (1995) estimates the group bases of party identification by state, finding, for instance, the extent to which wealthy individuals are more likely to be Republicans in some states compared with others. Instead of focusing solely on income when studying the cleavages straddled by the parties, he also looks at race, religion, education, gender, rural versus urban, and union membership. He then classifies state party systems into three groups: southern cleavage, where party support differs primarily by race; New Deal, where the parties divide over Protestant versus Catholic and income; and post–New Deal, which combines race- and income-based party cleavages. Brown suggests that only the New Deal states have party systems that organize around the classic issues of redistribution. Following Jennings, Brown finds that Democratic Party control corresponds with higher welfare expenditures in New Deal states, but not in other states.[17]

Thus, this evidence suggests that party systems polarized by income behave in a manner more consistent with some of the theories on redistribution. Further research into whether rising inequality leads to greater redistribution in polarized states, and into other related predictions, seems warranted. Rising inequality may also foster the development of the class-based party systems described by Jennings. However, as discussed earlier, the only research that has investigated this possibility at the national level finds no evidence that rising inequality has increased the association between income and partisan identification in the United States (McCarty, Poole, and Rosenthal 2003).

Although much research has investigated the relationship between income inequality and income redistribution at the cross-national level, very little has investigated this relationship at the state level in the United States. The evidence is somewhat mixed on whether inequality leads to higher or lower AFDC benefits. The literature reviewed in this section suggests primarily that there is much to be done. Some findings suggest that part of the explanation for the contradictory results is that rising inequality may not lead to more lower-income voters because poorer individuals are less likely to vote. Evidence that rising inequality has failed to lead to greater Democratic electoral success in U.S. states provides indirect support for this suggestion. The contradictory results may also arise because of the problematic assumption made by much of the theory in this area that elections focus exclusively on the issue of redistribution. Researchers have also yet to apply to AFDC policy much of the theory developed for and applied to cross-national data. For instance, researchers have yet to test theories about social affinity or mobility.

MEDICAID

Enacted in 1965, Medicaid is the primary vehicle for providing the poor and near-poor with access to health services. Medicaid is the third-largest source of health care insurance in the United States behind employer-based coverage and Medicare. In 1998 Medicaid covered 12 percent of the total U.S. population, up from 9.1 percent in 1978 (U.S. Department of Health and Human Services 2000, 6). States spent over 14 percent of their general funds and 44 percent of federal funds provided to them on Medicaid in 1999 (27). The federal government's share of Medicaid costs, which has ranged from about 50 to 77 percent of total state spending, is determined by a formula based on states' per capita incomes. States administer Medicaid within federal guidelines and receive federal funds contingent upon their compliance with federal standards regulating the type and amount of services, states' eligibility determination policies, and state provider payment policies. However, within those guidelines states can enact more generous Medicaid benefits by expanding their pool of recipients or by offering more services to each enrollee. Federal law requires states to cover all citizens who qualified for AFDC, so states could reduce Medicaid costs by trimming their welfare rolls. States can also choose to cover other groups, such as the medically needy.

There is less research on the relationship between inequality and Medicaid policy than on inequality and welfare policy. Early cross-sectional research on the determinants of state Medicaid policy was methodologically flawed: it examined Medicaid expenditures rather than policy. As Russell Hanson (1984, 313–15) argues, the aggregated spending measures used in these studies do not directly reflect policy decisions. Although Medicaid is one of a few key programs that redistribute income to the poor, researchers have not tested for a relationship between inequality and the generosity of Medicaid policy. Charles Barrilleaux and Mark Miller's (1988) review of this literature does not mention research on inequality as a determinant of state Medicaid policy.

As discussed earlier, income inequality could influence policy on redistribution either by changing the parties' policy positions or by increasing the likelihood that the party that represents those with lower incomes will gain control of government. However, the evidence presented in the previous section suggests that inequality does not increase the electoral success of Democratic candidates, even in states where Democrats are most likely to represent poorer individuals. Studies have also found mixed results on the relationship between party control and the generosity of Medicaid programs (Barrilleaux and Miller 1988; Hanson 1984; Kronebusch 1997). Using better measures of state policy on Medicaid, Colleen M. Grogan (1994, 1996) and Thad Kousser (2002) find some effect of party control of government.

Future research must further investigate the relationships between inequality and party control, but other research suggests that nonpolitical factors determine Medicaid policy. A number of researchers have suggested that interest groups, such as health providers, play a large role in determining Medicaid policy (Barrilleaux and Miller 1988; Grogan 1994, 1996). Barrilleaux and Miller (1988) find that the demand for Medicaid-paid health care, measured by the number of recipients, affects neither the supply of services nor the relative Medicaid spending efforts of states' citizens. Instead, the supply of services is the driving force in determining both demand and spending effort (see also Hanson 1984; Kronebusch 1997). They conclude that Medicaid budgets, which constitute large portions of state and national budgets, are at the mercy of relatively small and well-organized interests.

Medicaid policy provides a dependent variable well suited for studying the impact of inequality on redistribution because of the tremendous funds that state governments devote to this program and the discretion they have had, at least since the 1980s, in implementing Medicaid.

TAX PROGRESSIVITY

Unlike welfare and Medicaid programs, tax progressivity directly affects individuals in the middle of the income distribution. Although researchers have linked changes in the tax structure to rising inequality in other countries, such as the United Kingdom (Johnson and Webb 1993), as of the late 1990s researchers have apparently not made such a link in the United States. The research reviewed earlier provided some suggestion that inequality influences public policy decisions about redistribution. Does inequality influence tax progressivity?

Because of a lack of data over time on tax progressivity, little systematic research has investigated its determinants at the federal or state level. Public finance economists and other researchers have extensively studied tax burdens. They have not focused on what explains changes in tax progressivity (see, for instance, Katz, Mahler, and Franz 1983; Musgrave and Musgrave 1989; Pechman 1986).

Michael Allen and John Campbell (1994) have undertaken the only study that investigates the determinants of federal tax progressivity, but they do not consider the potential influence of income inequality and look only at income tax. Using data from 1916 to 1986, they measure progressivity as the difference between the effective tax rates paid by moderate-income and high-income families. (Low-income groups do not pay income tax.) Their results suggest that macroeconomic and government fiscal conditions primarily drive changes in tax progressivity, though often in unexpected directions. As with some of the literature on welfare and Medicaid, they conclude that the partisan composition of government has little influence on effective tax rates.

Although Allen and Campbell (1994, 181) do not explicitly address inequality, a few of their explanatory variables suggest indirect links. For instance, they find that increased unemployment corresponds with decreased tax progressivity. They suggest that political elites often reduce taxes on high-income groups, apparently to foster economic growth when unemployment rises. High unemployment tends to correspond with periods of higher inequality in the United States, suggesting a possible indirect relationship with income inequality.[18]

As discussed earlier, income inequality could influence policy on redistribution either by changing the parties' position on this issue or by increasing the likelihood that the party representing those with lower incomes will win elections. Allen and Campbell's (1994) work suggests that the latter is unlikely because Democratic control of Congress or the presidency has not corresponded with greater effective tax progressivity. Benjamin Page (1983, 49) argues that because the nominal tax rates published in the tax schedules are more progressive than the rates that individuals pay, the nominal rates are largely symbolic. Thus, partisan control may have stronger effects on the symbolic component of income tax in terms of nominal rates than in terms of effective rates, precisely the result found by Allen and Campbell (1994, 182–83). Although the coefficient for Democratic president suggests a modest positive effect on income tax progressivity, this and their other political variables have a stronger impact on symbolic tax progressivity, which they measure as the difference between the nominal and effective income tax rate paid by very high-income families. Thus, it seems unlikely that income inequality could influence effective tax progressivity by changing partisan control of the federal government.

Research has more explicitly addressed the influence of income inequality on state tax progressivity. Unfortunately, estimates of state-level tax progressivity exist for only a few periods; moreover, they depend on many assumptions about the distribution of tax burdens and often include local taxes, over which states exert some control (Hanson 1996, 64). Donald Phares (1973) calculated tax progressivity measures for 1962, and an organization called Citizens for Tax Justice (CTJ) calculated a measure for 1985, 1991, and 1996.[19] These measures suggest that taxes at the state level are regressive. In Phares's index, only Delaware had a progressive tax system. By the early 1990s, six states appeared to have progressive tax systems. Based on a family of four, the measures from 1991 suggest that the average state-level tax burden for the poorest quintile was 12.6 percent. For the wealthiest quintile it was 8.4 percent.

The Phares and Citizens for Tax Justice measures of state tax progressivity have spawned a few papers in the state-level literature on the determinants of progressivity. The only paper that tests for a relationship between state-level tax progressivity and income inequality is Jacobs and Waldman (1983). Using Phares's (1973) measure of tax progressivity for 1962 and a Gini measure (Hopkins 1965) for state-level inequality, they find that greater inequality is associated with more progressive tax systems.

Noting that greater income inequality corresponds cross-sectionally with greater tax progressivity but also—at least in some studies—with lower levels of welfare and Medicaid generosity, Jacobs and Waldman (1983, 561) speculate that pronounced economic stratification has fomented intense but fleeting populist movements that may have had a lasting effect on the tax code.

More recent analyses find conflicting results on the determinants of tax progressivity; none mention income inequality. Some studies find that party competition corresponds with increased tax progressivity (Lowery 1987; Martinez 1997), and others find no relationship (Morgan 1994).[20] A few studies find that states that are more conservative have less progressive tax structures (Erikson, Wright, and McIver 1993, 83–85; Martinez 1997).

A number of authors have suggested that political factors have less influence on tax progressivity than on other redistributive state policies because the history of state and federal tax policy appears to constrain changes in states' tax policy (Hansen 1983; Morgan 1994, 521–22). For instance, David Lowery (1987) finds that states that introduced an income tax before 1960 tend to have more progressive tax systems (see also Berch 1995). Income taxes are a more progressive alternative to property and sales taxes. After the introduction of the federal income tax, states became less likely to introduce their own income taxes, and thus they have remained less progressive. However, other research has failed to support this conclusion (Martinez 1997; Morgan 1994).

As with Medicaid, research has only begun to investigate the relationship between income inequality and tax progressivity. However, the results found by Lowery (1987), Hansen (1983), and Morgan (1994) suggest that historical accidents may restrict states' ability to alter the progressivity of their taxes. Thus, future research into tax progressivity, at least at the state level, may be less promising than research into welfare and Medicaid.

OTHER POLICIES

This review has not addressed a number of other policies that redistribute wealth. The reason for their exclusion varies by policy.

Although I have focused on state policies that redistribute through taxes and transfers, states may also influence the distribution of market incomes through a number of policies. One such policy is the minimum wage. As the real value of the federal minimum wage declined during the 1980s, thirteen states enacted minimum wages above the federal level. David S. Lee (1999) finds that these states, ceteris paribus, experienced less growth in inequality in the lower tail of the distribution, particularly for women (see also Card and Krueger 1995; DiNardo, Fortin, and Lemieux 1996). One study found that changes in the minimum wage explain about 25 percent of the overall increase in the wage dispersion for men and over 30 percent for women (DiNardo, Fortin, and Lemieux 1996). In 2003, ten states had a minimum wage above the federal level.[21] Unfortunately, researchers have not systematically studied the determinants of changes in the minimum wage. Since few states have made changes in their minimum wage laws, there may be too little variation for systematic analysis.

State governments can also redistribute income with unemployment insurance, a state program with federal minimum standards. In the 1940s almost 100 percent of unemployed individuals received some sort of unemployment insurance. However, this rate had dropped dramatically by the mid-1980s, falling below 50 percent, and it has remained just above that level since then (Matthews, Kandilov, and Maxwell 2002). Very little research has investigated or even noted this decline, with the exception of Blank and Card (1991) and Matthews and his colleagues (2002). The latter authors test for an effect of partisan control of government, but they find mixed results. Future research on unemployment insurance policy seems worth pursuing.

States may also be able to influence the distribution of market incomes with laws affecting levels of unionization. Some studies have linked growing inequality in the United States with the decline of unions. Martina Morris and Bruce Western (1999, 644) conclude from their review of the literature that the decline in unionization in the United States accounts for roughly 20 percent of the increase in earnings inequality since the 1970s. Right-to-work laws are one of the only relevant and easily observable union-related policies that state legislatures enact. Business interests have forcefully pushed for such laws, and labor interests have fought them vehemently (Gall 1988).

State governments can also redistribute income through education, housing benefits, energy aid, and other programs, but researchers have not yet explored the determinants of these policies and have only begun to investigate their impact on inequality.

With the exception of income taxes, this literature review has also ignored the influence of inequality on federal redistributive policy. Although states control a great deal of redistributive policy in the United States, the federal government continues to affect wealth inequality through a number of policies. For instance, of the more than $300 billion the federal government spent on income-tested programs in 2000, about 10 percent went to food stamps (U.S. Department of Commerce 2002, no. 515). State governments administer this program, but the U.S. Congress sets food stamp benefit levels, giving state governments no control. Future research could investigate whether inequality influences congressional voting on food stamp benefits.

CONCLUSION

Income inequality has increased markedly in the United States since the 1960s, but redistributive benefits appear to have decreased. Although scholars have developed many theories relating income inequality to redistributive policy, little research has attempted to explain the decline in welfare benefits. Unlike the cross-national literature, scholars have conducted few theoretically informed, politically oriented time-series analyses of the determinants of redistributive policy in the United States, and only a couple have included inequality as a causal factor. Much of the existing research focuses on state governments' welfare policies; it has not investigated the relationship between rising income inequality and either tax progressivity or Medicaid policy, to which states devote vast resources.

The research reviewed here presents contradictory evidence on the relationship between income inequality and redistributive policy: some evidence suggests that greater inequality has led to greater redistribution, and other research suggests the opposite. While income inequality has increased markedly in most U.S. states, state governments have made their welfare benefits less generous, not more so.

The most frequently employed theories linking inequality to redistribution suggest that greater inequality leads to greater redistribution. The research and preliminary results noted in this review suggest some problems with the mechanisms underlying such theories. For instance, most assume that greater inequality should lead to more lower-income voters, to whom candidates can appeal by promising redistribution. However, preliminary results suggest that greater inequality is not associated with increased electoral success by Democratic candidates, who more often promise redistributive policies. In part, the lack of such a relationship may arise because lower-income individuals are less likely to vote. Thus, inequality may lead to relatively more lower-income individuals, but not to more lower-income voters—and maybe even fewer.

Given the interest in this topic evident in cross-national research, it seems likely that interest in the U.S. case will rise. This literature review supplemented with preliminary analysis provides a basis for this future research.

NOTES

1. The results of Hacker and his colleagues (2003) are based on estimates of Gini coefficients for a subsample of the Luxembourg Income Study (LIS), 1981 to 1998, and include up to twelve nations in any given year; see also Kenworthy (1998).

2. Early examples of the application of the median voter theory to redistribution in the United States that do not address inequality include Orr (1976) and Roberts (1984, 1985).

3. Larry Bartels (2003) provides an example of political parties in the United States having an apparently profoundly different impact on income inequality. He finds that while Democratic administrations at the federal level have corresponded with little or no growth in income inequality, Republican administrations are associated with substantial increases. His analysis suggests that inequality, measured by the ratio of incomes at the eightieth percentile of the income distribution to those at the twentieth percentile, would actually have decreased slightly had Democrats controlled the White House throughout the last thirty years, while continuous Republican control would have caused inequality to increase more than 80 percent faster than it actually has. William Berry and his colleagues (1998) provide time-series measures of state, party, and ideology from 1960 to 2000. Their data are available through the Interuniversity Consortium for Political and Social Research (ICPSR) website, www.icpsr.umich.edu (search for study 1208).

4. The Gini coefficients are from Langer (1999) and are available from www.u.arizona.edu/~llanger/ replication—datasets.htm. She calculates the Gini coefficients from CPS data and thus must use the census definition of income, which excludes capital gains, poorly measures capital income, understates the amount of cash received by the poor, and subjects the data to top-coded maximum values. One might want to use the Gini coefficients for market or factor income, that is, income before taxes and transfers. Andrew Bernard and Bradford Jensen (1998) provide a similar analysis for census data, 1970, 1980, and 1990, on the 90–10 difference in the log of real wages controlling for education, experience, race, and other characteristics. Their paper also presents their estimates for each state for all three census years (table 6). A number of papers by economists have used other measures of inequality in U.S. states; see, for instance, Borjas and Ramey 1994, 1995; Lee 1999; Topel 1993.

5. Their paper claims to be the first of its kind, and a cited reference search suggests that no paper has since cited it.

6. Jacobs (1980) used measures of inequality that should have varied in their sensitivity to different parts of the income distribution. He found that a census-based measure of inequality, which is more sensitive to differences between low and middle incomes, correlates more highly with measures of public policy than does an income tax measure of inequality, which is more sensitive to differences between middle and high incomes.

7. A second literature has more directly compared the benefits of government spending with taxes paid by deriving an index of redistribution for each state; see DeLeon (1973) and Uslaner and Webber (1975). However, researchers have criticized these ratios and no longer appear to use them (Hanson 1984, 313–15; Jacobs and Waldman 1983). Only Hayes and Slottje (1989) report finding no relationship between state-level inequality and expenditures on welfare.

8. A welfare benefits dataset is available on Robert Moffitt's home page: www.econ.jhu.edu/People/Moffitt/DataSets.html.

9. A potential objection is that the federal government funded a majority of the AFDC program, rendering comparisons across states potentially problematic because federal funding varied to some extent by state income. However, federal funding should bias the results in favor of the median voter hypothesis because states that had high-income inequality also tended to be poor and thus received more federal funding.

10. Much of the data used in this paper and an expanded dataset from 1960 and 1998 are available on Moffitt's home page (see note 8). The Urban Institute's website (http://afdc.urban.org/AFDownload.html) has an archive of state-level AFDC data.

11. For instance, as they acknowledge, their median voter model assumes that people cast their votes based only on the issue of welfare generosity. They assume that policy converges to the position of the median voter, and they do not investigate the impact of party control of government.

12. For a list of their control variables, see Hill, Leighley, and Hinton-Andersson (1995, 78). Their dataset is available from: www.pubadm.fsu.edu/archives/1995/hill/hill1.html.

13. This estimate represents something of an average between the cross-sectional relationship and the across-time relationship. The cross-sectional relationship in any given year is larger.

14. Specifically, Husted and Kenny (1997) measure lower-income voter turnout at the county level as a state's average county median family income, weighted by the number voting in the county, divided by average county median family income, weighted by the county's voting-age population.

15. This result holds in regression analyses with fixed effects for states and years, and with varying lags on inequality.

16. For an excellent review of the research on party control of government and expenditures in U.S. states, see Besley and Case (2003).

17. There are some concerns, however, with Brown's (1995) analysis. He provides no standard errors or confidence intervals for his estimates of group support for parties, nor does he provide any time trends; these differences may simply arise by chance. More important, the classification of state cleavages into New Deal, post–New Deal, and southern seems somewhat arbitrary. He does not test whether states differ significantly from each other or from the national average. If one is primarily concerned with redistribution, as Brown is, why not primarily investigate cleavages by income?

18. Alan Blinder and Howard Esaki (1978) find that a 1.0-percentage-point rise in unemployment decreases the income share of the lowest quintile by 0.13 of a percentage point. Some evidence suggests that Democratic presidents are associated with lower income inequality in part because they pursue policies that increase employment (Bartels 2003; Hibbs 1987; Hibbs and Dennis 1988).

19. See the CTJ website at: www.ctj.org.

20. Michael Martinez's (1997) data on tax progressivity as well as his explanatory variables are available online at: www.pubadm.fsu.edu/archives1997/martinez/martinez1.html.

21. For a map noting variations in state minimum wages, see Department of Labor, Employment Standards Administration, Wage and Hour Division, "Minimum Wage Laws in the States," at: www.dol.gov/esa/minwage/america.htm. The January issues of the *Monthly Labor Review* from the Bureau of Labor Statistics contain an annual summary of the previous year's proposed and enacted state labor legislation (Lee 1999, 1019).

REFERENCES

Albritton, Robert. 1989. "Impacts of Intergovernmental Financial Incentives on State Welfare Policymaking and Interstate Equity." *Publius: The Journal of Federalism* 19: 127–41.

Alesina, Alberto, and Howard Rosenthal. 1995. *Partisan Politics, Divided Government, and the Economy.* Cambridge, U.K.: Cambridge University Press.

Allen, Michael Patrick, and John L. Campbell. 1994. "State Revenue Extraction from Different Income Groups: Variations in Tax Progressivity in the United States, 1916 to 1986." *American Sociological Review* 59: 169–96.

Barrilleaux, Charles, and Belinda C. Davis. 2003. "Explaining State-Level Variations in Levels and Change in the Distribution of Income in the United States, 1978 to 1990." *American Politics Research* 31(3): 280–300.

Barrilleaux, Charles J., and Mark E. Miller. 1988. "The Political Economy of State Medicaid Policy." *American Political Science Review* 82: 1089–1107.

Bartels, Larry M. 2002. "Economic Inequality and Political Representation." Unpublished paper. Princeton University.

————. 2003. "Partisan Politics and the U.S. Income Distribution." Unpublished paper. Princeton University.

Baumgardner, James R. 1993. "Tests of Median Voter and Political Support Maximization Models: The Case of Federal State Welfare Programs." *Public Finance Quarterly* 21(1): 48–83.

Becker, Gary S. 1983. "A Theory of Competition Among Groups for Political Influence." *Quarterly Journal of Economics* 98(3): 371–400.

Benabou, Roland. 1996. "Inequality and Growth." In *National Bureau of Economic Research Macro Annual,* edited by Ben S. Bernanke and Julio J. Rotemberg. Cambridge, Mass.: MIT Press.

Berch, Neil. 1995. "Explaining Changes in Tax Incidence in the States." *Political Research Quarterly* 48(3): 629–41.

Bernard, Andrew B., and J. Bradford Jensen. 1998. "Understanding Increasing and Decreasing Wage Inequality." Working paper 6571. Cambridge, Mass.: National Bureau of Economic Research.

Berry, William D., Evan J. Ringquist, Richard C. Fording, and Russell L. Hanson. 1998. "Measuring Citizen and Government Ideology in the American States, 1960 to 1993." *American Journal of Political Science* 42(1): 327–48. Available as study 1208 at: www.icpsr.umich.edu (updated April 17, 2001).

Besley, Timothy, and Anne Case. 2003. "Political Institutions and Policy Choices: Evidence from the United States." *Journal of Economic Literature* 41(1): 7–73.

Black, Duncan. 1958. *The Theory of Committees and Elections.* Cambridge, U.K.: Cambridge University Press.

Blank, Rebecca M., and David E. Card. 1991. "Recent Trends in Insured and Uninsured Unemployment: Is There an Explanation?" *Quarterly Journal of Economics* 106: 1157–89.

Blinder, Alan, and Howard Esaki. 1978. "Macroeconomic Activity and Income Distribution in the Postwar United States." *Review of Economics and Statistics* 60: 604–9.

Borjas, George J., and Valerie A. Ramey. 1994. "Time-Series Evidence on the Sources of Trends in Wage Inequality." *American Economic Review* 84(2): 10–16.

————. 1995. "Foreign Competition, Market Power, and Wage Inequality." *Quarterly Journal of Economics* 110(4): 1075–1110.

Brown, Robert D. 1995. "Party Cleavages and Welfare Effort in the American States." *American Political Science Review* 89(1): 23–33.

Brown, Robert D., and Gerald C. Wright. 1992. "Elections and State Party Polarization." *American Politics Quarterly* 20(4): 411–26.

Burnham, Walter Dean. 1992. *Partisan Division of American State Governments, 1834 to 1985.* Conducted by the Massachusetts Institute of Technology and the Interuniversity Consortium for Political and Social Research. Ann Arbor, Mich.: ICPSR.

Calvert, Randall. 1985. "Robustness of the Multidimensional Voting Model: Candidates' Motivations, Uncertainty, and Convergence." *American Journal of Political Science* 29: 69–95.

Card, David E., and Alan B. Krueger. 1995. *Myth and Measurement: The New Economics of the Minimum Wage.* Princeton, N.J.: Princeton University Press.

Council of State Governments. Various years. *The Book of the States.* Lexington, Ky.: Council of State Governments.

Cox, Gary W., and Matthew D. McCubbins. 1986. "Electoral-Politics as a Redistributive Game." *Journal of Politics* 48(2): 370–89.

Danziger, Sheldon, and Peter Gottschalk. 1995. *America Unequal.* Cambridge, Mass.: Harvard University Press.

DeLeon, Richard E. 1973. "Politics, Economic Surplus and Redistribution in the American States: A Test of a Theory." *American Journal of Political Science* 17: 781–96.

DiNardo, John, Nicole M. Fortin, and Thomas Lemieux. 1996. "Labor Market Institutions and the Distribution of Wages, 1973 to 1992: A Semiparametric Approach." *Econometrica* 64(5): 1001–44.

Dixit, Avinash, and John Londregan. 1996. "The Determinants of Success of Special Interests in Redistributive Politics." *Journal of Politics* 58(4): 1132–55.

Dye, Thomas, R. 1966. *Politics, Economics, and the Public.* American Politics Research Series. Chicago: Rand McNally.

————. 1969. "Income Inequality and American State Politics." *American Political Science Review* 63(March): 157–62.

Erikson, Robert S., Gerald C. Wright, and John P. McIver. 1993. *Statehouse Democracy: Public Opinion and Policy in the American States.* New York: Cambridge University Press.

Gall, Gilbert J. 1988. *The Politics of Right to Work: The Labor Federations as Special Interests, 1943 to 1979.* Contributions in Labor Studies 24. New York: Greenwood Press.

Grogan, Colleen M. 1994. "Political-Economic Factors Influencing State Medicaid Policy." *Political Research Quarterly* 47(3): 589–622.

————. 1996. "Correction Note: Political-Economic Factors Influencing State Medicaid Policy." *Political Research Quarterly* 49(3): 673–75.

Hacker, Jacob, Suzanne Mettler, Diane Pinderhughes, and Theda Skocpol. 2003. "Public Policy as a Cause and Effect of Inequality: The United States in Comparative and Historical Perspective." Background memoranda. American Political Science Association Task Force on Inequality and American Democracy (March 31, 2003).

Hansen, Susan B. 1983. *The Politics of Taxation: Revenue Without Representation.* New York: Praeger.

Hanson, Russell L. 1984. "Medicaid and the Politics of Redistribution." *American Journal of Political Science* 28: 313–39.

————. 1996. "Intergovernmental Relations." In *Politics in the American States: A Comparative Analysis,* edited by Virginia Gray, Herbert Jacob, and Kenneth N. Vines. Washington, D.C.: CQ Press.

Hayes, Kathy J., and Daniel J. Slottje. 1989. "The Efficacy of State and Local Governments' Redistributive Programs." *Public Finance Quarterly* 17(3): 304.

Hayes, Kathy J., Daniel J. Slottje, and Susan Porter-Hudak. 1991. "U.S. Federal Redistributive Income Policies." *Applied Economics* 23(7): 1193.

Hibbs, Douglas A. 1987. *The American Political Economy: Macroeconomics and Electoral Politics.* Cambridge, Mass.: Harvard University Press.

Hibbs, Douglas A., and Christopher Dennis. 1988. "Income Distribution in the United States." *American Political Science Review* 82(2): 467–90.

Hill, Kim Q., Jan E. Leighley, and Angela Hinton-Andersson. 1995. "Lower-class Mobilization and Policy Linkage in the United States." *American Journal of Political Science* 39(1): 75–86.

Hofferbert, Richard I. 1966. "The Relations Between Public Policy and Some Structural Environmental Variables." *American Political Science Review* 60: 73–82.

Hopkins, Thomas. 1965. "Income Distribution in Grant-in-Aid Equity Analysis." *National Tax Journal* 18(March): 209–13.

Husted, Thomas A. 1989. "Nonmonotonic Demand for Income Redistribution Benefits: The Case of AFDC." *Southern Economic Journal* 55(3): 710–27.

Husted, Thomas A., and Lawrence W. Kenny. 1997. "The Effect of Expansion of the Voting Franchise on the Size of Government." *Journal of Political Economy* 105(1): 54–82.

Jacobs, David. 1980. "Dimensions of Inequality and Public Policy in the States." *Journal of Politics* 42(1): 291–306.

Jacobs, David, and Don Waldman. 1983. "Toward a Fiscal Sociology: Determinants of Tax Regressivity in the American States." *Social Science Quarterly* 64(3): 550–65.

Jennings, Edward T. 1979. "Competition, Constituencies, and Welfare Policies in American States." *American Political Science Review* 73(2): 414–29.

Johnson, Paul, and Steven Webb. 1993. "Explaining the Growth in the U.K. Income Inequality: 1979 to 1988." *Economic Journal* 103(417): 429–36.

Katz, Claudio, Vincent Mahler, and Michael Franz. 1983. "The Impact of Taxes on Growth and Distribution in Developed Capitalist Countries: A Cross-national Study." *American Political Science Review* 77: 871–86.

Kenworthy, Lane. 1998. "Do Social Welfare Policies Reduce Poverty? A Cross-national Assessment." In *Luxembourg Income Study.* Working paper no. 188. Syracuse, N.Y.: Center for Policy Research and Luxembourg Income Study.

Key, V. O., Jr. 1949. *Southern Politics in State and Nation.* New York: Alfred A. Knopf.

Kousser, Thad. 2002. "Politics of Discretionary Medicaid Spending, 1980 to 1993." *Journal of Health Politics, Policy, and Law* 27(4): 639–71.

Kristov, Lorenzo, Peter Lindert, and Robert McClelland. 1992. "Pressure Groups and Redistribution." *Journal of Public Economics* 48(2): 135–63.

Kronebusch, Karl. 1997. "Medicaid and the Politics of Groups: Recipients, Providers, and Policymaking." *Journal of Health Politics, Policy, and Law* 22(3): 839–78.

Langer, Laura. 1999. "Measuring Income Distribution Across Space and Time in the American States." *Social Science Quarterly* 80(1): 55–67.

Lee, David S. 1999. "Wage Inequality in the United States During the 1980s: Rising Dispersion for Falling Minimum Wage?" *Quarterly Journal of Economics* 114(3): 977–1023.

Lidbeck, Assar, and Jorgen W. Weibull. 1993. "A Model of Political Equilibrium in Representative Democracy." *Journal of Public Economics* 51: 195–209.

Lowery, David. 1987. "The Distribution of Tax Burdens in the American States: The Determinants of Fiscal Incidence." *Western Political Quarterly* 40: 137–58.

Martinez, Michael D. 1997. "Don't Tax You, Don't Tax Me, Tax the Fella Behind the Tree: Partisan and Turnout Effects on Tax Policy." *Social Science Quarterly* 78(4): 895–906.

Matthews, Peter H., Ivan T. Kandilov, and Bradford Maxwell. 2002. "Interstate Differences in Insured Unemployment: Some Recent Evidence." *Applied Economics Letters* 9(14): 945–48.

McCarty, Nolan, Keith T. Poole, and Howard Rosenthal. 2003. "Political Polarization and Income Inequality." Working paper. New York: Russell Sage Foundation.

McKelvey, Richard D. 1976. "Intransitivities in Multidimensional Voting Models and Some Implications for Agenda Control." *Journal of Economic Theory* 12: 472–82.

Meltzer, Allan H., and Scott F. Richard. 1981. "A Rational Theory for the Size of Government." *Journal of Political Economy* 89(5): 914–27.

Milanovic, Branko. 2000. "The Median Voter Hypothesis, Income Inequality, and Income Distribution: An Empirical Test with the Required Data." *European Journal of Political Economy* 16(13): 367–410.

Moene, Karl O., and Michael Wallerstein. 2001. "Inequality, Social Insurance, and Redistribution." *American Political Science Review* 95(4): 859–74.

Moffitt, Robert. 1990. "Has State Redistribution Policy Grown More Conservative?" *National Tax Journal* 43(2): 123–42.

Moffitt, Robert, David Ribar, and Mark Wilhelm. 1998. "The Decline of Welfare Benefits in the United States: The Role of Wage Inequality." *Journal of Public Economics* 68(3): 421–52.

Morgan, David R. 1994. "Tax Equity in the American States: A Multivariate Analysis." *Social Science Quarterly* 75(3): 510–23.

Morris, Martina, and Bruce Western. 1999. "Inequality in Earnings at the Close of the Twentieth Century." *Annual Review of Sociology* 25: 623–57.

Musgrave, Richard A., and Peggy B. Musgrave. 1989. *Public Finance in Theory and Practice.* 5th ed. New York: McGraw-Hill.

Orr, Larry. 1976. "Income Transfers as a Public Good: An Application to AFDC." *American Economic Review* 66: 359–71.

Paddock, Joel. 1998. "Explaining State Variation in Interparty Ideological Differences." *Political Research Quarterly* 51(3): 765–80.

Page, Benjamin I. 1983. *Who Gets What from Government.* Berkeley: University of California Press.

Pechman, Joseph A. 1986. *The Rich, the Poor, and the Taxes They Pay.* Boulder, Colo.: Westview Press.

Peltzman, Sam. 1976. "Toward a More General Theory of Regulation." *Journal of Law and Economics* 19(2): 211–40.

Perotti, Roberto. 1994. "Income Distribution and Investment." *European Economic Review* 38(3–4): 827–35.

———. 1996. "Redistribution and Nonconsumption Smoothing in an Open Economy." *Review of Economic Studies* 63(3): 411–33.

Peterson, Paul, and Mark Rom. 1989. "American Federalism, Welfare Policy, and Residential Choices." *American Political Science Review* 83: 711–28.

Phares, Donald. 1973. *State-Local Tax Equity.* Lexington, Mass.: D. C. Heath.

Plotnick, Robert D. 1986. "An Interest Group Model of Direct Income Redistribution." *Review of Economics and Statistics* 68(4): 594–602.

Plotnick, Robert, and Richard F. Winters. 1985. "A Politico-Economic Theory of Income Redistribution." *American Political Science Review* 79: 458–73.

Plott, Charles R. 1976. "Axiomatic Social Choice: An Overview and Interpretation." *American Journal of Political Science* 20: 511–96.

Poole, Keith T., and Howard Rosenthal. 1997. *Congress: A Political-Economic History of Roll Call Voting.* New York: Oxford University Press.

Riker, William. 1980. "Implications of the Disequilibrium of Majority Rule for the Study of Institutions." *American Political Science Review* 74: 432–47.

Roberts, Kevin W. S. 1977. "Voting over Income Tax Schedules." *Journal of Public Economics* 8(3): 329–40.

Roberts, Russell D. 1984. "A Positive Model of Private Charity and Public Transfers." *Journal of Political Economy* 92(1): 136–48.

———. 1985. "Recipient Preferences and the Design of Government Transfer Programs." *Journal of Law and Economics* 28(1): 27–54.

Romer, Thomas. 1975. "Individual Welfare, Majority Voting, and the Properties of Linear Income Tax." *Journal of Public Economics* 42(2): 163–85.

Soss, Joe, Sanford F. Schram, Thomas P. Vartanian, and Evin O'Brien. 2001. "Setting the Terms of Relief: Explaining State Policy Choices in the Devolution Revolution." *American Journal of Political Science* 45(2): 378–95.

Stonecash, Jeffrey M. 1999. "Political Cleavage in U.S. State Legislative Houses." *Legislative Studies Quarterly* 24(2): 281–302.

Topel, Robert. 1993. "What Have We Learned from Empirical Studies of Unemployment and Turnover?" *American Economic Review* 83(2): 110–15.

Tweedie, Jack. 1994. "Resources Rather Than Needs: A State-Centered Model of Welfare Policymaking." *American Journal of Political Science* 38(3): 651–72.

U.S. Department of Commerce. U.S. Census Bureau. 2002. "Table F-4: Gini Ratios for Families, by Race and Hispanic Origin of Householder: 1947 to 2001." *Current Population Survey, Annual Demographic Supplements.* Available at: http://landview.census.gov/hhes/income/histinc/f04.html (visited 2002).

U.S. Department of Health and Human Services. Health Care Financing Administration. 2000. *A Profile of Medicaid: Chartbook 2000.* Available at: http://cms.hhs.gov/charts/medicaid/2Tchartbk.pdf (visited 2003).

Uslaner, Eric, and Ronald Webber. 1975. "Politics of Redistribution: Toward a Model of Policymaking in the American States." *American Politics Quarterly* 3: 130–70.

Verba, Sidney, Kay Lehman Schlozman, and Henry E. Brady. 1995. *Voice and Equality: Civic Voluntarism in American Politics.* Cambridge, Mass.: Harvard University Press.

Winters, Richard. 1976. "Party Control and Policy Change." *American Journal of Political Science* 20(4): 597–636.

Wittman, Donald. 1977. "Candidates with Policy Preferences: A Dynamic Model." *Journal of Economic Theory* 14: 180–89.

———. 1983. "Candidate Motivation: A Synthesis of Alternatives." *American Political Science Review* 77: 142–57.

Chapter 22

Income Distribution and Public Social Expenditure: Theories, Effects, and Evidence

Lars Osberg, Timothy M. Smeeding, and Jonathan Schwabish

Political irrelevance not withstanding, inequality is exacting a considerable cost on the society and turning attention to it would hardly be "frivolous."

—Eugene Smolensky, "Income Inequality: A Conversation with Bob Lampman" (2002)

What is the relationship between economic inequality and public social expenditure? Why might it matter?

Income distribution and social spending have long been analyzed by both economists and political scientists. More than seventy years ago, R. H. Tawney (1931/1964, 133, 121) discussed the growth and significance of public provision for education, health, and social services and noted that "the standard of living of the great mass of the nation depends, not merely on the remuneration which they are paid for their labour, but on the social income which they receive as citizens." He saw the expansion of such public spending for "purposes of common advantage" as the primary route to overcome inequalities of opportunity and circumstance. In his now-classic book, Gøsta Esping-Andersen (1990) has more recently argued that there are significant differences between countries in the processes that determine public social spending and that these socioeconomic forces are shaped by the nature of states and their differences.

This chapter represents an attempt to contribute further to this tradition. We begin with an overview of some recent literature and data on the relationship between inequality and public social expenditure. We follow the tradition of much of this research and focus on developed nations—developing and Third World countries are left in the background.[1]

Even among the world's affluent nations there are many different channels by which goods and services are distributed. Although non-excludable goods, such as national defense and clean air, are provided to all citizens of a nation and by their nature are not subject to social or economic standing within the nation, governments also take economic, social, and moral stances on the distribution of income or consumption among their citizens. These views help shape the actual inequality with which goods and services are distributed throughout the nation.

Throughout this chapter, we refer to two meanings of the terms "inequality" and "redistribution." Income redistribution through tax and transfer systems may alter the inequality of outcomes (as in the Temporary Assistance to Needy Families [TANF] program in the United States). As well, redistributive programs may attempt to equalize the prospective life chances of individuals from different racial, ethnic, and social class backgrounds—that is, reduce inequality of opportunity. Because the philosophical justifications for reducing inequalities of outcome or inequalities of opportunity are often quite different, the analytical distinction is worth making. However, as a practical matter, policies that affect outcomes also affect opportunities.

Because we are interested in how economic inequality affects social expenditures and how this differs among affluent nations, we use cross-national comparisons. The international data indicate that political and economic systems respond differently to market-driven and demography-driven changes in social and economic status. It is thus of interest to policymakers to see how policies are affected by socioeconomic change, especially in reaction to market-driven changes in poverty and economic inequality.

It is not our intent to evaluate and reconcile all of the different dimensions of distribution. We will consider, however, the social science research that has examined these issues on limited scales. There is a great deal of such research. Political science researchers, such as Karl Moene, Michael Wallerstein, and Torben Iversen, have summarized and modeled the different paths by which a nation's political system can affect its distribution of economic and social parameters. Sociologists such as Lane Kenworthy, Jonas Pontusson, and John Stephens have looked at these issues through a similar lens. And economists such as Anthony Atkinson, Peter Lindert, Lee Rainwater, and Alberto Alesina often look to multivariate analysis to understand more fully the correlations between distribution and social good provisions—but much remains to be done.

We begin by examining the data on economic inequality and noncash goods in a cross-national context. We then summarize a selection of key articles in the recent literature dedicated to these issues. We conclude with our own thoughts on where this literature now stands, where it needs to go, and the issues that need further research.

ECONOMIC INEQUALITY, CASH BENEFITS, AND PUBLIC NONCASH MERIT GOODS

European discussions of social policy sometimes refer to the concept of a "social wage"—or "family income package," shorthand for the aggregate value of the goods, services, and transfer payments that the state provides to all residents—as a basic right of citizenship (Sefton 2002). Since the economic resources necessary to deliver a social wage can be seen as (approximately) equivalent to a lump sum payment to all citizens, it is necessarily of much greater relative importance for those who are less affluent in market incomes (see Smeeding 2002a; Smeeding and Rainwater 2002).

This section discusses the differences between pre- and post-tax-and-transfer income and the impact of the varying size of the "social wage" on the distribution of real incomes across nations. We begin with a general discussion of economic resources and public goods and compare incomes and living standards cross-nationally. Then we explicitly investigate the differences in disposable (post-tax-and-transfer) income inequality. Next we turn to the relative well-being of children and the earnings gap between the top and bottom of the distribution. We then discuss noncash incomes and the effects of such benefits on general measures of income and distribution. Finally, we describe the differences in the provision of (net) public benefits and taxes for different nations.

Economic Resources and Public Goods

If cross-national differences in social expenditures and inequality were small, there would be little to discuss, so a useful first step is to assess the current extent of differences across jurisdictions in economic inequality. However, it is clear that societies differ in the extent of their public sectors and in the degree to which social policy is delivered through in-kind benefits or cash transfers. Thus, measures of inequality differ across societies depending on the measure of individual incomes; either pre- or post-tax and transfers (both monetary and in kind). The size and design of the social wage may also affect individual and labor market behavior and hence, over time, indirectly affect pre-tax-and-transfer inequality. However, we abstract from this latter behavior and focus instead on cross-national variation in income and inequality using standard pre- and post-tax-and-transfer income measures.[2]

Total social expenditures vary greatly across nations. In 1998 in the developed countries, total social expenditures as a percentage of gross domestic product (GDP) ranged from 15 percent in the United States to 26 percent in the United Kingdom to over 30 percent in Sweden (OECD 2002b).[3] The available evidence (Smeeding 2002a) indicates that social expenditures as a fraction of total government spending in OECD nations range from 0.67 in Australia to 0.90 in Denmark and Sweden. That is, 67 to 90 percent of all government spending is made up of redistributive cash or in-kind benefits.[4] Thus, our topic is about most of what governments actually do.

In this section, we trace cash and near-cash (food, housing) benefits for OECD countries over the past twenty years, using data from the OECD (2001). We present these estimates in comparable format in figure 22.1. In that figure, seventeen OECD nations—all of the major nations except for the central and eastern Europeans—have been grouped into six clusters: Scandinavia (Finland, Norway, Sweden); northern Europe (Belgium, Denmark, Netherlands); central and southern Europe (Austria, France, Germany, Italy, Luxembourg, Spain); the Anglo-Saxon nations (Australia, the United Kingdom, and Canada); the United States; and Mexico.[5]

The Scandinavians and northern Europeans follow similar patterns—high levels of spending that show responsiveness to the recession of the early 1990s in Sweden and Finland, followed by a tapering. The central and southern Europeans and the Anglo-Saxon nations show remarkably similar spending patterns—again rising in the early 1990s but overall at a level distinctly below the other two groups. The United States is significantly below all these others and by the late 1990s was spending at a level closer, in terms of GDP per capita, to Mexico than to the other richer OECD nations. These figures illustrate the wide differences in outcomes that we can find for money social spending, using figures that exclude financing of health care, education, and retirement for the elderly. They also correspond very closely to the measures of money and near-money income inequality used in the analytic literature in this area, including that presented later.

In general, publicly supplied goods are more important to the purchasing power of the poor than the rich because they are more equally distributed than income and because they are supplied relatively equally as government outlays per person (or per student) for both rich and poor. Although publicly provided social insurance programs may bring benefits to both rich and poor, the amount of payment is relatively more important to those who are less affluent in market income terms, and their probability of receipt is often greater. (For example, the greater employment insecurity of low-wage workers makes it likelier that they will receive unemployment insurance.) We therefore begin this chapter with some estimates

FIGURE 22.1   *Non-Elderly Social Expenditures in Seventeen Nations*

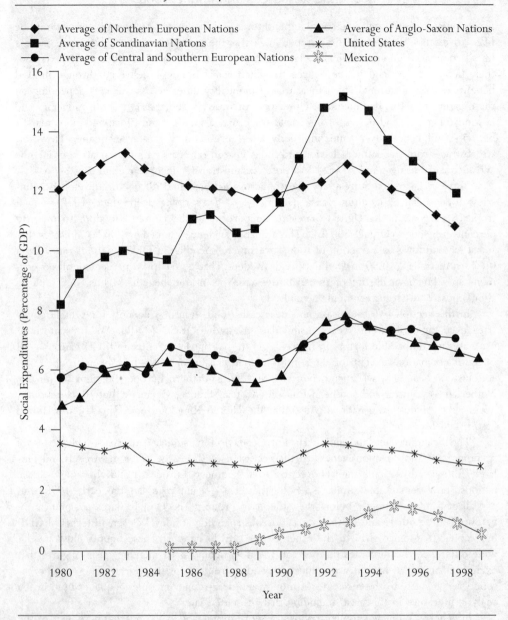

◆——— Average of Northern European Nations   ▲——— Average of Anglo-Saxon Nations
■——— Average of Scandinavian Nations   ✳——— United States
●——— Average of Central and Southern European Nations   ✳——— Mexico

Source: OECD (2002b).
Notes: Total non-elderly social expenditures include all cash plus near-cash spending (for example, food stamps) and public housing but exclude health care and education spending. Anglo-Saxon nations include Australia, the United Kingdom, and Canada; Scandinavia includes Finland, Norway, and Sweden; northern Europe includes Belgium, Denmark, and Netherlands; central and southern Europe includes Austria, France, Germany, Italy, Luxembourg, and Spain.

of the aggregate value of redistributive public expenditures and their impact across the income distribution.

Our basic question here is: What is the distribution of real income within countries? When we add between-country inequality to inequality within nations, a related question becomes: What is the real standard of living at each point in the income distribution? In particular, although the United States has the highest average income, it also has the highest income inequality. Might it be true that being poor in the United States is better than being middle-income in other rich countries (in the sense of having an absolutely higher standard of living)?

Timothy Smeeding (2002a) estimates the real purchasing power parity (PPP)-adjusted distribution of disposable cash and near-cash income, or disposable income, for a number of countries.[6] In general, comparisons of "real" economic well-being or "living standards" look very different across and within countries depending on whether we look at the relatively rich or the relatively poor.

Here we compare PPP-adjusted distributional measures of living standards for all households and for households with children. We separate disposable income into two components—market income (which includes earnings, income from capital, and private transfers) and the part that comes from redistributive government transfers, net of the direct taxes paid by citizens that fund these transfers. To these we add in noncash benefits in the form of education and health care for children. (We explore the impact of taxes in a later section.)

We present evidence on absolute and relative living standards across countries because there are two different perspectives on why inequality may matter for social outcomes. For example, if it is available material resources during a person's childhood that affect future social outcomes (such as adult earnings capacity), then greater present inequality of outcomes implies both an increase in current inequality of opportunity and in future inequality of outcomes because of the reduced material inputs available to low-income families. In this case, the absolute comparison of living standards across countries makes sense because a smaller share of a larger pie could add up to "more pie"—the relative disadvantage of poor households in a rich country could be counterbalanced by a (possibly) greater access to material goods. The other perspective sees the social pathology of deprivation playing itself out (at least within relatively affluent OECD nations) primarily in terms of the consequences of an inability to attain socially defined norms of consumption. From this perspective, it is *relative* income within countries that is all-important, and cross-country comparisons of the absolute living standards of specific income deciles are of little relevance.[7] We do not want to preclude either of these perspectives.

Some Results: Real Cash Income for All Persons

Combining PPPs and relative disposable income data for thirteen countries, we can compare the distribution of real incomes across nations and over the income spectrum (see figure 22.2). We compare real incomes adjusted for household size using the square root of family size and presented on a per person basis (expressed in PPP-adjusted 1997 U.S. dollars per equivalent person, weighted by the number of persons per household; see Smeeding and Rainwater 2002). We present not only relative incomes at both the tenth and ninetieth percentile income levels, but also real incomes. All percentiles are given as a fraction of the median U.S. equivalent disposable income per person ($28,005 in 1997 dollars). The reader should note the relative, within-nation comparisons as well as the "real income" comparisons, even though the focus of the figure is the real comparisons. (Figure 22A.1, in contrast, makes only relative comparisons within nations for a larger set of nations.)

Are people at the bottom of the income distribution in the United States "better off," in absolute income, than people at the bottom of the income distribution elsewhere? Apparently not—at the tenth percentile in figure 22.2, the United States has the third-lowest real income level relative to the median. Only in Australia and the United Kingdom (with average incomes and GDP per capita that are roughly 67 and 75 percent of the U.S. values, respectively) do low-income persons have a lower real living standard (in money terms) compared with that in the United States. All other nations have higher living standards for the average low-income person measured in equivalent disposable cash income terms, despite the fact that all have average real incomes (and average GDP per capita) far below those found in the United States (Smeeding and Rainwater 2002, tables 2 and 3). For instance, the average Dutchman has a real income 80 percent as large as that of the average American, but a low-income (tenth percentile) Dutchman has an income that is 10 percent greater than the income of a comparable low-income American. That is, Dutch real income at the tenth percentile is 43 percent of the U.S. median compared with 39 percent in the United States. And the Netherlands is quite typical—the thirteen-country average real income at the tenth percentile is 43 percent of the U.S. median.

At the other end of the spectrum, a high-income (ninetieth percentile) American has a living standard that is 209 percent of the living standard of the median American. The next nearest nation in this respect is Switzerland, at 185 percent of the U.S. median, and the third-highest is Canada, at 167 percent. On average, a person at the ninetieth percentile in the United States has a living standard that is 43 percent higher than that of a similar person in the other twelve nations (209 compared with 146).[8]

Combining these percentiles, we find two measures of economic distance: the decile ratio, and the real income gap between the tenth and ninetieth percentiles. The gap between rich and poor in the United States given by the decile ratio is the largest of all the countries at 5.36. The equivalent income (EI) of a low-income person is $10,927 (or 39 percent of $28,005), while that of a high-income person is $58,530 (209 percent of $28,005), producing a gap of $47,608. This amount is 1.64 times the average gap of $29,081, and more than $11,000 higher than the next nearest gap ($36,406 in Switzerland). The smallest gap ($17,643) is found in Sweden.

Real Living Standards for Children

The real incomes of children are of interest for two reasons. Because children are individuals, albeit "junior citizens," they have a right to consideration of any deprivation in their current consumption, and some would argue that their lack of control over the determinants of family income gives them a special claim (as "deserving poor") on society's sympathies. And second, because children are "potential adults," inequality in household income may also serve as an indicator of equality of opportunity and as a dollar measure of the types of life chances that a parent can provide for his or her child. Concern about economic inequality among children is therefore based on a mingling of concerns for both equality of outcome and opportunity (for a more complete discussion, see Phipps 1999).

Figure 22.3, which addresses the issue of real incomes for children, is constructed exactly the same as figure 22.2. All incomes are expressed as a fraction of the 1997 U.S. overall median adjusted disposable ($28,005) but with equivalent income person weighted by the number of children in each household. The percentiles differ from those in figure

FIGURE 22.2   *Economic Distance and Real Standards of Living in Thirteen Countries, 1992 to 1997*

	Tenth Percentile (Low-Income)	(Length of Bars Represents the Gap Between High- and Low-Income Individuals)	Ninetieth Percentile (High-Income)	Ratio of Ninetieth to Tenth Percentile (Decile Ratio)	Real Income Gap[b]
Switzerland, 1992	55%		185%	3.36	$36,406
Norway, 1995	50		143	2.86	26,044
Belgium, 1996	47		153	3.26	29,685
Germany, 1994	44		139	3.16	26,604
Denmark, 1995	43		123	2.86	22,404
France, 1994	43		148	3.44	29,405
Netherlands, 1994	43		133	3.09	25,204
Finland, 1995	41		110	2.68	19,323
Canada, 1994	41		167	4.07	35,286
Sweden, 1995	40		103	2.58	17,643
Australia, 1994	34		148	4.35	31,925
United Kingdom, 1995	33		142	4.30	30,525
United States, 1997[a]	39		209	5.39	47,608
Simple average	43		146	3.49	29,081

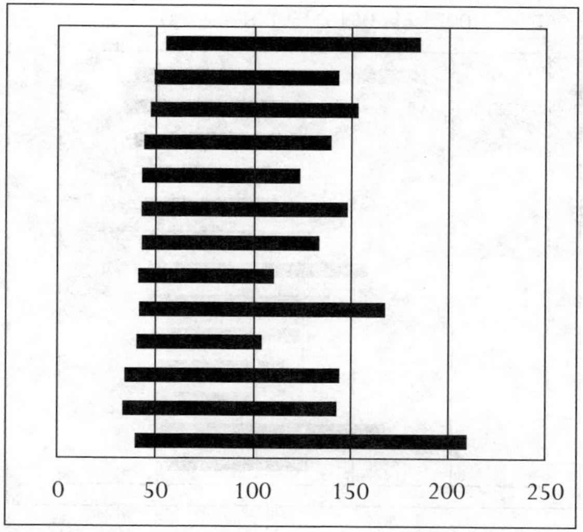

Source: Authors' calculations from Luxembourg Income Study.

Note: Numbers given are percentages of overall U.S. 1997 median equivalent income in PPP terms.

[a]The United States median income per equivalent person in 1997 was $28,005.

[b]Figures given are expressed in PPP-adjusted 1997 U.S. dollars per equivalent person, weighted by the number of persons per household.

FIGURE 22.3   Equal Opportunity and Fair Chance: Economic Distance and Real Standards of Living for Children in Thirteen Countries, 1992 to 1997

| | Fair Chance | Economic Distance | | Equal Opportunity | |
	Tenth Percentile (Low-Income)	(Length of Bars Represents the Gap Between High- and Low-Income Individuals)	Ninetieth Percentile (High-Income)	Ratio of Ninetieth to Tenth Percentile (Decile Ratio)	Real Income Gap[a]
Norway, 1995	55%		126%	2.29	$19,884
Switzerland, 1992	51		165	3.24	31,926
Sweden, 1995	48		97	2.02	13,722
Denmark, 1997	48		114	2.37	18,483
Finland, 1995	46		122	2.66	21,283
France, 1994	44		137	3.11	26,045
Canada, 1997	44		156	3.55	31,366
Belgium, 1997	44		127	2.89	23,244
Netherlands, 1994	42		110	2.62	19,043
Germany, 1994	40		121	3.03	22,684
Australia, 1994	36		124	3.44	24,644
United Kingdom, 1995	31		127	4.10	26,885
United States, 1997	35		180	5.15	40,327
Simple average	43		131	3.11	24,580

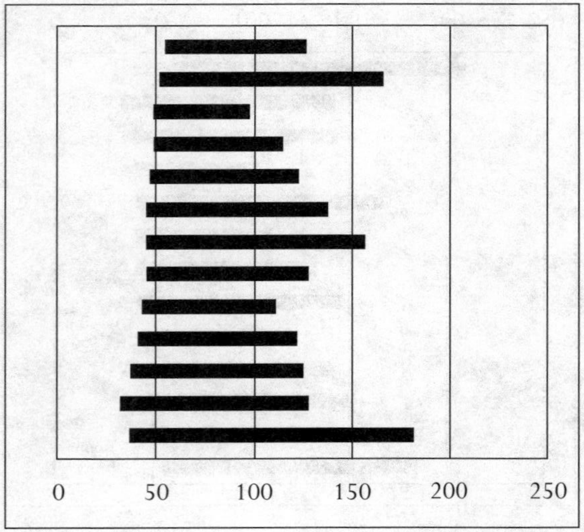

Source: Luxembourg Income Study and authors' calculations.

Note: Numbers given are percentages of overall U.S. 1997 median equivalent income in PPP terms.

[a]Figures given are adjusted dollars per equivalent-person 1997 U.S. dollars, weighted for the number of children in each unit size, and relative to the overall U.S. median of $28,005.

22.2 because figure 22.3 presents only the incomes for families with children, and because on average families with children have lower equivalent incomes than all families. On average, children's real incomes at the tenth percentile are the same as all persons' real incomes at the tenth percentile (43 percent of the median in figure 22.3), but the average incomes of families with children are less than those of all families, mainly because the ninetieth percentile for children (131 percent of the U.S. median in figure 22.4) is below that for the whole population (146 percent in figure 22.2). Thus, inequality as measured by the decile ratio is less than average for children, and the real income gap is also lower for children.

The nations with the highest tenth percentile offer their poor children the least deprivation and, to the extent that current resources enable future outcomes, the best economic chance for future success. We emphasize that the impact of childhood income on life chances is likely to be highly nonlinear: although a few dollars more may matter a lot for the severely disadvantaged, the same dollar amount is likely to have relatively little impact on the life chances of the already affluent. Susan Mayer (1997) and others have also argued that income alone is a poor proxy for life chances for middle-class households with children—another $100 or even $1,000 per child for middle-income or well-to-do families makes little difference to their children's overall life chances compared with other influences (parents, schools, communities, peers, and so on). But as Greg Duncan and his colleagues (1998) note, a child born into a family with very low income (roughly into a tenth percentile of 31 to 37 percent of the median) has significantly poorer overall life chances.[9] Thus, real income at the tenth percentile for children is a meaningful and important indicator of a fair life chance for those children who are least advantaged.

Based on real incomes alone, a low-income tenth-percentile child in the United Kingdom has less of a chance, at 31 percent of the median, than does a child in the United States, at 35 percent of the median. Australian children are at roughly the same level of living as American children, while the next nearest is unified Germany, at 40 percent. All other nations have children's living standards that are at or above the average standard of 43 percent, which is eight percentage points above the U.S. level, or almost one-fourth higher than the 35 percent U.S. value. In the United States this is a $2,250 per child deficit in 1997 PPP dollars. The United States is, *on average,* a rich nation. However, because income inequality is greater in the United States than in other nations, children in families at the bottom of the income distribution end up absolutely worse off than the worst-off children in other nations. Simply put, the inequality extant among American children is not offset by the overall richness of the nation.

At the other end of the scale, children in prosperous (ninetieth percentile) American households have living standards 80 percent above that of the median person in the United States. Similar Swiss children are also relatively better off (at 165 percent of the median). The average incomes of the ninetieth-percentile children in all thirteen nations are 131 percent of the median, while U.S. children are forty-nine percentage points above this level—or $16,635 per child better off than on average.

These percentiles translate into decile ratios and real income gaps for children that are similar to those found in figure 22.2. Here we interpret the economic distance measure as a measure of equality of opportunity or "equal chance." Nations with smaller economic distances (or lower real income gaps) provide more equal chances for all their children, including both high- and low-income children. The U.S. gap in decile ratio (5.11) and real PPP-adjusted per child terms is again the highest. Only one other nation (the United Kingdom) has a decile ratio above 4.00. The real income gap of $40,327 between rich and poor kids in the United States is by far the largest, with Switzerland and Canada the only others above

FIGURE 22.4 *Equal Opportunity and Fair Chance: The Impact of Combining Cash and Noncash Income on Economic Distance and Real Standards of Living for Children in Thirteen Countries, 1992 to 1997*

| | Fair Chance | Economic Distance | | Equal Opportunity | |
	Tenth Percentile (Low-Income)	(Length of Bars Represents the Gap Between High- and Low-Income Individuals)	Ninetieth Percentile (High-Income)	Ratio of Ninetieth to Tenth Percentile (Decile Ratio)	Real Income Gap
Norway, 1995	67%		123%	1.83	$19,889
Switzerland, 1992	58		148	2.56	31,964
Denmark, 1997	57		109	1.92	18,468
Sweden, 1995	54		93	1.71	13,851
Belgium, 1997	52		117	2.27	23,085
Finland, 1995	50		110	2.19	21,310
Canada, 1997	49		138	2.79	31,609
France, 1994	46		120	2.58	26,282
United States, 1997	46		162	3.51	41,199
Netherlands, 1994	43		97	2.24	19,179
Germany, 1994	43		107	2.50	22,730
Australia, 1994	40		112	2.82	25,572
United Kingdom, 1995	34		110	3.20	26,992
Simple average	49		119	2.47	24,861

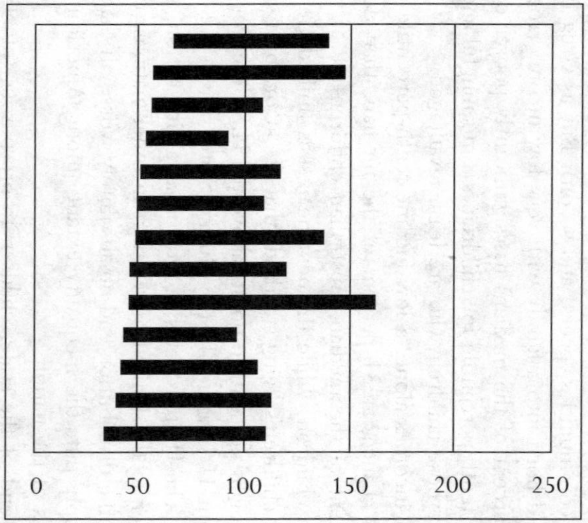

Source: Luxembourg Income Study and authors' calculations.

Notes: Figures given are percentages of overall U.S. 1997 median cash plus noncash income and expressed as adjusted dollars per equivalent person in 1997 U.S. dollars, weighted for the number of children in each unit size. The tenth and ninetieth percentiles are divided by the overall U.S. median of $35,516.

the $30,000 level; the other nations are near or below the $24,861 average difference. The above-average gaps between poor and rich children in these three nations must be seen in light of the fact that all three also have above-average ratios of the ninetieth to tenth percentile. The real income gap of $40,327 in the United States reflects the fact that low-income (tenth percentile) children have resources of $9,802 (assuming that all resources are evenly split among household members), while high-income (ninetieth percentile) families have $50,129 to spend on each child.

Overall, our conclusion is that there are significant differences in real income levels and inequality across the countries we have examined. If one uses the United States as a benchmark, it is clear that both low-income individuals and poor children are significantly worse off than their counterparts in most other developed countries, measured in dollars of equal purchasing power. However, up to this point we have not considered noncash benefits, a topic to which we now turn.

Public Versus Private Income and the Added Value of Noncash Benefits

The "social wage" can be paid partly in cash and partly in services—but how much do these different kinds of "payment" affect inequality among children? To examine this issue, we have added the PPP-adjusted value of public health care per child and the PPP-adjusted value of elementary education per child to the cash income figures from the Luxembourg Income Study, which are also based on OECD (2002a, 2002b) estimates and given in 1997 PPP-adjusted dollars. Health care spending for children is assumed to equal half of the government cost of health care per capita. Recent cross-national research on the cost of health care by age groups suggests that this is the average cost of providing insurance per child in rich nations (Smeeding and Freund 2002).[10] Education spending is estimated by the PPP-adjusted spending per elementary school child in every country. All benefits are assumed to be valued at government cost by the recipients of these benefits, a procedure that clearly understates the value of publicly provided education by implicitly ignoring the rate of return to education. We ignore publicly subsidized child care, secondary and tertiary education benefits, and all other noncash benefits for youth.

Smeeding and Rainwater (2002) are not able to directly allocate noncash government benefits across the distribution of disposable incomes here, but we assess their importance to children alone based on Smeeding (2002a). Table 22.1 indicates that only in Sweden, Finland, France, and the United Kingdom are cash benefits greater than noncash benefits for the median child.[11] Health care benefits are smaller than education benefits everywhere. The relative balance between spending on cash and noncash programs differs markedly across nations.

Why do some nations provide, for example, public housing while others provide cash (which could also be spent on needs such as food or on wants such as liquor) to enable low-income people to pay the rent? Although in-kind benefits are important for child welfare, economists have long argued on efficiency grounds for cash transfers. Presumably, the parents of affected children would prefer to receive the same amount that is being spent on noncash benefits as a cash transfer, because that would enable them to choose the utility-maximizing consumption bundle (from a set that includes the actual in-kind program) or they could choose a better alternative of equal cost. In such a case, taxpayers are no worse off and recipient families are potentially better off; as economists would say, it would clearly be a Pareto superior policy change. However, the crucial issue is one of agency—parents

TABLE 22.1   *Cash and Noncash Benefits at the Fiftieth Percentile for Eleven Countries[d] (1997 U.S. PPP Dollars)*

Country	Cash Transfers[a]	Health[b]	Education[c]	Total Noncash	Total Benefits Cash + Noncash
Australia	$2,175 (102)	$567 (37)	$3,530 (59)	$4,097 (55)	$6,272 (65)
Canada	2,678 (126)	720 (46)	4,500 (75)	5,220 (69)	7,898 (82)
Denmark	5,558 (261)	645 (42)	6,083 (102)	6,728 (90)	12,286 (127)
Finland	6,041 (283)	512 (33)	4,369 (73)	4,881 (65)	10,922 (113)
France	5,716 (268)	735 (47)	3,436 (58)	4,171 (56)	9,887 (103)
Germany	2,191 (103)	769 (50)	3,183 (53)	3,952 (53)	6,143 (64)
Netherlands	3,350 (157)	641 (41)	3,013 (51)	3,654 (49)	7,004 (73)
Norway	3,902 (183)	749 (48)	7,690 (129)	8,439 (112)	12,341 (128)
Sweden	8,925 (418)	663 (43)	5,194 (87)	5,857 (78)	14,782 (153)
United Kingdom	4,408 (207)	521 (34)	3,017 (51)	3,538 (47)	7,946 (82)
United States	2,133 (100)	1,550 (100)	5,961 (100)	7,511 (100)	9,644 (100)
Simple Average	4,280	734	4,543	5,277	9,557

Source: Smeeding (2002a).
Note: Numbers in parentheses indicate index position with United States equal to 100.
[a]Median cash benefits per child for all children taken from LIS and expressed in 1997 PPP-adjusted dollars.
[b]Public health expenditures per child from OECD in 1997 PPP-adjusted dollars, with adjustments for employer-provided health benefits in the United States (OECD 2002b).
[c]Public elementary school expenditures per school-age child in 1997 PPP-adjusted dollars (OECD 2002a).
[d]Belgium and Switzerland are not included in this table because they report only after-tax earnings.

may or may not spend cash transfers for the benefit of their children, and there is a potential cost from misallocation within the family. Hence, social policy designers have often preferred to deliver in-kind services rather than provide cash transfers—recognizing that the trade-off is the efficiency advantages that can be obtained from parental choice weighed against the degree to which parents can be trusted to act in the best interests of their children.

From the point of view of the child and from the point of view of the taxpayer, the large size of noncash benefits means that they have a large effect on child well-being. In our data, we have no way of estimating the impacts of the balance of cash transfers and in-kind service delivery programs—that is, the relative size of the efficiency benefits of devolution to parents compared with the potential agency costs of misallocation within the family. We therefore add together the dollar value of cash transfers and in-kind services; in doing so, we implicitly assume that these opposite influences offset each other.

In practice, the United States spends the least on cash benefits but the second-most on noncash benefits (see table 22.1). Only Norway spends more for noncash benefits than does the United States. In fact, many nations spend far below the average amount on noncash benefits, and most spend far less than the United States. When the two are added together, the United States spends close to the average of total benefits for all the nations combined, but in the United States much more is spent in ways that demonstrate little trust in parental decisionmaking. Measured by total benefits, Australia, the Netherlands, and Germany seem to be making the least effort; their education spending is particularly low (on this point, see Allmendinger and Leibfried 2002). Although these values differ by income quintile, the median benefit picture suggests that public noncash benefits are indeed important.

Since we are presuming that these in-kind services are equally distributed, their effect on the overall distribution of resources across families with children necessarily lessens the relative distance between the rich and poor child in each nation. Because health (everywhere but in the United States) and education benefits are assumed to be the same regardless of income level, the proportionate effect is greater on low-income children than on high-income children. Thus, the tenth percentiles rise on average by six points, or 14 percent, to 49 percent of the median. The ninetieth percentiles change by twelve points, or only 10 percent, to 131 percent of the median. The overall ratio of rich to poor falls from 3.11 based on cash alone (figure 22.3) to 2.47 when noncash benefits are also taken into account (figure 22.4). However, the dollar distances remain largely unchanged, since both rich and poor children are assumed to receive more or less equal benefits.

In low-cash-transfer nations, like the United States, noncash benefits raise the fair chance measures, pushing the tenth percentile to 46 percent of the median, which is still below average but puts American children on a par with French children and above German, Australian, and Dutch children. Rich (ninetieth percentile) American children are still far above the median, but the decile ratio is now 3.51, not 5.11. In Norway, Denmark, and Sweden, the ratio of rich to poor is under 2.0. Clearly, noncash benefits have an equalizing effect on the differences between rich and poor nations.

This result is highly sensitive to the assumption that noncash benefits have the same value for rich and poor children. In practice, children are at the receiving end of a series of decisions in which educational resources are allocated to school boards, to specific schools, and to classes within schools. If, for example, school spending is locally financed from the property tax or local income tax, as is partially the case in the United States, the revenues available from low-income neighborhoods may reduce educational spending for low-income children compared with high-income children. Both David Card and Abigail Payne (1998) and Kathryn Wilson (2000) find that public school spending in the United States may differ by 65 to 75 percent between rich and poor districts. (However, recent changes in school financing legislation have greatly equalized within-school spending [see Murray, Evans, and Schwab 1998; Corcoran et al. 2002].) In a recent paper, Kathryn Wilson, Kristina Lambright, and Timothy Smeeding (2003) also find that once school expenditures are assigned (at the school district level) to students ranked by family income, spending levels between the top and bottom quintiles varied by only 15 percent at most in 1998. Adjusting for the differential costs of providing education (according to local wage costs and other factors) reduces this difference to 8 percent. However, adjusting for student needs in terms of the extra costs of educating bilingual, disabled, and poor children increases the differences to 25 percent or higher. Thus, if poor children received education benefits not of $5,960 but rather $5,000, while rich children received $7,000 in benefits, the ratios of the ninetieth to the tenth percentile in the United States would be 43 and 165, respectively, in figure 22.4, and the results would be much the same as if only cash benefits were counted. In the United States the importance of the local property tax base for education funding still differs by locality even after states redistribute to reach minimally acceptable spending levels. But most of the other countries in our data are unitary states, with national government allocation of educational expenditures. In educational finance, each country has its own complexities, but there are some grounds for suspicion that national systems are less likely to have substantial differences in school resources than highly fragmented school systems.

Similarly, national systems of public health care are not precisely equal in actual program delivery, but they do have strong bureaucratic and political pressures pushing them toward comparable provision. On the other hand, we know that health care benefits are different in the United States—because the Medicaid program supporting low-income children in the United States is very different, in terms of outlays per child, from employer-subsidized programs for the middle class and well-to-do. These differences are not reflected in the estimates of figure 22.4 (see also table 22.2 and table 22A.1). Hence, within-country distributions of noncash benefits are crucial to the results obtained.

The larger issue here is the possibility that the rich might "drop out from the top." If inequality greatly increases, at some point the rich can afford to opt out of public programs and purchase substitute services in the private market, perhaps even finding it advantageous to do so. In all countries the fact that taxes increase with income while benefits are approximately a lump sum amount means that the rich pay more in taxes than they receive in value of public services—but the extent of the gap depends on the degree of inequality in market incomes. When the affluent can afford to forgo public benefits and purchase private alternatives not available to the poor, the underfunding of public services does not affect them personally. Indeed, their incentive to "go private" increases with the size of the disparities in market incomes. Part of this private-public substitution may occur at the firm level: employers may provide highly paid employees with health and retirement benefits that supersede government-provided benefits for the same purpose. But whether the mechanism is a firm-level benefit or a personal decision, when a society becomes more unequal, one question is increasingly asked: Why should high-income people support public programs?[12]

The Importance of Taxation and the Public Provision of Benefits

Inequality is much higher in the United States than in other countries with similar (and indeed lower) average incomes. Furthermore, American inequality differs noticeably from that in other rich countries primarily because of differences in relative income levels in the lower tail of the American income distribution. As we have observed, an American child at the tenth percentile of the U.S. income distribution has an adjusted disposable income that is just 35 percent of U.S. median income, and between 43 and 46 percent of the median when we count noncash benefits. In this context, government efforts on behalf of low-income children are crucially important. Table 22.2 presents net public benefits—cash and total (cash plus noncash) benefits received, net of direct taxes paid for social programs—as a percentage of income at the various percentile points of the income distributions in each nation (see table 22A.1 for details). Here we count not only the amount received by each child but also the direct taxes that the family pays to the government for all social benefits—for the elderly as well as for children. We estimate tax costs by assuming that all families pay equal proportions of their taxes for social expenditures (transfers in cash and in-kind) and for exhaustive government expenditures (defense, police, environment, and other public goods) in each nation. The share of every dollar of tax paid for social expenditures ranges from sixty-seven cents per dollar of tax in Australia to ninety cents per dollar in Norway. (The remainder is used to fund non-excludable public goods, which are not allocated here.)

On average, more than half (52.9 percent) of the total disposable incomes of low-income (tenth percentile) families with children come from public cash transfers—and up to 67.3 percent once noncash benefits are included (table 22.2). The fraction of total incomes that comes from public benefits varies more with earnings in the bottom of the income distribution than anywhere else. Countries with relatively large numbers of low-income children and families with little earnings, like the United Kingdom and Australia, find that public benefits are 80 or 90 percent of total incomes at the bottom of the distribu-

TABLE 22.2   *Government Support for Children in Eleven Countries, 1992 to 1997: Net Cash (and Noncash) Transfers (Benefits Minus Taxes) as a Percentage of Adjusted Income, by Percentile Point*

| Country | Year | Tenth Percentile | | Fiftieth Percentile | | Ninetieth Percentile | |
		Cash	(Noncash)	Cash	(Noncash)	Cash	Noncash
Australia	1994	82.8	(88.3)	−14.7	(9.3)	−31.2	(−8.1)
Canada	1997	64.0	(73.6)	−20.5	(5.7)	−24.6	(−4.8)
Denmark	1992	22.6	(45.4)	−26.1	(2.7)	−37.3	(−9.0)
Finland	1994	62.0	(72.2)	−4.4	(13.3)	−23.4	(−5.4)
France	1994	47.2	(60.6)	21.2	(33.1)	2.5	(13.0)
Germany	1994	38.1	(55.4)	−27.0	(−4.3)	−34.1	(−15.4)
Netherlands	1994	43.0	(60.6)	−23.2	(−2.1)	−42.2	(−18.0)
Norway	1995	44.6	(63.8)	−15.0	(11.3)	−23.4	(−0.3)
Sweden	1995	26.0	(50.7)	1.6	(25.0)	−27.6	(−1.2)
United Kingdom	1995	92.5	(94.4)	4.8	(19.9)	−34.7	(−15.8)
United States	1997	58.4	(74.7)	−10.3	(16.3)	−27.6	(−4.9)
Average		52.9	(67.3)	−10.3	(15.2)	−27.6	(−3.7)

Source: Table 22A.1 and figure 22.3.
Notes: Numbers given are for cash transfers and cash transfers plus education benefits at each level of income, net of direct taxes paid for social programs. Belgium and Switzerland are not included in this table because they report only after-tax earnings.

tion. Countries where low-income families work—even high-tax and high-benefit nations like Denmark and Sweden—find that public cash benefits are one-quarter or less of total cash incomes. Counting noncash benefits as well raises the fraction of income that is publicly supported in every nation to at least 50 percent, including both Denmark and Sweden. The variation in benefits at the bottom is also related to two other factors—the wage level and the generosity of benefits. For instance, low-income parents work more in the United States than in most other nations, but the wages they earn are much lower (Smeeding 2002a; Osberg 2002; Smeeding, Rainwater, and Burtless 2001). Also, public benefits in cash are less generous in the United States, Australia, and the United Kingdom than in most other nations, thus limiting the effects of transfers on low incomes (Smeeding 2002b).

The importance of the state in income redistribution is evidenced by the fact that public benefits make up more than half of total resources for low-income children in every country shown, once noncash benefits are included. Conversely, taxes paid exceed benefits received for upper-income groups. At the median, families pay almost as much in taxes for social programs as they receive back in cash benefits, and all families with children, save those in Britain, Sweden, and France, come out net taxpayers. But when noncash benefits are included, children in all countries except Germany and the Netherlands are net beneficiaries from the tax-benefit process. Thus, noncash benefits for children may be important elements of the calculus of support for social programs among families with children in these rich nations.

Because our data include only direct taxes, they give us an incomplete picture of net fiscal incidence. Nevertheless, well-to-do families with children are net taxpayers everywhere but in France. The deficit is very large—the average rich family pays over 25 percent more in direct taxes than it receives in benefits. Once noncash benefits are counted, families on average almost break even, though the balance is still in deficit for almost all nations.

In fact, public support for both cash and noncash benefits may be strongly affected by the income position of families. Although our estimates are rough, we find that high-income families, who can afford private substitutes for public services, have less incentive to vote for the funding of public services. Noncash benefits clearly play a large and equalizing role for most families, but with greater inequality, private health insurance and private schooling may become attractive alternatives to public-sector provision of health and educational benefits for high-income families. We consider this possibility in the next section, where we look at the literature that examines the degree to which the political economy of more unequal societies responds with lessened support for public services.

THE LITERATURE ON PUBLIC REDISTRIBUTIVE GOODS AND INEQUALITY

The literature on public goods and inequality can be categorized into three main threads, and we look at each in turn. The first looks at the relationship between specific measures of social capital and inequality (for example, Putnam 2001; Costa and Kahn 2001; Knack and Keefer 1997; Alesina and La Ferrara 1999, 2001).[13] (For useful annotated bibliographies on social capital and research on the connection between inequality and violence, see World Bank Group 1999, 2003.) The intent of this literature is to capture national or jurisdictional (U.S. state, for example, or Canadian province) tastes for redistributive and collective goods. The second literature tests the median voter hypothesis (and the closely related issue of social mobility) and other closely related hypotheses (specifically, the social affinity hypothesis), relating it to inequality and examining its effects on growth or on social spending within and across countries. These papers (Milanovic 2000; Bassett, Burkett, and Putterman 1999; Alesina and La Ferrara 2001; Kristov, Lindert, and McClelland 1992) are typically motivated by the relationships between measures of inequality (such as median income levels, share of the median income, and Gini coefficients) and growth, but they focus on the impact of inequality on the decisionmaking process of the median voter. There is also a much more robust and more recent literature on this topic and similar issues, including the works of Karl Moene and Michael Wallerstein (2001, 2002), Jonas Pontusson (forthcoming), David Bradley and his colleagues (2001), and Lane Kenworthy and Jonas Pontusson (2002). Finally, the third strand we identify is the literature on the impact of redistributive public spending on inequality and growth—specifically the effects of health and education benefits. This literature on inequality and redistribution and their interactions with economic growth includes papers by Roberto Perotti (1992, 1996), William Bassett and his colleagues (1999), Torsten Persson and Guido Tabellini (1994), Alberto Alesina and Dani Rodrik (1994), Lars Osberg (1995), Xavier Sala-i-Martin (1997), Roland Bénabou (1996, 2000), Amparo Castello and Rafael Domenech (2002), and, most recently, Frederick van der Ploeg (2003) and Thorvaldur Gylfason and Gylfi Zoega (2003).

A general comment to make about almost all of this literature is that "redistribution" and "inequality" are usually interpreted, fairly casually, in terms of annual money income. Inequality in lifetime income and year-to-year income insecurity is rarely mentioned. However, many of the cash transfers of the welfare state have a "social insurance" rationale, which is really about redistribution between contingencies rather than between individuals who may not be "rich" or "poor" in a lifetime income sense, even if their current income is depressed.[14]

In an insurance program, it is always the case in any given year that some policyholders receive net payouts (for example, fire insurance purchasers whose houses burned down) while others make net payments (the policyholders whose houses did not burn), but that does not imply that insurance is "redistributive" in a forward-looking sense. Social insurance programs are no different.

For example, in any given year workers' compensation systems pay benefits to those who are injured in workplace accidents. This can be seen as a transfer program that redistributes income from more affluent healthy workers to less well off injured workers. However, it could also be seen as an insurance program that provides all workers with the benefit of greater income security and may not redistribute expected lifetime income at all. Unemployment insurance benefits and income support programs can be similarly interpreted. Since those who are lucky one year may be unlucky in a subsequent year, the longer the accounting time frame the less the perceived redistributional impact of a social insurance program.

However, even those who turn out to be lucky every year (because their house never burns down, or they never have a workplace accident) are better off because of the availability of insurance. Hence, a better measure of redistribution is the difference among people in the net actuarial value of social insurance coverage. Since the lifetime income poor are more likely to be exposed to such shocks as unemployment or workplace injury, the actuarial value of coverage in social insurance programs *is* redistributive. However, the net value of redistribution is equal only to the predictable difference in expected value of benefits, *not* to the face value of benefits. Similarly, the measurement and the conceptualization of the "redistributive" element of in-kind public services (such as education and health care) depend heavily on methodological assumptions.[15]

Cross-State and Cross-National Research on Redistribution of Social Capital and Trust

We begin our review of the literature that investigates expenditures and inequality with a review of some of the studies that focus on social capital. In their investigations of issues related to trust, community participation, and general social organization, these authors are primarily interested in how individuals (and groups) interact with each other and government, in addition to how they broadly *perceive* society and government and the relationship between the two.

In the first line of research (Costa and Kahn 2001; Alesina and La Ferrara 1999), multiple regressions are run across the states of the United States using a wide variety of datasets, which are difficult to compile for a large number of countries (see table 22A.2). In Alesina and La Ferrara (1999), the authors use the General Social Survey (GSS) and census state data to construct inequality measures by U.S. states to determine the proportions of respondents involved in any number of social groups, including churches, fraternities, hobby clubs, sport clubs, youth groups, and literary groups. They construct a probit model where utility is gained from involvement in community activities and thus measured as a binary variable. Demographic controls include age, marital status, race, education, number of children, real income, full-time or part-time status, and controls for U.S. state dummies (see Alesina and La Ferrara 1999, tables 2 through 6). Predictors of participation typically enter as expected: lower education and younger children tend to reduce participation; women and younger people (below age thirty) participate less; and increases in income tend to increase participation. Additional results indicate that inequality and racial and ethnic fragmentation tend to lower participation in community activities.[16] Alesina and La Ferrara conclude that community heterogeneity, measured by fragmentation and inequality, decreases community participation statistically, significantly, and nontrivially.

Alesina and La Ferrara (2001, abs.) extend these ideas by addressing perceptions of economic and social mobility as they affect people's taste for redistribution within the United States. They report that "people who believe that the American society offers equal opportunities to all are more averse to redistribution in the face of increased mobility." Those who do not perceive there to be an equal chance or a great deal of mobility do not find social mobility to be a good substitute for redistributive policies. Thus, the political economy approach from the economists' point of view suggests that preferences for redistribution are tied to beliefs about equality of opportunity and social and economic mobility. However, we must emphasize that Alesina and La Ferrara are examining differences in attitudes within the United States—that is, within a common context of understanding of the acceptable domains of inequality and a common perception of basic human rights. In international comparisons, we cannot explain the unusual level of income inequality in the United States by some unusually high level of belief in equality of opportunity, since the responses of Americans to comparable questions in attitudinal surveys are often much the same as those of respondents in other countries (see Osberg and Smeeding 2003).

Also using the GSS for an analysis of U.S. states, Ichiro Kawachi and his colleagues (1997) relate social capital indicators, including trust, to mortality rates. They find that states with high levels of mistrust have higher rates of mortality, adjusting for age. In percentage terms, they claim that a "percentage increment in people agreeing that others would take advantage of them was associated with an increase in overall mortality of 6.7 deaths per 100,000" (1494). Replicating these types of studies cross-nationally would be a difficult task, primarily owing to data restrictions and consistency, although John Helliwell (2002) uses the World Values Survey cross-nationally in a similar manner.[17]

Drawing on a number of studies and data sources, Dora Costa and Matthew Kahn (2001) seek to explain the observed decline in social capital in the United States. They conclude that rising community heterogeneity and, in particular, rising income inequality explain the fall in social capital outside the home (see also Putnam 2001; Soroka, Johnston, and Banting 2002). Rafael La Porta and his colleagues (1997, 334) focus on the effects of trust on large organizations, measured by "government effectiveness, participation in civic organizations, size of the largest firms relative to GNP, and the performance of a society more generally." Similar to the findings in Costa and Kahn (2001), Alesina and La Ferrara (1999, 2001), Kawachi and his colleagues (1997), and Fukuyama (1995), the finding of La Porta and his colleagues is that trust raises civic involvement and government and social efficiency. All of these papers therefore find at least some evidence that social capital and the relationships between people or communities play at least some role in the growth of inequality.

Going further, Stephen Knack and Philip Keefer (1997) tie the differences in social capital to differences in trust and civic cooperation in a cross-national context (including developing nations), arguing that low social polarization and institutions that constrain governments from making arbitrary acts lead to higher levels of trust.[18] The links between inequality, trust, and social spending are clearly important here, and the large variation in countries gives perspective to our "rich country" efforts.

Closely associated with the social capital studies is the small literature that relates various measures of trust to economic outcomes. Recent work by Joel Slemrod and Peter Katuscak (Slemrod 2002; Slemrod and Katuscak 2002) uses the same data used in this study to look at the various impacts of trust. In the latter paper, the authors use the WVS data with additional controls for age and education to show that "on average, a trusting attitude has a positive impact on income, while trustworthiness has a negative impact on income" (abs.). Slemrod (2002) uses the first wave of the WVS to examine the relationship between the extent of tax-cheating and the size of government. Clearly, if trust is related to income and taxes, the effectiveness of government policies will be affected, and those outcomes, in turn, will have an impact on redistribution and social expenditure decisions. Using three-stage least squares, Slemrod claims that "tax cheating is lower in countries that exhibit more (not-government-related) trustworthiness." Additionally, when he considers the effects of prosperity levels, and how prosperity depends on government size and individual levels of trust, he finds some evidence "that both prosperity and government involvement are higher in more trusting societies" (abs.).

Other work in the area of trust and economic outcomes includes studies by Knack and Keefer (1997), Zak and Knack (2001), and Knack and Zak (2002), who come to similar conclusions. Knack and Keefer (1997) find that trust exhibits a strong and positive relation-ship to growth, while Zak and Knack (2001) introduce other influences on growth, includ-ing formal institutions, social distance, and discrimination. In the oft-referenced Zak and Knack (2001) paper, the authors' general equilibrium model matches consumers and bro-kers to test differences in trust across societies and the potential consequences of different levels of trust for the economy. In examining the relationship between trust and growth, the authors find that a 1 percent increase in trust increases a country's investment-GDP ratio by 0.2 percent and growth by 1.1 percent (elasticities calculated at the sample means).[19] In a second set of estimates, Zak and Knack look to explain the determinants of trust and find that higher levels of inequality (various measures), social distance, and economic discrimina-tion lower trust, while increases in "formal institutions" (contract enforceability and corrup-tion) serve as a positive force on levels of trust. The Zak and Knack (2001) study is a prime example of utilizing trust in a broad, cross-national framework, and there has been an increasing amount of work in this kind of research over the past few years.

Broadly expanding work on trust and social spending, Edward Glaeser, Jose Scheink-man, and Andrei Shleifer (2002) have constructed a model of "institutional subversion." The model aims to capture how people, particularly the wealthy, subvert legal, regulatory, and political institutions by using forms of influence such as intimidation and corruption. In their model, initial inequality in private resources enables some individuals to gain an illicit advantage in regulatory and legal processes, and that illicit advantage both accentuates subse-quent inequality and reduces future growth. This implies that institutional reform, especially in countries with weak legal and prosecution systems, may be both vital in addressing inequality concerns and difficult to implement. Other work in related areas has included institutional controls in an effort to measure such effects on inequality and other outcome measures.

We conclude that measures of trust in other individuals and trust in governments are important determinants of cross-national (and also cross-jurisdictional) institutions for redis-tribution. However, trust in government's ability to redistribute and a willingness to assign government the responsibility for redistribution may be perceived differently. Altruism to-ward one's neighbors and fellow citizens may not translate directly into enthusiasm for government as the mechanism for actualizing these wishes. The relationship between poli-tics, institutions, economics, and more social outcomes, such as trust, is especially compli-cated within a cross-national framework. The next section looks more closely at work that examines the relationship between inequality and public expenditures.

Inequality and Public Expenditures

In the second thread of economics research, the question of how inequality, public goods, and social mobility are related to one another and to economic growth is examined from a cross-national viewpoint. While the earlier literature refers almost exclusively to overall social spending and not as much to education or health care as separate entities with possibly different determinants and distributions, the newer literature explicitly addresses different types of spending (see, for example, Moene and Wallerstein 2002). We begin with the older literature.

Branko Milanovic's (2000) paper outlines one economic theory of social expenditures and inequality as follows:

> When individuals are ordered according to their factor (or market) incomes, the median voter (the individual with the median level of income) will be, in more unequal societies, relatively poorer. His or her income will be lower in relation to mean income. If net transfers (government cash transfers minus direct taxes) are progressive, the more unequal is the income distribution, the more the median voter has to gain through joint action of taxes and transfers, and the more likely he or she is to vote for higher taxes and transfers. With the median voter as decisive, more unequal societies will therefore choose greater redistribution. (368–9)

Milanovic uses the LIS dataset to analyze seventy-nine country observations (waves 1 through 4). Using fixed effects, he regresses three measures of inequality (either the Gini coefficient for factor incomes or the share of total factor income received by the bottom half [bottom quintile] of the population ranked by factor [market] income and the proportion of the population over sixty-five years old), on the extent of redistribution. (He defines the dependent variable as "how the share of [i] the bottom half and of [ii] the bottom quintile [ranked by factor income . . .] increases when we move from factor . . . to disposable income" [384].)

Milanovic's paper does not, however, present any data on median voters or their incomes compared with the average incomes in society. It is not generally true that the outcomes experienced by the median voter are reflected at all in changes in these different indices of inequality,[20] so there is only a very loose link between the model of voting behavior and the inequality measures he uses. In fact, more affluent voters may be better able to exert their influence through political contributions, greater political knowledge, or greater access to elected officials (see Ansolabehere, de Figueiredo, and Snyder 2003). Furthermore, the largest effects of greater inequality resulting in greater social spending by governments seem to come from social retirement expenditures.

There are strong arguments for distinguishing retirement income transfers from other issues. Societies with broad and deep social retirement programs, like those of Scandinavia and northern Europe, tend to have lesser amounts of private pension income or savings because of the high benefits from government. These countries therefore have higher pre-benefit inequality (Smeeding and Williamson 2001). In other countries, however, registered private pension plan contributions are tax-exempt, and the public sector contributes significantly, through tax expenditures, to the relative size of the private pension sector. However, we do not capture this past role of the public sector when we examine current pension receipts. Hence, in the area of old-age security, the true size of the public-sector role may be more imperfectly measured by current expenditures than is the case for other types of social expenditures. Moreover, the aggregate value of pensions paid relative to pension contributions received (for both the public and private sectors) necessarily depends crucially on the age structure of the population.

Another variant in the political economy vein is provided by Lorenzo Kristov and his colleagues (1992), who have proposed a variation on the "pressure group" model.[21] In their model, governments transfer income between different pressure groups, which are defined as groups that "form and expend their members' resources to promote or to fight any specific income-transfer proposal that has a serious chance of passage" (137). Instead of assuming that members of pressure groups "vote their pocketbooks," the authors develop a model: individuals first decide which group to join and then decide how much effort to expend on political activity. How individuals specifically translate their own economic status and their subsequent beliefs as to what social transfers should look like are determined at least in part by the economic climate of the society. Indeed, the authors note, "growth might be a negative influence on commitment to social transfers for a reason linked to the social-affinity hypothesis: the greater the recent rate of growth the stronger the perception of upward mobility, reducing sympathy with those presently poor" (152).

Readers will note that this formulation conflates societal and individual income growth—and income growth greatly complicates discussions of inequality. Individuals typically receive higher incomes as they grow older, and in general the year-to-year change in an individual's real income can be expressed as the sum of the change in (1) the change in average real incomes of all people, (2) their own personal *expected* change in *relative* incomes (for example, change due to greater age or experience), and (3) any *unexpected* year-to-year variability in personal income flows. Each component has different implications for inequality, and for attitudes.

As already noted, the relationship between growth in average income and redistribution has often been explained in terms of social spending as a normal good—hence, higher rates of growth of average income should lead to *higher* rates of public spending. However, changes in average incomes do not necessarily translate into individual experiences of income change. It is quite possible, for example, for individuals to experience over their own lifetimes a faster rate of change in their personal incomes even as aggregate growth slows if the age-earnings profile becomes sufficiently steeper.

But would a faster *predictable* rate of change of income with age necessarily represent greater "mobility"? Even in a caste society whose members never escape their origins, there is some payoff to job experience. In a caste society, steeper age-earnings profiles would certainly mean that, in a cross-section of individuals of all ages, more individuals move between income deciles—but by most criteria that would not imply greater "social mobility" or "equality of opportunity." Presumably the concept of equal opportunity refers to opportunities for access to income streams with different expected lifetime present value.

To the degree that age-related changes in income are predictable, individuals presumably make an approximate calculation of expected future lifetime income when they are young. Hence, we can think of such expectations as indicating an individual's social class origins. If so, it is the *unpredictable* component of incomes that is closer to what most people mean by "social mobility." But if "income mobility" and "income uncertainty" are much the same idea, how should we predict the voting behavior response to greater *uncertainty* in forecast income streams?[22] Predictions of the median voter response to greater *predictable* mobility in forecast income streams (that is, a steeper age-earnings profile) are similarly unclear.[23]

Econometrically, Kristov and his colleagues (1992) "test" social affinity theory by regressing a series of covariates that attempt to explain patterns in their dependent variable—social transfers as a share of GDP. They find that the larger the gap between the rich and the middle (the 90-50 ratio), the *greater* the redistribution that takes place, but the greater the gap between the bottom and the middle, the *less* the redistribution, presumably because of pressure politics. (These are exactly the opposite signs to those we hypothesize.) Kristov and his colleagues argue that willingness to engage in political activity and resulting redistribution depends on poverty (the clear net gainers from redistribution), social affinity, the growth rate of aggregate income, and income asymmetry (income inequality). Their paper focuses only on the period 1961 to 1980, when there was both growing equality and growing real incomes in most of the countries examined.[24] They find that the closer that the poor are to the middle class (or the higher is the mobility between middle and lower incomes), the higher is the willingness to redistribute. The same results may not hold in later periods—for example, 1980 to 2000—when not all incomes grew to the same extent, rising (not falling) economic inequality was the norm in some countries, and overall rates of wage and income growth were much less in most nations (Osberg 2003; Smeeding 2002a). While the paper by Kristov and his colleagues does not seem to support our hypothesis, we can applaud it for separating the effects of rich and poor on outcomes, and for not focusing on one simple summary measure of inequality.

The more recent literature on social spending and inequality is both diverse and rapidly expanding (see Moene and Wallerstein 2001, 2002; Kenworthy and Pontusson 2002; Bradley et al. 2001). These papers all purport to test the "median voter" model—for example, the differences being expressed as the difference between the mean and median incomes or voters—but they then use earnings inequality for all earners (not voters alone) to express this difference. Voting turnout is used as a measure of intensity of preferences, and institutions are represented by right or left government parties. Additional controls in the models found in these papers include demographic and economic characteristics and union and wage-setting institutions, among others (see also Kahn 2002).

The argument supporting the median voter hypothesis has received significant criticism. Some recent studies argue, as do we, that more affluent individuals may become less "public-spirited" as they become more distant from the middle and lower classes. At the same time, these individuals may also be better able to further their own interests through political contributions, greater political knowledge, higher probability of voting, or greater access to elected officials. A recent study by Larry Bartels (2002a) argues that constituents at the seventy-fifth percentile of the income distribution have almost *three times* as much influence on U.S. senators' voting patterns as those at the twenty-fifth percentile. Nolan McCarty, Keith Poole, and Howard Rosenthal (2003, 24) also look at the United States and speculate that "richer voters represented by both parties are . . . less likely to favor redistribution and social insurance than were the counterparts of these voters a half-century earlier." Although it is plausible that in all societies the power of the affluent exceeds that of the lower classes, the issue for comparative purposes is the slope of the gradient—*how much* of a difference there is between the effective political influence of the affluent and the poor in different countries.

Noting that even the most right-wing Canadian politicians feel compelled to support universal public health care and oppose "two-tier" medicine, we, being Canadian and American, are somewhat skeptical that "left" and "right" relative positions within nations have comparable meanings in a cross-national context—but some political scientists seem to accept this notion. On the other hand, values and tastes for redistribution are rarely used directly (which we think is unfortunate), and the new literature seems to dislike the use of union membership or centrally determined wages (perhaps owing to measurement issues) as a proxy for institutions that reflect public tastes for redistribution (Bradley et al. 2001). However, a positive development is that some of the newer papers are using LIS as well as published OECD data or secondary data; most of these sources are willing to share their data and variables, making replication and further analysis easier for researchers.

Jaejoon Woo (2003) has developed a model to measure the different degrees to which economic and political institutions affect public deficits. Woo's basic model relies on decade averages of variables for the 1970 to 1979 and 1980 to 1990 periods for fifty-seven developed and developing nations.[25] Including income inequality indicators, the author finds that income inequality positively (and statistically significantly) affects public deficits; the coefficients imply that "an increase in inequality of ten Gini points is associated with an increase in the public deficit of 1.5 to 1.9 percent of GDP" (403). With several sensitivity tests and specification modifications, Woo shows that economic factors—GDP, inflation, liquid liabilities in the system, and measures of trade—enter the model with signs as expected (positive, negative, negative, positive). All of the political variables incorporated, such as cabinet changes, changes in effective executive, coups d'état, and major constitutional change, enter the model with negative coefficients, though only the latter two are statistically significant. Hence, inequality has important consequences for social spending, not only through transfers, but also in how governments choose to balance spending in a broader framework.[26]

Moene and Wallerstein (2002) argue that investigations of the relationship of social expenditures to inequality should be carried out on a disaggregated basis because there is no a priori reason why national levels of welfare spending, unemployment insurance, health care, pensions, and education should all have the same determinants. Social insurance, targeted social assistance, and universal benefits programs (like child allowances) may reflect different tastes, values, and mechanisms for redistribution—indeed, countries may have different conceptualizations of whether a given program represents "redistribution," "insurance," or delivery of a basic citizenship right. These differences are particularly likely if the desired impact of redistribution differs: in some countries the "working poor" may be thought to be particularly worthy of transfers, while in others redistribution may aim at improving the lot of the least well off (who are usually outside the labor force).

In different countries, "redistribution" may have different intended beneficiaries and different mechanisms of delivery. As already noted, countries differ in their tastes for cash versus goods and services. The implication is that we should model demand for social goods on a policy-by-policy basis, although the danger is that we may ignore the built-in relationships between different programs that are a part of each nation's social history and institutions. In net, however, some disaggregation is to be preferred. In fact, Moene and Wallerstein find that higher levels of inequality in pre-tax earnings are associated with lower levels of spending for policies that insure against income loss for working persons (see also next section on regime models). Although they find different determinants for different types of social spending, they find no category of social spending that is positively related to income inequality.

Surveys of the literature include those of Roman Arjona, Maxime Ladaique, and Mark Pearson (2001) and William Scarth (2000). Although the high level of inequality and low level of redistribution in the United States is an important counterexample, Arjona and his colleagues find support for the hypothesis that higher levels of pregovernment ("market") income inequality lead to *greater* levels of redistribution. In suggesting that the form of additional redistribution also matters and that policies that reduce market income inequality directly, by raising the market incomes of the poor, may be good for growth, they raise the important point that a *general* correlation (plus or minus) between inequality and growth may be of very limited use in thinking about *specific* policy choices. (And governments always, in practice, have to consider specific policy choices.) The example they give is greater education for the poor, which produces lower market income inequality.[27]

An emerging literature on social spending transfers in cash and kind (for example, education), which has been reexamining the relationship between social policies, employment, and economic growth across a wide range of nations, supports this point of view (see van der Ploeg 2003; Gylfason and Zoega 2003). These studies include the OECD and also, to a lesser extent, the major developing nations. Both theoretical models and empirical evidence suggest that social policies may indeed promote economic growth as much as they harm them. Education may be a particularly important case where increased spending leads to more and better education and thereby promotes economic growth directly, as well as indirectly through increased social equality and cohesion. As yet, however, there is no general agreement in the literature on the effects of social policy on growth, negatively or positively, although the recent literature is much more supportive of a positive relationship.

While the recent literature on median voters, inequality, and redistribution has progressed in many ways, a basic question remains: Does more inequality produce voters and institutions that support more redistribution, or does greater equality produce support from labor and other institutions for more redistribution (for example, see Bertola, Blau, and Kahn 2002)? One possible reason for this uncertainty is that the new literature characterizes inequality with single value measures, (such as the Gini and the 90–10 ratio), not with measures of differences in inequality at both the top and bottom of the distribution. However, there is also a more institutional welfare state regime literature on social policy preferences and outcomes that may tell us more about this phenomenon.

The Institutional Political Science Literature on Inequality and Social Systems

The new literature on cross-national "social policy preferences" is typified by the work of Torben Iversen, David Soskice, and Peter Hall (Iversen and Soskice 2001, 2002; Hall and Soskice 2001; Iversen 1999). The approach, while akin to the earlier "worlds of welfare capitalism" work of Esping-Andersen (1990), offers a much more institutionally driven and sophisticated argument about national preferences for redistribution. The argument is that coordinated nations—those with a high degree of cooperation between business, industry, and labor—invest in human capital in different ways than nations with liberal market economies, where competition replaces consensus-seeking. Skill training is more specific (for example, vocational training), job tenure is longer, and job-changing is less frequent in these coordinated economies than it is in societies with more general training. In these latter types of economies, market competition rewards high skills with high, "winner take all" wages; labor is not an active political voice; and low skills are punished with low wages. They term this latter group of nations the riskier "liberal economies."

In the liberal economies, there is less employment protection and less wage protection. In the coordinated economies, strong employment protection and wage protection from within and outside companies is coupled with high unemployment benefits, adequate and early take-up social retirement, and various other trappings of the European welfare state. As a result, when market-based earnings inequalities grow, more redistribution takes place because of the built-in stabilizers in Western coordinated economies (see also Kenworthy and Pontusson 2002).

Robert Franzese (2001) also argues that since the wealthy are more active politically, the relatively less well off will suffer through changes to the tax and transfer systems. Christopher Jencks examines the views held by people at different points in the political spectrum. He particularly focuses on the contradictions in the United States between wanting low inequality, having high inequality, and doing relatively little to address the problem systematically. He states:

> If you are a hard-core Rawlsian who thinks that society's sole economic goal should be to improve the position of the least advantaged, European experience suggests that limiting inequality can benefit the poor. If you are a hard-core utilitarian, European experience suggests—though it certainly does not prove—that limiting inequality lowers consumption. But European experience also suggests that lowering inequality reduces consumption partly by encouraging people to work fewer hours, which many Europeans see as a good thing. If you care more about equal opportunity for children than about consumption among adults, limiting economic inequality among parents probably reduces disparities in the opportunities open to their children. (Jencks 2002, 64–65)

One of the difficulties in examining inequality cross-nationally, he argues, is the perception of what it means to be poor. Specifically, while Jencks argues that the United States does less than virtually every other developed nation to limit inequality, rich Americans can buy more than the rich in other nations and poor Americans can buy less.

If the coordinated nations have the least inequality (as is the case), then lessened inequality and greater social spending are the joint product of the broader systems of social and economic cooperation in coordinated societies (which can be called "business social capital"). This hypothesis is difficult to examine conclusively since clearly there must be some set of processes to generate any particular pattern of inequality, but a number of different processes might generate the same level of inequality. This question also raises the endogeneity issue, which we now address.

The Endogeneity Issue

Recently, Kenworthy and Pontusson (2002) have argued that household earnings inequality can be determined by employment and (household) income variables and that *changes* in redistribution are a function of *changes* in employment, unionization, GDP, trade, and other political controls. Pablo Beramendi (2003) and Bradley and his colleagues (2001) also argue that reductions in inequality can be at least partially determined by measures of social expenditures (overall social expenditures in the former and taxes and transfers in the latter). This is not a surprising view, since the goal of social expenditures and public goods is, at least in part, to reduce inequality.

These theories force us, however, to consider the possible reverse causality (endogeneity) of inequality in regression models. The key to resolving the causality issue is to find a variable that determines inequality but is exogenous to the social expenditure decision—and such instruments are hard to come by. The instruments proposed by Beramendi (2003) include government ideology (such as right- and left-leaning government legislative and executive bodies) and the ratio of the minimum wage to the average wage. Moene and Wallerstein (2002) use wage-setting institutions and political variables as instruments for inequality. (Their inequality measure is the logarithm of the 90–10 wage ratio.) The exogeneity of these factors to social expenditures, however, is sometimes a difficult case to make, especially if institutions directly affect wage levels (for example, minimum wages) and employment and training policy.

SUMMARY AND CONCLUSION

In this brief summary of the literature, we have not delved at all into the literature on education and health spending and inequality, leaving these for the time being to other projects within this broader effort (see, for example, Berkman et al. 2002 on health spending and Corcoran et al. 2002 on education finance). However, we are led to the following observations:

1. Inequality and poverty are different, and a single summary measure of inequality—such as the Gini or the 90–10 ratio—will not allow us to differentiate among explanations that hinge on the forces that affect different parts of the distribution of income or are affected by different parts of the distribution. Hence, we prefer measures of income inequality that distinguish the top and the bottom of the distribution—for example, the 90–50 and 50–10 percentile ratios.

2. The measurement of the "redistributive" element of "social insurance" transfer programs and of public services (such as education and health care) depends heavily on the frame of analysis and associated methodological assumptions (for example, the accounting period for income flows).

3. Because the relationship between economic inequality and social spending is one of mutual interdependency, it may be crucial to distinguish specific types of social spending, which are differentially affected by different aspects of inequality.

4. Many "political economy" models are of a reduced-form nature with little attention paid to desired levels of redistribution (or national differences in the taste for redistribution) in combination with the institutions and voting mechanisms (parties, lobbies, and so on) legitimizing these tastes. In fact, voting models are rarely employed (only assumed) in the median voter literature in economics.

5. There is a good deal of evidence for differing national interpretations of whether social spending—on health care, for instance—is perceived as redistributive. Hence, different types of social expenditures—in cash (income maintenance, social insurance) or on service (health or education)—may have different political determinants across and within different societies.

6. Huge leaps of analysis are often made in the current literature (such as the assumption that political preferences can be measured on a left-right domestic spectrum that is comparable internationally); these leaps are crucial to the models developed but seem to us to be questionable in a cross-national context.

7. The literature on the lobbying and buying of political influence is widely divergent in its veins. McCarty and his colleagues (2003) and Bartels (2002a, 2002b) all find increasing political polarization following economic polarization. Yet this responsiveness of political parties to even more divergent income groups is disputed by at least one recent paper (Ansolabehere, de Figueiredo, and Snyder 2003).

The literature on income inequality and social goods provision is rapidly growing, but large gaps remain. We have established why such spending is important, indeed necessary, for equality of opportunity and fair chances for children in modern society. However, the linkages between economic inequality and social goods provision are often tenuous and need more modeling and estimation. Clearly no one discipline—economics, sociology, or political science—can resolve this central issue alone.

APPENDIX

FIGURE 22A.1   "Social Distance": Relative Income Comparisons Across Twenty-One Nations in the 1990s (Decile Ratios for Adjusted Disposable Income)

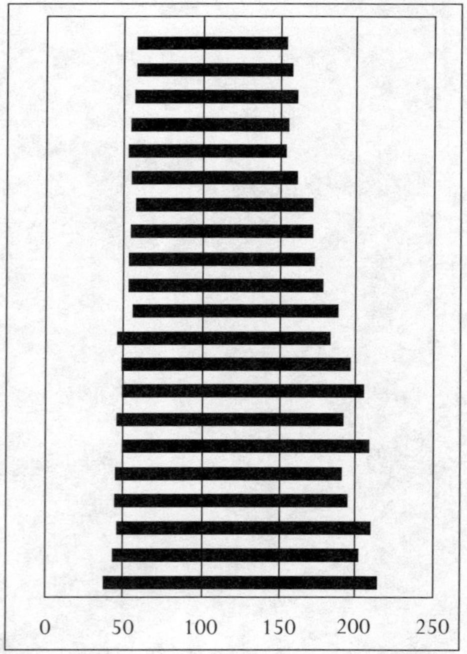

	Tenth Percentile (Low-Income)	(Length of Bars Represents the Gap Between High- and Low-Income Individuals)	Ninetieth Percentile (High-Income)	Ratio of Ninetieth to Tenth Percentile (Decile Ratio)
Sweden, 1995	60%		156%	2.59
Finland, 1995	59		159	2.68
Belgium, 1992	59		162	2.76
Norway, 1995	56		157	2.82
Denmark, 1992	54		155	2.84
Austria, 1987	56		162	2.89
Luxembourg, 1994	59		173	2.92
Netherlands, 1994	56		171	3.08
Germany, 1994	54		174	3.18
France, 1994	54		179	3.32
Taiwan, 1995	56		188	3.36
Canada, 1994	47		184	3.90
Spain, 1990	50		197	3.96
Israel, 1992	50		205	4.12
Japan, 1992	46		192	4.17
Ireland, 1987	50		209	4.20
Switzerland, 1992	45		192	4.22
Australia, 1994	45		195	4.33
United Kingdom, 1995	46		209	4.52
Italy, 1995	43		201	4.68
United States, 1997	38		214	5.64
Simple average	52		183	3.63

Source: Authors' calculations from Luxembourg Income Study; Japan taken from Ishikawa (1996).
Note: Numbers given are percentages of median in each nation.

TABLE 22A.1   Mean Amount for Children in Thirteen Nations at the Tenth, Fiftieth, and Ninetieth Percentile Point, in National Currency, 1992 to 1997

Country	Year	Disposable Personal Income	Market Income (Earnings)	Transfers	Taxes	Net Cash Transfers	Noncash Benefits Health	Noncash Benefits Education	Net Transfers[b]
Tenth percentile point									
Australia	1994	10,082	1,729	8,551	199	8,153	567	3,530	12,250
Belgium[a]	1996	12,322	3,592	8,730	0	8,730	765	5,205	14,700
Canada	1997	12,322	4,434	8,036	511	7,377	720	4,500	12,597
Denmark	1992	13,442	10,401	7,081	5,248	−2,206	645	6,083	4,521
Finland	1994	12,882	4,894	9,795	2,077	5,911	512	4,369	10,792
France	1994	12,322	6,511	5,866	55	5,757	735	3,436	9,928
Germany	1994	11,202	6,938	5,650	1,386	2,878	769	3,183	6,831
Netherlands	1994	11,762	6,699	8,453	3,467	1,596	641	3,013	5,249
Norway	1995	15,403	8,334	8,467	1,878	5,190	749	7,690	13,629
Sweden	1995	13,442	9,944	7,417	3,920	−422	663	5,194	5,435
Switzerland	1992	14,283	7,787	6,867	2,348	4,147	742	5,489	10,377
United Kingdom	1995	8,682	648	8,087	110	7,924	521	3,017	11,462
United States	1997	9,802	4,074	5,954	417	5,311	955	5,961	12,226
Fiftieth percentile point									
Australia	1994	22,964	26,331	2,175	3,752	−8,909	567	3,530	−4,813
Belgium[a]	1996	24,924	21,328	3,597	0	3,597	765	5,205	9,567
Canada	1997	28,565	34,430	2,678	5,964	−14,609	720	4,500	−9,389
Denmark	1992	26,605	33,548	5,558	11,386	−19,781	645	6,083	−13,053
Finland	1994	22,964	23,970	6,041	7,210	−9,107	512	4,369	−4,226
France	1994	24,364	19,191	5,716	440	4,604	735	3,436	8,775
Germany	1994	22,964	29,169	2,191	7,312	−14,600	769	3,183	−10,647
Netherlands	1994	22,964	28,293	3,350	7,552	−14,804	641	3,013	−11,151

TABLE 22A.1   (Continued)

Country	Year	Disposable Personal Income	Market Income (Earnings)	Transfers	Taxes	Net Cash Transfers	Noncash Benefits		Net Transfers[b]
							Health	Education	
Norway	1995	27,725	33,078	3,902	8,262	−14,970	749	7,690	−6,531
Sweden	1995	22,684	22,332	8,925	7,645	−8,258	663	5,194	−2,401
Switzerland	1992	30,245	37,058	0	6,104	−13,625	742	5,489	−7,395
United Kingdom	1995	19,604	14,059	9,408	3,274	1,363	521	3,017	4,901
United States	1997	28,005	30,900	2,133	3,841	−7,157	1,550	5,961	354
Ninetieth percentile point									
Australia	1994	34,726	45,567	571	7,821	−22,393	567	3,530	−18,297
Belgium[a]	1996	35,566	2,608	2,958	0	2,958	765	5,205	8,928
Canada	1997	43,688	54,449	2,116	9,701	−24,986	720	4,500	−19,766
Denmark	1992	31,926	43,827	5,101	15,294	−29,143	645	6,083	−22,415
Finland	1994	38,087	47,017	7,348	14,530	−25,256	512	4,369	−20,375
France	1994	38,367	37,417	2,935	1,575	−1,088	735	3,436	3,083
Germany	1994	33,886	5,436	2,283	12,048	−25,382	769	3,183	−21,430
Netherlands	1994	30,806	43,798	3,238	13,093	−29,420	641	3,013	−25,767
Norway	1995	35,286	44,965	3,939	12,490	−23,603	749	7,690	−15,165
Sweden	1995	27,165	34,671	5,163	11,406	−20,351	663	5,194	−14,494
Switzerland	1992	46,208	53,368	600	7,074	−15,055	742	5,489	−8,825
United Kingdom	1995	35,566	47,903	1,580	11,283	−26,747	521	3,017	−23,210
United States	1997	50,129	63,982	1,759	12,362	−30,742	1,700	5,961	−23,081

Source: Authors' calculations from the Luxembourg Income Study.

[a]After-tax earnings only.

[b]Net transfers = net cash transfers plus education plus health.

TABLE 22A.2   *Published Research on Social Capital*

Author(s)	Dataset	Survey Years	Variables	Use[a]
Costa and Kahn (2001)	American National Election Study	1952, 1972	Organization membership	T, A
	Americans' Use of Time	1964 to 1965, 1985	Time visiting friends; at parties; time spent in organization activity	T, A T, A T, A
	Current Population Survey	1974, 1989	Any volunteer work in past year/week; hours volunteered in past year (grouped)	T, A T, A
	DDB Life Style Survey	1975 to 1998 1975 to 1998	Frequency entertained in past year; frequency volunteering in past year; frequency family eats dinner together	T, A T, A T
	Five Nation Study	1960	Organization membership	T
	General Social Survey	Selected years 1974 to 1998	Frequency spent evening with friends; frequency spent evening with neighbors; frequency spent evening with relatives; organization membership	T T T, A T
	Giving and Volunteering in the United States	1988 to 1996	Any volunteer work in past year/week	T
	NPD Group Time Study Data	1992 to 1996	Time spent volunteering; time visiting family/friends	T T, A
	Political Participation in America	1967	Organization membership	T
	Time Use in Economic and Social Accounts	1975 to 1976	Time visiting friends; at parties; time spent in organization activity	T, A T, A
Alesina and La Ferrara (1999)	General Social Survey	1972 to 1994	Membership in organizations	T, A
	Current Population Survey	1996 to 1998	State-level Gini coefficients	T, A

TABLE 22A.2   (Continued)

Author(s)	Dataset	Survey Years	Variables	Use[a]
Alesina and La Ferrara (2001)	General Social Survey	1978 to 1991	Demographic/income variables	T, A
	Panel Study of Income Dynamics		Constructed mobility indices	T, A
Milanovic (2000)	Luxembourg Income Study	Waves 1 to 4	Age, factor/market income	T, A
Bassett, Burkett, and Putterman (1999)	World Bank (Deininger and Squire 1996)	Around 1965	Income shares	A
	Paukert (1973)	Around 1965	Income shares	A
	Perotti (1996)	Around 1965	Income shares, measures of democracy	A
	Penn World Tables	1960, 1970	GDP, income shares	A
	Barro-Lee	1970 to 1985	Age	A
Persson and Tabellini (1994)	Various sources	Various years	GDP, income shares, education, electorate	A
Kristov, Lindert, and McClelland (1992)	Organization for Economic Cooperation and Development	1960 to 1981	Transfers/GDP, unemployment, share of population over sixty-five, per capita GDP, relative price deflator, deadweight loss, GDP growth, two inequality gaps (log of prefiscal income ratio, top [middle] quintile to middle [bottom] quintile)	A

Source: Authors' compilation.
[a]T = trends; A = analysis.

The authors would like to thank the Russell Sage Foundation, the Institute for Social and Economic Research (ISER) at the University of Essex, and the Social Policy Research Centre (SPRC) at the University of New South Wales Social Policy Research Centre (UNSW), Sydney, Australia, for support while working on this paper. Helpful discussions were had with Christopher Jencks, Irv Garfinkel, Sara McLanahan, David Brady, Robert Haveman, David Soskice, and Robert Goodin, and good comments were made at seminars at the Australia National University, Canberra Australia, and at the Center for Advanced Study in March 2002. The authors wish to thank Kathryn Neckerman and an anonymous referee for helpful comments, and Andrea Johnson, Lynn Lethbridge, JoAnna Moskal, Mary Santy, Martha Bonney, and Kati Foley for their excellent help with manuscript preparation. All errors are our own.

NOTES

1. Conceptually, it is hard to argue that the economic processes and social institutions that affect income distribution and social goods provision are structurally similar in all nations—for example, in the United States and Afghanistan. However, the maintained hypothesis of structural similarity sits behind the cross-country regressions methodology. Practically, the lack of reliable data and consistent economic measurement and policy regimes make less-developed countries difficult to study in a comprehensive manner. However, we do in one place include comparable social spending in Mexico in figure 22.1 to illustrate the variance across major OECD nations.

2. This chapter makes use of three main data sources. The Organization for Economic Cooperation and Development (OECD) provides a wealth of information, ranging from national account data (GDP, social expenditures) to education data (expenditures, enrollment), to other demographic information (population, race, gender). The Luxembourg Income Survey (LIS) is a collection of household income surveys for almost thirty countries for various years. (Around 120 country-year surveys are currently available.) The different surveys are harmonized so that users can make easy comparisons of household income data across nations and time. Finally, in four separate waves of interviews, the World Values Survey (WVS) collects information on sociocultural and political change for more than sixty-five countries. The data available in the WVS range from religious affiliations to participation in community organizations to beliefs and trust in one's family, neighborhood, and society.

3. The variation in non-elderly total social expenditures is even more pronounced. The northern European (Belgium, Denmark, the Netherlands) and Scandinavian (Finland, Norway, Sweden) countries spend markedly more (as a percentage of GDP) on social expenditures for the elderly than do the Anglo (Australia, Canada, the United Kingdom, the United States) countries (OECD 2001).

4. We estimate this ratio by adding OECD "social expenditures" and OECD "final government outlays" and dividing this total into OECD "social expenditures." For more on this method, see Smeeding (2002a) and OECD (2001). Like the OECD, we do not include tax expenditures as public benefits in these calculations.

5. No comparable time series exists that includes both health care and education spending.

6. To compare living standards or other indicators across countries, PPP exchange rates compare the prices of comparable consumption baskets in different nations in order to translate per capita national incomes into a common currency.

7. To take a specific example, if the intergenerational inheritance of poverty is primarily due to the impact on life chances of such factors as low self-esteem or the cumulative impact of social exclusion, which are plausibly driven by a low *relative* consumption bundle, then differences in relative income are the crucial issue. Since these general phenomena are often best understood through specific examples, we can cite the anxiety of teens and preteens about going to school in unstylish clothes, their "need" to have a cell phone to contact their friends, or the equipment requirements of organized youth sports leagues. It is clear that the absolute cost and degree of newness needed to be "stylish," the socialization patterns of youth, and the local league requirements for sports gear differ substantially across countries and have varied considerably

over time within countries. However, if children who do not have enough to be part of the team or to join the mainstream social group absorb the impacts of that exclusion, then it is the *relative* income of their families that matters.

8. We note that these differences in money income across nations would be magnified if income were standardized for differences in labor supply, since cross-country differences in labor supply are relatively small at the top of the income distribution compared to the bottom. Simply put, the poor in the United States work much harder and still get less than the poor in other affluent nations (for details, see Osberg 2002, 2003).

    Christopher Jencks (2002) raises well-known questions about the appropriateness of such cross-national comparisons. We acknowledge these concerns but feel that such comparisons are useful in a global context.

9. Duncan and his colleagues (1998) find that American children who live in families with incomes at or below 75 percent of the U.S. poverty line (roughly 33 to 36 percent of the median income) do less well than other American children. Similar studies have not been done for other nations. Similar figures to those found here but from an earlier period can be found in Rainwater and Smeeding (2000).

10. In the United States, we also include the value of employer-provided health care benefits.

11. The values for the tenth and ninetieth percentiles are included in table 22A.1. The values in table 22.1 are averages per child for all children in cash and per school-age child for health and education.

12. Note that when it becomes common for elite bureaucrats and politicians to opt out of public education and health care, both their personal knowledge of these systems and their credibility with the wider public in proposing reforms diminishes. This is another argument for why the political economy of more unequal societies may be more dysfunctional.

13. Robert Putnam (1995, 67) defines social capital as follows: "By analogy with notions of physical capital and human capital—tools and training that enhance individual productivity—'social capital' refers to features of social organization such as networks, norms, and social trust that facilitate coordination and cooperation for mutual benefit."

14. David Moss (1996), for example, argues that from the first years of labor legislation in the United States, reforms were motivated primarily by the problem of worker insecurity.

15. For example, the health care services received by the elderly may be of greater dollar value than those received by the middle-aged, but if the middle-aged can expect to receive similar services in a few years, a lifetime perspective may be more appropriate. In the same vein, should we count the very ill as getting more "income" if they incur expensive hospital stays? Given that all citizens have a chance of illness, the expected value of health care services is a better indicator of benefits.

16. Alesina and La Ferrara's (1999, 16) racial and ethnic fragmentation variable is an index that "measures the probability that two randomly drawn individuals in area *i* belong to different races. Therefore, higher values of the index represent more racial fragmentation." They also include individual and state controls in some versions of the regressions; these prove to depress the coefficients on the variables of interest, but signs and statistical significance are maintained.

17. Helliwell (2002) uses three waves of the WVS for forty-eight countries to test what factors affect individual "satisfaction of life," as measured by the WVS. As in previous work, Helliwell provides some evidence that trust positively affects life satisfaction. He notes that "average well-being would increase by .03 on a ten-point scale for each 0.1 increase in the proportion of the population judging that people can in general be trusted" (19).

18. Social capital also erodes if individuals are increasingly too busy to participate in voluntary associational life. ILO data indicate that from 1980 to 2000 average actual working hours per adult (age fifteen to sixty-four) rose by 234 hours in the United States, to 1,476, while falling by 170 hours in Germany, to 973. Although Canada, France, Germany, Sweden, the United Kingdom, and the United States all had average actual hours of paid work per adult that clustered in a fairly narrow interval in 1980, by 2000 the differential in actual hours of paid work was quite dramatic. As Stephen Jenkins and Lars Osberg (2003) argue, the rise in average working hours of *other* people generally makes it harder for each individual to arrange a satisfying social life, thereby diminishing the marginal utility of their leisure and fueling a "vicious

circle" of subsequent increases in labor supply and declining utility and social capital (see also Osberg 2002).

19. The authors estimate both a linear ordinary least squares model and a two-stage least squares model. In the latter, religious variables (percentage Catholic, percentage Muslim, and percentage Eastern orthodox) are used as instruments for trust, with results almost identical to the OLS estimates.

20. For example, the median voter can easily be completely unaffected by changes in the share of income received by the bottom quintile.

21. Closely related methodologically is a paper by Robert Plotnick (1986), who constructs a similar model by individual U.S. states using AFDC (Aid to Families with Dependent Children) data.

22. Presumably it would be rational for risk-averse individuals to want to buy more social insurance, possibly through the public sector, as income risk rises. However, when income risk rises, the certainty equivalent income falls, and whether individuals want more or less redistribution as a result depends on whether such redistribution is a normal good. Unless individuals make systematic prediction errors, the stochastic component in income will be of mean zero—in other words, uncorrelated with growth.

23. If, for income streams of equal present value, the age-earnings profile steepens, there seems no obvious reason why the motive for redistribution to other households should change. However, public pensions and Social Security are a substantial part of public expenditures—which have often been seen as "forced savings" that people voluntarily impose on themselves. Such programs redistribute income over the life cycle, but again, predictions are ambiguous.

24. Note that during much of this period the study of economic inequality was said to be "as exciting as watching paint dry," owing to the relative constancy of aggregate measures, such as the Gini index of money income inequality. In international data it is the 1975 to 1995 period, particularly in the United Kingdom and the United States, that has seen much larger changes in inequality.

25. Note that most works, unless with a specific aim, do not include developing countries, owing to unavailable or unreliable data.

26. Riccardo Fiorito and Tryphon Kollintzas (2002) have developed a model that divides goods into merit and public goods. The latter category includes health, education, and other services that can be privately provided; this is the group we tend to focus on in our empirical paper. The former category includes defense, public order, and justice—the typical set of public goods. In all cases, they find that public goods are substitutes, while merit goods are complements to private consumption.

27. Clearly, we can also think of policy designs that imply that more redistribution causes lower market incomes (for example, social assistance rules that create poverty traps and lower labor supply) and reduced economic growth. Arjona and his colleagues (2001) conclude that they cannot say which interpretation best fits the data.

REFERENCES

Alesina, Alberto, and Eliana La Ferrara. 1999. "Participation in Heterogeneous Communities." Working paper 7155. Cambridge, Mass.: National Bureau of Economic Research (June).

———. 2001. "Preferences for Redistribution in the Land of Opportunities." Working paper 8267. Cambridge, Mass.: National Bureau of Economic Research (May).

Alesina, Alberto, and Dani Rodrik. 1994. "Distributive Politics and Economic Growth." *Quarterly Journal of Economics* 109(2, May): 465–90.

Allmendinger, Jutta, and Stephan Leibfried. 2002. "Education and the Welfare State." Unpublished paper. University of Bremen, Germany (June).

Ansolabehere, Stephen, John M. de Figueiredo, and James M. Snyder Jr. 2003. "Why Is There So Little Money in U.S. Politics?" *Journal of Economic Perspectives* 17(1, Winter): 105–30.

Arjona, Roman, Maxime Ladaique, and Mark Pearson. 2001. "Growth, Inequality, and Social Protection." Labor Market and Social Policy occasional paper 51. Paris: Organization for Economic Cooperation and Development.

Bartels, Larry M. 2002a. "Economic Inequality and Political Representation." Unpublished paper. Princeton University, Princeton, N.J. (November).

———. 2002b. "Partisan Politics and the U.S. Income Distribution, 1948 to 2000." Unpublished paper. Princeton University, Princeton, N.J. (September).

Bassett, William F., John P. Burkett, and Louis Putterman. 1999. "Income Distribution, Government Transfers, and the Problem of Unequal Influence." *European Journal of Political Economy* 15(2, June): 207–28.

Bénabou, Roland. 1996. "Inequality and Growth." In *National Bureau of Economic Research Macroeconomics Annual 1996,* edited by Ben S. Bernanke and Julio Rotemberg. Cambridge, Mass.: MIT Press.

———. 2000. "Unequal Societies: Income Distribution and the Social Contract." *American Economic Review* 90(1, March): 96–129.

Beramendi, Pablo. 2003. "Decentralization and Income Inequality." Doctoral dissertation. Juan March Institute, Madrid, Spain.

Berkman, Lisa, David Cutler, Ellen Meara, Dolorea Acevedo-Garcia, and Arnold Epstein. 2002. "Social Inequality and Health: The Impact of Social, Economic and Health Policies on Population Health." Unpublished paper. Harvard University, Working Group on Social Inequality, Cambridge, Mass. (June).

Bertola, Giuseppe, Francine D. Blau, and Lawrence M. Kahn. 2002. "Labor Market Institutions and Demographic Employment Patterns." Working paper 9043. Cambridge, Mass.: National Bureau of Economic Research (July).

Bradley, David, Evelyne Huber, Stephanie Moller, Francois Nielsen, and John Stephens. 2001. "Distribution and Redistribution in Post-industrial Democracies." Luxembourg Income Study working paper 265. Syracuse, N.Y.: Syracuse University, Center for Policy Research (May).

Card, David, and A. Abigail Payne. 1998. "School Finance Reform, the Distribution of School Spending, and the Distribution of SAT Scores." Working paper 6766. Cambridge, Mass.: National Bureau of Economic Research (October).

Castello, Amparo, and Rafael Domenech. 2002. "Human Capital Inequality and Economic Growth: Some New Evidence." *Economic Journal* 112(March): C187–200.

Corcoran, Sean, William N. Evans, Jennifer Godwin, Sheila E. Murray, and Robert Schwab. 2002. "The Changing Distribution of Education Finance: 1972–1997." Project review. Russell Sage Foundation, New York.

Costa, Dora L., and Matthew E. Kahn. 2001. "Understanding the Decline in Social Capital, 1952–1998." Working paper 8295. Cambridge, Mass.: National Bureau of Economic Research (May).

Deininger, Klaus, and Lyn Squire. 1996. "A New Data Set Measuring Income Inequality." *World Bank Economics Review* 10(3, August/September): 565–91.

Duncan, Greg J. W. Jean Yeung, Jeanne Brooks-Gunn, and Judith Smith. 1998. "How Much Does Childhood Poverty Affect the Life Chances of Children?" *American Sociological Review* 63(3, June): 406–23.

Esping-Andersen, Gøsta. 1990. *The Three Worlds of Welfare Capitalism.* Cambridge: Polity Press.

Fiorito, Riccardo, and Tryphon Kollintzas. 2002. "Public Goods, Merit Goods, and the Relation Between Private and Government Consumption." Discussion paper 3617. London: Center for Economic Policy Research (July).

Franzese, Robert J. Jr. 2001. "Political Participation, Income Distribution, and Public Transfers in Developed Democracies." Unpublished manuscript. University of Michigan, Ann Arbor.

Fukuyama, Francis. 1995. *Trust: The Social Virtues and the Creation of Prosperity.* New York: Free Press.

Glaeser, Edward L., Jose Scheinkman, and Andrei Shleifer. 2002. "The Injustice of Inequality." Discussion paper 1967. Cambridge, Mass.: Harvard University (August).

Gylfason, Thorvaldur, and Gylfi Zoega. 2003. "Education, Social Equality, and Economic Growth: A View of the Landscape." Working Paper 876. Munich, Germany: Center for Economic Studies and Institute for Economic Research (February).

Hall, Peter A., and David Soskice. 2001. *Varieties of Capitalism.* New York: Oxford University Press.

Helliwell, John F. 2002. "How's Life? Combining Individual and National Variables to Explain Subjective Well-being." Working paper 9065. Cambridge, Mass.: National Bureau of Economic Research (July).

Ishikawa, Tsureo. 1996. Data runs conducted by Japanese Ministry of Welfare. Personal communication. November 26, 1996.

Iversen, Torben. 1999. *Contested Economic Institutions: The Politics of Macroeconomics and Wage Bargaining in Advanced Democracies.* New York: Cambridge University Press.

Iversen, Torben, and David Soskice. 2001. "An Asset Theory of Social Policy Preferences." *American Political Science Review* 95(4, December): 875–93.

———. 2002. "Political Parties and the Time Inconsistency Problem in Social Welfare Provision." Unpublished paper. Harvard University, Cambridge, Mass. (March).

Jencks, Christopher. 2002. "Does Inequality Matter?" *Daedalus* 131(1, Winter): 49–65.

Jenkins, Stephen P., and Lars S. Osberg. 2003. "Nobody to Play With? The Implications of Leisure Coordination." ISER working paper 2003-19. Institute for Social and Economic Research, University of Essex (August 2003).

Kahn, Lawrence M. 2002. "The Impact of Wage-Setting Institutions on the Incidence of Public Employment in the OECD: 1960–1998." Working paper 757. Munich: Center for Economic Studies and Institute for Economic Research (July).

Kawachi, Ichiro, Bruce P. Kennedy, Kimberly Lochner, and Deborah Prothrow-Smith. 1997. "Social Capital, Income Inequality, and Mortality." *American Journal of Public Health* 87(9, September): 1491–98.

Kenworthy, Lane, and Jonas Pontusson. 2002. "Inequality and Redistribution in OECD Countries." Paper presented at Comparative Political Economy of Inequality Workshop. Ithaca, N.Y. (April 5–6, 2002).

Knack, Stephen, and Philip Keefer. 1997. "Does Social Capital Have an Economic Payoff? A Cross-Country Investigation." *Quarterly Journal of Economics* 112(4, November): 1251–88.

Knack, Stephen, and Paul J. Zak. 2002. "Building Trust: Public Policy, Interpersonal Trust, and Economic Development." In *Supreme Court Economic Review,* edited by Todd J. Zywicki. Chicago: University of Chicago Press.

Kristov, Lorenzo, Peter Lindert, and Robert McClelland. 1992. "Pressure Groups and Redistribution." *Journal of Public Economics* 48(2, July): 135–63.

La Porta, Rafael, Florencio Lopez-de-Silanes, Andrei Shleifer, and Robert W. Vishny. 1997. "Trust in Large Organizations." *American Economic Review, Papers and Proceedings* 87(2, May): 333–38.

Mayer, Susan E. 1997. *What Money Can't Buy: Family Income and Children's Life Chances.* Cambridge, Mass.: Harvard University Press.

McCarty, Nolan, Keith T. Poole, and Howard Rosenthal. 2003. "Political Polarization and Income Inequality." Working paper 201. New York: Russell Sage Foundation (February).

Milanovic, Branko. 2000. "The Median Voter Hypothesis, Income Inequality, and Income Distribution: An Empirical Test with the Required Data." *European Journal of Political Economy* 16(3, September): 367–410.

Moene, Karl O., and Michael Wallerstein. 2001. "Inequality, Social Insurance, and Redistribution." *American Political Science Review* 95(4, December): 859–74.

———. 2002. "Income Inequality and Welfare Spending: A Disaggregated Analysis." Unpublished paper. Oslo, Norway: University of Oslo.

Moss, David A. 1996. *Socializing Security: Progressive-Era Economists and the Origins of American Social Policy.* Cambridge, Mass.: Harvard University Press.

Murray, Sheila E., William N. Evans, and Robert M. Schwab. 1998. "Education-Finance Reform and the Distribution of Education Resources." *American Economic Review* 88(4, September): 789–812.

Organization for Economic Cooperation and Development (OECD). 2001. *Social Expenditure Database: 1980–1998, 3d.* Paris: OECD.

———. 2002a. *Education at a Glance: OECD Indicators 2002.* Paris: OECD.

———. 2002b. *OECD Health Care Data 2002.* Paris: OECD.

Osberg, Lars S. 1995. "The Equity/Efficiency Tradeoff in Retrospect." *Canadian Business Economics* 3(3, April–June): 5–19.

———. 2002. "Time, Money, and Inequality in International Perspective." Unpublished paper. Paper prepared for the International Workshop of the Bocconi University Centennial. Milano, Italy (May 30–June 1, 2002).

———. 2003. "Long-Run Trends in Income Inequality in the U. S. A., the U. K., Sweden, Germany, and Canada: A Birth Cohort View." *Eastern Economic Journal* 29(1, Winter): 121–41.

Osberg, Lars S., and Timothy M. Smeeding. 2003. "Attitudes to Inequality: International Comparisons of

Preferences for Leveling." Unpublished paper. Syracuse University, Center for Policy Research, Syracuse, N.Y. (January).

Paukert, Felix. 1973. "Income Distribution at Different Levels of Development: A Survey of Evidence." *International Labor Review* 108(2): 97–125.

Perotti, Roberto. 1992. "Income Distribution, Politics, and Growth." *American Economic Review* 82(2, May): 311–16.

———. 1996. "Growth, Income Distribution, and Democracy: What the Data Say." *Journal of Economic Growth* 1(2, June): 149–87.

Persson, Torsten, and Guido Tabellini. 1994. "Is Inequality Harmful for Growth?" *American Economic Review* 84(3, June): 600–21.

Phipps, Shelley. 1999. "Innis Lecture: Economics and the Well-being of Canadian Children." *Canadian Journal of Economics* 32(5, November): 1135–63.

Plotnick, Robert D. 1986. "An Interest Group Model of Direct Income Redistribution." *Review of Economics and Statistics* 68(4, November): 594–602.

Pontusson, Jonas. Forthcoming. *Social Europe vs. Liberal America: Social Protection, Employment, and Inequality in Comparative Perspective*. New York: Century Foundation.

Putnam, Robert D. 1995. "Bowling Alone: America's Declining Social Capital." *Journal of Democracy* 6(1, January): 65–78.

———. 2001. *Bowling Alone: The Collapse and Revival of American Community*. New York: Touchstone Books.

Rainwater, Lee, and Timothy M. Smeeding. 2000. "Doing Poorly: The Real Income of American Children in a Comparative Perspective." In *Crisis in American Institutions*, edited by Jerome H. Skolnick and Elliot Currie. Boston: Allyn and Bacon.

Sala-i-Martin, Xavier. 1997. "Transfers, Social Safety Nets, and Economic Growth." *International Monetary Fund Staff Papers* 44(1, March): 81–102.

Scarth, William. 2000. "Growth and Inequality: A Review Article." *Review of Income and Wealth* 46(3, September): 389–97.

Sefton, Tom. 2002. "Recent Changes in the Distribution of the Social Wage." CASE working paper 62. London: Center for Analysis of Social Exclusion, London School of Economics and Political Science (December).

Slemrod, Joel. 2002. "Trust in Public Finance." Working paper 9187. Cambridge, Mass.: National Bureau of Economic Research (September).

Slemrod, Joel, and Peter Katuscak. 2002. "Do Trust and Trustworthiness Pay Off?" Working paper 9200. Cambridge, Mass.: National Bureau of Economic Research (September).

Smeeding, Timothy M. 2002a. "Globalization, Inequality, and the Rich Countries of the G-20: Updated Results from the Luxembourg Income Study and Other Places." Unpublished paper. Syracuse University, Center for Policy Research, Syracuse, N.Y. (May).

———. 2002b. "Real Standards of Living and Public Support for Children: A Cross-National Comparison." Unpublished paper. Syracuse University, Center for Policy Research, Syracuse, N.Y. (May).

Smeeding, Timothy M., and Deborah Freund. 2002. "The Future Costs of Health Care in an Aging Society: Is the Glass Half Full or Half Empty?" Unpublished paper. Syracuse University, Center for Policy Research, Syracuse, N.Y. (February).

Smeeding, Timothy M., and Lee Rainwater. 2002. "Comparing Living Standards across Nations: Real Incomes at the Top, the Bottom, and the Middle." Luxembourg Income Study working paper 266, rev. Syracuse, N.Y.: Syracuse University, Center for Policy Research (February).

Smeeding, Timothy M., Lee Rainwater, and Gary Burtless. 2001. "United States Poverty in a Cross-National Context." In *Understanding Poverty*, edited by Sheldon H. Danziger and Robert H. Haveman. New York and Cambridge, Mass.: Russell Sage Foundation and Harvard University Press.

Smeeding, Timothy M., with assistance from James Williamson. 2001. "Income Maintenance in Old Age: What Can Be Learned from Cross-National Comparisons?" Luxembourg Income Study working paper 263. Syracuse, N.Y.: Syracuse University, Center for Policy Research (May).

Smolensky, Eugene. 2002. "Income Inequality: A Conversation with Bob Lampman." Fifth Annual Lampman Memorial Lecture. University of Wisconsin, Institute for Research on Poverty, Madison (June 25).

Soroka, Stuart N., Richard Johnston, and Keith G. Banting. 2002. "Ethnicity, Trust, and the Welfare State."

Unpublished paper. Paper presented to the conference Social Cohesion and the Policy Agenda: Canada in International Perspective. Queen's University at Kingston. Ontario, Canada (August 19–21, 2002).

Tawney, R.H. 1931/1964. *Equality*. 4th ed. London: Unwin Books.

van der Ploeg, Frederick. 2003. "Do Social Policies Harm Employment and Economic Growth?" Working Paper 886. European University Institute, Center for Economic Studies and Institute for Economic Research (CESifo) (March).

Wilson, Kathryn S. 2000. "Using the PSID to Examine the Effects of School Spending." *Public Finance Review* 28(5): 428–51.

Wilson, Kathryn, Kristina T. Lambright, and Timothy M. Smeeding. 2003. "School Finance and Equality of Opportunity: Equal Dollars or Equal Chances for Success?" Unpublished paper. Syracuse University, Center for Policy Research, Syracuse, N.Y. (April).

Woo, Jaejoon. 2003. "Economic, Political, and Institutional Determinants of Public Deficits." *Journal of Public Economics* 87(3, March): 387–426.

World Bank Group. 1999. "Inequality and Violence." Available at: www.worldbank.org/poverty/inequal/abstracts/violence.htm (last updated November 11, 1999).

———. 2003. "Social Capital for Development." Available at: www.worldbank.org/poverty/scapital/index.htm (last updated July 22, 2003).

Zak, Paul J., and Stephen Knack. 2001. "Trust and Growth." *Economic Journal* 111(470, April): 295–321.

Chapter 23

Politics, Public Policy, and Inequality: A Look Back at the Twentieth Century

Howard Rosenthal

For at least a century, the United States has enjoyed unbridled prosperity. True, there have been significant interruptions in the upward course of per capita growth, most notably during the Great Depression. Although we could not always answer positively to Ronald Reagan's famous 1980 presidential debate question, "Are you better off now than you were four years ago?" most of us are unambiguously better off than our grandparents were fifty years ago, or their grandparents fifty years earlier.[1]

The distribution of prosperity, however, unlike the aggregate, has not followed a monotonic path. The broad outline of what happened is easy to summarize. Inequality in income and wealth decreased for much of the twentieth century. The decrease in inequality appeared to fit the hypothesis of Simon Kuznets (1955): as industrialization led a larger fraction of the population to enter high-productivity activities, inequality fell. The fall in inequality, however, has been arrested and reversed. When inequality started to rise depends on which measure one uses, but the reversal did not start before the late 1960s and was clearly in full bloom before—not after—Reagan took office.

In this essay, I document that the long-run trend in inequality—decreasing for roughly the first three-quarters of the twentieth century and increasing thereafter—is matched by similar trends in public policy and political polarization, and I discuss the implications of these parallel trends. I focus on public policies, such as taxes and minimum wages, that are tied to inequality, since they are explicitly redistributive. For example, David Lee (1999, 979) finds that "almost all of the growth in the wage gap between the tenth and fiftieth percentile is attributable to the erosion of the real value of the federal minimum during the [1980s]." Estate taxes became more onerous for the first three-quarters of the century before reversing in the late 1970s. Top marginal income taxes increased before starting a decline in the 1960s. The federal minimum wage took root in 1938 and increased, in real terms, until the late 1960s but then declined precipitously. I later document in more detail how minimum wages and taxes closely tracked the secular pattern of inequality.

As inequality among Americans fell during the first two-thirds or three-quarters of the twentieth century, Americans also seemed to have grown closer together politically. In 1960 the sociologist Daniel Bell published *The End of Ideology: On the Exhaustion of Political Ideas in the Fifties*. A year later the political scientist Robert Dahl (1961) pointed to a nation moving from oligarchy to pluralism. Similarly, the new "rational choice" school in political science emphasized Tweedle-Dee-Tweedle-Dum parties focused on the median voter (Downs 1957) and members of Congress largely concerned with constituency service (Fiorina 1978) and universalism in pork barrel politics (Weingast, Shepsle, and Johnsen 1981). What these authors pointed to was echoed in analyses of roll-call voting patterns in the House and Senate. Put simply, the fraction of moderates grew and the fraction of extreme liberals and extreme conservatives fell from 1900 to about 1975 (Poole and Rosenthal 1997; McCarty, Poole, and Rosenthal 1997).

Just as inequality went from falling to rising in the last quarter of the century, we witnessed a turnaround in politics. Keith Poole and I have termed this "the polarization of American politics" (Poole and Rosenthal 1984; see also Krugman 2002a, 2002b). Moderates are nearly extinct. Extreme liberals and extreme conservatives have surfaced, particularly extreme conservatives in the Republican Party. What, more precisely, are the changes in partisan positions that underlie polarization? The Republican Party in Congress moves from a very conservative position in 1900 to a substantially more moderate position in the 1970s before rebounding to 1900 conservatism in 2000. The Democratic Party becomes more moderate until the 1950s and then drifts, relatively slowly, to a more liberal position. The net effect of these changes is that the differences between the parties—polarization—narrow until the 1970s and then expand.

My main focus—stimulated by the parallel trends in economic inequality, political polarization, and public policy—is on how politics and economic inequality relate and are coupled by economic policy. There is, in this respect, an abundance of alternative hypotheses about the rise of inequality. The list includes greater trade liberalization, increased levels of immigration, declining rates of trade unionization, the fall in the real minimum wage, a decline in progressive taxation, technological change increasing the returns to education, the increased rates of family dissolution and female-headed households, the aging of the population, pure racism, America's federal political system, gridlocked national politics, and the absence of proportional representation in elections (for an overview of some of these topics, see Atkinson 1997; see also Alesina, Glaeser, and Sacredote 2001).

Most of these factors are either directly political or potentially affected by public policy. Technological change, however, would appear to respond to many forces that are independent of government policy. Similarly, the decline of marriage is universal throughout the Western world. The roots of this may be just as much in technological changes that affect work in the household and in changes in lifestyle as in the changes in incentives produced through welfare and other public policies. Nonetheless, politics and public policy remain the focus of this essay.

An important aspect of the increase in inequality is that it has indeed taken place during a period of substantial economic growth. Although the quadrupling, from 1970 to 2000, of the proportion of the population who are incarcerated (Western, Kleykamp, and Rosenfeld, this volume) suggests that many African American males may not be better off than their grandparents, by and large the increase in inequality is not a matter of pauperization.[2] Although there is debate as to whether the lower end of the income distribution is somewhat worse off or has remained relatively stable in economic status, it has pretty clearly not gotten much worse off. Moreover, a substantial segment of the lower tail consists of immigrants who are much better off than they were in their nation of origin. At the same time, in the middle and at the top end of the income distribution, voters have become much richer. This is not just because the growth rate of income at each centile has been increasing in the centile. The poor who are eligible to vote increasingly vote less than the rich. In addition, nonvoting legal and illegal immigrants tend to be poor. Another factor, but quantitatively less important than immigration, arises from growth in the number of incarcerated Americans and ineligible ex-felons (on both criminals and immigrants in voter turnout, see McDonald and Popkin 2001).

Prosperity, immigration, and criminal justice policy combine to mute the political response to inequality. This chapter proposes an account of the political and institutional forces that are likely to blunt a movement toward redistributive economic policies. Rising wealth and incomes have created a sizable constituency with a vested interest in the status quo, while the growing share of noncitizens and disenfranchised ex-offenders reduces the political power of the poor. As I discuss later, these shifts in the electorate take place in the context of institutional features of the American political system that give economic policies a kind of "stickiness," particularly given the polarization discussed earlier. Once established, economic policies that affect the distribution of income tend to be slow to change.

The essay proceeds as follows. A theoretical overview of the political economy of inequality is provided in the next section. This section also briefly applies the theoretical perspective to an understanding of events in the twentieth century. In the following section, I make some international comparisons and highlight how the Great Depression, World War II, and the 1960s represented exceptional events for the United States. I suggest how politics might be relevant to differences in inequality across nations. In the next section, I document the polarization of politics in the United States. The following section links that political polarization to outcomes in income and wealth inequality and immigration. That is followed by a section in which I argue that increases in aggregate income and wealth and in immigration are acting to mute any political response to inequality. Finally, I show how changes in public policies on taxes and minimum wages correspond with changes in inequality and political polarization. This section also emphasizes that old-age insurance taxes follow an entirely different pattern from taxation that is explicitly redistributive.

THE POLITICAL ECONOMY OF INEQUALITY:
A THEORETICAL OVERVIEW

This essay attempts to tie together the complex social phenomena of inequality, public policy, and political polarization. I start with a theoretical perspective that draws from formal models in political science and economics.

Politics as Liberal-Conservative Competition

A basic premise is that public policy throughout the twentieth century was largely (but not entirely, because of race) a matter of political competition over a single liberal-conservative dimension.[3] In particular, in this theoretical overview I am assuming that the 435 members of the House of Representatives fall along a liberal-conservative continuum with the most liberal representative in position 1, the median representative in position 218, and the most conservative in position 435. Similarly, the 100 senators can be ranked from 1 to 100. In the 107th Congress that served in 2001 to 2002, the five most liberal senators were Feingold, Dayton, Corzine, Wellstone, and Boxer; the five most conservative were Ensign, Smith, Nickles, Gramm, and Kyl.[4] More information about how liberal-conservatism is measured is provided later in the chapter. The liberal-conservative cleavage captures the debate over income and estate taxes and minimum wages.

American Institutions, Gridlock, and Sticky Policies

This cleavage interacts, in turn, with the presence of checks and balances in the American political system. For starters, new legislation requires either passage in both houses of Congress and the president's signature or, in the case of a presidential veto, passage by two-thirds majorities in both houses of Congress. Policy change can also be impeded by the filibuster in the Senate. In addition, congressional committees have substantial power that enables them to structure or impede legislation. The upshot here is that no single individual is decisive in the policy process. The United States is not like the United Kingdom, where a single parliamentary election can easily lead to substantial policy change. In the United States a number of veto agents or pivots (Krehbiel 1998; Brady and Volden 1998) must be on board to engender legislative change. A large coalition must be created to defeat the status quo and change policy. In a nutshell, legislation in the United States tends to be very sticky.

There are several examples of sticky legislation for policies that are central to this essay.

1. Goldin (1994) documents how presidential vetoes withheld restrictive immigration legislation until the 1920s even though congressional majorities had favored it for several decades. The restrictive immigration laws of the 1920s remained largely intact for forty-five years, until the Immigration Act of 1965. Although Congress subsequently passed compromise immigration bills, the liberal 1965 policy essentially prevailed for the rest of the century.

2. The maximum estate tax rate remained fixed at 77 percent from 1940 through 1976 while the minimum estate subject to tax remained, in nominal dollars, fixed at $60,000 from 1942 through 1976.

3. Minimum wages changed more frequently, but because they are also defined in nominal dollars, the real value of the wage can erode sharply when, as happened from 1981 through 1989, no increase is enacted over a relatively long period.

4. Economic regulations adopted during the New Deal remained in effect for decades. Transportation and telecommunications were deregulated only in the late 1970s and 1980s. The separation of commercial and investment banking and other aspects of the Glass-Steagall Act remained in effect from 1933 until the passage of the Gramm-Leach-Bliley Act in 1999.

5. Welfare as an entitlement, known as AFDC (Aid to Families with Dependent Children), was initiated by the Social Security Act of 1935. The basic system remained in place and was extended until, over sixty years later, the passage of the Personal Responsibility and Work Opportunity Reconciliation Act (PRWORA) of 1996.

The power that institutions give to the status quo is important in assessing empirical studies of inequality. Because legislative adjustments are infrequent and nonincremental, the typical continuous responses embodied in econometric models are inappropriate. In short, the lumpiness of politics makes it all the more difficult to understand the interactions of the slew of factors, listed earlier, that affect inequality.

Overcoming the force of status quo policies—gridlock for short—typically requires both a dramatic change in economic or social conditions and strong majorities (for an opposing view, see Mayhew 1991). A recent example of a social shock changing policy was the terrorist attack of September 11, 2001, which led to the USA Patriot Act. The terrorist attack moved the status quo on civil liberties and privacy to the left on the liberal-conservative continuum. Existing constraints on law enforcement appeared to be too liberal. A more conservative policy became possible. (The policy can be safely interpreted as conservative in that of the sixty-six House votes against the act, sixty-two came from Democrats, largely on the left wing of the party.)[5]

The stickiness is especially likely to be overcome when the shocks lead to change that is favored by a party that controls both the White House and has majorities in Congress. The New Deal is, of course, the most pronounced example. The shock of the Depression changed how the status quo in economic policy mapped onto the liberal-conservative dimension, while the huge Democratic majorities made passing new programs easy. (The Democrats had an edge of eighty to sixteen in the Senate at one point.) The important policy changes of the 1960s discussed earlier occurred during unified Democratic government, with majorities reinforced by the Goldwater debacle of 1964. Similarly, the double-digit inflation before the 1980 election changed the status quo and led a Democratic-controlled House to concede the Reagan tax cuts of 1981, although as soon as inflation dropped, the Democrats declared later Reagan budgets "dead on arrival."[6]

The blocking of major policy change in the Reagan era once the inflation shock had passed illustrates the stickiness of policy in times when there are no great shocks and when political competition produces more even results than the huge majorities of the Depression era.[7] The possibilities for gridlock are further accentuated by political polarization. Institutions that lead to "pivotal politics" (Krehbiel 1998) or "revolving gridlock" (Brady and Volden 1998) interact with polarized politics to further restrict policy change.

Let me illustrate this point. With George W. Bush in the White House, a normal bill requires not only his assent but also the support of the liberal-conservative median in the House. Moreover, a bill also has to avoid a filibuster in the Senate. To get the necessary sixty votes for cloture, a bill has to be acceptable to the filibuster pivot. This is senator 41 in the ranking. (Johnson of South Dakota and Feinstein of California tied for this spot in the 107th Senate).[8] The Republicans cannot move any policy in a more conservative direction without the consent of this filibuster pivot. The other side of this coin is that Democrats cannot make more liberal policies without the agreement of majorities that would override a presidential veto. In the Senate an override requires support from senator 67 (DeWine of Ohio in the 107th Senate) in the liberal-conservative lineup. So no change is possible for any policies that fall in the gap between the filibuster pivot in the Senate and the veto override pivot in Congress. As moderates disappear, the pivots are more likely to be quite conservative or quite liberal. As politics become more polarized, this gap or "gridlock zone" becomes larger.[9]

The import of sticky politics is that trends in inequality can persist for a long time. If the New Deal enacted policies that reduced inequality, inequality was likely to fall for some time, even after preferences might have shifted in favor of a less egalitarian society. Similarly, the high degree of inequality at the beginning of the twenty-first century can be expected to persist—absent a devastating shock to the system, such as a Depression-like economic event. Persistence is all the more likely in the presence of polarized politics and an enlarged "gridlock zone." Federal legislation that would deal with inequality is highly unlikely.

The Political Economy of Redistribution

In contrast to the political science of legislation, with its emphasis on gridlock and the persistence of the status quo, the economics of redistribution largely relies on models in which the individual with median income dictates policy. The basic insight was developed by Duncan Foley (1967). Income distributions are skewed—that is, average income is above median income. Being below average, the median income voter should support redistribution. In fact, if taxes are proportional to income and redistribution is identical (lump-sum) for all, only the minority with incomes above the average would oppose redistribution. So simple majority rule should lead to redistribution.

Foley's basic insight has been tempered by subsequent work that emphasizes the restraints on redistribution that would result from diminished labor supply (Romer 1975, 1977; Roberts 1977), simple deadweight loss (Meltzer and Richard 1981; Bolton and Roland 1997), expectations of upward mobility (Benabou and Ok 2001), and credit market imperfections (Benabou 2000). Nonetheless, in median voter democracies some redistribution can be expected to occur. Redistribution, however, might be absent because the majority rule model is simply inappropriate. One factor that would make the model inappropriate is the median voter having, as indicated later in the chapter, an income much higher than that of the median individual in the income distribution. The other is that political institutions are distant from simple majority rule and, as indicated earlier, gridlock can block policy change.

The Impact of Inequality on Policy Formation

When policy change does occur, the nature of the change can be shaped by the inequality present in society. If the top half of the income or wealth distribution has a lot to lose, its members can be expected to fight hard to protect gains and to seize the opportunity to reverse or limit redistribution when in power. The dramatic increase of real income and wealth in the last half of the century and a dramatic increase in the fraction of the population invested, directly or indirectly, in equities (Duca and Saving 2002) may underpin the regressive tax policies of the Bush administration. Conversely, when inequality is high and incomes are low or falling, a unified left government may be more inclined to press for redistributive taxation of wealth and income, minimum wages, and income insurance programs.

Coalitions that reduce inequality can still be built, however, under conservative governments. As Claudia Goldin (1994) stresses, the restriction of immigration in the 1920s was a response not only to nativist and southern concerns with the distribution of political power but also to labor concerns about low-wage competition from immigrants. The Republican-sponsored laws of the 1920s are likely to have increased wages at the low end and stimulated black migration to the North (Collins 1997), at the expense of those denied entry. From a broader perspective, the rich can make redistributive concessions to the poor to secure the participation of the poor in wars (Ticchi and Vindigni 2003) or to avoid a revolution by the poor (Acemoglu and Robinson 2001). Avoidance of revolt or at least unrest does seem to have been an underpinning of the Great Society program.

Programs to reduce inequality might be tempered by two factors. First, I conjecture that, for a given level of inequality, redistribution becomes less likely at very high levels of per capita income. The basic logic is that at high levels of societal income the rich and middle classes rely on self-insurance and have less demand for redistributive social insurance. The middle classes become more risk-acceptant. Second, who votes affects redistribution. A perhaps unintended consequence of the largely unskilled immigration of the past thirty years is that poverty is concentrated among immigrants who have no voting rights. The lower turnout, in general, of the poor combines with immigration and the overall increase in income to reinforce the effect of gridlock in blocking public policies that would reduce inequality.

Other Events

Other events, particularly swings in technology, the business cycle, wars, social unrest, and racial politics, are somewhat independent and distinct from the trends in political polarization, public policy, and income inequality that are emphasized here. Some of these changes have direct effects on inequality. Racial biases in hiring may trap low-income African Americans. Technological change that generates increasing returns to education may have a direct effect on inequality that is not compensated by changes in public policy. The changes also have indirect effects through their influence on the political process by shifting the control of government and public policies. Thus, the Depression and World War II combined to produce high marginal tax rates that persisted into the postwar period.

Applying the Theoretical Framework

Let me, very speculatively, apply the theoretical perspective just developed to the unfolding of the twentieth century. In the first half of the century, inequality may have been decreased by a combination of technological factors of the Kuznets variety, the severe tightening of immigration in the 1920s, anticompetitive incumbent protection measures brought about by the Great Depression, and very high marginal tax rates on incomes and estates justified by war finance.[10] The huge congressional majorities enjoyed by the Democrats in much of the period from the 1930s to the 1970s permitted the passage of policies that may have contributed to lowering inequality. These policies, given the status quo bias in American politics, were likely to persist for a very long time.

By 1950, however, the aggregate economy was at an all-time peacetime high in terms of per capita output. (In contrast, per capita output in continental Europe and Japan remained well below its prewar highs.) As time progressed, pressure built for changing government policy in a direction that would promote competition and risk-taking through deregulation and place more reliance on self-insurance and less on social insurance.

These pressures continued in the 1960s, when the top half of the income distribution was earning much more in real terms than during the Roosevelt years. Memory of the Great Depression had faded for some and was nonexistent for others. Moreover, the Democratic Party turned away from issues of general social welfare and toward issues—race, gender, sexual preference, immigration from outside northern Europe—that were based on ascriptive characteristics of individuals (Gerring 1998). In promoting these antidiscriminatory measures, the party lost its dominance in the South. Among southern voters, conservatives—most notably well-to-do southerners (see McCarty, Poole, and Rosenthal 2002)—switched to the Republicans. In the House of Representatives, African Americans became concentrated in the left wing of the Democratic Party. As such, race ceased to be a distinct issue dimension in American politics and became embedded in the liberal-conservative conflict over redistribution.

The political pressure against egalitarian, redistributive policies came to the fore in the last quarter of the century. Perhaps the first marker was the antitax movement that led to the passage of Proposition 13 in California in 1978. During this last quarter-century, technology, globalization, and increased immigration may all have contributed to worsening income inequality. Nonetheless, new conservative strength both blocked compensating policy responses and, when given the opportunity, reduced the support for existing programs.

The parallel trends in inequality, public policy, and politics seem less explicable in terms of other factors. Race does appear related to the current absence of redistribution in the United States (Alesina, Glaeser, and Sacredote 2001) and to the absence of public spending in local communities (Alesina, Baqir, and Easterly 1999; Alesina and La Ferrara 2000, 2002). The claim that welfare expenditures in the United States are low because of race has been made by many authors, including Gunnar Myrdal (1960), Jill Quadagno (1994), and Martin Gilens (1999). But it is hard to see racism as hardening in the last quarter of the twentieth century when inequality increased. Racism and racial tension seem to have been at least as rife when inequality fell. Recall the lynchings and race riots in the first half of the century and the urban riots of the 1960s. Similarly, unionization has been declining since the 1950s, well before inequality worsened, and trade liberalization has been ongoing since the 1930s. So my focus in the rest of the essay will be on minimum wages, taxes, and immigration and the relationship between these policies and inequality.

SOME INTERNATIONAL COMPARISONS

Many observers have noted that income inequality in continental Europe and Japan is not as severe as in the United States, with Britain being something of an intermediate case. It is therefore important to examine the major distinctions in the historical experiences of the industrialized nations. I emphasize trends in aggregate economic experience, the 1960s, and institutions, in contrast to an older literature that roots "American exceptionalism" more in the organization of labor and the absence of Socialist and Communist parties (Lipset 1996; Sombart 2001). In a nutshell, I argue that the Great Depression may have allowed the United States to parallel other nations in the decline of inequality for most of the twentieth century, while the economic expansions of the first half of the century may have sown the seed for the current increase in inequality.

There were indeed dramatic differences in the pattern of aggregate growth between the United States and the six other major industrial nations that formed the G-7 (Canada, France, Germany, Italy, Japan, and the United Kingdom). Over the course of a century all seven nations did incredibly well. Angus Maddison (1995, 194–97) presents time series on GDP per capita in terms of 1990 Geary-Khamis dollars. In 1900 all the G-7 nations were below $4,700, and two, Italy and Japan, were below $1,800. By 1990 all had passed $15,600. The path of growth, however, was substantially different across these societies. The European nations involved in World War I all took a substantial hit. The United States and Japan did not. Germany never recovered until the advent of the command economy of Nazism. Germany did not surpass its 1913 GDP per capita until 1934. But perhaps the most important contrasts in economic growth occurred during the Depression and then during World War II.

The Great Depression

The United States was particularly hard hit by the collapse of the 1930s. The United States did not surpass its 1929 level of GDP per capita until 1940. The public policy effects of the

Depression in the United States were not just the introduction of social insurance and progressive taxes. The Depression furthered anticompetitive regulation in the form of the Motor Carrier Act, the Banking Act of 1933 (Glass-Steagall), the Civil Aeronautics Act, the Federal Communications Act, the Wagner Act, which strengthened unions, agricultural price supports and marketing boards, taxicab regulation at the local level, and so on. These were all reversals of capitalism that, as Raghuram Rajan and Luigi Zingales (2003a,b) have argued, were part of a worldwide response that cushioned incumbents from the shock of especially bad times. Incumbent protection coupled with progressive taxation is likely to preserve incomes at the low end while blocking the entrepreneurial creation of new fortunes and performance-based compensation at the high end.

War

World War II, however, represents the greatest distinction between the United States and the other major industrialized nations. On the one hand, the war led to tax policies with very high marginal rates. Inertia carried these policies forward for many years. On the other hand, the United States did not suffer the physical destruction and economic disruption that befell the countries, including G-7 members France, Germany, Italy, and Japan, that were defeated and occupied at one point in the war. Those countries experienced complete economic collapse by the end of the war. Per capita GDP in France in 1943, 1944, and 1945 was below the 1900 level. The 1946 and 1947 levels in Germany similarly fell behind the comparable figure for 1900. The Italian GDP per capita in 1945 was below that for 1905, while Japan in 1945 lagged behind the 1911 level. Per capita output in the United Kingdom in 1945 exceeded that at the flight from Dunkirk. But output soared the most in the United States. By 1945 the United States had more than doubled the 1938 level of output.

Clearly, the aftermath of World War II could be expected to have a great differential impact on how nations organized politically and implemented policies with respect to redistribution and social insurance. (For example, did old-age pensions in Europe have to be provided by the state because private firms had no capacity to provide them and individual savings had been wiped out in the war?) Thomas Piketty (2001) has argued that wartime wage policies in France and the destruction of wealth during two wars established a political lock-in of redistributive policies that have kept income inequality from rising there. In this respect, it is interesting that Britain and the United States were the major industrial nations with the greatest degree of inequality by the end of the century (see, for example, Atkinson 1997). Britain, as indicated earlier, is intermediate between the United States and Europe in the impact of the war; it is also intermediate with respect to inequality. It is the only European nation where elections could result in implementing and sustaining "reforms," first under Margaret Thatcher and then under Tony Blair.

There are two further distinctions between the United States and other nations that may relate to the rise of inequality in the last quarter of the twentieth century. These are the civil rights and immigration legislation passed in the 1960s and American institutions.

The 1960s

After World War II there were dramatic differences in the pattern of economic growth between the United States and the nations recovering from the war. There were also unique policy changes in the United States that occurred in the 1960s, including the Voting Rights

Act of 1965 and the Civil Rights Act of 1964. These policies capped a process that broke apart the old Democratic coalition of white southerners and northern non-Protestants.

From the end of Reconstruction to the mid-1930s, southern Democrats represented the left wing of the Democratic Party and were the force behind legislation, such as railroad regulation in the 1880s (Poole and Rosenthal 1993) and corporate taxation in the 1910s (Brownlee 1996), that had a redistributive aspect—from northern whites to southern whites. Starting in the 1930s, but most emphatically after the passage of civil rights legislation in the 1960s, the southern delegation in Congress moved substantially to the right and became hostile to redistribution.[11] Similarly, southern voters, including whites, who were once solidly Democratic are now split heavily along income lines (McCarty, Poole, and Rosenthal 2002). In other words, the enfranchisement of African Americans in the South shifted the policy debate from one of North-South or urban-rural redistribution among whites to one of white-black or rich-poor redistribution. The connection of redistribution to race may have made Americans relatively unfavorable to redistribution (see Alesina, Baqir, and Easterly 1999; Alesina and La Ferrara 2000; Alesina, Glaeser, and a Sacredote 2001; Alesina and La Ferrara 2002).

The 1960s also featured the development of affirmative action policies based on ascriptive characteristics of individuals. These policies reflected a shift, as mentioned previously, in Democratic Party platforms from an emphasis on general welfare to ascription (Gerring 1998). A recent theoretical model by David Austen-Smith and Michael Wallerstein (2003) suggests why race may now be linked to an increase in inequality even when it did not seem to be consistent with the fall in inequality earlier in the century. The distinction arises from the post-1960s availability of affirmative action as a social policy. In their model, there is neither racial discrimination in employment nor prejudice among voters. But they demonstrate, within the context of the model, that there will be less redistribution when there are two policy instruments—affirmative action and redistribution—than when redistribution is the only policy instrument.

In addition to civil rights legislation, the 1960s also featured the passage of the Immigration Act of 1965, which opened the United States to substantial legal immigration for the first time in over four decades. This immigration may well have exposed the domestic poor to wage competition (Borjas 1999; Bean and Bell-Rose 1999) and caused the lower-income brackets to become less represented in the voting population.

Institutions

As outlined in the previous sections, the United States has institutions that support gridlock and make policies sticky. Institutions, it can be suggested, helped lock in New Deal–type policies. They also may make it difficult to respond to the current increase in inequality. On the other hand, the institutional story should be taken with some caution. In addition to the institutional structure for legislation, there is another important difference between the United States and at least some continental European nations: it does not have politicized national labor organizations capable of organizing mass protests. If the United States can have gridlock in its national legislature, Europe can have it in the streets.

Inequality and Politics

I now turn to some comparative evidence on inequality. In figure 23.1, I show the percentage of total income that accrues to the top one-tenth of 1 percent of families in the United

FIGURE 23.1   *Top 0.1 Percent Income Shares in the United States, France, and the United Kingdom, 1913 to 1998*

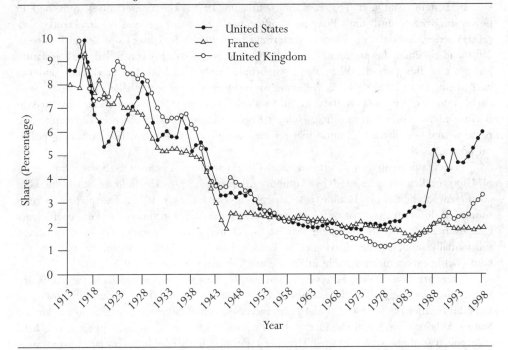

Source: Reproduced from Piketty and Saez (2003, fig. 12). See source for details of computation. © 2003 by the President and Fellows of Harvard College and the Massachusetts Institute of Technology. Reprinted with permission.

States, Britain, and France. The data, based on tax returns, are reproduced from Piketty and Saez (2003). Early in the twentieth century, one family in one thousand accounted for 8 percent or more of family income in all three countries. By the late 1960s this share had fallen dramatically to around 2 percent in all three countries. Without the data from the last quarter-century, it would be hard to find a role for politics—there were a mixture of left, right, and fascist regimes in the three countries—and easy to see support for the Kuznets notion of rising industrialization leading to a drop in inequality.

The divergence occurred in the last two decades. The share of the rich held at 2 percent in France but increased to over 3 percent in Britain and to 6 percent in the United States. It is easier to see the role of politics than of technology from this point on. Larry Bartels (2002), on the basis of regression analysis for 1948 to 2000, argues that Republican presidents are associated with the growth of income inequality and Democratic presidents with its reduction. The Bartels story does not say much about the general fall in inequality in the first half of the century, but politics does appear to have had an impact in the last half.

In the United States, Ronald Reagan took office in 1981. Concurrently, the Republican vote share and, with a lag, seat share for the House of Representatives was increasing (Duca and Saving 2002). Consequently, for the last twenty years of the century, the Republicans controlled either the presidency or both houses of Congress for all but two years (1993 and 1994). Starting with Nixon in 1969, the Republicans exercised the same level of control for all but six of the last thirty-two years of the century. This is precisely the period when inequality reversed.

In Britain, Margaret Thatcher took office in 1979. The conservatives remained in power in Britain until Tony Blair took office in 1997, near the end of the Piketty-Saez (2003) series. In contrast, François Mitterrand brought the Socialists to power in France in 1981 and retained the presidency until 1995. The Socialists also controlled the legislature for most of this period. When the right briefly controlled both the presidency and the parliament, from 1995 to 1997, "reforms" were blocked by massive labor disruptions. Similarly, reforms proposed in Italy by Silvio Berlusconi in 1994 were blocked by strikes; Berlusconi was forced from office. Helmut Kohl's sixteen years in office in Germany were perhaps facilitated by a realization that reforms were not consistent with maintaining political power.

The data presented by Piketty and Saez (2003) are largely echoed in shorter time series of Gini coefficients presented by Anthony Atkinson (1997). He indicates that the Gini coefficient of household income rose sharply in Britain after 1977. The picture here is somewhat different than that of Piketty and Saez, since Atkinson shows that Gini coefficients rose even more sharply in Britain than in the United States. Income, however, remained substantially more equally distributed in Britain than in the United States. In contrast, the Gini coefficients remained stable in France and Germany and even fell in Italy.

There are two caveats, however, to the simple story that recent trends in inequality are simply the consequence of the politics of the 1980s and 1990s. First, Atkinson shows that the Gini coefficients for Sweden and Japan increased about the same degree as in the United States. Although the Social Democrats did not hold office continuously in Sweden, it is hard to argue that there was a Reagan-Thatcher-type switch there. Similarly, Japan went away from complete Liberal Democratic Party (LDP) control in the 1990s. The other side of the coin is that Atkinson also shows that, as in France, inequality did not increase in Germany and Italy. In Germany the right governed, with Helmut Kohl, from 1982 to 1998. The Italian case is more mixed but certainly not one of a Mitterrand-type left-wing government. Second, as I show later on, in the United States many of the important policy changes that would be associated with an increase in inequality were initiated before the election of Reagan. Similarly, figure 23.1 shows that inequality in Britain began to increase before Thatcher's election.

Putting these results together, I suggest that technological and market forces are pushing toward increased inequality. So are the "reforms"—weaker unions, deregulation, free trade, and privatization—pushed by some business interests that would benefit from these forces. Such reforms are more likely to be pushed when the right has political power. Indeed, causality may be reversed. If inequality is produced by large increases in income in the top half of the income distribution, conservative or right governments may be as much the consequence of inequality as its cause (a point I argue in a later section).

The right, on the other hand, may not always be able to implement reforms. Powerful labor movements can block change from ever being put on the legislative table or veto change through strikes and mass demonstrations. The power of labor unions may be what ties together the lack of an increase in inequality in France, Germany, and Italy. Note that Margaret Thatcher's defining moment with labor was in facing down the coal miners in 1985; Reagan's was firing the air traffic controllers in 1981. In contrast, Jacques Chirac and Alain Juppé caved to the 1995–1996 strikes.

This comparative discussion highlights the distinctive historical context of the United States, including the social legislation of the Depression, the relative prosperity of the

World War II and postwar period, and the civil rights and immigration legislation of the 1960s. These historical events, I argue, are important influences on inequality as well as the associated trends in political polarization and economic policy that I discuss.

POLARIZATION

What do we mean by the "polarization of American politics"? We all recognize that members of Congress can be thought of as liberals and conservatives. Ted Kennedy is a liberal, Dianne Feinstein is a more moderate Democrat, John Breaux even more so, Olympia Snowe is a moderate Republican, and Trent Lott is a conservative Republican. The perception of liberal-conservativeness is commonly shared. There is a common perception because there is a predictability of behavior. If I know that Olympia Snowe will fight a large tax cut, I am pretty sure that all or almost all the Democrats will support her position. In fact, for the past quarter-century we can find a common ordering from liberal to conservative that, on average, "explains" over 90 percent of all the individual roll call votes cast by legislators. On a given vote, legislators break into two camps, one liberal and the other conservative. On some votes, with large conservative majorities, the break might come between Dianne Feinstein and senators to her right. On closer votes, Olympia Snowe might be at the break point. For any vote, we can find a break point that represents our "explanation."

A statistical method called DW-NOMINATE (McCarty, Poole, and Rosenthal 1997) permits us to assign to representatives numerical values for liberal-conservativeness. These values allow us to compare representatives across American history and study polarization.[12] Schickler (2000) has developed an interesting graph that we can use to portray polarization. I reproduce it as figure 23.2.

Figure 23.2 contains plots of three liberal-conservative measures against time. The graph in the middle is the position of the median House member, the member who ranks 218 out of the 435 representatives. Not surprisingly, the position of the median member of the Republican House delegation plots out as the top graph, above the overall median in a conservative direction. The median Democrat is the bottom graph.

It can be seen that the median position in the House does not track inequality (figure 23.1) particularly well. The overall House median is more volatile than either party median. Party ideology changes only slowly but elections can sharply shift the position of the House. This happened frequently before World War I, when elections to the U.S. House of Representatives reflected a competitive democracy rather than a gerrymandered welfare state for incumbents. Since World War I, there have been only two big shifts: the liberal move after the 1929 stock market crash and the conservative move with the "Contract with America" in 1994.[13] The overall volatility bears little relationship to the gradual decline in inequality from 1913 to 1975 shown in figure 23.1. In particular, the House moved in a conservative direction from 1913 to 1929 and from 1937 to 1948. Conversely, as inequality rose after 1975, the House became more liberal until 1994. Changes in the position of the median Democrat also fail to track changes in inequality.

What does track changes in inequality is the position of the median Republican. House Republicans, who were almost entirely northerners before the 1960s, moved in a liberal direction until the early 1970s and then moved back to being as conservative as they were before 1929. (The story for the Senate is similar to that for the House.)

How does figure 23.2 show polarization? We can think of polarization as the *difference* between the Republican median and the Democrat median. From 1913 to 1975, as inequality fell, polarization fell. Until 1937, not only did the Republicans become more liberal, but

FIGURE 23.2   *Floor and Party Medians, House of Representatives, 1865 to 1997*

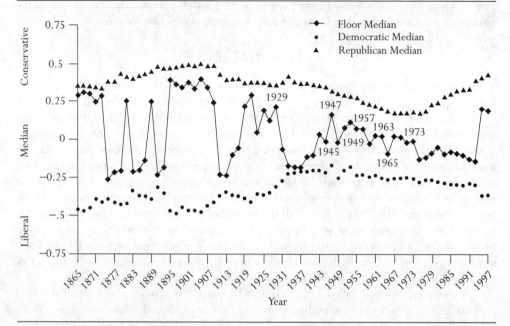

Source: Reproduced from Schickler (2000). The medians are computed using first-dimension DW-NOMINATE scores. © 2000. Reprinted with the permission of Cambridge University Press.

the Democrats became more conservative as the position of southern Democrats changed. After 1937 the Democrats became more liberal but at a very slow rate. So polarization continued to fall until 1975 because of the more rapid liberal movement of Republicans. In the last quarter of the century, both parties moved, particularly Republicans, to extreme positions. How we measure polarization is robust to alternative definitions. In the remainder of this chapter, rather than use the difference between medians, I use the average distance between Democrats and Republicans.[14]

It should be pointed out that the changing positions of the Republicans and the increase in polarization are not simply attributable to the changes in southern politics. There would be similar results if we analyzed the roll call votes of just northerners. The trend of House polarization is echoed by a separate analysis of presidents since 1955 done by Keith Poole.[15] The positions of presidents are pegged by having them "vote" on roll calls that *Congressional Quarterly* uses to compute presidential support scores. The basic story is that Reagan and George H. W. Bush appear as far more conservative than Eisenhower and Nixon, while Clinton was only slightly more conservative than his Democratic predecessors.

Polarization along liberal-conservative lines may be particularly relevant to the study of inequality because redistributive issues typically involve liberal-conservative splits (see, for example, Poole and Rosenthal 1991 on minimum wage). As the parties move apart on redistributive issues, voters may polarize more along income lines. McCarty, Poole, and Rosenthal (2002) show that partisan identification and presidential vote choice are increasingly stratified by income, with the top income quintile becoming overwhelmingly Republican supporters while the bottom quintile gives overwhelming support to Democrats.

POLITICAL POLARIZATION, ECONOMIC INEQUALITY, AND IMMIGRATION

The trend in polarization matches up with two other major reversals in American society: the shift from decline to increase in economic inequality (seen in figure 23.1) and the reversal in immigration.

Comparisons of the income share of the rich in figure 23.1 and either the position of the median Republican or the difference in the party medians disclose a high degree of congruence. I now show a similar result for the postwar period using two different measures. To measure inequality, I employ the widely used Gini coefficient. To measure polarization, I employ the average liberal-conservative (DW-NOMINATE) distance between Republicans and Democrats. The results are in figure 23.3. The correlation for 1947 to 2001 is 0.94.

A time series covering wealth inequality was developed by Edward Wolff (2002a). The fit to polarization for 1927 to 1990 is not as tight as with the Gini coefficients. The result is shown as figure 23.4. Wealth concentration into the top 1 percent declines as polarization declines through the 1970s and then, in the first half of the 1980s, begins to increase as wealth increases. Afterward, surprisingly, wealth inequality plateaus around 20 percent. More recent work by Wojciech Kopczuk and Emmanuel Saez (2003), based on estate tax returns from 1916 onward, shows a similar pattern. These authors find that the share of wealth held by the top 1 percent oscillated from 35 to 40 percent until 1929. Afterward, with the stock market crash and estate taxation, this share fell to the 21 to 23 percent range from 1940 until 1965, before dropping to just under 20 percent in the late 1970s. Afterward, wealth inequality increased, but only slightly, to about 22 percent. Of course, these reports can be biased by the ability of the rich to effectively transfer their estates to their heirs in a way that avoids reporting the wealth. Even so, a basic picture emerges. The long-term decline in the wealth of the rich was at the least halted and perhaps slightly reversed at a point close to when political polarization increased.

The pattern also holds with respect to immigration. The plot of the percentage foreign-born against polarization is shown in figure 23.5. The correlation of 0.95 was computed by matching the thirteen observations for the decennial census from 1880 through 2000 with the polarization index for the corresponding House. The percentage foreign-born is not the only way in which immigration might be measured. Frank Bean and Gillian Stevens (2003, 19) show that the flow of immigration fell dramatically in the 1910s as a result of World War I and fell through the 1920s and 1930s to nearly 0 after the passage of the national-origins quota immigration acts of 1921 and 1924. Immigration then increased in every decade from the 1940s through the 1990s. Thus, the flow of immigrants appears to have picked up sometime before the change in inequality.

But what of low-skilled immigrants, those with a potential impact on both inequality and polarization? The increase in immigration right after World War II was in large part a flow of refugees. Only in the 1960s, centered on the abolition of national quotas in the Immigration and Naturalization Act Amendments of October 3, 1965, did the number of immigrants from Asia and Latin America exceed those from Europe and Canada (Bean and Stevens 2003, 21). Third World immigrants began to strongly outnumber those from the First World only in the 1970s. Similarly, illegal immigration, as proxied by "apprehensions" by the Immigration and Naturalization Service (INS), did not become a major factor until the 1970s (Bean and Stevens 2003, 24). Consequently, it is plausible that low-skilled immigration became a major factor only in the late 1960s and in the 1970s—precisely the time period when polarization began to increase.

FIGURE 23.3   *Income Inequality and Political Polarization, 1947 to 2001*

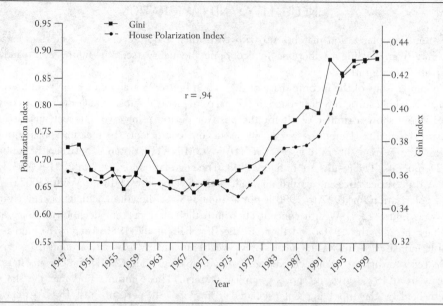

Source: Gini index, U.S. Census (2002), polarization, computation of average DW-NOMINATE distance between Republicans and Democrats by Keith T. Poole. There is one data point for each two-year Congress. The Gini index value is for the first year of the Congress. For example, the first data point is polarization for the 80th House, 1947–1948 and the Gini value for 1947.

FIGURE 23.4   *House Polarization and Percentage of All Wealth Held by Wealthiest 1 Percent, 1921 to 1997*

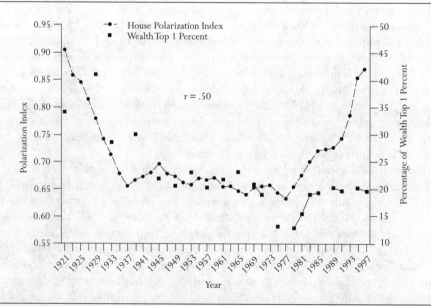

Source: For polarization source, see figure 23.3. Wealth source is Wolff (2002a, table A-1, 82–83). Wolff does not provide a wealth measure for every year.

FIGURE 23.5   *Percentage of Foreign-Born and Political Polarization, 1880 to 2000*

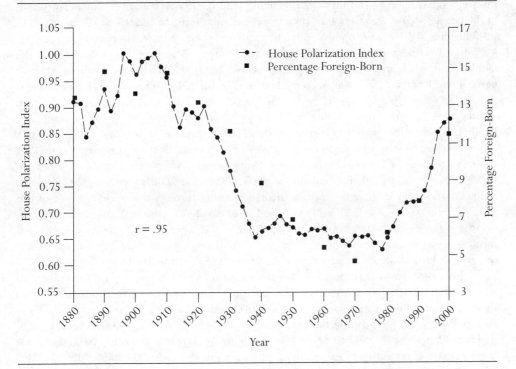

Source: For polarization source: see figure 23.3. For percentage foreign-born source: U.S. census, various years. Each percentage foreign-born corresponds to a decennial census. The corresponding polarization point is for the Congress that began service in the year preceding the census.

THE POLITICAL IMPLICATIONS OF ECONOMIC INEQUALITY

It is now time to reconcile the continual prosperity of the United States since the Great Depression, marked by an enormous increase in aggregate per capita output, with the increase in inequality from the 1970s onward (figures 23.1, 23.3, and 23.4) and to relate these observations to politics. I contend that economic prosperity, as reflected in growth in the incomes and assets of middle- and upper-income voters, weakens the political movement for redistributive policies. This shift is reinforced by the rising prevalence of noncitizens in the population, particularly among the poor.

Frank Levy's *The New Dollars and Dreams* (1998) drew attention to those Americans who had fallen behind at the bottom of the income distribution. But data presented in that study highlight a different point with respect to political implications. Let's characterize the poor as families with under $20,000 in 1997 dollars. Levy shows that, in 1949, 60 percent of American families, a strong majority, fit this definition of poor. At the other end, only about 3 percent had incomes over $60,000. *In 1949 there were, percentage-wise, almost no rich Americans.* We were all far from heaven. By 1973, near the time when the inequality curve began its reversal, the situation had changed dramatically. The poor under $20,000 had fallen to about 19 percent, and the relatively well-to-do above $60,000 had risen to well over 20 percent. This 20 percent that was truly middle-class and above would now represent a sizable segment of the population interested in retaining their wealth. They would be more politically powerful than their numbers would indicate, through voting, through making campaign contributions, and through interacting with their representatives. Not surprisingly, in the late 1970s a wave of tax limitation referenda went coast to coast, from Proposition 13 in California in 1978 to Proposition 2½ in the liberal bastion of Massachusetts.

By 1996 there had been further dramatic change. A slightly larger fraction of the families had fallen into the poor segment below $20,000, which rose from roughly 19 percent to 21 percent. The top category, however, continued to surge ahead. By 1996 about 32 percent of the population was above $60,000. Even if those families earning the high incomes were putting in more total hours owing to female entry into the labor force, the family unit would be likely to resist taxation on either incomes or wealth.

I have made somewhat different tabulations to use data that are closer to the present time and to take an intervening date close to the worst post–World War II recession. In figure 23.6, I look at household income in 1967, 1984, and 2000 in terms of 2000 dollars. A first observation is that real median income is rising through this period. It goes from $31,397 in 1967 to $35,568 in 1984 to $42,148 in 2000. Although incomes may have decreased somewhat at the bottom end, *a majority of Americans were better off* even though inequality was increasing. While the higher the centile was in the distribution, the higher the growth rate of income attached to that centile, even the median had real growth.

I have also shown percentages of households in income categories (in 2000 dollars) of $35,000 and above—types at or near the median and above it. The rightmost set of bars shows all households earning over $35,000. The other bars show breakdowns for finer income categories. As shown in the rightmost set, households over $35,000 increased steadily from 42 percent in 1967 to 58 percent in 2000. As shown in the other bars, there was an increase in every category except the bottom category of $35,000 to $50,000. That loss was more than offset by movement into higher income classes. In particular, Americans with incomes over $100,000 rose from about 3 percent in 1967 to over 13 percent in 2000. There are now lots of pretty rich households.

Very much the same story emerges if we look at after-tax incomes. Kevin Phillips (2002, 128) presents a chart that shows the inflation-adjusted, annual after-tax income of the two bottom quintiles from 1967 to 1997. The chart also shows the top 5 percent and the top 1 percent. The two bottom quintiles have been basically stable—we do not see pauperization. Inequality has grown because the top groups have reaped all the benefits of per capita economic growth. Similarly, even for the carefully chosen period 1977 (before the bad times of the late 1970s and early 1980s) to 1994 (after the recession of 1991 to 1992 and before most of the boom of the 1990s), Phillips shows family income in the middle quintile declining by only 1 percent.

The growth in median income and the much faster growth in high incomes is not a scenario that generates strong political demands for redistribution. Indeed, it is as if economic policy in the United States was successfully solving a maximization problem: let high incomes grow as much as possible subject to not making the median household worse off.

Changes in wealth holdings also show significant growth for households at the upper end of the distribution. It is true that consumer debt as a fraction of income has risen dramatically (see, for example, Phillips 2002, 134). It is also true that mortgage exposure has risen through an increase in the mortgage debt-to-loan value or debt-to-equity ratio (Bahchieva et al. 2003). But a much rosier picture emerges if we consider asset holdings and net worth, particularly those of the middle class.

The median net worth of households jumped from $56,900 (in 1998 dollars) in 1983 to $71,100 in 1998 (Bertaut and Starr-McCluer 2002, 186). From 1983 to 1995, the

FIGURE 23.6   *Household Income in 2000 Dollars, 1967, 1984, and 2000*

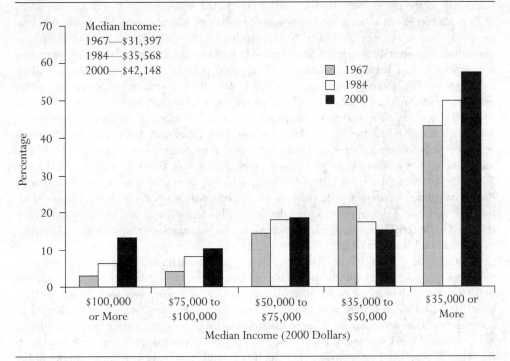

Median Income:
1967—$31,397
1984—$35,568
2000—$42,148

■ 1967
□ 1984
■ 2000

Percentage (y-axis)

Median Income (2000 Dollars) (x-axis): $100,000 or More; $75,000 to $100,000; $50,000 to $75,000; $35,000 to $50,000; $35,000 or More

Source: U.S. Department of Commerce (2000).

fraction of households owning mutual funds, tax-deferred equity, all types of bonds, and other financial assets all increased (Poterba 2002, 110). (There was a slight decline in directly held equity.) Particularly striking is the jump in households with tax-deferred equity, which went from 19.5 percent in 1983 to 30.4 percent in 1995. By 1995 nonhousing (for example, credit card) debt represented less than 10 percent of nonhousing assets for all age groups except those thirty-four and below (Poterba 2002, 115). Thus, many of those who were indebted could anticipate wealth accumulation during their life cycle. By 1998 citizens in the third wealth quartile had nearly half of their total assets in investments other than their primary residence, and their debt, other than mortgage and home equity debt, was less than 6 percent of their assets (Bertaut and Starr-McCluer 2002, 196–97). This quartile is almost certain to contain the pivotal voters.

John Duca and Jason Saving (2002) argue that the increase in equity holdings, brought about by 401(k) plans and lower mutual fund charges, explains the increase in the Republican vote share for the House of Representatives. Americans, far more than the citizens of other industrialized nations (Guiso, Haliassos, and Jappelli 2002), are into stocks. Duca and Saving's results do not control for the end of the one-party system in the South. But not only does later research (John Duca, personal communication, August 19, 2003) confirm this result for the Republican shares broken out by North and South, but part of the increased Republican support in the South can be attributed to the increase in incomes in the South. The Duca and Saving results suggest that voter sentiment against redistribution drives both the increase in inequality associated with postwar Republican administrations (Bartels 2002) and the more frequent election of Republicans since 1968.

The effect of rising incomes in the South illustrates how inequality and politics may be responsive to the unique federal structure of the United States, mentioned at the beginning of this chapter. When income inequality across families or households in the nation was low, inequality across states, particularly North-South, was high. As regional differences have diminished and overall inequality has increased, within-state inequality must be increasing more rapidly than national inequality.[16] Thus, state politics can become polarized along income lines. For instance, for years after World War II Pennsylvania had always had either one very liberal senator (Guffey or Clark) or one very conservative one (Edward Martin). By 1969, however, both of Pennsylvania's seats were in the hands of moderate Republicans, first Hugh Scott and Richard Schweiker and later John Heinz and Arlen Specter. The moderation closely followed the national path for House Republicans shown in figure 23.2. This moderate representation began to unravel when Heinz was killed in a plane accident in 1991. Heinz was replaced by Harris Wofford, a liberal Democrat who was then beaten by Rick Santorum, a conservative Republican. It is likely that when Pennsylvania's other senator, the moderate Arlen Specter, leaves the Senate, his replacement will not be a moderate. (In the 107th Senate, Specter was fifty-third on the liberal-conservative scale while Santorum was tied for eighty-fifth.)

If the rapid increase in within-state inequality finds an echo in Santorum-type conservatism, offsetting advocacy for the poor may be less forthcoming. Reinforcing this expectation, those with low incomes are disproportionately noncitizens, as shown in figure 23.7, which is based on research by Christine Eibner. She used the November 1998 CPS to compute the cumulative family income distribution for voters, nonvoters, and noncitizens. Both citizenship and voting are notorious for being overreported. It is not clear how over-reporting is correlated with income, but the bias is unlikely to overwhelm the import of her results. Median family income in 1998 for the entire sample of 74,631 was near $38,000. For voters, it was much higher, $45,000. Reported income for nonvoters had a lower median of about $34,000. For noncitizens, the median was only about $25,000. The median voting citizen takes in nearly twice as much as the median noncitizen. These results suggest one factor that militates against public policies that would reduce inequality. Those who vote have relatively high incomes. Those who are ineligible to vote have relatively low incomes. Moreover, immigrants, regardless of their citizenship status, are typically substantially better off than in their country of origin. Their advocacy for redistribution may be tempered by this relative evaluation of their economic attainment.

Thus, the political implications of immigration, which militate against redistributive politics, reinforce the economic consequences of immigration. Bean and Bell-Rose (1999, 13) summarize recent research on immigration:

> The most authoritative assessment of immigration's economic consequences has been carried out by the National Research Council. . . . The Council reached two major conclusions: Immigration exerts a positive effect on the U.S. economy overall but only a small adverse impact on the wage and employment opportunities of competing native groups; and immigration benefits high-skilled workers and the owners of capital but not low-skilled workers or those who do not own capital. . . . Recent immigration . . . appears to have exerted negative effects on the economic situation of African Americans. . . . This is perhaps not surprising given that . . . benefits [of immigration] were concentrated among the highly skilled and the owners of capital, both of which groups include disproportionately fewer African Americans than whites.

FIGURE 23.7   *Family Income by Citizenship and Voter Turnout in 1998*

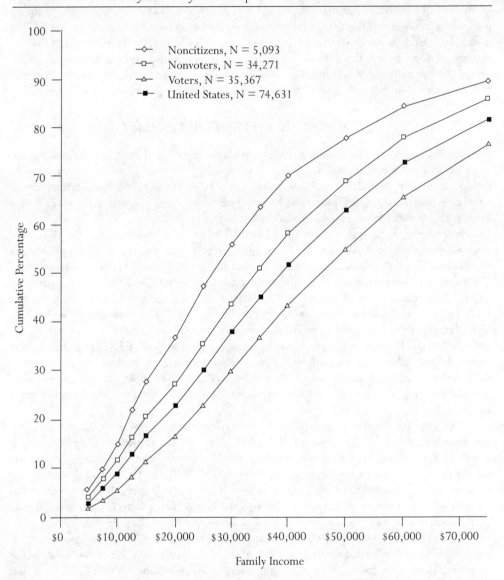

Source: Christine Eibner from November 1998 Current Population Survey. The points plotted correspond to the upper end points of the fourteen income categories used in the survey.

The Bean and Bell-Rose summary stresses small losses at the bottom of the economic hill and big gains at the top. This finding is consistent with the evolution of the overall income distribution that I noted earlier—stability or slight retrogression of real incomes at the bottom and large increases at the top. To the extent that low-skilled immigration has contributed to the increase in inequality, public policy, expressed in the abandonment of discriminatory national quotas and limited attention to illegal immigration, has been a driving force.

The economic effects of immigration summarized by Bean and Bell-Rose do not substantially differ from the summary presented by George Borjas (1999), who draws a strong policy implication from the data: admit more high-skilled immigrants and fewer low-skilled immigrants. Such a proposal would have not only a potential direct economic effect—through raising wages at the bottom—but also an indirect political effect. As current immigrants become naturalized and the flow of new immigrants is reduced, the income distribution of voters would come to more closely resemble the overall income distribution.

PUBLIC POLICIES AFFECTING INEQUALITY

Immigration policy is one policy that in a perhaps unintended way contributed to the worsening of economic inequality. Other policies might be thought of as contributing to income inequality directly. I focus on minimum wages, estate taxes, and income taxes, largely because I can report long time series of these policies. These policies reverse in a manner that parallels the reversals in inequality and in politics.

Federal minimum wages were introduced in 1938. The real value of the minimum wage follows a sawtooth pattern. The sawteeth reflect the fact that the wage is not indexed to inflation. When the current nominal wage is in the gridlock zone, the real wage declines. The Democrats attempted to index minimum wages in the 1960s and 1970s. On September 15, 1977, an amendment sponsored by Phil Burton of California to index the wage for five years failed by the relatively narrow margin of 232 to 191.[17] The vote was strongly along liberal-conservative lines, with moderate Democrats joining Republicans to defeat the amendment. Had Burton succeeded, the minimum wage today might be far higher in real terms. It may have been as difficult to pass deindexation as it is now difficult to pass meaningful increases. Since the wage is not indexed, deflation may help to reduce inequality if minimum wages are, as Lee (1999) argues, an important factor in determining wage inequality.

The sawteeth, however, are only temporary interruptions in an upward trend that persisted until 1968, at the very end of Lyndon Johnson's Great Society. This is shown in figure 23.8. Minimum wages initially failed to cover large categories of workers, largely as a matter of concessions to southern Democrats. Figure 23.8 also shows that coverage was expanded at the same time as the basic minimum wage was increasing. The postwar period was indeed one of generous increases. Although the largest increase occurred in the Truman years, there was a real increase even under Eisenhower, a Republican president.

The big change occurred when Richard Nixon took office. Even though there was some post-Watergate increase, minimum wages did not recover even half of the losses in the first six Nixon years. Increases in minimum wages were voted under President Carter, but they were quickly eroded by the high inflation at the end of his four years. In Carter's last year in office, 1980, real minimum wages were actually less than in Ford's last year, 1976. The Reagan years saw much further erosion of the minimum wage. The "kinder, gentler" increase accepted by George H. W. Bush restored very little of the losses. Bill Clinton was then barely able to better the Bush restoration.

Politically, the reversal in the minimum wage chart is consistent with an end to Democratic dominance in American politics that, as noted previously, can probably be dated from the Nixon election in 1968. But it is also possible that preferences on minimum wages have changed for individual legislators. Poole and Rosenthal (1991) did an admittedly crude calculation of preference shifts by comparing the votes of senators who had voted on minimum wages in both 1977 and 1989. They found that the real wage these senators would

FIGURE 23.8   *Real Minimum Wages 1910 to 2000*

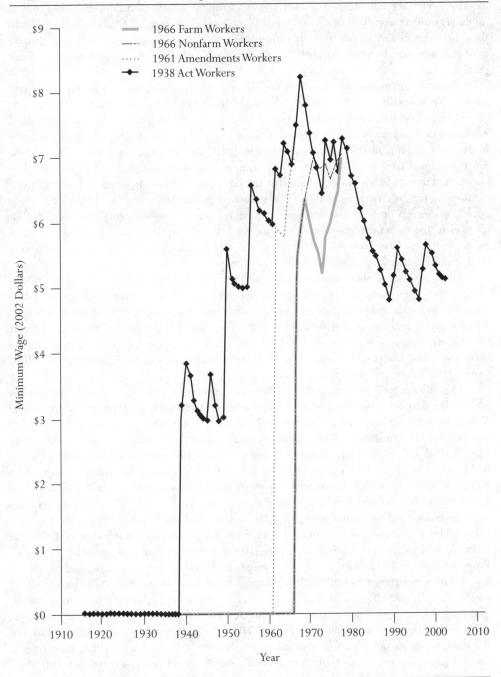

Source: U.S. Department of Labor Employment Standards Administration, Wage and Hour Division, "Federal Minimum Wage Rates Under the Fair Labor Standards Act," available at: www.dol.gov/esa/minwage/chart.pdf. Deflator: CPI-U.

support had fallen by 15 to 20 percent from 1977 to 1989. The decline in their support might reflect the academic debate over the employment effects of minimum wages, but it might also reflect a shift in the preferences of increasingly better-off citizens. Both a shift in these preferences and an overall shift to Republicans would be consistent with an electorate that was increasingly tilted toward the well-to-do by declines in turnout and by immigration.

The real minimum wage today is no higher than it was in the 1950s. But since real wages have generally risen, this wage is less and less a binding constraint on employers. It should be noted that nine states currently have higher minimum wages than the federal minimum of $5.15 an hour. The highest of these wages, $7.15 in Alaska, is still substantially below the real value of the federal minimum in 1968. The minimum wage in California, the most populous state, is $6.75.[18] Lee (1999) exploits the cross-sectional variation induced by state minimum wage laws to conclude that the fall in real minimum wages in the 1980s was a major source of wage inequality. The reduction in inequality in the 1950s and 1960s could, conversely, reflect the increase in real minimum wages during this period. But changes in the minimum wage obviously cannot account for all of the long-term trends in inequality: there was no minimum wage in the United States before 1938, yet, as figures 23.1 and 23.4 indicate, inequality fell during this period.

Thus, we should also consider taxation. The story is clearest for the estate tax. It is difficult to reduce complex tax codes to single numbers. I focus on two series for the estate tax. The first is the maximum estate tax rate—how much the super-rich would have to pay without giving away or sheltering their wealth. The second is the maximum estate without tax liability, that is, the minimum taxable estate. Both series are shown in figure 23.9. To make the series comparable with each other and with the various inequality graphs, I have graphed 1.0 minus the maximum tax rate.

The influence of partisan politics is even clearer for estate taxes than for minimum wages. The first taxes were introduced under unified Democratic government during World War I. More estates were subject to tax until a unified Republican government in 1926 both lowered the tax and increased the minimum estate subject to tax from around $500,000 to $1,000,000 (in 2002 dollars). Taxes were increased and the minimum was decreased when the Democrats took control of the House in the 1930 elections. Taxation of the wealthy increased in the Roosevelt years until the maximum estate tax rate reached 77 percent in 1940. Rates then remained unchanged for thirty-seven years until 1977. During this time inflation eroded the minimum until, by 1976, estates under $250,000 were subject to tax. (The failure to increase the minimum for so many years resembles the failure of California to adjust real estate taxes during the real estate price boom that preceded the passage of Proposition 13 in 1978. That failure broadened the base for an antitax movement.)

Estate taxes then reversed with legislation in 1976 (effective for 1977) passed under the Ford presidency. The reduction in rates and the increase in the minimum were minor. The phased-in minimum adjustments failed to outstrip inflation in the Carter years. Reagan did substantially lower taxes on large estates. His bill, which would have eventually lowered the top rate to 50 percent, was aborted when the Tax Reform Act of 1986, enacted in a time of large deficits, temporarily increased the rate from 55 percent to 60 percent. Clinton's legislation in 1993 made 55 percent, not 50 percent, permanent. Moreover, the minimum again decreased as a result of inflation. The minimum was stabilized, but not substantially increased, after the Republicans took control of Congress in the 1994 elections. Finally, a unified Republican government made drastic changes in 2001.

The picture just given—of gradual change from Ford through Reagan followed by a

FIGURE 23.9   *Estate Tax, 1916 to 2010*

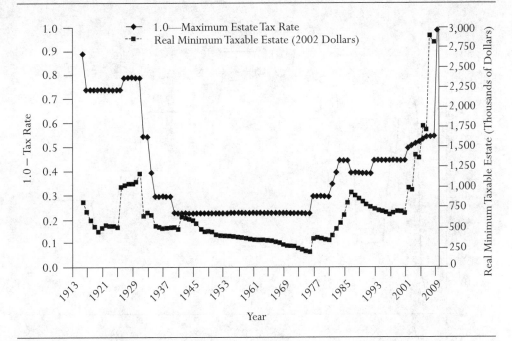

Source: Miller, Monson, Peshel, Polacek and Hoshaw (2002). Deflator: CPI-U.

"big bang" with Bush 43—is misleading to some degree. A generous exclusion of about $1,000,000 (in 1998 dollars) for a closely held business was introduced in 1977.[19] In 1986 the marital deduction was increased from 50 percent to 100 percent (see Carroll 2002, 393). "Family limited partnerships" for limiting estate taxes began to be mass-marketed, apparently in the late 1980s.[20] In other words, when we consider features of the tax other than maximum rates and minimum taxable estates, the changes in the 1970s and 1980s were more substantial.

A somewhat different story pertains to top minimum federal income tax rates, shown in figure 23.10. Marginal tax rates were increasing in the period of decreasing inequality. The Kennedy tax cuts, however, led to a decrease in marginal tax rates before the turnaround in inequality. As inequality has grown, however, top marginal tax rates have continued to fall.

Edward Wolff (2002b, 28) provides marginal rates on incomes of $135,000, $67,000, and $33,000 from 1947 to 2000 (in constant 2000 dollars). The story here is more in accord with the pattern I found for estate taxes. These marginal rates were fairly steady throughout the period of declining inequality after World War II. In 1980 the marginal rates on $135,000, $67,000, and $33,000 were 59 percent, 49 percent, and 28 percent, respectively, consistent with strong progressivity in taxation. By 1991 the three marginal rates were nearly equal—31 percent, 28 percent, and 28 percent, respectively.

The picture of income taxes drawn from marginal rates is echoed by the effective rate on the top 1 percent by income. The effective rate adjusts for shelters and other gimmicks used to reduce taxes. Christopher Carroll (2002, 393) presents data for various years from 1963 to 1995. The effective rates on the rich moved upward from 24.6 percent in 1963 to

FIGURE 23.10   *Top Marginal Tax Rates, Federal Income Tax, 1916 to 2003*

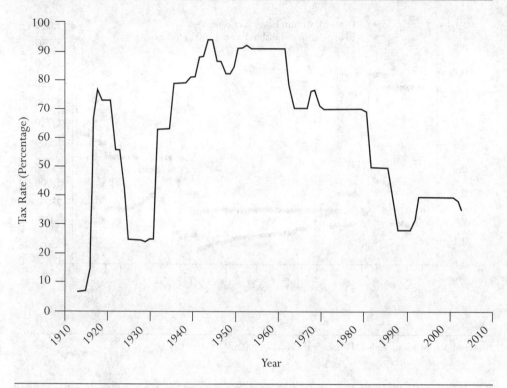

Source: 1916 to 1969, various sources. 1970 to 2003, Urban-Brookings Tax Policy Center, available at: www.taxpolicycenter.org.

27.8 percent in 1977 and then declined to 19.2 percent in 1985. Pressures to reduce the deficit thereafter led to an upward trend, but by 1995, after the Clinton bill of 1993, the effective rate had reached only 23.8 percent, still slightly below the 23.9 percent during 1980, Carter's last year in office. Kevin Phillips (2002, 96) presents effective rates for those earning more than $1 million from 1948 to 1970. These peaked in the period 1955 to 1960 at 85.5 percent and then declined to 66.9 percent in 1965. Phillips also shows rates with FICA tax included for 1977 onward. These declined during the Carter years, from 35.5 percent in 1977 to 31.7 percent in 1980. Under Reagan the rate dropped further, to 24.9 percent in 1985 before rebounding to 26.9 percent in 1988.

In summary, the three public policies of minimum wages, estate taxes, and income taxes are all characterized by the following:

- Consistent with the trend in inequality in the twentieth century, redistributive policies are first strengthened and then relaxed.

- The dates of a move away from redistribution are somewhat different—early 1960s for marginal tax rates, late 1960s for minimum wages, and mid-1970s for estate taxes and effective tax rates on the rich. Importantly, however, all of these shifts, like the tax revolts at the state level, preceded the election of Ronald Reagan. One might say that,

FIGURE 23.11   *Social Security Benefits and Taxes, 1930 to 2010*

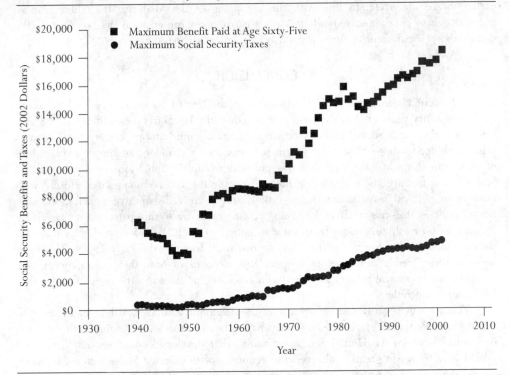

Source: Social Security Administration (2002, table 2.A3, 83, and table 2.A28, 116). Deflator: CPI-U.

by analogy to Andrew Jackson riding a wave of democratization to the presidency, Reagan rode a wave of antigovernment sentiment.

Social security, an extremely important public expenditure, has not suffered the same fate as minimum wages for the poor or taxes on the rich. The data are presented in figure 23.11. Social security is financed by a tax that, unlike the estate tax and the income tax, is openly regressive. Earnings above the cap are untaxed. Moreover, the tax is just a payroll tax; income from capital is untaxed. This tax, however, has grown. In an antitax era, Congress has supported, as evidenced in the figure, an increase in the maximum real amount that a wage earner can pay into the system. This has been accomplished by raising both the tax rate and the cap. At the same time, notwithstanding the perpetual "crisis" in social security, the maximum real amount that a worker gets out of social security has risen dramatically. Social security is formally called old-age insurance and was sold to the public, somewhat misleadingly, in that guise. Although the payments are mildly redistributive to lower-wage earners, it is largely a middle-class program that is not supported by taxes on high incomes or capital.

So far, in distinction to high taxes on the rich, social security taxes are being maintained. Similarly, Medicare has grown as inequality has grown. The cap on Medicare taxes, originally the same earnings level as social security taxes, was raised in 1991; Medicare taxes became totally uncapped in 1994. Because of the great variance in health care outcomes, health care consumption is far riskier than the rest of old-age consumption. Again, we see demand for a government program that offers broad insurance in old age as against earlier in the life cycle. In line with the uncapping of the Medicare tax, there is now political debate only about extending Medicare (to cover prescription drugs) whereas the debate about social security turns around retrenchment or privatization.

CONCLUSION

Although economic inequality fell about equally in the United States, France, and Britain in the first seventy years of the twentieth century, over the last thirty years the United States has followed an exceptional path, with inequality rising much more sharply there than in other developed nations. These long-term patterns pose a challenge to simple explanations of American inequality and motivate this political and institutional inquiry. In the United States I find that trends in economic inequality over the last century match closely with changes in political polarization, immigration, and many redistributive policies. Of economic policies that might affect inequality, estate taxes track this pattern for the entire century, as do minimum wages from their inception in 1938. Following a slightly different pattern, income taxes on the rich started a downward trend in the early 1960s. This essay lays out these trends and develops a speculative account of how they relate, noting the complex and reciprocal relationships between economic policies and the constituencies they both create and reflect.

This account is grounded historically in the economic and political history of the century. Although the Great Depression may have played a role, the origin of the striking differences between the United States and most other developed countries may have been World War II, which greatly enhanced the economy of the United States but led to widespread destruction elsewhere. The base present at the end of the war created the opportunity for growth to create a large class of well-to-do and left this class, unlike its counterpart in Europe, without much support for redistribution or social insurance. The "free market" orientation of a large segment of the population may have been buttressed by the spread of equity ownership in the last two decades of the century.

In addition, the current increase in conservatism and polarization follows the push by the Democrats in the 1960s to allow increased immigration and to end discrimination against African Americans. This led to the realignment of the South into a two-party system favorable to the Republicans. Furthermore, immigration has caused the income distribution of citizens to diverge from the income distribution of all households. The political changes have been substantial. Democratic control of the presidency and Congress was pervasive from 1932 to 1968 but sharply broken thereafter. One result has been major policy shifts in minimum wages, income taxes, and estate taxes.

This essay provides a sobering view of the prospects for change in current economic policies and thus in economic inequality itself. On the one hand, the widening economic disparity between the rich and the rest of the population could generate a movement for redistribution. On the other hand, the nature of American political institutions, now compounded by increasing polarization, makes economic policy difficult to change. As long as prosperity continues for voters in the middle to upper segments of the income distribution, we are unlikely to see a major shift in favor of sharply redistributive policies.

I thank Frank Bean, John Duca, Christine Eibner, Hank Farber, Keith Poole, Jim Poterba, Jean-Laurent Rosenthal, Andrea Vindigni, and seminar participants at Brown and Russell Sage for several insights. I thank Herman K. van Dijk and Rene Segers for pointing me to a data source. The editor of this volume, Kathy Neckerman, made particularly valuable contributions. Much of the work was carried out while I was a visiting scholar at Russell Sage and a fellow of the John Simon Guggenheim Memorial Foundation.

NOTES

1. Reagan quoted at www.cnn.com/ALLPOLITICS/1996/debates/history/1980/index.shtml. A video clip of Reagan making the statement is at www.cnn.com/ALLPOLITICS/1996/debates/history/1980/reagan. carter.debate.mov.

2. On the other hand, incarceration does not relate to inequality in any simple way. Incarceration rates showed relatively little variation during the fall of inequality in the first three-quarters of the twentieth century. Consider the rates in three years of relative prosperity, 1929, 1949, and 1969. The rates per 100,000 for these years were 98, 109, and 97, respectively; see *Sourcebook of Criminal Justice Statistics*, which can be downloaded at www.albany.edu/sourcebook/1995/wk1/t623.wk1, table 6.23. I thank Bruce Western for pointing me to this source.

3. See Poole and Rosenthal (1997) for a more detailed discussion of the dimensionality of congressional politics.

4. Rankings taken from "107th Senate Rank Ordering," available at: voteview.uh.edu/SEN107.htm.

5. Vote results taken from "Final Vote Results for Roll Call 398," Thomas website of Congress, available at: clerk.house.gov/cgi-bin/vote.exe?year = 2001&rollnumber = 398.

6. The expression is found in countless sources, such as Calmes (1985).

7. For a detailed study of how divided government deflected policy change in the Reagan era by preserving Conrail as an independent company, see Baldwin and Bhattacharyya (1991).

8. Rankings taken from "107th Senate Rank Ordering," available at: voteview.uh.edu/SEN107.htm.

9. The theory of how policy formation in one dimension is affected by the status quo was developed by Thomas Romer and Howard Rosenthal (1978, 1979), extended to Congress by Arthur Denzau and Robert Mackay (1983), and embedded in the theory of pivotal politics by Keith Krehbiel (1998). David Brady and Craig Volden (1998) illustrate how the theory applies to gridlock.

10. There is probably no single factor that can explain the fall of inequality from 1913 through the 1960s. The fall, for example, of the income share of the rich (figure 23.1) from 1913 to 1933 would seem to be greater than that which would be produced by the very limited federal income and estate taxation of the period (figures 23.9 and 23.10). Similarly, there was no dramatic increase in inequality following the Kennedy tax cuts of the 1960s. A federal policy of importance for wage inequality in recent years, the minimum wage, did not exist before 1938. The limited impact of federal fiscal and wage policies prior to the New Deal suggests important roles for immigration and technology.

11. The changing position of southern Democrats can be seen graphically in animations shown at voteview. uh.edu/default_nomdata.htm.

12. Jordan Ellenberg (2001) has presented a very accessible introduction to the method on *Slate*. A more extensive nontechnical discussion is Poole and Rosenthal (1997, ch. 2).

13. Recent work by Lewis and Poole (2003) shows that the standard error of the overall median is on the order of 0.04 for the Senate. The standard error for the House would be even smaller. Consequently, a move like that following the 1994 elections would be statistically significant at a very high level.

14. These distances are based on the two-dimensional DW-NOMINATE scaling (McCarty, Poole, and Rosenthal 1997). They thus avoid, unlike the difference in medians, any possibility that the changes in polarization are due simply to the rise and fall of the race issue.

15. Posted at voteview.uh.edu/default_recpol.htm.

16. Paul DiMaggio drew this point to my attention.

17.   Information found in the Voteview database available at voteview.uh.edu.
18.   Minimum wage data from U.S. Department of Labor, Employment Standards Administration, Wage and Hour Division, published May 13, 2003, at www.dol.gov/esa/minwage/america.htm.
19.   On the other hand, the generation skipping tax was introduced, something that made estate tax more onerous for very rich families.
20.   The late 1980s is indicated by www.falc.com/flp/flp.htm.

REFERENCES

Acemoglu, Daron, and James Robinson. 2001. "A Theory of Political Transitions." *American Economic Review* 91(September): 938–63.

Alesina, Alberto, Reza Baqir, and William Easterly. 1999. "Public Goods and Ethnic Divisions." *Quarterly Journal of Economics* 114(November): 1243–84.

Alesina, Alberto, Edward Glaeser, and Bruce Sacerdote, 2001. "Why Doesn't the U.S. Have a European Style Welfare State?" *Brookings Papers on Economic Activity* (Fall): 187–278.

Alesina, Alberto, and Eliana La Ferrara. 2002. "Who Trusts Others?" *Journal of Public Economics* 85(2, August): 207–34.

———. 2000. "Participation in Heterogeneous Communities." *Quarterly Journal of Economics* 115(3, August): 847–904.

Atkinson, Anthony. 1997. "Bringing Income Distribution in from the Cold." *Economic Journal* 107(441, March): 297–321.

Austen-Smith, David, and Michael Wallerstein. 2003. "Redistribution in a Divided Society." Unpublished paper. Northwestern University, Evanston, Ill.

Bahchieva, Raisa, Michael N. Schill, Susan M. Wachter, and Elizabeth Warren. 2003. "Mortgage Debt, Bankruptcy, and the Sustainability of Homeownership." Paper presented to the Princeton conference on Credit Markets for the Poor. Princeton, N.J. (May 2–3).

Baldwin, Corwin, and Sugato Bhattacharyya. 1991. "Choosing the Method of Sale: A Clinical Study of Conrail." *Journal of Financial Economics* 30(1, November): 69–98.

Bartels, Larry M. 2002. "Partisan Politics and the U.S. Income Distribution, 1948–2000." Working paper. Princeton, N.J.: Princeton University.

Bean, Frank D., and Stephanie Bell-Rose. 1999. "Introduction." In *Immigration and Opportunity: Race, Ethnicity, and Employment in the United States*, edited by Frank D. Bean and Stephanie Bell-Rose. New York: Russell Sage Foundation.

Bean, Frank D., and Gillian Stevens. 2003. *America's Newcomers and the Dynamics of Diversity*. New York: Russell Sage Foundation.

Bell, Daniel. 1960. *The End of Ideology: On the Exhaustion of Political Ideas in the Fifties*. Cambridge, Mass.: Harvard University Press.

Benabou, Roland. 2000. "Unequal Societies: Income Distribution and the Social Contract." *American Economic Review* 90(1, March): 96–129.

Benabou, Roland, and Efe Ok. 2001. "Social Mobility and the Demand for Redistribution: The POUM Hypothesis." *Quarterly Journal of Economics* 116(2, May): 447–87.

Bertaut, Carol C., and Martha Starr-McCluer. 2002. "Household Portfolios in the United States." In *Household Portfolios*, edited by Luigi Guiso, Michael Haliassos, and Tullio Jappelli. Cambridge, Mass.: MIT Press.

Bolton, Patrick, and Gerard Roland. 1997. "The Breakup of Nations." *Quarterly Journal of Economics* 112(4, November): 1057–90.

Borjas, George J. 1999. *Heaven's Door: Immigration Policy and the American Economy*. Princeton, N.J.: Princeton University Press.

Brady, David W., and Craig Volden. 1998. *Revolving Gridlock Politics and Policy from Carter to Clinton*. Boulder, Colo.: Westview Press.

Brownlee, W. Elliot. 1996. *Federal Taxation in America: A Short History*. New York: Cambridge University Press.

Calmes, Jacqueline. 1985. "Special Report: Congress and OMB Controlling the Budget Process: Stockman Left as His Legacy Enhanced OMB Involvement." *Congressional Quarterly Weekly Report*, September 14, 1809.

Carroll, Christopher D. 2002. "Portfolios of the Rich." In *Household Portfolios*, edited by Luigi Guiso, Michael Haliassos, and Tullio Jappelli. Cambridge, Mass.: MIT Press.

Collins, William J. 1997. "When the Tide Turned: Immigration and the Delay of the Great Black Migration." *Journal of Economic History* 57(3, September): 607–32.

Dahl, Robert A. 1961. *Who Governs: Democracy and Power in an American City*. New Haven, Conn.: Yale University Press.

Denzau, Arthur, and Robert Mackay. 1983. "Gatekeeping and Monopoly Power of Committees: An Analysis of Sincere and Sophisticated Behavior." *American Journal of Political Science* 27(4, November): 740–61.

Downs, Anthony. 1957. *An Economic Theory of Democracy*. New York: Harper & Row.

Duca, John V., and Jason L. Saving. 2002. "The Political Economy of the Mutual Fund Revolution: How Rising Stock Ownership Rates Affect Congressional Elections." Working paper. Dallas, Tex.: Federal Reserve Bank, Research Department.

Ellenberg, Jordan. 2001. "Growing Apart: The Mathematical Evidence for Congress' Growing Polarization." *Slate*, posted December 26, 2001. Available at: http://slate.msn.com/id/2060047/.

Fiorina, Morris. 1978. *Congress: Keystone of the Washington Establishment*. New Haven, Conn.: Yale University Press.

Foley, Duncan K. 1967. "Resource Allocation and the Public Sector." *Yale Economic Essays* 7: 45–98.

Gerring, John. 1998. *Party Ideologies in America, 1828–1996*. New York: Cambridge University Press.

Gilens, Martin. 1999. *Why Americans Hate Welfare: Race, Media, and the Politics of Antipoverty Policy*. Chicago: University of Chicago Press.

Goldin, Claudia. 1994. "The Political Economy of Immigration Restriction: The United States, 1890–1921." In *The Regulated Economy: A Historical Approach to Political Economy*, edited by Claudia Goldin and Gary Libecap. Chicago: University of Chicago Press.

Guiso, Luigi, Michael Haliassos, and Tullio Jappelli. 2002. *Household Portfolios*. Cambridge, Mass.: MIT Press.

Krehbiel, Keith. 1998. *Pivotal Politics: A Theory of U.S. Lawmaking*. Chicago: University of Chicago Press.

Kopczuk, Wojciech, and Emmanuel Saez. 2003. "Top Wealth Shares in the United States, 1916–2000: Evidence from Estate Tax Returns." Unpublished paper. Berkeley: University of California.

Krugman, Paul. 2002a. "America the Polarized." *New York Times*, January 4.

———. 2002b. "Far Richer." *New York Times Magazine*, October 20.

Kuznets, Simon. 1955. "Economic Growth and Economic Inequality." *American Economic Review* 45: 1–28.

Lee, David S. 1999. "Wage Inequality in the United States During the 1980s: Rising Dispersion or Falling Minimum Wage?" *Quarterly Journal of Economics* 114(3, August): 977–1023.

Levy, Frank. 1998. *The New Dollars and Dreams: American Incomes and Economic Change*. New York: Russell Sage Foundation.

Lewis, Jeffrey B., and Keith T. Poole. 2003. "Measuring Bias and Uncertainty in Ideal Point Estimates Via the Parametric Bootstrap." Working paper. Los Angeles: University of California, *Political Analysis*, forthcoming.

Lipset, Seymour Martin. 1996. *American Exceptionalism: A Double-Edged Sword*. New York: W. W. Norton.

Maddison, Angus. 1995. *Monitoring the World Economy: 1820–1992*. Paris: Development Center of the Organization for Economic Cooperation and Development.

Mayhew, David R. 1991. *Divided We Govern: Party Control, Lawmaking, and Investigations, 1946–1990*. New Haven, Conn.: Yale University Press.

McCarty, Nolan, Keith T. Poole, and Howard Rosenthal. 1997. *Income Distribution and the Realignment of American Politics*. Washington, D.C.: American Enterprise Institute.

———. 2002. "Political Polarization and Income Inequality." Working paper. New York: Russell Sage Foundation.

McDonald, Michael P., and Samuel L. Popkin. 2001. "The Myth of the Vanishing Voter." *American Political Science Review* 95(4, December): 963–74.

Meltzer, Allan H., and Scott F. Richard. 1981. "A Rational Theory of the Size of Government." *Journal of Political Economy* 89(5): 914–27.

Miller, Monson, Peshel, Polacek & Hoshaw (San Diego, Calif.). 2002. "Abbreviated Legislative History of U.S. Transfer Taxes." Available at: www.estate-plan.com/pdf/Art_History_Tax.pdf.

Myrdal, Gunnar. 1960. *Beyond the Welfare State: Economic Planning and Its International Implications*. New Haven, Conn.: Yale University Press.

Phillips, Kevin. 2002. *Wealth and Democracy: A Political History of the American Rich*. New York: Broadway Books.

Piketty, Thomas. 2001. "Income Inequality in France, 1901–1998." CEPR discussion paper 2876.

Piketty, Thomas, and Emmanuel Saez. 2003. "Income Inequality in the United States, 1913–1998." *Quarterly Journal of Economics* 118(1, February): 1–39.

Poole, Keith T., and Howard Rosenthal. 1984. "The Polarization of American Politics." *Journal of Politics* 46(4, November): 1061–79.

———. 1991. "The Spatial Mapping of Minimum Wage Legislation." In *Politics and Economics in the 1980s*, edited by Alberto Alesina and Geoffrey Carliner. Chicago: University of Chicago Press.

———. 1993. "The Enduring Nineteenth-Century Battle for Economic Regulation: The Interstate Commerce Act Revisited." *Journal of Law and Economics* 36(2, October): 837–60.

———. 1997. *Congress: A Political-Economic History of Roll Call Voting*. New York: Oxford University Press.

Poterba, James. 2002. "Taxation and Portfolio Structure: Issues and Implications." In *Household Portfolios*, edited by Luigi Guiso, Michael Haliassos, and Tullio Jappelli. Cambridge, Mass.: MIT Press.

Quadagno, Jill S. 1994. *The Color of Welfare: How Racism Undermined the War on Poverty*. Oxford: Oxford University Press.

Rajan, Raghuram G., and Luigi Zingales. 2003a. "The Great Reversals: The Politics of Financial Development in the Twentieth Century." *Journal of Financial Economics* 69(1, July): 5–50.

———. 2003b. *Saving Capitalism from the Capitalists: Unleashing the Power of Financial Markets to Create Wealth and Spread Opportunity*. New York: Crown Business.

Roberts, Kevin W. S. 1977. "Voting over Income Tax Schedules." *Journal of Public Economics* 8(3, August): 329–40.

Romer, Thomas. 1975. "Individual Welfare, Majority Voting, and the Properties of a Linear Income Tax." *Journal of Public Economics* 4(2, February): 163–85.

———. 1977. "Majority Voting on Tax Parameters: Some Further Results." *Journal of Public Economics* 7(1, February): 127–33.

Romer, Thomas, and Howard Rosenthal. 1978. "Political Resource Allocation, Controlled Agendas, and the Status Quo." *Public Choice* 33(4, November): 27–43.

———. 1979. "Bureaucrats Vs. Voters." *Quarterly Journal of Economics* 93(4): 563–87.

Schickler, Eric. 2000. "Institutional Change in the House of Representatives, 1867–1998: A Test of Partisan and Ideological Power Balance Models." *American Political Science Review* 94(2, June): 269–88.

Social Security Administration. 2002. *Social Security Bulletin: Annual Statistical Supplement*. Available at: www.ssa.gov/policy/docs/statcomps/supplement/2002/supp02.pdf.

Sombart, Werner. 2001. *Economic Life in the Modern Age*, edited by Nico Stehr and Reiner Grundmann. New Brunswick, N.J.: Transaction Publishers.

Ticchi, Davide, and Andrea Vindigni. 2003. "On Wars and Political Development: The Role of International Conflicts in the Democratization of the West." Unpublished paper. Stockholm University.

U.S. Department of Commerce. U.S. Census Bureau. 2000. "Money Income in the United States, 2000: Table A-1." Washington: U.S. Government Printing Office.

———. 2002. "Table F-4: Gini Ratios for Families, by Race and Hispanic Origin of Householder: 1947 to 2001 (families as of March of the following year)." Published September 30. Available at: 148.129.75.3/hhes/income/histinc/f04.html.

Weingast, Barry R., Kenneth A. Shepsle, and Christopher Johnsen. 1981. "The Political Economy of Benefits and Costs: A Neoclassical Approach to Distributive Politics." *Journal of Political Economy* 89(4, August): 642–64.

Wolff, Edward N. 2002a. *Top Heavy: The Increasing Inequality of Wealth in America and What Can Be Done About It*. New York: New Press.

———. 2002b. "Recent Trends in Living Standards in the United States." Unpublished paper. New York University.

Part VII

Inequality in Wealth

Chapter 24

U.S. Black-White Wealth Inequality

John Karl Scholz and Kara Levine

The distribution of wealth in the United States is highly skewed. In 1998 the top 1 percent of families held 34 percent of the wealth, and the top 10 percent of families held 68.7 percent of the wealth (Kennickell 2000). Wealth is distributed far more unevenly than income. The Census Bureau estimates that in 1998 households in the top 5 percent of the income distribution received 21.4 percent of annual income. Households in the top 20 percent of the income distribution received 49.2 percent of annual income (U.S. Department of Commerce, various years).

Wealth can affect economic well-being in a number of ways. It can be used for immediate consumption. It may allow families to better educate their children, live in safe neighborhoods, keep up their living standard during hard times, and maintain adequate consumption levels during retirement. High levels of wealth can facilitate access to the political process and other civic institutions. Extreme wealth disparities may result in differences across families in each of these aspects of economic well-being or opportunity.

Wealth inequality among households with young children may lead to unequal opportunities for those children. Educational attainment, labor force participation, welfare receipt, and early or out-of-wedlock childbearing have been linked to childhood factors such as neighborhood quality (Haveman and Wolfe 1994; McLanahan and Sandefur 1994). Wealth enables parents to provide better environments for their children, so wealth disparities may contribute to differences in children's economic success.

Differences in wealth holdings for households nearing retirement may also affect economic well-being. Without adequate savings, households may face large drops in consumption upon retirement or find their choices regarding living arrangements or medical care restricted.[1] Furthermore, wealth inequality at older ages implies that estate sizes may be unequal, perhaps contributing to wealth inequality in the next generation.

Determining how aggregate U.S. wealth inequality has evolved over time is not a simple task, owing largely to data limitations. Because wealth is so highly concentrated in the United States, surveys that do not have a significant oversampling of very high-income (or high-wealth) households will not provide accurate information on the distribution of wealth. This concern effectively rules out commonly used datasets such as the Panel Study of Income Dynamics (PSID) and the National Longitudinal Surveys (NLS).[2] Probate data have been used in several innovative studies of bequests (see, for example, Menchik and David 1983; Wilhelm 1996), but since only very wealthy families are subject to estate taxes,

TABLE 24.1   *Total Net Worth Held by Different Percentile Groups, 1989, 1992, 1995, and 1998 Surveys of Consumer Finances*

Survey Year	0 to 89.9 Percentile	90 to 99 Percentile	99 to 99.5 Percentile	99.5 to 100 Percentile
1989	32.7	37.1	7.3	22.9
	(3.1)	(3.5)	(1.2)	(2.8)
1992	33.0	36.9	7.5	22.6
	(1.7)	(1.9)	(0.5)	(1.4)
1995	32.2	33.1	7.6	27.1
	(1.8)	(1.4)	(0.7)	(2.0)
1998	31.3	34.7	8.2	25.8
	(1.7)	(1.7)	(0.5)	(1.8)

Source: Kennickell (2000, table 5).
Note: Standard errors due to imputation and sampling are given in parentheses.

strong assumptions need to be made when using estate tax data to make inferences about the evolution of wealth inequality.

One U.S. dataset is designed expressly to collect extensive, accurate information on wealth and its distribution. The Board of Governors of the Federal Reserve System, with other collaborators, has conducted Surveys of Consumer Finances (SCFs) every three years since 1983. The SCFs include a significant oversample of high-income taxpayers and hence have a more complete representation of the portfolios of very affluent people in the United States than do other data sources. Owing to differences in the SCFs prior to 1989, we will focus on developments between 1989 and 1998.[3]

Arthur Kennickell (2000) finds no statistically significant changes between 1989 and 1998 in the Gini coefficient, an index of inequality, for net worth across years.[4] As shown in table 24.1, the share of wealth held by households in the top 10 percent of the wealth distribution also remained very stable at around 68 percent. Changes across years within the top 10 percent are also not statistically significant.

These results differ from those presented by Edward Wolff (2000), who argues that wealth disparities continued to widen from 1989 to 1998. We have somewhat more confidence in Kennickell's conclusions than Wolff's, for the following reasons. Discrepancies in aggregate asset and liability totals in the Surveys of Consumer Finances and the Flow of Funds (FoF) accounts motivate Wolff to proportionally adjust SCF items to match FoF totals.[5] In some cases the adjustments are significant.[6] Rochelle Antoniewicz (1996) provides reasons why Wolff's adjustments may not be appropriate and suggests that the SCFs and FoFs, once adjusted to account for differences in definitions and coverage, are strikingly close.[7] Wolff's calculations also do not account fully for imputation and sampling variation.[8] As the standard errors in table 24.1 show, it is difficult to make strong statements about the evolution of wealth inequality over time. More work on the evolution of wealth in the 1980s and 1990s would clearly be worthwhile.

Several papers piece together wealth information covering longer time periods. John Karl Scholz and David Joulfaian (2003) report that between 1962 and 2001 the ratio of net worth between the ninety-fifth and fiftieth percentiles of the net worth distribution increased to 15.3 from 9.8. The ratio of net worth between the ninety-ninth and fiftieth percentiles of the net worth distribution increased to 68.8 from 35.8. Wolff (1998) reports

FIGURE 24.1   *Mean and Median Net Worth of White, Black, and Hispanic Households,*
by Age

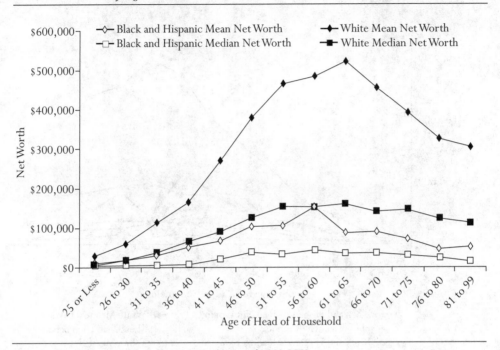

Source: Authors' calculations from 1989, 1992, 1995, and 1998 SCFS.

that in the 1970s wealth inequality in the United States was comparable to that of other developed countries, but by the 1980s the United States had become one of the most unequal economies in this group. James Smith (1999b) shows that wealth became significantly more unequal between 1984 and 1994 in the PSID.

Although there are many possible explanations for long-run trends in wealth inequality, there is no single dominant cause. Most of the academic literature on wealth inequality focuses on the large gaps between wealth levels held by black and white families. There are at least two reasons for this emphasis. To the extent that we care about racial aspects of economic inequality, wealth differences between blacks and whites are intrinsically interesting. More broadly, developing a better understanding of factors leading to the black-white wealth gap should enhance understanding of the factors driving wealth inequality more generally.

The facts about black-white wealth inequality that researchers have sought to explain are striking. Figure 24.1 shows mean and median net worth for different age groups for white households and for black and Hispanic households.[9] Wide net worth disparities are apparent at every age. At age fifty-one to fifty-five, for example, the mean (median) net worth of white households is $467,747 ($156,550), while for black and Hispanic households it is $105,675 ($33,170).

A natural explanation for the wealth disparities shown in figure 24.1 is that white families have higher incomes than black and Hispanic families, which leads to greater accumulations of net worth. However, even after splitting the sample by educational attainment, which is a common proxy for permanent income, figure 24.2 (for means) and figure 24.3

FIGURE 24.2   *Mean Net Worth of White, Black, and Hispanic Households, by Age and Education*

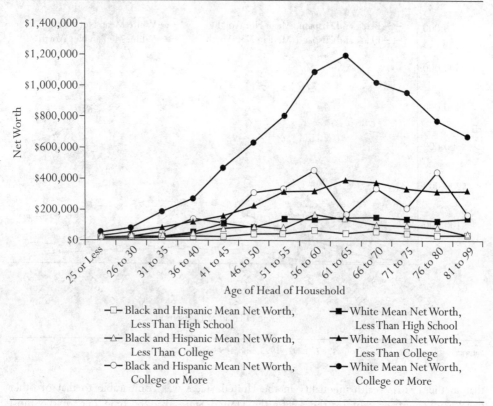

Age of Head of Household

—□— Black and Hispanic Mean Net Worth,   —■— White Mean Net Worth,
      Less Than High School   Less Than High School
—△— Black and Hispanic Mean Net Worth,   —▲— White Mean Net Worth,
      Less Than College   Less Than College
—○— Black and Hispanic Mean Net Worth,   —●— White Mean Net Worth,
      College or More   College or More

Source: Authors' calculations from the 1989, 1992, 1995, and 1998 SCFS.

(for medians) show that large wealth disparities remain when groups are defined by race or ethnicity. The net worth of black and Hispanic *college* graduates is similar to the net worth of white *high school* graduates, and the net worth of black and Hispanic high school graduates is similar to the net worth of white high school dropouts. The observed wealth differences are large and persistent across age groups and cannot be accounted for solely by differences in educational attainment across the groups.

Many researchers have examined the factors contributing to these wealth disparities. Our objective in this survey is to provide a critical review of this literature, sorting out what we know and what we still need to know about black-white wealth inequality. We use a simple life-cycle model to organize our review and to highlight a variety of factors that may influence wealth.

The basic premise of the life-cycle model is that over the course of its life a household smoothes the utility it derives from consumption.[10] A household's wealth at any point in time depends on the amount of resources that it has accumulated until then. Therefore, we can loosely divide the factors that affect wealth into two groups: those that determine available resources and those that affect the consumption choices (and hence the saving decisions) made by households.

Clearly the amount of labor income earned over the course of an individual's life affects

FIGURE 24.3   *Median Net Worth of White, Black, and Hispanic Households, by Age and Education*

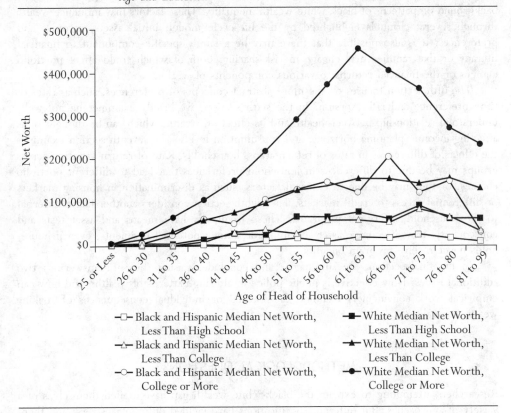

Source: Authors' calculations from the 1989, 1992, 1995, and 1998 SCFS.

the amount of household resources, as do other sources of income, such as financial transfers from family members or capital income. Rates of return on assets may also vary across households and hence contribute to household wealth differentials.

The consumption and saving choices are influenced by additional factors as well. For example, household "preferences" such as time preference (or "patience"), risk aversion, the length of financial planning horizons, and the desire to leave an inheritance influence the household saving rate. Preferences may also affect the asset portfolio composition chosen by a household, and asset portfolio composition may in turn affect the household rate of return on the assets mentioned earlier. Other factors may affect desired consumption directly, such as the number of people in the household or the need to pay for medical expenses. Finally, there may be external factors that affect household savings: the presence of a government safety net that relies on income and asset tests to determine eligibility may actually deter some households from saving.

This chapter examines the extent to which these various factors contribute to racial disparities in wealth accumulation and to observed wealth inequality. The first section provides a brief overview of the main methodological approaches taken by previous authors. The remaining sections examine the evidence of the importance of the factors just mentioned in explaining wealth inequality. In the second section, we consider labor income and demographic characteristics, which may affect preferences or desired consumption choices. The third and fourth sections focus on the effect of intergenerational transfers and family background on patterns of black-white wealth inequality. These factors may influence wealth through several channels highlighted by the life-cycle model: initial assets, income, and preferences. It is also possible that there may be a family-specific component to financial literacy or that families may engage in risk-sharing, both of which could affect portfolio choices or the financial returns to various components of wealth.

The fifth section focuses on the more abstract concepts of preferences, such as rates of time preference and risk aversion. In the sixth section, we briefly examine the not-well-understood relationship between health and its effect on wealth, which can be thought of as affecting income, planning horizons, and consumption levels. The seventh section examines the effects of differences in rates of return across households. Rate-of-return variation across groups may be due to differences in household preferences that lead to different portfolio choices, or they may be due to external factors, such as discrimination in housing markets or differential access to credit markets. The eighth section considers another factor external to the household, safety-net programs. These frequently have means and asset tests and consequently may discourage asset accumulation among potential recipients, even if households never receive program benefits.

In the final section, we summarize and conclude, raising (but not answering) two additional issues: How effective is public policy in altering patterns of wealth? And how can empirical work convincingly examine the societal or individual consequences of striking wealth inequality?

METHODOLOGICAL QUESTIONS

Researchers attempting to explain the black-white wealth gap have availed themselves of a variety of approaches. But different specifications have yielded different answers, and there is no consensus on the preferred empirical strategy. This section discusses the empirical approaches taken in the literature as well as the methodological questions raised by the analysis of the black-white wealth gap.

Table 24.2 summarizes the set of studies that are the primary focus of this research synthesis.[11] For each study we highlight the data that are used, the age group the study focuses on, the empirical approach adopted, the dependent and independent variables used in the empirical models, and whether the study provides separate estimates for married couples and for singles.

The first four studies listed in table 24.2 (Smith 1995; Oliver and Shapiro 1995; Hurst, Luoh, and Stafford 1998; and Conley 1999) estimate regression models of household wealth, including among the independent variables an indicator variable for race and/or ethnicity. Conditioning on other covariates, the coefficient on the indicator variable should reflect wealth differences across racial and ethnic groups that are unexplained by other factors. An insignificant indicator variable suggests that wealth differentials can be completely explained by factors such as income, education, and household composition rather than by race or ethnicity.[12]

The indicator variable approach is restrictive. A linear regression with an indicator implies that the slope of the wealth function with respect to all other covariates is the same for both races, and only the intercept of the function is shifted up or down. This restriction does not appear to hold based on evidence from other studies.[13]

Other researchers follow a regression decomposition approach, also known as the Blinder-Oaxaca method or means-coefficient analysis (see, for example, Blau and Graham 1990; Menchik and Jianakoplos 1997; Avery and Rendall 1997; Gittleman and Wolff 2000; Altonji and Doraszelski 2001). The underlying idea is that observed differences in wealth can be broken down into two parts: the portion that can be explained using differences in household characteristics and the portion that is unexplained. Using the observed relationship between wealth and individual characteristics for white households, researchers can simulate the expected wealth holdings for black households using their characteristics and the white regression coefficients. The deviation between simulated and observed wealth provides a measure of the unexplained black-white wealth gap. A similar analysis can be performed by using the regression coefficients estimated on black households to simulate the wealth of white households based on their characteristics.

A near-universal finding of the regression decomposition approach is that considerably more of the black-white wealth gap can be "explained" if the regression coefficients estimated on a sample of white households are used to predict wealth for black households than if the regression coefficients estimated on a sample of black households are used to predict wealth for white households. This discrepancy is unsatisfying, since there is no a priori reason to prefer one approach to the other.

Three recent studies of black-white wealth inequality using data from the PSID significantly advance the literature. Joseph Altonji and Ulrich Doraszelski (2001) provide an extremely thorough analysis using the regression decomposition framework. They perform separate analyses for married couples, single men, and single women; they use both mean and median regressions; and their dependent variables include the level of wealth, the log of wealth, components of wealth, and the wealth-to-permanent income ratio, the last of which allows for interaction between demographic variables and permanent income. They also estimate wealth accumulation models, using as dependent variables both changes in wealth and changes in the wealth-to-permanent income ratio over five-year periods. They incorporate many robustness checks, such as including third-order polynomials in income and using alternative measures of permanent income.

Altonji and Doraszelski (2001) are also among the first researchers to address a critical concern that arises when applying the regression decomposition framework. Because white and black households have different income distributions, using black wealth models to predict white wealth involves extrapolating out of sample, which may lead to unreliable results. Altonji and Doraszelski address this issue in two ways. First, they perform decompositions on subsets of the white and black populations that resemble each other. To choose these subsets, they use the wealth model from one group and use it to predict wealth for the other group; the 50 percent in each group with the lowest prediction errors are selected into these subsets. The underlying assumption is that those with low prediction errors must have characteristics similar to those in the other group. Second, they restrict the subsets by permanent income, eliminating households with income close to or below zero, and white households with permanent income above the maximum observed in the black sample. The results from these tests are broadly consistent with their initial analyses, which lead them to conclude that extrapolation out of sample is not the cause of the difference between white and black wealth models.

Robert Barsky, John Bound, Kerwin Charles, and Joe Lupton (2001) argue that the Blinder-Oaxaca decomposition is not an appropriate tool for studying the racial wealth gap given the nonlinear relationship between wealth and income and given that the income distribution of white households is shifted to the right relative to the income distribution of

TABLE 24.2   Summary of Studies Analyzing the Black-White Wealth Gap

Author(s) and Year	Data	Age Cohort	Estimation Type	Dependent Variable	Independent Variables	Estimate Separately for Married Couples and Singles?
Smith (1995)	Health and Retirement Study, wave 1, 1992	51 to 61	Linear mean and median regression	Level wealth	Family income quintile, health status, education, financial horizon, subjective probability of living until age seventy-five, labor force status, region, pension indicator, expectations regarding salary, bequest preferences, received inheritance dummy, inheritance amount, black, Hispanic	No
Oliver and Shapiro (1995)	Survey of Income and Program Participation	All	Linear mean regression	Level wealth	Race dummy, residence in South, education, age, work experience, white collar dummy (includes self-employed), number of workers in household, household income, male, children, widow dummy	No
Hurst, Luoh, and Stafford (1998)	PSID wealth supplements, 1984, 1989, 1994	All	Linear mean and median regression	Level wealth	Permanent income, African American dummy, age of head, education of head, married dummy, number of children, male, holding stock dummy, region	No
Conley (1999)	PSID, 1992 to 1994	18 to 30	Linear mean regression	Log wealth	Respondent characteristics: race, female, age, number of siblings, education, income in 1992; parental characteristics: age, number of years household was female-headed between 1980 and 1984, welfare receipt in 1984, education of head, occupational prestige of head, permanent income, indicator for positive wealth in 1984, net worth, primary residence equity, business equity, other illiquid assets, liquid assets	No

Study	Data	Age	Method	Dependent variable	Independent variables	
Blau and Graham (1990)	1976 and 1978 National Longitudinal Survey of Young Men and Young Women	24 to 34	Regression decomposition (linear mean regression)	Level wealth	Permanent income, transitory income, age of head, dummy if the head is a single woman, number of children, dummy if residence is in the central city, dummy if residence is in Standard Metropolitan Statistical Area (SMSA) outside of the central city, dummy if residence is in the South, number of weeks worked by wife	Yes
Avery and Rendall (1997)	Survey of Consumer Finances, 1989	25 and older	Regression decomposition (linear mean regression)	Log non-inherited wealth	Age, education, military service, health, number of children, number of siblings, current earnings (or Social Security pension income for older households), received inheritances	No
Menchik and Jianakoplos (1997)	National Longitudinal Study of Mature Men, 1976; Survey of Consumer Finances, 1989	58 to 72; all	Regression decomposition (linear mean regression)	Level wealth	NLS: permanent income, transitory income, age, number of children, predicted inheritance value, self-employment status, weeks spouse worked, bequest intent, residence in central city, residence in SMSA outside central city, residence in South, expected rate of return, pension wealth, Social Security wealth; SCF: permanent income, transitory income, age, number of children, inheritance value, self-employment status, female head, weeks spouse worked, bequest intent	Yes
Gittleman and Wolff (2000)	PSID wealth supplements, 1984, 1989, 1994	All	Regression decomposition (linear mean regression); Counterfactual simulations	Level wealth; change in wealth	Age, female head, single head, number of children, education, family income, small or large city	No

TABLE 24.2   (Continued)

Author(s) and Year	Data	Age Cohort	Estimation Type	Dependent Variable	Independent Variables	Estimate Separately for Married Couples and Singles?
Altonji and Dor-aszelski (2001)	PSID wealth supplements, 1984, 1989, 1994 (main files, marriage history file; childbirth and adoption file)	All	Regression decomposition (linear mean regression, linear median regression, mean regression index, median regression index)	Level wealth, log wealth, and wealth to income ratio	Current family income, permanent family income, age, region, weeks spouse worked, number of children both in and outside of household, children present dummy, health status, education, number and tenure of marriages, self-employment status, number of siblings[a]	Yes
Barsky, Bound, Charles, and Lupton (2001)	PSID, 1984, 1989, 1994	45 to 49	Nonparametric	Level wealth	Average household labor earnings over five-year period as a proxy for lifetime earnings	No

Source: Authors' compilation.
[a]For analysis of couples, measures are included for both head and spouse, where applicable.

black households. Assuming a parametric form under these conditions can lead to mis-specification errors that are unlikely to average to zero and may therefore bias results. They show that the typical regression decomposition approach overestimates the contribution of earnings to the wealth gap when using white coefficients; they also argue that using black coefficients to estimate white wealth involves extrapolation out of sample and overestimates the wealth gap at higher incomes, thereby underestimating the contribution of earnings to the wealth gap.

Barsky and his colleagues address these issues by performing a nonparametric analysis of the black-white wealth gap. Their approach is to reweight white households to make the earnings distribution of the white population resemble the earnings distribution of the black population. They then calculate the wealth distribution counterfactual rather than simply the counterfactual mean of wealth, as is done in regression decomposition studies. This counter-factual distribution can be used to calculate the contribution of earnings to the wealth gap at all points along the earnings distribution.[14]

Maury Gittleman and Edward Wolff (2000) look at wealth *accumulation* over a ten-year period.[15] Their strategy is to calculate, for a variety of factors, what average black wealth would have been if the characteristics or behavior of black households had been identical to those of white households over the previous ten-year period. They use this counterfactual estimate of wealth held by blacks to calculate by how much the wealth gap would have closed had their experiences been the same as those of white households. The specific factors they examine are earned income, saving rates, saving functions (where the saving rate increases with income), rates of return, portfolio composition, inheritance amounts, and changes in household composition.

The methods discussed in this section have been used to examine the extent to which several potential factors explain wealth inequality. The following sections examine these factors and assess the evidence on their importance.

LABOR INCOME AND DEMOGRAPHIC CHARACTERISTICS

Existing estimates of the effects of income, age, education, region of residence, and number of children on the black-white wealth gap vary greatly and, in the regression decomposition analyses, tend to depend on whether black wealth is predicted using coefficients estimated from a sample of white households or whether white wealth is predicted using coefficients estimated from a sample of black households. For example, point estimates in the studies we consider suggest that income and demographic factors can explain anywhere from 5 to 120 percent of the black-white wealth gap when white coefficients are used to predict black wealth. Most estimates, however, fall between 60 and 90 percent. When coefficients estimated from a sample of blacks are used to predict white wealth, estimates range between 12 and 84 percent, with most falling between 20 and 35 percent.[16]

Altonji and Doraszelski (2001) find that using coefficients estimated on a sample of black households to estimate *log* wealth for a sample of white households accounts for about the same fraction of the wealth gap as when the opposite is done (using white coefficients to calculate black log wealth). In both cases, estimates of the effects of income and demo-graphic factors range from 65 to 85 percent. As mentioned earlier, other studies present results outside this range. Thus, there is clearly considerable uncertainty regarding the magnitude of the overall effects of income and demographic characteristics on the racial wealth gap.

Barsky and his colleagues (2001) focus solely on the contribution of earnings to black-white wealth inequality. They note that the regression decomposition approach tends to overstate the importance of earnings in explaining the wealth gap when white coefficients are used to predict black wealth. This is due in part to the fact that the true wealth-income relationship is not linear, as assumed by the typical regression decomposition.[17] Rather than assume a particular relationship between wealth and income, these researchers adopt a new nonparametric approach; they conclude that earnings differences account for 64 percent of the mean wealth gap between whites and blacks.

For comparison, they also apply the regression decomposition technique to their data, first using only income to estimate wealth, then adding an income-squared term to better capture the nonlinear relationship between wealth and income. When income is the only explanatory variable, they find that it accounts for 97.5 percent of the black-white wealth gap; adding a quadratic income term yields an estimate of 72.1 percent. These results are consistent with the authors' discussion: if we take their estimate of 64 percent to be correct, both regression decomposition estimates overstate this amount, but the quadratic estimate is closer to the "true" value. Note that these latter two estimates are also consistent with the range of regression decomposition estimates found in the literature.

Barsky and his colleagues also find that the role of earnings is largest at the low end of the wealth distribution and decreases at higher wealth levels. According to their analysis, earnings explain 100 percent of the wealth gap at the tenth percentile of the wealth distribution, but only 55 percent of the wealth gap at the ninetieth percentile. Estimating white and black wealth distributions using the black earnings distribution shows similarities in wealth at the lower end of the distribution but not at the upper end: although the twenty-fifth percentile of the estimated white wealth distribution is equivalent to the 23.4 percentile of the black wealth distribution, almost the entire population of black households (99.6 percent) has less wealth than the amount held by the households at the sixtieth percentile of the estimated white wealth distribution.

The analysis of Barsky and his colleagues (2001) raises at least two important points. First, regression decomposition estimates may overstate (understate) the importance of earnings and perhaps demographics when white (black) coefficients are used to predict black (white) wealth. Second, the contribution of earnings apparently varies significantly across the income distribution. This highlights a possible limitation in studying only the mean wealth gap.

Assessment   Differences in labor income have a major effect on black-white wealth differentials. Additional work seeking to narrow the range of uncertainty about the magnitude of the effect could usefully be undertaken. Income appears to have a larger effect on wealth differentials than demographic characteristics. Although most studies report only the combined effect of income and demographic factors, several provide separate estimates (see, for example, Menchik and Jianakoplos 1997; Avery and Rendall 1997; Gittleman and Wolff 2000). They report that income differences account for 12 to 72 percent of the wealth gap and that demographic characteristics account for −7 to 17 percent.[18]

A troubling aspect of the older papers is that estimates of black wealth using coefficients estimated from a sample of white households resulted in the unexplained portion of the black-white wealth gap being much smaller than estimates of white wealth using the coefficients estimated from a sample of black households. This might indicate that behavior governing wealth accumulation in black households is fundamentally different than in white households. Alternatively, statistical or methodological issues may explain the discordant results.

Recent papers provide some clues. Evidence from Altonji and Doraszelski (2001) suggests that these discrepancies are not as acute when log wealth is the focus of the analysis. Both Altonji and Doraszelski (2001) and Barsky and his colleagues (2001) emphasize that relative to white families, black families have lower income. If wealth is a convex function of income (that is, if wealth increases with income at an increasing rate), the predicted wealth function using only the low end of the income distribution will be flatter—there will appear to be a weaker relationship between income and wealth—than we would observe when using households throughout the income distribution. Altonji and Doraszelski conclude that extrapolation out of sample is not the primary cause of the difference between white and black wealth models. Barsky and his colleagues seem to suggest otherwise.

It would be worthwhile to further explore the implications of the regression decompositions, focusing on wealth in levels and logs and restricting the sample to black and white families with similar wealth, income, and demographic characteristics. Research along these lines would help resolve the question of whether black households have fundamentally different wealth accumulation patterns than white households, or whether observed racial differences in wealth can be explained largely (or fully) by differences in observed characteristics.

Examining systematically how covariates, particularly demographic factors, influence regression results could also advance the literature. Because empirical specifications vary significantly across studies, it is difficult to understand how demographic variables influence wealth accumulation. Interpretation of coefficients is also complicated. For example, children may have several potential, competing influences on wealth accumulation. Consumption may increase (and saving decrease) with the number of children in the family. But saving may increase with the number of children if families are concerned about college costs. If the likelihood that parents will be taken care of in old age increases with the number of children in the family, there might be a negative correlation between wealth and the number of children, as long as people generally accumulate wealth for retirement or late-in-life medical expenses. Given these considerations, it is perhaps not surprising that estimates in the literature find conflicting results for the relationship between children and wealth.[19]

There are also intriguing differences where income and demographic characteristics tend to account for a larger fraction of the wealth gap for singles than for married couples. Learning the reason for the different wealth accumulation patterns of married and single households could be useful for understanding and modeling wealth inequality more generally.

INTERGENERATIONAL TRANSFERS

Inheritances and Gifts

Early studies of the black-white wealth gap that controlled for income and demographic characteristics left a large portion of the wealth gap unexplained, leading authors of earlier papers to speculate that family transfers are likely to play an important role (Blau and Graham 1990; Oliver and Shapiro 1995). Several researchers have since examined the importance of inheritances and gifts, including Smith (1995), Avery and Rendall (1997), Menchik and Jianakoplos (1997), Gittleman and Wolff (2000), and Altonji and Doraszelski (2001). Estimates of their importance range from less than 1 percent to 24 percent of the black-white mean wealth gap.[20] The evidence about the effect of inheritances on the median wealth gap is scant, although we suspect that inheritances have little or no effect on the wealth of the median household, instead playing a larger role at the upper end of the wealth distribution.[21]

The results from Smith (1995) suggest that inheritances contribute to wealth inequality at both the mean and median, although his estimates are not broken down by race. An increase in the present discounted value of an additional dollar of inheritances, if received, increases mean (median) net worth by $0.36 ($0.43). To the extent that inheritances are unevenly distributed across racial and ethnic groups, Smith's estimates suggest that they contribute to the wealth gap.[22]

Kerwin Charles and Erik Hurst (2002) show that 42 percent of white households in the PSID get help from their family in coming up with a down payment for a home. Fewer than 10 percent of black families get this help. This specific example suggests that there are racial differences in the likelihood that parents will help their children make high-return investments, and in their ability to do so.[23]

The regression decompositions performed by Menchik and Jianakoplos (1997) and Avery and Rendall (1997) give specific attention to the role of inheritances and gifts. Using data from the 1989 SCF, Menchik and Jianakoplos find that inheritances account for 19.3 percent of the wealth gap for married households and 11.6 percent of the wealth gap for single households. These estimates average the results from the two approaches in regression decomposition: estimating black wealth using white coefficients and vice versa.[24] Avery and Rendall (1997) find similar results.[25]

Gittleman and Wolff (2000) examine wealth accumulation over a ten-year period rather than wealth in levels. Using the PSID wealth supplements in 1984, 1989, and 1994, they find that inheritances played almost no role in the wealth gains of blacks over the period, but constituted as much as 10 percent of the increase in wealth for whites. Had black households inherited amounts similar to the inheritances of white households, the black-white mean wealth ratio in 1994 would have increased by five to eight percentage points, from 0.28 to between 0.33 and 0.36. This implies that between 7 and 11 percent of the approximately $120,000 mean wealth gap would have been closed. Because these simulations are based on wealth changes over a ten-year period, they ignore any differences in wealth due to inheritances made prior to the start of the period, and as a result they may be somewhat lower than estimates based on lifetime inheritances and gifts received.

Assessment   Financial transfers appear to contribute to the wealth gap, although they seem to matter much more at the mean than at the median. Estimates from regression decompositions and counterfactual simulations suggest that between 7 and 24 percent of the mean wealth gap can be explained by racial differences in received inheritances.[26] Intergenerational transfers are unlikely to be important for the median household given the infrequency of transfer receipt.

We raise two considerations for future work. First, the existing studies are somewhat dated, and the effect of inheritances on wealth inequality may differ over time. For example, as the fraction of the population receiving inheritances increases—especially as the parents of the baby boom generation die in increasing numbers—the impact of inheritances on the distribution of wealth may increase as a result.

Second, while the range of estimates in the literature appears to provide an answer to the question of how much inheritances and gifts contribute to the black-white mean wealth gap, it is not obvious that this is the best question to answer. Exploring how inheritances are translated into wealth and whether this mechanism differs by race might better illuminate the relationship between family transfers and wealth. As noted earlier, for example, Smith (1995) finds that an additional dollar of inheritance increases mean net worth by $0.36. Although we would not expect a dollar-for-dollar increase in wealth if inheritances were anticipated, it is not clear that we would expect $0.36 either. Both the anticipation and timing of bequests should determine how gifts affect wealth accumulation, and these factors might depend in turn on life expectancy or on how much households want to leave bequests. A related question is whether prospective inheritances offset wealth accumulation, in which case we might find that inheritances actually mitigate the measured wealth gap.

Bequest Motives

Differences across groups in the desire to leave an inheritance may contribute to black-white wealth inequality. Leaving race aside for the moment, bequests might affect wealth accumulation in at least two ways. First, bequests increase the wealth of recipients. The desire to leave bequests may also be learned behavior and would result in greater intergenerational persistence in wealth than in a world with no bequests. Second, the desire to leave a bequest may increase saving rates. Of course, bequests may be small or have no causal relationship with wealth.

There is considerable debate over the presence, frequency, strength, and nature of bequest motives. James Davies (1981) shows that a substantial amount of bequests occur in a standard life-cycle model even absent purposeful bequest motives, simply owing to uncertainty about the date of death. Michael Hurd (1987, 1989) compares the rates at which the elderly with children decumulate assets with the rates at which the elderly without children decumulate assets and finds essentially no difference. He concludes that households do not have purposeful bequest motives.

The behavior documented by Hurd is inconsistent with attitudinal measures elicited from surveys. In wave 1 of the Health and Retirement Study (HRS), for example, respondents were asked how important it was to them to leave an inheritance to their heirs: 22.8 percent said "very important," 42.9 percent said "somewhat important," and 29.4 said "not important at all."[27]

Menchik and Jianakoplos (1997) use similar attitudinal questions from the SCF to determine whether a family has a "bequest intent." They include this indicator variable in linear wealth regressions, and as we would expect if Hurd's results are correct, they find the coefficient on this attitudinal response to be generally insignificant. Not surprisingly, when they include "bequest intent" in their regression decompositions, they find essentially no contribution of this factor to the wealth gap.

In contrast, Smith (1995) uses the HRS to estimate mean and median wealth regressions, including indicator variables for those who feel that leaving an estate to their heirs is "very important" or "somewhat important," omitting the response "not at all important." He finds that respondents who believe that leaving a bequest is "very important" accumulate $86,000 more in assets than those who place no importance on leaving a bequest.[28] Smith also estimates wealth regressions separately by race and finds a large difference in the coefficient on the "very important" indicator variable: $123,575 for whites and $17,469 for blacks.

Smith calculates that racial differences in the coefficients on the bequest preference questions result in $53,000 lower net worth for blacks. This difference is apparently not due to a weaker desire to leave inheritances among black families; it may occur because blacks are less able to "afford" bequests. Interestingly, the desire to leave bequests appears to be stronger among blacks than it is among whites in the HRS. Of the black respondents, 35.0 percent think that leaving an estate is very important, compared with 20.3 percent of whites; 39.3 percent of blacks think it is somewhat important, while 43.7 percent of whites give this response; 21.6 percent of blacks think that leaving an estate is not at all important, compared with 31.0 percent of whites. Although these responses do not control for other factors, they suggest that, if anything, bequest preferences are somewhat stronger among blacks.

Given that Smith (1995) reports mean white wealth as $264,000 and mean black wealth as $72,000, we could interpret his results to mean that bequests and the desire or ability to leave them account for as much as 28 percent of the wealth gap ($53,000 lower wealth divided by $192,000, the raw wealth differential between mean black wealth and mean white wealth). However, this contribution to the wealth gap occurs not because whites are more likely to want to make bequests, but because they are better able to afford bequests and may save at a higher rate to accumulate an estate. The nonlinear relationship between income and saving exacerbates differences in bequest intent, widening the wealth gap.

Assessment   We are left with a somewhat unsatisfying conclusion about the importance of bequests in understanding wealth inequality. First, there is no strong empirical evidence that households have purposeful bequest motives—that is, there is no strong evidence that households either consume less or work harder in order to bequeath wealth. Second, it is clear that a large amount of money is frequently transferred to children and others upon the death of a wealthy household. Given existing racial disparities of wealth, these transfers disproportionately benefit white households relative to black households. Third, attitudinal questions suggest that bequests are at least as important to blacks as to whites, if not more so. Although many people report that they wish to leave bequests, it is still not clear how much that desire actually affects savings behavior, and to what extent preferences toward bequests vary over the income distribution. We think additional work on bequest motives, actual bequests, and wealth inequality could be valuable.

FAMILY BACKGROUND

The studies discussed thus far examine the importance of monetary inheritances and gifts actually received in explaining the racial wealth gap. These transfers are presumably received from family members, most likely from parents. Three additional studies test the importance of family background more generally. Conley (1999) estimates a mean regression of log 1994 wealth using a young cohort from the PSID (respondents age eighteen to thirty in 1992 to 1994). He finds that blacks had significantly less wealth than their white counterparts, even controlling for income and demographics. However, an additional control for parental wealth eliminates this significance of race in determining wealth. Conley contends that parental wealth is the most important predictor of wealth, with an individual's own income second. These predictors, along with other demographic characteristics, fully account for the black-white mean wealth gap.

Altonji and Doraszelski (2001) also use the PSID to look at the role of family background in understanding black-white wealth differences. They seek to determine whether the effects of family background can explain the finding that the wealth holdings of black households appear to be more weakly related to income and demographics than the wealth holdings of white households, as is shown by the fact that the unexplained portion of the wealth gap is consistently larger when using the black wealth function than when using the white wealth function. They hypothesize that blacks receive fewer intergenerational transfers than whites if the ability to accumulate and bequeath wealth differed for their parents and other antecedents; such differences are likely given historical factors such as slavery and subsequent racial discrimination. If inheritances and gifts differ by race and are correlated with income and demographics, this could explain the differences between the black and white wealth functions.

The authors' clever empirical strategy is to compare the degree to which the black-white wealth gap can be explained by standard models incorporating a rich set of demographic characteristics and income with the degree to which the black-white wealth gap can be explained by the same model with family-specific fixed effects. The key idea behind using this type of model is that the effect of family background on wealth should not differ for siblings; that is, family background is "fixed" within a given family. Using a fixed-effects model essentially nets out the common effect for siblings. Therefore, if family background (through transfers, adverse family history, and so on) has a significant impact on wealth accumulation, we should be able to account for this with the family fixed effect. As a result, the fixed-effects models estimated for whites and for blacks should not produce disparate estimates of the portion of the racial wealth gap explained by income and demographics if time-invariant family characteristics are responsible for the differences.

Altonji and Doraszelski (2001) find that the fixed-effects models yield estimates similar to those without fixed effects, and so they do not increase the portion of the wealth gap explained when using the coefficients of the black wealth function to estimate wealth held by white households. This leads them to conclude that family background and intergenerational transfers are not central to explaining differences in how black and white households accumulate wealth. They note, however, that family background appears to have an effect on the likelihood of self-employment, which is positively correlated with wealth. Furthermore, the authors do not rule out the possibility that family background affects the intercept of the wealth function. They suggest that future research focus on differences in rates of return and consumption (saving) behavior for explaining differences in the black and white wealth functions.[29]

Charles and Hurst (2003) report evidence consistent with the possibility that family background affects wealth through its influence on saving preferences. First they document the wealth correlation across generations using parents and children in the PSID and find an age-adjusted wealth correlation between 0.25 and 0.52. Second, they decompose the wealth correlation into two major components: the correlation between parent and child incomes and the residual (after controlling for measures of family risk-sharing, received gifts and bequests, and expected gifts and bequests). The residual can be interpreted as the correlation in saving preferences, which they find to be sizable: around 40 percent of the raw wealth correlation.[30]

Assessment   There is a sharp contrast between the conclusions reached by Conley (1999) and Charles and Hurst (2003) and those reached by Altonji and Doraszelski (2001). Conley's results—that parental wealth is the most important predictor of wealth—imply that differences in parental wealth, which are correlated with race, may explain much of the measured black-white wealth gap. Evidence from Charles and Hurst (2003) is consistent with this conclusion; they argue specifically that correlated saving preferences explain much of the positive correlation of intergenerational wealth.[31] Therefore, to the extent that saving preferences are "inherited," family background has an impact on wealth beyond the wealth effects of direct financial transfers. In contrast, the evidence presented by Altonji and Doraszelski (2001) reduces the role that family background plays in explaining the wealth gap relative to other studies. These conflicting results are puzzling; future research that reconciles them would be valuable.

There are several ways one might extend these results. An underlying assumption of the Altonji and Doraszelski (2001) fixed-effects strategy is that parents give equal financial amounts to their children. A number of studies document the fact that inheritances are evenly divided in most cases and are only weakly related to income when the division is uneven, at least in the United States in the twentieth century (Menchik 1980; Wilhelm 1996). Studies also show that while inter vivos transfers among siblings may be negatively related to income, discrepancies in gifts across siblings are still fairly small in magnitude (McGarry and Schoeni 1995; Altonji, Hayashi, and Kotlikoff 1996). But studies of the distribution of inter vivos transfers between children in the same family suffer from data limitations. They rarely consider parents' educational investments in children, which presumably influence the trajectories of future earnings. They have a difficult time accounting for the fact that transfers are likely to occur disproportionately at specific times, such as when children go to college, get married, buy a house, or have children themselves; if recipients of transfers are at different stages of the life cycle, it is thus hard to establish the equality of transfers. Hence, it is not clear that family background can definitively be accounted for by a fixed effect among siblings.

But Conley's (1999) work also has limitations. He examines only one regression with a dummy variable reflecting racial differences. As noted earlier, this approach assumes that wealth functions for blacks and whites have the same slope but differ in levels. Other analyses using regression decompositions suggest that in fact the black and white wealth functions differ substantially (Altonji and Doraszelski 2001).[32] We conclude that additional work on the role of parental background on black-white wealth inequality would be valuable.

Family Support Networks

Family support networks may also affect wealth accumulation, and we offer two opposing possibilities. First, strong family support networks may reduce precautionary saving for some individuals and therefore result in lower accumulated wealth (though higher consumption and well-being) than for those with weaker support networks, all else being equal. A second possibility is that if family support involves provision of household services like child care, transportation, and home maintenance, it might increase the wealth of those with support networks.[33]

Little is known about the effects of family relationships on saving behavior. There is suggestive evidence that households can rely on family members for assistance in times of need (McGarry and Schoeni 1995; Cox 1990). Joseph Altonji, Fumio Hayashi, and Laurence Kotlikoff (1997) find that reallocating a dollar from parental income to child income would reduce transfers from parents to children by only thirteen cents, rather than the full dollar predicted by models with complete intergenerational altruism. The literature suggests, therefore, that some families help out financially when households face low income. However, it does not address the more relevant question for our purposes of whether strong support networks affect wealth.

Because family members may be able to provide household services at or below market cost, well-developed family networks may allow households to *increase* rather than decrease saving. For example, when a retired grandparent offers free child care services, money that would otherwise have been spent on child care can be saved. An even more substantial possibility is that a grandparent's child care services sufficiently increases the marginal benefit to the parents of working that the household would be able to have two earners rather than one. As another example, when family members offer rides to work or assist with home maintenance projects, the beneficiaries of this help can save rather than spend money on transportation or home repairs.

Assessment   We are not aware of any evidence regarding the effects of family support, either financial or in-kind, on saving behavior, nor are we aware of evidence regarding the differences between black and white families in the relative strength of family support networks—again, whether in terms of financial transfers or services. For these channels to have important effects on the racial wealth gap, three things would need to be true. First, family support would need to influence saving behavior. Second, there would need to be racial differences in the strength of family support networks. And third, the effects would need to work in specific directions—for example, if networks reduce saving (through a decreased need for precautionary saving), blacks would need to have stronger networks than whites. Exploring these relationships might be an interesting area for additional research.

CONSUMPTION

Given the portion of the black-white wealth gap that remains unexplained by observable factors, there has been considerable speculation that racial differences in saving rates must be a contributing factor. Blacks do appear to save at lower rates than whites. But empirical evidence suggests that saving rates increase with income, and because blacks tend to have lower incomes than whites, it is not clear that apparent racial differences in saving rates are due to fundamental differences in saving behavior. Only one study attempts to account for the way in which differences in saving rates might contribute to racial wealth inequality. Gittleman and Wolff (2000) suggest that if black households had the same saving rate as whites over the previous ten-year period, the wealth gap would have been smaller by about 11 percent. However, the wealth gap would have narrowed by only 1 percent if saving had been made a function of income and the wealth of black households had been predicted by substituting the saving *function* estimated on a sample of white households. Their results suggest that there is little difference by race in saving behavior that is independent of income.

It is not surprising that racial differences in saving rates largely disappear once saving rates are allowed to vary with income: the relationship between permanent income and saving rates appears to be quite dramatic. Karen Dynan, Jonathan Skinner, and Stephen Zeldes (2000) estimate saving rates across income levels for forty-five- to forty-nine-year-olds in the United States using three different datasets: the Consumer Expenditure Surveys (CEX), the PSID, and the SCF. They find that estimated saving rates increase from less than 5 percent for the bottom quintile of earnings to more than 40 percent of income for the top 5 percent.[34]

This pattern contradicts the predictions from simple versions of the life-cycle model, which imply that consumption (and therefore saving) is proportional to lifetime income. Under some common specifications of preferences, all households will have the same saving rate, regardless of income. However, if time preference rates differ across households, if the rates of interest for households differ, if households face different amounts of uncertainty or if preferences are not homothetic (if they change disproportionately as income increases), then models predict that the saving rate will differ with income.

Consider the assumption that time preference rates vary by income group or by education. Suppose also that high-income households are more patient (or equivalently, have a lower time preference rate) so they value consumption tomorrow almost as much as consumption today. As a consequence, these households will save more than otherwise equivalent households that are less patient, in order to ensure adequate consumption levels in the future. These more patient households will therefore accumulate wealth faster. Similarly, if those with greater educational attainment are more patient, as suggested by their investment in human capital, they will save at a higher rate.

Emily Lawrance (1991) examines the relationship between time preference and income by looking at food consumption expenditures for families between 1974 and 1982. She finds that high-income, highly-educated households have faster growth rates of consumption than do low-income, less-educated households. This empirical pattern is consistent with a negative correlation between income and time preference, implying that higher-income households are more patient.[35] Although there are other possible interpretations, Lawrance argues that differences in time preference are the most reasonable explanation of her results. This result is controversial.[36]

Although they hardly provide definitive evidence, responses to a qualitative question in the SCFs suggest that household planning horizons, which may be correlated with patience, vary systematically across racial and ethnic groups. The question asks respondents to report how far in advance they (and their partner) tend to plan.[37] An ordered probit regression of the responses to this question suggests that respondents in black and Hispanic households have significantly shorter planning horizons than do other racial and ethnic groups, even after conditioning on education, age, and income.[38]

Families may also differ by levels of risk aversion. Households with a greater degree of risk aversion will save more to prevent low consumption in case of low earnings or a bad medical state than less risk-averse households, all else being equal. Risk aversion could also affect portfolio choices and household rates of return. However, to our knowledge, no empirical evidence exists regarding the relationship between measures of risk aversion and income or wealth.

Those who are more likely to experience low consumption may not want to hold wealth in riskier or less liquid forms. Blau and Graham (1990) argue that blacks' higher unemployment rates (and transitory income) result in their holding assets in a more liquid form, particularly at lower levels of income and wealth. There is also suggestive (but hardly definitive) evidence from the SCF that households may have systematically different preferences for risk, even after conditioning on observable characteristics, and that these preferences may be related to wealth. Respondents are asked to choose between four categories summarizing how much financial risk they are willing to take.[39] Like the planning horizon questions, an ordered probit regression of the responses to this question suggests that respondents in black and Hispanic households have significantly less willingness to take risk than do other racial and ethnic groups, even after conditioning on education, age, and income.[40]

Additional analyses suggest that both "planning horizon" and "willingness to take risk" indicator variables are positively and significantly correlated with net worth in regressions of net worth in both levels and logs.[41] These descriptive results raise a question about why planning horizons, impatience, and willingness to take risk might differ systematically across groups. As previously noted, Charles and Hurst (2003) suggest that saving preferences are in fact correlated across generations, and Lawrance (1991) cites evidence suggesting that "patience" is learned and fixed by adolescence. However, it may also be true that institutional or economic factors explain these differences in preferences. One area for future research might be to determine whether these apparent preference differences can be explained by other factors, such as health status, life expectancy, or the presence of a public safety net, or whether they seem to be genetically inherited or culturally determined.

Assessment   The evidence is clear that high-income households save a greater fraction of their resources than low-income households. This contributes significantly to racial wealth inequality because blacks tend to have lower household incomes than whites. The nonlinear relationship between income and savings suggests that linear regression decompositions may not be the best tool for explaining the wealth gap. As discussed in previous sections, Altonji and Doraszelski (2001) and Barsky and his colleagues (2001) have begun to explore less restrictive empirical approaches, but more research is needed in this direction.

A first step in clarifying the degree to which differences in saving patterns can explain black-white wealth differences would be to simulate the wealth accumulation of households accounting for differences in saving rates by income level. If it appears that differential saving rates by race, independent of income, are capable of matching patterns in the data, then work would naturally turn toward the more difficult task of determining the underlying explanation for saving rate differences. We think that new work examining the factors associated with differences in rates of time preference, risk aversion, and perhaps other factors related to preferences (such as time inconsistency) might help us better understand black-white differences in wealth and contribute to a more fundamental understanding of economic behavior.

HEALTH

There is a well-documented positive correlation between good health and wealth (Smith, 1999a). Evidence also suggests that blacks and Hispanics tend to have poorer health than whites (Smith 1995). Although we would like to know to what extent poor health contributes to racial wealth inequality, no estimates quantify the contribution of differences in health status to the racial wealth gap. Consequently, in this section we simply discuss the potential relationships between health, wealth, and race.

It is possible that health does not affect wealth at all. The documented correlation may reflect the fact that good health follows from high income and wealth. The wealthy presumably have more resources, enabling them to lead a healthy lifestyle, receive preventive care, and treat medical conditions. However, there are several possible ways in which the causation between health and wealth could work in the opposite direction. For example, a shorter expected life span associated with poor health would reduce the need for savings in retirement; this reduced need for savings could lead to lower lifetime wealth accumulation.[42] Poor health might negatively affect income through lower wages or through more frequent periods of unemployment for unhealthy individuals. A third potential mechanism is a change in the saving behavior of those in poor health: they may have a stronger precautionary motive for saving to pay for anticipated medical treatment or to maintain consumption in case of unemployment, among other things. Alternatively, the high cost of care and treatment may reduce saving.

Smith (1999a) provides evidence on some of these relationships. He finds that negative health shocks lead to a sizable reduction in saving. This is partly due to out-of-pocket medical expenses; lowered life expectancy and reduced earnings also contribute. This evidence suggests that good health is not simply a by-product of wealth. Furthermore, any precautionary saving motive, if it exists, appears to be offset by the higher out-of-pocket medical expenses of those in poor health.

These results do not offer any explanation for why whites tend to be in better health than blacks or Hispanics. New theories focus on the impact on health of early childhood factors, long-term stress, and income inequality. Differences in these factors by race and ethnicity could contribute to differences in health status, which could in turn affect wealth, but additional research is needed.[43]

Assessment The strong correlations between health and wealth and between race and health suggest that differences in health status have an important influence on wealth inequality. These relationships clearly need to be better understood, but the task will be difficult. A central impediment to making further progress is identifying plausible exogenous variation in health that can inform evidence on the direction of causality in the relationship between health and wealth.

RATES OF RETURN

Differences in rates of return on saving or on existing assets can contribute to wealth inequality. Families make different portfolio choices for a variety of reasons related to risk aversion, information, and the need for liquid assets, among other factors. With different investment choices, the overall rate of return for some households will be lower than for others. Existing evidence indicates that portfolio choices are probably more significant than asset-specific rates of return in understanding black-white wealth gaps. Although we deal with portfolio choices and asset-specific rates of return separately, together they determine a household's overall return on investments.[44]

Housing and Credit Markets

Available evidence suggests that differences in asset-specific rates of return are not responsible for the observed racial wealth gap. Put differently, black households appear to receive the same rates of return on their equity, housing, and other investments as do white households. Gittleman and Wolff (2000) calculate what black wealth would have been in 1994 had black households earned the rates of return on assets that whites did during the previous ten-year period, using household data from the PSID. They find that the black-white wealth ratio would in fact have been two to three percentage points *lower*—that is, the wealth gap would have been wider by 3 to 4 percent. According to their analysis, blacks actually earned a higher rate of return on capital than did whites from 1984 to 1994: 41 percent compared with 32 percent. Home prices increased faster for blacks than for whites, as did business equity, stocks, and real estate.

There remain striking black-white differences in housing, which is the largest component of wealth for most families. Blacks are less likely than whites to be homeowners, and the homes of black families tend to be less valuable than the homes of whites, even after conditioning on housing unit characteristics (Long and Caudill 1992). James Long and Steven Caudill (1992) conclude that housing market discrimination is not important for homeownership, but there may be subtle forms of discrimination that restrict the sizes, locations, and types of houses available to blacks, leading to lower-valued homes. Charles and Hurst (2002) show that blacks are less likely to apply for mortgage loans, perhaps because they expect to be rejected. And indeed, they find that blacks are almost twice as likely as whites to be rejected for a mortgage. However, conditional on a loan being granted, the terms of the mortgage appear to be the same.

There may also be racial differences in access to credit markets. According to data from the SCF, blacks and Hispanics are more likely to be turned down for credit: 31 percent of Hispanic families and 36 percent of black families had been turned down for credit or discouraged from borrowing in the five years prior to the time of the surveys, while only 14 percent of whites had been turned down for credit or discouraged from borrowing.[45]

A greater unavailability of credit to blacks might affect the likelihood of their becoming self-employed. Again, there are large black-white differences in self-employment (see Fairlie and Meyer 2000), and self-employment is positively correlated with wealth. Menchik and Jianakoplos (1997) suggest that differences in self-employment can account for 7 and 12 percent of the wealth gap of married and single households in the NLS, respectively. In the 1989 SCF, differences in self-employment account for 24 and 8 percent of the wealth gap of married and single households, respectively.

Portfolio Choices

Households hold many types of assets, including stocks, bonds, mutual funds, housing equity, other real estate, annuities, saving and checking accounts, money market funds, certificates of deposit, and business equity. Because these may produce different rates of return, systematic differences in household portfolio choices by race could lead to different overall rates of return and therefore different rates of wealth accumulation.

Three striking differences in portfolio choices have been documented in the literature. First, although whites are more likely to be homeowners, housing equity makes up a much greater share of wealth for blacks. According to Gittleman and Wolff (2000), between 63 and 66 percent of whites owned a home in the three years of the PSID wealth supplement, compared with 37 to 38 percent of blacks. Housing equity accounted for 31 to 35 percent of white wealth, compared with 53 to 64 percent of black wealth.[46] Second, whites are much more likely than blacks to own stock. According to Hurst, Luoh, and Stafford (1998), 8.3 percent of black "stable households" owned stock in 1989; this increased to 14.3 percent in 1994.[47] In comparison, 36.0 percent of stable white households owned stock in 1989; this increased to 44.8 percent in 1994. Third, blacks are much less likely than whites to own simple bank accounts. In 1989, 52.4 percent of black families held a bank account, compared with 88.5 percent of white families; these numbers fell in 1994 to 45.4 percent and 85.3 percent, respectively (Hurst, Luoh, and Stafford 1998).

As with asset-specific rates of return, only Gittleman and Wolff (2000) estimate the contribution of portfolio choices to the wealth gap. Their simulations suggest that substituting average white portfolio choices would have reduced the racial wealth gap in 1994 by between 7 and 11 percent. This is mostly due to differences in stock ownership: white households own stock at a much higher rate. Of course, the estimated effect would likely be larger if the data reflected the extremely strong stock market performance in the second half of the 1990s.

Hurst, Luoh, and Stafford (1998) find that stock ownership is a strong predictor of wealth and differs greatly by race. Although they do not present their results in terms of the wealth gap, rough calculations using their results suggest that differences in the likelihood of stock ownership account for 11 to 14 percent of the wealth gap.

Assessment   Evidence from these studies suggests that differences in portfolio composition are an important determinant of the racial wealth gap, with estimates ranging between 7 and 14 percent. These results leave an important question unanswered: What explains differences in portfolio choices? Perhaps they can be fully explained by black-white differences in income. Perhaps family support networks allow risk-sharing or encourage riskier behavior. Perhaps greater uncertainty about household stability, future employment, or future earnings causes some households to keep a higher percentage of their wealth in liquid assets. Perhaps lack of experience or knowledge about financial institutions limits portfolio choices. Or perhaps there are cultural differences in risk aversion. Further research is needed to uncover the forces behind racial differences in portfolio composition. Conditional on holding specific assets, there is little evidence that there are systematic differences in rates of return across racial and ethnic groups.

GOVERNMENT PROGRAMS

Means-tested government assistance programs typically have asset limits as part of eligibility requirements. These asset limits provide a direct incentive against asset accumulation. Since these types of programs are targeted toward the poor and income is correlated with race, these programs may have a differential effect by race on wealth accumulation.

If households are forward-looking, asset tests may be salient for any household expecting to draw benefits from the program in the future. Put differently, the existence of means-tested transfers with asset tests may inhibit precautionary saving among all families who think there is a positive probability of receiving program benefits in the future. In this sense, government programs may result in different saving rates between rich and poor families.

Glenn Hubbard, Jonathan Skinner, and Stephen Zeldes (1995) have constructed a sophisticated life-cycle simulation model that predicts, in the absence of asset testing, that low-income families would save considerably more than they actually do. They are able to closely match wealth-income ratios observed in the PSID by including stylized means-tested transfer programs in their model. Their results suggest that the presence of these government programs may indeed contribute to differences in saving behavior between high- and low-income families.

Jonathan Gruber and Aaron Yelowitz (1999) find that among the eligible population, Medicaid lowered wealth holdings by between $1,293 and $1,645 in 1993, and the expansions in Medicaid from 1984 to 1993 lowered wealth holdings by about 7.2 percent. David Neumark and Elizabeth Powers (2000) find mixed evidence that supplemental security income (SSI) affects wealth and saving but conclude that SSI reduces the saving of men nearing retirement. Powers (1998) finds modest, negative effects on wealth accumulation of AFDC asset tests.

James Ziliak (2001) suggests that government transfers have small but discernible negative effects on liquid asset accumulation. Hurst and Ziliak (2001) find consistent results and show that a policy that increases program asset limits would have, at best, a modest positive effect on savings, since it appears that most families eligible for welfare are not facing binding asset constraints. These results suggest that in the aggregate, wealth accumulation is not substantially affected by the asset limits and that asset-tested programs are unlikely to have a large impact on the racial wealth gap.

Assessment   The existing evidence, though somewhat sparse, suggests that the effects of antipoverty program asset tests are not large and that only a small percentage of the population is affected. In the absence of more evidence, we conclude that public assistance programs do not contribute significantly to racial wealth inequality.

CONCLUSIONS

Figures 24.4 and 24.5 summarize the existing empirical work examining black-white wealth inequality. Figure 24.4 presents those studies that have estimated, through a number of different methods, the extent to which racial differences in income and demographic variables contribute to the measured gap in average wealth between black and white households. Figure 24.5 presents results from studies that measure how other factors affect the racial wealth gap. These fall into one of three areas: family background or transfers, consumption and savings behavior, and household rates of return.

Figures 24.4 and 24.5 suggest that differences in income and demographic characteristics are the most important factors explaining black-white wealth differentials. Transfers and family background also appear to be important. Portfolio choices may play a modest role, particularly owing to differences in stock ownership. Finally, the evidence thus far, though scant, suggests that saving behavior, while related to income, is not otherwise strongly related to race and therefore does not contribute significantly to the black-white wealth gap.

The majority of these results are based on regression decompositions that estimate the contribution of various factors. There is clearly no consensus in the literature, except perhaps that differences in income and demographic characteristics explain much of the wealth gap. We believe that there are several methodological considerations that could help resolve some of the wide variation in estimates. We discuss six of them here.

First, it would be useful to further investigate the implications of the fact that whites and blacks do not share similar income distributions and that they may differ by other characteristics associated with wealth accumulation. As noted by Altonji and Doraszelski (2001) and Barsky and his colleagues (2001), these differences may bias regression decomposition estimates of the importance of certain factors in explaining the wealth gap. In particular, they may explain the common finding that more of the wealth gap can be accounted for when using white coefficients to predict black wealth than when using black coefficients to predict white wealth. Altonji and Doraszelski (2001) and Barsky and his colleagues (2001) come to different conclusions, however, about the relevance of this problem.

Altonji and Doraszelski (2001) address the problem by comparing their full sample results with those obtained by performing regression decompositions on subsamples of whites and blacks that have similar income and demographic characteristics. The results do not change, implying that the lack of overlapping characteristics does not explain the difference in black and white wealth functions. Barsky and his colleagues (2001) conclude the opposite, showing that regression decomposition estimates using white coefficients to predict black wealth overestimates the contribution of earnings to the wealth gap; using black coefficients to predict white wealth should underestimate the contribution of earnings. A limitation of this analysis is that it considers only earnings, while Altonji and Doraszelski's analysis conditions on many demographic control variables.

Second, studies might benefit from a more systematic examination of demographic variables. The specifications summarized in figures 24.4 and 24.5 are inconsistent in their inclusion or exclusion of various factors, and that inconsistency probably contributes to the

FIGURE 24.4   The Contribution of Income and Demographics to the Black-White Wealth Gap

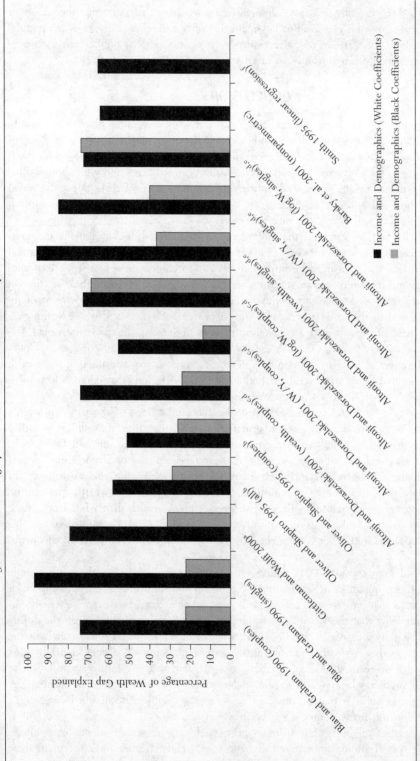

Source: Authors' compilation.

[a]Reported estimate is an average of regression decompositions performed for 1984, 1989, 1994. [b]Includes a dummy indicating self-employment or professional status; because self-employment could be considered an aspect of portfolio choice or rate of return, including it here could inflate the contribution of income and demographics. [c]Reported estimate is an average of mean and median regression analyses for couples. [d]Included are health status and self-employment measures; since these could affect saving and rate of return, respectively, including them here may inflate the estimate of the importance of income and demographics. [e]Reported estimate is an average of results from four analyses: mean and median regression for single men and women (equal weights). [f]Included in this estimate are measures reflecting health status, received inheritances, bequest preferences, and financial planning horizons; this could inflate the estimate of the importance of income and demographics relative to the importance of family transfers and saving behavior.

FIGURE 24.5   Factors Explaining the Black-White Wealth Gap: Looking Beyond Income and Demographics

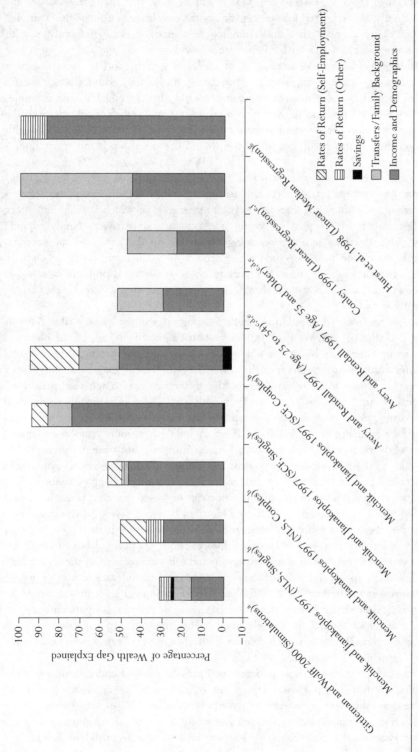

Source: Authors' compilation.
[a] Simulation based on ten-year wealth changes: black wealth is recalculated after substitution of relevant white parameter. [b] Estimates based on average of analyses using white and black coefficients to estimate wealth. [c] Includes measure of health status as part of demographics, although it could affect wealth through saving behavior. [d] Estimate based on white coefficients. [e] Savings and rates of return were not considered in this analysis. [f] Conley reports that parental wealth, income, and demographics together account for all of the wealth gap, with parental wealth being more important. For purposes of this figure, we assigned 55 percent to parental wealth and 45 percent to income and demographics. [g] These are not the actual percentages reported by the authors but were derived from: (1) their regression yields an insignificant coefficient on the indicator for black; this leads them to conclude that they can account for 100 percent of the wealth gap; (2) their results imply that "holding stock" may account for 11 to 14 percent of the wealth gap; and (3) all other covariates are income or demographic factors.

variation in estimates. Figures 24.4 and 24.5, for example, show that the regression decompositions consistently do a better job of explaining the wealth gap for singles than for married couples. This suggests that understanding how marital status interrelates with wealth accumulation would be useful for better understanding wealth inequality.

Third, although regression decomposition of the *mean* wealth gap (the most common approach) is informative, other approaches illuminating the factors that influence wealth accumulation at the tails of the wealth distribution would also be valuable. For example, although regression decomposition suggests that intergenerational transfers contribute to the mean wealth gap, much of the effect presumably takes place at the upper end of the wealth distribution, and these transfers do not affect the wealth of typical black and white households.

Fourth, a major issue in this literature is to determine to what extent family background and intergenerational transfers contribute to black-white wealth inequality. There is evidence that transfers matter, but there are several other ways in which families can affect wealth. Families may teach or pass on saving preferences and behavior; family support networks may either decrease or increase saving depending on the nature of the support; and families may affect the rate of return of households by influencing portfolio choices, perhaps through risk-sharing or exposure to certain types of assets. Altonji and Doraszelski (2001), Conley (1999), and Charles and Hurst (2002) have somewhat different views on the importance of these factors.

Fifth, another unanswered question is whether saving rates differ by race after controlling for income. Gittleman and Wolff (2000) suggest that most, if not all, of the observed difference in saving rates can be accounted for by differences in income. Their results suggest that after controlling for income, the saving rate for blacks may be slightly lower than for whites; according to their simulations, this difference over a ten-year period accounted for only about 1 percent of the racial wealth gap. There is little other empirical evidence comparing saving rates by race, yet many factors, some of which are known to differ by race, may influence saving behavior. These include government transfer programs, family support networks, health, risk aversion, bequest motives, and time preferences. We think a fruitful area for future research would be to examine whether saving behavior varies by race after controlling for income. If no evidence of differences in saving behavior by race is found, then mechanisms affecting saving behavior can be ruled out as a possible suspect for contributing to the racial wealth gap. If a relationship between saving behavior and race is found, however, then these individual elements could be explored further.

Sixth, the underlying reasons for apparent differences in portfolio choices by race are not well understood. Differences in stock ownership and self-employment in particular, both of which are less likely to occur among blacks, appear to have a moderate impact on wealth inequality. Determining whether these differences are institutional or cultural would be worth investigating, particularly because this distinction may be relevant for policymaking.

To address these six points, it will continue to be important to have datasets with sample sizes or sampling frames that include a large number of very high-wealth households. The SCFs are essential for this reason.

Further research progress on these six issues will provide a better understanding of racial wealth inequality, which is an important starting point for understanding the evolution of wealth inequality more generally. The persistence of the black-white wealth gap, and the fact that a significant portion may be unexplained, is a puzzle that, once solved, should give us a clearer picture of the mechanisms determining the wealth accumulation patterns of all households.

The literature surveyed in this chapter points to the importance of particular factors in predicting wealth and wealth inequality more generally. There is a consensus that labor income accounts for the majority of the racial wealth gap, which suggests that wealth inequality in the population is likely to be strongly related to inequality in labor income. In fact, it appears that over the long run, trends in wealth inequality have mirrored changes in income inequality, with both increasing fairly steadily over the last forty years (Scholz and Joulfaian 2003). We can also expect similar though perhaps weaker effects from other factors; for example, if the size and frequency of inheritances and gifts become more (less) similar across the population, we would expect measured wealth inequality to diminish (increase).

As this survey has suggested, more could usefully be learned to better understand the evolution of wealth inequality in the United States and how it affects households across different demographic groups. We close by briefly raising two issues that should be the subject of additional future work. First, how can empirical work convincingly examine the societal or individual consequences of striking wealth inequality? Inequality may lead to differential access to the political process and other civic institutions. It may lead to unequal opportunities for young children. It may affect the living standards of the elderly. And it may contribute to wealth inequality in the next generation. Second, how effective is public policy in altering patterns of wealth? Many policies attempt to increase wealth, ranging from individual development accounts (IDAs) targeted at low-income families to tax incentives for saving and pensions.[48] Yet there is considerable controversy over the efficacy of these policies. Resolving these debates will have important implications for the future direction of policy as it relates to wealth.

We are grateful to the Russell Sage Foundation for supporting our work, to participants of the Summer 2001 Inequality Workshop at Harvard, to Kathryn M. Neckerman, and to members of the Wisconsin Inequality Working Group—Betty Evanson, Bob Hauser, Bob Haveman, John Mullahy, Stephanie Robert, Gary Sandefur, and Bobbi Wolfe—for helpful comments on our work.

NOTES

1. See, for example, Banks, Blundell, and Tanner (1998) and Bernheim, Skinner, and Weinberg (2001). For a different view, see Engen, Gale, and Uccello (1999).

2. Several datasets have supported and will continue to support useful analyses related to wealth that do not depend on accurate representations of wealth holdings at the top of the wealth distribution. These include the Panel Study of Income Dynamics (PSID), which has special wealth supplements in 1984, 1989, 1994, and 1999; the Survey of Income and Program Participation (SIPP), which includes periodic wealth "topical modules"; the Consumer Expenditure Surveys (CEX), which contain a small set of wealth questions; and the National Longitudinal Surveys, which also contain a small set of wealth questions. Thomas Juster, James Smith, and Frank Stafford (1999) report that the wealth data in the PSID are quite comparable to those in the Survey of Consumer Finances, except in the top 5 percent of the wealth distribution.

3. The developers of the data warn that the 1983 SCF is different from the surveys beginning in 1989, and these differences might make it inappropriate to use for cross-year comparisons. The 1986 SCF was a telephone follow-up to the 1983 survey and is generally thought to be less accurate than the surveys of 1983, 1989, and subsequent years.

4. The Gini coefficients range from 0.781 to 0.794. Perfect equality would result in a Gini of zero, and perfect inequality would result in a Gini of one.

5. The Flow of Funds is published by the Federal Reserve Board and offers national balance sheet totals.

6. For example, stocks and bonds are scaled by a factor of 1.23 in the 1995 SCF.

7. Antoniewicz (1996) provides three reasons why it is difficult to accept Wolff's adjustments. First, the household sector in the FoF is computed as a residual, so it does not provide an unassailable benchmark. Second, it is difficult to match asset and liability categories in the SCFs and FoFs. Third, the household sector in the FoFs includes nonprofit institutions, so the FoF benchmark needs to be adjusted to account for this discrepancy. Given this reading of Antoniewicz's work, Wolff's adjustments do not seem compelling. Even if some change is needed, proportional adjustments implicitly assume there is uniform underreporting (in percentages) of the adjusted items. There is clearly no reason to believe misreporting takes this particular pattern. For an additional discussion, see Kennickell (1998).

8. In 1989 the creators of the SCFs began providing five separate imputed values for each missing variable. They also selected 999 sample replicates from the final data in a way that allows users to capture important dimensions of sample variation. Accounting fully for imputation and sampling variation generally increases standard errors when working with wealth data. (This observation arises from Scholz's experience with these issues drawn from his work on Bernheim, Lemke, and Scholz 2002.) This is likely to be a particularly important concern at the extremes of the wealth distribution and for subpopulations, such as disaggregated statistics by race or ethnicity.

9. The data are a pooled sample of the SCFs from 1989, 1992, 1995, and 1998. Dollar amounts are in constant 1998 dollars and the observations are weighted. Net worth is a comprehensive measure that includes housing assets less liabilities, business assets less liabilities, checking and saving accounts, stocks, bonds, mutual funds, retirement accounts, certificates of deposit, whole life insurance and other assets less credit card debt, and other liabilities. It excludes defined benefit pension wealth, defined contribution pension wealth held outside 401(k)s, Social Security, consumer durables, and future earnings. This concept of wealth is similar to those used by other studies discussed in this survey, although definitions of wealth sometimes vary slightly.

10. Economists typically think of households maximizing utility over time, where lifetime utility equals the discounted, additively separable stream of within-period utility (discounted by the factor δ), which in turn depends on consumption (that is, $V(C) = \sum_{t=0}^{T} \delta^t u(C_t)$). Consumers are constrained by lifetime resources. A simple representation of the household's budget constraint is $A_{t+1} = (1 + r_t)(A_t + Y_t - C_t)$, where A_t is assets, Y_t is income, C_t is consumption and r_t is the rate of return on assets.

    The solution to this intertemporal consumption problem, which maximizes well-being subject to lifetime resource constraints, is to equate the discounted value of the marginal utility of consumption across time. Saving in each period is the difference between income (defined to include revaluations of existing assets) and consumption. The discounted value of past and current saving across families is equal to the stock of wealth at any given time. The simple model provides an abstract representation of a wide range of economic and sociological phenomena influencing wealth and its evolution.

11. Melvin Oliver and Thomas Shapiro (1995) and Dalton Conley (1999) develop far-reaching sociological analyses of racial wealth inequality, but we focus on their empirical analyses of black-white wealth differentials.

12. The skewed wealth distribution has led some researchers to examine the log rather than the level of wealth; some also estimate median or quantile regressions in addition to mean regressions.

13. See, for example, Altonji and Doraszelski (2001), who find across several specifications that wealth is more weakly related to income and demographics among blacks than among whites.

14. Barsky and his colleagues (2001) focus only on income, so their study differs from the more comprehensive attempts to examine black-white wealth inequality. Their approach can be extended to multivariate analysis, which would be a worthwhile undertaking.

15. Gittleman and Wolff (2000) report results from a standard regression decomposition as well.

16. Regression decomposition estimates using white coefficients include Altonji and Doraszelski (2001), 5 to 120 percent; Gittleman and Wolff (2000), 77 to 81 percent; Blau and Graham (1990), 74 to 97 percent;

Oliver and Shapiro (1995), 58 percent; and Avery and Rendall (1997), 23 to 30 percent. Estimates using black coefficients include Altonji and Doraszelski (2001), 12 to 84 percent; Gittleman and Wolff (2000), 28 to 33 percent; Blau and Graham (1990), 22 percent; and Oliver and Shapiro (1995), 29 percent. Regression decomposition estimates where the results from using white and black coefficients are averaged include Menchik and Jianakoplos (1997), 44 to 93 percent. Estimates using linear regression include Hurst, Luoh, and Stafford (1998), 100 percent; and Smith (1995), 63 to 67 percent. Barsky and his colleagues (2001) find that income accounts for 64 percent of the black-white wealth gap.

17. Because of the nonlinear relationship between income and wealth, and because the white earnings distribution extends further to the right than the black earnings distribution, linear estimates of white wealth as a function of income are much steeper than linear estimates of black wealth. Using these linear estimates overestimates the black-white wealth gap at the upper end of the income distribution and therefore also overestimates the contribution of earnings to the wealth gap. Including a quadratic income term to take into account the nonlinear relationship between income and wealth should improve the estimate, but it continues to overstate the fraction of the wealth gap attributable to differences in income.

18. The range of estimates for income ignores the Avery and Rendall (1997) estimate of 6.3 percent, which applies to households whose head is fifty-five years or older.

19. Paul Menchik and Nancy Jianakoplos (1997) find mostly small, negative, but insignificant coefficients on number of children. In contrast, Francine Blau and John Graham (1990) find that wealth is positively related to the number of children in the household.

20. Back-of-the-envelope calculations using 1998 SCF data suggest that inheritances and gifts may account for a relatively small percentage of the racial gap in mean wealth. The mean net worth of white households in 1998 was $332,979; the mean wealth of black and Hispanic households was $68,473. Mean inheritance amounts received by white and black households are $30,345 and $8,248, respectively, when the value of inheritances is grossed up by a 5 percent nominal rate from the date of receipt. The gap in mean inheritance amounts is $22,097, which is 8.4 percent of the difference in mean wealth amounts, $264,506.

21. Fewer than half of all households in the SCF pooled sample reported having received an inheritance. Therefore, the median inheritance amount for both whites and blacks is zero.

22. Smith (1999b, 7) concludes, however, that "financial inheritances appear not to be quantitatively important in explaining wealth levels or wealth changes," based on his analysis of data from the PSID.

23. Housing can be considered a high-return investment because of the substantial tax preferences accorded to owner-occupied housing.

24. Menchik and Jianakoplos (1997) also present estimates from the 1976 NLS, where the contribution of inheritances is only 2.2 percent of the wealth gap for married couples. The SCF estimates are likely to be more reliable, because they are based on reported inheritances received rather than predicted inheritance amounts, which are used in the NLS estimates. Furthermore, the SCF is more recent and is likely to have better information on wealth.

25. Avery and Rendall (1997) examine mean regression decompositions using the 1989 SCF, but their dependent variable is log of non-inherited wealth rather than level of current wealth. Using coefficients estimated on a white sample to predict black wealth, they find that for twenty-five- to fifty-four-year-olds, received inheritances account for 21.8 percent of the racial wealth gap and for those over fifty-five years old, received inheritance accounts for 24.0 percent. These analyses account for earnings, age, marital status, and education. Because coefficients estimated from a white sample tend to explain a larger fraction of the wealth gap than the reverse, the results from Menchik and Jianakoplos (1997), which are averages, appear to be consistent with the Avery and Rendall results.

26. Here we ignore the estimates from the NLS provided by Menchik and Jianakoplos (1997); they are based on predicted rather than actual inheritances, and they do not seem consistent with other studies.

27. These percentages are based on weighted responses. Of the remaining respondents, 1.2 percent did not respond or did not know, and 3.7 percent disagreed with their spouse so an answer was not coded.

28. Those who believe that leaving an estate is "somewhat important" accumulate $56,000 more wealth than those who believe it is not important. For the median household, the differentials are much less, at $12,000 and $9,000. These results are all statistically significant at conventional levels.

29. Although their analysis was designed to test the importance of intergenerational transfers, the fixed effects model should control for *all* time-invariant unobservable aspects of family behavior. These include learned saving preferences and behavior, experience with financial institutions or types of assets, and potential risk-sharing.

30. Additional evidence from the PSID 1996 supplement supports the possibility that saving preferences are correlated across generations. Charles and Hurst (2003) find that preferences for risk aversion are similar between parents and children, particularly at the tails of the risk aversion distribution.

31. Charles and Hurst (2003) also find that several other factors account for the intergenerational correlation of wealth, such as correlation of income between parent and child, family risk-sharing, and received and expected bequests. These factors are all addressed in the literature and discussed in other sections of this chapter.

32. Altonji and Doraszelski (2001) also note that Conley (1999) excludes permanent income measures for adult children; his sample size is small; he does not control for family-specific effects; his sample may be questionable given the fact that he reports similar percentages of self-employed blacks and whites; and his standard errors are large.

33. Strong family support networks may also increase wealth by encouraging individuals to engage in riskier behavior or by enabling them to make certain investments, such as buying a home. Portfolio choices such as these are discussed in a later section.

34. Smith (1999b) also raises the possibility that increasing income inequality, coupled with the fact that high-income households save more than low-income households, could significantly increase wealth inequality. He concludes, however, that this is unlikely to be the most important factor in explaining the evolution of wealth inequality in recent decades.

35. Lawrance (1991) estimates Euler equations (equations governing the choice of consumption over time) derived from the utility function $V_{it} = E_t \left[\sum_{s=t}^{N} (1+\rho_i)^{t-s} U(C_{is}) \right]$. From this process she is able to estimate the time preference parameter ρ for different groups of households. According to one set of estimates, the time preference parameter for white, college-educated families in the top 5 percent of the labor income distribution is 0.10, compared with 0.19 for nonwhite families without a college education whose labor incomes are in the bottom fifth percentile (Lawrance 1991, table 1, 69). These suggest large differences in the "patience" of each group of households, where patience is defined as the extent to which households prefer to consume today rather than save in order to consume more in the future. A time preference of 0.10 implies that the value of consumption decreases by 90.9 percent each year into the future, while a value of 0.19 implies a decrease in the value of consumption of 84.0 percent each year. This means, for example, that households with a time preference of 0.19 will value consumption five years in the future at 41.8 percent of the same amount of consumption today; for households with a time preference rate of 0.10, this figure is 62.1 percent. Although other sets of Lawrance's estimates are smaller, such as those using the passbook saving rate rather than the Treasury bill interest rate to estimate the Euler equations, she finds that having high income, having a college education, and being white are all consistently associated with lower rates of time preference.

36. Dynan (1993) questions Lawrance's (1991) result and suggests that the faster growth of consumption among higher-income households is due to favorable wealth shocks not received by lower-income households. Dynan, Skinner, and Zeldes (2000) develop a sophisticated life-cycle simulation model and conclude that different time preference rates for low- and high-income households cannot properly account for observed savings patterns. Their simulations indicate that if high-income households have lower time preference rates, these households save more than their low-income counterparts when young, but spend more than low-income households when old; this is inconsistent with the empirical findings, which show that saving rates increase with income, even among the elderly.

37. The question reads, "In planning your family's saving and spending, which of the time periods listed on this page is most important to you and [if appropriate] your (spouse/partner)?" Potential responses include "next few months," "next year," "next few years," "next five to ten years," and "longer than ten years."

38. Controls include indicator variables for high school completion, some college, college degree and post-college training, five-year age intervals, income quintile, and survey year.

39. Specifically, the SCF asks the following question: "Which of the statements on this page comes closest to the amount of financial risk that you and your (spouse/partner) are willing to take when you save or make investments?" The four possible answers are: "take substantial financial risks expecting to earn substantial returns," "take above-average financial risks expecting to earn above-average returns," "take average financial risks expecting to earn average returns," and "not willing to take any financial risks."

40. The regressions include indicator variables for high school completion, some college, college degree and postcollege training, five-year age intervals, income quintile, and survey year.

41. We use an inverse hyperbolic sine transformation of net worth when looking at the log specification. This transformation allows us to account in a reasonable way for the fact that some SCF households have negative net worth. These analyses also confirm that, as expected, being black or Hispanic is negatively correlated with net worth after including the appropriate controls.

42. Blacks have shorter life expectancies than whites. For example, at age 20, white men are expected to live an additional 55.5 years, compared with 49.5 years for black men. Life expectancies for white and black women at age 20 are 60.8 years and 56.2 years, respectively (Anderson 2001).

43. For example, studies that document differences in race and ethnicity in the use of long-term care and home health care find that black families make less use of nursing homes and skilled nursing facilities (Cagney and Agree 1999; Wallace et al. 1998). It is not yet clear whether racial differences in wealth and income can account for these patterns.

44. One study estimates the combined effect of asset-specific rates of return and portfolio choices on the wealth gap: Menchik and Jianakoplos (1997), using data from the 1976 NLS, suggest that racial differences in the after-tax household rate of return account for 1 percent of the wealth gap for married households and 8 percent of the wealth gap for single households. These results average the results using white and black coefficients.

45. Because these results may simply indicate that blacks are more likely to apply for loans that exceed their ability to repay, they are only suggestive of the possibility that there is differential access to credit markets based on race.

46. Long and Caudill (1992) find a much smaller differential in rates of homeownership using the 1986 Current Population Survey; however, they restrict their sample to married households with the head over age twenty. Homeownership rates for black households and white households are 63.2 and 78.5 percent, respectively.

47. Stable households are those in which the head of household remained the same in the relevant time period—in this instance, between 1989 and 1994.

48. Wolff (2003, 354) provides a different perspective on the role of policy. He suggests that while wealth appeared to become more unequal in the United States during the 1980s, when Ronald Reagan was president, wealth also appeared to become more unequal in Sweden during a time when the government was (mainly) controlled by Social Democrats. In contrast, wealth appeared to become less unequal in the United Kingdom when Margaret Thatcher was the leader. Wolff concludes that "the differences in public policy alone cannot account for these trends in wealth distribution."

REFERENCES

Altonji, Joseph G., and Ulrich Doraszelski. 2001. "The Role of Permanent Income and Demographics in Black-White Differences in Wealth." Working paper 8473. Cambridge, Mass.: National Bureau of Economic Research.

Altonji, Joseph G., Fumio Hayashi, and Laurence J. Kotlikoff. 1996. "The Effects of Income and Wealth on Time and Money Transfers Between Parents and Children." Working paper 5522. Cambridge, Mass.: National Bureau of Economic Research.

———. 1997. "Parental Altruism and Inter Vivos Transfers: Theory and Evidence." *Journal of Political Economy* 105(6): 1121–66.

Anderson, Robert N. 2001. *United States Life Tables, 1998.* National Vital Statistics Reports 48(18). Hyattsville, Md.: National Center for Health Statistics.

Antoniewicz, Rochelle. 1996. "A Comparison of the Household Sector from the Flow of Funds Accounts and the Survey of Consumer Finances." Finance and Economics Discussion Series 1996-26. Washington, D.C.: Board of Governors of the Federal Reserve System.

Attanasio, Orazio P., and Martin Browning. 1995. "Consumption over the Life Cycle and over the Business Cycle." *American Economic Review* 85(5): 1118–37.

Avery, Robert B., and Michael S. Rendall. 1997. "The Contribution of Inheritances to Black-White Wealth Disparities in the United States." Working paper 97-08. Ithaca, N.Y.: Bronfenbrenner Life Course Center.

Banks, James, Richard Blundell, and Sarah Tanner. 1998. "Is There a Retirement-Savings Puzzle?" *American Economic Review* 88(4): 769–88.

Barsky, Robert, John Bound, Kerwin Charles, and Joe Lupton. 2001. "Accounting for the Black-White Wealth Gap: A Nonparametric Approach." Working paper 8466. Cambridge, Mass.: National Bureau of Economic Research.

Bernheim, B. Douglas, Robert Lemke, and John Karl Scholz. Forthcoming. "Do Estate and Gift Taxes Affect the Timing of Private Transfers?" *Journal of Public Economics*.

Bernheim, B. Douglas, Jonathan Skinner, and Steven Weinberg. 2001. "What Accounts for the Variation in Retirement Wealth Among U.S. Households?" *American Economic Review* 91(4): 832–57.

Blau, Francine D., and John W. Graham. 1990. "Black-White Differences in Wealth and Asset Composition." *Quarterly Journal of Economics* 105(2): 321–39.

Cagney, Kathleen A., and Emily M. Agree. 1999. "Racial Differences in Skilled Nursing Care and Home Health Use: The Mediating Effects of Family Structure and Social Class." *Journals of Gerontology*, series B 54(4): S223–36.

Charles, Kerwin Kofi, and Erik Hurst. 2002. "The Transition to Homeownership and the Black-White Wealth Gap." *Review of Economics and Statistics* 84(2): 281–97.

———. 2003. "The Correlation of Wealth Across Generations." *Journal of Political Economy* 111(6): 1115–82.

Conley, Dalton. 1999. *Being Black, Living in the Red: Race, Wealth, and Social Policy in America*. Los Angeles: University of California Press.

Cox, Donald. 1990. "Intergenerational Transfers and Liquidity Constraints." *Quarterly Journal of Economics* 105(1): 187–217.

Davies, James. 1981. "Uncertain Lifetime, Consumption, and Dissaving in Retirement." *Journal of Political Economy* 89(3): 561–77.

Dynan, Karen E. 1993. "The Rate of Time Preference and Shocks to Wealth: Evidence from Panel Data." Working paper 134. Washington, D.C.: Board of Governors of the Federal Reserve System, Economic Activity Section.

Dynan, Karen E., Jonathan Skinner, and Stephen P. Zeldes. 2000. "Do the Rich Save More?" Working paper 7906. Cambridge, Mass.: National Bureau of Economic Research.

Engen, Eric M., William G. Gale, and E. Cori Uccello. 1999. "The Adequacy of Household Saving." *Brookings Papers on Economic Activity* (2): 65–165.

Fairlie, Robert W., and Bruce D. Meyer. 2000. "Trends in Self-employment Among White and Black Men During the Twentieth Century." *Journal of Human Resources* 35(4): 643–69.

Gittleman, Maury, and Edward N. Wolff. 2000. "Racial Wealth Disparities: Is the Gap Closing?" Working paper 311. Annandale-on-Hudson, N.Y.: Bard College, Jerome Levy Economics Institute.

Gruber, Jonathan, and Aaron Yelowitz. 1999. "Public Health Insurance and Private Savings." *Journal of Political Economy* 107(6), pt. 1: 1249–74.

Haveman, Robert, and Barbara Wolfe. 1994. *Succeeding Generations: On the Effects of Investments in Children*. New York: Russell Sage Foundation.

Hubbard, R. Glenn, Jonathan Skinner, and Stephen P. Zeldes. 1995. "Precautionary Saving and Social Insurance." *Journal of Political Economy* 103(2): 360–99.

Hurd, Michael D. 1987. "Savings of the Elderly and Desired Bequests." *American Economic Review* 77(3): 298–312.

———. 1989. "Mortality Risk and Bequests." *Econometrica* 57(4): 779–813.

Hurst, Erik, Ming Ching Luoh, and Frank P. Stafford. 1998. "The Wealth Dynamics of American Families, 1984 to 1994." *Brookings Papers on Economic Activity* 1: 267–337.

Hurst, Erik, and James P. Ziliak. 2001. "Welfare Reform and Household Saving." Discussion paper 1234-01. Madison, Wisc.: Institute for Research on Poverty.

Juster, F. Thomas, James P. Smith, and Frank Stafford. 1999. "The Measurement and Structure of Household Wealth." *Labour Economics* 6(2): 253–75.

Kennickell, Arthur B. 1998. "Comments on 'Recent Trends in the Size Distribution of Household Wealth' by Edward Wolff. Available at: www.federalreserve.gov/pubs/oss/oss2/papers/jep.wolff.3.pdf.

———. 2000. "An Examination of Changes in the Distribution of Wealth from 1989 to 1998: Evidence from the Survey of Consumer Finances." Prepared for the Conference on Saving, Intergenerational Transfers, and the Distribution of Wealth, Jerome Levy Economics Institute, Bard College (June 7–9). Available at: www.federalreserve.gov/pubs/oss/oss2/papers/wdist98.pdf.

Lawrance, Emily. 1991. "Poverty and the Rate of Time Preference: Evidence from Panel Data." *Journal of Political Economy* 99(1): 54–77.

Long, James E., and Steven B. Caudill. 1992. "Racial Differences in Homeownership and Housing Wealth." *Economic Inquiry* 30(1): 83–100.

McGarry, Kathleen, and Robert F. Schoeni. 1995. "Transfer Behavior in the Health and Retirement Study: Measurement and the Redistribution of Resources Within the Family." *Journal of Human Resources* 30: S184–226.

McLanahan, Sara, and Gary Sandefur. 1994. *Growing up with a Single Parent: What Hurts, What Helps.* Cambridge, Mass.: Harvard University Press.

Menchik, Paul L. 1980. "Primogeniture, Equal Sharing, and the U.S. Distribution of Wealth." *Quarterly Journal of Economics* 94(2): 299–316.

Menchik, Paul L., and Martin David. 1983. "Income Distribution, Lifetime Savings, and Bequests." *American Economic Review* 73(4): 672–90.

Menchik, Paul L., and Nancy Jianakoplos. 1997. "Black-White Wealth Inequality: Is Inheritance the Reason?" *Economic Inquiry* 35(2): 428–42.

Neumark, David, and Elizabeth Powers. 2000. "Welfare for the Elderly: The Effects of SSI on Preretirement Labor Supply." *Journal of Public Economics* 78(1–2): 51–80.

Oliver, Melvin, and Thomas Shapiro. 1995. *Black Wealth/White Wealth.* New York: Routledge.

Powers, Elizabeth T. 1998. "Does Means-Testing Welfare Discourage Saving?: Evidence from a Change in AFDC Policy in the United States." *Journal of Public Economics* 68(1): 33–53.

Scholz, John Karl, and David Joulfaian. 2003. "Wealth Inequality and the Wealth of Cohorts." Working paper. Madison: University of Wisconsin.

Smith, James P. 1995. "Racial and Ethnic Differences in Wealth in the Health and Retirement Study." *Journal of Human Resources* 30: S158–83.

———. 1999a. "Healthy Bodies and Thick Wallets: The Dual Relation Between Health and Economic Status." *Journal of Economic Perspectives* 13(2): 145–66.

———. 1999b. "Why is Wealth Inequality Rising?" Working paper, Santa Monica, Calif.: RAND.

U.S. Department of Commerce. U.S. Census Bureau. Various years. "Historical Income Tables, 1967 to 2001—Households." Available at: www.census.gov/hhes/income/histinc/h02.html.

Wallace, Steven P., Lene Levy-Storms, Raynard S. Kington, and Ronald M. Andersen. 1998. "The Persistence of Race and Ethnicity in the Use of Long-term Care." *Journals of Gerontology*, series B, 53(2): S104–12.

Wilhelm, Mark O. 1996. "Bequest Behavior and the Effect of Heirs' Earnings: Testing the Altruistic Model of Bequests." *American Economic Review* 86(4): 874–92.

Wolff, Edward N. 1998. "Recent Trends in the Size Distribution of Household Wealth." *Journal of Economic Perspectives* 12(3): 131–50.

———. 2000. "Recent Trends in Wealth Ownership, 1983 to 1998." Working paper 300. Annandale-on-Hudson, N.Y.: Bard College, Jerome Levy Economics Institute.

———. 2003. "The Impact of Gifts and Bequests on the Distribution of Wealth." In *Death and Dollars: The Role of Gifts and Bequests in America*, edited by Alicia H. Munnell and Annika Sunde'n. Washington, D.C.: Brookings.

Ziliak, James P. 2001. "Income Transfers and Assets of the Poor." Discussion paper 1233-01. Madison, Wisc.: Institute for Research on Poverty.

Part VIII

Methods and Concepts

Chapter 25

Assessing the Effect of Economic Inequality

William N. Evans, Michael Hout, and Susan E. Mayer

The rise in income inequality over the past three decades has spawned a surge in research that examines the causes and consequences of this trend. Authors from a variety of disciplines have examined the impact of various measures of inequality on outcomes as diverse as mortality, health habits, self-reported health status, civic and voter participation, trust, marriage, crime, educational attainment, the size of local governments, self-reported happiness, and school spending. Regardless of the outcome, all research that tries to evaluate the causal impact of inequality empirically faces a common set of methodological issues. In this chapter, we attempt to catalog the most common of these issues and to describe how researchers have dealt with them. The topics we describe are by no means exhaustive, and because they are common issues, they will be familiar to many researchers.

TYPES OF INEQUALITY EFFECTS

The primary focus of this chapter is a discussion of the techniques and issues associated with research that use a measure of inequality as an explanatory variable in regression models. Inequality is a property of a population or subpopulation—not of the individual. For that reason, estimates of the effect of inequality require a different approach to data than estimates of the effect of an individual's attribute. In this section, we discuss four mechanisms through which inequality can affect an outcome. Each mechanism requires a different methodology to measure the causal impact of inequality.

Mechanical Consequences

If inequality in some attribute such as income, wealth, or consumption affects an outcome and the effect does not decline over time, as inequality in x increases, inequality in the outcome increases. Suppose the attribute (x) is related to an outcome of interest (y) by this equation:

$$y_i = a + \beta x_i + e_i \qquad (25.1)$$

for persons $i = 1, \ldots, N$, and where e_i is an error term that summarizes the accumulated influence of all sources of variation in y_i that are uncorrelated with income. In this model, the variance in y is related to the variance in x by the formula:

$$\sigma^2_y = \beta^2 \sigma^2_x + \sigma^2_e \qquad (25.2)$$

The impact of inequality illustrated by equation 25.2 is a mechanical relationship—if the variance of x increases and β does not change, the variance of y increases in proportion to the square of β.[1]

Given consistent estimates of the causal impact of x on y, quantifying this mechanical relationship between growing inequality in x and y is mostly an accounting exercise. This does not mean that the consequences of the relationship are trivial. For example, social scientists from a number of disciplines have established that fathers' and sons' earnings are correlated. In regressions of log earnings of sons (y) on log earnings of fathers (x), estimates of β are around 0.40 when earnings are averaged over several years (Solon 1992; Zimmerman 1992). Chinhui Juhn, Kevin Murphy, and Brooks Pierce (1993) note that between 1965 and 1988 the standard deviation of log weekly wages for prime-age working males increased from 0.45 to 0.59, meaning the variance of log wages increased by 0.14. If the impact of fathers' wages on their sons' wages can be thought of as causal, and if the relationship has not changed as inequality has increased (which some researchers suggest are both very big ifs; see Levine and Mazumder 2002; Fertig 2001; Mayer and Lopoo 2004; Harding et al., forthcoming), and using estimates of $\beta = 0.4$, the mechanical effect described in equation 25.2 suggests that the variance in the log wages of sons would have increased by 0.023 between the fathers' and sons' generation. If we assume the standard deviation of sons' log weekly wages is around 0.6 (which is close to current estimates), rising inequality in fathers' weekly wages would have increased wage inequality by 6.3 percent.

Relational Effects

Over time the basic relationship between the variables x and y outlined in equation 25.1 may change, and depending on the direction and magnitude of the change, there can be important consequences for inequality. For example, suppose that the parameter β is positive and its estimated value increases over time, but the distribution of x does not change. This could happen if, for example, the importance of parental income to children's outcomes increases during a period when income inequality is not increasing. By construction, the variance of y increases under these circumstances. We call this type of inequality effect a "relational" effect, highlighting the changing relationship between x and y as a cause of changing inequality in outcomes even when income inequality does not change.

Income became more salient for a wide variety of social outcomes as inequality rose between 1975 and the mid-1990s. As examples, consider income effects on voting and happiness. Affluent voters supported Republicans more than they had done before, and poor voters supported Democrats slightly more in the elections of 1988, 1992, and 1996 than they had in the past (Brooks and Brady 1999). The effect of income on several measures of subjective well-being rose between 22 and 42 percent between 1975 and 2000 (Hout 2003). Likewise, a growing literature suggests that the correlation between socioeconomic status and health may have increased over the past forty years (Feldman et al. 1989; Pappas et al. 1993; Preston and Elo 1995; Deaton and Paxson 1998; Evans, Ringel, and Stech 1999).

Maybe the most heavily researched example of a relational effect is in the literature on the causes rather than the consequences of changing inequality. David Autor and Lawrence Katz (1999) summarize the extensive literature on this subject and note that for males the Gini coefficient of male log weekly wages increased from 0.25 in 1965 to 0.343 in 1995, a 37 percent increase in twenty-three-years. About two-thirds of the change in wage inequality has been "within group"—that is, changes in wages for people defined by similar age, education, and racial groups. However, a large portion of the remaining one-third of the change in wage inequality is attributable to rising returns to skill. Since 1965 the education and job tenure skill premiums have increased considerably. Autor and Katz note that among college graduates the difference in wages between those with twenty-five and five years of experience increased from about 24 percent in 1963 to about 41 percent in 1995. The changes in the returns to education, however, have not been monotonic. Because of a glut in the number of college graduates, the wage gap between college-educated workers and those with a high school degree fell in the 1970s. However, between 1979 and 1995 the college–high school wage gap rose from 35 to 50 percent for all workers. Overall, Autor and Katz estimate, for males, 47 percent of the change in weekly wage inequality can be explained by these changes in skill premiums.

Functional Form Effects

In many cases, an outcome (y) is related to income in a nonlinear form, which in turn, produces a correlation between the level of y and the variance of x. Suppose that the nonlinear relationship between income and a variable of interest is represented by figure 25.1, where higher incomes produce larger values of y but the return to a higher income diminishes as income rises. In this case, a costless redistribution of x from high-x to low-x individuals increases the average level of y until x is equally distributed. Thus, if the relationship between x and y is concave downward, inequality in x is associated with a lower mean level of y. But if the relationship between x and y is linear, no amount of redistribution can change the mean level of y. Consider two communities in which the relationship between income and some outcome y is the same. In community A, all people have the same income I_a, and average outcome in this community is y_a. In contrast, community B has two equal groups of people, one with income I_1 and the other with income I_2, where the average income of community B (I_b) is equal to I_a. By construction, community B has more income inequality than A, and as a result, an analysis would conclude that even though average incomes across communities are the same, y is lower in community B.

Externality Effects

The final way in which inequality can alter outcomes is if inequality affects outcomes through externalities or other direct effects. Inequality can affect outcomes even when income and the outcome are unrelated. In this case, we say that the effect is due to an externality of inequality. Most of the previous empirical research that examines the consequences of rising inequality tries to examine these direct effects. We provide three examples of possible externalities of income inequality that have been addressed in previous research, although we make no claims that these externalities are actually present.

Psychological Effects   Social comparison theory assumes that individuals evaluate themselves relative to others. Relative deprivation theory is a special case of social comparison theory (Merton and Kitt 1950; Davis 1959; Runciman 1966; Williams 1975) that assumes that comparisons with others who are more advantaged make individuals feel relatively deprived.[2] As inequality increases, the opportunity for negative social comparisons increases because the distance between the rich and the poor increases. Relative deprivation theory assumes that individuals largely ignore others who are worse off than themselves.

FIGURE 25.1   *The Impact of Income at the Individual Level*

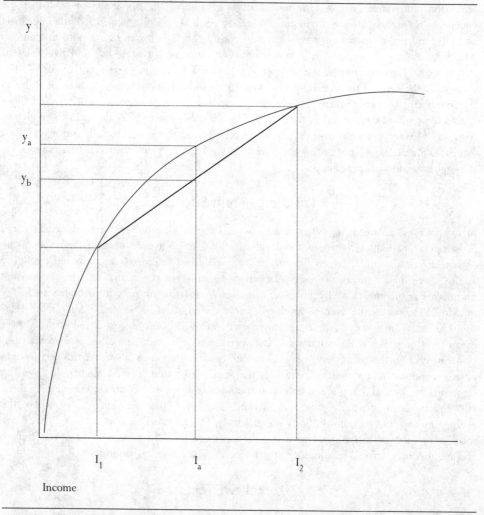

Source: Authors' compilation.

When people do compare themselves to others who are worse off, sociologists assume that they experience what they call "relative gratification" (Davis 1959). If individuals mostly compared themselves to the poorest people in society rather than to the richest, increases in inequality would make most people feel better, because the distance between themselves and the bottom would increase. If people mostly compared themselves to some real or imagined national average, increases in inequality would make the rich feel richer and the poor feel poorer. How this would affect the mean level of subjective well-being would depend on the functional form of the relationship between income and subjective well-being, which is unknown.

State Spending   Theory predicts that an increase in inequality could either raise or lower state spending for the poor. Most models of how governments spend revenue (Romer

1975; Roberts 1977; Meltzer and Richards 1981) assume that political competition makes the voter with the median income the decisive voter. As a result, the spending preferences of the median voter prevail. As inequality increases, median income falls relative to mean income, so the median voter feels poorer and demands policies to reduce the income gap. A second argument that predicts increased redistribution when inequality rises is that as inequality increases, the rich become increasingly fearful of the poor (Piven and Cloward 1993; Gurr 1970). To forestall crime and civil disturbances, they spend more to placate the poor. Other theories suggest that a rise in income inequality reduces government spending because as the rich get richer they gain political influence and as the poor get poorer they become more alienated from the political process. Some empirical research estimates the consequences of an increase in income inequality on state social spending (Mayer 2002; Perotti 1996; Alesina and Rodrik 1994; Kaplan et al. 1996).[3]

Social Organization   The effect of economic inequality is likely to depend to some extent on the geographic proximity of the rich to the poor. Indeed, this assumption is built into conventional measures of inequality, which describe the dispersion of income among all households in some geographic area such as a nation, a state, or a neighborhood. Both theoretical (Durlauf 1996) and empirical research (Mayer 2001) suggest that economic inequality increases economic segregation. Economic segregation has been associated with many outcomes, including children's health and educational attainment.[4] Thus, inequality could affect important outcomes through its effect on economic segregation. Several researchers have suggested that inequality affects trust, social capital, and social participation, which in turn affect important outcomes (Wilkinson 1997; Alesina and La Ferrara 2000, 2002; Costa and Kahn 2003; Kawachi et al. 1997).

In many research projects, it may be difficult to distinguish between mechanical, relational, functional form and the externality effects of inequality. For example, in a 1992 paper and a subsequent book, Richard Wilkinson (1996) argues that life expectancy is lower in nations with more unequal income distributions, and that this relationship cannot be attributed to country-specific factors such as diet and exercise. Subsequent studies show a similar correlation between income inequality and health across different countries, states in the United States, and smaller geographic regions such as metropolitan statistical areas (MSAs) (Waldmann 1992; Kaplan et al. 1996; Kennedy, Kawachi, and Prothrow-Stith 1996). However, data limitations make it hard to say whether this correlation is due to a relational, functional form or externality effect. Andrew Clarkwest and Christopher Jencks (2003) show that the correlation between income inequality and mortality occurred in recent decades but not earlier, suggesting the possibility that the correlation between mortality and income (or a correlate of income) may have changed over time. This would be a relational effect. Hugh Gravelle (1998) and Gregory Rodgers (1979) argue that the relationship between individual health and individual income is concave and therefore that the correlation is due to the functional form of the relationship. In contrast, many of the authors cited here argue for a externality effect, such as effects due to relative deprivation or stress arising from a decline in trust or social cohesion.[5]

Estimating the Consequences of Inequality

How we estimate the consequences of inequality depends on which kind of effect we anticipate. For example, mechanical and relational effects can be estimated with equations 25.1 and 25.2 if we have adequate data. In practice, however, the growing literature on the consequences of income inequality has focused on estimating the externality effects of inequality on outcomes as diverse as mortality, health habits, self-reported health status, civic and voter participation, trust, marriage, crime, educational attainment, the size of local governments, self-reported happiness, and public spending. Much of this chapter is based on the premise that researchers want to estimate externality effects. Therefore, we mainly examine the problems that researchers face when trying to isolate this causal relationship. In some cases, we have some practical solutions. In other cases, we have only words of caution.

To estimate the reduced-form effect of inequality, many researchers begin with a basic model that correlates a group-level outcome with some measure of inequality. A generic regression model of this type is:

$$Y_s = \alpha + \beta_i\, I_s + \beta_x\, X_s + e_s \qquad (25.3)$$

where Y is an outcome (such as mortality or happiness), I is a measure of inequality, X is a vector of covariates, and the subscript s indicates a geographical area such as a state or nation. In this particular case, observations vary in only one dimension—across geographical areas. In principle, this same model could be applied to variations over time, with s indicating year or some other time unit. This is by far the most popular model estimated in the literature. We will table for now whether this simple model can accurately measure a causal impact of I on Y and instead use it to highlight a few key features of this and more complex models.

MEASURING INEQUALITY

Even the simple model outlined in equation 25.3 requires that researchers confront a series of basic measurement questions. The first is how to measure inequality. Even if we confine our discussion to measures of economic inequality (rather than social, racial, gender, or other kinds of inequality), there are a variety of possible measures, and the choice of measure can in principle have important consequences for the results.

The Measure of Income

In choosing a measure of income inequality, we must decide what measure of income to use—for example, labor income, household income, or family income. Some research adjusts family income for family size while most does not. Income can be measured before or after government transfers and taxes and over different time periods. Different measures of income can yield different levels of inequality. For example, in 2000 the Gini coefficient for household income was .460 compared to .430 for family income, meaning that family income is somewhat more equally distributed than household income. The change in inequality can also depend on the measure of income. The Gini coefficient for household income increased from .394 in 1970 to .460 in 2000, an increase of .066, or 14.3 percent. The Gini coefficient for family income increased from .353 in 1970 to .430 in 2000, an increase of .077, or 17.9 percent. This means that there is more inequality in the incomes of unrelated individuals than in the incomes of related individuals living in households but that inequality increased more among related than among unrelated individuals over this period. Since the 1970s inequality in wages has increased more than inequality in household income.

The period over which inequality is measured is also important. Imagine a society in which everyone who is the same age has the same income but older people have higher incomes than younger people. Inequality estimated for any one year in such a society might be high, but lifetime incomes would be equal. In the Panel Study of Income Dynamics (PSID), the Gini coefficient of family income was 0.442 in 1993. The Gini coefficient for the same sample but based on income averaged between 1988 and 1993 was only .225. Thus, families' long-term incomes are much more equally distributed than their short-term incomes. Most research suggests that the extent to which income fluctuates across years has not changed much over time.[6] So the trend in the Gini coefficient of long-term income should be highly correlated with the trend in the Gini coefficient based on income measured in only one year.[7]

The relative deprivation hypothesis argues that when individuals compare themselves to others who are more advantaged, they feel bad, which might result in worse behavior, worse health, and greater mortality. People probably have worse information about the incomes than about the consumption of others, because they can observe others' homes, cars, vacations, and so on. This suggests that consumption inequality might be more relevant than income inequality for many outcomes. Datasets that measure income, however, are more readily available, larger, and capable of providing measures of inequality at smaller levels of aggregation than consumption-based datasets. Thus, practical research on the consequences of economic inequality are based on income rather than consumption.

The Measure of Inequality

Once the measure of economic status is defined, the measure of inequality has to be defined. Social scientists have developed dozens of different measures of inequality, all with distinct advantages and drawbacks (for a detailed discussions of various measures of inequality, see Cowell 1977). In this section, we describe the construction of and properties for some of the most common inequality measures. But this list is certainly not exhaustive of all possible measures. In what follows, we assume all measures will be constructed for a continuous measure of income x, from survey data that contain n respondents, where y_i is an outcome for respondent i.

The Gini coefficient is probably the most frequently used measure of inequality. It is based on the Lorenz curve, which is a plot of the cumulative share of income for households ranked from the poorest to the richest. If income is equally distributed in the population, the Lorenz curve would be a forty-five-degree line—10 percent of income would come from the top 10 percent of households, 40 percent of income would come from the top 40 percent of households, and so on. The greater the degree of inequality, the more the Lorenz curve departs from the forty-five-degree line. The Gini coefficient is constructed by calculating the area between the Lorenz curve and the forty-five-degree line and dividing it by the area under the forty-five-degree line. With individual-level data, the Gini coefficient can be calculated as:

$$G = \Sigma_i \Sigma_j \mid y_i - y_j \mid / 2n^2 \bar{y} \qquad (25.4)$$

where $\bar{y}$ is the sample mean of y. The Gini coefficient varies between zero and one, with higher numbers representing more inequality.

The Gini coefficient is computationally time-consuming to calculate compared to most other measures of inequality because it requires at a minimum the $[n(n + 1)/2 - n]$

unique comparisons of y_i and y_j. Although the speed of computing has increased considerably, calculating Gini coefficients from microdata can be time-consuming in large datasets. However, Branko Milanovic (1997) has demonstrated that an excellent approximation of the Gini coefficient can be obtained via one pass through the data and is given by the equation:

$$G = (1/\text{sqrt}(3))(s_y /\bar{y}) \rho (y,r) \tag{25.5}$$

where s_y and $\bar{y}$ are the standard deviation and mean of income, respectively, and $\rho(y,r)$ is the correlation coefficient between income and its ascending rank.

To demonstrate the accuracy of this approximation, we performed a simple simulation. Using data from the 1980 U.S. Census Bureau 5 Percent Public Use Micro Samples (PUMS), we find that the average family incomes at the state level are mostly between $15,000 and $30,000, while most state-level standard deviations of family income lie between $12,000 and $24,000. In a simulation exercise, we assume that the mean and standard deviation of family income are uniform over these ranges and draw at random the first two population moments for a state. Next, we draw one thousand incomes at random from a log-normal distribution with these moments. We then calculate the Gini coefficient for these one thousand families using equations 25.4 and 25.5. We perform this exercise ten thousand times, drawing new population means and standard deviations each time. Across all ten thousand random populations, the average differences between the actual Gini coefficient and the approximation from equation 25.5 is less than one-tenth of 1 percent, and the correlation coefficient between the two values is 0.9999. The approximation in equation 25.5 is incredibly accurate.

A second measure of inequality, the Theil index, is calculated according to the equation

$$T = \Sigma_i[y_i/n\bar{y}] \ln(y_i/\bar{y}) \tag{25.6}$$

where the term in brackets is the share of aggregate income for person i. Therefore, the Theil index is a weighted geometric average of relative incomes. Under perfect equality, $y_i = \bar{y}$ so $T = 0$, and in the extreme, if one person has all income and everyone else has none, then T approaches $\ln(n)$. Unlike the Gini coefficient, the Theil index can be decomposed into between- and within-group measures of inequality, which can be an advantage for some research.

Relatively simple measures of inequality include the coefficient of variation (CV) defined as (s_y/y) and the so-called Robin Hood index, often used by public health researchers. The Robin Hood index is the fraction of total income that has to be transferred from people above the mean income to people below the mean to have an equal income distribution. Another set of inequality measures compares incomes at different points in the income distribution. Wilkinson's (1992, 1996) investigation of the impact of income inequality on health, for example, uses the fraction of aggregate income coming from the poorest 70 percent of households. Other researchers use the ratio or log difference in incomes between observations at the top and bottom percentiles of the distribution, such as the ninety-fifth and fifth percentiles or the ninetieth and tenth percentiles.

Unlike the Theil index and the Gini coefficient, the Robin Hood index and measures that compare income levels at different percentiles are relatively easy to interpret. Knowing that 50 percent of income needs to be redistributed to families below the mean to achieve equality, or that 75 percent of income comes from the top 25 percent of families, is a more familiar way to think about income distributions than the numbers represented by the Gini coefficient or the Theil index.

The Gini coefficient, the Theil index, and the coefficient of variation satisfy Dalton's transfer principle: a transfer of income from person j to any lower-income person, holding all else constant, will reduce inequality. All other measures of inequality require specific transfers to change the level of inequality. All measures of inequality listed earlier are "mean-independent," meaning that a proportionate change in everyone's income will not change the level of inequality.

One last inequality measure that deserves mention is a measure of relative economic position or relative deprivation. The seminal definition of relative deprivation is accredited to W. G. Runciman (1966), who argued that an individual is relatively deprived if:

> (i) He does not have X, (ii) he sees some other person or persons, which may include himself at some previous or expected time, as having X (whether or not this is in fact the case), (iii) he wants X, and (iv) he sees it as feasible that he should have X.

Thus, we feel relatively deprived if others in our reference group possess something that we do not. Although the object of deprivation (X) could be measured using any number of attributes (physical strength, attractiveness, intelligence, personal possessions), we follow others in defining X as income (Yitzhaki 1979; Hey and Lambert 1980; Berrebi and Silber 1985). Schlomo Yitzhaki (1979) develops a measure of relative deprivation that is based on the comparison of person i's income (y_i) to the other N people in i's reference group and is calculated as:

$$RD_i = \frac{1}{N}\sum_j (y_j - y_i) \qquad \forall y_j > y_i \qquad (25.7)$$

This measure posits that relative deprivation for person i is driven by the incomes of people who earn more than y_i.[8] The summation in equation 25.7 is divided by the size of the reference group to make the measure invariant to the size of the reference group. Dividing by N can also be interpreted as adjusting for the probability of making a comparison. If person i and person j are alone on a desert island, N is low so the probability of making a comparison is high. In contrast, if person i and person j live in New York City, N is high so the probability of making a comparison is low.

It is important to note that a number of researchers have used the phrase "inequality" as a proxy for some other intrinsic characteristic about the population, such as relative deprivation. For example, Wilkinson (1992) suggests that "relative deprivation" is a likely cause for the observed negative cross-sectional correlation between income inequality and life expectancy at the national level. He argues that individuals who feel they are economically disadvantaged compared to their peers may be depressed and disgruntled, conditions that affect health both directly (through heart disease, high blood pressure, and suicide) and indirectly (through increased smoking, poor eating habits, and alcohol abuse). In his work, Wilkinson uses the phrases "income inequality" and "relative deprivation" interchangeably. In fact, the title to a 1997 letter to the editor of the *British Medical Journal* written by Wilkinson is "Comment: Income Inequality Summarizes the Health Burden of Individual Relative Deprivation."

Looking at the definition of relative deprivation in equation 25.7, and any of the income inequality measures described here, it is important to note that by construction, these variables are measuring different things. Income inequality is a group measure, while relative deprivation is specific to the individual. Two people living in the same state or country can be "exposed" to the same level of group inequality, yet they can experience different levels of relative deprivation. The variables, however, are clearly related. Yitzhaki (1979) shows that average relative deprivation in a community is mean income times the Gini coefficient. Although a society with more income inequality has more relative depriva-tion, it is difficult to formally test the relative deprivation hypothesis with a measure of inequality because any estimated effect of inequality could be due to mechanisms other than relative deprivation.

All inequality measures cited here, except those comparing income at different per-centiles, must be calculated with information about the entire distribution of income. This is problematic in datasets that top-code income data. For example, family and household income in the 1980 census PUMS data is top-coded at $75,000 and at $50,000 in the 1970 PUMS. Top-coding in the 1990 PUMS is much more complicated, and those interested should check documentation from the 1990 census for details. In any case, not correcting for top-coded values tends to understate the degree of income inequality. For example, we described a simulation in which we constructed ten thousand samples of one thousand families—each sample being drawn from a log-normal distribution with a different mean and variance of family income. For each of the samples, we artificially top-coded income at $75,000 and recalculated the Gini coefficients. Across all 10 million observations, 1.7 per-cent of incomes were top-coded, which is close to the average across samples for the 1980 PUMS. Using income with top-coded values reduced the Gini coefficient by an average of 3 percent. This does not seem like a large amount, but note that between 1980 and 1990 the Gini coefficient for household income rose by 7 percent. Thus, a 3 percent reduction in a calculated value due solely to measurement error is a large value. Measurement error is greater in samples with a higher fraction of top-coded wages.

Nevertheless, there is a quick and accurate "fix" for the problem of top-coded in-comes—these values can be replaced by an estimate of the mean income for those with top-coded values (Gastwirth 1972). Mean incomes for those with top-codes can be esti-mated using a variety of different techniques. One useful procedure is to exploit the proper-ties of the Pareto distribution, which is a cumulative density function (CDF) that has been shown in a number of contexts to mimic the properties of the right-hand tail of the U.S. income distribution. The probability density function (PDF) of the Pareto distribution is defined as:

$$f(x) = ab^a/x^{a+1}, \text{ for } b \leq x \leq \infty \qquad (25.8)$$

and the CDF is given as:

$$F(c) = \text{Prob}[x \leq c] = 1 - (b/c)^a. \qquad (25.9)$$

The Pareto has the nice property that the conditional expectation has a simple form:

$$E[x \mid x > k] = ka/(a - 1). \qquad (25.10)$$

Suppose that income is top-coded at $75,000 in the census and that incomes above $65,000 follow a Pareto distribution. If we know the value of the Pareto parameter a, then it is possible to replace the top-coded wages with the conditional expectation, $E[x \mid x > \$75,000] = \$75,000a/(a - 1)$.

The only question then is how to estimate a. First, let T be the value of top-coded income and assume that income above b follows a Pareto distribution. Pick b to be an income $10,000 to $15,000 below T. From equation 25.9, notice that $Prob(x > T) = (b/T)^a = P_t$. Estimate P, the fraction of people with incomes in excess of b who are top-coded. Therefore, $a = \ln(P_t)/[\ln(b) - \ln(T)]$. So if incomes above $60,000 are Pareto and half these values are top-coded, then $a = 3.106$ and $E[x \mid x > 75,000] = 75,000(3.106)/(2.106) = \$110,612$.

Returning to the simulation where we artificially top-coded incomes, if we allow the parameters of the Pareto distribution for high incomes to vary across samples and replace the top-coded values with conditional expectations, the Gini coefficient in this sample now is only 0.06 percent smaller than the actual Gini coefficient.

The Level of Aggregation

Researchers must decide the appropriate level of aggregation (city, county, state, or country) over which to measure inequality. They would ideally be guided by theory, but theory often provides little guidance on this issue. For example, some theories suggest that inequality increases feelings of alienation or relative deprivation. However, these theories typically do not specify which group people use as their reference group. Relevant reference groups could include neighbors, coworkers, people with similar levels of education, or people in the same geographical area, such as the state or county. If individuals' perceptions about their relative economic position are driven by personal observation, a local measure of inequality is preferred. Nevertheless, if individuals compare themselves to national standards, the nation is the right unit of observation.

The social psychology literature suggests that members of one's reference group are typically selected based on either similarity or geographic proximity (Singer 1981). While geographic proximity is relatively easy to determine, "similarity" is a more nebulous concept. Various studies report that individuals define reference groups along demographic lines such as gender, education, and race (Merton and Kitt 1950; Singer 1981; Bylsma and Major 1994). However, it is clear that there is no perfect formula for determining reference groups, and in fact individuals appear to have different reference groups for different kinds of comparisons. Critics assert that the Achilles' heel of social evaluation theory is the "failure to explain adequately how the relevant comparisons are selected in the first place" (Pettigrew 1978, 36).

Of course, determining the correct reference group is an issue only if inequality mainly affects outcomes through such comparisons. If inequality is related to important outcomes because of its effect on government spending, then political jurisdictions such as counties, school districts, or states are likely to be relevant units of analysis for inequality. If inequality is important because of nonlinearity in the relationship between income and the outcome, then we would face a different set of issues in determining the relevant unit in which to measure inequality.

In practice, however, the choice of aggregation and the measure of inequality are driven primarily by practical considerations such as data availability. The question then becomes, when we have a measure of inequality for the perfect reference group, how do we know whether the measure is adequate? In his work on the relationship between inequality and health, Angus Deaton (1999) acknowledges the limitations of using birth cohorts as a reference group but notes that cohorts include a higher ratio of relevant to irrelevant people than, say, a state. There is no guide, however, to how much "signal" must be contained in the measure to dampen the background noise produced by the irrelevant comparisons. Looking at the level of aggregation from the perspective of measurement error, if changing the level of aggregation removes irrelevant comparisons in a random, nonsystematic way, the correlation between inequality and the outcome of interest should increase in magnitude as the fraction of relevant to irrelevant comparisons in the reference group grows. This is a useful way to frame the issue if interpersonal comparison is the main mechanism through which inequality operates.[9]

One practical limitation to using income inequality at lower levels of aggregation is data availability. The U.S. Census Bureau reports aggregate measures of income inequality at the national level on an annual basis using data from the March Current Population Survey (CPS) and at the state level every ten years using data from the census long-form data. Although the March CPS has always reported the standard metropolitan statistical areas (SMSA) of residence—and starting recently, the county of residence for some counties— these data typically have too few observations to calculate Gini coefficients accurately at the substate level, unless we are willing to pool multiple surveys.

The census Public Use Micro Samples do report detailed data on household, family, and individual income and identify geography down to the PUMA (Public Use Microdata Area) level, which is a county group or subcounty collection of 100,000 people. However, if a county has fewer than 100,000 people, it is grouped with other counties. As a result, if researchers want to construct income inequality measures at the substate level, they must either not calculate the number for certain counties or use groups of counties as a single unit.

The census does report detailed data about income distributions in the form of counts of households, families, and individuals in income groups as part of the Summary Tape Files 3A. These counts are reported for all levels of geography down to the census block level, and these can be used to accurately estimate measures of income inequality.

A number of authors have postulated various flexible functional forms that describe the underlying distribution of income in the United States. Given parameter estimates of these distributions, we can calculate variables like the Gini coefficient from a closed-form representation. James McDonald (1984) summarizes the properties of a number of these flexible functional forms, including distributions based on the beta and gamma functions. One flexible form that performed well in his empirical tests, called a three-parameter distribution, was suggested as an approximation to the income distribution by Camilo Dagum (1980). This distribution did not perform as well as some four-parameter models, but in none of these more complicated models could one obtain a closed-form representation for the CDF. For a random variable z, the CDF of the three-parameter Dagum distribution is defined as:

$$F(z) = [1 + (b/z)^a]^{-p} \quad \text{for } z > 0 \text{ and } (b,a,p) > 0 \quad (25.11)$$

where the r'th moments of the distribution are defined as:

$$E(Z^r) = pb^{ra} B(1 - r/a, p + r/a) \quad (25.12)$$

and $B(\bullet,\bullet)$ is the evaluation of the complete beta function. McDonald (1984) and Dagum (1980) also show that the Gini coefficient for income inequality can be calculated as:

$$G = -1 + B(p,p)/B(p,p + 1/a). \tag{25.13}$$

Given this distribution for income, we can use the counts of households in income groups in such datasets as the Summary Tape Files 3A to estimate the underlying parameters of the income distribution. Suppose there are k income groups, N_k is the number of families in group k for a particular area, and the probability of observing a family in a particular income group is defined as $Pr(k)$ where $Pr(k) = F(a_k) - F(a_j)$ for people who report their incomes between a_j and a_k. The log-likelihood that can be maximized is simply $L = \Sigma_k N_k \ln[Pr(k)]$.

We have used this distribution and counts of families in income groups from the 1970, 1980, and 1990 census Summary Tape Files 3a to estimate state-specific parameter values and then used these to produce the state-specific estimates of the Gini coefficient. The correlation coefficient from the actual values reported by the census and our estimated values for these three years are 0.998, 0.996, and 0.98, respectively. This maximum likelihood model seems to do a good job of characterizing state-specific income distributions in each year. The plot of the actual Gini for 1980 at the state level, as reported by the Census Bureau on its website, and the number estimated by the Dagum model are reported in figure 25.2. The model tracks well except for the one outlier, which is the District of Columbia.

We have also used this procedure to estimate county-specific parameters of the Dagum distribution for 1970, 1980, and 1990. We are unable to compare a predicted Gini from the estimated parameters with an actual value because this measure is not on the Summary Tape Files. However, there are two measures of aggregate income in those files that we can compare to predictions from the Dagum model. First, for each county in 1980, the census reports the fraction of families with income in excess of $50,000. This value is easily predicted from the Dagum parameters as $1 - F(50,000)$, and in figure 25.3, we plot the actual reported probability with the predicted value based on the maximum likelihood estimates of the Dagum parameters. Notice that the points fall along the forty-five-degree line and the correlation coefficient between the actual and predicted values is 0.996. In figure 25.4, we plot the average family income by county, as reported by the census, with the predicted value, using the moment-generating function in equation 25.12. Notice once again that the points lie along the forty-five-degree line and that the correlation between the actual and predicted values is 0.997.

How Much Do These Measures of Inequality Differ?

Each of the measures of inequality described in this chapter has distinct properties. For example, in comparison to the Gini coefficient, the Theil index is much more sensitive to transfers between people near the middle of the distribution. In contrast, a transfer of income from someone at the top of the distribution to someone at the bottom tends to produce larger changes in the Gini coefficient than the Theil index. However, the correlation among these measures of inequality is high, and the correlations are robust to different levels of aggregation.

To document this point, we use data on household income from the 1980 census 5 percent Public Use Micro Samples to construct nine standard measures of income inequality at the state level: the Theil index, the Gini coefficient, the coefficient of variation (CV), the ln(95/5) ratio, the ln(90/10) ratio, the share of aggregate income received by the top 25 percent of households, and the Robin Hood index. Top-coded values were replaced using

FIGURE 25.2   *Gini Coefficient of Family Income at the State Level, 1980*

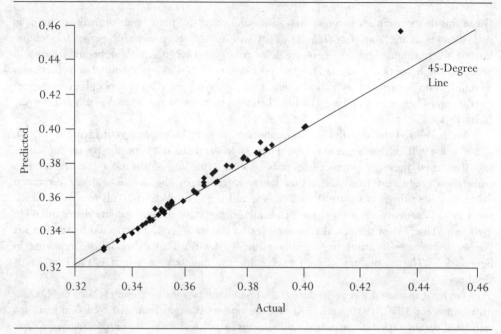

FIGURE 25.3   *Families with Income Greater Than $50,000, at the County Level, 1980 Census*

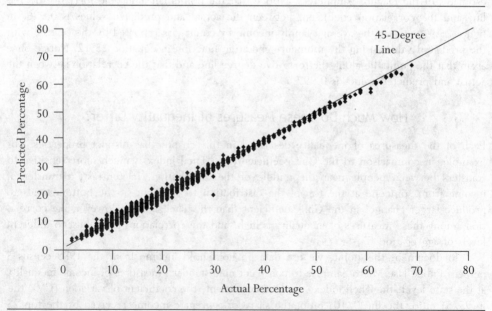

FIGURE 25.4   *Mean Income at the County Level, 1980 Census*

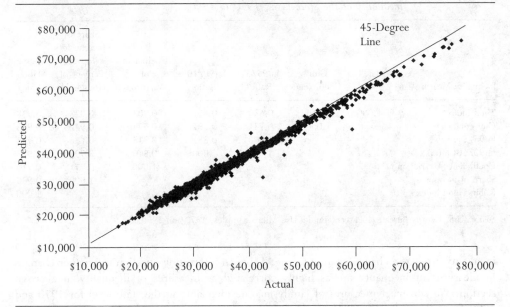

Source: Authors' compilation.

the procedure described earlier. In table 25.1, we report the correlation coefficients between each of these measures.

The Theil index, Gini coefficient, Robin Hood index, and share of income from the top 25 percent of households all are strongly correlated with correlation coefficients in excess of 0.98. The CV is more highly correlated with the Theil index and Gini coefficient than with the Robin Hood index or share of income measure. The ln(95/5) and ln(90/10) measures are highly correlated with each other, but in general are less highly correlated with the other measures of inequality.

As we illustrate later, a number of researchers estimate a model in which a change in

TABLE 25.1   *Correlation Coefficients for Various Measures of Household Income Inequality at the State Level, 1980*

Inequality Measure	Theil Index	Gini Coefficient	ln(95/5) Ratio	ln(90/10) Ratio	Coefficient of Variation	Share of Income for Top 25 Percent of Households	Robin Hood Index
Theil index	1.000	0.992	0.893	0.891	0.970	0.991	0.983
Gini coefficient		1.000	0.919	0.928	0.938	0.991	0.997
ln(95/5) ratio			1.000	0.973	0.776	0.877	0.783
ln(90/10) ratio				1.000	0.769	0.885	0.930
Coefficient of variation					1.000	0.954	0.921
Share of income						1.000	0.986
Robin Hood index							1.000

Source: U.S. Census Bureau 5 Percent Public Use Micro Samples, 1980.

TABLE 25.2   Correlation Coefficients for Changes in Various Measures of Household Income Inequality at the State Level, 1970 to 1990

Inequality Measure	Theil Index	Gini Coefficient	ln(95/5) Ratio	ln(90/10) Ratio	Coefficient of Variation	Share of Income for Top 25 Percent of Households	Robin Hood Index
Theil index	1.000	0.964	0.630	0.801	0.903	0.928	0.938
Gini coefficient		1.000	0.731	0.897	0.773	0.942	0.993
ln(95/5) ratio			1.000	0.851	0.318	0.668	0.754
ln(90/10) ratio				1.000	0.510	0.798	0.913
Coefficient of variation					1.000	0.771	0.719
Share of income						1.000	0.935
Robin Hood index							1.000

Source: U.S. Census Bureau, 1 Percent Public Use Micro Samples, 1970 and 1990.

inequality predicts a change in an outcome. Thus, an interesting question is whether changes in measures of inequality are as highly correlated as measures of inequality in a cross-section. We construct measures of family income inequality at the state level for 1970 and 1990 from the 1 Percent PUMS and difference the values. In table 25.2, we report the correlation between the various measures of change in inequality over the twenty-year period. The measures of inequality that were highly correlated in levels are also highly correlated in changes between 1970 and 1990. In particular, the Theil, the Gini, the share of income from the top 25 percent of families, and the Robin Hood index are the most highly correlated in changes, whereas the CV generally has the weakest correlation with other measures. In general, the correlations in changes are nowhere near as strong as the correlations in levels.

The results in tables 25.1 and 25.2 suggest a few key conclusions for researchers. First, deciding which measure of inequality to use, especially in models with a time-series component, may be important. This point is in fact brought out in a number of chapters in this book. In a number of cases, results are statistically significant when one measure is used but not with another. Running counter to this result is the fact that the Theil index, the Gini coefficient, the Robin Hood index, and the share of income from the top 25 percent are highly correlated in levels and changes.

To see whether the measures of inequality are as highly correlated at lower levels of aggregation as at the state level, we use the 1980 Summary Tape Files 3A to construct measures of inequality at the county level using the procedure outlined earlier. The procedure allows us to construct all measures except the Theil index. Similar data are available for the nearly fifteen thousand school districts in the United States in the 1980 Census of Population and Housing Summary Tape File 3F.

Correlations between various measures of household income inequality across counties and school districts are reported in tables 25.3 and 25.4, respectively. The correlation among the Gini coefficient, the Robin Hood index, and the share-of-income measures declines when we move to lower levels of aggregation. The CV has the weakest correlation with the other measures. These correlations suggest that as we move to lower levels of aggregation, deciding which inequality measure to use may become much more critical. In tables 25.5 and 25.6, we also report the correlation coefficients for the change in these

TABLE 25.3   *Correlation Coefficients for Various Measures of Household Income Inequality at the County Level, 1980*

	Gini Coefficient	ln(95/5) Ratio	ln(90/10) Ratio	Coefficient of Variation	Share of Income for Top 25 Percent of Households	Robin Hood Index
Gini coefficient	1.000	0.891	0.901	0.767	0.967	0.835
ln(95/5) ratio		1.000	0.999	0.585	0.748	0.499
ln(90/10) ratio			1.000	0.554	0.763	0.518
Coefficient of variation				1.000	0.820	0.812
Share of income					1.000	0.947
Robin Hood index						1.000

Source: U.S. Census Bureau, Summary Tape Files 3A, 1980

TABLE 25.4   *Correlation Coefficients for Various Measures of Household Income Inequality at the School District Level, 1980*

	Gini Coefficient	ln(95/5) Ratio	ln(90/10) Ratio	Coefficient of Variation	Share of Income for Top 25 Percent of Households	Robin Hood Index
Gini coefficient	1.000	0.860	0.873	0.444	0.963	0.826
ln(95/5) ratio		1.000	0.999	0.272	0.693	0.430
ln(90/10) ratio			1.000	0.284	0.711	0.452
Coefficient of variation				1.000	0.488	0.487
Share of income					1.000	0.945
Robin Hood index						1.000

Source: U.S. Census Bureau, 1980 census.

TABLE 25.5   *Correlation Coefficients for Changes in Various Measures of Household Income Inequality at the County Level, 1970 and 1990*

	Gini Coefficient	ln(95/5) Ratio	ln(90/10) Ratio	Coefficient of Variation	Share of Income for Top 25 Percent of Households	Robin Hood Index
Gini coefficient	1.000	0.780	0.798	0.429	0.941	0.758
ln(95/5) ratio		1.000	0.999	0.153	0.526	0.153
ln(90/10) ratio			1.000	0.168	0.660	0.219
Coefficient of variation				1.000	0.498	0.502
Share of income					1.000	0.932
Robin Hood index						1.000

Source: U.S. Census Bureau, Summary Tape Files 3A, 1970 and 1990.

TABLE 25.6   *Correlation Coefficients for Changes in Various Measures of Household Income Inequality at the School District Level, 1970 and 1990*

	Gini Coefficient	ln(95/5) Ratio	ln(90/10) Ratio	Coefficient of Variation	Share of Income for Top 25 Percent of Households	Robin Hood Index
Gini coefficient	1.000	0.804	0.819	0.342	0.938	0.733
ln(95/5) ratio		1.000	0.999	0.123	0.552	0.196
ln(90/10) ratio			1.000	0.136	0.575	0.223
Coefficient of variation				1.000	0.407	0.413
Share of income					1.000	0.921
Robin Hood index						1.000

Source: U.S. Census Bureau, *School District Data Book,* 1970 and 1990.

measures over the 1970 to 1990 period. The variables with the strongest correlation in levels are also those with the strongest correlation in changes. The variable with the weakest correlation between all others is again the CV.

ESTIMATION ISSUES

Besides measurement problems, the cross-sectional model outlined in equation 25.3 that relates inequality to outcomes also presents some estimation challenges. In this section, we discuss a number of common problems associated with inferences from models represented by equation 25.3.

The Ecological Fallacy

As we outlined earlier, one of the ways in which outcomes and inequality can be correlated is through the functional relationship between income and the outcomes. As figure 25.1 demonstrates, if the impact of income declines as incomes rise, then a simple regression of Y on a measure of inequality generates a positive relationship. In a simple cross-sectional model like that posed in equation 25.3 where the unit of observation is an aggregate outcome, it is difficult to distinguish an impact of inequality due to the functional form relationship from the other effects of inequality, because we cannot easily model the individual-level functional form of the relationship between income and the outcome in aggregate data.

A number of researchers have defined this problem as the ecological fallacy, by which they mean the possibility that covariance between inequality and an outcome of interest is driven *solely* by the nonlinear relationship between individual income and the outcome. Researchers from a variety of disciplines have demonstrated that measures of health, such as mortality rates or life expectancy, measured at the country, state, county, or MSA level are adversely related to income inequality. However, since the pioneering work of Evelyn Kitagawa and Philip Hauser (1973), it has also been known that mortality rates drop more sharply moving from $10,000 to $20,000 than when incomes move from $100,000 to $110,000 (Preston 1975; Deaton and Paxson 2001a, 2001b). Gravelle (1998) and Rodgers (1979) question whether the relationship between income inequality and aggregate measures of health is due to a systematic relationship between income inequality and mortality or to

TABLE 25.7   *Linear Probability Models, Outcomes for Males Age Twenty-Five to Sixty-Four, 1987 to 1991*

	Died in Five Years	Self-Reported Health Status	Current Smoker	Exercised in Past Thirty Days	Voted in 1988 Election	Can Trust People
Dataset	1988 to 1990 NHIS/MCOD	1988 to 1990 NHIS	1988 to 1991 BRFSS	1988 to 1991 BRFSS	November 1988 CPS	1987 to 1991 GSS
Observations	97,778	97,778	96,114	96,330	29,135	2,103
Sample mean	0.026	0.091	0.297	0.724	0.655	0.434
Income						
$10,000 to $20,000	−0.020	−0.130	−0.038	0.026	0.073	0.054
	(0.0027)	(0.0028)	(0.007)	(0.006)	(0.0097)	(0.039)
$20,000 to $30,000	−0.028	−0.185			0.131	0.098
	(0.0022)	(0.0038)			(0.0104)	(0.040)
$30,000 to $40,000	−0.033	−0.206			0.146	0.126
	(0.0022)	(0.0039)			(0.0107)	(0.042)
More than $40,000	−0.037	−0.224			0.165	0.123
	(0.0022)	(0.0038)			(0.0111)	(0.041)
$20,000 to $35,000			−0.065	0.071		
			(0.006)	(0.006)		
$35,000 to $50,000			−0.083	0.103		
			(0.007)	(0.007)		
More than $50,000			−0.102	0.141		
			(0.007)	(0.007)		

Source: Authors' compilation.
Notes: OLS standard errors are in parentheses. Other covariates include controls for age, education, race, ethnicity, and marital status, as well as, when appropriate, dummy variables for the year of the survey.

the functional form of the relationship between income and health. The concerns with the use of aggregate data have prompted many researchers to move towards models with individual-level data (Gravelle 1998; Fiscella and Franks 1997; Mellor and Milyo 2001, 2002; Deaton 2001).

The concern about the ecological fallacy is bolstered because many outcomes appear to have a nonlinear relationship to income. In table 25.7, we present simple linear probability estimates of various measures of health and social outcomes from a variety of nationally representative datasets. In all cases, we select as the sample males age twenty-five to sixty-four and choose a set of years near 1990 to hold constant the definition of nominal income. In columns 1 and 2, we use two outcomes from the 1987 to 1990 National Health Interview Survey (NHIS). The first indicator is whether a person died over the next five years, and the second is whether a person self-reported fair or poor health.[10]

In an important extension of the NHIS data, the Multiple Cause of Death (MCOD) data file was constructed by merging individual-level records from the 1986 to 1994 data files with the National Death Index. The MCOD/NHIS identifies whether individuals in the NHIS had died by the end of 1995, when they died, and the multiple causes of death. We pick the first four complete years of the MCOD file, 1987 to 1990. In columns 3 and 4, we add two measures of health habits from the 1988 to 1990 Behavioral Risk Factor Surveillance System (BRFSS) survey: an indicator for whether the person is a current smoker, and an indicator for whether the person has exercised at all in the past thirty days.[11] In column 5, the outcome we consider is an indicator for whether respondents reported they voted in the 1988 presidential election. This variable is taken from the special Voting Supplement to the November 1988 Current Population Survey. Finally, in the sixth column, we report results for a model that has as the dependent variable a response to a question from the 1987 to 1991 General Social Survey (GSS) about whether "most people can be trusted" or "you can't be too careful," and we identify respondents who indicate the former as people who are trusting. In each regression, we use a limited set of covariates, including a complete set of age effects, dummies for race (black and other race), education (less than nine years, nine to eleven years, twelve years, and thirteen to fifteen years), marital status (never married, widowed, separated and divorced), and, where appropriate, year. In the voter participation model, we also include dummy variables for whether the state had a Senate election and a gubernatorial election. In each survey, income is a categorical variable. We tried to create categories with equal dollar values. For the NHIS, CPS, and GSS datasets, we have income groups in $10,000 intervals, the final group being $40,000 and above. For the BRFSS, we have groups for less than $10,000, $10,000 to $20,000, $20,000 to $35,000, $35,000 to $50,000, and $50,000 and above. In each case, we use the lowest income group (less than $10,000) as the reference group.

Although we define the income categories in $10,000 increments, it is not clear that the average person in a particular category is $10,000 richer than the average person in the lower, adjacent group. Data from the 1990 census suggest that average incomes across the groups are in fact about $10,000 apart. Family income is a continuous value in the census, and using data from the 1990 census 1 Percent PUMS, we calculate average family income for people in the income groups that we use for the NHIS regressions in table 25.7. Average income for the less than $10,000, $10,000 to $20,000, $20,000 to $30,000, $30,000 to $40,000, and more than $40,000 are $5,300, $15,039, $24,777, $34,590, and $70,136, respectively.

The results in the table demonstrate an incredibly uniform pattern in the income effect across outcomes. Moving from having less than $10,000 in annual income to between $10,000 and $20,000 has large impacts on each outcome—usually of a magnitude that is equal to the sample mean. However, moving from the second highest to the highest income group usually has a marginal impact on the outcome. This is even more remarkable when we consider the fact that people in the highest group have on average $35,000 more income than people in the next highest group. The results in table 25.7 raise the suspicion that an estimate of equation 25.3 may simply capture the ecological fallacy. In the next table, we examine whether this concern is in fact real.

In table 25.8, we estimate four linear probability models for five of these same outcomes. In the first model, we estimate a simple bivariate regression of the outcome on the Gini coefficient of family income measured at the level of the state.[12] Next, we add demographic characteristics for the state such as average age, percentage black, percentage other race, fraction in various education groups, fraction married, and log mean income. This model is equivalent to a regression of state means on the outcomes and the Gini coefficient where each observation is weighted by the number of observations in the state. Next, we investigate the consequences of using individual-level data by replacing the state-mean characteristics with corresponding individual-level covariates, except that we keep state mean income in the model. Finally, we examine the ecological fallacy by replacing state mean income with a complete set of dummy variables for each income group.

TABLE 25.8   *Linear Probability Models, Outcomes for Males Age Twenty-Five to Sixty-Four: Parameter Estimates (Standard Error) on State Gini Coefficient*

	Died in Five Years	Self-Reported Health Status	Current Smoker	Exercised in Past Thirty Days	Voted in 1988 Election
Dataset	1987 to 1990 NHIS/MCOD	1988 to 1990 NHIS	1987 to 1991 BRFSS	1988 to 1991 BRFSS	November 1988 CPS
Observations	97,778	97,778	96,046	96,046	29,135
Sample mean	0.026	0.091	0.297	0.724	0.655
1. Gini only	0.140	0.548	0.172	−1.136	−0.907
	(0.024)	(0.043)	(0.059)	(0.058)	(0.125)
2. Add state means of demographic variables	0.097	0.464	−0.431	−0.399	−0.748
	(0.049)	(0.089)	(0.150)	(0.146)	(0.192)
3. Replace with individual-level data	0.101	0.217	0.037	−0.833	−0.832
	(0.024)	(0.042)	(0.060)	(0.058)	(0.125)
4. Add income dummy variables	0.107	0.223	0.061	−0.928	−0.861
	(0.024)	(0.041)	(0.060)	(0.053)	(0.125)
	[0.033]	[0.087]	[0.222]	[0.222]	[0.287]

Source: Authors' compilation.
Notes: OLS standard errors are in parentheses. The numbers in brackets are Huber/White standard errors corrected for within-state correlation in the errors. State demographic characteristics include average age, the fraction married, the fraction with less than nine, nine to eleven, twelve, and thirteen to fifteen years of education, the fraction black, fraction some other race, average family income, and, where applicable, year of survey dummy variables. The individual characteristics include a complete set of age, race, marital status, ethnicity, income, and year of survey fixed effects.

In three cases (self-reported health status, smoking, and exercise), the movement from aggregate to individual-level data has a large impact on the effect of the Gini coefficient: in two cases the coefficient falls in magnitude, and in one case it rises. Comparing models 3 and 4, the results demonstrate that adding a nonlinear specification for income hardly changes the effect of the Gini coefficient, except in the case of smoking. These results suggest two things. First, moving to individual-level data can have dramatic effects on the estimates. Second, the benefits of moving to individual data are not limited to the ecological fallacy. In fact, it appears that the ecological fallacy explains little of the effect of inequality. This is consistent with other recent research that has tried to control individual-level measures of income in estimates of the effect of inequality on low birthweight (Meara 1999) and educational attainment (Mayer 2001).

Design Effects

Individual-level data have a number of distinct advantages even if the ecological fallacy does not account for much of the effect of inequality. First, as we illustrate in table 25.8, individual-level data are more likely than aggregate data to have detailed demographic and socioeconomic variables that can be used as covariates. Second, many of these datasets have detailed location codes, allowing researchers to use measures of inequality for smaller geographic areas.

However, using individual-level data can complicate the statistical inference associated with traditional regression results. In particular, inequality is measured at a different level of aggregation than the outcome, and regression errors are typically correlated within a group. In this case, OLS standard errors tend to be understated. This problem is typically referred to in the theoretical literature on random assignment trials as a "design effect," and the problem arises when treatment randomization is done at the group level (for example, schools or communities) rather than at the individual level (Cornfield 1978). Consider an experiment that randomly assigns some high schools to an aggressive antismoking program while a second group of schools is the control. Because outcomes like smoking are highly correlated within a school, the effective number of observations within a school is typically lower than the number of people sampled.

The correlation in errors for a group can be modeled as a "random effect," and equations can be estimated through feasible generalized least squares. The random-effects specification is appealing because the properties are well known and the procedure is simple to perform in most econometrics packages. The model does have the drawback that it assumes equi-correlated errors across observations within a "cluster," an assumption that is probably violated in many datasets and is violated by construction in models where the outcome of interest is discrete. A more popular strategy in recent years has been to use the generalized estimating equation (GEE) model of Kung-Yee Liang and Scott Zeger (1986). GEE allows for unrestricted correlations in errors within "clusters" (for example, states or counties) and is preprogrammed in common software packages such as STATA and SAS. In STATA, for example, the "cluster" command in linear models implements a grouped version of the basic Huber (1967) and White (1980) variance covariance matrix. This procedure allows for an arbitrary covariance structure within a cluster that has been prespecified by the researcher.

In practice, the within-group correlation in errors is not trivial and can vastly change the effective standard errors in empirical work. In the final row of table 25.8, we add in brackets standard errors that allow for arbitrary covariance in the errors at the state level. Reading across the final row of the table, standard errors increase by 38, 121, 414, 580, and 130 percent.[13] All of these results suggest that controlling for within-state correlation in errors is critically important in this context.

There is an important caveat about using the GEE procedure. The standard error estimates are consistent as the number of clusters approaches infinity, so the procedure has poor properties when the number of groups is small. Jeffrey Wooldridge (2003) and Joshua Angrist and Victor Lavy (2002) note that some Monte Carlo evidence shows poor performance with forty to fifty clusters. There is concern therefore that our standard errors in table 25.8 are not consistent. There is no magic number for the number of clusters needed to implement this procedure. There is a good reality check, however: if the standard errors go down, one probably has too few clusters. With small numbers of clusters, Angrist and Lavy (2002) suggest aggregating the data down to the group level and running a between-group regression model. Unfortunately, we raise the issue of within-group correlations because researchers had important concerns about the between-group model!

Omitted Variable Bias

The primary concern with regressions such as equation 25.1 is that the estimated coefficient for inequality is subject to omitted variable bias. For the estimate of β_i in equation 25.3 to be an unbiased estimate of the true effect of inequality, all exogenous factors that cause inequality and are related to the outcome must be controlled. The suspicion of omitted variables bias is easy to raise in a cross-section because inequality is not randomly distributed across countries, states, counties, or MSAs. Regions with high inequality may differ in many respects from those with less inequality. Many of the same characteristics that lead to regional variation in income inequality also lead to persistent differences in outcomes. Many of the factors that explain state-to-state variation in outcomes such as mortality, crime, marriage rates, or voter participation are measurable, such as levels of education, racial composition, ethnic diversity, and the age distribution. However, it is usually not possible to measure all potentially relevant variables.

To motivate the concern of an omitted variables bias in a simple regression like equation 25.3, we return to the literature that examines the link between income inequality and mortality. This work began by looking at cross-country correlations in the two variables, then moved to an examination of income inequality and mortality across geographic boundaries in a single country. But because these papers seldom tried to control more than a few characteristics of states, a lingering question was whether the positive estimate for β_i in equation 25.3 represented a causal relationship or a spurious relationship, owing to an omitted state characteristic that affects mortality.

Figure 25.5 maps quartiles of age-adjusted mortality for 1990 across states, with darker colors representing more inequality. This is similar to the depiction found in Mellor and Milyo (2002). Figure 25.5 shows that states in the South have the highest mortality rates, while states in the plains and New England have much lower mortality. In figure 25.6, we examine a similar map for quartiles of income inequality in 1989 using the Gini coefficient for family income generated from the 1990 census as the measure of inequality. In this map, darker areas have higher income inequality. Notice in figure 25.5 that regions with high income inequality are roughly the same regions that have high mortality. This raises the suspicion that the relationship between inequality and health represents correlation rather than causation.

To illustrate the potential sensitivity of the estimated effects of the Gini coefficient to the inclusion of other state-specific variables in a regression, we rerun the basic models in table 25.9 and sequentially add a few more state-specific characteristics. The first variable we add is the fraction of people in the state who are black. Angus Deaton and Darren Lubotsky (Deaton and Lubotsky 2003) demonstrate that in cross-section models with aggregate data, the inequality-health relationship is incredibly sensitive to the inclusion of the fraction black in the regression. In particular, they find that including the fraction black reduces the qualitative importance and statistical significance of the inequality measure.

Including the percentage black has a dramatic impact on four of five outcomes. The coefficient on the Gini falls by half in the mortality and voting equations, by two-thirds in the exercise model, and switches signs in the current smoker equation. In the next line, we add another variable that has been suggested by some to have a "group" impact, namely, the fraction of people with less than a high school degree. Many outcomes are correlated with individual-level education, but some authors (Moretti 2002) have argued that there are externalities to living in an area with a more-educated population, although others find different results (Acemoglu and Angrist 2000). When we add the fraction with low education, the coefficients on the Gini in the fair/poor health and exercise equation drops by 75 percent, while the coefficient on the Gini in the current smoking equation actually doubles and becomes a statistically significant negative coefficient.

Although these results are for a limited number of outcomes and a limited number of covariates, they suggest that the estimated effect of inequality in standard equations is sensitive to the covariates included in the regression. This raises the concern that cross-

FIGURE 25.5   *State Family Income Inequality, 1989*

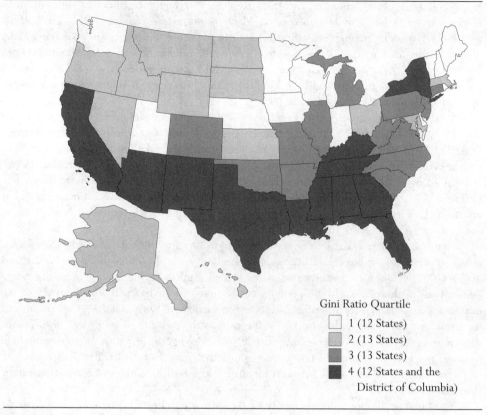

Gini Ratio Quartile

☐ 1 (12 States)

▨ 2 (13 States)

▨ 3 (13 States)

■ 4 (12 States and the
    District of Columbia)

Source: Authors' compilation.

sectional models like those in equation 25.3 are subject to an omitted variables bias. Researchers use a standard set of techniques to reduce omitted variable bias. Each technique has its strengths as well as its weaknesses. In the next two sections, we discuss two of the methods that have been used with increasing frequency in this field—fixed-effects estimation and instrumentals variables.

One approach to potential omitted variable bias is to control as many characteristics of states as possible. Because states with high and low income inequality are so distinct, most measures of inequality are strongly correlated with other state demographic characteristics. To give some indication of the strength of these relationships, table 25.10 shows the correlation between log median family income and the Gini coefficient at the state level and county levels with eight other observed characteristics. Notice that the Gini coefficient is much more strongly correlated with almost all the other variables than log median family income at both levels of aggregation. The strength of the correlation between most of these variables and the Gini coefficient raises the possibility of problems related to multi-colinearity when one simply controls a large number of state characteristics. A second problem is that some state characteristics may be endogenous with respect to inequality. For example, there is reason to think that educational attainment and even marital status might be endogenous.

FIGURE 25.6   *State Age-Adjusted Mortality Rate, 1990*

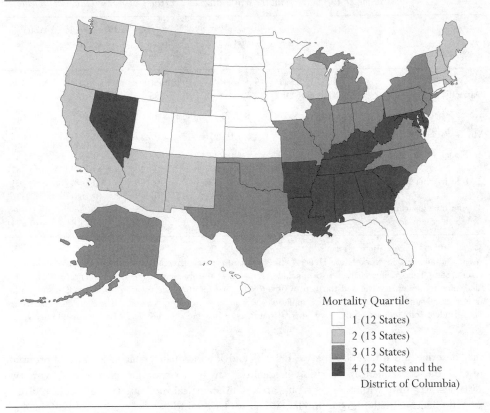

Mortality Quartile

☐ 1 (12 States)

▨ 2 (13 States)

▨ 3 (13 States)

■ 4 (12 States and the
District of Columbia)

Source: Authors' compilation.

Including more endogenous variables usually results in reducing the reduced-form effect of inequality.

REDUCING THE OMITTED VARIABLES BIAS

Because it is impossible to include all potentially relevant exogenous factors in a model and because some factors are partly endogenous, researchers have turned to indirect ways to control the relevant exogenous omitted variables. The two main techniques for doing this are fixed-effects and instrumental variables.

Reducing the Omitted Variables Bias Through Fixed-Effects Models

As we mentioned earlier, states with high levels of income inequality differ in many ways from states with low levels of income inequality. More important, the differences across states in inequality and other variables persist over time. The correlation coefficient between the 1990 and 1970 state Gini coefficient of family income is 0.78. The corresponding correlation for mortality is 0.85. Therefore, most of the differences in these variables are differences that persist over time. Given the impossible task of specifying all the variables

TABLE 25.9   *Linear Probability Models, Outcomes for Males Age Twenty-Five to Sixty-Four, Parameter Estimates [Huber/White Standard Errors] on State Gini Coefficient*

	Died in Five Years	Self-reported Health Status	Current Smoker	Exercised in Past Thirty Days	Voted in 1988 Election
Dataset	1987 to 1990 NHIS/MCOD	1988 to 1990 NHIS	1988 to 1991 BRFSS	1988 to 1991 BRFSS	Nov. 1988 CPS
Observations	97,778	97,778	96,046	96,046	29,135
Sample mean	0.026	0.091	0.297	0.724	0.655
1. Model 4 from table 25.8	0.107	0.223	0.061	−0.982	−0.861
	[0.033]	[0.087]	[0.222]	[0.222]	[0.287]
2. Add fraction black	0.048	0.219	−0.176	−0.248	−0.401
	[0.029]	[0.092]	[0.249]	[0.269]	[0.376]
3. Add fraction with less than a high school degree	0.051	0.045	−0.378	−0.056	−0.495
	[0.033]	[0.082]	[0.175]	[0.280]	[0.321]

Source: Authors' compilation.
Notes: The numbers in brackets are Huber/White standard errors corrected for within-state correlation in the errors. State demographic characteristics include average age, the fraction married, the fraction with less than nine, nine to eleven, twelve, and thirteen to fifteen years of education, the fraction black, fraction some other race, average family income, and, where applicable, year of survey dummy variables. The individual characteristics include a complete set of age, race, marital status, ethnicity, income, and year of survey fixed effects.

that describe the differences between high- and low-inequality states, a more appropriate test of the consequences of rising inequality may be to examine changes in these two variables over time within a geographic area. This statistical model is typically referred to as a fixed-effects or within-group model. When we have multiple observations of both inequality and the outcome within states over time, we can hold constant permanent differences across states by adding a set of state dummy variables. To control for factors that are

TABLE 25.10   *Correlation Coefficients Between Log Median Family Income and Gini Coefficient in Family Income and Other Characteristics, 1990*

	State-Level Data		County-Level Data	
	Log Median Family Income	Gini Coefficient in Family Income	Log Median Family Income	Gini Coefficient in Family Income
Percentage in poverty	−0.729	0.724	−0.739	0.822
Percentage on public assistance	−0.281	0.632	−0.606	0.690
Percentage black	−0.101	0.716	−0.113	0.494
Percentage Hispanic	−0.171	0.318	−0.041	0.300
Percentage with less than a high school degree	−0.434	0.624	−0.664	0.564
Percentage less than eighteen years old	−0.069	0.175	−0.221	0.140
Percentage more than sixty-four years old	−0.069	0.244	−0.407	0.051
Unemployment rate	−0.233	0.514	−0.443	0.510

Source: U.S. Census Bureau, 1990 census.

constant across all states but that vary over time, we also can add a set of year dummy variables.

For an outcome of interest $Y_s t$ that varies across states (s) and years (t), the basic econometric specification for a within-group model can be described as follows:

$$Y_{st} = \alpha + \beta_i I_{st} + \beta_x X_{st} + u_s + v_t + e_{st} \tag{25.14}$$

where X is a vector of time-varying state characteristics, I is the time-varying, group-specific measure of inequality, u_s is a state-specific effect, v_t is a time effect, and e_{st} is a random error. The state effects are designed to capture the characteristics of the state that vary across states but are constant over time, such as whether the state is primarily rural or urban, southern or northern, and so on. Likewise, the year effects are designed to capture those characteristics that are common to all states but vary over time. The coefficient of interest is on the variable I, which is a state-specific measure of inequality. This basic model can easily be adapted to accommodate individual-level data.

Fixed-effects models are frequently called "within-group estimators" because the parameter estimates are determined by the changes in the endogenous and exogenous variables within the group—or in this case, within a state—over time. The within-group estimator has a number of advantages, the chief one being the ability to purge from the analysis permanent state characteristics that might alter both outcomes and inequality. There are two primary disadvantages. First, most models do not explain why the key covariates—in this case, inequality—change in a state over time. For example, in a model like equation 25.14, where the outcome of interest is mortality, the key covariate is income inequality, and data vary across states and years, the fixed-effects model does not explain why some states have had higher-than-average growth in inequality. If the reason for this increase is also the reason mortality or voting or any other outcome of interest has changed, then we are back into the problem of omitted variables bias.

Second, most of the variation in variables that we would include in X or I tends to be across groups rather than within a group over time. As a result, the fixed-effects model uses much smaller variation in the data to identify parameters, greatly reducing the precision of the estimates. Therefore, standard errors tend to increase. In many cases, researchers are left with statistically imprecise but qualitatively large coefficients. In this case, we cannot reject the null hypothesis of "no effect," but we also must be concerned about whether the hypothesis has been given a fair chance, that is, whether there is enough sample variation left in the data to detect a precise relationship. For example, consider a researcher who wants to pool data on outcomes at the state level for the 1970 to 1990 period and to use data from the decennial census to construct state-specific Gini coefficients. In a fixed-effects model, there is little residual variation left in the Gini once state and year effects are added to the model. Just as an example, the R-squared produced in a regression of state-specific Gini coefficients for family income for 1969, 1979, and 1989 (yielding 153 observations) on state and year effects is 0.92. Therefore, only 8 percent of the variation in the covariate of interest is used to identify the model, greatly increasing standard errors.

The stark difference between the value and precision of parameter estimates in cross-sectional and fixed-effects estimates is illustrated with a simple example. Social scientists have been interested for a number of years in the impact of income inequality on criminal activity. A positive link between inequality and crime is predicted in Gary Becker's model of crime(1968), Robert Merton's (1938) strain theory, and the social disorganization theory of Clifford Shaw and Henry McKay (1942). Dozens of papers have included as a covariate in their regressions some geographically based measure of inequality. A recent example is the work of Morgan Kelly (2000), who regresses county-level crime in 1994 on a host of variables, including a measure of income inequality. Kelly finds a statistically significant and qualitatively strong positive link between county-level inequality and violent crime, but a small negative and statistically insignificant impact of inequality for property crime.

It is easy to reproduce the basic results in Kelly (2000), albeit with a smaller set of control variables. Using data from Evans and Topoleski (2002), we regress county-level violent and property crime rates (crimes per 100,000 residents) for 1995 and 1985 on the fraction of nonwhites, fraction in certain age groups, log per capita income, log weekly wage, employment to population ratio, and the county-level family income Gini coefficient. For 1995 (1985) we use data from the 1990 (1980) census to calculate the Gini coefficient. In table 25.11, we report the simple cross-sectional relationship between crime and inequality. In the top half of the table, we report results for violent crime, and in the bottom half we report numbers for property crime. Because of reporting inconsistencies in crime data across agencies, we have data on only 2,012 counties for both years. In both cross-sections there is a quantitatively large and statistically precise relationship between income inequality and both types of crime. For example, in 1985 the coefficient on the Gini is 1,785 and the t-statistic is in excess of 10. The standard deviation of the Gini coefficient across counties is 0.036, so an increase in the Gini coefficient equal to a two-standard-deviation movement is predicted to increase the crime rate by 128.5, which is 49 percent of the sample mean. In the 1995 property crime cross-section, the t-statistic on the effect of the Gini coefficient is again about 10, and a two-standard-deviation increase in the Gini would increase property crime by about 24 percent. When we pool the two cross-sections and add a year effect, the results are simply the arithmetic average of the first two columns.

There is reason to believe that the results in the first three columns are subject to an omitted variables bias. Income inequality at the county level tends to be highest in large urban counties where crime is also the highest. Most of the variation in crime and income inequality is across counties rather than across time within a county. Regressing violent crime rates, property crime rates, and the county-level Gini coefficient on county and year effects, the R-squareds are 0.87, 0.92, and 0.89, respectively, indicating that there is some but not much within-panel variation in the Gini to identify a fixed-effects model.

In the final column of the table, we add county fixed effects to the pooled model. Notice that the R-squared jumps considerably in both models. Notice, however, that the parameter estimates fall considerably from the pooled models—by 65 percent in the case of violent crime and by 95 percent in the case of violent crime. Because a smaller degree of variation is used to identify the fixed-effects model, the standard errors also increase considerably, nearly doubling in both cases. In this instance, the use of fixed effects in a panel dataset generates vastly different estimates than in the cross-sectional models.

Reducing Omitted Variables by Using Two-Stage Least Squares

A standard solution to the omitted variables bias problem is to use some instrumental variables (IV) procedure such as two-stage least squares (2SLS). In contrast to many fixed-effects models where there is unexplained variation in x within a group over time that identifies the model, IV estimation takes the opposite extreme and requires a more precise statement about the source of variation in the data. To set up the discussion for this section, it is easiest to start with a simple model such as the basic bivariate regression:

TABLE 25.11   *OLS and Fixed-Effects Estimates, Crime Rate Equations at the County Level, 1985 and 1995*

Year	1985	1995	Pooled	Pooled
Observations	2,012	2,012	4,024	4,024
Include county fixed-effects	No	No	No	Yes
Violent crime				
Mean of dependent variable	262	369	316	316
Coefficient on family income Gini	1785	1939	1867	659
	(150)	(182)	(119)	(209)
R-squared	0.477	0.472	0.471	0.881
Property crime				
Mean of dependent variable	2,917	3,173	3,044	3,044
Coefficient on family income Gini	5,890	10,525	7,563	370
	(913)	(1,060)	(744)	(989)
R-squared	0.505	0.506	0.408	0.923

Source: F.B.I. Uniform Crime Reports, 1985 and 1995.
Notes: OLS standard errors are in parentheses. The crime rate is defined as crimes per 100,000 people. State demographic characteristics include the log per capita income, log weekly wage, the employment to population ratio, the fraction of people in different age groups, and, in the final two columns, year effects.

$$y_i = \alpha + x_i\beta + \varepsilon_i. \tag{25.15}$$

In the context of this chapter, this could be a regression of state-level mortality or any number of other outcomes (y) on income inequality (x). We suspect that the realization of x conveys some information about the error term e_i, and that therefore OLS estimates of the parameters in equation 25.15 will be biased, so we consider an IV procedure. Implementation of IV requires a third variable (z), an instrument, that directly shocks x but has no direct impact on y. The implementation of a two-stage least squares model requires a "first-stage" regression of x on the instrument z, and then the second-stage regression (equation 25.15) is estimated by replacing x with its predicted value from the first-stage regression. Because the predicted value of x is a linear combination of factors uncorrelated with ε (the instrument z), the predicted value is by construction uncorrelated with the error term ε, and a consistent estimate is obtained.

It is sometimes useful to think of 2SLS as indirect least squares in the case where there is only one endogenous covariate and one instrument. If z impacts x, and x causes y, we should see a direct relationship between z and y. In this simple case, the ratio of these estimates reproduces the same estimate as 2SLS. Again, returning to equation 25.15, a first-stage regression of x on z generates an estimate of the coefficient dx/dz. Next, consider a reduced-form regression y on z. Since we assume that the only impact of z on y is through x, the units of measure on this coefficient are (dy/dx)(dx/dz). Dividing the reduced form by the first stages generates a coefficient with dy/dx as the units of measures. This coefficient is exactly the 2SLS result in this simple case.

The key assumption of this exercise, however, is that x has no direct impact on y. Even slight correlation between z and y can lead to errors in estimates. To demonstrate this point, we draw on results from others and examine the relative consistency of OLS and IV estimates. Suppose 25.15 can be estimated by OLS or IV, and let β_{ols} and β_{iv} be these estimates, respectively. It can be shown that the consistency of the instrumental variables relative to the OLS estimate is given by:

$$\text{plim}(\beta_{iv} - \beta)/\text{plim}(\beta_{ols} - \beta) = \rho(z_i,\varepsilon_i)/[\rho(x_i,\varepsilon_i)\rho(z_i,x_i)] \qquad (25.16)$$

where $\rho(a,b)$ is the correlation coefficient between a and b (Bound, Jaeger, and Baker 1995). This equation points out an important characteristic of instrumental variables estimates, namely, that in order for IV estimates to produce "more consistent" estimates, it must be the case that z_i and ε_i are correlated at a fraction of the rate that x_i and ε_i are correlated, where that fraction is determined by the strength of the first-stage relationship $\rho(z_i,x_i)$. If $\rho(z_i,x_i)$ is "low," say, 0.1, then $\rho(z_i,\varepsilon_i)$ must be one-tenth the size of $\rho(x_i,\varepsilon_i)$ in order for IV to produce an estimate that is "more consistent" than OLS. The fact that z and ε_i must be correlated at a fraction of the rate that x and ε_i is the impetus for the growth in the use of natural experiments or quasi-experimental variation as instrumental variables (Angrist and Krueger 2001). Natural experiments use changes in x produced by random or external events as instruments for x. These events are in most cases defined by some external source lessening the chance that z and ε_i are correlated.

A second problem with some 2SLS models is finite sample bias—or as it is commonly referred to in the literature, the problem of "weak instruments." In the 2SLS procedure, predicted values of x are used in equation 25.15 rather than actual values. The predicted values come from the first-stage regression of x on z. Because the variable x is used in the construction of the first-stage estimates of z, the predicted x does contain some information about the original variable x that lead to 2SLS. A number of authors have examined in detail diagnostic tests for finite sample bias, including Bound, Jaeger, and Baker (1995) and Staiger and Stock (1997). In a model with one endogenous variable, as in equation 25.15, and more than two instruments, the degree of finite sample bias is roughly proportion to one over the F-statistic for the joint test that the instruments are statistically distinguishable from zero in the first-stage regression. Holding the first-stage fit constant, finite sample increases linearly if more instruments are added to the model. Likewise, holding the number of instruments constant, finite sample bias is increased as the first-stage fit declines. (Measured by the partial F-test that the instruments can be excluded from the model.) In practice, the problems generated by finite sample bias have been in situations where 2SLS models are identified with dozens (or sometimes even hundreds) of instruments. Reducing the dimensions of the problem by using parsimonious specifications often does the trick. Other solutions are available even in models with weak instruments. For example, limited information maximum likelihood is median-unbiased even in the case of weak instruments.

The third problem with IV estimates is the sample sizes needed to construct meaningful inferences in these two-step models. Instrumental variables models rely on a second-stage relationship to infer casual relationships—in this instance, the instrument changes the measure of inequality and, as a result, indirectly changes outcomes. Therefore, the precision of any instrumental variables procedure is determined by the size of the first-stage relationship, the true impact of x on y, and the number of observations. A weaker first-stage relationship (in a qualitative sense, not a statistical one) produces a smaller reduced-form relationship and, as a result, a less precise estimate.

To illustrate this point, we want to make use of one stylized fact. In 2SLS models with one endogenous covariate and one instrument, the absolute value of the t-statistic on the 2SLS estimate of β is roughly equal to the t-statistic on the variable z in the reduced form (the regression of y on z). Next, consider the results in table 25.8, where we show that a simple cross-sectional regression of mortality on income inequality plus other covariates produces a coefficient of 0.101 for the Gini coefficient (row 4). In a simple cross-section of fifty states and the District of Columbia, the standard deviation of the 1990 Gini coefficient in family income is 0.025, which is 6.5 percent of the sample mean. Suppose a researcher is lucky enough to identify a discrete instrument that alters the Gini coefficient by 2.5 percentage points, which would be a large change. If the OLS estimate of 0.101 were true, a regression of y on z would produce an estimate of $(0.025)(0.101) = 0.002525$. The sample size needed to detect 2.5 thousandths of a change in the probability of death is staggering.

The criteria for successfully using 2SLS models are stringent in any case, but they are particularly troublesome in this instance. First, we need a plausibly exogenous form of variation. Second, we need a variable that is correlated with the unobserved component of the regression at a fraction of the rate of the potentially contaminated covariate. Third, we need an instrument that explains enough of the contaminated covariate to eliminate concerns of finite sample bias. Fourth, in most cases, we need an incredibly large sample to have any hope of identifying a statistically meaningful 2SLS relationship. Given these criteria, it should be no surprise that 2SLS has not been used much in models that examine the impacts of inequality. The largest obstacle is certainly finding exogenous variation in inequality that does not directly alter outcomes.

CONCLUSION

As income inequality has grown over the past thirty years, so too has the empirical literature interested in discerning the real impacts of this change. Researchers in the area come from a variety of disciplines, examine a host of outcomes, and use a wide range of techniques. In this chapter, we have tried to summarize some of the issues that any researcher faces when examining the social dimensions of inequality. Unfortunately, in attempting to answer some important questions, we have raised several new ones. To be sure, determining causal relationships is difficult in almost all non-experimental settings, but it is particularly hard in this context. The key covariate of interest in this chapter (income inequality) is the outgrowth of a detailed and complicated social and economic process. As a result, it is correlated with many observed factors and certainly with many unmeasured variables as well. Therefore, there is always the suspicion that the estimated effect of inequality may actually be measuring something other than the direct impact of inequality. Teasing out what is fact and what is fiction will take years and a variety of clever research designs.

NOTES

1. Note that because β is squared in equation 25.2, this statement is true whether β is positive or negative. Note too that the linear relationship in equation 25.1 is just a convenience that keeps the derivation tractable. The qualitative conclusion that rising variance in an independent variable raises the variance of the outcome does not strictly depend on this functional form. For simplicity, we simply assume that whatever the underlying relationship might be, we can find some transformation that will make it linear.
2. An important distinction is between individual relative deprivation, in which an individual compares his or her personal situation to the situation of other individuals, and group relative deprivation, in which a person compares his or her relevant group's situation with the situation of another group. Growing inequality can affect both sorts of relative deprivation, but here we emphasize individual comparisons, not group comparisons. Individual comparisons are more likely to lead to isolation and stress, while group comparisons are more likely to lead to collective action (Gurr 1970; Smith, Spears, and Hamstra 1999).

3. Under some circumstances, growing inequality leads to a "mechanical" increase in redistributive spending. If inequality increases while mean income stays the same, the poor almost always get poorer. The number of individuals and families who qualify for means-tested entitlement programs therefore tends to increase.

4. Research also suggests that racial segregation is associated with black infant mortality (Ellen 2000). However, economic and racial segregation need not be highly correlated, and in fact, as economic inequality increased over the last thirty years, economic segregation but not racial segregation increased.

5. It also may be difficult to distinguish between relational and externality effects when income is measured crudely with large, open-ended income categories for the rich. Categorizing income in this way makes it hard to get a reliable estimate of the variance of income. Researchers often create income groups based on percentiles of the income distribution. This rank-order information with a fixed number of ranks is useful for descriptive analysis, but it rules out the possibility of saying whether widening gaps between the top and bottom percentiles are due to growing variance in income or increased strength in the relationship between income and outcome. The distinction is nonetheless an important one that could orient our thinking about the consequences of growing inequality for the full range of outcomes that might be considered.

6. In the PSID, the inter-year correlation of income ranges between .86 and .89 in all years between 1968 and 1990. The correlation between income in 1991 and 1992 was .84, and the correlation drops to around .75 for 1992 to 1995. The correlation between income in a year and income five years later is between .71 and .75 for all years between 1968 and 1988. In 1988 this correlation drops to .66; it drops to .65 in 1989, and then to .74 in 1990.

7. However, one study (Krueger and Perri 2002) finds that while the amount that families report as income became more unequal, the amount that they report spending did not become more unequal. Between 1972 and 1998, their measure of income inequality increased by 20 percent, but their measure of inequality in expenditures increased by less than 2 percent. They argue that the increase in income inequality is partly due to an increase in income volatility. But at the same time income was becoming more volatile, the credit market improved to keep pace with the increase in volatility, allowing families to smooth income fluctuations over time and maintain a level of spending consistent with their permanent income. If this happened and if income inequality is important because it results in inequality in consumption, we might not observe any effect of the increase in income inequality. But income inequality could be important for reasons other than consumption inequality. When income volatility increases, risk-sharing becomes more attractive. This can cause private credit markets to expand, but it can also cause voters to demand the expansion of government income support programs.

8. Yitzhaki (1979) proposes an analogous relative satisfaction metric that is equal to $\mu - RD$. Since we are using reference-group fixed effects, this measure is a linear combination of the fixed effect and the relative deprivation measure. A second potential measure of relative satisfaction, $\{y_i - E(y \mid y < y_i)\} \times \text{prob}(y < \ln y_i)$, is a linear combination of RD, y_i, and μ.

9. If social comparisons are the main mechanism through which inequality operates, the issue of reference groups is even more complex. For example, it makes a difference whether social comparisons depend on rank or distance. If they depend only on rank, then increases in inequality that do not change ranks would not affect social comparisons. In addition, people change reference groups when comparisons become less favorable, and unfavorable comparisons can be motivating as well as alienating.

10. The NHIS is an annual survey of 100,000 people from 40,000 households designed to track illness and disability among the non-institutionalized population. Each NHIS has two components. The first is a household file that contains basic demographic information, self-reported health status, height and weight, lists of chronic and acute conditions, and counts of doctor visits and hospitalizations as well as a measure of family income for all household members. The second component of the NHIS comprises special-interest modules that survey samples of core respondents about current health topics. Modules vary in size and scope, and in many years there are numerous special topics.

11. The BRFSS is a stratified sample administered and supported by the Behavioral Surveillance Branch (BSB) of the National Center for Chronic Disease Prevention and Health Promotion (NCCDPHP) and the Centers for Disease Control and Prevention (CDC). The BRFSS collects yearly state-level data on health and risk behavior through random telephone surveys of private households. Only one adult per phone

interview is questioned. Calls are made during day and evening hours, seven days a week, within a two-week period every month. The survey questions include a combination of individual characteristics and health practices and risk behavior questions. State public health programs voluntarily participate in the survey, and each state is responsible for collecting data. The individual state files are then collected by the CDC and merged into a national sample. The number of participating states has increased from fifteen in 1984, the first year of the survey, to fifty states in 1995. In 2001, the BRFSS had over 200,000 respondents.

12. We attach to the data used in table 25.7 the state-level Gini coefficient of family income measured using 1990 census data. State codes are available in the public use versions of the BRFSS and CPS datasets. They are not available in the GSS or the NHIS. Christine Eibner and William Evans (forthcoming), however, have received permission to use restricted-use versions of the NHIS and the NHIS/MCOD at the NCHS data center, which provides them with access to state codes.

13. The incredibly large increase in standard errors for the BRFSS outcomes may be due to the unique nature of these data. State health departments field a common survey, but each state uses different sampling frames and contractors to conduct the survey. As a result, the common within-state correlation in errors may be larger for the BRFSS than in NHIS or CPS, which follow the same survey protocol in each state. It is interesting to note that in the case of the BRFSS data, the raw cross-sectional results between the outcome and the Gini coefficient are by far the most precise estimates, yet by row 4, with within-state correlation in errors, the coefficient on the Gini in the current smoker coefficient is statistically insignificant.

REFERENCES

Acemoglu, Daron, and Joshua Angrist. 2000. "How Large Are Human Capital Externalities? Evidence from Compulsory Schooling Laws." Macroannual 9-59. Cambridge, Mass.: National Bureau of Economic Research.

Alesina, Alberto F., and Eliana La Ferrara. 2000. "Participation in Heterogeneous Communities." *Quarterly Journal of Economics* 115(3): 847–904.

————. 2002. "Who Trusts Others?" *Journal of Public Economics* 85(2): 207–34.

Alesina, Alberto F., and Dani Rodrick. 1994. "Distributive Politics and Economic Growth." *Quarterly Journal of Economics* 109(2): 465–90.

Angrist, Joshua D., and Alan B. Krueger. 2001. "Instrumental Variables and the Search for Identification: From Supply and Demand to Natural Experiments." *Journal of Economic Perspectives* 15(4): 69–85.

Angrist, Joshua D., and Victor Lavy. 2002. "The Effect of High School Matriculation Awards: Evidence from Randomized Trials." Working paper 9389. Cambridge, Mass.: National Bureau of Economic Research.

Autor, David, and Lawrence F. Katz. 1999. "Changes in the Wage Structure and Earning Inequality." In *Handbook of Labor Economics,* vol. 3A, edited by Orley Ashenfelter and David Card. Amsterdam: Elsevier-North Holland.

Becker, Gary S. 1968. "Crime and Punishment: An Economic Approach." *Journal of Political Economy* 76(2): 169–217.

Berrebi, Z. Moshe, and Jacques Silber. 1985. "Income Inequality Indices and Deprivation: A Generalization." *Quarterly Journal of Economics* 100(3): 807–10.

Brooks, Clem, and David Brady. 1999. "Income, Economic Voting, and Long-term Political Change, 1952–1996." *Social Forces* 77(4): 1339–75.

Bound, John, David Jaeger, and Regina Baker. 1995. "Problems with Instrumental Variables Estimation When the Correlation Between the Instruments and the Endogenous Explanatory Variable Is Weak." *Journal of the American Statistical Association* 90(430): 443–50.

Bylsma, Wayne H., and Brenda Major. 1994. "Social Comparisons and Contentment: Exploring the Psychological Costs of the Gender Wage Gap." *Psychology of Women Quarterly* 18(2): 241–49.

Clarkwest, Andrew, and Christopher Jencks. 2003. "Inequality and Mortality in Rich Countries: Who Owns the Null Hypothesis?" Working paper. Cambridge, Mass.: Harvard University, John F. Kennedy School of Government.

Cornfield, Jerome. 1978. "Randomization by Group: A Formal Analysis." *American Journal of Epidemiology* 108(2): 100–2.

Costa, Dora L., and Matthew E. Kahn. 2003. "Civic Engagement and Community Heterogeneity: An Economist's Perspective." *Perspectives on Politics* 1(1): 103–11.

Cowell, Frank A. 1977. *Measuring Inequality.* Oxford: Philip Allan.

Dagum, Camilo. 1980. "Inequality Measures Between Income Distributions with Applications." *Econometrica* 48(7): 1791–1803.

Davis, James A. 1959. "A Formal Interpretation of the Theory of Relative Deprivation." *Sociometry* 22: 280–96.

Deaton, Angus. 1999. "Inequalities in Income and Inequalities in Health." Working paper 7141. Cambridge, Mass.: National Bureau of Economic Research.

————. 2001. "Relative Deprivation, Inequality, and Mortality." Working paper 8099. Cambridge, Mass.: National Bureau of Economic Research.

————. 2003. "Health, Inequality, and Economic Development." *Journal of Economic Literature* 41(1): 113–58.

Deaton, Angus, and Darren Lubotsky. 2003. "Mortality, Inequality, and Race in American Cities and States." *Social Science and Medicine* (March): 1139–53.

Deaton, Angus, and Christina Paxson. 1998. "Aging and Inequality in Income and Health." *American Economic Review* 88(2): 248–53.

————. 2001a. "Mortality, Education, Income, and Inequality Among American Cohorts." In *Themes in the Economics of Aging,* edited by David Wise. Chicago: University of Chicago Press for National Bureau of Economic Research.

————. 2001b. "Mortality, Income, and Income Inequality Among British and American Cohorts." Princeton, N.J.: Princeton University, Center for Health and Well-being.

Durlauf, Steven N. 1996. "Neighborhood Feedbacks, Endogenous Stratification, and Income Inequality." In *Dynamic Disequilibrium Modeling: Theory and Applications: Proceedings of the Ninth International Symposium on Economic Theory and Econometrics,* edited by William Barnett, Giancarlo Gandolfo, and Claude Hillinger. New York: Cambridge University Press.

Eibner, Christine E., and William N. Evans. Forthcoming. "Relative Deprivation, Poor Health, Habits, and Mortality." *Journal of Human Resources.*

Ellen, Ingrid Gould. 2000. "Is Segregation Bad for your Health? The Case of Low Birth Weight." *Brookings-Wharton Papers on Urban Affairs 2000*: 203–29.

Evans, William N., Jeanne S. Ringel, and Diana Stech. 1999. "Tobacco Taxes and Public Policy to Discourage Smoking." *Tax Policy and the Economy* 13: 1–55.

Evans, William N., and Julie Topoleski. 2002. "The Social and Economic Impacts of Native American Casinos." Working paper 9198. Cambridge, Mass.: National Bureau of Economic Research.

Feldman, Jacob J., Diane M. Makuc, Joel C. Kleinman, and Joan Cornoni-Huntley. 1989. "National Trends in Educational Differentials in Mortality." *American Journal of Epidemiology* 129(5): 919–33.

Fertig, Angela R. 2001. "Trends in Intergenerational Earnings Mobility." Working paper 2001–23. Princeton, N.J.: Princeton University, Center for Research on Child Well-being.

Fiscella, Kevin, and Peter Franks. 1997. "Poverty or Income Inequality as a Predictor of Mortality: Longitudinal Cohort Study." *British Medical Journal* 314: 1724–28.

Gastwirth, Joseph L. 1972. "The Estimation of the Lorenz Curve and Gini Index." *Review of Economics and Statistics* 54(3): 306–16.

Gravelle, Hugh. 1998. "How Much of the Relation Between Population Mortality and Unequal Distribution of Income Is a Statistical Artifact?" *British Medical Journal* 316: 382–85.

Gurr, Ted Robert. 1970. *Why Men Rebel.* Princeton, N.J.: Princeton University Press.

Harding, David J., Christopher Jencks, Leaonard M. Lopoo, and Susan E. Mayer. Forthcoming. "Trends in Intergenerational Economic Mobility: Theories and Estimates for the United States Since 1960." In *Unequal Chances: Family Background and Economic Success,* edited by Samuel Bowles and Melissa Osbourne. New York/Princeton, N.J.: Russell Sage Foundation/Princeton University Press.

Hey, John D., and Peter J. Lambert. 1980. "Relative Deprivation and the Gini Coefficient: Comment." *Quarterly Journal of Economics* 95(3): 567–73.

Hout, Michael. 2003. "Money and Morale: What Growing Economic Inequality Is Doing to What Americans Think of Themselves and Others." Paper presented to the Russell Sage Foundation Social Inequality Conference, Washington, D.C. (May) Available at: www.russellsage.org.

Huber, Peter J. 1967. "The Behavior of Maximum Likelihood Estimates Under Nonstandard Conditions." In *Proceedings of the Fifth Berkeley Symposium on Mathematical Statistics and Probability.* Vol. 1. Berkeley: University of California Press.

Juhn, Chinhui, Kevin M. Murphy, and Brooks Pierce. 1993. "Wage Inequality and the Rise in Returns to Skill." *Journal of Political Economy* 101(3): 410–42.

Kaplan, George A., Elsie R. Pamuk, John W. Lynch, Richard D. Cohen, and Jennifer L. Balfour. 1996. "Inequality in Income and Mortality in the United States: Analysis of Mortality and Potential Pathways." *British Medical Journal* 312: 999–1003.

Kawachi, Ichiro, Bruce P. Kennedy, Kimberly Lochner, and Deborah Prothrow-Stith. 1997. "Social Capital, Income Inequality, and Morality," *American Journal of Public Health* 87(9): 1491–98.

Kelly, Morgan. 2000. "Inequality and Crime." *Review of Economics and Statistics* 82(4): 530–39.

Kennedy, Bruce P., Ichiro Kawachi, and Deborah Prothrow-Stith. 1996. "Income Distribution and Mortality: Cross-sectional Ecological Study of the Robin Hood Index in the United States." *British Medical Journal* 312: 1004–7.

Kitagawa, Evelyn M., and Philip M. Hauser. 1973. *Differential Mortality in the United States: A Study in Socio-economic Epidemiology.* Cambridge, Mass.: Harvard University Press.

Krueger, Dirk, and Fabrizio Perroi. 2002. "Does Income Inequality Lead to Consumption Inequality." NBER working paper #9202. Cambridge, Mass.: National Bureau of Economic Research.

Levine, David I., and Bhashkar Mazumder. 2002. "Choosing the Right Parents: Changes in the Intergenerational Transmission of Inequality—Between 1980 and the Early 1990s." Working paper 2002–08. Chicago: Federal Reserve Bank.

Liang, Kung-Yee, and Scott L. Zeger. 1986. "Longitudinal Data Analysis Using Generalized Linear Models." *Biometrika* 73: 13–22.

Mayer, Susan E. 2001. "How Did the Increase in Economic Inequality Affect Educational Attainment?" *American Journal of Sociology* 107(1): 1–32.

———. 2002. "How Economic Segregation Affects Children's Educational Attainment." *Social Forces* 8(1): 153–76.

Mayer, Susan E., and Leonard Lopoo. 2004. "Trends in the Intergenerational Economic Mobility of Sons and Daughters." In *Generational Income Mobility in North America and Europe,* edited by Miles Corak. Cambridge: Cambridge University Press.

McDonald, James B. 1984. "Some Generalized Functions for the Size Distribution of Income." *Econometrica* 52(3): 647–64.

Meara, Ellen. 1999. "Inequality and Infant Health." Unpublished paper. Harvard University, Cambridge, Mass.

Mellor, Jennifer, and Jeffrey Milyo. 2001. "Reexamining the Evidence of an Ecological Association Between Income Inequality and Health." *Journal of Health Politics, Policy, and Law* 26(3): 487–522.

———. 2002. "Income Inequality and Individual Health: Evidence from the Current Population Survey." *Journal of Human Resources* 37(3): 510–39.

Meltzer, Allan, and Scott F. Richards. 1981. "A Rational Theory of the Size of Government." *Journal of Political Economy* 89(5): 914–27.

Merton, Robert. 1938. "Social Structure and Anomie." *American Sociological Review* 3(5): 672–82.

Merton, Robert K., and Alice Kitt. 1950. *Contributions to the Theory of Reference Group Behavior.* Glencoe, Ill.: Free Press.

Milanovic, Branko. 1997. "A Simple Way to Calculate the Gini Coefficient, and Some Implications." *Economics Letters* 56(1): 45–49.

Moretti, Enrico. 2002. "Estimating the Social Return to Higher Education: Evidence from Longitudinal and Repeated Cross-sectional Data." Working paper 9108. Cambridge, Mass.: National Bureau of Economic Research.

Pappas, Gregory, Susan Queen, Wilbur Hadden, and Gail Fisher. 1993. "The Increasing Disparity in Mortality Between Socioeconomic Groups in the United States, 1960 and 1986." *New England Journal of Medicine* 329(2): 103–9.

Perotti, Roberto. 1996. "Growth, Income Distribution, and Democracy: What the Data Say." *Journal of Economic Growth* 1(2): 149–87.

Pettigrew, Thomas F. 1978. "Three Issues in Ethnicity: Boundaries, Deprivations, and Perceptions." In *Major Social Issues: A Multidisciplinary View,* edited by J. Milton Yinger and Stephen J. Cutler. New York: Free Press.

Piven, Frances Fox, and Richard Cloward. 1993. *Regulating the Poor: The Functions of Public Welfare.* New York: Vintage Books.

Preston, Samuel H. 1975. "The Changing Relation Between Mortality and Level of Economic Development." *Population Studies* 29(2): 231–48.

Preston, Samuel H., and Irma T. Elo. 1995. "Are Educational Differentials in Adult Mortality Increasing in the United States?" *Journal of Aging and Health* 7(4): 476–96.

Roberts, Kevin. 1977. "Voting over Income Tax Schedules." *Journal of Public Economics* 8: 329–40.

Rodgers, Gregory B. 1979. "Income Inequality as Determinant of Mortality: An International Cross-Section Analysis." *Population Studies* 33(2): 343–51.

Romer, Thomas. 1975. "Individual Welfare, Major Voting, and the Properties of a Linear Income Tax." *Journal of Public Economics* 4: 163–85.

Runciman, Walter G. 1966. *Relative Deprivation and Social Justice: A Study of Attitudes to Social Inequality in Twentieth-Century England.* Berkeley: University of California Press.

Shaw, Clifford, and Henry McKay. 1942. *Juvenile Delinquency and Urban Areas.* Chicago: University of Chicago Press.

Singer, Eleanor. 1981. "Reference Groups and Social Evaluations." In *Social Psychology: Social Perspective,* edited by Morris Rosenberg and Ralph H. Turner. New York: Basic Books.

Smith, H.J., Russell Spears, and I.J. Hamstra. 1999. "Social Identity and the Context of Relative Deprivation." In *Social Identity,* edited by Naomi Ellemers, Russell Spears, and Bertjan Doosji. Oxford, U.K.: Blackwell.

Solon, Gary. 1992. "Intergenerational Income Mobility in the United States." *American Economic Review* 82(3): 393–408.

Staiger, Douglas, and James H. Stock. 1997. "Instrumental Variables Regression with Weak Instruments." *Econometrica* 65(3): 557–86.

Waldmann, Robert J. 1992. "Income Distribution and Infant Mortality." *Quarterly Journal of Economics* 107(4): 1283–1302.

White, Halbert. 1980. "A Heteroskedasticity-Consistent Covariance Matrix Estimator and a Direct Test for Heteroskedasticity." *Econometrica* 48: 817–30.

Wilkinson, Richard G. 1992. "Income Distribution and Life Expectancy." *British Medical Journal* 304: 165–68.

———. 1996. *Unhealthy Societies: The Afflictions of Inequality.* London: Routledge.

———. 1997. "Health Inequalities: Relative or Absolute Material Standards?" *British Medical Journal* 314(7080): 591–95.

Williams, R., Jr. 1975. "Relative Deprivation." In *The Idea of Social Structure: Papers in Honor of Robert K. Merton,* edited by Lewis A. Coser. New York: Harcourt Brace Jovanovich.

Wooldridge, Jeffrey M. 2003. "Cluster-Sample Methods in Applied Econometrics." *American Economic Review* 93(2): 133–38.

Yitzhaki, Shlomo. 1979. "Relative Deprivation and the Gini Coefficient." *Quarterly Journal of Economics* 93(2): 321–24.

Zimmerman, David J. 1992. "Regression Toward Mediocrity in Economic Stature." *American Economic Review* 82(3): 409–29.

Chapter 26

How Inequality May Affect Intergenerational Mobility

Michael Hout

Inequality and social mobility go together intuitively. For hundreds of years social observers have treated both as measures of a nation's ability to offer opportunity and to treat its citizens fairly. Robert Mare (2002) notes that the sociological study of social mobility is rooted in concerns with the causes of social inequality.[1] Closer inspection reveals that these core social indicators are far from equivalent. Though each does indeed reflect an aspect of opportunity and fairness, inequality and mobility are very different phenomena. Most important, they have different perspectives on time. Inequality refers to the contemporary differences in wages, incomes, and wealth at some point in time; mobility refers to the difference from one generation to the next in these and other indicators of standards of living. As such, there is no *necessary* connection between them.[2] This disconnect regarding time reveals itself in the research literature as a parallel disconnect between the literatures on inequality and mobility.

What, then, are we to make of the intuitive connection between inequality and mobility? Intuitions are often rooted in substance, and so it is with the connection between inequality and mobility. The literature may be thin, and the connection may not be necessary, yet it merits more consideration than it has gotten to date. Thus, I propose in this review an agenda for exploring the possibility that there is a *contingent* relationship between inequality and mobility.

TWO SENSES OF EQUALITY

One important source of the intuition that inequality and mobility ought to go together is the importance of *equality* in the formation of both concepts. Inequality is the negation of equality, plain and simple. Mobility is usually understood as "equality of opportunity"—the outcomes may be unequal, but everyone, regardless of starting point, can have the same opportunity to get a good result. Perfect mobility exists when the correlation between a person's current position and starting position is zero—that is, when that individual's income, occupational status, and education do not depend on how much income, occupational status, and education his or her parents had. The positive correlations observed in every study quoted here are imperfections when judged against this ideal.

Research in political sociology and public opinion shows that adults tend to tolerate inequalities of outcome, especially if they think that they come from unequal abilities or luck, but that they object to inequalities of opportunity (Bobo 1997). The game can have high stakes as long as it is fair to all players. So, as a tool for understanding the public's approach to these issues, the common distinction between overall inequality and inequality of opportunity can be useful. After granting that point, however, we must also accept that the outcome-opportunity pairing has not been very useful as a tool for theory-building. None of the empirical studies or theory papers over the past twenty-five years discuss a mechanism or process that might link inequality of outcome to inequality of opportunity. There is an oft-replicated generalization that nations that have less inequality of outcomes also have less inequality of opportunity. I am convinced that we will make more progress linking mobility to inequality if we think of perfect mobility from a slightly different angle—as equality in an imagined world where inequalities at any one time are undone by moving the dispossessed up and the privileged down over time. In this world, equality is achieved by taking turns being rich and poor, esteemed and scorned. Under this definition of perfect mobility, each individual experiences the full range of outcomes over her or his lifetime. The prevalent understanding of perfect mobility is statistical and diachronic. My alternative is narrative and approaches time as a continuum.

I have found no literature on this alternative definition of perfect mobility, so let me interject a story to illustrate the idea. Shortly after my family and I moved to Berkeley, one of the graduate students took us on a tour. Part of the tour included the expensive homes in the hills with their panoramic views of San Francisco Bay and the Golden Gate. Our guide capped off that segment of the tour with the observation that "after the Revolution,[3] we will all take turns owning these homes." The idea is, of course, that the landscape makes some locations more desirable than other locations. Unfettered, the market economy maps the income distribution onto the landscape. But even if a revolution erupts and levels the income distribution, it could not level the landscape. Nature's intrinsic inequality is beyond reach. The revolutionary accommodation to this natural inequality is to take turns enjoying the advantages of living in the prized locations. Mobility of this sort would, over a lifetime, ameliorate an inexorable inequality.

Never mind that no hitherto existing society has ever worked this way. And never mind the high probability that incumbents would try to overstay their allotted time in the desired spots.[4] Focus instead on the way in which a perfect mobility scheme reconciles two sets of averages: the averages across individuals at each point in time and the average for each individual over time. As long as people differ one from another at any time (period inequality), then there must also be some compensating mobility over time (personal or turn-taking inequality). Inequality at one time does not imply unequal lifetimes for individuals without the additional proviso that the lifetime circulation of people fails to offset it. Formally, we will be able to recognize whether turn-taking inequality offsets period inequality by comparing the variance of outcomes at any point in time with the variance of outcomes that people experience. If the two are equal, then the turn-taking is working to offset the inequalities among individuals; if period inequality exceeds the personal variance over a lifetime, then turn-taking is not offsetting inequalities among individuals.[5]

The housing parable invites us to think mostly in terms of mobility over a work life. But the equality of opportunity idea that motivates it is actually about freeing people from the constraints of having grown up in circumstances that offered few resources. So we need to stretch the parable back in time enough to encompass intergenerational as well as intragenerational turn-taking.

Further implications follow. Think of the incentive to pursue mobility as proportional to the difference between a person's current position and one that she or he could hope to attain. The incentive to pursue mobility (either individually or collectively) is proportional to the amount of cross-sectional inequality. As inequality approaches zero, the payoff to mobility does too. (The difference between two nearly equal positions is nearly zero, by definition.) In the same way, under conditions of great inequality, the incentive to pursue mobility is great for those who are initially disadvantaged (their payoff is large and positive), and the incentive to resist mobility is just as great for those who are initially advantaged (their payoff is also large but negative).

My initial thought was that this system also implies a negative correlation between level or position at one time and the next, but that is not true. Because individuals continually exit the system—through migration or death—we can imagine an age-graded mobility regime of steady upward mobility over the life cycle that is consistent with the idea of perfect mobility. Under such a scheme each individual starts out low and progresses ever upward until exit. A system like that could, in principle, entail perfect mobility so long as the span of levels or positions over the life cycle is as great as the span of levels or positions in each cross-section. (Other conditions must also be met.)[6] Among the interesting variants to be considered are conditions such as cumulative advantage—the idea that individuals with initial advantages or first movers might progress upward through an age-graded system faster than later movers (DiPrete 2001).

The image of inequality based in an inalterable natural landscape invites us to think of positions as fixed through time. But occupational, income, and wealth distributions experience real growth, which the mobility literature calls "structural mobility." This idea will have to be accommodated in any turn-taking model of perfect mobility.

In the next section, I review the literature on intergenerational mobility with an eye on its implications for the turn-taking perspective. More comprehensive reviews exist (Ganzeboom, Treiman, and Ultee 1991; Breiger 1995); I draw on them somewhat and direct the reader's attention to them. I then discuss in some detail a new approach to linking inequality and mobility that Gary Solon (2001) has proposed, and I compare it with what has come before and with what I have in mind. In the final section, I lay out the agenda of research implied by this review.

INTERGENERATIONAL OCCUPATIONAL MOBILITY

The study of intergenerational mobility has been a mainstay of sociology for over one hundred years. As early as 1927, Pitrim Sorokin compiled twenty-three intergenerational mobility studies from six countries. The studies ranged in size from just 62 naval officers and their sons to 24,442 "employed boys" in New York State. The earliest studies were two French samples from 1900, and the latest was Sorokin's own sample of Minneapolis businessmen in 1926. Only one drew a cross-sectional sample, although the vague information about the early French samples does not rule out the possibility that they too involved samples drawn from the general population. From his hodgepodge of data, Sorokin concluded that mobility varied according to origin, that there might be more inheritance of high-status than lower-status occupations, and that *contemporary occupational groups are far from being rigid, and the membranes between them are far from being impenetrable*" (419, Sorokin's emphasis).

Sorokin (1927, 424) was interested in finding a trend in mobility. Again, he found differences by origin. "[The evidence] suggests that within the same society there may be groups in which inheritance of occupation goes down, while within other groups it increases. This probably is the most correct picture of what is going on in reality." After seventy-five years of research, we can say that both of these vague generalizations were correct and that most of the variation among occupations turns out to be linked to what has come be understood as structural mobility. That is the way in which growth increases the probability that anyone, no matter her or his origins, will work in a growing occupation and, similarly, the way in which decline decreases the probability that anyone will work in a declining one. By extension, structural mobility increases the probability of intergenerational inheritance within growing occupations and decreases the probability of intergenerational inheritance within most declining occupations.[7]

Sorokin's motivating ideas were the distinctions between vertical and horizontal mobility and between individual mobility and collective mobility through broad social trends like economic growth and recession. Each affects opportunity. Sorokin argued that these parts change independently. He also set out to find a general trend in mobility but concluded that the independent movement of the subparts of the system work against general trends, suggesting that the "trendless fluctuation" in the data is a typical state for such a complex "system of interactions" (152).

How Mobility Depends on the Association Between Origins and Destinations

Mobility is actually a slant on the main concern of the academic literature. The mobility rate is just a by-product of how occupational success depends on social origins. Mobility is least when origins have a large effect on success; mobility would be very high if success ever turned out to be statistically independent of origins. So mobility researchers have focused far more on the origin-destination association than on its by-product—mobility—since these relationships were delineated by Otis Dudley Duncan and other important scholars in the 1960s.

Many scholars worked on mobility, but progress in understanding social stratification and inequality seemed elusive in the period from the 1920s to the 1960s. The problem was ultimately traced to the way in which those researchers framed the problem. By focusing on mobility instead of the association between origins and destinations, they effectively missed the underlying determinants and positioned themselves to see only indirectly the consequences of those determinants. To understand the limitations of this view, consider mobility in a simple society that has three strata of occupations—the best, the middle, and the worst. Classify each worker's social origins according to his or her father's occupation. People are upwardly mobile if they work in an occupation that has more status than their father's occupation had and downwardly mobile if they work in an occupation that has less status than their father's occupation had. They are immobile if their own occupation matches the status of their father's occupation. People with middle origins can experience all three mobility outcomes: they can be upwardly mobile, downwardly mobile, or immobile. But people from the best origins cannot be upwardly mobile, and people from the worst origins cannot be downwardly mobile. Viewing the problem from this oblique angle, researchers learned some important lessons but were continually baffled by observations such as the commonplace one that rising education does not improve mobility chances (see, for example, Boudon 1974).

An exception to the prevailing oblique view was Natalie Rogoff's work. Rogoff (1953, 1966) classified people according to their origins in the conventional way, but she ignored mobility and classified people directly according to their social destinations. She then compared, for each cell of the resulting table, the ratio of the actual count to the count expected under perfect mobility. Rogoff had made a fundamental conceptual breakthrough that subsequent work by Leo A. Goodman (1969) and Robert Hauser (1978) put on a firmer statistical base. In choosing a statistical counterfactual—perfect mobility—as the baseline for her analysis, she drew attention to the statistical association between origins and destinations. The significance of that move is easily lost on nonspecialists, but it paved the way for the major developments that came about between 1963 and 1973.

Otis Dudley Duncan and Robert W. Hodge (1963) made the conceptual shift from studying mobility as a subject of its own to studying how success depends on social origins and thinking about its consequences for mobility only after the primary relationship is worked out. Duncan (1966a, 1966b) followed with two methodological papers that spelled out how to apply the insights of the new perspective. In "Methodological Issues in the Analysis of Social Mobility" (1966a), he argued that the new approach was the appropriate one by noting that the social origins of a cross-section of contemporary workers do not refer to any specific point in the past. Prior to Duncan's intervention, researchers had usually thought of the origin distribution as "the past" and the destination distribution as "the present" (see, for example, Glass 1954). Duncan showed the fallacy of that view. Within any mobility analysis, the youngest workers may not even be out of their parents' home yet (they are still attached to their origins), while workers on the verge of retirement left home some forty years before. Even cohorts of workers of roughly the same age refer ambiguously to the past because some come from large families and others from small ones; the probability that a past worker is represented in a later labor force is proportional to his or her fertility (and childless workers from the past are never represented in an origin distribution). Thus, the only logically consistent approach to the mobility table is one that treats "father's occupation" or "family income while growing up" as a characteristic not of the past but of the present—as a characteristic of a person's own history that affects his or her present success.

Mobility tables are inherently bivariate. With "Path Analysis: Sociological Examples," Duncan (1966b) introduced the idea of causal chains. Origins may affect success directly, of course, but more likely there are "intervening variables" that are affected by origins and, in turn, affect success. The greatest of these intervening variables is, of course, education. Being born to parents who are highly educated, work in desirable jobs, and/or are rich bestows advantages in school, engenders the desire to pursue higher education, and facilitates one's own higher education by providing the means of paying for it. Educational success, once it is secured, improves the chances of occupational and economic success.

This work set the stage for the intellectual revolution that came with Blau and Duncan's *The American Occupational Structure* (1967). Chapter 5 of that classic articulates how the process of social stratification follows from origins through education to career beginnings and socioeconomic destinations.

As novel as the path-analytic approach was, there were important continuities with the past too. Duncan's innovations relied heavily on Sorokin's ideas about vertical mobility. Path analysis required scores. Blau and Duncan scored both occupational origins and occupational destinations on a single dimension of desirability. Rooted in prestige studies pioneered at the National Opinion Research Center (NORC) in the late 1940s and extended in the mid-1960s—just as the Occupational Changes in a Generation (OCG-I) project was under way—this approach to measuring occupational status was ideally suited to Sorokin's concept of a vertical hierarchy of occupations. Duncan's (1961) scale averaged the educational credentials that an occupation required and the wages it paid to derive that occupation's socioeconomic score.[8] Soon thereafter William H. Sewell, Robert Hauser, and others elaborated a number of other "intervening variables"—that is, steps along the way from origin to destination (Sewell, Haller, and Portes 1969; Sewell and Hauser 1975; Hauser 1973; for a full list, see Sewell et al. 2003).

In the late 1960s and early 1970s, not only were path analysis and the multivariate approach to understanding the origin-destination association developed, but good cross-national data also finally became available (see, for example, Lipset and Zetterberg 1956). A real problem arose, however, in analyzing these data: nations typically varied considerably in the prevalence of different occupations. When two nations had different mobility rates, researchers had trouble deciding whether variation in types of occupations accounted for all of the difference in mobility or whether the origin-destination association differed too. Leo Goodman's (1969, 1970, 1972, 1974, 1979, 1984) development of log-linear models solved that problem and set off a third generation of mobility studies (for example, Hauser 1978; Erikson and Goldthorpe 1987a).[9] Goodman's approach allowed for a specific test of the hypothesis that the association between origins and destinations is identical in two or more nations. If so, then any observed difference in mobility rates can unambiguously be attributed to the relative prevalence of different occupations; if not, then researchers knew that cross-national differences in the origin-destination association contribute to the cross-national differences in mobility rates.

David Featherman, Frank Jones, and Robert Hauser (1975) applied Goodman's innovation in an influential paper. They undertook a two-country comparison of Australia and the United States and found that the association between origins and destinations was the same in both countries. From their two-country comparison they advanced the bold conjecture that mobility differs but the association is the same in nations with a market economy and a nuclear family system (Featherman, Jones, and Hauser 1975, 340). This came to be known as the FJH hypothesis, and the model it implies—the log-linear model of no three-way interaction in the three-way table of origins by destinations by nation—came to be known as the model of "common social fluidity." The third generation of mobility studies was launched (Ganzeboom, Treiman, and Ultee 1991).

Erikson, Goldthorpe, and Portocarero (1979) were the first researchers to test the FJH hypothesis. Comparing England, France, and Sweden, they found that the association between origins and destinations in England and France was very similar—barely statistically significant in a test involving twenty thousand observations—but that the association in Sweden was significantly weaker. Over the years Erikson and his colleagues (1982, 1987a, 1987b; with an intervention by Hauser 1984a, 1984b) refined the analysis, but the principal finding stood: England and France were nearly identical, and Sweden was more open. As countries were added to the Comparative Analysis of Social Mobility in Industrial Nations (CASMIN) caseload, they were judged by the English-French pattern, which came to be called the "core" pattern. The German mobility pattern was very similar, but German classes exhibited more closure, which showed itself in the statistical analysis as a stronger association between origins and destinations (Müller and König 1986). Similarly, Irish mobility (both in the Republic of Ireland and in Northern Ireland) was restrained by an origin-destination association that was closer in magnitude to the German than the English or French association but similar to all of those other countries in the pattern (Hout and Jackson 1986; Hout 1989). Finally, Dutch mobility was found to conform to the familiar pattern at a weaker strength of association that differed little from the Swedish (Ganzeboom and De Graaf 1984). In Eastern Europe—Hungary and Poland—the pattern was different because communism ruled out self-employment, but otherwise these countries conformed to the results obtained in Western Europe.

Erikson and Goldthorpe (1987a, 1987b) brought all of these datasets together (and added Scotland to the analysis) in two papers that introduced their core model and its national variations. Their main conclusion was that the countries differed in the strength of association (or, inversely, openness) but that they exhibited a strong similarity in the pattern of association. In 1992 they introduced the "unidiff" model (Erikson and Goldthorpe 1992a; see also Xie 1992)—which expressed this idea formally as a log-multiplicative model—and found that their revision of the FJH hypothesis could not be rejected.

Several interesting countries could not be fitted into the CASMIN scheme because the unit-record occupational coding scheme could not be reconciled with the CASMIN standard one. Australia, Japan, and the United States, in particular, were left out of the core analysis, as were Czechoslovakia and Italy, because their data became available too late. Yet analyses by Erikson and Goldthorpe (1992a) indicate that the fundamental conclusion of *The Constant Flux* is validated by these cases. To the extent to which they can be compared with the other countries, they appear to differ only in the strength of association, not in its basic pattern. Indeed, as far as Erikson and Goldthorpe could tell, Australia and the United States more closely resembled Britain and France than any of the CASMIN nations did. Alan Kerckhoff and his colleagues (1989) also concluded that American and British mobility were very similar and that the association between origins and destinations was the same in the two nations. Japan more nearly resembled the stronger association of origins and destinations that characterized Germany (see also Ishida 1993; Ishida, Goldthorpe and Erikson 1991).

At the same time, researchers following Hauser's (1984a, 1984b) lead began to apply "vertical" models to the CASMIN data (Ganzeboom, Luijkx, and Treiman 1989; Hout and Hauser 1992; Wong 1992). They too found a common pattern of association—different from the core pattern specified by Erikson and Goldthorpe but common in the sense that it also did not vary from country to country—and again, it indicated that origin affected destination more in Germany and Ireland than in England or France (intermediate) or Sweden and the Netherlands (lower). The class and vertical perspectives on mobility were quite distinct. The class view—championed by Erikson and Goldthorpe—emphasized differences of kind among occupational categories. The employment relations that align the interests of service-class employees (managers and professionals) with the interests of their employers proffer advantages relative to the employment relations that typify wage work on a simple labor contract. The vertical perspective noted the even grading of prestige assessments, pay scales, and annual incomes. They saw occupations as differing in degree rather than kind. Attempts to adjudicate between these perspectives have not been definitive. The evidence is consistent with both points of view. Statistical tests usually imply a mixed model that includes elements of each approach (see, for example, Hout 1989, ch. 5). Most important for present purposes, however, is that both points of view support the conclusion that mobility patterns—whether they are rooted in class distinctions or a status hierarchy with fine gradation—differ among nations only in strength, not in type. Furthermore, the relative ordering of nations from most open to most closed is nearly identical (compare Erikson and Goldthorpe 1992a and Hout and Hauser 1992).

Researchers have added many nations to the pool of countries under study since the CASMIN study was completed: Spain (Rodriguez Menes 1993; Salido 1999), Austria and Czechoslovakia (Haller, Kolosi, and Robert 1990), Denmark (Hansen 1998), Finland (Pontinen 1984), Norway (Ringdal 1994, 2001), Canada (de Seve 1998; Wanner and Hayes 1996), Israel (Goldthorpe, Yaish, and Kraus 1997), China (Cheng and Dai 1995; Walder, Li, and Treiman 2000), Taiwan and South Korea (Phang and Lee 1996), Russia (Marshall, Sydorenko, and Roberts 1995; Gerber and Hout 2002), Slovenia (Ganzeboom, Kramberger, and Nieuwbeerta 2000), and Brazil (Wong 1992; Scalon 1999). And replications within countries have established that the pattern remains the same even where the trends point to change (Hout 1988; Ganzeboom et al. 1989; Breen and Whelan 1996; Schizzerotto and Pisati 1998; Ringdal 2001; Gerber and Hout 2002).[10]

These dozens of studies show a mobility pattern that is characterized by more social inheritance and short-distance mobility than would be expected by chance. There is socially and statistically significant persistence of advantage from one generation to the next. The models that dominate this literature do not reduce the association to a single number. On the other hand, methods developed about ten years ago (simultaneously) by Yu Xie (1992) and Erikson and Goldthorpe (1992a) allow us to summarize cross-national and over-time comparisons in a single parameter.

Those single-parameter contrasts suggest that Britain is near the center of the range of association and that other countries are between 20 percent more open and 20 percent more closed than Britain. If we accept that the association between origins and destinations in Britain corresponds (roughly) to a correlation coefficient of between .36 and .40, then the observed range of associations falls in a range of correlations between .29 and .48. While that nineteen-point range is quite broad, even the high end represents a great deal of turn-taking from one generation to the next. Finally, we might also want to adjust all these numbers upward in deference to measurement errors and to what Hout and Hauser (1992) characterize as the inherent downward bias in the most commonly applied models. If those errors and biases have led researchers to understate the association in Britain by as much as 20 percent—and that is probably high—then the range could be as high as .35 to .58. In the upper reaches of this range, we are beginning to see some impressive persistence of inequality from generation to generation. But for the most likely range of estimates, this research tradition has shown that exchange mobility rules the day. None of the observed data indicate more than modest persistence of social standing from origins to destination. It takes generous adjustments for measurement error and intrinsic downward biases in the most prevalent models to get sizable estimates for the most extreme countries.

These results suggest that mobility chances—as governed by the association between origins and destinations—improve when income inequality is reduced and may worsen when income inequality rises. Sweden, Norway, and the Netherlands have markedly less income inequality than other Western European nations and also have some of the weakest associations between origins and destinations. Likewise, Ireland has the highest income in-equality in Western Europe and a relatively strong association between origins and destina-tions. Britain and France are in the middle of the rank order of nations with respect to both inequality and origin-destination association. Finally, recent evidence about the post-Com-munist trends in Russia and perhaps Hungary indicate that the rapidly rising inequality in those nations has been accompanied by increases in origin-destination association.

Two observations about the United States weaken the claim that inequality within generations relates to inequality between generations. First, the United States stands out as by far the most unequal wealthy nation, yet the origin-destination association in the United States is about as strong as we find in Britain and France. Second, while income inequality grew rapidly in the United States between 1974 and 1985, the association between origins and destinations fell. Income inequality continued to rise through 1996, but the origin-destination association has not changed since 1985 (Hout and Beller 2003). Thus, the Amer-ican case greatly complicates the picture of inequality and mobility. I will try to sort through it after discussing, briefly, the role of so-called structural mobility in overall mobility.

Structural Mobility

Mobility reflects the imperfect relationship between origins and destinations, as we have seen, but occupational change also plays an important role. When the distributions of origins and destinations do not match perfectly, we can say with certainty that some mobility must have occurred; not everyone can stay in their class of origin and yet be distributed differently than their fathers were across the classes. The most important source of a discrepancy between the distributions of origins and destinations is change in the distribution of occupations, but differential fertility can also play a role. This component of overall mobility—referred to as structural mobility in the literature—brings together all the factors that contribute to success but are independent of social origins. These include the historical shifts from agriculture to manufacturing and on to post-industrial services as the dominant modes of production.

The great shifts of the last one hundred and fifty years are included under the structural mobility rubric. The industrial revolution moved millions of farm-origin workers off the land and into factories. Then the coming of post-industrial society, though less revolutionary, shifted the center of commerce from the factory to the office and the salesroom. The service sector of post-industrial employment has also expanded the roles of both professionals and menial workers in the economy. For over one hundred years these successive economic restructurings were an engine of social mobility, most of it upward (see, for example, Featherman and Hauser 1978; Goldthorpe 1980; Sewell 1984). But since the mid-1970s the momentum has abated. The cohorts that have left the U.S. labor force, for example, have been the last farm-origin cohorts. They have been replaced by the second post-industrial generation—sons and daughters of professionals and office workers who face a labor force with a profile not very different from the distribution of their origins. U.S. mobility would have slowed down in the 1980s had exchange mobility not increased enough to offset the falloff in structural mobility (Hout 1988).

The link between structural mobility and inequality would come from that component of inequality that exists between groups. Most directly, if there were large between-occupation components to the run-up in wage or income inequality, it would show here in structural mobility. Indeed, the arguments early in the debates about whether inequality was rising addressed these issues. Barry Bluestone and Bennett Harrison's arguments in *The Deindustrialization of America* (1982) and *The Great U-Turn* (1988) were of this variety. They noted that the growth of services was creating jobs at the top and the bottom of the occupational hierarchy while the shutdown of manufacturing was hollowing out the middle (see also Morris, Bernhardt, and Handcock 1994; Bernhardt, Morris, and Handcock 1995). This is structural mobility. Yet its centrality for understanding inequality—and the consequences of this engine of inequality for mobility—is compromised by two ambiguities. First, between-occupation inequality is a small part of the trend toward inequality in U.S. incomes and wages (see, for example, Bell and Freeman 1991). Second, the causal order here is very murky. Structural mobility is primarily used to explain growing inequality. But our focus here is on the social consequences of rising inequality—including its consequences for mobility chances.

A WORKING MODEL TO TIE INEQUALITY TO MOBILITY

This review of the literature has revealed hints of a relationship between inequality and mobility, but the evidence is indirect, qualitative, and ultimately inconclusive. In this section, I draw on recent work by Gary Solon that I find to be very promising and blend it with an insight that Peter Gottschalk and Robert Moffitt contributed. Together these pieces imply a testable proposition about how growing inequality can influence the association between origins and destinations in a mobility table.

Definitions and Notation

Let $y_{it}*$ be some outcome of interest (for example, wage, annual income, occupation, socioeconomic status, wealth) suitably scaled (maybe logged) for person i, observed in year t. Let μ_i represent i's relevant time-invariant attributes (note that there is no t subscript) such as gender, ancestry, nativity, family background, education (usually not varying much over time), the component of "ability" that does not vary over time, and time-invariant aspects of personality. For ease of exposition, further assume that these time-invariant items have been scaled so that the average within-cohort slope of their sum is unity.

Suppose $y_{it}*$ depends on μ_i within cohorts (indexed by b), with life-cycle effects proportional to age ($a_{it} = t - b_i$) and a disturbance term (ε_{it}):

$$y_{it}* = \alpha_b + \mu_i + \beta a_i + \varepsilon_{it} \tag{26.1}$$

where ε_{it} has a mean of zero and a homoskedastic variance.

The issue is to understand how time-invariant individual differences (μ_i) result in variation in outcomes ($y_{it}*$). We have used the convenient linear form in equation 26.1 because that is the functional form that results in a one-to-one correspondence between the variance of μ_i and the variance of $y_{it}*$, as shown in equation 26.2. The other two sources of variation in outcomes are life-cycle effects that improve individuals' outcomes (on average) as they age (βa_i) and transient individual differences (ε_{it}). If there is no autocorrelation in the ε (a reasonable assumption as long as we get all the time-invariant individual differences measured in μ_i) and μ, b, and ε are mutually uncorrelated (another reasonable assumption as long as we have measured all the time-invariant individual differences in μ_i), then at each time point t:

$$Var(y_t*) = Var(\mu) + \beta^2 Var(a_t) + Var(\varepsilon_t) \tag{26.2}$$

Solon (2001) is my source for equations 26.1 and 26.2. He draws three lessons from equation 26.2:

1. The life-cycle differences imply nothing that would be considered fundamentally inequitable, since all individuals who live long enough eventually experience the benefit of these differentials (the turn-taking equality mentioned earlier).

2. Over a lifetime, variation in μ—which represents the lifelong earnings gap between the chronic haves and the chronic have-nots—is more consequential for well-being than variation in ε because, while ε may have a high variance, the fact that both its mean and autocorrelation are zero makes it transitory and implies (by definition) a very small cumulative effect.

3. The first two lessons imply that nearly all lifelong inequality reflects the permanent differences among people captured by μ. In a cross-section, however, $Var(a_t)$ and $Var(\varepsilon_t)$ contribute to variance and can be as large as or larger than $Var(\mu)$.

In theory anyway, the growing inequality could stem from growing life-cycle variance due either to increased β or increased $Var(a_t)$ or both, or it could stem from growing $Var(\varepsilon_t)$ that has nontrivial, short-term, but tiny lifelong implications. Cross-sectional data cannot parse these three components. Add on the prospect of autocorrelation in ε (DiPrete's [2001] cumulative advantage hypothesis) and we have a very difficult problem that is well beyond the scope of this review. Thus, as a compromise that allows us to move forward, we assume no autocorrelation in ε and specify a tractable, functional form for the other kinds of changes.

Lawrence Katz (1994), Peter Gottschalk and Robert Moffitt (1994), and Gary Solon (2001) propose that we simplify the problem by giving the systematic part of equation 26.1 one time-sensitive weight (p_t) and the disturbance a different weight (q_t):

$$y_{it}* = p_t [\mu_i + \beta a_{it}] + q_t \varepsilon_{it} \tag{26.3}$$

This is a version of Xie's (1992) multiplicative layer effect for this kind of model. Under the model in equation 26.3, the variance of $y_{it}*$ for cohort b in year t is:

$$Var(y* \mid b\varepsilon_t) = p_t^2 \, Var(\mu) + q_t^2 \, Var(\varepsilon) \tag{26.4}$$

The advantage of equation 26.4 is that we can track systematic changes over time if we can figure out what the p_t are.[11]

Simplistic though it may be, the model in equation 26.3 is both powerful as a way of thinking through the problem at hand and well rooted in the substantive literature. Much of what has been written about the growing inequality of wages can be expressed as hypotheses about p_t or q_t. For example, according to the widely discussed "skill-biased technological change" hypothesis (see, for example, Fernandez 2001), modern (computer-related) technology is skill-intensive in a way that has raised the premium on education; that is a claim that computers have raised p_t. Meanwhile, discussions of the ways in which winner-take-all logic has swept labor markets (Frank and Cook 1995) imply that market pressures have raised the variance in outcomes for people with the same measured skills; that is a claim that q_t has risen over time. Thus, equation 26.3 gives us a simple but meaningful tool for relating changing inequality to the main components of mobility research.

Intergenerational Mobility

We can consider the implications of the models in equations 26.1 and 26.3 for intergenerational mobility. Think of the family background of an individual, i, as consisting of her parents' score on $y_{it}*$ while she was growing up. In sociology this is conventionally referred to as i's "social origin" to emphasize that we are thinking of it as an attribute of i, not of her parents. For simplicity, think of that individual's social origin as summarized in a single score. We can arrive at that fiction by assuming: (1) that both parents were born in the same year and (2) that we have some reasonable way of combining the mother's and father's μs to form a single μ to express i's social origin. In the literature, it is more common to assume that one parent dominated in setting the family's standard of living (see, for example, Erikson and Goldthorpe 1992a), but that assumption does not seem very realistic for recent cohorts. So for now let us assume that we know how to weight mothers' and fathers' contributions to background. When we get to the agenda, figuring out those weights will be number one on the to-do list.

If the life-cycle portion of equations 26.1 and 26.3 (βa) is small, then the first assumption is unimportant. The second assumption—that we know how to combine the two parents and how to combine different components of family background (including the transitions from two parents to one parent to parent-and-stepparent with possible effects of nonresident parents, and so on)—has been a major issue in the literature.

For right now let's keep the model as simple as possible. Think of intergenerational transmission of time-invariant effects as a one-dimensional transfer from one generation to the next:

$$\mu_i = \gamma + \delta \, v_i + \eta_i \tag{26.5}$$

where v represents the (weighted) sum of the parents' time-invariant attributes, γ indicates the uniform difference between origins and destinations, δ gauges the effect of origin on destination, and η is a disturbance. Let $\mathrm{cov}(v, \eta) = 0$. The intergenerational difference in endowments is then a function of both γ and δ (contra Solon, who cites only δ):

$$\mu_i - v_i = \gamma + (1 - \delta)v_i + \eta_i \tag{26.6}$$

γ is the difference expected for people with the origin scored zero (may not be observed). If $0 < \delta < 1$, then the expected difference decreases as origins increase. In the limiting case of $\delta = 0$, destination is independent of origin, and intergenerational change is the greatest. Substituting equation 26.5 into equation 26.1, we can see the relationship between single-year outcomes across generations:

$$y_{it}{}^* = \gamma + \delta \, v_i + \beta a_i + (\eta_i + \varepsilon_{it}) \tag{26.7}$$

We do not observe v_i, but we may observe $y_{is}{}^*$ for $s = b, \ldots, b + 18$. In any one year:

$$y_{is}{}^* = v_i + \beta(s - c) + \varepsilon_{is} \tag{26.8}$$

(where c is the parents' year of birth or the average of their years of birth). Averaged over the years from b to $b + 18$, we get:

$$y_i{}^{**} = v_i + \beta(9 + b - c) + \xi_i \tag{26.9}$$

where $y_i{}^{**}$ is the mean of $y_{is}{}^*$ over $s = b, \ldots b + 18$ and ξ_i is the mean of ε_{is} over the same period. Note that ξ_i will be very close to zero. Solving equation 26.9 for v_i and substituting the result into equation 26.7 yields:

$$y_{it}{}^* = \gamma + \delta y_i{}^{**} + \beta a_i - \delta \beta A_i + \eta_i + \varepsilon_{it} - \delta \xi_i \tag{26.10}$$

where $A = 9 + b - c$, that is, the parents' ages when the respondent is around nine years old. Destinations $y_{it}{}^*$ depend on origins, age, parents' ages at the subject's birth, and three kinds of disturbances: random attributes of people that do not change over time (η_i); year-to-year random fluctuations of outcomes (ε_{it}); and the parents' average random component (ξ_i), which, being an eighteen-year average of random shocks, is probably very close to zero.

Inequality and Mobility

Following Gottschalk and Moffitt (1994), let us suppose that rising inequality is driven by rising p_t and q_t, as in equation 26.3. This time we multiply equation 26.9 by p_{b+9} and q_{b+9}, then derive a new version of equation 26.10 and multiply its time-invariant portion by p_t and its time-varying portion by q_t. The result:

$$y_{it}* = p_t\gamma + \kappa_{bt}\delta y_i** + p_t\beta(a_i - \delta A_i) + p_t\eta_i - \kappa_{bt}q_{b+9}\delta\xi_i + q_t\varepsilon_{it} \quad (26.11)$$

where $\kappa_{bt} = p_t/p_{b+9}$ gives the implication of changing inequality for the association between origins and destinations. When κ_{bt} is greater than one, it amplifies the long-run parameter δ, decreasing mobility and increasing the intergenerational correlation. The κ term expresses the relative returns to attributes in the current generation compared with those returns in the parents' generation. If people face a labor market with higher returns to inheritable characteristics than their parents faced, then origins will become a more important influence on their attainment.

Education is the biggest component of both μ_i and v_i. So we can perhaps think more clearly about κ_{bt} if we think of it as the rate of return to education in the current generation compared with the return obtained by the parents' generation while today's workers were growing up. Think first about the generation that grew up in the Depression, fought in World War II, and had careers that spanned the years from 1945 to 1975. Their parents (their fathers mainly) experienced relatively low returns to education in the 1930s, so this cohort has a relatively low p_b denominator in comparison with earlier and later cohorts. Returns to education rose from 1950 to 1970 before tailing off as these people approached retirement. Equation 26.11 implies that they must have experienced a bigger effect of origins on destinations around 1970 than around 1950.[12] In contrast, the first wave of the baby boomers grew up in the 1950s and early 1960s as returns to education were rising and entered the labor force in the early 1970s when returns started to sag; they experienced first falling, then rising returns. Thus, for baby boomers the effect of origins on destinations should also rise as they age, though probably not as much as with the earlier Depression cohort.[13]

AGENDA

We can develop measures of $y_{it}*$ and y_i** by focusing on occupations. For example, occupations can be scored according to the well-known Duncan scale (which averages the percentage of occupational incumbents with twelve or more years of schooling and the percentage of incumbents with earnings above the national median) as well as the new scores developed by Hauser and Warren (1997). There are two reasons to do so. The first is practical. The data on occupational origins are better and more reliable than the data on income origins, and the literature is dominated by occupational mobility studies.

Important Questions

What are social origins? Among the many important social changes of the twentieth century, two have profound implications for the study of social mobility. The prevalence, early in the century, of two-parent, one-earner families allowed researchers like Blau and Duncan (1967) to assume a unitary social origin for each person working in the present generation.

Two-earner families, single-parent families, serial families, and other innovations have called that assumption into question. By studying, first, the effect of the mother's occupation on life chances and then the effect of family disruption on life chances, then both simultaneously, we hope to figure out how to use what we know about complex social origins to redefine what we mean by mobility. Timothy Biblarz and Adrian Raftery (1993, 1999; Biblarz, Raftery, and Bucur 1997) have demonstrated convincingly that the intergenerational association is stronger in two-parent families than in other families. The differentials and interactions related to family structure have not changed since the 1960s, even though nonstandard forms have become more prevalent.

When does a career start? This question vexed Blau and Duncan (1967), led to a revision of the way in which first occupations are measured (Featherman and Hauser 1978), and ultimately produced a "rupture" in the stratification literature. Recent efforts have begun to heal the rupture (Shavit and Müller 1997), but much work remains. A promising start includes the dynamic models of Aage Sørensen (for example, Sørensen and Morgan 2000) and Thomas DiPrete (2001).

Classes or continua? While my earlier exposition makes use of the scalability of occupations, most sociologists prefer to think of occupations not as points on a continuum but as discrete classes (see, for example, the earlier discussion in this chapter, as well as Erikson and Goldthorpe 2002). A controversy along these lines (see, for example, Hout and Hauser 1992) was never resolved. Work in progress (Hout and Beller 2003) revives it with the hope of reaching a resolution.

What should we have learned from the falling inequalities from 1945 to 1975? The link between inequality and mobility seems to be the ratio or difference of inequality in the current generation compared with the parents' generation. We could get a decent time series of returns to education back to the cohort born between 1898 and 1902 using the Blau-Duncan OCG-I survey for 1962 if we assume that cohort differences are more important than life-cycle or period differences. We would probably adjust the data for age effects. We could then use this time series and equation 26.11 to see whether there is an empirical link by (1) testing the specification and (2) getting estimates of the time and/or cohort effects.

CONCLUSION

This literature to date has offered surprisingly little evidence that links intergenerational difference and persistence (mobility and immobility) to economic or other inequality. Most writers use a presumed link to justify interest in the subject. Enormous effort has been invested in establishing and quantifying the intergenerational relationship. Myriad approaches have reached a common conclusion: the generations are not independent, but there is substantial mobility. Less consensus has emerged regarding changes over time or the magnitude of cross-national differences. There is consensus that however large the cross-national differences might be, they are within a narrow—not a wide—range. No observed countries lie outside a range that would correspond to correlations of magnitudes $.25 < r < .50$.

Solon's recent expression of how we might think about intergenerational associations offers the most promise for establishing a link between inequality and mobility. The research agenda sketched here would contribute to progress in this direction.

I am grateful to the Russell Sage Foundation for financial support; to Henry Brady, Neil Fligstein, Bob Hauser, Kathy Neckerman, Geno Smolensky, and an anonymous reviewer for helpful comments on an earlier draft of this chapter; and to Emily Beller and Aliya Saperstein for research assistance.

NOTES

1. Mare (2002) also notes, with disapproval, that the literature has strayed quite far from its roots in the past twenty-five years or so, and he calls for more interest in the links between mobility and inequality. This chapter is my attempt to think through how we might achieve that linkage.

2. In fact, the literature contains occasional reference to the idea that high mobility might, under the right circumstances, be the antidote to high inequality; see, for example, Lipset and Zetterberg (1956) and Cox and Alm (1996).

3. The year was 1985, so this phrase had a certain irony even then.

4. Once they leave, many will try to get back there again, as the RSF visiting scholars and CASBS fellows do.

5. It would, in theory, be possible for inequality to increase or decrease so much over time that personal variance could exceed period variance. But that is a complication that I will not get into here.

6. Christopher Jencks (2002) considers this kind of age-graded mobility and inequality briefly but moves on quickly to other topics.

7. For example, the decline of farming as a profession has decreased the percentage of farm-origin men and women who have grown up to work their own farms even though most farmers continue to come from farm origins; see, for example, Featherman and Hauser (1978), Hout (1988), and Erikson and Goldthorpe (1992a).

8. The history of socioeconomic measurement is beyond the scope of this review; see Hauser and Warren (1997).

9. See Ganzeboom, Treiman, and Ultee (1991) for a full discussion of this literature and an elaboration of the idea of generations of mobility studies.

10. Change almost always goes from less to more open. The only exceptions in the literature are Bolivia (Kelley and Klein 1977), Russia (Gerber and Hout 2002), and, perhaps, Hungary (Peter Robert, personal communication, 2002).

11. In this specification, we have a different p_t and q_t for each cohort. In empirical applications, we would probably want to relax that restriction in order to get more stable estimates of p_t and q_t by pooling across cohorts.

12. We can actually observe the men from this cohort in 1962 and 1973 using OCG-I and OCG-II and test this derivation.

13. We can observe both men and women from this cohort over time in the General Social Survey (GSS).

REFERENCES

Bell, Linda A., and Richard B. Freeman. 1991. "The Causes of Increasing Inter-industry Wage Dispersion in the United States." *Industrial and Labor Relations Review* 44: 275–87.

Bernhardt, Annette, Martina Morris, and Mark S. Handcock, 1995. "Women's Gains or Men's Losses? A Closer Look at the Shrinking Gender Gap in Earnings." *American Journal of Sociology* 101(2): 302–28.

Biblarz, Timothy J., and Adrian E. Raftery, 1993. "The Effects of Family Structure on Social Mobility." *American Sociological Review* 58: 97–109.

———. 1999. "Family Structure, Education, and Socioeconomic Success: Rethinking the 'Pathology of Matriarchy.'" *American Journal of Sociology* 105: 321–65.

Biblarz, Timothy J., Adrian E. Raftery, and Alexander Bucur. 1997. "Family Structure and Social Mobility." *Social Forces* 75(4): 1319–39.

Blau, Peter, and Otis Dudley Duncan. 1967. *The American Occupational Structure*. New York: John Wiley.

Bluestone, Barry, and Bennett Harrison. 1982. *The Deindustrialization of America.* New York: Basic Books.

——. 1988. *The Great U-Turn: Corporate Restructuring and the Polarization of America.* New York: Basic Books.

Bobo, Lawrence. 1997. "Race, Public Opinion, and the Social Sphere." *Public Opinion Quarterly* 61(1): 1–15.

Boudon, Raymond. 1974. *Education, Opportunity, and Social Inequality.* New York: John Wiley.

Breen, Richard, and Christopher T. Whelan. 1996. *Social Class and Social Mobility in Ireland.* Dublin, Ireland: Gill and McMillan.

Breiger, Ronald L. 1995. "Social Structure and the Phenomenology of Attainment." *Annual Review of Sociology* 21(1): 115–36.

Cheng, Yuan, and Jianzhong Dai. 1995. "Intergenerational Mobility in Modern China." *European Sociological Review* 11(1): 17–35.

Cox, W. Michael, and Richard Alm. 1996. "Time Well Spent: The Declining Real Cost of Living in America." Annual report of the Federal Reserve Bank of Dallas. Dallas, Tx.: Federal Reserve Bank of Dallas.

De Seve, Michael. 1998. "The Erikson and Goldthorpe Core Model of Social Fluidity in Canada: A Comparison with England and France." Paper presented to the meeting of the International Sociological Association. Montreal, Canada (August 1998).

DiPrete, Thomas A. 2001. "'Positional Capital' as a Mechanism for Earnings Inequality: Theory and Evidence." Paper presented to the semiannual meeting of the International Sociological Association Research Committee on Stratification. Berkeley, Calif.(August 2001).

Duncan, Otis Dudley. 1961. "A Socioeconomic Index for Occupations." In *Occupations and Social Status*, edited by Albert J. Reiss. New York: Free Press.

——. 1966a. "Methodological Issues in the Analysis of Social Mobility." In *Social Structure and Mobility in Economic Development,* edited by Neil J. Smelser and Seymour Martin Lipset. Chicago: Aldine.

——. 1966b. "Path Analysis: Sociological Examples." *American Journal of Sociology* 72: 1–16.

Duncan, Otis Dudley, and Robert W. Hodge. 1963. "Education and Occupational Mobility: A Regression Analysis." *American Journal of Sociology* 68(6): 629–49.

Erikson, Robert, and John H. Goldthorpe. 1987a. "Commonality and Variation in Social Fluidity in Industrial Nations. Part I: A Model for Evaluating the 'FJH Hypothesis.'" *European Sociological Review* 3(1): 54–77.

——. 1987b. "Commonality and Variation in Social Fluidity in Industrial Nations. Part II: The Model of Core Social Fluidity Applied." *European Sociological Review* 3(2): 145–66.

——. 1992a. *The Constant Flux: A Study of Class Mobility in Industrial Societies.* Oxford: Clarendon Press.

——. 1992b. "The CASMIN Project and the American Dream." *European Sociological Review* 8(3): 283–305.

——. 2002. "Intergenerational Inequality: A Sociological Perspective." *Journal of Economic Perspectives* 16: 31–44.

Erikson, Robert, John H. Goldthorpe, and Lucienne Portocarero. 1979. "Intergenerational Class Mobility in Three Western European Societies: England, France, and Sweden." *British Journal of Sociology* 30(4): 415–41.

——. 1982. "Social Fluidity in Industrial Nations: England, France, and Sweden." *British Journal of Sociology* 33(1): 1–34.

Featherman, David L., and Robert M. Hauser. 1978. *Opportunity and Change.* New York: Academic Press.

Featherman, David L., Frank L. Jones, and Robert M. Hauser. 1975. "Assumptions of Social Mobility Research in the United States: The Case of Occupational Status." *Social Science Research* 4(4): 329–60.

Fernandez, Roberto M. 2001. "Skill-biased Technological Change and Wage Inequality: Evidence from Plant Retooling." *American Journal of Sociology* 107: 273–320.

Frank, Robert, and Phillip J. Cook 1995. *The Winner Take All Society.* New York: Penguin.

Ganzeboom, Harry B. G., and Paul De Graaf. 1984. "Intergenerational Occupational Mobility in the Netherlands in 1954 and 1977: A Log-linear Analysis." In *Social Stratification and Mobility in the Netherlands,* edited by B. F. M. Bakker, J. Dronkers, and Harry B. G. Ganzeboom. Amsterdam: SISWO.

Ganzeboom, Harry B. G., Anton Kramberger, and Paul Nieuwbeerta. 2000. "The Parental Effect on Educational and Occupational Attainment in Slovenia During the Twentieth Century." *Druzboslovne Razprave* 16(32–33): 9–54.

Ganzeboom, Harry B. G., Ruud Luijkx, and Donald J. Treiman. 1989. "Intergenerational Class Mobility in Comparative Perspective." *Research in Social Stratification and Mobility* 8: 3–84.

Ganzeboom, Harry B. G., Donald Treiman, and Wout Ultee. 1991. "Comparative Intergenerational Stratification Research: Three Generations and Beyond." *Annual Review of Sociology* 17(1): 277–302.

Gerber, Theodore, and Michael Hout. 2002 "Tightening Up: Social Mobility in Russia, 1988 to 2000." Paper presented to the semiannual Meeting of the Research Committee on Social Stratification of the International Sociological Association. Brisbane, Australia (August 2002).

Glass, David V. 1954. *Social Mobility in Britain.* London: Routledge and Kegan Paul.

Goldthorpe, John H. 1980. *Social Mobility and Class Structure in Modern Britain.* Oxford: Clarendon Press.

Goldthorpe, John H., Meir Yaish, and Vered Kraus. 1997. "Class Mobility in Israeli Society: A Comparative Perspective." *Research in Social Stratification and Mobility* 15: 3–28.

Goodman, Leo A. 1969. "How to Ransack Mobility Tables and Other Kinds of Cross-classification Tables." *American Journal of Sociology* 75: 1–40.

———. 1970. "Multivariate Analysis of Qualitative Data: Interactions Among Multiple Classifications." *Journal of the American Statistical Association* 65(329): 226–56.

———. 1972. "Some Multiplicative Models for the Analysis of Cross-classified Data." In *The Sixth Berkeley Symposium on Mathematical Statistics and Probability,* edited by Lucien Le Cam et al. Berkeley: University of California Press.

———. 1974. "The Analysis of Systems of Qualitative Variables When Some of the Variables Are Unobservable: A Modified Latent Structure Approach." *American Journal of Sociology* 79: 1179–1259.

———. 1979. "Simple Models for the Analysis of Association in Cross-classifications Having Ordered Categories." *Journal of the American Statistical Association* 74(367): 537–52.

———. 1984. *The Analysis of Cross-classified Data Having Ordered Categories.* Cambridge, Mass.: Harvard University Press.

Gottschalk, Peter, and Robert A. Moffitt. 1994. "The Growth of Earnings Instability in the U.S. Labor Market." *Brookings Papers on Economic Activity* 2: 217–54.

Haller, Max, Tamas Kolosi, and Peter Robert. 1990. "Soziale Mobilitat in Osterreich, in der Tschechoslowakei und in Ungarn: Eine vergleichende Analyse der Effekte von Industrialisierung, sozialistischen Revolutionen und nationaler Eigen heit" (Social Mobility in Austria, Czechoslovakia, and Hungary: A Comparative Survey on the Effects of Industrialization, Socialist Revolution, and National Identity). *Journal fur Sozialforschung* 30(1): 33–72.

Hansen, Erik Jorgen. 1998. "The Intergenerational Social Mobility of Women: Experiences from Classification Problems and Problems of Interpretation of the Results in a Danish Longitudinal Study." Paper presented to the meeting of the International Sociological Association. Montreal, Canada (August 1998).

Hauser, Robert M. 1973. "Disaggregating a Socio-Psychological Model of Educational Attainment." In Structural Equation Models in the Social Sciences, edited by Arthur S. Goldberger and Otis Dudley Duncan. New York: Seminar Press.

———. 1978. "A Structural Model of the Mobility Table." *Social Forces* 56: 919–53.

———. 1984a. "Vertical Class Mobility in England, France, and Sweden." *Acta Sociologica* 27(2): 87–110.

———. 1984b. "Vertical Class Mobility in England, France, and Sweden." *Acta Sociologica* 27(4): 387–90.

Hauser, Robert M., and John Robert Warren. 1997. "Socioeconomic Indexes for Occupations: A Review, Update, and Critique." *Sociological Methodology* 27: 177–298.

Hout, Michael. 1988. "More Universalism and Less Structural Mobility: The American Occupational Structure in the 1980s." *American Journal of Sociology* 93(6): 1358–1400.

———. 1989. *Following in Father's Footsteps: Social Mobility in Ireland.* Cambridge, Mass.: Harvard University Press.

Hout, Michael, and Emily Beller. 2003. "Mobility Trends in the United States, 1972 to 2000: Class and Socioeconomic Status." Paper presented to the semiannual meeting of the International Sociological Association Research Committee on Stratification. Oxford, U.K.(March 2002, revised August 2003).

Hout, Michael, and Robert M. Hauser. 1992. "Symmetry and Hierarchy in Social Mobility: A Methodological Analysis of the CASMIN Model of Class Mobility." *European Sociological Review* 8(3): 239–66.

Hout, Michael, and John A. Jackson. 1986. "Dimensions of Occupational Mobility in the Republic of Ireland." *European Sociological Review* 2(2): 114–37.

Ishida, Hiroshi. 1993. *Social Mobility in Contemporary Japan.* Stanford, Calif.: Stanford University Press.

Ishida, Hiroshi, John H. Goldthorpe, and Robert Erikson. 1991. "Intergenerational Class Mobility in Postwar Japan." *American Journal of Sociology* 96(4): 954–92.

Jencks, Christopher. 2002. "Does Inequality Matter?" *Daedalus* (Spring): 49–65.

Katz, Lawrence F. 1994. "Comments and Discussion." *Brookings Papers on Economic Activity* 2: 255–61.

Kelley, Jonathan, and Herbert S. Klein. 1977. "Revolution and the Rebirth of Inequality: A Theory of Stratification in Postrevolutionary Society." *American Journal of Sociology* 83(1): 78–99.

Kerckhoff, Alan C., Richard T. Campbell, Jerry M. Trott, and Vered Krauss. 1989. "The Transmission of Status and Privilege in Great Britain and the United States." *Sociological Forum* 4(2): 155–77.

Lipset, Seymour Martin, and Hans Zetterberg. 1956. "A Theory of Social Mobility." *Transactions of the Third World Congress of Sociology*, vol. 3. London: International Sociological Association.

Mare, Robert D. 2002. "Observations on the Study of Social Mobility and Inequality." In *Social Stratification: Class, Race, and Gender in Sociological Perspective*, second edition, edited by David B. Grusky. Boulder, Colo.: Westview Press.

Marshall, Gordon, Svetlana Sydorenko, and Stephen Roberts. 1995. "Intergenerational Social Mobility in Communist Russia." *Work, Employment, and Society* 9(1): 1–27.

Morris, Martina, Annette D. Bernhardt, and Mark S. Handcock. 1994. "Economic Inequality: New Methods for New Trends." *American Sociological Review* 59(2): 205–19.

Müller, Walter, and Wolfgang Konig. 1986. "Educational Systems and Labour Markets as Determinants of Work-life Mobility in France and West Germany: A Comparison of Men's Career Mobility, 1965–1970." *European Sociological Review* 2: 73–96.

Phang, Ha-Nam, and Sung-Kyan Lee. 1996. "Structural Change and Intergenerational Class Mobility: A Comparative Study of Korea and Taiwan." *Han'guk Sahoehak (Korean Journal of Sociology)* 30(3): 575–604.

Pontinen, Seppo. 1984. *A Comparison of Social Mobility in Scandinavian Countries*. Helsinki, Finland: Sociological Institute.

Ringdal, Kristen. 1994. "Intergenerational Class Mobility in Postwar Norway: A Weakening of Vertical Barriers?" *European Sociological Review* 10(3): 273–88.

———. 2001. "Social Mobility in Norway, 1973 to 1995." Paper presented to the semiannual meeting of the Research Committee on Social Stratification of the International Sociological Association. Berkeley, Calif. (August 2001).

Rodriguez Menes, Jorge. 1993. "Movilidad social y cambio social en España" (Social Mobility and Social Change in Spain). *Revista Española de Investigaciones Sociologicas* 61: 77–125.

Rogoff, Natalie. 1953. *Recent Trends in Occupational Mobility*. Glencoe, Ill.: Free Press.

Rogoff Ramsoy, Natalie. 1966. "Changes in Rates and Forms of Mobility." In *Social Structure and Mobility in Economic Development*, edited by Neil J. Smelser and Seymour Martin Lipset. Chicago: Aldine.

Salido, Olga. 1999. "Women's Intergenerational Mobility in Spain: Two Generations in Contrast." Paper presented to the semiannual meeting of the International Sociological Association Research Committee on Social Stratification. Madison, Wisc. (August 1999).

Scalon, Maria Celi. 1999. "Social Mobility in Brazil." Paper presented to the semiannual meeting of the International Sociological Association Research Committee on Social Stratification. Madison, Wisc. (August 1999).

Schizzerotto, Antonio, and Maurizio Pisati. 1998. "La Mobilité sociale en Italie" (Social Mobility in Italy). *La Revue Tocqueville* 19(1): 159–72.

Sewell, William H., Jr. 1984. *Structure and Mobility: Men and Women of Marseille, 1820 to 1870*. New York: Cambridge University Press.

Sewell, William H., Archibald O. Haller, and Alejandro Portes. 1969. "The Educational and Early Occupational Attainment Process." *American Sociological Review* 34: 82–92.

Sewell, William H., and Robert M. Hauser. 1975. *Education, Occupation, and Earnings in the Early Career*. New York: Academic Press.

Sewell, William H., Robert M. Hauser, Kristen W. Springer, and Taissa S. Hauser. 2003. "As We Age: A Review of the Wisconsin Longitudinal Study, 1957 to 2001." *Research in Social Stratification and Mobility* 20. Forthcoming.

Shavit, Yossi, and Walter Müller. 1997. *From School to Work: Comparative Educational Qualifications and Occupational Destinations*. Oxford: Clarendon Press.

Solon, Gary. 2001. "Mobility Within and Between Generations." In *The Causes and Consequences of Rising Inequality*, edited by Finis Welch. Chicago: University of Chicago Press.

Sørensen, Aage B., and Stephen L. Morgan. 2000. "School Effects: Theoretical and Methodological Issues." In *Handbook of the Sociology of Education,* edited by Maureen T. Hallinan. New York: Kluwer/Plenum.

Sorokin, Pitrim A. 1927. *Social Mobility.* New York: Harper and Brothers.

Walder, Andrew, Bobai Li, and Donald J. Treiman. 2000. "Politics and Life Chances in a State Socialist Regime: Dual Career Paths into the Urban Chinese Elite, 1949–1996." *American Sociological Review* 65: 191–209.

Wanner, Richard A., and Bernadette Hayes. 1996. "Intergenerational Occupational Mobility Among Men in Canada and Australia." *Canadian Journal of Sociology* 21(1): 43–76.

Wong, Raymond S. 1992. "Vertical and Nonvertical Effects in Class Mobility: Cross-national Variations." *American Sociological Review* 57(3): 396–410.

Xie, Yu. 1992. "The Log-Multiplicative Layer Effect Model for Comparing Mobility Tables." *American Sociological Review* 57(3): 380–95.

Index

Boldface numbers refer to figures and tables.